AMERICAN GOVERNMENT
Your Voice, Your Future

Matthew R. Kerbel

Villanova University

Academic Media Solutions

Affordable - Quality Textbooks, Study Aids, & Custom Publishing

Cover photo: Onur ERSIN/Shutterstock.com

American Government—Your Voice, Your Future, 6th Edition, Matthew R. Kerbel

Paperback (black/white): ISBN-13: 978-1-942041-34-4
                                  ISBN 10-: 1-942041-34-9

Paperback (color):   ISBN-13: 978-1-942041-36-8
                                  ISBN-10: 1-942041-36-5

Loose leaf version (B/W): ISBN-13: 978-1-942041-35-1
                                  ISBN-10: 1-942041-35-7

Online version: ISBN-13: 978-1-942041-37-5
                                  ISBN-10: 1-942041-37-3

To Gabrielle and her generation,
so they may never lose the love of learning

Brief Contents

Contents

PART 1 WHY SHOULD WE CARE ABOUT AMERICAN DEMOCRACY? 1

1 Should We Care about Politics? 1

2 The Constitution and Federalism: Setting the Ground Rules for Politics 25

PART 2 CITIZENSHIP AND DEMOCRACY 55

3 Public Opinion: What Is It, and What Does It Have to Do with Me? 55

4 Political Culture, Socialization, and Participation 89

PART 3 CONNECTIONS BETWEEN CITIZENS AND GOVERNMENT 127

5 Mass Media: Influencing What We Think About   127

8 Interest Groups: Accessing Government through Common Membership 227

PART 4 INSTITUTIONS OF DEMOCRACY 257

9 Congress 257

10 The Presidency 297

11 The Federal Bureaucracy 337

12 The Judiciary 365

PART 5   WHAT GOVERNMENT DOES AND HOW WELL IT WORKS 399

13 Establishing Civil Rights   399

14 Protecting Civil Liberties 425

15 Domestic Policy and Policy Making 447

16 Foreign and Defense Policies 471

Appendices A-1

Preface

Understanding and Using This Book

Unifying Themes: Accessibility, Relevance, and Choice

For many of us, government seems distant and irrelevant—in part because it's so big, in part because it's hard to draw the connection between what political figures do and the things that have meaning in our lives. I constantly talk to students who don't care about the political world, don't see how it affects them, or don't wish to find out. Maybe you feel that way, too. If you do, it certainly doesn't help to have an American government text that portrays government as a far-away abstraction. Too often, I've heard my students complain about government texts being too plodding and inaccessible. I've heard similar complaints from professors.

Here, you'll be presented with an entirely different version of American government. Think of it as an up-close version, where abstractions give way to gritty fundamentals, revealing a government composed of all-too-ordinary people who share our daily concerns and priorities. Members of Congress struggle to fit in and find ways to get their homework done. Lobbyists struggle to beat out other lobbyists and make the case that will win over members of Congress. Supreme Court justices play high-stakes poker with their colleagues in an effort to shape their decisions on a case without realizing they've been influenced. The political system is filled with situations like these and with people trying to do their jobs under conditions of uncertainty and in the face of great time pressures.

If this sounds familiar, that's the point. Government cannot be relevant to our lives until we're able to see it in terms that make sense to us. This book will encourage you to experience American government in a way to which you can relate, because the truth is that when you strip away the generalizations and remove the distance, the people and situations you encounter in Washington or in your state capital are remarkably like those you encounter in any institution or social situation—including college.

Making government less mysterious and more real should make it easier for you to wrestle with the central question of the book: What do you want your relationship to government and politics to be? We all have a choice to participate in the political system or to opt out, and if we choose to participate, we also can decide how much and in what form we want to get involved. There are a lot of options, starting with voting and branching out to include reading about politics, signing an online petition, giving money to a political cause or candidate, sending email to an elected representative, engaging in protest demonstrations, and much more.

Because the choice of whether and how to participate is deeply personal, only you can make it, and by the time you've finished with this book, I sincerely hope you are interested in doing just that: deciding what you want your political role to be. I could spend sixteen chapters telling you why I believe it's important for you to participate—and I do believe it's important, or I wouldn't have bothered writing this book—but what's the point of that? It's far more important for you to decide for yourself what, if anything, you're going to do, to have ownership of your decision, and to feel comfortable with it. You may conclude that you don't want to have a role in politics or that it doesn't matter whether or not you get involved. With this book, I'll help you make an informed decision, whatever that decision may be.

How This Book Is Organized

Think of this book as a round-trip journey on which you are the navigator. It's a round-trip journey because if you were to read the book straight through, you'd find that in the last four chapters of the book, we're back to talking about some of the same issues we discuss in the first two, reconsidering them in light of everything we've learned along the way. In five parts encompassing sixteen chapters, *American Government: Your Voice, Your Future* 6e maps out a route designed to take you from understanding your place in the political system to how people connect with government, how the political system works and what it does, and finally—to come full circle—how responsive it is to your demands and desires.

Part 1 Why Should We Care about American Democracy?

We'll start with background on the fundamental concepts you'll need to understand if you're going to be able to make an intelligent decision about what you want your political role, if any, to be. Although this is the most abstract portion of the book, the concepts are illustrated with concrete examples. Think of this part as a presentation of the building blocks you'll need for the rest of the book and the place where you'll encounter foundational questions about the role and purpose of government that will set the tone for the discussions that follow.

Chapter 1 Should We Care about Politics? The question posed by the chapter title is one you will be able to answer for yourself by the time you've finished reading this book. It's a personal question with no correct answer, but an informed response necessitates understanding how government fits into everyday life—whether we care about politics or not. Chapter 1 addresses how societies come together to make choices about governing themselves, discussing the fundamentals of such things as authority, legitimacy, power, equality, and liberty.

Chapter 2 The Constitution and Federalism: Setting the Ground Rules for Politics The Constitution establishes the broad outlines for how American government operates, and federalism is one of the most important and distinctive features of the American system. Together, the Constitution and federalism shape the rules for American politics. We'll look at the origin, makeup, and evolution of both, keeping an eye on how the ground rules influence who is favored and who is disadvantaged in the political process.

Part 2 Citizenship and Democracy

Moving from a discussion of concepts to a discussion of their application, this section explores the parallel issues of how the United States developed as a nation and how individual Americans develop—or don't develop—into political creatures. We'll examine public opinion about politics and politicians, the elements of political culture that lead people to identify as Americans, aspects of political socialization that acquaint us with that culture while teaching the basics of civic involvement, and the kinds of political participation in which, once socialized, we may choose to engage.

Chapter 3 Public Opinion: What Is It, and What Does It Have to Do with Me? To answer the question posed in the chapter title, we'll look at three important components of public opinion: political knowledge, attitudes, and beliefs. Political knowledge is our factual understanding of politics, and we'll find that it tends to be not particularly extensive. Political attitudes encompass how we feel about politics, such as whether we feel distant from political figures and what they do. Political beliefs involve what we think is true about politics. Together, these elements of public opinion influence the way we relate to what politicians do.

Chapter 4 Political Culture, Socialization, and Participation By broadening the discussion of public opinion to include issues of national and individual identity, we consider ways that Americans unite as a nation, come of age as political individuals, and engage in political action. National self-identification is rooted in something we call political culture. The process of political socialization explores how important people in our lives shape our adult perspectives on politics and government. The political activities we might consider doing encompass a variety of forms of political participation—from voting to attending protest rallies.

Part 3 Connections between Citizens and Government

Once we have explored the nature of public opinion and the origins of political involvement, we'll look at three institutions that link us to the people who represent us in government: the mass media, political parties, and interest groups. When working properly, each of these institutions functions like the connective tissue of government by channeling citizen demands and concerns to political figures and information about political figures to citizens. As we'll see, sometimes these connections aren't as clear or as simple as you might expect.

Chapter 5 Mass Media: Influencing What We Think About The media comprise the first of the three linking institutions that we'll examine. Most everyone is familiar with media like television, radio, newspapers, and the Internet, but we may have thought of these media only as sources of entertainment. They also play a central role in politics by providing us directly and indirectly with information that can shape the way we think about our government and the people in it. We'll look at how they do it and evaluate how effectively the media keep us informed about politics and government.

Chapter 6 Political Parties: Connecting Us to the Electoral Process Political parties may be less familiar to us than the media, even though they help to organize a lot of political activity, particularly in terms of how candidates for office are recruited, funded, and ultimately elected. This is the case despite the fact that the Constitution does not provide for parties. We'll look at why the United States has only two major parties (most nations have more), explore how political parties have evolved through American history, and examine how parties are organized and what they do.

Chapter 7 Campaigns and Elections: Vehicles for Democratic Expression One of the most important functions of political parties is structuring the way we choose elected officials. We'll devote a chapter to examining this essential role of parties in connecting candidates and voters. We'll spend some time in the cutthroat world of political campaigns, where the stakes are high and the winner takes all, examining the process for selecting candidates, the strategies candidates use to try to win elections, and the vital role of money in the campaign process.

Chapter 8 Interest Groups: Accessing Government through Common Membership Probably the least familiar of our three linking organizations, interest groups are nonetheless vital to determining important national policies, as people who organize around common interests are the ones who are best positioned to be heard by elected leaders. We will consider what interest groups are, where they come from, why people belong to them, the resources they have to get the ear of government officials, and the way they use those resources to advance their agendas.

Part 4 Institutions of Democracy

The discussion of institutions that connect us with government will lead directly to Part 4, where we address the operation of the institutions that constitute government: Congress, the presidency, the federal bureaucracy, and the judiciary. Rather than regarding them as abstractions, we will treat these institutions as organizations run by people just like us, who (also just like us) have goals and objectives and a lot of work to do, and who try to advance their objectives as best they can with limited resources. We'll look at the world of Washington as a place where lots of people press to get all sorts of things done, looking for allies to help them, while trying to dodge the equally determined efforts of those who oppose them.

Chapter 9 Congress We will begin Part 4 by looking at Congress. Like any institution, including your college or university, Congress operates under a set of unspoken rules that attempt to promote civility and encourage compromise. We'll look at these rules and how Congress is organized to facilitate legislative work—a rather messy process in which it's far easier to frustrate someone else's initiative than it is to get something accomplished.

Chapter 10 The Presidency The presidency is probably the most visible office in the world, yet it can be surprisingly mysterious—and complex. There is a highly institutionalized side to the presidency composed of a web of offices and presidential advisors operating within the White House. At the same time, the presidency is the most personal of government institutions, responding more to the character of its chief occupant than any other political office. We'll look at how strong presidents have shaped the office and at the many—often contradictory—roles we ask the president to assume.

Chapter 11 The Federal Bureaucracy The president is the chief executive, and the branch of government he ostensibly heads is the executive branch, or the federal bureaucracy. Even though it may be less well known than the president himself, the federal bureaucracy has an important place in the functioning of Washington. Hierarchical and specialized, it is a sometimes explosive mix of lifelong civil servants and political appointees who serve at the president's pleasure. With the president as the head of the executive branch, you might think that bureaucrats would be responsive to him, but the reality is far more complicated. We'll explore why as we examine the functions bureaucrats perform.

Chapter 12 The Judiciary Perhaps the most mysterious branch of government, the judiciary can be just as political as any other institution—despite its dark-robed justices and secretive deliberations. From state courts to the federal courts, up to and including the United States Supreme Court, the judiciary faces a dilemma: It is charged with making judgments it has no power to enforce. As we look at how the court system is constituted, we will explore the informal mechanisms available to judges and justices that give them standing to confront others in the political system.

Part 5 What Government Does and How Well It Works

We ask our government officials to do two important things: (1) to protect the rights and liberties discussed in Part 1 and (2) to make policy on behalf of the country. We'll see how some policies are more controversial than others and how even the least controversial policies can have their detractors. Does discord mean government isn't responding well to our needs—or is it just a characteristic of being human that we're going to have disagreements about the policies government produces? We'll consider these issues by looking at policy from the standpoint of government responsiveness. We'll examine how effectively the officials we discussed in Part 4 listen to the voices expressed through the institutions we discussed in Part 3—voices reflecting opinions and participation styles of people like us, as we discussed in Part 2.

Chapter 13 Establishing Civil Rights Civil rights policies ensure that the law treats everyone equally and protects individuals from discrimination. We will explore the history and development of civil rights law as it pertains to the struggle for equal treatment fought for by groups that have historically experienced discrimination in America: African Americans, Native Americans, Latinos, women, Asian Americans, disabled individuals, LGBT individuals, and senior citizens.

Chapter 14 Protecting Civil Liberties Civil liberties are constitutional and legal protections against government infringement on personal freedoms. This encompasses a wide range of freedoms, almost all of which are universally accepted in principle but may be controversial in practice. For instance, the Constitution prohibits the government from restricting religious freedom, but does this right extend to permitting prayer in public places? The Constitution establishes the right of Americans to bear arms, but is this a relatively unrestricted personal right to own firearms or a collective right to form militias? We will explore questions like these, which illustrate the complexity of civil liberties.

Chapter 15 Domestic Policy and Policy Making Domestic policies include budgetary decisions, regulations, and legislation pertaining to how Americans resolve domestic problems. Regulatory policies give government a role in adjusting the marketplace in ways that would not otherwise occur, in order to minimize hazards created by a free market or to maximize its benefits. Domestic legislation comes in several forms, most notably distributive policies, which claim tax dollars for projects or programs that could potentially benefit anyone, and redistributive policies, which transfer resources from one group to another. Because domestic policy decisions have "losers" who bear the cost and "winners" who benefit, they can be controversial. We'll explore this controversy in detail.

Chapter 16 Foreign and Defense Policies Foreign policy is about how the United States conducts itself as a nation among other nations. It encompasses a host of economic, diplomatic, and military concerns, ranging from questions about global trade to relationships with other nations and how much to invest in maintaining a military. An extensive network of political advisors, diplomats, military personnel, and international leaders shape the direction of foreign policy and influence foreign policy decisions, which because of their life-and-death implications are among the most crucial decisions a nation has to make.

A Word on Critical Thinking

You'll find that the more you learn about how American government operates and affects your life, the more important it will be to have the skills to assess the many claims that politicians and elected officials make. Critical thinking skills make navigating the political process possible. With them, you can evaluate the content of news stories, determine if a policy proposal is in your best interest, assess whether claims made by your senator about her performance in office accurately represent her record—all things you'll need to do to have a meaningful political voice.

That's why this book approaches the American political system as a forum for developing critical thinking skills. From the outset, when we talk about the origins

and foundation of the political system, through the closing chapters that connect those foundations with policies that affect our daily lives, we'll never stop asking questions about how theory is connected to practice, or why citizens, politicians, reporters, lobbyists, and judges act the way they do, or whether an observation about government is rooted in opinion or fact. Questions like these will develop and sharpen the analytical tools that will make us better citizens—and students—and help us make intelligent decisions about whether and how to participate in politics.

Before You Start: How to Use This Book

Four things set *American Government: Your Voice, Your Future* 6e apart from conventional textbooks. They are:

- Student options: print and online versions
- Natural and relaxed writing style
- Modular presentation
- Ease of navigation and repetition

Here's a quick overview of each one.

Student Options: Print and Online Versions

American Government: Your Voice, Your Future 6e is available in multiple versions, offered online, in PDF, and in print. The content of each version is identical. The most affordable version is the online book, with upgrade options including the online version bundled with printable PDFs or paperback. What's nice about the print version is it offers you the freedom of being unplugged—away from your computer or device. The people at Academic Media Solutions recognize that it's difficult to read from a screen at length and that most of us read much faster from a piece of paper. The print options are particularly useful when you have extended print passages like this one to read. Then, you can turn to the online edition to take full advantage of the digital version, including search and notes. Use the search feature to locate and jump to discussions anywhere in the book. You can move out of the book to follow web links. You can navigate within and between chapters using a clickable table of contents. These features allow you to work at your own pace and in your own style, as you read and surf your way through the material. (See "Harnessing the Online Version" for more tips.)

Whether you're working in print or online, each chapter concludes with a set of features designed to reinforce and expand what you've learned, including a concise chapter review, a list of key terms and definitions, an annotated bibliography that lists readings you could consult for more details, and a list of notes with follow-up information.

Natural and Relaxed Writing Style

Conventional textbooks supply you with information. *American Government: Your Voice, Your Future* 6e is a book that can teach. It's not a substitute for the learning you do in class—no book can be—but it is a core learning tool in a way that traditional books cannot be. The difference lies in the way the material is presented to you. Some of this comes from the interactive capability of working online, but an important component of teaching is how information is presented. That's where the style of the book comes into play.

I'm sure you've already noticed that this book has an informal, open quality. That's by design. The intent is to have a conversation between author and reader, much like you would find in a first-person novel or an in-class lecture. The philosophy that guided the writing of this book is that learning is a dynamic process and that we learn best when we interact with the material—when we feel engaged in the story a book tells. In this regard, both the online and print versions are designed to be interactive learning devices. Both present a detailed and thoughtful account of the people, processes, systems, and institutions that comprise American government in an engaging, challenging, personalized, true-to-life manner that talks to you rather than down to you or past you.

Modular Presentation

Most of us are used to learning one chunk of information at a time. So *American Government: Your Voice, Your Future* 6e reduces information to its component parts for easier digestion. You may have noticed how this preface is broken into small, modular sections; in the online version, it's on several brief screens that you can move through quickly and easily. The entire book follows this format.

Moreover, the construction of this book permits some deviation from the traditional linear textbook model, where material is presented through a running text narrative offset with secondary material in boxes. In this book, the set-aside information is not secondary at all, but core text that appears in pedagogical boxes. These features may illuminate or elaborate on a point in the text, or they may use something in the text as a point of departure for a related discussion. They should be regarded as core material, not peripheral content you can ignore.

This is important to remember because it defies convention. You may have seen textbooks that are dotted with little bordered "boxes" that scream, "This is secondary material—don't read me!" Such is not the case with the boxes in this text. Far from it. As you navigate the book, you will find that these boxes supplement the core text by explaining complicated processes in simple terms, placing material about American government in a global context, and challenging you to think about issues and political events. In particular, you will encounter:

Demystifying Government boxes, which clarify things about American government that might otherwise seem cloudy or complex;

Global Topics boxes, which invite you to think comparatively about American government in an increasingly interconnected world; and

Biography boxes, which illustrate the lives of key political figures, helping you to figure out how they fit into the American political system.

You'll find glossary terms and footnotes in this material, just like you'll find in the body of a chapter. The only difference is in the way you navigate through them. Having material set aside like this permits you to read ahead and come back if you so choose. It's another way this book presents you with a nonlinear approach to the material. You just have to remember not to ignore it.

Ease of Navigation and Repetition

Whether you're working online or with print, you'll find that the design of the book allows you to move quickly and easily within and between chapters, jumping ahead to explore an essay or game that applies to what you're reading, bouncing back to a place you've already been to review something you haven't seen in a while. Because repetition is an important part of learning, key terms introduced early in the book are emphasized again when they appear in later chapters, and because we often forget some of what we learned weeks and months ago, key segments of early chapters are repeated for quick review when they are relevant to understanding material in later chapters. It's all part of the philosophy of having a book that teaches rather than simply presents information.

Harnessing the Online Version

The online version of *American Government: Your Voice, Your Future* 6e offers the following features to facilitate learning and to make using the book an easy, enjoyable experience:

- *Easy-to-navigate/clickable table of contents*—You can surf through the book quickly by clicking on chapter headings, or first- or second-level section headings. And the table of contents can be accessed from anywhere in the book.

- *Key concepts search*—Type in a term, and a search engine will return every instance of that term in the book; then jump directly to the selection of your choice with a click of your mouse.

- *Notes and highlighting*—The online version includes study apps such as notes and highlighting. Each of these apps can be found in the tools icon embedded in the Academic Media Solutions/ Textbook Media's online eBook reading platform (http://www.academicmediasolutions.com; http://www.textbookmedia.com).

- *Upgrades*—The online version includes the ability to purchase additional study aids that enhance the learning experience.

Instructor Supplements

In addition to its student-friendly features and pedagogy, the variety of student formats available, and the uniquely affordable pricing options designed to provide students with the flexibility that best fits any budget and/or learning style, *American Government: Your Voice, Your Future*, 6e comes with the following teaching and learning aids:

- *Test Item File*—An extensive set of multiple-choice, short answer, and essay questions for every chapter for creating original quizzes and exams.

- *Instructor's Manual*—An enhanced version of the book offering assistance in preparing lectures, identifying learning objectives, developing essay exams and assignments, and constructing course syllabi.

- *PowerPoint Presentations*—Key points in each chapter are illustrated in a set of PowerPoint files designed to assist with instruction.

Student Supplements and Upgrades (Additional purchase required)

- *Lecture Guide*—This printable lecture guide is designed for student use and is available as an in-class resource or study tool. Note: Instructors can request the PowerPoint version of these slides to use as developed or to customize.

- *Study Guide*—A printable version of the online study guide is available via downloadable PDF chapters for easy self-printing and review.

- *Online Video Labs with Student Worksheets*—A collection of high-quality, dynamic, and sometimes humorous video segments (contemporary and classic) produced by a variety of news, entertainment, and academic sources, accessed via the web. Organized by chapter, the video segments illustrate key topics/issues discussed in the chapters. Each video segment is accompanied by a student worksheet that consists of a series of discussion questions that help students connect the themes presented in the video segment with key topics discussed in the specific chapter. Instructors are provided with suggested answers for each worksheet (for questions not based on student opinion).

Reviewers

The scholars listed here have read and commented on this text, contributing valuable insights and suggestions, both large and small, that collectively shaped the book's content and presentation. I am indebted to them for permitting me to incorporate their ideas, and I am particularly grateful to the many specialists who contributed their insights into material that I appreciate only as a generalist. Their labors were critical to the completion of this project.

Evelyn Ballard
Houston Community College

Ken Baxter
San Joaquin Delta College

Joel Bloom
SUNY-Albany

Melanie Blumberg
California U of Pennsylvania

Robert Bradley
Illinois State University

Barry Burden
Harvard University

Amy Carter
Westminster College

Craig Curtis
Bradley University

Michael Good
California State University

Catherine Grott
Montana State University

Randy Hagerty
Truman State University

William Hall
Bradley University

James Hanley
Adrian College

James Harrigan
LeMoyne College

Marjorie Hershey
Indiana University

Donna Hoffman
University of Northern Iowa

James Ivers
Eastern Michigan University

Mark Joslyn
University of Kansas

Alice Kaiser-Drobney
Slippery Rock University

William Kelly
Auburn University

Jeffery Kraus
Wagner College

Paul Lermack
Bradley University

Norm Luttbeg
Texas A&M University

Tim Nokken
University of Houston

Mark Peterson
Washburn University

Rob Preuhs
The University of Denver

Beth Rosenson
University of Florida

Scot Schraufnagel
University of Central Florida

Mark Tiller
Houston Community College

David VanHeemst
Olivet Nazarene University

Joe Wert
Indiana University Southeast

Garry Young
George Washington University

Acknowledgments

This book has its origins in another age, when the Internet was first becoming functional and startup companies were popping up and failing everywhere as entrepreneurs tried to figure out how to work the new medium. Against this backdrop, I recall sitting in the restaurant of a generic conference hotel in Chicago—or maybe it was San Francisco—complaining to one of those entrepreneurs, Ed Laube, about the slow pace of negotiations with a Very Large Publisher over the rights to a concept book I was developing, which I described as a "book that can teach." I had known Ed for some time and I knew he was an original thinker who embraced unconventional approaches to conventional problems. We commiserated about the state of textbook publishing—the Very Large Publisher was holding up my concept project while it gobbled up a Not-So-Large Publisher and shuffled its editorial staff—and agreed that the conventional publishing model that produced carbon copies of bulky, oversized, uninteresting texts was in need of an overhaul.

It took two more conversations before we both realized that what Ed wanted to accomplish at his small start-up company meshed beautifully with what I wanted to do with my concept book. This sparked a collaboration with Ed that culminated in the original version of this book and continued through the first four editions. For everything he contributed—for his support, insight, and steadiness—Ed from the start made certain that this huge project would get done, and he did this without sacrificing creativity or compromising objectives. Today, Ed and I are partnered with Dan Luciano, who continues in the same tradition to develop this book to accommodate the growing capabilities of online publishing and social media. Along with the editorial talents of Vickie Putman, Dan has helped shape a volume that speaks to today's media-savvy readers. Countless others have made their mark on this book as it went through development and production, including, in previous editions, Tom Doran, Jean Privitt, and Mary Monner. Their contributions are embedded in the DNA of this edition. I have never experienced anything quite like the spirit and energy displayed by the people who contributed to this project, first at its original publisher, Atomic Dog, and now at Academic Media Solutions.

If not for my wife Adrienne, I may never have begun this odyssey by signing on to work with Atomic Dog. When I raised doubts about the wisdom of working with a publisher that had such an unconventional imprint, she looked at me the way someone who knows you better than you know yourself can look at you and said, essentially, if you don't write for them, who on earth will? I never looked back after that, and Adrienne never stopped supporting my efforts. This project is a labor of love on her part as much as mine, for the way she appreciated and nurtured my writing is a selfless expression of her love and a product of her unending support, without which I could not have taken on a manuscript of such massive scope.

If Adrienne was my sustenance for this project, my daughter Gabrielle was my inspiration. Every time I picked her up at kindergarten and watched her bubble over with excitement about what she had done in school that day, I redoubled my efforts to write a textbook that could tap into that innate love of learning that all too often dissipates with time. Back then, her youthful enthusiasm guided me to write a book that might inspire undergraduates. With the publication of the sixth edition, she is now an undergraduate herself and a contributor to this book as a research assistant. But my wish for her remains the same: that she and others can find a way to cherish or, if lost, rekindle the joy of exploration and knowledge that so easily gets buried in the daily grind of work and the pressure to get good grades. In this spirit, I dedicate this book to her.

Matthew R. Kerbel
Wayne, Pennsylvania

About the Author

Matthew R. Kerbel is professor and chair of the Department of Political Science at Villanova University outside Philadelphia, where he teaches and writes about the way the mass media influence American politics, especially national political campaigns and presidential governance.

He is the author, co-author, or editor of nine books, including *Next Generation Netroots: Realignment and the Rise of the Internet Left* and *Remote and Controlled: Media Politics in a Cynical Age*. His interest in political communication was sharpened by stints working in television news as a writer for the Public Broadcasting Service in New York City and in radio as an on-air news anchor in exceedingly small markets. He lives in Wayne, Pennsylvania, with his wife Adrienne and daughter Gabrielle.

Should We Care about Politics?

CHAPTER 1

Copyright: Deng/Shutterstock.com

Learning Objectives

When you have completed this chapter, you should be able to:

- Understand the difference between a direct and representative democracy.
- Distinguish between legitimacy and authority.
- Explain how legitimacy and authority are related to power.
- Identify political resources and why they are the tools of power.
- Define elitism and pluralism, and explain how each offers a different view of how resources are distributed in society.
- Differentiate equality of opportunity from equality of outcome.
- Relate political equality to equality of opportunity, and economic and social equality to equality of outcome.
- Define liberty, and explain the trade-offs between liberty and equality of outcome.
- Appreciate government as the arbiter in disputes between liberty and social responsibility.

1.1 Introduction

On November 8, 2016, Donald J. Trump was elected president of the United States.

The prospect of a President Trump was considered unbelievable when the businessman-turned-celebrity announced his candidacy in June 2015. Even as he rose to the top of a crowded field of Republican candidates in early 2016, few political professionals regarded Trump as a serious contender for his party's nomination. When he won the nomination, few thought that he had a chance of winning the general election.

Source: Joseph Sohm/Shutterstock.com.

Trump consistently trailed former Secretary of State Hillary Clinton in opinion polls, and his campaign had all the signs of a loser. His nominating convention failed to inspire the public. Survey data indicated he lost all three presidential debates.[1] He shook up his campaign leadership twice, inexplicably campaigned in states where the election was not competitive, and faced blistering allegations about his personal and professional behavior. On election night, the Clinton campaign rented a large convention hall suitable for a big celebration, whereas the Trump campaign gathered in a modest hotel ballroom. These disparate choices told the same story: both campaigns expected Trump to lose. The electorate, however, had other ideas.

When the votes were counted, Clinton ended up with a national plurality in excess of 2.8 million, or approximately 2.1 percent.[2] She won the popular vote by a larger margin than John F. Kennedy in 1960 and Richard Nixon in 1968. But in states that Democrats had won reliably for twenty-four years, Trump staged one of the greatest upsets in American political history. In Pennsylvania, Michigan, and Wisconsin, he mobilized white voters in rural and exurban counties in numbers few experts believed possible—just enough voters to give him slender victories in these states and more than enough votes in the Electoral College to claim the presidency.

Donald Trump is a pop-culture figure. He is a reality television star known for his real estate empire and a business mogul who crafted a public persona through careful branding. Unlike his predecessors, the presidency for him will be an entry-level job; he has never held an elected or military office. To his supporters, this is his appeal: at a time when so many Americans feel the country is off course, he is the outsider who promises to disrupt Washington. To his detractors, his lack of experience is a source of worry. After an election that was anything but normal, a Trump administration promises to be anything but typical.

Trump's election is the latest unexpected turn in a century filled with political turmoil and the second time in sixteen years when the popular vote runner-up was victorious. In 2000, Vice President Al Gore lost the presidency despite winning more votes than his opponent after the election went into a seven-week overtime period of ballot challenges that culminated in an unprecedented 5–4 Supreme Court decision effectively installing George W. Bush in the White House. No one had ever witnessed anything quite like it, and it was the first of a series of unprecedented events that would define politics in your lifetime.

Surprise terrorist attacks on the World Trade Center and the Pentagon on September 11, 2001, shocked the nation and thrust politics into the center of daily life. As anthrax-coated letters began appearing in the mail, Americans of all generations turned to elected leaders for reassurance and to government agencies for help. Such is the way of life in a crisis, when public decisions supersede private actions.

In the days following the attack, Americans experienced a wave of unity and national purpose, and political differences were briefly put aside. But the good feelings soon gave way to an era of partisan rancor, as America became involved in intractable wars in Afghanistan and Iraq. Initially backed by leaders of both major political parties and large majorities of Americans, support for these conflicts plummeted as they became bogged down by insurgencies and American casualties grew. Iraq, in particular, came to be re-

The twenty-first century has been filled with political surprises and turmoil, from a tied presidential election that was decided by the Supreme Court to the election of the first African American president to the unprecedented resistance that greeted his successor. Pictured: 2000 electoral vote loser Al Gore; Barack and Michelle Obama acknowledge their supporters. *Sources:* Left: Joseph Sohm/Shutterstock.com. Right: Everett Collection/Shutterstock.com

garded by many as an unnecessary war of choice justified by questionable claims about the security threat posed by the regime of Saddam Hussein.

Then came a deep recession and, in 2008, a financial crisis that rocked confidence in global markets and had some economists speculating about whether we were on the verge of a second Great Depression. Against this backdrop, promising to bridge partisan divisions and reshape America's direction, Barack Obama was elected the first African American president of the United States—a feat so remarkable that, until it happened, mainstream political commentators wondered whether it was possible despite polling evidence that suggested it was inevitable.

Although Obama's election defied history, his promise to bridge partisan differences fell short. Following a flurry of legislative activity during his first two years in office—including passage of a controversial law to extend health-care coverage to the uninsured—a reaction from the right by "Tea Party" patriots casting themselves in the mold of the original American revolutionaries resulted in Republicans regaining control of the House of Representatives in 2010, abruptly dashing the president's legislative plans and ushering in another round of angry partisan gridlock. Just when it appeared the Obama era would be short-lived, a reaction from the political left against the perceived excesses of the very wealthy took hold across the country in late 2011 as people took to the streets in solidarity with those who had built a permanent occupation in a park in New York's financial district. Although "Occupy Wall Street" had faded from the headlines by the following spring, the nation remained focused on economic inequality. This shift in the political narrative away from the anger generated by Obama's activist first two years, combined with a gradually improving economy, helped lift Obama to reelection in 2012, albeit with the continuation of divided government and partisan conflict.

Donald Trump was carried to victory in reaction to the events of the Obama years, when deepening inequality precluded many Americans from sharing the gains of a rebounding economy and when social progress for previously excluded groups produced a backlash that found voice in a candidate who promised to close the nation's borders to Muslims and deport millions of undocumented immigrants. Trump promised to hear the voices of those who feel that the economic changes of the young century have left them behind or who express anger and anxiety about America's growing multiculturalism. If he governs for these groups, then in fundamental ways, the Trump years promise a radical departure from the Obama years. But much more than a sea change in policy is likely to come out of a presidency born of the most disruptive campaign in memory, an election in which significant numbers of both candidates' supporters lived in fear of the outcome. Immediately following the election, 42% of Americans (and 72% of Clinton voters) said they were afraid of what was to come (whereas on the winning side, a comparable 40% described themselves as relieved).[3] This is not a typical reaction to an election and suggests that we are living through an unusually precarious moment.

Profound political, economic, and social change can be exhausting—or it can be energizing, depending on how we react. And our reactions can be critical to determining how political events will play out. Whether we pay a lot of attention to politics or ignore it completely, whether in times of comfort or times of distress, we live in a country where you can draw a straight line between your choice of whether or not to get involved and the kind of government we get. No one will make you vote if you don't want to, and no one will make you keep up with the news (well, your professor might, but you'll be back to having free choice over your news habits in a few months). You can make your own choices about what you know and whether or how much to get involved. Some combination of these individual decisions—and the choice to be apolitical is a decision—determines what happens in Washington, in your state capital, in your community, and to you.

So how much should you care about what happens in politics? How much does political participation mean to you personally? Wait—don't answer yet. Let's talk first about where you fit in—about the big and small ways being a citizen invites you to engage in the political process—before deciding whether it's worth your time and energy to give politics and government a second thought once you're done with this course. Let's use the quiz in Table 1.1 as a starting point.

1.2 Democracy and Everyday Life

Ever since grade school, we've had a pretty basic sense of what it means to live in a democracy. At the same time, we don't always know what democracy means in everyday life, except maybe for some of the obvious things like voting and making contributions to political candidates. These are the most direct and visible ways we interact with government and politics. Think, though, about some of the choices in the "Is it relevant?" quiz. We can also interact indirectly, passively, or without direct knowledge that we're in a political situation at all.

That's because a government as big and complex as ours has great reach in our lives—greater than we probably realize.

democracy: A government created by the people over whom it rules.

In any form, **democracy** entails a few basic things: participation by the people, the willing consent of the people to accept and live by the actions of government, and the recognition that we all have basic rights that government can't take away from us. These are the things Abraham Lincoln was talking about in the passage from the Gettysburg Address that mentions "government of the people, by the people, and for the people."

It's easy to imagine how these prerequisites for democracy might not always hold. We often choose not to participate—or may end up unknowingly participating without giving consent. At various times in our history, those who did not own property, people of color, women, and young people were denied the most basic political freedoms. Even today there are obstacles to voting that fall disproportionately on poor individuals and minorities (see Demystifying Government: When Laws Make It Hard to Vote).

1.3 Making Democracy Practical

L.O. Understand the difference between a direct and representative democracy.

Does this mean that the democratic ideals that our politicians like to praise at Memorial Day parades don't really work in America? Does it mean that they work, but unevenly? How much does government act poorly or inappropriately, simply because the principles it's based on don't fully translate to real-world conditions? No system is perfect, but which imperfections are you willing to live with, and which ones, if any, are intolerable? These are hard questions that don't invite a single answer. And they go to the heart of how we function as a people.

TABLE 1.1 Is It Relevant?

Here's a list of activities that may or may not constitute ways we can interact with the political process. Select the ones you believe have something to do with your relationship with government or politics.

1. Voting in a congressional election
2. Watching the *Daily Show* on Comedy Central
3. Joining AAA (American Automobile Association) for towing services
4. Trying to drive 10 miles over the speed limit to avoid getting a ticket
5. Making a $10 contribution to a candidate for mayor
6. Attending a private college or university
7. Camping out at Yosemite
8. Buying a Diet Coke
9. Buying a lottery ticket
10. Flushing the toilet

They're all "Yes" answers. Surprised? Here are the reasons why:

1. Easy question: voting is the most obvious way we participate in politics.
2. Political and social satire get us to think about what government is doing.
3. Even though it may not be why we join, organizations like AAA lobby elected officials over legislation.
4. Government officials write a lot of rules we live under, like speed limit laws, and enforce them with agents like police officers who determine whether 10 miles over the limit is bending the law too much.
5. Another easy one: money plays a big role in politics.
6. Whether it's adhering to national antidiscrimination policy on admission or hiring decisions, or administering federally subsidized student loans, even private schools find it hard to escape the influence of government.
7. National parks like Yosemite are preserved through government actions.
8. Almost every state imposes a sales tax on food items. If you live in Delaware or New Hampshire and you answered "no," go ahead and give yourself credit because they have no sales tax.
9. Lotteries are established and supported by state governments, and the proceeds are often used to pay for government programs.
10. You can't even find privacy from government actions here. Most places have a sewer system that wouldn't be there if not for the government.

Score Yourself: If you got 8–10 correct, you pay more attention than most people to politics and government. Odds are you know what C-SPAN is (and if you don't, go to www.cspan.org). If you got 5–7 correct, you have a pretty good feel for the role of government in our lives. If you got fewer than 5 correct—keep reading!

Democracy is both an imperfect system and a complex idea. In fact, the broad principles we're talking about can take on different forms depending on the circumstances—with different results. In the small towns of colonial New England, a form of **direct democracy** took hold that enabled everyone to have a personal say in what government did. On this small scale, it was possible for every citizen of a town to gather in a meeting place and directly influence the way the community governed itself. When you stop to consider the lines in the parking lot if a nation of 325,190,987 people[4] tried to do something like this, you realize why even when we were a much smaller country we decided to take a different course. Instead of direct democracy, we opted to choose people to represent our wishes in government decision making through the indirect mechanisms of **representative democracy**. This system—also called a republican system (you may have heard the United States referred to as a **republic** for this reason)—depends heavily on some familiar things, like holding free elections and keeping elected officials accountable to the voters. It's far more practical than direct democracy, but the trade-off is that it's also more complex.

1.4 Buying into Authority

For a democracy—or any political system—to function effectively, we have to buy into the basic principles it's based on. That's not always so automatic, especially in a large and diverse country like ours where we often disagree on what government should do and

direct democracy: Democracy without representation, where each eligible individual participates in decision making.

representative democracy: A form of democracy in which eligible individuals choose others to make decisions on their behalf.

republic: Any nation with provisions for the selection of representatives who make decisions on behalf of those who select them. James Madison said a republic was "a government in which the scheme of representation takes place," as compared to direct democracy.

L.O. Distinguish between legitimacy and authority.

When Laws Make It Hard to Vote

You probably won't face much of an argument if you claim that the only equitable way to represent everyone's voice is to make sure everyone has the same opportunity to vote. Voting isn't mandatory in America, but every eligible American is supposed to have unchallenged access to the ballot. As a practical matter, though, this isn't always the case. Some of us face obstacles that make voting difficult or even impossible and risk being **disenfranchised**—denied the right to cast a vote—because of hurdles that aren't in the way of other voters. In some instances, the government itself is the source of these roadblocks.

Voter ID laws, on the books in a number of states, are one possible source of disenfranchisement. If you pay attention to politics, you probably know that a debate has been ongoing about whether election outcomes are undermined by voter fraud, such as people voting multiple times or registering to vote in multiple locations. If the integrity of the vote is in doubt, then the simple solution is to require people to identify themselves at polling places. On the assumption that voter fraud is a problem, thirty-two states had some form of voter ID law in place during the 2016 election. Most states request voters to provide a form of identification, although nine require an ID, and seven of these require a photo ID, such as a driver's license.[T1]

Voter ID requirements sound like a simple way to protect the vote, but they run the risk of undermining it. That's because some groups are less likely than others to have the identification needed to vote. A 2014 report by the federal Government Accountability Office found that voter ID laws reduced turnout among young people and new voters,[T2] and other studies have found evidence of decreased turnout among Latino, African American, Asian American, and multiracial voters.[T3]

The politics of voter ID laws complicates things because support or opposition to the policy plays out along partisan lines. Individuals who are more likely to be disenfranchised by voter ID laws tend to be Democrats, and those promoting the laws tend to be Republicans. In close elections, even a small difference in turnout between Democrats and Republicans can be decisive, so the effects of ID laws can be profound. Some Republican officials have openly acknowledged this advantage. In 2012, the chair of the Florida Republican Party candidly admitted that voter ID laws were designed solely to reduce turnout among Democrats, a sentiment echoed in offhand comments by Republican officials in Pennsylvania and Wisconsin.[T4]

Complicating things further is the lack of support for the claims of widespread voter fraud used to justify the laws. Over a period of fourteen years, one investigator found only thirty-one cases of voter misrepresentation, the kind of fraud that voter ID could prevent. During this time, over 1 billion votes were cast in federal, state, and local elections.[T5] Although the evidence for widespread misrepresentation may not be there, people certainly believe voter fraud is a problem. The sentiment that voter fraud happens with great or some frequency was expressed by almost half the respondents to a *Washington Post*-ABC News poll taken before the 2016 election. Only 1 percent of respondents held the correct view that voter fraud almost never occurs.[T6] Beliefs like this could understandably lead people to support voter ID laws even if those laws do more to undermine our elections than does voter fraud.

---

disenfranchised: Losing or being denied the legal right to vote by intentional or unintentional means.

even on what society should look like. Some people want government to tax less, while others want it to spend more on social services; some people oppose the death penalty or legal abortion, while others feel differently. Some of these differences take on a moral dimension, where people hold views that they feel reflect the correct way to live or the way a just society should act. When feelings about these things become intense, people often don't want to give in. At the same time, governing ourselves in a democracy is all about finding room for compromise.

Against this backdrop of different values and objectives, there has to be some agreement on the rules of the game—on the way we're going to set up our democracy—or else the entire system could topple under the weight of our vast disagreements.

Let's say your candidate for president loses the election. What are you going to do about it? You may demonstrate against the winner, speak out against his actions, or work against him in the next election. Even before President Trump was inaugurated, opponents planned protests to coincide with his inauguration. But even if you think the winner is an incompetent swine, you're probably going to accept what he does as representing the official actions of the president of the United States.

authority: The right to act in an official capacity by virtue of holding an office like president or member of Congress.

That's because Americans generally respect the **authority** of a victorious candidate—his or her right to assume office and to carry out the responsibilities pertaining to that office. It's one of the rules of the game the vast majority of us accept, even if we some-times don't like it, and it makes democracy possible. There is nothing automatic about this response; many nations—even democratic ones—struggle to resolve contested claims to authority, sometimes to the point where a military coup results in the overthrow of a le-gitimately elected government.

Americans have a long history of avoiding violent conflicts over authority disputes. As a society, we've shown a preference for investing authority in officials we may not like on the understanding that there will be other elections that may produce outcomes more to our liking. The 2016 election was fraught with concerns by partisans on both sides that the winner would lead the country to ruin, and at times, the tensions this created spilled over into physical altercations at Trump campaign rallies, but Election Day transpired largely without incident. Hillary Clinton's supporters may have experienced shock and disap-pointment at the unexpected result, but they did not deny that an election had taken place and accepted that if the results could not be legally challenged, then Donald Trump would become president. During the summer of 2009, some demonstrators fearful that President Obama's call for health-care reform would lead to a government takeover of medical care stormed meetings with their congressional representatives and angrily confronted them, but they continued to protest within the system rather than attempt to overturn it. Similar-ly, maybe you don't like the way one of your professors exercises authority—perhaps you feel he or she grades arbitrarily—but you probably won't question the professor's right to assign course grades.

So, even a candidate elected by the slimmest margin assumes the jurisdiction to act with the authority of the office to which he was elected. More than half the electorate supported someone other than Donald Trump, as both he and Hillary Clinton finished with less than 50% of the vote in a field where minor candidates combined for several percentage points. But this is irrelevant to President Trump's claims to the authority of the presidency. By virtue of assuming the office, he gets access to the powers of the presiden-cy just as he would have if he had received majority support.

1.5 Inheriting Legitimacy

A grant of authority may automatically flow to the winner of an election, but it is up to the victor to determine how to exercise the authority of his or her office. In the case of a new president, prudence might call for considering protocol and tradition when deciding what actions to take and when to take them. Even incoming presidents who intend to move the country in a different direction than their predecessors generally try not to exercise au-thority in a disruptive way, although President Trump—who was elected on the promise to be disruptive—has not always exhibited such caution (see Demystifying Government: Trump, Authority, and Tradition).

The risk to an officeholder of pressing his advantages beyond customary limits is that it could diminish his **legitimacy**, the widespread acceptance of his actions. Diminished legitimacy, in turn, could make it harder for him to maneuver politically because of the resistance he would face from people who oppose him.

Legitimacy is a funny thing because, unlike authority, which is granted by virtue of holding an office, legitimacy is partly inherited and partly earned. One source of legit-imacy evolves over time and is rooted in the way we come to accept an office and by extension its occupant as being rightful and appropriate. The German sociologist Max Weber suggested this kind of legitimacy is rooted in tradition and law—that after hun-dreds of years, for instance, we have come to accept the presidential winner as the legit-imate occupant of that office for a period of four years, under a plan set up long ago in the Constitution. This is why most Americans who voted for someone else accept a new president who attains office through normal, legal, time-tested channels. Even his stron-gest opponents do not call for tanks in the streets.

The legitimacy an official inherits is usually on display at the start of a term of office through a "honeymoon" or grace period. This was the case with President Obama, who began his administration with the support of 70 percent of the country. But it was not the

legitimacy: Widespread public acceptance of the official standing of a political figure or institution.

Trump, Authority, and Tradition

Presidents are called upon to exercise their authority every day in response to a range of domestic and foreign policy concerns. That they *can* exercise authority is unquestioned—they have a right to do so by virtue of occupying the office. *How* they exercise their authority is a different matter. Certainly, the public will expect presidents not to exceed the limits of their office or to exercise authority arbitrarily or for personal gain. It is also assumed, but not stated, that presidents will exercise authority with caution. One way for presidents to assure that they do not overstep their boundaries is by acting in accordance with how their predecessors treated their authority during their time in office. Traditions and protocols developed over time in national and international affairs have guided past presidents and helped maintain continuity during presidential transitions.

But President Trump may be different from his predecessors on this score, as he comes from a non-political tradition and won the presidency on the express promise *not* to conduct business as usual. Shortly after his election, Trump engaged in a series of casual phone conversations with world leaders, including one with the president of Taiwan that was rebuked by China as a violation of long-standing American policy in the region (China does not recognize Taiwan as an independent nation, and no American leader had spoken with a Taiwanese leader since the United States recognized the People's Republic of China in 1979).[T7] That the incoming president had the authority to engage in the conversation was not in question. But that doesn't mean it was without ramifications for Sino-American relations. Actions generate reactions, and presidents acting within their authority but outside of long-established traditions can behave in ways that have unwanted or unexpected consequences.

Protesters push back against the election of Donald Trump. *Source:* Christopher Penler/Shutterstock.com.

case for President Trump, who was surrounded by unusually strong doubts about his legitimacy that prevented a significant upsurge of goodwill after his election. A divisive campaign resulting in a second-place finish in the popular vote created legitimacy issues for the new president as he assumed office against the backdrop of Facebook groups and Twitter hashtags proclaiming Donald Trump is #NotMyPresident.

Following a bitter campaign where he questioned the integrity of the electoral process and suggested it might be rigged against him, Trump remained a polarizing figure as he entered the White House and the least popular new president in the history of opinion polling. One month after his election, his favorable rating in the Gallup Poll was 42%, with 55% disapproving, a deficit of 13 points. This is far below levels of public support for Obama (68% approval), George W. Bush (59% approval), and Bill Clinton (58% approval) at comparable points in their transitions.[5]

Favorable Ratings of Recent Presidents-Elect

	Date	Favorable %	Unfavorable %
Donald Trump	Nov. 9–13, 2016	42	55
Barack Obama	Nov. 7–9, 2008	68	27
George W. Bush	Dec. 15–17, 2000	59	36
Bill Clinton	Nov. 10–11, 1992	58	35

Source: Jeffrey M. Jones, "Trump Favorability Up, but Trails Other Presidents-Elect," Gallup, November 17, 2016. http://www.gallup.com/poll/197576/trump-favorability-trails-presidents-elect.aspx?g_source=Politics&g_medium=newsfeed&g_campaign=tiles.

The discrepancy between Hillary Clinton's popular vote win and Donald Trump's comfortable electoral vote tally compounded the new president's legitimacy problems. We will learn in Chapter 7 that the Electoral College was designed by the Constitution's framers as a means to place the final decision for presidential selection in the hands of an elite. Most states award electoral votes as a unit to the candidate who wins the most popular votes, resulting in an electoral vote total that is in excess of the percentage of popular votes received. This usually serves to boost the winner's legitimacy by resoundingly ratifying his win. But when the winner of the electoral vote does not win the popular vote, the new president may experience a drag on his legitimacy as he operates under the shadow of having finished second.

This has happened four times in our history before 2016, typically producing a high degree of bitterness about the outcome. Three of these "minority" presidents served single terms: John Quincy Adams, selected by Congress in 1824 after finishing behind Andrew Jackson in a multiple-candidate contest where no one received a majority of electoral votes; Rutherford B. Hayes, who became president in the disputed election of 1876 by the vote of a divided congressional commission established to resolve a number of ballot irregularities; and Benjamin Harrison, who defeated Grover Cleveland in the Electoral College in 1888, only to lose to him in a rematch four years later. When it happened again in 2000, with George W. Bush defeating popular vote winner Al Gore, it took the terror attacks of September 11, 2001, and subsequent invasions of Iraq and Afghanistan to put to rest questions about the incumbent's legitimacy.

1.6 Earning Legitimacy

For our elected officials to act effectively—whether by addressing terrorist threats or trying to get Congress to approve a budget—we have to accept their actions as appropriate, even if we don't always approve of them. This means the president can ease or compound legitimacy issues through his words and actions. For President Trump, acknowledging the divisions responsible for a popular vote/electoral vote split and pursuing a restrained agenda free of controversial initiatives would be a time-tested way to expand popular support and build legitimacy. However, doing this would be at odds with his over-the-top public style and his promise to shake up Washington, even if it would be consistent with the pledge he made in his victory address to be president for all Americans.

Like Donald Trump, President Obama faced a high degree of resistance to his legitimacy, although not because of his actions. Those who questioned if he was rightfully born in the United States and doubted the validity of his birth certificate raised fundamental questions about his legitimacy to hold office in an effort to cast doubt on the legitimacy of his presidency. Other presidents experienced legitimacy crises because of their behavior. Bill Clinton's involvement with Monica Lewinsky and his subsequent impeachment diminished his legitimacy in the eyes of some. In the waning days of the Nixon administration, the president's legitimacy had been greatly diminished as a consequence of his role in the Watergate scandal.

Authority and legitimacy may seem like distant abstractions, but we deal with them almost every day. You're dealing with them in your classroom right now as you navigate your response to the way your professor has decided to structure this class. Before you enrolled, your professor chose to assign this text and made decisions about the work you would be required to do, the way grades would be calculated, how course material would be presented, whether you would have the opportunity to earn extra credit, how much emphasis to place on attendance and class participation, and a host of related items.

Other professors who teach this course probably would have made different choices because each professor has the authority to define the parameters of instruction—and you're left to contend with those choices. You may find that you like the professor's style of instruction and appreciate the course, and you may end up recommending it to your friends. Or you may take issue with anything from the reading load to how you're evaluated to the way lectures are delivered. In turn, you may find yourself acquiescing to things you dislike, or you may react by daydreaming during lectures, cutting classes, not reading the material fully, or engaging in any number of time-tested ways to rebel against academic authority figures. Regardless of your reaction, though, the chances are good that you will never question your professor's right to teach the course as he or she chooses. In other words, you accept your professor's authority to determine the contours of the course.

That is, unless your professor does something that you feel defies the boundaries of his or her authority. Let's look at a hypothetical example of this. Imagine that your professor randomly assigned everyone in your class to one of two groups and permitted everyone in the other group to skip this week's lectures, declaring that they would not be held accountable for the work they missed. You'd probably agree that your professor has the authority to determine if someone is entitled to an excused absence from class. To do so in an arbitrary manner, though, without explanation, feels wrong.

This capricious quality could well undermine your professor's legitimacy by making it seem as if he or she is acting unfairly. Randomly dismissing some classmates but not others is a heavy-handed thing to do, even if it's technically within your professor's authority to do it, which brings the legitimacy of the act into question. To be legitimate, you might expect everyone to be offered the option to miss the lectures or at least to be provided with a rationale for why some people will be exempt from attending.

When the legitimacy of authority figures is brought into question, it's natural to raise doubts about their right to act as they did, and your choice of how to respond may take on greater urgency than if you simply took issue with a professor's methods of evaluation or one of the many things a professor plainly has the authority to do. Do you accept it and move on, with the professor's legitimacy permanently diminished in your eyes? Do you take action by confronting your professor or by lodging a complaint with the dean? When you make your decision, how much do you take into account that you're dealing with someone who has some leverage over your future for the next few months—someone who will grade you at the end of the semester?

1.7 Power Surge

L.O. *Explain how legitimacy and authority are related to power.*

power: The ability to make others act in a way that they otherwise might not have done.

If you find yourself thinking you would probably not want to risk your grade in a confrontation with your professor, you would be giving up doing something you wanted to do in order to protect your GPA. In this case, you would be reacting to the **power** your professor has over you in your class. People have power when they can prevent you from doing something you want to do or make you do something you might not want to do. They can do it by coercing you through implied or overt threats or by influencing you with the promise of something you want or need. In the case of our fictional random dismissal from class, your behavior would be in response to a calculation about the likely cost of a confrontation with the professor. No words have to be spoken because the threat of a lower grade would be implied by the situation.

L.O. *Identify political resources and why they are the tools of power.*

In a raw, basic sense, power is about might rather than right. You could even say that, initially, the people who get to decide the right way of doing things—who determine how authority is constituted—are the ones who wield power most successfully. Power isn't simply the use of force, though. It's subtler than that. It's about convincing other people of mutually shared interests, or threatening them with the loss of something they want, or actually denying them something they want, or providing them with a favor, or any number of other things that might move individuals to act the way the person with power wants them to. In this regard, the person with power has tools in his or her arsenal—**resources** that may be used to change another person's behavior.

resources: Anything of value to others that can be used to sway another individual.

When the president says he'll veto an act of Congress in an effort to prevent its passage, he is exercising power over Congress, and the resource he's using is the threat of the veto. But the president can also exercise power by using personal charm or sharing the glow of his popularity—if he happens to have these resources at his disposal because he's charming or popular. Computer firms that make contributions to congressional candidates in an effort to influence their positions on high-tech matters exercise power with the use of money. Lawyers with expertise, lobbyists with information (see Demystifying Government: Information and Power in the Twenty-first Century), you with your ability to vote in elections—all have resources that are desired by others in the political process. Power is exercised when resources are used to achieve a desired outcome.

When you stop to think about it, we're involved in power relationships with other people all the time. Sometimes we are in the powerful position of being able to offer or

Information and Power in the Twenty-first Century

It's been widely said that knowledge is power. It's been just as widely said that we're living in the information age and that what we know defines our place in society. These may be overworked sayings, but they're overworked for a reason. The fact is that our world is so technical and so specialized that what we know really does go a long way toward determining how powerful we are. That's just another way of saying that information is one of the most important resources we'll encounter in our exploration of politics and government.

It shouldn't take too much thought to find places where information matters. Computers are obviously about information, and as we'll find out in a few weeks, the signature media of the twenty-first century, such as social media and twenty-four-hour cable television, play a huge role in how we understand political issues, how candidates get elected, and a host of other situations where power is at stake.

We'll also find information popping up (literally and figuratively) in less expected places. Members of Congress can't survive without it. Neither can bureaucrats. Next to money, it's the lifeblood of many interest groups. The president relies on all sorts of information about public preferences before making decisions that could affect his political career. So, when you think about power, think about information as one of the foremost tools of power.

---

withhold resources others want. Sometimes people have power over us because they control resources—such as grades—that matter to us. Any individual or group with resources can engage in a power relationship, and power relationships are among the most fundamental elements at every level of politics, from the White House to school boards. Quite often, maybe surprisingly, a mutually beneficial exchange of resources gets others to act in a way they might not have intended. In the American political system, the exercise of power is about mutual benefit a lot more than we might suspect.

When we start to think of power in terms of relationships, we're getting to the heart of what **politics** means. We all have things we want to accomplish and things we want to avoid. And we're always involved in relationships with other people. When you bring human desire and human relationships together, you have the essentials of a process that ultimately determines who gets what. When this process happens in a public sphere so that everyone in the country is potentially affected by what happens, we have politics of the sort that matters in government. Almost seventy years ago, a student of the process, Harold Lasswell, called politics "the study of who gets what, when and how."[6]

Some of us may be more powerful by virtue of having more resources (see Demystifying Government: Do I Have the Resources That Matter?); some of us may get heavily involved by virtue of our interest in what government does. But regardless of our level of power or interest in this process, we are all affected by it—even if you never had a single thought about politics before you registered for this course. That's because politics produces winners and losers on everything from whether we'll be sent to war to how much we'll have to pay in taxes to who gets to operate your favorite TV station to whether embryonic stem cells can be used for scientific research to whether you may legally drink beer. Think of something you encounter in your daily life, and the chances are that in some way it's influenced by politics.

politics: The process of determining who gets what, when, and how.

L.O. Define elitism and pluralism, and explain how each offers a different view of how resources are distributed in society.

1.7a Facts and Judgments

Before we go forward, let's determine how facts are distinguished from judgments. Throughout this course, we're going to be making observations based on analysis of information and observations based on our judgments or evaluations of circumstances. These are different kinds of observations. When we evaluate data or information, we make **empirical** or factual observations about the world around us. No value judgments are involved when we do this. When we say something like, "The president can use his veto power to prevent an act of Congress from becoming law," we're making an empirical observation based on our understanding of the president's powers under the Constitution.

empirical: Any statement based on the assessment of data or the analysis of information, without regard to value judgments.

Do I Have the Resources That Matter?

Everyone has resources, but you can argue—to borrow from George Orwell—that some resources are more equal than others. Some people believe that the resources that most influence political officials are concentrated in the hands of a few, giving this small group disproportionate power to determine political outcomes. Others point to the way Americans like to join groups and feel that the resources held by groups with broad memberships greatly influence the decisions that come out of the political process. Whether you believe the resources that move the political system are held by a few people or many people determines whether you believe political power is wielded by the few or the many.

You may know people who say there's no reason to vote because your vote really doesn't matter, since voting doesn't overrule the actions of powerful, unelected people with wealth, prestige, or access to sophisticated information who make decisions that affect our lives. People who think like this have a lot in common with people who say the political system is characterized by **elitism**, or the belief that government is in practice controlled by a small, centralized hierarchy of people with a wealth of resources at their disposal. Advocates of elitism believe that a stable, resource-rich, permanent elite drives political decisions in the United States, rendering the vast majority of Americans effectively powerless.

On the other hand, many Americans join groups like service organizations; mosques, churches, or synagogues; and other community groups—all sorts of organizations where we expend time (a resource) pursuing matters of interest to us. These groups operate in public, allowing us to voice our interests and concerns in a manner in which they'll be heard. As these groups compete with each other for public attention, it's possible that they shape the way government officials listen and respond. If you agree with this assessment, you're in line with those who say the political system is characterized by **pluralism**, or the belief that government in practice responds to the many (plural) voices expressed through group membership. One advocate of this position is political theorist Robert Dahl, who once wrote of the central role of "all the active and legitimate groups in the population," who "can make themselves heard at some crucial stage in the process of decision."

Obviously, pluralism and elitism present divergent and mutually exclusive ways of understanding who holds power, and sorting through the two approaches is not that simple because it's easy to see where each has merit. It may even be tempting to say that they both describe our political system, but you shouldn't lose sight of the fact that pluralism and elitism assume the system is structured in entirely different ways. Figure 1 (immediately below) illustrates the different ways elitists and pluralists describe the structure of the political system.

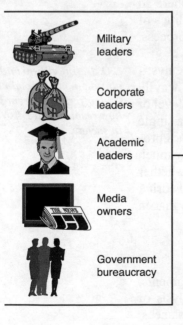

Military leaders

Corporate leaders

Academic leaders

Media owners

Government bureaucracy

The theory of *elitism* suggests that society is vertically or hierarchically organized, with those on top—corporate, military, academic, media, and bureaucratic leaders—controlling the resources to which government responds.

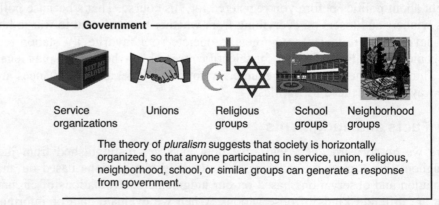

Government

Service organizations · Unions · Religious groups · School groups · Neighborhood groups

The theory of *pluralism* suggests that society is horizontally organized, so that anyone participating in service, union, religious, neighborhood, school, or similar groups can generate a response from government.

FIGURE 1 Elitism vs. Pluralism

But when we say something like, "It's a good thing for the president to veto an act of Congress," we're making a **normative** observation or value judgment that involves assessing a standard or making an evaluation. We could easily apply different norms or standards and argue that it's not a good thing for the president to issue a veto.

Let's do a quick check. Cover the right-hand column of Table 1.2 and see if you can figure out which of the statements in the left column are normative and which ones are empirical. If some of the statements appear to fit into both categories, it's because the line between a factual evaluation and a value judgment is not always as clean as you might think—which can be a source of misunderstanding in a political discussion if someone makes a value judgment that you take to be a statement of fact!

1.8 It's Not Fair!

Let's return one more time to the hypothetical example of your professor randomly dismissing part of your class. Whether you thought it was ridiculous that a professor would dismiss some of the class at random, or whether you thought it was wrong that someone else would get to be excused from work for what appeared to be no good reason, your reaction to the example was based on an assumption about how people should be treated. It must seem fairly obvious that if you're going to make an exception for someone, there had better be a good reason for it.

What may seem less obvious is that sentiment like this doesn't have to be automatic or universal. It's a value judgment, and we're going to find that people make all kinds of judgments about what seems right and fair—judgments that, in their scope and range, contribute to the complexity of political debate. If this sounds normative to you, then you were paying attention when you read Section 1.7a (and if this doesn't make sense, you might want to take a minute and review Table 1.2). Either way, before moving on, take a few minutes to look at Global Topics: Different Countries, Different Choices, where you'll learn an important distinction about normative judgments like this, which are based on values, and empirical observations based on fact.

Once you're clear about what constitutes a normative judgment, we can return to the matter at hand—fairness. Would it have been different if you and everyone else had been given the choice to stay or go? Perhaps that would seem less arbitrary and, accordingly, more acceptable. If it feels this way, you're tuned into a prominent way many Americans understand the notion of equality. It's called **equality of opportunity**, and it's about everyone having the same chance for advancement, free from obstacles that might limit some people from realizing their potential. This is essentially what Thomas Jefferson had in mind when he wrote in the Declaration of Independence that "all men are created equal," although his eighteenth-century perspective excluded women, African American slaves, and Native Americans from consideration. Over time, efforts have been made to

elitism: The theory that government responds to a small, stable, centralized hierarchy of corporate and academic leaders, military chiefs, people who own big media outlets, and members of a permanent government bureaucracy. People who subscribe to this position believe that the actions of regular citizens, like voting and joining groups, simply mask the real power exercised by elites.

pluralism: The theory that government responds to individuals through their membership in groups, assuring that government is responsive to a wide range of voices. People who subscribe to this position believe that the wide distribution of resources in society drives the decisions government officials make.

normative: Any statement that invokes a judgment or evaluation.

L.O. Differentiate equality of opportunity from equality of outcome.

equality of opportunity: One of several ways of understanding equality. This way values giving people comparable advantages for succeeding in life, regardless of the unequal outcomes that may result.

TABLE 1.2 Normative or Empirical?

The painting contains three shades of blue oil paint.	**Empirical:** the artist or art expert can factually distinguish paint shades.
The painting would be more dramatic if it contained nine shades of blue paint.	**Normative:** this is an opinion, not a statement of fact.
The painting would be more effective if it were displayed in a brighter light.	**Normative:** this is an opinion, not a statement of fact.
The United States may be classified as a republic rather than as a direct democracy because elected representatives make decisions on behalf of the public.	**Empirical:** this is based on facts as opposed to value judgments.
The United States is better suited to being a republic than a direct democracy because of the vast size of the country.	**Normative:** this is an opinion, not a statement of fact.

Different Countries, Different Choices

Why do Scandinavian countries provide far more extensive social services to their citizens than the United States? Why do their citizens agree to pay far more in taxes than most Americans would ever accept? Or, to put it another way, why do Scandinavians value equality of outcome so much more than Americans?

Political scientist John Kingdon has a theory. He speculates that the immigrants who settled the United States and influenced the development of its political system—groups we will discuss in detail in Chapter 4—were fundamentally different from the groups that determined the political rules in other nations. Starting with the original settlers from Great Britain who colonized North America, the United States has long attracted immigrants from other countries who were motivated by religious, economic, or political freedom to take up a new life in an unfamiliar place. These immigrants shared a mistrust of government, either because it stood in the way of worshiping as they pleased or posed an obstacle to self-betterment. They valued self-reliance and were risk-takers, willing to depart familiar surroundings to take a chance on a new life with unknown hazards. And, the choices they made based on the values they held were influential to the development of the United States. In contrast, Native Americans and African Americans who also populated North America and may have made different choices were denied political rights and therefore were shut out of decision making.

As a group, white immigrants to America were more likely than their counterparts who remained in Europe to believe that individuals can make better decisions for themselves than government can make on their behalf. They were more likely to regard government as a force that blocks individual initiative. In a land that lacked the rigid class structures prevalent in Europe, they were more likely to value opportunity and regard government as a potential obstacle to achieving it. These were not people who would look kindly on paying as much as Norwegians do in taxes (see Figure 15.3 for a comparison of tax revenues in the United States and Scandinavia), or would want government to provide the wide array of social services that Norwegians receive in exchange for their hefty tax payments.

The decisions made by these earliest of settlers structured the choices available to future generations and set the United States on a course that differs significantly from nations, like the countries of Scandinavia, where government is viewed as a source of lifelong social services and as a mechanism for correcting economic and social disparities.[T8]

---

incorporate groups Jefferson left out, but the basic idea that people are "created equal" still applies to where we start out in life, not where we end up—to the chances life affords us rather than to the results we achieve.

L.O. *Relate political equality to equality of opportunity, and economic and social equality to equality of outcome.*

political equality: Establishing political and legal rights on the basis of the individual, so that everyone has the same right to vote and is equal under the law. An alternative would be to grant political rights to elite individuals based on wealth or social standing.

equality of outcome: One of several ways of understanding equality. This way values leveling the social and economic inequalities among people, rather than attempting to give people comparable advantages for succeeding in life.

Valuing equality of opportunity is consistent with supporting government efforts to make the "starting line" more equal. That's why Americans usually support government programs to help underprivileged kids have access to higher education, because education is considered the gateway to opportunity. It's also why Americans generally value **political equality** and believe that everyone should have the same political and legal rights as everyone else. If all votes count the same and if everyone has the same rights in a court of law, the theory goes, then the playing field isn't tilted toward some groups and away from others. Everyone has the same opportunity to make the most of themselves without the political or legal system getting in the way. When you think about it this way, you can apply the language of equal opportunity to the issue we were discussing earlier about some groups of voters being disproportionately affected by voter ID laws.

To value opportunity is a choice, and it's a different choice than some other countries make. In places like Norway and Sweden, for instance, people place more emphasis than Americans do on **equality of outcome**, on diminishing economic and social disparities among people through government actions that try to level off differences between rich and poor by redistributing resources from top to bottom. If Americans as a group were as interested as Scandinavians in equality of outcome, then our government might provide cradle-to-grave health care, long stretches of paid maternity leave, and generous retirement benefits like they do in Norway and Sweden. Of course, we'd have to pay a lot more in taxes to support programs like these, and that would result in a lot of resources shifting around so that rich and poor alike would benefit equally. A country makes choices like that when it primarily values **economic equality** and **social equality**—both forms of equal outcomes—in which economic and social distinctions are minimized as a matter of policy and choice. When Occupy Wall Street protesters tried to draw attention to economic inequity in the United States in 2011, they were operating in a political context often unaccommodating to discussions of equality of outcome.

Just take a quick look at social and economic patterns in the United States, and you'll probably begin to realize how much equality of outcome takes a backseat to equality of opportunity. We're aware of the existence of social classes, of the great distance there is between the wealth of someone like software magnate Bill Gates and people who have to work for a living, to say nothing of people who can't find work at all or who live in poverty. But the size of the disparity might be even greater than you imagine. In 2013, the combined wealth of the six heirs to the Wal-Mart fortune—all members of the same family—equaled the combined wealth of *the bottom 40 percent of all Americans*.[7] The same disparity applies to income. Figure 1.1 shows that in 2014, the average annual income of the bottom 90 percent of American households was $33,000, whereas the top one-tenth of 1 percent averaged over $6,000,000. Figure 1.2 demonstrates how far this puts us from income equality. If we valued equality of income, the bars in this figure would be the same size. Instead, income disparities are large and have been growing for many years. Since 1979, American households in the top 1 percent have seen their income grow at four times the rate of that of the bottom one-fifth.[8] Nonetheless, although we'll find that some efforts are made to address these inequalities, as a matter of policy—and as a matter of choice—Americans tend to make the normative judgment that providing opportunity is generally preferred over equalizing outcomes.

Because we tend not to value equality of outcome, groups that have historically met with discrimination lag behind in their share of economic resources. The earning power of African Americans, Hispanics, and other minority groups falls below the earning power of whites—sometimes well below. For instance, according to the U.S. Census Bureau, in 2010, one in ten whites lived in poverty, compared with better than one in four African Americans and Hispanics.[9]

economic equality: A form of equality of outcome that values using government policy to minimize the economic disparities found in society.

social equality: A form of equality of outcome that values using government policy to minimize the social class distinctions found in society.

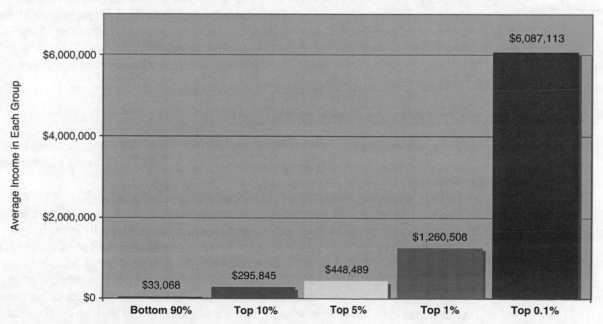

FIGURE 1.1 The Top Overshadows Everyone[T9]

The top 10 percent of the population dwarfs the bottom 90 percent in average income, and the top one-tenth of 1 percent overshadows everyone.

Source: Emmanuel Saez, "U.S. Income Inequality Persists amid Overall Growth in 2014," Washington Center for Equitable Growth, June 29, 2015. http://equitablegrowth.org/research-analysis/u-s-income-inequality-persists-amid-overall-growth-2014/.

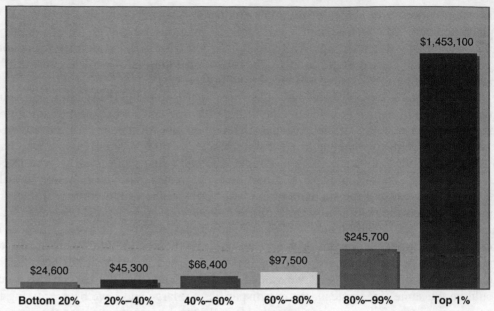

FIGURE 1.2 Income Inequality in America[T10]

If income were distributed equally across the population, then there would be no income classes. Each of the bars in this figure would be the same size. In reality, we're very far from this equal outcome in the United States.

Source: Congressional Budget Office, "The Distribution of Household Income and Federal Taxes, 2011." https://www.cbo.gov/sites/default/files/113th-congress-2013-2014/reports/49440-Distribution-of-Income-and-Taxes.pdf.

Similarly, the earning power of women is less than the earning power of men. In 2015, the median annual income for women was 80 percent of the median annual income for men, according to the Institute for Women's Policy Research, and had not improved since the start of the economic recession in 2008.[10] The federal government is quite aware of these disparities—there's even a Women's Bureau at the U.S. Department of Labor that in past administrations provided a checklist you could use if you were a working woman and you thought you were being unfairly compensated for your work.[11] Still the inequalities remain, as the statistics show, in violation of a primary assumption about how equality of opportunity should work.

1.9 Unequal and Different

The tendency in the United States to emphasize opportunity over outcomes raises important questions about the relationship between the condition of being unequal and simply being different.

Think of someone you know—perhaps a friend, significant other, or classmate. Start thinking of some of the outward differences between you. Maybe there are gender differences, or differences in eye, skin, or hair color. You could be different heights or weigh different amounts. The more you think about it, the longer the list of differences should become because so many factors contribute to the unique way we look.

You would no sooner want these physical differences to determine how others treat you than you would for your professor to randomly determine who gets to be excused from your next class. Neither, in a normative sense, is fair. Both undermine the central idea of equality of opportunity, which is that all people should be in a roughly comparable situation that permits them to express their talents and abilities.

In theory, we should have the same chance to succeed despite these many differences. Rather, our capabilities and interests should determine what we achieve. Some of us will become shopkeepers, while others become bookkeepers; there will be lawyers and landscapers and teachers and daycare providers and salespeople and waiters and chief operating officers. If we have an even shot at all these outcomes and reach the one we choose because of where we decide to direct our energy, you could say equality of opportunity is working well. There should be no relationship between the outcomes we choose and our surface differences, which have no bearing on our talents and interests.

The fact that we see disparities in outcome based on gender, racial, and ethnic characteristics is a sign that equality of opportunity does not work in practice the way it does in theory. Remember, the dilemma isn't that people end up in different places—that's to be expected—it's that people end up in different places for reasons that have no bearing on their talents or ability. It suggests that some groups face obstacles to achievement or are disadvantaged because they are different.

Consider how the economic inequalities we just discussed can disproportionately affect groups that have historically met with discrimination. If a rural Latino teenager who attends an underfunded public school scores lower on the SAT than a white suburban teenager who attends a well-funded public school, she likely will face a more limited set of college options. But is her score lower because she isn't as bright as her suburban counterpart, or is it because she didn't have access to resources such as academic counselors or SAT prep classes? Is it possible that if she had had the advantages of a wealthier school system, her SAT scores would have been higher, and she would have had the same educational opportunities as someone from an affluent suburb?

Other groups—such as African Americans facing hiring discrimination and women who are paid less money to do the same work as men—find the playing field tilted against them because of race and gender differences. At times in our history, these obstacles have become political issues, in that they became the focus of public debate. But the fact that the debate over advancing equality of opportunity needs to consider group differences says a lot about the tricky nature of how our society handles diversity and how diversity poses a challenge to the fundamental American idea that individuals should be provided opportunity free from arbitrary obstacles.

1.10 Equal and Free?

How much of your income would you be willing to pay in taxes if you received government benefits in return? Twenty percent? Thirty? Fifty? Eighty? At some point, it'll feel like a drag on your earning power and you'll resist. In America, we tend to reach that point pretty quickly. We see taxes—along with some of the government programs the taxes pay for—as an imposition on our ability to make choices for ourselves about what to do with our money. Many Americans prefer voluntary action to government mandates.

This resistance to being told what to do has deep roots in our country, which was born in a rebellion against a strong central government. It's about **liberty**, about having the freedom to act without others interfering with what we do, and it's at the center of so many of the choices we make when we govern ourselves. Americans place a premium on preserving liberty. It was the rationale for fighting two world wars and the cold war with the former Soviet Union, and it's the thing Americans most fear losing to terrorists. Hours after the World Trade Center was destroyed, President Bush told the nation, "Our way of life, our very freedom came under attack."[12]

In an absolute sense, if we had total liberty, there would be chaos because everyone would do whatever he or she wanted. So, we make choices. One of the biggest trade-offs we make is between liberty and equality. We've already seen how there are several ways to understand what it means for people to be equal. Certain types of equality are more compatible with having liberty, while others may only be attained by placing restrictions on liberty.

Let's see if you can identify the trade-offs between liberty and the five types of equality we've talked about: equality of opportunity, equality of outcome, political equality, social equality, and economic equality. Take a look at Figure 1.3 to gain a sense of the balancing act that has to be maintained in order to preserve both liberty and equality.

L.O. Define liberty, and explain the trade-offs between liberty and equality of outcome.

liberty: The ability to pursue your ends and objectives, tempered by socially defined boundaries and limited government impediments.

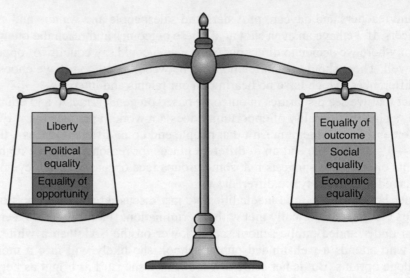

FIGURE 1.3 Balancing Liberty and Equality

1.11 Whose Choice?

We've been saying that society makes choices between liberty and equality, normative choices that involve judgments about what we value and what we're willing to trade off to achieve those values. And while this is the case, it's also very abstract. Who is society, after all, but you and me? We didn't write the rules of the game—other people for a complicated set of reasons made the choice to value liberty over equality of outcome long ago—but on an everyday basis, we're faced with lots of choices that we can affect.

We're constantly faced with situations where we are asked voluntarily by others or involuntarily by government to give up some of our liberty to act in order to benefit others. Sometimes, we do this with no problem; other times, it's inconvenient, and we gripe about it or perhaps take things into our own hands and resist the restrictions placed on us.

Take, for instance, the simple act of listening to music. Maybe you live in a dorm or apartment and have a roommate or two. If your roommate isn't around in the middle of the afternoon and you can't find your headphones, you can probably feel pretty good about blasting your music if you want to without having to think about how it affects anyone else. Your liberty to act is absolute. But if your roommate is there and you have different musical tastes, you've got a choice to make between doing what you want—exercising your liberty to listen to music—and imposing a restriction on your wishes in order to take your roommate's feelings into account. Some of us might factor our roommate's wishes heavily into our decision, whereas some of us might not consider them at all.

If our decision caused conflict, we may or may not be able to manage it privately and peacefully without a resident advisor in a dorm or the campus police intervening. If our decision entailed curtailing what we would have done if we were left alone, such as turning down the volume, we might grumble at our loss of liberty but accept it as a condition of having a roommate.

social responsibility: Concern for the protection of the rights of individuals in a community or society, at the expense of some degree of personal liberty.

On a larger scale, conflicts like this between personal liberty and the rights of others are the very things government tries to resolve every day. These conflicts involve trade-offs between liberty and **social responsibility**, or the concern for the rights of others in society. Because our actions constantly affect other people, and because it's human nature to want to pursue our desires and objectives despite this, we are continually asking government to resolve disputes between personal liberty and social responsibility. Essentially, we turn to government to draw the boundaries that determine where individual liberty stops and the needs of society start.

Obviously, not everyone will draw that line in the same place. Not everyone believes that government is always the appropriate arbiter, either, believing instead that individuals should work out their conflicts without government getting involved. A lot of political debate turns on these two facts.

Drinking laws are among those that you may have strong feelings about. As a society, as you're no doubt quite aware, we've decided that it is illegal to purchase or consume alcohol until you turn twenty-one. You probably know the rationale for this, which has to do with the desire to cut down on alcohol-related driving accidents. Essentially, if you are under twenty-one, your liberty (some would call it a right) to drink has been curtailed by government action in favor of the socially responsible position that it is more important to protect the lives of everyone on the roads. That's a choice that stems from a value judgment. You may agree with it or not. But it's the law.

So, what do you do about it? One option is to do nothing—to plan a big celebration on your twenty-first birthday and to do nothing before then. You might take this course of action if you agree with the law or even if you disagree with it but recognize its legitimacy. Another option is to violate the law and try not to get caught. You might do this if you disagree with the trade-offs behind the law, or if you feel drinking alcohol should be a matter of personal choice and not a matter for government to consider. There would be sanctions if you were caught because you would be breaking the law, not changing it. But that would be a consequence you would have to face.

The dual questions of when to give up liberty to protect the rights of others and whether government or private individuals should make the decision have a long history in our country's political debates. As you can probably see, when your liberty is at issue, feelings can get pretty intense. Also, as with all interesting political questions, there are winners and losers, which can make the result of what government does hard for some to swallow.

Compounding the issue is the great range of reactions we have to the tension between liberty and responsibility as well as other questions regularly placed before our political system. The great diversity of America that we were talking about before is both a strength and a complicating factor for our politics. It's a strength inasmuch as the expression of a wide range of viewpoints tends to enhance the decisions we make for ourselves, because a variety of voices coming from different vantage points can make for intelligent and gratifying solutions to problems, much like the blending of many ingredients can make food tastier and more satisfying.

At the same time, diverse perspectives can make it harder to reach a conclusion, complicating the process by which decisions are made. A system designed over two centuries ago to hear primarily the voices of white land-owning males has been required to expand to accommodate the views and desires of people with a wide range of backgrounds, perspectives, and beliefs. How it has managed to do this, and what it means in real terms for you and me, is part of the story you'll read in the next chapter.

1.12 So—Should I Care about Politics?

Whether you should personally care about politics is a normative judgment. It's also a personal matter that you'll probably approach differently from your friends. You'll make a judgment that depends in part on how much you think politics matters in your life. No one else can make that judgment for you.

We started out by asking whether it makes sense to care about the political system enough to engage in it because the question goes right to the heart of why you're in this course. If there's absolutely no reason to care about politics, then it's going to be a long semester or quarter! There are certainly reasons to get involved, but you may feel they don't apply to you. In the end, you may decide like many people that you're just not a political person. At that point, you'll be able to draw your conclusions with your eyes open to the evidence.

But before we can make an informed decision about whether and how much we should care about the public side of life, we should grow to understand it much better. There may already be things you know now that you didn't realize before you started reading this chapter, like how you're involved in power relationships at times when you're totally unaware of them—whether it's in the classroom with your professor or with a membership you may have in the American Automobile Association.

We've already seen that we can be involved in politics even if we don't care about it and even if we're not paying attention. We've talked about how the republican form of democracy we practice in this country reaches into things we may take for granted in our daily life, like having other people elected by us (or by our neighbors if we don't take part) make decisions on our behalf. We've talked about how we tend to act around authority figures, whether they're our professor or our president, and how their ability to wield resources can influence our lives—especially if we see their actions as legitimate.

We identified ways we're involved in power relationships with people every day—directly with people we work and live with, indirectly through the actions of political figures that make decisions on our behalf. We even looked at equity issues—matters of fairness—and how they balance the freedoms that a lot of us feel are extremely important in our lives. We talked about how liberty and equality are much more than abstractions. They're values, and as such, the extent to which we enjoy them, as well as the form they take, are the product of choices and trade-offs made by our society and shaped by government action. Whether we feel it's important to try to contribute to the political dialogue that shapes those trade-offs may be one part of the answer to our question about whether political involvement matters to us.

We've hinted at the idea that in order to make choices about who gets what, when, and how, we set up rules and then play by them (to a greater or lesser extent). In fact, a specific set of rules is in place that determines how politics works in this country. Some of the rules are legal in nature; a lot of them are set out in the Constitution. But even the Constitution has its roots in a struggle between different ways to define the political ground rules. As we understand those rules, we'll probably come to recognize a little more about where we come from as a nation, and how the resolution of some of our earliest political struggles shaped the political options before us today, some two centuries later. How can the struggles of people long gone be relevant to how we live our lives in the twenty-first century? Chapter 2 has some answers to that question.

Chapter Review

Understand the difference between a direct and representative democracy.

Even though people often speak of America as a democracy, it is best understood as a republic because we elect representatives to make decisions on our behalf. In that respect, our country is a representative democracy rather than a direct democracy, where people would make decisions on their own behalf. A representative democracy is far more practical for a nation as large as the United States, but it is also more complex and can be controversial inasmuch as there can be strong differences of opinion about what representatives should do in our name.

Distinguish between legitimacy and authority.

For a republic to function effectively, there has to be agreement on the principles on which it's based. Americans typically respect the authority of elected representatives to act in an official capacity by virtue of holding an office, and for the most part, grant legitimacy to elected officials even when they disagree with them. However, political figures can undermine their legitimacy through their actions because, unlike authority, legitimacy is partly earned.

Explain how legitimacy and authority are related to power.

Elected officials can use their authority and legitimacy to exercise power, although their ability to do so is hardly automatic. Power is about getting others to act the way you want them to, even if they prefer to act otherwise, in order to determine who gets what, when, and how.

Identify political resources and why they are the tools of power.

The tools of power are resources, which can encompass a wide range of things, such as a politician's personal charm, the information supplied to members of Congress by a lobbyist, or the promise of campaign money.

Define elitism and pluralism, and explain how each offers a different view of how resources are distributed in society.

Who gets to exercise power is an important—and open—question. Those who subscribe to the theory of elitism believe that a permanent, unelected elite of corporate and academic leaders, military chiefs, media operators, and bureaucrats holds the resources that matter in government decision making. Those who subscribe to the theory of pluralism believe that ordinary individuals can exercise power in a republic because the resources that matter to people in government are widely distributed in society.

Differentiate equality of opportunity from equality of outcome.

Many Americans value equality of opportunity, or trying to give people a fair start in life, knowing that people of different interests and abilities will end up in different places. Equality of opportunity comes at the expense of equality of outcome and produces economic and social disparities in the name of protecting individual initiative. Many value political equality on the assumption that ensuring everyone the same right to vote and equal rights under the law promotes equal opportunity.

Relate political equality to equality of opportunity, and economic and social equality to equality of outcome.

In truth, we have neither equality of opportunity nor equality of outcome in America, although we are much more likely to support government actions that promote the former. One place where equal opportunity breaks down is in the unequal economic and social outcomes of women and historically disadvantaged racial and ethnic groups be-cause unequal outcomes are supposed to be a product of our different talents, interests, and abilities, not our physical or ethnic differences.

Define liberty, and explain the trade-offs between liberty and equality of outcome.

There are also important trade-offs to be made between equality of opportunity and liberty, which is the ability to pursue our objectives, tempered by socially defined boundaries and limited government impediments. Liberty is consistent with equal opportunity because it supplies the freedom to make individual choices. Absolute liberty would generate chaos, so liberty is bounded by social responsibility, or the concern for the rights of others in society.

Appreciate government as the arbiter in disputes between liberty and social responsibility.

We turn to government to draw the boundaries that determine where individual liberty stops and the needs of society start. But we won't all draw that boundary in the same place, which can lead to political disputes over whether government should create boundaries or leave matters of social responsibility to individuals.

Key Terms

authority The right to act in an official capacity by virtue of holding an office like president or member of Congress. (p. 6)

democracy A government created by the people over whom it rules. (p. 4)

direct democracy Democracy without representation, where each eligible individual participates in decision making. (p. 5)

disenfranchised Losing or being denied the legal right to vote by intentional or unintentional means. (p. 6)

economic equality A form of equality of outcome that values using government policy to minimize the economic disparities found in society. (p. 15)

elitism The theory that government responds to a small, stable, centralized hierarchy of corporate and academic leaders, military chiefs, people who own big media outlets, and members of a permanent government bureaucracy. People who subscribe to this position believe the actions of regular citizens, like voting and joining groups, simply mask the real power exercised by elites. (p. 12)

empirical Any statement based on the assessment of data or the analysis of information, without regard to value judgments. (p. 11)

equality of opportunity One of several ways of understanding equality. This way values giving people comparable advantages for succeeding in life, regardless of the unequal outcomes that may result. (p. 13)

equality of outcome One of several ways of understanding equality. This way values leveling the social and economic inequities among people, rather than attempting to give people comparable advantages for succeeding in life. (p. 14)

legitimacy Widespread public acceptance of the official standing of a political figure or institution. (p. 7)

liberty The ability to pursue your ends and objectives, tempered by socially defined boundaries and limited government impediments. (p. 17)

normative Any statement that invokes a judgment or evaluation. Think of the word *norm*, which implies a standard for evaluating something. (p. 13)

pluralism The theory that government responds to individuals through their memberships in groups, assuring that government is responsive to a wide range of voices. People who subscribe to this position believe that the wide distribution of resources in society drives the decisions government officials make. (p. 12)

political equality Establishing political and legal rights on the basis of the individual, so that everyone has the same right to vote and is equal under the law. An alternative would be to grant political rights to elite individuals based on wealth or social standing. (p. 14)

politics The process of determining who gets what, when, and how. (p. 11)

power The ability to make others act in a way that they otherwise might not have done. (p. 10)

representative democracy A form of democracy in which eligible individuals choose others to make decisions on their behalf. (p. 5)

republic Any nation with provisions for the selection of representatives who make decisions on behalf of those who select them. James Madison said a republic was "a government in which the scheme of representation takes place," as compared to direct democracy. (p. 5)

resources Anything of value to others that can be used to sway another individual. (p. 10)

social equality A form of equality of outcome that values using government policy to minimize social class distinctions found in society. (p. 15)

social responsibility Concern for the protection of the rights of individuals in a community or society, at the expense of some degree of personal liberty. (p. 18)

Resources

You might be interested in examining some of what the following authors have said about the topics we've been discussing:

Dahl, Robert. *Preface to Democratic Theory*. Chicago: University of Chicago Press, 1956. Different approaches to American democratic theory, with special attention paid to majority and minority rule—things we're going to talk more about in Chapter 2.

Lasswell, Harold D. *Politics: Who Gets What, When, How*. New York: Meridian Books, 1958. A classic discussion of the meaning of power.

Machiavelli, Niccolò. *The Prince*. New York: Penguin Books, 1999. Written 500 years ago, it contains observations about power that still ring true.

You may also be interested in looking at these resource sites:

You can find a good starting place for information on the U.S. government and the people who work in it by going to http://www.usa.gov.

What was government like during its formative years? Frenchman Alexis de Tocqueville traveled America from one end to the other in search of true democracy, and you can find his observations at http://xroads.virginia.edu/~Hyper/detoc.

Notes

1 Jennifer Agiesta, "Hillary Clinton Wins Third Presidential Debate, According to CNN/ORC Poll," October 20, 2016. http://www.cnn.com/2016/10/19/politics/hillary-clinton-wins-third-presidential-debate-according-to-cnn-orc-poll/.

2 Cook Political Report. http://cookpolitical.com/story/10174.

3 Jim Norman, "Trump Victory Surprises Americans; Four in 10 Afraid," Gallup, November 11, 2016. http://www.gallup.com/poll/197375/trump-victory-surprises-americans-four-afraid.aspx?g_source=ELECTION_2016&g_medium=topic&g_campaign=tiles.

4 Population estimate as of December 25, 2016, from the U.S. Census Bureau's U.S. Population Clock, at http://www.census.gov/popclock/.

5 Jeffrey M. Jones, "Trump Favorability up, but Trails Other Presidents-Elect," Gallup, November 17, 2016. http://www.gallup.com/poll/197576/trump-favorability-trails-presidents-elect.aspx?g_source=Politics&g_medium=newsfeed&g_campaign=tiles.

6 Harold D. Lasswell, *Who Gets What, When, How* (New York: Meridian Books, 1958).

7 Presidential candidate Bernie Sanders frequently made this claim during the 2016 campaign. It originates with the work of economist Sylvia Allegretto of the Institute for Labor and Employment at the University of California–Berkeley. The media fact-checking organization Politifact rated the claim to be true. See Sean Gorman, "Bernie Sanders Says Walmart Heirs Are Wealthier than Bottom 40 Percent of Americans," Politifact Virginia, March 14, 2016. http://www.politifact.com/virginia/statements/2016/mar/14/bernie-s/bernie-sanders-says-walmart-heirs-are-wealthier-bo/.

8 IncomeInequality.org, at http://inequality.org/income-inequality/.

9 U.S. Census Bureau, *Statistical Abstract of the U.S., 2012* (Washington, D.C.: U.S. Census Bureau), p. 455.

10 Ariane Hegewisch and Asha DuMonthier, "The Gender Wage Gap: 2015; Annual Earnings Differences by Gender, Race and Ethnicity," Institute for Women's Policy Research, September 2016. http://www.iwpr.org/publications/pubs/the-gender-wage-gap-2015-annual-earnings-differences-by-gender-race-and-ethnicity.

11 You may access the Women's Bureau at the U.S. Department of Labor website, at http://www.dol.gov/wb/.

12 "Day of Infamy," *Time*, September 12, 2001.

Table, Figure, and Box Notes

T1 Jasmine C. Lee, "How States Moved toward Stricter Voter ID Laws." *New York Times*, November 3, 2016. http://www.nytimes.com/interactive/2016/11/03/us/elections/how-states-moved-toward-stricter-voter-id-laws.html.

T2 "Issues Related to State Voter Identification Laws," U.S. Government Accountability Office Report to Congressional Request-ers," September 2014. http://www.gao.gov/assets/670/665966.pdf.

T3 Zoltan L. Hajnal, "The Results on Voter ID Laws Are In—And It's Bad News for Ethnic and Racial Minorities," *Los Angeles Times*, September 8, 2016. http://www.latimes.com/opinion/op-ed/la-oe-hajnal-voter-id-research-20160908-snap-story.html.

T4 David Wright and Eugene Scott, "GOP Congressman: Voter ID Law Will Help Republican Presidential Candidate," CNN.com, April 6, 2016. http://www.cnn.com/2016/04/06/politics/glenn-grothman-voter-id-wisconsin-republican-2016/; James Bouie, "Republicans Admit Voter-ID Laws Are Aimed at Democratic Voters," *The Daily Beast*, August 28, 2013, http://www.thedailybeast.com/articles/2013/08/28/republicans-admit-voter-id-laws-are-aimed-at-democratic-voters.html; Kelly Cernetich, "Turzai: Voter ID Law Means Romney Can Win PA," *Politics PA*, June 25, 2012. http://www.politicspa.com/turzai-voter-id-law-means-romney-can-win-pa/37153/.

T5 Justin Levitt, "A Comprehensive Investigation of Voter Impersonation Finds 31 Credible Incidents out of One Billion Ballots Cast," *Washington Post*, August 6, 2014. https://www.washingtonpost.com/news/wonk/wp/2014/08/06/a-compre hensive-investigation-of-voter-impersonation-finds-31-cred ible-incidents-out-of-one-billion-ballots-cast/?utm_term=.183e9d430ad4.

T6 Emily Guskin and Scott Clement, "Poll: Nearly Half of Americans Say Voter Fraud Occurs Often," *Washington Post*, September 15, 2016. https://www.washingtonpost.com/news/the-fix/wp/2016/09/15/poll-nearly-half-of-americans-say-voter-fraud-occurs-often/?utm_term=.0e5a2ccb124b.

T7 Mark Landler and David E. Sanger, "Trump Speaks with Taiwan's Leader, an Affront to China," *New York Times*, December 2, 2016. http://www.nytimes.com/2016/12/02/us/politics/trump-speaks-with-taiwans-leader-a-possible-affront-to-china.html?_r=0.

T8 John W. Kingdon, *America the Unusual* (New York: Worth Publishers, 1999).

T9 Emmanuel Saez, "U.S. Income Inequality Persists amid Overall Growth in 2014," Washington Center for Equitable Growth, June 29, 2015.

T10 Congressional Budget Office, "The Distribution of Household Income and Federal Taxes," 2011.

The Constitution and Federalism: Setting the Ground Rules for Politics

Copyright: Painting by Howard Chandler Christy.

Learning Objectives

When you have completed this chapter, you should be able to:

- Address how actions taken by the British prior to the American Revolution were at odds with the colonial tradition of self-rule.

- State why postrevolutionary America first established a confederal system of government and why the Articles of Confederation were ineffectual.

- Identify the institutional safeguards to liberty contained in the Constitution.

- Describe the political battle over constitutional ratification between Federalists and Anti-Federalists, and explain the role of the Bill of Rights in winning support for ratification.

- Explain the concept of national supremacy.

- Discuss the tension between the federal and state governments in the period prior to the Civil War and how the concept of dual federalism was employed to avoid conflict.

- Understand how federalism evolved in the twentieth century and how it influences contemporary politics.

2.1 Introduction

Think back for a second to grade school. Try to remember what your classroom and playground felt like. For many, these places provided our first encounter with rules and structures in social situations. The restrictions generated by those rules may have been unpleasant. At the same time, it's not hard to imagine how chaotic things would have been without them.

This essentially describes the trade-off we face when we consider how to establish the ground rules for politics. Rules place limits on our liberty. But the total lack of rules is a recipe for chaos. A functional government rests somewhere between the extremes of no liberty and chaos—but precisely where is an open question that can cause some intense political disputes.

In the early days of the republic, political disputes over how to write the rules of the game were commonplace because there were different points of view about how deeply government should reach into everyday life. The differences were rooted in the experiences people had with government prior to and during the American Revolution. Some people were influenced by what felt to them like government repression under the British and were determined to avoid establishing a strong central government here. Others feared that if the central government were too weak, it would be impossible for the new nation to function. Out of this debate came America's first halting attempts at self-government.

The results weren't very pretty, at least initially. Many early decisions did not withstand the test of time, and there were ongoing, heated political debates as people on both sides of the strong government question jockeyed for political advantage. Because setting the rules is never a neutral exercise—some groups are inevitably favored at the expense of others—the question of how government should operate was a central issue that consumed American politics for years after the Revolution ended. It's a lively story with implications for how Americans live today because the rules that were settled on still favor some at the expense of others, more than 230 years after they were written. So, as we go back in time to revisit these events, we're really looking at the roots of how we make choices for ourselves in the twenty-first century.

2.2 Ground Rules for Revolution

L.O. Address how actions taken by the British prior to the American Revolution were at odds with the colonial tradition of self-rule.

The multiethnic, postindustrial America of the twenty-first century still operates under rules created by European male settlers in response to circumstances long forgotten by most of us. To understand what America is now we should understand what it was then— who settled this country, what they were looking for, how they were different from some of the people they left behind, and what they experienced in colonial America.

As we mentioned in Chapter 1, European settlers were risk takers, people willing to leave their homes and everything familiar in search of religious freedom or economic opportunity. If you imagine for a second what it would take for someone to cross a dangerous ocean in a small, precarious vessel on a journey of great uncertainty, you can probably get a sense of how those who came to America differed from those who decided not to make the trip. Notwithstanding the sense of community found in some of the religious groups that came here, there was certainly enough individualism to go around.

Risk-taking and self-reliance are consistent with the desire for government to do less so individuals can maintain more liberty and seek opportunities. From the start, America's white settlers were inclined to favor placing restrictions on government so they could preserve the freedom to go it alone—a freedom they found wanting in the Old World.

Their perspective mattered most to America's political development. In the eighteenth century, America's nonwhite settlers and natives were composed primarily of African American slaves and Native Americans, both of whom—to expand on a term from Chapter 1—were **disenfranchised** by Europeans by being kept out of the decision making that produced our constitutional and legal system.[1]

The inclination toward individualism exhibited by white settlers—which goes a long way toward explaining how the rules were written in America—was compounded by

disenfranchised: Losing or being denied the legal right to vote by intentional or unintentional means.

events in the decade leading up to the American Revolution, a time when many colonial settlers experienced British policy as heavy-handed and burdensome. Not surprisingly, a string of British legislative acts passed during this time were widely regarded as impositions on liberty. Table 2.1 illustrates some of the more salient actions.

The series of events depicted in the timeline, starting with the imposition of the Stamp Act and concluding with the First Continental Congress, represented a British crackdown on colonial life. True, the colonies had never been autonomous, but the vast ocean separating London and Boston effectively afforded the colonies a certain amount of self-rule. The King and Parliament were simply too far away and too preoccupied with other matters to maintain tight control on colonial life. So, for the better part of 150 years prior to the Boston Massacre, colonial settlers drafted constitutions to govern the colonies, created

TABLE 2.1 British Policy Prior to the American Revolution

Early 1760s: In the early 1760s, American colonists fought alongside the British in the French and Indian War. It was a long and expensive war, and the British turned to the colonies to help pay for the war through a series of Parliamentary acts.

1764: The American Revenue Act was passed in 1764. It was widely called the **Sugar Act** because of the tariff it placed on sugar, along with other goods. The Sugar Act was followed in short order by the **Quartering Act**, which forced colonists to shelter British troops, and the **Stamp Act**, which taxed everyday legal documents like marriage licenses and newspapers.

1765: The Stamp Act of 1765 created uproar in the colonies, leading some colonies to refuse to import British goods and to the outcry, "no taxation without representation." The protest led to the repeal of the Stamp Act, but in 1767 Parliament imposed a new round of taxes on goods imported from Great Britain, which led to a new boycott and growing tensions.

1770: The British sent troops to Boston to maintain order, but their presence inflamed tensions. On March 5, 1770, tensions erupted into a skirmish; shots were fired and five colonists were killed in what history remembers as the **Boston Massacre**.

The Boston Massacre[T1]

1773: When Great Britain imposed the Tea Act of 1773, giving the East India Tea Company a monopoly over the tea trade in North America, tensions rose again. In the protest known as the **Boston Tea Party**, a group of colonists masquerading as Native Americans boarded ships loaded with tea and dumped the contents into Boston Harbor.

The Boston Tea Party[T2]

1773: Parliament moved swiftly and severely in response to the Boston Tea Party, initiating what became known as the **Coercive Acts** (in the colonies, the Intolerable Acts). Loading and unloading ships in Boston Harbor was prohibited and the Quartering Act was revitalized.

1774: In response, representatives from most of the colonies gathered in 1774 at the **First Continental Congress** to protest the action, voting to boycott British goods. The Continental Congress lacked **authority**, but it represented a major step forward in forging among the colonists a sense of collective purpose and the ability for collective action.

The Continental Congress[T3]

Sugar Act: The first in a string of taxes levied by Great Britain on the American colonies. Formally called the American Revenue Act of 1764, it taxed a number of colonial imports, including sugar.

Quartering Act: An act of the British Parliament requiring colonists to house British troops; first imposed in 1765 and then again in 1774 as part of the Coercive Acts.

Stamp Act: A particularly vexing tax levied by the British on scores of legal documents, which led to a colonial boycott of British goods.

Boston Massacre: A precursor to the war that was still five years away, it was the first mortal conflict between colonists and British troops in Boston and resulted in the deaths of five colonists in 1770.

Boston Tea Party: A protest against the Tea Act of 1773 in which fifty colonists dressed as Native Americans boarded British trade ships loaded with tea and threw the contents into the water.

Coercive Acts: Called the Intolerable Acts in the colonies, the Coercive Acts represented the British attempt to clamp down on the colonies following the Boston Tea Party.

First Continental Congress: A gathering of representatives from twelve of the thirteen colonies in Philadelphia in 1774 to protest the Coercive Acts and chart a unified colonial response.

authority: The right to act in an official capacity by virtue of holding an office like president or member of Congress.

representative assemblies with the authority to draft laws, and held free elections. They had to share this authority with royal governors, but they had a taste of self-government, and they liked it. Against this backdrop, and considering their personal inclination toward preserving liberty, it's no wonder why so many of them found the Coercive Acts to be intolerable.

Within months of the First Continental Congress, the tense, cold standoff turned violent. Clashes between colonists and British soldiers at Lexington and Concord, Massachusetts, on April 19, 1775, marked the start of the American Revolution. One month later, the **Second Continental Congress** convened in Philadelphia to coordinate the war effort. One year later, it would declare American independence from Great Britain.

From the outset, the American Revolution differed from other revolutions in the sense that the objective was not to overthrow the existing order and replace it with something new. There was no talk of overthrowing the British monarchy, and the government of Great Britain continued to exist outside the former colonies after conceding defeat to the Americans. Instead, the American Revolution was more of a separation—perhaps the way some of us as teenagers move away from our parents and establish autonomy when we begin to see ourselves as adults and question parental authority. To Americans supporting the war, the purpose was to rebel against the existing order. The British crackdown in America had led some to begin to question British authority, and even though the idea of going it alone was far from universally popular in the colonies (many opposed revolution and hoped to reconcile their differences with the British), by 1775, it had become a viable option.[2]

2.3 Ground Rules for Independence

What gave Americans the right to separate from Great Britain? Law and tradition bound them to the British, who saw the Revolution as a profound act of treason. Supporters of the Revolution, though, believed the British had forfeited their right to govern the colonies when they began to deny colonists their liberty. In this idea, they had support from theorists who had written in the abstract about why governments form and under what circumstances they may be overturned.

The founders read widely and were influenced by theorists dating back to antiquity. You could turn to the theoretical influences of three Enlightenment thinkers in particular to find the origins of one of the key philosophical justifications for the Revolutionary War. The seventeenth-century British philosophers Thomas Hobbes and John Locke and the eighteenth-century Franco-Swiss philosopher Jean-Jacques Rousseau differed in their view of human nature and their prescriptions for how government should operate, but they spoke of government as being the product of a **social contract** among individuals.

Thomas Hobbes wrote that without governments, people existed in what he called the **state of nature**—a ruthless place where people can easily deny others their liberty and their lives by simple force. Hobbes had a negative view of human nature and painted a brutal picture of what life would be like if we permitted ourselves to exist in the state of nature. In a passage from his book *Leviathan*, Hobbes claims that life in the state of nature is "solitary, poor, nasty, brutish, and short."[3]

The only way to protect people from this ugly situation is for them to give up liberty in exchange for the security of a strong government (a "leviathan," representing government to Hobbes, is a big, powerful monster), essentially to form a social contract with others in which liberty is the price of protection. Hobbes believed that people had to give up most of their liberty—far more than colonial settlers would have been happy with—in exchange for the right to live, which is why he was a supporter of a strong and forceful monarchy.

Thomas Hobbes (1588-1679)
The seventeenth-century British social thinker and author of *Leviathan* who believed that people need to trade off liberty for a strong government that can protect their fundamental right to live.

Second Continental Congress: A gathering of representatives from the colonies in Philadelphia in 1775, necessitated by the need to coordinate planning during the Revolutionary War, that functioned as the first central government in colonial America.

social contract: The arrangement in which people agree to give up some of their liberty to establish a government that will protect basic rights that are threatened in the state of nature.

state of nature: The condition of total liberty in which people are free to act on their impulses, but where individual rights are afforded no protection.

John Locke (1632-1704)
A seventeenth-century British social contract theorist whose ideas about government getting its authority from the consent of the governed in order to protect fundamental human rights greatly influenced the leaders of the American Revolution.

Although he had a somewhat more upbeat view of mankind, John Locke also advocated for a social contract as the basis of civil society. Locke believed that in the state of nature people possess **natural rights**—to life, liberty, and property—which they enter into a social contract to protect. Since the purpose of government in this contract is to do more than provide physical safety, the reins of government shouldn't be as tight as in Hobbes' vision. To Locke, liberty is something for government to protect as much as it is what you give up to have government protect you. In other words, government needs to be strong enough to protect individual rights but not so strong that it becomes a threat to liberty, so there have to be limits on government that monarchy cannot provide.

Locke went much further than Hobbes, asserting that people form governments and people can dissolve them, through revolution if necessary, should they become too strong and violate individual rights. This was fairly radical thinking in an era of monarchy, when you consider that monarchs claimed their authority came from God. Locke rejected this "divine right of kings," arguing that governments receive their authority from the consent of the governed.

Locke's fingerprints are all over the **Declaration of Independence**, whose author, Thomas Jefferson, was heavily influenced by Locke. The idea that everyone is equal in the state of nature; that people are born with natural rights; that governments are formed to protect these rights; that individuals and not deities form governments; that governments must derive their authority from the people they govern; that people have the right to overthrow a government that fails to protect individual liberty—it's all there, and it all has its roots in Locke's writing.

Perhaps because of what was at stake in the Declaration of Independence, Jefferson can be forgiven for not footnoting Locke. And educated people in 1776 understood where Jefferson's ideas came from. The full text of the Declaration of Independence can be found in Appendix A.

For much of this country's history, Americans have subscribed to Locke's generally positive view of humanity. Having two great oceans to provide shelter from the conflicts of the rest of the world surely contributed to American optimism. But, at times of great stress, it may be easier to subscribe to Hobbes' view of the state of nature than to Locke's, and to ask government to step in and provide greater fundamental protection. There are indications that some people reacted this way in the aftermath of the September 11, 2001, terror attacks on the United States, turning to government for protection against a world that appeared to become dramatically more dangerous overnight. See Demystifying Government: Hobbes, Locke, and Terror.

For his part, Jean-Jacques Rousseau held a view of individuals that more resembled Locke's positive vision than Hobbes' dismal one. Rousseau was concerned with the relationship between rulers and those they rule, writing in *The Social Contract* that people submit to the rule of others only because their rights will be better protected by government than if left to the random brutality of the state of nature. But, Rousseau insisted that rulers are bound to protect everyone's rights, not simply the rights of the wealthy and powerful. In his view, rulers who failed to provide these fundamental protections have broken the social contract they have with the ruled.[4] This contractual view of rights is reflected in the list of offenses alleged against King George in the Declaration of Independence.

As with Hobbes and Locke, the theory of government espoused by Rosseau contributed to the rationale for independence and provided the theoretical underpinning for the republic that would arise from it. In this important respect, the ideas guiding the revolution and the republic that grew from it were not original. But the idea of founding a nation on them was a bold and ambitious experiment. The founders' work was radical because they dared to put theoretical abstractions into practice.

natural rights: Inalienable rights inherent to every individual that cannot be taken away by individuals or government, and that government should be designed to protect.

Declaration of Independence: The document drafted by Thomas Jefferson and approved by the Continental Congress in July 1776, stating the reasons for the Revolutionary War and declaring a formal break with Great Britain.

Jean-Jacques Rousseau (1712-1778)
An eighteenth-century Franco-Swiss philosopher whose political ideas about the contract between rulers and the public influenced the leaders of the American Revolution and are reflected in the Declaration of Independence.

Hobbes, Locke, and Terror

For two decades, political debate in the United States revolved around the question of whether government had grown so large as to be intrusive. After a period in the 1950s, 1960s, and 1970s in which the national government addressed problems of segregation, poverty, crime, women's rights, and a host of other social and economic dilemmas, debate turned to whether in the course of addressing these issues government had grown so strong as to infringe on personal liberties. Through the 1980s, the Reagan and George H. W. Bush administrations advocated the position that government is a problem more than a solution to problems. In the 1990s, Congress picked up this line of reasoning. You could draw a straight line from Jefferson and Locke to the contemporary argument that big government is a threat to personal liberty.

Then terrorists destroyed the World Trade Center and heavily damaged the Pentagon. Anthrax began showing up in the mail. American troops were dispatched to Afghanistan, and America shifted to a war footing. People stopped talking about government as an intrusion. The state of nature suddenly resembled Hobbes' dark views more than Locke's hopeful ones. People looked to government for aid and assistance in numbers not seen for decades. In keeping with Hobbes' prescription that a strong government is needed to keep us safe and alive, many Americans even began saying they would be willing to give up liberty in return for protection.

An article that ran in *The Philadelphia Inquirer* toward the end of 2001 discussed how "a new view of freedom" had settled into the national psyche, a view far more restrictive than what had been the norm for generations.[T4] It told of how trust in government shot up after the attacks because Americans had become "newly appreciative of safety" and therefore "willing to give [government] unusually broad powers to fight terrorists." Americans expressed willingness to "put up with more government" and give the president "a little more latitude to do what he thinks is right."

Immediately after the attacks, three in four Americans had reservations about immigration and wanted to make it harder for people of other nations to enter the United States, essentially limiting the free passage to America that has been one of the hallmarks of American liberty. Unease about foreigners settled into this nation of immigrants, with the call going out to government to do what was necessary to keep America safe.

Large numbers of people supported a Bush administration directive to try alleged terrorists in secret military tribunals, out of view of the public and apart from the normal judicial system—essentially denying these suspects the ordinary rights allowed others charged with crimes. One individual quoted in the article acknowledged, "That is kind of scary, taking away one of the freedoms Americans believe in." But, he added, "We are at war. I'm more tolerant of that at the moment."

By late 2005, the question of whether government had grown too intrusive seemed to have come full circle. That's when it became known that President Bush—who ran for office as a limited government conservative—had authorized eavesdropping on domestic telephone and e-mail communications without a court order. In other words, the government was monitoring the private conversations and e-mail messages of American citizens without their knowledge and without a warrant.[T5] Bush acknowledged the program, and defiantly said it would continue, justifying his actions on national security grounds. Opponents said it amounted to an illegal and possibly unconstitutional infringement on personal rights. Either way, it was clear that a conservative administration was directing the government to engage in the most intrusive of activities.

In the years since the Bush administration, many Americans continue to fear for their safety and worry about external threats. One of the messages of Donald Trump's presidential campaign was that individuals who are non-white and non-Christian, whether Muslims coming to the United States from abroad or Mexicans living in the United States without documentation, pose potential threats that require a strong government to repel. Those individuals who felt targeted by President Trump's rhetoric feared his administration would overstep traditional boundaries of restraint and target their personal liberties.

How tolerant should Americans be of the actions of the federal government in matters of personal security? How tolerant are you? Is a strong government necessary when we're faced with potentially devastating threats, and if so, what types of actions should the government take in order to keep us safe and secure? Is it appropriate to restrict immigration? Ban Muslims from entering the United States? Limit the rights of suspected terrorists? Engage in secret domestic surveillance without the consent of the courts? If you support a strong government for the purposes of protection from terrorist threats, do you also support government activity for the purpose of protection from other naturally arising social ills and injustices, like poverty and crime, or is physical protection different from these things? Your answer to these questions likely rests with whether you accept Hobbes' or Locke's view of human nature and their remedies for maintaining security.

2.4 Self-Governance—First Attempt

Almost immediately after declaring independence from Great Britain, the Continental Congress went to work to create a framework for collective government. It was a difficult job because the practical need for the new United States to act in concert was balanced by strong concerns about the individual states giving up too much authority to a distant national government that might not be responsive to local concerns. Fears were widespread that a strong national government would be an obstacle to liberty, especially in light of colonial experiences with British rule over the past generation. Furthermore, even though the Declaration of Independence announced a new United States of America, most citizens of this new country identified with their respective state rather than with the collection of states. People would refer to themselves as New Yorkers, Virginians, or Rhode Islanders—not as Americans. Why, then, would they accept a strong government of the United States?

L.O. State why post-revolutionary America first established a confederal system of government and why the Articles of Confederation were ineffectual.

At the same time, members of the Continental Congress knew that without a central government, they would not be able to maintain an army, negotiate treaties with other nations, or coordinate commerce among the states. The rules of the game would have to be written carefully.

When a framework did materialize in the form of the **Articles of Confederation,** which were adopted by Congress in 1777 and ratified by all thirteen states in 1781, the results were problematic. The Articles addressed the fear of a strong centralized government by creating a loose federation or "league of friendship" among the states in which "each state retains its sovereignty, freedom, and independence, and every power, jurisdiction, and right, which is not by this Confederation expressly delegated to the United States." In other words, the laws and actions of the individual states were supreme to the actions of the United States. The national government took its cues from the thirteen state governments.[5]

Articles of Confederation: The first constitution of the United States, which created a loosely functioning national government to which the individual states were supreme. It addressed concerns about a strong national government undermining individual liberty, but it created a national government that was unable to regulate commerce or conduct foreign policy and was abandoned in favor of the United States Constitution just eight years after it was ratified.

The Articles further protected the states by requiring that national action of any kind would have to win the approval of nine states. The national government was composed of a Congress in which each state had one vote, but any five states could keep the national government from acting. Because of concerns about centralized authority, there was no independent chief executive like the modern-day president. There was no national court system for resolving disputes. The Articles were inflexible: All thirteen states had to agree to amend the Articles; one lone dissenter could prevent change from happening.

These features conspired to create a national government that was weak and ineffective. The Articles of Confederation created a national government that would not undermine individual liberty, but it also created a national government that could barely act. It couldn't keep states from putting up barriers to trade with other states or resolve trade wars between them. It couldn't raise taxes. It could pass laws, but it couldn't make the states follow them. It was severely limited in its ability to conduct foreign affairs. Because changes had to be approved unanimously, it couldn't do much to fix these weaknesses, especially when groups in some states benefited from the rules as they were written in the Articles.

Small farmers and debtors, of whom there were many in the years following the Revolutionary War, appreciated the fact that the Articles kept politics close to home and receptive to local needs and were among the Articles' strongest supporters. But the Industrial Revolution was about to hit the new country with the force of a tidal wave, and anyone involved in banking or the trade or manufacture of merchandise was frustrated by the inability of the Articles to regulate commerce among the states and maintain stable international ties. From the standpoint of conducting normal relations with other countries, the Articles of Confederation was a disaster.

If that wasn't enough, hard economic times fell upon the new country following the Revolutionary War. Things were particularly bad in Massachusetts, where heavy taxes and an economic depression placed a disproportionate burden on small farmers, many of whom lost their land and landed in debtor's prison. Suffering farmers in western

Shays' Rebellion: A rebellion by debtor farmers in western Massachusetts, led by Revolutionary War Captain Daniel Shays, against Boston creditors. It began in 1786 and lasted half a year, threatening the economic interests of the business elite and contributing to the demise of the Articles of Confederation.

confederal system: An arrangement for establishing a government out of a set of component states, in which the national government is the creation of the states and subservient to them. The Articles of Confederation established a system like this in the United States. In today's world, the United Nations may be the most prominent example of a confederation.

Massachusetts blamed their plight on Boston merchants, who pressed for taxes so the state could repay the money it had borrowed from them during the war. In a case of borrowers rising up against unfair conditions they attributed to lenders, a group of debtor farmers took up arms to prevent Massachusetts courts from convening and sentencing debtors.

The insurrection was led by Revolutionary War officer Daniel Shays, and **Shays' Rebellion** started in August 1786 and lasted half a year until the Massachusetts militia put an end to it. It was typical of the type of rebellion that characterized this unsettled time. The national Congress had been powerless to deal with either the complaints or the actions of the debtors, and business groups who had previously been frustrated with the Articles of Confederation now worried that their fundamental interests were threatened.

It was 1787, and the ruling elite had seen enough. It was time to change the ground rules.

2.5 Self-Governance—Second Attempt

The rules of the game under the Articles of Confederation turned out to be bulky and unworkable. They were also unusual rules. Most nations do not establish a **confederal system** (see Figure 2.1). They are not a confederation of essentially independent states that band together to create a weak central union. Of course, there were special circumstances involved in trying to bring together thirteen largely autonomous colonies into a single nation, so the type of structure most common in the world—the **unitary system**—was never really an option. And when the framers of the government tried a second time,

 A *unitary system* is like a jigsaw puzzle made out of only one piece. Unitary contains the word *unit,* meaning one or singular. In the United States, each state is a unitary system with respect to its counties, cities, and townships. There are county governments, city governments, and township governments, but they're all chartered by the state and completely dependent on the state for their existence. Only the state can create a county or change county lines. Most nations of the world operate as unitary systems, where the national government creates all the local governments.

 A *confederal system* is like a jigsaw puzzle made up of many noninterlocking parts. The whole picture is the sum total of the pieces, but it isn't strong and can easily fall apart. In a confederation, the national government has only those powers granted to it by the states, like in the Articles of Confederation. If a small number of states disagree with what the national government wants to do, the national government is restricted from acting.

A *federal system* is like a jigsaw puzzle with interlocking parts. Each state can still act on its own, but it is bound to the others through a national government. Each piece is still important in its own right, and in a federal system, a lot of power is reserved to the states. But the federal government has a lot of power too and functions as its own entity, not simply as a creation of the states. There are powers denied to the states that only the federal government has, like negotiating treaties with other countries. But at the same time, the federal government cannot interfere with the internal actions of any state, eliminate a state, or redraw state boundaries like in a unitary system.

FIGURE 2.1 Unitary, Confederal, and Federal Systems

they again opted for an atypical structure in a **federal system**, still trying to find a way to balance the needs of the states with the need to function as a nation. This time, after a tough political debate, they fared much better. Figure 2.1 explores the differences among unitary, confederal, and federal systems.

Although by the spring of 1787 there was widespread sentiment that the Articles of Confederation had to be revised, there were different opinions about what that meant. Those benefiting from the rules of the game would fight hard to maintain their advantages. Others wanted a stronger and more functional central government that would dramatically change the rules. Most everyone was fearful of creating a system that could suppress liberty in the effort to make government more effective. Even if life under the Articles was chaotic, memory of British rule tempered the temptation to overreach in the other direction.

So, a delicate political challenge confronted the fifty-five men who gathered in Philadelphia in May 1787, ostensibly to revise the Articles. In what became known as the **Constitutional Convention**, delegates from every state but Rhode Island[6] assembled for the stated purpose of strengthening the confederation. (See Demystifying Government: Delegates to the Constitutional Convention.) It was clear from the start, though, that the convention was going to abandon the confederal system and replace it with something that might protect against chaos without burying individual liberties. The recognition of that goal was the easy part. Getting there—and getting political support for something new—would pose immense hurdles.

Despite widespread support for a federal system to replace the confederation, the convention nearly fell apart over two central issues: large versus small state representation in the new federal government and the legality of slavery.

Large, populous states like Virginia and Pennsylvania, mindful of their ability to dominate the new national government, advocated a method of representation based on population. Early in the convention, Edmund Randolph introduced what would be known as the **Virginia Plan**, which called for representation in the legislature based on population and a strong national government that would reign supreme over the states. Small states strenuously objected, and in turn, offered an alternative, the **New Jersey Plan**. Far less ambitious, it was essentially a stronger version of the Articles of Confederation, with representation based on states where each state would have one vote in the legislature.

In politics, it helps tremendously to set the agenda, and the Virginia group, by virtue of the fact that they were prepared with a plan, had the advantage of going first and structuring the course of the debate. The New Jersey Plan was offered in reaction to it, but it was voted down by the convention, as was a proposal by Alexander Hamilton that would have provided for an extremely strong central government with a powerful executive who served for life. With the rejection of the New Jersey Plan for a state-centered government and the Hamilton plan for what looked to many like a monarchy, it became clear that the Virginia Plan—soundly positioned between the two—would be the foundation for the new Constitution.

It was equally clear, however, that nothing was going to happen unless the small states were on board, and as structured, the Virginia Plan would never come close to winning broad-based support. The convention deadlocked over the issue, and as May turned into June, tension was as thick as the Philadelphia humidity. Delegates from states large and small didn't want to sacrifice their essential interests, although most everyone wanted to return home with something better than the Articles. In the long run, this created an environment where compromise was possible.

The logjam was broken by the **Connecticut Compromise**, which provided a bicameral or two-house legislature. Representation in the lower house—the House of Representatives—would be determined by population, and states would be equally represented in the upper house, or Senate. Voters would directly elect members of the House of Representatives, while state legislators would appoint senators. In this arrangement, the configuration of the House of Representatives would address the concerns of the large states, and the configuration of the Senate would address the concerns of the small states.

unitary system: The inverse of a confederal system, in which a centralized national government creates health care units like states, provinces, and counties, which derive their authority from the national government. Most nations are unitary systems. In the United States, the relationship between each individual state and its counties, townships, and cities is a unitary relationship, with the states creating and empowering the local governments.

federal system: The arrangement created by the United States Constitution, in which the national government and the states share authority over citizens. States may act autonomously to do such things as create school districts, levy taxes, or assemble a police force; at the same time, powers are reserved for the national government, which is supreme to state laws. In addition to the United States, only Canada, Germany, India, and a small group of other nations have federal systems.

Constitutional Convention: A meeting of representatives from twelve of the thirteen states held in Philadelphia in 1787, which produced the federal system of government outlined in the United States Constitution.

Virginia Plan: A proposal for the new Constitution, supported by large states, that would have based representation on population and provided for a centralized national government that could overrule the states.

New Jersey Plan: A proposal for the new Constitution, supported by small states, that would have provided for equal representation of large and small states in the national legislature, while limiting the power of the national government over the states.

Chapter 2 The Constitution and Federalism: Setting the Ground Rules for Politics

Delegates to the Constitutional Convention

The fifty-five delegates to the Constitutional Convention were an elite group of educated and privileged men. About half had had the rare opportunity to attend college. More than half were lawyers or had legal training, and almost one-quarter were businessmen or merchants. Several, like George Washington, were among the wealthiest people in the new nation, and many of the nation's most prominent families were represented. In keeping with their wealth and status, the delegate list read like a "who's who" of colonial and American politics. Although only eight delegates had signed the Declaration of Independence and only six had signed the Articles of Confederation, 80 percent had been members of the Continental Congress. Not surprisingly, the delegates would be a strong presence in the government they created. The convention boasted two future presidents (Washington and Madison), one future vice-president, four cabinet secretaries, five Supreme Court justices, nineteen senators, and thirteen House members.

Painting by Howard Chandler Christy.

A few delegates had an important influence on the proceedings. By presiding over the meeting, Virginia's George Washington supplied the gathering with an important element of **legitimacy**. As leader of the Continental Army during the Revolutionary War, Washington was easily the most heroic figure in America. Old and frail, the 81-year-old inventor, writer, publisher, and diplomat Benjamin Franklin said little at the convention, but his presence made an important public statement about the significance of the proceedings. His democratic sentiments were well known, but the elder statesman from Pennsylvania could work behind the scenes to facilitate compromise among the divergent perspectives held by the delegates.

One of the more critical voices was Virginia's George Mason, who, despite being a vocal and influential delegate, refused to sign the Constitution. His reservations centered on the concern that the government created by the Constitution would be too strong and might trample on the freedoms of those who created it. He feared the lack of a bill of rights (which was subsequently added by constitutional amendment) and the potential for abuses of power by Congress and the judiciary would hurt those without many resources and take power from the states.

The other end of the spectrum was represented by delegates who feared the new government wouldn't be strong enough. New York's Alexander Hamilton, who had married into an aristocratic family, was concerned about creating a strong central government that could pay its debts and function on the world stage. He unsuccessfully proposed to the convention something resembling the British monarchy.

Virginia's James Madison occupied the middle ground between these two perspectives, which helped to make him the most influential member of the convention. Although not an imposing figure or speaker, and despite being one of the younger delegates at age thirty-six, Madison had the greatest influence on the Constitution. An advocate of a stronger central government than what the Articles provided, Madison was a tireless campaigner and natural politician who was able to fashion compromise while successfully advocating his ideas.

Connecticut Compromise: A compromise between the Virginia and New Jersey Plans that broke the deadlock over representation at the Constitutional Convention by providing for a bicameral legislature. Large states would get their demand for representation based on population in the House of Representatives, while every state, regardless of size, would have two senators, which pleased small states.

Apart from the fact that senators are now also directly elected, the Connecticut Compromise established the structure for Congress that exists to this day.

With the Connecticut Compromise came the hope that the convention would bear fruit, but one serious problem remained. If representation in the House of Representatives was to be based on population, should slaves be among those counted? Delegates from southern states, where slavery was concentrated, argued they should be, even though slaves were denied all rights granted to free persons. Of course, counting slaves for purposes of representation would have enhanced the power of southern states in the new Congress.

Some delegates from outside the South would have been happy to outlaw slavery entirely in the Constitution. It wasn't difficult to see the ironic contrast between the language of the Declaration of Independence, justifying separation from Great Britain, and the practice of slavery. As a pragmatic matter, though, slavery was essential to the southern economy, and there would be no union of the states if the convention insisted on pursuing the matter. So, slavery would be left to fester like a raw wound in the body politic for generations as the price of establishing a federal system.

Northern delegates did strenuously object to the southern proposal to count slaves for representation purposes, but this matter was addressed in the **Three-Fifths Compromise**—a purely pragmatic attempt to split the difference between the two camps by counting each slave as three-fifths of a person for the purpose of determining representation in the House. As a reflection of the odious nature of the compromise, the final draft of the Constitution never mentions slaves, distinguishing instead between "free persons" (who would be counted fully) and "all other persons."

The summer of 1787 was coming to a close, and compromise was making possible a blueprint for a new federal government.

2.6 Ground Rules in Theory and Practice

If the Virginia Plan set the agenda for the Constitutional Convention, Virginia's James Madison developed the blueprint for some of the new government's most important features. Madison was an advocate of a strong central government, but he recognized that if it were to survive, it couldn't be so strong as to threaten individual liberties. Returning to the rationale for independence, Madison reasoned that the new government could be no more threatening to natural rights than American colonists believed the British government had been. That was a tall order to fill. It was one thing to declare independence on the basis of Locke's theoretical principles about the nature of government. It was quite another to design a functioning government that would uphold those principles.

For guidance, Madison turned to the writings of John Locke and eighteenth-century French political theorist Baron de Montesquieu. A supporter of democracy, Montesquieu believed that the best way to protect individual liberty was to make sure that power wasn't concentrated in any one place. He advocated separating powers into three distinct branches of government—an executive, a legislature, and a judiciary—each dependent on the others and therefore able to limit the powers of the others.

These ideas were incorporated into the design of the federal government. The Constitution provides for a system of **separation of powers**, whereby the executive (president), legislature (Congress), and judiciary (Supreme Court) are independent of one another. They represent different constituencies, are chosen by different means, perform distinct functions, and serve for terms varying from two years to life. Because nothing can get done unless they agree to work together, anyone can frustrate the initiatives of the other two, a process known as **checks and balances**. You can find a quick overview of the workings of separation of powers in Table 2.2.

It's human nature to want to get things done, but, as we've seen, separation of powers and checks and balances purposely make it difficult for the federal government to accomplish things. One way to think about this frustrating situation is that it's actually a feature of the Constitution designed to protect individual liberty. Here's how it works: Because Congress, the president, and the Supreme Court each can check the initiatives of the other

legitimacy: Widespread public acceptance of the official standing of a political figure or institution.

Three-Fifths Compromise: A compromise between northern and southern states that broke the deadlock over how slaves should be counted for purposes of representation. Three-fifths of slaves would be included in population totals, benefitting southern states that had the largest concentration of slaves by inflating their representation in the House of Representatives.

L.O. Identify the institutional safeguards to liberty contained in the Constitution.

separation of powers: The division of political power among several equal and independent branches of government to prevent power from being consolidated in any one branch.

checks and balances: The ability of any one of several equal and independent branches of government to keep the others from acting, designed to prevent power from being consolidated in any one branch. Because any branch can put a check on the others, government can only act when there is cooperation between the branches, a situation that necessitates compromise.

TABLE 2.2 The Three Branches

	Executive Branch	Legislative Branch		Judicial Branch
		House	Senate	
Represents	Entire nation	Small districts	States	The Constitution
Chosen by	Electoral College	The people	The people (originally state legislatures)	The president, confirmed by the Senate
Term	4 years, renewable once	2 years	6 years	Life
Function	Carrying out laws	Writing laws	Writing laws	Judging laws

two branches, things can only get done when they work together. Often, their interests won't line up, and one branch will put a check on everyone else—such as when the Supreme Court declares an act of Congress unconstitutional, the president vetoes a bill, or the Senate refuses to confirm a presidential appointee.

It's an inefficient way of trying to do business. Things happen much more slowly than they would if everyone worked together. When the branches continue to disagree, nothing gets done at all. In these situations, the whole process stalls. Everything grinds to a halt. No bill is passed, or the law is struck down, or the appointment doesn't happen.

At the same time, the process makes it hard for any one group or interest to achieve its goals at the expense of everyone else. It forces deliberation and compromise. That helps protect the wishes of those who otherwise might be overwhelmed by the quick actions of like-minded government officials. So, while it may be frustrating, the inefficiency of a decentralized system is also a safeguard. The Constitution's framers chose to create frustration as part of the price of protecting personal liberty.

Along with separation of powers and checks and balances, the Constitution contained other safeguards designed to protect citizens from the new government it created. As we saw in Chapter 1, the Constitution called for a **republic** or **representative democracy** in which the House of Representatives would consist of people selected by and accountable to voters. Representatives have to face the voters again after a fixed term of two years, and can be tossed out of office if their actions defy the wishes of the people they represent. Originally selected by state legislators, senators are now chosen in the same manner and serve a fixed term of six years.

Other safeguards followed from the ideas of John Locke. Representative democracy implies a government based on **popular sovereignty**, where the government is run by the people it is designed to serve based on the free expression of their will to be governed. Recall that Locke argued against the divine right of kings to rule, asserting that government gets its authority from individuals and must protect the natural rights of those it serves. By implication, if the new government had failed in this endeavor, it would have been appropriate for Americans to reject it and try again.

The Constitution also established a **limited government** by placing specific restrictions on what government can do. This, too, is consistent with Locke's thinking because it is based on the principle that the people rightly decide the appropriate role for government, and that Americans can restrict the government from acting in ways that they feel might jeopardize their liberty. So, for instance, Congress is prohibited—by constitutional amendment—from restricting religious freedom. Contrast this way of thinking with the traditional rationale for monarchy, in which a king's broad authority doesn't take into account restrictions on individual liberty.

A final safeguard—**federalism**—was more a product of necessity than design, but it serves the purpose of placing a check on the actions of government that can be just as strong as separation of powers, checks and balances, representative democracy, popular sovereignty, or limited government. We've already seen how a federal government contrasts with a confederal government, like the one created by the Articles of Confederation, and a unitary government, which is the model for most governments in the world. Federalism regards the bulky architecture of shared authority between the national (federal) government and the states as a feature of the republic. By assigning some functions to the federal government, others to the states, and still others to both, the framers of the Constitution ensured that there would be multiple centers of power.

Throughout our history, federalism has been the source of intense political disputes the likes of which you won't find in too many countries. We'll take a closer look at these disputes in Section 2.10, "Federalism: (Almost) Only in America."

For something so important, the Constitution is a simple document. It consists of seven articles and twenty-seven amendments, the first ten of which constitute the Bill of Rights (see Appendix B). Take a look at Table 2.3 to see what was in the original, unamended document.

republic: Any nation with provisions for the selection of representatives who make decisions on behalf of those who select them. James Madison said a republic was "a government in which the scheme of representation takes place," as compared to direct democracy.

representative democracy: A form of democracy in which eligible individuals choose others to make decisions on their behalf.

popular sovereignty: Rule by the people based on the consent of the governed.

limited government: The idea that power can be denied to government and the people who serve in it, in order to restrict those in positions of authority from infringing upon individual liberty.

federalism: The division of power between a sovereign federal government and sovereign state governments, which provides that some functions will be performed by the national government, some by the state governments, and some by both the national and state governments. As a feature designed to limit the strength of government, federalism works to decentralize power by creating dual levels of authority.

TABLE 2.3 What Was in the Original Constitution?

Article I	Establishes the legislative branch of government, with instructions for electing representatives and senators, and gives basic guidelines for how Congress should run and what it should do.
Article II	Establishes the executive branch or presidency. It says that the president shall be commander-in-chief of the armed forces, grants the president the power to make treaties, mandates that the president report to Congress from time to time on the state of the nation, and devotes a lot of attention to presidential selection.
Article III	Establishes the judiciary. It mandates the establishment of a Supreme Court, stipulating the matters over which it should have jurisdiction, and gives Congress the authority to set up lower courts.
Article IV	Addresses the relationship between the federal government and the states, including procedures for admitting new states to the union, and defines the relationship of each state to the others.
Article V	Sets up the mechanism for amending the Constitution.
Article VI	Transfers to the new government all outstanding debts acquired by the United States under the Articles of Confederation and establishes the Constitution as the supreme law of the land.
Article VII	Sets up the procedures for ratifying the Constitution.

2.7 "If Men Were Angels"

The clearest rationale for why the new nation might benefit from all these institutional safeguards appeared in a series of essays written after the Constitutional Convention by Alexander Hamilton, James Madison, and John Jay. First published anonymously between October 1787 and May 1788 in several New York newspapers under the name "Publius," which is Latin for "public man," the eighty-five essays that came to be known as *The Federalist* (to many today, *The Federalist Papers*) were meant to persuade a reluctant New York State of the advantages of the Constitution. Notwithstanding their political purpose, *The Federalist* remains one of the clearest expressions of how the Constitution was designed to work, not to mention the best surviving glimpse into the thinking of the Constitution's authors.

As a body of work, *The Federalist* addressed the "defects" in the Articles of Confederation (in a series of essays believed to have been written by Alexander Hamilton) and detailed how the new Constitution would correct them without costing citizens their liberty (in an argument made by Madison). Additionally, John Jay, who had experience in foreign affairs, authored a few essays dealing with constitutional structure and foreign relations.

Madison made the argument that the new government had to have numerous power centers in order to protect people from the worst motives of their neighbors, both in and out of government. "If men were angels, no government would be necessary," he wrote. "If angels were to govern men, neither external nor internal controls on government would be necessary." But common sense and knowledge of human nature tells us that we need to be cautious in social endeavors, especially when power is involved.

We've all at times questioned the motivation of people we've met. Maybe they were trying to sell us something, or trying to befriend us, and for whatever reason, the way they acted didn't feel right to us. Madison acknowledged these types of experiences happen all the time, and when you're trying to govern yourself as a nation, you run the risk that a group of people with malevolent motives will band together as a **faction** and work to impose their will on everyone. Even if they are small in number, a faction of highly motivated people can threaten the rest. Madison's fear was that if they were not controlled, factions could impose their will on others and produce **tyranny**, denying liberty to those who did not share the wishes of the faction.

Madison lays out the problem in detail and assesses the possible solutions to it in Federalist #10, ultimately explaining why the new Constitution provided the surest and safest

The Federalist: A collection of essays written by Alexander Hamilton, James Madison, and John Jay in an effort to persuade a reluctant public to support the Constitution.

faction: A group of individuals who are united by a desire that, if realized, would threaten the liberty of the larger community—in James Madison's words, individuals who are "united and actuated by some common impulse of passion, or of interest, adverse to the rights of other citizens, or to the permanent and aggregate interests of the community." A faction may be defined by size, such as when a majority of citizens threatens the liberty of the minority, or by intensity, such as when a minority of citizens with intensely held preferences threatens the liberty of a disinterested majority.

tyranny: The denial of liberty to individuals through the actions of a faction or through the actions of government itself.

way to address the dangers of faction. In Federalist #51, he goes on to detail how separation of powers and checks and balances work to protect against the danger of tyranny from the government.

In Federalist #10, Madison addresses alternative ways to deal with the dangers posed by factions. Here's a simple way of thinking about what he said. Let's say you wanted the liberty to dress in whatever style appealed to you. Further assume that there is a group of people—a faction—that wanted to impose a national dress code that would forbid the wearing of shorts and nose rings. They could be small in number but highly motivated, plotting to find ways to get you to dress like they do while you're busy going about your life, not giving a second thought to what you wear. Or, they could be large enough in number to overwhelm you. Either way, they could pose a threat to your free expression.

Madison looks at ways to prevent that from happening and considers two options: removing the causes of faction—the things that motivate others to gang up on you—or controlling their effects. Removing the causes of faction would require either removing liberty or giving everyone the same preferences and desires. Neither is a particularly attractive option. In the first case, what's the point of removing liberty if the objective is to preserve liberty? Madison says this remedy would be "worse than the disease" of faction itself. He likens liberty to air: We need it to breathe, and fire needs it to burn, but if you eliminated air just to put out fires, you'd be extinguishing life in the process. So, this solution is effective, but way too expensive.

What about giving everyone the same preferences and desires? That would result in a society where everyone would look, act, feel, and believe the same things—a place where, say, everyone wore shorts and nose rings. If you're having trouble imagining how this might come about, it's because this is not a practical solution. As long as people have liberty, different opinions will form, and with them, the risk that factions will form. "The latent causes of faction," Madison says, "are thus sown in the nature of man." It's a condition we simply have to deal with.

Madison concludes that if we can't regulate the causes of faction, we need to control their effects so that liberty can be protected. This is where the safety features of the Constitution come into play, starting with the establishment of a republican form of government. As we know, unlike direct democracy, a republic is characterized by elected representatives who are accountable to the people through popular sovereignty. In this depiction of events, our dress-code advocates can vote along with everyone else for representatives to Congress. Their intensely expressed wish for everyone to dress in a particular manner may result in the election of some representatives who share their views, which, in turn, will be expressed in Congress to other representatives who speak for different people who do not share their views. Because they are a faction, it will be hard for them to attain enough support in Congress to impose their wishes on others, although Congress will give them a forum for having their views heard. In a country as large as the United States, Madison speculated that there would be many factions concerned with a host of issues, none of which would be able to dominate the government.

To make things more secure, the Constitution makes it difficult for any one group to dominate the workings of government by separating powers into different branches and through checks and balances. Add staggered terms for elected representatives, different constituencies for elected representatives, and federalism—all the safeguards we talked about earlier—and it becomes difficult for a single faction to manipulate the machinery of government.

At the same time, Madison was sensitive to the need to protect the public from the government. In Federalist #51, he describes the benefits derived from separation of powers and checks and balances, which make it difficult for government to overwhelm individual liberty. By creating different institutions with separate and distinct roles, representing different groups in society, the three branches are likely to adhere to distinct agendas, which they cannot advance alone. As a consequence, each branch will have to moderate its wishes through compromise with the others or submit to the reality that nothing will get done. Either outcome protects the public from the threat of centralized power. "Ambition must be made to counteract ambition," Madison writes. "The interest of the man must be connected with the constitutional rights of the place."

Essays in *The Federalist* are not long, but they were written in the language of eighteenth-century America and should be read slowly. You can access the original text of Federalist #10 and Federalist #51 in Appendixes C and D, respectively.

2.8 Selling the Constitution

It may be strange to think of politicians writing essays in an effort to win a political battle, but that's essentially what *The Federalist* was about. Today, Hamilton and Madison would take to Twitter to build support for the Constitution. They would set up an organization to collect contributions from wealthy like-minded donors and use that money to buy thirty-second television ads in states where ratification of the Constitution seemed shaky. At the same time, even if their methods seem quaint by comparison, the bitter struggle over ratification was as partisan and nasty as anything in politics today.

L.O. Describe the political battle over constitutional ratification between Federalists and Anti- Federalists, and explain the role of the Bill of Rights in winning support for ratification.

Those who favored ratification cleverly called themselves "Federalists," leaving their opponents with the negative tag "Anti-Federalists." Since the way you characterize your political opponent goes a long way to structuring the debate (see Demystifying Government: The Politics of Language), this choice of label gave the Federalists the upper hand in the discussion because it's always better to be for something than to want to obstruct something. And if the Anti-Federalists were opposed to the Constitution, and people at large were widely opposed to the Articles of Confederation, then it was reasonable to wonder exactly what the Anti-Federalists were for.

In fact, the Federalists did have the advantage of being more organized than the Anti-Federalists, and of having a cohesive argument for ratification. They had the stature of national figures like Washington and Franklin behind them. They had frustration over the Articles to help their cause. What they didn't have was enough votes.

It was clear to the Federalists that ratification was in serious jeopardy in a number of states. Because state legislatures (rightly) feared losing power under the new constitutional arrangement, they were among the Constitution's strongest critics, and the Constitutional Convention shrewdly maneuvered to have ratification considered in state conventions rather than in the legislatures. But ratification still had to take place at the state level, where officials stood to lose a lot of power and could be counted on to lead the charge against the proposed new order.

To confront this difficulty, the Constitution's supporters opted to require ratification from only nine of thirteen states before the new constitutional arrangement would take effect—even though unanimity had been required to revise the Articles. They recognized that unanimity was an unrealistic objective, and were savvy enough to realize that if faced with the reality of the new government taking effect elsewhere on the continent, reluctant states would find themselves with no alternative but to go along.

There were other huge obstacles as well. Anti-Federalists made much of the apparent class bias at the Constitutional Convention, claiming that a group of lawyers and merchants had created a new government that would undermine the interests of farmers and

---

DEMYSTIFYING GOVERNMENT

The Politics of Language

Couching the ratification debate in the language of "Federalists" and "Anti-Federalists" is akin to how language is used in present-day debates over contentious policy issues. Think about the way each side in the abortion debate implicitly characterizes the other through the selection of the labels they claim for themselves. Abortion rights supporters call themselves "pro-choice," suggesting that their opponents—implicitly "antichoice"—stand in opposition to liberty. Those on the other side of the question label themselves "pro-life," with clear implications for what that makes the other side. Would anyone willingly claim to be "pro-death"?

debtors. Considering the conflicts between debtors and creditors that helped fuel the Constitutional Convention, it's not at all surprising that this argument carried a lot of weight. Add this to the sentiment that the country had just finished fighting a war to get away from a strong central government and the Anti-Federalists had a strong case.

In what would become typical of politics in America, the battle was spirited, impassioned—and dirty. Rumors flew in the newspapers. Pagans would control the government. Federal crimes would be punished by torture. The Pope would be elected president.[7]

The claims about punishment and torture stuck, and the Federalists found that they had to respond to charges that the Constitution did not protect people from fundamental abuses of liberty by the federal government. Their answer was a promise to amend the Constitution immediately in a way that would protect individuals from abuses by government. The result of this promise was the first ten amendments to the Constitution—the Bill of Rights—passed as promised by the First Congress and ratified by the states within two years.

The First Congress quickly took up the matter of a Bill of Rights as promised by the Federalists in their campaign to win ratification of the Constitution. On September 25, 1789, Congress passed and sent to the states twelve amendments designed to protect people from abuses of their liberty by the new government. The first amendment, which addressed the number of constituents each House member would represent, was not ratified. The second amendment, which set restrictions on congressional compensation, took 203 years to ratify and became the Twenty-seventh Amendment to the Constitution on May 7, 1992. The remaining ten were ratified December 15, 1791, and became known as the Bill of Rights. Table 2.4 describes each amendment included in the Bill of Rights.

The promise of a Bill of Rights turned out to be a particularly important maneuver by the Federalists. By January 1788, Delaware, Pennsylvania, New Jersey, Georgia, and Connecticut had ratified the Constitution, but the remaining states were either strongly opposed or too close to call. The outcome in Massachusetts was in question when its convention met in February, and the Bill of Rights concession is credited with making the difference in a narrow vote to approve. It would help make the difference in other narrow votes to come.

TABLE 2.4 The Bill of Rights

First Amendment	The First Amendment prevents government from interfering with several key personal freedoms, including the freedom to worship, speak, and assemble peacefully. It also prevents the government from restricting freedom of the press and the freedom to petition government.
Second Amendment	The Second Amendment protects the right to bear arms.
Third and Fourth Amendments	The Third and Fourth Amendments provide a right to privacy from government interference. The Third Amendment prevents government from forcing citizens to house soldiers during peacetime—addressing one of the complaints the colonists had against the British. The Fourth Amendment protects against unreasonable searches and seizures of property or personal effects.
Fifth through Eighth Amendments	The Fifth through Eighth Amendments establish a host of protections for individuals accused of a crime. These include the right not to be tried twice for the same crime, the right to be indicted by a grand jury before being tried for a capital crime, the right not to be forced to testify against yourself, the right to due process of law, and the right not to have property confiscated by government without compensation (all in the Fifth Amendment); and the right to a speedy and impartial trial, the right to be informed of charges against you, the right to call and confront witnesses, and the right to a lawyer (all in the Sixth Amendment); and the right to a jury in civil trials (Seventh Amendment); the right to be free from excessive bail and from the infliction of cruel and unusual punishments (Eighth Amendment).
Ninth and Tenth Amendments	The Ninth Amendment is a safety net establishing that any rights not specifically mentioned in the first eight amendments are not necessarily denied. The Tenth Amendment establishes that any powers not granted to the federal government or prohibited to the states are reserved for the states.

TABLE 2.5 Constitutional Timeline

It took time before the machinery created by the Constitution came on line. Some of it was being put into place while the ratification process was still playing out. Here's how the new government unfolded between June 1788 and June 1789.

June 21, 1788	The Constitution is adopted when New Hampshire becomes the ninth state to ratify.
September 1788	Congress sets dates for voting for president.
January 1789	Presidential electors are chosen in states that ratified the Constitution.
February 1789	Presidential electors meet and select George Washington as the first president.
March 3, 1789	The government established by the Articles of Confederation ceases to exist.
April 6, 1789	The first Congress of the United States meets to begin organizing.
April 8, 1789	Members of the House of Representatives take the oath of office.
April 30, 1789	George Washington is sworn in as the first president of the United States. The executive branch becomes operational.
June 1, 1789	The first act of Congress provides for senators to take an oath of office and recognizes the oath that House members took on April 8th as official.
June 3, 1789	Senators take the oath of office, and John Adams is sworn in as vice president. Congress becomes fully operational.
February 2, 1790	The Supreme Court meets in first full session. All three branches of the new government are now operational.

Source: National Archives at http://www.archives.gov

Things remained tenuous, though. New Hampshire was leaning against ratification, and in March, Rhode Island held a referendum that rejected the Constitution by a large margin. It was up to Maryland to regain the momentum for the Federalists, which it did in April with a vote to ratify. South Carolina soon fell in line, and when New Hampshire became the ninth state to ratify on June 21, 1788, the Constitution had been officially adopted.

Nonetheless, the battle continued. As a practical matter, the constitutional plan could not have been implemented without the blessing of two of the largest states, New York and Virginia. This was hardly forthcoming. Owing in part to the hard work and political skills of James Madison in Virginia and Alexander Hamilton in New York—of which the publication of *The Federalist* was a part—and in part to the relative disarray of the Anti-Federalists, these two populous states eventually ratified the Constitution, even though the vote in each case was harrowingly close (the margin in the New York convention was three votes of fifty-seven cast). It's quite likely that a majority of New Yorkers and Virginians opposed the Constitution at the time their states ratified it. Hamilton assumed a majority of Americans opposed it, but the Federalists had outmaneuvered their opponents. North Carolina would ratify the Constitution following Washington's inauguration as president. Rhode Island, the final holdout, would sign on almost two years after the document had become official, and there would be a federal republic in the United States. Table 2.5 details how the new government unfolded.

2.9 Changing the Constitution

The rules of the game set out in the Constitution have evolved over time, and much of that change has been gradual and evolutionary, rather than sudden and dramatic. Although there are formal mechanisms for amending the Constitution, the greatest change has come through differences in the way the Constitution is interpreted. This has afforded the Constitution the flexibility to respond to two centuries of dramatic social, economic, and political change.

Amendment Ratification

Amendments need to be proposed, then ratified. The Constitution allows the process to begin at either the federal or state level. At the federal level, an amendment is proposed if it is approved by a two-thirds vote of both the House of Representatives and the Senate. Every amendment to the Constitution has originated this way. It then follows one of two paths. The most typical path is for the amendment to be considered by the legislatures of the fifty states. The amendment is ratified if it is approved by three-fourths of the state legislatures. All but one amendment was ratified this way.

The lone exception was the Twenty-first Amendment, which repealed the Eighteenth Amendment outlawing the sale or manufacture of alcohol. The Twenty-first Amendment followed the other ratification path permitted by the Constitution: It was approved by special ratifying conventions in three-fourths of the states. These were like the state ratifying conventions that approved the original Constitution.

For an amendment to be proposed at the state level, two-thirds of the state legislatures would have to ask Congress to call a national convention, similar to the Constitutional Convention that produced the Constitution. Whatever amendment or amendments the national convention approved would then require the approval of three-fourths of either the state legislatures or state conventions for ratification. This method has never been used.

To review, amendments need to be proposed, then ratified. The Constitution provides two ways to propose amendments and two ways to ratify them. Every amendment in our history has been proposed by a two-thirds vote of both houses of Congress, and all but one has been ratified by a vote of three-fourths of the state legislatures. The one exception was approved by ratifying conventions in three-fourths of the states. Amendments may also be proposed if two-thirds of the state legislatures request a national constitutional convention. This method has never been used.

The Constitution's authors were determined not to repeat the mistakes of the Articles of Confederation, which were impossible to amend. At the same time, they wanted it to be difficult to change the supreme law of the land. They decided on two methods for proposing and ratifying amendments to the Constitution, which are described in Demystifying Government: Amendment Ratification.

Formally changing the Constitution has proved difficult. Since 1789, only twenty-seven amendments have been ratified—ten of which were the Bill of Rights. Many of the ratified amendments broadened the grant of constitutional rights or strengthened the power of the federal government. Table 2.6 provides an overview.

Because so many parties have to agree to amend the Constitution, a large number of efforts have failed. Some of the more significant proposals that never made it include:

■ A proposed Equal Rights Amendment that would have made sex discrimination unconstitutional. It was proposed in 1972 with a time limit for ratification. Three-fourths of the state legislatures failed to ratify it by 1982, and it expired.

■ Full congressional representation for the District of Columbia. This amendment was proposed in 1978 and expired, unratified, seven years later. To this day, residents of the nation's capital have no representation in the Senate and are represented in the House by a delegate who cannot vote.[8]

■ A proposal to allow Congress to limit child labor. Proposed in 1926, it remains ten states short of ratification and has no time limit. But no state has acted on the amendment since 1937.

Many more proposals of lesser note have been unsuccessful, typically unable to muster the congressional support necessary to send them to the states for ratification. Some of the failed attempts over the past few years would have established:

■ A constitutional right to health care.

■ A constitutional restriction against the early release of convicted criminals.

■ A constitutional right to own a home.

TABLE 2.6 Amendments to the Constitution

Apart from the Bill of Rights, the amendments to the Constitution—in order of appearance—did the following:

Eleventh (1795)	Limited federal court jurisdiction in suits against the states
Twelfth (1804)	Modified the method of selecting the president
Thirteenth (1865)	Abolished slavery
Fourteenth (1868)	Expanded the federal guarantees of equal protection of the law and due process of the law to the states
Fifteenth (1870)	Extended voting rights to African Americans
Sixteenth (1913)	Authorized a federal income tax
Seventeenth (1913)	Changed the method of choosing senators from selection by state legislatures to direct popular vote
Eighteenth (1919)	Abolished the sale and production of alcohol; repealed by the Twenty-first Amendment (1933)
Nineteenth (1920)	Extended voting rights to women
Twentieth (1933)	Established that presidential terms expire on January 20th and that congressional terms expire on January 3rd
Twenty-first (1933)	Repealed the Eighteenth Amendment (1919)
Twenty-second (1951)	Established presidential term limits
Twenty-third (1961)	Extended the right to vote in presidential elections to residents of the District of Columbia
Twenty-fourth (1964)	Abolished the poll tax in federal elections
Twenty-fifth (1967)	Provided procedures for handling presidential disability and for filling a vacancy in the vice presidency
Twenty-sixth (1971)	Extended voting rights to eighteen-year-olds
Twenty-seventh (1992)	Prohibited midterm congressional pay increases

The Thirteenth, Fourteenth, and Twenty-fourth Amendments expanded civil rights. The Fifteenth, Seventeenth, Nineteenth, Twenty-third, and Twenty-sixth Amendments expanded the right to vote.

It's pretty easy to see how difficult it would be to get all the necessary parties to come together to modify the Constitution around these relatively specific issues. It may be less obvious to see how profound changes have occurred through judicial interpretation and political circumstance. Rather than alter the physical document, changes of this nature alter the way we understand the physical document.

The courts have had to deal with countless disputes over constitutional interpretation, and in the process, they have shaped the way the Constitution is applied and understood, sometimes in ways its authors never could have imagined. The Supreme Court is the arbiter of constitutional disputes, but in a good example of how judicial interpretation has modified the Constitution, nothing in the Constitution itself actually grants this authority to the Supreme Court. As we will see in Chapter 12, early in its history, the Supreme Court interpreted the Constitution to say that the Court's power to review the Constitution was intended by the document's framers.

Changes in political circumstances have similarly shaped the Constitution in unintended ways. For instance, political parties are never mentioned in the Constitution, and with good reason—the Federalists equated parties with factions and saw them as a threat to liberty. Yet, the years immediately following the ratification of the Constitution saw the emergence of political parties, and they have been a central part of our political process ever since. The Constitution has been flexible enough to adapt to this change.

Soon we'll learn about the complex constitutional mechanism for presidential selection, called the Electoral College. It originally provided for an elite group of individuals, called electors, to debate the merits of the candidates and vote for the one they felt most qualified. Through natural evolution, political parties acquired that function. But the electors still exist, even though they only go through the motions of voting for president. The Constitution was flexible enough to adjust to a situation its authors simply couldn't anticipate.

2.10 Federalism: (Almost) Only in America

L.O. Explain the concept of national supremacy.

Federal systems are unusual in the world. A handful of countries, such as Canada, Germany, and Switzerland, have them, There has also been movement toward a federated Europe, although as Global Topics: American Federalism versus European Federalism explains, the joint decision making and collective politics practiced in Europe is a different thing entirely from American federalism. In the United States, federalism is one of the defining characteristics of political debate.

Having states and a federal government as independent power centers is an effective feature of the Constitution designed to keep power from being concentrated in a single set of hands. It is also an awkward design that has caused conflict throughout American history.

The dilemma focuses on which power center—the states or Washington, D.C.—gets to have the final word in American politics. There's no doubt that Madison intended the national government to be supreme to the state governments. But this was a point of contention at the Constitutional Convention that wasn't put to rest until the Civil War settled the matter some seventy years later by establishing that the South did not have a right to depart from the Union to form a new confederation.

The Constitution does contain wording that appears to support Madison's position. Article VI states, "This Constitution, and the laws of the United States which shall be made in Pursuance thereof . . . shall be the supreme Law of the Land." This seems to suggest that actions of the federal government should override actions of the states, but not everyone saw it this way at first. Only over time, through precedent and judicial interpretation, did this **supremacy clause** cement the position of the federal government as superior to the states. Even today, 150 years after the Civil War, the relationship between the states and the federal government reverberates through our politics. In 2009, with Congress assuming an activist posture in the first year of the Obama administration, Texas Governor Rick Perry even raised the prospect of secession from the union if Washington refused to rein in what he called its "oppression" of the states through what he regarded as the national government's failure to respect the states' Tenth Amendment right to all powers not granted to the federal government.[9] Governor Perry's words raised eyebrows across the country, as they echoed arguments from the Civil War era, although the sentiment he expressed is deeply rooted in the earliest and most fundamental constitutional battles between the states and the national government.

There are other hints that the Constitution's framers intended for the states to be subservient to the federal government. In Article I, Section 8, Congress is given the authority "To make all laws which shall be necessary and proper for carrying into Execution . . . all other Powers vested by this Constitution in the Government of the United States." Implicit in this statement is a large grant of power to the national government that, when broadly interpreted, gives Congress the ability to make laws that states would be obligated to follow.

The key word here is *interpreted*—and there are several different ways of understanding the intent of the Constitution's framers with respect to federalism that could be conveniently applied by people on both sides of the strong federal government question. Beyond giving the federal government the upper hand in its relationship with the states, the Constitution provides little guidance on how federalism is to operate in practice. Consequently, the specific relationship between the federal and state governments has varied at different points in our national history and has evolved over time.

Madison's vision was what might best be termed **nation-centered federalism**, whereby the Constitution was the supreme law of the land, the federal government was a cre-

supremacy clause: A constitutional provision (Article VI) establishing the relationship between the federal and state governments. The supremacy clause asserts that any conflict between the federal government and the states will be decided in favor of the federal government.

L.O. Discuss the tension between the federal and state governments in the period prior to the Civil War and how the concept of dual federalism was employed to avoid conflict.

nation-centered federalism: One of several perspectives on federalism, which argues for the supremacy of the Constitution and federal law over state actions.

American Federalism versus European Federalism

Federal systems are rare because federations typically form when a nation is forged from units with a history of political autonomy, like the thirteen American colonies. Few nations can claim a history like this. Switzerland is a centuries-old federation of small states called cantons, some of which date back to a time before Switzerland was a nation. German federalism united several previously independent states in the mid-nineteenth century. The Canadian federation permits the coexistence of English and French-speaking provinces in one nation.

Surrendering sovereign authority to a larger entity can be a complex and complicated affair. For instance, compare federalism in the United States with the movement to create a federated Europe, which has existed in some form since the end of World War II. The European Movement, an international organization that originated in 1947, is committed to the creation of a federal Europe through political, social, and cultural integration of European nations. Following a century of devastating European wars, founders of the European Movement believed that the integration of Europe around common political and economic interests was the only path to lasting peace and security on the European continent.[T6]

In 1948, delegates from across Europe participated in the Congress of Europe, where prospects for European integration were discussed by some of the continent's most prominent and powerful leaders.[T7] Two years later, the first steps toward economic integration took place when several European nations agreed to integrate their steel and coal industries. Integration of the nuclear power industry followed, and by 1967 a European Parliament was formed. In 1992, a formal European Union (EU) was created by the Treaty of Maastricht, and with it a greater degree of formal cooperation among the governments of member nations.[T8]

These steps produced common policies and led to joint decision making on a host of trade and economic matters and facilitated the development of a common European market through the relaxation of trade barriers. In the 1990s it became possible to travel between European countries without a passport, and today a common currency—the Euro—has replaced the national currency of seventeen EU member nations.[T9]

These developments have produced a host of policies and governing institutions that are binding on member nations. But, cooperation and integration are not the same as federalism. The political relationship among EU member states is quite different from the political relationship among the American states, and the relationship between member states and the EU is different from the relationship between the American states and the American federal government. Despite having coordinated economic policies and a common currency, the nations of Europe remain individually sovereign.

Even as EU membership grew to include Eastern European nations of the former Soviet bloc, steps toward greater integration—and possibly a single European nation—were resisted by those who view them as a threat to national sovereignty. Foreshadowing the 2016 "Brexit" vote in Great Britain to withdraw from the European Union, a concerted effort by supporters of a united Europe to win approval of a European Constitution faced a serious setback in 2005 when the people of France and the Netherlands rejected it, leading Great Britain and several other nations to postpone their ratification votes indefinitely. Among the objections voiced by opponents was that calling the document a Constitution rather than a treaty or agreement, and the creation of what they viewed as national institutions for Europe, suggested a degree of unification on par with a federal republic like the United States. In an argument reminiscent of claims made by early opponents of American federalism, European antifederalists questioned whether the EU exceeded its authority by, in their view, imposing changes through an illegitimate document that did not express the wishes of the European people.[T10] Instead in 2007, leaders of the twenty-seven member nations signed the Treaty of Lisbon, which streamlined and strengthened the institutions and procedures of the European Union without creating a constitutional government.

---

ation of the Constitution, and the states—despite their broad grant of authority—were subservient to both. But those favoring greater state and local control of politics advocated a form of **state-centered federalism**, which turned Madison's perspective on its head with the claim that the Constitutional Convention itself was a meeting of the states intended to revise the Articles of Confederation. Therefore, the Constitution it produced and the federal government it established were essentially a creation of the states, which should have the final say in disagreements over which level of government had the ultimate authority to act.

This might seem like an academic argument, but the implications were tremendous. When southern states seceded from the union during the period leading up to the Civil

state-centered federalism: One of several perspectives on federalism, which argues that the Constitution and the federal government are creations of the states and therefore can be overruled by the states.

War, they justified their actions on the basis of state-centered federalism—that the federal union was created by the states, who maintained the right to opt out. In turn, northern states opposed secession—and justified military action—on the basis of nation-centered federalism, that the union of the states was greater than the sum of its parts.

During the decades following the drafting of the Constitution, many took a middle perspective that worked as long as the states and the federal government didn't have to confront irreconcilable differences—the perspective of **dual federalism**, which contended the Constitution had given both the states and the federal government distinct authority over a broad range of matters. In other words, the grant of authority to the federal government could coexist with a different but equally broad grant of authority to the states, sidestepping the matter of which would win a battle of wills.

Dual federalism provided a reasonable way to manage the natural tension arising between the federal government and the states because, during the period stretching from the Constitutional Convention to the Civil War, the federal government and the states for the most part did operate in distinct spheres. Government at both levels was small by today's standards and didn't participate in a wide range of activities, so disputes could be minimized.

When the two clashed, though, they made a loud noise. The most notable conflict during this period came to a head in 1819, when the U.S. Supreme Court had to determine whether the federal government had the right to charter a federal bank and locate it, free of taxes, in one of the states. The decision, in the case *McCulloch v. Maryland*, was the first to clearly enumerate **national supremacy**, or the dominance of the federal government over the states. It's an important case, and it's discussed in Demystifying Government: *McCulloch v. Maryland* (1819).

If the Civil War established that states could not leave the federal union, it also ushered in a period of rapid growth in the United States, which posed new challenges for federal/state relations. As waves of immigrants flocked to American cities during a period of rapid industrialization, government at both the federal and state levels had to address a host of new social and economic concerns. By the start of the twentieth century, a new intergovernmental relationship was forged that lasted for the better part of seventy years. Dubbed **cooperative federalism**, it was characterized by federal-state partnerships, where federal funds were used to help states administer federal priorities at the state level.

The story of American government in the twentieth century is a tale of increasing demands on government through the first two-thirds of the century, followed by a reaction against central government activity in the latter one-third. It's a story with all kinds of implications for how government developed and how it works today, so we'll be coming back to it a lot. The discussion in Demystifying Government: Big Government, Fighting Words describes how the debate over big government that defines so much of our contemporary politics has its roots in federalism.

With the start of the Great Depression at the dawn of the 1930s, state governments were unable to handle the demands created by massive unemployment. With the election of President Franklin D. Roosevelt in 1932, the relationship between the federal and state

During the Great Depression, the federal government employed artists to paint public murals. William Gropper's "Construction of a Dam" (1939) is characteristic of much of the art of the 1930s, with workers in heroic poses laboring to complete a public project.[T11]

McCulloch v. Maryland (1819)

The dispute before the U.S. Supreme Court in *McCulloch v. Maryland* centered on two questions about the scope and reach of the federal government: Could the federal government engage in activities that were not expressly delegated to it in the Constitution, and does the federal government supersede the states when a conflict arises between them? In both cases, the verdict was a resounding yes, setting the stage for the future growth of national power and the eventual repudiation of state-centered federalism.

The particulars center on the establishment by the federal government of a Bank of the United States. First chartered by Congress in 1791 as a means for coining currency, making loans, and centralizing the financial affairs of the United States, the first Bank of the United States was controversial. Not surprisingly, supporters of nation-centered federalism, like Treasury Secretary Alexander Hamilton—always an advocate of a strong central government—were behind the idea. Hamilton justified the creation of the bank on the grounds that the Constitution gave Congress a broad grant of power that extended to just about anything not expressly denied to it. Just as predictable were the bank's opponents: debtor farmers (who still didn't trust the actions of lenders) and advocates of state-centered federalism, who felt Congress had grossly overreached its authority because the Constitution did not specifically give Congress the power to charter a national bank.

The charter on the bank expired in 1811, but the financial demands of the War of 1812 were justification for President Madison—the same James Madison who guided the development of the Constitution—to recommend that Congress revisit the charter. A second Bank of the United States was subsequently established, and it met with a heightened level of opposition. The state of Maryland imposed a tax on the Baltimore branch of the bank in 1818, which the bank's cashier, James McCulloch, refused to pay on the grounds that a state did not have the power to tax a federal entity. Shortly afterwards, the dispute landed in the U.S. Supreme Court.

The decision, written by Chief Justice John Marshall, backed both the power of Congress to establish the bank and the right of the federal government to do so without having to submit to taxes levied by a state. In so doing, Marshall invoked both the **"necessary and proper" clause** and the supremacy clause of the Constitution.

In ruling to support the right of the federal government to charter a bank, Marshall took a broad interpretation of the "necessary and proper" clause, arguing that the language of Article I, Section 8, gave Congress powers that were not specifically delegated to it in the Constitution—powers that were implied but not stated. This interpretation allowed Congress to act with great flexibility in future years, permitting the federal government to grow in authority in relation to the states.

In ruling against Maryland on the tax issue, Marshall invoked the reasoning of nation-centered federalism and a broad reading of the supremacy clause. He argued that as long as the federal government acted constitutionally, its actions were binding on the states. Since Marshall had already established that the bank charter was a "necessary and proper" move for Congress in its constitutionally enumerated capacity to regulate commerce, it followed that the states had no choice but to permit Congress to establish branches of the bank, tax free, wherever it wished.[T12]

---

governments changed dramatically. The programs of Roosevelt's **"New Deal"** produced an unprecedented expansion in the size and role of the federal government. For the first time, the federal government was involved in such things as unemployment compensation and social security. The federal government also took a bigger role in regulating the economy, and spent money on construction projects to get people back to work. With the New Deal, the federal government became a presence in the lives of American citizens like it never had before.

This active federal role reached its peak in the 1960s during the administration of President Lyndon B. Johnson. The **"Great Society"** initiatives of the Johnson administration took the philosophy of the New Deal one step further, seeking to use the federal government to solve broad social problems, like eliminating poverty and hunger in America. State governments became agents of a federal agenda, carrying out a large number of new social programs that were funded and regulated by Washington. The Great Society created a complex web of programs and regulations, some

President Lyndon Johnson signs the Medicare Bill as former President Truman looks on, July 30, 1965.[T13]

"necessary and proper" clause: A constitutional provision (Article I, Section 8) giving Congress a broad grant of authority to make laws that are binding on the states.

New Deal: The name given to the programs of President Franklin D. Roosevelt, which vastly expanded the role of the federal government in an effort to deal with the debilitating effects of the Great Depression on American society.

Chapter 2 The Constitution and Federalism: Setting the Ground Rules for Politics

Big Government: Fighting Words

It's said that the more things change, the more they stay the same. So it is with the debate over the size and role of the federal government. If you listen to some of the arguments for a smaller federal government that have been made over the past thirty years, you might think you were back at the Constitutional Convention. When President Reagan said in his inaugural address, "the federal government did not create the states, the states created the federal government," he was echoing the philosophy of state-centered federalism that had been advocated by those who feared strong federal control some two hundred years earlier—a philosophy that had been rebuffed by Chief Justice Marshall in *McCulloch v. Maryland*, discredited by the outcome of the Civil War, and forgotten in the activism of the New Deal and the Great Society.

When no less a spokesman than the president of the United States makes the case for a smaller, state-centered government, an argument long dead can come roaring back. By the time President Reagan made his pronouncement in 1980, the United States had already taken a few steps back from the activism that was the hallmark of the previous half-century. Subsequently, Reagan took the case much farther than most people imagined he could. Ever since the Reagan years, where you stand on the question of federal versus state power has been a defining question in political debate.

The issue has both practical and philosophical significance. As a practical matter, the more the federal government does, the more it costs—a price that must ultimately be paid in taxes. And, as a practical matter, how effectively government spends those tax dollars can have a bearing on how much people want government to do. A large, strong federal government was popular when it put people to work during the Great Depression, but less popular when it failed to cure social ills as Great Society programs promised it would.

As a philosophical matter, the big government debate raises the normative question of what government should do. Ronald Reagan was philosophically opposed to the federal government trying to cure social problems, and felt that government is most effective at the local level, where it is closer to the people. He saw a large federal government as the problem, not as the solution to other problems.

When George W. Bush took office in 2001, the large government/small government debate continued to define American politics. Bush cast himself in the Reagan mold, and advanced policies designed to limit what government could do. In his first months in of-fice, during a time of federal surpluses, he successfully advocated the largest tax cut in twenty years, which he argued was a matter of returning excess federal money to the public. Two years later, during a period of mushrooming deficits, he followed up with another substantial tax cut, arguing that it was necessary to get the economy moving again. Opponents argued that the Bush tax cuts would hamstring the ability of government to provide a wide range of programs and services. Supporters did not disagree—and did not complain.

President Obama articulated a different view of federalism, built around the idea that the federal government is and should be a positive force in American life. He expressed his belief in the value of a strong national government during a September 2009 address to a joint session of Congress, as he made the case for why the federal government should reform the American health care system:

Our predecessors understood that government could not, and should not, solve every problem. They understood that there are instances when the gains in security from government action are not worth the added constraints on our freedom. But they also understood that the danger of too much government is matched by the perils of too little; that without the leavening hand of wise policy, markets can crash, monopolies can stifle competition, the vulnerable can be exploited. And they knew that when any government measure, no matter how carefully crafted or beneficial, is subject to scorn; when any efforts to help people in need are attacked as un-American; when facts and reason are thrown overboard and only timidity passes for wisdom, and we can no longer even engage in a civil conversation with each other over the things that truly matter—that at that point we don't merely lose our capacity to solve big challenges. We lose something essential about ourselves.[T14]

President Obama made his case at a moment when many Americans were feeling vulnerable, but his advocacy on behalf of a national health care policy met stiff resistance from congressional Republicans, who stood united in opposition to any reform measures that imagined an expanded federal role. Far from a dull academic exercise, the debate over federalism involves a host of questions about what government will and should do, with real implications for who gets what, when, and how.

of which fell short of their goals. As a consequence, the latter one-third of the twentieth century witnessed a gradual reaction against the strong role of the federal government characterized by the New Deal and the Great Society.

In the late 1960s, President Richard M. Nixon attempted to simplify the federal government while shifting the balance of power in running government programs toward the states. He called the initiative **New Federalism**. One characteristic of Nixon's New Federalism was less federal regulation of federal money so that states could have more freedom to decide how to address social problems.

With the election of Ronald Reagan in 1980, the movement toward less federal involvement in everyday life begun in the Nixon administration took a dramatic turn with an effort to shift responsibility for social programs from Washington to the states. Though largely unsuccessful, it represented a bold departure from the New Deal and Great Society. The rhetoric and actions of the Reagan administration reflected the philosophy of those who advocated a limited role for the federal government some 200 years earlier, as Reagan sought to vastly limit the size and scope of the federal government.

President Ronald Reagan signs the Tax Reform Act of 1986.[T15]

President Bill Clinton took office in the wake of the smaller government debate of the Reagan years. Despite a natural inclination for a large, active federal government along the lines of Roosevelt and Johnson, Clinton found himself swimming against the strong Reagan tide. His response to New Federalism was to make the federal government smaller by making it more efficient. Clinton's **"Reinventing Government"** initiative met with modest success.

The small government argument remained popular through the start of the millennium, with George W. Bush as its most visible advocate. In the wake of the September 11, 2001, terrorist attacks on the United States, though, President Bush found himself in the position of advancing a larger role for the federal government in military matters and homeland security, as public sentiment took a turn toward renewed acceptance of a stronger role for Washington in security matters. At the same time, his tax-cutting policies raised speculation among critics that President Bush sought to starve the federal government of its funding in an attempt to return federal-state relations to what they were before the growth of the federal government during the New Deal.

The election of Barack Obama ushered in a sea of change in the federalism question, but did not put to rest questions about the appropriate size and scope of the federal government. In Obama, Americans had a president who advocated for an active federal role in solving major problems, departing from the philosophy that guided most of his recent predecessors.

President Obama signs legislation repealing the "Don't Ask, Don't Tell" policy, December 2010.[T16]

Great Society: The name given to the programs of President Lyndon B. Johnson, which elevated the federal government to the most prominent role it would play in the twentieth century. The philosophy of the Great Society was that government should try to solve large social problems like hunger and poverty.

New Federalism: The name given to the programs of Presidents Richard M. Nixon and Ronald Reagan, which started as an effort to streamline the federal government produced by the Great Society and ended up as a movement to reverse fifty years of federal growth by returning authority to the states.

Reinventing Government: The name given to President Bill Clinton's initiative to make the federal government smaller by making it more efficient.

2.11 Who Would Create a System Like This?

If you had set out to design a constitutional system, you probably never would have come close to creating the complicated mechanism in place in the United States. The combination of factors leading to the adoption of the Constitution was unparalleled, contributing to the development of a political system the likes of which had never been attempted.

Look at what the authors of the Constitution had to contend with. Any central government they created had to enter into a relationship with the states. For their creation to be viable, they had to produce a government that was strong enough to deal with the social unrest that the Articles of Confederation couldn't handle. If there was going to be any hope for constitutional ratification, they had to address the fears of small states that they would be dominated in the federal government by the commercial interests of the larger states. They had to face the fact that slavery ran the southern economy. They couldn't create a strong, centralized government or detractors would fear they were reproducing the type of system they had just fought to leave. And they had to do this knowing they were going to ask the states to ratify a document that diminished their power. Above all, they set about creating a system that would produce a new set of winners and losers from the power structure that was in place, and people are often reluctant to buy into new rules when they're not sure how or if they'll benefit.

To this effort, the Constitution's framers brought a keen understanding of key political writers and a willingness to put political theory into practice. The fact that *The Federalist* could articulate a constitutional philosophy is a good benchmark of how much abstract thought guided the writing of the Constitution. The safeguards to liberty built into the Constitution were a consequence of the belief that abstractions could be brought to life. You could call it a crazy belief because, throughout history, violence and not reason had been the hallmark of great changes in governments, where new rules meant new winners and losers. As experimental as the Constitution was in its day, the United States is still using the bulky, complex mechanism designed around the ideas of Locke and Montesquieu.

If the Constitution's authors created the playing field on which to go about the business of politics and government, it remains up to us how and how much we want to get into the game, if at all. We didn't create the rules of American democracy, but these rules shape the decisions we face about everything political, from the options available for political participation, to how we express our views about our leaders, to how we can have a role in deciding what government does or does not get done.

The political world may be all around us, and it may affect our everyday world in ways we may not readily recognize, but that doesn't mean our everyday world has a lot of room for the political world. The process of becoming politically aware and knowledgeable takes time and effort; having opinions about elected officials takes a certain level of interest that not everybody has. Let's take a look at public opinion—what we know, think, and believe about politics, and how it influences the way we relate to what politicians do. We'll have that discussion in Chapter 3, which opens Part 2 of the book, called "Citizenship and Democracy."

Chapter Review

Address how actions taken by the British prior to the American Revolution were at odds with the colonial tradition of self-rule.

Years before the American Revolution, conditions were building in the colonies for an eventual separation from Great Britain. The British imposed a series of acts that the colonists found restrictive, including taxes on tea and other goods through the Sugar Act and the Stamp Act, and a requirement that colonists house British soldiers through the Quartering Act. These actions clashed with a long colonial tradition of limited self-rule, including the free election of representative assemblies, and contributed to a growing feeling that something needed to be done—even though separation from Great Britain was far from universally popular.

State why postrevolutionary America first established a confederal system of government and why the Articles of Confederation were ineffectual.

The colonists were reluctant to give up too much liberty in exchange for security, so when they won their independence, they established a weak confederal system of government under the Articles of Confederation, in which the national government was a creation of the states. The Articles turned out to be ineffective, and the new United States had difficulty conducting foreign policy, regulating commerce, and even settling disputes among the states.

Identify the institutional safeguards to liberty contained in the Constitution.

The Articles were far from easy to revise, however, because concerns remained about the harmful effects of a strong central government, and because changing the structure of government would create a new—sometimes uncertain—set of winners and losers. Disputes centered on the competing interests of large and small states, and of free and slave states. Eventually, these differences were ironed out through compromise. The Constitution's framers also built a series of institutional safeguards into the new government, including separation of powers, checks and balances, popular sovereignty, limited government, and federalism. These addressed concerns that a strong central government would overwhelm personal liberty.

Describe the political battle over constitutional ratification between Federalists and Anti-Federalists, and explain the role of the Bill of Rights in winning support for ratification.

Because of the political controversy caused by changing the rules of the game, the Constitution was not easily ratified. Those who supported ratification called themselves Federalists. They engaged in a long and sometimes nasty debate with Anti-Federalists in an attempt to get the requisite nine states to endorse the Constitution. Federalists Alexander Hamilton, James Madison, and John Jay authored eighty-five essays known as *The Federalist*, which detailed how the Constitution would address the weaknesses of the Articles while protecting the public from tyranny at the expense of factions. One of the strongest arguments against ratification was that the new Constitution did not contain a Bill of Rights. A Federalist promise to add one as soon as the new government was established tipped the balance in favor of ratification.

Explain the concept of national supremacy.

Discuss the tension between the federal and state governments in the period prior to the Civil War and how the concept of dual federalism was employed to avoid conflict.

Although federalism is an institutional safeguard designed to disperse authority, it has also been a source of great controversy. Prior to the Civil War, the relationship between the federal and state governments was a matter of great controversy. In 1819, the Supreme Court supported national supremacy in *McCulloch v. Maryland*, ruling that

the interests of the federal government are supreme when they conflict with the interests of the states. Many still subscribed to the concept of state-centered federalism—the belief that the Constitution and the federal government it established are creations of the states, which maintain ultimate authority. Because the two levels of government typically addressed different matters, regular conflict could be avoided through the principle of dual federalism, which contended that the federal government and the states had their own distinct grants of authority. Dual federalism, however, was insufficient to avoid large conflicts like the one created by slavery.

Understand how federalism evolved in the twentieth century and how it influences contemporary politics.

The nature of federalism changed as government at both levels became more involved in everyday life in response to the growing complexity of America in the twentieth century. Joint endeavors between the federal government and the states, called cooperative federalism, characterized the relationship during the first two-thirds of the last century. In the 1960s, President Nixon introduced an initiative called New Federalism, the first step in an effort to limit the federal role in daily life that was accelerated in the Reagan administration and embraced by the Bush administration. Even though federalism was established over two centuries ago, dramatic changes since then in the relationship between the federal government and the states show how the rules of the political game are always evolving—with consequences for who gets what, when, and how.

Key Terms

Articles of Confederation The first constitution of the United States, which created a loosely functioning national government to which the individual states were supreme. It addressed concerns about a strong national government undermining individual liberty, but it created a national government that was unable to regulate commerce or conduct foreign policy and was abandoned in favor of the United States Constitution just eight years after it was ratified. (p. 31)

authority The right to act in an official capacity by virtue of holding an office like president or member of Congress. (p. 27)

Boston Massacre A precursor to the war that was still five years away, it was the first mortal conflict between colonists and British troops in Boston and resulted in the deaths of five colonists in 1770. (p. 27)

Boston Tea Party A protest against the Tea Act of 1773 in which fifty colonists dressed as Native Americans boarded British trade ships loaded with tea and threw the contents into the water. (p. 27)

checks and balances The ability of any one of several equal and independent branches of government to keep the others from acting, designed to prevent power from being consolidated in

any one branch. Because any branch can put a check on the others, government can only act when there is cooperation between the branches, a situation that necessitates compromise. (p. 35)

Coercive Acts Called the Intolerable Acts in the colonies, the Coercive Acts represented the British attempt to clamp down on the colonies following the Boston Tea Party. (p. 27)

confederal system An arrangement for establishing a government out of a set of component states, in which the national government is the creation of the states and subservient to them. The Articles of Confederation established a system like this in the United States. In today's world, the United Nations may be the most prominent example of a confederation. (p. 32)

Connecticut Compromise A compromise between the Virginia and New Jersey Plans that broke the deadlock over representation at the Constitutional Convention by providing for a bicameral legislature. Large states would get their demand for representation based on population in the House of Representatives, while every state, regardless of size, would have two senators, which pleased small states. (p. 33)

Constitutional Convention A meeting of representatives from twelve of the thirteen states held in Philadelphia in 1787, which produced the federal system of government outlined in the United States Constitution. (p. 33)

cooperative federalism One of several perspectives on federalism, popular during the first two-thirds of the twentieth century, which was defined by joint endeavors between the federal and state governments. Typically, state governments would carry out federal initiatives, using federal money and federal guidelines. (p. 46)

Declaration of Independence The document drafted by Thomas Jefferson and approved by the Continental Congress in July 1776, stating the reasons for the Revolutionary War and declaring a formal break with Great Britain. (p. 29)

disenfranchised Losing or being denied the legal right to vote by intentional or unintentional means. (p. 26)

dual federalism One of several perspectives on federalism, popular during the early years of the republic, which stated that the federal and state governments operated concurrently in separate arenas, and that each had the final say in those areas where it had a clear grant of authority. (p. 46)

faction A group of individuals who are united by a desire that, if realized, would threaten the liberty of the larger community—in James Madison's words, individuals who are "united and actuated by some common impulse of passion, or of interest, adverse to the rights of other citizens, or to the permanent and aggregate interests of the community." A faction may be defined by size, such as when a majority of citizens threatens the liberty of the minority, or by intensity, such as when a minority of citizens with intensely held preferences threatens the liberty of a disinterested majority. (p. 37)

federalism The division of power between a sovereign federal government and sovereign state governments, which provides that some functions will be performed by the national government, some by the state governments, and some by both the national and state governments. As a feature designed to limit the strength of government, federalism works to decentralize power by creating dual levels of authority. (p. 36)

The Federalist A collection of essays written by Alexander Hamilton, James Madison, and John Jay in an effort to persuade a reluctant public to support the Constitution. (p. 37)

federal system The arrangement created by the United States Constitution, in which the national government and the states share authority over citizens. States may act autonomously to do such things as create school districts, levy taxes, or assemble a police force; at the same time, powers are reserved for the national government, which is supreme to state laws. In addition to the United States, only Canada, Germany, India, and a small group of other nations have federal systems. (p. 33)

First Continental Congress A gathering of representatives from twelve of the thirteen colonies in Philadelphia in 1774 to protest the Coercive Acts and chart a unified colonial response. (p. 27)

Great Society The name given to the programs of President Lyndon B. Johnson, which elevated the federal government to the most prominent role it would play in the twentieth century. The philosophy of the Great Society was that government should try to solve large social problems like hunger and poverty. (p. 47)

legitimacy Widespread public acceptance of the official standing of a political figure or institution. (p. 34)

limited government The idea that power can be denied to government and the people who serve in it, in order to restrict those in positions of authority from infringing upon individual liberty. (p. 36)

McCulloch v. Maryland The 1819 Supreme Court case that established federal supremacy over the state governments. (p. 46)

nation-centered federalism One of several perspectives on federalism, which argues for the supremacy of the Constitution and federal law over state actions. (p. 44)

national supremacy The doctrine that the federal government has the final word in disputes with the states. National supremacy was established through court rulings, precedent, and the victory of the North in the Civil War, eventually resolving the conflict between nation-centered federalism and state-centered federalism in favor of the former. (p. 46)

natural rights Inalienable rights inherent to every individual that cannot be taken away by individuals or government, and that government should be designed to protect. (p. 29)

"necessary and proper" clause A constitutional provision (Article I, Section 8) giving Congress a broad grant of authority to make laws that are binding on the states. (p. 47)

New Deal The name given to the programs of President Franklin D. Roosevelt, which vastly expanded the role of the federal government in an effort to deal with the debilitating effects of the Great Depression on American society. (p. 47)

New Federalism The name given to the programs of Presidents Richard M. Nixon and Ronald Reagan, which started as an effort to streamline the federal government produced by the Great Society and ended up as a movement to reverse fifty years of federal growth by returning authority to the states. (p. 49)

New Jersey Plan A proposal for the new Constitution, supported by small states, that would have provided for equal representation of large and small states in the national legislature, while limiting the power of the national government over the states. (p. 33)

popular sovereignty Rule by the people based on the consent of the governed. (p. 36)

Quartering Act An act of the British Parliament requiring colonists to house British troops; first imposed in 1765 and then again in 1774 as part of the Coercive Acts. (p. 27)

Reinventing Government The name given to President Bill Clinton's initiative to make the federal government smaller by making it more efficient. (p. 49)

representative democracy A form of democracy in which eligible individuals choose others to make decisions on their behalf. (p. 36)

republic Any nation with provisions for the selection of representatives who make decisions on behalf of those who select them. James Madison said a republic was "a government in which the scheme of representation takes place," as compared to direct democracy. (p. 36)

Second Continental Congress A gathering of representatives from the colonies in Philadelphia in 1775, necessitated by the need to coordinate planning during the Revolutionary War, that functioned as the first central government in colonial America. (p. 28)

separation of powers The division of political power among several equal and independent branches of government to prevent power from being consolidated in any one branch. (p. 35)

Shays' Rebellion A rebellion by debtor farmers in western Massachusetts, led by Revolutionary War Captain Daniel Shays, against Boston creditors. It began in 1786 and lasted half a year, threatening the economic interests of the business elite and contributing to the demise of the Articles of Confederation. (p. 32)

social contract The arrangement in which people agree to give up some of their liberty to establish a government that will protect basic rights that are threatened in the state of nature. (p. 28)

Stamp Act A particularly vexing tax levied by the British on scores of legal documents, which led to a colonial boycott of British goods. (p. 27)

state-centered federalism One of several perspectives on federalism, which argues that the Constitution and the federal government are creations of the states and therefore can be overruled by the states. (p. 45)

state of nature The condition of total liberty in which people are free to act on their impulses, but where individual rights are afforded no protection. (p. 28)

Sugar Act The first in a string of taxes levied by Great Britain on the American colonies. Formally called the American Revenue Act of 1764, it taxed a number of colonial imports, including sugar. (p. 27)

supremacy clause A constitutional provision (Article VI) establishing the relationship between the federal and state governments. The supremacy clause asserts that any conflict between the federal government and the states will be decided in favor of the federal government. (p. 44)

Three-Fifths Compromise A compromise between northern and southern states that broke the deadlock over how slaves should be counted for purposes of representation. Three-fifths of slaves would be included in population totals, benefiting southern states that had the largest concentration of slaves by inflating their representation in the House of Representatives. (p. 35)

tyranny The denial of liberty to individuals through the actions of a faction or through the actions of government itself. (p. 37)

unitary system The inverse of a confederal system, in which a centralized national government creates subnational units like states, provinces, and counties, which derive their authority from the national government. Most nations are unitary systems. In the United States, the relationship between each individual state and its counties, townships, and cities is a unitary relationship, with the states creating and empowering the local governments. (p. 32)

Virginia Plan A proposal for the new Constitution, supported by large states, that would have based representation on population and provided for a centralized national government that could overrule the states. (p. 33)

Resources

You might be interested in examining some of what the following authors have said about the topics we've been discussing:

Hobbes, Thomas. *Leviathan*. New York: Oxford University Press, 1996. This version contains the original text and notes explaining Hobbes' reasoning.

Locke, John. *Two Treatises of Government*. New York: Cambridge University Press, 1994. This is a student version of the text of one of Locke's most influential works, including background on the author and his times.

McWilliams, Wilson C., ed. *Federalists, the Antifederalists, and the American Political Tradition*. New York: Greenwood Press, 1992. Seven essays explore the thinking and motivation of the people who fought on both sides of the constitutional ratification question, and examine the relevance of their observations to today's politics.

Millican, Edward. *One United People: The Federalist Papers and the National Idea*. Lexington, KY: University Press of Kentucky, 1990. If you're interested in *The Federalist*, this book explores the arguments of Hamilton, Madison, and Jay, and the many ways they have been interpreted over the years.

Rossiter, Clinton L. *1787: The Grand Convention*. New York: W.W. Norton, 1987. A richly detailed, illuminating account of the people, politics, and events that shaped the Constitution.

You may also be interested in looking at these resource sites:

You can find the Articles of Confederation at: http://www.usconstitution.net/articles.html.

The Library of Congress offers all of *The Federalist Papers* online at http://www.congress.gov/resources/display/content/The+Federalist+Papers.

Notes

1 See John W. Kingdon, *America the Unusual* (New York: Worth Publishers, 1999).

2 For an overview of the events of the Revolutionary War, courtesy of the History Channel, go to http://www.historychannel.com and type "American Revolution" at the search bar.

3 Thomas Hobbes, *Leviathan* (New York: Oxford University Press, 1996), 84. This edition contains the original text and notes explaining Hobbes' reasoning.

4 Jean-Jacques Rousseau, *The Social Contract*. New York: Oxford University Press, 1994.

5 You may access the text of the Articles of Confederation at http://www.usconstitution.net/articles.html#Preamble.

6 Rhode Island refused to send delegates because small farmers with large debts who feared the actions of a convention filled with wealthy creditors controlled the state politically.

7 You can read about these false allegations and the whole story of constitutional development in the article, "A More Perfect Union: The Creation of the New Constitution," at the National Archives website at http://www.archives.gov/national_archives_experience/charters/constitution_history.html.

8 The politics of full representation for the District of Columbia makes it unlikely that this situation will change any time soon, even though it may seem strange that people living in the nation's capital do not have the same rights to representation as everyone else. Because the District of Columbia is a heavily Democratic city, it would certainly send Democrats to the House and Senate—ensuring that Republicans will work to prevent this from happening.

9 Hilary Hylton, "What's All That Succession Ruckus in Texas?" *Time*, April 18, 2009.

Table, Figure, and Box Notes

T1 National Archives and Records Administration.

T2 National Archives and Records Administration.

T3 National Archives and Records Administration.

T4 *Philadelphia Inquirer*, December 26, 2001.

T5 For a discussion of the Bush program, see James Risen, *State of War: The Secret History of the CIA and the Bush Administration*. New York: The Free Press, 2006.

T6 See the European Movement website at http://www.europeanmovement.eu/index.php?id=5154.

T7 Ibid.

T8 See the European Union website at www.europa.eu.

T9 http://ec.europa.eu/economy_finance/euro/index_en.htm.

T10 See the European "No" Campaign website, at www.europeannocampaign.com/293.html.

T11 Photo courtesy of Department of the Interior.

T12 You can find the text of Marshall's ruling at http://supreme.justia.com/us/17/316/case.html.

T13 Photo courtesy White House Press Office.

T14 http://www.whitehouse.gov/the_press_office/Remarks-by-the-President-to-a-Joint-Session-of-Congress-on-Health-Care/.

T15 Photo courtesy of U.S. Federal Government.

T16 Photo courtesy of Chuck Kennedy, White House photographer.

Public Opinion: What Is It, and What Does It Have to Do with Me?

CHAPTER 3

Copyright: Vladimir Wrangel/Shutterstock.com

Chapter Outline

Learning Objectives

When you have completed this chapter, you should be able to:

- Define public opinion.
- Distinguish the empirical components of public opinion from its normative components.
- Explain how direction, intensity, and stability are elements of public opinion.
- Understand the possible ramifications of low levels of political knowledge.
- Identify political attitudes like trust, cynicism, and efficacy, and address how each is represented in the population.
- Distinguish attitudes from beliefs, and discuss the relationship between intensely held beliefs and political action.
- Explain the relationship between beliefs and ideology.
- Differentiate liberalism from conservatism in terms of the role each endorses for government.
- Identify and describe ideological positions other than liberalism and conservatism.
- Briefly explain random sampling, and understand how opinion polls work.

3.1 Introduction

L.O. Define public opinion.

Did you know that more than two in three Americans have a favorable impression of Britain's Queen Elizabeth?[1] That 16 percent of the U.S. population is actively disengaged at work?[2] That 32 percent of Americans say figure skating is their favorite Olympic sport while only 3 percent prefer luge?[3] How do we know this? *Why* do we know this? Why do we *want* to know this?

public opinion: A collection of opinions people hold on matters relating to government, politics, and society.

We know these and many other details about our society because we have at our disposal the means to gather information about **public opinion**—information that tells us what people think in matters relating to politics and society. We gather information about public opinion because it's of interest to lots of different groups—corporations looking for the best way to market a product, elected officials concerned with how their actions are being perceived by voters, and even political scientists who want to learn more about how government works.

We're not likely to be interested in everything there is to know about public opinion, but there's a highly attentive audience for every bit of information that's gathered. Maybe you find the high level of disengagement in the American workplace to be little more than an interesting factoid, but it could be valuable information to a corporation looking to boost its productivity. Perhaps you could live a contented life never knowing that Americans prefer figure skating to luge, but if you're an NBC television executive looking to maximize the size of the audience for the Olympics, this small kernel of public opinion is a golden nugget.

empirical: Any statement based on the assessment of data or the analysis of information, without regard to value judgments.

normative: Any statement that invokes a judgment or evaluation. Think of the word *norm*, which implies a standard for evaluating something.

Public opinion about politics encompasses a range of things—from what people know and understand about what's going on in Washington, D.C. or in their state capitals, to what people think government should and should not do, to how people evaluate the job elected officials are doing, and more. Public opinion in a representative democracy is a two-way street: It's the basis for officials to understand public concerns and for the public to gauge official actions.

Collecting public opinion is an **empirical** enterprise, in that it's based on systematic, scientific measurement of opinions. But the substance of public opinion has an important **normative** component. Public opinion measures the values people place on such things as the characteristics people desire in politicians or the policies people say government should pursue.

L.O. Distinguish the empirical components of public opinion from its normative components.

L.O. Explain how direction, intensity, and stability are elements of public opinion.

directional: An aspect of public opinion that measures whether people feel favorably or unfavorably toward a political figure, institution, or policy.

Before we look at the particulars of public opinion, there are a few things we could consider about its structure. At its most basic, public opinion often has a "thumbs up" or "thumbs down" quality. We tend to think that Congress is either doing a good job or a bad job. In other words, public opinion is **directional**—it can be positive or negative. We can think of this as an expression of people's preferences—good or bad, hot or cold—about a candidate for office, the performance of the president, or a policy idea that's being batted around in Congress. When we said that 68 percent of Americans have a favorable impression of Queen Elizabeth, we were making a statement about the direction of public opinion. The simplicity of positive and negative expressions allows us to get a quick sense of where the nation stands collectively on important political matters.

intensity: An aspect of public opinion that measures how strongly people feel toward a political figure, institution, or policy.

Public opinion is also characterized by **intensity**, by how deeply or strongly an opinion is held. If you're capable of living a happy and satisfied existence without thinking about which Olympic sport is your favorite, we'd say you have a low intensity of feeling about the issue. You may have an opinion, of course, but it wouldn't be a deeply held one. Many issues that surface in American politics are low-intensity issues.

A good example is campaign finance reform, or whether changes should be made to the way candidates for office raise money. For many years, Americans have generally supported the idea of campaign finance reform, meaning the direction of opinion on the issue was positive. At the same time, Americans ranked it as a low-level concern, meaning that they didn't feel strongly about it. Not coincidentally, without intense public support for change, Congress is reluctant to seriously consider meaningful campaign finance reform legislation.

High-intensity issues tend to be ones that hit home for people. They can be bread-and-butter domestic issues, such as whether the Affordable Care Act should be repealed, preserved, or expanded; fundamental foreign policy issues, such as whether the United States should have gone to war with Iraq; or social issues with personal or moral ramifications, such as whether same-sex couples should be allowed to marry. Beyond issues like these, Americans typically have lots of opinions but few strong opinions.

Finally, public opinion is fluid. People change their minds about things. Circumstances change, causing people to assess situations differently, which is why it is common for public opinion on the president's job performance to fluctuate widely over the course of an administration. This speaks to the **stability** of public opinion, or changes in the direction of public support for an official, candidate, institution, or policy. When opinions are less intensely held, they are susceptible to large swings.

Let's look at two figures that contrast stable public opinion with unstable public opinion. American attitudes toward religion, portrayed in Figure 3.1, were remarkably stable for the twenty-year period from 1984 through 2004. During that time, roughly four in five Americans said that religion is an important factor in their lives. Only in recent years do we see the start of a drop-off in this sentiment, as Millennials—a far less religious group than their parents and grandparents—have become a larger share of the population. But in the period before Millennials entered the adult population, public opinion about the role of religion in everyday life was about as stable as an opinion can be.

Now look at Figure 3.2, which measures public opinion about whether the economy of the United States had gotten worse during the previous year. Look at how the figure jumps around, as economic conditions varied wildly over time. The peaks in the figure

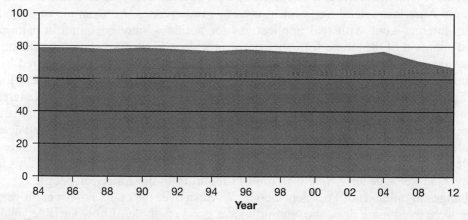

FIGURE 3.1 Percentage of Americans Saying Religion Is an Important Part of Life, 1984–2012[T1]

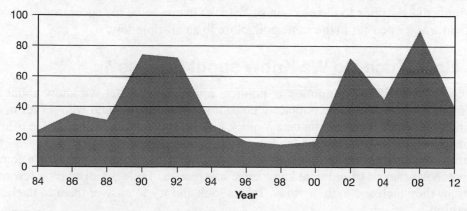

FIGURE 3.2 Percentage of Americans Saying the U.S. Economy Is Getting Worse, 1988–2012[T2]

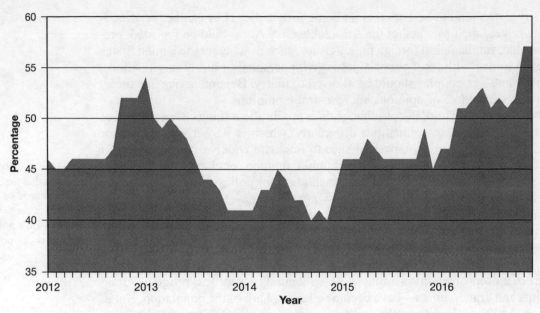

FIGURE 3.3 Approval of President Obama's Job Performance, 2012–2016[T3]

track the recessions that occurred at the start of the 1990s and the 2000s, with the largest peak coinciding with the "Great Recession" of 2008.

The direction, intensity, and stability of public opinion combine to create a barometer of where Americans stand on political issues as time passes. An example of how these factors interact—one with real implications for politics—may be found in patterns of public approval of the job performance of the president. Figure 3.3 shows the fluctuation in President Obama's job approval ratings during his second term as measured by the Gallup Poll. Despite being bogged down with approval ratings below 50 percent for the better part of 2012, Obama rebounded before Election Day, surging into positive territory in time to be re-elected that November before falling back into negative territory several months later. For the better part of 2014, the president's approval scores hovered near the 40 percent mark, low enough to portend big losses for his party in that year's congressional elections. His job approval ratings improved substantially toward the end of his term, however, and Obama left office with robust support from the American people.

Changes in opinions of President George W. Bush over the course of his eight years in office were even more dramatic, and provide a good example of how variable, shallow, and unstable opinions can be. Immediately following the September 11, 2001, terrorist attacks, President Bush had the approval of almost the entire country, topping out at 92 percent support in early October 2001 in the ABC News/*Washington Post* poll. In the days immediately prior to the election of Barack Obama to be his successor, Bush's job approval was 23 percent in the same poll, close to an all-time low.

3.2 How Much Do We Know about Politics?

L.O. Understand the possible ramifications of low levels of political knowledge.

One component of public opinion is political knowledge—what we know about how government is structured, the policies it considers or carries out, and who serves in or is running for elected office. Let's take a quick quiz to see how your knowledge of a few political items compares to what Americans as a whole know.

Some time ago, researchers Michael X. Delli Carpini and Scott Keeter took a comprehensive look at levels of political knowledge in America. Table 3.1 displays a few of the questions they included in their study. Take a look and try to answer them to the best of your ability.

So, how did you do? If you missed some of these questions, don't feel bad. You're in good company. As Delli Carpini and Keeter found, most people retain some political

TABLE 3.1 A Quick Political Knowledge Quiz[T4]

Test your knowledge of political institutions, processes, and policies:

1. Do you happen to know how many times an individual can be elected president?
2. What percentage vote of Congress is needed to override a veto by the president?
3. True or False: A district attorney's job is to defend an accused criminal who cannot afford an attorney.
4. True or False: Every decision made by a state court can be reviewed and reversed by the Supreme Court.
5. True or False: The Social Security tax money collected from an individual is set aside specifically for that person's retirement benefits.
6. Yes or No: Is the United States a member of NATO, the North Atlantic Treaty Organization?

Answers:

1. Twice (percentage answering correctly in 1990: 73)
2. Two-thirds (percentage answering correctly in 1985: 63)
3. False (percentage answering correctly in 1983: 47)
4. False (percentage answering correctly in 1983: 11)
5. False (percentage answering correctly in 1981: 75)
6. Yes (percentage answering correctly in 1989: 60)

knowledge, and some people have large reserves of political information, but many people are quite limited in what they know about politics. Some of us are totally lacking in knowledge of our political institutions and policies.[4]

People who are capable of rattling off the names of the starting pitchers on their hometown baseball team may be at a loss to recall the names of their U.S. senators. People who can readily identify Oprah Winfrey may go blank trying to place Loretta Lynch.[5] For many of us, it's a matter of priorities. Americans simply do not make politics a main concern.

This is not a new story. Low levels of political knowledge have characterized American public opinion for as long as anyone can remember. Delli Carpini and Keeter found that levels of political knowledge are essentially unchanged from what they were over a half century ago. Their findings reinforce a study of political knowledge that was conducted over sixty years ago, when three researchers named Bernard Berelson, Paul Lazarsfeld, and William McPhee set out to understand how people made up their minds when they voted in the 1948 presidential election. Their study included a look at how much voters knew about the issue positions of the candidates. The answer: like today, not very much. Only about one in three voters had an accurate perception of the candidates' positions on major issues.

If you think for a second about the sources of political information we have today that didn't exist in 1948—or 1968 or 2008—the consistency in our lack of political knowledge is noteworthy. We've lived through an information explosion since you were born, featuring twenty-four-hour cable news services, live television coverage of Congress, newspapers with websites, weblogs, Google, Facebook, Twitter, Snapchat—all sorts of facts and opinions conveniently available like never before. Yet, our low levels of political knowledge remain unshaken.

One explanation is that it's simply difficult to learn new information or to be motivated to learn new information. Another explanation is that it's possible to be exposed to too much information—to feel bombarded by 24/7 news and information and tune it out. A variation on this explanation is that it can be hard to make sense of the information we get, to put it together in a meaningful way, even to decipher what's truthful and what is not. A fairly widespread example of this phenomenon is discussed in Demystifying Government: More Information, Less Knowledge.

On the face of it, having a nation of people who don't know much about politics seems at odds with the underlying assumptions of a representative democracy that the Federalists

More Information, Less Knowledge

Berelson, Lazarsfeld, and McPhee's study of how people decide to vote found that knowledge of election issues and correct understanding of candidate positions on major issues were higher among those who paid close attention to media reports. This suggests that people who watch or read the news more often are likely to acquire more political information.

But how do we know that the information we're getting is entirely accurate?

News reports seem very authoritative when they're delivered by well-groomed anchors on television or when they appear in crisp print in the newspaper. The problem is, in a media environment dominated by cable news, talk radio, and social media, misinformation can spread quickly. So, it can be hard to spot misleading information, even if we know not to believe everything we see or read.

Here's an example that originates in 2009, when the Obama administration and Congress were debating the details of overhauling the health-care system, and survives today in our political discourse. Throughout the summer and fall of that year, news reports were filled with stories about the politics of health-care reform—a huge, complex, and controversial task—that included discussion of various proposals for how the health-care plan would operate. As is often the case in a fluid political situation, the specifics changed a lot as the president tried to find enough votes to get some version of a plan through Congress. This made the health-care story complicated to report and difficult to keep straight.

The situation was ideal for the spread of misinformation, and in fact, opinion polls taken in mid-2009 revealed a great deal of confusion—and concern—about what Congress was doing. One of the most celebrated untruths about the plan was that it would ration care through a government board that would determine the worthiness of a patient's health-care claims and deny expensive care to the very sick and the elderly. Termed "death panels" by the plan's detractors, it became a topic of widespread discussion in the summer of 2009, in part because prominent reform opponents such as former Alaska Governor Sarah Palin and former House Speaker Newt Gingrich implied the claims were true.

Politifact.com, a fact-checking project of the *St. Petersburg Times*, examined the "death panel" claims and found them to be emphatically false. The foundation of the claim was that the government planned to save money by rationing care, which would be done through a panel of bureaucrats who would decide who was worthy of getting treatment. The truth behind this charge is a lot more complicated and difficult to fit into a brief television news story, Facebook post, or tweet.

According to Politifact, the plan under consideration by Congress proposed subsidizing optional doctor visits for seniors receiving assistance from the government program Medicare to discuss living wills and other end-of-life treatments. It also proposed the creation of a government board to examine research on effective medical outcomes to improve diagnosis and treatment. And although the board could give guidance on such things as end-of-life care, it couldn't mandate or withhold it.[T5]

Politifact concluded there was no truth to Governor Palin's claim that a panel of bureaucrats would be able to determine who was worthy of receiving health care, saying it "sounds more like a science fiction movie ('Soylent Green,' anyone?) than part of an actual bill before Congress."[T6] But most people do not spend time browsing political fact-checking websites, so the notion of "death panels" continues to infuse discussion of health-care policy.[T7]

We can be surrounded by information and still be uninformed. If we were concerned about government getting too involved in something as personal and as important as our relationship with our doctors, we might take seriously a claim that Congress was going to interfere with that relationship, especially if the claim was discussed frequently in the press, finding ourselves with more information—but less knowledge.

advocated during the battle over ratification of the Constitution. After all, to have an effective democratic republic, it follows that those who elect representatives should have some knowledge of what they stand for, so there can be a meaningful connection between representative and represented. It makes sense that information is an important resource for connecting our interests to the actions of our representatives, to make sure they're acting according to our wishes. As Berelson and his colleagues put it:

> The democratic citizen is supposed to be well informed about political affairs. He is supposed to know what the issues are, what their history is, what the relevant facts are, what alternatives are proposed, what the party stands for, what the likely consequences are. By such standards, the voter falls short. Even when he has the motivation, he finds it difficult to make decisions on the basis of full information when the subject is relatively simple and proximate; how can he do so when it is complex and remote?[6]

Is democracy compromised if our political knowledge is far less than what democratic theorists suggest is necessary for us to be able to make complex political decisions? Berelson and company do not believe so. No place is political knowledge more important than in the decisions Americans make in the voting booth, but people are able to make those decisions all the time without detailed knowledge of the candidates or issues. As we'll see in Chapter 4, people use all kinds of shorthand methods to figure out how to vote. While levels of political knowledge in America may fall short of what John Locke would have found desirable, the argument can be made that the political process survives just fine without highly informed citizens.

Or does it? Here's another view: Delli Carpini and Keeter say that whites, males, older people, and financially well-off individuals tend to know more about politics than blacks, women, young people, and people with low incomes. Since informed people are better able to identify what they want from the political system, people who already have economic and social advantages may be better positioned to get the political system to respond to them. From this perspective, there is an "information elite" whose control of an important resource—information—gives it political power, while the lack of political knowledge serves as a detriment to those who need it the most.

3.3 Political Attitudes: From the Heart

If political knowledge is scarce in the population, political attitudes—another component of public opinion—are commonplace. People have attitudes about all sorts of things. **Attitudes** tap how people feel about politics or how people are oriented to political figures, institutions, issues, or events. Like any feeling, attitudes are something people experience; they cannot be right or wrong in a normative sense. Maybe you have an attitude about New Age music: You hate it, love it, or just don't get it. Or maybe you couldn't care less. That's an attitude, too. There's nothing inherently wrong or right about any of these positions—they're just how you feel. Political attitudes work the same way.

We have attitudes about a wide range of things. Let's look at a few and see how our attitudes compare with others in our class and with the nation as a whole. We'll consider our attitudes toward big government, levels of trust we place in government, political efficacy, and tolerance of diversity.

L.O. Identify political attitudes like trust, cynicism, and efficacy, and address how each is represented in the population.

attitudes: A component of public opinion that measures people's orientations toward politics.

3.3a Big Government

As we said in Chapter 2, the debate over how large and strong the federal government should be continues to divide people as much now as it did two hundred years ago. Table 3.2 contains a question pertaining to the matter of government power that has appeared for many years in the Gallup Poll, a major survey of American public opinion. Take a minute to think about the question and decide what option best reflects your attitude.

Age-old concerns about a strong federal government are apparent in contemporary attitudes. Almost twice as many people express concern that government is excessively powerful than are satisfied with the amount of government's power.

However, this has not always been the case. Worries about the power of government began rising during George W. Bush's second term, as the country became bogged down

TABLE 3.2 Big Government[T8]

Do you think the federal government has:
Too much power
About the right amount of power
Too little power
NATIONAL RESULTS
In 2015, 69 percent of respondents said that government is too powerful, whereas only 7 percent answered that government is not powerful enough. The middle position—about the right amount of power—was selected by approximately one-third of respondents.

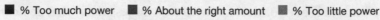

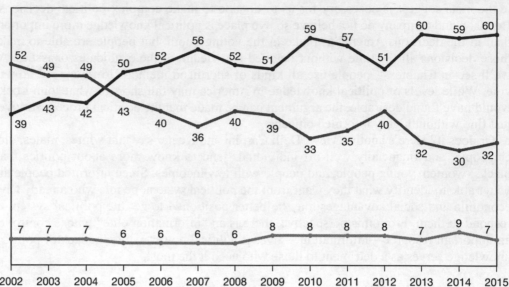

FIGURE 3.4 Attitudes about the Power of the Federal Government, 2002–2015[T9]

in conflicts in Iraq and Afghanistan, and spiked during the Obama years following a period of government activism that resulted in the controversial passage of the Affordable Care Act. There was a similar spike in the 1970s, in the aftermath of the abuses of power that characterized the Watergate scandal.[7] Only a small but constant percentage of Americans feel government is not powerful enough. The trend going back to 2002 is displayed in Figure 3.4.

Even when concerns about the power of government were at a low point in the early years of the century, a sizable percentage of Americans still felt that government was too strong. This is a reflection of how concerns about government creeping too far into daily life are both deeply rooted in American history and a prominent part of how Americans experience government. Perhaps the opinions of your classmates reflect this attitude as well.

It is also the case that not all groups of Americans share the same degree of concern about the power of the federal government. The American National Election Studies (ANES), a major survey of American public opinion, took a close look at how women and men, nonwhites and whites, and southerners/non-southerners felt about government power. They found some interesting differences.[8]

For both women and men, the level of concern about government moves up and down together. In other words, there are no gender differences in the direction of this attitude: during times when people feel government is too powerful, this concern is shared by women and men. But at every point, women express less concern than men about government encroachment on their personal lives.

One way of understanding this difference is to think of it in terms of the policies government produces and the way they're received by women and men. We know from opinion polls that women as a group tend to be receptive to policies that assist the poor, minorities, and the poorly educated, whereas men are more likely to question whether these are appropriate things for government to be doing—or whether the fact that government involvement in policies such as these is a sign that government is doing too much.

We see something similar when we look at racial differences, where nonwhites are far less likely to be concerned about the power of government than whites. This difference may be explained by the tendency for nonwhites as a group to be more receptive than whites to the policies of the federal government.

When we look at regional differences, a less stable pattern of public opinion emerges. Traditionally, the South has been highly sensitive to federal power. As we saw in

Chapter 2, southern states were the strongest early advocates of **state-centered federalism**, seceded from the Union prior to the Civil War, and were reconstructed after the war under federal authority. More recently, in the 1950s and 1960s, the federal government was responsible for desegregating the South through policies that some white southerners regarded as excessive use of government power.

state-centered federalism: One of several perspectives on federalism, which argues that the Constitution and the federal government are creations of the states and therefore can be overruled by the states.

Not surprisingly, during the 1960s, southerners were more likely than others to feel that the federal government was too powerful. Then something interesting happened in the 1970s. As the era of dramatic policy changes stemming from the civil rights movement began to wind down, attitudes about government power began to change as well. By 1972, regional differences virtually disappeared. Southerners even became incrementally less likely than others to express the opinion that the government is too powerful. As circumstances change, attitudes often follow.

3.3b Trust in Government

When your political history is infused with strong doubts about centralized authority, you might expect people to be somewhat hesitant to place their trust in government. When we look at how much trust Americans place in the federal government to do what's right, we in fact find an undercurrent of doubt—not enough to bring our support for the institutions of government into question, but doubt nonetheless. Although only a tiny fraction of Americans feel their government never does the right thing, a majority feels it does the right thing only some of the time. And only 4 percent feel that government just about always gets it right.

In Table 3.3, you'll find a question from the ANES, this one pertaining to the matter of trust in government.

Like opinions about government power, there has been a great deal of change over the years in this attitude as well, suggesting that Americans are not entirely predisposed to skepticism and that events can affect our disposition. Over the past several decades, the degree of trust we've placed in government has tracked very closely with the actions of prominent government officials, most notably the president. Figure 3.5 demonstrates how the amount of trust we've placed in government has taken a roller-coaster ride since 1964.

Back in the late 1950s and early 1960s, trusting government was almost a unanimous sentiment. That was a lifetime ago, before the Vietnam War and Watergate drained the well of universal trust. As the United States became deeply entrenched in Vietnam, the administration of President Lyndon Johnson purposely misrepresented the extent and likely duration of the war. His successor, Richard Nixon, assumed Johnson's misleading approach to Vietnam, then fell from office as a result of the Watergate scandal, during which he obstructed justice and concealed illegal activities. Gradually, Americans began to feel that their leaders were deceiving them as a matter of policy, and trust in government dropped accordingly—from a high of 76 percent in 1964 to only 36 percent by 1974.

TABLE 3.3 Trust in Government[T10]

How much of the time do you think you can trust the government in Washington to do what is right—just about always, most of the time, only some of the time, or none of the time?
Just about always
Most of the time
Only some of the time
None of the time
Don't know/no opinion
NATIONAL RESULTS
In 2012, 76 percent of respondents felt that government could be trusted to do what was right only some of the time, whereas 20 percent said that government could be trusted to do what was right most of the time. Only 2 percent answered that this was true just about always, and another 2 percent felt it was true none of the time.

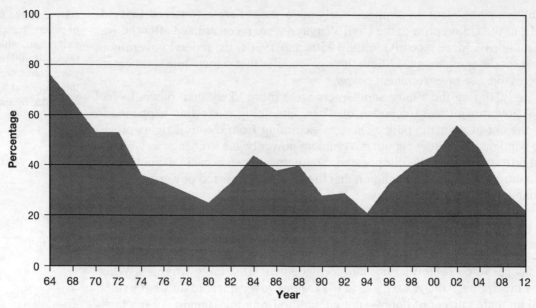

FIGURE 3.5 Americans Who Always or Usually Trust Government to Do What Is Right, 1964–2012[T11]

And trust continued to fall. President Gerald Ford pardoned Nixon for his role in Watergate, which at the time was widely regarded as a move that sheltered Nixon from accountability. President Jimmy Carter presided over what many considered a hapless administration characterized by a sour economy and frustration overseas. By the end of Carter's term in 1980, only one-quarter of Americans felt they could trust government to generally do what is right.

Feelings of trust recovered during the Reagan administration, but hardly to the optimistic levels reached in the early 1960s, then dropped again in the wake of widespread disappointment with President George H. W. Bush. In 1994, President Bill Clinton unsuccessfully attempted to make government more responsible for providing health care—after running as a moderate who downplayed the desire to create more government programs—and trust in government crashed to its modern-day low. Trust in government was buffeted again during the Clinton impeachment proceedings. During the fast economic times of the late 1990s, though, trust recovered to the modest levels of the Reagan years, peaking after the 2001 terrorist attacks, then declining sharply through the Bush and Obama administrations as the nation grew deeply divided.

The amount of confidence we have in the major institutions of government is consistent with our feelings of trust. In today's toxic political environment, all three branches of the federal government are viewed with disdain. But in what may be a case of familiarity breeding a bit of contempt, the two branches of government elected by the people—Congress and the presidency—are less trusted than the Supreme Court. In 2014, more than half the country had hardly any confidence in Congress, and in the middle of President Obama's second term, 44 percent felt the same about the presidency. The figures for the Supreme Court are slightly better, with about one-quarter of the country expressing a great deal of confidence in the Court and one-fifth expressing hardly any, although these attitudes are more negative than they were ten years earlier.

Overall, public trust in government institutions ranks below trust in nongovernmental institutions, such as those devoted to medicine and science (see Figure 3.6).

Another interpretation of what's happened since the early 1960s is that Americans have become more cynical about government. **Cynicism** is a pervasive feeling of mistrust or suspicion, and it can be distinguished from skepticism, which is having doubts or wanting proof before believing something. Skepticism offers the possibility of acceptance when one's doubts are satisfied, but cynicism holds no such promise. Skepticism is captured in Missouri's nickname—the "Show-Me" state: Prove it to me before you ask me to believe

cynicism: A pervasive attitude of mistrust about politics that may lead people to withdraw from political participation.

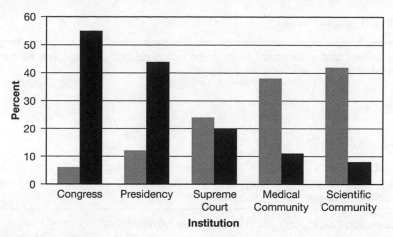

FIGURE 3.6 Percentage of Americans Expressing High and Low Levels of Confidence in Key Institutions, 2014[T12]

The light bars indicate the percentage of people who have a great deal of confidence in the listed institution, whereas the dark bars show the percentage who have hardly any confidence.

The degree of confidence that people have in Congress and the presidency is quite low. People are nine times more likely to have hardly any confidence in Congress and almost four times more likely to have hardly any confidence in the presidency than to express a great deal of confidence in these institutions. The Supreme Court is the only branch of government with more supporters than doubters—but not by much. In contrast, other social institutions command higher levels of public confidence. Scientists and doctors only have a smattering of detractors.

you. Cynicism is expressed when someone rolls his or her eyes, looks at the sky, and walks away.

The distinction is important because cynicism and skepticism can generate entirely different reactions to politics. We can be skeptical but still be engaged in the political process. It's probably fair to say that many of the framers of the Constitution were skeptical about creating a strong central government, but their reaction was to attempt to create a system that kept government under control. If they had been cynics, it's doubtful that they would even have tried.

When we're suspicious of something, we tend to withdraw from it or at least search for evidence to validate our suspicions. If we're cynical about government, we may find ourselves pointing out things we don't like about politicians or what they do and using this as justification for feeling cynical. Or we might just withdraw from politics entirely. Of course, if we do that, we're leaving the system to others who will engage it to advance their interests.

3.3c Efficacy

The flip side of cynicism is **efficacy**, or the sense that you can get results from the political system if you engage in political action. One way to measure the extent of cynicism is to assess the degree of efficacy people feel. The more efficacy people feel, the less cynical they're likely to be.

Efficacy can be hard to measure because it can be difficult for survey questions to distinguish someone who feels the system isn't responding to him or her from someone who feels totally alienated from government. For this reason, we'll approach efficacy from several directions by using three ANES questions (see Table 3.4) to determine how efficacious you feel.

As you can tell, we are not living in an age when people feel great efficacy about government and elected officials. Many people are confounded by the complexity of government, have doubts about the motives of elected officials, and feel powerless to control what government does.

> **efficacy:** The attitude that you can be effectual and effective in your dealings with government.

TABLE 3.4 Efficacy[T13]

> Sometimes politics and government seem so complicated that a person like me can't really understand what's going on.
>
> Agree
>
> Disagree
>
> Neither
>
> Don't know/no opinion
>
> NATIONAL RESULTS
>
> In 2012, 56 percent of respondents agreed with this statement, 29 percent disagreed with it, and 16 percent neither agreed nor disagreed.

> Public officials don't care much about what people like me think.
>
> Agree
>
> Disagree
>
> Neither
>
> Don't know/no opinion
>
> NATIONAL RESULTS
>
> Sixty-one percent of respondents agreed with this statement, 18 percent disagreed with it, and 21 percent neither agreed nor disagreed.

> People like me don't have any say about what the government does.
>
> Agree
>
> Disagree
>
> Neither
>
> Don't know/no opinion
>
> NATIONAL RESULTS
>
> Forty-eight percent of respondents agreed with this statement, 35 percent disagreed with it, and 17 percent neither agreed nor disagreed.

When we take a little closer look at this situation, something interesting pops out of the data. The degree of efficacy people feel turns out to have a lot to do with their social and economic situations, as captured by their levels of education and income. You can see this by looking at how people with different levels of education and income responded to the three questions you just answered. See Figure 3.7.

Figure 3.7 makes it pretty clear that people with less education and income have less efficacy. There are striking attitude differences between the wealthiest or most educated people and the poorest or least educated people. For instance, 72 percent of people whose education falls short of a high school diploma find politics too complicated. That figure falls to 52 percent in your group—people with some college education—and drops even further to 45 percent among college graduates and people with postgraduate education. Accordingly, almost two of three high school dropouts feel they have no say in what government does, compared with four in ten college graduates.

This suggests a relationship between having command of the kind of information and skills that come with formal education and the feelings we develop about our place in the political system. It makes sense that if something like government feels complicated because we don't understand it, we're probably not going to give it a big place in our lives. It also follows that people would feel disconnected from government if they don't understand it, and would also feel that elected officials don't care about them and that what they say doesn't matter. Even if formal education doesn't entail formal education about government—think of your friends who avoid taking courses in political science!—the skills that come with higher education can produce a sense of confidence that's associated with feeling efficacious about government.

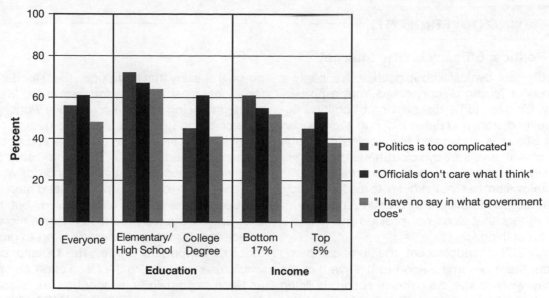

FIGURE 3.7 Different Perspectives on Efficacy[T14]

The income figures tell a similar story, with an important wrinkle for who gets what, when, and how. Look at the responses people give to the question about having a say about what government does. Over half the people in the bottom one-sixth of the income scale feel they have no say politically. Only 38 percent of the wealthiest Americans feel this way. It can make you wonder whether wealthy people feel more efficacy toward government because government really is responding to their interests with greater regularity.

Of course, if having information fuels empowerment, the Internet—which promises access to information and easy ways to link to other people—may offer a new way of building efficacy. Levels of efficacy remained low during the time when television dominated our politics, but there is some evidence that the Internet may offer an alternative to people who are interested in connecting with others through politics. Demystifying Government: Building Political Efficacy on the Internet explores this possibility by looking at two Internet-based presidential campaigns: the 2008 Obama campaign and the unsuccessful but instructive effort by Howard Dean four years earlier.

3.3d Tolerance

The 2016 campaign tested the limits of tolerance for individuals with diverse backgrounds as Donald Trump tapped into a vein of animosity and anger in American public opinion toward ethnic and religious minority groups, immigrants, and women. Running against the first female presidential nominee of a major political party to replace the first African American president, Trump gave voice to the resentment among some who resisted the growing presence and power of traditionally disadvantaged groups. At the same time, those advocating for diversity in America responded with equally impassioned voices. The result was a campaign that in part played out along a values divide that captured our tolerance of the changing demography of America.

Tolerance can be difficult to capture in opinion surveys because people generally do not like to express attitudes that may make them look bad. Still, there are as many ways to determine tolerance as there are different groups with which people identify. Table 3.5 demonstrates one with particular resonance for the politics of the last few years: Would you vote for a woman or an African American presidential candidate? When these questions were asked in the 2010 General Social Survey (GSS), a large biennial study of trends, changes, and constants in how Americans feel, think, and act conducted by social scientists based at the University of Chicago, you could see the effect of the recent presidential primary contest between a strong female (Hillary Clinton) and African American candidate. Overwhelmingly, Americans said that race and gender would not factor into their choice.

Building Political Efficacy on the Internet

When people feel cynical about politics, it's partly a consequence of feeling disconnected from a political community. It's easy to be disbelieving of political figures who seem distant and detached, and even though the United States is connected electronically through television, overall levels of cynicism have grown over the years since television became a central feature in our lives. Television has not proven to build efficacy, and may, in fact, undermine it by creating a false connection to others that does not provide the nourishment of the real thing.[T15]

Although still an adolescent medium compared to television, there is some reason to believe that the Internet may work in the opposite direction, building efficacy by building community. The first signs of this possibility appeared during the 2004 election cycle, when Democratic presidential candidate Howard Dean became the first political figure to test the potential of the Internet to bring people into the political process. Defying conventional wisdom that campaigns should be run on a top-down basis, the once-anonymous former Vermont governor built a viable political following by bringing people together online and listening to their suggestions for how to run his campaign.

Tapping into a nation that had become increasingly comfortable with the Internet, the Dean campaign created a space where supporters could interact virtually through weblogs (or "blogs") to discuss how to promote their candidate. His web page also directed supporters to a website called meetup.com, where people could sign up to attend campaign meetings in person on the first Wednesday of every month. Over the course of the year leading up to the election, tens of thousands of people joined these virtual and real communities, with the number involved in the Dean campaign growing steadily as word about what Dean was doing spread online.

Comments posted by users of Dean's official campaign blog suggested that people were reacting emotionally to the experience, expressing feelings of political efficacy that had eluded them for decades—or, for younger participants, for their entire lives. People reacted to being part of a community working together for a common goal, and they were getting out of their houses to get involved in the political process—many of them for the first time. Their comments suggested they were experiencing the full range of what politics can be—fun, exciting, purposeful, and meaningful.

Dean's presidential efforts failed, but four years later Barack Obama produced a larger, more sophisticated, and ultimately successful effort to organize and mobilize supporters online. The Obama campaign's web presence was like the Dean effort on steroids, or, as Dean's campaign manager Joe Trippi called it, the Apollo project compared to Dean's Wright brothers operation.[T16] The Obama website gave supporters a set of tools they could use to organize on behalf of the candidate, virtually and in the real world. And they responded, giving unprecedented amounts of time and money, enabling their candidate to defeat a better-known and well-funded primary opponent in then-senator Hillary Clinton, then defeat Senator John McCain in the general election. Like the Dean supporters, members of Obama's Internet constituency believed in and were motivated by their candidate.

Since 2008, we have seen people continue to engage in campaign politics via the Internet and social media, even as political conditions changed. President Obama was able to re-energize his supporters in 2012 and turn them out to vote in an election rooted more in the pragmatic realities of governance than the soaring rhetoric of hope. Many responded—both in support and opposition—to Donald Trump's Twitter campaign, which engaged and enraged people across the political spectrum during the wild and divisive 2016 election. In contexts ranging from sober to outrageous, online politics has served as a vehicle for political activism noticeably at odds with the cynicism typical of the television age.

This may seem unsurprising to those who have lived almost their whole adult lives with an African American president, but there was a time when this would have been unthinkable, as many Americans openly opposed the idea of a woman or a person of color serving as president. Accordingly, all of President Obama's predecessors have been white males, and all but one has been Protestant.[9] In 1984 when Democratic presidential nominee Walter Mondale chose Representative Geraldine Ferraro as his vice-presidential running mate, it was considered a historic and risky choice. But, when Senator John McCain selected Alaska Governor Sarah Palin as his running mate in 2008, it was clear that times had changed. McCain's selection of Palin—only the second female running mate of a major party nominee—guaranteed that either an African American or female candidate would win national office in 2008.

TABLE 3.5 Tolerance[T17]

If your party nominated a woman for president, would you vote for her if she were qualified for the job?
Yes
No
Don't know/no opinion
If your party nominated a black (African American) for president, would you vote for him if he were qualified for the job?
Yes
No
Don't know/no opinion
NATIONAL RESULTS In 2010, a resounding 95 percent of respondents answered yes to both questions, whereas only 4 percent said no.

Greater diversity among serious presidential candidates during the years prior to 2008 suggested that we may have been building to a watershed election.[10] In 2000, former transportation secretary and American Red Cross president Elizabeth Dole ran an unsuccessful but credible campaign for the Republican presidential nomination (she later won election to the Senate from North Carolina). Former Secretary of State Colin Powell was prominently discussed as a presidential candidate after emergence as a public figure during the Persian Gulf War. Al Gore was almost elected president in 2000, running on a ticket with Connecticut Senator Joseph Lieberman, the first Jewish national candidate in American history.

When we look beyond diversity in national candidates, though, our capacity for tolerance is more dubious, especially when people are asked to be lenient in less abstract settings. Respondents to the 2000 GSS were asked if they were comfortable allowing people whose ideas or values were not mainstream to speak publicly, to have books advocating their views on the shelves of public libraries, or to teach at a college or university.

Take a look at what they said. Figure 3.8 displays the responses people gave regarding four groups whose views could be considered outside the mainstream of American public opinion: gays, anti-religionists (people who oppose all churches and religions), Communists, and racists. The figure shows that most Americans would be willing to permit each of them to speak. But a sizable minority would not, ranging from 27 percent who would object to a gay speaker publicly advocating homosexuality to 39 percent who would have a problem with a racist speaker publicly proclaiming personal views on the inferiority of African Americans.

For most of our history, presidential politics was the exclusive province of white male Protestants. As more Americans have become accepting of diversity at the highest levels of government, real and would-be nominees from different backgrounds have begun to emerge. Left to right: Representative Geraldine Ferraro; Senator Elizabeth Dole; Secretary of State Colin Powell; Senator Joseph Lieberman; Governor Sara Palin; former President Barack Obama.[T18]

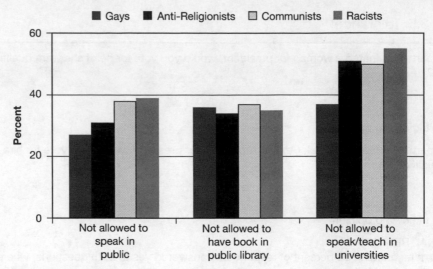

FIGURE 3.8 Putting Tolerance to the Test[T19]

Roughly one-third of Americans have a problem with library books proclaiming positions outside the mainstream, regardless of the position at issue. When it comes to permitting members of these groups to teach in colleges or universities, Americans are at their most intolerant. Although we think of universities as being places where dissenting opinions are welcomed, accepting diverse and perhaps distasteful discourse in the classroom requires a high level of tolerance, considering the authority claimed by professors—tolerance to a degree not exhibited by many Americans. These figures haven't changed much in the intervening years. The percentage of Americans who would preclude a Communist from teaching at a university or a racist from speaking in public has hardly budged since 2000.[11]

So, are we a tolerant people? Answering this question may be like asking if the glass is half empty or half full. From one perspective, the answer would seem to be yes. Most measures of tolerance won the support of majorities of Americans, even large majorities. Some circumstances, such as objecting to racist teachings, actually could be interpreted as being intolerant of an intolerant message, even though this position disregards the constitutionally protected freedom of the speaker in the effort to discard the message.

On the other hand, the number of people professing intolerant positions is significant. And there's always the possibility that data like these may not fully reflect the depth of intolerant attitudes. After all, it's not always easy to admit to having a position that many people would find unpopular, a topic we'll address in Demystifying Government: Saying the "Right" Thing.

3.4 Political Beliefs: From the Head

L.O. Distinguish attitudes from beliefs, and discuss the relationship between intensely held beliefs and political action.

beliefs: A component of public opinion that measures what people think is true about politics.

If political attitudes are plentiful and come from your heart, political **beliefs** are just as plentiful, but they're of an entirely different nature. Whereas attitudes stem from what people feel, political beliefs are things people think to be true about politicians, politics, and policy. You might say they come from our head or mind.

We said that attitudes could never really be wrong because they're simply a reflection of how we're oriented toward political people, institutions, and events. Beliefs are more complex. People can believe things that are not true, such as that Social Security isn't a government program (it is) or that 15 percent of the federal budget goes to foreign aid (the real figure is much less). Months after Saddam Hussein was overthrown, a majority of Americans incorrectly believed that the Bush administration had found a link between Iraq and al-Qaeda.[12] Though false, people hold to beliefs like these as if they are true, muddying the political decision-making process.

Beliefs can even influence attitudes. Some people believe there was a conspiracy to assassinate President Kennedy that included members of the government. It's not hard to

Saying the "Right" Thing

Some attitudes are simply easier than others to admit to, and as a result, we need to be a little careful about the face value of data on controversial attitudes like intolerance. What if you feel that gay people shouldn't be allowed to teach in universities, but you also feel that if you express this to a pollster, you're going to look narrow-minded? Or maybe you didn't support Hillary Clinton's presidential candidacy but felt admitting as much might make you appear sexist? Situations like this can give people strong motivation to cover up their antisocial attitudes and behaviors and report positions that don't reflect what they really feel. If enough people do this, pollsters won't get an accurate reading on the extent of social intolerance. Something called a **social desirability bias** results when public opinion polls reflect what people want others to believe instead of what they really believe.

During the 2008 presidential election, with the first African American nominee of a major party on the ballot, pollsters wondered whether social desirability bias would present itself in the form of what's known as the "Bradley Effect," named for former Los Angeles mayor Tom Bradley who lost his 1982 bid to become California governor despite pre-election polls that showed him ahead. Bradley, who was African American, lost to a white candidate, and one explanation for the discrepancy between the polls and the election result was that a percentage of white voters falsely told pollsters they intended to vote for the more experienced Bradley.

The Bradley Effect did not materialize in 2008, when final aggregate polling closely matched the outcome. One possible reason why is that the political agenda had changed in the intervening years, diminishing the importance of racially charged issues like welfare and crime. Another possibility is that it was easier for people who didn't want to vote for Obama because of his race to justify their decision on other grounds—such as McCain's greater experience in politics—resulting in an accurate accounting of their vote, albeit for the wrong reason.[T20] Social desirability bias will not emerge if people have comfortable ways of rationalizing unpleasant attitudes.

Questions about voting history can produce this kind of bias. All Americans know they're *supposed* to vote, but many people do not. It's easy to imagine some nonvoters telling pollsters they voted to avoid the social embarrassment of publicly admitting they didn't do something they felt they should have done.

Surveys of public opinion can anticipate this problem and try to mitigate it with questions worded to offset social desirability bias. For instance, questions about voting can start out with a disclaimer that many people don't vote because they lack the time or interest, suggesting that not voting is an acceptable behavior with no social consequences. In the end, of course, it's up to individuals to decide whether to admit to something that may cause them some discomfort.

---

imagine how having a belief like this could negatively influence attitudes like efficacy and trust in government.

Similarly, people may fiercely believe that something is right or wrong when in truth their belief cannot be supported by objective facts. Some people equate legalized abortion with murder because they believe that life begins at conception. Others endorse abortion rights with as much fervor because they believe that before a fetus is viable outside the womb it is part of the mother's body, and the mother has the right to make decisions affecting her body. As a matter of scientific principle, the question of when life begins eludes clear definition. An argument can be made for both positions, but neither can be proved. Of course, if you fervently hold to a belief, it might be impossible to convince you that it's a belief and not a fact. It will certainly seem factual to you.

Intensely held beliefs can motivate people to political action. Recall that one dimension of public opinion is intensity, which is perhaps most clearly visible when it comes to the public expression of beliefs. Sometimes political activity stems from the actions of an intense minority of citizens whose strong beliefs lead them to make demands on government, even if most of the population feels less strongly about the matter than they do. In cases like this, which might remind you a little of Madison's argument about the dangers of minority **factions**, the political system is supposed to diffuse the intensity of the feelings these groups express by providing them with an outlet for articulating their beliefs as part of a broader dialogue on the subject that concerns them.

Again, the abortion issue is an excellent example of this. It is prominently placed in the news, and a subject of widespread discussion, in part because of the efforts of activists on both sides of the issue. Over the years, there have been a series of legislative and judicial

social desirability bias: A form of error in public opinion polls, whereby opinions or behaviors that could be considered undesirable are not fully reported in the data.

faction: A group of individuals who are united by a desire that, if realized, would threaten the liberty of the larger community—in James Madison's words, individuals who are "united and actuated by some common impulse of passion, or of interest, adverse to the rights of other citizens, or to the permanent and aggregate interests of the community." A faction may be defined by size, such as when a majority of citizens threatens the liberty of the minority, or by intensity, such as when a minority of citizens with intensely held preferences threatens the liberty of a disinterested majority.

debates about the legal parameters of abortion. Many people view abortion as an emotional issue with complex moral dimensions.

This would suggest that abortion is a matter about which most Americans hold strong and intense beliefs. But it is not. Data from the 2000 GSS indicate that the abortion issue is one of the most important issues of the day to only 14 percent of the public. Another 14 percent say it is not at all important to them. And the rest fall somewhere in between, concerned about it perhaps but not in a deeply committed way. Not surprisingly, then, a 2016 Gallup Poll found that only 20 percent of Americans said that a candidate for office must share their views on abortion. Half said abortion is one of many important factors that shape how they vote. Twenty-eight percent said they really didn't care.[13]

The abortion issue also provides an excellent illustration of the complexity of beliefs. Sometimes during the course of trying to be persuasive in political debate, advocates can overly simplify an argument, even though public opinion may well be quite complicated. If pollsters were to ask people the deceptively simple question "Should abortion be legal?" they might get answers, but it's unlikely that these answers would reflect the complex array of beliefs people hold on the matter.

Support for the unqualified condition that abortion should be legal under any circumstances looks dramatically different if it is interpreted to mean at any point during pregnancy (a position held by 15 percent of Americans) or during the first trimester of pregnancy (a position held by 61 percent).[14] Figure 3.9 demonstrates how beliefs about abortion can change when people are asked to consider different circumstances under which abortion could be permitted. Far fewer people believe financial need or the possibility of birth defects should be reasons for legal abortion than if a pregnancy was caused by rape or incest or the physical health of the woman is endangered.

So it is with many issues: Beliefs can be more complex than any single measure indicates. This can make definitive statements about public opinion hard to come by. If you were affiliated with the Right to Life movement and wanted to make the case to legislators that there is strong antiabortion sentiment in America, you could claim that almost 65 percent believe that abortion should not be freely available under all circumstances. If you represented the abortion rights movement and wanted to make the case to legislators that most Americans are supportive of the principle of abortion, you could say that over four in five Americans support legal abortions under some circumstances. Both arguments would be accurate, at least to the degree that both arguments capture an element of public opinion on the issue.

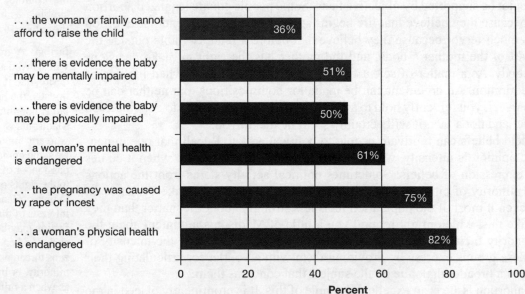

Abortion should be permitted if . . .

. . . the woman or family cannot afford to raise the child	36%
. . . there is evidence the baby may be mentally impaired	51%
. . . there is evidence the baby may be physically impaired	50%
. . . a woman's mental health is endangered	61%
. . . the pregnancy was caused by rape or incest	75%
. . . a woman's physical health is endangered	82%

Percent

FIGURE 3.9 Abortion Should Be Permitted If . . . [T21]

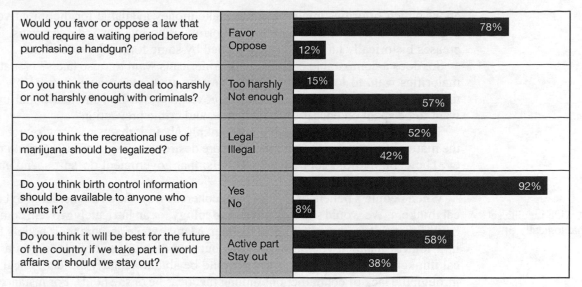

FIGURE 3.10 What Americans Believe[T22]

Several other prominent issues are listed in Figure 3.10. See if your sense of what Americans believe is in line with what Americans say they believe.

3.5 Ideology: Beliefs That Make Sense

Just like opinions are neither right nor wrong, nothing says people have to hold beliefs that make collective sense. It's pretty commonplace for people to be perfectly happy holding contradictory beliefs—even without realizing it.

L.O. Explain the relationship between beliefs and ideology.

For instance, when people are asked if they believe government is spending too much or too little on a host of domestic social programs, large numbers repeatedly say too little. Look at Figure 3.11 to see some of the things that majorities of Americans say are underfunded.

Spending more on any of these priorities means either taking money away from other things, going into debt, or raising taxes. While it's possible to imagine a spirited debate

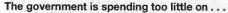

The government is spending too little on . . .

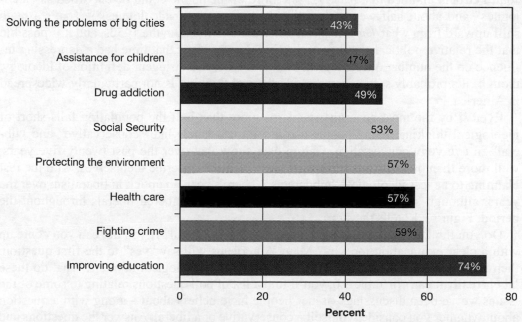

FIGURE 3.11 Consistent Beliefs?[T23]

about which priorities might be cut to make money available for the initiatives listed in Figure 3.11 or about the desirability of borrowing to live beyond our means, funding increases historically have been accompanied by some form of revenue hikes.

So, does a comparable percentage of Americans want to raise taxes? Not at all. Large majorities want to lower taxes. Hardly anyone advocates raising them. How exactly do those large majorities of people expect government to find the additional money they want to be spent on education, health care, and crime prevention?

The answer is they're probably not thinking about it that way. They're not connecting the matter of tax increases with their sincere desire to have government spend more money. They simply hold contradictory beliefs: that government doesn't spend enough, and that taxes are too high.[15]

When people's beliefs fit together in a coherent way, they're considered to be ideological thinkers. We would say they have an **ideology**, or an intricately woven, complex set of beliefs that fit together in a logical manner. Many people assume their beliefs fit together in a logical manner—perhaps you do—but that alone does not make you an ideological thinker. A dispassionate observer would be able to identify an ideological individual through the lack of contradictions among the ideas he or she holds. For instance, someone might be considered an ideological thinker if he or she supported a balanced budget and higher taxes or spending cuts to make it possible.

It's difficult to pinpoint the exact percentage of Americans who think this way, but the best evidence is that it's not very high. If you go back three generations, you'll find an influential study of how Americans reason about politics in a book called *The American Voter*. Angus Campbell and his colleagues set out to understand how Americans make sense of political parties and candidates for office, and as part of their inquiry, they isolated and identified ideological thinkers.[16] They found that back in 1956, less than 3 percent of the people they studied could be classified as "ideologues," in the sense that their beliefs were "functionally related" to each other. Another 13 percent could be termed "near-ideologues" for their tendencies to use ideological labels like "conservative" and "liberal" without demonstrating that they fully grasped the meaning of the terms. That meant that the remaining 85 percent of the public did not think about things ideologically.

One generation later, a different team of researchers working in a different era found that ideological thinking had increased dramatically since the late 1950s, perhaps as a consequence of the traumatic political and social events of the civil rights era and the Vietnam War. Writing in *The Changing American Voter*, Norman Nie, Sidney Verba, and John Petrocik claimed that by 1972, one-third of the public could be classified as "ideologues" and about half were either "ideologues" or "near-ideologues."[17] That's a huge shift upward from what *The American Voter* authors found in the 1950s, and it is possible that the relative political stability of the Eisenhower era at that time had a depressing influence on the number of ideological thinkers.[18] Given a stringent definition of ideology, though, it's probably safe to say that ideological thinking is not particularly widespread in America.

Even if by the most generous standards more than half the population falls short of ideological thinking, many people use ideological labels like "conservative" and "liberal" in everyday conversation. Gallup data show that over the past twenty-five years, well more than half of Americans used these labels to describe themselves, with the rest claiming to be less ideological "moderates." There's been an uptick in liberalism over the years, although self-professed conservatives have outnumbered liberals throughout the period. Figure 3.12 tells the story.

L.O. Differentiate liberalism from conservatism in terms of the role each endorses for government.

Do you think of yourself as being conservative or liberal? If you do, can you come up with a clear explanation for why? Many Americans will say "yes" to the first question, then struggle with the second. If most people aren't ideological thinkers, what do these labels really mean? In Table 3.6, you'll find a list of poll questions relating to some of the issues we've been discussing—issues people have beliefs about—along with a question about whether you consider yourself a conservative or a liberal. Answer the questions and then evaluate how reliably you take liberal or conservative positions.

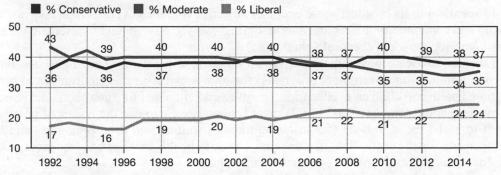

FIGURE 3.12 Liberal-Conservative Self-Identification, 1992–2015[T24]

TABLE 3.6 Are You Ideological?

1. We hear a lot these days about liberals and conservatives. Where would you place yourself? Would you say you are liberal, conservative, moderate, or you don't know?

   A. Liberal
   B. Conservative

   C. Moderate
   D. Don't know/no opinion

2. Are we spending too much, too little, or about the right amount on the environment?

   A. Too much
   B. Too little

   C. About right
   D. Don't know/no opinion

3. Are we spending too much, too little, or about the right amount on health care?

   A. Too much
   B. Too little

   C. About right
   D. Don't know/no opinion

4. Are we spending too much, too little, or about the right amount on child care?

   A. Too much
   B. Too little

   C. About right
   D. Don't know/no opinion

5. Do you favor or oppose the death penalty for persons convicted of murder?

   A. Favor
   B. Oppose

   C. Don't know/no opinion

6. Are we spending too much, too little, or about the right amount on improving the nation's education system?

   A. Too much
   B. Too little

   C. About right
   D. Don't know/no opinion

7. Would you oppose or favor a law that would require a person to obtain a police permit before he or she could buy a gun?

   A. Oppose
   B. Favor

   C. Don't know/no opinion

8. Are we spending too much, too little, or about the right amount on Social Security?

   A. Too much
   B. Too little

   C. About right
   D. Don't know/no opinion

9. Are we spending too much, too little, or about the right amount on dealing with drug addiction?

   A. Too much
   B. Too little

   C. About right
   D. Don't know/no opinion

EVALUATE YOUR ANSWERS

The CONSERVATIVE answer to each question is A.

The LIBERAL answer to each question is B.

The MODERATE answer to each question is C.

Do you fall most often in the liberal, conservative, or moderate category?

liberalism: An ideology that advocates the use of government power to address economic and social problems, like unemployment and environmental protection, while limiting government involvement in moral matters like abortion rights and prayer in public schools.

conservatism: An ideology that advocates limits on government power to address economic and social problems, relying instead on economic markets and individual initiative to address problems like health care and education while promoting government involvement in moral matters to, for instance, minimize or eliminate abortions or permit prayer in public schools.

Liberalism in its broadest sense endorses an active role for government in addressing social and economic problems and a more limited role for government in refereeing matters involving personal or moral values.

Liberals advocate government activism (which in a practical sense translates into spending money on government programs) for such social issues as environmental protection, health and child care, education, and drug addiction and for such economic issues as welfare and Social Security. In this regard, liberals seek to use the power of government to assist those in need (for instance, through welfare and drug programs) and to compensate for the inequities (like unequal access to health care) or consequences (like air and water pollution) of the economic marketplace.

At the same time, liberals typically believe government should stay out of matters that they consider to be of a moral nature. Consequently, liberals may oppose using government power to limit abortion rights, impose the death penalty, or require prayer in public schools (however, they may be quite comfortable engaging the government to protect abortion rights and defend against school prayer). Liberals may also favor gun control laws, limits on military spending, and tax laws that benefit lower-income people.

Conservatism applies different principles to arrive at mirror-image positions. In its broadest sense, conservatism values the power of the marketplace to address economic concerns and individual initiative to confront social problems, therefore advocating a limited role for government power in economic and social matters. Contemporary conservatism for many years accepted the reality of America's social welfare programs, although more recently, some conservatives have aggressively attempted to roll back or privatize programs such as Obamacare, Medicare, and Social Security (all of which were in the crosshairs of congressional Republicans at the start of the Trump administration). Conservatives tend to be suspicious of government programs that are not subjected to what they regard as the beneficial self-correcting forces of the marketplace and that take money out of taxpayer's pockets that could be put toward free enterprise.

Consequently, conservatives advocate less involvement in (and less money for) government programs on environmental protection, health and child care, education, and drug addiction. They regard welfare as a program that can undermine individual initiative, and they have been successful in restructuring government welfare benefits to orient the program toward getting people to find jobs. Unlike liberals, conservatives would like Social Security to be a market-oriented program.

Where conservatives seek to keep government out of economic and social matters, a hallmark of American conservatism since the Reagan administration has been an attempt to use government power to advance positions with a clear moral dimension. This, too, is a mirror image of liberalism, and it leads conservatives to seek government intervention to restrict or eliminate legal abortion, legalize the death penalty, permit prayer in public schools, and forbid gay marriage. Conservatives may also oppose gun control laws, value military spending, and favor tax laws that benefit those at the top of the income scale out of the belief that it helps them produce wealth for society.

Chances are, if you call yourself a liberal or conservative, your positions on all of these issues do not align perfectly with the prescribed ideological positions advocated by the "left" (the traditional designation for "liberals") or the "right" (the designation for "conservatives"). If that's the case, you're not alone. Just like the authors of *The American Voter* discovered, most people don't hold internally consistent beliefs. That may not stop us from using the conservative or liberal labels to describe ourselves. It just means that using the labels doesn't make us ideologues. For instance, while liberals in general favor more spending than conservatives on social and economic concerns, majorities of conservatives support the liberal position on such issues as protecting the environment, providing health care and child care, improving education, and combating drug addiction.

In fact, the terms are loose enough that what it means to be a liberal or a conservative has changed over time. We said that some conservatives support a limited role for government. But think back to our discussion of John Locke in Chapter 2. You may remember that we encountered the idea of limited government when we discussed Locke and the ideas that influenced the early Federalists. We said that in Locke's time, the idea of **limited government** was pretty radical stuff. In its day, Locke's writing was considered quite liberal because it advocated protecting the rights of the individual from encroachment by either government or the cruelty of the state of nature.

Today, Locke is regarded as a classical liberal, as someone who was a liberal in the context of the time in which he lived, and his writing is viewed as an expression of **classical liberalism**. He regarded monarchy, the strong central government of his day, as an obstacle to the advancement of individual rights and liberties.

As American government has grown in size, scope, and function, particularly in the twentieth century, liberals and conservatives have switched some of their philosophical clothes. Liberals have emerged as those who advocate using government power because they regard contemporary government social programs as a means to the traditional goals of protecting individual rights. Conservatives disagree, and they have emerged as those who seek to maintain the once radical ideas of limited government advocated by classical liberals two centuries ago.

Although most Americans are not ideological thinkers, and most ideological dialogue in the United States takes place between conservatives and liberals, there are other ideological positions as well. If you think of ideologies as being points on a line, with liberals on the left and conservatives on the right (remember, we said that liberals are commonly referred to as being "left" or "left-wing" and conservatives as "right" or "right-wing"), and you extend the line in both directions, you'll arrive at these other positions.

To the left of liberalism, you'll find **socialism**, which applies some of the principles of liberalism to a different conclusion. American liberals place a premium on **equality of outcome**, but they strive to enhance outcomes at the margins while accepting the American preference for **equality of opportunity**. Socialists, on the other hand, strive for equality of outcome over equality of opportunity, and they view government power as a critical instrument for getting there. Socialists would advance what they consider a common, collective interest and believe that the creation of wealth should serve the common good instead of going to make a small number of people rich. Bernie Sanders hails from a version of this political tradition.

To the right of conservatism, you'll find **fascism**, the ultra-nationalistic ideology of the far right that favors developing a strong military and police apparatus to defend the interests of the state. A militant ideology, fascism endorses the concentration of power by any and all means and rejects liberal notions of individual rights.

Libertarianism is typically placed far to the right as well, but it can be harder to place on a left-right continuum. It covers a range of political and economic theories, but the basic intent of libertarians is to advance individual liberty free from government interference. In this regard, libertarians take the ideas of classical liberalism beyond where conservatives would go. Kentucky Senator Rand Paul, who ran unsuccessfully for president in 2016, casts himself in this tradition, although he does not go as far as some libertarians, who would roll back all but the most basic functions of government, such as defense and some elements of criminal justice. As a Republican, Paul also refrained from advocating some libertarian social positions that are typically rejected by conservatives, such as legalizing abortion, drugs, and prostitution.

3.6 Measuring Public Opinion

It puzzles a lot of people exactly how we can know what a large nation believes about gun control or feels about political efficacy. You may be wondering this yourself: Where do these precise-looking figures in opinion polls come from, and how much faith should we place in their accuracy? When the Gallup Organization tried to find out about people's confidence in the work of pollsters—essentially by conducting a poll about polls—it found that despite widespread sentiment that polling produced accurate results, most people said it simply was not possible to get reliable data about a whole nation by talking to only one thousand or so people. In other words, people believe polls work even as they doubt the science that makes them work.

limited government: The idea that power can be denied to government and the people who serve in it, in order to restrict those in positions of authority from infringing upon individual liberty.

classical liberalism: A term given to the philosophy of John Locke and other seventeenth- and eighteenth-century advocates of the protection of individual rights and liberties by limiting government power.

L.O. Identify and describe ideological positions other than liberalism and conservatism.

socialism: A left-leaning ideology centered on the use of government power to advance equal outcomes.

equality of outcome: One of several ways of understanding equality; this way values leveling the social and economic inequities among people, rather than attempting to give people comparable advantages for succeeding in life.

equality of opportunity: One of several ways of understanding equality; this way values giving people comparable advantages for succeeding in life, regardless of the unequal outcomes that may result.

fascism: A militant, ultra-nationalistic ideology of the extreme right that rejects liberal ideas about personal rights.

libertarianism: An ideology centered on the reduction of government power to advance personal liberty.

L.O. Briefly explain random sampling, and understand how opinion polls work.

That's not so hard to understand when you consider that it's not intuitive how a poll of a tiny number of people can accurately capture the beliefs and opinions of many millions. It's not an easy thing to explain either. Maybe the best way to think about it is to imagine a bowl of hot soup. If you put a spoon in the bowl, mix it around, take a spoonful to your mouth, and spit it out because it's too hot and making your tongue blister, you don't need to finish the whole bowl to know that it's boiling hot. That little sample told you everything you had to know, and you got an accurate measure as long as you mixed up the soup so you weren't taking it from a part of the bowl that might have been cooler, like the edge or the top.

Polls work pretty much the same way. The key to conducting a good poll is making sure that the "soup" is all mixed up or, to put it another way, that everyone in America (or whatever group you're polling) has the same chance of being selected for the poll. If you only taste from the edge of the bowl where perhaps the soup is always cooler—or if you only talk to a select group of people with the same set of characteristics—you can end up misjudging the broader group. The soup you eat has to be representative of the soup in the bowl, just like the people you talk to in your survey have to be representative of the people in the country.

Early political polls ran into this problem. A magazine called the *Literary Digest* had been conducting opinion polls on how Americans were going to vote for president, and between 1916 and 1932, it had called every presidential election correctly using a method whereby millions of people were contacted and asked to fill out sample ballots. The *Literary Digest* got the names of these people from phone books and automobile registration lists, and they operated on the (flawed) assumption that the more people you contact, the more accurate the results. To continue our analogy, they wanted to finish off about one-third of the soup before deciding they had enough information to conclude that the soup was hot.

Their approach worked for many years. Then, in 1936, with Franklin Roosevelt facing re-election, the *Literary Digest* got it wrong, predicting a lopsided win for challenger Alf Landon, when in fact, Roosevelt won in a landslide. It seems the phone books and automobile registration lists came back to haunt them. With Roosevelt's New Deal policies assisting people hurt by the Depression, the votes of those who couldn't afford phones and cars differed wildly from the votes of the wealthy and middle class who were not as affected by the Depression and were more likely to pay for than to benefit from Roosevelt's programs. This group was much less likely to support Roosevelt, and their opinions were given disproportionate weight. Without realizing it, the *Literary Digest* was sampling from only one part of the soup bowl.

That same year, the Gallup Organization predicted the election outcome correctly by talking to only a few thousand people. It was as big a win for scientific polling methods as it was for Roosevelt because it demonstrated the inherent accuracy of taking small, careful samples and discredited methods that reached out to large numbers of people. It also made a name for George Gallup, who put his reputation and a lot of money on the line by betting that his results would be more accurate than the *Literary Digest* results.[19]

Randomization is the key to being able to discern the opinions of many people by contacting only a few. A scientific survey is based on a **random sample** of individuals, meaning that everyone contacted for an opinion poll had the exact same chance of being contacted as everyone else. What the *Literary Digest* did was comparable to what happens when we ask our friends their opinions. We'll get a response, but it will only tell us about the opinions of the people we talked to—we won't be able to apply their opinions to what a larger group might say because our friends are self-selected. They just aren't representative of a larger group because we don't choose our friends at random.

If everyone has an equal chance of being selected for a poll, it turns out you don't have to talk to many people before you generate an accurate view of public opinion. This can be confusing because it seems counterintuitive, but it's what makes scientific polling possible. After only several hundred interviews with randomly selected individuals, pollsters can begin to speak with some degree of accuracy about how well the opinions they collected reflect national public opinion. Statistical models can tell them how likely it is that a survey of, say, one thousand people represents the opinions of the larger group they were sampled from.

random sample: The basis for a scientifically accurate public opinion poll, in which everyone in the community being polled has an equal chance of being selected to give their opinions to pollsters. In a poll of national opinion, everyone in the country would have an equal chance of being selected to participate in it.

For all the mathematical sophistication that goes into designing and conducting public opinion polls, the degree of accuracy they return depends at least as much on the human element as scientific acumen. Both science and art go into the process of writing questions, ordering questions in a survey, and asking questions in an impartial manner. It's not always easy to anticipate how seemingly simple changes in the wording of a question can dramatically alter the answers people give, or how small voice modulations can unconsciously direct someone toward a particular response.

For instance, take a look at this question from the General Social Survey: "Are you in favor of the death penalty for persons convicted of murder?" Straightforward and simple, it generated a "yes" response of 60.3 percent. Now look at this equally straightforward variation on the question from the same survey: "Do you favor or oppose the death penalty for persons convicted of murder?" It sounds like exactly the same question, but in this form, 73.8 percent said they "favor" the death penalty, a nontrivial increase of 13.5 percentage points.

Why such a noticeable difference? One possibility lies in a subtle variation in how the two questions are constructed. The first question asks people to consider the death penalty in the affirmative, simply asking them if they favor it for persons convicted of murder. The second question asks people to make a thumbs up/thumbs down choice on the same matter, inviting them to consider whether they favor the death penalty in the context of whether they may also oppose it. It's possible that when people are invited to think about support for the death penalty in the context of opposition to the death penalty, more of them voice their support than when they're not encouraged to think about the possibility of opposing it.

At this point, you could be forgiven for wondering how pollsters can figure out how to word questions at all if something as seemingly simple as the addition of a couple of benign words can significantly alter the response to a question. In fact, a lot of attention is paid to precision in question wording because the effects can be so strong. Pollsters with a long history of conducting surveys can rely on the results they have gathered over time to fashion questions in a way that they are confident will generate accurate results. New questions are routinely tested in several forms in order to identify and weed out leading or misleading wording.

Likewise, reputable polling firms are attentive to the sequence of questions in a survey, to the fact that asking questions about one topic could unintentionally prompt people to think about subsequent topics in the context of the earlier questions. For instance, a battery of questions about the war in Afghanistan placed immediately before a question about President Obama's job performance at the height of the war's unpopularity might unintentionally lead some people to think about Obama's job performance in terms of the Afghanistan War, yielding lower performance scores than if the job performance question had been asked first.

Similarly, people who administer surveys over the telephone are trained in techniques for asking questions in a balanced and neutral fashion. Without careful attention to how questions are asked, the beliefs or biases of those reading the questions could influence how a respondent answers, and neither questioner nor respondent might be aware of what's going on.

For all these reasons—question wording, sequencing, and delivery—opinion polls should be regarded as imperfect mechanisms that, even in the best of cases, are susceptible to human error. Good surveys minimize the problems, but when you add human error to the statistical error present in surveys, it should be easy to see why survey results need to be approached with some caution. Surveys are a powerful tool, and they can sketch a remarkably accurate picture of public opinion. Still, they're best approached as a snapshot of opinion that's accurate within a narrow range.

3.7 Measuring Public Opinion in Politics

Early in his campaign for re-election, Bill Clinton consulted with one of his political advisors about a weighty and critical issue: where he should take his vacation. It seems the president and those who helped him make political decisions felt it was important to use the vacation as a vehicle for sending the right image of the commander-in-chief to undecided voters. So, Clinton's advisors commissioned a public opinion poll. It turned out that taking the First Family to a wealthy friend's compound in the exclusive Massachusetts retreat Martha's Vineyard, as Clinton had done in the past, smacked of elitism to those swing voters who might determine the outcome of the next election. Polls showed these voters preferred camping trips.

So, the president took his family to Wyoming.

Polling has become so prevalent in politics that it's hard to find a part of the political system that polling hasn't touched. Public officials at all levels of government have come to depend on polls for a host of purposes, from figuring out what legislation to promote to crafting a public image. Candidates use polls for every facet of their work, from determining what issues to talk about to figuring out what slogans to use. Interest groups—which we'll discuss in Chapter 8—use polls showing public support for their positions to win the votes of legislators. The media build stories around polls, especially during election campaigns when reporters turn to them as a source of hard data for assessing likely winners and losers.

3.7a Candidates and Opinion Polls

There was a time when politicians relied on their innate sense of public opinion to shape how they talked to voters. As polling developed as a science, it became commonplace for candidates to employ pollsters to assist with campaign strategy. By the 1990s, polling had become such a prominent element of campaigns that candidates stopped making decisions before consulting their pollsters.

Consider the 1996 election, in which Bill Clinton sought a second term against Republican Senator Robert Dole. During that election, it seemed as if no item was too small to avoid being subjected to opinion polls that would guide the two national campaigns in what they said and how they said it. For instance:

- The Clinton campaign polled four different versions of a campaign slogan before arriving at "Building a Bridge to the Twenty-First Century," which was preferred by far more people than the self-serving alternative, "Building a Bridge to a Second Term."

- The Dole campaign, looking for a way to talk about conservative values without scaring away moderate voters, conducted an opinion poll and found that an anti-Hollywood theme would do the trick with people who worried about the movies and music their kids were exposed to.

- When polling showed that 80 percent of Americans favored a balanced budget, Clinton's pollsters urged him to endorse the idea, to the chagrin of some of his more principled liberal advisors who simply thought it was bad policy. (Clinton eventually sided with the pollsters.)

- Both the Dole and Clinton campaigns used polls to shape their television commercials. Ideas for ads were frequently "mall tested" by pollsters, meaning that prototype ads were shown to people in shopping malls who were then polled for their reactions.

- The Clinton campaign conducted a poll to end all polls—a "neuropersonality poll" that asked questions about every facet of people's lives in order to put together a blueprint of the electorate. From this poll, Clinton's aides were able to discern precisely which messages would appeal to the voters they needed. It played a major role in shaping the strategy that carried Clinton to victory.[20]

There are two schools of thought about the polling phenomenon. You could argue that polling at this level is consistent with the way representative democracies are meant to function, with candidates finding out exactly what the public wants to know so they can closely align themselves with public opinion. You could also contend that there's something a little spineless about candidates relying on opinion polls to decide how to act and what to say. Think about whether the heavy reliance by candidates on polls seems like the ultimate expression of representatives responding to what people say they want, or whether it suggests a craven willingness for candidates to twist themselves like claymation figures into whatever shape pollsters say people want to see.

3.7b The Political Value of Misleading Polls

You may not have much familiarity with interest groups at this point (that will change soon), but the important thing to know is that they are organizations that try to get government officials to promote their views on issues they care about. Since elected officials tend to perk up when they hear that large numbers of people (read: potential voters) hold a particular viewpoint, an interest group can be persuasive if it can demonstrate widespread public support for a position it's promoting. Public opinion polls are one way for interest groups to make their case.

Remember what we said about the artistic component of polling? Scientific polls like the ones conducted by the Gallup Organization regard the nuances of question wording and question order as potential obstacles to producing accurate and reliable results. Polls commissioned by interest groups may be less inclined toward objectivity and more oriented toward demonstrating public support for the group's position—whether or not it really exists. In other words, pollsters working for interest groups may be intentionally "creative," wording questions in such a way as to generate the response that the group desires.

For instance, a group promoting widespread tax cuts might conduct a poll with questions like, "Would you support tax relief in the form of a government effort to return hard-earned money to people through a capital-gains tax cut?" It's hard to be against "tax relief" or "returning hard-earned money" to people, so questions like these could easily produce results that exaggerate the level of support for the tax cut. Where pollsters looking to accurately capture public opinion would avoid loaded phrases like these, interest groups might deliberately include them because it serves their political purposes.

Push polls are the most unethical example of using surveys to produce an outcome rather than measure opinion. With push polling, people who sound like they work for a professional polling firm but who really work for a political candidate call potential voters to ask questions that are highly biased against the candidate's opponent. The purpose is to trash the opposition by leaving people with a negative impression of them.[21]

push polls: Surveys that appear legitimate but in fact are a dirty campaign trick designed to generate negative opinion about an opponent in a political contest.

The moral of the story is: When you're looking at poll numbers, remember the motivation of the people who commissioned the poll.

3.7c Media and Opinion Polls

Whereas candidates, elected officials, and interest groups use public opinion to try to gain political advantage, the media use public opinion as an easy and convenient way to tell political stories. Media outlets conduct polls about all sorts of social and political issues and use results they find interesting to fashion stories for newspapers or television news programs.[22]

Media polls are most prevalent during presidential election years, when campaign news is saturated with poll results about how the race is shaping up. On television, tracking polls—which show a daily running average of support for major candidates—are a fixture in the weeks leading up to an election.

On election nights, the major television networks rely on exit polls for early predictions of the outcome. Exit polls are based on interviews with randomly selected voters as they leave the polling place. These voters are asked a small number of questions, including questions about how they voted in the day's most prominent contests. Because most respondents can accurately recollect how they voted just moments earlier, exit polls can be a reliable source of information. Consequently, networks use them to help predict the outcome of races before all the votes are counted.

Survey methods have become so reliable, in fact, that in races that are not close, network television personnel sometimes know the results of an election hours or even days

Too Much Information?

One of the bizarre twists of polling technology is that in some instances, it's possible to know the outcome of an election before anyone votes. When Barack Obama hinted to a rally on the election eve 2008 that a celebration was in their near future, he wasn't being overconfident; detailed opinion polling told him he was going to win. In 1980, Jimmy Carter's chief pollster informed the president that he was not going to be re-elected several days before the polls opened. In 1992, George H. W. Bush experienced the same surreal fate. Not a vote had been cast, but the outcome was assured.

From what we know about polling, it's not too hard to understand how this can happen. Obama scored an easy victory in 2008, and the 1980 and 1992 elections produced lopsided defeats for the incumbents—all well beyond the margin of error of good opinion surveys. As people put the finishing touches on their voting intentions several days before the election, pollsters captured the one-sided nature of their decisions and had a high degree of confidence in the findings.

Media outlets had access to the same information, but unlike the losing candidates (whose only use of the poll numbers was to brace themselves for what was about to happen to them), news executives confronted a serious dilemma about what to do with the information. There are a lot of pressures on journalists and news executives to report valuable information, such as the winner of a presidential election, as quickly as possible. Releasing that information before Election Day, though, poses a serious threat to the democratic tradition of one person–one vote because if the winner is announced before the votes are cast, it would be reasonable for people to ask why they should go to the polls at all, especially if they intended to vote for the eventual loser. Because news organizations want to avoid the appearance of undermining democratic processes, they studiously avoid calling the outcome of elections before people get a chance to cast their

vote, despite strong pressures to quickly release important information.

But what about on election night itself? Television networks try to hold back on making predictions about an election until all the polls have closed, but competitive pressures to make a fast call have led to some unfortunate consequences. In lopsided presidential contests, exit poll results permit the projection of enough eastern states to make the general trend of the election clear to people living in the West. In 2008, once Barack Obama won the state of Ohio, pollsters and political reporters knew he was going to be elected president because the states he had already won in conjunction with western states where pre-election and Election Day polls showed him comfortably ahead totaled enough electoral votes for victory. But, Ohio was called in the middle of the evening on the East Coast, a couple of hours before polls closed out West. In an effort to avoid calling the election while people were still voting, the major television networks struggled to avoid definitive language about the outcome—and Obama himself refrained from making a victory statement—until after polls closed in California at 11 p.m. Eastern time.

In 2000, the major television networks used exit polls to declare that Al Gore had won the presidential vote in the state of Florida, even though the polls were still open in a small portion of the Florida panhandle that's in the Central Time Zone. Then, in an embarrassment of unprecedented proportion, the networks one by one retracted the call as the actual votes began to indicate the exit polls might be incorrect. Late on election night, the networks awarded the Florida presidential vote to George W. Bush—only to retract that call when the final vote tally turned out to be too close to call. It was an ugly case of competitive pressures producing hasty judgments about what to report.

before anyone has voted. This has generated intense discussion among network television officials and political observers about the appropriate use of opinion polls to predict election outcomes, which we discuss in Demystifying Government: Too Much Information?

When we don't have an election going on, media organizations rely on the information in opinion polls to write stories about whether people feel the country is going in the right direction, their degree of support for highly visible policies or policy proposals debated by Congress, and how much they approve of the job the president is doing.

3.8 What Should We Make of Public Opinion?

Like any tools, opinion polls can be of value if you know how to use them. That means remembering both what they can and cannot tell us. Experienced political advisors know a great deal about the science and art of polling and can discern the currents of public opinion quite effectively.

On the other hand, journalists, who are not schooled in the ways of opinion polls, sometimes do a sloppy job of interpreting them. We know that polls present us with a good bet that public opinion reflects the numbers in the poll, but there is always a margin of error. When journalists forget to include the margin of error in their interpretation of polls—which happens frequently—they run the risk of misinterpreting what's going on. For instance, a poll with a margin of error of three points that shows one candidate three points ahead of the other is telling us that the contest is a dead heat. But it's not uncommon for journalists to inaccurately report that one candidate holds a three-point lead.

Even when polls are accurately interpreted, they still need to be handled with care. We know that Americans often do not hold strong or stable opinions about things. It's a mistake to accept poll data as a measure of deeply held or carefully considered attitudes and beliefs when in fact polls may be measuring opinion that's weak or fleeting. Polls are of limited value if the opinion they're measuring is soft or poorly developed, or if people are poorly informed about the matter in question. People will give all sorts of answers to pollsters' questions, but that doesn't automatically make their answers thoughtful or meaningful.

Even for public officials who are advised by the most sophisticated professionals, there is a difference between being responsive to public opinion and making responsible public decisions. Sometimes, simply doing what the public wants can produce policy with undesirable outcomes. During the Reagan administration, the president wanted to cut taxes and spending on domestic policies; majorities in Congress wanted to maintain or increase spending on domestic programs, although a majority was also willing to go along with cutting taxes. So, the president got his way on tax cuts while Congress got its way on maintaining domestic spending. This split reflected public opinion fairly well, but it was problematic as the government soon began spending more money than it was taking in. Many years of large budget deficits followed, and while each side blamed the other for this outcome, a case can be made that the president and Congress were being more responsive than responsible.

An important component of effective leadership involves following public opinion. Another important component can be making unpopular decisions if, in the view of elected officials, public opinion is ill conceived. Governing through polls doesn't typically encourage this type of leadership.

Making decisions for a large, diverse population is a difficult proposition anyway, with or without opinion polls. From a largely homogeneous population at the turn of the eighteenth century, today's America is a multiethnic place where a rich variety of traditions support a range of sometimes incompatible approaches to how Americans should live and be governed.

We're going to explore this cultural terrain next. We'll look at how people become political creatures—to the extent that we know or appreciate politics at all—by examining some of the influences that shape political development. We'll also explore the possibilities available to us for participating in politics if we are so inclined. All of this lies ahead in Chapter 4.

Chapter Review

Define public opinion.

Distinguish the empirical components of public opinion from its normative components.

Public opinion is information that tells us what people think about matters relating to government, politics, and society. Because public opinion is gathered through careful scientific measurement, it is derived from empirical means. But public opinion also has an important norma-

tive component because it tells us what people value about government and politics.

Explain how direction, intensity, and stability are elements of public opinion.

There are several elements to the structure of public opinion. The direction of public opinion gives us a "thumbs up/thumbs down" reading on the degree of support people feel for a political individual, institution, or action. The intensity of public opinion tells us how strongly people hold to an opinion. The stability of public opinion tells us whether an opinion is fleeting or endures over time.

Understand the possible ramifications of low levels of political knowledge.

One component of public opinion is knowledge. Americans have never exhibited high levels of political knowledge, probably because politics is not a high priority for many Americans. Some argue this lack of knowledge does not prevent people from making intelligent political decisions. Others decry what they call an "information elite" of resource-rich individuals whose relatively high levels of political knowledge permit them to effectively identify what they want from government—and get it—while the poor have relatively less knowledge and therefore achieve less from government.

Identify political attitudes like trust, cynicism, and efficacy, and address how each is represented in the population.

Another component of public opinion is attitudes, or how people feel about political figures, institutions, issues, or events. People hold attitudes on a wide range of things. For instance, many Americans say that the government is too strong, a view predominantly held by men, whites and, until the 1970s, southerners. Over the years, trust in government has declined from its pre-Vietnam highs. Cynicism has increased, and efficacy has declined. However, efficacy remains generally higher among people with higher levels of education and income, suggesting the possibility that wealthy people feel greater efficacy because government is more likely to respond to their wishes.

Distinguish attitudes from beliefs, and discuss the relationship between intensely held beliefs and political action.

Beliefs address what people think is true about politics. While attitudes can never be incorrect because they reveal how people feel, it is possible to hold incorrect beliefs. Strongly held beliefs can motivate people to political action. Beliefs may also be quite complex and hard to capture with a few survey questions.

Explain the relationship between beliefs and ideology.

When beliefs fit together in a logical order, we call it an ideology. Most people in America are not ideological thinkers.

Differentiate liberalism from conservatism in terms of the role each endorses for government.

The most frequently used labels are liberal and conservative. In its broadest sense, liberalism endorses an active role for government in addressing social and economic problems and a more limited role for government in refereeing matters involving personal or moral values. In its broadest sense, conservatism values the power of the marketplace to address economic concerns and individual initiative to confront social problems, therefore advocating a limited role for government power in economic and social matters.

Identify and describe ideological positions other than liberalism and conservatism.

There are other ideological positions as well. For instance, socialism subscribes to some of the same principles as liberalism but carries the desire for equal outcomes much further. Libertarianism subscribes to the conservative desire for freedom from government action, but also endorses moral positions conservatives would likely reject.

Briefly explain random sampling, and understand how opinion polls work.

The most efficient way to measure the opinion of a large group like a nation is to take a random sample of the opinions of a small subset of that group, making sure that everyone in the nation had an equal chance of being selected for questioning. Opinion polls can provide an account of public opinion if they are conducted and interpreted properly. Officials, candidates, interest groups, and the media utilize opinion polls to determine or demonstrate how Americans react to public events, although there is a difference between being responsive to public opinion and making responsible public decisions. Sometimes simply doing what the public wants can produce policy with undesirable outcomes.

Key Terms

attitudes A component of public opinion that measures people's orientations toward politics. (p. 61)

beliefs A component of public opinion that measures what people think is true about politics. (p. 70)

classical liberalism A term given to the philosophy of John Locke and other seventeenth- and eighteenth-century advocates of the protection of individual rights and liberties by limiting government power. (p. 77)

conservatism An ideology that advocates limits on government power to address economic and social problems, relying instead on economic markets and individual initiative to address problems like health care and education, while promoting government involvement in moral matters to, for instance, minimize or eliminate abortions or permit prayer in public schools. (p. 76)

cynicism A pervasive attitude of mistrust about politics that may lead people to withdraw from political participation. (p. 64)

directional An aspect of public opinion that measures whether people feel favorably or unfavorably toward a political figure, institution, or policy. (p. 56)

efficacy The attitude that you can be effectual and effective in your dealings with government. (p. 65)

empirical Any statement based on the assessment of data or the analysis of information, without regard to value judgments. (p. 56)

equality of opportunity One of several ways of understanding equality; this way values giving people comparable advantages for succeeding in life, regardless of the unequal outcomes that may result. (p. 77)

equality of outcome One of several ways of understanding equality; this way values leveling the social and economic inequities among people, rather than attempting to give people comparable advantages for succeeding in life. (p. 77)

faction A group of individuals who are united by a desire that, if realized, would threaten the liberty of the larger community—in James Madison's words, individuals who are "united and actuated by some common impulse of passion, or of interest, adverse to the rights of other citizens, or to the permanent and aggregate interests of the community." A faction may be defined by size, such as when a majority of citizens threatens the liberty of the minority, or by intensity, such as when a minority of citizens with intensely held preferences threatens the liberty of a disinterested majority. (p. 71)

fascism A militant, ultra-nationalistic ideology of the extreme right that rejects liberal ideas about personal rights. (p. 77)

ideology A wide-ranging set of beliefs that logically fit together. (p. 74)

intensity An aspect of public opinion that measures how strongly people feel toward a political figure, institution, or policy. (p. 56)

liberalism An ideology that advocates the use of government power to address economic and social problems, like unemploy-

ment and environmental protection, while limiting government involvement in moral matters like abortion rights and prayer in public schools. (p. 76)

libertarianism An ideology centered on the reduction of government power to advance personal liberty. (p. 77)

limited government The idea that power can be denied to government and the people who serve in it, in order to restrict those in positions of authority from infringing upon individual liberty. (p. 77)

normative Any statement that invokes a judgment or evaluation. Think of the word *norm*, which implies a standard for evaluating something. (p. 56)

public opinion A collection of opinions people hold on matters relating to government, politics, and society. (p. 56)

push polls Surveys that appear legitimate but in fact are a dirty campaign trick designed to generate negative opinion about an opponent in a political contest. (p. 81)

random sample The basis for a scientifically accurate public opinion poll, in which everyone in the community being polled has an equal chance of being selected to give their opinions to pollsters. In a poll of national opinion, everyone in the country would have to have an equal chance of being selected to participate in it. (p. 78)

social desirability bias A form of error in public opinion polls, whereby opinions or behaviors that could be considered undesirable are not fully reported in the data. (p. 71)

socialism A left-leaning ideology centered on the use of government power to advance equal outcomes. (p. 77)

stability An aspect of public opinion that measures how much change or variability there is in the way people feel toward a political figure, institution, or policy. (p. 57)

state-centered federalism One of several perspectives on federalism, which argues that the Constitution and the federal government are creations of the states and therefore can be overhauled by the states. (p. 63)

Resources

You might be interested in examining some of what the following authors have said about the topics we've been discussing:

Berelson, Bernard R., Paul F. Lazarsfeld, and William N. McPhee. *Voting: A Study of Opinion Formation in a Presidential Campaign.* Chicago: University of Chicago Press, 1954. A classic study of how people in the upstate New York city of Elmira decided how to vote in the 1948 elections, with important observations about political knowledge and the subject of our next chapter, political participation.

Campbell, Angus, Philip E. Converse, Warren E. Miller, and Donald E. Stokes. *The American Voter.* New York: John Wi-

ley and Sons, 1960. A seminal study on how Americans vote, with an interesting section on ideological thinking in 1950s America.

Delli Carpini, Michael X., and Scott Keeter. *What Americans Know about Politics and Why It Matters.* New Haven: Yale University Press, 1996. A thorough account of political knowledge in America.

Nie, Norman H., Sidney Verba, and John R. Petrocik. *The Changing American Voter.* Cambridge, MA: Harvard University Press, 1979. One generation after *The American Voter*, this book challenges some of the assumptions about how people understood politics during the relatively sleepy 1950s.

1 The exact figure is 68 percent, from a December 1998 Gallup Poll cited in Darren K. Carlson, "Queen Elizabeth: 50 Years of Public Opinion," *Gallup Poll News Service*, February 6, 2002.

2 Add to this an additional 55 percent of the population that's simply not engaged, and you have a picture of a turned-off workforce. Kenneth A. Tucker, "A Passion for Work," *Gallup Management Journal,* February 18, 2002.

3 Not too many Americans enjoy ski jumping either. The figures are from a February 2002 Gallup Poll cited in Jeffrey M. Jones, "Figure Skating Tops List of Americans' Favorite Winter Olympic Events," *Gallup Poll News Service*, February 8, 2002.

4 Michael X. Delli Carpini and Scott Keeter, *What Americans Know about Politics and Why It Matters* (New Haven: Yale University Press, 1996).

5 She was President Obama's attorney general.

6 Bernard R Berelson, Paul F. Lazarsfeld, and William N. McPhee, *Voting: A Study of Opinion Formation in a Presidential Campaign* (Chicago: University of Chicago Press, 1954), 308.

7 "The American National Election Studies Guide to Public Opinion and Electoral Behavior," Center for Political Studies, University of Michigan, November 5, 2015. http://www.election studies.org/nesguide/toptable/tab4a_1.htm.

8 Ibid. The survey covered the period 1964–2000 and was in response to the question, "Some people are afraid the government in Washington is getting too powerful for the good of the country and the individual person. Others feel that the government in Washington is not getting too strong." (The wording of the question varied in different years, as follows: 1964, 1966, 1970: "has not gotten too strong for the good of the country"; 1964–1972: "Have you been interested enough in this to favor one side over the other?"; 1976–1992: "Do you have an opinion on this or not?") In all years, the follow-up question was, "What is your feeling—do you think the government is getting too powerful, or do you think the government is not getting too strong?"

9 John F. Kennedy was the only Catholic president.

10 Up to a point, at least. The GSS also finds that one-third of Americans feel that most men are better suited emotionally for politics than most women.

11 Data from the 2016 General Social Survey, at https://gss dataexplorer.norc.org/projects/18607/variables/256/vshow and https://gssdataexplorer.norc.org/projects/18607/variables/252/ vshow.

12 Steven Kull, Americans on Iraq: WMD, Links to al-Qaeda, Reconstruction. The PIPA/Knowledge Networks Poll, July 1, 2003, 4.

13 Gallup Poll, at http://www.gallup.com/poll/1576/abortion .aspx.

14 Ibid.

15 This is not a new story, either. In 1935, after two years of Franklin D. Roosevelt's New Deal policies, the Gallup Organization reported that six in ten Americans thought the federal government was spending too much money on programs designed to bring relief from the Great Depression. At the same time, nine in ten supported the Social Security program.

16 Angus Campbell, Philip E. Converse, Warren E. Miller, and Donald E. Stokes, *The American Voter* (New York: John Wiley and Sons, 1960), 216–255.

17 Norman H. Nie, Sidney Verba, and John R. Petrocik, *The Changing American Voter* (Cambridge, MA: Harvard University Press, 1979).

18 It is also possible that the authors of *The Changing American Voter* were more lenient in the standards they used to classify ideologues, inadvertently inflating the number of ideological thinkers in their study.

19 The story of early scientific polling is an interesting one that you can read about in transcripts from the PBS program, "The First Measured Century," which you can access online at http://www.pbs.org/fmc/segments/progseg7.htm.

20 Richard Stengel and Eric Pooley, "Masters of the Message: Inside the High-Tech Machine That Set Clinton and Dole Polls Apart," *Time*, November 6, 1996. You may access the full article at http://cgi.cnn.com/ALLPOLITICS/1996/elections/time.special/ pollster/. It's colorful and fast moving, filled with accounts of power, personal jealousies, infighting, backstabbing, an ill-timed rendezvous with a prostitute—and enough opinion polls to make your head spin.

21 See "Push Polling," BBC News, February 22, 2000, at http:// news.bbc.co.uk/2/hi/in_depth/americas/2000/us_elections/glos sary/n-p/652168.stm.

22 One way to get a sense of the wide range of topics in media polls is to check out pollster.com at the *Huffington Post*, http:// www.huffingtonpost.com/news/pollster/.

Table, Figure, and Box Notes

T1 Data from American National Election Studies, at http:// www.electionstudies.org/nesguide/toptable/tab1b_3.htm.

T2 Data from American National Election Studies, at http:// www.electionstudies.org/nesguide/graphs/g4e_1_3.htm.

T3 Source: Gallup Poll, responses to the question, "Do you approve or disapprove of the job Barack Obama is doing as president?" taken from the first monthly survey of the Gallup rolling average of 1,500 adults nationwide. See http://www.gallup.com/ poll/116479/Barack-Obama-Presidential-Job-Approval.aspx.

T4 Michael X. Delli Carpini and Scott Keeter, *What Americans Know about Politics and Why It Matters* (New Haven: Yale University Press, 1996).

T5 Angie Drobnic Holan, "Palin 'Death Panel' Claim Sets Truth-O-Meter Ablaze." Politifact.com, at http://politifact.com/ truth-o-meter/article/2009/aug/10/palin-death-panel-remark -sets-truth-o-meter-fire/.

T6 Ibid.

T7 See, for instance, Kimberly Leonard, "Is the 'Death Panel' Debate Dead?" *US News and World Report*, July 9, 2015. http:// www.usnews.com/news/articles/2015/07/09/medicare-rule -revisits-death-panel-issue.

T8 Data from 2016 American National Election Studies. American National Election Studies, Center for Political Studies, University of Michigan. Electronic resources from the ANES World Wide Website (www.umich.edu/~nes). Ann Arbor, MI:

University of Michigan, Center for Political Studies [producer and distributor], 1995–2000. These materials are based on work supported by the National Science Foundation under Grant Nos.: SBR-9707741, SBR-9317631, SES-9209410, SES-9009379, SES-8808361, SES-8341310, SES-8207580, and SOC77-08885. Any opinions, findings, and conclusions or recommendations expressed in these materials are those of the author(s) and do not necessarily reflect those of the National Science Foundation.

T9 Jim Norman, "Public Remains Wary of Federal Government's Power. Gallup, October 9, 2015. http://www.gallup.com/poll/186065/public-remains-wary-federal-government-power.aspx?g_source=government%20is%20too%20powerful&g_medium=search&g_campaign=tiles.

T10 Data from 2016 American National Election Studies. American National Election Studies, Center for Political Studies, University of Michigan. Electronic resources from the ANES World Wide Website (www.umich.edu/~nes). Ann Arbor, MI: University of Michigan, Center for Political Studies [producer and distributor], 1995–2000. These materials are based on work supported by the National Science Foundation under Grant Nos.: SBR-9707741, SBR-9317631, SES-9209410, SES-9009379, SES-8808361, SES-8341310, SES-8207580, and SOC77-08885. Any opinions, findings, and conclusions or recommendations expressed in these materials are those of the author(s) and do not necessarily reflect those of the National Science Foundation.

T11 Data from 2016 American National Election Studies, at http://www.electionstudies.org/nesguide/toptable/tab5a_1.htm.

T12 Data from 2016 General Social Survey, at https://gssdataexplorer.norc.org/projects/18607/variables/455/vshow.

T13 Data from 2016 American National Election Studies. American National Election Studies, Center for Political Studies, University of Michigan. Electronic resources from the ANES World Wide Website (www.umich.edu/~nes). Ann Arbor, MI: University of Michigan, Center for Political Studies [producer and distributor], 1995–2000. These materials are based on

work supported by the National Science Foundation under Grant Nos.: SBR- 9707741, SBR-9317631, SES-9209410, SES-9009379, SES- 8808361, SES-8341310, SES-8207580, and SOC77-08885. Any opinions, findings, and conclusions or recommendations expressed in these materials are those of the author(s) and do not necessarily reflect those of the National Science Foundation.

T14 Data from 2016 American National Election Studies, at http://www.electionstudies.org/nesguide/toptable/tab5b_1.htm; http://www.electionstudies.org/nesguide/toptable/tab5b_2.htm; and http://www.electionstudies.org/nesguide/toptable/tab5b_3.htm.

T15 For an interesting account of this phenomenon, see Roderick P. Hart, *Seducing America: How Television Charms the Modern Voter* (Sage Publications Thousand Oaks, CA 1999).

T16 Joe Antonio Vargas, "Obama's Wide Web," Washingtonpost.com, August 20, 2008.

T17 Data from 2014 General Social Survey, at https://gssdataexplorer.norc.org/projects/18607/variables/590/vshow and https://gssdataexplorer.norc.org/projects/18607/variables/400/vshow/.

T18 All photos in the public domain and all sourced from the U.S. government, with the exception of the Sarah Palin photo, which is in the Creative Commons and sourced by Therealbs2002.

T19 Data from 2000 General Social Survey, at http://www.icpsr.umich.edu/GSS/.

T20 See Nate Silver, "Debunking the Bradley Effect," *Newsweek*, October 21, 2008.

T21 Data from Gallup Poll, at http://www.gallup.com/poll/1576/abortion.aspx.

T22 Data from 2006, 2012, and 2014 General Social Survey.

T23 Data from 2014 General Social Survey.

T24 Lydia Saad, "Conservatives Hold on to Ideology Lead by a Thread," Gallup, January 11, 2016. http://www.gallup.com/poll/188129/conservatives-hang-ideology-lead-thread.aspx.

Political Culture, Socialization, and Participation

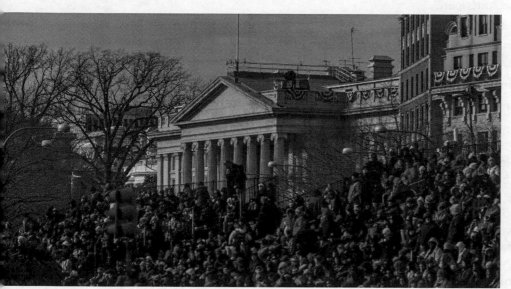

Copyright: Christopher Parypa/Shutterstock.com

Learning Objectives

When you have completed this chapter, you should be able to:

- Appreciate American political culture as a set of shared values.
- Understand how immigration has both challenged and helped define American political culture.
- Identify how immigration, migration, and aging are changing American population demographics.
- Define political socialization.
- Describe how political socialization is a lifelong process, and identify primary and secondary agents of political socialization.
- Explain the relationship between political socialization and the circumstances of one's upbringing.
- Discuss multiple ways in which people participate in politics and several factors that influence the likelihood that someone will participate.
- Identify reasons why people vote, despite time and information costs.
- Explain several common ways people arrive at their voting decisions.

4.1 Introduction

Are you an American?

Easy question, right? If you were born in or live legally in this country, your answer is probably "sure" (otherwise, it's probably "no"). Still, if you are an American, when you think about your identity, is "American" qualified with something else?

Irish American?

African American?

Italian American?

Chinese American?

Cuban American?

German American?

Native American?

Vietnamese American?

Mexican American?

Those qualifiers tell us about where we came from. Many people think of themselves as Americans while simultaneously seeing themselves in terms of their heritage. This helps explain why American politics can be so complex while saying a lot about the richness of the American identity.

On one hand, Americans are many different people with deep roots in a variety of diverse, sometimes conflicting traditions, and at times, this has been a source of political conflict and division. On the other, Americans share a common set of values, attitudes, and beliefs, which together form an American **political culture**. Those values tend to be about "buying in" to the idea of America and how it operates, which is essential in order for the United States to function as a nation.

political culture: The common set of attitudes, beliefs, and values that provide the foundation of support for a political system.

During moments of great change, the fundamental question of what it means to be an American can be up for debate. We are living through one of those moments now. Generational shifts and immigration are changing the demography of the country, making it less white and less Anglo. This is not a new phenomenon—America has seen moments like this before, when new groups emerge in large numbers and bring with them different social and cultural values. The Millennial generation—which is your generation if you are a college-aged reader—is less religious and more socially liberal than older generations, representing a historic break with the past.[1] But the "former" America has not yet exited the stage. Many older, whiter, less urban, and more conservative individuals looking to preserve a country they see disappearing found resonance in Donald Trump's promise to "make America great again." This set up what promises to be one of the defining conflicts of the Trump era, between different appreciations of American political culture.

The strength of that culture will help determine how smoothly and effectively we address our conflicts. We saw in Chapter 3 just how much disagreement there is in America on specific issues of policy. At the same time, there's a lot of agreement on how to set up the political rules of the game. A basic accord supplies the framework for American political culture. It encompasses things like:

- Acceptance of representative democracy and capitalism as default political and economic arrangements
- Acceptance of the rule of law for resolving disputes and determining political winners and losers
- Belief in compromise with others as a way of achieving objectives
- Agreement on the rules for electing representatives
- Approval of the fundamental choice of liberty and opportunity over equal outcomes (which we talked about in Chapter 1)

These bedrock qualities of the American political culture help to maintain the legitimacy of the system, but during times of stress, they can come under assault. We have already seen them strained by the weight of the political moment. Candidate Trump's flirtation with the possibility that he would not concede defeat if he lost defied custom and tradition, contravening accepted methods for settling elections. Bitterness from years of partisan wrangling in Congress between representatives from different sides of the cultural divide makes compromise difficult. A chaotic information environment and relaxed limitations on money in politics, among other things, are complicating the relationship between voters and representatives.

At the same time, political culture can provide the means for working through differences by emphasizing the common ground that defines us as a nation. Perhaps the items on this list seem so basic as to make you wonder, "Who wouldn't agree with these things?" That's a natural reaction; we can be so deeply enmeshed in political culture that its tenets just seem obvious. In practice, there is no reason to believe people will automatically accept these principles, and individuals in many other cultures do not (see Global Topics: Political Culture in Comparative Perspective). That many Americans might do

---

GLOBAL TOPICS

Political Culture in Comparative Perspective

The American political culture is so universally accepted that when we talk about it, you may just think we're stating the obvious. That's not uncommon for something that's part of a core identity—it seems obvious because it's so deeply ingrained. This tends to make it difficult to imagine that the political cultures of other nations may look quite different because of the human tendency to believe that others fundamentally think like we do and want what we want. Because of this, American political culture may be best understood in a comparative perspective, in which we're open to the possibility that people in other nations have a different relationship to their government and to what constitutes acceptable political action.

Have you ever heard someone say that something is "un-American," like "It's un-American not to reward someone for hard work"? Now try to imagine someone saying something is "un-Canadian" or "un-Vietnamese." Most likely, you'll never hear anything like that because thinking about one's nation in terms apart from others is not a part of all political cultures. That's not to say that people of other nations do not notice cultural differences, but they don't necessarily define and describe themselves in terms of those differences. In the United States, though, it's probably not necessary to explain what it means for something to be un-American because, as vague as that phrase is, for many Americans, it encompasses a set of ideas associated with what it means to be an American. In that respect, it is both a part of the political culture and a way of reflecting that culture to others.

Political culture may be understood as the product of a nation's formative political experiences—whether a nation has a long history of democracy or repression or corruption or incompetent leadership. In the early 1960s, researchers Gabriel Almond and Sidney Verba wrote a pioneering study comparing political cultures of different nations, taking into account these historical differences. In *The Civic Culture*, they attempt to explain differences in the levels of political attachment by people in different nations and identify the characteristics that motivate people to political action.

They found mid-twentieth-century Italy to be an alienated political culture, where people had low levels of national pride and lacked confidence in their ability to influence what government did. Almond and Verba attribute these tendencies to a history fraught with tyranny and ineffective efforts at democratic self-governance. In Mexico, they found a sense of isolation from politics and mistrust of authority mixed with great national pride and aspirations toward democracy. They characterize the German political culture, one generation removed from the trauma of World War II, as one where people are knowledgeable about politics and actively engaged in formal political activity like voting, while feeling detached and cynical about politics. And they see the political culture of England as being highly developed, with engaged, interested citizens who take emotional satisfaction from political participation.

These patterns differ from the political culture of the United States, which Almond and Verba regard as a participant civic culture where, in contrast to the other four nations, people are frequently exposed to political messages, feel obligated to participate in their communities and feel competent to do so, tend to voluntarily join groups in large numbers, get emotionally involved in political campaigns, and take great pride in the political system.[T1]

Does this description conform to the way you see America? Would describing it any other way seem—un-American?

so without thinking about it addresses how political culture works: It is composed of assumptions that are fundamental to the point of being almost invisible.

Accepting this broad framework doesn't imply that everyone agrees with the specific choices made in America on matters of policy—far from it, as we saw in Chapter 3. But it does mean that there's a sense of acceptance and even pride in the American system that is a basic part of the identity of many Americans, regardless of their origin.

In this chapter, we're going to explore American political culture in order to get a sense of who Americans are and how American political culture affects politics. Then, we'll move from the collective portrait of a diverse nation to political socialization, the processes that shape our individual awareness of and relationship to politics. Finally, we'll put these general observations together with the individual ones when we look at how political culture and political socialization relate to participation in the political arena in ways large and small.

4.2 Political Culture: Who Are We?

L.O. Understand how immigration has both challenged and helped define American political culture.

If you paid attention to the 2016 campaign, you could be forgiven for thinking that the major presidential candidates were speaking to two different nations. To listen to campaign rhetoric was to hear incompatible narratives about the United States in 2016, each appealing to a distinct set of Americans. Donald Trump painted a dark vision of a decaying country in need of salvation. Hillary Clinton spoke of a strong nation whose challenges could be surmounted by working together. Her America is young and multicultural; his is older and white. Her America benefits from the technological changes brought by the information economy; his America has been left behind in shuttered plants and factories. Her America is coastal, urban, and suburban; his is landlocked, rural, and exurban. These two Americas share the same borders, but they are at odds with each other and threatened by the thought of the other governing them. They are emblematic of the economic and cultural changes bearing down on our political institutions and pressuring our politics.

Donald Trump and Hillary Clinton rallied distinct groups of Americans around different and ofgten incompatible visions of gthe country. *Sources:* Top photo: George Sheldon/Shutterstock.com. Bottom photo: JStone/Shutterstock.com.

One of the great challenges of our time will be finding peaceful ways to manage the forces unleashed by great social and economic change. As a nation of immigrants, where just about everyone can trace his or her lineage to someplace else, many generations have had to figure out how to live alongside those whose customs and practices seemed alien. Our time is no different.

Barack Obama spoke to our common experience on his way to becoming the first African American president, a theme embraced by Hillary Clinton's campaign slogan, "stronger together," as she sought to become the first woman elected to the presidency. Donald Trump denounced Mexican immigrants as "rapists" who are "bringing drugs" and "crime,"[2] and spoke of banning Muslims from entering the country.[3] Both of these sentiments—about inclusion and differences—are part of the American cultural fabric, and they define the parameters of our present-day divide.

Moments such as ours strain the political culture by accentuating our differences at the expense of sentiments about which we overwhelmingly agree. A few years ago, the Institute for Advanced Studies in Culture at the University of Virginia attempted to identify some of the constants in American political culture. They discovered nearly unanimous buy-in among Americans for what they

FIGURE 4.1 Shared American Ideals?[T2]

Percent Agreeing	
87%	America from the beginning has had a destiny to set an example for other nations.
94%	America's contribution is one of expanding freedom for more and more people.
95%	America is the world's great melting pot, in which people from different countries are united into one nation.
96%	With hard work and perseverance, anyone can succeed in America.
95%	Democracy is only as strong as the virtue of its citizens.

call the "American creed"—ideals about the public life of America. Take a second to see how much you subscribe to the "American creed" by answering the five brief questions in Figure 4.1.

Pretty clearly, Americans overwhelmingly are proud of their country, believe in its goodness and the goodness of its citizens, and even feel that America has a mission to serve as an example for the rest of the world. These elements of political culture may seem abstract, and in one important sense, they are: The nearly universal acceptance of others in *theory* does not translate into universal tolerance for the *practice* of people expressing unpopular ideas, as we saw in Section 3.3d, "Tolerance," in Chapter 3. Political culture is manifested through abstract perceptions about self and nation, rather than through specific attitudes, beliefs, and actions that may be at odds with how many Americans view themselves. This infuses political culture with a generous portion of mythology.

We saw the connection many Americans have to their political culture at work in the public reaction to the terror attacks of September 2001. American flags and American flag stickers blossomed overnight on homes, office buildings, and cars. The near-universal sentiment that *we* had been attacked was an expression of an attitude about identifying as an American. At that moment, being conservative or liberal didn't matter, nor did the national origin of one's ancestors. (One unfortunate and important exception to this involved Americans of the Muslim faith and of Middle Eastern origin, who experienced increased discrimination that reflected the worst elements of the hybrid American culture.)

We saw the contours of our political culture during the Cold War as well, even during times of great unrest as a result of strong differences of opinion about such things as the civil rights movement and the Vietnam War. For a while in the 1960s, the American flag became a symbol adopted by those who supported American policy in Vietnam. Some on the other side of this issue burned the American flag as a way of expressing their views, a manifestation of our cultural acceptance of dissent. We know from Chapter 3 that dissent is something people don't embrace quite as strongly as the "American creed." In this regard, everyone may not always accept all cultural values.

Still, even at a moment of great divisions over policy, Americans expressed attitudes and beliefs rooted deep in the political culture. Although vocal minorities at times have advocated the overthrow of the American system, an overwhelming number of Americans—including many who opposed the Vietnam War—continued to feel a patriotic attachment to the American system and rejected the Communist system of the Soviet Union as an inferior alternative.

The flag is a powerful symbol of American political culture. Top: The flag flying in official capacity. Bottom: The flag as a symbol of free expression *Sources:* Top photo: Orhan Cam/Shutterstock.com. Bottom photo: Andrew Selman via Wikimedia.

Chapter 4 Political Culture, Socialization, and Participation

4.2a Group Membership and Tolerance

The tendency for Americans to join organizations is one characteristic of American political culture that separates it from the political cultures of other nations. Observers of American culture have noted this characteristic for centuries. In 1831, the French nobleman Alexis de Tocqueville spent the better part of a year touring the United States, an experience that culminated in publishing his observations in the two-volume work, *Democracy in America*, in 1835 and 1840. In it, he made the observation that America is a nation of joiners and that through participating in groups with fellow citizens, Americans learned the fundamentals of compromise necessary to a functioning democracy.[4] Tocqueville noted how, "Americans of all ages, all stations in life, and all types of disposition are forever forming associations. There are not only commercial and industrial associations in which all take part but others of a thousand different types—religious, moral, serious, futile, very general and very limited, immensely large and very minute."[5] Today, we would call these voluntary groups: civic and religious organizations, political clubs, sports leagues, neighborhood associations, charitable and service organizations, and educational and cultural groups. They need not be expressly political in order to teach how to tolerate and work with others; in fact, most of these groups are not political, and they may be devoted to pursuits as recreational and ordinary as intramural sports or playing trumpet in the band or working on the school newspaper.

Recent research confirms what Tocqueville saw over 185 years ago: Americans tend to join groups more frequently and more widely than people in other nations.[6] The more groups we join, the more experience we get in the give-and-take with other people that teaches us how to be tolerant. Therefore, people who join more groups tend to be more tolerant of the rights of others. It is the isolated individual who is likely to be the least tolerant of all.[7]

However, there are indications that we have been living through a period of diminished civic activity. Historically, there have been peaks and valleys in the degree to which Americans engage in group activities, and evidence suggests that for the past several decades, we have been in one of the valleys. Political scientist Robert D. Putnam writes that over that period, Americans have become increasingly isolated from one another by joining fewer organizations and spending less time with neighbors and friends. As a consequence, Putnam argues that Americans have become detached from the relationships that reinforce basic democratic and civic values. The title of his book, *Bowling Alone*, refers to the disappearance of bowling leagues that once provided a social connection for many people, while providing a visual metaphor for the isolation that characterizes the leisure and work lives of so many people who spend their days living in places where they don't know their neighbors, working alone in cubicles, commuting alone in cars, and recreating alone in front of the television.[8]

Putnam sees in these trends the loss of social capital—the connections we make with each other when we spend our time in association with others. The value of social capital is in its ability to nurture trusting relationships, through which we learn how to compromise and reciprocate with others. These values are associated with having a rich civic life and stand in sharp contrast to the isolation from one another that, according to Putnam, characterizes our time and makes us feel detached and alienated from each other, our communities, and our government.[9]

To reverse these trends, Putnam advocates the daunting task of creating social capital through renewed civic engagement in all facets of life: promoting family-friendly workplaces; designing communities with common areas that promote socializing with neighbors; encouraging clergy to spark a spiritual awakening that will promote religious tolerance; developing Internet activities that engage people in communities; and participating in social and political activities.[10] For some, this would require changing the fundamental patterns of our lives—from joining groups to spending less time in the car. The benefit to individuals could be greater personal fulfillment. The benefit to the political culture would be a deeper investment in the bonds that help a republic endure. Demystifying Government: Virtual Civic Engagement considers whether social media might help make something like this possible.

DEMYSTIFYING GOVERNMENT

Virtual Civic Engagement

There are many opinions about whether the bonds of virtual relationships formed on the Internet are comparable to friendships formed in person. But the Internet has created intriguing possibilities for meeting people in the real world—possibilities that could contribute to the formation of social capital by creating a way to find interesting and like-minded people who otherwise would be unknown to us. Obvious examples of this are online dating sites, which can be a source of personal enrichment. But sites geared toward connecting groups of people with shared interests offer intriguing possibilities for renewed civic engagement.

Consider the example of Meetup, a service that enables people to find others online who share their interests and arrange in-person get-togethers. People looking to reach out to others can go to meetup.com and search the database of topics until they find what they're looking for. Topics cover the range of civic and personal interests that Putnam identified as central to community life: books, films, games, health, music, pets, hobbies, work, and politics—everything from Audi owners to ferret lovers. You can scan today's list of groups by going to https://www.meetup.com.

Site users can join an existing group or suggest a topic for the purpose of attracting others with the same interest. When a topic attracts enough people in the same geographic area, members vote on a time and a place for a meeting and get together in person, typically in an informal location like a bar, café—or bowling alley.

Meetup was created with social activities in mind, but it unexpectedly developed an important political function in 2003, as supporters of Democratic presidential hopeful Governor Howard Dean began using the website to organize on behalf of their candidate. The official campaign rapidly recognized the value of Meetup for national grassroots organizing, and in early 2003, placed a Meetup link on the candidate's website. Shortly thereafter, Dean's Meetup numbers started to soar, growing from several hundred in January to over 65,000 in July, to better than 180,000 before Dean ended his presidential bid the following February.

The first Wednesday of every month became the designated day for Dean meetups, at which thousands of volunteers at hundreds of locations across America would gather in small groups to plan strategy for the Dean campaign. The Dean website trumpeted this activity as the first true grassroots presidential campaign of the Internet era, and attributed the sharp rise in Dean's profile during 2003 to the high degree of interest the candidate generated through Meetup. As a civic matter, Meetup became the vehicle by which people who were previously detached from or passive about politics could get involved in a presidential campaign—many for the first time in their lives. It foreshadowed the online-driven civic engagement that would become the hallmark of Barack Obama's 2008 presidential campaign, offering a tantalizing glimpse of how the Internet can bring people together in the real world to work for a political cause—a far cry from the couch-potato politics of passive observation and detachment offered by television.

4.2b Immigration

Because one component of political culture is the belief that America is an open place accepting of others in need—the idea symbolized by the welcoming torch of the Statue of Liberty—America has been able to incorporate numerous subcultures that immigrant groups have brought with them to this country. This simultaneously makes American government more interesting—and more complicated. It brings texture to the American tapestry while assembling a much wider set of values than those subscribed to by the Anglican males who wrote the Constitution, making governing the country a challenge, especially at a moment like ours when immigration is at the forefront of political debate.

L.O. Identify how immigration, migration, and aging are changing American population demographics.

Changes in political culture—and politics—may be anticipated through the changing face of diversity in America. Cultural changes have also been driven in recent years by shifting migration patterns and the growing number of senior citizens in America. Let's look a little closer at these factors. We'll examine America's long history of immigration and the nature of American cultural diversity, recent patterns of geographic mobility, and the aging of America.

It's probably not overstating things to say that America is a place where just about everybody comes from someplace else. Even the Native American civilizations that European settlers encountered when they came to North America were likely populated by individuals whose origins may be traced to Asia, and to a long walk over what thousands of years ago was a land bridge across the Bering Straits between Alaska and Russia.

Between 1820 and 2000, a total of 66 million immigrants came to the United States, changing the tenor of American life. Of these, better than half (58 percent or 38,460,000) came from Europe. Much of the immigration from Europe came in waves, starting with British and Irish immigrants in the early to mid-nineteenth century, German immigrants following the Civil War, and immigrants from Eastern Europe in the first decades of the twentieth century.

One of the first waves of immigration came from the British Isles, especially Ireland. Between 1830 and 1860, almost 2 million Irish immigrants came to America, representing 40 percent of all immigrants to the United States during that period. Almost another 1.5 million arrived between 1860 and 1890. Many Irish immigrants were Catholic, adding a religious mix to what had been an overwhelmingly Protestant nation.

Germany was the next big departure point. Between 1850 and 1900, following the initial wave of Irish immigrants, a large group of German immigrants came to the United States. The peak was in the 1880s, when 1,450,000 German immigrants represented more than 25 percent of all immigrants during that time. A large influx of immigrants from the Scandinavian countries overlapped the wave of German immigrants. Over 1.5 million Scandinavians, many of them Norwegians and Swedes, came to America between 1870 and 1910.

The turn of the twentieth century witnessed a large influx of Italian immigrants—over 3 million between 1900 and 1920—representing 20 percent of all immigrants during that time. The same period was a peak time for Eastern European immigrants. Three million Russians arrived between 1890 and 1920, 1.2 million Hungarians arrived between 1900 and 1920, and 250,000 Poles arrived during the 1920s. This wave of immigration included a large number of Jews, Russian Orthodox, and other non-Protestants. Notice how as time passed, European immigration moved clockwise, from western to central to eastern Europe (see Figure 4.2).

European immigration trailed off sharply in the 1930s. When immigration picked up again in the 1970s, it had a decidedly more global quality, featuring Asian immigrants from China, Japan, and Veitnam; Latino immigrants from Mexico, the Caribbean, Central and South America; and African immigrants, whose numbers have dobuled every decade since the 1970s.

Americans' tolerance has been tested after each great wave of immigration, from the present day back to the first influx of Irish immigrants in the 1840s. Nativist Protestants opposed to the foreign, "contaminating" influences of Roman Catholics formed secret

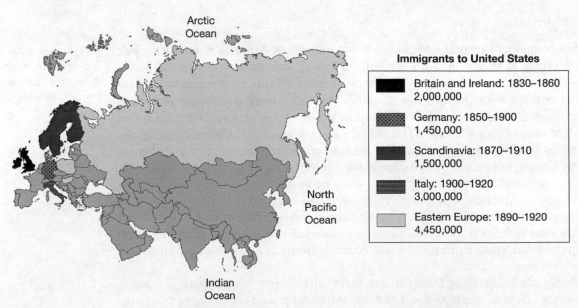

FIGURE 4.2 Native Countries of Immigrants to the United States, 1830–1920[T3]

societies with names like "The Order of the Star-Spangled Banner" in an effort to combat citizenship for Irish immigrants. Because these organizations operated in secrecy, with their members never claiming to know anything about the leadership, the anti-Catholic crusade was dubbed the **"Know-Nothing"** movement. It survived as a national movement for almost twenty years, until it dissolved over differences about slavery just prior to the Civil War.

The "Know-Nothing" movement showed how tolerance can be tested when some people feel threatened by large-scale changes to their way of life. This regrettable chapter in American history has been repeated several times, as people with different religious practices, skin colors, and native languages came to America and, by virtue of their numbers, modified the cultural and political landscape. Jews arrived in large numbers in the early twentieth century to widespread anti-Semitism. The wave of German immigrants was subsiding around World War I, but American involvement in the war generated public hostility to immigrants of German descent, just as participation in World War II produced hostility toward Japanese Americans. During the 1990s, the most recent wave of American immigrants produced a "close-the-borders" backlash aimed at Latinos, an attitude that is even more pronounced today than it was twenty years ago. We are also witnessing an increase in anti-Muslim sentiment and a renewed hostility in some corners to groups that have been here for a long time, such as African Americans and Jews.

Turn over this picture, however, and you'll find the beneficial side of immigration. People from different cultures bring variety to everything from the arts to politics, adding richness to the things people consider uniquely American. Individuals willingly coming to the United States tend to embrace the "American creed," which provides a common sense of self-identification. Many immigrants—even from vastly different political cultures—instinctively subscribe to key elements of the American approach to government and society. For instance, Irish immigrants who came to America to escape poverty accepted the idea of opportunity as an avenue toward self-betterment. Contemporary immigrants from Cuba who came to America to escape the repression of the Castro regime fiercely embrace the American values of liberty and limited government.

Every generation of immigrants brought with them the myth of the American dream, that their children would find a better life despite the hardships and discrimination that might await them. However glorified this myth may be, to a certain extent, Americans have eventually accepted groups that in their day were derided as dangerously threatening to the established social order.

4.2c Diversity

With immigration comes variety. Just look at the 2010 Census. The Constitution requires that a **census** be taken every ten years, in which everyone in the country is supposed to be counted. The census says a lot about the composition of the United States and tells us how it has changed since the last census was taken a decade ago. Demystifying Government: Slipping through the Cracks tells why an accurate census is so important.

Figures from the 2010 Census confirm the story of America's immigrant past and present. Although more than six in ten Americans are non-Hispanic whites, roughly one in eight is African American, slightly more than one in six is of Hispanic origin, and one in twenty is Asian American. Also, just as immigrant groups have traditionally settled in specific states or regions, the Census reveals that the South, Southwest, and portions of the Northeast are the most diverse regions of the country. The Latino population is largest in California, Nevada, Arizona, New Mexico, Colorado, Texas, Florida, New York, and New Jersey. The Asian American population is greatest in the states of the Pacific Rim and along the East Coast from New York to Virginia. African Americans are most numerous in the states of the deep South and in the large industrial states of the East and Midwest. In contrast, northern New England and the Great Plains states tend to have the highest percentage of white residents.

If diversity influences politics, then it should be pretty easy to imagine that national politics is far from a singular phenomenon. Although political activity is about much

"Know-Nothing" movement: An anti-Catholic movement that formed in the 1840s as a reaction to the first large wave of Irish immigration.

census: An accounting or, as Article I, Section 2 of the Constitution puts it, an "actual Enumeration" of the residents of the United States, taken every ten years by constitutional decree to assess population growth and population shifts. Census figures are used to determine representation in Congress, as states that lose population between censuses stand to lose House seats to states that gain population.

Slipping through the Cracks

As you can probably imagine, it's impossible to count *everybody* in a nation as vast as the United States. Some people live in remote areas; others are homeless; many others simply elude the reach of census takers. In fact, the Census Bureau estimates that in 2010, census takers missed hundreds of thousands of people. Latinos, African Americans, Native Americans, and people who rent homes are more likely to be undercounted than whites, older people, and homeowners, who are more likely to be overcounted.[T4]

This probably doesn't sound like a big deal unless you're really compulsive about record keeping, but from a political perspective, it's huge. Real resources ride on the outcome of the census—big dollars and real power. Some policies provide for federal money to be allocated to states based on population, so states where a disproportionate percentage of the population was undercounted will lose funds they would otherwise be eligible for, while still having to provide for the undercounted people. When we talk about Congress in Chapter 9, we'll see that the census is used to determine which states will gain or lose seats in the House of Representatives, so states where a disproportionate percentage of the population was undercounted, along with undercounted groups in those states, will lose representation to which they're entitled. Compounding the political tension is the fact that undercounted groups are more likely to support Democrats, lending a partisan element to the outcome of the census count.

It turns out that there's a remedy for this disparity, but it's highly controversial. The Census Bureau can estimate the true population using statistical methods, correcting the errors produced by the actual head count.

This possibility generated a huge political battle in the days leading up to the 2000 Census. Because underrepresented groups tend to disproportionately support Democrats, any statistical adjustment to the census would likely result in the creation of more congressional districts favorable to Democratic candidates. Not surprisingly, Republicans ferociously opposed the statistical estimate, claiming it would amount to a mere guess at the true population—a far cry from the hard numbers required by the Constitution. They argued that even a flawed head count was better than an estimated count and closer to what the nation's founders had in mind. In 1999, the Supreme Court put its stamp on this reasoning, claiming that using estimated figures for determining congressional representation was unconstitutional.[T5]

But the matter of sampling did not go away. In 2009, President Obama appointed Robert Groves, a statistical sampling expert, to head the Census Bureau. Groves had been an advocate of sampling during the 2000 Census, and some congressional Republicans feared he would rekindle the sampling conflict in advance of the 2010 Census, a concern Groves put to rest at his confirmation hearing by asserting he would not use the methodology.[T6] But the political stakes are high enough that it would not be surprising for the issue of sampling to arise again during the 2020 Census.

---

more than racial or ethnic identification, it still stands to reason that states and regions with greater diversity are likely to voice different concerns and interests than states and regions with less diversity. The politics of New York is different from the politics of Idaho, in part because of the different groups that settled there.

Some of these differences go back to the distinctions between liberals and conservatives that we talked about in Chapter 3, although this too can be oversimplified. You can review the concepts of liberalism and conservatism in Demystifying Government: Review: Liberalism and Conservation.

For instance, we mentioned that African Americans are more likely to express the liberal position supporting government activity in economic and social matters—adding a liberal bent to politics in regions with large African American communities. Not every minority group has liberal inclinations, though. Older Cuban Americans, for instance, can be quite conservative politically, lending a conservative quality to regions with large Cuban American communities, like southern Florida.

Probably the biggest story in the 2000 and 2010 Census is the emerging majority of minority groups, so to speak. Those figures we were just talking about from the 2010 Census are simply a snapshot of America at a given time. It's also possible to look at trends in immigration patterns and birth rates and try to estimate what America will look like in the years ahead. The Census Bureau has developed a projection like this, and you can see the results in Figure 4.3.

Review: Liberalism and Conservatism

Liberalism in its broadest sense endorses an active role for government in addressing social and economic problems and a more limited role for government in refereeing matters involving personal or moral values.

Liberals advocate government activism (which in a practical sense translates into spending money on government programs) for such social issues as environmental protection, health and child care, education, and drug addiction and for such economic issues as welfare and Social Security. In this regard, liberals seek to use the power of government to assist those in need (for instance, through welfare and drug programs) and to compensate for the inequities (like unequal access to health care) or consequences (like air and water pollution) of the economic marketplace.

At the same time, liberals typically believe government should stay out of matters that they consider to be of a moral nature. Consequently, liberals may oppose using government power to limit abortion rights, impose the death penalty, or require prayer in public schools (however, they may be quite comfortable engaging the government to protect abortion rights and defend against school prayer). Liberals may also favor gun control laws, limits on military spending, and tax laws that benefit lower-income people.

Conservatism applies different principles to arrive at mirror-image positions. In its broadest sense, conservatism values the power of the marketplace to address economic concerns and individual initiative to confront social problems, therefore advocating a limited role for government power in economic and social matters. Contemporary conservatism for many years has accepted the reality of America's social welfare programs, although more recently, some conservatives have aggressively attempted to roll back or privatize programs such as Obamacare, Medicare, and Social Security (all of which were in the crosshairs of congressional Republicans at the start of the Trump administration). Conservatives tend to be suspicious of government programs that are not subjected to what they regard as the beneficial self-correcting forces of the marketplace, and that therefore take money out of taxpayers' pockets that could be put toward free enterprise.

Consequently, conservatives advocate less involvement in (and less money for) government programs on environmental protection, health and child care, education, and drug addiction. They regard welfare as a program that can undermine individual initiative, and they have been successful in restructuring government welfare benefits to orient the program toward getting people to find jobs. Unlike liberals, conservatives would like Social Security to be a market-oriented program.

Keep in mind that this is an estimate based on current trends, and if immigration or birth rates should change, the estimates could be off. Nonetheless, the most notable thing about the projection is that during your lifetime, the white majority that has always characterized this country will become a numerical minority. By the year 2060, non-Hispanic whites are projected to dip below the 50 percent mark in total population, remaining the largest group in America but shrinking from a majority to a plurality of the population, as Hispanics, African Americans, and Asian Americans will together constitute a numerical majority of Americans.

For a nation that's always seen itself as primarily Anglican, these changes promise to create an entirely different identity—one with potentially profound political implications. The questions are speculative, but interesting, even if the answers are unknowable. What would it mean for whites to be just another minority under these new circumstances? Would whites see themselves as a minority? As the largest minority? Or still as a majority? Would they continue to control a disproportionate amount of economic resources by virtue of having been a majority group for so long? Would greater diversity in the population translate into greater diversity among elected representatives, and if so, what might that mean for the direction of our politics?

4.2d Migration

In addition to being an immigrant nation, America has always been a mobile nation. As large numbers of people move around within the United States, politics is inevitably affected. Once an agrarian country centered on rural concerns, America was redefined by industrialization, which brought about massive movement toward urban centers in the

liberalism: An ideology that advocates the use of government power to address economic and social problems, like unemployment and environmental protection, while limiting government involvement in moral matters like abortion rights and prayer in public schools.

conservatism: An ideology that advocates limits on government power to address economic and social problems, relying instead on economic markets and individual initiative to address problems like health care and education while promoting government involvement in moral matters to, for instance, minimize or eliminate abortions or permit prayer in public schools.

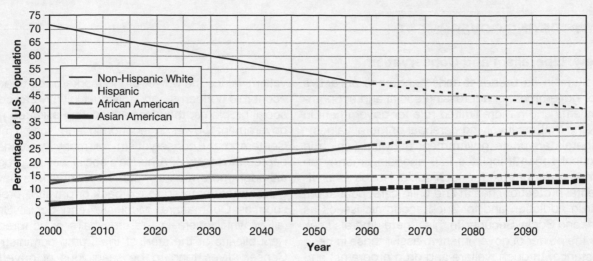

FIGURE 4.3 Projected Ethnic Group Demographics for the Twenty-first Century[T7]

As the white population steadily shrinks in size and the African American population holds steady, the Hispanic population is projected to double from turn-of-the-century levels by 2045 or 2050, while the Asian American population doubles by 2040. Projecting to the turn of the next century, only four in ten Americans will be white. One-third of the population will be Hispanic.

late nineteenth and early twentieth centuries. With urban development, political attention turned to urban issues like transportation, sanitation, labor laws, and a host of matters that were irrelevant in an earlier time.

In recent decades, there have been two politically meaningful population shifts: regionally from the old industrial cities of the Midwest and Northeast to the South and Southwest, and nationally from cities to suburbs.

The regional shift is evident when you compare where people lived in 1920 with where they lived in 1960 and 2000. Ninety-odd years ago, the most populous states were in the industrial centers of the Midwest and Northeast that in recent years have been dubbed the "Rust Belt" region, after the aging industries of twentieth-century America that were once their crowning jewels. By 1960, the move to warmer "Sun Belt" states had already begun, and by 2000, America's center of gravity had shifted to the South and West. Figure 4.4 illustrates these population shifts.

The ascendancy of conservative national politics coincided with this migration. Through the 1960s, heavily populated industrial centers were the engine of liberal politics, a key base of political support for presidents like Franklin Roosevelt and Lyndon Johnson who, as we noted in Chapter 2, presided over a large expansion in the role of the federal government. These regions lost political clout as they lost population to the Sun Belt states, which traditionally have been more socially and economically conservative.

Now it's easy to overstate the relationship between population shifts and changes in political currents—there's a lot more to it than where people move, as we'll see as we go along. For instance, liberal presidents like Roosevelt and Johnson drew support from

America at Night: A Portrait of Urban Sprawl[T8]

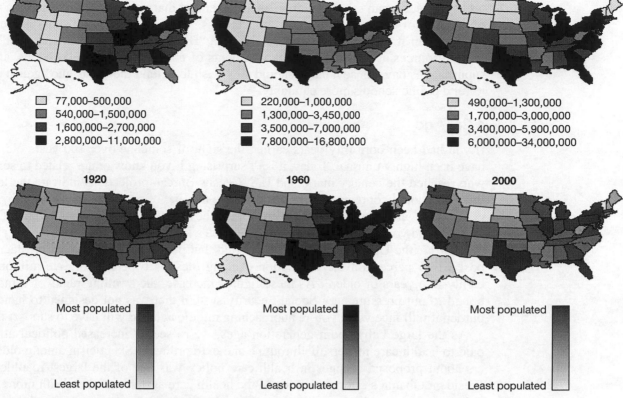

FIGURE 4.4 Population Shifts, 1920–2000[T9]

outside their base in the Rust Belt. And, in recent years, immigration patterns have started to eclipse the effects of domestic migration, as an influx of more liberal Latino voters has softened the conservative leanings of the Sun Belt and made several Western and Southwestern states fertile ground for Democrats. Still, as people move, congressional districts move with them, and national officials take notice of where the votes are.

The other meaningful migration in recent years has been the steady nationwide exodus of city dwellers to ever-expanding rings of suburbs. The urban exodus began after World War II, and by 2000, a country that originated as a rural nation and experienced urban migration in the twentieth century had become suburbanized. A glimpse of the nation at night, with lights radiating out from core cities, communicates a sense of how America's population spreads out for miles from downtown.

When we think of suburbs, we tend to think of affluence, and it is true that part of the motivation for the post-war migration from inner cities by people with resources was to escape growing urban decay. Today's suburbs are more complex than this; some older suburbs have predominantly working class neighborhoods, and in some places, suburbs are starting to become ethnically diverse.

Once more conservative than residents of urban areas, suburbanites have undergone a political transformation. In the 1996 election, political analysts made a lot out of the phenomenon of "soccer moms"—suburban women with young kids (whom they shuttled to soccer games, hence the name). These voters tended to be social moderates who were attracted in large numbers to the policies of President Clinton, permitting the Democratic president to make inroads through traditionally conservative suburban areas. In 2004, those same analysts labeled these voters "security moms" concerned with terrorism, who were more likely to support President Bush. But by 2008, the suburbs had become a rich source of votes for Barack Obama and his message of inclusive "post-partisan" politics. In 2016, Democrats regarded suburbanites as a key component of Hillary Clinton's coalition.

The politics of affluence does play a role in some urban-suburban issues, however, like education. Public schools in many states are supported by property taxes, meaning affluent suburban communities of private dwellings are able to collect more money to spend on education. This can create wide disparities in the educational opportunities available to urban and suburban schoolchildren, an arrangement that challenges the American notion of equality of opportunity but that, nonetheless, will be defended by suburbanites who benefit from it. As we will see in Section 4.6, "Black and White, Rich and Poor," with more resources at their disposal than residents of poorer urban neighborhoods, affluent suburbanites have an advantage should they wish to defend the status quo against efforts to fund public schools more equitably.

4.2e Age

If you had been born fifty years earlier, the sight of someone over 100 years old would have been highly unusual. Today, it isn't surprising if you know or are related to someone who reached the century mark, and U.S. Census Bureau projections indicate the longevity trend should continue. Add to this the huge number of people in the aging baby boom generation—all those people who were born in the twenty years following the end of World War II—and you have the makings for age to be a key political divide in the years ahead.

In 2012, the U.S. Census Bureau reported that people sixty-five years or older composed 13.5 percent of the population. Among these, 1.6 percent or five million were eighty-five years or older.[11] As these figures increase, the swelling ranks of seniors are bound to put pressure on a Social Security system that was not designed to handle the burden it will face when you're approaching middle age and will have to support it.[12]

As the large baby boom generation ages, we're seeing increased political attention paid to health care matters, both routine and extraordinary. Skepticism among older voters about proposed changes in health care policy was one of the largest roadblocks to President Obama's efforts to overhaul the health care system in 2009. With more Americans requiring medical assistance in their advanced years, a heated political debate has emerged over the question of how much government will be asked to do to defray the costs, especially for those who cannot afford medical services or prescription drugs. And, we're witnessing an intense ethical debate over emerging medical technologies like cloning and performing research using stem cells from human embryos—research that has the potential to advance treatments for diseases like Alzheimer's that affect people later in life but that, by its very nature, raises controversial questions about what constitutes life itself.

4.3 Political Socialization: How We Become Political Creatures

L.O. Define political socialization.

political socialization: The process by which we acquire political knowledge, attitudes, and beliefs.

cognitive: A factual awareness or appreciation of someone or something. Cognition implies knowledge and the ability to exercise judgment. This is why we would say that a young child's understanding of the president is not cognitive because kids' awareness of the president as an important figure lacks appreciation of what the president does and why he is important.

affective: Existing in the realm of emotion or feeling.

How do we become political creatures? That may be a strange question to ask after spending so much energy in Chapter 3 talking about how many of us simply aren't political creatures. The fact is, though, that while we are often not very political by choice, we're still exposed to a multitude of political influences, starting from the time we're very young, through the process of **political socialization**.

Take a minute and think back. Try to identify your earliest political memory—the first time in your life that you can remember being aware of a politician or a political event. It can be about an election, a national event—anything where a political figure was involved.

Chances are, the event you remembered took place when you were between six and ten years old, around the time kids begin to open up to the larger world. And chances are also that it involved the president. For most kids, the president is the first political figure we're aware of, our gateway to appreciating politics. Of course, when kids become aware of the president, it's in the simple way you would expect kids to process information. They really don't understand what the president does, even as they recognize that he is someone important. In other words, young kids will have a limited **cognitive** or factual understanding of the president. Instead, their relationship to the president will be highly **affective** or emotional.[13]

Initial impressions of the president are that he is powerful and good. This was the case in 1958, when presidential scholar Fred Greenstein examined the impressions of President Eisenhower held by fourth- through eighth-graders,[14] and it was the case in 2000 when Greenstein's study was replicated on the same age groups with respect to impressions of President Clinton.[15] With the exception of eighth-graders in the 2000 study, kids in 1958 and 2000 ranked the president as more important than a host of authority figures they knew firsthand, including teachers, principals, doctors, police officers, and religious leaders.[16] In both years, kids were inclined to view the president in positive terms as well, although the 2000 study reveals a tendency for today's generation to hold less positive views overall than kids did in the late 1950s.

This could be the result of greater negative media coverage of the president, or of kids having access to the Internet at a young age, where they are exposed to a wider variety of political messages. The 2000 study revealed that 81 percent of fourth- through eighth-graders used the Internet, changing patterns of socialization by accelerating exposure to adult political messages.[17] It has long been the case that as kids age, they abandon the generally positive affect toward political leaders that characterizes early socialization, precisely because age exposes us to a more adult appreciation of the political world and, with it, a less childlike view of politicians. Attitudes like **cynicism** that we discussed in Chapter 3 traditionally develop during adolescence when a more complex understanding of politics sets in.

Political socialization doesn't just happen passively as we age, though. There are forces that act on us, shaping the way we become political as we venture beyond our childhood homes. These **agents of socialization** are many and varied, and they work on us from birth through early adulthood because political socialization is a process that plays out over a long period of time. There are several important agents of socialization, starting with our parents and siblings in our home as we grow up, continuing with our friends as we get older, our teachers in school, our coworkers when we get a job, and the media throughout our lives.

4.3a Family and Friends

Maybe you heard your parents talking about Bill Clinton's involvement with Monica Lewinsky, or about whether they thought the president should have been impeached for his actions. Perhaps you have older sisters or brothers who were involved in a cause and liked to talk about it. If your parents voted, maybe they took you to the polls when you were very young. Or you may remember them talking about the Iraq War or the price of gas or food or how high taxes are and blaming it on one politician or another.

It doesn't take much for kids to learn about politics from parents and siblings. The home can be a laboratory for young kids, who absorb an awful lot of information just from the tone of their parents' voices and from what their parents say about political figures and issues. Kids don't even have to be involved in the conversation; they're pretty good at putting together what they hear to figure out how the world works—or, at least, how the world works based on the way it looks at home. Because kids interact heavily with their families, and because families are where kids figure out who they are by the way others relate to them, parents and siblings are considered a **primary agent of socialization**.[18]

One's childhood home is the place where people experience early life socialization. It's where we internalize a set of values about how the world works that will structure our relationship to politics as we age. From their parents and families, young children learn messages about authority, order, trust, tolerance, cooperation, and obedience. If you grew up in a home with strict parents, you likely internalized different values than if you grew up in a permissive home.

Such early learning is very important because it sets the stage for the continuing socialization of our later years, when we develop a mature sense of our political selves. By no means does this suggest that we become a carbon copy of our parents—far from it. In fact, for all the power of the family to socialize us to politics, you can probably think of many ways you're different from your parents politically. At the very least, you probably hold different positions on many political issues.

Instead, the strongest relationship between parents and kids tends to be on the general level of **party identification**, or the political party you identify yourself with. You could

cynicism: A pervasive attitude of mistrust about politics that may lead people to withdraw from political participation.

agents of socialization: External influences that shape the way we are socialized to politics, including parents and siblings in the home, friends and coworkers outside the home, and institutions like schools and the media.

L.O. Describe how political socialization is a lifelong process, and identify primary and secondary agents of political socialization.

L.O. Explain the relationship between political socialization and the circumstances of one's upbringing.

primary agent of socialization: Parents and siblings exert disproportional influence on the political development of children by virtue of the initial influence they have on kids, giving the family a primary role in the process of political socialization.

party identification: An individual's association with a political party. The most common parties Americans identify with are the two major parties, Republican and Democrat. Party identification—also called party I.D.—varies in intensity such that it may be strong or weak. Those who do not identify with any party are typically called independents.

think of party identification as being socialized much like religious identification. In other words, chances are you identify with the same religious group as your parents. At the same time, you may hold different attitudes about the nature or importance of religious worship, or about some of the specific positions of your religious group. This is analogous to holding the same party identification as your parents but disagreeing on particular political issues.

One major study on how effectively party identification is socialized showed that six in ten children had the same partisanship as their parents when both parents had the same partisanship—both were Republicans or both were Democrats.[19] While this is a large percentage—much larger than anything else that's socialized from parent to child—consider that it also means that four in ten children whose parents share a partisan attachment end up identifying with a different party or not identifying with any party. Furthermore, not every child comes from a home where the parents share partisanship. You can pretty much flip a coin to determine the partisanship of kids who come from homes where their parents do not have the same party identification because they are equally likely to be Democrats or Republicans.[20]

From childhood through college and beyond, friendship groups rival the family as an important socializing agent, taking on a central role in political socialization during adolescence. Because peer groups are interpersonal, they are a primary agent of political socialization. But, unlike our families, we get to choose our friends. As teens and even now, we may look for friends who help us fit in at school. If we do, we look for friends who are a lot like us. This means that for many people, peers reinforce rather than challenge existing political beliefs—to the extent that politics enters into friendships at all.

As we get older and the initial influence of family socialization fades, we may be more open to a broader spectrum of opinion in our friendships. If this happens, peers can actually challenge our earlier political learning and serve as an agent for change.[21] This typically does not happen while we're still young, though.

4.3b Schools and the Media

It's pretty obvious that a lot of formal learning about politics happens in school. After all, it's happening right now. And it starts in preschool, where we begin to learn about the president and about holidays commemorating political figures. In this regard, schools are an excellent source of political information and a fairly direct agent of political socialization.

Perhaps the strongest contribution of schools to political socialization is a bit less obvious. If you grew up in the United States, do you remember what your kindergarten classroom looked like? Was there a flag over the chalkboard? Did you pledge allegiance every morning, to one nation, "invisible"? Was the room decorated in paper cutouts of turkeys and Pilgrims in November, Lincoln and Washington in February, or were there paper ballots with the names of real candidates on Election Day? Exposure to political symbols and engaging in patriotic rituals work to develop a national identity, making the classroom a subtle but important source of political socialization.

How thoroughly do the schools act as an agent of socialization? Not as thoroughly as family and friends, with whom we are engaged in close interpersonal relationships. Although schooling can give us a basic civic education, for

Much of the political socialization that occurs in school may be found in the trappings of the classroom rather than in the curriculum. Try to remember how prominently the flag was displayed in your elementary classrooms. *Source:* michaeljung/Shutterstock.com

many kids the amount of political learning that occurs in secondary school is limited—you probably remember from Chapter 3 that levels of political knowledge tend to be low among adults. Also, while kindergartners may be taken by stories of how George Washington could not tell a lie, we saw in Chapter 3 that adults are more cynical about politicians, meaning that attitudes learned in school eventually change, beginning in adolescence when we start to see the political world as a complex place.

For these reasons, we may think of school as a **secondary agent of socialization**. Schools matter to our political development, but not as much as parents, siblings, and peers, with whom we have strong and regular interpersonal relationships.

The same may be said of the media, even though common sense may tell us that the media exert a strong influence on our development by virtue of how pervasive the Internet, television, radio, and newspapers are in our daily life. Like schools, the media can be a source of political learning. As we'll see in Chapter 5, we live in an information environment so cluttered with noise that it's often hard to make good judgments about what's factual and what's simply opinion. This limits the ability of the mass media to serve as a reliable source of political information.

The media are also surprisingly limited in their ability to shape our political attitudes. The primary reason for this is media messages are impersonal and have trouble competing with family and friends. We're more likely to pay attention to or believe media messages that reinforce our existing attitudes while ignoring others—a phenomenon called **selective exposure**. We may even unconsciously filter out messages that don't conform to our prevailing attitudes, through a process called **selective perception**. Between consciously being uninterested in messages that conflict with our attitudes and unconsciously filtering messages that conflict with our attitudes, the way we use the media puts the brakes on its effectiveness as a socializing agent.

The media are not without effect, however. They may have a socializing influence through their ability to set the boundaries of what we're aware of politically, determining the issues and people we think about. This process is called **agenda setting**. It can be a powerful effect in the sense that things that are not on our agenda will have no place in public political discussion, making them less likely to be considered for political action. The power of agenda setting is limited, though, to influencing what's on our mind. Remember, agenda setting is different from generating opinions—we're not saying that the media have the kind of reach into our lives necessary to formulate opinions on our behalf.

Agenda setting influences what we think about, rather than the attitudes and opinions we hold about the things on our mind.[22] If you find yourself talking to your friends about terrorism or global warming or other topics you know about because they're in the news, you could say that the media helped place those topics on your personal agenda. Your attitudes and opinions about these topics are less likely to be shaped by the media—although we will see that when television commentators consistently portray a politician or an issue in a particular light, our thinking tends to follow from what they say. That, too, is covered in Chapter 5—so stay tuned.

secondary agent of socialization: Schools and the media have an effect on political socialization, but the effect is less than from primary agents like the family because we do not form close interpersonal bonds with either institution.

selective exposure: The tendency to pay attention to messages that are consistent with existing attitudes or beliefs while overlooking messages that conflict with them.

selective perception: An unconscious process by which we filter information that we deem irrelevant, uninteresting, or inconsistent with our attitudes and beliefs while absorbing information that conforms to our self-perception.

agenda setting: The tendency for topics given great weight by the media to be given equally great weight by those who use the media, such that the people and events considered important by those who determine media coverage will become the people and events that the public considers important.

4.3c Other Influences on Political Socialization

Not everyone is socialized under the same circumstances, which means there may be sharp differences among us in the way we come to understand the political world, even though we will all be exposed to the same agents of socialization. African Americans and women, for instance, have for a long time been socialized differently than whites and men.

Generations of African Americans have had to contend with a political system that produced obstacles to participation, and have had to face the dilemma of how to become socialized to a system that was in some important respects unwelcoming.[23]

Studies indicate that as early as grade school young girls begin to react to messages that suggest they should be less interested in political life than young boys, despite demonstrating greater proficiency with language and greater maturity than boys of the same age.[24]

These varying experiences with political socialization help explain why some African Americans may feel conflicted about embracing the shared experiences of American political culture that we talked about earlier, or why, despite recent gains, women remain disproportionately underrepresented in elected offices with respect to their numbers in the population. They may also help explain why it is possible for us to talk about patterns of public opinion that are distinct to African Americans and women. In the aggregate, African Americans are much more likely to support government solutions to social problems and Democratic candidates for public office than the population as a whole. The tendency for women to hold more liberal positions on social issues than men may also have its origins in the different ways men and women are socialized.

The things that happen when you're young and as you reach adulthood can also shape the way you're socialized to politics. Imagine that you were born into a home that was hit hard by the Great Depression, where food and money were scarce and you had to live from day to day with what little you could find. Perhaps your great-grandparents came of age in an environment like this. It's not too difficult to imagine that the development of their political attitudes could have been driven by issues of scarcity, and perhaps an attachment to government assistance to help mitigate the painful effects of poverty.

generational effects: Historical influences felt by an entire generation during their formative years, which shape the way they are socialized to politics.

Maybe your parents or grandparents had to contend with the Vietnam War when they were younger. Perhaps they had to confront a decision about whether to go to Vietnam or to resist the draft—a common experience for young people in the middle and late 1960s and early 1970s. Perhaps they were influenced by counterculture demonstrations against the war, which were politically and socially anti-establishment in nature. Intense social experiences like these can have as great an impact as the Depression on shaping the relationship an entire generation develops toward politics. Such **generational effects** on political socialization help explain why large groups of people, like the baby boomers born in the twenty years after World War II, move through life with a commonly held set of political and social attitudes developed from their formative experiences.[25]

At the same time, where you are in life can interact with how you respond to the formative political events of your generation and alter the way you relate to politics as you age. Baby boomers like Bill Clinton, who protested the system when in their twenties, were hardly radical in their approach to government when their turn came to run things twenty years later. Maybe you have strong ideals right now about what you hope to do with your life, or how you can contribute to society. That wouldn't be unusual because many people have strong ideals when they're in college, and are really open to the idea of social change.

life cycle effects: Changes to the way we relate to politics and society that naturally occur during the course of aging, which typically leave us less open to political and social change as we get older.

That's not to suggest you won't have strong ideals twenty years from now—the last thing you need is someone older than you telling you that you're going to outgrow idealism—far from it! You may instead find your idealism living side by side with a growing sense of pragmatism. **Life cycle effects** studied in older people point to the emergence of a kind of practical outlook on things when people acquire jobs, families, and the other trappings of middle age. As you might expect, the older we get, the less open we become to political and social changes. Still, it will be interesting to see how life cycle effects compete with generational effects as the Millennial generation ages and to see if generational influences remain with you into old age.

4.4 Political Participation: Getting Involved

L.O. Discuss multiple ways in which people participate in politics and several factors that influence the likelihood that someone will participate.

Fresh from the process of childhood political socialization, armed with a sense of our political selves, we can go forward into the adult world of politics and participate in a variety of political activities.

Or not.

The truth is, while some people are heavily engaged in politics, it's not all that unusual to find people whose participation is limited to voting—or less. Just like the civic activities we discussed in Section 4.2a, "Group Membership and Tolerance," involvement in a range of political activities is relatively low.

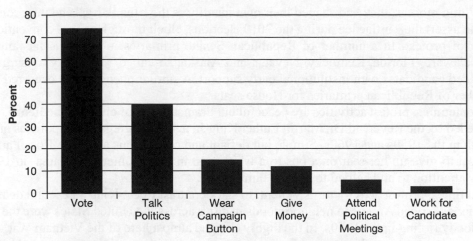

FIGURE 4.5 Percentage of People Who Claim to Participate in Six Types of Political Activities[T10]

To many people, **political participation** only means voting. However, it can be a lot more than going to the polls. If you take a look at Figure 4.5, you'll find a list of six different ways we can participate in politics. Take a second and think about which of these activities you've done in the last year. This should begin to give you a sense of just how much—or how little—Americans get involved politically beyond the voting booth.

4.4a Conventional Participation

According to the United States Elections Project, an estimated 60 percent of eligible voters cast a ballot in the 2016 election, in which the presidency was vacant and one-third of the Senate and the entire House of Representatives was up for grabs. During "midterm" elections—the elections that fall during the middle of a presidential term in which congressional and gubernatorial seats are the biggest draw—turnout is typically much lower. In 2014, it was just over 36 percent.[26]

That's roughly comparable to the percentage of Americans who claim they talk about politics from time to time, perhaps with the intent of influencing others. Talk may not be cheap, but it is relatively inexpensive compared to other forms of participation, and as the amount of effort involved in an activity increases, the number of people engaged in that activity predictably declines. So it is that only 15 percent will wear a campaign button, put a bumper sticker on their car, or display a sign in front of their house in support of a political candidate. Fewer will contribute money to a political candidate, attend political meetings, or volunteer time to work for a political candidate.

4.4b Unconventional Participation

Even fewer will get involved in less conventional forms of political participation, like engaging in a protest or demonstration, even though American history is replete with examples of protest activity. From the Boston Tea Party prior to the Revolution to Shays' Rebellion during the period of the Articles of Confederation, small but intensely committed groups of dissenters have sought to bring about political change through acts of defiance. The day after Donald Trump's inaugural, millions participated in a Women's March on Washington and affiliated marches across the country to protest the new president and his agenda. The demonstrations were compared by some to an uprising in the spring of 2009, when individuals opposed to the spending policies of the new Obama administration organized a protest inspired by the Boston Tea Party. Playing on the historical symbolism of colonial-era rebellion, they organized on the Internet to mail tea bags to their elected representatives and the president, along with notes explaining the nature of their concerns. Then, on April 15—tax day—they held rallies in cities across the country to protest what they viewed as the intrusive nature of big government.

political participation: The range of activities people can engage in to influence the political process. While voting is the most commonly performed political act, participation encompasses a host of things—from writing letters to public officials to contributing time or money to a campaign or protesting the actions of government.

Within months, they had shaped their own identity as the "Tea Party," and they continued to assert their influence during the 2010 elections, albeit through a more conventional form of protest. In a number of Republican Senate primaries in states as far-ranging as Delaware, Florida, Kentucky, Nevada, and Alaska, so-called "Tea Party" insurgents upended candidates with institutional party support. A similar phenomenon occurred in a number of Republican primaries for House seats.

Sometimes, protest activities are peaceful but dramatic acts of **civil disobedience**, like those led by the Reverend Dr. Martin Luther King Jr. against segregationist policies in the South in the 1950s and 1960s. Simple but defiant and courageous acts, like Rosa Parks's refusal to give up her seat on a bus to a white man in Montgomery, Alabama, in 1955, drew attention to and helped to change unjust laws.

At times, protest activity turns violent. In stark contrast to Dr. King's peaceful demonstrations, African American neighborhoods in cities across the United States were the site of bloody rioting in the 1960s. In the highly charged atmosphere of the Vietnam War, college campuses across the country became centers of sometimes violent protests. At Kent State University in 1970, police killed four students and wounded nine others during a protest against President Nixon's decision to escalate the war. The 1960s also witnessed political assassination as a tool of protest, including the murders of President John F. Kennedy, his brother Senator Robert F. Kennedy, and Dr. King.

civil disobedience: A peaceful means of protest whereby individuals draw attention to laws they consider unjust by disobeying them and being arrested for their actions.

4.5 Young and Old, Men and Women

OK, so maybe you looked at the list of activities in Figure 4.5 and thought, "I don't wear campaign buttons. I don't give money to political candidates. I'm not into meetings and rallies, and I don't know anyone who is." That wouldn't be very surprising. Not only are these types of political activities not widespread, but they're also especially uncommon among young adults. All forms of political participation are—and with good reason.

Think of the things that are on your mind right now or that have been on your mind at one time or another since you started school. Maybe you're worried about your grades, or how you're going to pay for your education. Friendships and relationships might take up a lot of your time. You could be preoccupied with where you're going to live next semester, or maybe you've got an issue with a roommate that's taking a lot of your energy. Perhaps you have some unresolved matters with your family. You could just be thinking about the plans you have for this weekend or for after you stop reading about political participation.

Grades, money, friends, dating, housing, roommates, family, social plans—some or all of these things are typical of what we spend our time thinking about as young adults. That doesn't leave a lot of time for joining political campaigns, especially if politics feels so much more remote than these other immediate things. For this reason, political analysts questioned whether Barack Obama would suffer during the 2008 presidential campaign because some of his strongest support came from young people. Similar questions were raised about Bernie Sanders during the 2016 Democratic primaries, as much of his support came from Millennials.

After a while, this starts to change for many of us. We graduate from college and find work. Many people find a long-term partner and settle down in an apartment or house that they rent or own. Life takes on a new rhythm, a more settled rhythm conducive to greater political involvement. For some, this newfound appreciation of political engagement is interrupted briefly as the responsibilities of having young children encroach on time available for civic activity. Otherwise, the tendency to participate in politics builds through middle age, as having the time to get involved coincides with having interests to protect—like a family, a job, or a house—and growing responsibilities like loans and an ever-increasing tax bill. We still have a lot going on like when we were younger, but the things we're doing are more likely to be the sorts of things that lend themselves to political action.

Political participation begins to trail off as we get older and begin to slow down, although senior citizens are among the most politically active of any group when it comes to voting. Even though there is a drop-off in voting after people reach retirement age, the

The Rise of Women in Elected Office

Hillary Clinton fell short in her quest to become the first female president. But the fact that a major political party could nominate a woman for president is a sign of how far women have come in politics in a very short time. One way to gauge the level of political activity by women is to look at how many women have run for and served as governors and senators. The first two women governors followed their husbands in office—Miriam Ferguson in Texas and Nellie Ross in Wyoming, both elected in 1925. After them, fifty years passed before Connecticut's Ella Grasso became the first woman elected to a governorship without following a spouse. By 2002, women were serious contenders in half of that year's thirty-six gubernatorial contests. In 2009, eight states had female governors, or 16 percent of the total, although that number declined to six in 2016.[T11]

A similar picture emerges when you look at the Senate, where fifty women have served between 1922 and 2017. Initially, a number of these women, too, were appointed to fill seats left vacant by their husbands. But, Hattie Wyatt Caraway of Arkansas was the rare exception: Having been appointed to the Senate in 1931, she ran for and won election to her seat the following year. It took until the 1990s for women to become a regular presence in the Senate. In 2017, there were a record twenty-one female senators representing eighteen states (California, New Hampshire, and Washington have two female senators).[T12] These figures, of course, are well below the percentage of women in the population, a sign of how long it took for the political climate to change enough for female candidates to be regarded as serious political contenders.

decline is gradual. People in their eighties are still far more likely to vote than people in their twenties!

It has also been the case historically that women have tended to participate less than men. Some of this is no doubt because women were denied the right to vote until 1920. In recent years, women have demonstrated greater political involvement, particularly in the areas of voting and running for elective office. The women's vote has been especially important in recent years—in fact, if only men voted, Barack Obama would have lost the 2012 election. Additionally, women are starting to serve in elected office at a higher rate than ever before. See Demystifying Government: The Rise of Women in Elected Office.

Even in places where women appear to participate less than men, some of the disparity can be understood in terms of differences in education. In fact, how much education you have has a lot to do with how likely it is for you to get involved politically.

If you look at Figure 4.6, you'll find the percentage of men and women who told the General Social Survey that they engaged in several types of political participation—attending political events, contributing to candidates, and contacting government officials. In each category, you can see that men are slightly more likely to get involved than women, which might lead you to conclude that men participate more than women.

But watch what happens to the differences between men and women when you look at their levels of participation in terms of how much education they have. Participation rates rise steadily for men and women as they amass more years of schooling, really shooting up for college grads. As participation rates go up, gender differences shrink or disappear. College-educated women are just as likely as college-educated men to contribute to political campaigns, almost as likely to contact government officials, and somewhat more likely to attend political rallies.

4.6 Black and White, Rich and Poor

If President Obama's electoral prospects were dependent in part on support from young people, who traditionally participate at lower levels than middle-aged and older people, it was equally problematic that he also depended on the engagement of African Americans, who participate in some—but not all—political activities at lower rates than white. There are multiple reasons for this discrepancy, including a legacy of institutional restrictions against African American voting, and a complex relationship among participation, social and economic resources, and psychological factors that adversely affects African Americans. Just as differences in political participation rates between men and women can be

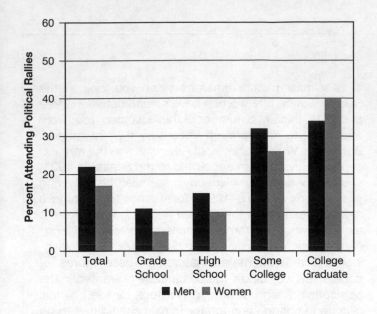

Men **Women**

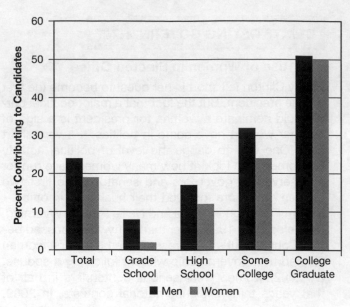

Men **Women**

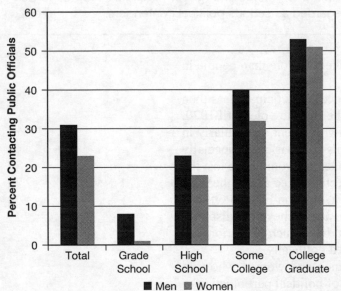

Men **Women**

FIGURE 4.6 Gender, Education, and Participation[T13]

Gender differences in participation depend heavily on education. As education levels increase, gender differences disappear in rates of attending political rallies, contributing to political candidates, and contacting public officials.

explained by education rather than gender differences, participation differences between African Americans and whites defy simple racial explanations.

In 1972, political scientists Sidney Verba and Norman Nie published a ground-breaking study of American political participation, in which they found that a greater share of African Americans are entirely uninvolved politically than their numbers in the population would suggest. At the same time, Verba and Nie found that African Americans vote at about the same rate as whites and are about even with the rest of the population among the small group of people who are highly active politically. In other words, blacks opt out of the political process at a higher rate than whites, but those that are highly involved are about as active and engaged politically as whites.[27]

The fact that we don't find significant racial differences in voting patterns is noteworthy when you consider the obstacles to voting that African Americans faced in the South until very late in the twentieth century. Although granted the legal right to vote following the Civil War, it took a century before those rights were more than words on a piece of paper.

The years immediately following the Civil War gave few hints that it would take a century before one-time slaves would be free to embrace the political rights promised to them during Reconstruction.[28] A string of federal acts promised to immediately enfranchise African Americans. In rapid succession:

- *The Military Reconstruction Act of 1867* required all southern states to give former slaves the right to vote as a condition of being readmitted to the Union.

- *The Fourteenth Amendment*, ratified in 1868, extended citizenship to former slaves.

- *The Fifteenth Amendment*, ratified in 1870, specifically forbade states to deny the vote to someone on the basis of race, color, or the fact that they were once a slave.

- *The Enforcement Act of 1870* imposed criminal penalties on anyone who would try to deny blacks the right to vote.

- *The Force Act of 1871* shifted the right to oversee elections from the states (some of which vehemently resisted black voting rights) to the federal government.

Initially, hundreds of thousands of former slaves flocked to the political process. African Americans voted in large numbers and were elected to offices at all levels of government. However, as Reconstruction ended and federal troops withdrew from the South in the late 1870s, whites who vehemently opposed black involvement in politics did everything they could to lock them out of the process. Using a combination of violence and political tactics, white southerners ruthlessly put an end to black participation. As northern troops departed the region, southern whites employed violent attacks against African Americans as an intimidation tactic designed to keep them from voting. By the 1890s, with whites back in control of state legislatures, many southern states passed a series of laws designed to make it impossible for blacks to vote. These included:

- *Literacy tests*, which required voters to demonstrate knowledge of the Constitution that might be advanced for you, even if you've already read Chapter 2 of this book. Because many African Americans lacked formal education, literacy tests were an effective way to disenfranchise them. (See Demystifying Government: How Well Would You Do on a Literacy Test?)

- *Poll taxes*, which required voters to pay a tax in order to exercise their right to vote. Although the tax was generally nominal, it had the practical effect of disenfranchising countless black voters who were too poor to pay it.

- *Grandfather clauses*, which exempted whites—many of whom were as uneducated as African Americans—from having to take literacy tests or pay poll taxes because they were eligible to vote or were descended from someone who was eligible to vote in 1867—before passage of the Fourteenth Amendment.

- *"White primaries,"* which circumvented the Fifteenth Amendment by keeping African Americans from voting in Democratic Party primaries by declaring the Democratic Party to be a private organization exempt from laws requiring equal participation. In southern states dominated by the Democratic Party, primary winners invariably won elections, and exclusion from primary voting was an effective way to disenfranchise blacks.

These discriminatory laws remained on the books for decades. Although the Supreme Court ruled grandfather clauses unconstitutional in 1915[29] and "white primaries" unconstitutional in 1944,[30] southern states continued to disenfranchise African Americans until the Supreme Court and Congress actively intervened in the 1960s. By then, African Americans had to overcome the effects of having been locked out of the political process in the South for four generations.

For African Americans who choose not to participate in politics, the underlying causes start with the relationship between race and class. Verba and Nie found that people with higher **socioeconomic status (SES)**—well-educated people with high incomes and high-status jobs—are more likely to have resources that facilitate political participation, and that African Americans are less likely to be represented in the high-SES group. These resources include time, money, and information about politics.

Verba and Nie speculate that there is an intricate relationship between having resources, having the motivation to use them, and getting results. They contend that this relationship explains who is likely to participate and why African Americans are less likely to be

socioeconomic status (SES):
A measure of an individual's social position based primarily on education, income, and occupation. High socioeconomic status individuals are more likely to have advanced education, high incomes, and occupations that award high status and demand great responsibility, like professional or managerial work.

How Well Would You Do on a Literacy Test?

For decades, African Americans had to endure hardship and humiliation in order to register to vote. It was not uncommon for voter registration offices to be open only a few days a month, during work hours. White employers who permitted black workers to take time off to register were subjected to organized economic retaliation designed to threaten the jobs of African Americans who registered. At the Registrar's Office, it was common for local deputies to harass, threaten, and intimidate blacks who tried to register. Information on African American applicants would likely find its way from the registrar to the Ku Klux Klan, which would use violence or the threat of violence against blacks who dared to try to register.[T14]

If would-be voters actually made it to the literacy test, they faced an exam designed for them to fail. A case in point is the Alabama Literacy Test, which consisted of three parts: a reading of a portion of the Constitution, which the applicant had to interpret orally to the registrar, and two written sections on constitutional, federal, and state law that were evaluated in secrecy by a Board of Registrars. Here are some questions from that test. See if you can answer them:

- If a person charged with treason denies his guilt, how many persons must testify against him before he can be convicted?
- At what time of day on January 20 each four years does the term of the president of the United States end?

- If the United States wishes to purchase land for an arsenal and have exclusive legislative authority over it, consent is required from _____.
- Name one area of authority over state militia reserved exclusively to the states.
- The power of granting patents, that is, of securing to investors the exclusive right to their discoveries, is given to the Congress for the purpose of _____.
- In what year did Congress gain the right to prohibit the migration of persons to the states?[T15]

As you can see, these questions are challenging (or trivial) even for people with a formal education. They would only humiliate and discourage someone with no education. The combination of legal roadblocks, physical threats, and violence was effective; in many southern counties, the African American registration rate was zero, and it remained this way for decades.

By the way, the answers are: Two persons must testify against someone charged with treason; the president's term ends at noon on January 20; consent for purchasing land for an arsenal has to come from the legislature; the states have exclusive authority over the appointment of officers to militia; Congress grants patents for the purpose of promoting progress; Congress gained the right to prohibit the migration of persons to the states in 1808. Be honest—how many of these did you get right?

---

represented among political participants.[31] The process works something like that shown in Figure 4.7.

The economic disparity that distinguishes high-SES individuals from low-SES individuals is associated with a psychological divide. People with more resources to use in the political process, a group in which African Americans are less well represented than whites, are more likely to be oriented toward the political process. They're more likely to be aware of and concerned about the political process, and have a high sense of political **efficacy**, which you may recall from Chapter 3 is the feeling that you can get results if you enter the political arena. This should make sense: If you start out with the necessary tools, you're more likely to feel you can get the job done. You feel motivated. You participate.

efficacy: The attitude that you can be effectual and effective in your dealings with government.

We've already talked about how participation is linked to getting results when we said in Chapter 1 that not participating is always a choice but that people who participate are more likely to get results from government. This works to reinforce the psychological drive to participate because when you actually accomplish something by participating, it's natural to feel like you can get the system to respond to your wishes. You've already done it! To the degree that what people get through participating is tangible, which it often is, participating also works to bolster their supply of political resources that were the catalyst for participating in the first place.

You can probably see how the tangible and psychological rewards that come from participating work to reinforce the tangible and psychological advantages that high-SES individuals start with. So, if African Americans are underrepresented in the high-SES

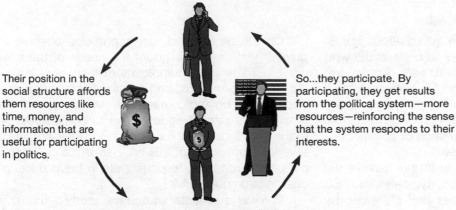

High socioeconomic status individuals are people with higher education, high incomes, and high-status jobs.

Their position in the social structure affords them resources like time, money, and information that are useful for participating in politics.

So...they participate. By participating, they get results from the political system—more resources—reinforcing the sense that the system responds to their interests.

Having resources makes them more likely to want to use them and to believe the system will respond to them if they do. This is a psychological factor that stems from their socioeconomic condition.

FIGURE 4.7 Resources, Psychological Factors, and Participation

group, they will ultimately be less likely to participate and less likely to believe that participating will make a difference. That's because the process can work in reverse to keep low-SES individuals from wanting to engage in political activity. Low SES means having fewer resources that are useful for participating in politics, which can reinforce the psychological orientation that political participation is a waste of time because the system will not be responsive. This low sense of efficacy discourages participation—and is self-fulfilling.

You can probably also see how participation can reinforce social status, independent of race. With people from higher socioeconomic groups participating more, the political system is going to be more responsive to their interests, which you can probably imagine are different from the interests of people with lower socioeconomic status. For instance, the political interests of unemployed people for job training or unemployment insurance are worlds apart from the concerns of high SES individuals, but the unemployed are not oriented to participate in large numbers in the political process, so they are in a weakened position to make demands on the system.[32] Political officials will be more sensitive to the needs of high-SES individuals, who will be well positioned to reap the rewards of government. For more on the relationship between resources and motivation, see Demystifying Government: Revisiting Resources That Matter.

4.7 I Couldn't Care Less!

Maybe you couldn't care less about who participates and what happens to them. There's a word for that. It's called **apathy**. It's a word that is widely used in the media and in conversation to describe the way many people relate—or fail to relate—to politics. Americans are widely perceived to be apathetic as a result of having low levels of political knowledge and involvement. People who are apathetic avoid political participation because they genuinely don't care about it. (They might want to avoid reading about it, too.)

Or do they? Some research on the topic points to a different conclusion, based on observations of people in social settings who avoided talking about politics. This line of thought suggests that people seem apathetic not so much because they don't care about what's going on but because they feel powerless to do anything about it. Big political problems, even those that could affect us directly, are just that—big—and they can leave us feeling overwhelmed.[33]

In the face of this, and to avoid the social embarrassment that could come from making it appear that we actually believe our opinion might matter or that we could exercise some control over the situation, a lot of people resort to saying "I'm not interested" or "I'm just

apathy: A sense of indifference to or lack of interest in politics.

Revisiting Resources That Matter

Remember in Chapter 1 when we talked about **pluralism** and **elitism** as different ways to understand who gets what, when, and how? (If not, take a quick trip back to Section 1.7, "Power Surge," in Chapter 1.) In a way, when we talk about the connection between having resources and having the motivation to participate in politics, we're revisiting the question of whether political power is held by many or few.

Let's look a little more closely at the case of the long-term unemployed population, typically low-SES individuals who lack the resources and therefore the motivation to participate politically. If political officials are more sensitive to the needs of people who participate, and unemployed individuals tend not to participate, you could make the case that the political system will not be responsive to their interests, choosing instead to respond to the interests of a smaller group of resource-rich, high-SES individuals. You'd be making an argument in support of an elitist perspective of American government, in which few people with a lot of resources exercise power. This conclusion seems to be supported by the claim that people without many resources and who lack efficacy are unlikely to be able to get political figures to respond to their needs.

On the other hand, we might also observe that government does not ignore the needs of the unemployed. There are unemployment insurance policies, job-training programs, and economic plans during periods of high unemployment designed to lower the unemployment rate. Presidents like to boast about how many new jobs were created under their administration. Why does any of this happen when unemployed people are not likely to participate in the political process in large numbers?

Political scientists who have studied this question[T16] claim that other groups will speak for the unemployed in the political system. For instance, unions and civil rights groups, out of self-interest or social justice concerns, may advocate policies that benefit unemployed people. Is this consistent with the pluralist perspective that resources are distributed widely enough for many to wield political power? Is it simply a modification of an elitist argument because unemployed people inadvertently benefit from the convergence of their interests and the interests of a powerful elite? Is it possible that government would respond more quickly or lavish more attention on the needs of the unemployed if they participated in the political process?

---

pluralism: The theory that government responds to individuals through their memberships in groups, assuring that government is responsive to a wide range of voices. People who subscribe to this position believe that the wide distribution of resources in society drives the decisions government officials make.

elitism: The theory that government responds to a small, stable, centralized hierarchy of corporate and academic leaders, military chiefs, people who own big media outlets, and members of a permanent government bureaucracy. People who subscribe to this position believe the actions of regular citizens, like voting and joining groups, simply mask the real power exercised by elites.

L.O. Identify reasons why people vote, despite time and information costs.

not paying attention." They strike an apathetic pose, and they resist political involvement, even on issues that hit home, like rapidly increasing tuition costs, where they're quite aware that what happens does matter to them.

Doing this takes work. We have to try hard to be apathetic because it's so natural to care about what happens to us and to those around us. And apathetic periods come in cycles. There was a great deal of interest in the 2008 election, and record crowds estimated at close to two million people gathered in Washington in January 2009 for President Obama's inaugural.

You may have noticed that this section on apathy is a lot shorter than others in the book. Do you care?

4.8 Why Vote?

Bad jokes about apathy aside, when you look at the most commonly engaged form of participation—voting—it's reasonable to ask why anyone would take the time to do it at all. When you look at what you have to do in order to vote in an election in this country, you might reasonably ask how our turnout can be as *high* as 60 percent in a presidential election year. Some countries, like Australia, have close to perfect turnout. In these countries, voting is compulsory because it is regarded as an obligation rather than a right. There's actually a fine for not voting. Under those circumstances, plenty of people manage to find their way to the polls. It doesn't happen that way in the United States, though, where the process is much more complex and there is no monetary cost to not participating.

First, you have to register to vote. This typically involves satisfying age and residency requirements, although the specifics vary by state. Alabama, for instance, makes you affirm your allegiance to the Constitution and swear that you have no plans to overthrow the legally elected government of the state.

If you live in North Dakota, you have it easy because there's no registration requirement there—you can just skip to the part where you show up at the polls on Election Day. If you live in any other state, you have to be aware of the need to register, know the registration deadline in order to register in time to vote in the next election (it's typically a couple of weeks or so before Election Day), and know how to register.[34]

Until recently, registering to vote in most states involved locating and visiting a state office, like your County Board of Elections. Things got easier with the passage of the **National Voter Registration Act** of 1993. It's commonly called the "Motor Voter Act," because of a provision that makes it possible for you to register to vote when you apply for or renew your driver's license.

The Motor Voter Act has other provisions, also designed to make registration more convenient. All states except for Minnesota, Wyoming, Wisconsin (and, of course, North Dakota) must accept mail-in registration forms, including a national mail-in voter registration form made available by the Federal Election Commission. Agencies that provide public assistance, like Medicaid and food stamps, or services to people with disabilities are also required to provide voter registration services. Some states, like California, let you register online, while others let you download application forms off the Internet.

The Motor Voter Act makes registration easier than it used to be—if you know about it. If you're like many people, though, you didn't know about it until about a minute ago, unless you stumbled across it when you got your driver's license. It still requires the expenditure of a valuable resource—time—to complete the registration form, and turnout figures suggest it has not significantly boosted voter turnout.

Also, don't forget that registering to vote is only the first step in the process. You then need to find and get directions to your polling place—information that will take time to get—and arrange to take time out of your day to vote. Polls open early in the morning in most states, and they typically remain open until seven, eight, or nine in the evening, giving people who work during the day the opportunity to vote without taking time away from their jobs. However, this can mean the added inconvenience of having to get up a little earlier or delay an evening activity and possibly wait in long lines.

In recent years, a number of states have made voting easier by opening the polls prior to Election Day to permit people to vote on their schedule. In 2008, thirty-two states permitted some form of early voting, where votes were cast (but not counted) before Election Day.[35] If you live in Oregon or Washington, you can mark your ballot in the comfort of home and mail it to the county elections office or place it in a drop box. As long as it's received by Election Day, it counts.[36] Oregon even permits voters with disabilities to vote by iPad.[37]

However, legislative efforts to make voting easier started facing pushback in 2012, notably in competitive states with Republican governors and legislatures, giving the issue of easing voting restrictions a decidedly partisan cast. Ohio eliminated four of five weekend early voting periods, a move that civil rights groups claimed would disproportionately hurt African American voters. Florida cut its early voting period from fourteen to eight days, and Governor Rick Scott refused to extend the early voting period in the face of long lines and frequent delays.[38] These efforts continued in 2016, along with the implementation in a number of states of the voter ID laws we discussed in Chapter 1. Together, they make the costly act of voting even costlier by adding hurdles to participating.

Even in states with few obstacles and early voting opportunities, it still takes resources to vote, and in states that still do it the traditional way, voting can be a pain. It requires work and time, and the sacrifice of something else you might want to be doing, like sleeping or going out or being with your family. It may seem particularly burdensome if you're one of those low-efficacy Americans who feel the political system is not going to respond to your wishes and interests anyhow. If you believe your vote does not matter, or politicians are all just a bunch of hypocrites, you're not likely to invest your resources in registering and voting.

So, if voting is such a hassle, why does anyone want to do it? You'll find a few explanations in Demystifying Government: Why People Vote.

National Voter Registration Act: Passed in 1993 to simplify and standardize voter registration requirements, the "Motor Voter Act" allows residents of most states to register to vote at the same time as they apply for or renew their driver's license. It also provides for a standardized, national registration form that can be downloaded from the Internet.

Why People Vote

Why do you vote? Some people say:

- Because it's my obligation to vote
- Because it makes me feel good
- Because I feel that I can influence what's happening

If you say, "I vote because I feel it's my obligation to vote," then you're expressing a sentiment about **civic responsibility**, the sense that there are certain things we're obligated to do as citizens of a democracy. Some people feel that the inconvenience of voting is part of the price we pay to maintain privileges like the freedom to speak our mind or to complain when we don't like something.

If you say, "I vote because it makes me feel good," then you know that you don't have to make the differ-ence in an election to feel like you've made a differ-ence. It's efficacy again, in a specific form that relates to voting. Some people get a sense of efficacy from voting because they feel like their voice will be included in the mix of voices expressed on Election Day. Also, it can be gratifying to speak up.

If you say, "I vote because it gives me the feeling that I can influence what's happening," then you are trying to shape your world. Influence is a different type of feeling than efficacy. Some people feel that vot-ing equals influence, regardless of the outcome of an election. They see voting as a way to shape the future course of politics, either by contributing to a candi-date's winning margin or by making a show of support for the loser.

---

civic responsibility: A sense of duty or obligation to society that some people believe comes along with citizenship.

Because the mathematics of voting makes the likelihood of casting the deciding vote in an election remote, many people vote because of the attitudes they have about living in a democracy. People vote because they feel they should, or because it makes them feel good, or because it gives them the sense that they have a voice in public affairs.

4.9 How Can I Decide?

L.O. Explain several common ways people arrive at their voting decisions.

Chances are some people in your class have voted in a real election, others are eligible but have never voted, and still others may be ineligible to vote in the United States because they're not 18 years old or American citizens. So, to make sure everyone has had a voting experience (or something close to it) before we move on, let's take a minute and cast a vote in a hypothetical congressional election. Imagine you're in a voting booth, staring at the ballot that appears in Figure 4.8. You're trying to decide how to vote in a con-gressional race between Republican Leonard Fitzsimmons and Democrat Marjorie Carp. Because you know their names and their party affiliations, you have exactly the same information you would have in a real voting booth. Imagine there are other people in line behind you, so try not to linger too long over your decision.

So, what was your decision? Did you make a choice? Or did you go for the "no vote" option? Maybe you were thinking, "I don't know any of these people. How can I vote?" And, of course, you don't know anything about them—which precisely mirrors the situa-tion of many people who cast ballots in real elections. They still manage to vote. Perhaps you did too. Let's look at how they do it.

OFFICIAL BALLOT, U.S. CONGRESS

INSTRUCTIONS: To vote for a candidate, mark an X in the oval beside the candidate you prefer.		
	Leonard Fitzsimmons (Republican)	⬭
U.S. Congress (vote for **ONE** candidate)	**Marjorie Carp** (Democrat)	⬭
	(No vote)	⬭

FIGURE 4.8 Sample Ballot

4.9a Party I.D. Voting

One of the few clues you had to guide you was party affiliation, so if you identify as a Republican, you may have voted for Leonard Fitzsimmons, or if you identify as a Democrat, you may have voted for Marjorie Carp. Even without knowing anything else about these candidates, this is a reasonable thing to do because a simple party label can convey a lot of information. Perhaps you assumed that the Republican candidate is the more conservative of the two. Often, you would be correct. Perhaps you reasoned that you don't know what Carp's positions are on issues that matter to you, but if you're a Democrat, the chances are that she's closer to your beliefs than Fitzsimmons. That seems like a pretty reasonable assumption as well.

You may even have voted for the candidate who shares your partisanship without even wondering what the candidate stands for, simply because you're a strong partisan. Remember, party identification is socialized more strongly than political attitudes and beliefs, and if we're predisposed to thinking of ourselves as Republicans or Democrats, it's natural to gravitate to a candidate who shares our identification.

So, party identification can help strip away the confusion of an unfamiliar ballot and provide a reasonable guideline for how to vote. It wouldn't be surprising if many of your classmates voted this way, just as it wouldn't be surprising to find many Americans voting this way in real elections. In recent years, party identification has been a good way to predict how people will vote.

At the same time, party identification may not be quite as strong as it was many years ago. In 1952, 47 percent of Americans claimed to be Democrats and 28 percent identified themselves as Republicans, according to the American National Election Studies (ANES). Half of these called themselves strong partisans. That left one-quarter of the electorate as either independent or apolitical.

Compare that to 2012, when the ANES reported only 35 percent identified themselves as Democrats and 27 percent as Republicans, leaving 38 percent of us as independents or apolitical.[39] Although about one-third of the independents said they "lean" toward the Democratic Party and an equal number "lean" toward the Republican Party, we find that people who identify loosely with a political party are a bit more likely than strong supporters to shop around when they vote.[40]

More independents and fewer strong partisans in the electorate can produce **ticket splitting** among voters, where people vote for, say, a Democratic candidate for president and a Republican candidate for Congress. This type of voting pattern can generate divided government, where one party controls the White House and the other controls at least one house of Congress, like we saw during twenty-eight of the thirty-six years between 1981 and 2017.

ticket splitting: Voting for candidates of different parties for different offices, rather than voting a "party line" for all Republicans or all Democrats. Ticket splitting, which has increased in recent years, is a sign of how Americans have been growing independent from political parties.

4.9b Candidate Characteristics

Did you think about voting for Leonard Fitzsimmons because he has an Irish-sounding name? Maybe you cast your vote for Marjorie Carp because she is the only woman on the ballot.[41] Ethnic and gender identification can be other useful voting shortcuts. In fact, candidates with ethnic-sounding names may count on votes from people who will identify with their background. A particularly unusual case of identity voting is discussed in Demystifying Government: The Surprising Success of Victor Morales.

Candidate character, as well as characteristics, may also play a role in voting. Sometimes the character of candidates—their integrity, or the way they handle their personal or public life—can factor into whether people will vote for them. Hillary Clinton struggled with voters who felt her use of a private e-mail server while secretary of state raised questions about her judgment. Her husband, Bill Clinton, conducted his personal life in a way that lost him the respect—and in some cases, the votes—of people who otherwise approved of his performance in office. Anthony Wiener, a member of Congress from New York who resigned his post in 2011 amidst evidence that he had used social media to send sexually explicit photos of himself to women, attempted to make a comeback two years

The Surprising Success of Victor Morales

It's not every day that someone with no political experience, hardly any money, and no backing from the political establishment can make a credible run for a Senate seat from a major state. However, that's exactly what high school geography teacher Victor Morales did in Texas—twice—as the nominee of the Democratic Party for the Senate in 1996 and as the runner-up in a three-way race for the same nomination in 2000.

To the political establishment, Morales came out of nowhere in 1996, riding around Texas on a shoestring budget in an old pickup truck, to defeat two members of the U.S. Congress for the Senate nomination in a race he lost to incumbent Republican Senator Phil Gramm. Four years later, using the same low-budget strategy, he came in second in a field of three candidates, only to lose a head-to-head runoff with Ron Kirk, the well-funded, party-endorsed former mayor of Dallas.

Part of Morales' success no doubt stemmed from the fact that he was a maverick outsider in a state that likes anti-politicians, and an underdog who achieved a kind of celebrity status through news coverage of his seemingly impossible quest. But Texas Democratic Party leaders promoting Kirk were sensitive to the fact that Morales could count on a large turnout among Latino Democrats, a force in Texas politics, because of his roots in the Latino community. They feared Latino support would not be enough for Morales to be elected to the Senate, but it might just be enough to defeat Kirk for the Democratic nomination.

Eager to avoid a second Morales nomination, Democrats supporting Kirk's candidacy arranged for high-profile endorsements from gubernatorial nominee Tony Sanchez and former San Antonio mayor and U.S. Secretary of Housing and Urban Development Henry Cisneros. The extent to which these endorsements from high-profile Latino figures helped Kirk win the Democratic nomination may never be known, but it illustrates how much political leaders believe voters will support candidates with backgrounds similar to their own.

---

later by running for mayor of New York City, but his candidacy derailed when additional pictures surfaced during the campaign. Former South Carolina governor Mark Sanford, once considered a possible presidential contender, saw his national ambitions dissipate in 2009 after he admitted to having an affair with an Argentine woman after mysteriously disappearing for five days without explanation, telling his staff that he was taking personal time to hike the Appalachian Trail (however, South Carolina voters forgave him four years later when they elected him to the House of Representatives).

Of course, these are high-profile cases of politicians in the news. Voting for or against candidates because of their personal characteristics requires having more information about them than their last name or their party identification, and information can be costly to acquire. This limits the circumstances under which people will find themselves in a position to vote on a candidate's character.

4.9c Issue Voting

issue voting: Choosing a candidate in an election on the basis of his or her proximity to your position on an issue or issues you consider important.

More limited still may be the opportunity to vote on the positions a candidate takes on issues. **Issue voting** requires satisfying several conditions, which involve having fairly specific information about the candidates running for an office and the motivation to use it to determine how you'll vote. To cast a vote on an issue, you must:

- Have enough awareness of an issue to have a position on it.
- Be aware of where the candidates stand on the issue.
- Differentiate the candidates' positions on the issues.
- Vote for the candidate whose position is closest to yours.

Take a second and try it. Imagine that our two congressional candidates have announced their position on a hypothetical second stimulus bill similar to the one Congress passed in 2009 providing close to $800 billion to stimulate the economy through a mixture of government spending and tax cuts. Most of the plan entailed spending measures in areas such as education, green energy technology, and highway construction, with about one-third of the spending reserved for individual and business tax cuts. Supporters argued the stimulus was needed to jump-start an economy facing its deepest downturn since the

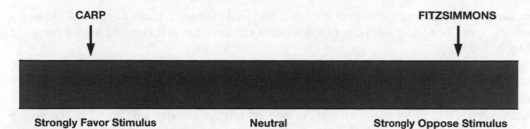

FIGURE 4.9 Issue Voting: Positions of Two Hypothetical Congressional Candidates on $800 Billion Stimulus Package

Great Depression. Opponents claimed that the program was an inappropriate use of tax dollars—a wasteful giveaway to special interests that would dramatically expand the federal budget deficit. In the upcoming election, let's assume that supporters and opponents are making the same arguments.

Figure 4.9 displays the positions of our two hypothetical congressional candidates. Leonard Fitzsimmons opposes the initiative, saying it's a huge mistake to believe we can "spend our way out of recession." Marjorie Carp strongly supports it with some minor reservations, saying "bold action is needed to get the economy on track" while urging more tax breaks and fewer spending projects.

To cast an issue vote, you would vote for a candidate based on this issue, regardless of where he or she stands on all other issues, and regardless of his or her party identification.

Clearly, you'd have to feel pretty strongly about the issue to do this, and some people do feel that strongly about some issues. Perhaps caring deeply would then motivate you to be informed about the issue, but information can be difficult to come by or complicated to wade through for even the most dedicated voter.

When a team of political scientists investigated voters' decision-making processes in 1956, they found that no more than one-fifth to one-third of voters could satisfy the informational requirements for issue voting.[42] A later study of this question found that, in 1992 and 1984, more people—on average, better than half—were able to navigate the informational requirements necessary for issue voting on a host of issues, including government spending, crime, job policies, the environment, aid to minorities, and women's rights.[43]

However, the figure was lower in 1988, 1980, and 1976, jumping around a bit from election to election. This could reflect how the information environment isn't always the same from issue to issue or from year to year. Some issues are more complex than others, and sometimes it's just harder to differentiate where the candidates stand. In fact, political candidates eager to reach as many voters as possible may intentionally take broad or vague positions, complicating our ability to place ourselves clearly in one camp.

4.9d Retrospective Voting

Issue voting is prospective in nature because we're looking ahead and making judgments about what candidates are likely to do after they're elected. Some people make decisions about candidates by looking at the past. When an incumbent is running for reelection, it's fairly typical for voters to view the election as a referendum on his or her job performance. **Retrospective voting** provides an opportunity for people to look back and evaluate how the official has performed in office to determine whether the incumbent should be retained or replaced.[44]

We might take any number of things into account when making a retrospective evaluation about an official. The candidate's actions on a particular issue or set of issues could be prominent in our thinking, particularly if it's an issue that affects us personally like the economy, or something the candidate made a big deal about when running for office the last time. We might take character into account when making a retrospective evaluation and ask if the official is worthy of our continued support.

It's hard to know exactly what people will look for, but incumbents assume that voters will be judging their actions and record and try to be prepared as best they can. They can never control the timing of events, though. President Obama believed voters would

retrospective voting: Evaluating the past performance of an incumbent to make a judgment about the future—whether the incumbent should be retained or replaced.

evaluate his overall economic performance and find enough to their liking to award him a second term. But there was no way to know for certain what events might have intervened before Election Day.

When Hillary Clinton sought the presidency in 2016, she ran as a de facto incumbent, strongly endorsed by Barack Obama. The president's job approval was strong, and economic indicators were robust, but many people felt they were not participating in the economic recovery. Large majorities of Americans felt the country was going in the wrong direction, and some were looking to make a change. To these voters, the endorsement of an incumbent president—even a popular one—was a reminder that Secretary Clinton represented the status quo.

George W. Bush also faced re-election when a majority of Americans said they felt the country was going in the wrong direction. Normally, this spells difficulty for an incumbent, and throughout 2004, President Bush ran even with his challenger, Massachusetts Senator John Kerry. Although President Bush was re-elected, the country remained divided on his performance to the end, handing the president a narrow three-point victory with a slim majority in the Electoral College.

4.10 A Look Ahead: Apathy, Efficacy, and the Media

Remember a little while back, in Section 4.7, "I Couldn't Care Less!" when we were saying that apathy might be about powerlessness? That people may come across as uncaring because problems seem so overwhelming that we might actually feel uneasy suggesting that we believe we can do something about them? It's possible that the media contribute to this situation.

That's because the choice to participate in politics is made in a prevailing climate of public opinion, which is influenced by the media. In the 1960s, when getting involved was cool, the prevailing climate of public opinion supported political participation, even activism and protest—some of the less conventional forms of participation we talked about earlier.

The climate was quite different in the 1980s and 1990s, and this was reflected in the way society was mirrored back to us on television and in newspapers. If those messages preach conformity, it's possible that we'll feel reluctance to express ourselves, especially if our opinions differ from the norm. We may be discouraged from talking about politics, from participating in political campaigns, possibly even from voting. We'll seem and act apathetic, not just because we may feel overwhelmed by the magnitude of the problems we face, but because we're reacting to a social climate perpetuated by media messages that are unsympathetic to political participation.[45] We're apathetic because we want to fit in.

Media coverage of political events may have an impact on feelings of efficacy as well. From Internet websites to talk radio to television news shows, we're bombarded with lots of information about politics and government, but we don't have a clear way to make sense of it all. It's easy to get lost or confused in the free market of messages, where everyone seems to have a point of view and it can be hard to figure out whom to believe. As we'll see in Chapter 5, even "credible" media sources like network and local news programs play on our fears and doubts, inviting us to anticipate the worst possible outcomes from events or to accept that our political leaders are motivated by the basest instincts. There's evidence that as television replaced newspapers as our primary source of information, feelings of efficacy began to decline—a pattern that began taking shape more than a generation ago.[46]

The tone of our political discussion just makes things worse. To call it "discourse" or "debate" risks putting a refined label on political coverage that's often harsh and shrill. In an environment where there are so many information sources that everyone has to yell to get our attention, how can we know what's truthful, what's partially truthful, what's rumor, and what's totally fabricated? The answer is, very often we don't have a reliable way of navigating through the noise.

Sometimes, we end up believing things about our public officials that aren't entirely true. Sometimes, we just turn the noise off altogether. These are both reasonable responses to our twenty-first-century media environment. Neither does much to facilitate feelings of efficacy.

Of course, it's easy to blame the media for everything from political apathy and inefficacy to why there was no hot water in the shower this morning. The media are so pervasive that they make an easy target, and even though there are places where the media play a critical role in the way the political system operates, it is possible to exaggerate the extent of that role. We'll be sure to aim carefully as we begin to explore the role the media play in connecting us to—or distancing us from—the political world. That's the matter we'll take up next, in Chapter 5.

Chapter Review

Appreciate American political culture as a set of shared values.

American political culture comprises a widely held set of values, attitudes, and beliefs that people have about the United States. It unifies America as a nation despite its great diversity by giving people a sense of an "American creed" that most Americans subscribe to, despite differences about how America should be governed.

Understand how immigration has both challenged and helped define American political culture.

Holding these shared values can ease the strain caused by diversity. Throughout history, periods of heavy immigration have typically produced an intolerant reaction, like the anti-Catholic "Know-Nothing" movement of the mid-1800s and, more recently, anti-Latino sentiments. New groups put a strain on resources and bring different customs and traditions that may seem alien and threatening to those who were here before them, although immigrant groups typically embrace American political culture, and over time contribute to the diversity that is one hallmark of that culture.

Identify how immigration, migration, and aging are changing American population demographics.

Changes in our political culture—and our politics—may be anticipated through the changing face of diversity, migration patterns, and the growing number of senior citizens in America. As Asians and Hispanics replace Europeans as the largest immigrant groups, whites are steadily becoming a smaller percentage of the population, and census projections estimate that whites will be a minority by the middle of the twenty-first century.

Define political socialization.

Political socialization is the process by which we acquire knowledge about politics, along with the attitudes and beliefs that we carry into adulthood.

Describe how political socialization is a lifelong process, and identify primary and secondary agents of political socialization.

Socialization is a lifelong process facilitated by a series of agents, primary among them our parents, siblings, and friends. Although parents are the most important single agent of political socialization, many parental attitudes and beliefs are not socialized between generations, with party identification the most widely acquired parental characteristic. Secondary agents of socialization include schools and the mass media, which influence political discourse through agenda setting.

Explain the relationship between political socialization and the circumstances of one's upbringing.

Political socialization is also affected by the circumstances of our upbringing, with African Americans and women confronting a political environment that has not always embraced their participation; by large-scale events that shape our generation; and by where we are in the life cycle.

Discuss multiple ways in which people participate in politics and several factors that influence the likelihood that someone will participate.

There are many ways beyond voting that people participate in politics, like working for a candidate, contacting public officials, contributing money to a campaign, talking about politics, or participating in a protest or an act of civil disobedience. Of these, voting is the most common political activity, although only slightly more than half the eligible voters have participated in recent presidential elections. The likelihood of participating in politics is influenced by age, education, socioeconomic status, and efficacy.

Identify reasons why people vote, despite time and information costs.

Participation takes effort, and given time and information costs, you can make the case that it's sensible not to vote. Still, people find the motivation to vote because they feel it is their civic responsibility, they get a sense of efficacy from voting, or they believe that voting gives them some influence over politics.

Explain several common ways people arrive at their voting decisions.

Voting decisions may be based on party identification, attributes of the candidate, issues, or retrospective evaluations of candidate performance.

Key Terms

affective Existing in the realm of emotion or feeling. (p. 102)

agenda setting The tendency for topics given great weight by the media to be given equally great weight by those who use the media, such that the people and events considered important by those who determine media coverage will become the people and events that the public considers important. (p. 105)

agents of socialization External influences that shape the way we are socialized to politics, including parents and siblings in the home, friends and coworkers outside the home, and institutions like schools and the media. (p. 103)

apathy A sense of indifference to or lack of interest in politics. (p. 113)

census An accounting or, as Article I, Section 2 of the Constitution puts it, an "actual Enumeration" of the residents of the United States, taken every ten years by constitutional decree to assess population growth and population shifts. Census figures are used to determine representation in Congress, as states that lose population between censuses stand to lose House seats to states that gain population. (p. 97)

civic responsibility A sense of duty or obligation to society that some people believe comes along with citizenship. (p. 116)

civil disobedience A peaceful means of protest whereby individuals draw attention to laws they consider unjust by disobeying them and being arrested for their actions. (p. 108)

cognitive A factual awareness or appreciation of someone or something. Cognition implies knowledge and the ability to exercise judgment. This is why we would say that a young child's understanding of the president is not cognitive because kids' awareness of the president as an important figure lacks appreciation of what the president does and why he is important. (p. 102)

conservatism An ideology that advocates limits on government power to address economic and social problems, relying instead on economic markets and individual initiative to address problems like health care and education, while promoting government involvement in moral matters to, for instance, minimize or eliminate abortions or permit prayer in public schools. (p. 99)

cynicism A pervasive attitude of mistrust about politics that may lead people to withdraw from political participation. (p. 103)

efficacy The attitude that you can be effectual and effective in your dealings with government. (p. 112)

elitism The theory that government responds to a small, stable, centralized hierarchy of corporate and academic leaders, military chiefs, people who own big media outlets, and members of a permanent government bureaucracy. People who subscribe to this position believe the actions of regular citizens, like voting and joining groups, simply mask the real power exercised by elites. (p. 114)

generational effects Historical influences felt by an entire generation during their formative years, which shape the way they are socialized to politics. (p. 106)

issue voting Choosing a candidate in an election on the basis of his or her proximity to your position on an issue or issues you consider important. (p. 118)

"Know-Nothing" movement An anti-Catholic movement that formed in the 1840s as a reaction to the first large wave of Irish immigration. (p. 96)

liberalism An ideology that advocates the use of government power to address economic and social problems, like unemployment and environmental protection, while limiting government involvement in moral matters like abortion rights and prayer in public schools. (p. 99)

life cycle effects Changes to the way we relate to politics and society that naturally occur during the course of aging, which typically leave us less open to political and social change as we get older. (p. 106)

National Voter Registration Act Passed in 1993 to simplify and standardize voter registration requirements, the "Motor Voter Act" allows residents of most states to register to vote at the same time as they apply for or renew their driver's license. It also provides for a standardized, national registration form that can be downloaded from the Internet. (p. 115)

party identification An individual's association with a political party. The most common parties Americans identify with are the two major parties, Republican and Democrat. Party identification—also called party I.D.—varies in intensity such that it may be strong or weak. Those who do not identify with any party are typically called independents. (p. 103)

pluralism The theory that government responds to individuals through their memberships in groups, assuring that government is responsive to a wide range of voices. People who subscribe to this position believe that the wide distribution of resources in society drives the decisions government officials make. (p. 114)

political culture The common set of attitudes, beliefs, and values that provide the foundation of support for a political system. (p. 90)

political participation The range of activities people can engage in to influence the political process. While voting is the most commonly performed political act, participation encompasses a host of things—from writing letters to public officials to contributing time or money to a campaign or protesting the actions of government. (p. 107)

political socialization The process by which we acquire political knowledge, attitudes, and beliefs. (p. 102)

primary agent of socialization Parents and siblings exert disproportional influence on the political development of children by virtue of the initial influence they have on kids, giving the family a primary role in the process of political socialization. (p. 103)

retrospective voting Evaluating the past performance of an incumbent to make a judgment about the future—whether the incumbent should be retained or replaced. (p. 119)

secondary agent of socialization Schools and the media have an effect on political socialization, but the effect is less than from primary agents like the family because we do not form close interpersonal bonds with either institution. (p. 105)

selective exposure The tendency to pay attention to messages that are consistent with existing attitudes or beliefs, while overlooking messages that conflict with them. (p. 105)

selective perception An unconscious process by which we filter information that we deem irrelevant, uninteresting, or inconsistent with our attitudes and beliefs, while absorbing information that conforms to our self-perception. (p. 105)

socioeconomic status (SES) A measure of an individual's social position based primarily on education, income, and occu-pation. High socioeconomic status individuals are more likely to have advanced education, high incomes, and occupations that award high status and demand great responsibility, like professional or managerial work. (p. 111)

ticket splitting Voting for candidates of different parties for different offices, rather than voting a "party line" for all Republicans or all Democrats. Ticket splitting, which has increased in recent years, is a sign of how Americans have been growing independent from political parties. (p. 117)

Resources

You might be interested in examining some of what the following authors have said about the topics we've been discussing:

Almond, Gabriel A., and Sidney Verba. *The Civic Culture: Political Attitudes and Democracy in Five Nations*. Newbury Park, CA: Sage Publications, 1989. This study of several countries lends a comparative perspective to political culture.

Clark, Terry Nichols, and Vincent Hoffmann-Martinot, eds. *The New Political Culture*. Boulder, CO: Westview Press, 1998. This edited volume of essays on comparative political culture reflects contemporary thinking on the subject.

Dawson, Richard E., and Kenneth Prewitt. *Political Socialization: An Analytic Study*. Boston: Little, Brown, 1969. As the name suggests, this volume is a good overview of political socialization, containing a particularly good discussion of the agents of socialization.

Eliasoph, Nina. *Avoiding Politics: How Americans Produce Apathy in Everyday Life*. New York: Cambridge University Press, 1998. An interesting and surprising take on the widely held belief that Americans do not participate in politics because they are apathetic.

Fiorina, Morris P. *Retrospective Voting in American National Elections*. New Haven, CT: Yale University Press, 1988. For those who want to learn more about the evaluations people make about incumbents running for reelection and how those evaluations factor into how people vote.

Putnam, Robert D. *Bowling Alone: The Collapse and Revival of American Community*. New York: Simon and Schuster, 2000. This influential book presents an impressive array of data to support the argument that Americans have become increasingly detached from each other, weakening the civic bonds on which a vital democracy depends.

Tocqueville, Alexis de. *Democracy in America*. New York: Vintage Books, 1945. One of the first and most perceptive observers of American civic life, Tocqueville comments on the American tendency to join groups—a characteristic of American political culture that still holds true.

You may also be interested in looking at this resource site:

If you would like a copy of the national voter registration form, you can find it at http://www.fec.gov/votregis/vr.shtml

Notes

1 For an excellent overview of Millennial attitudes and preferences, see the Pew Research Millennial project, at http://www.pewresearch.org/topics/millennials/.

2 "Here's Donald Trump's Presidential Announcement Speech," *Time*, June 16, 2015. http://time.com/3923128/donald-trump-announcement-speech/.

3 Jeremy Diamond, "Donald Trump: Ban All Muslim Travel to US," CNN, December 8, 2015. http://www.cnn.com/2015/12/07/politics/donald-trump-muslim-ban-immigration/.

4 Alexis de Tocqueville, *Democracy in America* (New York: Vintage Books, 1945).

5 Cited in Robert D. Putnam, *Bowling Alone: The Collapse and Revival of American Community* (New York: Simon and Schuster, 2000), 48.

6 Gabriel A. Almond and Sidney Verba, *The Civic Culture* (Newbury Park, CA: Sage Publications, 1989).

7 Allan Cigler and Mark R. Joslyn, "The Extensiveness of Group Membership and Social Capital: The Impact on Political Tolerance Attitudes," *Political Research Quarterly* 55:1 (March 2002), 7–25.

8 Putnam, *Bowling Alone*, 15–28.

9 Ibid., 18–24.

10 Ibid., 402–414.

11 "Age and Sex Composition in the United States: 2012." U.S. Census Bureau, 2012. https://www.census.gov/population/age/data/2012comp.html.

12 If you work or have worked, you've already started to support the Social Security system. As you age, there will simply be fewer workers contributing to the system and more retirees claiming benefits, so your share of the burden will increase.

13 Fred I. Greenstein, "Children and Politics," in Greenberg, Edward S. (ed.), *Political Socialization* (New York: Atherton Press, 1970), 56–63.

14 Fred I. Greenstein, "The Benevolent Leader: Children's Images of Political Authority," *American Political Science Review* 54 (1960): 934–943.

15 Amy Carter and Ryan L. Teten, "Assessing Changing Views of the President: Revisiting Greenstein's Children and Politics,"

Presidential Studies Quarterly 32: 3 (September 2002): 453–462.

16 Eighth-graders in the 2000 group ranked doctors ahead of the president as the most important authority figures.

17 Carter and Teten, "Assessing Changing Views of the President."

18 Richard E. Dawson and Kenneth Prewitt, *Political Socialization: An Analytic Study* (Boston: Little, Brown, 1969), 105–126.

19 Frank Sorauf, *Party Politics in America*, 2nd ed. (Boston: Little, Brown, 1972), 144.

20 Ibid.

21 Dawson and Prewitt, Political Socialization, 127–142.

22 Maxwell McCombs and Donald Shaw, "The Agenda-Setting Function of the Mass Media," *Public Opinion Quarterly* 36 (Summer 1972): 176–187.

23 Dwaine Marvick, "The Political Socialization of the American Negro," in Dawson and Prewitt, *Political Socialization*, 151–177.

24 Greenstein, "Children and Politics," 59.

25 The term "baby boomers" applies to the generation born during the years 1945–1965, the older members of which came of age during the Vietnam War. See M. Kent Jennings and Richard G. Neimi, *Generational Politic*s (Princeton, NJ: Princeton University Press, 1982).

26 United States Elections Project, at http://elections.gmu.edu/index.html.

27 Sidney Verba and Norman Nie, *Participation in America: Political Democracy and Social Equality* (New York: Harper and Row Publishers, 1972), 125–137.

28 Material discussed here may be found in greater detail in "Introduction to Federal Voting Rights Laws," United States Department of Justice, Civil Rights Division, Voting section website. To learn more, go to http://www.justice.gov/crt/.

29 *Guinn v. United States*, 238 US 347 (1915).

30 *Smith v. Allwright*, 321 US 649 (1944).

31 Verba and Nie, *Participation in America*, 125–173 and 334–343.

32 Kay Lehman Scholzman and Sidney Verba, *Injury to Insult: Unemployment, Class, and Political Response* (Cambridge, MA: Harvard University Press, 1979).

33 Nina Eliasoph, *Avoiding Politics: How Americans Produce Apathy in Everyday Life* (New York: Cambridge University Press, 1998).

34. You can find registration deadlines for your state from electionline.org, at http://www.pewcenteronthestates.org/initiatives_detail.aspx?initiativeID=34044.

35. National Conference of State Legislatures, at http://www.ncsl.org/LegislaturesElections/ElectionsCampaigns/AbsenteeandEarlyVoting/tabid/16604/Default.aspx.

36 http://www.co.multnomah.or.us/dbcs/elections/election_information/voting_in_oregon.shtml.

37 Mackenzie Weinger, "Oregon iHappy with iPod Voting," *Politico*, November 9, 2011.

38 Emily Bazelon, "Why No One Should Have to Wait Two Hours to Vote," Slate.com, November 12, 2012.

39 Data from 2016 American National Eletion Studies (ANES), at http://www.electionstudies.org.

40 The NES Guide to Public Opinion and Election Behavior, which may be accessed at http://www.electionstudies.org/. Figures do not sum to 100 percent because of rounding error.

41 Or maybe because you like fish?

42 Angus Campbell, Philip E. Converse, Warren E. Miller, and Donald E. Stokes, *The American Voter* (New York: John Wiley and Sons, 1960), 168–187.

43 Paul R. Abramson, John H. Aldrich, and David W. Rhode, *Change and Continuity in the 1996 and 1998 Elections* (Washington, D.C.: Congressional Quarterly Press, 1999).

44 Morris P. Fiorina, *Retrospective Voting in American National Elections* (New Haven: Yale University Press, 1988).

45 Elisabeth Noelle-Neumann, *The Spiral of Silence* (Chicago: University of Chicago Press, 1984).

46 Michael J. Robinson, "Public Affairs Television and the Growth of Public Malaise: The Case of the Selling of the Pentagon," *American Political Science Review* 70 (June 1976): 409–432.

Table, Figure, and Box Notes

T1 Gabriel A. Almond and Sidney Verba, *The Civic Culture: Political Attributes and Democracy in Five Nations* (Newbury Park, CA: Sage Publications, 1980).

T2 1996 Survey of American Political Culture, University of Virginia Institute for Advanced Studies in Culture (IASC).

T3 Immigration and Naturalization Service Fiscal Year 2000 Statistical Yearbook.

T4 "Census Bureau Releases Estimates of Undercount and Overcount in the 2010 Census," U.S. Census Bureau, May 22, 2012. https://www.census.gov/newsroom/releases/archives/2010_census/cb12-95.html. See also Haya El Nasser and Paul Overberg, "Census Continues to Undercount Blacks, Hispanics, Kids," *USA Today*, May 23, 2012.

T5 The case was *Department of Commerce et al. v. United States House of Representatives et al.*, 98–404 (1999).

T6 Timothy J. Alberta, "Census Nominee Rules Out Statistical Sampling in 2010." *The Wall Street Journal*, May 15, 2009, at http://online.wsj.com/article/SB124241977657124963.html.

T7 Source: U.S. Census Bureau.

T8 Ibid.

T9 Data courtesy Marc Imhoff of NASA GSFC and Christopher Elvidge of NOAA NGDC. Image by Craig Mayhew and Robert Simmon, NASA GSFC.

T10 Data from 2000 American National Election Study. American National Election Studies, Center for Political Studies, University of Michigan. Electronic resources from the ANES World Wide Website (www.umich.edu/~nes). Ann Arbor, MI: University of Michigan, Center for Political Studies [producer and distributor], 1995–2000. These materials are based on work supported by the National Science Foundation under Grant Nos.:

SBR-9707741, SBR-9317631, SES-9209410, SES-9009379, SES-8808361, SES-8341310, SES-8207580, and SOC77-08885. Any opinions, findings, and conclusions or recommendations expressed in these materials are those of the author(s) and do not necessarily reflect those of the National Science Foundation. Data for percentage who voted from official turnout figures from the 2000 election.

T11 National Governors Association, at http://www.nga.org/portal/site/nga/menuitem.42b929b1a5b9e4eac3363d10501010a0/?vgnextoid=d54c8aaa2ebbff00VgnVCM1000001a01010aRCRD&vgnextfmt=curgov.

T12 U.S. Senate, at http://www.senate.gov/artandhistory/history/common/briefing/women_senators.htm.

T13 Data from 2000 General Social Survey.

T14 See "Voting Rights," from the Civil Rights Movement Veterans, at http://www.crmvet.org/info/lithome.htm.

T15 To see the complete literacy test, go to http://www.crmvet.org/info/litques.htm.

T16 Kay Lehman Scholzman and Sidney Verba, *Injury to Insult: Unemployment, Class, and Political Response* (Cambridge, MA: Harvard University Press, 1979), 333–356.

Mass Media:
Influencing What We Think About

CHAPTER **5**

Source. Scanrail1/Shutterstock

Learning Objectives

When you have completed this chapter, you should be able to:

- Define mass media, and explain why the media can both enhance and confound our ability to make enlightened decisions about politics and government.

- Identify the gatekeepers of news in the traditional press and on the Internet.

- Explain the evolution of the press in America—from the party press to the penny press to the mass media era.

- Define "infotainment," and explain how it complicates the media environment.

- Assess the risks posed by the concentration of media power.

- Explain agenda setting.

- Discuss the conflict between politicians and journalists that emerged in the mass media era over control of news messages.

- Speak intelligently about media bias, and explain why bias can be difficult to identify.

- Address the possible relationship between news messages and cynicism in the traditional media and the problem of finding truthful information on the Internet.

Chapter Outline

5.1 Introduction

L.O. Define mass media, and explain why the media can both enhance and confound our ability to make enlightened decisions about politics and government.

On September 12, 2009, a crowd estimated at close to two million people gathered in Washington to protest the policies of the Obama administration.

Or maybe it was 60,000.

Wouldn't it be easy to tell the difference? After all, the discrepancy between these two figures is so vast that anyone in attendance would have been able to tell which was closer to the truth. But if you heard or read about it in the media, your impression of the crowd would have depended on where you turned to get your information.

The confusion over the size of the crowd can be traced to a public claim made by one of the event organizers that ABC News was reporting between 1 and 1.5 million people in attendance. In fact, ABC News.com had reported a crowd estimate of between 60,000 and 70,000, the figure supplied to them by the Washington, D.C. fire department. The organizer who used the outsized figure subsequently apologized for misrepresenting the ABC News estimate.[1]

But not before the larger figure began circulating through the conservative blogosphere—an amalgamation of conservative blogs and websites—in what resembled a cyber-version of the kid's game "whisper down the lane." Michelle Malkin, one of the most widely read conservative bloggers, inflated the ABC News figure to two million, which, owing to her great popularity, was noticed and repeated by other conservative bloggers. Before long, the right blogosphere was abuzz with news about the record crowds on the Washington Mall.

At the same time, the left side of the blogosphere pushed back, with progressive bloggers like Glenn Greenwald saying the two million figure "was literally invented out of whole cloth" and "bears no relationship whatsoever to reality."[2]

His objective, along with other liberals, was to prevent the conservative blogosphere's estimate from becoming established conventional wisdom and sparking a larger, lasting story about the size of the opposition to the Obama administration.

And what about readers who don't frequent the blogosphere? Their understanding of what happened in Washington that day might have depended on what news sources they read as well. On that score, *Time* magazine would have been of little assistance, telling its readers that:

> If you get your information from liberal sources, the crowd numbered about 70,000, many of them greedy racists. If you get your information from conservative sources, the crowd was hundreds of thousands strong, perhaps as many as a million, and the tenor was peaceful and patriotic. Either way, you may not be inclined to believe what we say about numbers, according to a recent poll that found record-low levels of public trust of the mainstream media.[3]

Welcome to the twenty-first century world of news and information.

In an ideal world, if you were inclined to participate in the political process, you'd be able to get all the information you need to make intelligent political decisions from the wide variety of **mass media** at your disposal: newspapers, television, radio, magazines, and the Internet (see Demystifying Government: Just Passing Through). What you'd learn from these information sources would be clear and valid, believable, and easy to understand. Facts would be neatly distinguished from opinion, they would be accurate, and there would be no rumors or half-truths. You'd wade your way through this information until you learned what you needed or wanted to know. Your information environment would offer you both clarity of content and diversity of ideas.

The real world of mass media falls far short of this ideal.

The mass media of your parent's generation offered more clarity than the mass media of our time, but it, too, had its shortcomings. In that world, only a small number of people—newspaper editors, television news producers, select prestigious journalists, and evening news anchors—were the decision makers or **"gatekeepers"** of news content, making the choices about what to cover and what not to cover. Even today, the same small number

mass media: Vehicles, such as television, radio, newspapers, magazines, and the Internet, capable of rapidly communicating information to large numbers of people over large distances. Note that *media* is the plural form of *medium*: Television is a medium, whereas television and the Internet *are* media.

gatekeepers: Television producers, newspaper editors, and prestigious reporters and anchors who make the decisions about what stories will be published or aired. Think of the imagery of a guard who decides who will be allowed to pass through a gate. In this case, news gatekeepers determine which information will be allowed to pass through the medium.

L.O. Identify the gatekeepers of news in the traditional press and on the Internet.

Just Passing Through

The word *media* is the plural form of the word *medium*, which is defined as an element through which something passes. In the spiritual world, a medium is the person at a séance who claims to be able to receive and relay messages from the dead to the living. In the world of communication, a medium is a tangible element like a newspaper, television, radio, computer, book, movie, CD, or DVD—anything that can transmit information, which is the thing that passes through the medium.

The media in the previous list would all be considered mass media because they're capable of passing information to large numbers of people. In contrast, hand-printed newspapers or books of which only a few copies were produced would still be media, but not in a mass sense. It's easy to associate mass media with technology because technological innovations like radio, television, cable, and the Internet have profoundly enhanced the reach of contemporary media. For this reason, our "information age," as it is sometimes called, could accurately be termed an age of mass media.

We tend to use the words *media* and *press* interchangeably—you'll even see a little of that in this chapter—but they're really different. *Press* evokes journalism, or the process by which information is gathered, whereas *media* evokes the methods of communicating the information journalists gather. There can also be a normative difference between the terms, with *press* suggesting the careful gathering of factual information, and *media* implying something faster, flashier, and perhaps more slipshod. "I'm a journalist" can have a more substantive ring than "I'm with the media."

---

of highly influential editors and producers make decisions about news content for the traditional media, like newspapers and television news programs.

The choices they made in that earlier time tended to be stable and consistent, which had its advantages and disadvantages. On the plus side, the stable choices of traditional gatekeepers offered a clear view of key political officials and candidates, which could be pretty helpful in evaluating their performance, deciding how to vote (retrospectively or on issues), and figuring out exactly what Congress, the president, the courts, and state and local officials were up to. You might even say that this kind of linkage between people and their political leaders could be a valuable political resource because the media are a major source of political information, which we know can be critical to informed political involvement.

But there was a price to be paid for this stability. Because gatekeepers traditionally made predictable story choices, typically favoring recurring news themes and relying on the same set of official sources, there were limits on the range of ideas available to think about. The information may have been clear, but it was limited in scope. What was gained in clarity was lost in diversity.

Today, the media environment is hardly limited, but it is murky. It's like a noisy bazaar, where literally hundreds of media outlets are clamoring for a few seconds of your attention. Anyone with a web address can be a gatekeeper. Nonstop cable news demands interesting around-the-clock content. How can you be sure that they're giving you reliable information? Which media outlets are exaggerating the truth, or trading in rumor and innuendo? How can we be intelligent news consumers and reasonably informed citizens when we can't easily answer these questions? This is what we'll be talking about as we go through Chapter 5.

Political theorist Robert Dahl points to two criteria for effective democratic processes that can guide us as we attempt to figure out how well we're served by the media. They are "effective participation" and "enlightened understanding." The first of these entails assuring that we have an equal and effective opportunity to participate in political decision making (which is already complicated, as we saw in Chapter 4, by unequal patterns of participation resulting from the unequal distribution of resources). Enlightened understanding makes effective participation possible in that, unless we have a way to understand the terms of political debate, we won't be able to arrive at sensible decisions. In other words, in order to have a flourishing democracy, we have to have access to good information. Suppress critical information, and people may well make different—and inferior—decisions.[4]

As we examine the role of the media in the political process, we'll keep returning to the question of how well they promote—or how much they discourage—effective participation and enlightened understanding. First, we'll look back on the media through history to see how they have evolved from being a limited factor in early politics to a major player today. Then, we'll try to figure out exactly what counts as news now and talk a little about how privately owned newspapers and television stations and the like came to play such an important role in public life.

We'll try to figure out how we can differentiate information from entertainment, both in coverage of elections and news coverage of people in office, while exploring the paradox that an ever-expanding menu of media choices has developed alongside an ever-diminishing pool of media owners. Finally, we'll examine the effect the mass media can have on the public beyond setting the political agenda and raise the question of whether there is bias in coverage. When we're finished, we may or may not be better positioned to draw on the mass media for useful information about politics and government, but we should have a better idea of how to approach news coverage.

5.2 Political History of the Media: From Colonial Press to Global Media

L.O. Explain the evolution of the press in America—from the party press to the penny press to the mass media era.

The United States is a media-saturated nation where sources of information too numerous to count are available through the click of a mouse or television remote control. It certainly didn't start out that way. The timeline in Table 5.1 illustrates the evolution of the press by detailing key moments in American media. In colonial America, there wasn't

TABLE 5.1 Three Hundred Years of Media Development[T1]

TIMELINE 1700–1950	
Colonial Press (1700–1790)	
1704	The weekly *Boston Newsletter* debuts as the first continuously published newspaper in the American colonies. It depended on foreign newspapers for much of its news content, even though those papers were months out of date.
1784	The *Pennsylvania Packet and Daily Advertiser* becomes the young nation's first daily newspaper.
Party Press (1790–1830)	
1789	John Fenno publishes the *Gazette of the United States*, which becomes the first Federalist Party newspaper, frequently featuring the writing of Alexander Hamilton.
1791	James Madison and Thomas Jefferson persuade writer Philip Freneau to establish the first Republican (anti-Federalist) Party newspaper, the *National Gazette*.
Penny Press (1830–1880)	
1833	Benjamin Day publishes the *New York Sun* for the remarkably low sum of one cent, using advertising revenue to make up the balance of his costs.
1841	Horace Greeley establishes the *New York Tribune* as an intelligent alternative among penny newspapers.
Yellow Journalism (1880–1920)	
1883	Joseph Pulitzer acquires the *New York World*, dramatically increasing its circulation with sensational coverage and crusading journalism that appealed to immigrant readers.
1895	William Randolph Hearst purchases the *New York Journal* and enters into fierce competition with Pulitzer as the period of "yellow journalism" reaches its peak.

TABLE 5.1 Three Hundred Years of Media Development[T1] *(continued)*

TIMELINE 1700–1950 *(continued)*	
Emerging Mass Media (1920–1950)	
1920	KDKA/Pittsburgh becomes America's first commercial radio station and the first radio station to report the results of a presidential election. (In case you missed the broadcast, Harding defeated Cox.)
1926	NBC radio begins operation as two networks: the Red Network and the Blue Network (which eventually became ABC). CBS radio followed one year later.
1947	The first regularly scheduled television newscast appears on NBC. The *Camel News Caravan*, sponsored by Camel cigarettes, featured an announcer at a desk and a cigarette constantly burning in an ashtray.
TIMELINE 1950–Present	
Age of Television (1950–1980)	
1954	Broadcaster Edward R. Murrow uses his television program *See It Now* as a platform for exposing the anticommunist crusade of Senator Joseph McCarthy as a hollow smear campaign.
1960	John F. Kennedy and Richard Nixon hold the first televised presidential debate.
1968	CBS anchorman Walter Cronkite goes to Vietnam and reports that the best outcome the United States could expect in the Vietnam War was "stalemate." President Lyndon Johnson interprets Cronkite's commentary as a sign that he has lost the support of mainstream America.
1974	Richard Nixon becomes the first American president to resign from office after his involvement in the Watergate scandal and cover-up is revealed by investigative reporters Bob Woodward and Carl Bernstein and in widely viewed television congressional hearings.
Age of New Media (1980–present)	
1982	Satellite technology makes possible the national publication of *USA Today*.
1991	CNN provides real-time worldwide coverage of the Persian Gulf War.
1996	Internet users top sixty million worldwide, as major daily newspapers begin to maintain websites.
2003	Obscure Vermont Governor Howard Dean momentarily becomes the front-runner for the Democratic Party's presidential nomination behind an unprecedented Internet fund-raising and organizing effort.
2008	Illinois Senator Barack Obama perfects the Dean model for Internet fund-raising and mobilization and successfully reaches the White House.
2016	Donald Trump uses Twitter to make outrageous comments that set the campaign agenda when amplified by conventional media and rides a populist wave to the presidency.

much of a press, and what there was didn't concentrate much on political issues until just before the Revolutionary War. The colonial press needed government approval to operate, and under British law, any publisher who circulated material that criticized the government was subject to prosecution for seditious libel. So, newspaper publishers tended to avoid hot-button political issues, and the British authorities more or less left them alone.[5]

Then came the **Stamp Act**, which you may recall from Chapter 2 placed a tax on newspapers. With their interests at stake, publishers used their newspapers to defy the Stamp Act, in the process transforming newspapers into vehicles for arousing public opinion. Newspapers sympathetic to the revolutionary cause played an important role in setting the agenda for the war by recounting stories of British corruption and war atrocities, and of the colonists' military resistance.[6]

Stamp Act: A particularly vexing tax levied by the British on scores of legal documents, which led to a colonial boycott of British goods.

party press: Newspapers functioning as an arm of a political party, communicating information about partisan politics from party leaders to their supporters. Newspapers functioned in this capacity from the inception of political parties in America around 1790 through the 1830s.

penny press: High-circulation newspapers, emerging after 1830, that kept costs down by selling advertising. These newspapers brought in large numbers of readers with lurid and sensational reporting.

yellow journalism: The term given to the sensational newspaper coverage prevalent during the turn of the twentieth century, noteworthy for its emphasis on violence, sex, human-interest stories, and exposés of official corruption.

muckraking: Investigative reporting prevalent during the turn of the twentieth century, which centered on uncovering corruption in government and industry for the purpose of promoting progressive reforms.

The emergence of political parties following the Revolutionary War ushered in the era of the **party press**. From about 1790 through the 1830s, newspapers became an important vehicle for reaching and "educating" the party faithful in order to advance the political objectives of party leaders. No longer apolitical, the press had become a mouthpiece for the views of party leaders, which meant that newspapers also weren't objective. However, press objectivity wasn't highly valued in the early nineteenth century, and it wasn't important to the survival of newspapers, which had a built-in readership from party faithful, who loved partisan rhetoric.[7]

Newspapers of this time were expensive, costing upwards of six cents. Most people couldn't afford the price, but most people couldn't vote. So, party newspapers were limited in circulation and purchased by a small, loyal following. As the 1830s approached and voting rights were extended to men who didn't own property, political parties became larger, mass political activity emerged, and newspapers became an important link between party leaders and their growing legions of loyalists.

Major technological changes were taking place at this time as well, lowering printing costs and creating new markets for manufactured goods that had to be advertised. The **penny press** emerged in response to these conditions. Starting in the early 1830s, publishers found they could sell newspapers to readers for a penny if they also sold advertising to manufacturers interested in alerting emerging mass markets about their products.[8] The marriage of publisher and advertiser had begun.

Not coincidentally, so had the marriage of media and entertainment. In order to bolster advertising revenues, penny newspapers required large circulation figures, just like today's newspapers. The best way to sell papers to a large number of readers was to emphasize sensational stories and tell them in lurid detail—just like today. In 1835, the *New York Herald* ran a series of stories telling in graphic detail of the ax murder of a prostitute, and circulation figures soared. If this sounds like something from today's cable news programs, it's because stories about sex and violence have always commanded an audience.

The penny press did not put the party press out of business, and partisan publications continued to survive even as they were pushed aside by mass publications. But the necessity of reaching a large audience argued against outright partisanship in coverage. Publishers who wished to have their political views represented began relegating them to the editorial page. Also, while many penny publications focused on fires and murders, the penny press provided a forum for the emergence of the journalism of ideas. Horace Greeley, a well-known political activist and writer in the mid-nineteenth century, published the *New York Tribune* as an intelligent alternative to sensational journalism. A number of reputable journalists of that era found their start under his tutelage; he even hired Karl Marx as a foreign correspondent.

The period that followed witnessed the emergence of newspapers as big businesses. The immigrant influx at the turn of the twentieth century created new markets for newspapers, which began to increase in value. Trends in newspaper ownership anticipated the corporate mergers which, as we will shortly learn, are characteristic of our era, with declining competition, owners buying newspapers in multiple cities to form chains, and businessmen buying existing papers to get into the newspaper business. Publishers like William Randolph Hearst and Joseph Pulitzer engaged in ferocious competition with each other, while amassing enormous fortunes and great power. In this competitive climate, much like today, newspapers began to figuratively scream for attention, offering sensational human-interest stories about crime and sex, large headlines, photographs, and comic strips set off with yellow ink—hence the term **"yellow journalism."**[9]

The age of yellow journalism also ushered in a period of reporting on corporate abuses and political corruption, subjects with great appeal to members of the lower classes. Dubbed **"muckraking,"** this investigative reporting was the engine behind an era of progressive reforms, which included child labor laws, food inspection, and land conservation.

As newspapers became big business, journalism became a profession. Schools of journalism began to appear on college campuses, and journalists enjoyed a high level of prestige. As yellow journalism diminished after World War I, professional journalists ushered in a period of objectivity, which placed a premium on detached, balanced reporting. The ideal story presented a compilation of facts without a theme, as reporters saw themselves as purveyors of details rather than as storytellers. This continued until competition from television pushed the pendulum back to thematic storytelling in the 1970s.

Of course, the twentieth century was also the time when mass communication emerged in its numerous forms, including telephones, movies, radios, and eventually television. The rise of radio as a national medium in the 1930s began a transformational period in which emerging media networks integrated the nation. The NBC radio network premiered in 1926, CBS in 1927, and by the 1940s, better than 60 percent of radio stations were network affiliates.[10] With them came the first evidence of what we now take for granted: When electronic media become a routine part of life, they have the power to connect and move an entire society.

Even though newspapers had long reached large audiences, before radio there was nothing close to what we now call mass media. On October 30, 1938, Americans learned how profoundly and how immediately people could be touched by mass media. The forum was a radio adaptation of H.G. Wells' science-fiction story "The War of the Worlds," about a Martian invasion of earth. It was presented as a Halloween show by the gifted young director Orson Welles (no relation), who decided to tell the story as a real-time "newscast," with announcers appearing to break into regular programming with bulletins describing a supposed Martian invasion transpiring in New Jersey (that's right, New Jersey). There was a disclaimer at the start of the show that everything you were about to hear was a dramatization, but not everyone heard it. Imagine how you would react if you turned on your radio that night and heard the urgent report in Figure 5.1, believing it was real.

People panicked. They ran, hid in basements, or covered their noses to protect themselves from Martian poison gas. Believing the realistic reports of a Martian invasion were in fact real reports of a Martian invasion, they moved quickly to defend themselves from what they believed was a dangerous and imminent threat. It wasn't until later that people learned—through real radio news reports about the panic—that the invasion was just part of a radio play. And it wasn't until much later that people realized they had lived through an accidental demonstration of something we now experience every day: the power of the mass media to dramatically influence massive numbers of people.

Although television entered the scene in the late 1940s, its potential wasn't felt until the 1950s, when news reporters and political figures began to recognize how profoundly the visual medium could stir public opinion. For the next three decades, television news dominated the media landscape, filling our homes with images of political events like civil rights violence, urban riots, political assassination, war, and scandal, while changing the way candidates run for and act in office. Television remains a potent but altered force

In the competition between Hearst's *New York Journal* and Pulitzer's *New York World*, the publishers tried to arouse public opinion to ignite a war with Spain. Pictured is the sensational way the *World* covered Admiral Dewey's victory at the Battle of Manila during the Spanish-American War.

AUDIO TEXT: "Ladies and gentlemen, this is the most terrifying thing I have ever witnessed. Wait a minute. Someone or something I can see is turning out of that black hole through luminous disks—the eyes, it might be a face. Good heavens, something's wriggling out of the shadow like a gray snake. Now it's another one, and another one and another one. They look like tentacles to me. There, I can see the thing's body now. It's large as a bear and it glistens like wet leather. But that face. It—it's, ladies and gentlemen, it's indescribable. I can hardly force myself to keep looking at it, it's so awful. The eyes are black and they gleam like a serpent. The mouth is kind of V-shaped with saliva dripping from its rimless lips that seem to quiver and pulsate. The monster or whatever it is can hardly move. It seems weighed down by possibly gravity or something. The thing is rising up now and the crowd falls back. They've seen plenty. This is the most extraordinary experience, ladies and gentlemen. I can't find words. I'll pull this microphone with me as I talk. I'll have to stop the description so I can take a new position. Hold on, will you please, I'll be back in a minute."

MP3 file/Source: www.u.s.archive.org

FIGURE 5.1 The Power of Mass Media: Uniting—At Times Scaring—A Nation

today, thanks to the emergence of satellite and cable technology, which gave birth to multiple channels and around-the-clock programming. Of course, television now shares the media spotlight with the Internet, whose full potency as a political tool is still emerging.

Both the Vietnam War and the Watergate scandal initially aroused interest in investigative reporting. Then, after many years of official government sources lying to journalists as a matter of policy, investigative reporting gave way to a kind of aggressive journalism that redefined the relationship between reporters and officials and lent a negative cast to political coverage that's still with us today. Add to this the swirl of new technology and an increasingly competitive media marketplace, and you have an information environment that resembles the yellow journalism period of one hundred years ago, only faster-paced and all-encompassing We'll examine how to make sense of news reporting in this environment, sort out the way reporters and officials interact, and clarify what coverage of politics and government looks like, and why.

5.3 How Do We Know If It's News?

The printed word makes things seem so—authentic. So does the smooth, polished voice of a news anchor. Of course, we know that we should never believe everything we read or hear, but how can we know which media reports to accept, reject, or question?

Take a look at the statements in Table 5.2. Each one circulated freely on the Internet and caught the attention of mainstream news outlets. Can you tell if they are factually correct?

Every one of these quotes sounds reasonable at face value. They cite facts or statistics and are spoken in authoritative language. We would be forgiven if we thought they were truthful.

But none of them are.

The first quote comes from Tennessee Republican Rep. Diane Black, who based her figures on the worker participation rate rather than the unemployment rate. But according to fact-checkers at the *Washington Post*, the worker participation rate, or the percentage of people in the labor force, declined largely because of the retirement of baby boomers, a demographic factor that no administration could control. They add that the "prediction" of 5 percent unemployment was a projection made by economic advisors to President Obama before he took office, and they conclude that Black uses statistics and word choices to create the misleading impression that unemployment under Obama was worse than it really was and not as good as the administration promised it would be.[11]

Donald Trump made the statement about the murder rate at a campaign rally in Cedar Rapids, Iowa, on October 28, 2016, and repeated it at other rallies over the next several days. But the facts say the exact opposite. According to the *Washington Post*, statistics from the Federal Bureau of Investigation (FBI) show that the homicide rate in 2016 was the *lowest* it had been in fifty-two years. What had jumped was the single-year increase in homicides. That increase was the highest in forty-five years, but according to criminal justice

TABLE 5.2 Is It True?

QUOTE 1: "If the same percentage of people were in the labor force today [in 2014] as there were in 2009, our unemployment rate would be an astronomical 10.8 percent. This is in stark contrast to the [Obama] administration's prediction that [President Obama's] 'stimulus' legislation would have lowered unemployment to just 5 percent today."[T2]
QUOTE 2: "You won't hear this from the media: We have the highest murder rate in this country in 45 years. You don't hear that from these people. They don't want to talk about it. The highest murder rate in the United States in 45 years."
QUOTE 3: "Hillary Clinton surged the trade deficit with China 40% as Secretary of State, costing Americans millions of jobs."
QUOTE 4: "Back in the Great Recession, when millions of jobs across America hung in the balance, Donald Trump said rescuing the auto industry didn't matter very much."[T3]

experts cited by the *Post*, such year-to-year figures are insufficient to conclude anything about long-term trends, and even with the increase, the overall crime rate had held steady.

According to the *Tampa Bay Times* fact-checking group Politifact, the third quote—a June 21, 2016, tweet from Donald Trump about the trade deficit—uses what they characterize as "cherry-picked" facts (the 40 percent figure is accurate but includes the aftermath of the 2008 recession, which started under Obama's predecessor) to make a dubious claim about Clinton, in that the secretary of state has little influence over trade deficits.[12]

Politifact also takes issue with the fourth quote, a charge by Hillary Clinton that Donald Trump opposed President Obama's bailout of the American automobile industry. Although Trump may have disagreed with Obama on how to rescue the auto industry, he has said on record multiple times that something had to be done to save it.[13]

How are we supposed to make our way through an information environment this complicated—and deceptive? Even if we were inclined to read with skepticism, without the ability to challenge a relentless barrage of facts and assumptions, it can be close to impossible to know whether information is true, misleading, or false. Mainstream news organizations such as the *Washington Post* and *Tampa Bay Times* and research organizations such as the Annenberg Public Policy Center at the University of Pennsylvania provide fact-checking websites where you can probe what you're hearing and reading and get a third party's judgment on the level of veracity behind widely circulated claims. But this requires time, effort, and interest, and we know that few people are concerned enough about politics to pay full attention to the things they're hearing, no less care enough to study the truthfulness of the facts behind the claims.

Social media gives all sorts of information—including misinformation—the ability to circulate quickly and freely, making the matter of being accurately informed particularly acute in our time. But the problem didn't begin with the Internet. Consider this news story, which ran on a television news broadcast and is typical of television news content:

> "Turbulence is often no more than a minor bump in flight, but there are some times when it can take you on a roller-coaster ride at 30,000 feet. Veteran flyers insist that it's nothing to be afraid of . . . but that's little comfort when you're being tossed around in the cabin."[14]

Or consider this story, which also ran on a television news broadcast:

> "Car theft is America's most expensive property crime, one every 23 seconds, adding up to almost 1.5 million stolen cars a year. And while that number is down over the past decade, police actually recover fewer cars now. One-third of them are never found."[15]

If you didn't think too hard, it might seem like these news stories were actually informative. But the first story is literally about nothing. It was a local television news story about how airplane turbulence is almost always harmless ("often no more than a minor bump in flight" . . . "nothing to be afraid of")—but because knowing that is "little comfort when you're being tossed around in the cabin," it's the kind of thing that might capture your attention and get you to watch the news report. The second story is just deceptive, suggesting that car theft is a worrisome crime when the statistics say that it is "down over the past decade." Wrap the same statistics in different words, and you'll see that two-thirds of a smaller number of stolen cars are returned. Both stories confuse more than they illuminate, raising concerns in order to get our attention.

Empty and misleading news is a product of ferocious competition for your attention, which has grown along with the number of news and information options. A big part of the problem of navigating the information environment is that the traditional rules for what constitutes news have changed to accommodate this competition.

A journalist working for a newspaper in the mid-twentieth century would have approached news coverage from a factual standpoint, ferreting out a series of answers to questions about what happened, when it happened, where it happened, and who was involved. He or she then would have attempted to evaluate the significance of these facts and report them in **inverted pyramid** fashion, so named because the most salient facts would be reported at the top of a story, with smaller, less critical facts noted in subsequent

inverted pyramid: A style of reporting typical of twentieth-century newspaper coverage, in which stories were constructed with the most important factual material in the first paragraph, followed by successively less important facts.

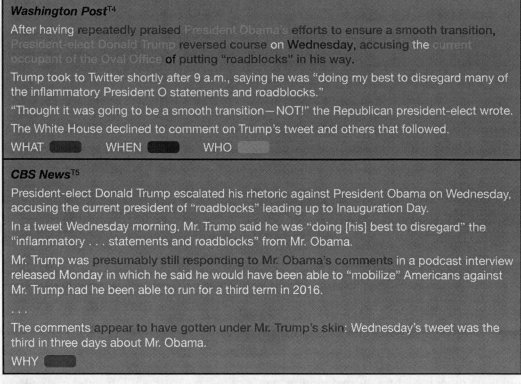

FIGURE 5.2 Just the Facts—or a Lot More?

paragraphs. You could read the first few paragraphs and be fairly well informed, and if you were interested, you could read more and fill in smaller details. After you read the first paragraph, though, you could stop at any time and be fairly certain that you had covered the most critical factual material.

Some (though far from all) newspaper stories are still written in the inverted pyramid style. Figure 5.2 shows an example from the *Washington Post*. Notice how the journalist puts the most important "what," "when," and "who" facts in the first paragraph. Subsequent paragraphs fill in the story with secondary facts.

Television news and some print journalism outlets do it differently. Television news reports tell a story in the classic sense of the word. They have a beginning, middle, and end, and a theme to tie them together. Because television news is thematic, it has to be about something more than the basic what, when, where, and who facts of the inverted pyramid story. Typically, "why" questions cement television news stories together. That's because why questions are analytical in nature; they permit the reporter to probe the subject, offering a hypothesis or a theory about what's happening in the news. In so doing, the reporter's perspective becomes inseparable from the facts of the story.

This makes things tricky for us because we're probably not aware of the fact that we're being shown information that's being filtered through a prism of the reporter's choosing. When you read the CBS News version of the presidential transition story that's transcribed in the bottom of Figure 5.2, you can see how the reporter gives you a way to understand the interplay between Trump and Obama. She places the president-elect's complaints about the transition in the context of an earlier comment by the outgoing president regarding his potential ability to have defeated Trump had he been allowed to run for a third term. The reporter theorizes that Obama's comments "appear to have gotten under Trump's skin." In contrast, the *Post* story simply reported the facts of what had transpired. If you found yourself thinking about a motive for Trump's tweet after reading the *Washington Post* version of the story in the top of the figure, it would be because you had formulated the theory yourself.

Television reporters don't have to reach far from traditional ways of doing business to find the themes for their reports. Journalists have long used a set of standards to determine if a story is **newsworthy**—that is, if it has enough news value to be published or broadcast. Media scholar Doris A. Graber says newsworthy stories typically exhibit a mix of the following five characteristics:

- **Conflict:** Natural or man-made disasters, scandals, or accidents hold the interest of news audiences.
- **Proximity:** People are more likely to be interested in things that happen close to home or that can affect their lives.
- **Timeliness and originality:** News should have happened recently, and it should involve something that doesn't happen every day.
- **Relevance:** We like stories that have some relationship to our lives, that have an impact on our lives, or that we can identify with. This is why a small earthquake in the United States would receive more news coverage than a devastating earthquake in China.
- **Familiarity:** We are drawn to familiar situations and people, which can extend to celebrities and public figures that we "know" through the media.[16]

newsworthy: The conditions under which a story warrants publication or dissemination, based on a set of values applied by newspaper editors and television producers. Newsworthy stories typically have conflict, proximity and relevance to the audience, timeliness, and familiarity.

If you think about it, these characteristics are likely to make news stories appeal to readers and viewers more than they are likely to reflect a story's political, social, or educational value.[17] What makes a story newsworthy, then, does not always stem from normative judgments by journalists and their editors and producers about what information the audience should have. It is not uncommon for traditional news stories to be selected for their audience appeal rather than for their ability to keep us informed about important political and social events. Although it is possible to capture our attention and inform us at the same time, not every informative story contains conflict or feels like it's close to home. So, a story about, say, congressional deliberation over farm subsidy legislation probably wouldn't have the staying power to compete for airtime with a good scandal or a shooting spree.

The stories that do make it on television rely on conflict to support reporter analyses of political figures and events that can be negative or cynical. After all, that's what's going to draw our interest. It's a far more interesting story if President Trump is having a thin-skinned reaction to a perceived slight than if he's just off tweeting about the presidential transition. Public figures acting irresponsibly are always fun to read about, so if the facts can be used to suggest that a politician behaved poorly, television news will naturally gravitate to this perspective.

5.4 Infotainment and Its Implications

If this sounds to you like the news media are in the business of entertaining us, you're right on target. At the same time, the news media are charged with the vital civic responsibility of keeping us informed so that we can make intelligent decisions about what government does. These responsibilities can easily conflict, often to the detriment of our ability to have the information we need to understand political events.

L.O. Define "infotainment," and explain how it complicates the media environment.

Because newspapers, television and cable stations, and many Internet sites are privately owned, they strive to maximize their profits. If they don't make money, they don't last long. They make money by attracting advertisers, who in turn seek large or targeted audiences for their products. Audiences, in turn, are drawn to interesting, entertaining, and dramatic stories.

When public events naturally generate drama—such as during the September 11, 2001, terror attacks—the media's need to attract us coincides with their responsibility to inform us. Often, the two do not overlap, though, leading to a problematic outcome: The ever-present pressure to make a profit encourages the media to emphasize dramatic stories that arguably are not central to our civic lives while downplaying or ignoring dull but important political and policy issues. Federal Reserve Board decisions on interest rates may directly affect the size of your credit card payments and the possibility that you will be able to afford to buy a home, but they're not as interesting as Kim Kardashian.

When the media give us a lot of information about the latter and precious little about the former, we risk becoming entertained spectators without the information we need to make intelligent public choices.

5.4a Distinguishing News from Entertainment

Sometimes it's hard to draw the line between information and entertainment. After all, many people in their late teens and early twenties grew up getting their news from fake news host Jon Stewart on *The Daily Show* and fake pundit Stephen Colbert on *The Colbert Report* on Comedy Central.[18] In a saturated media environment like ours, with so many information options available to us, news organizations have to shout very loud or say very outrageous things to be noticed over all the noise. Sometimes, news content can be so sensational—or sensational programs can look so much like news programs—that it's hard to tell where information stops and entertainment begins. Some media critics use the term **infotainment** to describe this phenomenon, which captures the entertainment value of information and the blending of news and entertainment programs.

Take a program like *Entertainment Tonight*, with its reporters and stories that resemble the evening news. At times, like during the Monica Lewinsky scandal in the Clinton administration, it even covered some of the same stories as the evening news. Does that make *Entertainment Tonight* a news program? Not in the traditional sense, but it is infotainment.

Traditional journalists would probably explain infotainment by saying that it resides in the realm of **soft news**, which shares some of the values of newsworthiness with **hard news**, but without the requirements of proximity, timeliness, or even relevance. Soft news stories are sometimes called feature stories because they're about things that could have happened at any time, without specific connections to the recent events that serve as the basis for hard news, like the type of story you'd find on *Entertainment Tonight*. You could classify the airplane turbulence and car theft stories we read about earlier as soft news (and these ran on evening newscasts). So, it really is hard to make the distinction between news programs that entertain and entertainment programs built around information.

Infotainment can overtake traditional journalism when straight news reporting is infused with large doses of celebrity culture. Political figures once resided exclusively in the world of the serious and celebrities in the world of entertainment, but as the distinction between the two has evaporated, it has become natural for us to regard politicians as celebrities, breaking down distinctions between the sober and the frivolous. When an incumbent president slow jams the news with Jimmy Fallon on the *Tonight Show*,[19] and a Democratic nominee for president gives a deadpan comedic performance on Zach Galifianakis's mock Internet talk show *Between Two Ferns*,[20] political leaders become indistinguishable from other pop-culture figures.

With the popularity of reality television programs, which put real people in carefully planned, unnatural situations in order to capture the appearance of spontaneity,[21] the blending of the serious and the absurd has become a staple of popular culture. On this basis, it may be unsurprising that someone who owes his celebrity status in large part to the fame he acquired as a reality television host could find his footing as a presidential candidate. Many traditional journalists may not have taken Donald Trump seriously, but he was able to make the transition to the political world with remarkable success.

It may not be much of a stretch to say that 2016 was the year when presidential politics fused with reality television. When a pop-culture figure becomes a presidential nominee, the merger of news and entertainment becomes irresistible. When that nominee is skilled in the methods of building and holding an audience, the merger of news and entertainment becomes inevitable.

The Trump campaign did not do many of the things we expect traditional campaigns to do. The candidate rarely held press conferences. He featured Trump properties and products at campaign events, conflating running for office with product placement. His rallies were revival events, where supporters were treated to accounts of the candidate's primary victories or favorable poll numbers rather than policy ideas and where opponents

---

infotainment: News reports and information-based programs that use information to entertain by playing on sensational topics, such as celebrities, violence, and the like.

soft news: Feature stories, stories about celebrities, and other news items that do not derive their news value from proximity, timeliness, or relevance to the reader or viewer.

hard news: Traditional news items that derive their value from recent, relevant events that have some bearing on the lives of readers or viewers.

were denounced with harsh and sometimes ominous words. The Trump campaign was a traveling spectacle, and like any reality TV show, people tuned in to see what would happen next. Ratings climbed by 50 percent at CNN, where it seemed every Trump event was worthy of being broadcast in its entirety, and whose president called 2016 "the best year in the history of cable news."[22]

Trump lived on social media as he lived on cable television, with Twitter being the candidate's medium of choice. For the first time in history, a presidential candidate communicated with his followers at the rate of 140 characters at a time. Sometimes Trump's tweeting got him in trouble. After Hillary Clinton challenged him for his alleged mistreatment of former Miss Universe Alicia Machado, Trump went on a late-night Twitter rant in which he criticized Machado's appearance and insinuated (incorrectly) that she had made a "sex tape."[23] Toward the end of the campaign, his senior staff took away his Twitter account to prevent late-night explosions.[24]

Donald Trump's ubiquitous social media presence allowed him to set the agenda for the 2016 campaign.
Source: txking/Shutterstock.com

Still, his social media use kept him in the spotlight and proved to be an effective way to set the agenda for the campaign. Trump was so outrageous that Clinton had no choice but to react to him, and traditional journalists couldn't avoid covering his tweet storms. This permitted Trump to sidestep the reporters, editors, and producers who are the traditional gatekeepers of information and become a gatekeeper himself. Candidates of the television age, who often had a contentious relationship with the journalists who controlled the news agenda, would have given anything for the means to do what Trump was able to do with his skillful use of social media.

5.4b The Profit Motive

Because entertaining stories provide the media with the most expedient way to build the audience they need to attract advertisers, they can be an irresistible source of news content. Newspapers and television networks make money from advertising in a manner that links advertising dollars to audience size. You may have heard about television ratings, which measure the size of the audience for television programs. Circulation figures (explained in Demystifying Government: How Circulation Figures Work) do the same for newspapers and are the key to profitability.

Television ratings can be a bit complicated to determine. An organization called Nielson Media Research estimates many people are watching television and what they are watching at any given time, using statistical techniques similar to those we discussed in Chapter 3 when we looked at how pollsters could assess public opinion by only talking to a small but carefully selected random sample of people.

DEMYSTIFYING GOVERNMENT

How Circulation Figures Work

It's fairly easy to determine how many people read a daily newspaper because publishers adjust the number of copies they print to meet the demand for their product. This is captured in circulation figures, which will vary by the popularity of the paper and by the size of the metropolitan area (commonly called a market) served by the newspaper.

For instance, in 2008 the circulation of the *Memphis Commercial Appeal* for a weekday edition aver-

aged 145,800. The *Boulder Daily Camera*, serving a smaller community, had an average daily circulation of 29,700.[T6] The circulation of the Memphis paper is more than four times the circulation of the Boulder daily. But that's roughly consistent with the population difference between the two cities. In 2008, metropolitan Memphis had 1.3 million people, more than four times Boulder's 290,000.[T7]

The two most important figures for advertisers—and, therefore, for everyone associated with a television production—are the ratings and share figures. Ratings measure the percentage of households with a television that have the television turned on to a program. The share is the percentage of that group with the television on that is tuned in to a particular program. A program with a large share of a large audience can command higher advertising rates, just like a paper with healthy circulation figures. Of course, programs that cannot maintain a large enough audience to cover their production costs and turn a profit come under careful scrutiny by media ownership. This includes news and information programs.

Ratings and circulation figures are a central part of our discussion of the media because the vast majority of news outlets in the United States are privately owned, for-profit ventures. The United States is unusual in this respect. Newspapers in many Western democracies are run by or maintain strong links to political parties (the way the American press operated in its early days) and receive government subsidies or tax breaks to offset their costs. Governments of all other industrialized democracies, such as Great Britain, Japan, Canada, Italy, France, and Germany, exercise some form of ownership over broadcast media. This translates into all or a portion of operating revenue coming from public money rather than advertising dollars and coincides with government regulations that range from requiring mandatory coverage of Parliament sessions, to free air time for candidates, to requirements that political programming demonstrate balance and facilitate democratic debate.[25]

The closest the United States comes to taxpayer-supported media is a public television and radio network, neither of which is entirely public. Both are supported in part by public money and in part by corporate and private contributions. The Corporation for Public Broadcasting (CPB) is a private nonprofit corporation created by Congress in 1967 to serve the public interest through educational, news, public affairs, and cultural programming that might not be found on commercial broadcasts. It supports National Public Radio (NPR) and the Public Broadcasting Service (PBS), which you may recognize if you spent any time as a kid watching Big Bird on *Sesame Street*.

5.4c Media Regulation and Deregulation

Beyond that, the United States is not entirely without regulation of the media, although what regulation exists pertains mostly to electronic media, pales in comparison to what we find in other democracies, and is less than it was two generations ago.

There are **libel** laws that prohibit all media from printing or broadcasting baseless material that could damage someone's reputation or defame their character. But libel is difficult to prove in court, especially because the Supreme Court has said the standard for proving libel requires demonstrating malice by the press.[26] In other words, to demonstrate libel, you have to prove malevolence on the part of the press, not simply incompetence.

There is also an independent government agency called the **Federal Communications Commission (FCC)**, established by Congress as part of the **Federal Communications Act of 1934**, to make sure the public interest was represented in the emerging radio (and later, television and cable) industry. The point of regulating the airwaves was to use government authority to counterbalance the profit motive and to make sure that private broadcast companies serve the public interest in the way they operate. The FCC has the authority to license radio and television stations, giving it leverage over broadcast outlets to enforce its public interest requirements.

The most important of these regulations is Section 315 of the Federal Communications Act, known as the **equal time provision**. In order to make sure a full range of political views would receive just treatment, the equal time provision directed broadcast outlets to make an equal amount of commercial time available to all candidates running for elected office.

In 1949, the FCC established the **fairness doctrine** to make sure that broadcasters devoted airtime to the discussion of controversial public issues, obligating them to present opposing views. Because anyone can start a magazine or newspaper without govern-

libel: The legal restriction against the malicious publication of material that knowingly damages an individual's reputation.

Federal Communications Commission (FCC): The federal agency responsible for regulating broadcast communications, including radio, television, wire, satellite, and cable transmissions. The FCC is directed by five commissioners who are appointed by the president and confirmed by the Senate for five-year terms.

Federal Communications Act of 1934: The act of Congress that established the Federal Communications Commission (FCC) and the equal time provision.

equal time provision: The federal requirement that broadcast outlets selling commercial time to a political candidate must make equal time available to other candidates running for office.

fairness doctrine: The FCC requirement, no longer in force, that electronic media provide a balanced forum for controversial public discourse.

ment approval, the government posed no obstacles to those who wanted to establish a print forum for their ideas (the fact that not everyone has the resources to publish a magazine or newspaper is another matter). However, since you need government licensing to run a radio or television station, the fairness doctrine was designed to ensure a balanced and vigorous public debate among the relatively few electronic media outlets. Regardless of this rationale, broadcasters opposed the fairness doctrine as a burdensome obligation not required of their print brethren, and in 1987, a sympathetic FCC agreed and revoked the measure.

By 1987, a trend toward media deregulation that had started in the late 1970s was in full swing. In addition to the fairness doctrine, a number of other FCC provisions were eliminated or relaxed, permitting broadcasters greater leeway to operate without government input. These include:

- Eliminating guidelines limiting broadcasters to eighteen minutes of commercials per hour.

- Eliminating a rule requiring broadcasters to devote a fixed percentage of time for local, public affairs, and non-entertainment programming.

- Lengthening of the term of broadcast licenses to five years for television and seven years for radio, reducing the frequency of government review.

- Increasing the number of television and radio stations that could be owned by a single broadcast organization.[27]

In addition, the deregulation trend led to the passage of the **Telecommunications Act of 1996**, the first major revision of telecommunication law since the FCC was founded. The purpose of the legislation was to foster competition in the emerging electronic marketplace of cable, satellite, and Internet communications by removing government barriers to ownership.

Overall, deregulation provides owners of electronic media with greater flexibility to serve the public interest as they see fit, without input or restrictions from government—and that returns us to the dilemma posed by privately operated media in a democracy. On one hand, media organizations seeking profitability behave just like corporations that manufacture cars and refrigerators. If entertainment is what brings in the audience, gets high ratings, and enables media corporations to charge top dollar for advertising, self-interest and an obligation to stockholders mandates that media owners bring on the infotainment. On the other hand, because the news media carry a civic responsibility, they are qualitatively different from manufacturers of cars and refrigerators.

After all, newspapers (and, over time, all news media) are the only private institutions afforded constitutional protection. It's there in the First Amendment, where it says "Congress shall make no law . . . abridging the freedom of speech, or of the press."

This protection is warranted because it's expected that privately owned media would serve the public good by providing a platform for the advancement of public discussion. The Code of Ethics of the U.S. Society of Professional Journalists puts it this way: "The primary purpose of gathering and distributing news and opinion is to serve the general welfare by informing the people and enabling them to make judgments on the issues of the time."[28] To do that responsibly can mean presenting exactly the kind of metered, sober (read: boring) material that can turn away audiences. This is the reason broadcasters resisted the fairness doctrine for so many years. In the wake of government deregulation of the industry, though, media organizations have less incentive to supply the type of news that provides the information we need to make intelligent political judgments.

Telecommunications Act of 1996: Legislation that overhauled the Federal Communications Act of 1934 by deregulating a range of communications technologies in an effort to promote competition in the development and provision of telecommunications services. If your local telephone company now offers long-distance service, or if your cable television provider also offers high-speed Internet access, it's because the opportunity for them to do so was made possible by this law.

5.5 More Choices, Fewer Options?

Some say the solution to this dilemma rests with competition. They point to the proliferation of media options that the marketplace has given us in your lifetime. If a wide array of ideas is available to us through cable television or the Internet, perhaps it matters less if any single outlet provides a detailed or balanced treatment of political and social issues.

L.O. Assess the risks posed by the concentration of media power.

We can find pretty much anything if we just look for it. In part, this approach guided the deregulation movement that crystallized with the Telecommunications Act of 1996.

5.5a Lots of Channels

There's no question the media are more diversified than they were a generation ago, with the Internet being the obvious but not the only example. When you were born, the system that would grow into the Internet we use today was an obscure network used mainly by scientists doing research. By the start of 2001, an estimated 361,000 people were online worldwide. And by mid-2016, that figure had mushroomed to 3,675,824,813—to the point where half the globe is now connected, including almost nine out of ten people in North America.[29] See Figure 5.3 for a detailed breakout of worldwide usage.

Maybe you've heard your parents or grandparents tell stories about how they had to actually walk over to the television and turn a dial to move from channel to channel, the sum total of which probably numbered anywhere from three to possibly eight, if they were lucky. Today, there are that many programming choices from HBO alone.[30] According to the Internet and Television Association, there are over 900 general and premium channels available from cable and satellite television providers.[31] These providers routinely include a search engine so you can sort through everything available to you.

This includes a lot of familiar channels, such as CNN, MTV, and ESPN, that are available through most services, as well as more obscure offerings such as the California Channel, the American Heroes Channel, and the Pursuit Channel.[32] The proliferation of television channels permits specialized programming, or **"narrowcasting,"** that appeals to small but interested audiences.

narrowcasting: Programming oriented to a small segment of viewers, like that found on cable television stations. It contrasts with broadcasting, like that found on traditional television networks, which seeks to reach a larger audience with programming that has wide appeal.

With the availability of high-speed Internet, cable providers are beginning to feel pressure from streaming video services such as Netflix, Amazon Prime, and Hulu. These services offer users the ability to stream a wide variety of network and cable content, including original content not available anywhere else, giving consumers more flexibility and choice and making media use even more personalized. Smart TVs offer apps linking directly to these services, or you can bypass television completely and stream content on a computer or personal device, offering unprecedented diversity in the way we watch video. Media consumption, which was once a centralized experience with content determined by a few networks, is now a highly personalized endeavor.

The media explosion is not limited to television or the Internet, either. Radio experienced something of a rebirth in the 1990s with the growth of talk radio programs, and in the early years of this century with the advent of satellite technology that made national radio broadcasts possible. Once the exclusive province of music, radio has been redefined as a platform for talk programs that feature celebrity hosts and listener call-ins. In 2016, there were 6,613 FM stations and 4,728 AM stations in the United States.[33] By one recent estimate, about 10 percent included talk programs on their schedules.[34]

Although Rush Limbaugh may be the most recognized talk radio host, the airwaves are filled with talkers who incite their listeners to call in and share their political perspectives—sometimes by making outrageous and incendiary political claims that stir the passions of sympathetic listeners. Talk radio programs offering a conservative per-

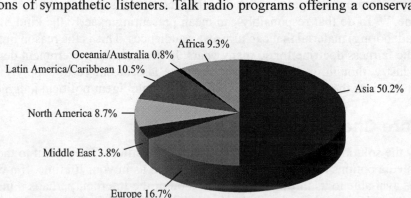

Africa 9.3%

Oceania/Australia 0.8%

Latin America/Caribbean 10.5%

Asia 50.2%

North America 8.7%

Middle East 3.8%

Europe 16.7%

FIGURE 5.3 Worldwide Internet Usage, 2016[T8]

spective, like Limbaugh's, have been the most durable. Well-known liberal figures like comedian Al Franken (now a senator from Minnesota) and Jesse Jackson have tried their hand as talk radio hosts, but most have failed to produce high ratings.

Even newspapers, which died off in large numbers due to their inability to compete with network evening news broadcasts in the 1970s and 1980s, have had something of a resurgence. Readership began declining fifty years ago as people preferred to come home to news from network television anchors Walter Cronkite and David Brinkley, the forerunners of Lester Holt, Scott Pelley, and David Muir. However, a countertrend has emerged in the past twenty years, with the growth of morning newspapers and Sunday editions. When you take everything into account, the total number of newspapers in the United States is essentially what it was in the 1960s.

As newspapers have held their own and adjusted to changing patterns of news usage, they also have dramatically changed their look and approach to reporting. Soft news, once the domain of feature sections in the "back" of the paper, appears more prominently, and in a trend that emulates television news reporting, thematic coverage is creeping into stories that once would have been presented in the inverted pyramid fashion. Technology that enables the printing of color pictures has brightened up the look of newspapers. Even the staid *New York Times* and the stuffy *Wall Street Journal*, the last of the traditional black-and-white newspapers, succumbed to the demand for color images that permit newspapers to capture the up-tempo appearance of video news.

USA Today is perhaps the most successful example of using television news techniques to market a newspaper. Colorful and fast-paced like a television news program, it features headline-length stories; pages of "factoids" from every state, designed to attract local readers; prominently placed pictures of celebrities; a statistics-laden sports section; feature-rich health, living, and technology sections; and a bright, detailed weather map. Even the curbside box that it's sold from has something in common with vintage television. Take a look next time you pass one.

Unlike those traditional, boxy newspaper vending machines, *USA Today*—the newspaper that tries to be TV news on the printed page—is sold from a slick receptacle that evokes a traditional television set.[T9]

5.5b Very Few Owners

Nonetheless, there is an ironic flip side to this proliferation of media resources. At a time when more information outlets are available than ever before, the free market fostered by deregulation has concentrated media ownership in very few hands. Passage of the Telecommunications Act of 1996 accelerated a process of media mergers and acquisitions that had begun in the 1980s during the Reagan administration, some of the highlights of which are:

- Capital Cities Corporation purchases the ABC television network.
- Loews Corporation purchases the CBS television network.
- General Electric purchases the NBC television network and its parent company, RCA.
- Australian media magnate Rupert Murdoch's News Corporation purchases Metromedia Television and forms the Fox Television Network.
- Time, Inc. buys Warner Communications in a $14.1 billion deal to create Time Warner.
- Viacom purchases Paramount Communications and Blockbuster Video.
- Gannett, America's largest newspaper chain, purchases Multimedia, Inc., to increase its newspaper, television, and radio holdings.
- Disney buys Capital Cities, which had previously bought ABC, for $19 billion.
- CBS television gets a new corporate parent as Westinghouse Corporation buys it for $5.4 billion.
- Time Warner buys Turner Communications[35] (and is itself later bought by America Online and for a brief time is known as AOL Time Warner).

FIGURE 5.4 The Mouse That Roars: What Disney Owns

Television, Radio, and Publishing	ABC Television Group/ABC Television Network/ABC Entertainment Group/ABC News/ABC Family/ABC Studios/A&E Television Networks (50%)/The Biography Channel/History/Hungama/Lifetime Entertainment Services (50%)/SOAPnet/ABC-Owned Television Stations Group (eight television stations)/ESPN/Disney Channels Worldwide/thirty radio stations/ESPN Radio/Hyperion Books/Disney Publishing Worldwide/ESPN Books
Parks and Resorts	Disneyland Resort/Walt Disney World Resort/Tokyo Disney Resort/Disneyland Paris/Hong Kong Disneyland/Shanghai Disney Resort/Disney Cruise Line/Adventures by Disney/Disney Vacation Club/Walt Disney Imagineering
Film and Music	Walt Disney Studios Motion Pictures/Walt Disney Studios Home Entertainment/Marvel Studios/Touchstone Pictures/LucasFilm/Disneynature/Walt Disney Animation Studios/Pixar Animation Studios/DisneyToon Studios/Disney Theatrical Group/Hollywood Records/Walt Disney Records
Disney Consumer Products	Disney Store/Disney Apparel/Disney Accessories and Footwear/Disney Fashion and Home/Disney Food/Disney Health and Beauty/Disney Stationary/Disney Toys
Other	Baby Einstein Company/Club Penguin/Disney Interactive Media/El Capitan Theatre/The Muppets Studio/Playdom/Rocket Pack/UTV Software Communications

Source: Columbia Journalism Review, http://www.cjr.org/resources/?c=disney

Remember, this was all before the Telecommunications Act was signed into law and deregulated the industry.

The consequence of this centralization is the emergence of what political scientist Dean Alger calls "megamedia," a few giant corporations that dominate media ownership and control the means of mass communication: conglomerates like Disney, Time Warner, General Electric, News Corporation, and Microsoft. Let's take a look at one of those conglomerates—Disney—in Figure 5.4 to get a sense of its size, scope, and reach.

What of this centralized ownership? Even though we have an enormous number of media options, the fact that very few corporations control so many of those choices may work to undermine our enlightened understanding of politics if, instead of presenting many perspectives, the media are presenting one perspective through many outlets. Alger writes:

> If a few megamedia corporations control most of the major print, broadcast, cable, and other media that most of the public relies on as their main sources of information, opinion, and creative expression, then this fundamental pillar of democracy is likely to be seriously threatened. Indeed, the Florida Supreme Court concluded:
>
>> The right of the people to know all sides of a controversy and from such information to make an enlightened choice is being jeopardized by the growing concentration of ownership of the mass media into fewer and fewer hands, resulting in a form of private censorship (*Miami Herald v. Tornillo*).[36]

Notwithstanding Alger's warning, media deregulation efforts continued into the Bush administration, with a controversial ruling in 2003 by the Federal Communications Commission that permitted even greater concentration of media ownership by further relaxing restrictions on the number of media outlets that a single corporation could own in any media market. The ruling met with stiff public opposition, leading Congress to weaken but not entirely roll back the FCC ruling. Donald Trump has signaled his sympathy for further deregulation efforts in his administration.

When we talked about the media's role in **agenda setting** in Chapter 4, we said that we tend to think about things that are covered prominently in the news. If an issue is not covered, then unless we or our friends are directly involved in the issue, there is no easy way to form an opinion on it, much less an informed opinion. In one instance that happened when General Electric (GE) was the parent company of NBC, an expert on consumer boycotts was invited to appear on the *Today* show, NBC's morning news and

agenda setting: The tendency for topics given great weight by the media to be given equally great weight by those who use the media, such that the people and events considered important by those who determine media coverage will become the people and events that the public considers important.

L.O. Explain agenda setting.

entertainment program, and was asked to talk about "the biggest boycott going on right now." When he suggested a boycott of GE's production of nuclear weapons, he was told by a program producer, "We can't do that one."[37]

It would seem this is a case where Alger's concern for enlightened choice is undermined by corporate pressures. Then again, had it happened today, it might be possible to find out about the boycott somewhere else, especially given the proliferation of information on the Internet.

5.6 The Politics of Entertainment I: Elections

Have you ever had a love-hate relationship with someone? You know, a situation where you always seem to be arguing with them, but you can't bear the thought of life without them? That may be the best way to think about how reporters and political figures relate to each other. Their relationship is adversarial, inasmuch as it is defined by conflict. However, it is also symbiotic, in that it is a relationship of mutual benefit and dependence. The consequence of this relationship is fierce competition for command of the news agenda, where candidates and reporters vie to control each other in a dance that shapes the news in a way that—like deregulation and centralized media ownership—may leave the viewer and reader without the most useful information for making an informed political choice.

L.O. Discuss the conflict between politicians and journalists that emerged in the mass media era over control of news messages.

Reporters and politicians are professionally joined at the hip. Reporters depend on politicians, especially important ones, to be sources for their stories. Politicians need coverage to keep their names in front of the public. This is what's typically called **free media** because all major candidates know they can count on the publicity that comes from being newsworthy without having to use any campaign money to get it.

Of course, candidates don't just want free coverage—they want favorable free coverage that will advance their political interests. This conflicts with reporters' professional autonomy in determining what the content of stories should be. That's the source of the struggle.

The other portion of a candidate's media exposure comes from, not surprisingly, **paid media**. These are the advertisements that candidates purchase on television, radio, and the Internet to promote their campaign—or to disparage their opponents. Paid media gives campaigns far more control over their message, as they can craft their own ads, but it doesn't give them the legitimacy that comes with messages communicated by journalists, so candidates need to engage journalists for coverage no matter how much money they have available to spend on buying commercials. Instead of struggling for message control, the major strategic challenges facing candidates when it comes to paid media are finding an effective message and raising the money to pay for ads. Television ads are expensive—they can be extremely expensive in large media markets—and are the biggest reason why the cost of running for office has become so high.

free media: The news coverage that major candidates for high office can expect to receive on a regular basis. Although free, candidates cannot control the content of this coverage or guarantee that it will be favorable.

paid media: Radio and television ads paid for and produced by political campaigns.

In 2016, Donald Trump leveraged his pop-culture celebrity status and skillful use of social media to generate unprecedented amounts of free media. Hillary Clinton spent three times as much as Trump on paid media. But Trump was so entertaining that he was able to command media attention by tweeting outrageous statements and making over-the-top pronouncements at his rallies. By one estimate, the free advertising he received was valued at $5 billion.[38]

5.6a The Candidate's Perspective

Candidates and reporters each have resources at their disposal to try to get the upper hand in coverage. Good campaigns are disciplined. They develop a message they want to communicate to the public and repeat that message constantly so that people learn it. Candidates who stay "on message" are generally able to set the agenda for the election because they make it difficult for reporters to deviate from what they are being told by campaign officials. By doing so, however, candidates communicate information about themselves that is more rhetorical than substantive—empty messages that serve the candidate's interests but leave voters without a sound basis for making an electoral choice.

Donald Trump's campaign message was simple and had great appeal to his followers, who found resonance in his promise to "make America great again" (a slogan first used by Ronald Reagan in his campaign for the presidency).[39] He repeated it constantly in his public statements and marketed it on hats that became an iconic symbol of his candidacy, garnering the attention of his opponents. In response to Trump's plans to skip one of the Republican primary debates, Texas Senator Ted Cruz manufactured hats that said, "Make Trump Debate Again."[40] Former president Bill Clinton called the slogan a racist dog whistle.[41] But the more other candidates and their surrogates drew attention to the slogan, the more it reinforced Trump's message.

In 2008, then-Senator Barack Obama wanted voters to perceive him as someone who could usher in a new direction for the country at a time when many people were tired of the Bush years. He accomplished this in part by marketing himself as the candidate of "hope" and "change"—admittedly vague terms that can mean a wide range of things, depending on what one might hope for or what one is looking to change. In this regard, Obama's message was more rhetorical than substantive, more about image-building than promoting a specific agenda. Obama's advisors calculated that if they could repeatedly associate the candidate with the words "hope" and "change," reporters would begin to use those phrases to characterize the Obama effort. The strategy worked, owing in large part to the candidate's discipline with the message, enabling Obama to define the contest on his terms.

Candidates have a few tools at their disposal to assist them with "message control." They can get the attention of reporters by staging **media events**—activities that appear to be news but that in fact are produced by the campaign to get reporters to give them free coverage of their message. Media events work if they are convenient for journalists to cover, if they offer good pictures for television, and—in the era of infotainment—if they are interesting or fun to watch.

Because the Trump campaign was so controversial, and because he could make an incendiary comment at any time, his campaign rallies became media events and were covered extensively on cable news networks. When Barack Obama ran for president, he staged a week-long tour of the Middle East and Europe to build his stature as an international figure and communicate that although he had only served a brief time in the Senate, he was ready to assume a global leadership position. During a stop in Berlin, his campaign advisors sought permission to allow him to speak at the Brandenburg Gate, a symbol of Germany's division and reunification where Presidents Reagan and Kennedy once spoke. Obama's advisors recognized the powerful symbolic imagery that would be communicated by such an event—as did the German leadership, which was divided over whether permitting the candidate to speak there would amount to taking sides in the American presidential campaign. Because of the controversy, Obama ultimately spoke in a different location, but the international journey was successful as a media event because it was the source of ongoing positive press for the candidate.[42]

Candidates know that if they give the media a chance to get a picture of them in an appealing setting, editors and producers will find the images irresistible. So, campaigns look for **photo opportunities**, where they can project an image of the candidate consistent with the message they want to communicate. In 1980, Ronald Reagan wanted to associate himself with the American values we discussed in Chapter 4, so he staged a photo opportunity in front of the Statue of Liberty. Vice President Al Gore gave his wife a long, lingering kiss before making his acceptance speech at the 2000 Democratic National Convention—a photo opportunity designed to communicate the message that Gore was more of a family man than Bill Clinton. Four years later, Senator John Kerry surrounded himself with Vietnam veterans and greeted his convention supporters by saying he was "reporting for duty," in an attempt to communicate that he would be strong on national defense issues. In each case, the resulting pictures played widely in the press and favorably for the candidate. Had Obama's Brandenburg Gate speech occurred, it would have provided a photo opportunity communicating Obama's claim to the mantle of international leadership associated with Kennedy and Reagan.

Of course, not all campaign experiences go the candidate's way. Following the Brexit referendum in which the United Kingdom voted to leave the European Union, Donald

media events: Activities staged by campaigns or political officials that have enough news value to draw press attention to a message the politician wants to communicate.

photo opportunities: Staged appearances by politicians in visually appealing settings designed to produce images that will be widely disseminated in the press.

Ronald Reagan was a master of the photo opportunity. By posing in front of the Statue of Liberty, as he did in this 1980 picture, he associated himself with a set of patriotic values designed to convince voters to see him in a positive light. Al Gore wanted to contrast his marital loyalty with incumbent president Bill Clinton by giving his wife an exaggerated kiss before accepting his party's presidential nomination.[T10]

Trump appeared in Scotland at one of his resorts and inexplicably declared the vote a "great thing"—even though Scotland had voted to remain—to the scorn and derision of the local population.[43] In 2012, Mitt Romney took a tour of Europe and the Middle East in an attempt to emulate the positive press generated by Obama's international travels four years earlier. However, Romney couldn't seem to get out of his own way on the trip, insulting the British by questioning how effectively they had prepared for the Olympics and managing to anger both Israelis and Palestinians with remarks about Jewish culture and the Palestinian economy that each group found insensitive.

When campaigns find themselves facing negative coverage, they often try to **spin** events to their liking, characterizing things in the best possible fashion in the hope that the press will report events the way the campaign wants them reported. (The term *spin doctor* is generally applied to political aides who work on reporters to accept their version of events.) In Romney's case, his spokesperson insisted that the candidate's remarks had been "grossly mischaracterized" and weren't nearly as bad as some had been suggesting.[44] In 1992, Bill Clinton finished in second place in the important New Hampshire primary, but he didn't want reporters saying that he had lost. Since opinion polls taken before the vote indicated that it was possible for him to have finished as low as third place, he told supporters at a rally after the votes were counted that he was the "comeback kid"—a characterization that implied he had won. The press picked it up, and Clinton was on his way to the Democratic Party nomination. He was able to successfully spin a loss into a victory.

Campaigns need to be vigilant about the way they employ these techniques. With so many media outlets competing for information and with some operating around the clock, the shelf life for information is very short. The time between when a candidate does something and when it ends up in the news, or the **news cycle**, is so short as to be in some cases instantaneous (for example, you can turn CNN on any time, and social media is a nonstop phenomenon). The continuous, never-ending news cycle means campaigns have to be on guard all the time, always staying on message, always thinking about ways to get their message in the news. It can easily strain their relationship with reporters, especially because reporters have resources of their own to battle the campaign's "message control," including technological advantages that fuel the news cycle.

Competition among media is part of what accelerates the news cycle. There are so many news outlets that the demand for original information is ferocious; the presence of twenty-four-hour news services means the demand for information never ends. This demand could not be satisfied without the appropriate technology. Satellites that make it possible to beam information around the world in real time; videotape that can be easily recorded and viewed immediately; cell phones that permit instantaneous communication from remote locations—these are at the technological heart of today's mass media. Consider that during the Vietnam War, battlefield footage was recorded on film, which had to be shipped by airplane to New York for development before it could be edited and aired—a process that took days. Twenty-five years later, when allied forces began their

spin: A technique used by political figures to characterize events in a favorable way in order to get the media to report them in a favorable way—regardless of what the facts of a story may indicate.

news cycle: The time between when an event happens and when it gets press coverage. With twenty-four-hour news services setting the pace, the demand for new information is enormous and immediate, greatly accelerating the news cycle.

attack on Iraq in the Persian Gulf War, people around the world could watch the events on CNN as they were happening.

While it's probably true that television reporters can't resist a great photo opportunity, that doesn't mean that they will spin the story the way the campaign wants it. No one likes to feel controlled, but that's exactly the way reporters feel in the wake of campaign news management techniques. Their defense is that they get to decide what goes into the story.

5.6b The Reporter's Perspective

To most journalists, simply relating a candidate's message makes them feel like a mouthpiece for the campaign. Giving in to that feels like an abandonment of their responsibilities. To battle back, reporters can choose a **frame** or context for their stories that sidesteps the message the campaign is trying to present. Frames give meaning to factual information by putting it in a perspective that the reporter chooses. Three popular reporter frames are the strategy a campaign is using, the campaign's prospects for winning and losing, and the candidate's character flaws. Each of these permits the reporter to cover the campaign on his or her own terms.

One way some reporters avoid feeling controlled is by reporting on how the campaign is trying to control the media message, rather than discussing the message. In other words, reporters will focus on the candidate's strategy for controlling the message rather than on the message itself, talking about how the campaign engages in spin or crafts media events in order to manipulate reporters and, by extension, everyone. Arguably, this information is not very useful to a voter trying to decide among the candidates.

Another favorite approach of election reporters is to cover the contest for president—who's up and who's down—rather than the substance of what the candidates are saying. This emphasis on the **horserace** aspect of the campaign protects reporters from the candidate's agenda-control efforts by explaining what the candidate is saying and doing in terms of the candidate's electoral prospects. Although voters learn about likely winners and losers, horserace coverage (like stories about how candidates manipulate reporters) offers little information on how best to vote (unless you simply want to vote with the likely winner).

The logic of horserace coverage says that any action of a candidate who is trailing in public opinion polls should be reported as an effort to climb back into the race, and any action of a candidate who is leading in opinion polls should be reported as an effort to extend that lead or protect against backsliding (regardless of whatever nonstrategic explanations there may be for the candidate's behavior). In either case, the actual content of what the candidate does or says is of secondary importance, permitting the journalist control of the message, but on terms that might not benefit the public.

Sometimes, events occurring outside the campaign become the subject of horserace scrutiny. For instance, days before the 2012 election, Hurricane Sandy struck the mid-Atlantic coast, devastating large portions of New York City and the New York metropolitan area, including large stretches of the New Jersey shore. Although damage from the storm was a human tragedy and posed a policy emergency, the timing of the event inevitably infused it with horserace considerations as well. Political reporters wondered aloud if voters would rally around the president during the emergency, and if a clean response by the administration would help improve Obama's re-election prospects. These musings were magnified when Republican New Jersey Governor Chris Christie effusively praised the Democratic president for working with him to bring quick relief to portions of his state hit hardest by the storm, offering a rare moment of bipartisanship for a president who had campaigned four years earlier on the desire to bring Republicans and Democrats together.

Finally, reporters can make the character of the candidate the centerpiece of their coverage. Before the investigative reporting of the Watergate period turned into aggressive reporting, the private lives and actions of public figures were off limits to reporters. Today they play a central role in political coverage. Sometimes, candidates give reporters good reasons to focus on their character. When a tape surfaced of Donald Trump having what the *Washington Post* called an "extremely lewd conversation" about his treatment of women that described what amounted to sexual assault, it dominated coverage of the

frame: The frame of reference for a news story, or the context around which the facts of a story are organized. If a news story is thematic, like most television news stories, the frame determines what the specific theme of the story will be.

horserace: That element of a political campaign that deals with winning and losing, whether a candidate is leading or trailing an opponent, and what the candidate may be doing to improve or solidify his or her electoral prospects.

2016 election, and the Trump campaign struggled for a way to respond as his support in public opinion polls cratered.[45]

When a story broke several days before the 2000 presidential election that George W. Bush had many years earlier been arrested for driving while impaired, it ran on every media outlet nationwide. During the 1992 campaign, Bill Clinton faced a barrage of stories about his character, including whether he had avoided the draft, smoked pot, and engaged in extramarital affairs.

Character can also be an overriding theme in news coverage that's ostensibly about issues and events. Late in the 2012 campaign, anonymous release of a video of Mitt Romney decrying 47 percent of Americans as victims who depend on government to take care of them generated unrelenting coverage of whether the remarks, recorded without the candidate's knowledge at a function with wealthy contributors, accurately portrayed Romney as cold, heartless, and aloof. Similarly, during the financial meltdown that immediately preceded the 2008 election, mainstream media storylines focused on Senator Obama's calm demeanor as he addressed the problem, contrasting it with McCain's supposedly unpredictable temperament. This framework served to communicate the idea that Obama was "presidential" and reinforce the Obama strategy of characterizing McCain as erratic.

Sometimes, when a character story hits the airwaves, reporters pile on it and cover it at the expense of everything else. When this happens, it's as if the candidate is under attack by the press for something he or she allegedly did, and aggressive reporting becomes **attack journalism**, where reporters latch on to the hint of a candidate indiscretion and, in the words of political scientist Larry Sabato, "go after a wounded politician like sharks in a feeding frenzy."[46] Sometimes, media critics refer to this as "gotcha!" journalism because the point of coverage appears to be catching a politician in a compromising situation, and reporters can seem to be playing a vengeful role.

attack journalism: A form of aggressive coverage in which reporters latch onto an allegation of misdoing by a candidate or public official and engage in a "feeding frenzy" in which they cover it intensely and to the exclusion of other news.

Apart from providing reporters with a way to maintain control of the news agenda, strategy, horserace, and character stories have the advantage of being entertaining. Strategy stories bring us inside the campaign and can make us feel like we're privy to information we wouldn't normally have. Horserace stories have the appeal of a high-stakes race or playoff game, complete with the dramatic tension that winning and losing provides. Character stories are of innate interest in much the same way that many people enjoy reading gossip about the personal lives of celebrities. Even feeding frenzies can have an appeal not unlike looking at an accident on the side of the road. So, reporters are certainly not doing a disservice to media owners by framing campaigns in a way that's inherently interesting.

They may be doing a disservice to the audience, though, when the information is used more to entertain than inform. Even in some of their coverage, reporters acknowledge that in their attempt to wrestle control of the news agenda from the candidate, they may be getting in the way of what the audience needs.

Political scientist Tom Patterson says there is a difference between the things that interest reporters and the things that interest ordinary people, claiming the public wants to know about issue-oriented material, whereas journalists are more focused on matters of strategy, horserace, and character. He claims reporters simply have a different framework for processing information about the election than the public does, built around the attitude that the election is a game. Their perspective is reflected in the stories they report.[47]

Patterson claims this difference leaves us lacking in information that we need to make intelligent political choices. In particular, the emphasis journalists place on strategy, horserace, and character frames means:

- *More negative news.* By Patterson's count, negative news stories more than doubled between 1960 and 1992.[48] Negative framing can weaken the bonds between the public and politicians by undermining our confidence in those who run for office.

- *More cynical perspectives on politics.* In the course of their struggle with candidates for control of the news agenda, reporters communicate the message that candidates will do anything to win and that everything they do is designed to help them win. This cynical perspective can leave us feeling like candidates are empty shells who make hollow, self-serving promises.[49]

- *Less issue coverage.* As reporters emphasize the horserace, stories about issues and policies are squeezed out. This leaves us with less information about where the candidates stand on issues, should we want to use this information to decide how to vote. By one count, issue stories on network evening news programs fell 26 percent between 1996 and 2000, while horserace stories increased by an almost identical percentage.[50] By another, as the number of horserace stories on the front page of the *New York Times* doubled between 1960 and 1992, the number of policy stories fell from over 50 percent to only 20 percent.[51]

5.7 The Politics of Entertainment II: Governing

The dynamics of election coverage also apply to coverage of elected officials, with the important exception that once in office, politicians have more resources at their disposal to try to manage the news message. They still engage in media events, hold photo opportunities, and spin the news to their advantage whenever possible. Once in office, though, they are even more newsworthy than when they were running for office. This is particularly true for the president. It means the struggle with the press can be heightened as well.

5.7a The President

Reporters approach stories about the president as if they were covering a campaign, placing presidential actions in the context of strategy, horserace, and character. In a political reporter's characterization of governing, presidents look to score political points by racking up victories over Congress as they work for approval of their legislative program. Discussion of the merits of the president's proposals is often supplanted by discussion of the political necessity of getting a legislative "win." Strategy stories address the tactics used by the White House to engineer legislative victories. As in a campaign, a feeding frenzy can happen at any time.[52] All in all, this type of news can be quite entertaining while sending the message that the political values of a campaign (that is, winning at all costs) are what serving in public office is all about. See Demystifying Government: The Health-Care Horserace.

Presidential efforts at image and message control date back over a century. Teddy Roosevelt, serving at the turn of the twentieth century, predates the mass media by a generation, but he could be viewed as a prototype for his media-savvy successors. Roosevelt actively cultivated reporters to advance his political purposes. As photography was central to selling newspapers during the period of yellow journalism that coincided with his administration, Roosevelt shrewdly cast an image of a strong and engaged president in order to sell an activist agenda to an American public that would never meet him personally or hear his voice.

Thirty years later, Franklin D. Roosevelt would have radio at his disposal for crafting a media image and engaging in a message control campaign that knew no equal in its time. He was not the first president to have radio as a tool, but FDR was the first to realize its political potential. In a world where most Americans had never heard a president's voice, Roosevelt realized that he could use radio to achieve a level of familiarity his predecessors never had, deliberately crafting an image of himself that to millions would be inseparable from the office he held (and, not coincidentally, that he would be elected to four times). He mastered the medium the way today's presidents try to conquer television, through strong, reassuring performances during times of peril—the Great Depression and World War II. A CBS radio bureau chief dubbed these talks **"fireside chats"** for their intimate, personal nature, and the name stuck.[53]

fireside chats: The term given to Franklin Roosevelt's radio addresses to the American public, which demonstrated Roosevelt's ability to master the medium and build a sense of rapport with ordinary Americans.

Before Franklin D. Roosevelt, presidential speeches were long, impersonal orations. Roosevelt's fireside chats were brief and delivered directly to the American people as though the president was talking personally to everyone in the radio audience (see Figure 5.5). He addressed listeners as "my friends," and spoke in a familiar manner that

The Health-Care Horserace

President Obama's proposed overhaul of the American health-care establishment entailed a tremendous political effort. If you followed press coverage of the initiative, you might have thought he was running for president all over again.

Winning and losing was a prominent theme running through mainstream coverage of the health-care events of 2009 and early 2010. The terms for success were clear: Congressional approval of anything resembling the president's package would constitute a "win" for the White House; compromise resulting in something less than the president wanted would register as a loss. Complete failure to win legislative approval for health-care reform would go down as a major setback, a sign of the president's weakness akin to losing an election, and a big enough defeat to cripple the president's future legislative plans.

Notwithstanding the fact that separation of powers and checks and balances necessitate compromise if anything is going to get done in Washington, framing the development of health-care policy as a political horserace sidesteps questions about the merits of the policy under consideration. After all, whether or not the president gets Congress to reform the health-care system doesn't address empirical questions about what's in the legislation or normative questions like whether or not the legislation is beneficial. It simply addresses whether the president is a political winner or loser.

Every step of the way, news audiences were treated to the strategic logic of the Obama health-care team's effort to "sell" its health-care plan. For instance, when the president decided to give a high-profile speech on health care to a joint session of Congress in the fall of 2009, it was widely portrayed as a dramatic attempt to use the trappings of office to generate momentum for reform.[T11]

Media events like town-hall-style meetings with citizens, which President Obama periodically held at venues around the country, were covered, not for their informational content, but as strategic attempts to put pressure on congressional representatives by building public support for the Obama plan.

Throughout the summer and fall, mainstream reporters asked variations of the basic horserace question: Will Obama "win" by getting Congress to pass a bill? As in presidential campaigns, polling on the president's job approval and on public support for elements of health-care reform provided real-time background for the horserace frame. When anti-reform protesters emerged in full force during the summer months, storming meetings held by members of Congress to ask angry questions about reform efforts, reporters wanted to know if the buzz they generated in the press would permanently damage the president's initiatives. When legislation seemed to bog down in the Senate, reporters speculated about whether Obama's dogged determination to win bipartisan support from a reluctant Republican Party was slowing his momentum. As congressional attention turned to a controversial proposal for a public health-care option that would be operated by the government, horserace-oriented reporters asked aloud whether Obama would reject the proposal—not because he thought it was a bad idea, but because doing so could win him the votes of a reluctant set of Democratic senators.

Coverage like this can be exciting, but it treats important policy considerations as though they were pawns in a political game, and governing as if it were running for office. And that makes it difficult to get the information we need to reach a judgment about the desirability of the policy being considered, while reducing the policymaking process to its lowest political terms.

AUDIO TEXT

The New Deal: "I pledge myself to a New Deal for the American people."

Destiny: "There is a mysterious cycle in human events. To some generations, much is given; of other generations, much is expected. This generation of Americans has a rendezvous with destiny."

Fear: "So, first of all, let me assert my firm belief that the only thing we have to fear is fear itself."

MP3 file/Source: Franklin D. Roosevelt Library and Digital Archive, http://www.fdrlibrary.marist.edu/audio.html

FIGURE 5.5 How FDR Sounded to a Worried Nation

inspired listeners to feel as if they personally knew this distant figure. Careful not to undermine the power of his message through overexposure, FDR resisted public calls for more fireside chats, giving only four during his first year as president and only twenty-six in the next eleven years. He chose his topics carefully, speaking primarily about the Depression, his New Deal economic recovery program, World War II, and national security issues.[54]

It's probably hard to imagine what it was like to hear the strong voice of the president say, "I pledge myself to a New Deal for the American people," or to reassure you that "The only thing we have to fear is fear itself," just as it may be difficult to imagine facing the extreme hardship of the Great Depression and the tremendous sacrifice and uncertainty of World War II. If you can use your imagination, try to envision how comforting it could have been, especially to those who had never before heard a president's voice.

It certainly would have been inconceivable to many Americans hearing those words from their radios that they were delivered by a man confined to a wheelchair, the result of adult polio. Ever aware that Americans in the 1930s and 1940s could perceive his wheelchair-bound presence as a sign of weakness, FDR worked assiduously to keep this basic fact about himself hidden from view. He carefully cultivated reporters, maintaining an open relationship with the White House press corps and permitting them access to power.[55] The relationship was symbiotic without being adversarial, and it paid off in the form of largely sympathetic coverage of FDR and his agenda. It was an era when reporters didn't consider it a sign of weakness on their part to acquiesce to White House requests not to write about or photograph the president in his wheelchair.

As media politics began to change in the generation that followed FDR, presidents began to employ different tactics to achieve the same objectives of news management and message control that the two Roosevelts accomplished so effectively in their time. John F. Kennedy won the loyalty of reporters by granting them access to his administration in much the same way as FDR, but he also implemented a strategy built around television to communicate an image of leadership directly to American homes that circumvented the traditional press. As Kennedy once remarked to a reporter, "When we don't have to go through you bastards, we can really get our story out to the American people."[56]

Both FDR and JFK held regular **press conferences**, meetings with journalists that allowed them to ask direct questions of the president on matters of policy. Kennedy permitted television cameras to broadcast these events live to the public in prime time, transforming press conferences from events designed to brief journalists to TV shows designed to showcase the president's quick wit and command of detail. A knowledgeable man with a good sense of humor, Kennedy commanded the stage at televised press conferences and used the conferences to construct an image of a substantive leader in charge of his administration and world events.[57] Barack Obama also excelled in the press conference format and resurrected it as a communication vehicle. President Trump is not one to dwell on the details of policy and has shied away from formal meetings with reporters.

A generation after Kennedy, presidential message control efforts increased in intensity, to the point where they came to resemble the love-hate struggle characteristic of election campaigns. Ronald Reagan used his acting skills coupled with strict control of information to create a likeable, strong persona who could dominate the news agenda. Unlike FDR or JFK, Reagan limited access to the reporters covering him. His media operations were tightly controlled by advisors, who would begin each day by deciding what they wanted coverage to look like on the evening news, and then would spend the rest of the day creating media events, producing sound bites, and spinning the statements necessary to realize their vision.[58]

The Reagan team was so successful in crafting and selling its message that Reagan became known in press circles as the "Teflon president," because even bad news seemed to slide right off of him. For the better part of his eight years in office, President Reagan was viewed positively by large numbers of Americans.[59] His success made his operation the model for those who followed him in office, and even if none of his successors has matched his level of effectiveness, they have all employed the tools of message control that have long since institutionalized the skeptical stance presidents and journalists have toward one another.

5.7b Congress

If the single occupant of the presidency is a natural focus for television's personalizing qualities, Congress poses something of a dilemma for a medium that thrives on telling individual stories. With a combined 535 senators and representatives, Congress is an unwieldy branch of government that doesn't offer its occupants easy entrée to television news. To compound matters, much of what happens in Congress occurs in committees and private meetings, which are largely out of the reach of cameras, and Congress is a deliberative branch of government where progress happens slowly; television, as we know, demands action and drama.

What is often visible to cameras is the infighting that's inevitable even among members of the same political party when political interests collide. This is sometimes sufficient to supply the drama otherwise missing from staid hearings and floor speeches, and it plays naturally on the strategy and horserace frames typical of presidential coverage.

So, members of Congress are not immune to the kind of "sky is falling" coverage that presidents experience when their proposals are not sailing along through the legislative process. At the same time that reporters were covering President Obama's health-care initiative as a political horserace, they were painting the legislative branch in similar tones, addressing infighting among liberal and conservative Democrats, between Democratic leaders of the House and Senate, and between Democrats and Republicans. As with presidential coverage that emphasizes the horserace aspects of governing, principled ideological differences are not reported to be the source of the conflict so much as petty partisanship and great clashes of egos.

When politics interferes with action and Congress fails to act, reporters are quick to cover the **gridlock** that ensues. Gridlock is typically reported as a problem, rather than as a natural institutional response to complicated problems. The expectation among reporters is that Congress *should* be able to report out legislation rather than fall victim to inaction, despite the fact that, by constitutional design, it is a place where passions and interests that might be adverse to the wishes of much of the country are frustrated or subjected to compromise (as we saw in Chapter 2 and as we'll see again in Chapter 9). Coverage of Congress in gridlock is the legislative equivalent to coverage of a president's failure to win a policy horserace, taking the inability to achieve an outcome as a sign of weakness independent of the merits of the policy under discussion.

> **gridlock:** The term given to legislative inaction, when members of Congress are unable to reach agreement and legislation stalls.

For many years, Congress was reluctant to open its proceedings to public view. The Senate, especially, with its long tradition as an exclusive club, was determined to maintain its privacy from the cameras that today seem to define public life. But as television naturally gravitated to the president, and presidents learned how to manipulate television coverage, some members of Congress grew concerned that their relative obscurity in the mass media was facilitating a flow of power toward the far more visible presidency.[60] By the late 1970s, the House of Representatives permitted cameras to broadcast its floor proceedings. The Senate followed suit in the 1980s. Today, you can view major House floor debates and key committee meetings on C-SPAN, and Senate proceedings on C-SPAN2.[61]

5.7c The Court System

Maybe Congress has become less private in the face of television cameras. Not the federal court system. The Supreme Court may be equal by design with Congress and the president, but its refusal to permit cameras in its proceedings and deliberations places it a clear third in the media's picture of the federal government.

Lack of press access to court activities has forced coverage of the Supreme Court to emphasize places where the Court's actions rub against the other, more observable federal institutions. Court rulings on matters of great visibility, like affirmative action or abortion rights, receive media scrutiny that typically explores how groups on different sides of the issue will be affected by the Court's decisions. This can include analysis of how these groups might petition the president or members of Congress, or what their next move might be in light of how the court ruled. This perspective fits nicely with the policy-as-strategy approach the press takes in its coverage of the president and Congress.

In a similar fashion, a recurring story involves how the ideological balance of the court shifts in response to presidential judicial appointments. This, too, is fundamentally a political horserace story, in which the president seeks to preserve (in the case of Trump) or alter (in the case of Obama) the Supreme Court's conservative tendencies. The side that's "winning" the horserace is determined in part by the alignment of justices who "swing" between the court's conservative and liberal factions—whether they're consistently siding with one group or the other. Unlike private deliberations, the votes of justices are a matter of public record, available to reporters who wish to speculate on how tightly conservatives maintain their grip on the institution.

5.8 Beyond Agenda Setting

So, what difference does it make if the media insist on framing politics and policy making in terms of winners and losers, strategies and tactics, and personalities and scandals? If the struggle between reporters and candidates or officials results in news coverage that does not enhance informed decision making, how much of this coverage gets through to the public and how do people process it?

In Chapter 4, we saw how the media can have an important influence over what we think about through their agenda-setting ability, tempered though it may be through **selective exposure** and **selective perception**. Now, perhaps, we have a better sense of what those things are that we're invited to think about.

Beyond agenda setting, there's evidence to suggest that the media can turn up the volume on a particular issue by covering it more intensively and affect the way we think about political figures by the context in which they're presented. Political scientists Shanto Iyengar and Donald Kinder performed a creative experiment in which they showed people television news reports that had been manipulated to emphasize stories about specific policy concerns. In most cases, people were more sensitized to the manipulated issue following exposure to the news reports than they were beforehand, attaching greater importance to it after being exposed to it in the news.[62]

Furthermore, exposure to stories featuring political figures in favorable contexts had the effect of bolstering people's impressions of them. News reports were found to unintentionally produce this **priming** effect, whereby the manner in which a politician was discussed in the news cued viewers to think about the politician in terms defined by that context.

Months after the September 11 attacks, President Bush continued to ride a wave of unparalleled popularity that can be explained in part by how the media covered him in the context of his efforts to fight terrorism, for which he received vast public support. When questions began to surface in May 2002 about whether the president had done everything possible to prevent the attacks, the White House acted swiftly to change the subject to terrorist threats that still remained, seeking to get the press to portray the president in a context where he was widely regarded as competent and to avoid reminders about some of the doubts people had about Bush's capability to serve as president prior to September 11.

The same thing happened in September 2005, following the administration's slow response to the catastrophe caused when Hurricane Katrina devastated New Orleans. In this instance, top White House officials attempted to avoid criticism by arguing that playing "the blame game" was irresponsible while the crisis was still unfolding, even as they attempted to blame state and local officials for permitting the city to flood. Just like three years earlier, the administration's concern was that if people were primed to think about President Bush's competence or integrity, they would begin to evaluate him in a critical light.

5.9 Media Bias?

There's a widely held belief that mainstream media are biased toward liberal positions. During the 1990s, some conservatives derided CNN as the "Clinton News Network," and Fox News deliberately presents a perspective on the news that is acceptable to conservatives in a self-described effort to counter what it perceives as a liberal bias elsewhere.

selective exposure: The tendency to pay attention to messages that are consistent with existing attitudes or beliefs while overlooking messages that conflict with them.

selective perception: An unconscious process by which we filter information that we deem irrelevant, uninteresting, or inconsistent with our attitudes and beliefs while absorbing information that conforms to our self-perception.

priming: A media effect whereby the context in which a political figure is presented in the news can create a positive or negative cue for how viewers think about and evaluate that figure.

L.O. Speak intelligently about media bias, and explain why bias can be difficult to identify.

Critics point to the personal beliefs of journalists, many of whom admit to being liberal, and argue that it is impossible for journalists to keep their worldview out of coverage, claims of objectivity notwithstanding. Conservative organizations, such as the Media Research Center, seek to publicize instances of liberal bias in mainstream reporting.

Those who have attempted to take an objective look at the issue are typically hard pressed to find *systematic* ideological bias in the news. It's not always the case, but people tend to find bias against the positions they hold, be they conservative or liberal, and when we try to quantify bias in the news, we're drawing a line between our view of the world and the news message. Coming up with an objective understanding of bias can be difficult because what's perceived as bias may depend partly on where we stand ideologically.

In fact, there's a left-wing critique of the media that claims there's a bias *toward* conservative institutions and ideas. From this point of view, the media support the interests of those who own the media, not those who report the news. This perspective includes an uncritical acceptance, for instance, of free enterprise, American military might, and American foreign policy interests. In specific terms, such critics might argue that patriotic coverage of the Iraq War, in which reporters presented American interests as "our" interests, ignored the perspective that the conflict served the needs of large oil companies and put business considerations ahead of regard for human life.[63] Consistent with this critique, it became an article of faith among many liberal critics that George W. Bush did not get the same level of press scrutiny as Bill Clinton.

There's a third perspective on bias that sidesteps ideological positioning to find a **structural bias** in the news—that is, a tendency for the media to cover the same limited set of individuals and institutions. When gatekeepers decide what's newsworthy, they're not starting out by looking at an infinite set of events to cover. Most events that could potentially be reported never even make it into the discussion.[64] However, events involving high-level elected officials, entertainment and business leaders, and other well-known individuals are never far from their radar screen. Consequently, these individuals and the institutions they represent are disproportionately featured in media coverage.[65]

structural bias: The possibility that news stories are skewed toward the limited set of sources and topics selected by gatekeepers for publication and broadcast.

Although news organizations appear to be ready to cover news anywhere it's happening at a moment's notice, in fact the process of making news is cumbersome and requires a lot of planning. High-ranking government officials, political party leaders, the heads of a few prominent interest groups, and academic experts offer gatekeepers a ready supply of reliable sources, giving their perspectives disproportionate media play. From this point of view, bias is not introduced because the media report on Donald Trump more than Hillary Clinton or Hillary Clinton more than Donald Trump but because they cover both Trump and Clinton far more reliably than they cover sources without official positions or high standing.

5.10 Making Sense of Media Coverage

What happens, then, when the media's desire to entertain us clashes with their obligation to inform us; when the proliferation of media give us more news options than our parents could have dreamed of but less clarity about who's doing the gatekeeping; when news cycles turn over at the speed of light? Under these circumstances, it's understandable if we're a bit confused, or feel like tuning out. Fox News uses the slogan, "We report, you decide," but is the process really that simple in an era where the volume, speed, and spin of information makes it nearly impossible to know how to sort through it all?

L.O. *Address the possible relationship between news messages and cynicism in the traditional media and the problem of finding truthful information on the Internet.*

There is no easy solution to this dilemma. Even professional media critics have a hard time coming up with suggestions for how to make good sense of the world as it appears in the media. Political communication specialist Roderick Hart makes the point that the pervasiveness of mass media, particularly television, has changed the way we feel about politics. Remember the cynicism and disillusionment we said so many Americans feel about government? Hart lays a lot of it at television's doorstep, claiming that while watching television can make us *seem* closer to our world, in reality it creates a false sense of intimacy that can leave us feeling empty. He would have us get more involved in the political world we can touch, relying less on the mass media for our information and more on the immediate attachments we can find in our communities, from which real satisfaction can flow.[66]

That's one solution—one that requires effort and desire on our part, and the ability to look past the messages in mainstream media that confound clear and informed understanding of political events. But looking past mainstream messages still leaves us with the dilemma of knowing how to sort through Internet and social media claims that might be false or only partly true. The mediated world is pervasive and freewheeling, and during the 2016 election, facts were a regular casualty of this freeform, free-for-all information environment. Without a centralized mainstream media like we had in the television age to provide a counterbalance, we can be at the mercy of information that substantiates our preconceptions, even if the things being said are false. This complicates the demographic and values differences that are dividing us politically, as discussed in Chapter 4, because when we confuse beliefs with facts, we lose the common framework for engaging those with different perspectives.

Earlier, we mentioned fact-checking websites such as Politifact and factcheck.org, where third-party analysts evaluate claims made by political candidates to determine if they are true, partly true, or demonstrable lies. As self-appointed neutral referees, these sites do not have to be balanced in their criticism of politicians, and in Donald Trump, they found a candidate who kept them busy because of his tendency to speak off the cuff without full regard for the truth. One fact-checker for a Canadian newspaper called the Trump campaign "a daily avalanche of wrongness," unique among politicians who are guilty of misleading to some degree, and acknowledged "the limited power of truth to reach people who are sure they already know it."[67] Politifact agreed. While calling claims made by Hillary Clinton about her private e-mail server "false and distorted," the fact-checkers at Factcheck.org reserved their greatest criticism for Donald Trump, whom they said was in "a league of his own" when it comes to telling falsehoods. Table 5.3 lists ten of their top Trump falsehoods from the 2016 campaign.

Lists like this are designed to correct the official record, but in a decentralized media environment, they can be perceived as being similar to the way football fans dispute calls

TABLE 5.3 Donald Trump's Top Ten False Claims According to Factcheck.org[T12]

1. The unemployment rate was 42 percent. TRUTH: It was 4.9 percent.

2. Ninety-six million people who gave up looking for jobs want to work. TRUTH: According to the Bureau of Labor Statistics, the figure was 5.5 million.

3. The murder rate is the highest in 45 years. TRUTH: At 4.9 per 100,000 people, the murder rate was far lower than it had been 45 years ago.

4. The U.S. ambassador to Libya "was left helpless to die as [then secretary of state] Hillary Clinton soundly slept in her bed." TRUTH: Trump later admitted the claim was baseless.

5. Clinton wanted to raise everybody's taxes massively. TRUTH: According to the nonpartisan Tax Policy Center, almost all of her proposed tax increases were for the top 10 percent of taxpayers.

6. Trump opposed the Iraq War before it started and had "25 different stories" to prove it. TRUTH: He never produced the stories.

7. Sen. Ted Cruz's father was linked to the Kennedy assassination. TRUTH: The claim was from an unsubstantiated *National Enquirer* story based on a photo of someone who looked like Ted Cruz's father.

8. Obama is "letting people pour into the country so they can go and vote." TRUTH: Only citizens can vote, and there are lengthy residency requirements for immigrants before they can apply for citizenship.

9. The terror group ISIS is making millions of dollars selling oil to Libya, and Iran is taking over Iraqi oilfields. TRUTH: There is no evidence for either claim.

10. Trump University had an "A" rating from the Better Business Bureau. TRUTH: It had a "D" rating in 2010, when it stopped admitting students.

against their team by referees. Trump supporters might understandably reject these judgments about their candidate, especially if they have encountered his claims elsewhere on websites they trust.

With so much false information going viral, it can be especially challenging to achieve the standard of enlightened understanding that Robert Dahl contends is essential for making sensible political decisions. But just as the Internet can be a source of rumor and innuendo dressed up as hard news, it can also be a source of ways to debunk falsehoods. The website Snopes.com disproves urban legends, validates or discredits Internet rumors, and keeps an account of fake news websites.[68] Factcheck.org has several commonsense steps to take to help identify and weed out false information and fake news stories, including the following:

- Consider the source—some websites actually tell you they're fiction.
- Look beyond the headline—sometimes the text is so outrageous that you will know it's fake.
- Check the author—a click or two on the author page can tell you if the author is real.
- Click links for supporting evidence—if they don't look real, they probably aren't.
- Examine the date—a new story shouldn't be supported by old facts.
- Think about the writer's intent—and remember that satire is supposed to sound real.
- Challenge your biases—and remember that we want to believe things that confirm our beliefs.
- Consult expert sites—Factcheck.org, Politifact.com, the *Washington Post* Fact-Checker, and Snopes.com may have already done the work for you.[69]

If, as Dahl contends, democracy is threatened by the lack of access to good information, it is especially important to sort through the clutter and, as best as possible, make intelligent decisions about what information to believe.

Chapter Review

Define mass media, and explain why the media can both enhance and confound our ability to make enlightened decisions about politics and government.

The mass media—encompassing newspapers, television, radio, magazines, and the Internet—are an important link between the public and government, although the variety of media messages and their sometimes uncertain origins can make it challenging to distinguish truth from half-truth, rumor, and gossip. This can confound our ability to make enlightened political choices by presenting us with inadequate or irrelevant information about politics and government.

Explain the evolution of the press in America—from the party press to the penny press to the mass media era.

For many years, we didn't have anything resembling mass media. During the Revolutionary War, newspapers found they could move public opinion, and with the establishment of political parties after 1790, newspapers became vehicles for rallying the party faithful. In the 1830s, the penny press emerged as an alternative to the party press. By the end of the nineteenth century, newspapers had become big businesses, drawing audiences with sensational "yellow jour-

nalism" and widely popular "muckraking" investigations of political and corporate corruption. The era of mass media followed in the twentieth century, first with radio, then television, cable, satellite, and Internet communication.

Identify the gatekeepers of news in the traditional press and on the Internet.

Traditional media like major newspapers and television news programs employ editors and producers to act as gatekeepers of news content and determine the stories that appear in print or on the air. On the Internet, things can be more confusing; anyone with a web address is a potential gatekeeper, and it can be hard to know if the material being reported is factual. Historically, gatekeepers have applied a set of standards to determine if a story is newsworthy, centering on characteristics like conflict, proximity to the news audience, timeliness, a sense of the unusual, relevance, and familiarity.

Define "infotainment," and explain how it complicates the media environment.

The blending of information with entertainment, or "infotainment," complicates the media environment. Feature-laden "soft news" has become a large part of mainstream coverage, and gossip programs share news subjects with newspapers and television news shows because they draw widespread attention, which serves the commercial needs of media operators.

Assess the risks posed by the concentration of media power.

This is happening at a time when the government is actively deregulating the media industry, which is facilitating the concentration of media ownership in the hands of a few "megamedia" organizations. The risk of such concentration of power is that stories threatening to these corporate interests will not be exposed in the news, undermining the level of information we need to make intelligent political decisions.

Discuss the conflict between politicians and journalists that emerged in the mass media era over control of news messages.

As mass media became a central part of our lives, it became a key resource for candidates and elected officials and the source of a struggle between politicians and journalists over control of the news message. Candidates try to get their version of events in the news by staging media events for the press, holding photo opportunities, and spinning news items in a favorable direction. Reporters have the last say in how a story is framed or the context in which it is presented. In recent years the techniques of campaign coverage have filtered into coverage of how officials gov-

ern, turning the process of governing into a kind of horse-race with political winners and losers.

Explain agenda setting.

Media coverage influences what we think about. Additionally, through priming, news stories can invite us to think about and evaluate political figures in specific ways.

Speak intelligently about media bias, and explain why bias can be difficult to identify.

Some people believe the news media are ideologically biased, although bias is a difficult thing to prove. A structural critique of news coverage argues that bias is not ideological so much as it is about the disproportionate attention centered on a small set of well-known individuals.

Address the possible relationship between news messages and the problem of finding truthful information on the Internet.

Making your way through the freewheeling, decentralized news environment can be difficult, and even professional media critics have a hard time coming up with suggestions for how to make sense of the world as it appears in the media. News messages may encourage cynicism and create a false sense of intimacy about the political world that ultimately leaves us feeling empty. At the same time, it can be difficult to figure out whether information on the Internet is accurate. Fact-checking sites can help but require levels of time and interest that many people do not have.

Key Terms

agenda setting The tendency for topics given great weight by the media to be given equally great weight by those who use the media, such that the people and events considered important by those who determine media coverage will become the people and events that the public considers important. (p. 144)

attack journalism A form of aggressive coverage in which reporters latch onto an allegation of misdoing by a candidate or public official and engage in a "feeding frenzy" in which they cover it intensely and to the exclusion of other news. (p. 149)

equal time provision The federal requirement that broadcast outlets selling commercial time to a political candidate must make equal time available to other candidates running for office. (p. 140)

fairness doctrine The FCC requirement, no longer in force, that electronic media provide a balanced forum for controversial public discourse. (p. 140)

Federal Communications Act of 1934 The act of Congress that established the Federal Communications Commission (FCC) and the equal time provision. (p. 140)

Federal Communications Commission (FCC) The federal agency responsible for regulating broadcast communications, including radio, television, wire, satellite, and cable transmissions. The FCC is directed by five commissioners who are

appointed by the president and confirmed by the Senate for five-year terms. (p. 140)

fireside chats The term given to Franklin Roosevelt's radio addresses to the American public, which demonstrated Roosevelt's ability to master the medium and build a sense of rapport with ordinary Americans. (p. 150)

frame The frame of reference for a news story, or the context around which the facts of a story are organized. If a news story is thematic, like most television news stories, the frame determines what the specific theme of the story will be. (p. 148)

free media The news coverage that major candidates for high office can expect to receive on a regular basis. Although free, candidates cannot control the content of this coverage or guarantee that it will be favorable. (p. 145)

gatekeepers Television producers, newspaper editors, and prestigious reporters and anchors who make the decisions about what stories will be published or aired. Think of the imagery of a guard who decides who will be allowed to pass through a gate. In this case, news gatekeepers determine which information will be allowed to pass through the medium. (p. 128)

gridlock The term given to legislative inaction, when members of Congress are unable to reach agreement and legislation stalls. (p. 153)

hard news Traditional news items that derive their value from recent, relevant events that have some bearing on the lives of readers or viewers. (p. 138)

horserace That element of a political campaign that deals with winning and losing, whether a candidate is leading or trailing an opponent, and what the candidate may be doing to improve or solidify his or her electoral prospects. (p. 148)

infotainment News reports and information-based programs that use information to entertain by playing on sensational topics, such as celebrities, violence, and the like. (p. 138)

inverted pyramid A style of reporting typical of twentieth-century newspaper coverage, in which stories were constructed with the most important factual material in the first paragraph, followed by successively less important facts. (p. 135)

libel The legal restriction against the malicious publication of material that knowingly damages an individual's reputation. (p. 140)

mass media Vehicles, such as television, radio, newspapers, magazines, and the Internet, capable of rapidly communicating information to large numbers of people over large distances. Note that media is the plural form of medium: Television is a medium, whereas television and the Internet are media. (p. 128)

media events Activities staged by campaigns or political officials that have enough news value to draw press attention to a message the politician wants to communicate. (p. 146)

muckraking Investigative reporting prevalent during the turn of the twentieth century that centered on uncovering corruption in government and industry for the purpose of promoting progressive reforms. (p. 132)

narrowcasting Programming oriented to a small segment of viewers, like that found on cable television stations. It contrasts with broadcasting, like that found on traditional television networks, which seeks to reach a larger audience with programming that has wide appeal. (p. 142)

news cycle The time between when an event happens and when it gets press coverage. With twenty-four-hour news services setting the pace, the demand for new information is enormous and immediate, greatly accelerating the news cycle. (p. 147)

newsworthy The conditions under which a story warrants publication or dissemination, based on a set of values applied by newspaper editors and television producers. Newsworthy stories typically have conflict, proximity and relevance to the audience, timeliness, and familiarity. (p. 137)

paid media Radio and television ads paid for and produced by political campaigns. (p. 145)

party press Newspapers functioning as an arm of a political party, communicating information about partisan politics from party leaders to their supporters. Newspapers functioned in this capacity from the inception of political parties in America around 1790 through the 1830s. (p. 132)

penny press High-circulation newspapers, emerging after 1830, that kept costs down by selling advertising. These newspapers brought in large numbers of readers with lurid and sensational reporting. (p. 132)

photo opportunities Staged appearances by politicians in visually appealing settings designed to produce images that will be widely disseminated in the press. (p. 146)

press conferences Scheduled meetings between reporters and political figures like the president, which give the press access to the official and an opportunity to ask him or her questions firsthand. (p. 152)

priming A media effect whereby the context in which a political figure is presented in the news can create a positive or negative cue for how viewers think about and evaluate that figure. (p. 154)

selective exposure The tendency to pay attention to messages that are consistent with existing attitudes or beliefs, while overlooking messages that conflict with them. (p. 154)

selective perception An unconscious process by which we filter information that we deem irrelevant, uninteresting, or inconsistent with our attitudes and beliefs, while absorbing information that conforms to our self-perception. (p. 154)

soft news Feature stories, stories about celebrities, and other news items that do not derive their news value from proximity, timeliness, or relevance to the reader or viewer. (p. 138)

spin A technique used by political figures to characterize events in a favorable way in order to get the media to report them in a favorable way—regardless of what the facts of a story may indicate. (p. 147)

Stamp Act A particularly vexing tax levied by the British on scores of legal documents, which led to a colonial boycott of British goods. (p. 131)

structural bias The possibility that news stories are skewed toward the limited set of sources and topics selected by gatekeepers for publication and broadcast. (p. 155)

Telecommunications Act of 1996 Legislation that overhauled the Federal Communications Act of 1934 by deregulating a range of communications technologies in an effort to promote competition in the development and provision of telecommunications services. If your local telephone company now offers long-distance service, or if your cable television provider also offers high-speed Internet access, it's because the opportunity for them to do so was made possible by this law. (p. 141)

yellow journalism The term given to the sensational newspaper coverage prevalent during the turn of the twentieth century, noteworthy for its emphasis on violence, sex, human-interest stories, and exposés of official corruption. (p. 132)

Resources

You might be interested in examining some of what the following authors have said about the topics we've been discussing:

Alger, Dean. *Megamedia: How Giant Corporations Dominate Mass Media, Distort Competition, and Endanger Democracy.* Boulder, CO: Rowman & Littlefield, 1998. Alger presents a clearly constructed analysis of how very few organizations own most of our favorite media outlets, and what that means for the quality of information we get.

Graber, Doris A. *Mass Media and American Politics*, 8th ed. Washington, DC: Congressional Quarterly Press, 2009. A thorough overview of media politics.

Hart, Roderick P. *Seducing America: How Television Charms the Modern Voter*. New York: Oxford University Press, 1994. Hart offers an original and thoughtful analysis of how television misleads us into feeling clever and involved when in fact it has the effect of making us cynical and detached.

Patterson, Thomas E. *Out of Order*. New York: Alfred A. Knopf, 1993. It's the political system that Patterson claims is out of order, owing to the misplaced role of the media as the primary link between candidates and voters.

Sabato, Larry J. *Feeding Frenzy: How Attack Journalism Has Transformed American Politics*. New York: The Free Press, 1991. An account of the rise of attack journalism, including many examples of feeding frenzies from the recent past.

Iyengar, Shanto, and Donald R. Kinder. *News That Matters*. Chicago: University of Chicago Press, 1987. A creative approach to capturing media effects beyond agenda setting.

You may also be interested in looking at similarities and differences in how the news is portrayed by these major outlets: CNN (www.cnn.com); NBC (www.msnbc. msn .com); ABC (http://abcnews.go.com); CBS (www. cbsnews .com); and FOX (www.foxnews.com).

Notes

1 "ABC News Was Misquoted on Crowd Size," ABC News. com, September 13, 2009. http://abcnews.go.com/Politics/pro test-crowd-size-estimate-falsely-attributed-abc-news/story ?id=8558055.

2 Glenn Greenwald, "*Time* Magazine: The Liberal Bias of Facts," salon.com, September 17, 2009.

3 David Von Drehle, "Mad Man: Is Glenn Beck Bad for America?" Time.com, September 17, 2009.

4 For a full discussion of these points, see Dean Alger, *Megamedia: How Giant Corporations Dominate Mass Media, Distort Competition, and Endanger Democracy* (Boulder, CO: Rowman & Littlefield, 1998), 4–20.

5 Richard Davis, *The Press and American Politics: The New Mediator* (White Plains, NY: Longman Publishing, 1992), 43–45.

6 Ibid., 47–49.

7 Richard L. Rubin, *Press, Party, and Presidency* (New York: W. W. Norton, 1981).

8 Ibid.

9 Davis, *Press and American Politics*, 70–79.

10 Ibid., 92.

11 Glenn Kessler, "Are There 91 Million Americans 'On the Sidelines' Looking for Work?" *Washington Post*, January 30, 2014. https://www.washingtonpost.com/news/fact-checker/wp/2014/ 01/30/are-there-91-million-americans-on-the-sidelines-looking -for-work/?utm_term=.41c6a10d6bba.

12 Louis Jacobson and Taylor Leighton, "Donald Trump Exaggerates Hillary Clinton's Role in Growing Trade Deficit with China," Politifact.com, June 28, 2016. http://www.politi fact.com/truth-o-meter/statements/2016/jun/28/donald-trump/ checking-donald-trump-hillary-clintons-role-growin/.

13 Lauren Carroll, "Clinton Twists Trump's Words on Rescuing the Auto Industry during Recession," Politifact, October, 18, 2016. http://www.politifact.com/truth-o-meter/statements/2016/ oct/18/hillary-clinton/clinton-twists-trumps-words-rescuing -auto-industry/.

14 WXYZ-TV-Detroit, February 26, 1997, cited in Matthew R. Kerbel, *If it Bleeds It Leads: An Anatomy of Television News* (Westview Press, Boulder, CO, 2000), 36–37.

15 NBC Nightly News, June 15, 1999, cited in Kerbel, *If It Bleeds It Leads*, 108.

16 Graber, *Mass Media*, 116–120.

17 Ibid., 120.

18 See The Pew Research Center for the People and the Press. "Survey Reports: Public Knowledge of Current Affairs Little Changed by News and Information Revolutions." April 15, 2007, at http://people-press.org/report/319/public-knowledge -of-current-affairs-little-changed-by-news-and-information -revolutions.

19 Spencer Kornhaber, "Obama's Last Slow Jam," *Atlantic*, June 10, 2016. http://www.theatlantic.com/entertainment/ archive/2016/06/obamas-last-slow-jam/486575/.

20 Josh Rottenberg, "Zach Galifianakis on Hillary Clinton's 'Between Two Ferns' Comedy Chops and Donald Trump's 'Psychosis,'" *Los Angeles Times*, September 24, 2016. http://www .latimes.com/entertainment/tv/la-et-st-zach-galifianakis -clinton-between-two-ferns-20160924-snap-story.html.

21 "Michael Ventre, "Just How Real Are Reality TV Shows?" Today.com, April 14 2009.

22 Michael O'Connell, "Jeff Zucker Talks Trump TV and CNN's Ratings Hot Streak: We've 'Outshined Everybody,'" *Hollywood Reporter*, October 27, 2016. http://www.hollywoodreporter .com/news/jeff-zucker-talks-trump-tv-cnns-ratings-hot-streak -weve-shined-everybody-941575.

23 Louis Nelson, "Trump Assails Former Miss Universe and Clinton in Early Morning Tweet Blitz," *Politico*, September 30, 2016. http://www.politico.com/story/2016/09/trump-alicia -machado-clinton-tweet-attack-228940.

24 Maggie Haberman, Ashley Parker, Jeremy W. Peters, and Michael Barbaro, "Inside Donald Trump's Last Stand: An Anxious Nominee Seeks Assurance," *New York Times*, November 6, 2016. http://www.nytimes.com/2016/11/07/us/politics/ donald-trump-presidential-race.html?_r=0.

25 Davis, *Press and American Politics*, 128–134.

26 The case is *New York Times Co. v. Sullivan*, 376 US 354 (1964).

27 Davis, *Press and American Politics*, 122.

28 Alger, *Megamedia*, 4–20.

29 Internet Usage Statistics, at http://internetworldstats.com/stats.htm. If you're interested, you can find a brief and interesting Internet timeline at http://www.webopedia.com/quick_ref/timeline.asp.

30 These include HBO, HBO2, HBO Signature, HBO Family, HBO Comedy, HBO Zone, and HBO Latino.

31 National Internet and Television Association, at https://www.ncta.com/industry-data.

32 You can find a full list of cable selections from Zap2it.com, a supplier of television and movie information and a division of Tribune Media Services.

33 U.S. Radio and TV Directory, at http://www.100000watts.com.

34 Carla Gesell-Streeter, "Talk Radio History," at http://www.radiotalk.org/history.html.

35 Alger, *Megamedia*, 5–10.

36 Ibid., 20, emphasis in original.

37 Todd Putman, "The GE Boycott: A Story NBC Wouldn't Buy." Extra!, January/February 1991. Extra! is published by an organization called FAIR (Fairness and Accuracy in Reporting), a media watchdog group with a liberal tilt, which works to expose news organizations when it believes they are suppressing important information. The author is an expert who was contacted to appear on *Today*. All quotations in this section come from this article. You can read the whole article on the FAIR website at http://www.fair.org/extra/best-of-extra/ge-boycott.html.

38 Jason LeMiere, "Did the Media Help Donald Trump Win? $5 Billion in Free Advertising Given to President-Elect," *International Business Times*, November 9, 2016. http://www.ibtimes.com/did-media-help-donald-trump-win-5-billion-free-advertising-given-president-elect-2444115.

39 Matt Taibbi, "Donald Trump Claims Authorship of Legendary Reagan Slogan; Has Never Heard of Google," *Rolling Stone*, March 25, 2015. http://www.rollingstone.com/politics/news/donald-trump-is-americas-stupidest-person-has-never-heard-of-google-20150325.

40 Bradford Richardson, "Cruz Sells 'Make Trump Debate Again' Hats, *The Hill*, January 27, 2016. http://thehill.com/blogs/ballot-box/presidential-races/267227-cruz-selling-make-trump-debate-again-hats.

41 Sam Levine, "Bill Clinton Says 'Make America Great Again' Is Just a Racist Dog Whistle," *Huffington Post*, September 8, 2016. http://www.huffingtonpost.com/entry/bill-clinton-make-america-great-again_us_57d06ccfe4b0a48094a749fc.

42 Nicholas Kulish and Jeff Zeleny, "Prospect of Obama at Brandenburg Gate Divides German Politicians." *New York Times*, July 10, 2008.

43 "Donald Trump in Scotland: 'Brexit a Great Thing,'" BBC News, June 24, 2016. http://www.bbc.com/news/uk-scotland-glasgow-west-36606184.

44 Sebastian Fischer and Christina Hebel, "Tour de Gaffes: Romney Flops in Europe," *Spiegel* Online, July 31, 2012.

45 David A. Fahrenthold, "Trump Recorded Having Extremely Lewd Conversation about Women in 2015," October 8, 2016.

https://www.washingtonpost.com/politics/trump-recorded-having-extremely-lewd-conversation-about-women-in-2005/2016/10/07/3b9ce776-8cb4-11e6-bf8a-3d26847eeed4_story.html?utm_term=.01106b05d1bd.

46 Larry J. Sabato, *Feeding Frenzy: How Attack Journalism Has Transformed American Politics* (New York: Free Press, 1991), 1.

47 Thomas E. Patterson, *Out of Order* (New York: Alfred A. Knopf, 1993), 53–93.

48 Ibid., 20.

49 Ibid., 78–81.

50 "Campaign 2000: More News, Less Filling," Center for Media and Public Affairs, September 21, 2000.

51 Patterson, *Out of Order*, 73–74.

52 Kerbel, *Remote and Controlled*, 102–129.

53 Betty Houchin Winfield, *FDR and the News Media* (Urbana: University of Illinois Press, 1990).

54 You can skim though the text of Roosevelt's fireside chats, archived at the Franklin D. Roosevelt Presidential Library, at http://www.mhrcc.org/fdr/fdr.html.

55 Graham J. White, *FDR and the Press* (Chicago: University of Chicago Press, 1979).

56 Mary Ann Watson, *The Expanding Vista: American Television in the Kennedy Years* (New York: Oxford University Press, 1990), 76.

57 You can read transcripts of some of Kennedy's press conferences through the John F. Kennedy library at http://www.jfklibrary.org/jfk_pressconf_menu.html.

58 Mark Hertsgaard, *On Bended Knee: The Press and the Reagan Presidency* (New York: Farrar, Straus and Giroux, 1988). Hertsgaard says the objective of the Reagan media team was "not simply to tame the press but to transform it into an unwitting mouthpiece of the government," and quotes NBC anchorman Tom Brokaw as calling the Reagan staff "killers" for their ability to get the coverage they wanted on a regular basis (p. 5).

59 *NBC Nightly News*, May 18, 1994. Cited in Kerbel, *Remote and Controlled*, 122.

60 Norman J. Ornstein, "The Open Congress Meets the President," in Anthony King (ed.), *Both Ends of the Avenue: The Presidency, Congress, and the Executive Branch in the 1980s* (Washington, DC: American Enterprise Institute, 1983).

61 Curious about what's on now? Check out the C-SPAN schedule at http://www.c-spanvideo.org/schedule.

62 Shanto Iyengar and Donald R. Kinder, *News That Matters* (Chicago: University of Chicago Press, 1987).

63 Calvin Exoo, *Politics of the Mass Media* (West Publishing Company, 1994). Exoo makes this point about the Persian Gulf War.

64 See, for instance, Gay Tuchman, *Making News: A Study in the Construction of Reality* (New York: Free Press, 1978).

65 Herbert J. Gans, *Deciding What's News: A Study of CBS Evening News, NBC Nightly News, Newsweek, and Time* (New York: Vintage Books, 1980).

66 Roderick P. Hart, *Seducing America: How Television Charms the Modern Voter* (New York: Oxford University Press, 1994).

67 Daniel Dale, "Confessions of a Trump Fact-Checker," *Politico*, October 19, 2016. http://www.politico.com/magazine/story/2016/10/one-month-253-trump-untruths-214369.

68 See Snopes.com, at http://www.snopes.com/info/aboutus.asp.

69 Eugene Kiely and Lori Robertson, "How to Spot Fake News," Factcheck.org, November 18, 2016. http://www.factcheck.org/2016/11/how-to-spot-fake-news/.

Table, Figure, and Box Notes

T1 Library of Congress and Richard Davis, *The Press and American Politics: The New Mediator*, 3rd ed. (Upper Saddle River, NJ: Prentice Hall, 2001).

T2 Rep. Diane Black (R-Tenn.), *The Tennessean*, January 28, 2014, cited in Glenn Kessler, "Are There 91 Million Americans 'On the Sidelines' Looking for Work?" *Washington Post*, January 30, 2014.

T3 Cited in Lauren Carroll, "Clinton Twists Trump's Words on Rescuing the Auto Industry during Recession," Politifact.com, October 18, 2016. http://www.politifact.com/truth-o-meter/statements/2016/oct/18/hillary-clinton/clinton-twists-trumps-words-rescuing-auto-industry/.

T4 John Wagner, "Trump Accuses Obama of Putting Up 'Roadblocks' to a Smooth Transition," *Washington Post*, December 28, 2016. https://www.washingtonpost.com/news/post-politics/wp/2016/12/28/trump-accuses-obama-of-putting-up-roadblocks-to-a-smooth-transition/?hpid=hp_hp_top-table-main_trumproadblock-1010am%3Ahomepage%2Fstory&utm_term=.0df1ddcdd59d.

T5 Emily Schultheis, "Donald Trump Accuses President Obama of 'Roadblocks' During Transition," CBS News, December 28, 2016. http://www.cbsnews.com/news/donald-trump-accuses-president-obama-of-roadblocks-during-transition/.

T6 The E.W. Scripps Company, at http://www.scripps.com/newspapers/locations. The Scripps Company owns both newspapers.

T7 U.S. Census Bureau, Metropolitan Statistical Areas of the United States, 2008.

T8 Figures from http://internetworldstats.com/stats.htm. Table designed by Annie Dunnigan, LLC.

T9 Photo courtesy of Ron Monner.

T10 Reagan photo courtesy Ronald Reagan Library. Al Gore photo courtesy Joseph Sohm/Shutterstock, Inc.

T11 For instance, see DoBias, M., and J. Lubell, "A POTUS proposal." *Modern Healthcare*, September 7, 2009, 8–9.

T12 Eugene Kiely, Lori Robertson, and Robert Farley, "The Whoppers of 2016," Factcheck.org, December 19, 2016. http://www.factcheck.org/2016/12/the-whoppers-of-2016/.

Political Parties: Connecting Us to the Electoral Process

Source: Peeradach Rattanakoses/Shutterstock

Learning Objectives

When you have completed this chapter, you should be able to:

- Define political parties.
- Explain why America's two-party system is consistent with its electoral mechanisms and public opinion.
- Identify third parties as either ideological, single-issue, or splinter parties, and explain why they rarely compete successfully for elected offices.
- Define the term *party system*, and identify the key characteristics of the five party systems that have arisen since parties emerged in the late eighteenth century.
- Identify the relationship between realignments and the demise of party systems.
- Explain why the post-1960s political era may be understood as a period of dealignment.
- Distinguish between the party in government and the party in the electorate.

6.1 Introduction

L.O. Define political parties.

What exactly is going on in the photo below? It's the serious business of formally ratifying the selection of a candidate who will seek to become the most powerful person in the world and crafting the positions on which he will campaign. So, why is this person wearing an Uncle Sam costume? Because politics in America is and always has been a blend of fun and responsibility, spectacle and power, sideshow and serious deal making.

This individual was among many who streamed into Cleveland for the 2016 Republican National Convention. His outfit may not exactly seem presidential, but it allows him to get involved in the fun of politics. If the essence of democracy is self-expression, then political party conventions like this one are bastions of democracy. It may not always be dignified, but you can probably see how political parties can provide an important link between ordinary people and the political process.

political party: An organized group of individuals with common interests seeking to gain power in government by electing officials to public office.

electorate: The portion of the public eligible to vote in elections.

A **political party**, in the words of political scientist Leon Epstein, is "any group, however loosely organized, seeking to elect government officeholders under a given label."[1] There are other definitions as well, but they hold in common the idea that parties are organized groups that share the desire to win power by contesting elections. If you take away the requirement about trying to elect officeholders, and instead talk about organized groups that try to influence the political process, you'll end up with something closer to the interest groups we'll be talking about in Chapter 8. Parties are about political competition, about winning and losing, and through our involvement in that competition, they can connect us to the electoral process.

Even though political parties are organized groups, that doesn't mean that they're tightly integrated. Parties exist at all levels of our federal system, and state and local parties can exercise a fair amount of autonomy from national parties. There are also different venues for parties, where they perform unrelated functions: in government, where Republicans and Democrats want to fulfill different legislative agendas, and among ordinary people in the **electorate**, where Republicans, Democrats, and a host of smaller parties run campaigns to compete in elections. So, it's fair to say that parties are organizations, but not hierarchical ones.

In the United States, two parties dominate the political landscape. That's not the case in other countries, though, and we're going to take a look at why. In fact, two parties have competed in elections in this country since its founding, and we're going to take a look back at that history to lend some perspective to where today's parties come from. Once we do that, we'll talk about the government and campaign venues where parties do most of their work, to get a sense of how they're set up and how they operate.

Since a big part of party activity is running political campaigns and competing in elections, we'll also take some time to look at how that works. Campaigns are complex, multistage enterprises that engage political parties and the mass media, and therefore require a lot of attention and explanation. So, we'll devote Chapter 7 to examining them.

A participant displays his patriotic feelings at the 2016 Republican National Convention.
Source: a katz/Shutterstock, Inc.

L.O. Explain why America's two-party system is consistent with its electoral mechanisms and public opinion.

6.2 Why Two Parties?

There's something that seems natural about the idea of two parties in competition, like two baseball or basketball teams facing off against each other. But, in truth, two political parties competing against each other is something that doesn't happen in most nations. Great Britain has three parties: two major ones and an active minor one. Twelve parties won seats in the 2013 Israeli parliamentary election. Italy boasts more than one dozen parties. You can find an overview of the wide range of viable political parties competing for power in governments around the world in Global Topics: Other Political Systems.

So, what is it about the United States that supports just two parties in regular competition? There are several explanations.

6.2a Winner-Take-All Elections

What would happen in a basketball game if we decided to award a partial victory to the team that scored the second-largest number of points? Suddenly, you wouldn't have to

Other Political Systems

Five parties? Seven parties? You can find nations around the globe boasting many actively engaged political parties that participate in elections with the expectation that they will share in governing. Zero parties? You can find that too (notice nations in the Middle East where political parties are forbidden to form). What you can't find much of is what we have in the United States—two parties competing against each other in a system where no other party has a realistic chance of governing.

Likewise, there is no apparent relationship between the size of a nation and the number of political parties it has. Tiny Iceland has multiple parties. So does Haiti. But, China only permits one party, as did the former Soviet Union.

Look at Figure 6.1 and notice how many political systems either clamp down on the formation of political parties or have a large number of functioning small parties. It should give you a sense that a system of two major parties competing for power is unusual, even though it feels natural to many Americans.

---

win in order to be competitive. If we extended the rule to award a partial victory, say, to any number of teams that could score at least fifty points, we might end up with a lot of basketball teams on the same court trying to score their points before the clock ran out.

Sound silly? Perhaps—but that's pretty much the way election rules work in nations with **proportional representation**, where voters select the party of their choice, and representation in the legislature is awarded in rough equivalency to each party's percentage of the total. Proportional representation systems feature **multimember districts**, meaning several people, typically of different parties, represent one district. Any party receiving more than a minimum percentage of the vote—which may be as low as 10 percent—is eligible for representation in the legislature, so it makes sense that many parties will take a shot at electoral competition. Proportional representation systems are popular in Europe, which helps explain why so many European nations have **multiparty systems**, with a large number of active parties successfully competing for a role in government.

The United States does things differently. The American **two-party system** discourages many parties from forming because the standard for being represented in government is nothing short of complete electoral victory. Unlike proportional representation systems, the American **winner-take-all system** awards all the representation to the candidate of the party that wins a **plurality** of votes, which simply means that the candidate has to win the most votes. He or she doesn't even need to win a **majority** of votes or more than half. In a winner-take-all system, just win one more vote than the next candidate, and you get to be the lone representative from your **single-member district**, which is represented only by the candidate of that winning party.

There's a pronounced difference between winner-take-all rules and proportional representation rules. Take a look at Table 6.1, where five fictional parties are competing in a hypothetical legislative district. The voting between the top two parties was close, with only a handful of votes separating the first-place Centrist Party from the second-place Conservative Party. The remaining three parties lagged behind.

If a proportional representation system with multiple-member districts were in place, several people would have the opportunity to represent the district. For the sake of example, let's say the district would have six representatives. Assume also that any party with at least 10 percent of the vote would be eligible for representation. Based on the proportion of the vote won by each party, the first-place Centrist Party and the second-place Conservative Party would each be awarded two seats and would be able to send two of their members to serve in the legislature. The third-place Labor Party and fourth-place Green Party would each get to send one of their members to the legislature because each party received close to one-sixth of the vote and cleared the 10 percent threshold for representation. Only the last-place Socialist Party, with 7 percent of the vote, would be shut out entirely.

proportional representation: Electoral systems that encourage the participation of many parties by awarding representation on the basis of the share of the vote won by each party in an electoral district.

multimember district: The structure of electoral districts in proportional representation systems, in which each electoral district sends several representatives to the legislature.

multiparty system: Political systems in which more than two parties have a realistic chance to win representation in government.

two-party system: A political system, like ours in the United States, in which only two parties have a realistic chance to win most elections.

winner-take-all system: The electoral system in use in the United States, whereby the candidate of the party receiving the most votes in an electoral district gets to represent that district.

plurality: Winning the most votes in an election, or at least one more vote than the next closest candidate or party.

majority: Winning more than half the votes in an election, or 50 percent plus one.

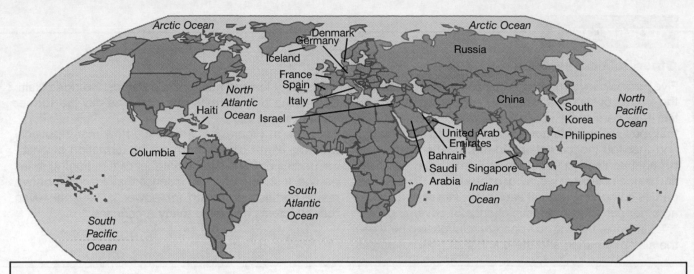

FIGURE 6.1 Other Political Systems

Bahrain: Bahrain does not allow political parties.

China: China's political party is the Communist Party of China. This party allows so-called democratic subparties, but all of their functions are handled by the primary party.

Colombia: Columbia's parties include the Social Party of National Unity, the Columbian Liberal Party, the Columbian Conservative Party, and the Democratic Center, among others.

Denmark: Denmark's parties include the Social Democrats, the Danish People's Party, the Venstre, and the Socialist People's Party, among others.

France: France's parties include the Socialist Party, Republicans, the National Front, the Centrist Alliance, the Christian Democrats, the Greens, and the Communist Party, among many others.

Germany: Germany's parties include the Social Democrats, the Christian Democrats, the Greens, and the Free Democrats, among others.

Haiti: Haiti's parties include Patriotic Unity, PHTK, the Christian Movement, the Christian National Union, the Democratic Alliance, and many others.

Iceland: Iceland's parties include the Independence Party, the Social Democratic Alliance, the Progressive Party, and Bright Future, among others.

Italy: Italy's parties include Forward Italy, the Liberal Popular Alliance, Conservatives and Reformists, Lega Nord, and Communist Refoundation, among many others.

Israel: Israel's parties include Likud, Labor, Zionist Union, Kalanu, Meretz, and Shas, among others.

Philippines: The Philippines' parties include the Philippine Democratic Party, the National People's Coalition, the Liberal Party, the Nationalist Party, and many others.

Russia: Russia's parties include United Russia, the Communist Party, the Liberal Democratic Party, A Just Russia, and many others.

Saudi Arabia: Saudi Arabia does not allow political parties.

Singapore: Singapore's parties include the People's Action Party, the Worker's Party, and the Singapore Democratic Alliance, among others.

South Korea: South Korea's parties include the Saenuri Party, the Democratic Party of Korea, the People's Party, and NCPR, among others.

Spain: Spanish parties include the People's Party, the Spanish Socialist Worker's Party, United We Can, Citizens, and the Basque Nationalist Party, among others.

United Arab Emirates: The United Arab Emirates does not allow political parties.

single-member district: The structure of electoral districts in winner-take-all electoral systems, in which each electoral district sends only one representative to the legislature.

If the American winner-take-all system were in place, the same results would produce a radically different outcome. With only 34.5 percent of the vote, the candidate of the Centrist Party would win the right to be the sole representative for the district, taking 100 percent of the representation, despite the fact that almost two-thirds of the voters preferred someone else. Furthermore, because the winner takes everything, small shifts in support can produce dramatically different results. Had the Conservative Party managed only a handful of votes separating the first-place Centrist Party from the second-place Conservative Party. The remaining three parties lagged behind.

6.2b Election Laws

If the electoral system discourages competition from minor parties, election laws compound this inequity by stacking the deck in favor of Republicans and Democrats. Candidates running under a major party label are guaranteed a spot on the ballot. Candidates of

TABLE 6.1 Change the Rules, Change the Outcome

PROPORTIONAL REPRESENTATION SYSTEM				
Party	**Number of Votes**	**Percentage of Votes**	**Number of Legislative Seats Won**	**Percentage of Representation**
Centrist Party	3,450	34.5%	2	33.3%
Conservative Party	3,375	33.8%	2	33.3%
Labor Party	1,275	12.8%	1	16.7%
Green Party	1,200	12.0%	1	16.7%
Socialist Party	700	7.0%	0	0.0%
TOTALS	**10,000**	**100.1%** (rounding)	**6**	**100.0%**

WINNER-TAKE-ALL SYSTEM				
Party	**Number of Votes**	**Percentage of Votes**	**Number of Legislative Seats Won**	**Percentage of Representation**
Centrist Party	3,450	34.5%	1	100.0%
Conservative Party	3,375	33.8%	0	0.0%
Labor Party	1,275	12.8%	0	0.0%
Green Party	1,200	12.0%	0	0.0%
Socialist Party	700	7.0%	0	0.0%
TOTALS	**10,000**	**100.1%** (rounding)	**1**	**100.0%**

smaller parties often have to earn their way on by collecting signatures from a sufficient number of voters to demonstrate their viability. The effort and expense required to do this discourage poorly organized and poorly financed third parties from trying.[2] In order to qualify for his third-party presidential run in 1992, businessman Ross Perot needed to file petitions in all fifty states, an enormous undertaking that required money, coordination, legwork, and legal assistance in interpreting the fifty individual state election laws in place across the country.

In 1980, Republican Representative John Anderson lost out to Ronald Reagan for the nomination of his party but decided to run as an independent candidate against Reagan and incumbent Democrat Jimmy Carter. Like Perot, Anderson had to overcome election laws designed to discourage this kind of insurgent candidacy. Unlike Perot, Anderson could not self-finance the effort to qualify on fifty state ballots, and the money it took simply to get into the game left him with limited resources to run a general election campaign.

The problems Anderson faced weren't restricted to money, either. By the time he had made the decision to run as an independent in late April 1980, the deadline for filing to get on the ballot had already passed in five states: Kentucky, Maine, Maryland, New Mexico, and Ohio. Anderson had to set up a separate petition drive in every state and in the District of Columbia. To qualify for the ballot in California, he needed 100,000 signatures, but he needed more than half that number in the much smaller state of Georgia. Qualifying for all fifty-one ballots in 1980 required a total of 1.2 million signatures gathered under fifty-one different sets of rules.[3]

6.2c Public Opinion and Party Flexibility

Back in Chapter 3, we said that, by and large, Americans agree on the rules of the political game. It's been a characteristic of American politics that, for all our disagreements on particular issues, most of us tend to prefer democracy, capitalism, liberty, and equality of opportunity to their alternatives. We also traditionally support moderate positions, such as those balancing individual liberty with social responsibility, over extreme positions. As a consequence, parties advocating socialism, communism, fascism, or libertarianism simply haven't found a big audience in America.

Because public opinion in normal times tends toward the political center rather than the political extremes, Republicans and Democrats typically are most successful when they craft moderate positions. After all, parties and their candidates have to go where the votes are. The centrist nature of public opinion dovetails with the winner-take-all electoral system, as both forces move political parties to embrace broad, mainstream political messages in the effort to capture the most votes.

Of late, some national Republican figures, including President Trump, have taken positions closer to their core supporters than to the mainstream on high-profile matters. This is unusual, and prior to 2016, it was not always an effective political strategy. A number of Senate races in 2010 and 2012 were lost to Republicans when they nominated Tea Party–backed candidates who ended up losing winnable seats in states like Delaware, Nevada, Missouri, and Indiana for taking out-of-the-mainstream positions on issues like women's health, immigration, and the economy. One of the more widely reported examples is former Missouri Representative Todd Akin, who lost a winnable Senate race in 2012 by saying that "legitimate rape" could not result in pregnancy. By 2013, some high-profile Republicans like former Bush strategist Karl Rove were concerned that the party would become increasingly marginalized if establishment leaders didn't challenge some of the more extreme sentiments expressed by the party's base.[4] This is because moderation generally wins elections, especially in large statewide and national electorates. And in the rare case when moderation doesn't win elections, it sets up potential conflict between the winner and more moderate voters. This is one reason why Donald Trump arrived at the White House as a polarizing figure with strong support from his base but deep dislike from large numbers of Americans.

You could say that both major parties function best when they act like big umbrellas containing several factions, which would probably go their own way in other nations where the electoral system rewarded multiple small parties.[5] The Republican Party is composed of several conservative factions that have different interests and agendas, including:

- *Religious conservatives* concerned about moral issues, but not economic issues.
- *Business conservatives* favoring free enterprise, who are not particularly concerned about moral questions.
- *Small government conservatives* whose laissez-faire views on social issues may conflict with the direction religious conservatives want government to take.

Similarly, the Democratic Party is composed of several relatively liberal factions that also have different and at times competing agendas:

- *Economic liberals*, centered around unions, who are concerned with wages, benefits, job creation, and the interests of workers.
- *Social liberals*, such as African Americans and many Jews, with a liberal social agenda, including concern for minority rights.
- *Social and economic moderates* ("New Democrats" as Bill Clinton called them), especially suburbanites and women concerned with crime, education, and the environment, whose support of globalization and free trade may conflict with the interests of union workers.

Even within these groups, there can be flexibility and overlap. Union workers with conservative social values were dubbed "Reagan Democrats" when they were persuaded to vote Republican in the 1980s. Business leaders in the entertainment field who have liberal social agendas often support Democratic candidates.

Because of the fluid and diverse nature of the groups that identify with the two major parties, Republicans and Democrats need to engage in the process of **interest aggregation** to bring together a wide variety of sometimes-conflicting demands, in order to enter into successful electoral competition. What makes U.S. parties interesting in this respect is that interest aggregation takes place *within* the party *before* it contests an election. In multiparty systems, where many narrow parties are represented in government, the process of negotiating among interests takes place when multiple victorious parties bargain with each other after the election for a place in the new government. The result of this negotiating is a **coalition** government made up of multiple parties.[6]

Because the groups that make up the two large parties are always negotiating with each other (or fighting among themselves) to get the party to represent their agendas, the parties are pretty adept at moving to where the votes are as public opinion shifts. In the 1980s, as public opinion took a conservative turn, the Republican Party shifted rightward and began a successful electoral run. Eventually, following a protracted battle among its more liberal constituencies (which tend to participate disproportionately in the process of selecting presidential candidates), the Democratic Party shifted rightward as well in the 1990s, only to revisit its earlier struggles following Bill Clinton's departure from the White House. During the second Bush administration, the Republican Party lost touch with a large number of voters in the political center and lost control of Congress and the White House. Barack Obama's rise to the presidency appeared to herald the resurrection of liberal groups in the Democratic Party, although internal battles persisted with economic moderates who remained a significant presence in Congress. Donald Trump's capture of the Republican nomination represented the continuation of a race to the right that took hold in the party during the Obama years.

This flexibility also permits the major parties to move into space occupied by smaller parties, should they begin to make electoral inroads. Ross Perot's economic pragmatism appealed to enough voters to make him a force (if not a factor) in the 1992 presidential contest. Over the next four years, both major parties deliberately made appeals to Perot supporters, and by 1996, they were able to cut the maverick Texan's vote-getting ability in half.

Figure 6.2 should give you a picture of what public opinion typically looks like in the United States and how the two major parties respond to it. The curved line captures the

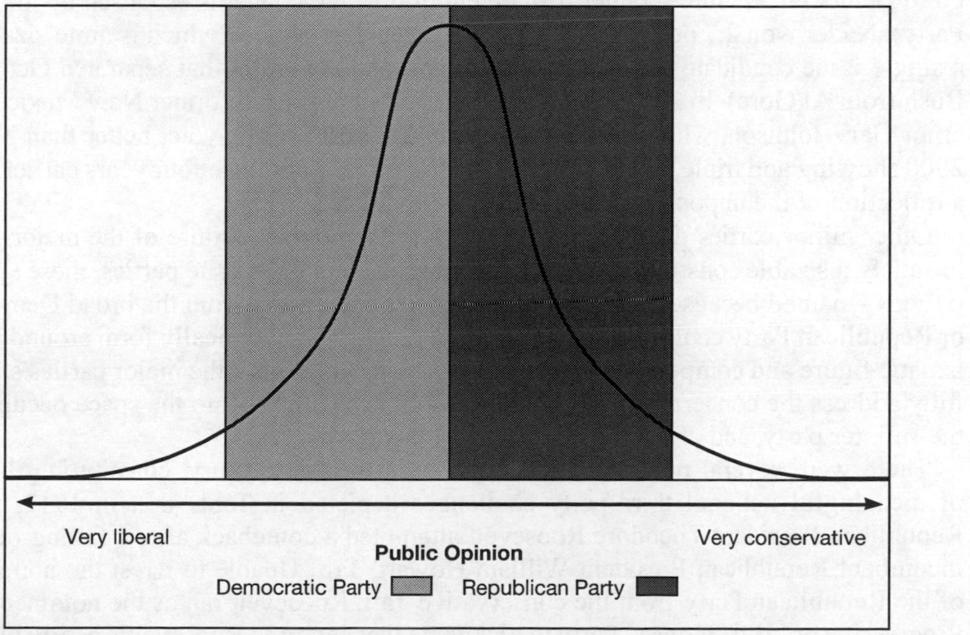

interest aggregation: The process by which groups with different and potentially conflicting agendas are brought together under the umbrella of a political party.

coalition: A government formed as a partnership among several victorious parties in a multiparty system, following negotiations about the agenda that each party will be allowed to pursue in exchange for its participation in the new government.

Very liberal   Very conservative

Public Opinion

Democratic Party ▢   Republican Party ▮

FIGURE 6.2 The Two Large Parties Maintain Their Dominance

distribution of opinions people hold, from very liberal to very conservative. It bulges in the middle, meaning that most people hold moderate views. If you think of this line in terms of votes, there are more votes where the line peaks. Public opinion may shift over the years to the (conservative) right or the (liberal) left—today you would find more of a bulge on the right than has been typical—but it tends to avoid extremes. As it shifts, the parties follow, like two big, wobbly Jello molds, capturing as many votes as they can while squeezing out smaller parties that could try to capitalize on changing public attitudes. This is why the Republican Party has moved to the right along with its voters, but in the process, it runs the risk of losing voters in the middle.

6.2d Third and Minor Parties

L.O. Identify third parties as either ideological, single-issue, or splinter parties, and explain why they rarely compete successfully for elected offices.

ideological parties: Third parties that form around a broad ideology not represented by the two major American parties. They endure from election to election despite the fact that they rarely achieve electoral success.

single-issue parties: Third parties that form to advance a specific issue agenda, like environmentalism, that members feel is not being adequately addressed by the two major American parties. They endure from election to election despite the fact that they rarely achieve electoral success.

splinter parties: Third parties that split away from one of the major parties in protest against the direction taken by the Republicans or Democrats. They often form around a charismatic leader and last a short time, after which the major parties address their concerns, and they lose their reason to continue.

With the rules stacked against them, you might think that third parties and minor parties simply wouldn't form at all. However, throughout our history, parties that have been unsuccessful at winning elections have repeatedly formed, and some of them have flourished. What's with that?

There are a couple of answers to this question. In some cases, winning is less important than giving party identifiers a place to go. Communists may not win too many elections in the United States, but if you're a Communist, then neither of the two major parties is going to represent your beliefs. That's why **ideological parties** like the Communist Party, Socialist Party, and Libertarian Party have a long history in the United States, complete with fielding candidates for office. Even though almost all ideological party candidates go down to defeat, having the opportunity to publicize their views can be a goal in its own right, apart from electoral victory.[7]

In a similar vein, some parties that endure from election to election formulate around a concern for a particular issue rather than a broad ideology. Such **single-issue parties** operate like ideological parties in that they compete in elections largely to draw attention to the issue they espouse. For instance, a Right-to-Life Party appears on the ballot in New York State elections. Nationally, the Green Party is a single-issue party devoted to the cause of environmentalism.

In 2000, the Green Party nominated noted consumer advocate Ralph Nader as its presidential candidate. Given the media's natural affinity for personality and celebrity, Nader's candidacy generated more media attention for the Green Party than a single-issue party normally would attract (although much of this centered around the horse race elements of Nader's candidacy—whether Nader would claim liberal votes that might otherwise go to Democrat Al Gore—rather than on environmental concerns espoused by the Green Party). Nader won 2.7 percent of the national presidential vote, which is quite sizable for a single-issue candidate (and quite a bit more than the margin that separated George W. Bush from Al Gore). In 2016, the Libertarian Party nominated former New Mexico Governor Gary Johnson, who captured more than 3 percent of the vote, better than Nader's 2000 showing and triple what he won as the Libertarian nominee four years earlier, likely a reflection of the unpopularity of the major candidates.

Other minor parties develop in reaction to the temporary failure of the major parties to satisfy a sizable constituency. Unlike ideological or single-issue parties, these **splinter parties**—named because of their propensity to splinter away from the broad Democratic or Republican Party coalitions—tend to be pragmatic. They typically form around a charismatic figure and compete for one or two election cycles until the major parties successfully address the concerns of the group that split away, move into the space occupied by the splinter party, and effectively put it out of business.

There were several notable splinter parties in the last century, constituting the bulk of meaningful national third-party challenges depicted in Table 6.2. In 1912, former Republican President Theodore Roosevelt attempted a comeback after a falling-out with incumbent Republican President William Howard Taft. Unable to wrest the nomination of the Republican Party from the conservative Taft, Roosevelt ran as the nominee of the Progressive or "Bull Moose" Party (a nickname that captured Roosevelt's hearty physical characteristics). On the strength of his personal popularity, Roosevelt secured more than

TABLE 6.2 Significant Third-Party and Independent Candidates of the Twentieth Century[T1]

Year	Candidate	Party	Type of Third Party	Percentage of Votes	Electoral Votes
1912	Theodore Roosevelt	Progressive/Bull Moose	Splinter	27.4%	88
1992	Ross Perot	Independent	Splinter	18.9%	0
1924	Robert M. LaFollette	Progressive	Splinter	16.6%	13
1968	George C. Wallace	American Independent	Splinter	13.5%	46
1996	Ross Perot	Reform	Splinter	8.4%	0
1980	John B. Anderson	Independent	Splinter	6.6%	0
1912	Eugene V. Debbs	Socialist	Ideological	6.0%	0

one-quarter of the vote, better than any third-party or independent candidate of the twentieth century. However, his presence on the ballot drained Republican votes from Taft and enabled the election of Democrat Woodrow Wilson.

After the election, the Republican Party absorbed the disaffected progressives, and the Progressive Party faded away. It reemerged briefly in 1924 under the leadership of one of its original founders, Senator Robert M. LaFollette of Wisconsin, whose showing was less impressive than Roosevelt's. LaFollette died shortly after the election, and although the Progressive Party continued to function for a while, it never again competed effectively in national elections.

In the mid-twentieth century, it was the Democratic Party's turn to see a faction walk out and compete against it. The issue of civil rights split southern Democrats from the rest of their party, as first Harry S Truman and then John F. Kennedy and Lyndon B. Johnson took increasingly progressive positions on race relations. In 1948, President Truman beat back a challenge by disaffected "Dixiecrats," who unsuccessfully ran Democratic South Carolina Governor Strom Thurmond as a regional alternative to Truman. Thurmond won only 2.4 percent of the vote, although he polled ahead of Truman in four southern states.[8]

A more serious split occurred in 1968, when fiery Alabama Governor George C. Wallace, a Democrat, received 13.5 percent of the vote as the candidate of the American Independent Party, on a platform of racial segregation. With the national Democratic Party supporting policies promoting civil rights for African Americans, Wallace's defection heralded the departure of white southerners as a Democratic Party constituency. Socially conservative white southerners eventually found a new home in the Republican Party, and the American Independent Party faded from the scene.

John Anderson's 1980 independent run for president and Ross Perot's 1992 independent bid were born more from widespread doubts about the major party nominees than from disagreements over the direction of a major party. In 1980, Republicans nominated former California Governor Ronald Reagan to face incumbent Democrat Jimmy Carter. At the time, Reagan was widely regarded as being more conservative than mainstream America and highly belligerent toward the Soviet Union, while Carter was saddled with a sour economy and a lingering crisis in which Americans were being held hostage in Iran.

In this environment, where one candidate did not inspire trust and the other was perceived to lack competence, undecided voters were looking for an alternative. Anderson, a previously obscure Republican congressman from Illinois who had lost his party's nomination to Reagan, presented himself as someone trustworthy and competent. Although his campaign received a fair amount of press interest because of its potential to complicate the horserace, Anderson's independent bid fell way short and, as many Americans warmed to Reagan during his first term, there was no rationale for Anderson to try again four years later.

Building a Viable Third Party—for a Few Months

If splinter parties gain momentum from charismatic figures, certainly Ross Perot fits the mold. The feisty self-made Texas billionaire surprised political observers when, during an appearance on CNN's *Larry King Live* in February 1992, he announced that he would put his considerable fortune behind an independent presidential run if people would circulate petitions sufficient to get his name on the ballot in all fifty states. They did. Perot coordinated and financed the effort—and advertised it by appearing on other television talk shows.

Perot was an unconventional candidate. He understood television and used the media to maximum effect. By late June, he was running neck-and-neck with his major party opponents—only to drop out of the race at a time when questions about his character threatened to foment into a feeding frenzy. Then, just as suddenly, Perot reentered the contest with just weeks to go before the election. His personal fortune permitted him to pick up where he had left off, albeit with a smaller base of supporters. Perot spent heavily to purchase thirty-minute-long "infomercials" focusing primarily on economic issues that interested his supporters. A combination of money, media, and misgivings about the major candidates contributed to his strong showing.[T2]

After the election, Perot remained a visible figure, energizing his followers and encouraging them to begin a third-party movement. As disaffection with the major parties continued into the first years of the Clinton administration, the Perot-backed organization "United We Stand America" became the basis for the Reform Party, which was organized with Perot's support in 1995. Leaders of the new party hoped to run candidates for numerous offices and to build on Perot's impressive showing in the 1992 presidential election.

However, the Reform Party faltered as the political climate changed. After a halting start, President Clinton began to connect with a large segment of the population. By 1996, a lot of the anger from four years earlier had dissipated, and with it, more than half of Perot's vote. Because the Reform Party had been built from the top down—around Perot's dynamic television persona—rather than from the bottom up, there was little to sustain it once Perot's television "act" grew stale. In 1998, the Reform

Reform Party Founder
Ross Perot

Party captured a major office when former professional wrestling star Jesse Ventura was elected governor of Minnesota in a tight, three-way race, but Perot's legions were learning how hard it is to build a viable third party in the United States.

By 2000, the national Reform Party had split into two camps: one loyal to its founder and one supportive of conservative television commentator Patrick Buchanan, who had been denied the nomination of the Republican Party and who was looking for a ready-made platform from which to launch a presidential campaign. Perot supporters cried foul and accused Buchanan of hijacking their organization. In a raucous and testy convention, the two camps nominated different candidates (the Perot group supported physicist Dr. John Hagelin), and it was left to the courts to decide who would be the official nominee. In September 2000, a federal judge declared Buchanan to be the Reform nominee. Buchanan turned out to be a candidate who did not resonate with the times, and his campaign went nowhere. In 2002, Ventura decided not to seek a second term as Minnesota governor, and the once high-flying Reform Party was left battered and irrelevant.

In a similar fashion, Perot offered himself as an alternative to unpopular incumbent Republican George H. W. Bush and scandal-plagued Democrat Bill Clinton. Unlike Anderson, Perot could bankroll his campaign with the considerable fortune he had acquired as the founder of Electronic Data Systems, a multibillion-dollar corporation. In a year when many voters were disillusioned with the major nominees, Perot's candidacy polled almost 19 percent of the vote. He tried to organize his independent bid into a permanent third-party organization, but as disaffected voters returned to the major parties, Perot's **Reform Party** candidacy did less well in 1996, and by 2000, the third-party movement had effectively run out of steam. Demystifying Government: Building a Viable Third Party—for a Few Months discusses the Perot effort in more detail.

Even though a number of third-party and independent presidential candidates performed admirably at the polls, they rarely had any traction in the Electoral College, which ultimately decides who becomes president (no third-party or independent candidate has won any electoral votes since George Wallace in 1968). In Chapter 7, we'll explore how the Electoral College works, but for now, the important thing to know is that in contempo-

Reform Party: The organization built by businessman Ross Perot in a mostly unsuccessful attempt to create a competitive third party.

rary elections, it takes 270 electoral votes to be elected president, which are awarded state by state on a winner-take-all basis. When you look at how even the more successful third-party and independent candidates did over the last hundred years, it's clear that none of them came close (review Table 6.2). Even in Perot's case, because his support was evenly spread throughout the country, he was unable to dent the Electoral College.

6.3 Party Systems

So, America has a two-party system and always has. From the time the Constitution went into effect, with the formation of rudimentary political parties, there have been two parties in regular competition with each other. In a **party system**, the *same* parties enter into regular competition with each other year after year, and although the number of parties has been stable over the past two centuries, party labels and the groups identifying with the parties have changed several times.

We can divide our history into five distinct periods, each characterized by a party system with a uniquely constituted pair of major parties competing against each other. Within each of these five party systems, the groups identifying with the two parties remained stable. But between each period, there was a **realignment**, or a significant, lasting, long-term shift in the groups that identified with the parties in the previous system, precipitating the change to the new system. Typically, realignments have followed a major social upheaval, like war or depression, which created new social cleavages that the existing parties were simply unable to address. Political scientist V. O. Key noted that each realignment followed what he called a **critical election**, in which large numbers of voters shift their allegiances in what turns out to be lasting fashion.[9]

The story of these five party systems and the realignments that fashioned them is in one respect the story of the major events that shaped American political history. Let's look briefly at that story, paying special attention to some of the key figures who emerged during these periods to get a sense of the foundation beneath the parties we know today as Republican and Democrat.

6.3a Formation of a Party System, 1796–1824

The framers of the Constitution did not look kindly on political parties and did not anticipate their existence. If you look at the Constitution, you'll find that parties aren't mentioned anywhere. That's because parties were perceived to be synonymous with **factions**, and you probably remember how poorly factions were regarded. Regardless, the fact that parties were feared as organizations that could produce **tyranny** didn't stop some of the same people who wrote negatively of them from organizing what would become the first party system.

George Washington, in his farewell address of 1796, spoke directly of "the baneful effects of the spirit of party:"

> It serves always to distract the public councils and enfeeble the public administration. It agitates the community with ill-founded jealousies and false alarms; kindles the animosity of one part against another; foments occasionally riot and insurrection. It opens the door to foreign influence and corruption, which finds a facilitated access to the government itself through the channels of party passion.[10]

All well and good, but at the same time Washington was urging his countrymen to put aside partisan differences, others—notably others who served in Washington's administration, like Alexander Hamilton and Thomas Jefferson—were at work forming what would soon become America's first political parties. By 1800, two factions in Congress had developed around the major issue of the day: the strength of the federal government relative to the states. Supporters of Hamilton's position in favor of a strong federal government with a strong national bank formed the camp that would eventually be known as the Federalists. Followers of Jefferson's position on states' rights would become known as the Democratic-Republicans (they were also called Anti-Federalists, Republicans, Jeffersonian Democrats, and even sometimes simply Jeffersonians).

party system: The regular, over-time competition of the same major political parties, composed of the same groups of identifiers.

L.O. Define the term **party system**, *and identify the key characteristics of the five party systems that have arisen since parties emerged in the late eighteenth century.*

L.O. Identify the relationship between realignments and the demise of party systems.

realignment: A shift from one party system to another, the result of a lasting, long-term adjustment in the groups that identify with the major political parties.

critical election: An election that heralds a realignment, during which large numbers of voters deviate from their traditional party allegiances in what turns out to be a lasting change.

faction: A group of individuals who are united by a desire that, if realized, would threaten the liberty of the larger community—in James Madison's words, individuals who are "united and actuated by some common impulse of passion, or of interest, adverse to the rights of other citizens, or to the permanent and aggregate interests of the community." A faction may be defined by size, such as when a majority of citizens threatens the liberty of the minority, or by intensity, such as when a minority of citizens with intensely held preferences threatens the liberty of a disinterested majority.

tyranny: The denial of liberty to individuals through the actions of a faction or through the actions of government itself.

In 1800, the two groups, or caucuses, began acting and looking like political parties. The Democratic-Republican congressional caucus nominated Thomas Jefferson for president, while congressional Federalists lent their support to the incumbent (and eventual loser) John Adams. Congressional partisans also began building connections with supporters in the states.[11] Despite widespread apprehension about political parties, the first party system was in full swing.

The Federalists never organized as effectively as the Democratic-Republicans, and John Adams was the only president who would wear their label. The Democratic-Republicans, with strength in the rural South, elected a succession of Virginians to the presidency between 1800 and 1824: Jefferson, James Madison, and James Monroe. In fact, the Federalists had such a hard time of it that by 1816 they stopped nominating presidential candidates altogether. From the time the Federalists called it quits until 1824, the country went through a brief period when there was little party activity at the national level.[12] This so-called "Era of Good Feelings" masked conflicts that were rumbling below the surface, however. It was only a short period of time before party competition would be back.

6.3b The Second Party System: Jackson Democrats vs. the Whigs, 1828–1856

The electorate was changing in the 1820s as states began removing property ownership as a requirement for political participation. This led to conditions that supported the emergence of the mass political parties that we know today. More than anyone else, Andrew Jackson—backwoodsman, lawyer, congressman, senator, and charismatic general in the War of 1812—would surface as the architect of the new political party (see biography).

"Old Hickory" was a popular, strong, and divisive figure, determined to democratize government and bring ordinary people into the political process. Elected to the presidency in 1828 as a Democratic-Republican, Jackson was a polarizing force who expanded Jefferson's party to include newly enfranchised voters while sending disaffected Jeffersonians into the opposition as National Republicans, or Whigs. Leaders of the new Whig Party—people like Henry Clay and Daniel Webster—feared Jackson's form of democracy meant trampling individual liberties. For its part, Jackson's party began competition under the abbreviated name "Democrats"—a label meant to capture the broad-based nature of the party and the same label it uses today.[13] In fact, the modern-day Democratic Party is the nation's oldest continually operating political party, tracing its roots back to Jefferson and Jackson.

Under Jackson's leadership, the Democrats held their first national nominating convention in 1832—the forerunner of the conventions we talked about at the start of the chapter—replacing the congressional caucuses that had selected previous presidential candidates. It was more democratic, and it drew more people into the political process. Presidential campaigns, once dominated by a congressional elite, became mass exercises. Something resembling modern political parties had been born.[14]

The Democrats drew their strength from the rural southern and western elements of Jefferson's party, but they were a national party with a base in New York led by the pragmatic Martin Van Buren, who would follow Jackson in the White House. The Whigs were also national in scope, and more of an elite party, supported by southern plantation owners and northern commercial interests. For three decades, they entered into regular competition with each other, with the Democrats winning most of the presidential contests (the two Whig victories were with military figures William Henry Harrison in 1840 and Zachary Taylor in 1848, both of whom promptly died in office not long after their inaugurations).

However, as the 1850s approached, the national coalitions in both parties came under enormous strain. Abolitionist sentiment grew in the northern and frontier states, while public debate over extending slavery to new western states intensified divisions over the issue of slavery. Northern Whigs aligned with strong antislavery forces and split from southern Whigs, who had been promoting compromise positions designed to preserve the union while maintaining the institution of slavery. Northern Democrats, who long

ANDREW JACKSON

Andrew Jackson was born in the Waxhaws area near the border between North and South Carolina on March 15, 1767. At age thirteen he joined the Continental Army as a courier, and in 1781 he was briefly taken prisoner by the British. In 1784, Jackson went to Salisbury, North Carolina, where he studied law for several years. His public service career began in 1788 with an appointment as prosecuting officer for the Superior Court in Nashville, Tennessee, which at that time was a part of the Western District of North Carolina. In 1796, Jackson was elected to Congress from the newly created state of Tennessee. The following year, the Tennessee legislature elected Jackson to serve in the U.S. Senate, but he held the seat for only one session before resigning to serve for six years as a judge on the Tennessee Supreme Court. In the years to follow, Jackson would rise to the rank of major general in the U.S. Army, and became a national hero during the War of 1812 following his defeat of the British at the Battle of New Orleans in January 1815. During this period he earned the nickname "Old Hickory." Jackson returned to the U.S. Senate in 1822, and two years later resigned his seat when the House of Representatives denied him the presidency despite winning the popular vote. He was subsequently elected twice, in 1828 and 1832. Following his second term, Jackson retired to his home near Nashville, where he died on June 8, 1845.[T3]

differed with their pro-slavery southern counterparts, found themselves in alliance with northern Whigs, and in the middle 1850s, they joined forces to create the Republican Party as an antislavery party.

The Whigs and the Democrats had originally organized around common economic perspectives. But their internal similarities were irrelevant to the issue of slavery, and as slavery became the overriding political concern, regional differences within each party pulled them apart. The realignment that ensued left the Democrats as a southern, pro-slavery party. It destroyed the Whigs entirely. And it enabled the emergence of the Republicans, the only "third" party ever to attain major party status.[15]

Based in Wisconsin, Michigan, Ohio, and Illinois, the Republican Party began competing successfully in statewide elections, as it spread through the Midwest eastward to anti-slavery regions of the North. By 1856, state Republican parties had unified, and the first Republican national convention was held. In 1860, the Republican Party elected its first president, Abraham Lincoln, ushering in secession, Civil War, and the third party system.[16]

6.3c The Third Party System: Ascendancy of a New Party, 1860–1892

From 1860 on, Republicans and Democrats engaged in regular competition with each other. Even though the labels haven't changed in over 145 years, the issues the parties have confronted and the groups aligning themselves with each party have shifted dramatically over the years.

The Republican Party dominated national politics during this era of the third party system, when the parties were organized over divisions stemming from the Civil War and Reconstruction of the Union. The Democratic Party had become a southern conservative party, while the Republican Party was essentially a northern party devoted to extending rights to freed slaves.

Still, just like the second party system had been organized around economic groups and fell apart when the parties weren't able to address the issue of slavery, the third party system, organized around the issue of slavery, was unprepared to address emerging economic concerns as the nation headed into the industrial era.

In the West, farmers became politicized in opposition to an eastern financial class that they felt had a tight grip over the economy. In cities, workers in the new industrial economy were concerned with issues of trade, wages, and as the century progressed, monopoly ownership of business. Neither party responded adequately to their complaints, which rose in volume over the latter third of the nineteenth century until they came to dominate national politics. The coming division in American politics would pit East against West, bankers and lenders against farmers and laborers, much as the previous conflict had divided North and South.[17]

6.3d The Fourth Party System: Republicans Again, 1896–1928

In 1893, the country plunged into economic depression. The Democratic Party was split down the middle between eastern forces of commercialism that favored the stability of a gold standard for currency, and western forces of populism—rural advocates of currency backed by silver, which by virtue of its greater availability would have a devaluing effect that would assist rural debtors.

By 1896, the agrarian forces had emerged victorious within the Democratic Party, which nominated Nebraskan William Jennings Bryan for president on a platform of "free silver" (see biography). The Republicans, with the strong support of commercial interests, cast Bryan as a radical and stoked fears of a populist takeover of the government that resonated in the industrial Northeast and Midwest. Banks and corporations heavily funded the Republican nominee, William McKinley (see biography). The nation was polarized.

BIOGRAPHY

WILLIAM JENNINGS BRYAN

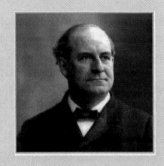

William Jennings Bryan, the fiery populist who secured three presidential nominations only to be turned away each time by the voters, was born in Salem, Illinois in 1860. After moving to Lincoln, Nebraska in 1887, he was elected to Congress in 1890 and reelected two years later. By 1896, he had become a national figure as an advocate of free silver as an alternative to the gold standard for American currency, which would have worked to the benefit of debtors and laborers over creditors and industrialists. At age 36, Bryan won the presidential nomination of the Democratic Party and delivered what became known as the "Cross of Gold" speech for its admonition not to "crucify mankind upon a cross of gold." Despite his oratory, Bryan lost the presidency to William McKinley in 1896 and again in 1900. He won a third Democratic nomination in 1908 but was defeated by William Howard Taft, making him the only party standard-bearer in history to run unsuccessfully for the presidency three times. In his later years, Bryan served as secretary of state under Woodrow Wilson and was active as an orator, author, and lecturer. He was the lead prosecuting attorney for the state of Tennessee in the 1925 "Scopes Monkey Trial" on the teaching of evolution. Bryan died in Tennessee of a heart attack, days after the conclusion of the trial.[T4]

BIOGRAPHY

WILLIAM MCKINLEY

William McKinley was born in Niles, Ohio on January 29, 1843, the seventh son of William and Nancy Allison McKinley. At age 18, he enlisted in the Ohio Infantry and served in the Civil War. McKinley was elected to Congress in 1876 as a Republican from the eighteenth district of Ohio, and despite constant gerrymandering of his district, he served as congressman from 1876 to 1890, with the exception of a period in 1884-1885, when he was unseated in a contested election. Congress passed the McKinley Tariff Act in 1890, but it hurt the Republican Party in the 1890 election, and McKinley lost his seat. He was elected governor of Ohio the following year, however, and reelected in 1893. In 1896, McKinley defeated William Jennings Bryan and was elected president. In 1898, McKinley asked Congress to declare war on Spain. During the brief Spanish-American War, he maintained direct control over the armed forces, making many decisions himself. After the war, McKinley made the decision to retain the Philippines and Puerto Rico, thus launching the global expansion of the United States. He was reelected president in 1900. The following year, McKinley was shot in Buffalo, NY. He died on September 14, 1901, from complications resulting from his wounds.[T5]

For the first time in over a generation, a presidential election offered a stark choice over economic issues long ignored by the major parties.

McKinley's victory in the critical election of 1896 cemented Republican control of national politics through the first one-third of the twentieth century. Even though the Republicans had been the majority party before, the 1896 vote revealed an entirely new set of allegiances for the two parties that would hold for decades. McKinley's victory was concentrated in the commercial centers of the Northeast and the industrial Midwest. Bryan swept the South and the West.[18]

The Republican Party established itself as the party of bankers, industrialists, urban laborers, and African Americans (who remained loyal to the party of Lincoln). The Democrats emerged as the party of rural interests and southerners (whose attachment to the Democratic Party was as strong as it had been since the Civil War). These two groups would compete against each other for more than thirty years, with the Republicans maintaining a clear advantage. Between 1896 and 1928, in a time marked by rapid immigration and industrialization, Republicans would lose the White House only in the wake of Teddy Roosevelt's third-party challenge in 1912 and again in 1916.

That is, until the next great economic depression.

6.3e The Fifth Party System: Democrats Emerge as Liberals, 1932–1964

Herbert Hoover, the last in the line of Republican presidents who served during the fourth party system, no doubt had little sense of what was coming (see biography). The Great Depression hit suddenly and ferociously in 1929, ending a decade of prosperity. Hoover spent the rest of his term unsuccessfully grappling with an economic downturn that proved deeper and more enduring than he had initially anticipated.

With the unemployment rate soaring above 20 percent, voters were ready for a change. In what emerged as a campaign of the powerful versus what Democratic nominee Franklin D. Roosevelt called the "forgotten man at the bottom of the economic pyramid," the Democratic Party won a landslide victory in 1932 that would establish it as the majority party for over three decades (see biography). Roosevelt himself would claim the presidency four times—breaking with the two-term tradition established by Washington—and between 1932 and 1964, popular General Dwight D. Eisenhower would be the only Republican to crack the Democrat's lock on the White House.[19]

After the election, Democrats embraced government activism to ease the burden felt by an increasingly angry and despondent America. In office, Roosevelt moved swiftly

---

FRANKLIN D. ROOSEVELT

Franklin D. Roosevelt was born into a life of privilege in Hyde Park, New York on January 30, 1882. His parents and private tutors provided him with almost all his formative education until 1896, when he attended Groton, a prestigious preparatory school in Massachusetts, followed by Harvard and Columbia University. In 1905, he married a distant cousin, Anna Eleanor Roosevelt, who was the niece of President Theodore Roosevelt. They had six children, one of whom died in infancy. Roosevelt began his political career in 1910 when he was elected to the New York State Senate as a Democrat. He was appointed assistant secretary of the navy by President Wilson in 1913 and held the post until 1920, when he was the vice-presidential nominee of the Democratic Party on a ticket that lost in a landslide to Warren Harding. The following year, Roosevelt contracted polio and permanently lost the use of his legs. In 1928, Roosevelt was elected governor of New York. Four years later, he won the nomination of the Democratic Party for president, and he defeated incumbent Herbert Hoover by a lopsided margin. Roosevelt would serve longer in the presidency than anyone in history, winning reelection three times. During his tenure, Roosevelt initiated a series of "New Deal" social welfare programs designed to address the effects of the Great Depression, and he presided over American involvement in World War II. He served until his death in 1945.[T7]

New Deal: The name given to the programs of President Franklin D. Roosevelt, which vastly expanded the role of the federal government in an effort to deal with the debilitating effects of the Great Depression on American society.

New Deal coalition: The political coalition composed of urbanites, ethnic and racial minorities, unions, liberals, and southerners that made the Democratic Party the majority party during the fifth party system.

to enact an agenda that was far more activist than the one on which he had campaigned. Working in tandem with Democratic majorities in the House and Senate, Roosevelt implemented the **New Deal** policies that would cement the electoral changes evident in the critical election of 1932. Key members of what would be termed the **New Deal coalition** included:

- Urbanites, particularly in the North, many of whom were first-time voters.
- Jews, many of whom were urbanites, and who were among the Democrats' strongest supporters.
- Catholics, many of whom were first drawn to the Democratic Party in 1928, when its nominee was New York Governor Al Smith, the first Catholic presidential nominee of a major party.
- African Americans, who abandoned the party of Lincoln after seventy years of affiliation.
- Organized labor, who benefited greatly from Roosevelt's New Deal reforms.
- Liberals, whose ideas were well received in FDR's reformist administration.
- Southern whites, who remained true to the party of the Civil War, despite conservative voting patterns that were out of sync with the progressive reforms of the New Deal.[20]

Fair Deal: The name given to the domestic policies of President Truman, which built on the popularity of the New Deal.

Great Society: The name given to the programs of President Lyndon B. Johnson, which elevated the federal government to the most prominent role it would play in the twentieth century. The philosophy of the Great Society was that government should try to solve large social problems like hunger and poverty.

Following Roosevelt, Harry S Truman maintained the New Deal coalition with his **Fair Deal** policies that built on popular New Deal programs by, for instance, raising the minimum wage and increasing Social Security benefits (see biography). The only Republican president elected during the fifth party system, Dwight D. Eisenhower served in the 1950s during a conservative interlude to the activist governments of his predecessors and successors (see biography). In the 1960s, Lyndon B. Johnson presided over a second wave of government activism ushered in by his **Great Society** programs aimed at conquering poverty and extending civil rights protection to African Americans (see biography).

However, Johnson's emphasis on civil rights alienated white southerners, and his prosecution of the Vietnam War deeply divided elements of the New Deal coalition. Although Democrats would continue to compete successfully in southern statewide elections, they no longer dominated. Republicans were emerging as a competitive force on the statewide level and, gradually, as a dominant force in presidential elections. Richard Nixon exploited cracks in the Democrats' southern base during his presidential campaign of

HARRY S TRUMAN

Harry S Truman was born in Lamar, Missouri on May 8, 1884. During his youth, Truman worked as a timekeeper for a railroad construction contractor, bank clerk, farmer, and clothing store owner before being elected judge and, in 1926, presiding judge of the Jackson County Court. In 1934, he won election to the U.S. Senate as a Democrat from Missouri, and in 1944 Truman was elected vice president on a ticket with Franklin D. Roosevelt. He became president 82 days after his inauguration upon Roosevelt's sudden death. In office, he approved the use of the atomic bomb against Japan, oversaw the founding of the United Nations, and presided over the start of the Cold War, issuing the Truman Doctrine in 1947 to support nations struggling against communism. Truman narrowly won an uphill reelection battle against Republican Thomas E. Dewey in 1948. His second term saw America wage an undeclared war in Korea. He retired to Independence, Missouri in 1953, and died on December 26, 1972.[T8]

DWIGHT D. EISENHOWER

Dwight D. Eisenhower, the World War II military leader who would become president of the United States, was born in Denison, Texas on October 14, 1890. In 1892, the Eisenhower family moved to Abilene, Kansas, where Eisenhower graduated from Abilene High School. In 1911, Eisenhower entered West Point, followed in 1925 by Command and General Staff School and the Army War College in 1927. He rose rapidly through the military ranks, serving as executive officer to the assistant secretary of war (1929 to 1933), chief military aide to Army Chief of Staff General Douglas MacArthur (1933 to 1935), then during World War II as commander-in-chief of Allied Forces in North Africa (1942), supreme commander of the Allied Expeditionary Forces (1943), commander of the Normandy invasion force, and five-star general (1945). After the German surrender in 1945, Eisenhower was appointed military governor of the U.S. Occupied Zone in Frankfurt and was designated army chief of staff. In 1948, Eisenhower became president of Columbia University, a position he held until he was named Supreme Allied Commander of the North Atlantic Treaty Organization in 1950. He retired from active service in 1952 to run successfully for president as a Republican. During his two terms in office, Eisenhower oversaw the end of the Korean War and the initial construction of the interstate highway system. He retired to his farm near Gettysburg, Pennsylvania after leaving office and died on March 28, 1969.[T9]

1968, and by 1972, Nixon swept the South against antiwar Democrat George McGovern, who was perceived as too liberal to be in touch with southern political sentiment.

Nonetheless, Democrats maintained control of the House of Representatives until 1994, and of the Senate until 1980. They would regain control again in 1986 and hold it on and off thereafter, at one point getting it back when Vermont Republican Senator Jim Jeffords left his party over disagreements with the policies of George W. Bush in 2001, throwing his support to Democratic leaders and breaking a rare 50–50 Senate tie. Throughout this period, more Americans still claimed to be Democrats than Republicans. There had been no political earthquakes on the scale of depression or civil war, and no obvious critical elections to usher in the start of a new political system. Yet, clearly, something had changed. What was it?

6.3f Divided Government in a Conservative Era, 1969–Today

In the wake of the social turmoil of the turbulent 1960s, large numbers of people who previously identified with one of the political parties were shaken from their partisan moorings. As the majority party in the fifth party system, the Democrats felt this shift

L.O. Explain why the post-1960s political era may be understood as a period of dealignment.

LYNDON B. JOHNSON

Lyndon B. Johnson was born August 27, 1908, in Stonewall, Texas. After high school, Johnson performed odd jobs, including work as an elevator operator and as part of a road construction gang, janitor, and office helper. He graduated from Southwest Texas State Teachers College in 1930 and worked as a secondary school teacher before being selected as legislative secretary to a U.S. congressman. In 1937, he won a special election for an open congressional seat and remained in the House of Representatives until 1948. While in Congress, Johnson enlisted in the navy and volunteered for active duty, earning a Silver Star for his role in an aerial combat mission. Johnson was elected to the U.S. Senate from Texas in 1948, became the youngest person to hold the post of Senate majority whip in 1951, and became Senate minority leader in 1953 and majority leader in 1955, where he was instrumental in the passage of the Civil Rights Act of 1957. He ran unsuccessfully for the Democratic presidential nomination in 1960 against John F. Kennedy, but Kennedy selected Johnson as his running mate, and he was elected vice president. Johnson became president after Kennedy was assassinated. During his administration, Johnson signed the Civil Rights Act of 1964, promoted "Great Society" social programs, and escalated the War in Vietnam. He was reelected in a landslide in 1964, but with the Vietnam War raging he chose not to run for reelection in 1968. Johnson retired to his Texas ranch where he died on January 22, 1973.[T10]

dealignment: The weakening of party affiliation, signified by an increase in the number of people who call themselves independents.

more strongly than the Republicans. The percentage of people claiming to be independent of party identification has increased since the 1960s, and the percentage of Democrats has declined (see Figure 6.3). This suggests a **dealignment** in American politics: not the establishment of a new party system so much as a weakening of the existing system.

One source of this possible dealignment is the weakening attachments of some of the original members of the New Deal coalition. Southern whites, for sure, as well as Catholics—both groups that were never ideologically liberal—over time relinquished their support for the Democratic Party. Part of the movement away from the Democrats came in reaction to the political dialogue of the twentieth century's last two decades, which was markedly different from the New Deal and Great Society periods. With the

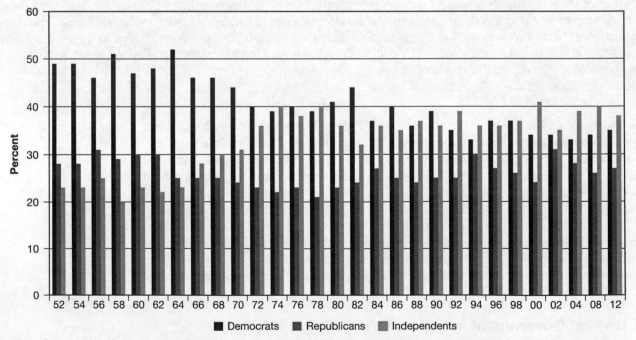

FIGURE 6.3 Weakening Party Ties[T11]

The percentage of independents increased dramatically in the late 1960s, while Democrats declined in strength and Republicans held their own. (Note: Independents include people who lean slightly toward one of the major parties.)

election of Ronald Reagan in 1980 on a platform of social conservatism, issues like abortion rights and gun ownership came to the forefront of debate.

However, while divisive, these issues have not proved to be of enough importance to voters to serve as the basis for realignment. The history of realignments since the Civil War has been that deeply felt economic issues have been the engine of political change, and the history of the late twentieth century has been that during times of economic difficulty, discussion of social issues tends to disappear.[21]

Additionally, while some groups moved away from the Democratic Party since Reagan, the "New Democrats" we mentioned earlier have shifted in the opposite direction. Middle-class suburbanites have become less strongly affiliated with the Republican Party over this period, as have women, whose lukewarm response to cultural conservatism is apparent in a **gender gap**, whereby women have supported Republican presidential candidates by a much lower margin than men.

gender gap: A difference in the voting pattern of men and women, evident since 1980, whereby men are more likely than women to support Republican presidential candidates.

Scholars who study political parties do not universally agree that the United States has gone through a dealignment, especially because the percentage of independents in the electorate began to stabilize in the late 1980s. If you want to make the case that dealigning forces have influenced party affiliation over the past two generations, though, it's easy to see where you would claim the trend started. It coincides with the fraying of the New Deal coalition during the Johnson administration in the mid-1960s. In Figure 6.3, check out the way the percentage of independents, which had hovered around 20 percent in the 1950s and early 1960s, shot up to 30 percent in 1968 and to 40 percent in 1974.

Since 1980, at the national level, it would only be exaggerating things a little to say that Republicans have been the "Male Party" and Democrats have been the "Female Party." When Ronald Reagan defeated Jimmy Carter that year, 54 percent of men supported Reagan, while only 46 percent of women did—a gap of eight points. There has been a gap of at least this magnitude in almost every subsequent presidential election. The 2016 gender gap was a record 24 points, 4 points larger than the gender gap that favored Barack Obama four years earlier. If only women could vote, Hillary Clinton would have been elected president in a 12-point rout. Of course, if only men could vote, Donald Trump would have won by the same margin.[22]

This is not to suggest that women vote as a unit or that there aren't important differences among women voters. Socially conservative and married women tend to support Republicans, for instance, whereas single women lean toward Democratic candidates. But it does point to the tendency for women more than men to be supportive of the activist agenda promoted by the Democratic Party and to the importance of women as an electoral force.[23]

Loosening political ties mean people are less likely to vote for the candidate of the same party for every office on the ballot, something that was quite commonplace during earlier periods of strong party allegiance. As we noted in Chapter 4, since 1968, we've been much more willing to engage in **ticket splitting**, dividing our vote between the parties. This can result in **divided government**, in which one party controls the White House while the other party controls at least one house of Congress.

ticket splitting: Voting for candidates of different parties for different offices, rather than voting a "party line" for all Republicans or all Democrats. Ticket splitting, which has increased in recent years, is a sign of how Americans have been growing independent from political parties.

Perhaps more than anything, divided government characterizes the politics of our recent past. In the forty-nine years from 1968 to 2017, the same party has controlled the White House and both houses of Congress only five brief times: during the four years of the Carter administration, during the first two years of the Clinton administration, during the first few months of the George W. Bush administration (prior to the defection of Republican Senator James Jeffords of Vermont), between the congressional elections of 2002 and 2006, and during the first two years of the Obama administration, when Democrats had large majorities in the House and Senate. During President Bush's first term, the margin of Republican control in the House and the Senate was slim, although Republican strength in the Senate did increase with the president's reelection. In 2010, voters decided to slam on the brakes after two extremely active years with Democrats in charge, returning to divided government following doubts about the substance and speed of implementation of the Democrats' agenda.

divided government: Partisan division of the national government, in which each of the two major parties can claim control of one branch (or one legislative house) of the federal government.

To put this in perspective, when Republican Dwight D. Eisenhower was reelected president in 1956, Democrats won control of both houses of Congress, marking the first time in over a century (since Zachary Taylor's election in 1848) that an election had produced a president of one party and a Congress of another.[24] As we identify less with political parties, we feel more freedom to pick and choose among individual candidates, regardless of party label. Presidents no longer have **coattails**, carrying senators and representatives into office on the strength of their victory. If anything, representatives and senators commonly have reverse coattails—outpolling the presidential nominee of their party. In 2016, Republicans lost seats in the House and Senate even as they recaptured the White House. As a consequence, governing becomes more ad hoc, and more difficult.

That's one reason why this period of divided government has often been characterized by the **gridlock** we talked about in Chapter 5. When voters place majorities of different ideological persuasions in the White House and Congress, officials will naturally disagree, and those checks and balances designed to slow progress kick into high gear. Without strong party ties, this has happened with great frequency over the past four decades. Once Republicans recaptured the Senate in 2002, Congress and the Bush White House at times were able to work effectively to move the president's legislative agenda, but even one-party control is not a recipe for moving legislation through the system. Democrat Barack Obama struggled mightily to fashion congressional support for health-care policy changes amidst deeply held party divisions over how to structure and pay for reform. Jimmy Carter and Bill Clinton (in his first two years) had comfortable House and Senate majorities but had limited success winning legislative approval for their major agenda items.

Today, President Trump has Republican majorities in the House and Senate, although the stability of this arrangement is likely to be tested by the deep divisions in the country that make this a particularly tricky time to govern. The atypical characteristics of the 2016 election raise questions about the ability of the current party system to address the demands of economic and social change. Anti-elite populist sentiment on both sides of the aisle is a sign of a restless electorate. Whether that suggests a long-term turn to Trump's populism of the right or something completely different, the stable party alignment of the past several decades occupies a precarious perch.

We've covered a lot of ground talking about 220 years of party history. Let's stop for a second and take a look at Figure 6.4, which summarizes the main points about partisan realignment and party systems. The majority party in each system is the one in bold type.

6.4 The Party in Government

"Do something!"

That's the cry heard for years from Americans frustrated with the inability of the federal government to make quick progress on important issues. But that doesn't mean we agree on the details of what should be done. Democrat Barack Obama was elected on a platform of change that included some huge promises—stabilizing the economy and ending the deepest recession since the 1930s, extending health-care coverage to uninsured Americans while bringing down health-care costs overall, combating global warming, improving public education—and his supporters expected that Democrats in Congress would work with him to move his agenda forward. But members of Congress have their own constituencies and their own views about how to approach these problems, leading to inevitable disagreement among congressional Democrats and between Congress and the president.

Some of these fault lines were evident even before Obama took the oath of office. The incoming president had asked Congress to prepare legislation designed to stimulate the economy, largely by using tax money to fund government projects that would quickly create jobs. His original plan was to have a bill ready for his signature on the day of his inaugural. But as Congress started work on the measure, disagreements quickly emerged on how much to spend and how to spend it. Some members worried about the size of the price tag, which could have exceeded one trillion dollars. Others wanted more money spent on tax relief and less on job creation. There were disagreements over which projects merited funding. The new president's insistence that the final product have bipartisan support further confounded a complex political situation.

Party System Number	Dates	Main Issue	Parties			Major Figure
1	1796–1824	Federalism	Federalists	vs.	**Anti-Federalists (Democratic-Republicans)**	Jefferson
2	1828–1856	Expansion	Whigs	vs.	**Democrats**	Jackson
3	1860–1892	Slavery/ reconstruction	**Republicans**	vs.	Democrats	Lincoln
4	1896–1928	Industrialization	**Republicans**	vs.	Democrats	McKinley
5	1932–1964	New Deal	Republicans	vs.	**Democrats**	F. D. Roosevelt
?	1968–present	(Dealignment?)	Republicans	vs.	Democrats	Reagan

Bold Denotes majority party in each system

FIGURE 6.4 Party Systems

Spurred by a sense of urgency stemming from the crisis atmosphere of the moment, and buoyed by the support of a new president fresh off a significant electoral victory, Congress eventually passed a stimulus package—one month later than Obama had requested, containing less money than he desired and appropriating more of it for tax cuts than he had wished.

It was by all measures a legislative victory for the young administration, but it also served as an early warning sign of the hazards that lay ahead for a president with ambitious goals, despite the presence of large congressional majorities. That's because, from this first initiative, President Obama had marched headlong into the limitations of partisanship in our institutions of government. When we talk about the **party in government**, we're talking about an elite group: the members of the Republican and Democratic Parties who serve in our governing institutions. We can contrast this with what we call the **party in the electorate**, which involves all of us who through our party identification make up rank-and-file party membership.

The party in government is an interesting and sometimes confounding entity. Remember, the Constitution established Congress and the presidency as institutions that would be filled by people who did not carry party labels. Nonetheless, both institutions are infused with partisanship. In Congress, party strength determines who runs the institution and who controls the agenda. Individual members, though, still have the freedom to go their own way, regardless of party membership. That's how Senator Jeffords' defection from the Republican party could upend President Bush's agenda and why Presidents Clinton and Carter were frustrated by members of Congress who shared a common party affiliation but not always common political interests.

6.4a How Parties in Government Function

Even when we don't have divided government, it can be difficult for members of the same party in Congress and the White House to work as one because of the way political parties function in government. They're flexible. They're not ideological. They're not **responsible parties**, which is simply to say that party leaders cannot impose an agenda

party in government: That component of political parties composed of elected officials that organizes and runs our governing institutions like Congress, the presidency, state governorships and assemblies, and the like.

party in the electorate: Party identifiers who make up the rank-and-file membership of the political parties.

responsible parties: Political parties whose legislative members act in concert, taking clear positions on issues and voting as a unit in accordance with their stated positions.

Responsible Parties

In some countries, political parties act cohesively in the legislature. Great Britain is a good example. Candidates run for office on a party platform, and when in office, leaders of the majority party advance that platform with the unified support of its members. Leaders of the minority parties will also vote as a unit, forming a reliable opposition group.

The British system offers incentives for responsible party behavior that don't apply to the American system. The British prime minister is selected by the majority party in the House of Commons and remains in office only with the continuing support of a legislative majority. If the prime minister loses the support of the majority, the government falls. So, it's in the interest of members of the majority party to act in concert in order to maintain their majority status. Separation of powers and fixed terms of office in the American system do not give legislative parties in the United States the same incentive to unify, as legislative majority status is conferred by the voters every two years, whether or not members of a party vote together.[T12]

In theory, there are advantages to having responsible parties. Campaigns run around clearly articulated programs would accentuate the choices between the parties and provide voters with the information they need to base their vote on the kind of policy they want government to make. There would be no fudging or fuzziness to the candidate's positions of the sort that can complicate **issue voting** like we talked about in Chapter 4—what you see would be what you get. All candidates of a party would run on the same program and in office would be accountable to that program. The party winning the most seats in the legislature would therefore be expected to move ahead and implement its program, while the minority party would play the role of loyal opposition.

For these reasons, responsible parties have had their advocates in the United States. Over a half-century ago, the American Political Science Association issued a report in which it advocated responsible parties for the United States.[T13] Although responsible parties would present voters with clear policy choices and make it easier for elected officials to claim a mandate for action, the decentralization of American politics discourages the collective action necessary to make it happen.

In 1994, the Republican Party attempted to impose a responsible party model on its candidates in that year's congressional elections, organizing its congressional campaigns around a platform it called "The Contract with America." Republican candidates signed a document pledging that, if elected as a legislative majority, they would work collectively to implement a carefully articulated set of policies, what they called "a detailed agenda for national renewal." It included provisions for how the House would operate and listed ten bills that would be considered during the first one hundred days of the congressional session on such things as a constitutional amendment requiring a balanced budget, a crime bill, a welfare reform proposal, and congressional term limits.[T14]

The idea of coordinating congressional campaigns around a national party theme was novel: Congressional campaigns are typically waged independent of each other, revolving around local rather than national concerns. Nonetheless, Republican congressional candidates endorsed the "Contract with America" with the discipline you'd expect to find in a system that has responsible parties.

However, it can be difficult to maintain strict party discipline in a system that requires power sharing in all but the most exceptional political circumstances. For the last two years of President Obama's first term, House Republicans abided by the informal "Hastert rule," stating that only measures supported by a majority of the majority would come to the floor for a vote. Named for former Republican House Speaker Dennis Hastert, the rule was an attempt to prevent Democrats from joining with a handful of Republicans to pass legislation. Although good for maintaining discipline, the "Hastert rule" made governing impossible by precluding compromise with Senate Democrats and President Obama, even when action was urgent. Following President Obama's reelection, political pressures on Republicans to act on a set of looming fiscal issues became impossible to ignore. With taxes set to rise for all Americans on January 1, 2013, House Speaker John Boehner agreed to set aside the rule and let the House vote on a Senate proposal to permit taxes to go up only on income over $400,000. The measure passed with a minority of Republicans and an overwhelming number of Democrats, preventing the country from going over what journalists called the "fiscal cliff." Party unity was the price of compromise, proving that when it comes to responsible parties, the United States just isn't like Great Britain.

issue voting: Choosing a candidate in an election on the basis of his or her proximity to your position on an issue or issues you consider important.

on their members in the House or Senate, and legislators will not automatically heed the wishes of a president of their party. To say we do not have responsible parties in the United States is not to suggest that parties act irresponsibly; rather, it is to say that members of a party do not act as one unit as parties often do in parliamentary systems. Global Topics: Responsible Parties puts the American system in an international perspective.

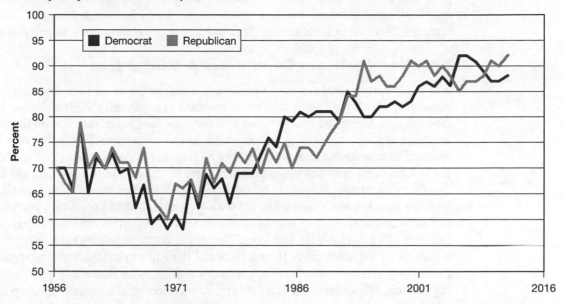

Party Unity in the House of Representatives

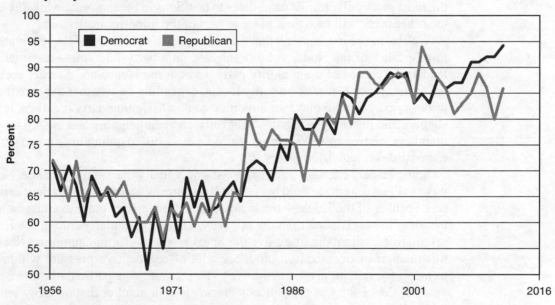

Party Unity in the Senate

FIGURE 6.5 Party Unity in Congress, 1955–2013[T15]

Party unity among Democrats increased greatly in the 1980s, while Republicans became a very cohesive party when they took over Congress in 1995 following the "Contract with America" election. By the start of this century, Democrats and Republicans had become so unified in their voting that bipartisanship became difficult to attain.

Because our political parties are those large, catch-all groups we were talking about earlier, it shouldn't be surprising to find members of the same party disagreeing with each other and coming down on different sides of an issue. Perhaps the most pronounced example of this is southern Democrats, who are typically more conservative than the rest of their party and often vote their own way. In fact, you could say that when you take into account how broad-based the parties are and how hard it is for party leaders to impose discipline, it's remarkable how much party cohesion there is in Congress.

In recent years, Democrats and Republicans have been able to get large majorities of their members to stick together on votes where the parties take a position. As you can tell from the party unity scores in Figure 6.5, in the 1960s and 1970s, Republicans were somewhat more unified than Democrats as conservative southern Democrats crossed over to vote with Republicans. In the 1980s, during the Clinton administration, there was growing polarization in the priorities of the parties, leading to greater internal cohesiveness in voting.[25] By 2003, partisanship had intensified to the point where *Congressional Quarterly* reported the most polarization in its five decades of keeping track of party unity scores.[26]

6.4b How Parties in Government Are Organized

Although party members may not always come together to vote on policy issues, they invariably speak with one voice when it comes to organizing the legislature. Parties organize the U.S. Congress and forty-nine of the fifty state legislatures, with the party holding the most seats commanding the power to set the rules (only Nebraska, which has a unicameral or one-house legislature, elects its representatives on a nonpartisan basis). We'll see in Chapter 9 how this gives majority party members many advantages if they can stay together and control the organizational process. So, when it comes to organizational matters, it's in everyone's interest to get with the program and vote along party lines.

Let's use the U.S. Congress as an example of how parties organize legislatures. Before the start of each two-year session of Congress, party members meet in groups closed to members of the other party (Democrats call their group a "caucus" and Republicans call their group a "conference"), to select their candidates for leadership positions in the coming session. It's understood that the candidates selected in caucus will receive the backing of all party members later on, when leadership votes are held in the full House or Senate. At that point, with individuals falling in line behind their party's choices, the party with the most seats will elect its candidates to positions in the majority, while the candidates of the other party will take their place as part of the minority leadership.

We'll also see in Chapter 9 that the leadership of the House of Representatives is vested in a Speaker of the House, who is selected on a party-line vote—essentially, as the top leadership choice of the majority party. In both the House and Senate, each party has a leader (majority leader or minority leader, depending on whether they are the majority or minority party), who plays an important role in assigning party members to committees, shaping and moving the legislative agenda, and campaigning and raising money for party members. There are also several "whips," who work to maintain as much party discipline as possible on legislative votes.[27]

Some leaders exercise power more strongly than others—for instance, Newt Gingrich went to great lengths to hold his fellow Republicans accountable for their actions when he was Speaker of the House—but in any event, the majority party exercises a lot more control over the legislature than the minority. This is particularly true in the House of Representatives, where the rules give the Speaker a lot of formal authority. Not surprisingly, this manner of organization produces a lot of competitive pressure within both parties to attain (or remain in) the majority.[28] The pressure was particularly intense in the early years of the century as the parties were so close in number that majority status remained within the reach of both.

6.5 The Party in the Electorate

political socialization: The process by which we acquire political knowledge, attitudes, and beliefs.

party identification: An individual's association with a political party. The most common parties Americans identify with are the two major parties, Republican and Democrat. Party identification—also called party I.D.—varies in intensity such that it may be strong or weak. Those who do not identify with any party are typically called independents.

Are you a Democrat? A Republican? If so, do you have your party membership card stored carefully in your pocketbook or wallet?

Can't find it? Don't spend too much time looking. There are no membership cards for American political parties, just like there are no meetings to attend and no dues to pay. You can be a Republican simply by virtue of identifying with Republicans, a Democrat with no more effort than it takes to think, "I guess I'm a Democrat." In some states, when you register to vote, you may be asked if you want to register with a party so you can participate in that party's primary election contests (we'll go into more detail on this in Chapter 7). But you can change your registration any time you want, and you can consider yourself a party member without ever registering.

When we talked about **political socialization** in Chapter 4, we said that **party identification** was the most well-socialized political phenomenon and that many of us hold to our party affiliation in a manner similar to the way many people are attached to a religious affiliation. This gives party identification a psychological component unrelated to whatever policy agreements we may have with the party we call our own. Through these associations, be they emotional or policy-based, we align ourselves with a party and become a small portion of that party's base of support. In effect, we are the party in the electorate—any of us who wish to claim allegiance to a political party, for whatever reason.

Now, there's a connection between us—the party in the electorate—and the party in government, inasmuch as party supporters typically want their candidates to succeed politically, or to have an effect on public policy making, or both. The extent to which the electorate acts on these wishes often depends on how much the electorate is motivated or mobilized. The composition of the party in government depends on how much we indulge our partisan instincts through the kinds of political participation we talked about in Chapter 4—contributing funds, campaigning, or voting for members of our party.

6.5a Who Makes Up the Party in the Electorate?

Because we don't have to declare our partisan allegiances, the composition of the Democratic and Republican Parties in the electorate will shift and change. Nonetheless, there are differences in the relative attachments of various groups of Americans to the two parties. Republicans are more likely to be older, white, southern, less well educated, and religious. Democrats tend to be younger, ethnically diverse, well educated, and secular (see Figure 6.6).

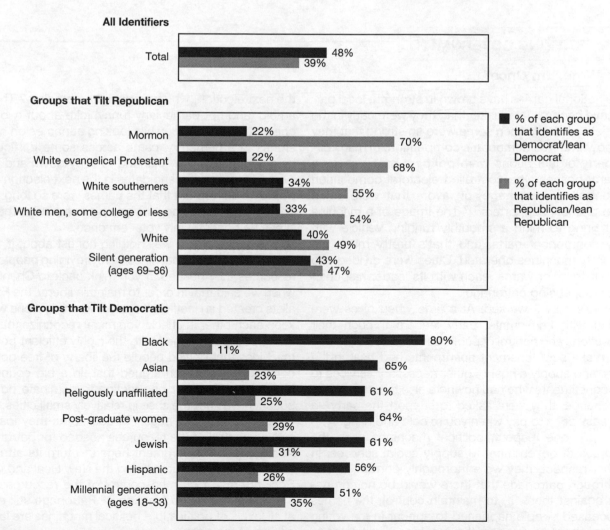

FIGURE 6.6 Democrats and Republicans in the Electorate[T16]

6.5b How Are Political Parties Organized to Reach the Electorate?

As much as party organizations inside the legislature are structured and hierarchical, party organizations that don't perform a legislative function are more decentralized. Instead of imagining a singular, cohesive, national Republican or Democratic Party, try to picture each party with several national organizations, fifty statewide organizations, and lots of local organizations, connected to each other but not organized from top to bottom. Each has a slightly different perspective on the same goal: electing Republicans or Democrats to office. From the standpoint of what they're about, party organizations outside the legislature are concerned with contesting elections—getting us to the polls to vote for their candidates—not with governing or advancing legislation. They share political interests with the party in government, but they operate separately.

Nationally, each party has three organizations: a national committee (the Democratic National Committee, or DNC, and the Republican National Committee, or RNC), run by a national committee chair, and House and Senate campaign committees.

The national committees govern the national parties and include among their members representatives from the state parties. The party that controls the White House typically finds that the president exercises a great deal of control over the actions of the committee, from selecting the chair to setting the goals and objectives for the national party. The party that is not in the White House typically finds that the national chair is an important force in establishing the direction of the party and laying the groundwork to contest the next national election.[29]

political machines: The name given to urban political parties that used patronage to overrun their competition and maintain power.

patronage: Jobs, favors, and other resources that party officials provide in exchange for people's political support.

DEMYSTIFYING GOVERNMENT

"Only Vote 'Em Once"

While national parties have grown in strength, local parties have become far weaker than they were early in the twentieth century, when some were so strong that they overpowered free democratic competition. In many cities, party organizations were **political machines** run by party bosses who controlled electoral competition by controlling **patronage**, or favors that were doled out to political supporters.[T17] The image of a machine might bring to mind a smoothly running vehicle with many component parts, and that's pretty much the way party machines operated. Cities were divided into small districts or wards, each with its leader responsible for dispensing patronage.

Here's how it worked: At a time when cities were flooded with immigrants, party leaders through their connections and control of public services could provide jobs, make sure tenement apartments had heat in the winter, and supply a host of other necessary services to poor constituents who had nowhere else to turn for help. In exchange, they were asked to support the party—a fairly easy price to pay when you're cold and hungry.

So, in one respect, political machines used the resources of government to supply social services. In another respect, they were thoroughly corrupt, ensuring through patronage that there would be no competition against them. If, to maintain control, the names of deceased people happened to appear in the voting logs prepared to support the machine candidates in

the next election, who was going to complain? There's an old (and not particularly funny) joke about two machine politicians who, while looking at names on headstones in a cemetery, came across some particularly long names that they planned to copy down and have "vote" for machine candidates in the next election. One politician blurted out that the names were so long, they could vote them twice, to which his companion replied, "Let's be honest. Only vote 'em once."

Of course, there was nothing honest about it, even though the political machines were providing people with resources they needed. If you think back to Chapter 2, when we said that in order to maintain liberty, the Federalists created an inefficient system where factions would keep each other in check, you might recognize that just the opposite happened with the highly efficient political machines that denied people the liberty of free political competition. Madison argued that, in a big country, it would be difficult for one faction to dominate politics, but such was not the case in relatively small cities.

Party machines began to decline as they lost exclusive control of the resources needed for patronage. As the federal government began to turn its attention to social welfare needs during the New Deal and Great Society eras, it claimed control of the resources that machines needed to function.[T18] Patronage still exists at all levels of politics, but political machines are largely a thing of the past.

As the main national organization for their respective parties, the DNC and RNC are responsible for arranging their party's national convention. However, the parties only meet in convention once every four years, for the purpose of nominating a presidential and vice-presidential candidate. On a more regular basis, the national committees are responsible for raising money for campaigns, establishing the guidelines for nominating presidential candidates, and helping state parties recruit candidates, develop campaign strategies, and build their organizations (you can probably imagine how the state parties perform parallel functions to the national committees). On the fund-raising front, the national committees are joined by the four congressional committees—the National Republican Congressional Committee (NRCC) and Democratic Congressional Campaign Committee (DCCC), which raise money for House candidates, and the Democratic Senatorial Campaign Committee (DSCC) and National Republican Senatorial Committee (NRSC), which do the same for Senate candidates.[30]

For a long time, national party organizations were weak, victims of campaigns that had become candidate-centered. With the growth of television as a central campaign tool, the locus of campaigning shifted from the national committees to the candidates and their personal campaign organizations. As we'll see in Chapter 7, political consultants, hired by the candidates to run campaigns and direct fund-raising techniques, made the national party organizations less important to candidates. In recent years, the national party organizations have rebounded, owing in large part to the ability of the national parties to provide candidates with resources like political information and technical knowledge, and as they became more proficient in raising money, they became stronger and more relevant.[31] Demystifying Government: "Only Vote 'Em Once" discusses the concurrent declining role of local parties. We'll get a deeper sense of how parties operate as we take a closer look at political campaigns and elections, the subject we'll discuss in Chapter 7.

Chapter Review

Define political parties.

Political parties are organized groups that link us to government through the role they play in recruiting and running candidates for elected office. We have two major parties in the United States; many nations have more than that.

Explain why America's two-party system is consistent with its electoral mechanisms and public opinion.

A two-party system is consistent with our electoral mechanisms that award representation on a winner-take-all basis to the plurality vote winner of an election. Election laws and the moderate tendencies of American public opinion also encourage two parties, although they are broad parties made up of groups that sometimes disagree.

Identify third parties as either ideological, single-issue, or splinter parties, and explain why they rarely compete successfully for elected offices.

When these disagreements become pronounced, a faction might temporarily leave and form a splinter party that competes as a third party against the Democrats and Republicans. Typically, one of the major parties is able to capture the allegiance of the disaffected faction in a future election, and the third party disappears. Third parties built around an ideology or single issue endure from election to election but rarely win public office.

Define the term *party system*, and identify the key characteristics of the five party systems that have arisen since parties emerged in the late eighteenth century.

Since parties emerged in the late eighteenth century, we have had five party systems in which two parties have faced each other in regular competition. Each party system gave way to a new one when a major issue arose that shattered the prevailing party coalitions, causing a realignment to a new party system following a critical election.

Identify the relationship between realignments and the demise of party systems.

Explain why the post-1960s political era may be understood as a period of dealignment.

The most recent realignment coincided with the emergence of the fifth party system under the leadership of the Democratic Party during the Great Depression, but since the 1960s, some observers say we've witnessed a period of dealignment characterized by weak party ties, more independent voters, and divided government.

Distinguish between the party in government and the party in the electorate.

We can understand political parties by distinguishing between the party in government and the party in the electorate. The party in government is composed of elected officials who serve in government, and our legislative branch is organized around parties, with the majority party controlling leadership positions and exercising great influence over the legislative agenda. Even though party leaders often have an agenda, party members do not always follow it because we do not have responsible parties that would obligate members to vote the party line. The party in the electorate is composed of those of us who identify as Democrats or Republicans, although American parties do not require formal membership.

Key Terms

coalition A government formed as a partnership among several victorious parties in a multiparty system, following negotiations about the agenda that each party will be allowed to pursue in exchange for its participation in the new government. (p. 169)

coattails The ability of a victorious presidential candidate to sweep congressional candidates of the same party into office on the strength of people voting for one political party. (p. 182)

critical election An election that heralds a realignment, during which large numbers of voters deviate from their traditional party allegiances in what turns out to be a lasting change. (p. 173)

dealignment The weakening of party affiliation, signified by an increase in the number of people who call themselves independents. (p. 180)

divided government Partisan division of the national government, in which each of the two major parties can claim control of one branch (or one legislative house) of the federal government. (p. 181)

electorate The portion of the public eligible to vote in elections. (p. 164)

faction A group of individuals who are united by a desire that, if realized, would threaten the liberty of the larger community—in James Madison's words, individuals who are "united and actuated by some common impulse of passion, or of interest, adverse to the rights of other citizens, or to the permanent and aggregate interests of the community." A faction may be defined by size, such as when a majority of citizens threatens the liberty of the minority, or by intensity, such as when a minority of citizens with intensely held preferences threatens the liberty of a disinterested majority. (p. 173)

Fair Deal The name given to the domestic policies of President Truman, which built on the popularity of the New Deal. (p. 178)

gender gap A difference in the voting pattern of men and women, evident since 1980, whereby men are more likely than women to support Republican presidential candidates. (p. 181)

Great Society The name given to the programs of President Lyndon B. Johnson, which elevated the federal government to the most prominent role it would play in the twentieth century. The philosophy of the Great Society was that government should try to solve large social problems like hunger and poverty. (p. 178)

gridlock The term given to legislative inaction, when members of Congress are unable to reach agreement and legislation stalls. (p. 182)

ideological parties Third parties that form around a broad ideology not represented by the two major American parties. They endure from election to election despite the fact that they rarely achieve electoral success. (p. 170)

interest aggregation The process by which groups with different and potentially conflicting agendas are brought together under the umbrella of a political party. (p. 169)

issue voting Choosing a candidate in an election on the basis of his or her proximity to your position on an issue or issues you consider important. (p. 184)

majority Winning more than half the votes in an election, or 50 percent plus one. (p. 165)

multimember district The structure of electoral districts in proportional representation systems, in which each electoral district sends several representatives to the legislature. (p. 165)

multiparty system Political systems in which more than two parties have a realistic chance to win representation in government. (p. 165)

New Deal The name given to the programs of President Franklin D. Roosevelt, which vastly expanded the role of the federal government in an effort to deal with the debilitating effects of the Great Depression on American society. (p. 178)

New Deal coalition The political coalition composed of urbanites, ethnic and racial minorities, unions, liberals, and southerners that made the Democratic Party the majority party during the fifth party system. (p. 178)

party identification An individual's association with a political party. The most common parties Americans identify with are the two major parties, Republican and Democrat. Party identification—also called party I.D.—varies in intensity such that it may be strong or weak. Those who do not identify with any party are typically called independents. (p. 186)

party in government That component of political parties composed of elected officials that organizes and runs our governing institutions like Congress, the presidency, state governorships and assemblies, and the like. (p. 183)

party in the electorate Party identifiers who make up the rank-and-file membership of the political parties. (p. 183)

party system The regular, over-time competition of the same major political parties, composed of the same groups of identifiers. (p. 173)

patronage Jobs, favors, and other resources that party officials provide in exchange for people's political support. (p. 188)

plurality Winning the most votes in an election, or at least one more vote than the next closest candidate or party. (p. 165)

political machines The name given to urban political parties that used patronage to overrun their competition and maintain power. (p. 188)

political party An organized group of individuals with common interests seeking to gain power in government by electing officials to public office. (p. 164)

political socialization The process by which we acquire political knowledge, attitudes, and beliefs. (p. 186)

proportional representation Electoral systems that encourage the participation of many parties by awarding representation on the basis of the share of the vote won by each party in an electoral district. (p. 165)

realignment A shift from one party system to another, the result of a lasting, long-term adjustment in the groups that identify with the major political parties. (p. 173)

Reform Party The organization built by businessman Ross Perot in a mostly unsuccessful attempt to create a competitive third party. (p. 172)

responsible parties Political parties whose legislative members act in concert, taking clear positions on issues and voting as a unit in accordance with their stated positions. (p. 183)

single-issue parties Third parties that form to advance a specific issue agenda, like environmentalism, that members feel is not being adequately addressed by the two major American parties. They endure from election to election despite the fact that they rarely achieve electoral success. (p. 170)

single-member district The structure of electoral districts in winner-take-all electoral systems, in which each electoral district sends only one representative to the legislature. (p. 166)

splinter parties Third parties that split away from one of the major parties in protest against the direction taken by the Republicans or Democrats. They often form around a charismatic leader and last a short time, after which the major parties address their concerns, and they lose their reason to continue. (p. 170)

ticket splitting Voting for candidates of different parties for different offices, rather than voting a "party line" for all Republicans or all Democrats. Ticket splitting, which has increased in recent years, is a sign of how Americans have been growing independent from political parties. (p. 181)

two-party system A political system, like ours in the United States, in which only two parties have a realistic chance to win most elections. (p. 165)

tyranny The denial of liberty to individuals through the actions of a faction or through the actions of government itself. (p. 173)

winner-take-all system The electoral system in use in the United States, whereby the candidate of the party receiving the most votes in an electoral district gets to represent that district. (p. 165)

Resources

You might be interested in examining some of what the following authors have said about the topics we've been discussing:

Hershey, Marjorie R. *Party Politics in America*, 14th ed. New York: Longman, 2010. This is a good source if you're looking for a comprehensive overview of American parties and party systems.

Hetherington, Mark J., and Bruce A. Larson. *Parties, Politics, and Public Policy in America*, 11th ed. Washington, DC: CQ Press, 2009. Like *Party Politics in America* by Marjorie Hershey, a good, comprehensive overview of political parties.

Maisel, L. Sandy, ed. *The Parties Respond: Changes in American Parties and Campaigns*, 4th ed. Boulder, CO: Westview Press, 2002. A recommended assortment of essays assessing the role and status of contemporary political parties.

Rosenstone, Steven J., Roy L. Behr, and Edward H. Lazarus. *Third Parties in America: Citizen Response to Major Party Failure*, 2nd ed. Princeton, NJ: Princeton University Press, 1996. A thorough review of third parties and third-party voting from the nineteenth century through Ross Perot.

Sundquist, James L. *Dynamics of the Party System: Alignment and Realignment of Political Parties in the United States*. Washington, DC: Brookings Institution, 1983. A good place to turn for a descriptive and theoretical discussion of party realignments in American history.

Wattenberg, Martin P. *The Decline of American Political Parties, 1952–1996*. Cambridge, MA: Harvard University Press, 1996. An interesting source to turn to on the phenomenon of dealignment.

Notes

1 Leon D. Epstein, *Political Parties in Western Democracies* (New Brunswick, NJ: Transaction Books, 1980), 9.

2. William J. Keefe, *Parties, Politics, and Public Policy in America*, 8th ed. (Washington, DC: Congressional Quarterly Press, 1998), 60.

3 Steven J. Rosenstone, Roy L. Behr, and Edward H. Lazarus, *Third Parties in America: Citizen Response to Major Party Failure* (Princeton, NJ: Princeton University Press, 1996), 21.

4 Liz Mariantes, "Karl Rove Take on the Tea Party. Is a GOP Civil War Looming?" *Christian Science Monitor*, February 4, 2013.

5 See Theodore J. Lowi, *The End of the Republican Era* (Norman, OK: University of Oklahoma Press, 1995); Richard S. Katz and Peter Mair, eds., *Party Organizations* (London: Sage Publications, 1992), 871–876; Steven B. Wolinetz, ed., *Parties and Party Systems in Liberal Democracies* (New York: Routledge, 1988), 272–279.

6 Epstein, *Political Parties*, 283.

7 Rosenstone, et al., *Third Parties in America*, 88–92. If you're interested in the positions of a few ideological parties, and want to know more about the issues that concern them, check out the websites for the U.S. Communist Party at http://www.cpusa.org/; the U.S. Socialist Party at http://sp-usa.org/; the U.S. Green Party at http://www.gp.org/; and the U.S. Libertarian Party at http://www.lp.org/.

8 For the political junkies among us, if the name Strom Thurmond sounds familiar, it's because the "Dixiecrat" who ran for president in 1948 is the same Strom Thurmond who retired from the Senate in 2003 at the age of 100. First elected to the Senate in 1954, he switched parties and became a Republican in 1964.

9 James L. Sundquist, *Dynamics of the Party System* (Washington, DC: Brookings Institution, 1983), 1–18.

10 You can read the full text of Washington's farewell address at the U.S. Department of State website, http://www.state.gov/usa/infousa/facts/democrac/49.htm.

11 Larry J. Sabato, *The Party's Just Begun: Shaping Political Parties for America's Future* (Glenview, IL: Scott, Foresman, 1988), 32–33.

12 Ibid.

13 If you'd like to read a brief but interesting biography of Andrew Jackson, you can find one at the White House website, http://www.whitehouse.gov/about/presidents/andrewjackson.

14 Paul Allen Beck, *Party Politics in America*, 8th ed. (New York: Longman, 1997), 23.

15 Sundquist, *Dynamics of the Party System*, 50–105.

16 The modern-day Republican Party rightfully claims to be the party of Lincoln, tracing its roots to the election of 1860.

17 Sundquist, *Dynamics of the Party System*, 106–146.

18 Ibid., 146–169.

19 Ibid., 198–214.

20 Sabato, *The Party's Just Begun*, 34.

21 Sundquist, *Dynamics of the Party System*, 412–449.

22 Danielle Paquette, "The Unexpected Voters behind the Widest Gender Gap in Recorded Election History," *Washington Post*, November 9, 2016. https://www.washingtonpost.com/news/wonk/wp/2016/11/09/men-handed-trump-the-election/?utm_term=.e6f93a93a5a1.

23 Martin P. Wattenberg, *The Decline of American Political Parties: 1952–1992* (Cambridge, MA: Harvard University Press, 1994), 162–167.

24 Beck, *Party Politics in America*, 321–322.

25 Isaiah J. Poole, "Party Unity Vote Study: Votes Echo Electoral Themes," *Congressional Quarterly*, December 11, 2004.

26 Responsible parties have had their advocates in the United States. Over a half-century ago, the American Political Science Association advocated responsible parties for the United States in a report called "Toward a More Responsible Two-Party System," *American Political Science Review* 44:3 (1950); online at http://www.apsanet.org/~pop/APSA_Report.htm.

27 For a more detailed account of the leadership positions in each house, by party, as well as the names and backgrounds of the current occupants of these positions, go to The Congressional Institute website at http://www.conginst.org/index.php?option=com_content&task=view&id=55&Itemid=, and click on any of the four boxes on the right-hand part of the screen (House Republican Leadership Positions; House Democratic Leadership Positions; Senate Democratic Leadership Positions; Senate Republican Leadership Positions).

28 Keefe, *Parties, Politics, and Public Policy*, 218–236; and Beck, *Party Politics in America*, 305–311.

29 Beck, *Party Politics in America*, 85–91.

30 Paul S. Herrnson, "National Party Organizations at the Century's End," in L. Sandy Maisel, ed., *The Parties Respond*, 3rd ed. (Boulder, CO: Westview Press, 1998), 50–82.

31 Ibid.

Table, Figure, and Box Notes

T1 William J. Keefe, *Parties, Politics, and Public Policy in America* (Washington, DC: CQ Press, 1998), 60.

T2 Steven J. Rosenstone, Roy L. Behr, and Edward H. Lazarus, *Third Parties in America: Citizen Response to Major Party Failure* (Princeton, NJ: Princeton University Press, 1996), 231–268.

T3 Information Services Branch of the State Library of North Carolina, Andrew Jackson, at http://statelibrary.dcr.state.nc.us/nc/bio/public/jackson.htm; Leonard W. Levy and Louis Fisher (eds.), *Encyclopedia of the American Presidency* (New York: Simon & Schuster, 1994); H. W. Brands, *Andrew Jackson: His Life and Times* (New York: Doubleday, 2005); Donald B. Cole, *The Presidency of Andrew Jackson* (Lawrence, KS: University Press of Kansas Press, 1993); Sean Wilentz, *Andrew Jackson* (New York: Times Books, 2005).

T4 Speer Memorial Library, Williams Jennings Bryan: Biographical Resources, at http://www.mission.lib.tx.us/exhibits/bryan/resource/bio/time.htm; Leonard W. Levy and Louis Fisher (eds.), *Encyclopedia of the American Presidency* (New York: Simon & Schuster, 1994); Robert W. Cherny, *A Righteous Cause: The Life of William Jennings Bryan* (Norman, OK: University of Oklahoma Press, 1994); Michael Kazin, *William Jennings Bryan: A Godly Hero* (New York: Knopf, 2006).

T5 Everett Walters, William McKinley Biographical Resources, at http://www.ohiohistory.org/onlinedoc/ohgovernment/governors/mckinley.html; Leonard W. Levy and Louis Fisher (eds.), *Encyclopedia of the American Presidency* (New York: Simon & Schuster, 1994); H. Wayne Morgan, *William McKinley and His America* (Kent, OH: Kent State University Press, 2003); Kevin Philips, *William McKinley* (New York: Times Books, 2003).

T6 Herbert Hoover Presidential Library and Museum, at http://hoover.archives.gov/education/chronology.html; Leonard W. Levy and Louis Fisher (eds.), *Encyclopedia of the American Presidency* (New York: Simon & Schuster, 1994); George H. Nash, *The Life of Herbert Hoover* (New York: W.W. Norton, 1983); Joan Hoff Wilson. *Herbert Hoover: Forgotten Progressive* (Prospect Heights, Ill.: Waveland Press, 1992).

T7 Franklin D. Roosevelt Presidential Library and Museum, Franklin D. Roosevelt Biography, at http://www.fdrlibrary.marist.edu/fdrbio.html; Leonard W. Levy and Louis Fisher (eds.), *Encyclopedia of the American Presidency* (New York: Simon & Schuster, 1994); Roy Jenkins, *Franklin Delano Roosevelt* (New York: Times Books, 2003); George McJimsey, *The Presidency of Franklin Delano Roosevelt* (Lawrence, KS: University Press of Kansas, 2000); Allan M. Winkler, *Franklin D. Roosevelt and the Making of Modern America* (New York: Pearson/Longman, 2006).

T8 Truman Presidential Museum and Library, Biographical Sketch, at http://www.trumanlibrary.org/hst-bio.htm; Leonard W. Levy and Louis Fisher (eds.), *Encyclopedia of the American Presidency* (New York: Simon & Schuster, 1994); Robert H. Ferrell, *Harry S Truman: A Life* (Columbia: University of Missouri Press, 1994); Alonzo L. Hamby, *Man of the People: A Life of Harry S Truman* (New York: Oxford University Press, 1995); David McCullough, *Truman* (New York: Simon & Schuster, 1992).

T9 Dwight D. Eisenhower Presidential Library & Museum, at http://www.eisenhower.archives.gov/ddebio.htm; Leonard W. Levy and Louis Fisher (eds.), *Encyclopedia of the American Presidency* (New York: Simon & Schuster, 1994); Peter G. Boyle, *Eisenhower* (New York: Pearson/Longman, 2005); Geoffrey Perret, *Eisenhower* (New York: Random House, 1999); Tom Wicker, *Dwight D. Eisenhower* (New York: Times Books, 2002).

T10 Lyndon Baines Johnson Library and Museum, President Lyndon B. Johnson's Biography at http://www.lbjlib.utexas.edu/johnson/archives.hom/biographys.hom/lbj_bio.asp; Leonard W. Levy and Louis Fisher (eds.), *Encyclopedia of the American Presidency* (New York: Simon & Schuster, 1994); Thomas W. Cowger and Sherwin J. Markman (eds.), *Lyndon Johnson Remembered: An Intimate Portrait of a Presidency* (Lanham, MD: Rowman & Littlefield, 2003); Robert Dallek, *Lone Star Rising: Lyndon Johnson and His Times, 1908–1960* (New York: Oxford University Press, 1991); Irwin Unger and Debi Unger, *LBJ: A Life* (New York: Wiley, 1999).

T11 Data from American National Election Studies, at http://www.electionstudies.org/nesguide/toptable/tab2a_1.htm.

The American National Election Studies, Center for Political Studies, University of Michigan. Electronic resources from the NES World Wide Web site (http://www.electionstudies.org). Ann Arbor, MI: University of Michigan, Center for Political Studies [producer and distributor], 1995–2012. These materials are based on work supported by the National Science Foundation under Grant Nos.: SBR-9707741, SBR-9317631, SES-9209410, SES-9009379, SES-8808361, SES-8341310, SES-8207580, and SOC77-08885. Any opinions, findings and conclusions or recommendations expressed in these materials are those of the author(s) and do not necessarily reflect those of the National Science Foundation.

T12 Paul Allen Beck, *Party Politics in America*, 8th ed. (New York: Longman, 1997), 303.

T13 Responsible parties have had their advocates in the United States. Over a half-century ago, the American Political Science Association issued a report in which it advocated responsible parties for the U.S. The report is called "Toward a More Responsible Two-Party System." It can be found in the *American Political Science Review* 44:3 (1950).

T14 You can read the full text of the Republican proposals at http://www.house.gov/house/Contract/CONTRACT.html.

T15 Congressional Quarterly, CQ Roll Call's Vote Studies—2013 In Review, February 3, 2014, http://media.cq.com/votestudies/.

T16 "A Deep Dive into Party Affiliation," Pew Research Center, April 7, 2015, http://www.people-press.org/2015/04/07/a-deep-dive-into-party-affiliation/.

T17 Martin and Susan Tolchin, *To The Victor: Political Patronage from the Clubhouse to the White House* (New York: Random House, 1971), 5.

T18 John F. Bibby, "State Party Organizations: Coping and Adapting to Candidate-Centered Politics and Nationalization," in L. Sandy Maisel, ed., *The Parties Respond*, 3rd ed., 23–49.

Campaigns and Elections: Vehicles for Democratic Expression

Source: Joseph Sohm/Shutterstock, Inc.

Learning Objectives

When you have completed this chapter, you should be able to:

- Understand how candidates are chosen to compete in elections through the nomination process.
- Contrast primaries with caucuses.
- Appreciate how and why candidate selection evolved from an elite to a mass-based process.
- Explain the role of money in waging successful campaigns.
- Identify key efforts to regulate campaign finance, and explain why they have fallen short of their stated goals.
- Discuss the relationship between momentum and expectations in presidential primary campaigns.
- Identify key strategic approaches to waging election campaigns.
- Explain how the Electoral College works and why it turns presidential campaigns into a small number of statewide elections.

7.1 Introduction

Imagine that you got up at 5:30 this morning, and you won't get to bed until after 1:00 tonight. You eat bad food whenever you have a second to grab some, which is rarely, because from the time you wake up until the time you go to sleep, you're constantly on the move, flying in and out of places so fast you lose track of where you are. In between, you go to meeting halls and auditoriums, where you're either talking to ten yawning people at a time or, if you're lucky, you're swamped by crowds and overwhelmed by reporters, leaving you no time to think for yourself. Either way, you find yourself repeating the same speech over and over until it feels like a stale, meaningless mantra. And when you're done speaking, you ask everyone you can find for money—people you know, people you don't know, it doesn't matter. You just keep asking for money—and lots of it.

Now imagine doing this every day for two years—more if you're not particularly well known. Think you can handle it?

Good. You're ready to run for president.

The process of running for president doesn't ensure that we'll send the brightest or most experienced candidates to the White House, but it does guarantee that they'll be durable. Running for president means making the sacrifice of personal time and family life for several years in the long-shot gamble that you'll be the last one standing on Election Day. "Running" for president is an appropriate term because the system in place for attaining the office is a marathon that can devour the weak.

We'll see that it incorporates some things we're already familiar with, like the media strategies that we talked about in Chapter 5. We'll also find that the Electoral College, an arcane and often misunderstood structure that usually has the last word on who is elected president, invariably drives general election strategies. Later in the chapter, we'll try to make sense of it.

As we proceed, we'll try to assess whether the process by which we select people for high office adequately provides us with a real and significant opportunity to have input to policy decisions, as we would expect if political parties are to function as effective linkages between citizens and officials. The point is not so much to determine if you would want to try your hand at running for president as it is to see if campaigns can engage you in politics in a meaningful way.

Our discussion of campaigns will focus on presidential races because they're by far the most complex, encompassing a two-step process of winning a party nomination and engaging a candidate of the other major party in the general election. This two-phase process is typical of campaigns for other offices as well, but only the presidential campaign lasts years and is always hotly contested. Many congressional seats, in contrast, are uncontested because the incumbent has successfully scared off possible challengers by raising large sums of money (something that congressional incumbents have an easier time doing than challengers who do not hold power), or because congressional district lines have been drawn to protect incumbents by including a disproportionate number of Democratic or Republican partisans within their boundaries. Both parties attempt to draw district lines in this fashion, creating as many "safe seats" as possible.

7.2 Decisions, Part I: The Selection Process

L.O. Understand how candidates are chosen to compete in elections through the nomination process.

nomination: The official endorsement of a candidate by a political party, making that candidate the one whose name will appear on the ballot next to the party label in the next general election.

There are two stages in the marathon process of choosing a president: the selection stage, which takes place within the political party, and the election stage, in which party candidates are pitted against each other. We'll look at them in that order, illustrating how the process unfolds, the strategies candidates use to advance their campaigns, and the importance of money and media to winning the race.

7.2a The Ground Rules

The end point of the selection process occurs when one candidate receives the **nomination** of a political party, formally making that candidate the official choice of the party. The race for the presidential nomination is really fifty-one individual contests (counting the

District of Columbia). To win the presidential nomination of a major political party, a candidate needs to compete in these contests, called primaries or caucuses, which are held in every state to select delegates to the party's national convention, held the summer before the presidential election. The candidate who receives a majority of the votes of the delegates at the convention wins the nomination of the party.

Because of the influence of federalism, election laws are state laws, leaving each state to determine its own rules for how its delegates will be chosen. Most states select their convention delegates in a **primary**, which is an election open to party identifiers for the purpose of selecting among candidates for an office. In states that hold primaries, Republicans and Democrats hold separate contests. In presidential primaries, voters select delegates pledged to support a candidate at the national convention. For lower offices, voters select the candidate directly; in most instances, the plurality winner receives the party's nomination.

A **caucus** works quite differently from a primary. It's a series of open meetings, starting at the local level and progressing over a period of time to meetings covering larger jurisdictions, like counties or congressional districts. At each stage of the process, party members select representatives pledged to a variety of candidates to attend the next caucus stage. At the last stage of the process, representatives are selected to attend a state convention, where delegates are chosen to attend the national convention. Unlike a primary, which is a secret ballot, caucus participants make their preferences public.[1] Picture the first stage of a caucus as being small groups of people meeting simultaneously in school buildings, lodges, and social halls across a state, discussing or even debating their presidential preferences with one another. It's a lot different than going to a voting booth and making your choice in private.

The number of states holding primaries has grown steadily, to the point where primaries are now by far the preferred method of delegate selection. In 2016, thirty-nine states and the District of Columbia held presidential primaries.[2] In 1968, only fifteen states held primaries, and the Democratic nominee, Vice President Hubert Humphrey, didn't enter any of them.[3]

In 2016, many states clamored to schedule their primaries and caucuses as early as possible in order to maximize their influence over the selection process. A brief look at the 2016 primary calendar in Table 7.1 shows how many states pressed to get into the action during the first month of the primary season. Take special note of what happened on March 1!

A cluster of states held their contests following the first events—the Iowa caucus, held in early February, and the traditional first primary in New Hampshire, held one week later. The marathon stretch culminating in the "Super Tuesday" contests on March 1 were designed to winnow the field quickly so that each party could rally around a nominee and begin planning for the general election. This happened in 2012, when the early primaries

L.O. Contrast primaries with caucuses.

primary: A method of candidate selection in which party identifiers vote for the candidate who will run on the party label in the general election. In presidential primaries, voters select delegates to the national convention.

caucus: A method of candidate selection in which party identifiers gather in a series of meetings to select delegates to the national convention.

TABLE 7.1 The Early 2016 Primary and Caucus Calendar[T1]

Date	Primary/Caucus
February 1	Iowa caucus
February 9	New Hampshire primary
February 20	Nevada caucus (Democratic); South Carolina primary (Republican)
February 23	Nevada caucus (Republican)
February 27	South Carolina primary (Democratic)
March 1	Alabama primary; Alaska caucus (Republican); Arkansas primary; Colorado caucus (Democratic); Georgia primary; Massachusetts primary; Minnesota caucus; Oklahoma primary; Tennessee primary; Texas primary; Vermont primary; Virginia primary

Chapter 7 Campaigns and Elections: Vehicles for Democratic Expression

and caucuses narrowed the Republican field and assured that former Massachusetts governor Mitt Romney, despite reservations about his conservative credentials from Republican voters, would be the only viable candidate for the Republican nomination. (Incumbent Barack Obama was running unopposed, so there was no question about the outcome of the Democratic contest.) Things didn't work out this way in 2016, as an unusually large field of Republican candidates with Donald Trump in the lead remained unsettled for months, while Vermont Senator Bernie Sanders's challenge to former Secretary of State Hillary Clinton endured well into the spring. Although both Trump and Clinton led their respective fields, neither nomination was settled until late in the primary process.

If you think it's silly to select a presidential nominee by compressing the primary schedule into a few hectic weeks, you're not alone. Politicians and pundits regularly second-guess the primary system, and party leaders have been tinkering with the rules for over thirty-five years. During this period, dramatic changes have occurred in the way we select presidential nominees, many of them occurring in the name of reform.

7.2b Reforming the Ground Rules

L.O. Appreciate how and why candidate selection evolved from an elite to a mass-based process.

In Chapter 6, we said that presidential candidates in the first party system were selected by a caucus of the members of their party in government. This system allowed a small, tightly controlled congressional elite to determine presidential nominees. As Jacksonian democracy came into vogue with the second party system, the congressional caucus fell out of favor and was replaced by the more open system of selecting nominees at national party conventions. So, ever since the 1830s, parties have been holding nominating conventions, but the way convention delegates are selected has changed over the years.

For much of the nineteenth century, state conventions, state party committees, or even state governors chose delegates. Initially, this reform permitted states to have a hand in the selection process, but the system remained elite-based, permitting state party bosses to exercise a heavy hand over which delegates were chosen. By the turn of the twentieth century, reformers complained that rank-and-file voters should have more say over the nomination process.

Enter the presidential primary. By 1916, more than half the states held them, but in the ensuing years, their popularity waned as party leaders objected to them, candidates ignored them, voters didn't turn out for them, and states didn't want to pay for them.[4] This permitted party bosses to continue to exercise leverage over the process and explains how Hubert Humphrey could enter the 1968 convention with the support of the Democratic Party elite and win the nomination without having contested any primaries.

The 1968 Democratic Convention was no ordinary gathering, though. Fighting in Vietnam was at a crescendo—the result of the policies of President Lyndon Johnson, a Democrat. An antiwar faction composed mostly of young activists planned to protest what was expected to be Johnson's renomination in Chicago that August. Even though Johnson dropped out of the race months before the convention, the antiwar faction of the Democratic Party marched in protest through the streets of Chicago, putting them at odds with the law-and-order Democratic Party boss, Chicago Mayor Richard Daley.

While the convention nominated Vice President Humphrey, the choice of party insiders, over the vocal protests of antiwar delegates, demonstrators clashed with police outside the hall. Scenes of mayhem and violence—of tear gas, arrests, and police beatings—appeared on television screens nationwide, portraying a divided and torn Democratic Party. Humphrey's candidacy failed, and the cry went out to change the nomination system in

In the late 1960s, anti-war protests like this one enveloped the country and disrupted the Democratic National Convention in Chicago.[T2]

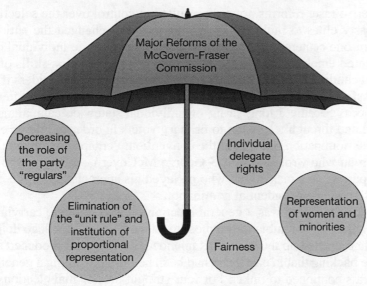

Fairness	All rules must be open and posted.
Elimination of the "unit rule" and institution of proportional representation	A state delegation cannot vote by majority rule to cast all its votes as a bloc. The final delegation should reflect choices made at the district levels.
Decreasing the role of the party "regulars"	The number of delegates the party committees of each state can send is limited, and elected officials do not receive automatic slots in the state delegation.
Individual delegate rights	No delegate can be compelled to cast a vote that was not the delegate's choice when selected.
Representation of women and minorities	Delegations from the states should reflect the racial and gender makeup of the state.

FIGURE 7.1 Major Reforms of the McGovern-Fraser Commission

a way that would shift control to rank-and-file Democrats from the party elites who had supported Humphrey.[5]

The reforms that changed the way party nominees are selected came between 1969 and 1971 from the Democratic Party Commission on Party Structure and Delegate Selection, commonly called the **McGovern-Fraser Commission** after its chairs, Senator George McGovern of South Dakota and, later, Representative Donald Fraser of Minnesota. The commission made the delegate selection process more open, egalitarian, and mass-based, making it harder for party elites to control the nomination. Major reforms of the McGovern-Fraser Commission are shown in Figure 7.1.

Like so many well-intentioned efforts, there were unexpected consequences to the McGovern-Fraser reforms. Although the commission didn't expressly advocate the expansion of primaries, many states found that moving to a primary system was the easiest way to implement the letter if not the spirit of the reforms. Because these changes were being made on a state-by-state basis, the Republican Party soon followed suit. This shifted the arena for candidate selection in both parties to the primaries and away from the national conventions, which became vehicles for ratifying the victorious primary candidate, rather than deliberative forums for selecting the candidate.[6] Even in 2016, when a substantial number of Republicans refused to rally around Donald Trump, there was little question that he would be nominated at the Republican Convention after emerging victorious in the primaries, and since 1968, the only convention to convene with the identity of the eventual nominee still in doubt was the 1976 Republican Convention, where incumbent President Gerald Ford had yet to secure enough delegates to brush back a spirited challenge from Ronald Reagan. Absent a meaningful role in the selection process, conventions have become staged **media events** showcasing the victorious nominee to the nation.

McGovern-Fraser Commission: The commission organized by the Democratic Party following its 1968 convention to democratize the process of delegate selection to party conventions.

media events: Activities staged by campaigns or political officials that have enough news value to draw press attention to a message the politician wants to communicate.

Chapter 7 Campaigns and Elections: Vehicles for Democratic Expression

The McGovern-Fraser reforms not only resulted in control over the selection process passing from party elites to rank-and-file voters, but they changed the entire nominating process from one centered in the party to one centered in the individual campaigns, with unprecedented emphasis on the personality and communication skills of the candidate. Successful candidates no longer had to be champions of party insiders if they could compete successfully in primary races by appealing directly to voters. After 1968, the nominating process became a long string of individual statewide campaigns, in which candidates appealed through television to primary voters in order to pile up enough delegates to win the nomination outright at the convention. Perhaps no one understood this better than the man who wrote the rules—George McGovern—a liberal who lacked the backing of the party's deal makers but who parlayed his appreciation of the new system into the 1972 Democratic presidential nomination.

The McGovern candidacy was a general election disaster, though, carrying only one state and the District of Columbia in the most lopsided Electoral College defeat to date. The new rules had opened up the system as intended, but they had produced a candidate without the elite backing that in past years had been helpful in winning a general election. So, the Democrats continued to tinker. For four straight presidential elections following McGovern's defeat, Democrats convened commissions to revise the rules. Each commission reacted to the perceived flaws of the one that came before, as all but one led to electoral failure.

The outcome of these commissions, and the political results they produced, are summarized in Table 7.2. The Mikulski Commission attempted to avoid a repeat of the McGovern debacle by ensuring that delegates more accurately represented the preferences of primary voters. This opened the process to a little-known, one-term ex-governor of Georgia, Jimmy Carter, who never would have had a chance at the presidential nomination under the old rules and who might have been locked out under the McGovern procedures.

When Carter took hold of the Democratic Party apparatus as president, he attempted through the Winograd Commission to solidify his position through changes making it harder to challenge his renomination, such as by binding delegates to support the candidate they were selected to represent. Carter survived a nomination challenge by Massachusetts Senator Edward Kennedy but was denied a second term. Party insiders blamed Carter's defeat and the shortcomings of his administration on the fact that he had been an inexperienced outsider, and a movement began to return elite control to the selection process. The Hunt Commission introduced "superdelegates"—state and local party leaders, members of Congress, and other elected officials—who would represent 14 percent of convention delegates and serve to throw the nomination to an experienced candidate acceptable to the party elite if needed. And in 1984, the Democrats nominated a candidate with a long résumé—former Vice President Walter Mondale—who promptly took his party to its second forty-nine-state loss in twelve years.

Candidates who had lost to Mondale in the 1984 primaries, like the less established Colorado Senator Gary Hart, argued for reforms that would make it easier for challengers to compete in the primaries. Democrats responded with the "Fairness" Commission, which instituted proportional representation methods designed to make this happen. The result was as planned: In 1988, Democrats nominated Massachusetts Governor Michael

TABLE 7.2 Changes Made to McGovern-Fraser Reforms

Commission	Year	Objective	Major Change	Result
Mikulski	1972	No McGoverns	Delegates better represent voter preferences	Carter elected
Winograd	1978	Re-elect Carter	Bind delegates on first ballot	Carter defeated
Hunt	1982	No Carters	Elite "superdelegates"	Mondale defeated
"Fairness"	1986	No Mondales	No "winner-take-all" primaries	Dukakis defeated

Dukakis, who was not one of his party's better-known national figures. He had marginally more success than Mondale, but his inexperience showed in the national campaign he waged, and Democrats once again lost the general election.[7]

The experiment with formal commissions ended in 1986, but the selection process continues to evolve. After the 2016 primaries, Bernie Sanders and his supporters successfully pressed the Democratic Party for a dramatic reduction in the number of superdelegates in order to level the playing field for an insurgent candidacy like his.[8] By virtue of her deep roots in the party, Hillary Clinton had claimed an overwhelming share of superdelegates in her contest with Sanders, padding her lead to a degree that Sanders was unable to surmount.

During the past few years, one of the most notable changes in the selection process has been the compression of the primary schedule that we mentioned earlier. The reason for this movement has to do with the political advantages to states of holding their primaries or caucuses early. Not all primaries and caucuses carry the same importance, and a state's position on the calendar is more important in the scheme of things than its population or diversity. By custom, Iowa holds the nation's first caucus, typically in late January, and New Hampshire follows with the nation's first primary roughly one week later. Throughout all the years of reform, this custom remains untouched. Both are small, sparsely populated states without urban centers, demographically atypical of much of the country. But they receive a disproportionate share of media attention over all other primaries and caucuses because they're first. Horserace-centered reporters, hungry for real voters to make real decisions, magnify the results of these first contests disproportionately.

In the primary-centered selection process that the McGovern-Fraser Commission set into motion, candidates get a critical boost coming out of Iowa and New Hampshire, and larger states began to realize that the closer they could schedule their primaries to the early contests, the more influence they would have over the outcome. Conversely, the closer they were to the end of the primary calendar, the greater the risk of being cut out entirely, as challengers dropped out and the eventual nominee became clear.

Jockeying among states for favorable primary calendar positions is an ongoing issue. After the 2004 election, representatives from western states like Colorado and Nevada said there should be at least one early western primary, perhaps even before Iowa and New Hampshire, and factions inside the Democratic Party battled over the question of whether to deny New Hampshire its traditional leadoff role. In 2008, the Democratic Party agreed to hold one early contest from every region of the country, with Nevada and South Carolina joining Iowa and New Hampshire on the early portion of the schedule.

As for those of us who would wish to influence the presidential selection process, geography is destiny. If you live in a state that held its 2016 primary or caucus after March 1, you faced a more limited choice than if you lived in Iowa, New Hampshire, Nevada, and South Carolina, especially if you are a Republican, as twelve candidates had already exited the race. Even though it is the product of reforms designed to democratize the selection process, the system in place through 2012 offers disproportionate influence to voters in the states that go first.

7.2c Money

As campaigns became primary-centered, they also became incredibly expensive to wage. One of the greatest costs in a primary campaign is television advertising, and as political parties have lost control of the nominating process to individual candidates, it is arguably the most critical resource for a campaign to have. To win primary votes, candidates have to reach those rank-and-file voters that reformers wanted to bring into the process. That means advertising and lots of it—which of course means raising a lot of money.

The rules that govern how money can be collected in a presidential campaign have experienced two significant legislative changes during the period since the McGovern-Fraser reforms and have had as much influence on how campaigns operate as changes in the delegate selection rules. Both were campaign finance reform laws. The first was instituted in 1974, the second in 2002.

L.O. Explain the role of money in waging successful campaigns.

Political Action Committees

PACs are organizations formed by special-interest groups of the sort we will be discussing in Chapter 8 for the purpose of contributing money to political candidates. Most PACs represent business groups, labor unions, or organizations with an ideological agenda—all of which have an interest in affecting public policy. Because PACs get their money directly from group members rather than from the organization's funds, they were technically legal before the implementation of the 1974 Federal Election Campaign Act because the language of the law prohibited contributions directly from unions and businesses.

The first PAC was formed in 1944 by the Congress of Industrial Organizations (CIO) for the purpose of collecting voluntary contributions from union members to support the reelection of Franklin D. Roosevelt. After 1974, PACs became officially sanctioned, and limits were placed on how much they could contribute. From that point, the number of PACs (and PAC dollars) grew astronomically. According to the nonpartisan Center for Responsive Politics, in 1974, 608 PACs were registered with the Federal Election Commission, and they had contributed a combined $15 million to presidential and congressional candidates.[T3] In 2016, 2,408 Super PACs—organizations free to raise and spend unlimited sums of corporate, union, or private cash to influence elections—had spent over $1.12 billion.[T4]

In Chapter 8, we'll take a closer look at who organizes and contributes to PACs, and how much they influence the decisions of victorious politicians.

L.O. Identify key efforts to regulate campaign finance, and explain why they have fallen short of their stated goals.

Federal Election Campaign Act: The 1974 act aimed at limiting the influence of big-money contributions on political campaigns.

Federal Election Commission (FEC): The federal regulatory agency that administers and enforces campaign finance laws.

political action committees (PACs): Organizations formed by interest groups such as labor unions, businesses, and ideological groups for the purpose of contributing money to political candidates.

As a consequence of illegal contributions to President Nixon's reelection campaign brought to light during the Watergate scandal, Congress turned its attention to reforming the way candidates solicit money. The result was the **Federal Election Campaign Act**, passed in 1971 and revised and strengthened several times during the following eight years. It set limits on campaign contributions, set practices for public disclosure of campaign contributions, established a method of partial public funding of presidential campaigns, and created the **Federal Election Commission (FEC)** to oversee the process. In an attempt to keep the FEC nonpartisan, its six commissioners are equally divided between Republicans and Democrats. Under the law, limits were placed on how much individuals and **political action committees** or **PACs** could contribute to candidates and party organizations. Demystifying Government: Political Action Committees discusses PACs in more detail.

Individuals could contribute no more than $1,000 to a candidate for federal office, and PACs could contribute no more than $5,000. The limits were applied to each election, with primaries and general election campaigns regarded as separate contests. Also, there were restrictions on contributions that could be made to party organizations and annual limits on individual giving. These limits were modified in 2002, then subsequently adjusted for inflation, resulting in the funding limits shown in Table 7.3.

In presidential campaigns, a system of matching public funds was first administered in 1976 to place voluntary limits on spending, while tightening the bonds to the political system for those of us interested in participating through contributing money. The idea was to give ordinary voters who might not think to make political contributions a convenient way to participate in the political process, while democratizing fund-raising at the margins by limiting the amount of big-dollar contributions in the system.

Here's how it works: The government retains a Presidential Election Campaign Fund financed by those of us who check a box on our tax return authorizing $3 of our tax payment to go to the fund (checking the box simply allocates the money—it doesn't increase

TABLE 7.3 Annual Federal Campaign Contribution Limits, 2015–2016[T5]

	To a Candidate (Per Election)	To a National Party Committee	To State, District, or Local Party Committees
Individuals	$2,700	$33,400	$10,000 (total)
PACs	$5,000	$15,000	$5,000 (total)

the tax payment). Money from the fund can go to candidates who demonstrate broad-based support by raising $5,000 in small contributions in each of twenty states. Once a candidate qualifies, the government matches up to $250 in contributions made by individuals; PAC contributions are not matched. In turn, the candidate agrees to a spending limit, which in 2016 was $48.1 million for the primaries and $96.1 million for the general election. During the primaries, there are also spending limits candidates must adhere to within individual states.[9]

If a candidate doesn't accept matching funds, he or she is still bound by the campaign contribution limits in Table 7.3, but not by the spending limits. A candidate able to amass large numbers of contributions or rely on a personal fortune would find spending limits burdensome. But, for many years, most candidates did not fall into either category, and matching funds were originally a great windfall for campaigns that lacked the means to raise equivalent amounts of money on their own. So, most candidates were willing to adhere to voluntary spending limits in return for a great infusion of cash. Between 1976 and 1996, only two independently wealthy candidates declined matching funds—former Texas Governor John Connelly, in an unsuccessful attempt to win the 1980 Republican presidential nomination, and businessman Steve Forbes, in an unsuccessful attempt to win the 1996 Republican nomination. Forbes tried to self-finance his way to the White House again in 2000, but his efforts were equally ineffective.

However, starting in 2000, a greater number of candidates and—importantly—several successful candidates began opting out of the public financing system. George W. Bush in 2000 and 2004 assembled a remarkably proficient fund-raising organization that shattered all fund-raising records to date to fuel two successful Republican nomination bids. His opposite number in 2004, Democrat John Kerry, secured his party's presidential nomination without public money. For the first time, spending limits were regarded as a hindrance to effective campaigning, rather than a jackpot that candidates could not refuse.

And that was before the Internet became the effective fund-raising medium that it is today. Former Vermont Governor Howard Dean in 2003 set fund-raising records for a Democrat and propelled a long-shot effort to credibility by relying on the Internet—a previously untapped source—before his campaign deteriorated in early 2004.[10] By 2008, the Internet had matured to the point where Barack Obama could raise three-quarters of a billion dollars for his presidential bid, an unprecedented sum bolstered by a tsunami of small online contributions from individual supporters. According to the *Washington Post*, the Obama primary and general election campaigns combined to raise over $500 million from 6.5 million online contributions, 6 million of which were $100 or less.[11] In 2012, 57 percent of contributions to Obama's re-election campaign were $200 or less,[12] on the strength of over 1 million more online contributions than he raised in 2008.[13] The Internet gives candidates with passionate supporters more attractive alternatives than public funds and makes it strategically foolish for them to forgo this advantage to accept public funding and stay within spending limits set by law.[14]

In fact, candidates had been trying to work around the public financing system from the beginning. Despite the best intentions of the reformers, there were loopholes in the system that could be exploited even by candidates who accepted matching funds, and given the pressure candidates felt to spend money on media (and travel and consultants), it wasn't long before spending dramatically increased. Campaigns were becoming expensive prior to the establishment of the FEC, but take a look in Figure 7.2 at how spending shot up after public financing went into effect in 1974.

What went wrong? Campaign finance limits restricted what's often called **hard money**—contributions made directly to candidates. They did not cover **soft-money** contributions, or money donated to state and local party committees or to the national parties' nonfederal accounts. The Federal Election Campaign Act left soft-money contributions unregulated, on the assumption that funds from these accounts would be used for state elections, voter registration, get-out-the-vote drives, and other "grassroots" activities.

This, in turn, provided parties and contributors with a loophole for circumventing campaign finance limits. With a little creativity, it's easy to see how the parties could spend soft money on, say, campaign overhead, permitting candidates to spend more of their hard

hard money: Funds contributed directly to candidates or national parties by individuals or PACs for the purpose of electing candidates to federal office. Federal law regulates hard-money contributions.

soft money: Funds contributed to state and local parties or to national parties for the purpose of running state elections or conducting local "grassroots" political activity.

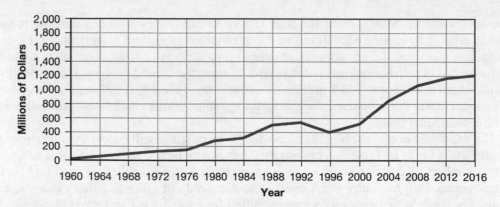

FIGURE 7.2 Presidential Campaign Spending before and after Campaign Finance Reform[T6]

The amount of money spent by presidential candidates more than doubled between 1964 and 1972, fueling campaign finance reform efforts. However, these efforts failed to hold down spending. In recent election cycles, campaign spending has flown off the charts. Remember, the figures shown are in millions of dollars.

money on campaign commercials and other political functions. One of the more popular uses of soft money was for what are euphemistically called "issue ads" by political professionals. These are commercials produced on behalf of a candidate, which appear to advocate the candidate's election (or the defeat of his or her opponent) by spotlighting an aspect of the candidate's record (typically by putting an opponent's record in a negative context). As long as these ads do not expressly advocate the election or defeat of a candidate, they are considered educational and can be paid for with unlimited soft money.[15]

For a long time, Congress has wrestled with changing the campaign finance structure to make contributing to presidential campaigns more democratic, but it's been a hard sell. Incumbent members of Congress of both parties have been reluctant to change a system that brought them to power, and although finance reform is a widely popular issue, it's not the sort of thing that gets most people out of their homes on Election Day (recall our discussion in Chapter 3 of how campaign finance reform is a low-intensity issue). Finally, in 2002, the political climate worked in favor of reform. By a narrow margin, both houses of Congress passed a version of campaign finance reform advocated by Republican Senator John McCain and Democratic Senator Russell Feingold, and a reluctant President Bush signed it into law.

The major feature of the Bipartisan Campaign Reform Act of 2002, commonly called the **McCain-Feingold Act**, is a prohibition of the use of soft money in federal elections, including a ban on "issue ads" funded with soft money. In exchange, after the 2002 elections, the annual limit that individuals can contribute in hard-money contributions to candidates and party organizations doubled—to $2,000 and $10,000, respectively.

Even after passage, McCain-Feingold met with resistance. Although ardent reform activists felt it was little more than a Band-Aid over a gaping wound, just about everyone directly influenced by the changes resisted them. Both major parties immediately searched for ways to circumvent the soft-money restrictions, while some PACs argued it went too far, challenging soft-money limitations as restrictions on free expression.

Detractors included four of the six FEC commissioners who were in office at the time the law went into effect. Because they were responsible for interpreting and enforcing the law, they were able to weaken some of the law's reforms, restoring large portions of the soft-money loophole that McCain-Feingold was designed to fill and providing exceptions under which federal candidates could still collect soft-money contributions. That led to a fight with Senator McCain, who vowed to undo the FEC action. The law got a boost in December 2002, when a divided Supreme Court upheld the soft-money ban, but McCain-Feingold was unable to prevent massive soft-money expenditures in the 2004 contest.[16]

McCain-Feingold Act: The name commonly used to describe the Bipartisan Campaign Reform Act of 2002, which prohibits the use of soft money in federal elections in an attempt to close a loophole in the 1974 Federal Election Campaign Act.

Then, in the landmark 2010 case *Citizens United v. Federal Election Commission*, a more conservative Supreme Court effectively gutted the McCain-Feingold Act, ruling that corporations were entitled to First Amendment rights similar to those held by individuals. In the Court's view, money is a form of expression and cannot be restricted by Congress. The ruling permitted corporations to spend unlimited sums on elections, which they promptly did in 2010 and 2012. Reaction to the ruling followed ideological and party lines, with conservative groups and Republican officials generally hailing it as a boost for free expression, whereas liberal groups and Democratic officials condemned it as a boon for special interests and a blow to the ability of ordinary people to influence government officials. Within five years of the ruling, campaign contributions by outside groups and individuals more than doubled, with nearly 60 percent of the increase coming from fewer than 200 people.[17]

7.2d Off to the Races: Money, Media, and Momentum

L.O. Discuss the relationship between momentum and expectations in presidential primary campaigns.

Perhaps the most accurate way to characterize the presidential selection season is to say it's a marathon leading up to the primaries, then a fast sprint to the nomination (followed by another marathon to the fall election for the primary winners). The strategy followed by candidates is dictated partly by the realities of the calendar and partly by the resources at their disposal.

Every potential president starts out with advantages and disadvantages, but not in equal amounts. As the 2016 Democratic presidential contest began to take shape, a potential candidate like Hillary Rodham Clinton, the former secretary of state, senator from New York, and First Lady, held one obvious advantage over, say, Lincoln Chafee.

Who's Lincoln Chafee? That's the advantage. If you live in Rhode Island, you probably know that he was recently your governor (and before that, your senator). But for the millions of Americans who do not live in Rhode Island (and who do not pay close attention to American governors), he had a lot of catching up to do when it came to **name recognition** because, as chief executive of a relatively small New England state, he was not exactly a household name. You may not have even known that he was a candidate for the 2016 Democratic nomination.

name recognition: An informal measure of how much the public is aware of a candidate or elected official, based on how widely people are able to identify the candidate or official.

Name recognition gives candidates credibility; no one is going to question whether Clinton could mount a viable presidential campaign the way one might raise that question about, say, Jim Webb.[18] (Look at the endnote if you don't know Jim Webb.) With credibility comes the ability to attract resources. It's easier to raise money if you look like you can mount a serious campaign. You'll attract seasoned campaign advisors. The media will pay more attention to you.[19]

By far, the greatest benefit of name recognition is the advantage it gives a candidate in attracting donors. Long before a single primary vote is counted in New Hampshire, well in advance of the snowy Iowa caucuses, the primary race takes shape as prospective candidates travel the country looking for financial support. This preprimary phase, which could legitimately be called the "money primary," can stretch out for a year or two for candidates with name recognition, even more for candidates who are less well known. It is not too much of an exaggeration to say that potential candidates for the presidency in 2020 will be making exploratory phone calls to potential donors before all the bills are paid for the 2016 contest. Considering the cost of buying television commercials in large states that now hold their primaries early in the process, raising large amounts of money is essential to any candidate who hopes to have a serious chance of making the race.

Once money is committed to a candidate, it's out of play for everyone else, and with the frontloading of expensive contests, money raised early counts the most. In the days following the McGovern-Fraser reforms, candidates could expect to be able to raise money during the long primary season if they experienced early success. Today's compressed primary calendar makes that impossible. A campaign is doomed without an early infusion of cash, either in the form of a large network of reliable donors, a committed supply of soft money, or a demonstrated ability to bring in large numbers of small contributions.

Candidates with large donor networks can use their fund-raising advantage to clear the field of poorly financed opponents before the voting starts. George W. Bush pursued this strategy to great effect. Aided by his connections to the oil industry, a key source of Republican money, Bush raised a staggering (at that time) $37.2 million for his campaign more than half a year before the first primary and caucus votes were cast. In contrast, a few high-profile contenders had raised far less. Former Vice President Dan Quayle and former Labor Secretary Elizabeth Dole had "only" been able to raise $3.5 million each, and former Tennessee Governor Lamar Alexander had raised $1 million less than that.[20] All three would call it quits several months before the Iowa caucus, recognizing that they simply did not have a realistic chance of attracting the kind of dollars they would need to compete.

As with a primary schedule that allocates political influence unevenly, there's a big irony in the way campaign finance regulations have restricted political competition. The reforms that produced today's primary system were intended to democratize the selection process, giving voice to the wishes of the party's rank-and-file voters. As candidates drop out before the voting starts when they can't raise the money necessary to compete, candidate selection shifts from people willing to go to the ballot box to people willing—and able—to open their checkbooks.

In addition to cash, viable campaigns need qualified staff and try to assemble a team of advisors with proven track records. A successful campaign needs organization, and potential staff members will want to place their professional futures in the hands of candidates who seem to be going somewhere. That's why candidates with name recognition are in a better position to attract the people who make a campaign run: fund-raisers, pollsters, speechwriters, and political consultants who can organize a national strategy, an advance staff to organize events, and grassroots political teams in key primary and caucus states who can get out the vote.[21] The emergence of Internet campaigning hasn't changed these realities, although it has created new positions for people skilled in using data to target and reach voters, as you can see in the Demystifying Government box, Hillary's Big Data.

The more a candidate demonstrates the ability to amass resources in the year or so before the primaries begin, the more seriously political reporters and pundits will regard the candidate. Achieving a high level of notice from the press is as critical as raising money because a campaign that depends on reaching voters on a state-by-state basis cannot survive without media attention. Press coverage then begets press coverage in a kind of self-fulfilling cycle: A candidate who gets press coverage is taken seriously by reporters, who react by bestowing even more press coverage on the candidate (in a modification of this formula, Donald Trump relied on his celebrity status and ability to command social media to draw the attention of reporters, even when they did not take him seriously). Of course, press attention helps the candidate raise more money and build a better organization. This process can work in reverse as well, with struggling candidates facing longer odds as the press ignores them.

But with the benefits of an effective early-stage campaign come the pressures of high **expectations**. Horserace coverage comes early to a campaign marked by a long march to raise money and establish credibility, and reporters will handicap the odds against each contender well before primary voters have their say.[22] When reporters see that candidates with name recognition are succeeding at fund-raising and attracting a professional staff, they will treat them as serious contenders who are expected to perform well once the voting begins. This can put pressure on candidates as well; for example, consider former Florida Governor Jeb Bush, who entered the 2016 campaign with every traditional political advantage and the high expectations they bring, only to exit the race early when his performance could not match what was expected of him.

On the Democratic side, as the candidate with the most early money, endorsements, and name recognition, Hillary Clinton began the 2016 primary contest as the **front-runner**—the candidate reporters said everyone had to beat. Accordingly, she carried the burden of having the highest expectations. If she stumbled, the failure to live up to expectations could have threatened her front-runner status, especially if she fell behind a candidate like Bernie Sanders, who entered the contest with none of Clinton's advantages. Sanders was the quintessential **long shot**, with little name recognition, no money, a skeletal staff, and a

DEMYSTIFYING GOVERNMENT

Hillary's Big Data

Have you noticed how ads for products similar to ones you recently purchased or searched for tend to pop up on the websites you view? That's because your browsing and purchasing history can be used by marketers to identify other items you might be interested in based on your past behavior. You can probably see why this information would be incredibly valuable to vendors looking to identify customers with specific interests and preferences. It's just as valuable to political campaigns because it allows them to locate persuadable voters and figure out the best way to speak to them about their candidate.

Both the Clinton and Trump campaigns invested heavily in such microtargeting efforts. Building on a methodology developed and refined during the previous two election cycles, the Clinton people relied on huge databases of voters that contained public information about everyone who is registered to vote and whether they registered with a political party. This information was supplemented with other publicly available data on things such as charitable giving patterns, home ownership, group memberships, magazine subscriptions, and social media footprints, permitting the campaign to assemble an extended profile of each voter. This information could then be blended with data gathered by phone surveys to help the campaign iden-

tify likely levels of support from individuals or voters sharing demographic traits, and the campaign could then design a portrait of each voter offering a precise estimate of the things that motivate and concern him or her. The campaign used this information to develop carefully refined messages for different voters, which were then employed in targeted advertising appeals and by canvassers knocking on doors.[T7] It enabled campaign workers to know where their likely voters were and develop persuasive ways to speak to the unconvinced to get them to come on board.

The Clinton campaign was visibly identified with its Big Data techniques, in part because the campaign was very public about building on the highly successful efforts of the two Obama campaigns. More quietly, the Trump campaign outsourced a fairly extensive data analytics effort to a British firm.[T8] One lesson of the 2016 campaign is that data analytics have become an essential component of contemporary campaigns, adding a sophisticated scientific spin to the age-old craft of political persuasion. Another lesson is that identifying the best ways to reach voters may be a necessary condition of winning an election, but it is not sufficient. Technology may help campaigns figure out what voters want, but candidates still need to make the sale.

message to the left of the political mainstream. He could afford to run well behind Clinton in opinion polls during the months leading to the Iowa caucus without suffering negative press coverage. However, once Sanders started showing strength in opinion polls, and especially after he played Clinton to a draw in Iowa and defeated her handily in New Hampshire, reporters started to take him seriously. He emerged as the main (and only) challenger to Clinton's nomination, and press expectations of his performance in future primaries increased accordingly.

Whether you're a front-runner, main challenger, or long shot, your strategy is largely dictated by your position in the race and the media-generated expectations that follow from it. When the primaries begin, a campaign generates **momentum** by meeting or exceeding expectations. This puts the greatest pressure on the front-runner to win early and often, while long shots simply need to do better than expected. In fact, a long shot who surprises reporters by finishing close to the top of the pack in the Iowa caucuses or New Hampshire primary can receive a gold mine of media coverage—even if he or she doesn't finish first. In that case, a candidate can win in the media without winning with the voters. But Iowa and New Hampshire have also put an early end to many candidacies. The logic of horserace coverage places so much weight on Iowa and New Hampshire that trailing candidates must exceed expectations in these early contests if they hope to survive.

Should long shots beat their expectations, they're no longer long shots, and reporters will require that they begin to win, and win soon. Failure to meet newly elevated expectations can stall momentum just as surely as a front-runner who underperforms runs the risk of being tossed from the race. Momentum has tangible rewards because resources follow winners, and if you're presented as a winner in the press, the money and organization you'll attract might just be enough to validate what reporters are saying about your campaign.

momentum: The ability of a presidential campaign to maintain viability by meeting or exceeding press-generated expectations during the long primary period.

Of course, candidates can be propelled all the way to victory by winning contests they're "expected" to lose. Rick Santorum showed surprising strength in Iowa in 2012, emerging from the field's bottom tier to edge Mitt Romney and establish himself as a credible contender. John Kerry came out of nowhere to beat Howard Dean in Iowa in 2004; when he finished first the following week in New Hampshire, his campaign got such a media boost that Kerry was able to ride the momentum it generated to the Democratic nomination.

Since 1972, no candidate has won a nomination after finishing below third place in either state.[23] Former New York City mayor Rudy Giuliani, a candidate for the 2008 Republican nomination, learned the hard way that if you skip over Iowa and New Hampshire because your prospects look brighter in subsequent states, you take yourself off the stage during the critical first weeks of the primary season when voters—and reporters—are sorting out winners and losers. Giuliani's defeat in Florida and his rapid demise as a candidate thereafter was rooted in his decision to downplay the Iowa and New Hampshire contests.

While campaigning in primary and caucus states, candidates fashion a message that can define their campaigns. Along with investing resources in the early contests, developing an effective message is a key part of attaining viability because it's not enough to tell people you're running for president simply because you want to be president. Candidates need to give people a reason to vote for them.

Typically, candidates try to do two things: They want to distinguish themselves from their rivals, which is sometimes difficult to do in a selection contest where your rivals come from within your party and probably agree with you more than they disagree. They also need to appeal to the people who are likely to turn out to vote.

One way candidates can draw distinctions with their opponents is by positioning themselves to the "right" or "left" of the opposition. For instance, in 2004, Howard Dean took a stand against the Iraq War, positioning himself as a more liberal candidate than John Kerry, even though Kerry had a more liberal record. George W. Bush used the term *compassionate conservatism* to portray a conservative philosophy with a moderate temperament that suggested unity and inclusiveness.

Even as Bush sought the middle ground, it was the middle ground within his party. Primary voters are more likely than general election voters to be closer to the poles of public opinion. Republicans are likely to be more conservative than the general population; Democrats are likely to be more liberal. Candidates need to reach these voters in order to be selected as the nominee of the party, so it's not uncommon for Republican hopefuls to sound more conservative during the primary race and for Democrats to sound more liberal until they secure their respective nominations and shift their campaign rhetoric toward the center of public opinion, where most voters lie, and where general elections are won and lost.

For the most part, this did not happen in 2016, just one of several ways in which it was uncharacteristic of presidential elections. The 2016 Republican primary campaign was a highly unusual contest in which Donald Trump openly appealed to relatively extreme sentiment in his party and was rewarded for it. Trump then refused to modulate his tone or his rhetoric in the general election campaign, and he was rewarded for that as well. He was an unlikely candidate who better fit the mold of previous "boutique" candidates than the profile of a party nominee, no less a president.

Defying expectations, Trump became the de facto front-runner for the Republican nomination long before the press acknowledged that he had staying power, whereas other candidates who might have been successful in a more typical year were cast aside. Contenders the press took seriously—at first—include the following:

- Former Florida Governor **Jeb Bush**, son of President George H. W. Bush and brother of former President George W. Bush
- Large-state Senators **Ted Cruz** of Texas and **Marco Rubio** of Florida
- Outspoken New Jersey Governor **Chris Christie**
- Libertarian-leaning Kentucky Senator **Rand Paul**
- Wisconsin Governor **Scott Walker**

As the primary field took shape, Bush was widely regarded as the candidate to beat, with the other five positioned to emerge as main challengers if Bush stumbled. A second tier of candidates featured individuals with national name recognition and credible claims to the nomination—had their campaigns taken off. They include the following:

- Governor **John Kasich**, who started in the back of the pack but became a significant figure with staying power after winning the primary in his home state of Ohio
- Three former candidates: **Rick Perry**, one-time Texas governor and unsuccessful candidate for the Republican nomination in 2012; former Pennsylvania Senator **Rick Santorum**, the runner-up for the 2012 nomination; and **Mike Huckabee**, who ran and lost in 2008
- Two-term Louisiana Governor **Bobby Jindal**
- Long-time South Carolina Senator **Lindsey Graham**

Several candidates with relatively thin claims to the nomination were also in the mix. These candidates were considered the longest of long shots—although the same could have been said of Donald Trump. They are as follows:

- Neurosurgeon and author **Dr. Ben Carson**
- Former Hewlett-Packard CEO **Carly Fiorina**
- Former New York Governor **George Pataki**
- Former Virginia Governor **Jim Gilmore**

Figure 7.3 portrays the Republican field in the reverse order of disappearance from the race, with the candidates who left first at the bottom.

How was a political novice able to beat back so many seasoned political figures and emerge from out of nowhere to claim the Republican nomination? The answer to that question rests with understanding the national mood in 2016, when there was a lot of dissatisfaction in the electorate and anger at political leaders—a factor that also drove Bernie Sanders's insurgent candidacy on the Democratic side.

Donald Trump is a Republican, but he ran for president by opposing the leadership of the Republican Party. Hillary Clinton won the nomination of the Democratic Party but had to make significant policy concessions to Sanders, the Vermont socialist who was not even a Democrat until he decided to oppose Clinton in the primaries. Party elites were under siege in 2016 as restlessness with business as usual took hold among voters across the political spectrum.

Trump told Republican voters that their leaders had betrayed them. He spoke directly to older, white, less-well-educated individuals who would form the core of his coalition, contending that Republican leaders didn't have their economic concerns at heart and were hapless in their efforts to take on the legacy achievements of the Obama years, such as the Affordable Care Act. Trump's rhetoric positioned him as a populist, someone who would empower ordinary people in his base and make their lives better by upending a Washington establishment he claimed didn't work for them. He had an uncanny ability to channel their economic and social grievances, and they were hungry to support someone who spoke their language. That Trump is a billionaire real estate investor and thus part of an economic elite did not undermine the potency of his message; instead, he was able to present himself as a "winner" who would make winners out of supporters who cheered the candidate's promise to blow up the Washington establishment. Trump's base was so loyal that he told a campaign audience in Iowa he could "stand in the middle of Fifth Avenue and shoot somebody and [he] wouldn't lose voters."[24] He was probably right.

Trump played the unusually large field of Republican candidates to his advantage during a string of debates that punctuated the primary calendar. Jeb Bush, in particular, proved to be a perfect foil for Trump. Other than the Clintons, no family is more associated with the politics of the past thirty-five years than the Bushes. Trump understood that a share of the Republican electorate saw Bush as the embodiment of everything they detested about Washington, and he used Bush's privilege as a weapon against him. With trademark swagger, Trump swatted away Bush as a politician bought and paid for by

FIGURE 7.3 The Crowded Field of 2016 Republican Presidential Candidates

The 2016 Republican primary field was the most crowded in memory. The candidates are pictured here in the reverse order of their departure from the race, with the winner, Donald Trump, occupying the top spot.

The candidates in the second row, John Kasich and Ted Cruz, dropped out after the May 3rd Indiana primary, won by Donald Trump, when it became evident that they could no longer prevent Trump from winning enough delegates to claim the nomination.

Marco Rubio and Ben Carson, in the third row, dropped out in March, in Rubio's case after losing his home state of Florida to Trump.

Jeb Bush, Jim Gilmore, Chris Christie, and Carly Fiorina are pictured in the fourth row. All departed in mid-February, with the one-time front-runner Bush exiting after a string of disappointing showings in the early contests, capped by a distant fourth-place finish in South Carolina.

Rand Paul, Rick Santorum, and Mike Huckabee, pictured in the fifth row, were casualties of poor performances in Iowa.

George Pataki, Lindsey Graham, Bobby Jindal, Scott Walker, and Rick Perry, in the sixth row, suspended their campaigns before the primary season began.

Sources: DONALD TRUMP, Joe Seer/Shutterstock.com; JOHN KASICH, Juli Hansen/Shutterstock.com; TED CRUZ Joseph Sohm/Shutterstock.com; MARCO RUBIO, Crush Rush/Shutterstock.com; BEN CARSON Joseph Sohm/Shutterstock.com; JEB BUSH, Joseph Sohm/Shutterstock.com; JIM GILMORE, Christopher Halloran/Shutterstock.com; CHRIS CHRISTIE, L.E.MORMILE/Shutterstock.com; CARLY FIORINA, Andrew Cline/Shutterstock.com; RAND PAUL, Christopher Halloran/Shutterstock.com; RICK SANTORUM, Christopher Halloran/Shutterstock.com; MIKE HUCKABEE, Christopher Halloran/Shutterstock.com; GEORGE PATAKI, Andrew Cline/Shutterstock.com; LINDSEY GRAHAM, Albert H. Teich/Shutterstock.com; BOBBY JINDAL, Christopher Halloran/Shutterstock.com; SCOTT WALKER, Andrew Cline/Shutterstock.com; RICK PERRY, Christopher Halloran/Shutterstock.com.

The 2016 Republican primary field was so large that it was difficult to fit all the candidates on one debate stage. *Source:* Joseph Sohm/Shutterstock.com.

special interests, establishing dominance over the former governor by dismissing him with scorn and derision. This put Bush—and other Republicans who would later fall by the wayside—in a defensive position that made them appear weak and hapless.

Republican leaders initially disregarded Trump's campaign as little more than a side-show, even though he performed well in opinion polls. It was easy to dismiss someone with no political experience and a makeshift campaign as unserious—until he started winning primaries. At that point, various "Never Trump" efforts began to materialize, but because they were swimming against the year's populist tide, they had the feel of a party establishment attempting to shape the process for their benefit. When Trump character-ized these efforts as an attempt to rig the primaries for elite interests at the expense of the people, he deepened his support with the largest and most animated group of Republican primary voters. Although a majority of Republicans supported other candidates, their loyalties were spread across a large field, and efforts to block Trump from the nomination proved fruitless.

While the large, unruly Republican field was succumbing to Donald Trump, populist sentiment was also roiling the waters in the smaller and more sedate Democratic pri-mary campaign. Like Republican leaders who expected Bush to emerge as their party's standard-bearer, Democratic leaders had essentially cleared the field for Hillary Clinton, whose advantages of fame, money, connections, and experience matched those held by the former Florida governor.

Bernie Sanders did not have any of these advantages. A relatively unknown senator from a small state, Sanders was elected as an independent but caucused with Democrats, which means he supported Senate Democratic leaders and relied on them for his com-mittee assignments even though he was not a party member. The Democratic Party was closer to his ideological leanings, but he characterized himself as a democratic socialist[25] and had often been critical of the Democratic Party.

Sanders had a long record of criticizing wealthy individuals and corporations for hijacking government and preventing it from working for regular people. Unlike Pres-ident Trump, who promised to shake up Washington with the strength of his presence, Senator Sanders proposed using the power of government to break up banks that were too big to fail, redistribute the tax burden upward, and rewrite campaign rules to reduce

Bernie Sanders' message of using government power to address the needs of ordinary people generated intense loyalty among his supporters. *Source:* J. Bicking/Shutterstock.com.

L.O. Identify key strategic approaches to waging election campaigns.

platform: The official document produced at the major party conventions that serves as a philosophical and policy blueprint for the party's presidential nominee.

the influence of big money. In this regard, Sanders's campaign was aligned with a progressive populism of the left. He shared with his right-leaning counterpart the diagnosis of a system designed by elites to work in their favor, but his solutions were quite different.

This message, coupled with the authentic way he delivered it, resonated with disaffected progressive voters, especially Millennials, who gravitated to his campaign in large numbers. From nowhere, Sanders emerged as a viable challenger to Clinton, and although he lacked the delegate strength he needed to win the nomination, his challenge was robust enough to engage Clinton on the issues that mattered to him and his supporters. He ended his campaign as one of the central figures in his newly adopted party, where he is a voice for the progressive left.

7.3 Decisions, Part II: The Election Process

When a roll call of the delegates at the national convention ratifies the primary victor, the candidate becomes the official party nominee, and the general election campaign begins. Typically held in late summer before the November election, conventions are a four-day gathering that in recent years has been a protracted "infomercial" for the party nominee.

Stage-managed by the victorious campaign, conventions produce made-for-television balloon-and-streamer-filled pictures that candidates love. Celebrities join political figures to speak or perform at the convention podium in order to boost press interest. Everything is designed to play well on television and to maximize positive exposure for the candidate, who may have been in politics (or on television) for years but who is "introducing" himself or herself to the American public as a future president. It's typical for each newly minted nominee to get a "bounce" in the polls from favorable reaction to four days of positive press exposure.

In 2008, Barack Obama capitalized on his ability to draw huge crowds and staged his Denver acceptance speech in a football stadium, complete with a stadium-sized stage set.[26] In 2004, John Kerry surrounded himself with veterans who had served with him in Vietnam to communicate the message that, in a time of war, he would be a strong commander-in-chief. In 2000, the Republican Convention studiously featured minority supporters, like General Colin Powell and former Oklahoma Representative J. C. Watts, in an effort to portray the party as diverse and inclusive.

Behind the scenes, delegates perform serious work in the form of writing the **platform** on which the nominee will run. The platform is a long document listing the principles that the party stands for under the leadership of its presidential nominee. So, if you were to read the party platforms, you would notice the philosophical differences separating the nominees and probably have a good sense of how each one would govern. Of course, few of us even think to do this, but that doesn't diminish the value of the platform as a blueprint for the next administration's priorities.

The platform is written under the direction of the winning campaign. However, platform writing can be a forum for uniting the party after a difficult primary contest if work needs to be done to win the allegiance of a vanquished candidate's supporters. At the Democratic Convention in Philadelphia where Clinton became her party's nominee, Bernie Sanders demanded and won a number of planks in the party platform, which then served as Clinton's official philosophical and policy blueprint for the fall campaign. This put the Democratic Party on record in support of such things as a setting a $15 minimum wage, providing free public college tuition for middle-class families, closing corporate tax loopholes, and expanding Social Security, a demonstration of the strong response to Sanders's ideas by voters in the Democratic primaries. The Sanders campaign characterized it as the most progressive Democratic Party platform in history.[27]

Because the party activists who become convention delegates and help shape the platform are generally more ideological than rank-and-file party adherents, it shouldn't be surprising that the Democratic and Republican platforms reveal differences in priorities and in approaches to problems. Perhaps no place is the difference between the two parties more clearly defined than in these documents.

In Table 7.4, take a look at a few "planks" from the 2016 Democratic and Republican platforms and see if you can spot some of these differences.

TABLE 7.4 Party Differences

2016 Platform Planks	
Democratic Party	**Republican Party**
"At a time of massive income and wealth inequality, we believe the wealthiest Americans and largest corporations must pay their fair share of taxes. Democrats will claw back tax breaks for companies that ship jobs overseas, eliminate tax breaks for big oil and gas companies, and crack down on inversions and other methods companies use to dodge their tax responsibilities. We will make sure that our tax code rewards businesses that make investments and provide good-paying jobs here in the United States, not businesses that walk out on America."	"American businesses now face the world's highest corporate tax rates. That's like putting lead shoes on your cross-country team. It reduces companies' ability to compete overseas, encourages them to move abroad, lessens their investment, cripples job creation here at home, lowers American wages, and fosters the avoidance of tax liability—without actually increasing tax revenues. We propose to level the international playing field by lowering the corporate tax rate to be on a par with, or below, the rates of other industrial nations."
"Democrats believe that health care is a right, not a privilege, and our health care system should put people before profits. Thanks to the hard work of President Obama and Democrats in Congress, we took a critically important step toward the goal of universal health care by passing the Affordable Care Act, which has covered 20 million more Americans and ensured millions more will never be denied coverage because of a pre-existing condition. Democrats will never falter in our generations-long fight to guarantee health care as a fundamental right for every American."	"Any honest agenda for improving healthcare must start with repeal of the dishonestly named Affordable Care Act of 2010: Obamacare. It weighs like the dead hand of the past upon American medicine. It imposed a Euro-style bureaucracy to manage its unworkable, budget-busting, conflicting provisions. It has driven up prices for all consumers. It must be removed and replaced with an approach based on genuine competition, patient choice, excellent care, wellness, and timely access to treatment."
"To build on the success of the lifesaving Brady Handgun Violence Prevention Act, we will expand and strengthen background checks and close dangerous loopholes in our current laws; repeal the Protection of Lawful Commerce in Arms Act (PLCAA) to revoke the dangerous legal immunity protections gun makers and sellers now enjoy; and keep weapons of war—such as assault weapons and large capacity ammunition magazines (LCAMs)—off our streets."	"We support firearm reciprocity legislation to recognize the right of law-abiding Americans to carry firearms to protect themselves and their families in all 50 states. We support constitutional carry statutes and salute the states that have passed them. We oppose ill-conceived laws that would restrict magazine capacity or ban the sale of the most popular and common modern rifle. We also oppose any effort to deprive individuals of their right to keep and bear arms without due process of law."
"Democrats applaud last year's decision by the Supreme Court that recognized that LGBT people—like other Americans—have the right to marry the person they love. But there is still much work to be done. LGBT kids continue to be bullied at school, restaurants can refuse to serve transgender people, and same-sex couples are at risk of being evicted from their homes. We will fight for comprehensive federal non-discrimination protections for all LGBT Americans, to guarantee equal rights in areas such as housing, employment, public accommodations, credit, jury service, education, and federal funding."	"Traditional marriage and family, based on marriage between one man and one woman, is the foundation for a free society and has for millennia been entrusted with rearing children and instilling cultural values. We condemn the Supreme Court's ruling in *United States v. Windsor*, which wrongly removed the ability of Congress to define marriage policy in federal law. We also condemn the Supreme Court's lawless ruling in *Obergefell v. Hodges*. In *Obergefell*, five unelected lawyers robbed 320 million Americans of their legitimate constitutional authority to define marriage as the union of one man and one woman."

Because conventions are no longer the scene of high-stakes balloting or factional jockeying, the only real surprise to emerge from contemporary conventions is the identity of the nominee's vice presidential running mate (who is selected by the nominee and ratified by the convention delegates). And even that bit of suspense has been removed in recent election cycles as nominees have chosen to unveil their choices at media events prior to the conventions to prolong the free media coverage they get during convention week. Both Donald Trump and Hillary Clinton announced their running mates before their conventions began.

Nominees typically choose to run with people who promise to balance them on such factors as ideology, experience, or geography. Hillary Clinton's choice of Virginia Senator Tim Kaine was made with an eye toward locking up the strategic state of Virginia. Outsider Donald Trump tapped Indiana Governor Mike Pence, a former member of Congress, because of his governing experience and ties to Washington. In 2012, Mitt Romney's choice of conservative Wisconsin Representative Paul Ryan was designed to convince core Republican voters that Romney, a one-time governor of a liberal state, was ideologically in line with his party. In 2008, Barack Obama's choice of Delaware Senator Joseph Biden gave the relatively inexperienced Illinois senator a veteran running mate with strong foreign policy credentials.

As far as excitement goes at party conventions, that's about it. The primary victor's name is placed in nomination. The delegates vote. They vote for the nominee's vice presidential selection. The nominee makes a big speech and tries to stir excitement among the party faithful. Balloons and streamers drop from the rafters. Then the other major party does the same thing. And the general election campaign begins.

7.3a Organization, Media, Information, and Endurance

It's tempting to begin this section with a disclaimer because here we are talking about how political parties form a link between us and our elected officials—we've already witnessed places where that link is problematic, from the primary calendar to campaign fund-raising—and what you are about to read may at times seem coldly calculated to manipulate our voting patterns more than to engage us in spirited political discourse. What you're going to read about is, frankly, an example of why many people are turned off by politics. So, if you can, try to keep an open mind, and remember that running for president is an intense ordeal, where the biggest political prize on Earth hangs in the balance.

From the convention to Election Day, party nominees have roughly seventy-five days to bring their case for election to the American people. It's hard work—and it's big business, requiring a more extensive campaign structure than the candidate had during the primary season, careful attention to paid and free media, an effective information-gathering apparatus, and, as always, the ability to remain sharp with little sleep.

Today's campaigns are an amalgam of professionals brought in to manage different components of the effort, meaning the candidate becomes a client to a series of political "hired guns" responsible for plotting and executing campaign strategy.

In addition to a campaign manager to handle the daily responsibilities of the effort, the campaigns hire media consultants, pollsters, fund-raisers, press officials, and staff members in much larger numbers than they had during the primary campaign. Their work entails designing, planning, and executing campaign events; testing themes for and developing television ads (media consultants); gauging and responding to public reaction to the candidate (pollsters); raising money (fund-raisers); and working to get reporters to cover the candidate's message (press secretary).

Much of this effort revolves around maximizing results from the **paid media** and **free media** we discussed in Chapter 5. In successful campaigns, the messages communicated in ads and in the press work together, are simple, and target groups of voters that the campaign needs to be victorious. As they did during the primaries, successful presidential candidates will go around the country giving essentially the same speech several times a day, hitting the same themes and staying "on message" in the hope that news stories will

paid media: Radio and television ads paid for and produced by political campaigns.

free media: The news coverage that major candidates for high office can expect to receive on a regular basis. Although free, candidates cannot control the content of this coverage or guarantee that it will be favorable.

reflect the theme crafted by the campaign. Only now, they will come under even greater press scrutiny.

In a savvy campaign, the same themes will appear in the candidate's paid advertising, allowing for a potentially powerful reinforcement tool because political professionals believe that if people hear a consistent message, they're more likely to absorb it. We know from Chapter 5 that reporters often rebel against this kind of message control by retaining the last word in framing news stories. Nonetheless, when a campaign can sustain a coordinated message in paid and free media, it can typically wage the election on its terms.

In order to determine which groups of voters the candidate needs to win over and what messages will reach them, professional pollsters conduct public opinion surveys throughout the campaign. Initial polls reveal a wealth of information that can be used to plot strategy, especially information about how voters view the candidates' strengths and weaknesses. By looking closely at survey results, pollsters can identify groups that strongly support the candidate, strongly support his opponent, and all-important "swing" groups that are within the candidate's reach and that could determine the outcome of the election.

Typically, campaigns will gather more information on how targeted groups of voters are reacting to the candidate by conducting **focus groups**, which bring together a small number of people sharing a targeted demographic, like suburban women or southern white men, to "talk" about the candidate. Unlike opinion polls, which you may recall consist of random samples in which theoretically anyone can be contacted, focus groups are nonrandom and nonscientific. They can quickly and inexpensively produce a wealth of useful details for the campaign about how the selected group feels about the candidate that can help them fine-tune their strategy.

focus group: A small group of voters chosen by a political campaign for their demographic similarities who are brought together to gauge how the group they represent feels about the candidate.

Getting out the message requires travel—and lots of it. In the early days of the republic, it was customary for presidential candidates to stay home and say nothing; anything more was considered undignified. Nothing could be farther from the description of today's general election campaigns, which feature nonstop travel by the candidate and his entourage, who crisscross the country at jet speeds in a test of endurance that taxes all but the strongest constitutions. Candidates watch the country go by in a blur as they are chauffeured about in what some describe as a "bubble" of advisors, advance people (who arrange the events), reporters, and the electronic gear of twenty-first-century politics: television cameras, microphones, wires, and the like.

7.3b Strategy Again

With an infinite number of possible events to attend and a finite amount of time, campaign strategists need to set the candidate's agenda for maximum political benefit. This is accomplished by identifying where the candidate needs to shore up strength among voters.

As we'll soon see when we talk about the Electoral College, presidential elections are decided on a state-by-state basis. Each state is accorded electoral votes, awarded as a bloc to the candidate who carries the state, and a candidate must win a majority of electoral votes (270) to be elected. This fact drives fundamental strategic decisions. Where the candidate visits and where he or she purchases commercial airtime is determined by the states that campaign operatives believe they need to carry to win the election.

Each campaign's fundamental strategic decisions are based on dividing the map into three groups: states the campaign feels it will lose no matter what it does (where there's no realistic chance to win electoral votes); states the campaign feels it will win no matter what it does (where it feels assured of winning electoral votes); and competitive states, which get the most attention. Many of these can be determined by recent voting patterns. For instance, in 2016, the Trump campaign knew that most states in the deep South and in the Rocky Mountain West reliably support Republican candidates. Likewise, the Clinton campaign knew it could count on California, New York, and most New England states. So, there was no point for either campaign to devote resources to those states.

The remaining states make up the campaign battleground. These are "swing" states that have a history of supporting Democrats or Republicans in recent elections, and which

Vote Swapping

Candidates aren't the only ones who can engage in election-year strategy. In 2000, when consumer advocate Ralph Nader was the presidential candidate of the Green Party, some Nader voters living in battleground states faced a dilemma: They were concerned that if they voted for Nader (their first choice) instead of Democrat Al Gore (their second choice), the loss of a vote for Gore would boost the prospects of Republican George W. Bush (their third choice). In a close race, they were concerned that a vote for Nader would be a vote for Bush.

The solution: Trade votes with Gore voters in states where the outcome wasn't in doubt. In an example of spontaneous, grassroots political involvement, Internet sites emerged that allowed Nader voters in battle-ground states to find Gore voters in states where one candidate or the other was sure to win so they could agree to "swap votes." The Nader voter in the battleground state would agree to cast a vote for Gore, believing that a Gore voter in a state where the race wasn't close would cast a vote on their behalf for Nader. Of course, these "agreements" were unenforceable, and neither voter would ever know if the other carried out the agreement. Still, it demonstrates that it's not just the professionals who can be sophisticated strategists in a presidential election and that, given the opportunity to reach others via the Internet, it's possible for ordinary people to play with the electoral rules in order to maximize their political expression in presidential campaigns.

both candidates feel could break in either direction. The more populous of these become key to the strategies of both campaigns. In reality, the national campaign for president isn't a national campaign at all; it plays out mostly in these swing states. If you live in places like Ohio, North Carolina, and Florida, you are showered with candidate visits and campaign promises and commercials, as both campaigns advance a strategy that will move them toward Electoral College victory. If you live in a state that's reliably in one column or the other, you're more of a bystander to a contest being played out elsewhere (see Demystifying Government: Vote Swapping).

Once target states have been identified, the campaign's pollsters go into action to assess the strength of the candidate and his or her opponent. The result of this assessment determines how resources are allocated. Campaigns will start with the electoral votes of their "base"—the states they can count on—and subtract that number from 270 to arrive at the number of electoral votes they need to win the election. They can identify where these votes might come from by looking at the number of electoral votes in the states that are up for grabs. From the survey data, they can determine which of the battleground states are likely to be the most competitive and devote the most resources to them.

Pollsters constantly take the temperature of the race in battleground states, and campaigns use the data to modify where they allocate resources. If the campaign's polls indicate that a state is starting to tip one way or another, resources can be pulled from that state and reallocated to a more competitive state.

In the closing weeks of the 2016 contest, when Clinton's polling indicated that her support was starting to lag in states where she had been leading throughout the campaign, she modified her schedule to make last-minute appearances in places like Michigan and New Hampshire. Her campaign downplayed these appearances in order to avoid the suggestion that she might be in trouble in states she was counting on to reach 270 electoral votes. But where a campaign sends a candidate in the last few days of a presidential campaign is always strategic and usually a good indication of what the campaign thinks of its prospects. Clinton ended up struggling in both states, and her loss in Michigan turned out to be decisive in the Electoral College.

7.3c Going Negative

It's always tempting for campaigns to use television commercials to define their opponent's character or record in negative terms through the use of negative ads (euphemistically called "comparative ads" by campaign professionals because they aim to highlight the positive qualities of the candidate by dragging down the candidate's opponent). The reason is simple: Advertising specialists believe they work. They permit the candidate to focus attention on the weaknesses of the opponent that the candidate's polling indicates will matter to undecided voters. If an opponent is relatively unknown, negative advertising can define the opponent in the most critical light to viewers who have no basis for challenging the assessment. Because Trump and Clinton were very well known, their negative ads were designed to reinforce preexisting impressions about their opponents. Clinton spent far more money on traditional advertising than Trump, hammering home questions about her opponent's character and fitness for office.

Opponents cried foul when the Johnson campaign juxtaposed this little girl's image with footage of a nuclear explosion in an ad suggesting that Barry Goldwater couldn't be trusted to avoid nuclear war. The Johnson campaign agreed and pulled the ad, something unimaginable today.[T9]

The environment produced by pervasive negative advertising can drive people away from politics, depressing turnout and increasing cynicism. However, political consultants bent on winning an election for their client will not be concerned with these serious systemic effects, and the fact is negative advertising exists because it's effective. People tend to remember negative messages, especially if they are repeated enough or left unchallenged. Even if they are challenged, the response from the opposing candidate can make him look defensive. Some campaigns actually anticipate negative ads and answer the charges before they're made in order to avoid looking defensive and "inoculate" the public against a charge they believe is coming.

Because people are repelled by negative messages even as they internalize negative allegations, negative ads can be risky to use. They can backfire by making the candidate who runs them appear mean-spirited. For this reason, negative ads will typically be shown first to focus groups to get a sense of how people from targeted demographic categories react to them. When they run, pollsters monitor public reaction closely, and campaigns will quickly pull negative ads at the slightest hint that they are hurting the campaign.[28]

Negative ads are not new to American politics, although in recent years, the threshold for what we seem to be willing to accept has gone up. For a good sense of how we've become more open to negative campaigning, consider the infamous "Daisy Commercial" run on behalf of Lyndon Johnson. It's still one of the most controversial in our history, even though it ran back in 1964. President Johnson's opponent, Republican Senator Barry Goldwater, generated concerns among many people that he might be trigger-happy and too willing to use nuclear weapons. To reinforce those concerns, the Johnson ad portrays a little girl pulling petals from a daisy while counting backward, fading into audio of a launch countdown, followed by an image of a nuclear explosion. Although that sounds heavy-handed, consider that Goldwater is never mentioned by name, and his policies are never discussed.

Almost fifty years later, it's still powerful. When the "Daisy Ad" ran, the Goldwater campaign cried foul, saying it unfairly implied that its candidate was a threat to world peace. Johnson agreed, and the ad never ran a second time. In today's charged political environment, unless the ad began to backfire politically, it's hard to imagine a campaign responding the same way.

7.3d Televised Debates

Presidential debates have become part of the quadrennial fall campaign ritual, but that wasn't always the case. They only date back to 1960, when John F. Kennedy and Richard M. Nixon squared off in a television studio in Washington, D.C. Presidential candidates had not debated before then. That's because it's unusual for the strategic interests of both candidates to lead them into a high-stakes confrontation with each other on the same stage in front of a huge national audience. Typically, one candidate will have more to gain by participating, leading an opponent to believe it is in his or her best interest to opt out. As you will see when you read Demystifying Government: The First Debate, both Kennedy and Nixon felt they had more to gain than lose by debating.

The First Debate

The first televised debates between Kennedy and Nixon occurred in part because both candidates stood to benefit from them. The race was close when Kennedy issued his debate challenge to Nixon, so neither candidate had the luxury of avoiding a direct confrontation by sitting on a large lead. Kennedy was knowledgeable and quick on his feet, and believed he could use the debate forum to dispel the idea that his youth was a liability in a contest against an incumbent vice president. Nixon knew that he wasn't the most trusted politician and believed that a strong performance could give him an opportunity to erase that impression. Besides, he had a record as a good debater, and to refuse Kennedy's invitation would make it appear that he was running scared.

Nixon's debating skills turned out to be of limited value, though. He failed to grasp what Kennedy's media consultants understood: that the debates would be about television. Kennedy's advisors knew that people are more likely to look at the pictures than listen to the words. They were savvy about the use of makeup to present a healthy image, and the inviting impression made by a blue shirt on a black-and-white television

screen. They could coach their candidate to look into the camera and talk to the voters, not to his opponent on stage. In short, they knew how to make Kennedy appear "telegenic," and in so doing, to invite a positive emotional reaction to the candidate.

That Nixon was recovering from an illness, looked pale, needed to shave, and perspired too much simply served to underscore the different impressions made by the two candidates. Perhaps the most valuable lesson of the Kennedy-Nixon debates was what the debates taught about the power of pictures more than words to communicate a message on television.

But the circumstances in 1960 were unusual, which is why it took sixteen years before presidential debates resumed. In 1964, President Johnson was so far ahead in opinion polls that he could simply refuse to debate Barry Goldwater. With Nixon on the ballot again in 1968 and 1972, there was probably no way that debates were going to happen, considering his bad experience in 1960.

It wasn't until 1976, when imperiled incumbent Gerald Ford was locked in a tight race with Jimmy Carter, that both sides felt it was in their interest to debate. Ford, whom Nixon appointed to the vice presidency after Spiro Agnew resigned in scandal, was elevated to the Oval Office following Nixon's resignation, making him the only president ever to serve without winning a national election. Two years into his brief term, Ford was still trying to convince Americans that he was up to the job, and his campaign operatives felt a televised debate would give him that opportunity. For his part, Carter was relatively unknown, and his campaign handlers felt a debate would give him positive exposure and a chance to show off his command of details.

Four years later, the political dynamics again favored a debate. This time, Carter was the imperiled incumbent, and Ronald Reagan was the challenger who needed a way to reassure Cold War voters that he would not act like a cowboy with America's nuclear arsenal.

Both debates worked to the advantage of the challenger, who received a boost by appearing on stage with the president. In 1984, with Reagan far ahead in opinion polls, his campaign calculated that it would make the president look magnanimous if he debated his opponent. This established the expectation that after three consecutive presidential elections with candidate debates, future campaigns would be expected to engage in debates as well. By 1988, debates had become the norm, and reluctant candidates found that the cost of looking like they were ducking their opponent had become too high for them to resist debating.

If you're on the debate team at school or if you know someone who is, you may be surprised at how little actual debating takes place at presidential debates. They tend to be more like joint press conferences, where both candidates repeat the same messages they've been talking about at campaign events. This can create a disconnected feeling, where candidates talk past each other or avoid questions in order to jump to their campaign talking points. In 2004, the Bush campaign went so far as to insist on guidelines that precluded the candidates from addressing each other directly. The name of the media game is to control the message by staying "on message," and that's how political advisors instruct candidates to approach televised debates.

They also instruct candidates to speak to the camera and try to relax. Because we react to what we see more than to what we hear, candidates who are unable to come across naturally in televised debates can find themselves at a disadvantage. In the 2000 debates, Al Gore was eager to show off his detailed policy knowledge, believing that it would show him to be more presidential than his less worldly opponent, George W. Bush. This turned out to be an incorrect assumption. Opinion polls conducted by both campaigns revealed that Gore turned off many undecided voters by coming across as somewhere between a bully and the smartest kid in the class. Gore may have won most of the debating points, but Bush appeared at ease and more likeable. Impressions like these can linger and factor into how people vote.

7.4 The Electoral College: Is This Any Way to Elect a President?

It's safe to say that no institution like the Electoral College has ever been created anywhere. It's been with us since the Constitutional Convention of 1787, modified once to account for political party competition, and has been the object of numerous reform proposals over the centuries, all of which have failed to materialize. It's complex, often misunderstood, and difficult to explain. Yet, it is almost always the final arbiter of who will enter the White House. First, let's make sure we understand how it works—see Demystifying Government: The Electoral College.

L.O. Explain how the Electoral College works and why it turns presidential campaigns into a small number of statewide elections.

7.4a Who Would Create a System Like This?

Although it may seem like the Constitution's framers created the Electoral College to make life miserable for government students, in truth, it was a compromise that solved a few key dilemmas. The framers wanted an elite to identify the most qualified presidential candidates rather than leave the choice to voters, but they didn't want presidents to be beholden to the elite that selected them. They didn't want to undermine separation of powers by simply having Congress select the president, and they needed a scheme for presidential selection that could win the support of slave and free states. In the Electoral College, the framers created a mechanism for assembling an elite that would go out of business as soon as its work was done, meaning it wouldn't be in a position to ask anything of the new president. And electoral votes are based partly on House districts, where the overrepresentation of slave states by virtue of the three-fifths compromise carries over to presidential selection. As complex as it is, the Electoral College is consistent with federalism by giving the states a key role in presidential selection, and separation of powers, by putting the choice of the president in the hands of Congress as a matter of last resort.

In its original incarnation, the Electoral College was really established as a mechanism that would perform the selection function that soon became the province of political parties. Electors were to identify the worthiest candidates in their respective states, and if a majority could not agree on a single best choice, the House of Representatives would settle the matter. By 1800, the selection process was already being performed through party nominations, and the mechanics of the Electoral College had to be changed.

In its original form, electors cast two votes, one for a candidate from another state in an effort to avoid parochial choices. The runner-up in electoral votes would become vice president. With the advent of two-party competition, it quickly became apparent that this meant the vice president could be the losing presidential candidate of the opposition party. As parties started nominating separate candidates for president and vice president,

The Electoral College

The president and the vice president are chosen by the Electoral College consisting of electors allocated to each state and (by virtue of the 23rd Amendment) the District of Columbia, which gets three electors. Electors are allocated by adding the number of senators (two) to the number of representatives in each state. Since the least populous states have one representative, the smallest number of electors a state can have is three.

In total, there are 538 electors in the Electoral College. Each gets one vote. The map below shows how many electors are allocated to each state. When you vote for a president and a vice president, you're really selecting the electors pledged to vote for the candidates you selected.

Electors are real people, chosen by the state party leaders in numbers equal to the electoral vote of each state. So, since Illinois has twenty electoral votes, the Illinois Republican Party selects twenty loyal Republicans to act as electors, and the Illinois Democratic Party selects twenty loyal Democrats to act as electors.

Independents and third parties that qualify to be on the ballot also get to field a slate of electors. We determine which slate of electors represents our state when we go to the polls to vote for the president. Our votes for the president are called the **popular vote**. The party of the candidate receiving **plurality** of popular votes for its slate of electors wins all the electors in the state.

In 2000, Al Gore won 366 more popular votes than George W. Bush in New Mexico, out of a total of 598,605 votes cast. It was less than a majority, but Gore's slim plurality was enough to give him all five of the state's electoral votes. Maine and Nebraska have the only exceptions in the winner-take-all rule. In those states, two electors are awarded to the plurality winner of the popular vote, and the rest are awarded to the plurality winner of the popular vote within each of the state's congressional districts. In 2016, Hillary Clinton won the overall popular vote of Maine while losing the popular vote of one of Maine's two congressional districts, so Donald Trump won one of Maine's electoral votes despite losing the state.

On the Monday following the second Wednesday in December, the winning slate of electors gathers in the state capital to cast their votes for president and vice president. In some states, election law requires the electors to vote for the state's popular-vote winner. Other states do not have this restriction, making it possible for a **faithless elector** to vote for a different candidate. Because electors are strong partisans and devoted a lot of time and energy to their party, few ever deviate from supporting their party's candidate.

The electoral votes are sent from the states to Washington, D.C., where on January 6, the vice president, acting in his constitutional capacity as president of the Senate, records the votes. The presidential and vice-presidential candidates receiving an outright majority of electoral votes—270—are elected. If no candidate receives 270 electoral votes, which could happen with a third-party candidate in the mix, the House of Representatives selects the president from the top three electoral-vote recipients. The Senate selects the vice president from the top two electoral-vote recipients.

The House votes for the president by state delegation, with representatives from each state together getting one vote. The candidate who receives a majority of the fifty state delegations is elected. In the Senate, each senator casts one vote for the vice president. The candidate who wins the majority is elected.

The Electoral College after redistricting based on the 2010 census.

---

popular vote: The votes individuals cast in a presidential election. Technically, these are votes for a slate of electors representing the candidate. A candidate who wins a plurality of the popular vote in a state gets all the electoral votes allocated to that state.

the possible outcomes became even more bizarre. In 1800, the Democratic-Republicans nominated Jefferson for president and Aaron Burr for vice president, resulting in an Electoral College tie as Democratic-Republican electors cast one vote each for Jefferson and Burr. The resulting complications led to passage of the Twelfth Amendment, providing for separate electoral tallies for president and vice president.[29]

In its time, the Electoral College was intended as a deliberative body, but as candidate selection shifted to the congressional caucus, then party conventions, then primaries, the functions of the Electoral College became much more automatic. Today, network anchors

DEMYSTIFYING GOVERNMENT

The Hamilton Electors

In early December 2016, while Donald Trump was assembling a new government, most Americans thought he had already been elected president. He had not. That didn't happen until electors met in their state capitals and the District of Columbia on Monday, December 19, to cast their votes, which meant there was still a chance for forces opposed to Trump's presidency to prevent it from happening—at least in theory.

Donald Trump received 306 electoral votes. That meant if at least 37 electors in Republican states voted for another candidate, he would have been denied the absolute majority of 270 needed to be elected, throwing the contest to the House of Representatives and giving Trump's opponents one last opportunity to stop him. And if those electors voted for a different Republican, such as Ohio Governor John Kasich—one of the last remaining primary candidates—then Kasich's name would be in the mix in the House, where the Constitution calls for the candidates with the three highest electoral vote totals (which presumably would include Kasich) to be considered for the presidency.

Could so many electors defect? Like everything else about the Electoral College, it's complicated, because a number of states bind their electors to vote for the state's popular vote winner. Would they defect? It would have been challenging for them politically because electors are partisans with strong incentives to act in the interest of their party, even if that interest conflicts with their view of what is best for the country. But should they defect? If you listen to the words of the people who brought us the Electoral College, the answer appears to be yes.

Alexander Hamilton, writing in Federalist 68, envisioned a deliberative body of electors who would take into account the popular will but exercise their superior judgment and make a wise decision. If faced with a candidate skilled in what he called "low intrigue, and the little arts of popularity"—qualities that would appeal to factions in the electorate—the electors would, in Hamilton's opinion, turn instead to someone who offered "a different kind of merit."

Electors opposed to Donald Trump felt this was the situation they faced in 2016. Calling themselves "Hamilton Electors," they made it their cause to call on other electors to join them in acquitting their responsibilities as Hamilton envisioned and cast their votes for someone other than Donald Trump. The Hamilton Electors faced huge obstacles. There was the problem of organizing action among electors meeting in disparate places and getting them to commit to rebelling against the wishes of their party on the expectation that others who have pledged to do so would follow through. They also faced stiff resistance from Trump supporters who did not take kindly to the prospect that an elite, albeit a constitutionally sanctioned one, would upend the anti-elite populist wave that had propelled Trump to the White House. Ultimately, they understood that even if they mustered the strength to send the election to the House, they would face tremendous opposition from Republican leadership. And it didn't help that Governor Kasich announced before the vote that he did not want to assume the presidency under circumstances that threatened to further divide the country.[T10]

This is why, when the electoral votes were cast, only two Trump electors voted for other candidates (in fact, more electors—five—abandoned Clinton). Members of the Hamilton faction later revealed that they believed they were close to the thirty-seven electors they needed to bottle up the election, but that a number of would-be allies demurred out of concern for the consequences of defying the voters. Still, seven faithless electors in one election is the largest number in over one hundred years, an indicator of the instability of politics in 2016. It also illustrates that the Electoral College, a mechanism few understand, can exercise tremendous influence over American politics—at least in theory.

---

talk about electoral votes as if they were coupons you clipped from a newspaper. On election night, they sit in front of big maps, rapidly assigning electoral votes to one candidate or another as soon as the popular vote from a state is determined. As the map fills in—red states for the Republican nominee, blue states for the Democrat—it becomes a race to 270, no more than a mathematical exercise. That is, until the bizarre election of 2016, when for a brief moment, the Electoral College became the focus of a last-ditch attempt to prevent Donald Trump from becoming president. You can read about the intrigue created by a small group of would-be faithless electors in Demystifying Government: The Hamilton Electors.

plurality: Winning the most votes in an election, or at least one more vote than the next closest candidate or party.

faithless elector: A member of the Electoral College who does not cast a vote for the plurality winner of the popular vote in his or her state.

7.4b Changing the Electoral College

Opponents of the Electoral College question the wisdom of retaining a system that could produce a president who finished second in the popular vote, as it has done twice in the twenty-first century and four times in our history. A fifth disputed election involved the House bypassing the electoral vote winner:

- **1824:** In a disputed election that wound up in the House of Representatives, John Quincy Adams was chosen president, despite the fact that Andrew Jackson had won more electoral votes.

- **1876:** In another disputed election involving questions about the accuracy of the vote in three southern states, Rutherford B. Hayes was elected president, despite having lost the popular vote to Samuel Tilden by three percentage points.

- **1888:** In an undisputed election, Grover Cleveland won a majority of popular votes but lost the electoral count to Benjamin Harrison.

- **2000:** In the closest election of our time, George W. Bush narrowly prevailed in the Electoral College on the basis of a contested victory in Florida, despite finishing second in the national popular vote count.

- **2016:** Hillary Clinton finished comfortably ahead of Donald Trump in the popular vote but lost the Electoral College and the presidency by virtue of popular vote losses in Pennsylvania, Michigan, and Wisconsin.

Not surprisingly, every time the popular vote and the electoral vote go in different directions, there's renewed call for Electoral College reform. However, if history is a guide, the odds aren't very good. Electoral College reform is a highly charged, big-stakes partisan issue; changing the rules will inevitably favor one side or the other and, quite possibly, could introduce unintended effects that everyone would be reluctant to face. Following their loss in 2012, Republicans in Florida, Pennsylvania, Virginia, Michigan, and Wisconsin toyed with the idea of eliminating the winner-take-all allocation of electoral votes in their states in favor of a proportional system that would have greatly aided Mitt Romney's candidacy. But they abandoned the idea when some state Republican officials decided it might be viewed as an effort to give them an unfair advantage. The Twelfth Amendment is the only successful alteration to the process in over two hundred years and more than one thousand attempts.[30]

Also, consider that even if these aberrant outcomes produced challenges to the legitimacy of the eventual winner, they didn't create a legitimacy crisis for the system. There was even something of a self-correction involving the first three disputed winners: Each served only one term, in two cases (1824 and 1888) to be followed in office by the candidate he had "defeated" four years earlier.

7.5 Leading or Following?

As a linkage between the public and the candidates who will become our public officials, political parties should be a vehicle for channeling our preferences to those who wish to lead us. The most important function they perform in this capacity is contesting elections. Whether parties carry out this function effectively in the electoral arena is a matter of some discussion. On one hand, through careful attention to public opinion polls and focus groups, candidates are acutely sensitive to political currents. But to what end? Is it leadership to listen to what people want and give it to them? Or does this amount to campaigning without principle?

Harry S Truman, who was president in an age before professional political consultants dominated campaigning, mused that he "wondered how far Moses would have gone if he had taken a poll in Egypt." The former president saw polls as interfering with the judgments politicians are hired to make, distinguishing *popular* decisions from *good* decisions. The natural remedy for officials who make decisions that their constituents dislike is to vote them out of office. Yet, politicians may use public opinion polls to guide their actions so as to maximize their chances of staying in office, making it harder for elections to perform a corrective function. Perhaps this is as it should be, or perhaps it comes at the cost of establishing principled links between voters and officials.

Add to this the explosion in campaign spending, and you have another potential strain on the connections parties can supply voters. Campaign finance reforms designed to strengthen the bonds between individuals and candidates by maximizing the role of small individual contributions have been undermined by the soft-money loophole. As large contributions from wealthy individuals and organizations flood the political process, it's reasonable to ask how much political influence is returned in the bargain, and to what effect. A disproportionate share of campaign money goes to incumbents who can use it to create a lopsided advantage in reelection contests. Like polls that can be used by candidates to stake out safe and popular ground, big money flowing to incumbents can drain the competition from elections.

As we noted earlier, political money is channeled through PACs that operate on behalf of organized interests. In turn, organized interests are established to represent constituencies, functioning like parties as a linkage to government. How strong and effective is this connection, and how closely do interest groups represent the wishes of people like us? Is all that PAC money advancing the agendas of people who identify with and support interest groups, or is it largely serving an elite? We'll turn to these questions next, in Chapter 8.

Chapter Review

Understand how candidates are chosen to compete in elections through the nomination process.

Contrast primaries with caucuses.

Appreciate how and why candidate selection evolved from an elite to a mass-based process.

One of the most important functions of political parties is competing in elections. Party nominees for all elected positions are selected in primaries or caucuses, depending on the state; presidential candidates enter a series of primaries and caucuses to win delegate support at the party's nominating convention. For many years, party elites selected presidential nominees at party conventions, but following 1968, a series of reforms instituted by the Democratic Party led to the proliferation of primaries and a shift away from elite control of the nominating process. Today, would-be nominees can secure enough delegates to win the nomination by competing in primaries, provided they can acquire enough resources—money, staff, and media attention—to remain viable.

Explain the role of money in waging successful campaigns.

Money is particularly critical for waging successful campaigns, and candidates typically spend years raising it.

Identify key efforts to regulate campaign finance, and explain why they have fallen short of their stated goals.

The 1974 Federal Election Campaign Act attempted to regulate campaign contributions, but a loophole permitted unlimited soft-money contributions. The McCain-Feingold Act was designed to close that loophole, but parties can still find ways to raise and spend large sums, and the 2010 Supreme Court ruling in *Citizens United v. Federal Election Commission* worked to undermine it.

Discuss the relationship between momentum and expectations in presidential primary campaigns.

A candidate emerges as the nominee by raising sufficient money and maintaining momentum through the primaries by meeting or beating performance expectations generated by reporters.

Identify key strategic approaches to waging election campaigns.

Nominees are introduced to the country at a national convention that has largely become a media event, and organize a professional staff of campaign aides who, with the use of opinion polls and focus groups, develop a strategy for allocating the candidate's time and money. Strategies may include running negative commercials in order to undermine support for the candidate's opponent; in recent years, nominees have faced off in televised debates.

Explain how the Electoral College works and why it turns presidential campaigns into a small number of statewide elections.

Strategy is largely shaped by the demands of the Electoral College, which makes the presidential race a state-by-state endeavor. The candidate who wins a plurality of the popular vote in enough states to win a majority of the electoral vote becomes president.

Key Terms

caucus A method of candidate selection in which party identifiers gather in a series of meetings to select delegates to the national convention. (p. 197)

expectation The benchmark for how well a campaign needs to perform in presidential primaries in order to receive positive horserace coverage, based on reporter assessments of the campaign's viability. (p. 206)

faithless elector A member of the Electoral College who does not cast a vote for the plurality winner of the popular vote in his or her state. (p. 220)

Federal Election Campaign Act The 1974 act aimed at limiting the influence of big-money contributions on political campaigns. (p. 202)

Federal Election Commission (FEC) The federal regulatory agency that administers and enforces campaign finance laws. (p. 202)

focus group A small group of voters chosen by a political campaign for their demographic similarities who are brought together to gauge how the group they represent feels about the candidate. (p. 215)

free media The news coverage that major candidates for high office can expect to receive on a regular basis. Although free, candidates cannot control the content of this coverage or guarantee that it will be favorable. (p. 214)

front-runner The presidential candidate who leads the primary horserace, based on media assessments of the campaign. (p. 206)

hard money Funds contributed directly to candidates or national parties by individuals or PACs for the purpose of electing candidates to federal office. Federal law regulates hard-money contributions. (p. 203)

long shot A presidential candidate who is not expected to fare well in the primary horserace, based on media assessments of the campaign. (p. 206)

McCain-Feingold Act The name commonly used to describe the Bipartisan Campaign Reform Act of 2002, which prohibits the use of soft money in federal elections in an attempt to close a loophole in the 1974 Federal Election Campaign Act. (p. 204)

McGovern-Fraser Commission The commission organized by the Democratic Party following its 1968 convention to democratize the process of delegate selection to party conventions. (p. 199)

media events Activities staged by campaigns or political officials that have enough news value to draw press attention to a message the politician wants to communicate. (p. 199)

momentum The ability of a presidential campaign to maintain viability by meeting or exceeding press-generated expectations during the long primary period. (p. 207)

name recognition An informal measure of how much the public is aware of a candidate or elected official, based on how widely people are able to identify the candidate or official. (p. 205)

nomination The official endorsement of a candidate by a political party, making that candidate the one whose name will appear on the ballot next to the party label in the next general election. (p. 196)

paid media Radio and television ads paid for and produced by political campaigns. (p. 214)

platform The official document produced at the major party conventions that serves as a philosophical and policy blueprint for the party's presidential nominee. (p. 212)

plurality Winning the most votes in an election, or at least one more vote than the next closest candidate or party. (p. 220)

political action committees (PACs) Organizations formed by interest groups such as labor unions, businesses, and ideological groups for the purpose of contributing money to political candidates. (p. 202)

popular vote The votes individuals cast in a presidential election. Technically, these are votes for a slate of electors representing the candidate. A candidate who wins a plurality of the popular vote in a state gets all the electoral votes allocated to that state. (p. 220)

primary A method of candidate selection in which party identifiers vote for the candidate who will run on the party label in the general election. In presidential primaries, voters select delegates to the national convention. (p. 197)

soft money Funds contributed to state and local parties or to national parties for the purpose of running state elections or conducting local "grassroots" political activity. (p. 203)

Resources

You might be interested in examining some of what the following authors have said about the topics we've been discussing:

Cramer, Richard Ben. *What It Takes: The Way to the White House.* New York: Random House, 1992. A firsthand account of the 1988 presidential contenders, written like a novel, that explores the character and motivation of those who roll the dice to enter the high-risk, marathon presidential sweepstakes.

DiClerico, Robert E., and James W. Davis. *Choosing Our Choices: Debating the Presidential Nominating Process.*

Lanham, MD: Rowman & Littlefield, 2000. The pros and cons of the way we select our presidential nominees, with suggestions for how we might do it differently.

Michael Nelson, ed. *The Elections of 2008*. Washington, DC: CQ Press, 2009. The 2008 election was one for the history books, and this book examines it from a variety of perspectives.

Polsby, Nelson W., and Aaron Wildavsky. *Presidential Elections: Strategies and Structures of American Politics*, 12th ed. Lanham, MD: Rowman and Littlefield, 2007. A comprehensive overview of campaigns and elections.

Notes

1 Paul R. Abramson, John H. Aldrich, and David W. Rohde, *Continuity and Change in the 1996 and 1998 Elections* (Washington, DC: CQ Press, 1999), 16.

2 Federal Election Commission 2016 Presidential Primary Filing Dates, at http://www.fec.gov/pubrec/fe2016/2016pdates.pdf.

3 Robert E. DiClerico and James W. Davis, *Choosing Our Choices: Debating the Presidential Nominating Process* (Lanham, MD: Rowman & Littlefield, 2000), 22.

4 Ibid., 3–6.

5 If you'd like to read more about what happened that August week in Chicago, CNN/Time offers a summary at http://www.cnn.com/ALLPOLITICS/1996/conventions/chicago/facts/chicago68/index.shtml.

6 DiClerico and Davis, *Choosing Our Choices*, 28–29.

7 Ibid., 14–23.

8 Tina Sfondeles, "Democrats Changing Superdelegate Rules; A Sanders Win," *Chicago Sun-Times*, July 24, 2016. http://chicago.suntimes.com/news/democrats-changing-superdelegate-rules-a-sanders-win/.

9 Federal Election Commission website at http://www.fec.gov/pages/brochures/pubfund_limits_2016.shtml.

10 DiClerico and Davis, *Choosing Our Choices*, 16–17.

11 Jose Antonio Vargas, "Obama Raised Half a Billion Online," washingtonpost.com, November, 20, 2008. http://voices.washingtonpost.com/44/2008/11/20/obama_raised_half_a_billion_on.html.

12 *New York Times*, at http://elections.nytimes.com/2012/campaign-finance.

13 Nicholas Confessore and Jo Craven McGinty, "Obama, Romney and Their Parties on Track to Raise $2 Billion, *New York Times*, October 25, 2012. http://www.nytimes.com/2012/10/26/us/politics/obama-and-romney-raise-1-billion-each.html.

14 Libby Watson, "Why Did Only One Presidential Candidate Take Public Financing?" Sunlight Foundation, January 27, 2016. http://sunlightfoundation.com/2016/01/27/why-did-only-1-presidential-candidate-take-public-financing/.

15 For a sense of who has been giving the most soft money to candidates in recent years—and how much they give—return to the Center for Responsive Politics website, at http://www.opensecrets.org/bigpicture/softtop.php?cycle=2002.

16 Center for Responsive Politics Statement on McCain-Feingold Decision, December 10, 2003.

17 Ian Vandewalker, "Election Spending 2014: Outside Spending in Senate Races since *Citizens United*, Brennan Center for Justice, 2015. http://www.brennancenter.org/sites/default/files/analysis/Outside%20Spending%20Since%20Citizens%20United.pdf.

18 Jim Webb is a former Virginia senator who ran for the Democratic presidential nomination in 2016.

19 Nelson W. Polsby and Aaron Wildavsky, *Presidential Elections*, 10th ed. (New York: Chatham House, 2000), 199–201.

20 Ibid., 100.

21 Gurbaksh Chahal, "Election 2016: Marriage of Big Data, Social Data Will Determine Next President," *Wired*, 2016. https://www.wired.com/insights/2013/05/election-2016-marriage-of-big-data-social-data-will-determine-the-next-president/; Meta S. Brown, "Big Data Analytics and the Next President: How Microtargeting Drives Today's Campaigns," *Forbes*, May 29, 2016. http://www.forbes.com/sites/metabrown/2016/05/29/big-data-analytics-and-the-next-president-how-microtargeting-drives-todays-campaigns/#2208c23d1400.

22 Matthew R. Kerbel, "The Media: Old Frames in a Time of Transition," in Michael Nelson, ed., *The Elections of 2000* (Washington, DC: CQ Press, 2001), 109–132.

23 Polsby and Wildavsky, *Presidential Elections*, 10th ed., 109–110.

24 Jeremy Diamond, "Trump: 'I Could Shoot Somebody and I Wouldn't Lose Voters,'" CNN, January 24, 2016. http://www.cnn.com/2016/01/23/politics/donald-trump-shoot-somebody-support/.

25 Okla Elliott, "What Does Sanders Mean by 'Democratic Socialism'?" *The Hill*, March 4, 2016. http://thehill.com/blogs/congress-blog/presidential-campaign/271652-what-does-sanders-mean-by-democratic-socialism.

26 Paul S. Herrnson, "National Party Organizations at the Dawn of the Twenty-First Century," in L. Sandy Maisel, ed., *The Parties Respond*, 4th ed. (Boulder, CO: Westview Press, 2002), 19–46.

27 "Democrats Adopt Most Progressive Platform in Party History," Berniesanders.com, July 10, 2016. https://berniesanders.com/democrats-adopt-progressive-platform-party-history/.

28 Hernson, "National Party Organization," 190–193.

29 Donald Lutz, "The Electoral College in Historical and Philosophical Perspective," in Paul D. Schumaker and Burdett A.

Loomis, eds., *Choosing a President* (New York: Chatham House Publishers, 2002), 31–51.

30 Lutz, "The Electoral College in Philosophical Perspective."

Table, Figure and Box Notes

T1 Politico, "2016 Elections Schedule," at http://www.politico.com/2016-election/schedule.

T2 By David Wilson. https://www.flickr.com/photos/davidwilson1949/6056934707/in/photolist-5coszA-aeenEK-2CqzzK-8QZ5mo, CC BY 2.0, https://commons.wikimedia.org/w/index.php?curid=48476311.

T3 Opensecrets.org, at http://www.opensecrets.org/pacs/superpacs.php.

T4 OpenSecrets.org, at https://www.opensecrets.org/outsidespending/summ.php?chrt=V&type=S.

T5 Federal Election Commission, at http://www.fec.gov/pages/brochures/contrib.shtml#Chart.

T6 Nelson W. Polsby and Aaron Wildavsky, *Presidential Elections*, 13th ed. (New York: Chatham House Publishers, 2012), 54; and OpenSecrets.org, at https://www.opensecrets.org.

T7 Kate Brannelly, "Trump Campaign Pays Millions to Overseas Big Data Firm," NBC News, November 4, 2016. http://www.nbcnews.com/storyline/2016-election-day/trump-campaign-pays-millions-overseas-big-data-firm-n677321.

T8 Polsby and Wildavsky, *Presidential Elections*, 10th ed., 101.

T9 Photos courtesy LBJ Library.

T10 Steve Peoples and Andrew Welsh-Huggins, "John Kasich's Blow to Hamilton Electors: Ohio Governor Says He Doesn't Want to Be Written In," *Salon*, December 7, 2016. http://www.salon.com/2016/12/07/ohio-governor-tells-electors-not-to-vote-for-him-over-trump/.

Interest Groups: Accessing Government through Common Membership

Source: RomanR/Shutterstock

Learning Objectives

When you have completed this chapter, you should be able to:

- Define interest groups, and distinguish them from political parties.
- Define lobbying.
- Identify key economic and noneconomic interest groups, and be familiar with some of the issues they promote.
- Distinguish purposive benefits from selective benefits, and explain why interest groups may use selective benefits to boost membership.
- Discuss some of the inside and outside strategies lobbyists use to advocate on behalf of interest groups.
- Explain how hard and soft money contributions from political action committees can influence lobbying.
- Identify "iron triangles," and appreciate how lobbying can be more cooperative than adversarial.
- Understand how issue networks develop around complex policy matters.
- Relate the interest group system to our earlier discussion of pluralism and elitism.

8.1 Introduction

Early in the administration of George W. Bush, an economic crisis was building in America. The stock market was in a free fall as investors lost confidence in corporate leadership following a string of revelations about wrongdoing at corporations like Enron, WorldCom, and the accounting firm Arthur Anderson. The sting of scandal reached the Bush White House, as questions emerged about whether the president and vice president engaged in illegal or unethical practices when they were businessmen. Older Americans who were depending on investments to cushion them in retirement began to worry that market losses would undermine their living standards or make it impossible to retire. Members of the House and Senate, most of whom would face the voters in a few short months, leaped into action and legislated different versions of corporate reform, then tried to hammer out language that would be acceptable to both chambers.

As representatives of the House and Senate met to address their differences, representatives of the American Institute of Certified Public Accountants (AICPA) went into overdrive to make sure the final product was as soft as possible on CPAs. They were facing the possibility of legislation that would impose greater government regulation and tighter accounting standards, changing the way accountants operate and, they feared, adversely affecting their bottom line.

So, the AICPA sprang into action to defeat what it saw as the most restrictive provisions of the emerging legislation, pressing senators and House members to water it down while simultaneously urging their own members to pressure Washington to guard their interests. In an email to its members, AIPCA wrote, "We cannot allow . . . the fierce search for blame [in the corporate scandals] to taint the 350,000 CPAs in this country who stand for integrity, competence and objectivity."[1] Translation: Your future is in danger—protect your turf.

You probably didn't know there was an American Institute of Certified Public Accountants, did you? Don't feel badly—not many people do. AICPA is not a high-profile organization. It seldom makes news. However, with one-third of a million members, it can speak with a pretty loud voice to defend its interests.

So, a group you might not have heard of is trying to influence legislation that will reverberate through the economy, potentially affecting your personal finances and your job prospects after graduation. Do you share their concerns? If you want to make your living one day as an accountant, you probably do. If not, or think Congress should tighten accounting procedures to shore up confidence in business and help the economy, you probably don't. In that case, who is developing strategies to represent your interests to those who make laws?

Welcome to the world of interest groups, which, like the mass media and political parties, provide us with a way to access and influence our government. Unlike the media, which are all around us, and parties, which are pretty visible, interest groups are the least discernible link between government and us. There is probably a lot we don't know about interest groups because we'd have to pay close attention to government to be aware of how they operate, and we know that most people don't. Interest groups complement political parties by giving people another way to make demands on government. Where parties permit access to the system by fielding candidates for us to choose among, interest groups provide access through membership in a group that presses its agenda on government officials.

The thing for us to figure out is whether the system of interest groups in place in America provides a strong and direct link to government that serves individual interests. We'll do that by looking at whose interests are being represented as we explore what interest groups do.

8.2 Factions Again?

L.O. Define interest groups, and distinguish them from political parties.

Will we ever stop bringing up the subject of factions? Eventually, but it makes sense to think back for a minute to what we said about factions in Chapter 2 because it should make the whole concept of interest groups easier to understand.

Remember in Chapter 6 when we said that there are no mentions of political parties in the Constitution because the framers equated them with factions and felt they were to be avoided? Interest groups can be regarded as factions as well—as the groups people naturally form to promote interests that are potentially detrimental to others. **Interest groups** are organizations of individuals with common objectives who seek to advance those objectives through the political process. Unlike parties, interest groups operate outside the formal political system, even as they work closely with elected representatives inside the system to advance their agenda. Unlike parties, which are broad organizations, interest groups form around narrowly defined issues. And, unlike parties, which were not anticipated by the framers, groups like these were expected to form naturally. The key thing is that they're supposed to compete with each other, and out of that competition should come compromises that serve the general interest. The question is—does it work that way?

Interest groups are sometimes called **pressure groups** because of the perception that they achieve their objectives by putting pressure on politicians. In fact, one of the main purposes of an interest group is **lobbying** government officials, trying to exert influence on the way they develop public policy. Interest groups are also called **special-interest groups** because of the narrowly defined nature of their objectives. These terms capture key characteristics of interest groups, which act on the political system from the outside to advance agendas that serve specialized needs rather than broad, common interests.

How specialized? How about:

- The Beer Institute.
- American Society of Home Care Inspectors.
- National Milk Producers Federation.
- American Ceramic Society.
- Hosiery Association.[2]

Beer? Ceramics? Hosiery? That's pretty narrow. They're all interest groups whose industries can benefit from favorable government action on things like taxes and trade policy. Other groups may not be affiliated with business but can have interests that are just as narrow.

Now, if the system is working the way Madison imagined it would, all these narrow groups will engage in competition with each other for government action, and out of that competition will come compromise, which in the long run will serve collective interests because no one will be positioned to get everything they wanted. This perspective is consistent with **pluralism**, where a wide distribution of resources in society is reflected in the large number of individual special-interest groups competing for the attention of government officials. It's a pretty clear example of how interest groups can link us to government through political action.

However, you may also remember the competing perspective, called **elitism**, that says ordinary people do not have a say in making important political decisions. Take the competition among interest groups out of the political process, and you have something that looks more like an elitist perspective on government than what Madison envisioned. If interest groups can find a way to hook into the political system, the argument goes, they can cozy up to officials and get what they want without having to compete with other groups. Small groups like the National Milk Producers Federation ("Connecting Cows, Cooperatives, Capitol Hill, and Consumers"[3]) can win small victories this way. Large interests like huge corporations, foundations, and professional associations with disproportionately more resources, though, stand to win large victories that can dictate the way public policy is made—like what the CPAs were after when they tried to block changes in accounting procedures.

So, as we become familiar with what interest groups are and how they work, let's try to keep in mind this question about whether they fit in the pluralist or elitist camp. We'll revisit the question later on, after we get a better feel for the different types of interest groups that are out there, and whose interests are served and whose are not.

interest groups: Organized associations that seek to promote common objectives through government action.

L.O. Define lobbying.

pressure groups: Another term for interest groups that emphasizes the demands interest groups make on the political system.

lobbying: Attempting to influence the content of policy by exerting influence on government officials.

special-interest groups: Another term for interest groups that emphasizes the narrow scope of their concerns.

pluralism: The theory that government responds to individuals through their memberships in groups, assuring that government is responsive to a wide range of voices. People who subscribe to this position believe that the wide distribution of resources in society drives the decisions government officials make.

elitism: The theory that government responds to a small, stable, centralized hierarchy of corporate and academic leaders, military chiefs, people who own big media outlets, and members of a permanent government bureaucracy. People who subscribe to this position believe the actions of regular citizens, like voting and joining groups, simply mask the real power exercised by elites.

8.3 Types of Interest Groups

L.O. Identify key economic and noneconomic interest groups, and be familiar with some of the issues they promote.

Just like clothing, interest groups are not one-size-fits-all. Consistent with the pluralist perspective, there are a wide variety of interests that cover a host of agendas that operate in Washington and in state capitals to promote their objectives to officials who can help group members get what they want. Most are organized to enhance their self-interest, although some work for the collective good or to promote a particular vision of society.

Some of these groups seek to advance economic objectives, such as business, professional, agricultural, and labor interest groups. Others advance noneconomic interests, such as ideological, civil rights, public interest, and single-issue interest groups.[4]

8.3a Economic Groups

If you're just looking at it in terms of raw numbers, economic groups compose by far the largest number of organized interests. Of these, business groups make up the largest share, followed by professional associations and unions.[5] You can take a look at some examples of economic groups in Table 8.1, along with how much money they put into the political system.

Business groups are among the most prevalent of interest groups; by one count, they constitute over seven of every ten registered lobbying organizations.[6] They are largely funded by businesses themselves, which hire professional **lobbyists** in an effort to achieve or—more often—protect favorable regulatory and tax rules.

lobbyists: Professionals hired by interest groups to influence the political process on behalf of the group.

Additionally, there are groups that speak for broad business concerns. The first such organization was the United States Chamber of Commerce—a name you may be familiar with but perhaps never thought of as an interest group. The Chamber of Commerce was founded in 1912 as a federation of state and local organizations committed to the advancement of free enterprise. Accordingly, it lobbies for business tax relief, against federally mandated wage and benefit requirements for workers, and against the expansion of social welfare programs.[7] The Chamber of Commerce was particularly active in 2016, spending more than any other organization on lobbying (almost $80 million) and $29 million on behalf of mostly Republican candidates it felt would advance its agenda.[8]

trade associations: Groups that advance the concerns of specific business interests, such as banks, energy companies, real estate firms, and car manufacturers.

In a more specialized vein, **trade associations** lobby on behalf of businesses that are widely regarded as trades, like bankers, manufacturers, and retailers. The American Bankers Association is the voice of the banking industry, the National Association of Manufacturers speaks for the manufacturing industry, and the National Association of Convenience Stores works on behalf of retail outlets. You may not have heard of these groups unless you know someone involved in the trade in question, but trade associations are often well-funded and important players in Washington, protecting and advancing the interests of their members.

Professional groups are powerful organizations representing the interests of professionals like doctors, lawyers, and educators. With large memberships and deep pockets, groups like the American Medical Association, the American Bar Association, the Association of Trial Lawyers of America, and the National Education Association are as influential as large business and trade groups.

It's not exaggerating to say that the road to creating or changing health-care policy runs through the American Medical Association (AMA) offices. President Clinton found that out the hard way in the 1990s, when the AMA led the charge against his ambitious attempt to change the way health care is provided. When President Obama tried again in 2009, he made an effort to bring doctors on board in order to prevent them from using their lobbying power against reform.

When it comes to the matter of placing limits on the liability of health-care providers, however, other powerful voices take a position at odds with the AMA. The American Bar Association (ABA) has lobbied for the expanded right of individuals to sue their health-care plans for damages resulting from being turned down for medical treatment, claiming it would result in few lawsuits and marginal increases in health-care costs. Not surprisingly, the AMA warns against frivolous lawsuits that would result in much higher

TABLE 8.1 Economic Lobbies, 2016[T1]

Sector	Select Industries	Total Contributions	To Democrats	To Republicans
Agribusiness	Crop Production Dairy Poultry Tobacco	$104,263,809	26%	74%
Communications	TV/Movies/Music Telecom Internet Publishing	$276,780,854	68%	32%
Construction and Manufacturing	Home Builders Contractors Building Materials Construction Services	$99,670,216	32%	67%
Defense	Aerospace Electronics	$28,546,526	42%	57%
Energy and Natural Resources	Oil and Gas Mining Utilities Waste Management	$161,803,416	27%	72%
Finance	Banks Securities Insurance Real Estate	$1,017,812,355	44%	55%
Health	Health Professionals Health Services Hospitals Pharmaceuticals	$258,402,597	45%	54%
Transportation	Airlines Automotive Trucking Railroads	$83,668,986	31%	69%
Other Business	Food and Beverage Retail Recreation Textiles	$445,728,788	41%	58%
Lawyers and Lobbyists		$223,958,048	70%	30%
Labor	Trade Unions Industrial Unions Public-Sector Unions	$178,835,378	86%	14%

medical premiums. It would also like to limit lawsuits against doctors, claiming too many physicians are losing their liability insurance as costs are driven up by expensive legal judgments.[9]

This debate tends to divide the political parties as well, with Democrats generally favoring expanded legal protections and Republicans favoring limits on medical malpractice awards. Consistent with this is the tendency for money from the legal community to be more likely than health-care money to find its way into the hands of Democrats. In 2008, anticipating a Democratic victory and a subsequent battle over health-care reform, slightly under two-thirds of the contributions from health-care professionals went to Democratic presidential candidates—with $11.7 million going to Barack Obama alone. This reversed the pattern from 2004, when over 60 percent of the political contributions from the medial field went to Republicans. But it still paled in comparison to the nearly 80 percent of contributions from the law profession that flowed to Democratic presidential candidates.[10]

Unions are the political counterparts to large business interests. Born of the discontentment workers felt with conditions in the industrial plants of late nineteenth-century America, the labor movement remains a powerful political force, although the declining number of union workers has diminished its standing considerably since the 1940s and 1950s. The AFL-CIO is the premier voice of organized labor, representing 12.5 million workers in the United States, ranging from electricians to plumbers to teachers to musicians. The AFL-CIO mission emphasizes establishing economic and social justice in the workplace, focusing on traditional bread-and-butter issues like wages, benefits, and working conditions, as well as such things as equal pay for women, trade policy, job retraining in emerging industries, and giving workers a greater say over production.[11]

Other large, influential unions include the Teamsters (which represent truckers, airline employees, and others in the transportation field), the United Auto Workers, the United Mine Workers of America, and the American Federation of State, County and Municipal Employees (AFSCME).

If business interests generally show a preference for supporting Republican candidates, unions have traditionally been an important source of support for Democrats. During the 2016 election, labor political action committees (PACs) channeled 85 percent of their presidential campaign contributions to Democrats.[12]

Agricultural groups have been organized for almost a century and a half, dating back to the establishment of the national Grange some 130 years ago. Today, with small family farms dwindling, agricultural interests largely represent "agribusiness:" large corporations involved in farming as well as the processing and trade of food products. Umbrella organizations like the American Farm Bureau Federation lobby on behalf of broad agricultural interests, such as farm price supports (a government subsidy to farmers forced to sell crops at a market price that's below their targeted price), federal worker safety laws, and government pesticide controls.[13] Organizations like the International Dairy Foods Association (and the National Milk Producers Federation) represent specialized agricultural industries.

One of the biggest spenders in the agricultural sector is the tobacco industry, whose status as producers of a hazardous product puts it in an unusual lobbying position. For years, the tobacco lobby spent considerable sums to prevent restrictions on cigarette advertising, particularly to teenagers, and federal health and safety regulations of firsthand and secondhand smoke. It fought having to put health warnings on cigarettes, and when warnings were mandated, it fought to keep the wording mild and innocuous. In recent years, the industry has been engaged in a battle against government lawsuits alleging the tobacco industry willfully misled Americans about the addictive nature of nicotine. Despite its funding and clout, the tobacco lobby has found itself on the defensive, in part because of changing public attitudes about smoking. As the industry's situation evolved, its lobbying approaches and objectives changed accordingly.

8.3b Noneconomic Groups

Interest groups organized around noneconomic matters generally do not command the big dollars that economic interests channel into the political system. However, you'll still find a strong political influence exerted by single-issue groups, government groups, civil rights and public interest groups, and ideological groups. Table 8.2 gives you a sample of some of the interests promoted by noneconomic groups, along with a sense of how much money they're spending on their cause.

Most *single-issue groups* are fairly small, but there are a lot of them, and they can be surprisingly effective. In part, this is because of the dedication of group members to their

TABLE 8.2 Noneconomic Lobbies, 2016[T2]

Groups	Examples	Total Contributions	To Democrats	To Republicans
Ideological Groups	Republican/Conservative	$79,478,820	1%	99%
	Liberal/Democratic	$77,962,435	99%	1%
	Republican Leadership PACs	$36,480,995	0%	100%
	Democratic Leadership PACs	$23,409,507	100%	0%
Single-Issue Groups	Foreign/Defense	$2,646,908	50%	50%
	Pro-Israel	$16,287,401	58%	42%
	Women's Issues	$36,041,979	98%	2%
	Human Rights	$16,627,727	92%	8%
	Environment	$97,697,946	96%	4%
	Gun Control	$1,258,653	98%	2%
	Gun Rights	$5,431,334	2%	98%
	Anti-Abortion	$1,786,624	3%	97%
	Abortion Rights	$3,514,812	98%	2%

cause, whether it be heartfelt support for or opposition to abortion laws, gun ownership, environmental protection, or a host of other specific issues. Single-issue group representatives may not mobilize politically around any other issue, but the issue that compels them to action does so totally, and the intensity of the beliefs of single-issue group members makes them a powerful force. One example of how this works is discussed in Demystifying Government: Lobbying the Abortion Issue.

So far, we've addressed groups organized around the promotion of economic self-interest or single issues. But *civil rights* and *public interest groups* promote objectives whose benefits extend far beyond group members to the broader society. If the American Medical Association is able to scuttle changes to health-care policy that would end up costing doctors money, the primary beneficiaries of their action are AMA-member doctors. However, if a public interest group like Public Citizen is able to get the federal government to impose tighter standards for child seatbelt restraints on automobile manufacturers, then all car owners with kids are the potential beneficiaries.[14] Similarly, if a civil rights group like the American Civil Liberties Union successfully petitions government to protect the anonymity of Internet users,[15] many who are not directly involved with the interest group stand to gain—including you, if you ever send personal data over the web.

Why the selflessness? Contemporary civil rights and public interest groups trace their origins to the social and political turmoil of the 1960s, to the antiwar, civil rights, and women's movements, when the social and political *status quo* was being challenged and questioned. That's why groups of this nature focus on issues of equal opportunity, minority and women's rights, environmental protection, racial equality, religious liberty, the rights of people with disabilities, and consumer safety.

The popularity of reforming the system and giving voice to the concerns of those lacking representation gained expression in the late 1960s through the political party reforms of the **McGovern-Fraser Commission** we talked about in Chapter 7. The interest group

McGovern-Fraser Commission: The commission organized by the Democratic Party following its 1968 convention to democratize the process of delegate selection to party conventions.

Lobbying the Abortion Issue

Public opinion polls suggest that while many of us have opinions about abortion policy, most of us do not hold opinions intense enough to drive us to political action. However, for the few who feel passionately about the matter, it's a single issue that's strong enough to motivate intense political activity—and conflict. For many engaged in the abortion debate, the outcome has a moral as well as a policy dimension, with some feeling that it is simply wrong to terminate a pregnancy and others believing that it is wrong to deny women the right to determine what to do with their bodies.

Complicating matters is the fact that the legal status of abortion procedures is debated as a **zero-sum policy**, in that any gains for one side come at the expense of the wishes of the other side. This adds to the ferocious quality of lobbying by groups on opposite sides of the issue. Note how the zero-sum characteristic of the abortion issue breaks along party lines, with most spending in support of abortion rights going to Democrats and most spending on the anti-abortion side going to Republicans. Policy debates that don't have a zero-sum quality—which is to say most policy debates—leave open the possibility for compromise. The abortion debate pits two dramatically different perspectives on the issue—and the two political parties—against one another in an all-or-nothing battle.

Look at how two powerful interest groups on opposing sides of the abortion issue frame the debate.

The National Right to Life Committee believes that abortion ends life and takes the position that it "carries out its lifesaving mission by promoting respect for the worth and dignity of every individual human being, born or unborn, including unborn children from their beginning." The mission statement of the National Right to Life Committee includes a reference to the Declaration of Independence, stating, "Our Founding Fathers emphasized the preeminence of the right to 'Life' by citing it first among the unalienable rights this nation was established to secure."[T3]

To Planned Parenthood, a fetus is part of the mother's body, and maintaining a legal right to abortion is a matter of human dignity and personal choice. The mission statement of Planned Parenthood asserts that "Planned Parenthood believes in the fundamental right of each individual, throughout the world, to manage his or her fertility, regardless of the individual's income, marital status, race, ethnicity, sexual orientation, age, national origin, or residence. We believe that respect and value for diversity in all aspects of our organization are essential to our well-being. We believe that reproductive self-determination must be voluntary and preserve the individual's right to privacy. We further believe that such self-determination will contribute to an enhancement of the quality of life and strong family relationships."[T4]

---

zero-sum policy: A policy debate in which any victory by one side comes at the expense of the opposing side, negating the possibility of compromise.

counterpart to this movement was a program by the Ford Foundation that offered start-up money to law firms willing "to advance necessary social change constructively."[16] Just as McGovern-Fraser engaged the Democratic Party on a path that diminished the authority of party elites, the Ford grants produced sixteen public interest law firms with a parallel objective: to open the political system to a broad range of public interests that were not being advocated by the powerful elite groups that had the ear of elected officials. These firms used the judicial system to press for change in the way government did business that would serve the broad public interest. As they achieved success, they were able to attract more contributors to the idea of challenging the system from within.[17]

Before he became a perennial presidential candidate, Ralph Nader achieved national prominence as a crusader for public interest causes. You can read about how he drew a lot of his supporters over the years from college campuses, in Demystifying Government: Ralph Nader and the Politics of Public Lobbying.

Civil rights and public interest groups are unique in a couple of important ways. They are pluralistic in character, expending resources on behalf of others who may not hold a lot of resources, even if those others are not group members. In contrast, the economic interest groups and some of the noneconomic interest groups we discussed are elitist in nature, channeling resources collected from a closed group of members into government action designed to aid those members. Also, where much of the lobbying that's done by business, trade and professional groups, agribusiness, and unions is aimed at preserving benefits already in place, civil rights and public interest groups engage in the (far more difficult) process of changing the law. From their inception as organizations designed to reform the political process, civil rights and public interest groups have positioned

Ralph Nader and the Politics of Public Lobbying

More than anyone else, Ralph Nader has been the face of the public interest movement over the past forty years. Nader emerged on the national scene in 1965 with the publication of the book *Unsafe at Any Speed*, which challenged General Motors' commitment to automobile safety. When it became public that GM had hired a private investigator to tail Nader and dig up dirt from his background, congressional hearings ensued, and the serious lawyer became a media star. Cast in the role of the defender of the little person, Nader became something of a folk hero and bankrolled his fame into the interest group Public Citizen, which engages in public action on behalf of such things as health and safety measures and environmental protection.[T5]

In the 1970s, when there was a lot of campus activism, Nader used colleges as sort of a farm system for public advocates. He sponsored Public Interest Research Groups—or PIRGs—on campuses all over the country (you may have one at your school) and encouraged young lawyers, dubbed "Nader's Raiders," to join him in the pursuit of government action they felt promoted the greater public good.

Today, organizations devoted to public lobbying post the results of their efforts on the Internet. If you're interested in seeing what public interest watchdogs are saying about lobbyists and interest group reform, you can check out websites for groups like Public Citizen (www.citizen.org) and the Center for Public Integrity (www.publicintegrity.org).[T6]

themselves in opposition to powerful elites, fighting battles that most likely would not be waged without an organized voice to speak out against entrenched interests.

If civil rights and public interest groups want to protect the general public from inequality and hazardous conditions, *ideological interest groups* seek to restructure society around a set of ideas about how they believe it should work. Like civil rights and public interest groups, their ends are nonmaterial and derived from an idea about the proper relationship between government and its citizens. Unlike civil rights and public interest groups, ideological interests are rooted more in a philosophy than in a cause. Their perspectives may be conservative, liberal, or otherwise, but in any case, they draw their energy from supporters who believe strongly in the organization's agenda.

Think back to when we were talking about **libertarianism** in Chapter 3. We said libertarians subscribed to an ideological perspective whose basic intent is to advance individual liberty free from government interference. The Cato Institute is an ideological group that reflects a libertarian agenda. Although it does not engage directly in lobbying or actively support political candidates, its mission is to "originate, disseminate, and increase understanding of public policies based on the principles of, individual liberty, limited government, free markets, and peace."[18]

libertarianism: An ideology centered on the reduction of government power to advance personal liberty.

Off to the left of the political spectrum, you'll find groups like People for the American Way Foundation. Their goals are quite a bit different than those of the Cato Institute's. Note how Cato emphasizes individualism through liberty and limited government, while People for the American Way focuses on community through equality and diversity: "Our vision is a vibrantly diverse democratic society in which everyone is treated equally under the law, given the freedom and opportunity to pursue their dreams, and encouraged to participate in our nation's civic and political life. Our America respects diversity, nurtures creativity and combats hatred and bigotry."[19]

Groups on the right try to advance a different view of America, particularly groups affiliated with the **"Religious Right,"** with conservative evangelical religious roots. This would include the Christian Coalition of America, a powerful, religious-based organization with a sweeping conservative agenda at odds with the goals of PFAWF. Founded by Pat Robertson (whom you may recognize from his cable television program on the Christian Broadcasting Network), the Christian Coalition describes itself as a "pro-family citizen action organization" established to promote Christian values in government and as "one of the largest conservative grassroots political organizations in America."[20]

Religious Right: Ideological interest groups promoting a conservative political agenda consistent with an evangelical religious perspective.

The different worldviews described by PFAWF and the Christian Coalition should give you a pretty good idea of just how strongly these two ideological groups clash.

Calling itself "America's leading grassroots organization defending our Godly heritage," the Christian Coalition is on a self-described moral mission. It defends traditional views of heterosexual marriage, opposes legalized abortion, and favors the use of tax money for private schools. People for the American Way, in contrast, is on a mission to limit the reach of the Christian Coalition. It supports gay rights, legalized abortion, improved public education, and religious freedom not defined in terms of Christian values or teachings.[21]

8.4 Would You Join an Interest Group?

L.O. Distinguish purposive benefits from selective benefits, and explain why interest groups may use selective benefits to boost membership.

In Chapter 6, we said that you don't have to join a political party to consider yourself a Republican or Democrat. Not so with interest groups, which rely on membership fees for their lobbying efforts. So, what might lead you to join? For the sake of argument, let's say you're concerned about the environment. Many of us are, so the chances are it's not too much of a stretch for you to imagine being at least a little concerned about fresh air, clean water, or open forests, to say nothing of global warming. You're probably not going to consider joining a lot of groups; for many people, one would be enough (possibly too much). You look around, and the first thing that surprises you is how many environmental interest groups are out there. Maybe you know about some of the big ones, like the National Wildlife Federation, the Sierra Club, the Audubon Society, or Greenpeace. Maybe you're surprised to learn that your options include smaller, more targeted groups like Pheasants Forever and the National Wild Turkey Federation.[22] How can you decide?

One easy way is to indulge your particular concern for the fate of pheasants or turkeys and join the group that's tailored to your interests. Assuming you don't have a strong passion for fowl that leads you to one of these options, you'll probably choose among the groups you know about and decide whether it's worth your while to become a member.

You look at the Sierra Club, where an introductory membership is $25. It turns out the Sierra Club offers a few incentives to ease you into membership, which are listed in Table 8.3. Take a look at the options, figure out which (if any) appeal to you, and decide whether you're going to join.[23]

selective benefits: Incentives offered exclusively to interest group members as a means of getting people to join.

If you decided to join the Sierra Club because of the trips or the messenger bag, you gave in to the lure of **selective benefits**—tangible goods that flow only to members after

TABLE 8.3 Do I Join the Sierra Club?

Answer YES or NO to each of the following questions to see if there are any conditions under which you would join the Sierra Club:		
1. I'll get a one-year subscription to *Sierra Magazine*, complete with great nature photography and articles on hot environmental issues. Is this worth $25 to join?	YES	NO
2. I'll get a free Sierra Club field messenger bag. Do I want this enough to spend $25 to join?	YES	NO
3. I'll be eligible to go on Sierra Club outings and service trips, like ski tours and visits to archeological sites. Is that worth $25 to me?	YES	NO
4. I'll have the satisfaction of knowing I'm doing something good for the planet. Do I want this enough to pay $25 to join?	YES	NO

If you responded . . .	
NO to all four questions . . .	None of the incentives were sufficient to get you to join the Sierra Club.
NO to the first three questions and YES to Question 4 . . .	You have decided to join the Sierra Club because of the satisfaction you feel from contributing to a cause you believe in, rather than because of any of the tangible incentives the club offers to members.
YES to at least ONE of the first three questions . . .	You have decided to join the Sierra Club because you want the benefits that you can only get by being a member.

Interest Groups for People Who Teach about Interest Groups

Even professors have special interests.

Find out if your professor is a member of the American Political Science Association, a professional association that lobbies on behalf of the interests of academic political scientists (you may not have thought of political scientists as a professional group, but they are). If he or she is a member, find out why. Chances are it's because membership includes a subscription to the *American Political Science Review*, a leading source of current academic research; *P.S.*, a journal that offers lots of professional information about what's happening in the field of political science; and *Perspectives on Politics*, offering reviews of academic books by political scientists. This information can be really helpful to political scientists engaged in research and teaching. If that's not enough, membership also includes a break on admission to the association's annual professional meeting—and a car rental discount.

Think for a minute about the causes that interest you. Can you think of a membership experience you've had with an organized group, small or large? Examples might include political, social, or religious groups—even organizations associated with your major.

---

they pay their dues. Many interest groups offer selective benefits to members because group leaders realize that not everyone will join a group simply because they share the group's objectives. Some selective benefits are just material goods with widespread appeal that have nothing to do with the group's lobbying objectives, like car rental discounts and inexpensive life insurance. Even your professor may be an interest group member because of the selective benefits he or she receives. See Demystifying Government: Interest Groups for People Who Teach about Interest Groups.

Here's the thing: Without the appeal of selective benefits, it makes perfect sense for people not to pay dues to an interest group, even if they share the group's objectives. Think about it: If the Sierra Club is successful in reducing pollutants in water, it can't restrict access to clean water to Sierra Club members. The clean water is a **collective good**—something everyone is free to enjoy, whether or not they join the interest group that worked to bring it about.

This poses a problem to interest groups that wish to expand their membership because sympathetic, would-be members can enjoy the benefit of the collective good without paying a penny. Economist Mancur Olson calls this a **"free rider"** problem because the would-be member gets to benefit from the work of the group without making a contribution and argues that groups need to rely on selective benefits to get people to sign up.[24] In large groups, which are going to survive with or without your membership dollars, the free rider problem can be a real dilemma—hence, the need for particularly attractive membership incentives if they're going to maximize their membership size.

However, it is also the case that quite a few groups manage to thrive without offering selective benefits to members.[25] How do they make it? One possibility is that Olson's attention to tangible goods as a means of attracting members overlooks other, less tangible rewards. Remember **efficacy**—that sense that you can get government to respond to your interests? Plenty of people get satisfaction from being part of a cause they believe in or from feeling they've expressed their ideas—something called a **purposive benefit**. It's what would lead someone—maybe you—to join the Sierra Club because of the satisfaction created by pitching in to help a worthwhile cause (if you, in fact, feel the Sierra Club does worthwhile things). In fact, for a brief time the Sierra Club sweetened the pot to attract new members by offering a free backpack—then giving new members the option to give it back in the name of efficacy, so that "all of my contribution goes towards protecting the environment."[26] Purposive benefits help explain the appeal of membership in a civil rights or public interest group: The collective good produced by the group may be enough to compel people to belong.

There's one other reason why people join interest groups. Have you ever worked at a plant or company that was unionized? Perhaps a relative of yours does. If so, you might have encountered a twist on the incentive structure we've been talking about in order to

collective goods: Benefits stemming from the work of an interest group that are available to everyone, whether or not they join the group.

free rider: Someone who is sympathetic to the objectives of an interest group and enjoys the benefits produced by that group without making a contribution. Accordingly, he or she "rides free" on the backs of dues-paying members.

efficacy: The attitude that you can be effectual and effective in your dealings with government.

purposive benefit: The gratification an interest group member gets by contributing to a cause.

entice people to join groups. Many unions operate as "closed shops," strengthening their numbers by compelling workers to pay union dues.[27] Because unions derive their benefits from collective bargaining, and because benefits flow to all workers, it's in the interest of unions to represent everyone at a work site and often in the interest of workers to join. However, the use of coercion to compel membership takes away the choice, making unions unique among interest groups in the manner in which they go about getting members.

8.5 Lobbyists and Lobbying

One obvious reason why interest groups want to encourage membership is that lobbying costs money. A less obvious reason is because there's power in numbers. Any interest group that can claim to speak for a lot of people simply has more clout. For instance, there's a group called the American Association of Retired Persons, which now goes by its initials, AARP. If you go to the membership page on their website, you'll find that it says, "Anyone over fifty can get all the great benefits of membership in AARP."

Anyone over fifty? In an organization dedicated to retired people?

That's not a misprint. By opening group membership to people fifty and over instead of moving the cutoff closer to the standard retirement age of sixty-five, AARP can expand its membership base and claim to speak for far more people—over 38 million in all—making it second only to the Roman Catholic Church as the nation's largest organization.[28] When a group representing that many people speaks, official Washington tends to listen. In 2009, AARP contributed momentum to President Obama's efforts to overhaul the health-care system when it came out in favor of the general principle of reform—provided that it did not reduce Medicare benefits for seniors.

Money and membership numbers are key resources used in lobbying. So is information because, as we'll see, one reason officials listen to lobbyists is because they can supply them with information they need in order to do their jobs intelligently. Interest groups have other important resources, too. Larger groups can depend on the media as a resource for publicizing their aims and objectives, and lobbyists rely on **access** to public officials—the ability to contact them on a regular, ongoing basis and know they'll be welcome.

With these resources—money, membership, information, media, and access—interest groups engage in a host of strategies to achieve their ends. We can group them into **inside strategies**, where direct personal contacts with officials or their staffs are the source of lobbying efforts, and **outside strategies**, where groups appeal to their membership in an indirect effort to get officials to respond to their wishes.

8.5a Inside Strategies

A lot of lobbying involves face-to-face interaction between lobbyists and officials. In fact, the term *lobbying* derives from the way interest group representatives would gather in the lobby of the legislative chamber—they aren't allowed inside—waiting to corner representatives as they emerged from the legislature.

Lobbying can take a lot of specific forms, but it tends to involve the same collection of activities. By one count, some of the most widely utilized inside strategies are:

- Making direct personal contacts with officials.
- Presenting technical information to officials.
- Helping to draft legislation.
- Testifying at legislative hearings.
- Making campaign contributions.[29]

Inside strategies involve the use of access, information, and money to advance group goals. That sounds pretty abstract, but in reality, inside lobbying is about building relationships.

Just take a look at some of the inside strategies in the previous list to get a feel for how it works. Direct personal contacts, targeted at members of Congress, their staff, and people who serve in the many agencies that constitute the executive branch of govern-

access: The ability to maintain personal contact with public officials. Many lobbying strategies depend on maintaining an open door to contacts in the legislative and executive branches.

inside strategies: Lobbying approaches that rely on direct relationships between lobbyists and officials.

outside strategies: Lobbying approaches that rely on mobilizing group members to influence the actions of officials.

L.O. Discuss some of the inside and outside strategies lobbyists use to advocate on behalf of interest groups.

ment, happen regularly and frequently. They can be made formally or at social gatherings. Official Washington loves to socialize, and it can be impossible to distinguish business from pleasure because when lobbyists are at a restaurant or social function with members of Congress, they are maintaining the personal contacts that make their job possible (yes, there's actually a career where part of the job description involves going to parties). In an important respect, lobbying is forever: It's an endless, ongoing process of cultivating relationships because interest groups are constantly engaged in the process of seeking what they want and protecting what they have.[30]

Because interest groups are also called pressure groups, it would make sense that personal contacts are used to twist the arms of legislators who stand in the way of the group's goal. That's the picture of lobbyists that a lot of people have in their heads—people who are always working whatever angle they can find to change the minds of opponents—and to a point this happens. However, maybe the more interesting contacts take place between lobbyists and officials who are sympathetic to the group's goals. You might think that interest groups don't have to lobby their friends, but in fact, sympathetic officials form an important base of support that groups constantly nurture, and interest groups commonly target friendly or undecided officials before they invest their time into trying to change people's minds.[31]

In this vein, lobbyists provide a service to sympathetic officials when they supply them with technical information and assist representatives and senators in drafting legislation. It's the business of interest groups to be familiar with the policy details of the interests they represent, and that expertise is incredibly valuable to busy officials who simply don't have the time to immerse themselves in the particulars of a legislative area. Of course, lobbyists who help draft legislation will do so with their interests liberally represented, but this doesn't cause a problem to allied legislators who will introduce the bill (and it in no way guarantees that the legislation they draft will pass through Congress in the form in which it is written, if it passes through Congress at all).

Information also comes into play when lobbyists testify at legislative hearings, where they get to display their expertise as members of Congress deliberate the merits of legislation. Hearings provide lobbyists with a forum for making the case for their position while showing off what they know, and because the substance of hearings is often covered by the press (even if it's an industry newsletter or trade publication), the lobbyist can use a hearing as a source of free publicity, playing the role of expert to set the press agenda in a manner that's favorable to the group's cause.[32]

8.5b Outside Strategies

While inside strategies are about networking, outside strategies are about mobilizing group supporters to demonstrate political demand for the group's position. Some of the most widely used outside strategies are:

- Contacting the press.
- Mobilizing grassroots members.
- Publicizing legislative voting.
- Advertising and public relations efforts.
- Endorsing candidates.
- Engaging in protests or demonstrations.[33]

Outside strategies entail the use of media and membership to advance group goals, expanding the arena in which interest groups can gain momentum for their cause beyond official Washington. The purpose is to get officials to take notice of an issue, either by demonstrating that group members are energized by it (meaning it might influence how they vote in November) or by publicizing it through the media.[34]

Outside strategies can be as routine as organized interest group efforts to get members to write to their representatives about an issue, but on occasion, outside strategies can be dramatic. There's a terrific story about a group of seniors in Chicago who long ago were mobilized to protest a tax on catastrophic health-care insurance, endorsed by AARP and guided through the House by powerful Congressman Dan Rostenkowski. With big interests lined up behind it, Congress approved the tax. However, smaller senior citizen interests opposed it, such as the National Committee to Preserve Social Security and Medicare. For more than a year, the smaller lobby ran television ads framing the tax as unfair to seniors, helping to make seniors aware of the tax and raise the visibility of their antitax position to legislators.

When Rostenkowski agreed to meet with a group of seniors in his district about the measure, the Committee to Preserve Social Security and Medicare went into action. Playing on the ire of their members, they recruited angry seniors to attend the meeting with signs protesting Rostenkowski's support of the measure. They were energized, and—prompted by interest group leaders—they wanted the congressman to talk to them personally. Rostenkowski left the meeting without doing so. Indignant, a group of about twenty seniors surrounded the congressman's car, in full view of television cameras and reporters—who had been tipped off to the potential for good pictures by interest group leaders. They were led by sixty-nine-year-old Leona Kozien, who to that point had never been involved in political action of any kind and certainly never dreamed that her name would end up in an American government textbook:

> The seniors stood in front of the car and waved placards. The congressman's driver honked the horn and moved the car a few inches. The front bumper brushed against Kozien's thigh, and she staggered a bit. Some man shouted, "You knocked her down! You hurt her!" This same man then turned to Kozien and said quietly, "Lay down under the car."

> "Are you crazy? No way, he'd run me over!" retorted Kozien, who was barely over five feet tall. The car moved again, and this time Kozien fell on the hood of the car. Her face was inches from Rostenkowski's, with glass separating them. She was still carrying her placard, and from inside the car, Rostenkowski saw her placard, her face, and her body sprawled across the windshield.

> "Killer! Killer!" the crowd shouted.

> Rostenkowski then got out of the car and ran through a parking lot, while angry seniors chased after him. The driver maneuvered through the crowd, drove around the block, and caught up with Rostenkowski down the street.[35]

Considering what we know about the media, it's not hard to imagine that pictures of a senior citizen hanging in protest from a congressman's car got national play—which is exactly what the group organizers had hoped for. The results were remarkable. It thrust the catastrophic health-care tax on the national agenda. Interest group leaders used it as a rallying point to motivate seniors across the country to write letters to their representatives urging Congress to repeal the tax. The effort culminated in an about-face by Congress, which voted overwhelmingly to ax the tax just one year after it had instituted it (even AARP changed its position). Working from the outside, strategically using media and membership, a small but determined interest group succeeded in getting Congress to reverse itself.

Although the outside strategies we listed previously are often employed independently, the case of the angry seniors combined most of them into a coordinated campaign. An organized public relations effort incorporating television advertising paved the way for the protest by making the issue of the catastrophic health-care insurance tax visible to seniors and officials.

Grassroots members were mobilized to attend the meeting with Rostenkowski, something they might not have done without encouragement when you consider that these were seniors who did not have a record of social activism or even tremendous political participation.

The press had been contacted about the event and informed by group leaders about the potential for great pictures to support a good story line (senior citizens with placards confront powerful House member). The media showed up because the promise of seniors picketing a congressman was too hard to resist.

Then, of course, there was the protest itself, which took place with more than a little coaching from organizers, who were out to get the pictures they knew could catapult their cause into national headlines. When they succeeded, more grassroots mobilizing took place in the form of an organized letter-writing campaign from seniors to representatives from districts across the country.

The two outside strategies on our list that didn't come into play in the catastrophic health-care tax example—publicizing legislative voting and endorsing candidates—serve a similar purpose to the strategies that did. Earlier, we talked about how ideological interest groups rate members of Congress based on how they vote on key issues in order to direct the support of members toward sympathetic representatives or to get them to work against representatives deemed hostile to their cause. Interest groups with large memberships may publicize legislative voting records as a way of putting pressure on members of Congress by publicly stating that the group is watching what they're doing. The implication, of course, is that members of Congress who don't act in accordance with group goals will face the wrath of interest group members at the polls. When the National Rifle Association (NRA) notified senators that it was going to publicize or "score" their vote on a 2013 proposal requiring background checks for gun purchases, it used its leverage to pressure legislators from supporting a measure supported by upwards of 90 percent of Americans but opposed by gun manufacturers. The proposal stalled on procedural grounds when an insufficient number of senators supported bringing it up for a vote.

Endorsing candidates works much the same way. Powerful interest groups with lots of members like the NRA or the AFL-CIO will target candidates for defeat, while showering supportive candidates with PAC money and working to get rank-and-file members out to the polls to vote for them.

Officials who hold significant influence over how the laws are written are often the beneficiaries of the largess of those interests in their jurisdiction. Senator Orrin Hatch, for instance, is the chair of the powerful Senate Finance Committee, with jurisdiction over federal health programs. Not surprisingly, two of the top five industries contributing to his senatorial campaigns between 2011 and 2016 were health-care professionals and pharmaceutical companies.[36]

That said, there are limits to outside strategies. Members of Congress can often tell if the cards and email they're getting are the product of an orchestrated effort (see Demystifying Government: "Dear Senator Surname"), and if so, they're easier to discount than a more spontaneous outpouring of discontent. Interest groups can go to a lot of effort to

---

DEMYSTIFYING GOVERNMENT

"Dear Senator Surname"

How can members of Congress or their staff tell if an interest group orchestrates a seemingly spontaneous outpouring of sentiment? One way is by looking at what's in the letters and emails arriving at the representative's office. Effective emails appear original and unrehearsed, and effective letter-writing campaigns will try to generate the appearance of spontaneity by offering guidelines for how supporters might craft their letters without imposing uniformity.

However, in the interest of generating as many letters with as little effort as possible, groups may use "sample" letters to coach their members on what to write. It's not unreasonable to expect people simply to copy the sample letter verbatim and send it to their member of Congress. So, if duplicate copies of the same letter start showing up, members know that they're dealing with an organized effort.

There are other easy clues to representatives that a letter is part of an organized campaign and should be discounted. Some people have been known to make it easy for members of Congress to figure out what's going on by enclosing the sample along with their rewritten copy in the envelope they mail to Washington, D.C. And some sample letters can be taken too literally, like this sample from the American Society of Radiologic Technologists, which begins: "Dear Senator (Surname) or Representative (Surname):" When members of Congress start getting letters addressed to "Senator Surname"—and while such letters may not come from radiologic technologists, they do happen—they may not look all that spontaneous.

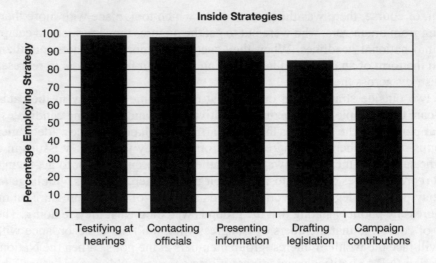

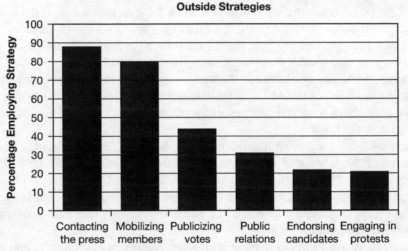

FIGURE 8.1 Inside vs. Outside Strategies[T7]

Interest groups widely employ almost every inside strategy available to them, whereas outside strategies are used more selectively—or rarely, as in the case of public relations, endorsing candidates, and protesting.

get members to write to their representatives, but, ironically, they'll be more effective if they can generate a big response with little prodding.[37] Of course, that only happens when group members are already upset about an issue, something group leaders cannot easily manufacture.

And not every group is like the NRA, with large numbers of motivated members that cast their votes with the group's agenda in mind. The senior citizen protest, although highly effective, is an unusual tactic to employ: Interest groups tend to shy away from protests and demonstrations. For that matter, if the great pictures of Leona Kozien dangling from the hood of Congressman Rostenkowski's car had not materialized, it's unlikely that there would have been national media coverage of the issue.

On the whole, lobbying is an insider's game. In a survey of interest groups, almost all of them claimed to engage in key inside strategies: contacting government officials, testifying at hearings, and presenting officials with technical information. By comparison, they relied less heavily on outside strategies, as Figure 8.1 demonstrates.

8.5c More Money

L.O. Explain how hard and soft money contributions from political action committees can influence lobbying.

Looking at interest group strategies permits us to revisit the matter of PACs from the perspective of where all that money is coming from. For starters, not every PAC is formed by an interest group and not every interest group has a PAC. Some PACs are organized and run by single individuals or small groups, like PACs organized to support presidential candidates. Still, many are the money-giving arms of organized interests. They tend to be formed by interest groups that are heavily engaged in advancing policy goals in a competitive political environment, where lobbying can get expensive and contributions to political officials are thought to be productive.[38]

Business interests are most likely to have PACs—by one count, better than 40 percent of PACs are affiliated with corporations. Ideological groups compose the next largest group of PACs, with organizations like the American Conservative Union and People for the American Way raising large sums of money in an attempt to influence a broad political agenda. Labor unions and trade associations are also big players in the use of PAC money to advance their interests.[39]

A list of the top twenty PAC contributors from the 2015–2016 midterm political cycle (see Table 8.4) gives you a pretty good idea of who the biggest players are. Here's how the top of the top shakes down: Coming in at number one overall is the National Association of Realtors, with total contributions of over $3,900,000. The International Brotherhood of Electrical Workers PAC is the top union contributor. The biggest-spending corporate PAC is AT&T ($3,100,750), followed closely by Honeywell International ($2,785,864).[40]

TABLE 8.4 Top PAC Contributors to Federal Candidates, 2015–2016[T8]

Rank	PAC Name	Amount	Percent to Democrats	Percent to Republicans
1	National Association of Realtors	$3,912,200	42%	58%
2	National Beer Wholesalers Association	$3,515,700	42%	57%
3	AT&T	$3,100,750	38%	62%
4	Honeywell International	$2,785,864	40%	60%
5	National Automobile Dealers Association	$2,747,250	28%	72%
6	Lockheed Martin	$2,600,750	38%	62%
7	Blue Cross/Blue Shield	$2,585,898	36%	64%
8	American Bankers Association	$2,524,507	22%	78%
9	Credit Union National Association	$2,462,350	46%	54%
10	International Brotherhood of Electoral Workers	$2,413,200	97%	3%
11	National Association of Insurance and Financial Advisors	$2,312,400	33%	67%
12	Operating Engineers Union	$2,270,903	74%	26%
13	Comcast Corporation	$2,264,200	37%	63%
14	United Parcel Service	$2,218,203	34%	66%
15	Northrop Grumman	$2,149,500	39%	61%
16	Boeing Corporation	$2,086,000	42%	58%
17	Machinists/Aerospace Workers Union	$2,084,500	92%	8%
18	Majority Committee PAC	$2,076,513	0%	100%
19	New York Life Insurance	$2,029,200	43%	57%
20	National Association of Home Builders	$2,028,125	16%	84%

The top twenty is also a stable group; eight of the top ten PAC contributors of 2009 appear on this list.[41]

Corporations, unions, associations, and individuals are also allowed to form "Super PACs" for the purpose of influencing elections without violating campaign spending restrictions. Unlike regular PACs, Super PACs cannot contribute directly to or coordinate with a campaign, but they are free to advocate on behalf of a candidate and can raise and spend unlimited amounts of money. Most competitive candidates in the 2016 presidential race were supported by a Super PAC, such as Priorities USA Action (Hillary Clinton), Right to Rise USA (Jeb Bush), and Conservative Solutions PAC (Marco Rubio). Collectively, 2,408 Super PACs raised a total of $1.7 billion and spent $1.1 billion during the 2016 campaign.[42]

In addition to PAC contributions, campaign funds also come in the form of **soft money**. Technically, soft-money contributions are made to national, state, or local political parties rather than to candidates, but campaigns rely heavily on soft money to supplement direct contributions. Donors use soft-money contributions to circumvent the strict limits on contributions to candidates because soft money is unregulated. Traditionally, Republicans had been the disproportionate beneficiaries of soft money. Beginning in 2004, Democrats began to bridge the money gap with Republicans through the active fund-raising of advocacy groups or "527 Committees"—named for the section of the tax code under which they are authorized. These groups are chartered to advocate issues and mobilize voters, for which they can raise unlimited amounts of soft money.[43]

8.5d Lobbying the Executive Branch

The inside and outside strategies we've discussed can, for the most part, be applied to lobbying the legislative and executive branches. Although some approaches, like advertising voting records and endorsing candidates, apply specifically to Congress, lobbyists find themselves heavily engaged in trying to influence the executive branch.

That's because the game isn't over once a group has successfully gotten Congress to act in its interest. Any new legislation that Congress creates is interpreted and put into effect by the **executive branch**, or the **bureaucracy**. As we'll see in Chapter 11, bureaucrats in the executive branch have a lot of freedom over how to implement acts of Congress, which means lobbying efforts extend to getting them to interpret the law in ways that are sympathetic to the group's wishes. As it turns out, bureaucrats can be influenced by the organizational clout of interest groups or benefit from the expertise interests groups can offer.

We hinted at the importance of how laws are interpreted in Chapter 7, when we mentioned that the Federal Election Commission (FEC) had weakened key provisions of the McCain-Feingold campaign finance reform law, making it possible for political parties to collect soft money in apparent contravention of the spirit of the law. If you don't remember the discussion, here it is, repeated from Chapter 7 (Section 7.2c, "Money"):

Even after passage, McCain-Feingold met with resistance. Although ardent reform activists felt it was little more than a Band-Aid over a gaping wound, just about everyone directly influenced by the changes resisted them. Both major parties immediately searched for ways to circumvent the soft-money restrictions, while some PACs argued it went too far, challenging soft-money limitations as restrictions on free expression. Detractors included four of the six FEC commissioners who were in office at the time the law went into effect. Because they were responsible for interpreting and enforcing the law, they were able to weaken some of the law's reforms, restoring large portions of the soft-money loophole that McCain-Feingold was designed to fill, and providing exceptions under which federal candidates could still collect soft-money contributions.

In this instance, the FEC is an independent regulatory agency with members appointed by the president and confirmed by the senate, charged with putting into effect the campaign finance law passed by Congress. Interest groups concerned with closing the soft-money loophole, like public interest groups that work for campaign reform, found it

---

soft money: Funds contributed to state and local parties or to national parties for the purpose of running state elections or conducting local "grassroots" political activity.

executive branch: The institutional component of the branch of government we think of as the presidency, charged with carrying out laws passed by Congress. Sometimes, the executive branch is referred to as the bureaucracy.

bureaucracy: Another name for the executive branch of government, the institutional component of the presidency, which is charged with carrying out laws passed by Congress.

necessary to lobby the FEC to press for a strict interpretation of the law, despite having already spent years trying to get Congress to pass the law in the first place.

In the case of McCain-Feingold, key public interest groups employed an outside strategy in order to pressure the FEC into a strict interpretation of the law. The effort was not lost on FEC commissioners, who, according to the *Washington Post*, "bristled" at the tactics, complaining that "the leaders of such groups as Common Cause and Democracy 21 were trying to influence commission decisions by lobbying through the news media."[44]

The executive-branch parallel to the interest group strategy of trying to influence congressional elections is trying to influence bureaucratic appointments. Because it's always easiest to lobby someone sympathetic to your cause, groups may support or oppose presidential appointees based on how closely an appointee's philosophy matches the group's objectives. In the case of the FEC, you would expect Common Cause and Democracy 21 to push for commissioners who are sympathetic to campaign finance reform as vacancies emerge on the commission.

8.6 Who Are These Guys?

If you pick up a copy of *Washington Representatives*, a comprehensive source of information on lobbyists, you'll find listings for around 20,000 individual lobbyists and 2,500 lobbying firms representing over 10,000 clients.[45] That's enough lobbyists to fill a small city. Who are these guys?

For starters, lobbyists are guys, or at least they have been traditionally, although women are becoming more visible as lobbyists. It's a profession that disproportionately draws well-off middle-aged Protestants, with Catholic and Jewish lobbyists more likely to represent unions and professional associations. Politically, Democrats are more likely to represent such areas as energy and labor, whereas Republicans are more likely to be drawn to business and agricultural issues.

Lawyers are also heavily represented among lobbyists, as are people with deep roots in Washington, D.C. This makes sense if you consider that lawyers are well situated to understand the ramifications of making changes to legislation. Being well connected in Washington helps open the doors that lobbyists need to walk through in order to implement inside strategies. In fact, it's not at all uncommon to find among the ranks of lobbyists former members of Congress and the executive branch, who can offer interest groups easy access to the corridors of powers and familiarity with how official Washington works.[46]

If lobbying is about implementing a variety of strategies designed to win the support or neutralize the opposition of officials toward an issue, then lobbyists are first and foremost strategists. Good lobbyists recognize the resources they have to work with and can design and implement an approach to convert those resources into the outcome they seek. To do this effectively, lobbyists need to know which officials can help them, then be thorough and follow through. Just like success in college, effective lobbying involves doing a lot of homework.[47] Demystifying Government: The "Five Commandments" of Lobbying offers a few basic tips on how good lobbyists maintain their clients and preserve their reputations.

iron triangle: The ongoing, mutually beneficial relationship among an interest group, members of Congress sharing the interest group's objectives, and bureaucrats in federal agencies responsible for carrying out legislation pertaining to the interest group's field. Iron triangles can develop in any policy area, and many distinct iron-triangle relationships form because the federal government is responsible for a large number of policies.

subgovernments: Another term for iron triangles, which captures the specialized (and often hidden) relationship among lobbyists, members of Congress, and bureaucrats, who share mutual professional and policy interests and objectives.

8.7 Competition . . . or Cooperation?

You're probably starting to get the idea that for all the competition between groups and for all the arm-twisting and threats to endorse political opponents, interest groups benefit from having a lot in common with the people they lobby. While it's true that some groups engage in zero-sum competition with other groups, a lot of the positions that groups advance are encouraged by like-minded officials who benefit magnificently from their relationships with lobbyists.

The term **"iron triangle"** describes the exchange of mutual self-interest among interest groups, legislators, and bureaucrats in the executive branch. Also called **"subgovernments"** for their highly specialized nature, iron triangles are enduring relationships based

L.O. Identify "iron triangles," and appreciate how lobbying can be more cooperative than adversarial.

The "Five Commandments" of Lobbying

Bruce C. Wolpe and Bertram J. Levine, two students of the process, offer five "commandments" for effective lobbying.

1. *Tell the truth.* A lobbyist's reputation lasts forever, and failing to provide lawmakers with a full appreciation of the obstacles they face could lead to political embarrassment for the legislator and professional oblivion for the lobbyist.

2. *Never promise more than you can deliver.* As tempting as it is to make grandiose claims, if you promise a legislator that you're going to enact a grassroots letter-writing campaign to other members of Congress, you better deliver. This is why it's important for lobbyists to know their resources.

3. *Listen and understand.* Words from an official that sound like a commitment could turn out to be much less, and a good lobbyist can tell the difference. So, if legislators say, "I want to help you," or "I believe you have a good case," they're expressing their support—but not their commitment to your cause.

4. *Work with staff.* In Chapter 9, we'll see just how busy members of Congress are. Their schedules make them dependent on their staff for decision making and processing a heavy workload. Personal relationships with members of Congress are important and may be an ego boost, but working with their staffs can clear the way to get things done.

5. *Spring no surprises.* Politicians hate surprises. Their staff members hate surprises. And lobbyists who do their homework can avoid unpleasant surprises.[T9]

on the mutual gratification of the needs of the three participants, and they can spring up around any policy area, no matter how tiny. Iron triangles capture the way interest groups can inject themselves into the heart of policy making, and they define the way interest groups held sway over government for the latter portion of the twentieth century (as we'll see in a little while, the iron lock started getting rusty as the twenty-first century approached). They're "iron" because, with each participant getting something they need from the others, there's no incentive for anyone to leave, either voluntarily or through persuasion. Figure 8.2 should give you a good idea of how they work.

As you look at the images in Figure 8.2, try to imagine lots of these iron triangles, encompassing all sorts of policy areas, and you can perhaps get a feel for how subgovernments could easily become their own little mutually beneficial worlds, operating autonomously from all other subgovernments.

Where's the competition in a system like this, the clash of interests that Madison said was supposed to produce policy to serve the greater good? Critics say it isn't there. For instance, it's easy to imagine that there are common interests among, say, Lockheed Martin Corporation (a top PAC contributor and a major manufacturer of missile systems), the Pentagon, and members of the House and Senate Armed Services Committees. Lockheed Martin has a commercial interest in selling its systems to the military, and the Pentagon has a professional interest in expanding and upgrading its stockpile of weaponry. Members of Congress serving on the Armed Services subcommittee that handles acquisitions of military hardware have a political interest in having expensive weapons systems constructed in their districts because it means jobs for their constituents.[48]

revolving door: A consequence of the close relationships between interest groups and government officials that makes it possible for lobbyists to become government officials charged with regulating the organizations they once worked for, or for government officials to become lobbyists who influence friends in their former agency.

Mutual interest keeps this small community together. Mutual expertise stemming from a shared knowledge base, combined with the natural, human enterprise of networking, can perpetuate the community through a **"revolving door"** in which it would not be uncommon for officers of Lockheed Martin to be prime candidates for service as ranking Pentagon officials (where human nature says they would look favorably on projects developed by their former employer), or for former Pentagon officials or Armed Services committee staff and members to use their expertise and connections to become lobbyists for Lockheed Martin, working closely with their one-time associates in government to promote corporate interests. In 2016, Lockheed Martin employed 86 lobbyists, 58 with government experience on their résumés.[49] This is why iron triangles are sometimes called "cozy triangles."

Among their many resources, interest groups have the persuasive power of **organized membership**, sometimes in large numbers. They have **money**, which can be channeled through PACs to political campaigns. And they have access to detailed **information** about their field. But interest groups need **legislation passed and implemented** in order to be successful.

Members of Congress can collectively **pass legislation**. Because legislation is shaped in committees, iron triangles are typically said to operate through the congressional committee structure. But, individually, members of Congress need the votes of large numbers of people, **money** to run for re-election, and **information** to do their committee work intelligently and effectively.

Similarly, bureaucrats in the executive branch have the authority to **implement legislation**. Implementing legislation can be detailed, technical work, and like members of Congress, bureaucrats in the executive branch need information to do their jobs intelligently and effectively.

Furthermore, members of Congress and the executive branch who share a policy interest will find themselves naturally aligned. Legislators who support a policy have an interest in seeing it implemented according to their wishes, just as bureaucrats invested in enhancing their agency will often listen to leading congressional voices as they enact policy.

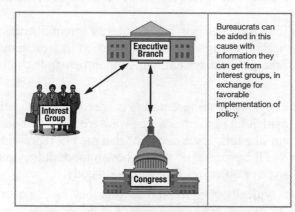

Bureaucrats can be aided in this cause with information they can get from interest groups, in exchange for favorable implementation of policy.

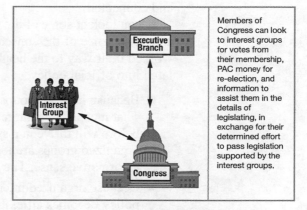

Members of Congress can look to interest groups for votes from their membership, PAC money for re-election, and information to assist them in the details of legislating, in exchange for their determined effort to pass legislation supported by the interest groups.

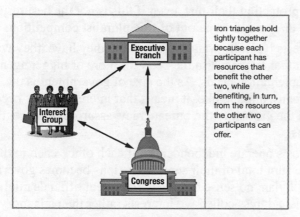

Iron triangles hold tightly together because each participant has resources that benefit the other two, while benefiting, in turn, from the resources the other two participants can offer.

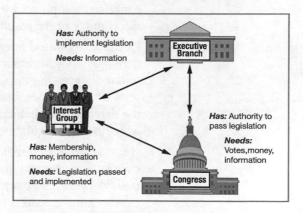

Has: Authority to implement legislation

Needs: Information

Has: Authority to pass legislation

Needs: Votes, money, information

Has: Membership, money, information

Needs: Legislation passed and implemented

FIGURE 8.2 Here's Why They Call Them "Iron"

You can look to the Obama cabinet for a good example of how the revolving door can work in the executive branch. President Obama appointed Lawrence H. Summers to head his National Economic Council and Steven Rattner to be a chief advisor to the Treasury Department, making them central decision-makers in the banking and automotive crises that were raging when Obama became president. Summers had rotated among high-level jobs in government, serving as President Clinton's treasury secretary; academia, where he was president of Harvard University; and the private sector, where he was part-time director of a lucrative hedge fund. Before he became Treasury secretary, Summers was deputy and protégé to Robert Rubin, who had his own revolving door experience, coming to the Treasury from the investment firm Goldman Sachs, then directing the financial services

Chapter 8 Interest Groups: Accessing Government through Common Membership

company Citigroup after his departure from government. Rattner came from Wall Street, where he had been an investment banker.

Although a background in the financial sector could be considered an asset in understanding the nuances of an arcane and complex world, it could also be viewed by critics as facilitating a worldview sympathetic to Wall Street that would limit the range of policy options they would consider. So, for instance, the Obama administration's high-level links to the banking community proved problematic amidst public outrage over billions of dollars in bonuses paid to Wall Street executives during the financial crisis, at a time when unemployment was climbing and the economy was on shaky footing.

Through cooperation, mutual interests are protected and everyone in a small, closed, iron-triangle community can get something they want. Nonetheless, it's reasonable to have doubts about whether the common good is best served by decisions made in this manner. Political scientist Theodore J. Lowi calls the system of subgovernments "interest group liberalism," a contorted version of pluralism in which public policy becomes the sum total of the combined self-interested actions of interest groups that can lock in to the political system. To Lowi, self-serving interests replace—but do not speak for—collective interests, which ultimately silences our voices in favor of the voices of the organized and connected.

If you look at some of the following characteristics of "interest group liberalism," you can get a sense of the consequences of the iron-triangle system, as interest groups have worked their way to the heart of the political system, where their demands can be translated into official policy.

- Because interest groups are organized, representation is based on organization. That means large interests with a lot of the resources we were talking about before will thrive in a system like this. Issue concerns that are not represented by organized groups are losers in the process, no matter how important they may be in a normative sense: They can have no voice if they have no body.

- Because organized interests typically want to protect what they have, government policy becomes inflexible. With well-positioned friends in government, groups can exercise their power by protecting their turf, even if this is not the best result for the country or the result that would come out of true pluralist competition.

- Because organized interests typically want more of what they have, they will make demands on government that can result in the need for more or bigger agencies to handle growing implementation needs. As the size of government is the sum total of its agencies, bureaus, and the like, it means that interest groups become the driving force behind the growth of the bureaucracy, assuring new programs, agencies, and regulations.

- Because organized interests operate independently of each other, each in their own subgovernment, the sum total of their separate actions becomes government policy. There's no overall plan, no sense of how government officials might make overarching decisions that address collective interests rather than a laundry list of individual interests.[50]

As an example of how interest groups can frustrate broad national interests, take the matter of "big government," which we know is an idea that's not part of American political culture. Many Americans complain about large government bureaucracies, and opinion polls invariably demonstrate wide support for cutting back the bureaucracy. Every president for the past thirty years has pledged to make government more efficient (Carter) or smaller (both Bushes), or saw it as the enemy (Reagan), or promised to reinvent it (Clinton) or put it to work for ordinary people (Obama). These positions generated popular support.

However, the bureaucracy has not gotten smaller—in large part because no president can undermine subgovernments without alienating the members of Congress who derive important political resources from the interest groups that would lose out if the president's popular plan were enacted. As we'll see in Chapter 9, no president can afford to do this on a wide enough scale to make a meaningful difference to the size and scope of government. So, a broadly held collective interest falls victim to the logic of "interest group liberalism."

8.8 Triangles or Networks?

If you were reading carefully earlier, you might have picked up the reference to the iron lock getting rusty as the twenty-first century approached. This doesn't mean that subgovernments have disappeared, or that revolving doors have stopped rotating. However, the interest group community has become more diverse, broad issues have drawn interest groups into policy areas they once ignored, new public interest groups have emerged, and many iron triangles have given way to more broadly defined **issue networks**. In an issue network, there are more players, and sometimes more light comes in from the outside. Interest groups with competing agendas have access to the system, opening the range of possibilities for how government will respond to an issue.

What brought this about? For one thing, as the problems that government addresses became more complex, the needs of interest groups became more complicated, causing them to expand their relationships with officials. Many smaller triangles by necessity became larger webs.

Add to this the emergence in your lifetime of greater diversity among interest groups—most notably the rise of public interest groups—and you have the makings of a more complex system. At one time, environmental policy would not have been made with input from groups like the Environmental Defense Fund and Population Zero because they simply did not exist. Today, agendas of groups like these are included in broader policy networks that in a previous generation would have been restricted to the agendas of groups lobbying to avoid the cost of environmental regulation.[51] For further discussion, see Demystifying Government: The Expanded Community of Abortion Lobbying.

Does this mean that the interest group system has become more pluralistic? At the very least, it means it has grown more fluid. Does this mean it has become more open and representative?

L.O. Understand how issue networks develop around complex policy matters.

issue network: A fluid policy community permeable to a wide range of interest groups, permitting a broad array of policy outcomes.

DEMYSTIFYING GOVERNMENT

The Expanded Community of Abortion Lobbying

The abortion issue provides a good example of how groups have been pulled into an issue area that was once exclusively the province of a few single-issue advocates primarily concerned with abortion law.

Traditionally, single-issue groups, like the ones we discussed earlier when we talked about abortion as a zero-sum issue, were the only players in the abortion lobby. "Pro-life" groups like the National Right to Life Committee lobbied against "pro-choice" groups like Planned Parenthood. The ramifications of abortion policy have since seeped into other areas of policy, particularly as medical technology has advanced, bringing new groups into the mix.

Interest groups concerned with health-care policy became engaged in abortion lobbying as it arose as a topic in discussions about reforming the health-care system. The Committee for the Separation of Church and State became involved in the issue—despite not having a position on abortion rights, women's rights, or

health-care issues—when it became concerned that a religious dimension to some abortion lobbying jeopardized the church/state boundary.

Doctors and researchers engaged in addressing infertility became intertwined with the abortion issue when their medical approaches became entangled with abortion legislation. Abortion procedures can be involved in infertility approaches that include implanting or using drugs to produce, then selectively terminate, multiple embryos. As a consequence, interest groups representing doctors, nurses, hospitals, and medical schools have engaged in lobbying in the abortion arena in an effort to represent the interests of those involved in reproductive medicine. Questions over medical research using stem cell tissue have thrust a new community of scientists into the abortion debate[T10] The result is a wide-ranging policy community involving a wealth of organized interests whose primary concerns are matters other than abortion rights.

Writing in 1960, political scientist E. E. Schattschneider said that interest groups simply do not represent most people because the number of groups is exceedingly small, especially when you compare it with the range of interests and concerns that people have. Because, as we know, those with more resources are more likely to participate, he says the interest group system is both narrow and tilted toward the interests of well-to-do individuals. This is especially so when you compare the interest group system to broad-based political parties, which appeal to a more general range of concerns.[52]

Interest groups walked into the void created when party reform unintentionally undermined the controlling grip of party elites.[53] They now work closely with political parties and often coordinate their efforts, with business groups and religious conservatives aligning with the Republican Party and unions aligning with the Democrats. Reliance on campaign contributions and voter mobilization efforts, commonplace among such groups as the Christian Coalition for Republicans and the AFL-CIO for Democrats, blends interest group tactics with party politics.

Does this lead to more broad-based representation? It doesn't change the fact that interest groups remain narrowly focused and speak for defined segments of the population. It does return an element of competition to the system that was missing when subgovernments were more prominent. It's up to you to decide whether the system is broad-based enough to be considered pluralistic.

8.9 Does Access Equal Influence?

L.O. *Relate the interest group system to our earlier discussion of pluralism and elitism.*

influence: The ability to shape political outcomes to your liking.

One way to approach the pluralism question is to determine whether the access interest groups have to the political system translates into influence over politicians—or more specifically, how much influence it permits over politicians. We already know that access is a group's ability to open doors to political officials, and there should be no doubt that between PAC contributions and the exercise of mutual interests, officials grant access to interest groups. Influence is another matter, though. To have **influence** is to have the ability to shape the decisions of political officials. Influence when successfully applied means getting things you want, and it's what all those PAC contributions are *intended* to produce.

There's evidence that this happens, at least some of the time. Journalist Jeffrey H. Birnbaum has covered money and politics for over twenty years, and he tells of the role interest groups played when Republicans became the majority party in the House of Representatives for the first time in forty years following the 1994 "Contract with America" election:

> When Republicans took control of the House of Representatives in January 1995 after forty years in the minority, they reached out to their most loyal backers—in large measure their financial backers—and rewarded them with seats at the table. And they, in turn, used that position to help House Republicans pass Newt Gingrich's Contract with America, which was, in effect, their wish list, ranging from limits on corporate lawsuits (a favorite of the U.S. Chamber of Commerce) to an increase in tax breaks for stay-at-home moms (beloved by the Christian Coalition). The point is that moneymen are players. They aren't figures lurking in the background, plotting political intrigue. They are central to the drama. They make a difference in the way laws are made and implemented.[54]

Birnbaum says interest groups may have the greatest sway over those few but important policy decisions that are not determined by local concerns (a senator from Kansas could never vote against wheat interests) or by clear partisan divisions. When representatives do not have an unambiguous direction on how to vote, Birnbaum says interest groups provide them with the crucial road map.[55] That, by definition, is influence.

While you're questioning how well the pluralist model applies to the interest group system, you might want to go back to the lists of top PAC contributors in Table 8.4 and think about who's likely to be influential in Washington. Does the influence trail seem long and varied or, as Schattschneider suggests, is influence concentrated in the hands of the few? Think also about public interest groups and whether they fill in enough gaps to compensate for the possibility that issues of widespread concern do not otherwise have an organized voice. Ask yourself if they provide sufficient balance to special-interest influences.

Also, think about whether having influence always means getting results. In some instances, like the reluctance of the Obama administration to take on the big-bonus culture of Wall Street, it's easy for critics to draw a line from access to influence to results. In other cases, connections are not as strong. All the business PAC money in the world—which, as you know, is a big number—could not keep Congress from passing a package of corporate reforms that business opposed. Sometimes, access equals influence, but it does not equal effective influence.

Even if influential interest groups do not always get what they want, you might ask if the sum total of what interest groups accomplish equals some version of the national interest. Supporters of the system might say that when we add everything up, we get policy that approximates what most people want. With self-interest, special interests, single interests, and public interests all having their say, the process may not be pretty to watch, but the outcome represents a mix of salient items on the public agenda. They could point to the rivalry within issue networks as evidence of ambition counteracting ambition in a competition among groups that doesn't explain all interest group interactions with government, but that characterizes how things work in large and important policy areas. And they might point to policy areas where interests on both sides of the question can claim policy victories.

Detractors would argue that we get policy that approximates what a select group of people want, most notably that group with a lot of resources, who may not get everything they're after but who get an awful lot. The effectiveness of public interest groups notwithstanding, they might point to the strong track record of moneyed groups in preserving a status quo that's beneficial to them. In the process of defending what they already have, the argument goes, these groups are responsible for preempting an open debate on our national direction—a debate that could well lead to changes that entrenched groups would find expensive. Critics could point to the powerful role money plays in keeping officials from seeking this debate, noting how incumbents are reluctant to act boldly out of the (reasonable) fear that it will cost them precious campaign dollars. From this perspective, interest groups not only fail to represent the greater good, they're responsible for making the political process stall out.

We could also look at the trend toward partisan **dealignment** that we talked about in Chapter 6 in the context of the entrenchment of special interests in the political system. As party allegiance weakens, we know there are more nonaligned voters who will not automatically vote for one party or another. As parties and interest groups become more intertwined, it's possible that candidates become more responsive to the concerns of the interest groups that help them with the resources they need to get elected rather than to the concerns of nonaligned voters.

dealignment: The weakening of party affiliation, signified by an increase in the number of people who call themselves independents.

As we understand more about how the major branches of government operate, we'll be better positioned to decide what results when interest groups interact with government officials and what the ramifications are for how those officials act. We've suggested that members of Congress, for instance, are overburdened with work and that a lot of what lobbyists do can greatly simplify their lives. This is surely a good thing for representatives. But is it a good thing for us? We're ready to turn now to Part 4, where we'll find the background we need to consider a question like this, as we put a human face on the institutions of the federal government, starting in Chapter 9 with Congress.

Define interest groups, and distinguish them from political parties.

Interest groups are specialized organizations of individuals with common purposes who seek to advance their objectives in the political process. Unlike political parties, their objectives are narrowly defined, and they operate outside the political system.

Define lobbying.

Interest groups engage in lobbying legislators and bureaucrats, attempting to exert influence over the shape of public policy.

Identify key economic and noneconomic interest groups, and be familiar with some of the issues they promote.

Groups promoting economic self-interest constitute the largest number of interest groups, with business, trade, and professional groups leading the way. Business groups generally support Republicans, while unions provide a vital source of support for Democrats. Noneconomic groups promote a variety of single issues and ideological concerns and include civil rights and public interest groups that advocate agendas designed to advance the public good.

Distinguish purposive benefits from selective benefits, and explain why interest groups may use selective benefits to boost membership.

Some people will elect to join interest groups for the purposive benefit of being part of something they believe in, but many will not. Because the benefits of interest group membership are often collective goods that are not limited to members, many groups offer incentives in the form of selective benefits to get people to join. Unions operating closed shops can get members to join through coercion.

Discuss some of the inside and outside strategies lobbyists use to advocate on behalf of interest groups.

Professional lobbyists do the work of interest groups, employing a range of inside and outside strategies. Inside strategies revolve around face-to-face interactions with officials and can include such things as testifying at congressional hearings, helping to draft legislation, presenting technical information to legislators and bureaucrats, or generally remaining in touch through direct personal contact. Outside strategies involve mobilizing members to pressure officials and can include a range of activities from engaging in public relations efforts to publicizing legislative voting records to endorsing candidates to, in unusual cases, engaging in protests or demonstrations.

Explain how hard and soft money contributions from political action committees can influence lobbying.

Financial contributions of hard and soft money made through PACs comprise an important part of lobbying as well. Unions are prevalent among PAC contributors, while businesses top the list of soft-money contributors.

Identify "iron triangles," and appreciate how lobbying can be more cooperative than adversarial.

Lobbying often brings to mind the application of pressure by interest groups on members of Congress (interest groups are sometimes called pressure groups for this reason), but a lot of lobbying is cooperative. Iron triangles, or subgovernments, describe mutually beneficial relationships among lobbyists, legislators, and bureaucrats who share legislative interests. Each has resources needed by the others, leading them to form lasting bonds of mutual self-interest.

Understand how issue networks develop around complex policy matters.

The emergence of public interest groups and the growing complexity of policy questions have picked the lock on some iron triangles, opening some policy areas to broader issue networks. Nonetheless, interest groups continue to use access to the political process to wield influence over political decision making.

Relate the interest group system to our earlier discussion of pluralism and elitism.

Those who feel interest groups do not exercise undue influence over the process point to the fact that even the most powerful and wealthy groups do not get everything they want, and that enough interests have a place in the system to provide a rough approximation of the public interest. Critics say interest groups exercise too much influence and, through the lack of direct competition between groups, undermine the pluralist ideal of policy development stemming from competition over ideas.

Key Terms

access The ability to maintain personal contact with public officials. Many lobbying strategies depend on maintaining an open door to contacts in the legislative and executive branches. (p. 238)

bureaucracy Another name for the executive branch of government, the institutional component of the presidency, which is charged with carrying out laws passed by Congress. (p. 244)

collective goods Benefits stemming from the work of an interest group that are available to everyone, whether or not they join the group. (p. 237)

dealignment The weakening of party affiliation, signified by an increase in the number of people who call themselves independents. (p. 251)

efficacy The attitude that you can be effectual and effective in your dealings with government. (p. 237)

elitism The theory that government responds to a small, stable, centralized hierarchy of corporate and academic leaders, military chiefs, people who own big media outlets, and members of a permanent government bureaucracy. People who subscribe to this position believe the actions of regular citizens, like voting and joining groups, simply mask the real power exercised by elites. (p. 229)

executive branch The institutional component of the branch of government we think of as the presidency, charged with carrying out laws passed by Congress. Sometimes, the executive branch is referred to as the bureaucracy. (p. 244)

free rider Someone who is sympathetic to the objectives of an interest group and enjoys the benefits produced by that group without making a contribution. Accordingly, he or she "rides free" on the backs of dues-paying members. (p. 237)

influence The ability to shape political outcomes to your liking. (p. 250)

inside strategies Lobbying approaches that rely on direct relationships between lobbyists and officials. (p. 238)

interest groups Organized associations that seek to promote common objectives through government action. (p. 229)

iron triangle The ongoing, mutually beneficial relationship among an interest group, members of Congress sharing the interest group's objectives, and bureaucrats in federal agencies responsible for carrying out legislation pertaining to the interest group's field. Iron triangles can develop in any policy area, and many distinct iron-triangle relationships form because the federal government is responsible for a large number of policies. (p. 245)

issue network A fluid policy community permeable to a wide range of interest groups, permitting a broad array of policy outcomes. (p. 249)

libertarianism An ideology centered on the reduction of government power to advance personal liberty. (p. 235)

lobbying Attempting to influence the content of policy by exerting influence on government officials. (p. 229)

lobbyists Professionals hired by interest groups to influence the political process on behalf of the group. (p. 230)

McGovern-Fraser Commission The commission organized by the Democratic Party following its 1968 convention to democratize the process of delegate selection to party conventions. (p. 233)

outside strategies Lobbying approaches that rely on mobilizing group members to influence the actions of officials. (p. 238)

pluralism The theory that government responds to individuals through their memberships in groups, assuring that government is responsive to a wide range of voices. People who subscribe to this position believe that the wide distribution of resources in society drives the decisions government officials make. (p. 229)

pressure groups Another term for interest groups that emphasizes the demands interest groups make on the political system. (p. 229)

purposive benefit The gratification an interest group member gets by contributing to a cause. (p. 237)

Religious Right Ideological interest groups promoting a conservative political agenda consistent with an evangelical religious perspective. (p. 235)

revolving door A consequence of the close relationships between interest groups and government officials that makes it possible for lobbyists to become government officials charged with regulating the organizations they once worked for, or for government officials to become lobbyists who influence friends in their former agency. (p. 246)

selective benefits Incentives offered exclusively to interest group members as a means of getting people to join. (p. 236)

soft money Funds contributed to state and local parties or to national parties for the purpose of running state elections or conducting local "grassroots" political activity. (p. 244)

special-interest groups Another term for interest groups that emphasizes the narrow scope of their concerns. (p. 229)

subgovernments Another term for iron triangles, which captures the specialized (and often hidden) relationship among lobbyists, members of Congress, and bureaucrats, who share mutual professional and policy interests and objectives. (p. 245)

trade associations Groups that advance the concerns of specific business interests, such as banks, energy companies, real estate firms, and car manufacturers. (p. 230)

zero-sum policy A policy debate in which any victory by one side comes at the expense of the opposing side, negating the possibility of compromise. (p. 234)

Resources

You might be interested in examining some of what the following authors have said about the topics we've been discussing:

Birnbaum, Jeffrey. *The Money Men: The Real Story of Fund-Raising's Influence on Political Power in America*. New York: Crown Publishers, 2000. An easy-to-read journalist's account of money in politics, which bridges our discussions of interest groups and political parties.

Cigler, Allan J., and Burdett A. Loomis, eds. *Interest Group Politics*, 7th ed. Washington, DC: CQ Press, 2006. A good overview of topics related to interest groups from a wide range of perspectives.

Kollman, Ken. *Outside Lobbying: Public Opinion and Interest Group Strategies*. Princeton, NJ: Princeton University Press, 1998. If you're interested in knowing more about the outside strategies interest groups employ, this is a good choice.

Lowi, Theodore. *The End of Liberalism: The Second Republic of the United States*, 40th Anniversary edition. New York: Norton, 2009. An interesting and influential argument about how interest groups have emerged as central to the political system and the consequences this poses for democracy.

Mahood, H. R. *Interest Groups in American National Politics*. Upper Saddle River, NJ: Prentice Hall, 2000. This well-written overview of interest group activity includes, among other topics, a discussion of PAC influences, an analysis of the strategies interest groups employ, and a review of elitist and pluralist perspectives on interest groups.

Olson, Mancur. *The Logic of Collective Action: Public Goods and the Theory of Groups*. Cambridge, MA: Harvard University Press, 1971. This seminal work on interest group formation considers the question of why people join interest groups if they can be a "free rider" and benefit without joining.

Schattschneider, E. E. *The Semisovereign People: A Realist's View of Democracy in America*. New York: Wa, 1975. Another seminal work addressing how the nature of organizations limits political involvement and input.

Wolpe, Bruce C., and Bertram J. Levine. *Lobbying Congress: How the System Works*, 2nd ed. Washington, DC: CQ Press, 1996. If you ever thought you'd want to be a lobbyist (and even if you never did), this book offers a practical guide to the basics.

Notes

1 "Accountants Attack Senate Reform Bill," *Los Angeles Times*, July 19, 2002.

2 All are registered as interest groups, although the Hosiery Association recently disbanded. For a complete list, go to https://www.opensecrets.org/industries/alphalist.php and click on the list of industries for the names of specific groups and how much they spent on lobbying activities in 2016.

3 National Milk Producers Federation, http://www.nmpf.org/about-nmpf.

4 H. R. Mahood, *Interest Groups in American National Politics: An Overview* (Upper Saddle River, NJ: Prentice Hall, 2000), 26–28.

5 Kay Lehman Schlozman and John T. Tierney, *Organized Interests and American Democracy* (New York: Harper & Row, 1986), 70.

6 Ibid., 70–71.

7 Mahood, *Interest Groups*, 32–34.

8 Opensecrets.org, at https://www.opensecrets.org/orgs/summary.php?id=D000019798.

9 You can track the issue by going to the American Bar Association website at http://www.abanet.org/poladv/priorities/mpl/. The AMA's side of the story may be found at http://www.ama-assn.org/ama/pub/advocacy/current-topics-advocacy/practice-management/medical-liability-reform.shtml.

10 Opensecrets.org, at http://www.opensecrets.org/pres08.

11 See the AFL-CIO website, at http://www.aflcio.org/aboutus/faq/.

12 Opensecrets.org, at https://www.opensecrets.org/pacs/sector.php?txt=P01&cycle=2016.

13 Mahood, *Interest Groups*, 29–30.

14 Public Citizen has recently been involved in such an action, as you can see by going to its website at http://www.publiccitizen.org/publications/release.cfm?ID=7172.

15 Such an action is ongoing, as you can see by going to the American Civil Liberties Union website at http://www.aclu.org/technology-and-liberty/internet-privacy.

16 Jeffrey M. Berry, *The New Liberalism: The Rising Power of Citizen Groups* (Washington, DC: Brookings Institution Press, 1999), 25–28.

17 Ibid.

18 You can access the Cato Institute at https://www.cato.org/mission.

19 You can access the People for the American Way Foundation website at http://www.pfaw.org/about-us/our-mission-and-vision.

20 You can access the Christian Coalition website at http://www.cc.org/about_us.

21 James L Guth and others, "Thunder on the Right? Religious Interest Group Mobilization in the 1996 Election," in Allan J. Cigler and Burdett A. Loomis, eds., *Interest Group Politics*, 5th ed. (Washington, DC: CQ Press, 1998), 169–192.

22 No, I'm not making this up. See Paul E. Johnson, "Interest Group Recruiting: Finding Members and Keeping Them," in Cigler and Loomis, *Interest Group Politics*, 36.

23 By the way, if you want to seriously consider joining the Sierra Club, you can get more information online at https://sierra.secure.force.com/donate/rc_connect__campaign_designform?id=70131000001LkO5AAK&formcampaignid=70131000001LWbDAAW&gclid=CM2c1PL8ntECFdiLswod7rgEnA#!form=00P3100000SKGDKEA5.

24 Mancur Olson Jr., *The Logic of Collective Action: Public Goods and the Theory of Groups* (Cambridge, MA: Harvard University Press, 1965).

25 Jack Walker, *Mobilizing Interest Groups in America: Patrons, Professions, and Social Movements* (Ann Arbor, MI: University of Michigan Press, 1991).

26 Sierra Club website, at https://secure2.convio.net/sierra/site/Donation2?idb=0&df_id=7040&7040.donation=form1&autologin=true&s_src=J09WOT0400&s_subsrc=JRG.

27 Olson, *Logic of Collective Action*, 75–76.

28 Burdett A. Loomis and Allan J. Cigler, "The Changing Nature of Interest Group Politics," in Cigler and Loomis, eds., *Interest Group Politics*, 5th ed., 12.

29 "AARP Reacts to President's Health Care Townhall," August 11, 2009, at http://www.aarp.org/aarp/presscenter/pressrelease/articles/prez_townhall_reaction.html.

30 Schlozman and Tierney, *Organized Interests*, 150.

31 Bruce C. Wolpe and Bertram J. Levine, *Lobbying Congress: How the System Works*, 2nd ed. (Washington, DC: CQ Press, 1996), 63–64.

32 Beth L. Leech and Frank R. Baumgartner, "Lobbying Friends and Foes in Washington," in Cigler and Loomis, eds., *Interest Group Politics*, 5th ed., 217–233.

33 Ernest Wittenberg and Elisabeth Wittenberg, *How to Win in Washington: Very Practical Advice about Lobbying, the Grassroots, and the Media* (Cambridge, MA: B. Blackwell, 1990), 109–110.

34 Schlozman and Tierney, *Organized Interests*, 150.

35 Ken Kollman, *Outside Lobbying: Public Opinion and Interest Group Strategies* (Princeton, NJ: Princeton University Press, 1998), 109–110.

36 Opensecrets.org, at https://www.opensecrets.org/politicians/summary.php?cid=N00009869&cycle=2016.

37 Kelly Patterson, "The Political Firepower of the National Rifle Association," in Cigler and Loomis, eds., *Interest Group Politics*, 5th ed., 136.

38 Kollman, *Outside Lobbying*, 75.

39 Mahood, *Interest Groups*, 71–77.

40 Opensecrets.org, at http://www.opensecrets.org/pacs/toppacs.php.

41 Opensecrets.org, at https://www.opensecrets.org/pacs/toppacs.php.

42 OpenSecrets.org, at https://www.opensecrets.org/pacs/superpacs.php.

43 Opensecrets.org, at http://www.opensecrets.org/bigpicture/stats.php?cycle=2008&Type=A&Display=T.

44 Thomas B. Edsall, "FEC to Allow 'Soft-Money' Exceptions," *Washington Post*, June 21, 2002, sec. A.

45 *Washington Representatives*, http://www.lobbyists.info/washington-representatives.

46 Mahood, *Interest Groups*, 48–49.

47 Wolpe and Levine, *Lobbying Congress*, 10–11.

48 Mahood, *Interest Groups*, 16–17.

49 OpenSecrets.org, https://www.opensecrets.org/orgs/summary.php?id=D000000104.

50 Mahood, *Interest Groups*, 16–17; and Theodore J. Lowi, *The End of Liberalism: The Second Republic of the United States*, 2nd ed. (New York: Norton, 1979), 57–61 and 310–313.

51 Mahood, *Interest Groups*, 20–21.

52 E. E. Schattschneider, *The Semisovereign People: A Realist's View of Democracy in America* (New York: Holt, Rinehart and Winston, 1960).

53 Burdett A. Loomis and Allan J. Cigler, "The Changing Nature of Interest Group Politics," *Interest Group Politics*, 1–32.

54 Jeffrey H. Birnbaum, *The Money Men: The Real Story of Fund-Raising's Influence on Political Power in America* (New York: Crown Publishers, 2000), xiii, emphasis in original.

55 Ibid., 11.

Table, Figure, and Box Notes

T1 Opensecrets.org, at https://www.opensecrets.org/industries/slist.php.

T2 Opensecrets.org, at https://www.opensecrets.org/industries/slist.php.

T3 You can read more about their position at http://www.nrlc.org/about/mission/.

T4 You can read more about their position at https://www.plannedparenthood.org/about-us/who-we-are/mission.

T5 For a look at the full range of issues on the Public Citizen agenda, go to http://www.publiccitizen.org.

T6 Jeffrey M. Berry: The New Liberalism: *The Rising Power of Citizen Government Groups* (Washington, DC: Brookings Institute Press, 1999), 25–28.

T7 Data from Kay Lehman Schlozman and John T. Tierney, *Organized Interests and American Democracy* (New York: Harper & Row, 1986), 150 (Table 7.1).

T8 Opensecrets.org, at https://www.opensecrets.org/pacs/toppacs.php.

T9 Bruce C. Wolpe and Bertram J. Levine, *Lobbying Congress, How the Systems Works*, 2nd ed. (Washington DC, CQ Press, 1996) 13–19.

T10 Laura R. Woliver, "Abortion Interests: From the Usual Suspects to Expanded Coalitions" in Allan J. Cigler and Burdette A. Loomis, eds., *Internet Group Politics*, 5th ed (Washington, DC: CQ Press, 1998, 327–342).

Congress

Copyright: turtix/Shutterstock.com

Learning Objectives

When you have completed this chapter, you should be able to:

- Discuss how the way congressional districts are drawn can determine who gets elected to Congress.

- Describe the demographic makeup of Congress, and explain how it differs from the population at large.

- Identify key congressional norms, and explain the purpose they serve for the institution.

- Contrast the organization of the House of Representatives with the organization of the Senate.

- Discuss ways in which minority rights are protected by Senate procedure.

- Identify key congressional leadership positions, and explain the role of leadership in Congress.

- Discuss how members of Congress manage their work expectations.

- Explain why members of Congress pay close attention to the votes they cast.

- Speak about the relationship between members of Congress and their constituents.

- Evaluate whether the perks of serving in Congress outweigh the disadvantages.

9.1 Introduction

You don't spend a lot of time thinking about Congress, do you? You're not alone. Many people are capable of having a great day without giving any thought to the workings of Congress, the presidency, the bureaucracy, or the court system. You may well be one of them. However, because we tend not to pay too much attention to our political institutions, it's easy to misinterpret what they do and how they do it.

A place like Congress can seem totally unrelated to our everyday experiences, when, in fact, in many important ways, it's a lot like places that are very familiar to us—your college or university, for instance—filled with people doing their best to find a way to fit in, manage their time amidst great pressure to do way too much, and avoid making mistakes that could hurt their future careers. If this sounds a little bit like some of what you face in school, it's because you have a lot more in common with members of Congress than you probably think.

In the pages ahead, we'll explore some of those similarities. We'll look at who gets to serve in Congress—the people who choose to run in elections and the characteristics of those who win. We'll examine how new members (called freshmen, just like in school) adjust to unfamiliar surroundings. We'll take some time to figure out what members of Congress do: what it means to serve in Congress, to be part of the congressional leadership, and to handle an unbelievable amount of work—way more than anyone can do at any one time (this may sound familiar to you, too). For some members, the work is just too much, and they decide to drop out, despite the thrill and privilege of serving in Washington. We'll figure out why.

When people do take the time to think about Congress—or when pollsters ask them to think about it—responses are typically negative, at least when they think about Congress as a large, disorganized group of 435 representatives and 100 senators. A 2013 survey found Americans hold Congress as an institution in lower regard than cockroaches, colonoscopies and head lice.[1] In another survey taken that same year, 74 percent of those responding wanted to see most congressional representatives defeated in the 2014 election.[2] However, only 38 percent said they wanted to see their own representative defeated.[3] So, when we put a single human face on the institution, we're much more likely to react positively. As we'll see, Congress is a complex and chaotic place, but it can be appreciated as the scene of hundreds of individual human dramas.

9.2 Getting to Congress: Who Wins and Why?

Many things determine the composition of that relatively small group of people who represent us in Congress. Candidates have to be motivated to run. They need to be willing to put everything in their lives on hold for up to a year so they can knock on doors, make phone calls, plead for money, give speeches, eat large quantities of mediocre chicken, and engage in all the campaigning activities we talked about in Chapter 7. Even if potential candidates have the passion to serve, they still may not run if they're not a good match to their district—say, if the candidate is a Democrat in a heavily Republican area.

9.2a Drawing the Lines

L.O. Discuss how the way congressional districts are drawn can determine who gets elected to Congress.

The first step in determining who gets to Congress happens before a single candidate decides to run, when lines are drawn on a map that determine the partisan composition of each district that will send someone to Congress. Congressional districts are drawn every ten years following the release of the decennial census. The Constitution requires that each state have at least one House district, with each district represented by a single member (each state, of course, also has two senators). In states with more than one House district, each district has to include roughly the same number of people.

redistricting: The process by which congressional districts are redrawn every ten years following the release of new census data.

This sounds pretty uninteresting and straightforward, but in fact, the way district lines are drawn can go a long way to determining who gets elected, so the process of **redistricting** is the basis of some pretty intense political battles. For starters, states that

When Incumbents Collide

In California, redistricting forced Representative Howard Berman, the top Democrat on the powerful House Foreign Relations Committee, into the same district as fifteen-year veteran and fellow Democrat Brad Sherman. Though both Democrats, the two faced off in November because of a California law that puts the candidates who poll first and second in the primary on the fall ballot, even if they represent the same party. Absent redistricting, both would have been reelected comfortably. But forced to compete head-to-head, the race between them turned bitter and ugly—to the point where a fistfight nearly broke out between them during a debate.[T1]

The two representatives were quite different in substance and style. With his important committee assignment and the backing of high-ranking fellow Democrats, Berman could present himself as a national figure with influence over significant policy discussions. Sherman, on the other hand, was less the team player in Washington and more attuned to parochial matters of concern to his Southern California constituents.[T2] In the end, constituent service beat out national endorsements: Sherman defeated Berman, ending the congressional career of one of the House's more senior members.

gain or lose large numbers of residents in the ten years since the previous census may gain or lose congressional seats.[4] Other states may see significant shifts in their populations, like from cities to suburbs. New lines need to be drawn to reflect these changes, a process that can lead to redrawing the boundaries of many or all previous districts.

If redistricting were a neutral exercise, it would be pretty dull, but it can be a highly political process when performed by officials with an interest in stacking the deck in favor of their party. District lines can be drawn in lots of ways to satisfy the population requirement, and the governors and legislators who are responsible for redistricting in many states look for the best ways to divide the opposition while maximizing their electoral prospects.

Redistricting is a complex process that takes place in several rounds and draws a lot of attention from interested parties. Because of federalism, each state has its own procedures for redistricting. A few rely on nonpartisan boards to draw the lines, but most commonly, the governor and state legislators draw district boundaries. Because of the stakes, interest groups may get into the act and lobby for boundaries that will help sympathetic candidates. Often, the courts have the final say, either because the governor and legislators couldn't arrive at a plan or because there's a question about the legality of the new districts. It's not uncommon for the courts to completely overturn the work of the legislature. It's also not impossible for a group challenging a redistricting plan to seek relief in a court that's historically supportive of their position.[5]

When states lose House seats, unless an incumbent retires, it's inevitable that two incumbents are going to be thrown together in a newly redrawn district, forced to fight against each other for their political lives. Depending on which party has the political advantage in drawing the new districts, incumbents of the same party could be forced to battle it out in a primary, or incumbents of different parties could be pitted against each other in the general election. In 2012, we saw both types of spectacles, and it got ugly. (See Demystifying Government: When Incumbents Collide.) Because (as we'll see) incumbents can generally depend on an easy ride back to Congress, redistricting can cause a sudden and unexpected end to a House career.

9.2b It Looks Like Some Kind of Serpent

When the dust settled on the 2012 election, Democrats found themselves once again in control of the White House and Senate and with a commanding lead of 1.3 million votes in the aggregate vote for the House of Representatives. But Republicans maintained control of the House chamber because of how those House votes were distributed—the first time in sixteen years that a party held the House while losing the combined popular House vote. The reason rests with where Republican and Democratic voters live and how congressional

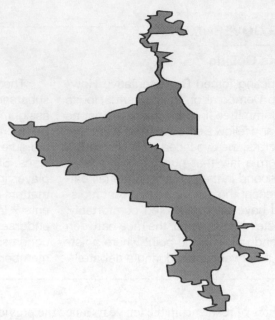

FIGURE 9.1 Is It a Serpent?

Actually, it's a congressional district. Specifically, it's Florida's Third Congressional District, stretching through parts of nine counties, in some cases not much wider than a highway. But it sure looks like a serpent.

district lines in some states were drawn around them.[6] With Democratic voters concentrated in urban areas, it's possible to draw boundaries that cluster those voters into a few districts while creating a far larger number of districts that favor Republicans. All that's needed to do this is partisan control of the line-drawing machinery. Republicans in states like Pennsylvania, Ohio, Wisconsin, Michigan, and North Carolina had this control after big statewide victories in 2010 left them in charge of governorships and state legislatures at the time when redistricting was constitutionally mandated following the 2010 census. So, in Pennsylvania, a state President Obama carried by a comfortable five points, Republicans won thirteen of eighteen congressional districts. In Ohio, which Obama won by two points, Republicans managed wins in twelve of the state's sixteen districts.[7] Because of how district lines were drawn, it took twice as many votes to elect a Democrat to the House in Michigan than it took to elect a Republican. In North Carolina, the ratio was over 3:1.[8]

Sometimes partisan state legislators go out of their way to construct districts shaped like the one in Figure 9.1 in order to give one party a distinct edge, pulling voters from small enclaves of partisan supporters and allowing district lines to meander over a wide range of territory in the most unlikely fashion. It's called **gerrymandering**, and it's an age-old political practice that predates the actions of nineteenth-century Massachusetts Governor Elbridge Gerry, who in 1811 signed off on a salamander-shaped district (hence the name gerrymander) designed to be a safe haven for Jeffersonian Democrats. Does it work? A case can be made that strong candidates from the disadvantaged party are discouraged from running in gerrymandered districts.[9] Certainly, partisans continue the practice because they believe it gives them an edge. For the better part of a decade, Republicans at the federal and state levels have benefitted from gerrymandered districts in states where Republicans controlled the redistricting process in 2010.

Since 1990, some states have engaged in the controversial practice of **racial gerrymandering**, drawing district lines that group together far-flung populations of African American or Hispanic voters for the purpose of assuring representation for these groups. The effort began in response to language added to the Voting Rights Act in 1982 prohibiting states from diluting the voting power of racial minorities, which was interpreted broadly in some states as a green light to gerrymander in order to bolster the influence of minorities.

gerrymandering: Drawing district lines in a way that favors the electoral prospects of the party in power.

racial gerrymandering: Drawing district lines in a way that combines disparate populations of minority groups in order to guarantee representation by those groups in Congress.

The effects of racial gerrymandering cut two ways. Although the districts it created sent generally liberal African American and Hispanic representatives to Congress, neighboring districts that lost these voters became more conservative. In 1992, seven districts represented by Democrats lost at least 10 percent of their African American constituents to racial gerrymandering. By 1996, all seven were represented by Republicans—enough to help Republicans hold the majority in Congress.[10] Ironically, a procedure designed to enhance minority representation in Congress had the effect of diluting minority influence because, as we will see, influence in Congress flows to those in the majority.

Because it's so controversial, racial gerrymandering has been the subject of court challenges. A divided Supreme Court has voted to curtail the process on multiple occasions, overturning some of the more far-reaching districts on the grounds that they represented an effort to segregate voters.[11] By the end of the 1990s, a number of states reacted to the Court's position by redrawing the boundaries of racially gerrymandered districts to reduce the concentration of minority voters.

9.2c Who Runs for Congress—And Who Makes It?

Against this backdrop of partisan maneuvering over district boundaries, a potential candidate needs to take a good, long look in the mirror before embarking on an expensive and time-consuming public campaign that could easily come to nothing. If you were thinking of running, you'd want to take a look at who lives in the district and assess how closely your background and political views match your would-be **constituents**. You would also need to make sure the timing is right for a run, especially if you have to abandon a lower office where you could probably win reelection.

A big part of this calculation involves whether or not you will have to face an **incumbent**. Challengers don't like to face incumbents, and for a good reason. With the contacts they have and with their ability to raise large sums of money, incumbents are hard to topple. Since World War II, better than nine in ten incumbent representatives and almost eight in ten incumbent senators seeking reelection have been victorious. Incumbents may play to their strength by raising large sums of money in an effort to scare off strong competition,[12] and the strategy is likely to work, unless the nation is going through an economic downturn or experiencing a moment when voters are unhappy with the status quo (as they have been a lot since 2006).

Some candidates are self-starters who make the judgment to run on their own, although to have a chance at success it helps if they have a high level of **name recognition** from a previous job. This favors amateurs who've previously worked as television commentators, actors, athletes, or at other high-visibility jobs. Many candidates are encouraged to run by political party operatives, who (as we mentioned in Chapter 6) engage in candidate recruitment as one of the formal functions of political parties.

As a constitutional requirement, you have to be at least twenty-five to serve in the House of Representatives, a resident of the state from which you're seeking election, and an American citizen for seven years. You don't have to live in the district you represent as long as you live in the same state, although as a practical matter, it's bad politics to ask people to vote for you when you live somewhere else. To be a senator, you have to be at least thirty and an American citizen for nine years.

On paper, this appears to open membership in Congress to most of us (at least in a few years). However, with the emphasis on wealth and popularity in candidate recruitment, it shouldn't be too surprising that Congress is far from a mirror of American society. (See Demystifying Government: Changes to the All-Male Club.) What may be surprising is how different it is from the country as a whole on such things as occupation, education, religion, race, and gender. Remember our earlier discussion about **pluralism** and **elitism**? When it comes to the characteristics of congressional members, background similarities favor some groups over others, even though Congress is a less homogeneous place than it was when you were born. Check out Figure 9.2 for some demographics on the 115th Congress that convened in 2017.

L.O. Describe the demographic makeup of Congress, and explain how it differs from the population at large.

constituents: Individuals living in a district represented by an elected official.

incumbent: An official presently serving in office.

name recognition: An informal measure of how much the public is aware of a candidate or elected official, based on how widely people are able to identify the candidate or official.

pluralism: The theory that government responds to individuals through their memberships in groups, assuring that government is responsive to a wide range of voices. People who subscribe to this position believe that the wide distribution of resources in society drives the decisions government officials make.

elitism: The theory that government responds to a small, stable, centralized hierarchy of corporate and academic leaders, military chiefs, people who own big media outlets, and members of a permanent government bureaucracy. People who subscribe to this position believe the actions of regular citizens, like voting and joining groups, simply mask the real power exercised by elites.

...nber of women were
...ress dubbed the "Year
...ough the vast majority
...een a notable female
...viously functioned as

...akers has made some
...ss. Legislative matters
..."women's issues," like family leave
during pregnancy and illness, funding for breast cancer
research, and workplace discrimination, have found their
way onto the agenda.[T3] Some have made it into law.

It takes time to accumulate power in Congress, and
more than a decade later, some women were beginning
to do just that. In 2001, Representative Nancy Pelosi became the first woman elected to a leadership position in
Congress when she was chosen to be the House Democratic whip; one year later, she became House Democratic leader. And in 2007, she became the first female
Speaker of the House, a job she held for four years.

As in any institution, though, change can be slow
and those who are there at the start can find it frustrating. Marjorie Margolies-Mezvinsky, a member of

the Class of 1992, stated that she and her female colleagues suffered indignities from congressional workers and some male members who treated them as
second-class citizens. She recalls an experience she
had during a presidential State of the Union Address
to a joint session of Congress, which she felt provided
a good measure of how far women in Congress had
come—and how far they still had to go:

> I remember sitting with my colleagues, looking
> around at all 435 of us. The women stood out in a
> truly dramatic fashion, and I thought, my gosh, peo-
> ple are going to turn on the tube tonight and see us
> and they're going to realize that the rest of the nation
> has begun to inch itself into this body. I was sitting
> next to North Carolina Democrat Martin Lancaster,
> who was trying to point out somebody on the other
> side of the aisle, and he said, "He's the guy with
> the receding hairline, gray hair." And I said, laugh-
> ing, "You've eliminated nobody!" My point is that the
> people who have always been outside of the sys-
> tem are now beginning to infiltrate it. There aren't
> enough of us, but we're working on it—all the time.[T4]

FIGURE 9.2 Who Gets to Serve?[T5]

Gender	Once a nearly exclusive male club, Congress has seen an influx of women in recent years. Still, at about one-fifth the membership of the House and Senate, women are well under-represented with respect to the population.
Race	Even with advances by minority groups in recent years, the 115th Congress is still overwhelmingly white. Of the 535 members of the House and Senate, 49 are African American, 38 are Hispanic, and 15 are Asian American.
Occupation	Not too many organizations can claim that almost 40 percent of its members are lawyers (apart from law firms, of course), but that's the case in Congress, where lawyers and business people far outnumber all other professionals. Remember when we said celebrities make good candidates? Recent Congresses have included several astronauts, including former Senator John Glenn; former football players like Representative Steve Largent; former baseball players like Jim Bunning, who once pitched a perfect game in the major leagues; and comedian Al Franken, best known for his work on "Saturday Night Live."
Sexual Orientation	There are seven openly gay members of Congress, all Democrats, including Tammy Baldwin of Wisconsin, the first openly gay or lesbian person to serve in the Senate.
Religion	Congress is an overwhelmingly Christian place where almost everyone has a religious affiliation. The 115th Congress includes thirty Jewish members, four Hindus, three Buddhists, and two Muslims.

substantive representation:
The ability of a legislator to
represent the agenda or interests of a group to which he or
she does not personally belong.

So, what of these apparent inequities between congressional members and the populations they represent? If Congress is largely a professional, white, male, straight, and Protestant bastion, can it function as a representative institution? The answer depends on how
we look at the idea of representation. As a descriptive matter, the answer would have to
be no because the congressional class picture doesn't look very much like the portrait of
America. As a substantive matter, the answer could still be yes. To engage in **substantive
representation**, a member of Congress has to be able to act in the interests of groups to

which he or she does not belong. If you believe that a white representative can promote the interests of African Americans or Latinos, that a male representative can advance the agenda of women's groups, or that a college-educated lawyer can advocate the concerns of blue-collar workers, then you may be able to make the case for Congress as a representative institution, despite the fact that it draws its members from a nonrepresentative elite group of Americans.[13]

9.3 Adjusting to Congress

L.O. Identify key congressional norms, and explain the purpose they serve for the institution.

Think back for a minute to college orientation, to what it felt like to be in a new place surrounded by new people. Maybe you traveled far from home, and everything looked new. Maybe you're a commuter, or going to a local school, and you had to confront new ways of doing things and new people as you made the transition from high school to college. Remember how you felt? Many people experience moments of frustration or confusion, even sadness or homesickness, during those first crazy days of college. You want to fit in, but everything is new, and you're not always sure how to do it.

As distant and remote as Congress may seem, new members are human and experience many of the same feelings. No place can compare with Congress (just like nothing exactly compares with college), so arriving there several months after experiencing the thrill of being elected (much like arriving at school several months after the excitement of getting that acceptance letter) can leave a person bewildered.

One member relates the story of getting to her new office to find it unfurnished. She was advised by a senior member to roam through the office building corridors looking for discarded furniture. So, she did, furnishing her office with stuff other people had cast off, not unlike the way some people furnish an off-campus apartment.[14]

One way we try to fit into a new place, be it college or Congress, is by learning the ways of the institution, the **norms** people live by as they try to get along with each other. Norms are unspoken and unwritten rules of behavior. No one has to teach us about them—we observe norms and internalize them, and if we violate them, we'll probably hear about it from a friend or from someone in a position of authority. For instance, it may be okay for you to get a visit from a friend at midnight while you're living at school. The norm for late-night visits when you're back at home with your parents over the summer could be something quite different. No one has to tell you this—you know what's going on— although your parents probably will say something if you violate the norm.

norms: Unspoken rules of behavior that people adhere to in an institution like Congress that allow people to fit in and help the institution run smoothly.

Norms help people ease into a new institution, but they also serve the institution by helping it run more smoothly. Many people don't get to choose their first-year roommate, and sometimes, things don't work out too smoothly, but by observing the norms for good roommate behavior, you can make the best of a bad situation. In much the same way, members of Congress do not get to choose their colleagues—voters in other districts do— but they have to find a way to work together. Norms help smooth the way for members who might not choose each other as colleagues if they had the option.

The five norms in Table 9.1 have existed in Congress for decades. Take a look at the table for a definition of each norm and an explanation of how it benefits members of Congress.

The last norm you looked at—reciprocity—can assume a couple of specific forms. The example in the table, where members trade support for each other's pet projects, is called **logrolling**, evoking the kind of cooperation people exhibit when they stand on a log and try to roll it down a river.[15] Logrolling helps members get the kind of projects for their home districts that constituents love—and that can only help their reelection prospects—although as Demystifying Government: The Golden Fleece points out, it's often the case that one member's beneficial project is a case of wasteful spending to those in other districts who do not benefit.

logrolling: A form of reciprocity in which members of Congress exhibit mutual cooperation for each other's pet projects.

compromise: A form of reciprocity in which members of Congress exhibit flexibility over their legislative objectives in exchange for future flexibility from their colleagues.

Reciprocity can also be expressed through **compromise**, or flexibility, over an issue that a member may feel strongly about—like the wording of legislation. Since what goes around comes around, members have an investment in compromising with each other, with the expectation that at some later time, others will offer the same courtesy to them.

TABLE 9.1 Congressional Norms

Norm	Definition	Example	Benefit
Specialization	**specialization:** The legislative norm that members of Congress should become experts in a legislative field.	Becoming an expert on global warming	Congress addresses a range of complex issues and needs members' expertise to handle them intelligently.
Legislative Work	**legislative work:** The legislative norm that members of Congress should stay on top of the work required by the committee that deals with their area of specialization.	A subcommittee chairman being prepared for a hearing	If some members are not prepared, the burden of their negligence is passed to other members.
Courtesy	**courtesy:** The legislative norm that members of Congress should treat each other with respect and avoid personal attacks, regardless of how much they may disagree.	Referring to a member you may personally dislike as "honorable" or "distinguished" during floor debate	Kind words cool the heat of conflict and keep debate moving forward.
Institutional Patriotism	**institutional patriotism:** The legislative norm that precludes members of Congress from acting or speaking in ways that would discredit the institution.	Avoiding getting entangled in a bribery scheme	Discredit brought upon the institution undermines every member's base of power.
Reciprocity	**reciprocity:** The legislative norm that encourages members of Congress to support each other's initiatives, even if there is no direct political benefit in doing so.	An urban senator voting for crop subsidies in return for a rural senator supporting mass transit aid	When everyone reciprocates, everybody benefits; if no one reciprocated, no one would benefit.

integrity: A key component of reciprocity in which members of Congress are expected to keep their word with each other and honor their commitments.

The same is true with **integrity**, which is a critical component of reciprocity. You probably know from personal experience how you feel about a friend who promises something and doesn't deliver. As one member put it, "You don't have to make these commitments [to other members], . . . but if you do make them, you had better live up to them."[16]

Remember, norms are enforced by the people in the institution, and stay in effect because the institution benefits along with its members. So, specialization is held in place by virtue of the tremendous amount of detailed work that Congress has to handle and the fact that it's in everybody's interest for the work to get done, which can best be accomplished if every member contributes. Likewise, the norm of doing legislative work is held in place by the fact that everyone benefits if everyone does a small share of the heavy lifting. If you've ever been in a group project where not everyone contributed equally (but everyone was in the same boat when it came to getting graded), you can probably appreciate how easily resentment could be generated toward those who did less work. Since congressional legislative work is like a big group project, specialization keeps the institution moving forward while minimizing those resentful feelings.

Of course, if norms no longer benefit those involved, they can evolve out of existence. One norm that's not in Table 9.1 is **apprenticeship**, even though it was a hallmark of how Congress did business for the better part of the twentieth century. Freshmen members were expected to refrain from voicing their opinions in committees, introducing legislation, or drawing attention to themselves as they learned the ropes from senior members and acclimated to the ways of Congress. Apprenticeship maintained institutional stability and was a great way for new members to learn other norms.

apprenticeship: The legislative norm that says freshmen members of Congress should limit their activity and defer to senior members as they learn the ways of the institution. Apprenticeship is no longer enforced in Congress.

If you happen to be a freshman, you probably don't think much of a norm that has you speaking only when you're spoken to and holding back on what you came to Congress to accomplish. If you had a large enough group of like-minded peers, you might want to do something about it.

That's essentially what happened to apprenticeship in Congress. In 1974, in the wake of the Watergate scandal that rocked the Nixon administration, a huge freshman class of 103 young, reform-minded newcomers was elected to Congress. They felt they had a mandate to change things in Washington, and they weren't about to be quiet or wait their turn. Backed by the strength of their large numbers, they fashioned themselves as a new type of member, more entrepreneurial and outspoken, as they brushed aside apprenticeship as an antiquated norm.[17]

In recent years, a decline in the number of members with long institutional memories and an increase in partisan sentiment have continued to change the ways of Congress and strain some of the other norms. Members have become more media-savvy and self-promotional; some (especially in the Senate) devote great energy to positioning themselves to run for president. In the process, they may be absent from Congress more than in the past, and fail to keep up with their legislative work the way you may at times let extracurricular activities cut into the time you devote to your homework.[18]

There have also been testy moments between the two parties reflecting the divisions we see in popular opinion about the direction of the country, and as partisanship produces tension in Congress, norms that for years have worked to the benefit of the institution come under pressure. For instance, in 2016, a group of 170 Democratic members staged a sit-in on the floor of the House to protest inaction on gun control legislation, faulting Republican leaders for not permitting a vote on legislation requiring background checks for gun purchases. The sit-in represented a dramatic departure from the decorum normally exhibited by members, violating the norm of courtesy. Republicans reacted angrily and tried to end the sit-in by rapidly adjourning Congress. House Speaker Paul Ryan accused Democrats of causing "chaos" in his chamber.[19]

pork barrel: Wasteful or unnecessary spending that can result from logrolling. Whether something is a pork-barrel project or a valuable use of taxpayer dollars may depend on whether you stand to benefit from it.

9.4 Serving in Congress: How Congress Works

New members of Congress arrive at an institution that's been shaped by centuries of history, but the broad contours of what Congress does—and what members are expected to do in Congress—can be traced to the parameters established in the Constitution.

Article I of the Constitution establishes a **bicameral** legislature with a House of Representatives (created in Section 2) and a Senate (created in Section 3) as the two branches. As constitutional articles go, it's pretty long because it takes great pains to spell out exactly what the Congress would do. The powers specifically granted to the House and Senate are

L.O. Contrast the organization of the House of Representatives with the organization of the Senate.

bicameral: A legislature composed of two houses.

enumerated powers: Powers directly granted to Congress by the Constitution.

called **enumerated powers**, and they go well beyond what the national legislature could do under the Articles of Confederation.

Enumerated powers include the power to tax, with all revenue bills required to originate in the House of Representatives, the body designed to be closer to the people. Other important enumerated powers include the ability to regulate commerce among the states and with other nations, coin money, raise a military, declare war, establish post offices and roads, and create a court system below the Supreme Court (which is itself established by the Constitution).

Then Article I gives Congress the ability "To make all Laws which shall be necessary and proper for carrying into Execution the foregoing Powers, and all other Powers vested by this Constitution in the Government of the United States, or in any Department or Officer thereof." This "necessary and proper" clause has been interpreted over the years as a broad grant of **implied powers**, which has allowed Congress to consider matters that could not have been anticipated by the Constitution's authors.

implied powers: The broad constitutional grant of power to Congress that allows it to make all the laws that are "necessary and proper" to carry out its enumerated functions.

Despite going into detail on a range of congressional responsibilities, the Constitution leaves it up to each house to determine how it's going to put into place the procedures to do its job. The Constitution dictates that a majority of members of a house is required to form a quorum (which is the number of members required for a legislative body to meet and do business) and that each house has to keep a record of its public votes and proceedings, but it leaves to each house the ability to determine how to do business. As a consequence, the two houses operate under different sets of rules.

standing committees: Permanent congressional committees that handle matters related to a specific legislative topic.

subcommittees: Subunits of standing committees that do the detail work involved in writing legislation.

iron triangle: The ongoing, mutually beneficial relationship among an interest group, members of Congress sharing the interest group's objectives, and bureaucrats in federal agencies responsible for carrying out legislation pertaining to the interest group's field. Iron triangles can develop in any policy area, and many distinct iron-triangle relationships form because the federal government is responsible for a large number of policies.

9.4a How the House Works

In a simpler time, the first Congresses (see Demystifying Government: How Congresses Get Their Numbers) debated important matters as a group, and if legislation was deemed appropriate, a committee was established to discuss the nuts and bolts. However, it didn't take long before the need to process a growing workload led to the establishment of permanent or **standing committees**, which were organized to deal with ongoing matters like budgetary or military concerns. By the 1820s, standing committees would debate legislation before it was brought before the full House.

Because most legislation needs to go through the committee process to make it to the floor for a vote, many of the thousands of proposals introduced each session for consideration never get a hearing and simply die on the vine. The few proposals that make it to committee are typically sent to one or more **subcommittees** of the standing committee. The detail work of legislating takes place in subcommittees, which are specialized units suited to ongoing relationships with interest groups of the sort we talked about in Chapter 8 when we discussed **iron triangles**. Together, twenty-one standing House committees support 100 subcommittees, each with its own chairperson and agenda (the Senate's six-

---

DEMYSTIFYING GOVERNMENT

How Congresses Get Their Numbers

Maybe the phrase "the first Congresses" in the first paragraph of Section 9.4a sounded a little funny to you. If it did, it's because you're probably used to thinking of Congress as a singular (albeit bicameral) entity. It is, of course, but when we talk historically about Congress, we classify each group that serves together as "a Congress," and we give it a number.

So, the First Congress served from 1789–1791, with the first year constituting the first "session" of the First Congress and the second year constituting the second session. Why two years? That's the stretch between congressional elections. The entire House of Representatives is up for election every two years (a short period designed to keep representatives responsive to public opinion). One-third of the Senate is also up for election every two years (a full Senate term is six years). When they reconvene in January following the election, the new collection of members—the "new Congress"—gets a new number.

The 115th Congress was elected in November 2016 and sworn in on January 3, 2017, to serve until January 2019.

TABLE 9.2 House Committees and Subcommittees, 2016[T6]

Committee	Members	Subcommittees
Agriculture	45	6
Appropriations	51	12
Armed Services	61	7
Budget	36	0
Education and the Workforce	38	4
Energy and Commerce	54	6
Ethics	10	0
Financial Services	59	6
Foreign Affairs	42	6
Homeland Security	30	6
House Administration	9	0
Intelligence	22	4
Judiciary	39	3
Natural Resources	43	5
Oversight and Government Reform	42	7
Rules	13	2
Science, Space, and Technology	39	5
Small Business	22	5
Transportation and Infrastructure	59	6
Veterans' Affairs	24	4
Ways and Means	39	6

teen standing committees support seventy-four subcommittees). Table 9.2 lists the names of the standing committees of the House, along with the number of House members serving on the committee and the number of subcommittees each committee had in 2016 (the names and sizes of committees and subcommittees will vary slightly from Congress to Congress). Notice how some of these committees have more people in them than an upper-division political science class!

If a bill fails to clear a subcommittee, it dies; otherwise, it's sent back to the full committee where it can again die if it fails to win passage. Even if it wins full committee approval, it's not out of the woods yet. That's because the House places restrictions on the terms of debate and on what bills get to move to the floor for final consideration. As with the development of standing committees, House rules on debate evolved over the years. Initially, House debate was fluid and unlimited. As the House grew in size and legislation grew in complexity, the House began placing limits on how long members could speak, and procedures were instituted to control the flow of legislation.

In the late nineteenth century, the House established a process by which legislation would be channeled from standing committees through a **Rules Committee** before it

Rules Committee: The committee of the House that channels legislation to the floor for debate and a vote on passage.

could come to the floor for debate and a vote. Despite the fact that a standing committee may have worked for months or longer on legislation, if it failed to be assigned a "rule" from the Rules Committee, it would simply disappear from legislative consideration. If the Rules Committee decides to assign a rule and bring a measure to the floor, it can set the terms of the debate, including whether amendments can be offered that would change the bill. If a bill is brought to the floor with a rule that prohibits amendments, then members have only the choice to vote the bill up or down as it's written. This gives the Rules Committee—and the political party controlling it—enormous power to set the terms of the House agenda.[20]

select committee: A House or Senate committee established on a temporary basis to review a specific matter. Typically, select committees make recommendations but do not move legislation.

If an issue lends itself to short-term review, the House may establish a **select committee** (also called a special committee) to investigate. Senate rules permit the establishment of select committees as well. Select committees are established for one congressional session and then expire. Instead of reporting bills like a standing committee, they usually review a matter and make recommendations for action. For instance, the Senate Select Committee on Ethics investigates alleged rules violations against senators or staffers and, pending their investigation, recommends disciplinary action if deemed appropriate.[21] In 2014, the House established a select committee to investigate the official response to attacks against U.S. personnel that took place in Benghazi, Libya, on September 11, 2012.[22]

A member introduces legislation in the House by literally dropping it in a wooden box at the front of the chamber. Any member can do it for any reason—to advance a personal priority or the priorities of constituents or interest groups. At that point, the bill is referred to a committee or, in some cases, multiple committees that have jurisdiction over the content of the proposal. For most bills, that's the end of the line. A select few undergo the generally slow process of moving through subcommittee, where hearings are held that shape the content of the emerging bill or determine whether it will ever come to a committee vote.

These are the textbook procedures for moving legislation through Congress and, well, this is a textbook, so what better place than here to describe it? Not every bill travels that route, however. There are House procedures that allow the leadership to circumvent the committee process entirely, which they may do in politically sensitive situations. It happened in 1996, when House Republican leaders moved a last-minute budget resolution directly to a floor vote following an unsuccessful confrontation with President Clinton over spending priorities. There's also a procedure called a **discharge petition**, which, if signed by half the membership (218 representatives), plucks a bill from committee and brings it to the House floor for a vote. It's usually very difficult to get half the House to go along with a discharge petition. In 2012, Minority Leader Nancy Pelosi tried to use a discharge petition to force a floor vote on a Senate-approved bill to lock in Bush-era tax rates for income under $250,000 a year but couldn't find Republicans willing to buck their leadership and go along. Reluctance to disobey the wishes of party leaders makes it unlikely for discharge petitions to succeed, but they can in rare cases—like in 2001, when supporters of campaign finance reform forced a vote on the campaign reform bill that would eventually become the McCain-Feingold Act.[23]

discharge petition: A House procedure that forces a floor vote on legislation stalled in committee. To succeed, a discharge petition must be signed by half the House membership.

filibuster: The strategy available to senators to delay or derail legislation by refusing to relinquish their time on the Senate floor. The filibuster is possible only in the Senate, where rules permit unlimited time for debate.

9.4b How the Senate Works

L.O. Discuss ways in which minority rights are protected by Senate procedure.

The early Senate operated like the early House, first as a deliberative body then through the work of standing committees. Owing to its smaller size, it never faced quite the same pressures as the House to limit debate or control the flow of legislation. So, the Senate doesn't channel legislation through a Rules Committee, and senators maintain the privilege of unlimited debate time. This gives each senator a legislative weapon not available to their House colleagues: the **filibuster**, or the ability to prevent a measure from coming to a vote by refusing to consent to end the debate. A filibuster can only be ended by a vote of **cloture**, which requires a supermajority of three-fifths, or 60 percent of the Senate to enact. This means a minority of 41 senators can block a bill if they stick together and refuse to support cloture. The filibuster can be a powerful procedure in the hands of a determined Senate minority—and a tool of last resort for outnumbered senators—

cloture: The procedure for ending a filibuster. A cloture vote requires a 60 percent majority of the Senate.

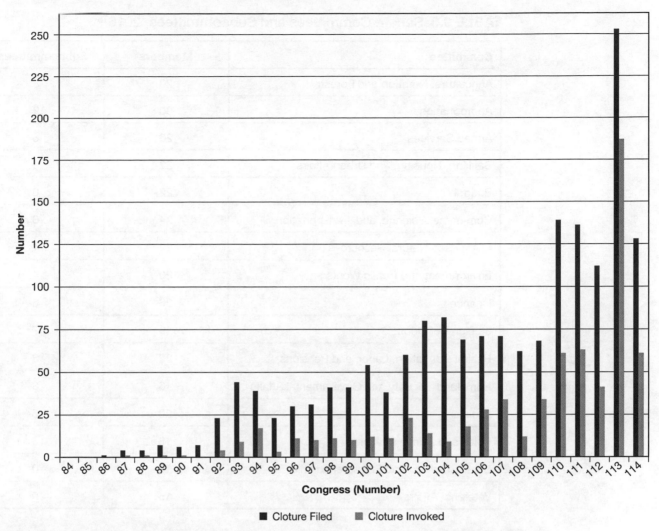

Number

Congress (Number)

■ Cloture Filed ■ Cloture Invoked

FIGURE 9.3 Explosion of the Filibuster, 84th through 114th Congress (1955–2017)[T7]

because it gives a minority of the Senate the opportunity to delay or prevent legislation they oppose despite the presence of majority support.

Although the picture of a senator stalling the chamber by reading from a telephone book or talking about his or her grandchildren may seem funny (and, yes, it's really happened), in recent years, filibusters have been sustained simply through the failure of cloture votes. This has coincided with an explosion of filibusters, as Figure 9.3 attests. The darker bars indicate the number of cloture motions filed to end filibusters, and the lighter bars indicate the number of those motions that succeeded.

Through the 1950s and 1960s, the filibuster was used strategically and selectively. It was a favorite tool of conservative senators opposed to civil rights legislation. A seventy-four-day filibuster delayed the landmark Civil Rights Act of 1964 from coming to a vote, and South Carolina Senator Strom Thurmond personally held the Senate floor for over twenty-four hours (a Senate record) in an unsuccessful effort to block the earlier Civil Rights Act of 1957.[24]

The routine use of the filibuster in recent years reflects entrenched partisan sentiment in the Senate. Notice the outsized darker bars on the right of Figure 9.3 corresponding to the 111th through 114th Congresses (2009–2017), where legislation routinely faced blocking tactics, for the first six years by a Republican minority that saw the filibuster as an effective way to slow or stop the Obama administration's agenda, then by minority Democrats seeking to keep the Republican Congress in check. That's why when President Obama and Senate Democratic leaders plotted strategy to reform the health-care system in 2009, their working assumption was that they would need 60 votes to pass anything in the

TABLE 9.3 Senate Committees and Subcommittees, 2016[T8]

Committee	Members	Subcommittees
Agriculture, Nutrition and Forestry	20	5
Appropriations	30	12
Armed Services	26	6
Banking, Housing, and Urban Affairs	22	5
Budget	22	0
Commerce, Science, and Transportation	24	6
Energy and Natural Resources	22	4
Environment and Public Works	20	4
Finance	26	6
Foreign Relations	19	7
Health, Education, Labor, and Pensions	22	3
Homeland Security and Governmental Affairs	16	3
Judiciary	20	6
Rules and Administration	18	0
Small Business and Entrepreneurship	19	0
Veterans' Affairs	15	0

Senate, because the Republican minority was unanimous in its opposition to Democratic proposals and planned to use the filibuster to stop them. And, it's why progressives in the Senate Democratic caucus agitated for filibuster reform prior to the start of the 113th Congress—with some success, as Democrats removed the supermajority requirement for confirming executive and judicial nominees (excluding nominees to the Supreme Court).

Apart from the protection of minority rights, the Senate operates much like the House. The standing committee, subcommittee, and select committee structure is the same, although with fewer members, there are more committee and subcommittee leadership opportunities. Virtually every senator has a leadership role somewhere, even newly elected senators. Table 9.3 lists the names of the standing committees of the Senate, the number of senators serving on each committee, and the number of subcommittees associated with each committee in 2016. Notice how much overlap there is between House and Senate committees, even though each house organizes its standing committees independently.

In some cases, the House and Senate establish **joint committees** to commonly investigate or study a matter that concerns both houses. Much of what joint committees do is routine and detailed. For instance, the Joint Taxation Committee pools House and Senate staff to help with the technical details of writing tax legislation.[25]

In an entirely different context, the two houses of Congress will form conference committees when they pass different versions of the same legislation. The Constitution requires that the House and Senate pass identical legislation before it's sent to the president for consideration, but it's probably easy to see how that's not likely to happen when legislation has to pass separately through the network of rules and committees in each house. So, when both houses pass their own version of a bill, they form a **conference committee** made of up of representatives and senators that tries to hammer out differ-

joint committees: Committees composed of members of the House and Senate that consider matters of interest to both houses.

conference committees: Committees made up of members of both houses of Congress, assembled when the House and Senate pass different versions of the same legislation. If the conference committee can iron out the differences, a compromise version of the legislation is sent back to both houses for final passage. If it cannot arrive at a compromise, the legislation dies.

ences between the two versions of the legislation, writing compromise language that committee members believe will be acceptable to majorities in both chambers. If they fail to do so, the legislation dies. If they succeed, the bill they produce still has to be approved by both houses.

Introducing a bill in the Senate works pretty much the way it does in the House. However, because the Senate is less formal and "clubbier" than the House, individual senators have more range to influence the path of legislation. In contrast to the formal discharge petition required by the House to bypass the committee process and bring a bill to a floor vote, any senator can request that a bill go directly to the floor (in reality, though, a senator would need the support of the Senate leadership to be successful). Because the Senate doesn't use a Rules Committee to prohibit a bill from being modified during floor debate, any senator can introduce an amendment to a bill being debated on the floor—forcing the Senate to act on the amendment even if it has nothing to do with the legislation being discussed. This privilege effectively circumvents the committee process. If a senator wishes to introduce a civil rights amendment to a bill on veteran's benefits, the rules allow it.[26]

Figure 9.4 provides an overview of the whole process of how a bill becomes law. Despite procedural differences between the two houses, notice the parallel structures in place between the House and the Senate for considering legislation. Notice, also, how each step in the process provides opponents with an opportunity to derail legislation. When you think for a second about all the places where proposals can die, it's not surprising that thousands of proposals flood into Congress but only a handful become law.

9.5 Serving in Congress: What Congress Does

As the legislative branch of government, Congress has its hands in the development of both domestic and foreign policy. Of course, power is separated among the branches of the federal government, so Congress is continually engaged in a push-pull relationship with the president, sometimes spearheading the national agenda and sometimes following the president's lead. Generally speaking, Congress is more assertive about domestic issues and follows presidential leadership in foreign affairs.

Every president comes to office with a domestic policy agenda—President Trump, for instance, wanted to cut taxes and boost infrastructure spending—but members of Congress can be fairly vocal about putting their imprint on the president's ideas, rejecting the president's agenda, or advancing an agenda that's entirely different than the president's. This may be an issue at times in the Trump administration because the president ran against the Republican establishment as much as he ran against Hillary Clinton, and his populist ideas can be at odds with policies congressional Republicans have supported over the years on key issues such as trade. During his transition, the new president indicated through his words and cabinet appointments that he would be open to supporting traditional Republican economic ideas, but it remains to be seen how President Trump plans to reconcile differences between his campaign promises and the long-standing policy aspirations of his legislative party.

Even when the president wants to work with a Congress of his own party, shared party affiliation is not a guarantee of success, as we noted in Chapter 6. President Clinton failed to marshal support for the largest initiative of his first term—an overhaul of the health-care system—despite having party control of both houses of Congress. It was sixteen years before another president would try again, and even though President Obama's Democrats also controlled both houses of Congress, he, too, found it difficult to broker agreement around any one approach to health-care reform.

When Congress and the president are of different parties, congressional leaders can be in a position to steer the national agenda. After Democrats briefly regained control of the Senate in 2001 when Vermont Senator Jim Jeffords bolted the Republican Party to become an independent aligned with the Democrats, the Senate immediately discarded President Bush's agenda to consider items that the president had no interest in pursuing, like campaign finance reform.

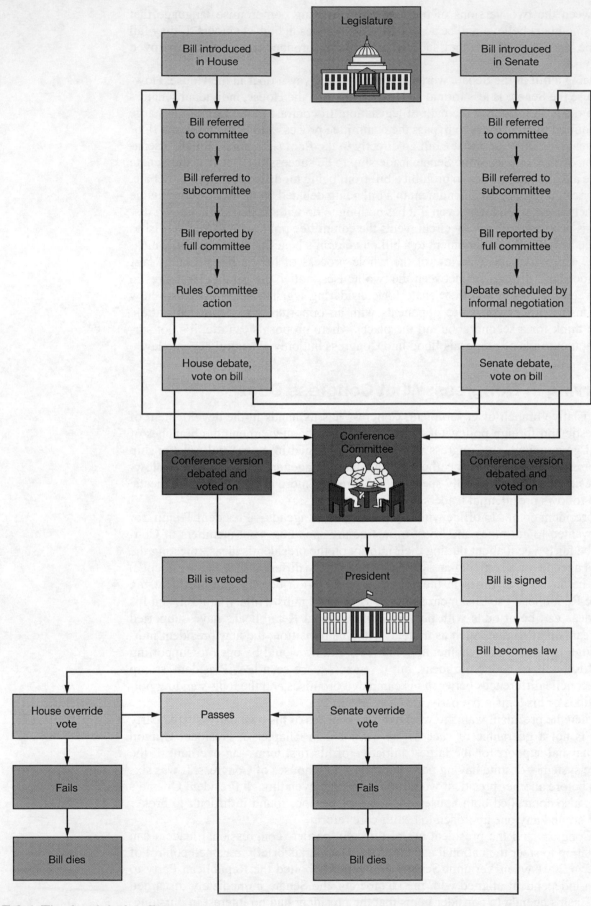

FIGURE 9.4 The Legislative Process

The Iraq Vote

In late summer 2002, rumors percolated through Washington that the Bush administration had made up its mind to conduct a military strike against Iraq in the not-too-distant future. The president himself fueled these rumors, as he spoke in increasingly belligerent tones about the dangers posed by Iraqi President Saddam Hussein's efforts to stockpile biological, chemical, and nuclear weapons.

The idea of a military campaign against Hussein was controversial. Among America's allies, only Great Britain expressed public support (a position not shared by a large portion of the British public), and some members of Congress expressed concern about the United States moving ahead without the United Nations' involvement. Others in Congress felt an unprovoked attack on Iraq would constitute a serious and potentially dangerous departure from the American position to use military options in self-defense, possibly giving cover to other nations to use force against their adversaries. Still others raised questions about the risks and costs of an all-out assault, whether the administration had a workable vision for a post-Hussein Iraq, and if war with Iraq would deflect resources and attention away from the campaign against terrorism.

Against this background, the Bush administration began sending signals that it might consider taking action without congressional backing. As commander-in-chief, Bush was in a strong constitutional position to order an attack on Iraq even without congressional approval. But this possibility generated a firestorm of congressional criticism, and in September, President Bush relented: He would not take action against Iraq without first consulting Congress.

Although members insisted on being included in the decision-making process, it was not easy for Congress to defy the president's wishes. Typically, members of Congress like to support the president on military matters, in deference to his role as commander-in-chief. This is particularly true for a popular president, which President Bush was in late 2002. Members also try to avoid being labeled as "soft" on something as important as national security. On the other hand, representatives know that it can be even more devastating to an official's career to support a war that bogs down in heavy fighting, produces a lot of American casualties, emboldens anti-American terrorists, damages the economy, or unleashes unexpected and unwanted side effects—such as the use by Iraq of chemical or biological weapons against American troops.

The capture of Baghdad would be quick, American casualties would be light, and Saddam Hussein would not use weapons of mass destruction against American troops, but the American occupation of Iraq after the war would be difficult and costly in lives and dollars, and one of the most compelling justifications offered by the administration for supporting the war—the existence of Iraqi weapons of mass destruction—would turn out to be faulty. By mid-2005, Americans had become restless with what had become an unpopular war, and in 2008, Barack Obama would win the presidency in part on a promise to end it. But in 2002, large bipartisan majorities felt they had no choice but to fall in line behind the president and overwhelmingly approve the resolution authorizing the use of force in Iraq.

Foreign affairs are another matter. The Constitution gives Congress important tools for the conduct of foreign policy, but it also gives a broad grant of authority to the president, and over time, the president has emerged as the premier voice in international matters. Congress has the power to declare war (something it has not done since World War II), and the Senate has the power to confirm ambassadors and ratify treaties. In turn, the president is commander-in-chief of the armed forces, and, as we'll see in Chapter 10, best positioned to move public opinion in times of international tension. As a consequence, Congress typically defers to presidential leadership on foreign and defense issues. As you will see in Demystifying Government: The Iraq Vote, Congress often has very little choice but to go along with the president.

On the other hand, Congress plays a central role in several important government activities: making budgets, overseeing the actions of the bureaucracy, confirming a wide range of presidential appointments, and removing other officials from office. Let's look at each one in turn.

9.5a Making Budgets

If you've ever tried to save for something or figure out how you're going to spend limited funds on a bunch of needs, then you know how tricky it can be to write a budget. Add the individual wishes of hundreds of members of Congress and the president into the mix, and it shouldn't be hard to see how writing a budget is one of the most complex, sensitive, and important things Congress has to do. Members who sit on committees with a hand in budget writing find that they are rarely lonely.

Budget writing is an annual affair that typically takes an entire year to complete. A number of committees get into the act, in keeping with the decentralized way the House and Senate function. The process has been more coordinated, though, ever since the passage of the **Congressional Budget and Impoundment Control Act of 1974.**[27] A lot of the action happens in the House and Senate Appropriations Committees, which are charged with reporting bills that determine how much money government agencies and programs will have to spend (**appropriations** refer to legislation authorizing the government to spend money).

The procedure is complex, but it follows this outline: First, the House and Senate budget committees set guidelines and budgetary priorities. Then the appropriations committees are supposed to allocate money in line with those priorities. They approve spending bills to cover the variety of items in the federal budget. If the sum of these expenditures exceeds the budgetary guidelines, the expenditures are brought into line with the budget targets through a process called **reconciliation**. For both houses to end up with the same budget, differences between them are resolved in a conference committee, after which final approval on a budget can be sought in both houses.[28]

If budget guidelines necessitate changes in tax law, the House Ways and Means Committee and the Senate Finance Committee get into the act. As the tax-writing committees of Congress, they draft legislation specifying which taxes will be raised and by how much.

Because so much money is at stake, and because real policy changes can be made by the act of budgeting, there are always a lot of congressional fingerprints on the final act. We'll take a closer look at budgeting when we talk about domestic policy in Chapter 15.

9.5b Oversight of the Bureaucracy

Congress may pass laws, but as we discussed in Chapter 8 and as we'll see in greater detail in Chapter 11, the bureaucracy is responsible for implementing laws, or carrying them out. This gives the bureaucracy a lot of freedom to interpret the intent of Congress, although Congress does have a function that can allow it to retain some control over how the bureaucracy implements legislation. It's called **oversight**, the process by which Congress reviews the actions of the bureaucracy to see that laws are being enacted as Congress intended. Most congressional oversight is carried out through the committees and subcommittees that share jurisdiction over a policy area with agencies and departments in the bureaucracy.

This sounds fairly neutral, but in fact, congressional oversight can be politically charged. The bureaucracy is part of the executive branch, and the president's political opponents in Congress can try to interfere with agencies they feel are implementing the law in accordance with the president's wishes instead of their own. Oversight can be a weapon for members of Congress who seek to undermine programs they don't like. During the budgeting process, oversight can have dramatic consequences for government programs, as Congress can reduce (or threaten to reduce) funds to agencies, or put restrictions on how money is spent, all set against the backdrop of competing political and ideological agendas about what government should and should not do. Republicans in recent years have cut the budgets of entities they felt did not warrant government spending, such as Amtrak and public broadcasting.

At the other end of the spectrum, oversight can be anything but acrimonious. The cooperative nature of iron-triangle relationships can turn oversight into something of a lovefest between bureaucratic agencies and the congressional committees supposedly overseeing them, fueled by mutual friendships with like-minded interest groups. When this happens, congressional committees work to protect agencies from scrutiny, investigations, and loss of funding.[29] Sometimes even representatives or senators who in other instances are vocal critics of government spending will work to protect agencies that benefit interest groups with cooperative ties to their office.

Congressional Budget and Impoundment Control Act of 1974: An act designed to centralize the congressional budgeting process, which established current procedures and timetables for writing a budget.

appropriations: Legislation permitting the government to spend money that determines how much will be spent and how it will be spent.

reconciliation: A procedure in the budget-writing process, whereby appropriations made in a number of congressional committees and subcommittees need to be brought in line with spending targets established early in the process.

oversight: The process of congressional review of the bureaucracy.

9.5c Confirming Presidential Appointments

The Constitution simply gives the Senate the responsibility to offer "advice and consent" when the president nominates people to fill vacancies in the bureaucracy and the court system. In reality, the function of confirming presidential appointees can be an institutional and ideological tug-of-war between the legislative and executive branches, as we saw when we were discussing the filibuster—especially when senators and the president have dramatically different ideas about how conservative or liberal appointees should be.

When a presidential nomination is made, it is referred to the appropriate Senate committee for deliberation, and if approved, to the floor for a final vote. The committee holds hearings on the nominee, which are often smooth and uneventful, although they can be contentious if there is a philosophical rift between the nominee and committee members.

Presidents are most likely to win approval for major cabinet-level appointments made as they come into office, on the grounds that a president has the right to appoint people of his choosing to key positions. However, even this is not guaranteed if an appointment is controversial. Democrats opposed a number of President Trump's cabinet nominees because of their lack of the requisite qualifications or conflicts of interest with the positions they were nominated to fill. Because Democrats could not filibuster them—they had eliminated that possibility when they reformed the filibuster rules when they held the Senate majority—they instead aired their complaints through congressional hearings in the hope that public pressure would force the president to relent or get several Republicans to join them in opposition.

In 2005, when the filibuster still applied to executive appointments, Democrats blocked President George W. Bush's appointment of former Undersecretary of State John Bolton to be the ambassador to the United Nations, contending Bolton lacked the diplomatic skills necessary for the post. In response, President Bush took the unusual step of circumventing the Senate and appointing Bolton to a temporary term using a constitutional provision enabling the president to make interim **"recess appointments"** while Congress is out of session.

Recess appointments don't require approval, and those appointed can only serve until the end of the congressional session—but they're highly controversial. Recess appointments anger senators, who see the appointments as a way for the president to circumvent the normal legislative process.

Traditionally, Senate hearings center on the nominee's qualifications for office, but in recent years, almost anything goes: moral issues, personal or family background, financial dealings, medical history—any or all of these could be open for discussion. Senators looking for justification to turn down a nominee can turn almost anywhere for a rationale to vote no.[30] This is particularly true for judicial nominations, which tend to be more contentious than other presidential nominations. You'll find a good example of just how contentious things can get in Demystifying Government: "Bork" Becomes a Verb.

Senators can also place "holds" on nominees they dislike. Until 2013, "holds" could be made anonymously, permitting obstructing senators to shield their identities. Senate Democrats accused Senate Republicans of using these tactics during the Obama and Clinton administrations to block liberal judicial appointees; Senate Republicans accused their Democratic counterparts of dragging their heels on a host of President Bush's bureaucratic and judicial nominees when they controlled the process. When the Senate fails to act on a nomination, unless the president takes the unusual step of making a "recess appointment" or appointing the nominee on an "acting" basis, the position simply remains vacant. After ten months in office, President Obama had won Senate confirmation for only six of his appointees to the lower federal courts, compared to 28 for President George W. Bush and 27 for President Clinton in their respective first years in office.[31]

9.5d Impeachment

No political power is greater than the power to throw someone out of office, and the Constitution grants that power exclusively to Congress. **Impeachment** is a two-step process involving both houses. The House of Representatives can impeach any federal official,

recess appointments: The constitutional power granted to the president to make nominations while Congress is out of session that do not require Senate approval. The appointments stand until the end of the congressional term.

impeachment: The power granted to Congress to remove from office the president, vice president, judges, and other federal officials.

"Bork" Becomes a Verb

It's hard to pinpoint when the Senate confirmation process became so ugly—it wasn't always that way—but one place to look is President Reagan's 1987 nomination of Robert Bork to the Supreme Court. Under intense pressure from liberal interest groups who feared Bork's constitutional philosophy was too conservative, and with the ideological direction of the Court hanging in the balance, Democratic senators subjected the nominee to rigorous questioning about his philosophical perspective, pronounced him unfit to sit on the Supreme Court, and voted down his appointment. Many conservatives were livid. They claimed that a nominee's philosophy had never been grounds for Senate action, that the president had the legitimate right to appoint someone who shared his ideological outlook, and that liberal senators had distorted Bork's record. Civility in the nomination process fell by the wayside as an ideological war of sorts was declared; "Bork" entered the language as a verb. To many conservatives, to be "Borked" meant to be ambushed and destroyed politically through misrepresentation and lies, and they vowed to be more media savvy and proactive next time.

Things got worse four years later, when President George H. W. Bush nominated Clarence Thomas to the Supreme Court. Thomas, a conservative African American judge, would replace liberal justice Thurgood Marshall—the first African American to sit on the Court—guaranteeing a shift in the Court's ideological center. Again, interest groups on both sides of the ideological spectrum geared up for full-scale battle, determined to win at any cost.

When the hearings began, little appeared to stand in Thomas's way. A southerner who began life in pov-

erty, Thomas's story was a compelling one, and his judicial record, though undistinguished to critics, didn't raise any red flags. Then word leaked to the press of sexual harassment charges leveled against him by a former employee, University of Oklahoma law school Professor Anita Hill, and the hearings took a bizarre turn. The Senate Judiciary Committee, run by Democrats, opted to explore the sexual harassment charges as the television cameras rolled. Conservative groups charged that it was a setup; Thomas himself pointedly called it a "high-tech lynching" of an African American nominee by white senators.

Today, sexual harassment is widely discussed and understood (in part, because of the Thomas hearings), but at the time, many Americans were not familiar with the topic, so it hit with tremendous force. Hill leveled her accusations as Thomas defended against them in what was arguably the most thorough exploration of the issue to date. All the while, it was hard to separate partisanship from the discussion, as evidenced by the pattern of Thomas's Democratic detractors grilling the nominee as his Republican supporters put Hill's credibility on trial. Ostensibly, the subject was sexual harassment, but the subtext was clearly politics and power.

Thomas was confirmed, 52–48, in one of the closest Senate votes ever for a Supreme Court nominee, and he took his seat on the Supreme Court under a cloud of controversy, but the bitterness of the battle never fully dissipated. As we will see in Chapter 12, Republicans responded to a 2016 Supreme Court vacancy by going one step further and refusing to hold hearings or a vote on President Obama's nominee.

including the president, vice president, Supreme Court justices, and federal court judges. Impeachment requires a majority vote of the House and is similar to an indictment in court in that it charges the official with one or more counts of misconduct. Once articles of impeachment are approved, a trial is held in the Senate, where evidence is presented to support each accusation. With the chief justice of the Supreme Court presiding, the impeached official is permitted to offer a defense against the charges. At the conclusion of the trial, each senator casts one vote on each article of impeachment, with a two-thirds majority required to remove the official from office.

The Constitution is especially vague on what constitutes an impeachable offense, stipulating only "Treason, Bribery, or other high Crimes and misdemeanors." Through the years, it has fallen to others to determine what this means. Invariably, the interpretation is political because, although the impeachment process looks like a trial, the jurors are elected officials responsive to public opinion. Regardless of the merits of the case, it's politically difficult to impeach and convict an official who has a lot of popular support.

It's also the case that impeachment doesn't happen very often. It's a complicated process with a low likelihood of conviction, designed that way so that political adversaries wouldn't routinely employ it. Only seventeen officials have been impeached since the Constitution was ratified, and only seven were convicted—all federal judges.[32]

TABLE 9.4 Comparing House and Senate

	House	Senate
Number of Members	435	100
Districts	Congressional districts	States
Member Terms	2 years	6 years
Elections Held	Every 2 years for everyone	One-third every 2 years
Distinctive Functions	Originate revenue bills Write articles of impeachment	Ratify presidential appointments Hold impeachment hearings Ratify treaties
Most Powerful Committees	Appropriations Budget Commerce Rules Ways and Means	Appropriations Armed Services Commerce Finance

There have been only two presidential impeachment trials—Andrew Johnson in 1868 and Bill Clinton in 1998—and both took place against the backdrop of partisan politics. Johnson, a southerner who took office upon the assassination of Abraham Lincoln, was strongly at odds with a Congress unsympathetic to the South in the period following the Civil War. When Congress passed the Tenure of Office Act, requiring congressional approval before a presidential appointee could be removed from office, Johnson ignored it, believing it to be unconstitutional. The House rushed to impeach him, eager to see Johnson removed for political reasons. He prevailed in the Senate by one vote.

President Clinton's impeachment grew out of charges that he perjured himself when he lied under oath about his sexual relationship with White House intern Monica Lewinsky. Since the charges did not stem from an issue related to the president's official conduct of his office, reporters, political analysts, and constitutional scholars questioned whether President Clinton's alleged offenses were impeachable. These questions were reinforced by the political nature of the proceedings, as the House voted almost along party lines to impeach. A dramatic Senate trial concluded in Clinton's acquittal on one count of perjury and one count of obstruction of justice. Both counts failed to produce even a simple majority of senators supporting conviction.

Richard Nixon is the one president who likely would have been convicted, on charges related to his conduct during the Watergate scandal, but he circumvented the impeachment process by becoming the first president to resign from office. Nixon faced removal in the wake of evidence pointing to a broad pattern of abuse of power stemming from his participation in and cover-up of events surrounding a break-in at Democratic Party headquarters. When a bipartisan majority of the House Judiciary Committee voted to recommend that the full House impeach the president, it became apparent that Nixon lacked the votes to avoid impeachment in the House or conviction in the Senate. Had the proceedings continued, it would have been the only time in history that the gravity of the charges against a president would have compelled significant numbers of his own partisans to vote to remove him from office.

This is a good time to stop for a second and review the broad outlines of what we've been discussing. Let's do it by briefly comparing a few key elements of the House and Senate—see Table 9.4.

9.6 Leading Congress

When the authors of the Constitution left it up to each house to figure out how it was going to function, they didn't imagine a role for political parties because, as we know,

L.O. Identify key congressional leadership positions, and explain the role of leadership in Congress.

they viewed parties as factions and assumed (or hoped) that they would never develop. As it turns out, parties mean everything in Congress. They determine who gets to lead Congress, control congressional committees, set the agenda, and set the rules. Power flows to the majority party; frustration visits the minority. For this reason, congressional leaders are highly motivated to attain and keep majority status.

In both houses, the majority is simply the party with the most seats. However, just like in congressional elections where all the representation goes to the winner, all of the leadership benefits go to the majority party. Even a slender two-seat advantage like Senate Republicans had following the 2016 election permits the majority party to have a majority of its members on all committees, to have its members chair all committees and subcommittees, and to have its leader set the legislative agenda. That's how Senator Jim Jeffords could turn a 50–50 Senate on its head by defecting from the Republican Party during the 2001 legislative session, becoming an independent who voted with Democrats on leadership issues. Overnight, (mostly liberal) Democrats replaced (generally conservative) Republicans as leaders and committee chairs, bringing with them an entirely different set of legislative priorities and the power to have them heard.

9.6a Leadership Structure

The different traditions and procedures in the House and Senate translate into differences in the degree to which the majority party can clamp down on the minority. The Senate offers more opportunities to members of the minority party to express their will through the filibuster and through courtesies extended individual members. It operates on the principle of **minority rights**, whereby deference is granted to the concerns of those whose party does not control the chamber.

The House, in contrast, functions on a **majoritarian principle** that frustrates dissent. After more than a century of dealing with rules that permitted legislative minorities to derail legislation, the House, around the turn of the twentieth century, instituted rules that give the leadership of the majority party tight control over all proceedings.

The **Speaker of the House** is the foremost leader in the chamber. Chosen by a caucus of the majority party, then ratified by a party-line vote of the full House, "Mister Speaker" as he is addressed (or, in the case of Nancy Pelosi, "Madam Speaker") is one of the premier leaders in Washington (not to mention second in line for the presidency after the vice president). The Speaker has both formal and informal powers, which allow the Speaker to advance his or her priorities and the priorities of the Speaker's party, regardless of the wishes of the minority. Formally, the Speaker presides over the House, resolves disputes as they arise, decides which committees will consider legislation, and determines who will serve on conference and select committees. Informally, the Speaker can influence the Rules Committee (affecting the scheduling of debate and votes on legislation), reward members for their loyalty (or punish members for their independence), influence assignments to standing committees, and function as the spokesperson for the House of Representatives in the press.[33]

Unlike other congressional leadership offices, the position of Speaker of the House is mandated by the Constitution. Article 1, Section 2 says that "The House of Representatives shall choose their Speaker and other Officers," leaving the rest of the leadership structure to evolve through custom and practice. What the Constitution does not say is that the Speaker has to be a member of a majority party (remember, no parties are mentioned in the Constitution) or even a member of the House. However, every Speaker has been a House member, and every contemporary Speaker has been a majority party member with many years of service in the House.

The Speaker is assisted by the rest of the majority party leadership, which, like the Speaker, is selected by a caucus of the majority party at the start of each congressional session. The key positions are the **majority leader** and the **majority whip**. The majority leader is the floor leader for the majority party, responsible for doing the everyday work of moving the party's legislative agenda through the House: lining up the support of committee chairs, gauging levels of support among House members, and persuading members

minority rights: Procedures, such as those in place in the Senate, that permit members of the minority party the opportunity to resist legislative actions they oppose.

majoritarian principle: Procedures, such as those in place in the House of Representatives, that limit the ability of the minority party to influence the shape of legislation or the direction of the legislative agenda.

Speaker of the House: The leader of the majority party in the House of Representatives who exercises control over the operation of that branch through formal and informal means.

majority leader: The number-two leadership position in the House of Representatives and the number-one leadership position in the Senate. In the House, the majority leader is the chief assistant to the Speaker; in the Senate, the majority leader is the chief leader on a par with the House Speaker.

majority whip: The number-three leadership position in the House of Representatives and the number-two leadership position in the Senate. In both instances, the whip is responsible for mobilizing party members to support the leadership on key issues.

to vote the party position. The majority leader is assisted in this effort by the majority whip. The name suggests whipping up or rounding up votes, which is a good description of what the whip does. The whip reminds party members of key votes, counts heads to determine if the party position is likely to prevail, and when necessary, leans on members to vote with the leadership.

Because, as we mentioned in Section 6.4a, "How Parties in Government Function," we do not have **responsible parties** in government, members—even powerful committee chairs—cannot be assumed to support the positions of leadership, and legislators will not automatically heed the wishes of a president of their party. This fact has been the cause of a lot of anguish over the years as party leaders have tried—some more successfully than others—to keep their members in line.

For example, in 2003, President Bush and Republican congressional leaders faced a revolt by a few congressional representatives of their own party over legislation to add a prescription drug benefit to Medicare. Republican leaders kept the final vote on the measure going all night in a frantic effort to convince enough recalcitrant conservatives to give their president a victory. One reporter recalled feverish efforts by House Speaker Dennis Hastert and his lieutenants:

> The House's reigning Caesars were running around in circles, going back once, twice, and three times to conservatives who were clearly hard "no's" and had been that way for days. Tom Feeney, R-Fla.? No thanks. Steve Chabot, R-Ohio? Didn't like the means-testing provision. Todd Akin, R-Mo.? The [Republican] whip, fellow Missourian Roy Blunt, had him out in the Speaker's lobby all alone and was getting nowhere.[34]

It took close to three hours and a few personal phone calls by the president to round up enough votes to secure passage of the measure. In time, however, the victory raised serious questions about the tactics used by the House leadership and the administration—including the prospect that Republican leaders had employed threats to change the votes of reluctant members, and that the White House knowingly withheld the true cost of the measure to keep conservatives on board—in an extreme example of what can happen because congressional representatives are free to go their own way.

The minority party counterparts to these leadership positions are the **minority leader** and **minority whip**. As leaders of the party out of power, their roles parallel their counterparts in the majority but without the ability to shape the legislative agenda. So, the minority leadership advocates the policy alternatives of the minority as they look for opportunities to develop alliances with wayward members of the majority in an effort to frustrate the majority party's agenda.

Leadership in the Senate operates a little differently. There is no counterpart to the Speaker of the House. Instead, the Constitution makes the vice president of the United States the presiding officer of the Senate, where his formal title is president of the Senate, and his one formal power is the ability to cast tie-breaking votes. However, unless it looks like the Senate is heading for a tie vote, you probably won't find the vice president anywhere near the Senate. In his absence, the chore of presiding over the Senate falls to the **president pro tempore**, a mostly honorary position that typically goes to the longest serving member of the majority party. Apart from being third in line for presidential succession behind the vice president and the Speaker of the House, the president pro tempore has no formal powers and typically finds the job of presiding over the Senate to be as dull as the vice president does. That's why, on any given afternoon, it's not unusual to find junior senators presiding over the proceedings, not as an honor but as an obligation assumed by those with the least standing in the chamber.

In the absence of a powerful figure like the House Speaker, the Senate is led by the majority leader and majority whip. They determine the items on the legislative agenda and work to keep their majority in line. It can be a harder job than what befalls their House counterparts because of the Senate's less hierarchical traditions that permit individual senators to go their own way. The minority leader and minority whip function much like their House counterparts. Figure 9.5 shows the House and Senate leaders after the 2016 election.

responsible parties: Political parties whose legislative members act in concert, taking clear positions on issues and voting as a unit in accordance with their stated positions.

minority leader: The number-one leadership position for the opposition party in the House of Representatives and Senate, whose responsibilities mirror those of the majority leader but without the ability to set or advance the legislative agenda.

minority whip: The number-two leadership position for the opposition party in the House of Representatives and Senate, whose responsibilities mirror those of the majority whip.

president pro tempore: The senator charged with the honorary duty of presiding over the Senate in the absence of the vice president of the United States.

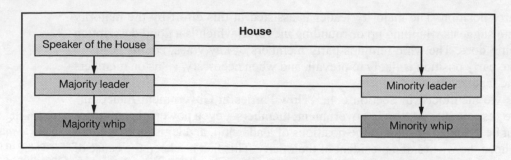

House

Speaker of the House → Majority leader → Majority whip

Minority leader → Minority whip

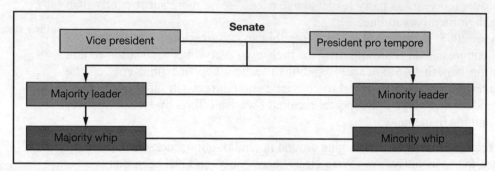

Senate

Vice president — President pro tempore

Majority leader → Majority whip

Minority leader → Minority whip

House Speaker
Paul Ryan (R-Wisconsin)
Elected to the House in 1998
Previous Occupation: Government service
Primary Function: Presides over House

House Majority Leader
Kevin McCarthy (R-California)
Elected to the House in 2006
Previous Occupation: Small business
Primary Function: Advances majority agenda

House Majority Whip
Steve Scalise (R-Louisiana)
Elected to the House in 2008
Previous Occupation: Louisiana politics
Primary Function: Lines up votes for majority

House Minority Leader
Nancy Pelosi (D-California)
Elected to the House in 1986
Previous Occupation: California politics
Primary Function: Advocates for opposition

House Minority Whip
Steny Hoyer (D-Maryland)
Elected to the House in 1981
Previous Occupation: Maryland politics
Primary Function: Mobilizes opposition

Senate Majority Leader
Mitch McConnell (R-Kentucky)
Elected to the Senate in 1984
Previous Occupation: Government service
Primary Function: Advances majority agenda

Senate Majority Whip
John Cornyn (R-Texas)
Elected to the Senate in 2002
Previous Occupation: Law
Primary Function: Lines up votes for majority

Senate Minority Leader
Chuck Schumer (D-New York)
Elected to the Senate in 1998
Previous Occupation: New York politics
Primary Function: Advocates for opposition

Senate Minority Whip
Richard Durbin (D-Illinois)
Elected to the Senate in 1996
Previous Occupation: Law
Primary Function: Mobilizes opposition

President Pro Tempore
Orrin Hatch (R-Utah)
Elected to the Senate in 1976
Previous Occupation: Law
Primary Function: Ceremonial

FIGURE 9.5 House and Senate Leadership[T9]

Maybe you're getting the sense that political parties have emerged as the organizations that hold Congress together, structure its operations, and help to centralize an institution staffed by hundreds of ambitious people from different regions of the country with varying personal agendas and objectives. Without parties to provide structure, it's quite possible that the legislative branch would be a much harder place to run—particularly in the Senate, where customs and procedures give voice to individual and minority opinions.

The other side of this coin is that during times of intense partisan division like we've experienced over the past few years, the efforts of party leaders can serve to heighten philosophical differences between the two camps, leading to hard-fought battles over legislation and, more broadly, the general direction of the country. Even with Democrats holding large majorities in the House and Senate following the 2008 election, party leaders found themselves with surprisingly little margin for error in carrying out their legislative plans. With Republicans almost unanimous in their opposition to Democratic proposals for a stimulus package aimed at jump-starting the economy in 2009 and legislation to reform health care—the two largest domestic items on President Obama's first year agenda—Democratic leaders could afford to lose few of their members if they hoped to advance their objectives. This was particularly so in the Senate, where all sixty Democrats were needed to end filibusters staged by all forty Republicans, so there was intense pressure on leadership to keep members in line. Under the circumstances, things got nasty.

There are a number of things the leadership can do to appeal for party cohesion. Leaders can listen to members and incorporate their interests as legislation is formulated. They can help them get committee assignments that will promote their career goals—by putting them on committees that afford them power in Congress or that address their personal legislative interests or the interests of their constituents. They shower members with rewards for adhering to the party line on key votes, although this tactic has fallen out of favor in recent years. Leaders can go to member districts and campaign for them, and use their clout to raise money for member reelection efforts.

Any or all of these things can just as easily be withheld from members who cause trouble for the leadership, but only to a limited extent. Remember, it's in the leaders' self-interest to help party members win reelection because holding the majority fulfills the promise of power in Congress, and every reelected member brings an incumbent or would-be majority leader closer to that goal.

9.6b Party Structure

For the congressional member who is not part of the leadership, party business is conducted primarily through participation in the **party caucus**. Each party in each house has a caucus, which conducts leadership elections and finalizes committee assignments at the start of each new Congress, and provides a forum for discussion of policy issues and party legislative strategies. The caucus is the place where House Republicans, House Democrats, Senate Republicans, or Senate Democrats can articulate their interests or concerns about the positions the party might take, in an effort to build general agreement for the positions that the leadership will move forward. (Although it's the same term, this use of caucus should not be confused with a caucus that meets to elect delegates to a political party convention, like the Iowa caucus we talked about in Chapter 7.)

party caucus: The group of all members of a political party in the House or Senate that meets to discuss and formulate legislative priorities.

Complementing the relatively informal caucus are party committees (see Table 9.5) that help coordinate the political and policy interests of the parties. Because these committees serve partisan purposes rather than institutional purposes, they're different and apart from the standing committees and subcommittees we talked about earlier. These committees give partisan advice on developing legislative strategy, recommend committee assignments by matching members with committees that can help them politically, and help party members with reelection needs.

A quick glance at a couple of these committee websites could give you a richer sense of how they operate and what they do. For instance, the Senate Republican Policy Committee (RPC) bills itself as "helping shape the GOP game plan:"

> The committee advances Republican policies by providing positions on legislation, floor debate, and votes. RPC also provides in-depth analysis on specific issues, policy solutions and alternatives, and strategic guidance. We also provide a recorded vote analysis and run the internal RPC TV broadcast.

> The RPC provides a forum for Republican Senators for policy discussions. This is principally carried out through the weekly policy lunch. RPC also hosts Republican Staff Directors and Legislative Directors to discuss the Senate committees and floor agenda.[35]

The Senate Democratic Steering and Outreach Committee, in addition to its committee assignment function, works to coordinate the Senate Democratic legislative strategy with Democratic allies outside Congress:

TABLE 9.5 Party Committees and Their Purposes[T10]

	Committee	Purpose
House	Republican Policy Committee	Build consensus for party policy positions
	Democratic Steering and Policy Committee	Build consensus for party policy positions Assign Democrats to committees
Senate	Republican Policy Committee	Research and draft party policy positions
	Democratic Policy Committee	Develop party positions and priorities
House	Republican Steering Committee	Assign Republicans to committees
Senate	Republican Committee on Committees	Assign Republicans to committees
	Democratic Steering and Outreach Committee	Coordinate party policy agenda Assign Democrats to committees
House	National Republican Congressional Committee	Elect Republicans to the House
	Democratic Congressional Campaign Committee	Elect Democrats to the House
Senate	National Republican Senatorial Committee	Elect Republicans to the Senate
	Democratic Senatorial Campaign Committee	Elect Democrats to the Senate

The Senate Democratic Steering and Outreach Committee is dedicated to fostering dialogue between Senate Democrats and community leaders from across the nation. Each year, the Steering Committee hosts numerous meetings with advocates, policy experts, and elected officials to discuss key priorities and enlist their help in the development of the Senate Democratic agenda. The Committee serves as a liaison between Senate Democratic offices, advocacy groups and intergovernmental organizations.[36]

Beyond these committees, members can find numerous opportunities to gather in less formal or smaller partisan group settings to discuss goals, map strategies, and mediate disputes. Congressional parties in both houses occasionally hold retreats (typically in a pleasant setting outside Washington) for the purpose of boosting party unity. Like on a college campus, there are plenty of extracurricular groups you can join in Congress, where you'll find other people with similar partisan or ideological interests. For instance, the Republican Study Committee is a House Republican group dedicated to advancing a small-government, socially conservative agenda. The Congressional Black Caucus and the Congressional Hispanic Caucus are organized around identity politics. The Blue Dogs are a group of moderate-to-conservative House Democrats that tries to build bridges between liberal Democrats and Conservative Republicans.

9.6c Committee Structure

Congressional leadership and party structures play big roles in the organization of the committee system. There are so many committees—the structure is so decentralized—that parties step in to hold things together. We've already talked about how committees are organized around parties and how leadership plays a critical role in making committee assignments, attempting to match members with committees that will advance their careers.

However, there are a few things we haven't addressed about the committee structure that are important to the way they operate. One is how the ratio of Republicans to Democrats is determined. Another is how member preferences are matched to committees. Then, there's the all-important matter of seniority.

We've said that the majority party receives a majority of seats on all committees, but the magnitude of that advantage will vary, depending on how many seats the majority party occupies. In a closely divided legislature of the sort we saw during the first years of the century, the majority party will command only a small advantage on most committees, but there can be exceptions. For instance, the majority party may demand disproportionate representation on the House Rules Committee, allowing majority leadership to control the flow of legislation to the floor. When one party controls a comfortable majority of seats in the House or Senate, as Republicans did after the 2014 House elections, their numerical advantage on each committee grows as well.

At the start of every Congress, new members will seek committees on which they want to serve and will typically lobby their leadership to get them. Members are goal-directed, and see committee service as an opportunity to advance career objectives. Those interested primarily in making laws will gravitate to policy-oriented committees, like the House Foreign Affairs Committee or the Senate Health, Education, Labor, and Pensions Committee. Those seeking to climb the leadership ladder in Congress will be drawn to committees where they can exert influence on the congressional agenda, like the Ways and Means Committee or the Rules Committee in the House. Members from competitive districts with reelection on their minds will want to join committees where they can benefit from the perks of pork, like the House Transportation and Infrastructure Committee.[37]

Although leaders try to accommodate assignment requests, not everyone gets what they want. Just like in many universities, where seniors have priority over freshmen when enrolling for courses, **seniority** gives long-serving members an edge in having their committee requests fulfilled. Seniority also plays an important role in committee leadership. As a long-standing matter of custom, each **committee chair** is the member of the majority party with the longest continuous service on the committee. The longest-serving member of the minority party is the **ranking minority member**. Although there have been a few cases over the past several decades of a party caucus granting a committee chair to someone other than the longest-serving member, the seniority custom is rarely violated.

Because most legislation first goes to committee for a hearing, a committee chair can have enormous power over the legislative process. Committee chairs are no longer the iron-fisted dictators of an earlier time, although they can still influence the committee's agenda, budget, and staff, and may have influence over determining subcommittee memberships. They can decide how—or whether—to route legislative proposals to subcommittees. They can decide when—or whether—to schedule a vote to send legislation on for consideration by the full chamber. By delaying action on a bill they don't like, chairs can keep the rest of Congress from considering it, even if the bill has widespread support. As a result, chairs are well positioned to fashion committees to suit their interests.[38]

Health-care reform was such a complicated legislative task that it fell under the jurisdiction of five separate committees—three in the House and two in the Senate. Each had to approve a reform measure before the entire House or Senate could vote.[39] Four of the five committees completed their work quickly, but the Senate Finance Committee took a lot longer as the committee chair, Senator Max Baucus, attempted to craft a proposal that Republicans could support. Considering the high degree of opposition among congressional Republicans to any health-care reform, this was a monumental task, but it was within the chairman's discretion to pursue it, and the entire process came to a halt for several weeks while the rest of Congress waited for Baucus to unveil his committee's measure.

seniority: The custom of awarding committee chairs on the basis of length of service.

committee chair: The member of Congress responsible for running a committee, who can have great influence over the committee agenda and, by extension, the legislative process.

ranking minority member: The minority party counterpart to the committee chair, but without the power to influence the direction of the committee.

9.7 Working in Congress: Washington

Okay, see if this sounds familiar to you. It's final exam week. You have four tests in the next three days, and while you've done your best to keep up with most of the reading, you realize you're facing a few long days and nights.

Now imagine that finals week goes on forever, and you'll have a sense of what the workload is like for members of Congress. There's always more to do than can get done, and just like you're always aware that you'll be getting graded at the end of each term, every member keeps an eye on when their term ends and they have to face the voters again.

L.O. Discuss how members of Congress manage their work expectations.

Members have to fulfill a number of obligations, all with implications for how well they'll do on Election Day. When they cast a vote on legislation, when they do work on committees, when they address the concerns and complaints of constituents, they realize they're doing things with the potential to assist—or undermine—their re-election prospects. It's a lot to cover, and it's probably not exaggerating things too much to say that a big misstep, or a lot of small missed steps, could put their future in jeopardy.

9.7a On the Job

Representatives can be easily overwhelmed. They need to make judgments about a wide range of issues, many of them detailed and technical. With the exception of perhaps one or two issues, members are limited in their level of expertise. It would be like taking a series of liberal arts courses in everything from biology to art history to sociology to psychology, and feeling a sense of command only in your major subject—except, where you probably take no more than five courses per term, representatives are inundated with many more than five complex issues they need to address.

Members of Congress typically spend more time in committee rooms than you spend in classrooms; just like the job of learning takes place in class, the detail work of Congress takes place in committee. Between committee and subcommittee assignments, members are regularly overbooked and have to make choices about which hearings to attend. It would be as if you registered for seven, 3-credit courses and some of them met at the same time.

More than committee work pulls members in competing directions. They need to meet with lobbyists and constituents, they're expected to spend time on the floor of Congress debating and voting on legislation, they have to pay attention to their public image by devoting time to the media and by making public speaking engagements, and they are presented with a steady supply of social functions that offer opportunities to "network" and conduct business. It's not unusual for a representative's day to begin early and end late in the evening.

Then there's the commute. Members must return to their districts regularly or they risk losing touch with their constituents at the grass roots. Some members who live close to Washington are able to divide their time between the Capital and their district, spending long weekends at home or even driving or taking the train if they're very close. Others have a much longer way to go: Imagine if you represented California—or Hawaii. Once home, members keep working, often on weekends, taking care to meet with constituents, locally based interest groups, and financial supporters.

9.7b Staff to the Rescue

Of course, they don't have to do it alone. The typical House member has a full-time staff of up to eighteen paid employees and nine college interns. The typical senator has a paid staff of between thirty and thirty-five and nine college interns. Typically well educated, young, and willing to trade off higher pay elsewhere for the thrill of working with powerful people and the ability to make important professional contacts, staffers help manage the workload by performing a number of important roles:

- *Administrative assistants (AAs)* help manage the Washington office, provide political advice to the representative or senator, and function as an intermediary in dealings with constituents, lobbyists, and other members.
- *Legislative assistants (LAs)* help manage the member's committee work by writing speeches and bills, analyzing legislative proposals, and following up on committee and subcommittee meetings the member misses.
- *Caseworkers* devote their time to helping constituents with problems and work either out of Washington, D.C., or out of one of the member's home offices. Representatives on average have two or three "branch offices" in their districts; senators average four offices in their state.

- **Press aides** are responsible for the member's media relations, including communicating the member's message to the press and managing communications with constituents through newsletters, social media, and, in some cases, surveys of constituent opinion.[40]

Take a look at some of the things a member of Congress might face on a typical day. You'll find them in Demystifying Government: A Day on the Hill. This is a fictional composite, but it's based on the real thing. Imagine you're the representative with the scheduling conflicts shown (in some cases, this will require a lot of imagination): a conservative, pro-business Democrat from a competitive district in the Northeast with an interest in affordable housing, alternative energy (particularly offshore wind power), and homeland security—all of which are important to the constituents who support you. During much

---

DEMYSTIFYING GOVERNMENT

A Day on the Hill

Conflicts in congressional schedules are the rule, rather than the exception. Every decision disappoints some groups. The conflicts listed below are typical of what you would have to face if you served in Congress. Take a look at each one and figure out, in each case, which options you would choose.

Conflict 1

- 7:50 A.M. Breakfast with Chamber of Commerce officials from home district to discuss business interests and the Chamber's political support for your reelection campaign
- 8:00 A.M. Breakfast meeting with fellow Blue Dog Democrats to discuss centrist legislative strategies

Consider: Meeting with lobbyists connected to your district instead of going to a regularly scheduled meeting with other conservative Democrats is the less risky choice. Maintaining good relationships with sympathetic groups will help you earn their money and support for your next reelection effort. You can always meet with the Blue Dogs next week.

Conflict 2

- 8:55 A.M. A long, impromptu meeting with a Republican colleague who wants your vote for a bridge construction project in her district; she is willing to support construction of a military helicopter in your district in return
- 9:00 A.M. Meeting with computer company lobbyists about adding funding to combat cyberterrorism in the homeland security bill

Consider: This is a tough call with no obvious good choice. The tradeoff you're arranging with your colleague will help you bring an important pork-barrel project back to your constituents. However, the computer lobbyist you're neglecting is a potential political supporter who wants to talk about an important legislative matter.

Conflict 3

- 10:15 A.M. Meeting with a postal worker from your district who is retiring after 50 years of service without ever calling in sick
- 10:20 A.M. Floor vote on designating an official "National Asparagus Day"

Consider: The meeting will matter to the postal worker (who may turn out to vote in the next election), it will likely get you favorable coverage in the local papers back home, and you'll build up good will with the postal workers in your district. The vote, on the other hand, is symbolic; missing it would be a problem only for a member from a district that produces asparagus.

Conflict 4

- 10:45 A.M. Hearing on wind and solar power (Committee on Energy and Commerce Subcommittee on Energy and Power)
- 11:00 A.M. Hearing on possible public/private expedition to Mars (Committee on Science, Space and Technology Subcommittee on Space)

Consider: You can't go to every hearing. Of the two, the hearing on wind and solar power is probably the more important one to you because your constituents will have a direct interest in the possibility of offshore wind farms. Your legislative assistant can keep tabs on the meeting you missed.

Conflict 5

- 1:15 P.M. Floor debate. Prepared remarks (two minutes) on proposed homeland security bill
- 1:20 P.M. Unscheduled visit by elementary school group from home district looking for personalized tour of Congress
- 1:20 P.M. Hearing on affordable housing: Committee on Financial Services Subcommittee on Housing and Insurance, on which you are ranking minority member

(continued)

A Day on the Hill (continued)

Consider: It makes sense that you'd want to deliver your remarks on an important measure like homeland security, but it's difficult to miss a meeting of a subcommittee where you're the ranking member without violating the norm of doing your legislative work. You could always have your remarks entered in the permanent record without actually presenting them. As hard as it is to overlook school kids from home—remember, their parents may be voters—the visit was unannounced and can be handled by your staff.

Conflict 6

- 3:00 P.M. CNN Interview on affordable housing
- 3:00 P.M. Floor vote on raising the minimum wage by 20 cents an hour

Consider: This is another tough call. You want the publicity that CNN can give you, but your opponent in the next election could raise questions about why you are not doing your job if you do not vote on an important measure like the minimum wage.

Conflict 7

- 8:00 P.M. Evening reception in Georgetown with lobbyists from Greenpeace
- 8:00 P.M. Evening function at the White House honoring the Canadian prime minister
- 8:00 P.M. Quiet time with family

Consider: The Greenpeace reception would allow you to mix with sympathetic lobbyists who support your environmental concerns. However, it means giving up an event at the White House. All of this weighs against time with your family, which is always a tough choice to make.

of the day, scheduling conflicts make it impossible for you to be everywhere and do everything you would like. You'll have the chance to decide how you will resolve these conflicts by selecting the events you're going to attend and those you're going to miss from a set of available options. Remember, some of what you miss can be taken care of by your staff—but not everything.

Also, remember that there's a potential cost every time members of Congress fail to show up for an event that a staff member can't cover, either in the form of a lost opportunity, an angry constituent, a violated congressional norm—or the appearance that they are just not doing their job.

9.7c Voting on Legislation

L.O. Explain why members of Congress pay close attention to the votes they cast.

If you felt it was an intrusion on your busy schedule to have to vote on legislation creating a "National Asparagus Day," you can probably get a sense of the range of things—big and small—that representatives are called upon to decide. Maybe which way to vote on something like an honorary holiday is a no-brainer (you support it!), but there are a lot of more substantive votes a member has to cast and—let's face it—with so many technical issues to decide, members have to cast plenty of votes on things they know nothing about.

cue taking: Looking to other members of Congress for guidelines on how to cast a vote on a technical or unfamiliar matter.

So, they need voting strategies. To simplify what could be confusing decisions on unfamiliar matters, members of Congress engage in **cue taking**, looking to other members for reliable signals on how to vote. There are several commonsense shortcuts that members might take. They could turn to a colleague who shares their philosophical outlook and vote the way the colleague is voting. They could seek advice from a member with expertise on the legislation being considered, such as a member of the committee that held hearings on it. If they are junior members, they might look for someone with seniority who has been around long enough to be familiar with the matter at hand. If they are in the House, they could turn to a member of their state delegation, someone from their area who is known and trusted. This sort of cue makes particular sense if the legislation could have an impact back home, like a measure that could affect an industry in the member's state.[41]

If a member's vote on the issue is important to other members but does not concern the member or his or her constituents, it would probably be an appropriate time to engage in logrolling, where the member would exchange his or her vote for future support on something that does matter to the member. Logrolling can be accomplished informally before a final vote on legislation, and it can involve a number of members. One former senator, sounding a whole lot like anyone who has ever called in favors from a friend, explained how he put together majority support for a bill: "Maggie said she talked to Russell, and Tom promised this if I would help him on Ed's amendment, and Mike owes me one for last year's help on Pete's bill."[42]

Cue taking is necessary when a lawmaker doesn't know much about the legislation on the table, and logrolling is effective when the outcome of a vote doesn't matter to the representative. Every so often, though, members have to cast votes that matter to their constituents on things their constituents are aware of and feel intensely about. These are the votes that get noticed, the votes that could influence how constituents react the next time they see the member's name on a ballot. Perhaps it's a vote involving an industry that employs a lot of people back home, like the automobile industry in the Midwest or the tobacco industry in the South. Maybe it's a vote about something that touches people's lives in a direct way, like tax increases, health-care costs, Social Security benefits, or education. These votes require extra care.[43]

Likewise, members will take notice when an issue mobilizes elite groups in their districts. Issues of this nature tend to be narrow and don't involve large numbers of constituents, but they can matter strongly to the group with a stake in the outcome—for instance, cigarette manufacturers facing a new surcharge on their product. Because elites are politically active, resource-rich groups that can use their clout to help or hinder a member's reelection prospects, they can command a lot of notice despite their size.

On occasion, these votes can be tricky, depending in part on how strongly representatives feel about the matter at hand, whether their position is at odds with the position of their constituents, and if they believe they should vote their mind rather than the preferences of the people who elected them. Demystifying Government: Burke's Dilemma explains.

It's unusual for a single vote to mean the difference between political life and death. Often, members will consider their overall voting record as they look toward the next campaign, rather than worry about any particular vote. They'll try to avoid casting what political scientist John Kingdon calls a "string of votes" against a series of constituent interests that could form the basis for a future campaign against them. They'll also try to be conscious of ways to explain the more controversial parts of their voting record to their

trustee: A philosophy of representation that says officials are elected for their wisdom and to exercise their judgment of the national interest, even when it is at odds with their constituents' wishes.

delegate: A philosophy of representation that says officials are elected to carry out constituent interests, even when these interests conflict with what the representative believes is the right thing to do.

DEMYSTIFYING GOVERNMENT

Burke's Dilemma

Before you get the sense that legislators try to make everyone happy all the time, you should consider a couple of things. Legislators have values, and sometimes they want to cast votes on principles that could contradict constituent wishes. Some legislators believe that they were hired to vote their conscience and experience, to do what they felt was best for the nation even if it contradicts the views of their constituents. These considerations can factor into their voting decisions, depending in part on how they view the notion of representation.

Edmund Burke, eighteenth-century political philosopher and member of the British Parliament, espoused the view of representatives as **trustees** who are elected to exercise their best judgment of the national interest. His perspective conflicts with the more widely held contemporary American view that representatives are **delegates** of the people who put them in office and are thereby obligated to vote their constituents' wishes. Both are legitimate ways to understand representation.

Most of the time, the difference between the trustee and delegate approaches to representation isn't relevant. Because most votes are not controversial, and because the personal philosophy of candidates recruited to run for office typically matches the prevailing views of the district, significant differences between representative and constituent do not emerge often or can get lost in the shuffle of legislation.

However, should members face a rare, highly visible vote on a matter where their best judgment puts them at odds with their constituents' wishes, they face a dilemma. In fact, they face "Burke's Dilemma," as Burke himself found his view of the national interest in conflict with the wishes of his constituents.

It's probably easy to see how the trustee view of representation can have its political costs. On matters of principle, it's also easy to see how representatives might wish to risk these costs and vote against their constituents' wishes in order to do what they feel is best for the nation.

constituents, perhaps by pointing to other actions more in line with constituent wishes or by finding shelter for their votes in the supportive words of the president or other authorities their constituents might respect.[44]

They do these things because they recognize that while most votes will be inconsequential, there will always be a handful of votes on salient issues that can generate political risk. The riskiest type of vote is on a highly visible and unpredictable matter that the member cannot avoid, like the decision members of Congress had to face in 2002 over whether to support military action against Iraq. As we discussed earlier, members had no way of knowing how the war would turn out or how their votes would be regarded in time.

9.8 Working in Congress: Back Home

L.O. Speak about the relationship between members of Congress and their constituents.

Whether members regard themselves as delegates or as trustees, the folks back home arc the ones who will decide whether they get to return to Washington for another term. Legislative voting is, of course, one of the determining factors that constituents might use when they decide whether to reelect an incumbent. There's another side to the job that's more personal and often more mundane than what a member does in Washington. It's about constituent service, and it's a key part of what members of Congress do to keep their voters satisfied with their performance.

Constituent service can help the entire district at once or serve one constituent at a time. Members are always looking out for things to bring back to their districts—tangible items like public projects or federal jobs. These are the fruits of logrolling, and since every member needs them, every other member is sympathetic to the need to trade off favors for favors. Remember the $1.2 million historical sewer in Trenton, New Jersey, that we mentioned in Demystifying Government: The Golden Fleece? That represents a $1.2 million federal outlay to a congressional district. The replica of the Great Wall of China in Bedford, Indiana? That's a $20,000 outlay to a congressional district. Members can point to them at reelection time as concrete evidence of their effectiveness in serving community interests and needs.

casework: Service performed by members of Congress for constituents with individual problems or complaints that they would like the government to address.

On a more individual level, members (with an important assist from their staff) regularly perform **casework** for constituents who have problems they would like to see handled by the federal government. Casework is homework in the literal sense of the word because it requires members to use their legislative positions to address requests from people back home that can be serious and important—as well as mundane or tedious. Just like the relationship that so many of us have to doing homework, it's fair to say that most legislators do not find this to be the most fulfilling part of their job. However (just like our homework assignments), it's important to do (your grade—and their reelection prospects—hinge on doing it), and the work never stops pouring in.

Some casework involves problems constituents have with government agencies. For instance, a constituent having trouble getting his Social Security check or veteran's benefits might contact a member of Congress for help. Someone having trouble getting a passport also could turn to his or her member for assistance. So might somebody whose child wants a congressional nomination to attend West Point.

Not all casework is about navigating the bureaucracy. Lots of people contact their member of Congress because they want to receive a flag that was flown over the Capitol (flags are raised and lowered over the dome with great frequency in order to provide this service).[45] Many are interested in arranging a tour of the House, Senate, or White House during their family trip to Washington.

Other requests are just downright odd. Members have been asked for recipes, transportation on military aircraft, help changing a grade in a college course (don't bother trying—it can't be done), and all sorts of unusual, personal items. These requests are granted if possible, or turned down gently, but they're always taken seriously because there's no point in antagonizing a potential voter, even though responding to these requests takes time.

All constituent requests may get a hearing, but members of Congress do not regard all constituents the same way, especially as they think about the next election. Members try to be alert to the groups of constituents they can count on to vote for them, those they can

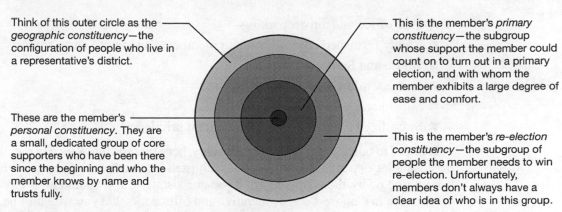

Think of this outer circle as the *geographic constituency*—the configuration of people who live in a representative's district.

This is the member's *primary constituency*—the subgroup whose support the member could count on to turn out in a primary election, and with whom the member exhibits a large degree of ease and comfort.

These are the member's *personal constituency*. They are a small, dedicated group of core supporters who have been there since the beginning and who the member knows by name and trusts fully.

This is the member's *re-election constituency*—the subgroup of people the member needs to win re-election. Unfortunately, members don't always have a clear idea of who is in this group.

FIGURE 9.6 Constituencies inside Constituencies[T11]

count on to support them intensely, and those whose support they probably can never win. The strong supporters can be pretty easy to identify, but at the margins, many representatives will confess to some fuzziness in their picture of whom they can rely on politically.

Political scientist Richard E. Fenno uses the term **home style** to describe the way members approach these different constituency groups. The way representatives size up the political inclinations of people in their district can affect the way they allocate staff resources in the district, how they fashion their trips home, and how they explain to their constituents what they do in Washington.[46]

Fenno says members—without being fully conscious of it—divide their districts into a set of overlapping constituencies based on perceptions of political support. From this perspective, a relatively small number of people can have a disproportionate influence on the member's approach to the whole district. Figure 9.6 illustrates the different layers of constituents that make up a member's district. Imagine that the circles in the figure represent different constituent groups in a district. Consider that constituents who are closer to the "bull's-eye" have more influence with their representative.

home style: The way legislators approach constituents, determined partly by how they size up their support in the district.

9.9 Staying in Congress

It shouldn't be too hard to figure out that when you add up the cost of all those staff members and the price of travel back to the district, members of Congress have a number of perks that ease the burden of their jobs and help grease the way towards reelection. The truth is, we haven't even scratched the surface of the rewards members of Congress get when they serve.

L.O. Evaluate whether the perks of serving in Congress outweigh the disadvantages.

9.9a Perks

You can start with the prestige of office (which is greater for senators but not so shabby for representatives). Tack on an annual salary in 2016 of $174,000.[47] Then, there are the professional and personal perks, such as the following:

- Allowances averaging $1,268,000 in the House and between $6 and $8 million in the Senate for
  - Legislative, administrative and clerical staff
  - Office expenses
  - Travel to and from home district or state based on distance from Washington
  - Franking (postage)
- Government subsidized health and life insurance
- Pension plan (typical lifetime benefit with retirement at age 60 after 20 years: $1,000,000)
- Recording studio
- Automobile leasing privileges

- Free office and airport parking
- Richly furnished offices for senior members and secret Senate "hideaway" offices
- House and Senate gymnasium
- House Child Care Center
- Subsidized haircuts (Senate only)
- Subsidized House and Senate restaurant privileges[48]

It's hard to put an exact figure on the salary, benefits, and allowances a member receives because a lot depends on sliding scales adjusted by the distance a member has to travel from home or by the population of a senator's state. But it should be pretty easy to see that service in Congress can be lucrative and offer perks that you wouldn't be able to find in many other jobs.

Compensation has grown in recent years. Take the salary figures as an example. In 1990, congressional salary was $98,400, which means it increased by $75,600 in two decades (it was last raised in 2009). That's a steep increase in a relatively short time—and quite a change from the $6 per day members earned in the First Congress.

More importantly, much of what members get in the form of taxpayer-subsidized benefits helps them stay in office. Travel allowances enable members to return to their districts to bolster support among their primary and reelection constituencies. The "franking" privilege, which allows members to substitute their signature for postage, enables them to send newsletters to constituents at no charge—newsletters that keep constituents familiar with their members' name and accomplishments (as told from the perspective of the member, of course). Access to video and audio recording equipment enables media-savvy members to take their positions to constituents in a more visible way.

9.9b Media Access

In fact, the media-saturated environment in which all political figures operate gives members of Congress a number of opportunities to keep their images and messages in front of constituents in a way that most political challengers would find hard to match. Your representative and senators have websites where you can go to find the latest "news" about what they've been up to, packaged to present your member in the most favorable light. Websites also facilitate casework by giving constituents an easy way to make frequently asked requests. Social media permit members (or their staffs) to reach constituents through Facebook, YouTube, and Instagram and to tweet messages on a regular basis (of course, their challengers are free to do the same).

It's worth taking a second to check out one of your representative's websites. Go to http://senate.gov and click on "find your senators" to locate the senators from your home state. If you're not from the United States, you could select the state your school is in, or any state you like. Click on their name and you'll be directed right to their website. Take a minute to look around, especially at the way they present themselves. What's your reaction?

Members of Congress also have easy access to conventional media. By virtue of their position in Congress, members are **newsworthy** and can command the attention of local radio and television in their districts with little effort. Senior members can attract national media as well. Committee chairs presiding over an issue in the news will find themselves in demand, as will members of the leadership of both parties and practically any senator, regardless of the story.

Everyone in Congress can take advantage of C-SPAN, the cable service that provides coverage of floor debate and key hearings on three channels operating 24/7. If a member wants to make points with the folks back home, a two-minute appearance from the floor of the House or Senate broadcast on C-SPAN offers an opportunity that wasn't available to earlier generations.[49]

The value of all this media attention rests with the ability it gives members to publicize themselves and their actions. Members naturally want to claim credit for doing things they know their constituents will support, and the media (supplemented by member web-

newsworthy: The conditions under which a story warrants publication or dissemination, based on a set of values applied by newspaper editors and television producers. Newsworthy stories typically have conflict, proximity and relevance to the audience, timeliness, and familiarity.

sites, social media, and newsletters) provide a natural way to do this. Leaders want to do the same thing for their party and will use the media to communicate whatever messages they feel give them an advantage over their adversaries, even to the point of staging media events to draw attention to their message.

9.9c The Incumbency Advantage

Even though party control of Congress shifted to the Democrats in 2006, to Republicans in the House in 2010, and to Republicans entirely in 2014, incumbents continue to hold a dramatic advantage over challengers and are reelected in overwhelming numbers. Prior to the 2016 election, Republicans controlled 247 House seats, meaning Democrats needed to pick up 30 seats to claim a majority. If all 435 seats were competitive, this wouldn't sound like a difficult task, but in fact, most House seats were never in play. There are several reasons for this. One is the strategic use of the perks of office by incumbents. Gerrymandering and the clustering of Democratic voters is another. Looming over everything is money. PAC money flows more freely to those who hold the reins of power than to those who wish to replace them, and Chapter 8 showed us just how much money now floods the political system.

Incumbents overall are able to far out-raise their challengers—in some cases, acting preemptively to raise so much money well in advance of the election that strong challengers never make the race. Challengers looking at an incumbent with name recognition, access to the perks of office, and a huge wallet are acting rationally if they think they'll never be able to catch up, and in the process, never be able to communicate their message and structure the agenda of the race. (This also explains why both parties will look to wealthy candidates who can self-finance campaigns against incumbents.)

The ability to raise large sums of money has a darker side. Members know they have to raise money to maintain their advantage, and they have to raise it in large quantities as campaign costs are high and continue to soar higher. Imagine serving in the House and having to run for reelection every two years. You'd never be done with your fund-raising. Senators have six years between contests but have to run statewide—a more expensive proposition, except in small states.

Money may be easy to come by, but members still have to ask for it. Some find the process distasteful. If you think about it for a second, no matter how big your ego or how much you feel you're worth it, many people cannot glide easily into a room filled with strangers, give a five- or ten-minute presentation about how important their reelection is to everyone in attendance, and then ask for large sums of cash. Calling potential donors on the telephone is hardly any better.

Herein lies a key dilemma of twenty-first-century legislative politics. Members of Congress are showered with perks. They have power and visibility. Once elected, the likelihood of keeping their job is greater than at any time in memory.

But the job has become more distasteful than ever before.

Between constant fund-raising, intense partisan bickering, endless casework, and long hours away from home and family, members can be forgiven for wondering whether the demands of such a seemingly glamorous occupation are worth it. In an era when it is more possible than ever to make a long career out of serving in the national legislature, it's not unusual for members to ask themselves whether it pays to serve.

Would you stay? It's a difficult question to answer if you've never put in the effort to run for office, just like it's hard for you to say if you'd go to college again until you've been through it once. It might seem easy to say no to staying in Congress, but if you were elected to one term in the House, you have already spent two years campaigning and raising money before you were sworn in, and another two years in office doing more campaigning and raising more money for your anticipated reelection campaign. That's four years of campaign work in order to serve two years in office. It's hard to walk away from an investment like that.

So, while some walk away, many stay despite the complaints—and some of them strive for higher office. For those who see elected office as a career, an eye is often turned to the next level of the political food chain. House members with long-term ambitions will wait for a Senate seat to become vacant. Many senators look in the mirror at some point in their careers and see a future president.

And why not? Even though the Constitution makes Congress the centerpiece of the political establishment, in the contemporary world no one is more visible than the American president. As an office, the presidency is quite different from Congress—less deliberative, less collaborative, and far more dependent on the actions and even the personality of one individual. It's also hard to make a successful bid for the presidency from Congress, even though so many members have tried. In this regard, Barack Obama is the exception to the rule. Given the huge differences between the two offices, maybe it's not surprising that only Obama, John F. Kennedy, and Warren Harding successfully made the move down Pennsylvania Avenue to the White House. Let's turn to Chapter 10 and see what they found waiting for them when they got there.

Chapter Review

Discuss how the way congressional districts are drawn can determine who gets elected to Congress.

People tend to hold negative opinions of Congress but positive opinions about their representative, which in some ways, is fitting for an institution that in recent years has become much more personalized. Before you can get to Congress, you have to run for election, and the way House district lines are drawn is a political matter that can dramatically influence who wins elections (senators, elected statewide, don't face this issue). Gerrymandering is the process of drawing district lines for political purposes, to bolster the prospects of one party at the expense of the other.

Describe the demographic makeup of Congress, and explain how it differs from the population at large.

With the high cost of campaigning, wealthy candidates who can finance their own race have become popular in recent years. Although women have been elected to Congress in larger numbers than ever before, members are still overwhelmingly male. Most members of Congress are white, college-educated professionals.

Identify key congressional norms, and explain the purpose they serve for the institution.

Like any institution, Congress has informal norms of behavior that members learn as they become familiar with the institution. Congressional norms emphasize flexibility, compromise, and civility—qualities that might not arise spontaneously in the often-contentious legislative environment.

Contrast the organization of the House of Representatives with the organization of the Senate.

Discuss ways in which minority rights are protected by Senate procedure.

The House and the Senate are organized differently, with the House less likely to tolerate minority dissent. Where the House places strict limits on debate, the Senate is respectful of the individual wishes of its members to the point that a single senator can filibuster legislation unless sixty colleagues vote to terminate debate. Both houses are organized around standing committees and subcommittees that hold hearings on legislative matters. Among the important functions Congress performs are writing an annual federal budget and overseeing the actions of the bureaucracy. The Senate confirms presidential appointments, and both houses play a role in the impeachment of federal officials.

Identify key congressional leadership positions, and explain the role of leadership in Congress.

A parallel leadership structure is in place in both chambers, with the majority party responsible for determining the legislative agenda and chairing committees. The leader of the majority party in the House is the Speaker, who presides over the chamber. The vice president of the United States presides over the Senate, but this is largely a ceremonial role with the important exception of being able to cast tie-breaking votes. Both parties have leaders and whips. With few exceptions, committee leadership is determined by seniority.

Discuss how members of Congress manage their work expectations.

Members of Congress face an intense legislative workload and the responsibility for handling constituent problems. Staff members help manage the work, but members still rely on shortcuts like cue taking from other members to figure out how to vote on a wide range of issues they know nothing about.

Explain why members of Congress pay close attention to the votes they cast.

Voting is a particularly important concern for members, who need to avoid casting a string of votes against different constituent groups, who might oppose them in the next election.

Speak about the relationship between members of Congress and their constituents.

Members tend not to see their district as a uniform entity, instead focusing their energy on maintaining good relationships with voters they believe are most likely to renominate and reelect them. It can be a demanding job.

Evaluate whether the perks of serving in Congress outweigh the disadvantages.

For all the perks of office that give incumbents an electoral advantage over challengers—including access to media resources that help them boost their name recognition and communicate messages to voters—the demands of casework and fund-raising can make the job a taxing one. This leads some members to walk away from public service, although many make a career out of running for and serving in Congress.

Key Terms

apprenticeship The legislative norm that says freshmen members of Congress should limit their activity and defer to senior members as they learn the ways of the institution. Apprenticeship is no longer enforced in Congress. (p. 264)

appropriations Legislation permitting the government to spend money that determines how much will be spent and how it will be spent. (p. 274)

bicameral A legislature composed of two houses. (p. 265)

casework Service performed by members of Congress for constituents with individual problems or complaints that they would like the government to address. (p. 288)

cloture The procedure for ending a filibuster. A cloture vote requires a 60 percent majority of the Senate. (p. 268)

committee chair The member of Congress responsible for running a committee, who can have great influence over the committee agenda and, by extension, the legislative process. (p. 283)

compromise A form of reciprocity in which members of Congress exhibit flexibility over their legislative objectives in exchange for future flexibility from their colleagues. (p. 263)

conference committees Committees made up of members of both houses of Congress, assembled when the House and Senate pass different versions of the same legislation. If the conference committee can iron out the differences, a compromise version of the legislation is sent back to both houses for final passage. If it cannot arrive at a compromise, the legislation dies. (p. 270)

Congressional Budget and Impoundment Control Act of 1974 An act designed to centralize the congressional budgeting process, which established current procedures and timetables for writing a budget. (p. 274)

constituents Individuals living in a district represented by an elected official. (p. 261)

courtesy The legislative norm that members of Congress should treat each other with respect and avoid personal attacks, regardless of how much they may disagree. (p. 264)

cue taking Looking to other members of Congress for guidelines on how to cast a vote on a technical or unfamiliar matter. (p. 286)

delegate A philosophy of representation that says officials are elected to carry out constituent interests, even when these interests conflict with what the representative believes is the right thing to do. (p. 287)

discharge petition A House procedure that forces a floor vote on legislation stalled in committee. To succeed, a discharge petition must be signed by half the House membership. (p. 268)

elitism The theory that government responds to a small, stable, centralized hierarchy of corporate and academic leaders, military chiefs, people who own big media outlets, and members of a permanent government bureaucracy. People who subscribe to this position believe the actions of regular citizens, like voting and joining groups, simply mask the real power exercised by elites. (p. 261)

enumerated powers Powers directly granted to Congress by the Constitution. (p. 266)

filibuster The strategy available to senators to delay or derail legislation by refusing to relinquish their time on the Senate floor. The filibuster is possible only in the Senate, where rules permit unlimited time for debate. (p. 268)

gerrymandering Drawing district lines in a way that favors the electoral prospects of the party in power. (p. 260)

home style The way legislators approach constituents, determined partly by how they size up their support in the district. (p. 289)

impeachment The power granted to Congress to remove from office the president, vice president, judges, and other federal officials. (p. 275)

implied powers The broad constitutional grant of power to Congress that allows it to make all the laws that are "necessary and proper" to carry out its enumerated functions. (p. 266)

incumbent An official presently serving in office. (p. 261)

institutional patriotism The legislative norm that precludes members of Congress from acting or speaking in ways that would discredit the institution. (p. 264)

integrity A key component of reciprocity in which members of Congress are expected to keep their word with each other and honor their commitments. (p. 264)

iron triangle The ongoing, mutually beneficial relationship among an interest group, members of Congress sharing the interest group's objectives, and bureaucrats in federal agencies responsible for carrying out legislation pertaining to the interest group's field. Iron triangles can develop in any policy area, and many distinct iron-triangle relationships form because the federal government is responsible for a large number of policies. (p. 266)

joint committees Committees composed of members of the House and Senate that consider matters of interest to both houses. (p. 270)

legislative work The legislative norm that members of Congress should stay on top of the work required by the committee that deals with their area of specialization. (p. 264)

logrolling A form of reciprocity in which members of Congress exhibit mutual cooperation for each other's pet projects. (p. 263)

majoritarian principle Procedures, such as those in place in the House of Representatives, that limit the ability of the minority party to influence the shape of legislation or the direction of the legislative agenda. (p. 278)

majority leader The number-two leadership position in the House of Representatives and the number-one leadership position in the Senate. In the House, the majority leader is the chief assistant to the Speaker; in the Senate, the majority leader is the chief leader on a par with the House Speaker. (p. 278)

majority whip The number-three leadership position in the House of Representatives and the number-two leadership position in the Senate. In both instances, the whip is responsible for mobilizing party members to support the leadership on key issues. (p. 278)

minority leader The number-one leadership position for the opposition party in the House of Representatives and Senate, whose responsibilities mirror those of the majority leader but without the ability to set or advance the legislative agenda. (p. 279)

minority rights Procedures, such as those in place in the Senate, that permit members of the minority party the opportunity to resist legislative actions they oppose. (p. 278)

minority whip The number-two leadership position for the opposition party in the House of Representatives and Senate, whose responsibilities mirror those of the majority whip. (p. 279)

name recognition An informal measure of how much the public is aware of a candidate or elected official, based on how widely people are able to identify the candidate or official. (p. 261)

newsworthy The conditions under which a story warrants publication or dissemination, based on a set of values applied by newspaper editors and television producers. Newsworthy stories typically have conflict, proximity and relevance to the audience, timeliness, and familiarity. (p. 290)

norms Unspoken rules of behavior that people adhere to in an institution like Congress that allow people to fit in and help the institution run smoothly. (p. 263)

oversight The process of congressional review of the bureaucracy. (p. 274)

party caucus The group of all members of a political party in the House or Senate that meets to discuss and formulate legislative priorities. (p. 281)

pluralism The theory that government responds to individuals through their memberships in groups, assuring that government is responsive to a wide range of voices. People who subscribe to this position believe that the wide distribution of resources in society drives the decisions government officials make. (p. 261)

pork barrel Wasteful or unnecessary spending that can result from logrolling. Whether something is a pork-barrel project or a valuable use of taxpayer dollars may depend on whether you stand to benefit from it. (p. 265)

president pro tempore The senator charged with the honorary duty of presiding over the Senate in the absence of the vice president of the United States. (p. 279)

racial gerrymandering Drawing district lines in a way that combines disparate populations of minority groups in order to guarantee representation by those groups in Congress. (p. 260)

ranking minority member The minority party counterpart to the committee chair, but without the power to influence the direction of the committee. (p. 283)

recess appointments The constitutional power granted to the president to make nominations while Congress is out of session that do not require Senate approval. The appointments stand until the end of the congressional term. (p. 275)

reciprocity The legislative norm that encourages members of Congress to support each other's initiatives, even if there is no direct political benefit in doing so. (p. 264)

reconciliation A procedure in the budget-writing process, whereby appropriations made in a number of congressional committees and subcommittees need to be brought in line with spending targets established early in the process. (p. 274)

redistricting The process by which congressional districts are redrawn every ten years following the release of new census data. (p. 258)

responsible parties Political parties whose legislative members act in concert, taking clear positions on issues and voting as a unit in accordance with their stated positions. (p. 279)

Rules Committee The committee of the House that channels legislation to the floor for debate and a vote on passage. (p. 267)

select committee A House or Senate committee established on a temporary basis to review a specific matter. Typically, select committees make recommendations but do not move legislation. (p. 268)

seniority The custom of awarding committee chairs on the basis of length of service. (p. 283)

Speaker of the House The leader of the majority party in the House of Representatives who exercises control over the operation of that branch through formal and informal means. (p. 278)

specialization The legislative norm that members of Congress should become experts in a legislative field. (p. 264)

standing committees Permanent congressional committees that handle matters related to a specific legislative topic. (p. 266)

subcommittees Subunits of standing committees that do the detail work involved in writing legislation. (p. 266)

substantive representation The ability of a legislator to represent the agenda or interests of a group to which he or she does not personally belong. (p. 262)

trustee A philosophy of representation that says officials are elected for their wisdom and to exercise their judgment of the national interest, even when it is at odds with their constituents' wishes. (p. 287)

Resources

You might be interested in examining some of what the following authors have said about the topics we've been discussing:

Davidson, Roger H., and Walter J. Oleszek. *Congress and Its Members*, 12th ed. Washington, DC: CQ Press, 2009. A comprehensive overview of topics relating to the operation of Congress, including congressional structure, leadership, and decision making.

Dodd, Lawrence C., and Bruce I. Oppenheimer, eds. *Congress Reconsidered*, 9th ed. Washington, DC: CQ Press, 2008. A selection of essays covering a variety of topics related to the operation of Congress.

Fenno, Richard F. *Home Style: House Members in Their Districts*. New York: Longman, 2009. The author traveled with members of Congress to see how they approach their constituents as they work for reelection.

Kingdon, John W. *Congressmen's Voting Decisions*, 3rd ed. Ann Arbor, MI: University of Michigan Press, 1992. A pioneering study of how members of Congress decide to vote.

Margolies-Mezvinsky, Marjorie. *A Woman's Place: The Freshmen Women Who Changed the Face of Congress*. New York: Crown Publishers, 1994. A former member of Congress discusses how the institution was changed by the largest influx of female representatives in its history.

Ornstein, Norman J., Thomas E. Mann, and Michael J. Malbin. *Vital Statistics on Congress*, 2008. Washington, DC: Brookings Institution Press, 2008. A thorough source of data on Congress.

You may also be interested in looking at your senators' websites. Go to www.senate.gov and enter your home state in the "Find Your Senators" window in the upper-right. Check out your home state senators' voting records, personal backgrounds, and other information. You can also view the Senate floor schedule, recent vote results, and Senate news.

Notes

1 "Congress Less Popular than Cockroaches, Traffic Jams," Public Policy Polling, January 8, 2013. http://www.publicpolicy polling.com/pdf/2011/PPP_Release_Natl_010813_.pdf.

2 "Record Anti-Incumbent Sentiment ahead of 2014 Elections," The Pew Research Center for the People and the Press, October 15, 2013. http://www.people-press.org/2013/10/15/record-anti -incumbent-sentiment-ahead-of-2014-elections/.

3 Ibid.

4 States can even gain population and lose seats if their growth was slower than population growth in other states.

5 Roger H. Davidson and Walter J. Oleszek, *Congress and Its Members*, 7th ed. (Washington, DC: CQ Press, 2000), 48–49.

6 "Geography, Not Gerrymandering, May Explain GOP's Hold on House," National Public Radio, November 15, 2012. http:// www.npr.org.

7 David Weigel, "How Ridiculous Gerrymanders Saved the House Republican Majority," Slate.com, November 7, 2012.

8 Adam Serwer, Jaeah Lee, and Zaineb Mohammed, "Now That's What I Call Gerrymandering!" *MotherJones*.com, November 14, 2012.

9 Linda L. Fowler, *Candidates, Congress, and the American Democracy* (Ann Arbor, MI: University of Michigan Press, 1993), 84–87.

10 Davidson and Oleszek, *Congress and Its Members*, 64–69.

11 Ibid., 56–59. The central cases were *Shaw v. Reno* 509 US 630 (1993) and *Miller v. Johnson* 515 US 900 (1995).

12 Davidson and Oleszek, *Congress and Its Members*, 53–56.

13 Hannah Pitkin, *The Concept of Representation* (Berkeley, CA: University of California Press, 1967).

14 Marjorie Margolies-Mezvinsky, *A Woman's Place: The Freshmen Women Who Changed the Face of Congress* (New York: Crown Publishers, 1994), 35. The member this happened to is Representative Jennifer Dunn, a Washington State Republican.

15 Sure, people roll logs down rivers. Check out http://uslogroll ing.com/. The origin of the term, though, is believed to be in the nineteenth-century custom of neighbors cooperatively rolling logs to build a fire.

16 David W. Rhode, Norman J. Ornstein, and Robert L. Peabody, "Political Change and Legislative Norms in the U.S. Senate, 1957–1974," in Glenn R. Parker (ed.), *Studies of Congress* (Washington, DC: CQ Press, 1985), 151; emphasis in original.

17 Burdett Loomis, *The New American Politician* (New York: Basic Books, 1988), 6–19.

18 David W. Rhode, Norman J. Ornstein, and Robert L. Peabody, "Political Change and Legislative Norms in the U.S. Senate, 1957–1974," in Glenn R. Parker (ed.), *Studies of Congress* (Washington, DC: CQ Press, 1985), 181–184.

19 Deirdre Walsh, Manu Raju, Eric Bradner, and Steven Sloan, "Democrats End House Sit-In Protest Over Gun Control," CNN, June 24, 2016. http://www.cnn.com/2016/06/22/politics/john -lewis-sit-in-gun-violence/.

20 Barbara Sinclair, *Unorthodox Lawmaking: New Legislative Processes in the U.S. Congress* (Washington, DC: CQ Press, 1997), 5–6.

21 U.S. Senate Select Committee on Ethics, at http://www .ethics.senate.gov/public/index.cfm/frequently-asked-ques tions1.

22 House Select Committee on Benghazi, at http://benghazi .house.gov/about.

23 Sinclair, *Unorthodox Lawmaking*, 9–31.

24 U.S. Senate, at http://www.senate.gov/artandhistory/history/common/briefing/Filibuster_Cloture.htm.

25 You can read about the Congressional Budget and Impoundment Control Act of 1974 online at http://budget.senate.gov/democratic/commhist.html.

26 Sinclair, *Unorthodox Lawmaking*, 63–69.

27 Davidson and Oleszek, *Congress and Its Members*, 205–206.

28 Sinclair, *Unorthodox Lawmaking*, 32–50.

29 Davidson and Oleszek, *Congress and Its Members*, 324–330.

30 Ibid., 314–317.

31 "For Obama Judicial Nominees, Confirmation is Slow Process," LATimes.com, November 16, 2009.

32 Davidson and Oleszek, *Congress and Its Members*, 328.

33 Ibid., 165.

34 Mike Viqueira, "Medicare Vote Got Surreal in House," MSNBC News, November 24, 2003.

35 Senate Republican Policy Committee, at http://www.rpc.senate.gov/about.

36 Senate Democratic Steering and Outreach Committee, at http://www.dsoc.senate.gov.

37 Richard Fenno, *Congressmen in Committees* (Boston: Little, Brown, 1973).

38 Christopher J. Deering and Steven S. Smith, *Committees in Congress*, 3rd ed. (Washington, DC: CQ Press, 1997), 124–182.

39 The reform measures passed by the three House committees were merged into one bill considered by the entire House, and the measures passed by the two Senate committees were merged into a separate bill considered by the entire Senate.

40 Davidson and Oleszek, *Congress and Its Members*, 153–155.

41 John W. Kingdon, *Congressmen's Voting Decisions*, 3rd ed. (Ann Arbor: University of Michigan Press, 1989), 75–96.

42 Davidson and Oleszek, *Congress and Its Members*, 279.

43 Kingdon, *Congressmen's Voting Decisions*, 29–45.

44 John W. Kingdon, *Congressmen's Voting Decisions*, 3rd ed. (Ann Arbor: University of Michigan Press, 1989).

45 If you're interested in obtaining one, keep in mind that there's a charge and you should allow six weeks for delivery.

46 Fenno, *Congressmen in Committees*, 1–53.

47 As of 2016. Data from the House of Representatives, at https://pressgallery.house.gov/member-data/salaries.

48 Figures are as of 2016 and are compiled from Davidson and Oleszek, Congress and Its Members, 153–155; the National Taxpayer's Union; and Ida A. Brudnick, "Congressional Salaries and Allowances: In Brief," Congressional Research Service, July 14, 2016. http://www.senate.gov/CRSpubs/9c14ec69-c4e4-4bd8-8953-f73daa1640e4.pdf.

49 If you're curious about who's on C-SPAN right now, just go to their website at http://www.c-spanvideo.org/schedule.

Table, Figure, and Box Notes

T1 "Berman Concedes to Sherman in Bitter House Race," *USA Today*, November 7, 2012.

T2 Ian Lovett, "Two Democrats, Two Incumbents and One Tough House Race," *New York Times*, September 28, 2012.

T3 Roger H. Davidson and Walter Oleszek, *Congress and Its Members*, 7th ed. (CQ Press, Washington, D.C.1999), 130–31.

T4 Marjorie Margolies-Mezvinsky, *A Women's Place: The Freshmen Women Who Changed the Face of Congress* (New York: Crown Publishers, 1994) 38–39.

T5 Christina Marcos, "115th Congress Will Be Most Racially Diverse in History," *The Hill*, November 17, 2016. http://thehill.com/homenews/house/306480-115th-congress-will-be-most-racially-diverse-in-history.

T6 United States House of Representatives, at http://www.house.gov/committees/.

T7 United States Senate, at https://www.senate.gov/reference/clotureCounts.htm.

T8 United States Senate, at http://www.senate.gov/committees/committees_home.htm.

T9 Ibid. Paul Ryan: Christopher Halloran/Shutterstock.com. Kevin McCarthy: Jaguar PS/Shutterstock.com. Steve Scalise: U.S. Congress. Leader Nancy Pelosi: Ryan Rodrick Beiler/Shutterstock.com. Steny Hoyer: Albert H. Teich/Shutterstock.com. Mitch McConnell: Christopher Halloran/Shutterstock.com. John Cornyn: Christopher Halloran/Shutterstock.com. Chuck Schumer: stocklight/Shutterstock.com. Richard Durbin: United States Senate of the House of congress. http://durbin.senate.gov/page_images/Durbin002.jpg. Orrin Hatch: stock_photo_world/Shutterstock.com.

T10 Roger H. Davidson and Walter Oleszek, *Congress and Its Members*, 13th ed. Washington, DC: CQ Press, 2009, 168.

T11 Richard F. Fenno, *Home Style: House Members in Their Districts*. New York: Longman, 2009.

The Presidency

CHAPTER 10

Copyright: Orhan Cam/Shutterstock.com

Learning Objectives

When you have completed this chapter, you should be able to:

■ Explain the difficulty presidents have living up to public expectations.

■ List the key formal powers of the presidency, and contrast them with informal presidential powers.

■ Understand the role of persuasion in presidential power.

■ Describe how and why contemporary presidents use public relations methods to bolster public support.

■ Appreciate why presidents may find themselves in competition with news reporters.

■ Identify and explain the key functions of the president's major roles, including chief executive, chief legislator, chief of state, chief diplomat, commander-in-chief, and chief of party.

■ Discuss the development of the institutional presidency.

■ Understand the changing role of the vice president.

■ Assess the balance of power between the president and Congress over foreign policy, as well as the general ebb and flow of presidential influence.

10.1 Introduction

L.O. Explain the difficulty presidents have living up to public expectations.

The presidency is fundamentally different from the world of Congress. Five hundred and thirty-five people give way to a single individual with a large supporting cast. The decentralized, institutional feel of the legislative arena disappears in favor of the personal mystique of a powerful man who lives and works in the shadows of the few others who have served before him.

Many of us have emotional reactions to the president that we don't have toward Congress. He can generate strong feelings in us—both positive and negative. We can be quick to comment about the job he's doing. His personal life is on display for us to judge. His quirks and foibles are magnified by television. Comedians make fun of him. We compare him to others who held the job, even presidents long ago that we don't personally remember, and have opinions about how he stacks up. We measure him for greatness, even as we are critical of his actions.

Many of us also have specific ideas about the qualities we want in our presidents (something we probably never think about in relation to members of Congress), personal characteristics we expect them to have. Take a second to think about this. Table 10.1 contains qualities that some people look for in the president.

If you're so inclined (or if you're asked by your professor), compare notes with your classmates about what they want in a president. Chances are, many of them have a long wish list. Are they looking for honesty? Integrity? Intelligence? Decisiveness? Strength? Determination? Flexibility? Experience? The ability to bring people together? Legislative skills? Communication skills? Good looks? These are just a few things people commonly say they expect their presidents to have. Does Donald Trump have all these qualities? Did Barack Obama? Of course not—it's such a demanding set of characteristics that we're much more likely to find them in a comic-book superhero than a person. But demand we will—and we feel disappointed when our presidents let us down.

Political scientist George Edwards sums up the dilemma by noting that "all" we want from our presidents is "leadership yet responsiveness, flexibility yet firmness, statesmanship yet political skill, openness yet control, and empathy for ordinary people yet uniqueness. In other words, the president is expected to be all things to all people."[1]

If in reality presidents don't have all of the personal characteristics we want them to, you might wonder why we maintain such high expectations of them. Maybe it's that past

TABLE 10.1 Things I May Want in a President

Here are a number of characteristics people may say they want in a president. Look them over and decide how many of these characteristics are on your list, and whether there are other qualities you would want that are not listed here.

Characteristic		
Brave	Good communicator	Life experience
Can unite people	Good legislative skills	Open to ideas
Curious	Good-looking	Politically savvy
Decisive	Good politician	Responsive
Determined	Honesty	Sensitive
Empathetic	Integrity	Strong
Faithful	Intelligent	Thoughtful
Firmly held convictions	Leadership skills	Understands people
Flexible		

TABLE 10.2 Criticism of Recent Presidents

President	Popular Criticism	Criticism Also Leveled Against
George W. Bush	Secretive Not substantive Not bright	George Washington
Bill Clinton	Duplicitous Deceptive Inconsistent	Thomas Jefferson
Richard Nixon	Disregards Constitution Ignores personal liberties	Abraham Lincoln

presidents set our expectations, and we want our recent ones to measure up. As part of our socialization to politics in elementary school, we internalize legends about the giants who held the office long ago, people like Washington, Jefferson, and Lincoln. In contrast, we hear so much criticism of recent presidents. Table 10.2 lists criticisms widely leveled against three recent presidents in the press and in public opinion.

Comedians regularly made fun of George W. Bush's intelligence. Lots of people—even his friends—felt Bill Clinton flip-flopped on important things and was deceptive when it suited his purposes. And Richard Nixon—during the Watergate scandal—was widely criticized by members of both political parties for disregarding personal liberties and trampling on the Constitution. Maybe you made these connections, maybe not.

What you may not have realized is that these are *exactly* the things that critics said about some of our more respected presidents, long before their faces were depicted on currency. It may surprise you to know that the things some people say about George W. Bush were also said about George Washington. Thomas Jefferson thought the first George wasn't particularly bright. Alexander Hamilton thought Washington craved power and control. His critics thought Washington paid way too much attention to his image and not enough to substance.

The things people said about Clinton echo what critics said of Thomas Jefferson, who was widely mistrusted, even by his allies, and believed to be someone who would say one thing and then turn around and say something contradictory if it suited his purposes.

Trampling on the Constitution? It was said about Lincoln as well as Nixon, by critics who watched Lincoln shut down opposition newspapers, arbitrarily arrest political dissenters, and deny prisoners who felt they were unlawfully incarcerated the right to petition for their release.

So, how did Washington, Jefferson, and Lincoln end up on Mount Rushmore if in their day they were criticized like our current presidents? The answer partly lies in the difference between myth and reality. Time has a way of making mortals heroic, of glossing over the flaws that make people human, especially if those mortals served at a critical time in our history like during the establishment of the constitutional system or the Civil War (our recent presidents did not have the opportunity to lead the United States to victory in the Revolutionary War, draft the Declaration of Independence, or emancipate the slaves). As a nation, we crave our heroes, and because of the psychological attachments people have to the presidency, our past presidents naturally fill the role. We know Washington didn't chop down that cherry tree, but deep down, many of us want to believe in leaders who could not tell a lie.

Besides, the presidency is the one office where greatness is the yardstick of performance. For many years, historians led by Arthur M. Schlesinger have been classifying past presidents as great, near great, average, below average, and failures.[2] Table 10.3 shows an updated composite ranking of the presidents, compiled from several sources. Some names remain affixed at the top—Lincoln, Washington, Franklin D. Roosevelt. Others are hopelessly in the cellar—Grant, Buchanan, Harding. What's interesting is that some presidents move around the rankings over time. Dwight D. Eisenhower was

TABLE 10.3 Ranking the Presidents[T1]

Top	Middle		Bottom
Lincoln	Reagan	Clinton	B. Harrison
F. Roosevelt	Polk	Carter	Arthur
Washington	Jackson	Ford	Grant
T. Roosevelt	Monroe	Taft	Hoover
Truman	McKinley	Nixon	Fillmore
Wilson	J. Adams	Hayes	Tyler
Jefferson	Cleveland	Coolidge	W. H. Harrison
Kennedy	Madison	Taylor	Harding
Eisenhower	J. Q. Adams	Garfield	Pierce
L. Johnson	G. H. W. Bush	Van Buren	A. Johnson
			Buchanan

ranked twenty-first in Schlesinger's 1962 survey (low average) but rose to tenth (high average) when his son replicated the exercise in 1996. Recent presidents like Clinton, George H. W. Bush, Carter, and Ford are all bunched in the middle. Will they still be there twenty-five or fifty years from now? Like most everything else, presidential performance looks different when viewed through the prism of time.

Presidents and presidential candidates, of course, are well aware that greatness is the standard by which they will be measured, and they play to it. You never hear presidential candidates promising to be the next Herbert Hoover. If there is a reason for caution in all this, it's that the Mt. Rushmore myth can influence the expectations we have of our presidents, elevating them to a place that's out of proportion to the realistic expectations of a complex and complicated office.

President Ford recognized this and played against the myth when he was elevated to the presidency upon Richard Nixon's resignation. "I'm a Ford, not a Lincoln," he told the nation, explicitly lowering expectations about his performance. It's only when we're offered the promise of a Lincoln that we can be set up for disappointment, because even Lincoln wasn't the Lincoln of myth when he walked the earth.

The wide-ranging and wildly unrealistic characteristics we look for in our presidents coincide with equally unrealistic and contradictory performance expectations. Just look at some of the things we expect the president to deliver:

- **Policy leadership:** On fundamental issues, we look to the president rather than Congress for leadership and direction. More than anyone else in the political system, we expect the president to keep us prosperous and safe, and we tend to punish presidents who fail to deliver. We hold these expectations despite the fact that the president is subject to forces beyond his control in the conduct of economic and foreign policy.[3]

- **Global leadership:** We expect the president to be the embodiment of America in the world, projecting a strong and compassionate image in line with how many of us like to view our global presence. In relations with other countries, the president is expected to act both wisely, as a statesman, and shrewdly, as a politician, despite the fact that this would require playing a unifying and divisive role simultaneously.

- **Crisis management:** The president is the person we turn to in a crisis, and we expect him to be in command. We expect the president to use his expertise and political skills to end a crisis successfully and in short order, with minimum harm to Americans, even though confusion may reign in the White House, information about what's happening may be incomplete, situations may change swiftly and unexpectedly, and good options may not be available.

- *Symbolic leadership:* We expect the president to be someone we can look up to and identify with, almost like a parent is to a young child. We want to be moved when he speaks. We want him to embody the best of us, and through his words and actions, project those positive characteristics back to us. Symbolically, we want him to be the image on Mount Rushmore, and many of us are sorely disappointed when he projects his human flaws rather than his idealized strengths.

- *Legitimacy for the system:* The president is as close as we get to a monarch, and like a king, we want the president to confer legitimacy on our collective sense of ourselves. We want him to act honorably so that his actions reflect well on American democracy and so that we may regard him as a unifying force. We want this despite the fact that the presidency is a political job, and politics is inherently divisive.

So, the myth of presidential greatness encourages a series of performance expectations that are at best contradictory and at worst impossible to fulfill. Presidents attempt to deal with this by compartmentalizing what they do, acting out different roles at different times, making a rousing speech for public consumption at a summit meeting with other world leaders while working outside the spotlight on the divisive politics of policy making. The compartmental approach can work up to a point, but presidents inevitably run up against their limitations and the many roadblocks built in to the federal system. Some presidents simply play one or two of these roles better than others. President George W. Bush received high marks for providing crisis management following the September 11, 2001 terrorist attacks (although his widely criticized response to Hurricane Katrina undermined his reputation). President Clinton was considered a strong policy leader. President Reagan provided a lot of people with symbolic leadership. It's a lot to expect them to perform all these roles at the same high level. But we do.

10.2 Growth of the Presidency

What's more, we have high expectations for performance in a presidential office that, on paper, doesn't have very much substance. The presidency started out as a poorly defined second cousin to Congress. Only time, precedent, and the actions of some of its more aggressive occupants have shaped the presidency into the powerful branch we know today.

Take a look at Article II of the Constitution, which establishes the presidency (you can find the full text in Appendix B and a discussion of the highlights in Demystifying Government: You Want to Be President?). Notice how short it is compared to Article I, which establishes Congress. It's only four sections (compared to the ten sections composing Article I)—and if you take away the material on the president's term of office, presidential elections, eligibility requirements, compensation, the oath of office, the requirement that the president make a State of the Union address to Congress, and **impeachment**, you're left with a grand total of two paragraphs dealing with what the president is supposed to do.

Article II opens with the declaration: "The executive Power shall be vested in a President of the United States," but it doesn't elaborate. The executive power? What's that supposed to be?

The authors of the Constitution were purposely vague about this central point. In colonial America, they had been pretty familiar with strong executives, both in the form of the King of England and the royal governors he appointed to oversee the colonies—who were widely regarded as corrupt officials who abused their power. In contrast, as we saw in Chapter 2, freely elected colonial legislatures served as a democratic check on these executives. The experience led them to conclude that strong legislatures were the best

impeachment: The power granted to Congress to remove from office the president, vice president, judges and other federal officials.

You Want to Be President?

You'd better be thirty-five years old. And you must be a natural-born citizen of the United States who's lived here fourteen years. So says the Constitution.

Here are a few other procedural matters pertaining to the presidency that are set down in Article II:

- The presidential term is four years.
- Congress establishes the president's salary but can't change it while he's in office.
- If the president dies or resigns, the powers and duties of the office "devolve on the Vice President." The Twenty-fifth Amendment, ratified in 1967, allows the president to temporarily assign his powers to the vice president if he is going to be incapacitated, such as if he's going under general anesthesia during an operation. It also provides for the vice president and a majority of Congress or the president's cabinet to make the vice president "Acting President" if they judge the president to be unable to function; and

it permits the president to fill a vacancy in the vice presidency, subject to confirmation by a majority vote of both Houses of Congress.

- The president has to "from time to time" give Congress "Information of the State of the Union," but it doesn't have to be in a formal speech.
- The president and vice president may be removed from office if impeached for and convicted of "Treason, Bribery, or other high Crimes and Misdemeanors." We discussed impeachment in Chapter 9 (Section 9.5d, "Impeachment").
- At his inauguration, the president is required to take the following oath: "I do solemnly swear (or affirm) that I will faithfully execute the Office of President of the United States, and will to the best of my Ability, preserve, protect and defend the constitution of the United States." George Washington added: "So help me God." So has everyone who came after him.

way to protect personal liberties.[4] So, they created a strong legislature in Article I, paying detailed attention to how it would function. Secondarily, they created the office of the president, whose grant of executive power was meant to be more vague than broad.

From these beginnings, the office of the presidency grew erratically, strengthened by precedent and by a few opportunistic presidents inclined to use ambiguous constitutional language to enhance their power. George Washington established expectations for the office by instituting standards for everything from how the president should be addressed (he preferred the constitutional designation of, simply, "the President of the United States" to Vice President John Adams' more regal, "His Highness the President of the United States and protector of their Liberties"), to procedures for how the executive branch would conduct business, to how long the president should serve (two terms, long before it was mandated by constitutional amendment).[5]

Andrew Jackson, who took office in 1829, was the first to assert a direct presidential connection to the people, strengthening the office with respect to Congress, which had previously played that role. Abraham Lincoln claimed unilateral power for the presidency as he led the Union through the Civil War. Following a period of congressional reemergence in the second half of the nineteenth century, a succession of presidents from Grover Cleveland to William McKinley to, most notably, Theodore Roosevelt, contributed to the expansion of presidential power.[6] Echoing Jackson, Roosevelt articulated his philosophy of a presidency limited only by what the Constitution prohibited him from doing (which, admittedly, is not much), calling himself "a steward of the people bound actively and affirmatively to do all he could for the people."[7]

The twentieth century witnessed a line of presidents who exercised aggressive leadership. Woodrow Wilson sought to be a strong party leader who could move public opinion and, with it, command congressional support. Franklin D. Roosevelt, governing during the Great Depression and World War II, was a proactive leader who presided over unprecedented expansion in the size and scope of the executive branch. Lyndon Johnson dominated Congress, establishing the center of policy making in the White House. Richard Nixon went to war with Congress over his attempts to expand presidential prerogatives, impounding funds for congressional initiatives he disliked and acting unilaterally in his prosecution of the Vietnam War. Ronald Reagan used the force of his personality and strong communication skills to move public opinion and congressional opponents.[8]

10.3 Sources of Presidential Power

Over the last century, success in the presidency came to hinge on the ability to articulate a message and establish a bond with voters. The advent of mass media made direct communication with the public more possible—and more necessary. Today, it's unthinkable for a day to go by without the president appearing in, or even dominating, the news agenda. The ubiquitous president is a late twentieth-century phenomenon that's worked to supplement the president's limited formal powers with a wealth of informal powers—for those presidents who know how to use them.

10.3a Formal Presidential Powers

Apart from giving the president that vague grant of "executive Power" and the equally vague (or broad) mandate to see to it that "the Laws be faithfully executed," the Constitution gives the president very few formal powers. The only specific powers expressly granted to the president are:

L.O. List the key formal powers of the presidency, and contrast them with informal presidential powers.

- **Appointments:** The Constitution gives the president the power to appoint ambassadors, Supreme Court justices, and other federal officers, like federal court judges, cabinet secretaries, and agency heads. The Senate has to confirm the president's nominees.

- **Treaties:** The president can negotiate treaties with other nations, subject to ratification by two-thirds of the Senate.

- **Commander-in-chief of the army and navy:** The Constitution makes the president the civilian commander of the military.

- **Veto power:** The president can veto an act of Congress, though Congress can override the veto with a two-thirds vote of both houses.

- **Recess appointments:** Presidential appointments made while the Senate is out of session do not require ratification, and stand until the end of the congressional session. We discussed them in Section 9.5c, "Confirming Presidential Appointments" in Chapter 9.

- **Convene Congress:** The president may call a session of Congress at any time.

- **Receive ambassadors:** The president officially greets representatives of other nations on behalf of the United States.

- **Pardon power:** The president may pardon anyone suspected, accused, or convicted of any crime for any reason without explanation (see Demystifying Government: Pardon Me?). Presidential pardons are final and cannot be overturned.

veto power: The constitutional power granted to the president to block an act of Congress. It takes a two-thirds vote of both houses of Congress to override a presidential veto.

recess appointments: The constitutional power granted to the president to make nominations while Congress is out of session that do not require Senate approval. The appointments stand until the end of the congressional term.

pardon power: The unilateral power of the president to grant unconditional clemency to anyone for any reason.

Time and tradition have supplemented the president's constitutional powers. For instance, the Constitution never mentions **executive privilege**, and Congress has never fully accepted it, but presidents have been known to use it freely. It's the power to keep material originating in the executive branch confidential. Although presidents find it helpful—and convenient—to be able to designate material as "privileged," executive privilege is far from an absolute power and can best serve as a defensive maneuver against Congress.

Typically, presidents have claimed executive privilege on matters surrounding national security, on the grounds that public exposure would undermine sensitive government operations—a position that's been upheld by the courts. Presidents have relied on executive privilege to keep members of the executive branch from testifying at congressional hearings and to prevent the release of sensitive documents.

executive privilege: The power of the president, established by custom, to keep Congress, the courts, and the public from having access to presidential documents and communications.

They have also claimed executive privilege in political circumstances to avoid the release of politically damaging information. President Nixon tried unsuccessfully to use executive privilege as a rationale to prevent the release of tapes of Oval Office conversations that implicated him in the Watergate affair.

The Bush administration, arguing that an important principle and not politics was involved, claimed executive privilege to prevent the release of information related to

Pardon Me?

The presidential pardon power has its origins in the traditional right of kings to be the final arbiter of disputes, which is why it is an absolute power. In fact, it's something of an anomaly: No other elected federal official can unilaterally grant clemency. This can cause controversy if a president is viewed as issuing pardons for political purposes.

On his last day in office, President Clinton ignited a scandal by issuing 140 pardons, some of them controversial pardons of political supporters, including a pardon of fugitive international financier Marc Rich, who was wanted by the Justice Department on fraud charges, and a pardon of his half-brother Roger, who faced allegations of illegal lobbying.

Perhaps the most famous use of the pardon power was President Ford's full pardon of his predecessor Richard Nixon for all actions taken by Nixon while he was in office. The pardon eliminated the possibility that the former president would be tried as a private citizen for illegal activities stemming from the Watergate scandal. Ford contended the pardon was necessary because a criminal trial of a former president would prevent the nation from healing. Critics contended the pardon placed Nixon above the law, shielding him from facing responsibility for his actions. There was even speculation at the time that Ford had agreed to pardon Nixon in exchange for the latter's resignation, but if this was so, it exacted a great political cost from Ford, who narrowly lost election to the presidency two years later. Also, it should be remembered that a president has the power to pardon anyone: Before he resigned, Nixon easily could have pardoned himself.

meetings between the vice president and energy company officials regarding the development of the administration's national energy policy—even though the vice president isn't the chief executive.

When you add up the president's formal powers, there's not a whole lot a president can use on an everyday basis that will help him politically. Most of the powers are situation-specific and only come into play when the president is faced with treaties he can negotiate, ambassadors he can receive, legislation he can veto, or individuals he can pardon. Recess appointments can only be made during those few weeks when Congress is out of session, and as we said in Chapter 9, the Senate regards them as hostile acts, so many presidents have been reluctant to make them. The appointment power can be formidable and can enable the president to put his mark on the executive branch and the judiciary—but it's only one aspect of the president's job. Likewise, commanding the military is an awesome power, but much of the president's involvement in domestic and foreign affairs doesn't involve military matters. The constitutional powers granted the president simply do not have a lot of day-in, day-out value.

10.3b Informal Presidential Powers

L.O. Understand the role of persuasion in presidential power.

Unlike formal powers, the prerogatives of the presidency can be enormously helpful to a president who wants to put his imprint on politics and policy. Political scientist Richard Neustadt distinguished formal, constitutional powers from informal means of exercising political power, saying the president may not occupy the strongest constitutional position with respect to Congress (which has the final word in overriding vetoes, confirming appointments, and even impeaching the president), but a skillful president can dominate Washington politically through careful use of the informal advantages his office provides. In fact, we will see that most of the president's power comes from informal sources. Neustadt recognized that the doctrine of separation of powers created three branches of government that need to find common ground in order to get anything accomplished. In this environment, a skilled and determined president can emerge as a political leader.[9]

persuasion: An informal source of presidential power that gives skilled presidents the opportunity to influence the decisions of members of Congress and others in Washington whose support the president needs to accomplish his political objectives.

He does it by using **persuasion**, by convincing others in Washington whom the president needs to get things done that his interests are their interests. There is no strict formula for doing this, but Neustadt claims the president can have maximum leverage if he enjoys a strong professional reputation in Washington and a high level of public prestige. Maintaining these requires creating favorable impressions of his ability and support.

A president's **professional reputation** is the judgment of him made by others in Washington, based on what he says and what he does. A president who rises above what is expected of him, acts consistently, and stands behind his beliefs is in a solid position to bargain for what he wants.[10] Immediately following the terrorist attack of September 2001, many in Washington who previously doubted whether he was up to the job perceived President Bush as steady, firm, and reassuring. His political stock soared as Bush erased impressions that he was a political lightweight. For several years, President Bush enjoyed the reputation of being a strong, decisive leader. Then, following the administration's halting response to Hurricane Katrina in 2005—which came at a time when the president was experiencing numerous political troubles—that reputation was replaced with far more critical assessments of his managerial and political acumen.

A president's **public prestige** is the impression formed by others in Washington of his standing with the public, and like the president's reputation, high levels of prestige can enhance his persuasiveness by making him a political force to be dealt with. In this regard, the president's public prestige and professional reputation can reinforce each other.[11] When President Bush asked Congress for approval to use military force against Iraq in September 2002, his strong public standing on matters of security and defense made it difficult for some members of Congress to oppose the request, despite their doubts about the advisability of the Iraq mission.

If President Bush had been an unpopular president at the time, congressional opponents of the Iraq War might have found it easier to voice their disapproval without worrying that their constituents would blame them for defying the president. Similarly, low standing with the public can undermine a president's professional reputation. Following the Hurricane Katrina fiasco, the president's popular support fell dramatically, reinforcing the growing perception in Washington that his professional reputation was not what it once had been.

10.3c Malleable Public Opinion

Writing over forty years ago, Neustadt saw the president's personality and popularity as secondary factors in determining the president's prestige. Today, anyone who works as a political advisor to the president would pay a great deal of attention to these things. Earlier presidents could take their **mandate** to lead from the election results, but contemporary presidents have to contend with a never-ending barrage of public opinion polls commissioned by independent research firms, major newspapers and television networks, political parties—even the White House—that measure presidential approval on an ongoing basis.

This gives the president a sliding mandate—a pliable environment for governing that can make him more or less persuasive as his term progresses.[12] President Obama was elected in 2008 by a wide popular- and electoral-vote margin during an economic emergency and could claim a mandate to move aggressively to address it, but Congress successfully blocked him from taking bold action later in his term when the president's public support lagged. Following his reelection victory, President Bush declared that the judgment of the voters had given him a new well of political capital, which he intended to use to restructure the Social Security system—a massive and politically risky undertaking. However, the president's mandate for change never materialized, owing to the fact that his reelection victory was narrow and he had said very little about his plans for Social Security during the campaign, making it difficult for him to claim a direct mandate to make changes to the program. President Trump spoke of having a mandate after he was elected, even though he finished second in the popular vote and entered office with historically low public approval. If history is a guide, his ability to claim a mandate later in his term will depend on how effectively he governs.

Because public support is neither steady nor reliable, presidents can have a difficult time mobilizing the public. Even a president with a high standing in public opinion polls can find that it is an effort to rally Congress and the public behind his policies. Much depends on the substance and style of his approach, and on events beyond his control that

professional reputation: The sense among Washington officials of the president's political skills and abilities. It is one of the keys to effective persuasion, as it enhances the president's ability to bargain.

public prestige: The sense among Washington officials about whether the president is well regarded by the public. It is one of the keys to effective persuasion, as it enhances the president's ability to bargain.

mandate: A directive by voters to the president to move ahead with the program he promised when he was a candidate. A large mandate produced by a lopsided vote gives the president a strong bargaining position with respect to Congress to set and advance the agenda in Washington.

might independently move public opinion away from him. Starting in late summer 2009, with public support for overhauling the health-care system eroding, President Obama embarked on a concerted drive to rally the public behind his reform efforts with a barrage of public appearances, including one before a joint session of Congress, that was credited by Washington observers with turning the tide of opinion back in his direction. Sometimes, the best the president can hope to do is move public opinion at the margins, getting some people who were opposed to become indifferent, or some who were indifferent to be supportive. Sometimes, small movements in public opinion are enough to secure the results the president wants—for instance, getting a wavering senator or two to support the president—while at other times, they fall short.[13]

The possibility of moving public opinion at the margins factored into President Obama's health-care strategy, as it became evident in mid-2009 that Senate Republicans were standing firmly against the president's reform push. Facing potential defections from a few Democrats representing conservative states, the president tried to rally public opinion behind health-care reform in the hope of influencing Olympia Snowe and Susan Collins, two Republican senators from the politically moderate state of Maine. But, overall support for Obama's efforts slipped as the complex legislative process played out. Senator Snowe broke with her party and was the only Republican to support the legislation on the Senate Finance Committee, but made it clear that her vote in committee might not reflect her vote on final passage of the bill. "My vote today is my vote today," she said, in a nod to the complexities of public opinion on the matter in her home state. "It doesn't forecast what my vote will be tomorrow."[14] Several months later, despite White House efforts, Snowe announced she would not buck her party and voted against the bill, along with the rest of the Senate Republican caucus.[15]

The summary figure that president-watchers (and presidents) look at to gauge presidential effectiveness is support for the president's performance in office: the percentage of Americans who approve and the percentage who disapprove. However, the polling environment is complex because pollsters ask so many questions—about individual policies, hypothetical approaches to problems, approval of the president as an individual, and much more.[16] We talked about this in Chapter 3, specifically in Section 3.6, "Measuring Public Opinion." Demystifying Government: When Do Polls Get in the Way of Governing? demonstrates how data on presidential performance are used.

With all the variables involved in opinion polls, there is one constant to the shape of presidential job approval that applies to almost all contemporary presidents: It goes down with time. Flush with the excitement and great expectations produced by a winning campaign, new presidents often come to office with a reservoir of goodwill that translates into a **honeymoon** period with the press and the public.[17] Trading on the unrealistic expectations of the presidential myth, new presidents offer the promise of great things; even people who supported the losing candidate are typically willing to give the new president a chance.

It doesn't take long for reality to set in. After a few weeks or months, unrealistically high expectations give way to the reality of governing, where hard choices by necessity begin to alienate groups of constituents. This is particularly the case during difficult economic times, which are generally blamed on the person in the White House. Presidential approval falls. The honeymoon becomes a distant memory.[18] President Obama's initial job approval numbers were in the high 60-percent range immediately after his inauguration. By the fall of 2009—after a whirlwind eight months of governing—they were in the low 50s, close to the margin he had been elected with a year before, and for much of the balance of his first term, less than half the country approved of his performance in office. Figure 10.1 shows the unmistakable downward trend in presidential job performance scores in presidents dating back to Lyndon Johnson.

Even though the general trend in presidential approval is downward, events can conspire to bolster a president's public standing. Typically, if a president is reelected, there is a brief "second honeymoon" characterized by an uptick in public approval. Immediately after his reelection victory, President Obama enjoyed his highest public approval ratings in almost four years.

honeymoon: The initial weeks of a new presidential administration when enthusiasm and good press typically translate into high public-approval ratings.

When Do Polls Get in the Way of Governing?

In film and on television, hypothetical presidents make decisions from the heart or the gut without obsessing over the details of polling data. Real presidents are far more likely to keep trusted pollsters as close advisors and rely on their counsel when deciding what positions they should take and how they should act. There are a couple of ways to view this reliance on survey data, which mirror the different legislative roles we discussed in Chapter 9—the **delegate** and the **trustee**.

When the president keeps his finger on the pulse of public opinion, it could be argued that he's acting like a delegate to govern as the public wishes. However, more than members of Congress, presidents are valued for their wisdom and leadership abilities, characteristics of the trustee role, which include the ability to set a national direction and build support when it's lacking. This is a daunting task for presidents who rely heavily on the safety of public approval.

Polling data can be used to help shape how the president presents his agenda to the public. George W. Bush's pollsters advised the president to stop using the word "privatization" to describe his proposal to restructure Social Security because polls showed that voters equated privatization with risk at a time when the stock market was volatile. Instead, they urged him to talk about "personal accounts"—which people associated with the security of ownership. Whether this shift in framing seems like a deceptive way to hide the risk inherent in the president's proposal or a shrewd way to shape public opinion depends in large part on how you view the president's role (and possibly whether you support his policy). When we see the president changing or shading positions in response to polls, it can work against the desire some people have to view the president as an independent leader. True, part of this desire is rooted in those sometimes unrealistic expectations of the president that we talked about earlier. Unrealistic or not, though, expectations can translate into attitudes. In theory, we might like to see the president move boldly on principle against the tide of public opinion. In practice, the president's political advisors would most likely say it's not worth the risk of alienating the electorate.

Not every president will listen to this advice. Despite the primacy of polling data in White House decision making, presidents have been known to buck the suggestions of their pollsters when facing problems that demanded risky, unpopular solutions. President George H. W. Bush violated his most prominent campaign pledge—"read my lips: no new taxes"—and supported a tax increase in order to win congressional support for an economic package he felt on the whole was best for the economy. That position triggered a political backlash that undermined his reelection prospects.

It is also quite commonplace for traumatic national events to produce a **rally effect**, whereby people turn to the president for leadership, temporarily bolstering his support scores in the process. The interesting thing about a rally effect is that it tends to happen regardless of what the president does, how well he performs, or whether he does anything at all. After President Reagan was shot in a failed assassination attempt in 1981, his job approval went up seven points. Early in his administration, President Kennedy ordered a failed assault on Cuba known as the Bay of Pigs invasion. It was a fiasco, the president admitted it was a mistake—and his job approval ratings went up. Americans were taken hostage in Iran during the Carter administration, the president did nothing, and his approval scores went up, too.[19] But gravity inevitably takes its toll on rallies. In Carter's case, as the Iranian hostage crisis dragged on for 444 days, his public support took a nosedive.

President George W. Bush experienced an unconventional pattern of public support in the early years of his administration because of the unusual way he came to power and the dramatic impact of the 2001 terror attacks. Instead of coming to Washington awash in good feelings, Bush had a stunted honeymoon following his contested election. Then the tragic events of September 11, 2001, united the public around the president, who saw his job approval top 90 percent—an unprecedented level commensurate with events. Bush's job approval scores remained high one year later, even as large numbers of Americans expressed concern about the direction of the economy. It seems that many people were willing to forgive the president for falling stock prices and a poor job market, either because they blamed the terror attacks for bad economic times or because their support for Bush's work in foreign affairs weighed more heavily in their overall assessment of his job performance.

delegate: A philosophy of representation that says officials are elected to carry out constituent interests, even when these interests conflict with what the representative believes is the right thing to do.

trustee: A philosophy of representation that says officials are elected for their wisdom and to exercise their judgment of the national interest, even when it is at odds with their constituents' wishes.

rally effect: The tendency for Americans to unite around the president during a crisis, temporarily bolstering his job-approval ratings.

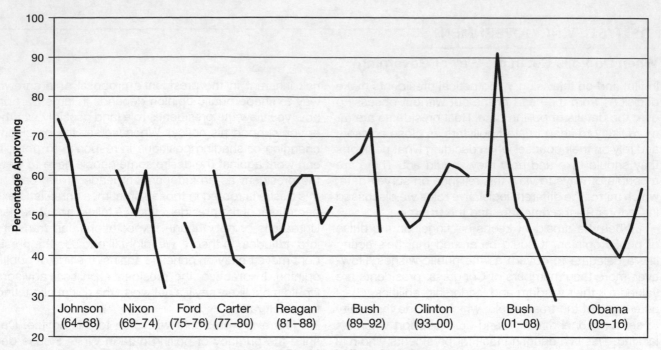

FIGURE 10.1 Down They Go

The general direction of presidential job performance scores is down. Of the nine presidents to hold office before Donald Trump, only Ronald Reagan and Barack Obama left office on the upswing, and only Reagan, Obama, and Bill Clinton left with a majority of the public approving of their performance.[T2]

In his second and third years, President Bush experienced a more customary pattern of public support. The president continued to realize a decline in popular support into his second year as unemployment mounted. This decline was halted by another rally event—the Iraq War—which briefly produced a surge in presidential approval that dissipated over the summer of Bush's third year, when American troops faced violence in postwar Iraq and the job market remained weak. The capture of Saddam Hussein in late 2003 produced another temporary bump in support for President Bush, but he faced strong political opposition throughout the 2004 presidential campaign as his approval rating sagged into the high 40 percent range.

Then, in his fifth year, President Bush experienced something of the mirror-image to the dynamics in play early in his first term. Although presidential second terms are customarily marked by an over-time decline in public approval, the Bush presidency lost support more quickly and to a greater degree than most of his recent predecessors. One year after he won reelection, Bush's performance was embraced by less than 40 percent of Americans, bogged down by the ongoing war in Iraq, soaring fuel costs, and the indictments of high-level Republican officials. Such unusually low support, realized so quickly in the president's second term, was the bookend to Bush's unprecedented high approval ratings early in his first, marking for the second time in five years an unusual extreme in presidential approval.

Rally effects aside, presidents labor—often unsuccessfully—to keep their performance ratings up in an effort to marshal their power. Political scientist Theodore Lowi, writing during the Reagan administration, saw a democratic dilemma in what he calls the personal presidency, where presidential power is built on popular support for things the president realistically can't deliver because the constitutional system is designed to frustrate his initiatives, not advance them. Only rarely can a president prevail over institutional checks and balances—like during a national crisis when he can rally Congress to his side. These are the exceptions—but we expect them to be the rule, an expectation that's inflated by our mythical notion of what the president can do and by presidents who play to that myth for political reasons, making promises that are hard to deliver.

Lacking the institutional powers necessary to play to public expectations, Lowi claims presidents engage in sales efforts to convince the public that they've met those expectations. He says that following a sincere effort to keep their promises, presidents spend their terms trying to create the illusion of success. Appearance replaces performance, sending performance expectations further out of whack with reality.[20]

With the personal side of the presidency playing such a large role in how the president governs, the makeup of the president's character can be important. Admittedly, character takes into account a lot of factors—it can be hard to pin down exactly what it is, much less figure out how it relates to presidential performance. One provocative approach to understanding presidential character is considered in Demystifying Government: Presidential Character.

DEMYSTIFYING GOVERNMENT

Presidential Character

Political scientist James David Barber suggested that one way to think about presidential character is to assess whether a president has an energetic, active approach to his job or a removed, passive style, and then to determine if the president takes pleasure in his activity or feels burdened by it. By crossing these two characteristics (activity and self-esteem), Barber arrives at four presidential character "types" or patterns into which every president can be classified.

The four types are displayed below: "active-positive;" "active-negative;" "passive-positive;" and "passive-negative."[T3]

Barber was heavily influenced by the behavior of Presidents Johnson and Nixon, whom he considered dangerous because of what he saw as "an energy distorted from within." Both were "active-negative" types who deceived the press and public, Johnson during the Vietnam War and Nixon during the Watergate scandal.

Barber claims that presidents with different character profiles would have behaved less compulsively and self-destructively, and he says we need to be aware of character issues before "hiring" a new president in order to avoid future troubles. However, his work is not without controversy. He admits to a preference for active-positive presidents (a categorization that even *sounds* more appealing than "passive" or "negative"), who display the energy of a Johnson or a Nixon but who are flexible and adaptive. However, this choice could be said to favor a governing model in which the president is an activist, rather than one where the president delegates the particulars of a limited agenda. Furthermore, because Barber's categories are broad, classifying presidents using his framework leaves room for a fair amount of interpretation.

Do you think Barber's typology would be useful for understanding the character of President Trump?

Active-Positive	Active-Negative
Examples: Franklin D. Roosevelt John F. Kennedy • Flexible and adaptive • Develops and grows over time • Feels capable of meeting job challenges • Well-grounded • Results-oriented	*Examples:* Lyndon B. Johnson Richard M. Nixon • Compulsive and insecure • Distorted ambition, which compensates for low self-esteem • Trouble managing aggressive feelings • Unable to correct misguided actions • Dangerous power-seeker
Passive-Positive	**Passive-Negative**
Example: Ronald Reagan • Compliant • Reacts to events rather than asserts himself • Nice guy searching for affection • Low self-esteem • Often disappointing in public office	*Example:* Dwight D. Eisenhower • Does little and enjoys little of what he does • Motivated by duty and service • Inflexible • Withdraws from conflict • Could lead the nation adrift

10.4 The Media as a Presidential Resource

L.O. Describe how and why contemporary presidents use public relations methods to bolster public support.

It's easier for presidents to sell the idea that they're performing than it is to actually perform because they have greater access to tools that allow them to speak effectively than to act effectively. Belying the chronic drop-off in public support that awaits most presidents is the fact that they have considerable resources at their disposal in their ongoing efforts to keep the public behind them. Most noteworthy is the megaphone the president can use to amplify his voice above the din of official Washington and command the attention of the press: There are 535 members of Congress, and the nine Supreme Court justices operate largely out of public view; the president is the only officer who alone can speak for a branch of government, an administration, or the nation. In this regard, the president can depend on the media to be an important source of informal power that enables him—if he is skillful—to elevate the importance of a constitutionally weak office.

10.4a The "Bully Pulpit"

Teddy Roosevelt called the president's elevated vantage point the "bully pulpit" ("bully" in Roosevelt's day meant wonderful), and presidents who have been skillful communicators (or who have had shrewd and skillful communications aides) have been able to command it with some success. Roosevelt served during the height of mass-circulation newspapers, and he shrewdly recognized the president's ability to use the mass media to reach out to the public and advance his agenda.[21] Subsequent presidents have mastered radio, television, and the Internet as vehicles for reaching the public with their messages. But all contemporary presidents who routinely engage in media strategies can trace their efforts to what Teddy Roosevelt started over one hundred years ago.

going public: The presidential strategy of using the media to appeal directly to the public to support presidential initiatives.

One of the more typical ways that presidents use the "bully pulpit" is by appealing directly to Americans through the media to support their agenda. Political scientist Samuel Kernell calls this strategy **"going public,"** and although it can be traced back in some fashion to Teddy Roosevelt, it has become the centerpiece of modern presidential governing styles.[22] President Obama telegraphed his intention to use the strategy to pressure Congress to consider his second-term agenda. The president "goes public" every time he makes a televised speech, appears at events around the country or the world, or employs **media events** to draw attention to and build support for an initiative. Today, presidents will go so far as to talk about policy initiatives in front of a backdrop bearing a slogan that tersely reinforces his main point—something like "Protecting Worker's Rights" or "Preserving Precious Natural Resources." It may seem cheesy and more suited to a salesperson than a national leader, but when the president goes public, he in effect becomes salesperson-in-chief.

media events: Activities staged by campaigns or political officials that have enough news value to draw press attention to a message the politician wants to communicate.

Even casual attention to television or the Internet would reveal that presidents frequently engage in public sales efforts. The point is to put pressure on members of Congress, while circumventing them at the same time. In Neustadt's terms, "going public" involves the president leveraging public prestige by moving voters to his position, rather than bargaining with members of Congress directly. Because these are the same voters who pass judgment on members of Congress, the strategy can be effective.

10.4b Media Operations

As objectionable as it may be to some people, public relations and advertising campaigns have become an integral part of White House operations and an essential part of being president. A large number of high-level White House staff members devote their time to developing, managing, and communicating the president's message on a daily basis. In the Obama White House, the key players resided in the **Communications Office**, contributing to the strategic planning of the president's policy agenda by formulating daily messages and planning media events designed to get the press to discuss the president's agenda and to do so in the way the president desires. In effect, the Communications Office tries to set the agenda for the agenda-setters in the press.

Communications Office: The White House office responsible for coordinating the president's media operations, including speechwriting and liaison with national and local reporters.

As part of this effort, the Communications Office coordinates the following communications functions:

- **Contact with national reporters.** The **press secretary** is the conduit between the president and the press. He or she manages requests for interviews with White House officials and holds regular **press briefings** with national newspaper, television, radio, magazine, and wire-service reporters who cover the White House, answering their questions—or avoiding them if doing so is in the president's interest. In recent administrations, the press secretary has worked to keep tight control over the flow of information.

- **Contact with local reporters and special interest media.** The Media Affairs Office is responsible for handling requests by local television and radio stations, newspapers, and specialized media, such as business, religious, and sports publications, for interviews with White House personnel and official information. The Media Affairs Office also maintains the White House website at http://www.whitehouse.gov.

- **Speechwriting.** The president employs a number of people who put words in his mouth, scripting everything from formal addresses to talking points for presidential appearances.[23]

The point of the effort is to get the White House to speak with one carefully crafted voice, which is often difficult to accomplish. The job of coordinating a single message can be daunting because so many people work with and around the president, all of whom have personal agendas that are not always the same as the president's. Administration officials routinely circumvent the official communications operation by giving news leaks to the press when it serves their purposes, even if it undermines the president's official message. Some White Houses are "leakier" than others. The Obama White House was tightly run, whereas the Clinton White House was known for its lack of discipline. The George W. Bush White House was highly intolerant of **news leaks**, unless they were put out on purpose with the blessing of the Communications Office to test public reaction to a policy move the White House was planning.[24] Their discipline had meaningful consequences for policy.

Presidents also have a couple of other tools to get their message to the public through the press. Presidents skilled in structured question-and-answer formats have relied on **press conferences** with reporters who cover the White House to disseminate the official line on topics of importance to the administration. Press conferences can either be

press secretary: The liaison between the White House and the national press covering the president.

press briefings: Formal exchanges of information between the press secretary and the national press covering the president.

news leaks: The tactic used widely by White House officials of releasing information to the press on an anonymous basis when it serves their interests to have the information publicized. Some leaks are unauthorized and unwanted by the White House.

press conferences: Scheduled meetings between reporters and political figures like the president, which give the press access to the official and an opportunity to ask him or her questions firsthand.

Presidents have been "going public" for years, and in media-savvy ways that have changed as communication technology grew up. Franklin D. Roosevelt (left) used his command of radio to give "fireside chats" that made people feel like he was a visitor in their living rooms. Ronald Reagan (center) used visual devices like charts in his televised addresses from the Oval Office. President Obama's weekly addresses (right) were made available as streaming videos on the Internet.[T4]

conducted privately or staged as television events. President Kennedy, for instance, was fond of televised press conferences because he could use them to speak directly to the public, in effect turning them into media events where reporters were props.[25]

Presidents generally cannot control what happens at a press conference, of course, but press conferences don't have to be risky ventures for them. They can take questions from reporters known to be friendly to the administration. Presidential advisors can usually anticipate the major questions reporters will ask, and speechwriters can craft responses in advance. Even if a question isn't about something he wants to address, the president can give a quick and general response and move rapidly to something he wants to talk about. Because reporters customarily are limited in their ability to follow up, it can be hard for them to get the president to address something he doesn't want to talk about. All this restricts how informative press conferences can be.[26]

President Obama addressed the press regularly. President Clinton held press conferences less frequently than some of his recent predecessors; President George W. Bush rarely held them, opting instead to let his press secretary interact with reporters. However often they held formal press events, every president since Franklin D. Roosevelt has held background briefings or **"backgrounders,"** where reporters are given information "off the record"—meaning they can use it as long as they don't attribute it to its source. Any administration official may hold a backgrounder, and unlike press conferences, they can be a good source of information for reporters. The administration can use backgrounders to float a policy idea without having the president's fingerprints on it in case it flops with the public (much like the way news leaks can be used), or even to send messages to other nations about possible foreign policy initiatives without yet having to defend them as official policy.[27]

backgrounders: Off-the-record exchanges between the president or administration officials and reporters. Whatever a reporter learns at a backgrounder can be used in a story, but the source of the information cannot be revealed.

10.4c Tensions with Reporters

L.O. Appreciate why presidents may find themselves in competition with news reporters.

As presidents have come to view the press as a tool in a public relations campaign, reporters have pushed back by looking critically, even cynically, at the president's motives and by reporting his actions accordingly. Today, presidential news is more likely to be about the motivation underlying what the president said or did than simply about his words or actions. By reporting on the presidential public relations machine, reporters try to dilute its effects by drawing attention to it.

It may be hard to believe that for a period before the Vietnam War, the president was widely regarded by the press as a public servant who spoke for the nation, and reporters would pass his words on uncritically. That was before the Johnson administration lied to reporters about American progress in Vietnam and the Nixon administration lied about the president's involvement in Watergate. Media advisors to Presidents Obama, George W. Bush, Clinton, and Reagan relentlessly stage-managed the president's image, leading reporters who felt they had been lied to by Johnson and Nixon to experience the additional burden of feeling controlled by the White House. The cumulative product of these experiences was the creation of an adversarial relationship between reporters and the president, in keeping with the relationship between reporters and political figures that we discussed in Chapter 5.

For a period of several years following the September 11, 2001 terrorist attacks, reporters covering President Bush assumed a more respectful and less critical tone reminiscent of coverage in the early days of television, in keeping with widespread calls for national unity. But, when the administration's slow response to Hurricane Katrina undermined the president's reputation as a decisive leader and capable manager, reporters who witnessed the bungled response first-hand began to revert to the more confrontational position they had taken toward President Bush's immediate predecessors.

Once again, the contours of a complex relationship between reporters and the president came into view. Presidents want to control the timing and content of news stories. So do reporters. Because the president's ability to persuade the public and official Washington depends so heavily on the media, he can't do without the reporters who cover his actions. At the same time, because the prestige and career advancement of those who cover his actions depend on having access to the White House, reporters can't do without the president.[28]

Because it's an ongoing relationship, both parties typically find a way to cooperate, although reporters will find some administrations to be more forthcoming than others, and levels of cooperation change over the course of time. Political scientists Michael Grossman and Martha Kumar identify three distinct phases in the relationship between the president and the press, starting with a period of alliance when an administration is new and reporters are engaged in developing relationships with new people in the president's press operation. It's a time when reporter and administration self-interest calls for cooperation, as both groups benefit from covering the administration in a favorable light.

It usually doesn't last long. Once the administration gets down to the business of governing, conflicts and controversies are inevitable. Reporters, seeing these items as **newsworthy**, diverge from the White House view of how (or whether) the story should be covered. A phase of competition sets in, leading reporters and White House officials to engage in manipulative actions for control of the agenda. The competition phase can endure for a long time before giving way to detachment, when the administration gives up on trying to build support for its agenda, abandoning its most intensive efforts to control the press. During the detachment phase, the president more or less avoids the press, and his schedule is tightly controlled.[29] Detachment is likely to set in during the final years of a president's second term, when reporters find greater newsworthiness in the race to replace the incumbent. In the Bush administration, the phase of competition left reporters griping that the Communications Office controlled information so tightly that, in the words of one reporter—uttered long before the devastation of Hurricane Katrina—"If the National Hurricane Center were as stingy with its information, there would be thousands dead."[30]

newsworthy: The conditions under which a story warrants publication or dissemination, based on a set of values applied by newspaper editors and television producers. Newsworthy stories typically have conflict, proximity and relevance to the audience, timeliness, and familiarity.

10.5 Chief Executive

For an officer with a brief constitutional job description, the president performs a wide range of policy and political roles: chief executive, chief legislator, chief of state, commander-in-chief, and chief of party. We'll look at each one in turn. Although we will find in these roles the occasional constitutional power like the ability to make appointments, the veto power, and the power to negotiate treaties, almost every tool the president wields has developed through custom and practice, placing them in the realm of informal powers—like the president's use of the media—that have expanded the capacity of a constitutionally limited branch.

L.O. Identify and explain the key functions of the president's major roles, including chief executive, chief legislator, chief of state, chief diplomat, commander-in-chief, and chief of party.

When we talk about the president as the **chief executive**, we mean he's the chief executive officer of the United States, as well as the chief of the executive branch of government, or the bureaucracy (which we'll be talking about in Chapter 11). In this capacity, he exercises "the executive Power" in a number of specific ways.

chief executive: The role the president plays as head of the executive branch, in which he carries out the constitutional directive to "take Care that the Laws be faithfully executed."

10.5a Making Appointments

We said in Section 10.3a ("Formal Presidential Powers") that presidents have the formal power to make appointments to key federal positions, which are subject to Senate confirmation. A big part of his role as chief executive rests with the appointments the president can make to upper-level positions in the bureaucracy. These include top appointments to the departments, agencies, and commissions that comprise the federal bureaucracy—and there are a lot of them, from large departments like Defense, Justice, and Treasury, to more narrowly focused agencies like the Federal Election Commission, the Federal Trade Commission, and the Nuclear Regulatory Commission.

There are serious limits to the president's appointment power. All in all, over 2.6 million people were employed in the executive branch in 2014.[31] Of these, the president appointed only a few thousand. The rest are civil servants, who get and hold their jobs independent of political considerations and, as we'll see in Chapter 11, are not indebted to the president. Furthermore, there are limits to the president's ability to remove people

TABLE 10.4 The Obama Cabinet, 2016

Department	Created	2015 Obama Cabinet
State	1789	Secretary of State John Kerry
Defense	1789	Defense Secretary Ashton Carter
Treasury	1789	Treasury Secretary Jack Lew
Justice	1789	Attorney General Loretta Lynch
Interior	1849	Interior Secretary Sally Jewell
Agriculture	1862	Agriculture Secretary Thomas Vilsack
Commerce	1903	Commerce Secretary Penny Pritzker
Labor	1913	Labor Secretary Thomas Perez
Health and Human Services	1953	HHS Secretary Sylvia Mathews Burwell
Housing and Urban Development	1965	HUD Secretary Julian Castro
Transportation	1966	Transportation Secretary Anthony Foxx
Energy	1977	Energy Secretary Ernest Moniz
Education	1979	Education Secretary John King
Veterans' Affairs	1988	Secretary of Veterans' Affairs Robert McDonald
Homeland Security	2002	Homeland Security Secretary Jeh Johnson

cabinet: The name given to the collection of secretaries of the executive departments. Despite commonly held beliefs to the contrary, the cabinet rarely serves as an advisory body to the president.

he appoints. The president cannot remove appointees who have fixed terms of office, like members of the Federal Communications Commission or the Federal Reserve Board, just as he can't remove judicial appointees. He has a lot more latitude over political assistants and cabinet members, whom he can remove at will.

The Constitution does not give the president the power to appoint a **cabinet**. It doesn't even mention one. However, every president has had one. George Washington had four cabinet secretaries: State, War, Treasury, and Justice. Today, there are fifteen (see Table 10.4).

In the Obama administration, eight other people also had cabinet "rank." They were: the vice president, the president's chief of staff (Denis McDonough), the United States trade representative (Michael Froman), the United States Ambassador to the United Nations (Samantha Power), the chair of the Council of Economic Advisers (Jason Furman), and the directors of the Environmental Protection Agency (Gina McCarthy), Office of Management and Budget (Shaun L. S. Donovan), and Small Business Administration (Maria Contrearas-Sweet).[32] Cabinet rank is assigned at the president's discretion, so these other individuals will vary from administration to administration. Several of these other cabinet-level officials in the Obama administration were part of the White House staff, or what is more formally called the **Executive Office of the President (EOP)**—the large, sprawling staff that assists the president in making political and policy decisions on a wide range of matters. We'll look more closely at the EOP in Section 10.10, "The Institutional Presidency."

Executive Office of the President (EOP): The large staff of advisors to the president that comprises the president's political and policy operation.

Contrary to widely held popular belief, presidents rarely convene their cabinets to get advice and make decisions because cabinet members function first as the head of their respective departments and only second as presidential advisors.[33] More often, communication in cabinet meetings flows in one direction: from the president to the cabinet secretaries, on whom the president relies to advance administration policies. It would be frustrating for the president to try to do otherwise because cabinet secretaries, as specialists in their own areas of expertise, have little in common with each other. As the heads of large departments, they may also have conflicting interests and agendas—something that doesn't lend itself to a frank and open exchange of ideas and advice.

10.5b Preparing Budgets

Congress has the power of the purse, but as chief executive, the president has a hand in formulating the budget. Like the cabinet, this role is not mentioned in the Constitution, but as the federal government took on more responsibilities in the twentieth century, the executive branch grew in size (revisit Table 10.4 to see how many cabinet departments were created after 1900). The president as chief executive naturally assumed a larger role in creating the budgets for these departments.

This role was formalized in the **Budget and Accounting Act of 1921**, which detailed the president's responsibility in the budget process. Among its key provisions are:

- The requirement that the president submit an annual budget proposal to Congress, reflecting his spending priorities and estimating how much money it's going to take to keep the executive branch operational for another year.
- The establishment of the **Office of Management and Budget (OMB)**, formally the Bureau of the Budget, which assists the president in formulating his budget.
- The establishment of a congressional investigative office, the Government Accountability Office (GAO), previously known as the General Accounting Office, designed to ensure the accountability of the executive branch.

The president's budget proposal is just a recommendation, and in a Congress controlled by the opposition party, it's likely to be "dead on arrival." However, because the president gets to draft a formal proposal, he gets to be a player in the budget debate that takes place in Congress. At a minimum, he has a forum for presenting his priorities. If he's dealing with a sympathetic Congress, he'll find that his recommendations are given serious consideration.

Budget and Accounting Act of 1921: The act providing the legal basis for presidential participation in the budget process, by requiring the president to submit an annual budget to Congress for its consideration.

Office of Management and Budget (OMB): The executive office responsible for developing the president's annual budget proposals by evaluating requests for funding among departments and setting the president's spending priorities.

10.5c Issuing Executive Orders

The Constitution instructs the president to "take Care that the Laws be faithfully executed," but without a road map showing how to do this, presidents since Washington have used **executive orders** to make directives to the bureaucracy that do not require congressional approval and that carry the force of law. Executive orders are another informal presidential power because they are based on a broad interpretation of the Constitution. They permit the president to act unilaterally on matters that are not itemized in the Constitution, and the courts have generally upheld the president's right to issue them.

Most executive orders are procedural or of little interest, but on occasion, presidents have used executive orders to do an end run around Congress and create policy. President Truman used an executive order to desegregate the armed forces (which are part of the executive branch). President Johnson used an executive order to require that private businesses receiving federal contracts (through executive branch departments) implement affirmative action policies. President Reagan used an executive order to ban abortion counseling in federally supported clinics. President Clinton used an executive order to overturn it.[34]

executive orders: Presidential directives to the bureaucracy that are legally binding and do not require congressional approval.

10.6 Chief Legislator

In addition to being chief executive officer and presiding over the executive branch, the president plays a central role in the legislative process by shepherding an agenda through Congress. Or, more accurately, every president tries to get Congress to approve his initiatives. In making the president **chief legislator**, the Constitution gives the president the vantage point from which to lead Congress but offers no guarantee of success. Much of the capital a president accumulates by developing a strong professional reputation and

chief legislator: The role the president plays when he offers a legislative agenda and attempts to win congressional approval for it.

enhancing his public prestige goes to convincing Congress to support his legislative initiatives. Win or lose, presidents know their leadership skills will be evaluated in the next election on the basis of how well they moved their program through Congress.

10.6a Proposing an Agenda

The origins of a president's agenda may be found in the election campaign—in the platform drafted at the party convention where the president was nominated and the rhetoric of his campaign speeches—and in the issues the president makes a priority upon taking office. In his second inaugural address, President Obama made the case for a progressive second-term agenda based on the positions he took during the 2012 campaign, including higher taxes on the wealthy, immigration reform, attention to global warming, and in the wake of the school shooting in Newtown, CT, gun control. However, advancing an agenda can be difficult, as presidents meet with mixed degrees of success in converting their priorities into congressional priorities. Sometimes, this is because what the president wants to accomplish is simply not what the congressional leadership wants to do. President Obama found himself in this situation with a Republican House and a Republican Senate minority willing to filibuster initiatives it disliked. Sometimes it's because presidents set out too many priorities for Congress to handle and find that their effort to accomplish a lot of things results in little or nothing getting done. President Clinton met with this fate when he tried to make four huge issues—health care, trade, spending, and taxation—his top priorities in his first term.

It's often hard to predict how effectively a president is going to manage his role as chief legislator. President Nixon faced resistance from an opposition Congress, but so did President Reagan, and Reagan was able to get Congress to accept his agenda, whereas Nixon was not. President Clinton tried unsuccessfully to get a Congress controlled by his own party to do a lot; President Johnson faced the same situation and was largely successful.

The differences? They can be explained in part by the situation surrounding the president's rise to power. President Johnson took office upon John F. Kennedy's assassination, and a year later won a lopsided election victory over a weak opponent. President Reagan won only slightly more than half the popular vote but carried better than 90 percent of electoral votes. Even though Reagan's election was in part a repudiation of incumbent Jimmy Carter, the press interpreted the election as a mandate for Reagan's legislative agenda, and that helped shape the public's response. The same interpretation followed Johnson's election, with similar results. Whether or not either interpretation was warranted, it had the effect of creating a climate in which the new president could place his agenda at center stage. Neither Nixon nor Clinton had this advantage.[35]

10.6b Lobbying Congress

Still, a mandate—or the appearance of a mandate—is simply a tool. Presidents need to maximize their resources of persuasion if they're going to put this tool to good use. They and their aides need to quickly identify their top legislative priorities. They need to organize staff members who will be responsible for **legislative liaison**—maintaining ongoing contact with Congress and lobbying for the president's proposals at every step of the legislative process. They need to develop a strategy about how they're going to do this. They need to access and absorb volumes of technical information on their policy priorities so they're ready for the inevitable questions or problems that will arise with Congress. They need to have insight into the ways of the federal government, or be clever enough to surround themselves with others who do. They need to persevere through the long and often frustrating legislative process, despite the emotional or physical toll it may take.[36]

If the administration has its priorities straight, is organized, efficient, strategic, informed, familiar with Washington, and tireless, it can approach Congress from a position of strength. Then, if the president has capital by virtue of his electoral mandate, professional reputation, and public prestige, he has a chance of seeing his legislative priorities move through Congress. At least, that's the way it would work in an ideal world.

legislative liaison: White House lobbyists who maintain regular contacts with members of Congress and congressional committees, in order to help guide the president's legislative agenda.

Everything could be in place for the president, and circumstances might still work against his best efforts. If an international crisis arises, it's likely that the president's domestic agenda will get sidetracked. If members of Congress are gearing up for reelection, it's possible that little legislating will get done because members will be more interested in drawing partisan distinctions than in making the compromises necessary to advance legislation.

That's why the timing of a president's actions is so important. There's a good reason we've been talking about legislative efforts during the early days of a presidential administration—during the honeymoon—when official Washington is typically most open to listening to what the president has to say. Time is the president's enemy if he wishes to lead Congress. This is why President Obama moved swiftly to get Congress to enact the largest and most difficult components of his domestic agenda in his first months and why he moved equally quickly on his second-term agenda following his second inaugural.

One presidential aide put it this way: "You've got to give it all you can that first year. Doesn't matter what kind of majority you come in with. You've got just one year when [members of Congress] treat you right and before they start worrying about themselves."[37] Another presidential assistant picks apart the typical four-year presidential administration like this: "You should subtract one year for the reelection campaign, another six months for the midterm [elections], six months for the start-up, six months for the closing, and another month or two for an occasional vacation. That leaves you with a two-year presidential term."[38]

10.6c Vetoing Legislation

Perhaps the president's strongest legislative weapon is negative. The Constitution gives the president the formal power to veto legislation sent to him by Congress, which has to muster a two-thirds vote in both houses to **override** the veto and make the legislation into law without the president's approval. The veto can be a strategic tool that a president can use to try to shape legislation to his liking and can be particularly useful to presidents who face a Congress controlled by the opposing party. If the president threatens to veto legislation while it's being considered by Congress, and the threat is credible—meaning members of Congress believe the president will go through with it—they could decide to re-shape elements of the legislation to the president's liking. Considering how hard it is to muster two-thirds majorities in both houses to override a veto, such shifting might make sense to legislators who would at least come out with some of what they want. It also means that a president doesn't always have to use the veto for it to be a potent weapon; the mere threat of action sometimes will suffice. Demystifying Government: Some Constitutional Tricks discusses other options the president has when considering how to act on legislation.

override: The congressional power to overturn a presidential veto by a two-thirds vote of both houses of Congress.

pocket veto: The presidential prerogative to veto a bill without taking action. Presidents may issue pocket vetoes only if Congress has passed legislation within ten days of adjournment. A pocket veto cannot be overridden.

DEMYSTIFYING GOVERNMENT

Some Constitutional Tricks

The Constitution lets the president pull a nifty maneuver if Congress passes legislation he doesn't want to sign and then adjourns within ten days of acting. It's called a **pocket veto**, and it lets the president veto a bill by doing absolutely nothing. Because Congress is out of town, a presidential veto could not be delivered to Congress for its consideration. So, the Constitution under these circumstances gives the president two options: Sign the bill, or put it in your pocket and forget about it. After the ten-day window is over, if the bill doesn't have the president's signature, it dies. This makes a pocket veto absolute—it cannot be overridden.

On the other hand, if Congress is in session and the president receives legislation he doesn't particularly like but has decided not to veto, he has the option of leaving it on his desk for ten days, at which point, it becomes law without his signature. A president might do this as a way of signaling that he recognizes he doesn't have the support to sustain a veto, but because he dislikes the legislation, he's going to let the bill become law without his name on it.

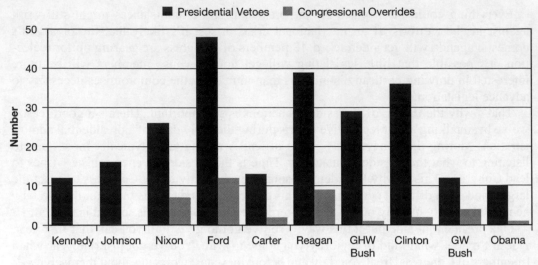

FIGURE 10.2 Presidents and Their Vetoes[T5]

If a president does veto a bill, the odds are great that the veto will hold up. Of 1,506 regular vetoes[39] cast between 1789 and 2016, only 111 have been overridden—about 7 percent. Presidents only have to worry about an override if they veto a bill that has widespread public support or if they're up against a Congress dominated by the other party. The latter situation is rare, although it has happened. President Ford, a Republican, faced overwhelming Democratic House and Senate majorities, which kept passing legislation he did not support. Ford's response was to use the veto pen forty-eight times in two and a half years, only to see twelve of them, or 25 percent, overridden—a rate of override about three and a half times the presidential average.[40] Under the circumstances, the strategy of using the veto as a way to get Congress to bend to the president's wishes was unavailable to President Ford. His only viable strategic option was to use the veto to send a message of disapproval to the legislature. Figure 10.2 shows how many vetoes the presidents since John F. Kennedy have cast.

President Obama only vetoed ten bills and President George W. Bush vetoed twelve during their respective eight-year terms. As Figure 10.2 indicates, these figures are historically low for recent administrations, although the Bush figure reflects the president's reliance to an unprecedented degree on signing statements—written pronouncements by the executive accompanying his signature on legislation. Other presidents have issued signing statements, but not to the same extent as President Bush and largely for the purpose of clarifying their views on the legislation they were signing. By one count, President Bush issued close to 800 signing statements in his first six years, besting by 200 the total number issued by all his predecessors *combined*.

And Bush's use of signing statements was highly controversial, because he employed them to qualify and in some cases nullify the contents of the bills he had signed into law, thereby greatly expanding the power of the executive with respect to the legislature. In 2006, a bipartisan task force convened by the American Bar Association came out strongly against Bush's use of signing statements, and the philosophy that suggests a president can interpret laws to his liking and sign—then gut—laws he does not like. The Bar Association flagged this as a serious violation of separation of powers and checks and balances, and urged Congress to prohibit the president from issuing signing statements without making a full report to Congress offering a legal basis for disregarding the law he has signed. They also urged the president to simply use his constitutional veto if he does not agree with an act of Congress.

10.7 Chief of State and Foreign Policy Leader

If the president's chief executive and chief legislator roles are marked by the strategic allocation of resources in an ongoing, often frustrating tug-of-war with Congress, the president as **chief of state** lives a much more charmed existence. A chief of state is a nation's official envoy to the world, a nation's symbolic and ceremonial head. The chief of state greets foreign dignitaries and has formal state dinners in their honor. The chief of state gets to light the official White House Christmas tree and grants honorary recognition to celebrities. He speaks for the nation and is the nation's representative around the globe.

If you think about it, this is an odd combination of roles, with the chief executive and chief legislator engaging in gritty political maneuvering while the chief of state rises above the political fray. Although there is substance to the president's responsibilities as chief of state, many of the functions he performs in this capacity are symbolic. That's why so many nations separate the roles, leaving the political stuff to a head of government and permitting a nonpartisan figure to assume the ceremonial role (see Global Topics: Chief of State vs. Head of Government).

Because we roll all these roles into one job, we ask the president to unify us as our symbolic representative and move us forward as our government leader—even though politics is, by definition, a divisive business. This can lead to some interesting wrinkles in the way presidents act and in the way we relate to our presidents. For instance, while opinion polls repeatedly showed large percentages of Americans approved of Bill Clinton's policy agenda, the litany of finance and sex scandals that pockmarked his administration marred his performance as chief of state. Some who saw Clinton as unprincipled or shady objected to him being the official voice of the United States, preferring instead someone they could relate to or be proud of.

George W. Bush tapped this desire when he campaigned for office as someone whom people would be proud to have as their symbolic leader. Following the 2001 terror attack, President Bush continually emphasized his role as chief of state, both to unify the nation and, subsequently, to leverage the support he was receiving for his partisan political battles with Congress. For Bush, being a successful chief of state became a resource in his role as chief legislator.

chief of state: The role the president plays as ceremonial head of the United States.

GLOBAL TOPICS

Chief of State vs. Head of Government

In Great Britain, a partisan prime minister, selected from the majority party in Parliament, performs the functions that are comparable to our chief executive and chief legislator. But Queen Elizabeth is the chief of state, the ceremonial leader who can rise above politics and represent Great Britain to the world. This type of arrangement, where an elected official runs the government while the head of state is a royal figure, is not uncommon around the world. In Denmark, Queen Margrethe reigns as chief of state while Prime Minister Lars Lokke Rasmussen runs the government. Belgium's King Philippe is head of state, but leaves the governing to Prime Minister Charles Michel.

Other nations divide the chief of state and head of government functions between a president and prime minister, maintaining a republican form of government in a parliamentary system.[T6] President Rebelo de Sousa greets official visitors to Portugal, while Prime Minister Antonio Costa takes responsibility for running the government. Austria, Italy, Germany, Ireland, the Czech Republic, and Hungary are among the nations that also have this arrangement.[T7] China has a separate president and premier but without the constitutional underpinnings of republican government.[T8]

In practice, the range of constitutional models is wide. In some systems, presidents have more than a symbolic role and play a part in governing, potentially posing a challenge to the prime minister. France and some Latin American nations have such "semi-presidential" systems.[T9] The issue of the governing role taken by a chief of state can be a difficult one. On one hand, the chief of state needs to offer legitimacy to a nation and serve as a source of political stability. On the other, presidents can clash with prime ministers in parliamentary systems should they claim to have an independent source of legitimacy and political support.[T10] Because of this, systems that separate the chief of state function from the head of government function may find themselves facing difficulties which, while different from those confronting the American president in a system that combines the two functions, are nonetheless problematic.

By the way, if you live in Canada or Australia, you too have prime ministers running the government. But your chief of state? Queen Elizabeth II of England—even today—through an emissary known as a governor general.

Chief Diplomat

The pageantry and pomp that serve as the trappings of the chief of state can mask a substantive role accorded the president. Think of him as the **chief diplomat**—as the person the Constitution makes responsible for receiving "Ambassadors and other public Ministers." Officially, this means that before ambassadors of other countries can set up shop in the United States, they must present their credentials to the president. This apparently ceremonial function gives the president the right to extend American **diplomatic recognition** to other nations—to decide whether the representative of a nation has legitimacy in the eyes of the United States.

Recognition by a major power like the United States can build instant global credibility for a new nation or a regime that takes power following a revolution or uprising. Situations like this don't come around often, but when they do, decisions about whether or when to extend diplomatic recognition can reverberate globally. For instance, in the confusion surrounding the demise of the Soviet Union, the United States faced the prospect of recognizing a host of self-declared independent states that previously had been part of one nation.

chief diplomat: A constitutional role of the president, in which he has the power to recognize ambassadors from other nations.

diplomatic recognition: Formal acceptance of the legitimacy of another nation or its representatives.

When Barack Obama ran for the presidency, he emphasized that having a person of color assume the presidency would send an important message to other nations. Attuned to the symbolism of the office, Obama has made reference to his historic election as emblematic of a change in America's posture toward the rest of the world, which had become strained during the Bush years. In what could be interpreted as a symbolic response, President Obama was awarded the Nobel Peace Prize just nine months into his presidency.

In addition to the pomp and ceremony of the chief-of-state role, the president performs key foreign policy functions, making him the paramount voice in American foreign affairs. One of his more important roles is diplomatic (see Demystifying Government: Chief Diplomat). He is also responsible for formulating the nation's foreign policy, overseeing intelligence activities, and functioning as commander-in-chief of the armed forces.

10.7a Formulating Foreign Policy

In keeping with the general tendency for the chief-of-state role to be less contentious than the president's domestic policy roles, the president typically finds himself with more leeway in foreign affairs than he does when he engages in the inevitable domestic clashes with Congress. This distinction led political scientist Aaron Wildavsky to contend that there are "two presidencies" with distinct patterns of political support—a domestic policy presidency, where presidential initiatives often get bogged down in the thistle of congressional opposition, and a foreign and defense policy presidency, where a determined president can almost always have his way.[41]

The key place Wildavsky looks for evidence of the two presidencies is in the record of success presidents have had in the formulation of policy. Where presidents have had mixed results moving domestic proposals through Congress, succeeding most thoroughly in the rare instances when they are propelled by a major crisis (like Franklin Roosevelt during the Great Depression) or when their party comprises an overwhelming congressional majority (like Lyndon Johnson in the 1960s or Barack Obama during his first two years), Wildavsky finds that presidents who wanted to pursue a foreign or military course typically succeeded.

Wildavsky finds several reasons for this. Unlike domestic policy, foreign policy is dangerous; events can move quickly and the consequences can be monumental. This tends to focus the public on the president's foreign policy actions and motivate presidents to devote a lot of resources to foreign policy formulation. No one else in Washington can rival the administration's investment in foreign policy expertise or its ability to speak with one voice.[42]

Wildavsky wrote during the heightened tensions of the cold war, leading some to reevaluate his argument with the passage of time.[43] Today, in a world where protection from terrorist threats dominates the foreign policy agenda, we can find some anecdotal evidence that the president again may have a relatively free hand in formulating foreign policy. It took only a few weeks in 2002 for President Bush to convince a reluctant Congress to endorse his plans to invade Iraq if that nation refused to permit open inspection of its weapons programs. Yet, at about the same time, the president remained unable to advance key elements of his domestic agenda.

10.7b Negotiating Treaties and Making Executive Agreements

The president's formal constitutional prerogative to negotiate treaties with other nations seems on the surface to contradict the idea that it's smooth sailing for presidents in foreign affairs. Because treaties have to be ratified by a two-thirds vote of the Senate, presidents may find that the negotiating they have to do with the legislative branch is much more difficult than the negotiating they had to do with the other nation or nations involved in the treaty. Historically, the Senate has not been shy about defeating even high-profile treaties with strong presidential backing; probably the most notable twentieth-century example is

President Obama meets with India's Prime Minister Manmohan Singh at the White House.[T11]

the defeat of the Versailles Treaty by the Senate following World War I, which kept the United States out of the League of Nations.

However, as is often the case with the president, there is an informal mechanism available to him that circumvents the constitutional complexity of navigating treaties through the Senate. Presidents can avoid a resistant legislature by issuing **executive agreements**, which do not require congressional action. The president can negotiate executive agreements with leaders of other nations, a practice with a long history even though it is not provided for in the Constitution. Once signed, executive agreements have the force of law. This gives the president great latitude in foreign policy negotiations, provided those nations are willing to forego the stature of a treaty.

executive agreements: Legally binding presidential agreements with other nations that do not require congressional approval.

10.7c Supervising Intelligence Activities

Since September 11, 2001, many of us have become more aware than before of our intelligence operations and the complex business of gathering information about groups or individuals who might pose a threat to national security. The secretive world of intelligence gathering falls under the auspices of the president through the director of central intelligence, whom the president appoints with Senate approval. It's been that way since the National Security Act of 1947 established the Central Intelligence Agency (CIA), the organization responsible for providing the president with information on security threats, under the supervision of the director of central intelligence.[44]

The CIA also reports to the **National Security Council (NSC)**, the primary body for assisting the president with security-related decisions. In addition to the president's national security advisor, the NSC includes select cabinet officials (including the secretaries of state, defense, and treasury) and receives military briefings from the chairman of the **Joint Chiefs of Staff**, the president's primary military advisor.[45]

In response to the attacks on the World Trade Center and the Pentagon, President Bush proposed and established a cabinet-level Department of Homeland Security, which

National Security Council (NSC): The group of senior policy advisors responsible for helping the president shape national security policy.

Joint Chiefs of Staff: The group of military advisors comprised of the heads of the army, air force, navy, and marines.

entailed conducting the largest reorganization of the federal government since Franklin D. Roosevelt was president. The new department combined a host of security-related and information-gathering organizations under one administrative umbrella in an effort to create a coordinated agency charged with border security, emergency preparedness, and antiterrorist intelligence gathering.

10.8 Commander-in-Chief

The Constitution gives Congress the power to declare war, but it gives the president the power to wage war. In the eighteenth-century world of the Constitution's framers, where troops were committed to battle following a formal declaration, the president's military powers were expected to be secondary to Congress. In a twenty-first-century world, where the military response to crisis is often swift and troops are sent into battle without formal declarations, the president's power as **commander-in-chief** of the armed forces looms large.

commander-in-chief: The president's constitutional role as civilian leader of the armed forces.

The president has several advantages over Congress in the conduct of military affairs. He has the formal power to move American forces overseas and commit them to battle. As we just noted, he has an intelligence and advisory structure that can keep him abreast of international developments, providing him with information that Congress does not have. He can act unilaterally and swiftly. Informally, he can move public opinion behind him once he acts.

The swelling of the president's military resources follows the growth of the United States as a world power. Until about seventy years ago, presidents had access to very limited advice and data for making military judgments, as there was little in the way of a defense establishment like we have today.[46] That was before the commander-in-chief was responsible for a nuclear arsenal, and before America's permanent military establishment ballooned in size and reach in response to the country's central place in world affairs. Although presidents have claimed the power to commit troops without congressional authorization since John Adams sent the navy to do battle with France, the scope, magnitude, and extent of American involvement overseas have made presidents serving since the middle of the twentieth century the central figures in military affairs.

In the 1970s, Congress tried to fight back. In the wake of the divisiveness of the Vietnam War, many members of Congress felt Presidents Johnson and Nixon had overstepped the boundaries of their role as commander-in-chief, and they were determined to reassert their constitutional prerogative over military matters. The result was the **War Powers Act of 1973** (which passed over President Nixon's veto), the intent of which was to limit the president's ability to initiate military action without congressional approval. It does this by requiring in the absence of a declaration of war that the president consult with Congress before taking action and periodically while troops are in the field. If Congress does not ratify the president's action within sixty days, the president has to bring the troops home (this may be extended to ninety days if the president claims immediate withdrawal poses a risk to the troops).

War Powers Act of 1973: A congressional attempt to reassert the role of the legislature with respect to the president in military affairs by restricting the president's ability to wage war.

The promise of the War Powers Act was that balance in military affairs would be reestablished between Congress and the president, but it hasn't quite worked out that way. Presidents have ignored the War Powers Act, choosing instead to continue to commit troops as they always did—and Congress hasn't tried to reign in the president. There are good political reasons why. As Vietnam faded into memory, passions subsided, and subsequent Congresses weren't eager to confront the president. If Congress pressed the point and the president decided to challenge the constitutionality of the War Powers Act, it's not at all clear that the act would hold up to scrutiny if the Supreme Court decided that it provides Congress with a veto over the president's actions (this would be considered a "legislative veto," and the Constitution only grants veto power to the president). As a practical political matter, because the president can typically rely on the public rallying behind him at least briefly when he sends troops abroad, it's difficult for Congress to stand up to the president when he's engaged in the role of commander-in-chief.

10.9 Chief of Party

It's nowhere to be found in the Constitution, but by custom, the president is the head of his political party. We found out in Chapter 6 that political parties are decentralized organizations built from the ground up. Despite this structure, as the highest elected national official, the president is well positioned to give a face and a voice to his party and, if he enjoys popular support, contribute heavily to party campaigning and fund-raising functions. It's an advantage the party out of power simply can't match.

Particularly when it comes to raising money, the president can be a party's biggest weapon. President Obama frequently e-mailed his supporters with requests for money during his reelection campaign. When President Clinton was in office, he routinely barnstormed the country, headlining fund-raisers that brought in record sums of money for the Democratic Party. President George W. Bush exceeded Clinton's fund-raising records to the benefit of the Republican Party, raising over $260 million for his reelection campaign.

Being party chief is not without its complications. An unpopular president can leave a party effectively leaderless, and because no one else commands the national stage like the president, no one else can step in as party leader if a president lacks popular support. Candidates for other offices will not want to be seen on the same stage with him for fear that their association will cost them votes. President Bush was so unpopular during the congressional elections held in the middle of his second term that he became a powerful political weapon for the *opposition* party. More than one Republican running for Congress conveniently found himself with something else on his schedule when word came that the president wanted to campaign for him.

Even popular presidents may find that there are limits to their political reach. In 2016, with his approval ratings in the mid-50% range, President Obama visibly threw his support behind Hillary Clinton and made an impassioned case to voters to elect her as his replacement, only to find that presidential approval is not transferrable. Two generations ago, when more people voted strictly by party, presidential candidates routinely carried members of Congress into office on their **coattails**. Today, as we saw in Chapter 6, people are more likely to split their ticket, voting for Republicans for some offices and Democrats for others.

coattails: The ability of a victorious presidential candidate to sweep congressional candidates of the same party into office on the strength of people voting for one political party.

The president may also face problems reconciling the blatant partisanship of the party-leader role with the president's other responsibilities. President Bush wrestled with this dilemma right before the 2002 congressional elections as he tried to remain above politics as chief of state while campaigning for Republican candidates as chief of party.[47] The balancing act was particularly delicate: The president tried to look serious and statesmanlike as he moved the nation closer to a conflict with Iraq, while also hopping around the country unleashing partisan rhetoric at political rallies. In his chief-of-state role, he was trying to unify the nation and prepare the world for military action, but the chief-of-party role required the president to get down into dirty, divisive partisan muck in order to rally the faithful and win votes for Republicans. The strategy carried risks for Bush's professional reputation, which would have been undermined had he appeared too partisan or divisive at such a somber moment.

You could say that Bush's problem reflects the crosscutting expectations we place on our presidents. It illustrates the dilemma that presidents face as they juggle contradictory roles.

10.10 The Institutional Presidency

It seems as though the more we ask the president to do, the more help he requires—and the more assistance he gets in the form of a large, bureaucratic staff centered around the Oval Office. In Section 10.5a ("Making Appointments"), we briefly made note of this staff in our passing reference to the Executive Office of the President (EOP). When the presidency was a fairly small office prior to the major expansion in federal functions that occurred during Franklin D. Roosevelt's administration, the White House staff was equally small. By way of comparison, Roosevelt left behind a personal staff of fifty-three

L.O. Discuss the development of the institutional presidency.

people, which had swollen to over 350 by the time Bill Clinton took office. During the same period, the president's budget advisors almost doubled in number, and his national security staff more than tripled.[48]

10.10a Inside the Executive Office of the President

White House Office: That portion of the Executive Office of the President organized to serve the president's immediate needs.

chief of staff: One of the president's top political advisors and the formal head of the White House staff.

Every administration organizes the EOP a little differently, but there are a number of constants that have endured from administration to administration. Every recent president has organized the **White House Office** around a **chief of staff**, who coordinates the workings of the White House Office and serves as a key advisor with intimate access to the president. The White House Office typically includes the president's personal secretary, legal advisors, political advisors, and in recent administrations has grown to include the Communications Office and offices that handle contacts between the White House and Congress, interest groups, and the president's political party.[49]

The inner circle of the White House Office contains the president's most trusted and influential confidants. Typically, these people are the president's longtime associates or personal friends, including people who worked with the president when he held lower offices and people who had high-level positions in the president's election campaign.

The rest of the EOP is just as compartmentalized, containing offices that assist the president on things ranging from budgetary to security matters.

10.10b The Office of the First Lady

The Executive Office of the President is housed in the West Wing of the White House. Across the way, in the East Wing, you'll find the offices of the first lady. There's no official role for the first lady, but the wife of the president is an important symbolic figure in American life, especially in an era when television cameras make her a public figure (whether or not that's her wish). Jacqueline Kennedy was the first to play the role of national hostess on television, projecting an air of youth and glamour akin to her husband's televised persona.

Traditionally, the first lady has played a social role, hosting guests at the White House. However, a few presidential spouses have seen themselves as more than official greeters. Eleanor Roosevelt, wife of Franklin, played an active role in her husband's administration. Ahead of her time, anticipating the revolution in women's roles that would begin twenty years after she left the White House, Eleanor Roosevelt lobbied her husband on behalf of the social issues she advocated. She wrote a newspaper column and was a media presence, promoting causes like rights for women and minorities.

Nancy Reagan maintained a far more traditional public image, but behind the scenes, she was influential in her husband's administration. People who worked in the Reagan White House understood the importance of being on good terms with the president's wife, and her close relationship with the president made her an important, though informal, advisor. Once, when reporters were shouting questions at President Reagan that he was unable to hear against the din of background noise, television microphones picked up Nancy Reagan whispering an answer in her husband's ear, which promptly came out of his mouth. It was a rare glimpse of how involved she was in the workings of the administration.

Hillary Clinton took the role of first lady to a place none of her predecessors had been—directly into the West Wing, where she set up shop with a personal staff. An attorney with experience as a congressional aide, she came to the White House with the résumé of someone who might have applied for work in the Executive Office of the President. As a candidate, Bill Clinton joked about his wife's ability and influence by saying that they offered voters a "buy one, get one free" option—a line foreshadowing her own run for president twenty-four years later.

In office, it came to pass. Bill Clinton put his wife in charge of a task force exploring proposals for restructuring the way Americans receive health care, a role so out of sync with the traditional work of a first lady that it sparked a national debate. When the Clinton health-care proposal tanked, Hillary Clinton shared the blame with her husband and never again took a visible policy role in her husband's administration. Nonetheless, she continued to be an influential advocate in the White House, and in the last year of the Clinton administration, she became the only first lady to be elected to public office when she won a Senate race in her adopted state of New York. In 2001, as President Clinton was moving out of the Oval Office, Senator Clinton was settling into her new workspace on the other end of Pennsylvania Avenue. Seven years later, after losing out to Barack Obama for the Democratic presidential nomination, her one-time rival saw fit to ask her to join his cabinet, where she served as secretary of state.

When Hillary Clinton left the White House, she was replaced in the East Wing by Laura Bush, a more traditional first lady who kept a lower and less controversial profile. Like many contemporary first ladies, she became a public advocate for a cause—in this case, literacy and childhood education—which she had promoted since her days as a teacher and librarian in Texas.[50]

Michelle Obama positioned herself somewhere between her two immediate predecessors. Acutely aware of her symbolic role, she kept a high profile as the mother of two young daughters—the first thing you would see on her webpage was the statement: "first and foremost, she is Malia and Sasha's mom."[51] But she is also a Princeton- and Harvard-educated lawyer with an impressive résumé in community service work, and she paired her professional and family backgrounds to speak out on the importance of community service and balancing work and family responsibilities.

10.11 Second in Command

Here's a job description for you to consider: You get to attend the occasional funeral for a head of state, preside over the Senate (where no one will complain that you hardly ever show), and otherwise make yourself available just in case something happens to your boss. For this, you will be well compensated with a good salary and a nice house in a great location.

L.O. Understand the changing role of the vice president.

Perhaps, you find the prospect of a job like this appealing, but many of the people who have served as vice president have commented on the remarkable emptiness of a position that is, after all, the only other nationally elected office in the United States. The first vice president, John Adams, bemoaned, "My country has in its infinite wisdom contrived for me the most insignificant office that ever the invention of man contrived or his imagination conceived." Thomas Marshall, vice president under Woodrow Wilson, compared his situation to "a man in a cataleptic fit: He cannot speak; he cannot move; he suffers no pain; he is perfectly conscious of all that goes on, but has no part in it." John Nance Garner, Franklin D. Roosevelt's first vice president, put it more succinctly: "The vice presidency isn't worth a pitcher of warm spit."[52]

It's probably not surprising that ambitious men could feel hamstrung in the vice presidency, or that the office itself was a late addition to the Constitution, where it was never more than a pencil sketch of an institution. The vice presidency gave the Constitution's authors a method of presidential succession that didn't violate separation of powers by relying on a congressional officer, and it resolved the issue of who would preside over the Senate and cast tie-breaking votes when necessary. It also created a dilemma for its occupants, who are given little authority and no power, and who until recent administrations have been reduced to waiting around in case something happened to the president (Demystifying Government: Moving from Second to First looks at the fate of a couple of recent vice presidents with presidential aspirations).

Throughout the nineteenth century and well into the twentieth, vice presidents were frequently the object of ridicule or neglect. Selected by party leaders to provide geographic or ideological balance to the presidential nominee, qualifications for the number-two office rarely advanced beyond the ability to carry a state or a voting group that the presidential candidate could not. As political circumstances evolved from year to year, necessitating a different balance in the next election, vice presidents found themselves highly expendable commodities: No nineteenth-century vice president was renominated for a second term by a major political party. After Martin Van Buren in 1836, none was nominated for president.[53]

The revamped, contemporary vice presidency is viewed as a stepping-stone to the presidency, but how successful have recent vice presidents been in achieving that ambition? When George H. W. Bush was elected president immediately after serving eight years as vice president to Ronald Reagan, he became the first vice president to take that step on his own since Martin Van Buren succeeded Andrew Jackson in 1836.

Al Gore tried to replicate the feat in 2000 but fell short. His troubles illustrate how the vice presidency can cut both ways when its occupant seeks the top prize. As a visible national figure, Gore had no trouble raising money and winning the nomination of his party. At the same time, he was saddled with the scandals of the Clinton years, and as a member of the administration, he had trouble distancing himself from them. Journalists wrote of Gore's dilemma trying to emerge from President Clinton's shadow, but the reality of the vice presidency is that it's hard for its occupant to run for president as his own person.

Since seeking the office wasn't much of a career move, it didn't draw the interest of big political names. Daniel Webster rejected overtures from Whig Party leaders to be their vice-presidential nominee in 1848, saying facetiously, "I do not wish to be buried until I am dead."[54] The nomination went instead to Millard Fillmore, who apparently didn't mind. So, most vice presidents were second-tier political figures who spent their time looking for something useful to do. Some didn't even bother to stay in Washington. Van Buren's vice president, Richard M. Johnson, left town in 1837 to operate a tavern.[55]

Circumstances changed dramatically in the middle of the twentieth century, making the modern vice presidency a much more desirable office both substantively and politically. When Harry Truman became president upon the sudden death of Franklin D. Roosevelt in 1945, World War II was ending. America and its allies were drawing plans for the shape of the postwar world, and the United States had been secretly developing an atomic bomb, but Truman was uninvolved in and largely unaware of these efforts. When he became president, he had to come up to speed quickly and was left to make life-and-death decisions that affected the future shape of the world. From that point on, it became clear that the vice president had to be someone who could step into a role that now had global implications.

That didn't mean that vice-presidential candidates didn't still have to give political balance to a ticket. But after 1945, presidential candidates needed to assure the country that they were running with someone who had the capability and experience to become president at a moment's notice. Their choice would come to be seen as an example of their judgment and leadership ability.

This applied in 1976 when Jimmy Carter selected Senator Walter Mondale to be his running mate. The liberal Mondale, a midwesterner and Washington insider, provided natural political balance to Carter's more conservative southern base. Mondale's four years as vice president turned out to be historic, as Carter offered him more policy responsibility than any vice president in history to that point. He had a West Wing office, access to presidential information, and met regularly with the president, serving as a key advisor. Al Gore played an even larger role in the Clinton administration, as the president made him primarily responsible for making decisions in a range of policy areas, including the environment, technology, and telecommunications.[56] Dick Cheney followed Gore as vice president and played a highly influential role, serving as one of President Bush's most trusted advisors with arguably more input to policy decisions than any vice president in history. Vice President Joe Biden, selected by President Obama to add experience and gravitas to a ticket headed by a young senator, was an important advisor to the president and proved to be a key negotiator with Congress, drawing on the relationships he built over the years in the Senate. Vice President Pence was selected for his experience as a former governor and member of Congress, providing governing experience for a running mate who was a political novice.

But can a vice president capitalize on this experience? Table 10.5 shows just how difficult it is to move up to the top spot from the vice presidency.

TABLE 10.5 Did They Become President?

Vice President	President Served	Became President through Presidential Death or Resignation	Ran for President, Won	Ran for President, Lost
Nixon[T12]	Eisenhower		YES	YES
Johnson	Kennedy	YES		
Humphrey	Johnson			YES
Agnew[T13]	Nixon			
Ford	Nixon	YES		
Rockefeller[T14]	Ford			
Mondale	Carter			YES
G. Bush	Reagan		YES	
Quayle[T15]	G. Bush			YES
Gore	Clinton			YES
Cheney	G. W. Bush			
Biden	Obama			

10.12 The Ebb and Flow of Presidential Influence

As an institutional matter, the president and Congress have long been in a tug-of-war befitting two institutions dependent on each other to get things done. The early presidents who stretched the reach of the presidency through a broad interpretation of the presidential role—presidents like Thomas Jefferson, Andrew Jackson, and Abraham Lincoln—did so at the expense of Congress. This is why we've seen strong presidencies followed by periods where Congress grabbed back some of the authority that it felt rightfully belonged to the legislature.

L.O. *Assess the balance of power between the president and Congress over foreign policy, as well as the general ebb and flow of presidential influence.*

The War Powers Act was passed during such a time, following a string of presidential administrations considered "imperial" for their regal tone and extensive claims of authority. If Franklin D. Roosevelt forever enhanced the role of the president when his administration dramatically increased the sweep of federal authority, the advent of America's global influence and the nuclear tension of the cold war gave late twentieth-century presidents godlike power over life and death. We looked to them to protect civilization and keep us safe from nuclear annihilation, giving them unprecedented opportunities to use their informal powers to strengthen the office. People started calling them the "leader of the free world." That's why the "imperial presidency" reached its height under Presidents Kennedy, Johnson, and Nixon, in the frostiest days of the cold war.[57]

It's not too hard to see how presidents serving under these conditions might take on imperial characteristics. The president has always had personal privileges, but the office assumed regal qualities under cold war circumstances. Imagine how you'd feel if you never had to wait in line for anything. You never had to drive a car, and you never got stuck in traffic because roads were closed off when you were coming. Every time you walked into a room, people would stand. Military bands would play "Hail to the Chief" when they spotted you. Airplanes would take off within thirty seconds after you boarded. It would be hard for most people not to let this go to their heads. Now consider what happens when they're also calling you the "leader of the free world." The effect would be to create a sense of privilege befitting an emperor.

As the president took on the characteristics of a monarch, the Executive Office of the President took on the air of a court. George Reedy, who served as press secretary to President Johnson, compared the situation in the White House to one you'd find in a palace, where courtiers cater to the king's ego, fight among themselves for the leader's attention, and engage in petty acts to undermine each other in the larger pursuit of winning the king's favor.

What did not happen in this atmosphere was an honest, hard-hitting exchange of ideas. Aides felt pressed to say yes to the president, regardless of how much they privately disagreed with what he was doing. To disagree was to risk the wrath of the chief executive and to be displaced from power. No one felt they could do what Reedy believed was necessary to reestablish a healthy atmosphere in the White House: Occasionally tell the president to "go soak his head."[58]

Bad ideas can be hatched in such an insular environment, without dissent to sharpen the president's thinking—and they were. The prosecution of the Vietnam War proceeded as President Johnson listened to advisors who assured him that escalating the conflict was the best policy, partly because they feared punishment if they dissented. This effectively trapped Johnson inside a gilded echo chamber, where the failure to hear dissenting voices kept him from recognizing that he was losing the support of the public. President Nixon's administration was secretive to a fault—the chief of staff tightly controlled all contact with Nixon—and in his imperial seclusion, Nixon believed he could get away with illegally thwarting his political opposition. He was, after all, the "leader of the free world."

That was when Congress fought back—with the War Powers Act and with impeachment proceedings against Richard Nixon, stemming from illegal activities conducted in a climate of White House secrecy. A period of congressional dominance followed, coinciding with the weak presidencies of Gerald Ford and Jimmy Carter.

Recognizing that presidential grandeur had taken the presidency too far away from its political roots, Gerald Ford followed Richard Nixon in office with a deliberate effort to make the president ordinary. Naturally unaffected and down to earth, Ford fit the role perfectly. In his first days in the White House, he held a media event designed to communicate the message that this president would not be an emperor: There in the kitchen was the new president in a bathrobe, making his breakfast toast. We had entered a period of the anti-imperialist president, the president of the people. Ford did away with the pomp that surrounded his predecessors, even to the point of requesting at times that "Hail to the Chief" be replaced by the fight song of his alma mater, the University of Michigan.

His successor also used populist symbols to communicate the message that his presidency was the antithesis of Johnson's and Nixon's. President Carter broke with tradition by leaving the limousine that carried him to the White House after his inauguration, choosing to walk the parade route, hand-in-hand with his wife. He wore cardigan sweaters instead of suits and ties. He invited people to call him "Jimmy."

Interestingly, the public eventually tired of this folksy presidential style, in no small part because of how it became intertwined with downsized presidential performance. It's impossible to know if Ford would have become a folk hero—the ordinary man in the White House—had he not generated so much ill will by pardoning President Nixon for his Watergate-related crimes or presided over an ailing economy. Likewise, the image of a plainspoken peanut farmer might have become Jimmy Carter's presidential legacy had he been able to tackle the rampant inflation that undermined the nation's standard of living and crises abroad that left many feeling that America had become a weak nation.

Ironically, despite the wrenching experiences of Vietnam and Watergate, the events of the Ford and Carter administrations left some people yearning for a return to the imperial presidency. Ronald Reagan promised to restore pomp and glitter to the office as part of a broader message of regaining a sense of national strength and pride. For many, it was the right message at the right time, playing to the enduring wish that the president provide a king-like legitimacy to the American system.

Events continued to shape the office after Carter's term, facilitating the conditions for a return to the imperial presidency, punctuated by an interlude defined by more down-to-earth politics. With the cold war still raging, many Americans found security in the regal trappings of the Reagan years. At the same time, the Reagan administration advocated policies that, for the first time since Franklin Roosevelt, assumed government was the source of our problems, not the solution to our problems. There was a profound transformation in the political debate, which for the first time in generations made it acceptable to consider shifting power away from Washington. In the process, President Reagan undermined one of the two pillars on which the imperial presidency had been built: the sense that the president, as the chief executive of the national government, was ultimately responsible for providing a huge range of services that could not be had elsewhere. As power began to flow out of Washington and to the states, the president's royal position was inevitably diminished.

Then the Berlin Wall came down, the Soviet Union crumbled, the cold war ended, and the other pillar supporting the imperial presidents—the fact that each was the "leader of the free world"—lost its currency. Without having to assume the posture of someone faced with decisions of global life and death, Bill Clinton could reach out to voters as a pop-culture figure rather than as a regal figure. He could appear on a late-night television variety show wearing shades and playing the saxophone, as he did during his presidential campaign. He could turn up on MTV and answer a question about the kind of underwear he prefers. In their day, no one could have imagined Presidents Johnson or Nixon answering a question about whether they liked boxers or briefs. For that matter, no one could have imagined either man being in a situation where the question would have been asked.

The office had returned to pre-imperial dimensions. Congress reasserted itself to the point where in the months following the 1994 Republican takeover of the House and Senate, the president briefly became secondary to Congress in political importance. Several years later, an energized Congress impeached but failed to convict President Clinton for his actions stemming from the Monica Lewinsky scandal.

Perhaps, things would have continued on this path had America not been the object of a major terrorist attack. Having elected in George W. Bush, a president with admittedly no foreign policy experience, foreign affairs ironically became the focal point of his administration. With this came a return to the serious business of being global leader, and not coincidentally, a return to some of the trappings of the cold war administrations: increased secrecy and the reassertion of presidential authority over Congress. The decision to invade Iraq was made in this climate. Years later, as the details of how those decisions were made began to become public, echoes of the Johnson and Nixon administrations reverberated through questions raised by administration critics about whether the failure to listen to dissenting voices resulted in critical errors of judgment about the rationale for war.

Donald Trump exhibits some of the characteristics of past imperial presidents through his larger-than-life persona, small circle of trusted advisors, and penchant for secrecy (recall that he was the first presidential nominee in forty years who did not release his tax returns). At the same time, he lacks the long history of political ambition that characterized presidents like Johnson and Nixon. Demystifying Government: President Trump discusses some of the challenges he faces as he transitions to the presidency.

Even at its most imperial, one of the ironies of the modern presidency is that the one branch that the president seems to have the least influence over is his own. There are interesting reasons why the "leader of the free world" often comes across as the head of the bureaucracy in name only. In reality, things are often different than what you'd expect from an organizational chart of the executive branch that has the president's name at the top. We'll look at the peculiar relationship between the chief executive and the executive branch as we turn to Chapter 11.

President Trump

It can be difficult to know how Donald Trump will approach the presidency because in important ways he defies comparison with previous occupants. Trump campaigned as a disruptive figure and arrived in Washington with the intention to shake things up. He assumed the presidency without prior political or military experience, entering politics at the highest level. His outsider sensibilities and lack of political training could lead him to bristle at the boundaries imposed by the office, especially if the urge to disrupt is curbed by the numerous requirements and expectations of the job.

It's probably fair to say that Donald Trump is not used to being constrained. He will be familiar with executive decision making from his private-sector experience, and one of his most heralded claims is his experience in making deals, but he may not be used to negotiating with others on an equal footing, such as other heads of state or even leaders of a separate branch of government. We have discussed how presidents inevitably find that the key to a successful tenure rests with their ability to win the support of other Washington players who have their own autonomous base of power and may not share the president's objectives. Governors and legislators learn by necessity how to build coalitions, but Trump comes from a background where he is more used to giving orders. As Harry Truman said of his successor, General Dwight Eisenhower, "He'll sit here, and he'll say, 'Do this! Do that!' *And nothing will happen.* Poor Ike—it won't be a bit like the Army."[T16]

Like any president, Trump will need to prioritize his governing objectives. He may have to decide how much initiative over the legislative agenda to concede to Congress or delegate to his aides, especially if he does not take interest in the details of governing. Some presidents have found delegating to others to be an effective management style. In that case, the skill and experience of the people surrounding him will be critically important.

Trump did campaign on several large-scale ideas, but they are controversial and problematic. He promised to build a wall on the Mexican border and have Mexico pay for it, and he promised draconian deportation measures and a ban on Muslims entering the country, all of which are likely to generate stiff opposition from outside groups, Democrats, and some mem-

Source: Evan El-Amin/Shutterstock.com

bers of his own party. His desire to repeal and replace Obamacare—which he shares with congressional Republicans—may be harder to do in practice than it sounded during the campaign, and Trump promised as president-elect to preserve some of the more popular elements of the measure, such as protection from being denied coverage for preexisting conditions. Like all presidents, he will have limited political capital, and he will have to decide how to spend it.

To that end, his popularity or lack thereof could turn out to be the strongest predictor of his effectiveness. Public support is a president's best friend because presidents share voters with members of Congress, making it harder for them to push back against a popular incumbent. We noted earlier that President Trump was elected with historically low public support that did not improve appreciably in the weeks following the election. As the winner of a contentious election in a divided country, success would normally depend on his ability to win over those who strongly opposed his candidacy, unless he pursues a strategy designed to appeal to base voters in congressional districts with boundaries drawn to favor Republicans.

Every president undergoes a form of on-the-job training because nothing is comparable to the presidential office, but President Trump may face a particularly steep learning curve. It remains to be seen if the presidency will change him or if he will change the presidency.

Explain the difficulty presidents have living up to public expectations.

Because the presidency is the only federal office that's personified by an individual, it's the only office where performance expectations are elevated to unrealistic heights. It's not uncommon for people to evaluate the president against a mythical ideal derived from the presidency's vast folklore, nor is it unusual for people to feel disillusioned when presidents do not live up to this standard.

List the key formal powers of the presidency, and contrast them with informal presidential powers.

Understand the role of persuasion in presidential power.

The Constitution gives the presidency few formal powers, initially designing it to be secondary in importance to Congress. Over time, through the efforts of strong presidents who mostly served during crises, the office has greatly expanded in size and influence. This permits savvy and skillful presidents to exercise the informal prerogatives of their office and wield power by effectively persuading others in the Washington community to support their interests. Cultivating a strong professional reputation and high levels of public prestige can bolster presidential persuasion.

Describe how and why contemporary presidents use public relations methods to bolster public support.

Appreciate why presidents may find themselves in competition with news reporters.

Contemporary presidents rely heavily on public relations to boost public approval—they have a Communications Office to do the work—though despite their best efforts, most presidents lose support over time. Their office gives them a big megaphone for influencing the news agenda, and presidents like to stage media events in order to take their message to the public on their own terms. However, journalists typically struggle against the president's desire to set the agenda, causing friction that's part of the competitive relationship between the White House and reporters.

Identify and explain the key functions of the president's major roles, including chief executive, chief legislator, chief of state, chief diplomat, commander-in-chief, and chief of party.

The multiple and mutually exclusive roles the president must play contribute to the complexity of the office. As chief executive, the president is in charge of the government's executive branch or bureaucracy, and is responsible for executing the laws passed by Congress. As chief legislator, the president can propose a legislative agenda and attempt to persuade Congress to accept it, relying on his legislative liaison staff to lobby Congress. The president also plays the largely symbolic chief-of-state role,

whereby he attends official functions and hosts foreign dignitaries. As chief diplomat, the president has the ability to extend diplomatic recognition to leaders of other nations, lending credibility to their regimes.

As commander-in-chief, the president is the civilian head of the armed forces. This gives him the power to commit troops and to wage war. Congress retains the power to declare war, but because contemporary wars are often waged without being declared, the military balance between the two branches has shifted heavily toward the president. In 1973, Congress tried to regain some of its military authority by passing the War Powers Act, requiring the president to get congressional approval to commit troops for more than sixty days, but presidents have largely ignored the measure.

The president's most divisive role is chief of party. Being the most prominent and powerful member of his party gives the president a platform for raising campaign money and stumping for his party's candidates for lower office. Contemporary presidents have rarely had coattails, though, limiting their influence over other races.

Discuss the development of the institutional presidency.

Over the past seventy years, the presidency has grown into a multifaceted institution centered in the Executive Office of the President. The White House Office contains the president's closest aides and coordinates the daily workings of the White House. Other offices handle national security issues, domestic policy, trade and budget issues, and environmental matters.

Understand the changing role of the vice president.

The vice presidency has evolved as well. Once a ceremonial office, modern vice presidents have become trusted White House policy advisers. Presidential candidates now select running mates for the political advantages they bring to the ticket and with an eye toward how their number two can help them in the increasingly complex job of governing.

Assess the balance of power between the president and Congress over foreign policy, as well as the general ebb and flow of presidential influence.

The president and Congress historically duel with each other for dominance in the federal system. The executive branch became ascendant with the New Deal programs of Franklin Roosevelt's presidency and the importance of the president as global leader during the cold war. The end of the cold war and a shift in public support toward a philosophy of less government growth permitted Congress to reassert itself in the 1990s. The shift in national priorities following the 2001 terror attacks has again revitalized the presidency.

backgrounders Off-the-record exchanges between the president or administration officials and reporters. Whatever a reporter learns at a backgrounder can be used in a story, but the source of the information cannot be revealed. (p. 312)

Budget and Accounting Act of 1921 The act providing the legal basis for presidential participation in the budget process, by requiring the president to submit an annual budget to Congress for its consideration. (p. 315)

cabinet The name given to the collection of secretaries of the executive departments. Despite commonly held beliefs to the contrary, the cabinet rarely serves as an advisory body to the president. (p. 314)

chief diplomat A constitutional role of the president, in which he has the power to recognize ambassadors from other nations. (p. 320)

chief executive The role the president plays as head of the executive branch, in which he carries out the constitutional directive to "take Care that the Laws be faithfully executed." (p. 313)

chief legislator The role the president plays when he offers a legislative agenda and attempts to win congressional approval for it. (p. 315)

chief of staff One of the president's top political advisors and the formal head of the White House staff. (p. 324)

chief of state The role the president plays as ceremonial head of the United States. (p. 319)

coattails The ability of a victorious presidential candidate to sweep congressional candidates of the same party into office on the strength of people voting for one political party. (p. 323)

commander-in-chief The president's constitutional role as civilian leader of the armed forces. (p. 322)

Communications Office The White House office responsible for coordinating the president's media operations, including speechwriting and liaison with national and local reporters. (p. 310)

delegate A philosophy of representation that says officials are elected to carry out constituent interests, even when these interests conflict with what the representative believes is the right thing to do. (p. 307)

diplomatic recognition Formal acceptance of the legitimacy of another nation or its representatives. (p. 320)

executive agreements Legally binding presidential agreements with other nations that do not require congressional approval. (p. 321)

Executive Office of the President (EOP) The large staff of advisors to the president that comprises the president's political and policy operation. (p. 314)

executive orders Presidential directives to the bureaucracy that are legally binding and do not require congressional approval. (p. 315)

executive privilege The power of the president, established by custom, to keep Congress, the courts, and the public from having access to presidential documents and communications. (p. 303)

going public The presidential strategy of using the media to appeal directly to the public to support presidential initiatives. (p. 310)

honeymoon The initial weeks of a new presidential administration when enthusiasm and good press typically translate into high public-approval ratings. (p. 306)

Joint Chiefs of Staff The group of military advisors comprised of the heads of the army, air force, navy, and marines. (p. 321)

impeachment The power granted to Congress to remove from office the president, vice president, judges, and other federal officials. (p. 301)

legislative liaison White House lobbyists who maintain regular contacts with members of Congress and congressional committees, in order to help guide the president's legislative agenda. (p. 316)

mandate A directive by voters to the president to move ahead with the program he promised when he was a candidate. A large mandate produced by a lopsided vote gives the president a strong bargaining position with respect to Congress to set and advance the agenda in Washington. (p. 305)

media events Activities staged by campaigns or political officials that have enough news value to draw press attention to a message the politician wants to communicate. (p. 310)

National Security Council (NSC) The group of senior policy advisors responsible for helping the president shape national security policy. (p. 321)

news leaks The tactic used widely by White House officials of releasing information to the press on an anonymous basis when it serves their interests to have the information publicized. Some leaks are unauthorized and unwanted by the White House. (p. 311)

newsworthy The conditions under which a story warrants publication or dissemination, based on a set of values applied by newspaper editors and television producers. Newsworthy stories typically have conflict, proximity and relevance to the audience, timeliness, and familiarity. (p. 313)

Office of Management and Budget (OMB) The executive office responsible for developing the president's annual budget proposals by evaluating requests for funding among departments and setting the president's spending priorities. (p. 315)

override The congressional power to overturn a presidential veto by a two-thirds vote of both houses of Congress. (p. 317)

pardon power The unilateral power of the president to grant unconditional clemency to anyone for any reason. (p. 303)

persuasion An informal source of presidential power that gives skilled presidents the opportunity to influence the decisions of members of Congress and others in Washington whose support the president needs to accomplish his political objectives. (p. 304)

pocket veto The presidential prerogative to veto a bill without taking action. Presidents may issue pocket vetoes only if Congress has passed legislation within ten days of adjournment. A pocket veto cannot be overridden. (p. 317)

press briefings Formal exchanges of information between the press secretary and the national press covering the president. (p. 311)

press conferences Scheduled meetings between reporters and political figures like the president, which give the press access to the official and an opportunity to ask him or her questions firsthand. (p. 311)

press secretary The liaison between the White House and the national press covering the president. (p. 311)

professional reputation The sense among Washington officials of the president's political skills and abilities. It is one of the keys to effective persuasion, as it enhances the president's ability to bargain. (p. 305)

public prestige The sense among Washington officials about whether the president is well regarded by the public. It is one of the keys to effective persuasion, as it enhances the president's ability to bargain. (p. 305)

rally effect The tendency for Americans to unite around the president during a crisis, temporarily bolstering his job-approval ratings. (p. 307)

recess appointments The constitutional power granted to the president to make nominations while Congress is out of session that do not require Senate approval. The appointments stand until the end of the congressional term. (p. 303)

trustee A philosophy of representation that says officials are elected for their wisdom and to exercise their judgment of the national interest, even when it is at odds with their constituents' wishes. (p. 307)

veto power The constitutional power granted to the president to block an act of Congress. It takes a two-thirds vote of both houses of Congress to override a presidential veto. (p. 303)

War Powers Act of 1973 A congressional attempt to reassert the role of the legislature with respect to the president in military affairs by restricting the president's ability to wage war. (p. 322)

White House Office That portion of the Executive Office of the President organized to serve the president's immediate needs. (p. 324)

Resources

You might be interested in examining some of what the following authors have said about the topics we've been discussing:

Barber, James David. *The Presidential Character: Predicting Performance in the White House*, 4th ed. Englewood Cliffs, NJ: Prentice Hall, 2008. Barber's effort to understand presidential performance by systematically classifying presidential character is as interesting as it is controversial.

Burke, John P. *The Institutional Presidency: Organizing and Managing the White House from FDR to Clinton*, 2nd ed. Baltimore: Johns Hopkins University Press, 2000. A look at the way the institutional White House is structured.

Edwards, George C. *Presidential Approval: A Sourcebook*. Baltimore: Johns Hopkins University Press, 1990. Edwards examines how popular support influences what the president is able to do.

Jones, Charles O. *The Presidency in a Separated System*, 2nd ed. Washington, DC: Brookings Institution, 2005. Do we expect too much from our presidents, considering the limits the Constitution places on the office?

Lowi, Theodore J. *The Personal President: Power Invested, Promise Unfulfilled*. Ithaca, NY: Cornell University Press, 1985. Lowi explores the president as a symbolic figure who fills a complex emotional role with the public.

Milkis, Sidney, and Michael Nelson. *The American Presidency: Origins and Development, 1776–1998*, 5th ed. Washington, DC: CQ Press, 2007. An historical account of growth and change in the presidency.

Nelson, Michael, ed. *The Presidency and the Political System*, 9th ed. Washington, DC: CQ Press, 2009. A wide-ranging set of essays covering important topics about the presidency.

Neustadt, Richard E. *Presidential Power: The Politics of Leadership*. New York: The Free Press, revised 1991. In a seminal work on presidential power, Neustadt makes the case that personal persuasion, not formal authority, is the key to presidential effectiveness.

You may also be interested in looking at these resource sites:

The White House, at http://www.whitehouse.gov

National Security Council, at http://www.nsa.gov

Office of Management and Budget at http://www.whitehouse.gov/omb

Council on Environmental Quality, at http://www.whitehouse.gov/ceq

Department of Homeland Security, at http://www.dhs.gov/

Office of the Vice President, at http://www.whitehouse.gov/vicepresident

Office of Administration, at http://www.whitehouse.gov/oa

Office of National Drug Control Policy, at http://www.whitehousedrugpolicy.gov

Office of Science and Technology Policy, at http://www.ostp.gov

Office of the United States Trade Representative, at http://www.ustr.gov

Council of Economic Advisors, at http://www.whitehouse.gov/cea

Notes

1 George C. Edwards III, *The Public Presidency: The Pursuit of Popular Support* (New York: St. Martin's Press, 1983), 188.

2 Arthur M. Schlesinger, Sr., who published a list of great presidents in 1948, initiated presidential rankings. Lincoln came in first, followed by Washington and FDR. Grant and Harding pulled up the rear.

3 Edwards, *The Public Presidency*, 187–191.

4 Sidney M. Milkis and Michael Nelson, *The American Presidency: Origins and Development: 1776–1998*, 3rd ed. (Washington, DC: CQ Press, 1999), 2–3.

5 Ibid., 66–84. Washington might have served a third term if he hadn't wanted to retire so badly. After his successor, John Adams, became the first president to be voted out of office, Thomas Jefferson honored the two-term tradition, and it stood until Franklin D. Roosevelt sought and won four terms in office starting in 1932. The Twenty-second Amendment (ratified in 1951) makes the two-term limit a constitutional requirement.

6 Ibid., 85–221.

7 Ibid., 196. This was most evident in international affairs, where Roosevelt exercised strong leadership independent of Congress—a model for American presidents of the twentieth century who served during America's emergence as a global power. See also 206–212.

8 Ibid., 222–241, 262–276, 307–327, and 340–353.

9 Richard E. Neustadt, *Presidential Power: The Politics of Leadership* (New York: The Free Press, revised 1991), 42–63.

10 Ibid., 64–87.

11 Ibid., 88–106.

12 Paul Brace and Barbara Hinckley, *Follow the Leader: Opinion Polls and the Modern Presidents* (New York: Basic Books, 1992), 18–19.

13 George C. Edwards III, *At the Margins: Presidential Leadership of Congress* (New Haven: Yale University Press, 1989), 142–143.

14 Gail Russell Chaddock, "Olympia Snowe Gives Healthcare Reform Its First Republican Vote," *Christian Science Monitor*, October 13, 2009.

15 David H. Herszenhorn and Robert Pear, "Final Votes in Congress Cap Battle on Health Bill," *New York Times*, March 25, 2010.

16 If you want to get a sense of the variety of matters that pollsters get into, take a look at the home page of one polling firm, Gallup, at http://www.gallup.com/Home.aspx.

17 Not every president gets the benefit of a honeymoon period. George W. Bush didn't have much of a honeymoon because of the raw feelings left by the unprecedented events surrounding how he came to office. Bill Clinton's early difficulties securing approval for key cabinet appointees and his controversial early steps supporting gays in the military energized Republicans to oppose him immediately.

18 Brace and Hinckley, *Follow the Leader*, 22–27.

19 Ibid., 27–30.

20 Theodore Lowi, *The Personal President: Power Invested, Promise Unfulfilled* (Ithaca, NY: Cornell University Press, 1985), 1–21.

21 Milkis and Nelson, *The American Presidency*, 200–202.

22 Samuel Kernell, *Going Public: New Strategies of Presidential Leadership* (Washington, DC: CQ Press, 1986), 1–4.

23 You can read more about the Communications Office at http://www.whitehouse.gov/government/off-descrp.html.

24 Edwards, *At the Margins*, 141–146. If an administration is considering a policy and wants to see how the press would react to it, they can leak the information anonymously and see if reporters shoot down their "trial balloon" before the president officially announces it.

25 Ibid., 112–115.

26 Ibid., 115–119.

27 Ibid., 119–121.

28 Michael Baruch Grossman and Martha Joynt Kumar, *Portraying the President: The White House and the News Media* (Baltimore: Johns Hopkins University Press, 1981), 3–13.

29 Ibid., 273–298.

30 Jim Rutenberg, "White House Keeps a Grip on Its News," *New York Times*, October 14, 2002. The *New York Times* discussed the conflict as it played out in the Bush White House, which included press complaints about the lack of presidential press conferences and news leaks.

31 U.S. Office of Personnel Management, at https://www.opm.gov/policy-data-oversight/data-analysis-documentation/federal-employment-reports/historical-tables/total-government-employment-since-1962/.

32 If you're interested in what these folks look like, you can find their pictures at http://www.whitehouse.gov/administration/cabinet.

33 George Washington tried to rely on his cabinet for advice, but found it to be ineffective because of sharp differences among its members. Subsequent presidents didn't fare much better.

34 You can find a list of recent presidential executive orders at http://www.whitehouse.gov/briefing-room/presidential-actions/executive-orders/.

35 Charles O. Jones, *The Presidency in a Separated System* (Washington, DC: Brookings Institution, 1994), 147–181.

36 Paul Charles Light, *The President's Agenda: Domestic Policy Choice from Kennedy to Carter* (Baltimore: Johns Hopkins University Press, 1982), 13–25.

37 Ibid., 13. Attributed to Harry McPherson, aide to President Johnson.

38 Ibid., 17.

39 The figure does not include pocket vetoes. If you include all vetoes, the total for the period is 2,572. See http://history.house.gov/Institution/Presidential-Vetoes/Presidential-Vetoes/.

40 Ford issued a total of sixty-six vetoes. This total includes eighteen pocket vetoes. See http://clerk.house.gov/art_history/house_history/vetoes.html.

41 Aaron Wildavsky, "The Two Presidencies," *Trans-Action* 4 (December 1966), 7–14.

42 Ibid.

43 See Donald A. Peppers, "The 'Two Presidencies' Thesis: Eight Years Later," in Steven A. Shull, ed., *The Two Presidencies: A Quarter Century Assessment* (Chicago: Nelson-Hall Publishers, 1991), 26–35; and Richard Fleisher and John Bond, "Are There Two Presidencies? Yes, But Only for Republicans," in Shull, *The Two Presidencies*, 119–142.

44 You can read more about the Central Intelligence Agency online at https://www.cia.gov/about-cia/index.html.

45 To read more about the National Security Council, go to http://www.whitehouse.gov/nsc/.

46 Wildavsky, "The Two Presidencies," 7–14.

47 See "Bush Feels Heat of U.N. Debate, U.S. Elections," *Washington Post*, October 27, 2002.

48 John P. Burke, *The Institutional Presidency: Organizing and Managing the White House from FDR to Clinton*, 2nd ed. (Baltimore: Johns Hopkins University Press, 2000), 13–18.

49 Ibid., 14–15.

50 For an overview of all the first ladies, see http://www.whitehouse.gov/about/first-ladies.

51 You can read more about Michelle Obama at http://www.whitehouse.gov/administration/first-lady-michelle-obama.

52 Milkis and Nelson, *The American Presidency*, 401–407. That last quote is commonly circulated but not exactly accurate. Garner, salty Texan that he was, actually compared the office to a different bodily fluid.

53 Ibid., 404.

54 Ibid.

55 Ibid., 405.

56 Ibid., 410–416.

57 Arthur M. Schlesinger Jr., *The Imperial Presidency* (Boston: Houghton Mifflin, 1973).

58 George E. Reedy, *The Twilight of the Presidency: From Johnson to Reagan* (New York: New American Library, 1987).

Table, Figure, and Box Notes

T1 Sources: Reuters; Tim H. Murray and Robert K. Blessing, *Greatness in the White House: Rating the Presidents from George Washington through Ronald Reagan* (University Park: Pennsylvania State University Press, 1994); and Harold W. Stanley and Richard G. Niemi, *Vital Statistics on American Politics 1999–2000* (Washington, DC: CQ Press, 2000).

T2 Lyn Ragsdale, *Vital Statistics on the Presidency*, revised edition (Washington, DC: Congressional Quarterly, 1998) and http://www.gallup.com.

T3 James David Barber, *The Presidential Character: Predicting Performance in the White House*, 4th ed. (Englewood Cliffs, NJ: Prentice Hall, 2008).

T4 All three images in the public domain and property of the U.S. Federal Government.

T5 Source: Office of the Clerk; U.S. House of Representatives, at http://clerk.house.gov/art_history/house_history/vetoes.html.

T6 CIA World Factbook.

T7 Ibid.

T8 John Higley and Rhonda Evans Case, "Australia: The Politics of Becoming a Republic," *Journal of Democracy* 11:3 (2000), 136–150.

T9 CIA World Factbook.

T10 Arend Lijphart, "Constitutional Design for Divided Societies," *Journal of Democracy*, 15:2 (2004).

T11 Image is in the public domain and property of U.S. Federal Government.

T12 Nixon ran and lost when he was an incumbent vice president in 1960; he ran again and won eight years later.

T13 Agnew resigned the vice presidency under a cloud of scandal and was replaced by Ford.

T14 Rockefeller had been an unsuccessful presidential candidate before Ford selected him to serve as vice president; he did not run for president afterward.

T15 Quayle ran in the Republican primary in 2000, eight years after leaving office. He did not win the nomination.

T16 Neustadt, *Presidential Power: The Politics of Leadership*, p. 9 (emphasis in original).

The Federal Bureaucracy

Copyright: Joe Gough/Shutterstock.com

Learning Objectives

When you have completed this chapter, you should be able to:

- Identify the federal bureaucracy as hierarchical and specialized, as well as fragmented and decentralized.
- Explain the relationship between political appointees and career civil servants.
- Discuss why political appointees can have divided loyalties between the presidents who appoint them and the departments or agencies they run.
- Identify key cabinet-level departments, independent agencies, independent regulatory commissions, and government corporations, and understand key differences in what they do and how they are structured.
- Define implementation, regulation, and administration.
- Explain why implementation can be a complex bureaucratic function.
- Demonstrate how the bureaucracy developed from a patronage system to a system based on neutral competence.
- Show how Congress and the courts attempt to exercise influence over the bureaucracy.

11.1 Introduction

When we imagine the bureaucracy, many of us picture something like this: waiting in long lines to speak with a bureaucrat working on the other side of a desk. It's an unpleasant and familiar image for many of us, which can lend a negative cast to our impressions of bureaucracy.[T1]

Chances are, at some point, you've had a close encounter with some sort of bureaucracy. Maybe it was in a government office, like the Department of Motor Vehicles if you've gone for a driver's license. Perhaps you've had to fill out forms or wait in line to process a college loan application. Most of us can't get through college without dealing with some type of "street level" bureaucracy,[1] either surrounding financial aid or course registration or at the bursar's office.

So, what comes to mind when you think about bureaucracy? Long lines? Paperwork? Inefficiency? Workers who could stand to be a little more, say, pleasant or concerned?

Impressions like these influence the way a lot of us think about bureaucracies. When we specifically think about the *federal* bureaucracy, seemingly so distant and far away, some people would add cold, heartless, and unfeeling to the description. If our personal encounters with bureaucrats confirm these ideas, they may be hard to shake.

Negative images of the bureaucracy may be compounded by the way bureaucracy is treated as an object of ridicule in the popular culture. The media, always looking for sensational stories to hold our attention, periodically find maddening or ridiculous bureaucratic breakdowns that they know will capture our attention, like these unearthed by public administration scholar Charles T. Goodsell:

- A Chicago woman undergoing chemotherapy applied for Medicare. She received a computer-produced letter indicating she was ineligible since she had died the previous April.
- A chronic alcoholic was arrested and mistaken for another man. When he protested, his claims of misidentification were diagnosed as paranoia and schizophrenia, and he was committed to a mental hospital.
- The Department of Energy set out to declassify millions of documents inherited from the Atomic Energy Commission. Eight of the released documents contained the basic design for the hydrogen bomb.
- A unit of what is now the Department of Health and Human Services sent fifteen chimpanzees to a Texas laboratory for the purpose of launching a chimp-breeding program. All were males.[2]

newsworthy: The conditions under which a story warrants publication or dissemination, based on a set of values applied by newspaper editors and television producers. Newsworthy stories typically have conflict, proximity, and relevance to the audience, timeliness, and familiarity.

Of course, since we understand what makes something **newsworthy**, we know that the press was drawn to these incidents precisely *because* they were exceptional. Ordinary stories of bureaucratic functioning wouldn't be very interesting because they would be about what happens when things go smoothly.

You say you're still not convinced because your encounters with bureaucracy tell you otherwise? Fair enough. But read on. There are a number of widely held beliefs about the bureaucracy that simply aren't true because there's more to the federal bureaucracy than what we occasionally see in the press. In truth, the bureaucracy is staffed by people—millions of them—who are multidimensional and far more dedicated than we may give them credit for: people much like us, many of them knowledgeable about their field and passionate about what they do.

See if you can accept the possibility that:

- Bureaucracies don't always cause more problems than they solve. Much of the time the bureaucracy functions without incident, exactly as it's intended to operate. If you don't want to take my word for it, look at public opinion surveys. Large majorities of people who've had bureaucratic encounters came through them feeling positive. Even the postal service gets good reviews from three-quarters of the public.[3]

- Bureaucracies aren't always inefficient. The key word here is *always*. Sure, there's waste, although as we'll see, some waste is in the eye of the beholder, and some of it is the result of political forces operating outside the bureaucracy. Many departments and agencies are actually efficient and effective. Of course, they don't draw attention to themselves.

- Bureaucrats care about ordinary people. In fact, they *are* ordinary people. And they're not forced to do what they do. They choose to do it for the same reason that so many of us choose our jobs: because they're interested in their field and they enjoy their work.[4]

If our myths about our presidents are unrealistic because we expect too much, perhaps our myths about the bureaucracy are unrealistic because we expect too little. It just may be that the bureaucracy is more beneficial than we imagine.

11.2 What's the Bureaucracy Really Like?

The executive branch or the federal **bureaucracy** is a large web of departments, agencies, and bureaus charged with carrying out the laws and regulations passed by Congress and signed by the president. To handle the complexity of this task, the bureaucracy is organized in a way that would look recognizable to any of us familiar with a university, the military, or the workings of a large corporation. The German sociologist Max Weber noted these characteristics of bureaucratic structures:

- *Hierarchy*—Authority is clearly structured in bureaucracies, and is designed to operate on a top-down basis.

- *Specialization*—Bureaucrats function in specific capacities, dictated by their place in the organization.

- *Formalization*—Rules and procedures are made clear, and everyone doing business with the bureaucracy is subject to the same set of rules.

- *Permanent staff*—Bureaucrats make a career of service to their organization, making them accountable to the institution rather than to prevailing political tides.[5]

Taken collectively, these characteristics lend a sense of the impersonal to bureaucracies, and in fact, that's the point of Weber's model. Organization is supposed to ensure efficiency and protect against favoritism. If you don't put faces and personalities to the people in the bureaucracy, it's easy to confuse impersonal structures with impersonal individuals. In truth, bureaucrats do a lot more than go to meetings and write memos.

The bureaucracy is highly *specialized*, and many bureaucrats are skilled policy experts. "Bureaucrats," says Goodsell, "operate bridges, investigate crimes, manage forests, program computers, arbitrate labor disputes, counsel teenagers, calculate cost-benefit ratios, operate sea-rescue cutters, run libraries, examine patent applications, inspect meat, negotiate contracts, and so on and so forth."[6]

It's also misleading to think of the bureaucracy as a single, massive entity. Departments and agencies dealing with diverse, unrelated concerns in practice have nothing to do with one another. This lends a *fragmented* and *decentralized* quality to the federal bureaucracy. Someone in the Department of Energy has interests and expertise in entirely different issues than someone in the Department of Justice. There would be no reason for their paths to cross, and there would be no common area of overlap if they did.

Furthermore, each department has its own way of doing things. Over time, departments develop distinct *organizational cultures*, which distinguish them from other departments, even to the point of making them incompatible with one another.

It's hard to define organizational culture. The scholar James Q. Wilson calls it "a persistent way of thinking about the central tasks of and human relationships within an organization."[7] He compares organizational culture to individual personality traits, as something passed along through generations, resistant to change.

L.O. Identify the federal bureaucracy as hierarchical and specialized, as well as fragmented and decentralized.

bureaucracy: Another name for the executive branch of government, the institutional component of the presidency, which is charged with carrying out laws passed by Congress.

You've probably had experiences with different organizational cultures if you've visited friends at other universities. Maybe you noticed that their approaches to work and play were a little different from what you're used to—seemingly little things, like how at some schools no one would think of studying on a Thursday night and at other schools no one would think of partying on Thursdays. Things like this reflect the way people at different schools experience college, and they tend to be passed along as each freshman class acclimates to the college or university.

In the bureaucracy, the comparable effect could be like what Wilson found in the Department of State among bureaucrats trained mostly as diplomats, who by virtue of what they do value openness and communication over secrecy and security. As a consequence of these tendencies, Wilson found the culture of the State Department to be a culture of openness, where people in charge of the secretive business of maintaining security lose out in the battle for money, staff, and status, and where security in general is regarded as an annoyance.[8] It shouldn't be too hard to imagine other agencies made up of people with different approaches to the world—those doing intelligence work, for instance—making different choices in a different environment.

It also shouldn't be too difficult to imagine what could happen if something threatened to uproot an organization's culture—like the changes that occurred to agencies that were folded into the Department of Homeland Security, which was created by restructuring and reorganizing a host of existing bureaucratic entities. Bureaucrats brought to the new department an established understanding of how to approach their work that put them in conflict with bureaucrats from other agencies who wanted to apply to the new department different approaches developed in *their* organization's culture. The urge to do so is embedded in human nature, but it can pose a serious obstacle to merging bureaucratic operations.

11.3 Who's in the Bureaucracy?

L.O. Explain the relationship between political appointees and career civil servants.

political appointees: Top-level bureaucratic officials whom the president appoints, typically pending Senate confirmation, and who serve at the pleasure of the president.

civil servants: Career employees who staff the bureaucracy in a wide range of positions and who get their jobs independent of political considerations.

If you were to visualize the bureaucracy as a big pyramid with the president at the top (it is, after all, the executive branch), as you worked your way down, you'd find layers of top-level executives, followed by a large assortment of specialists holding just about every white-collar and blue-collar job imaginable. The top executives are **political appointees**, consisting of roughly 3,000 people, including the department secretaries who serve in the president's cabinet, their undersecretaries and assistant secretaries, and bureau chiefs. The remaining employees, several million in number, are **civil servants**—the workers who permanently staff the bureaucracy. See Figure 11.1.

11.3a Political Appointees

One of the first tasks facing a new president is the responsibility—or opportunity—to fill top bureaucratic posts with people of his choice. Senior appointments are invariably

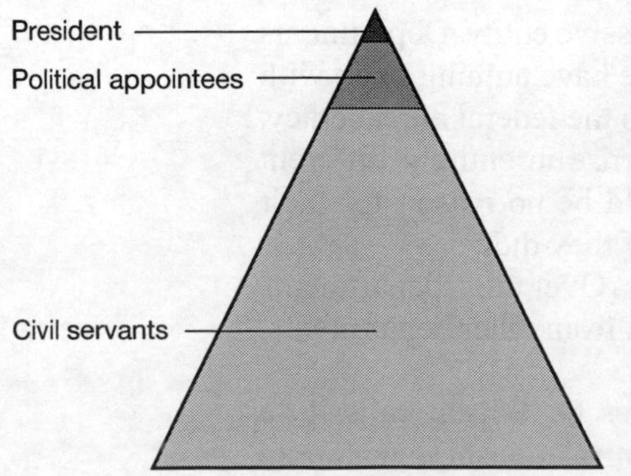

President ——————
Political appointees ——————
Civil servants ——————

Political appointees are the top-level department and agency heads. At the highest level, they are people who are close to the president and may have assisted in the president's election. At every level, they can be expected to share the president's philosophy of government. With few exceptions, political appointees stay no longer than the president, making their maximum service eight years. In practice, many serve far less than the maximum.

Civil servants make up the vast majority of bureaucratic positions. They get their jobs on the basis of their qualifications and by law are not permitted political connections to the presidential administration. After a period of time, they are civil servants from shifting political winds.

FIGURE 11.1 Staffing the Federal Bureaucracy

the subject of great speculation in Washington, and the choices a president makes can send a clear message about the type of administration he intends to conduct. President Trump appointed Exxon Mobil chief executive Rex Tillerson to be secretary of state and billionaire investor Carl Icahn as his special advisor on regulatory reform, signaling his administration would take a business-friendly approach to governing. President Obama, who campaigned on building bridges across the partisan divide, was determined to have several Republicans fill important, high-level positions in his administration. President Clinton said he wanted the top levels of the bureaucracy to "look like America," underscoring the importance he placed on diversity.

Appointments below the top two or three positions in a department are generally subject to a national search of candidates, although cabinet secretaries may bring in associates to fill some of these jobs, and large political contributors have been known to land appealing spots in government like ambassadorships. Vacant bureaucratic posts that need to be filled by presidential appointment are publicly listed in something called the Plum Book. Take a look at Demystifying Government: The Plum Book for details.

Historically, presidential appointees have been overwhelmingly white, male, affluent, middle-aged, educated individuals from high-status occupations. Perhaps the most important characteristic they share is their tendency to come to government with limited public-sector experience, and to leave after a relatively brief period of time, often never returning to serve another administration. During the short time they are in government service, political appointees spend time in their department or agency, but not with each other. This makes political appointees a detached, disconnected group and a fairly transient elite.[9]

> **Plum Book:** The congressional publication listing all top-level political positions in the bureaucracy.

11.3b Career Civil Servants

Their transience also sharply distinguishes political appointees from career civil servants, where the term "career" should be a strong clue as to their length of service in the bureaucracy. While political appointees come and go, typically more quickly than the presidents who appoint them, civil servants stay much longer, often serving in a department or agency until retirement. Although between one-quarter and one-third of political appointees can expect to be working elsewhere within a year of assuming their job,[10] the average civil servant in 2015 had started working in the bureaucracy in 2001.[11]

As a group, civil servants are middle-aged and male, better educated than the population as a whole and more Anglo, although since 1990 the ranks of women and minorities have increased somewhat. Figure 11.2 tells the story, comparing civil servant demographics from 1990 and 2015.

What do career civil servants do? Anything and everything—more than you can probably imagine. The range of civil-service work is unbelievably far-reaching: You could literally run a city with the variety of skills and specialties represented by civil servants. Between civil servants who work in Washington and those who work for the

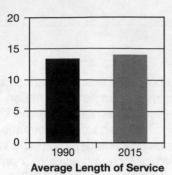

Average Length of Service

Civil servants have always been known for their staying power, and between 1990 and 2015, that staying power increased a bit.

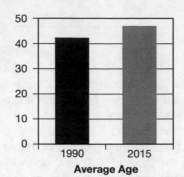

Average Age

If civil servants were middle-aged when the 1990s began, they grew a bit older by 2015.

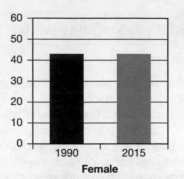

Female

Women comprised a minority of the permanent bureaucracy in 1990 and remained a minority in 2015.

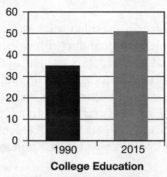

College Education

College-educated workers increased noticeably, from 35% in 1990 to 51% in 2015.

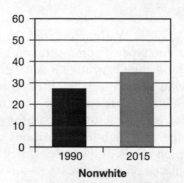

Nonwhite

African Americans, Hispanics, Asian Americans, and Native Americans grew from more than one-quarter of the civil service workforce to over one-third between 1990 and 2015.

FIGURE 11.2 Who Are the Civil Servants?[T2]

federal government across the country and around the world, you can find a full palette of white-collar and blue-collar specialties. Of course, there are letter carriers and park rangers and the folks who answer questions at the Social Security Administration, but the government also employs:

- Clerical workers
- Health-care workers
- Engineers
- Accountants and budget specialists
- Investigators
- Lawyers and legal workers
- Artists and information specialists
- Mathematicians and statisticians
- Librarians and archivists
- Plumbers and pipe fitters
- Machinists
- Cooks
- Chaplains
- Nuclear materials couriers
- Sociologists
- Clothing designers
- Funeral directors
- Beauticians
- Bartenders[12]

The main reason why civil servants stick around for so long is that after a probationary period many of them are eligible for **tenure**. Much like tenure in a university that protects your professors from losing their jobs if they publish controversial research, tenure in the civil service protects employees from being penalized by changing political currents. It also makes it difficult to let them go.[13]

The same logic of protection from political influences explains how white-collar civil servants get their jobs. Employment is merit based, keeping it outside the political process. Typically, applicants take an objective civil service exam, which forms the basis for

tenure: Job security afforded to civil servants following a probationary period, to protect them against losing their jobs for political reasons.

Federal Pay Grades

White-collar civil servants are covered by a detailed pay scale designed to reflect the complexity and difficulty of the jobs they perform. The **General Service (GS)** classification contains eighteen grades (GS1 to GS18); the higher the grade, the more specialized the work and the higher the pay. There are ten steps for advancement within the first fifteen grades, allowing employees pay raises without changing grades. The Civil Service Reform Act of 1978 created the **Senior Executive Service (SES)** for a small group of top-level policy experts and managers, including some political appointees. Blue-collar civil servants are covered by the **Federal Wage System (FWS)**, which typically pays the customary rate for services in the region of the country where the civil servants are employed.[T3]

their eligibility. Jobs are publicly posted, along with a description of responsibilities and a clearly defined pay grade. Federal pay grades are very specific, as Demystifying Government: Federal Pay Grades indicates.

Things weren't always like this. In Section 11.6b ("From the Spoils System to the Merit System"), we'll see that standardized hiring, pay, and promotion procedures were a reform designed to protect the bureaucracy from undue political influence.

General Service (GS): The system of eighteen grade levels (GS1 through GS18) that determines the pay level of white-collar civil servants.

11.3c Appointees vs. Careerists: Going Native　　*ω*

So, civil servants serve for years, are protected by tenure, and are experts in their respective field, while political appointees come and go, serve at the president's pleasure, and share no common political bonds. This can make things challenging for political appointees. In private bureaucracies, like the ones you find in large corporations, lines of authority work from the top down. Things are different in the executive branch, regardless of what may be suggested by the bureaucratic organizational pyramid. After all, how effective can a manager be if his or her tenured subordinates know they'll be there long after the manager leaves? That's the case in the federal bureaucracy, and it can turn traditional authority structures upside down. See Figure 11.3.

Given this environment, the president may choose to approach the bureaucracy strategically, to maximize his influence and the influence of his appointees. One place where the president can attempt to assert his will is through the approach he takes to making appointments. This is, after all, one area where he has a fair amount of leeway. Some presidents make loyalty a key criterion when selecting high-level appointees, hoping to find people who will resist the temptation to **"go native"** and become advocates for the department they run at the expense of the president's agenda.

However, presidents have to make their selections carefully because beyond the upper echelon of appointees, there are limitations to how broadly the law permits the president to remove the people he has appointed. Presidents often find it easier to lean on sympathetic appointees by reminding them of past loyalties than by threatening dismissal for noncompliant behavior, as you can see by looking at Figure 11.4.

11.3d The Administrative Presidency

A more extreme version of the presidential appointment strategy entails naming deeply ideological individuals committed to the president's goals to as many bureaucratic levels as the president can appoint people. This strategy assumes that the philosophical commitments of "true believers" will outweigh the temptation for them to "go native," and that strategic appointments reaching below the highest echelon of agencies and departments give the president more leverage with career civil servants.

This approach was used by President Nixon and replicated by President Reagan, both of whom faced a bureaucracy that housed a large number of liberals philosophically opposed to the president's objectives. It was part of a broader strategy of implementing an **administrative presidency** designed to maximize the president's ability to achieve

L.O. Discuss why political appointees can have divided loyalties between the presidents who appoint them and the departments or agencies they run.

Senior Executive Service (SES): The payment scale used for a small group of upper-level government managers and technical experts. Most positions covered by the Senior Executive Service are in the civil service, although the SES covers select political appointees whose jobs do not require Senate confirmation.

Federal Wage System (FWS): The system used to determine salaries for blue-collar civil servants.

"go native": The tendency for political appointees to adhere to the organizational culture of the department they are sent to run, making them advocates of the department rather than advocates of the president.

administrative presidency: A strategic approach to the bureaucracy relying on ideological political appointees and tight presidential management to combat the tendency for political appointees to "go native."

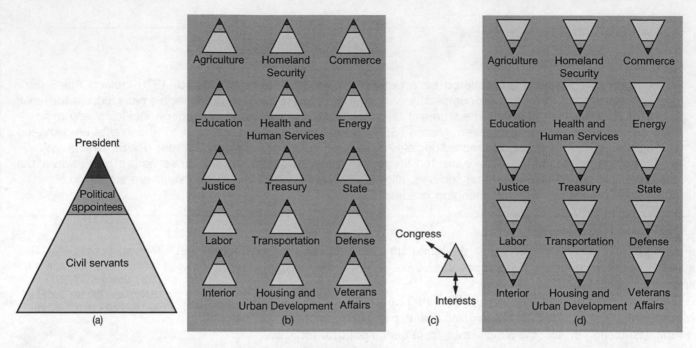

(a) This is the pyramid representing the structure of the federal bureaucracy that we saw in Figure 11.1, with the president and political appointees ostensibly on top.

(b) However, we now know that the bureaucracy isn't one integrated mass, but a group of unrelated departments and agencies. These fifteen represent only the major departments and don't include independent agencies, independent regulatory commissions, and government corporations.

(c) Since each department has its own organizational culture, each one is a little like a "native village" where civil servants, who have longevity, define the culture. They're engaged in long-term relationships with members of Congress and interest groups with whom they share concerns and interests—the ones we talked about when we discussed iron triangles. These enduring relationships define their everyday experiences. Political appointees have no such relationships: They are essentially outsiders in the village.

(d) With no ties to bind them to each other, political appointees find that their best option is to join the village—to "go native"—and identify with the culture of the department they were selected to run. As they do, they leave behind whatever mandate they got from the president to lead the department, becoming instead a spokesperson for the agency's interests. They become followers, in a sense, as traditional lines of command are upended. Real bureaucratic power rests with the careerists who would appear to be at the bottom of the organizational chart.

FIGURE 11.3 The Structure of the Federal Bureaucracy: A Second Look[T4]

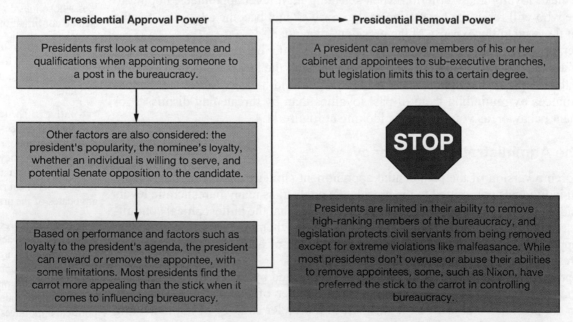

FIGURE 11.4 Presidential Means of Controlling Bureaucracy through the Appointment Power

policy objectives through tight administrative control of the bureaucracy, counteracting the strong tendencies of political appointees to become advocates for their agencies by:

- Requiring all agencies and departments to submit funding requests through the president's Office of Management and Budget (OMB), to try to short-circuit the close relationships civil servants have with the congressional allies who fund them.

- Requiring all agencies and departments to submit proposed rules changes to OMB to make sure they're in line with the president's program.

- Exploiting loopholes in the law to transfer or demote career civil servants who stand in the way of political appointees.

- Having lower-level appointees loyal to the president's program carry out functions typically reserved for high-level career civil servants.[14]

How well did it work? In the Reagan administration, the results were mixed, but in many respects positive. Career civil servants were largely responsive to Reagan's administrative presidency in the sense that there were few observable attempts to undermine the president's policies. However, the level of responsiveness varied by department, partly in reaction to how each department treated dissent. For instance, in the Food and Nutrition Service and the National Highway Traffic Safety Administration, the prevailing attitude among civil servants was that they were there to serve the president, and even if they didn't agree with what he was trying to do, they kept quiet and did their work. In the Civil Rights Division, there was vocal disagreement between appointees and careerists, and a number of resignations and threats of resignation.[15]

There was variation in the responsiveness of bureaucrats within individual bureaucratic units as well. In the Environmental Protection Agency, many civil servants complied with the president's policies while others strenuously resisted them. Often, the ones that went along did so out of the sense that it was better to acquiesce to the administration's wishes than to risk limiting career prospects, at least for the immediate future.[16]

A determined president, then, can expect to have some success counteracting the forces that, if left to their own devices, put control of bureaucratic units in the hands of career civil servants. Of course, it's also possible for an administration to take its efforts to control the bureaucracy too far. During the George W. Bush administration, an inspector general's report found that Monica Goodling, a White House liaison and senior counsel to the attorney general, had employed discriminatory practices in the hiring of senior careerists in the Justice Department. The report found that Goodling, in her zeal to shape the Justice Department in the political image of her boss, had inappropriately employed ideological and political criteria in an attempt to screen out candidates for high-level career positions who did not adhere to the president's conservative views.[17]

11.4 Departments, Agencies, Commissions, and Corporations

Let's take a minute and figure out the maze of departments, agencies, commissions, and corporations that make up the bureaucracy.

L.O. Identify key cabinet-level departments, independent agencies, independent regulatory commissions, and government corporations, and understand key differences in what they do and how they are structured.

11.4a Departments

In Chapter 10, when we talked about the president's cabinet, we said that the cabinet secretaries each head a department in the executive branch. The largest portion of the bureaucracy is composed of the fifteen departments headed by those cabinet secretaries (see Table 10.4).

Although departments and agencies have offices that are scattered around the country, the nerve center of the federal bureaucracy is located in a remarkably small section of Washington, D.C., where cabinet department headquarters are clustered in a narrow power corridor centered on the White House and Congress. Three of the oldest departments—Treasury, Justice, and State—are fairly close to the center of executive power, the White

House. Some of the departments that serve specific political constituencies, like Labor, Education, and Health and Human Services, are closer to the Capitol.

On paper, each of these departments is organized in a top-down fashion that seems to defy the upside-down power dynamics we were just talking about. Remember, though, organizational charts simply detail how the component parts of an institution fit together, not how it actually operates. It's worth looking at an organizational chart or two in order

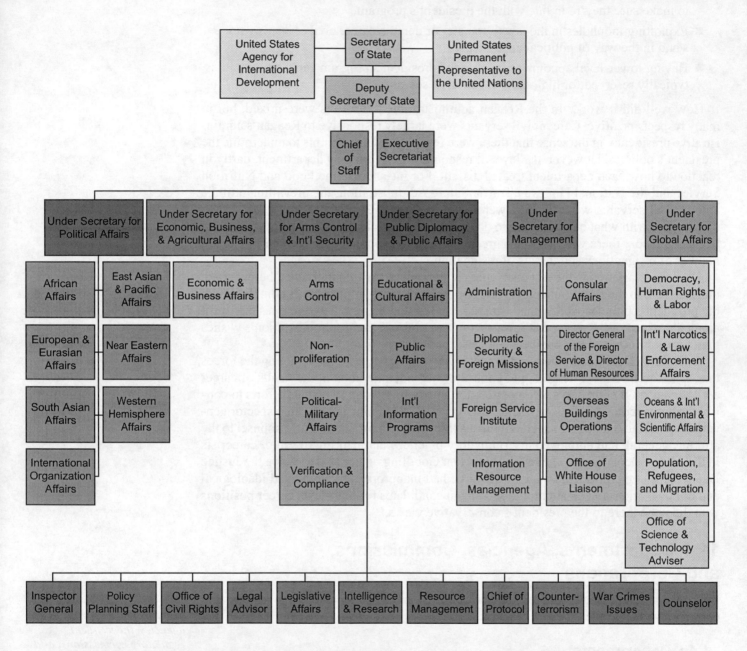

The Department of State is headed by the secretary of state, who is served by a deputy secretary of state. An executive secretariat coordinates the internal workings of the department's bureaus and offices. The United States ambassador to the United Nations reports directly to the secretary of state, who gives foreign policy direction to the director of the United States Agency for International Development. Six under secretaries report to the secretary of state. The under secretaries are specialists and are served by assistant secretaries who preside over bureaus that do the work of that specialization. For instance, the under secretary for political affairs is a crisis manager who troubleshoots problems involving the United States and different regions of the world.

The under secretary for political affairs is served by seven assistant secretaries, each of whom runs a bureau specializing in a geographic region. The same structure is in place for the remaining five under secretaries, who handle matters ranging from international trade and agricultural policy to arms control policy and strengthening democratic institutions abroad. In addition, ten offices report directly to the secretary of state. They cover a range of matters, from lobbying Congress to reviewing intelligence information to providing legal advice to the department.

FIGURE 11.5 State Department Organizational Chart[T5]

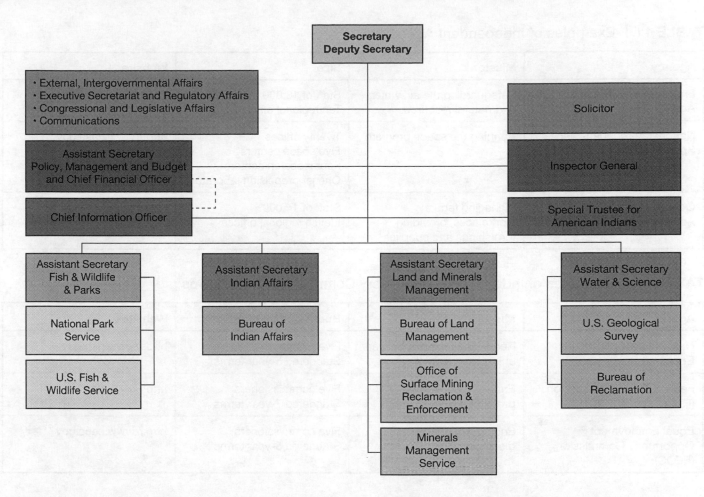

Every federal department is organized in a similar fashion, although the complexity of the organizational chart is a function of what it does and how far it reaches, not necessarily how large it is. Notice how the Interior Department organizational chart looks slender compared to the organizational chart of the State Department? But don't be fooled: The Interior Department employs three-and-a-half times as many people!

FIGURE 11.6 Interior Department Organizational Chart[T6]

to get a sense of the wide-ranging functions each department performs. You can find the State Department organizational chart in Figure 11.5 and the Interior Department organizational chart in Figure 11.6.

11.4b Independent Agencies

Beyond the fifteen cabinet departments lies an array of agencies and commissions. **Independent agencies** exist outside the cabinet departments—hence the name "independent." They report directly to the president, and are run by administrators who are appointed by the president and confirmed by the Senate. Independent agency heads also serve at the pleasure of the president, which means they can be removed from office at any time. Some examples of independent agencies are shown in Table 11.1.

11.4c Independent Regulatory Commissions and Boards

Like independent agencies, **independent regulatory commissions and boards** report to the president, and are headed by commissioners who are appointed by the president with Senate approval. However, they are more independent of the president than independent agencies because their members serve fixed terms and cannot be removed from office by the president. In fact, they're designed to be as free of political control as possible. By law, they are composed of a fixed number of members, typically between five and ten, and appointees must be divided between the two major political parties.

independent agencies: Bureaucratic organizations that report directly to the president rather than through cabinet secretaries, and whose administrators serve at the pleasure of the president.

independent regulatory commissions and boards: Panels designed to oversee the conduct of various segments of the economy. Members are appointed by the president and confirmed by the Senate. They serve fixed terms and cannot be removed by the president.

TABLE 11.1 Examples of Independent Agencies

Agency	Mission	Size	Website
Environmental Protection Agency (EPA)	Safeguarding the air, water, and natural resources	Staff of 18,000 Ten regional offices	http://www.epa.gov
National Aeronautics and Space Administration (NASA)	Running the space program	Twenty offices Five space centers Four research centers One jet propulsion laboratory	http://www.nasa.gov
General Services Administration (GSA)	Managing federal workplaces, providing furnishings and supplies	Staff of 14,000 Eleven regional offices	http://www.gsa.gov

TABLE 11.2 Examples of Independent Regulatory Commissions and Boards

Agency	Mission	Board Composition	Website
National Labor Relations Board (NLRB)	Regulating relations between unions and employers	Five members Staggered 5-year terms	http://www.nlrb.gov
Federal Trade Commission (FTC)	Enforcing consumer protection laws	Five commissioners Staggered 7-year terms	http://www.ftc.gov
Equal Employment Opportunity Commission (EEOC)	Ending workplace discrimination	Five commissioners Staggered 5-year terms	http://www.eeoc.gov

These commissions perform a regulatory function, which means they oversee a sector of society like banking, commerce, or communications, and are expected to act in the public interest. That's why they're supposed to be sheltered from political pressures. They have the authority to make and enforce rules, which makes them quite powerful. For instance, the Federal Reserve Board (FRB) has the authority to set interest rates, the Federal Communications Commission (FCC) licenses multimillion-dollar television and radio stations and regulates the Internet, and the Securities and Exchange Commission (SEC) oversees the stock market.

Other prominent independent regulatory commissions and boards are shown in Table 11.2.

Because independent regulatory commissions wield so much power, they are the focus of great attention from the groups they regulate. In some cases, a "revolving door" can develop between commissioners and the industries they regulate, whereby commissioners are selected from the regulated industry and then return to it after their term of service expires. Although it makes sense that commissioners would need the sort of technical expertise that working in industry provides, close ties could bring into question the independence or at least the sympathies of a commissioner. Ironically, a bureaucratic structure designed to be independent of political pressures runs the risk of being influenced by the very industries they were designed to regulate.

11.4d Government Corporations

government corporations: Corporations established by Congress to perform important services, like delivering the mail and operating rail lines, which could not be or were not profitably provided by private corporations.

Like private corporations, **government corporations** provide services to customers. Like private corporations, they typically have a board of directors. Like private corporations, they charge for their services. However, unlike private corporations, they do not seek to make a profit, are subsidized by Congress, and typically provide their services for less than what a private corporation would charge.

TABLE 11.3 Examples of Government Corporations

Government Corporation	Mission	Interesting Fact	Website
United States Postal Service (USPS)	Providing mail delivery	Largest government corporation	http://www.usps.com
Amtrak (National Railroad Passenger Corporation)	Providing passenger rail service	Created in 1971 from troubled private rail lines	http://www.amtrak.com

Congress creates government corporations when the private sector cannot profitably provide an important service. The first government corporation was the Tennessee Valley Authority (TVA), created as part of Franklin D. Roosevelt's New Deal to control flooding and produce inexpensive electricity for poor, depression-era residents of Tennessee and neighboring states. It still functions, selling low-cost power to its customers.[18]

Some government corporations are highly visible, although you probably don't think of them as government corporations (see Table 11.3).

Government corporations can be politically controversial. For a long time, the postal service ran up huge deficits, which required Congress to make up the difference. Amtrak continues to frustrate lawmakers who find themselves faced with subsidizing a service that has not found a way to break even. This is a particular irritant to members of Congress who feel they should not be in the business of running a railroad.

Members of Congress take some political cover from the fact that expenditures on public corporations are "off budget," meaning money spent on them doesn't count against official government budget figures. So, when the postal service was created from what had been a cabinet-level department called the U.S. Post Office, Congress could spend to cover its shortfall without appearing to dip into general revenues.

11.5 What the Bureaucracy Does

The bureaucracy performs three fundamental functions: implementation, regulation, and administration. Collectively, these functions give bureaucrats an enormous amount of influence over the shape of public policy.

L.O. Define implementation, regulation, and administration.

11.5a Implementation

When Congress passes and the president signs a bill, they approve words on a piece of paper. It's up to the executive branch to give life to those words. **Implementation** is the process by which departments and agencies enact the law, turning legal language into functioning policies. We briefly visited the concept of implementation when we were talking about the iron triangle in Chapter 8, when we said the power to implement legislation was one of the resources the bureaucracy has that interest groups want.

implementation: The bureaucratic function of taking the legal language of legislation and turning it into functioning programs.

Because the people who write the laws are different from the people who put them into effect, implementation is not a straightforward process. In theory, bureaucrats would implement legislation exactly as Congress intended. In practice, the intent of Congress is often not intelligible in the wording of legislation. Quite often, there is no single intent; rather, there are multiple perspectives of what the legislation would be from the members who voted to make it law. None of this is reflected in the wording of a bill. It falls to bureaucrats to put their imprint on legislation by deciding how it should be carried out. There's a saying that it's easy to agree on broad principles, but "the devil is in the details." Implementation is about the details.

L.O. Explain why implementation can be a complex bureaucratic function.

So, bureaucrats go about the business of formulating the rules that give shape to policy, resting decisions that shape policy in the hands of individuals who never face voters at the polls. In the most clear-cut cases—say, a presidential executive order, a carefully written congressional statute, or a detailed court decision—bureaucrats are given sufficient direction on how to act that the rules they create are little more than instructions on how

What Does It Mean?

When the president, in his capacity as commander-in-chief, issues an order to move troops, there's no room for interpretation. When he formally recognizes another nation in his capacity as chief of state and instructs the United States to commence diplomatic relations, it gets done.

But what does it mean when Congress passes legislation "to assure so far as possible every working man and woman in the Nation safe and healthy work conditions?"[17] That language comes directly from the Occupational Safety and Health Act. It fell to the administering agency, the Occupational Safety and Health Administration (OSHA), to create rules that it felt captured the intent of the words "as far as possible," "safe," and "healthy." Obviously, these terms can be interpreted in a multitude of ways, and the manner of interpretation determines how far-reaching the legislation will be. Then, once OSHA gave legal meaning to these legislative abstractions, it was up to the agency to determine how broadly the act would be applied by figuring out exactly when and how health and safety could be—and should be—protected.

With so much latitude, bureaucrats can shape public policy in ways elected officials never intended. In the extreme, they can gut legislation by the way they implement it. That's the charge that was leveled against the Federal Election Commission (FEC) by supporters of the McCain-Feingold Campaign Finance Reform Act. Senator John McCain was a vocal critic of the way the FEC interpreted the legal language in the bill, asserting they intentionally took the teeth out of it, but there was little he could do beyond trying to draw media attention to the issue or challenging the FEC in court. His name may appear on the bill, but once the legislation left Congress, the shape it assumed was out of his hands.

to follow through on the order, statute, or decision. However, ambiguity often clouds the process. When Congress provides bureaucrats with few details, bureaucratic rule making determines what those policies will look like.[19] Similarly, bureaucrats are the ones who reinterpret policies created in the past as new when unforeseen conditions arise, such as when laws regulating radio and television communication suddenly need to be applied to the Internet. This ambiguity can be a great source of bureaucratic influence (see Demystifying Government: What Does It Mean?)

Beyond ambiguity, a host of factors conspire to make implementation a complex process. Political scientist George C. Edwards points out several impediments to effective implementation, including problems with communication, insufficient resources, attitudes of bureaucrats, obstacles posed by standard operating procedures, and the fragmentation of the bureaucracy.[20]

Communication

For starters, you can't assume that bureaucrats responsible for implementing policy understand what they should be doing. Lines of communication between policy makers and bureaucrats are not always clear and open. Many agencies are very large and, as you can probably imagine from having looked at the organizational chart for the Department of State, messages often have to be communicated through multiple bureaucratic layers. The result can be like a game of "telephone," where a message whispered from person to person gets distorted in transit.

Even when messages are communicated clearly, they may not always be welcome. Remember, career civil servants can have strong views about their policy area, and may disregard or alter directions from policy makers if they're at odds with the civil servant's preferences or beliefs.[21]

Insufficient Resources

Everywhere we've turned, we've seen the relationship between resources and effectiveness, and the relationship certainly holds true for bureaucrats. It's difficult for bureaucrats to implement policy effectively when they're lacking these resources:

- *Staff*—When Americans complain about the size of government, as many tend to do, they're looking for a reduction in the size of the bureaucracy. In practical terms, this would mean reducing the size of the staff that's available to implement policy. Ironically, many departments and agencies find themselves calling out for more assistance, not cutbacks. In addition to sheer numbers, workers have to be skilled and effectively trained. If you don't know how to monitor food-processing plants, for instance, you'll be of little use to the Food and Drug Administration, which has to check the conditions of tens of thousands of plants using only four thousand food inspectors.

- **Information**—Bureaucrats need to know how to put a policy into effect, and the information required to do so can be technical and complex. If you're in the Environmental Protection Agency and Congress tells you that you're supposed to come up with standards for clean air, you'd better have some basis for determining how to do it. Because information is so critical to bureaucrats, they're happy to turn to sympathetic interest groups for assistance. As we saw in Chapter 8, this can cement a relationship of mutual dependence and tilt implementation decisions in the group's favor.

- **Facilities**—It may sound basic, but if a department or agency lacks the space to work effectively, or lacks supplies and equipment, it will have trouble getting things accomplished.[22]

Attitudes of Bureaucrats

When bureaucrats and lawmakers see eye-to-eye on a policy, implementation typically goes smoothly. When they do not, things can get interesting. Largely because career civil servants do not have to indulge the wishes of their politically appointed superiors, they can act with some discretion when it comes to making decisions about how something is to be done.[23]

Standard Operating Procedures

Bureaucrats are guided in their work by **standard operating procedures (SOPs)**, which are routines that are put in place to direct everyday decision making. If your task is to determine if someone is eligible for welfare benefits, for instance, established practices help you make the decision. Recorded in thick manuals, SOPs (as they're called) can play on the stereotyped image of bureaucrats mindlessly following a protocol that seems—well, bureaucratic. In most cases, though, SOPs make perfect sense to the people following them, and the ability to standardize decision making across a huge government lends an element of fairness to the implementation process. It also keeps bureaucrats from having to start from scratch every time they're faced with a new task. On the downside, SOPs may contribute to agency inflexibility when faced with a new mission that doesn't fit neatly within existing procedures.[24]

standard operating procedures (SOPs): Guidelines that provide uniformity to bureaucratic decision making.

Fragmentation

Because the bureaucracy developed in a piecemeal fashion in response to a host of unrelated political demands, it is highly fragmented. It's not uncommon for multiple agencies to have overlapping responsibilities. For instance, no less than a dozen agencies share responsibility for implementing legislation that prohibits discriminatory lending practices. This makes it difficult—at times, impossible—for implementation to proceed in a coordinated manner, and it contributes to the widely held sentiment that the bureaucracy is inefficient.

However, fragmentation serves a political purpose. Remember, for every bureaucratic function there is a corresponding congressional committee engaged in policy making, and those committees are centers of congressional power. Widening the scope of responsibility for any piece of legislation is a way of spreading around the resources. This makes bureaucratic reorganization a daunting task because congressional toes (and those of companion interest groups) will get badly bruised in the process.[25] It took a national crisis to get Congress to agree to the biggest bureaucratic reorganization in generations, changing the jurisdiction of all or part of the twenty-two security-related agencies that were combined to form the Department of Homeland Security.

11.5b Regulation

When lead contamination was found in drinking water in Flint, Michigan, in 2014, environmental advocacy groups charged that the city's water system—and many others around the country—violated federal safety standards and had not been caught.[26] It's the bureaucracy's job to impose standards to maintain safe water and food, clean air, and a wide range of other things. This is called **regulation**, and although there may not be a lot of dissension about the value of some things regulations attempt to protect, regulation is one of the bureaucracy's more controversial functions.

regulation: The bureaucratic function of placing standards or restrictions on the actions of private individuals or companies in order to protect the general welfare of the public.

That's because regulation is about control, with implications for personal liberty. Everyone values clean air. Not everyone wants to be told they have to pay for an expensive annual automobile emissions test, or for a catalytic converter when they buy a car. Corporate polluters will not appreciate being told they have to pick up the tab for maintaining a particular level of air or water quality. It's a source of tension that often plays out in our politics, as we'll see when we talk about domestic policy making in Chapter 15.

Regulations are also pervasive, which in its own right can be a source of political conflict. Some people simply object to the long regulatory reach of the federal government. Beyond food, water, and air quality, the bureaucracy has a hand in regulating workplace safety, consumer products, toxic waste disposal, business practices, highway safety, discriminatory hiring practices, cable television rates, and many less salient matters.

Federal Register: A publicly available list of all proposed and existing federal regulations.

When an agency proposes a new regulation, it is publicly posted in the **Federal Register** in advance of public hearings to solicit feedback. When a regulation goes into effect, it is published in the Federal Register as well. You can get a sense of the range and extent of federal regulations by browsing through the Federal Register online. The next time you log on, go to http://www.archives.gov/federal-register/index.html#at, and click on "Today's Federal Register" under the "Government Actions" heading. You'll get a list of every new regulation that was proposed or put into effect today, in alphabetical order, by agency.

deregulation: The lifting of federal regulations that had been previously imposed on private industry.

Political pressures against government regulation have resulted in the occasional **deregulation** of some industries. Deregulation arose out of the sentiment that government reaches too far into the activities of the private sector, and that the marketplace rather than government is an adequate mechanism for regulating corporate behavior. Although this perspective gained currency during the Reagan administration and is favored by congressional Republicans, one of the first major efforts at deregulation occurred in 1978, during the administration of Democrat Jimmy Carter, with deregulation of the airline industry.

Prior to deregulation, airlines had to adhere to strict bureaucratic guidelines for setting airfares and routes. Following deregulation, airlines had more freedom to set fare and route structures. Lower fares and new low-budget airlines emerged as the industry was deregulated. As a consequence, air travel became more affordable, and many people who used to rely on ground transportation found they could take to the skies. However, a deregulated airline industry also encountered a host of consumer complaints that hadn't existed before, among them long lines at airports, frequent delays, an inequitable fare structure, and insufficient service to remote locations.

If you've ever traveled by airplane, or if you have friends or relatives who have, you're probably familiar with what it's like. You can shop for bargain fares, and often you can find them—unless you want to fly during popular travel periods, like over Thanksgiving or Christmas. Chances are, the people sitting on either side of you paid a different price than you did for their tickets—possibly a lot more, conceivably a lot less. Even before additional security restrictions were imposed following the 2001 terror attacks, it wasn't uncommon to wait for a long time at airports to check your bags and to board the plane. On-time arrivals and departures on many routes are rare occurrences, especially if you're traveling during "rush hour," or if you're leaving from or going to a "hub" airport where one airline monopolizes air traffic. Air travel under today's system gets you there, but a number of indignities and inconveniences may be included in the (sometimes low, sometimes not so low) price.

Now, try to imagine a system that's quite different from the one you're used to. When you get to the airport, you find it busy but not frenetic. Lines move swiftly. Your flight leaves on time and arrives on time. You don't have to rearrange your plans to travel at off-hours to get a lower fare. In fact, if you change your mind about your travel plans, you just cancel your ticket and get your money back. You don't have to pay extra to check your bags. On board, you're treated to a hot meal on flights that are scheduled during the time most people eat breakfast, lunch, or dinner. The food probably isn't great, but at least it's more than pretzels or peanuts, and it's included in the price of your fare.

However, you paid a fair amount of money for your ticket—far more than the discounts you're used to paying if you fly home during midsemester break.

Which option do you prefer? Lower fares and more flights are a direct result of deregulation. So, are the inconveniences of contemporary air travel. To get you to fly, airlines will offer some seats at deep discounts. At the same time, they'll try to recoup some of their losses by putting restrictions on your ticket and by offering fewer services. In cities dominated by one airline, competitive pressures are limited, meaning fares are higher and there's little incentive to sell service.

Each system entails trade-offs. It's up to you to decide whether you prefer relative affordability with more hassles and fewer services or higher prices and fewer flights with better services. The way you answer this question may determine whether you believe the federal government should be in the business of regulating the airlines.

President Trump's philosophy of government is sympathetic to deregulation. President Obama's was not. In 2010, Obama signed into law the Dodd-Frank Wall Street Reform and Consumer Protection Act, designed to overhaul the financial regulatory system following the 2008 banking crisis. Supporters of the legislation contend that government regulation of the sort championed by the Dodd-Frank measure will encourage stability in the financial world. However, not everyone finds government regulation beneficial. Opponents would rather see the market take its course, uninhibited by government interference. The Bush administration was highly sympathetic to this view and put its weight squarely behind deregulation efforts in areas ranging from telecommunications to energy to environmental concerns.

11.5c Administration

One of the least glamorous but more critical functions of the bureaucracy is **administration**—carrying out the routine tasks that any organization must conduct in order to function on a daily basis. The bureaucracy has the responsibility to administer the policies it implements and the regulations it enacts. If Social Security is to function, someone has to print and distribute the checks. If reserves are going to be called to serve during a conflict in Iraq, Afghanistan, or Bosnia, someone has to notify them, someone has to train them, and someone has to equip them. Someone has to put the mail in your mailbox. Someone has to maintain national monuments. We may not like tax audits, but they're a fact of life, and someone has to conduct them, too.

There are countless administrative functions that the government is responsible for performing, with countless bureaucrats participating in the process. It is the end result of executing the law, the realm where things actually happen. Implementation and regulation may be where the bureaucracy has the most say over the shape of public policy, but without people to carry out administrative routines, nothing would get done.

administration: The bureaucratic function of tending to the details of executing public policy.

11.6 How the Bureaucracy Has Changed

Since the founding of the republic, the bureaucracy has exploded in size and scope, and has gravitated from being a source of presidential payback for political supporters to an organization structured to keep politics at arm's length. Despite the fact that it hardly resembles the bureaucracy of a hundred (or even sixty) years ago, chronic dissatisfaction with bureaucratic procedures or performance has fueled a merry-go-round of reforms that continue today.

L.O. Demonstrate how the bureaucracy developed from a patronage system to a system based on neutral competence.

11.6a Bureaucratic Growth

The bureaucracy grew dramatically but not steadily during the nineteenth and twentieth centuries, with the greatest bursts of growth coming in response to expansions in the role of the federal government in American life and the place of America in the world. Before the Civil War, the role of the bureaucracy was small because the federal government performed a limited set of functions and, apart from the Postal Service, experienced little expansion. Except for mail delivery and wartime military service, people had little direct contact with Washington.

Social changes following the Civil War and concurrent westward expansion produced the first burst of bureaucratic growth in the period immediately following 1860. Industrialization and economic expansion in the late nineteenth century fueled this trend. The Department of Agriculture, established in 1862, set the stage for the industrial-era Departments of Commerce (1903) and Labor (1913).

The federal bureaucracy grew sharply during World War I as America geared up for the war effort, but that was a temporary condition. When the war was over, the bulk of the bureaucracy that had been put in place during mobilization was dismantled. Not so a generation later, when the changes put into effect by Franklin D. Roosevelt's New Deal policies gave birth to permanent social welfare programs for the first time in American history.

Figure 11.7 tells the story of what happened to the bureaucracy as a result. Even after the United States dismantled what had been the largest wartime mobilization in its history following WWII, the bureaucracy never returned to pre-Depression era levels. The United States had emerged from the war as a global power with a large, permanent military and social welfare bureaucracy.

The 1960s brought the Johnson administration's Great Society programs, which extended the New Deal philosophy of a government-sponsored social welfare safety net to include programs designed to alleviate social ills. New bureaucratic units followed new social programs in areas like housing, nutrition, and human services.

The federal bureaucracy diminished in size to a small degree at the end of the twentieth century, largely in response to a decrease in career civil servants working in the Department of Defense following the end of the cold war. Even with this decline, civilian bureaucratic workers in the federal government comprised 2.1 percent of the domestic workforce in 1997, compared with less than 1 percent a century earlier.

Add state and local government bureaucracies to the mix and you'll get a sense of just how bureaucratic activity took off in the 1960s and 1970s. One reason why state and

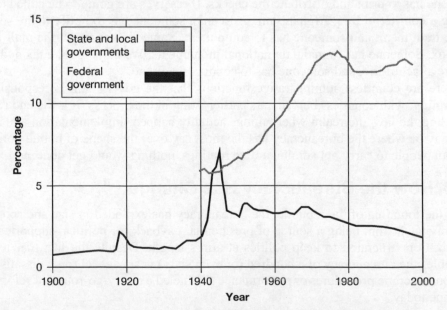

FIGURE 11.7 The March of Bureaucracy in the Twentieth Century[T8]

local bureaucracies appear to have grown so much more than the federal bureaucracy is because the federal bureaucracy utilizes a lot of consultants to do its work, something that states and localities tend not to do. If you were to include all the planning, training, research, development, and design activities that the federal government outsources to private firms, you'd have a more complete picture of just how large the federal bureaucracy is and how much it has grown since World War II.

Notwithstanding the reductions in bureaucratic personnel that followed both world wars, the clear tendency among bureaucracies is to grow. Once a department or agency is established, it takes on something of a life of its own apart from its mission. The natural human tendency toward self-preservation eventually sets in as people affiliated with a department or agency look for ways to maintain the organization that gives them work, and in which they have a long-term investment. Even if a bureaucratic entity successfully achieves its original objectives, its employees will readily alter the organization's goals rather than simply declare victory and go out of business.

This is especially true when careerists like civil servants staff organizations. Important professional benefits like salary, seniority, and rank accrue to people who have been with an organization for a long time. Long-term workers have developed expertise that may not be easily transferable to a position outside the organization. It's difficult and often undesirable to look for work in mid- or late career. People get used to the organizational culture and don't want to change the way they operate. These self-protective mechanisms contribute to what organizational specialist Anthony Downs calls the "Law of Increasing Conservatism," that organizations tend to become more conservative with age when they are staffed by people with many years of service. Unless there's a period of turnover or the organization grows rapidly in size to incorporate people without an investment in the status quo, bureaucratic entities tend toward a self-fulfilling sluggishness that perpetuates their existence while distorting their purpose and reducing their responsiveness.[27]

11.6b From the Spoils System to the Merit System

Individual bureaucratic units may be resistant to change, but the bureaucracy as a whole has undergone revolutionary alterations over the past two centuries. When the nation was young and the bureaucracy was small, federal positions were staffed with the president's political supporters. With little more than several thousand positions to fill—most of them outside Washington in such capacities as postal clerks, surveyors, or land office clerks— early nineteenth-century presidents could strengthen the bonds between national office-holders and local supporters that formed the basis for fledgling mass political parties.

Andrew Jackson used this system of political **patronage** to build the Democratic Party into the first mass-based national political organization. In exchange for a position in the federal bureaucracy, party supporters would kick back a small percentage of their pay to the political party.[28] The ability to offer such enticing rewards to political supporters was considered a perk of winning elections, the spoils of victory. That's why this method of staffing the bureaucracy is called the **spoils system**.

The spoils system had obvious advantages for the party in power, but it had its disadvantages for the operation of the bureaucracy. Changes in political power caused an upheaval to the system as workers loyal to the losing party would be kicked out by the winners. Workers loyal to the president did not have to be people of skill or merit. Also, as the federal government became larger and more specialized following the Civil War, making appointments started to become more of a burden to the president than a reward.

People looking for work hounded each new president. By 1881, President Garfield had 100,000 patronage positions at his disposal, four times the number available just thirty years earlier, reducing him to something of an employment agent for friends and supporters—a clerk who appointed other clerks.[29] As fate would have it, the undignified business of doling out goodies turned out to be the least of his worries. That year, Garfield was assassinated by a disgruntled office seeker who was overlooked for a patronage position.

Something had to give, and it soon did. In 1883, President Chester A. Arthur signed into law the **Pendleton Act**, ending the spoils system and creating the merit-based

patronage: Jobs, favors, and other resources that party officials provide in exchange for people's political support.

spoils system: The method of staffing the federal bureaucracy, commonplace in the nineteenth century, in which the president offered patronage appointments to political supporters.

Pendleton Act: The 1883 law requiring that merit-based criteria be used to hire public employees, ending the tradition of patronage appointments.

procedures we use today. It established the **Civil Service Commission** to oversee the process of hiring public employees, taking appointments out of the hands of elected officials and greatly reducing the spoils available to political parties. A **merit system** would replace politics as the basis for hiring government workers. Foremost among the reforms included in the Pendleton Act were the use of objective testing for hiring public employees, the establishment of pay grades, and the restriction against firing civil servants for refusing to support or endorse any political activity. In a further effort to de-politicize the bureaucracy, the **Hatch Act** of 1939 restricted federal workers from engaging in political activity while on the job.[30]

The prevailing philosophy about government embodied in the Pendleton Act is that politics can be taken out of implementation and administration. It's the principle of **neutral competence**, which says that bureaucrats selected for their ability or expertise will provide the best service because an efficient bureaucracy should function apart from the political decisions made elsewhere in government. So, political considerations should not guide the hiring of civil servants, and civil servants should be neutral to political considerations in the performance of their work. To the extent that civil servants are hired on a merit basis, this approach has been successful. However, because we can find politics in any relationship, including the relationships between civil servants and their constituent groups, the expectation that there's a neutral way to conduct bureaucratic business is not always realized.

11.6c Recent Reforms

The Pendleton Act and the Hatch Act weren't the last word on civil service reform. Far from it: For the past half century, every presidential administration has proposed tinkering with the bureaucratic machinery to make it more responsive. Ideas that have been floated during this period include greater disclosure of what the bureaucracy does through "sunshine laws," policing government spending to cut down on waste, introducing incentives to improve the performance of public workers, stimulating competition to produce performance pressures like you'd find in the private sector, using management principles to control and unify the bureaucracy, and making the bureaucracy more efficient by making it client centered.[31]

Clearly, these approaches tackle bureaucratic reform from numerous perspectives. The problem is, every administration has endorsed a different approach, and every approach has a constituency, giving voice to a host of opposing solutions, all of which manage to find their way into new laws and regulations. Instead of a coordinated approach to bureaucratic reform, we've seen piecemeal efforts, which satisfy constituencies with different philosophies about what an overhauled bureaucracy should look like.

The Clinton administration promoted a high-profile, large-scale effort at bureaucratic reform. It was dubbed "Reinventing Government," borrowing from the title of a 1992 book about applying entrepreneurial principles to the federal bureaucracy to make it more responsive to the shifting demands of a complex and changing economy. Among its core principles, the "Reinventing Government" approach to bureaucratic reform sees the recipients of bureaucratic services—us—as customers, much like a business would, and presents methods that bureaucrats can use to get feedback from the public to create a more "user-friendly" bureaucracy.[32]

The Reinventing Government project was rolled out with great fanfare in 1993 at a big media event on the White House lawn and was promoted as a key administration initiative. Five years after its inception, the Brookings Institution undertook a review of the Reinventing Government campaign. Its conclusion: Despite an "A+" for effort, and some notable improvements in "customer service," the overall result was inconsistent.

11.7 Bureaucratic Inefficiency

We've said all along that American government was not engineered to be efficient. Quite the opposite: The institutional design of the federal system slows progress and frustrates initiatives to attain the higher goal of resisting public passions and blocking the wishes of large or motivated groups. When it's working as planned, things take a long time to get done.

Now consider the place of the bureaucracy in that system. You might think that any organization engaged in policy implementation, regulation, and administration would be constructed to function efficiently and effectively. At the same time, we've seen how the federal bureaucracy is part of the federal system, even if it wasn't imagined as part of the original federal design. The result is a set of pressures that can work to undermine rational procedures and cost-effective operations.

In real terms, this means the bureaucracy will do things that may appear to some of us as wasteful and inefficient. Waste may take the form of money spent to implement programs that result from the **pork barrel** politics we talked about in Chapter 9.

Remember, though, that "wasteful" is in the eye of the beholder: It's easy to target spending on programs or projects that benefit others as wasteful, while accepting spending on programs or projects that benefit us as valuable—especially if jobs or tangible benefits come our way as a result.

Sometimes, waste will take the form of outsized government expenditures for ordinary household items, like the fabled $435 hammers and $3,000 coffeepots that get a lot of media attention (although there is a reasonable explanation for these charges—as you can see in the Demystifying Government: The $435 Hammer and the $3,000 Coffeepot box). When bureaucrats responsible for overseeing the expenditure of public money have an interest in the result, they have an incentive to engage in **"goldplating"** their purchases by seeking costly, top-of-the-line items.

So, how wasteful is the bureaucracy in absolute terms? Politicians of both parties are fond of calling for "cutting the fat" out of federal spending, offering it as the way to pay for other programs or to help balance the budget. When you take into account that a lot of what seems like fat has a constituency that presidents dare not offend, how much is left to cut? Figure 11.8 shows how the findings of one commission charged with determining how the federal government might save billions of dollars through greater bureaucratic efficiency could be countered by a close examination of the commission's recommendations. Though the particulars happened a long time ago, the example is just as relevant today as it was when the original claims and counterclaims were made because the same arguments about government waste and inefficiency are still being made.

In fact, a lot of what draws complaints about bureaucratic inefficiency is the product of more subtle forces than civil servants willfully spending hundreds of dollars for small hardware items. These forces include pressure to spend agency money, professional

pork barrel: Wasteful or unnecessary spending that can result from logrolling. Whether something is a pork-barrel project or a valuable use of taxpayer dollars may depend on whether you stand to benefit from it.

goldplating: Government purchasing of top-of-the-line items at maximum cost, which can happen when bureaucrats overseeing purchasing decisions have an interest in the items being purchased.

DEMYSTIFYING GOVERNMENT

The $435 Hammer and the $3,000 Coffeepot

One student of the bureaucracy offers the following explanations for two seemingly outrageous examples of wasteful government spending that have achieved the status of an urban legend: the $435 spent by the navy on a hammer and the $3,000 it spent on a coffeepot.

- The $435 hammer is an example of how billing procedures used by the military can make an item appear to be inflated beyond its actual value. The real cost of the hammer was nominal, but it was shipped along with very expensive equipment. The organization that supplied this equipment to the Navy was permitted to bill for overhead incurred in the manufacture of each of the items. Rather than calculate a separate overhead figure for each item, federal accounting guidelines directed the supplier to calculate

one overhead cost and then divide it equally over each of the items supplied. The resulting figure made it appear that some of the more complex equipment commanded relatively low overhead costs, but it also produced a billing statement with a $435 hammer.

- The coffeepot really did cost $3,000. But it wouldn't fit on your kitchen counter: It was designed to make coffee for over three hundred soldiers on a navy transport plane. Similar coffeemakers are used by commercial airlines, which often pay a much higher price.[T9]

No doubt, journalists would be more attracted to the outrageous dollar figures than to the rational explanations for them, perpetuating the impression that the government brazenly wastes our money. What do you think of these sober and more complex explanations?

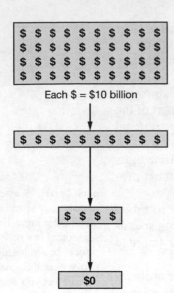

Each $ = $10 billion

In 1984, the Reagan administration established the President's Private Sector Survey on Cost Control, commonly called the Grace Commission. It recommended ways for the government to save $400 billion through more efficient management of the bureaucracy.

Subsequently, the General Accounting Office (GAO) and the Congressional Budget Office (CBO) issued a joint analysis of items where savings were counted twice and suggestions where no savings would be realized at all. Their revised figure was $100 billion in savings.

But, the report took issue with the claim that the remaining $100 billion could be classified as savings from running the bureaucracy more efficiently. The GAO and CBO found that about $60 billion in savings would require policy changes like taxing welfare benefits and restricting Medicare benefits. This left $40 billion in savings.

And most of that came from such things as collecting more taxes owed the government by hiring more Internal Revenue Service agents—a worthy goal, perhaps, but one with a price tag of its own. All told, the GAO and CBO found the actual efficiency savings in the Grace Report to be close to zero.

FIGURE 11.8 How Much Can Be Cut?[T10]

disincentives to operating efficiently, a lack of competition in the bureaucracy, and the political climate under which bureaucrats operate.

11.7a Pressure to Spend

Using a kind of perverse logic, the best way for an agency or department to demonstrate its value is to spend the budget it's been given. This creates a situation where there's greater pressure to spend money than there is to conserve it. The best way to demonstrate the value of a bureaucratic unit to congressional appropriators is to show that every item budgeted was necessary, and because future budget requests will take into account whether present appropriations were necessary, the natural urge to protect agency funding leads bureaucrats to the conclusion that they had best find a way to spend what they've been given.

Often this is not a problem; spending happens naturally. As the fiscal year winds down, though, budgets with unspent funds can pose a problem. Not wanting to give Congress a reason to cut back funding for their agency or office, bureaucrats can find themselves in a situation where they have to "use it or lose it"—spend the funds they have or risk being cut in size the next year. In a counterintuitive exercise that critics claim is quintessential bureaucratic thinking, conserving funds brings on punishment while spending (even for the sake of spending) is rewarded.

11.7b Professional Disincentives to Efficiency

In private enterprise, employees are commonly encouraged to find cost-saving measures, and those who realize effective ways to save money characteristically find themselves in line for advancement. Such incentives are unusual in the federal bureaucracy. People who make decisions about procurement, or purchasing goods and services, are not at the high end of the compensation scale and are not rewarded for doing their job in a way that saves money. Unlike in private businesses, efficiency is not professionally valued.[33]

11.7c Lack of Competition

Businesses respond to competitive pressures by looking for ways to cut costs when they find themselves in a disadvantageous competitive position. There is no analogy for this in the bureaucracy, no competitive situation that would require a bureau or agency to trim down. In fact, a set of contrary forces is at work. We've seen how individual bureaucratic units exist in isolation from each other, and how their congressional and interest group allies are invested in maintaining them and boosting their budgets. We've seen how the best way to garner a budget increase is through making sure the present budget is expended. These factors contribute to a noncompetitive environment without a mechanism for instigating bureaucratic efficiency.

11.7d Political Climate

Lack of competition can also mix with political pressures to influence the way agencies go about making procurement decisions. Take the case of weapons procurement, which constitutes a large portion of federal expenditures. Things like aircraft carriers and long-range missiles don't have a market outside the government, so defense contractors would have nowhere else to turn if they did not have government contracts. Corporations involved in military work have already invested a lot of overhead in developing the capacity to produce weapons, and they employ a lot of people in a lot of congressional districts, which means they and their employees would suffer a great hardship if the flow of federal dollars disappeared. Since members of Congress (and the corporate interests themselves) do not want to see this happen, there's a strong political imperative for keeping contractors supplied with work. Unlike a marketplace where competition would determine how contracts are awarded, strong political pressures underscore the need to maintain or increase military spending.[34] Political pressures are not limited to the Department of Defense. Literally every bureau or agency has congressional patrons who will maintain spending pressures to keep constituents happy. Again, there is no private sector parallel.

11.8 Congressional Influence on the Bureaucracy

You may be getting a sense of how strongly bureaucratic and congressional activities are intertwined. The relationship between Congress and the bureaucracy is in fact quite complex. On one hand, congressional constituents directly profit from services and benefits implemented by the bureaucracy, and as we have seen, much bureaucratic growth is the result of congressional action. On the other hand, because the bureaucracy is so wide-ranging and large, it is hard for Congress to manage and control it. Congress has several tools at its disposal to try to influence the bureaucracy, and while they are not inconsiderable, they are not without their shortcomings.

L.O. Show how Congress and the courts attempt to exercise influence over the bureaucracy.

11.8a Appointments

Some political appointees are subject to Senate approval, which gives senators an opportunity to hold hearings and express their views on the president's nominees. In cases where a nominee is particularly controversial, it's possible for the Senate to withhold action on the nomination in an effort to get the president to withdraw it, but this is a rare occurrence, which points out one of the limitations of Senate consent. Most nominees eventually win approval; some do not require approval at all. Once on the job, appointees are not directly accountable to members of Congress, so regardless of what may have transpired in their confirmation hearings, they can go their own way without fear of congressional reprisals.

11.8b Budgets

The ability of Congress to fund the bureaucracy is more significant than its role in the appointment process. A department or agency's authority to spend money and its actual budget is determined by congressional committees with parallel jurisdiction to the bureaucratic unit. So, for instance, funding for the Department of Agriculture has to pass through the House Agriculture Committee and the Senate Agriculture, Nutrition, and Forestry Committee.

At first glance, this would seem to give Congress enormous leverage over the bureaucracy, but when you consider that members of Congress often want to see department and agency budgets increased because of the political benefits they derive from government programs, congressional budgetary authority seems less compelling. A more likely consequence of the congressional role in the budget process is that Congress will direct an agency or department to spend money in a specific way by including legislative language that removes any doubt about what bureaucrats are supposed to do. This is typically done when a powerful member of a congressional committee successfully advances a legislative provision directly benefiting his or her district. Although the amount of money involved may be significant, this type of pork-barrel legislating offers at best piecemeal congressional control of the bureaucracy.

11.8c Oversight

oversight: The process of congressional review of the bureaucracy.

Congressional **oversight** is one of the most important functions performed by the legislative branch in its dealings with the bureaucracy. Technically speaking, oversight is the method Congress uses to ensure that legislation is implemented the way Congress intended. Setting aside for the moment that it's often impossible to say exactly what Congress intends when it passes a bill, oversight activities give members of Congress perhaps their best opportunity to influence bureaucratic activity.

Those same congressional committees whose jurisdictions dovetail with departments and agencies provide the forum for most oversight work. Informally, committee members and their staff communicate regularly with bureaucratic personnel, enabling them to forge and maintain close and influential working relationships. Formally, committees hold hearings on the actions of departments and agencies within their jurisdiction. These provide members of Congress with an opportunity to voice their opinions on how programs are being implemented, a matter of great concern to bureaucrats who are often responsive to members' concerns.[35] As one subcommittee chair said of the agencies in his oversight jurisdiction, "You just have to demonstrate some serious interest . . . serious thoughtful interest, and make suggestions. On the whole, they welcome them. . . . They know that they need you to go to bat for them [in the budgetary process]. So, it can be a very mutually supportive and pretty constructive relationship."[36]

11.8d Judicial Influence on the Bureaucracy

Like the actions of Congress, the president, or state officials, bureaucratic activity is subject to review by the courts. Agencies and bureaus end up in court when someone charges they are acting arbitrarily, failing to carry out the law, or overstepping their authority. More than in the past, the courts have shown a willingness to permit public challenges to bureaucratic actions, and Congress has at times written language permitting court challenges into legislation creating new programs. So, for instance, the Clean Air Act contains a provision permitting anyone to sue the Environmental Protection Agency for failure to properly implement the specific requirements of the act.[37]

The broad range of individuals who can bring suit against departments and agencies has made the courts an influential forum for shaping the way policies are implemented and regulations are enacted. In a manner that the president and Congress cannot match, courts can order written directives mandating bureaucrats to act in a stated fashion. Even so, unless those orders are simple and direct, they may not meet with easy compliance.[38] This is because, for all their authority, courts cannot march in and take over an agency. Ultimately, they have to rely on bureaucratic enforcement of court orders.

The lack of direct enforcement powers has broader implications for the place of the courts in the political process. In fact, the dependency of the courts on the bureaucracy to enforce court rulings mirrors a wider problem facing the judiciary, and anticipates a dilemma that has shaped the way courts have acted since the dawn of the republic. We'll visit that issue, among others, in Chapter 12.

Chapter Review

Identify the federal bureaucracy as hierarchical and specialized, as well as fragmented and decentralized.

The executive branch or the federal bureaucracy is a large web of departments, agencies, and bureaus charged with carrying out the laws and regulations passed by Congress and signed by the president. It is hierarchical and specialized, but also fragmented and decentralized, with numerous bureaucratic units handling unrelated tasks.

Explain the relationship between political appointees and career civil servants.

Political appointees fill the top administrative spots. They get their jobs through presidential appointment and generally serve at the pleasure of the president. Civil servants fill the vast majority of bureaucratic positions. They get their jobs by scoring well on objective exams. Once tenured, they can serve as long as they wish.

Discuss why political appointees can have divided loyalties between the presidents who appoint them and the departments or agencies they run.

The transient nature of political appointees generally leaves them unfamiliar with the organizational culture of the bureau or agency they are sent to run. This, coupled with the stability of career civil servants, can place political appointees in the position of "going native" and acquiescing to the ways of the department or agency, upending traditional lines of command. It can frustrate the president's desire to exercise control of the bureaucracy. Determined presidents can attempt to circumvent this by placing deeply loyal and ideological appointees at every available leadership level in the bureaucracy. Presidents like Reagan who have followed this strategy and implemented an administrative presidency have achieved some success.

Identify key cabinet-level departments, independent agencies, independent regulatory commissions, and government corporations, and understand key differences in what they do and how they are structured.

Fifteen cabinet-level departments make up the largest organizational component of the bureaucracy. Independent agencies, like the Environmental Protection Agency (EPA) and the National Aeronautics and Space Administration (NASA), operate outside the cabinet structure, reporting directly to the president. Independent regulatory commissions and boards, like the Federal Trade Commission (FTC), also report directly to the president, but are more independent than the independent agencies. They are composed of a fixed number of members, divided between the two major parties, who serve for a fixed term and cannot be removed by the president. Government corporations, like the U.S. Postal Service, are structured like private corporations and provide a service, though they do not seek to make a profit.

Define implementation, regulation, and administration.

Explain why implementation can be a complex bureaucratic function.

Bureaucracies engage in three primary functions: implementation, regulation, and administration. Implementation entails giving shape to policies, and it can be a complex process, hampered by ambiguous legislative intent, unclear communication between bureaucrats and legislators, insufficient resources, bureaucratic resistance, inflexible standard operating procedures, and bureaucratic fragmentation. Regulation entails monitoring the actions of the private sector to protect the general welfare by maintaining safe water, food, air quality, and the like. Administration involves carrying out routine organizational tasks required to keep the government functioning, like printing Social Security checks and maintaining national monuments.

Demonstrate how the bureaucracy developed from a patronage system to a system based on neutral competence.

The bureaucracy has grown as the federal role has expanded. Once largely a patronage system, it became a merit system in the twentieth century with the creation of a professional civil service based on the philosophy of neutral competence. Numerous efforts to reform the bureaucracy have been prevalent over the past half-century. Some reformers want to reduce bureaucratic inefficiency, which is maintained by a set of forces that include professional disincentives to efficiency, lack of competition in bureaucratic decision making, and political pressures from Congress to spend money.

Show how Congress and the courts attempt to exercise influence over the bureaucracy.

Congress, for its part, exercises some influence over the bureaucracy through Senate confirmation of some presidential appointees, the ability to fund bureaucratic agencies and departments, and oversight provisions. Since members of Congress benefit politically from bureaucratic activity, their ability to influence the bureaucracy is limited. The courts can also influence bureaucratic behavior by ruling that an agency or department acted arbitrarily, failed to carry out the law, or overstepped its authority. In recent years, the ability to bring suit against the bureaucracy has greatly expanded, in many cases to include ordinary citizens, giving the judiciary additional influence over what the bureaucracy does.

Key Terms

administration The bureaucratic function of tending to the details of executing public policy. (p. 353)

administrative presidency A strategic approach to the bureaucracy relying on ideological political appointees and tight presidential management to combat the tendency for political appointees to "go native." (p. 343)

bureaucracy Another name for the executive branch of government, the institutional component of the presidency, which is charged with carrying out laws passed by Congress. (p. 339)

civil servants Career employees who staff the bureaucracy in a wide range of positions and who get their jobs independent of political considerations. (p. 340)

Civil Service Commission The commission established by the Pendleton Act to oversee the hiring of career civil servants. (p. 356)

deregulation The lifting of federal regulations that had been previously imposed on private industry. (p. 352)

Federal Register A publicly available list of all proposed and existing federal regulations. (p. 352)

Federal Wage System (FWS) The system used to determine salaries for blue-collar civil servants. (p. 343)

General Service (GS) The system of eighteen grade levels (GS1 through GS18) that determines the pay level of white-collar civil servants. (p. 343)

goldplating Government purchasing of top-of-the-line items at maximum cost, which can happen when bureaucrats overseeing purchasing decisions have an interest in the items being purchased. (p. 357)

"go native" The tendency for political appointees to adhere to the organizational culture of the department they are sent to run, making them advocates of the department rather than advocates of the president. (p. 343)

government corporations Corporations established by Congress to perform important services, like delivering the mail and operating rail lines, which could not be or were not profitably provided by private corporations. (p. 348)

Hatch Act Legislation enacted in 1939 that prohibits civil servants from engaging in political activities. (p. 356)

implementation The bureaucratic function of taking the legal language of legislation and turning it into functioning programs. (p. 349)

independent agencies Bureaucratic organizations that report directly to the president rather than through cabinet secretaries, and whose administrators serve at the pleasure of the president. (p. 347)

independent regulatory commissions and boards Panels designed to oversee the conduct of various segments of the economy. Members are appointed by the president and confirmed by the Senate. They serve fixed terms and cannot be removed by the president. (p. 347)

merit system Procedures for hiring civil servants based on objective evaluations of their performance rather than on their political connections. (p. 356)

neutral competence The philosophy guiding nineteenth-century civil service reform, which states that bureaucrats should be chosen strictly for their ability to perform their job, without political criteria influencing their selection or their actions. (p. 356)

newsworthy The conditions under which a story warrants publication or dissemination, based on a set of values applied by newspaper editors and television producers. Newsworthy stories typically have conflict, proximity, and relevance to the audience, timeliness, and familiarity. (p. 338)

oversight The process of congressional review of the bureaucracy. (p. 360)

patronage Jobs, favors, and other resources that party officials provide in exchange for people's political support. (p. 355)

Pendleton Act The 1883 law requiring that merit-based criteria be used to hire public employees, ending the tradition of patronage appointments. (p. 355)

Plum Book The congressional publication listing all top-level political positions in the bureaucracy. (p. 341)

political appointees Top-level bureaucratic officials whom the president appoints, typically pending Senate confirmation, and who serve at the pleasure of the president. (p. 340)

pork barrel Wasteful or unnecessary spending that can result from logrolling. Whether something is a pork-barrel project or a valuable use of taxpayer dollars may depend on whether you stand to benefit from it. (p. 357

regulation The bureaucratic function of placing standards or restrictions on the actions of private individuals or companies in order to protect the general welfare of the public. (p. 352)

Senior Executive Service (SES) The payment scale used for a small group of upper-level government managers and technical experts. Most positions covered by the Senior Executive Service are in the civil service, although the SES covers select political appointees whose jobs do not require Senate confirmation. (p. 343)

spoils system The method of staffing the federal bureaucracy, commonplace in the nineteenth century, in which the president offered patronage appointments to political supporters. (p. 355)

standard operating procedures (SOPs) Guidelines that provide uniformity to bureaucratic decision making. (p. 351)

tenure Job security afforded to civil servants following a probationary period, to protect them against losing their jobs for political reasons. (p. 342)

Resources

You might be interested in examining some of what the following authors have said about the topics we've been discussing:

Aberbach, Joel D. *Keeping a Watchful Eye: The Politics of Congressional Oversight*. Washington, DC: Brookings Institution, 1990. A look at how Congress attempts to influence the bureaucracy, and at how congressional oversight has changed over the past decades.

Golden, Marissa Martino. *What Motivates Bureaucrats? Politics and Administration during the Reagan Years*. New York: Columbia University Press, 2000. President Reagan came to office espousing a philosophy of smaller government, putting him at odds with many bureaucrats. Golden looks at the ways bureaucrats responded to—and resisted—presidential directives they did not agree with.

Goodsell, Charles T. *The Case for Bureaucracy: A Public Administration Polemic*, 4th ed. Washington, DC: CQ Press,

2003. Many of us have negative associations with bureaucracies. Goodsell presents reasons why we might want to reconsider them.

Heclo, Hugh M. *A Government of Strangers: Executive Politics in Washington*. Washington, DC: Brookings Institution, 1977. A look at the sometimes surprising relationship between political appointees and career bureaucrats.

Hill, Michael, and Peter Hupe. *Implementing Public Policy*, 2nd ed. Thousand Oaks, CA: Sage, 2009. A comprehensive overview of issues related to implementation.

Kerwin, Cornelius M., and Scott R. Furlong. *Rulemaking: How Government Agencies Write Law and Make Policy*, 4th ed. Washington, DC: CQ Press, 2010. Congress sends laws to bureaucrats, who have to turn laws into policy. Kerwin and Furlong explain how they do it.

Wilson, James Q. *Bureaucracy: What Government Agencies Do and Why They Do It*. New York: Basic Books, 1991. A wide-ranging look at bureaucratic operations.

You may also be interested in looking at the Plum Book from the presidential transition in 2008, at http://www.transitionjobs.us/.

Notes

1 Researcher Michael Lipsky defines "street level" bureaucracy as the "schools, police and welfare departments, lower courts, legal services offices, and other agencies whose workers interact with and have wide discretion over the dispensation of benefits or the allocation of public sanctions." See Michael Lipsky, *Street-Level Bureaucracy: Dilemmas of the Individual in Public Services*, (New York: Russell Sage Foundation, 1980), xi.

2 Charles T. Goodsell, *The Case for Bureaucracy: A Public Administration Polemic* (Chatham, NJ: Chatham House Publishers, 1983), 3. This is a direct quote from the book.

3 Ibid., 16–37. Data on the postal service may be found on p. 30.

4 Ibid., 82–109.

5 H. H. Gerth and C. Wright Mills, eds., *From Max Weber: Essays in Sociology* (New York: Oxford University Press, 1946).

6 Goodsell, *Case for Bureaucracy*, 83.

7 James Q. Wilson, *Bureaucracy: What Government Agencies Do and Why They Do It* (New York: Basic Books, 1989), 91.

8 Ibid., 93–95.

9 Hugh M. Heclo, *A Government of Strangers: Executive Politics in Washington* (Washington, DC: Brookings Institution, 1977), 84–112.

10 Ibid., 102–105.

11 U.S. Office of Personnel Management, at https://www.opm.gov/policy-data-oversight/data-analysis-documentation/federal-employment-reports/reports-publications/profile-of-federal-civilian-non-postal-employees/.

12 See Federal Civilian Workforce Statistics, Occupations of Federal White-Collar and Blue-Collar Workers, September 30, 1999, Tables W-A2 and B-A2, at http://www.opm.gov/feddata/ocwcbc99.pdf.

13 Ronald N. Johnson and Gary D. Libecap, *The Federal Civil Service System and the Problem of Bureaucracy* (Chicago: University of Chicago Press, 1994), 4–5.

14 Marissa Martino Golden, *What Motivates Bureaucrats? Politics and Administration during the Reagan Years* (New York: Columbia University Press, 2000), 5–8.

15 Ibid., 151–155.

16 Ibid., 153–160.

17 See Dan Froomkin, "What Monica Doesn't Know," Washingtonpost.com, May 23, 2008; and Michael Isikoff and Thomas Evans, "Bush's Monica Problem," *Newsweek* (June 4, 2007): 24; and Joe Plazzolo, "The Goodling Report: How Aides Took Control of DOJ Hiring," *Legal Times*, November 28, 2009.

18 You can visit TVA online at http://www.tva.gov/.

19 Cornelius M. Kerwin, *Rulemaking: How Government Agencies Write Law and Make Policy* (Washington, DC: CQ Press, 1994), 1–6.

20 George C. Edwards, *Implementing Public Policy* (Washington, DC: CQ Press, 1980), 1–14.

21 Ibid., 17–51.

22 Ibid., 53–87.

23 Ibid., 89–97.

24 Ibid., 125–124.

25 Ibid., 134–141.

26 Arthur Delaney, "Our Drinking Water Regulation Is So Weak Even Flint's Water Got a Pass," *Huffington Post*, June 28, 2016. http://www.huffingtonpost.com/entry/flint-water-lead_us_57727d8be4b0f168323ae089.

27 Paul C. Light, *Thickening Government: Federal Hierarchy and the Diffusion of Accountability* (Washington, DC: Brookings Institution: Governance Institute, 1995), 34–36.

28 Johnson and Libecap, *Federal Civil Service System*, 14–15.

29 Ibid., 17–18.

30 Donald F. Kettl, and others, *Civil Service Reform: Building a Government That Works* (Washington, DC: Brookings Institution Press, 1996), 87–89.

31 Light, *Thickening Government*.

32 David Osborne and Ted Gaebler, *Reinventing Government: How the Entrepreneurial Spirit Is Transforming the Public Sector* (New York: Addison-Wesley, 1992).

33 James Q. Wilson, *Bureaucracy: What Government Agencies Do and Why They Do It* (New York: Basic Books, 1989), 320–322.

34 Ibid., 323–325.

35 Joel D. Aberbach, *Keeping a Watchful Eye: The Politics of Congressional Oversight* (Washington, DC: Brookings Institution, 1990), 130–144.

36 Ibid., 196.

37 Wilson, *Bureaucracy*, 279–281.

38 Ibid., 290–294.

Table, Figure, and Box Notes

T1 Photo: Long Island City Post Office, 46-02 21st Street; Source: U.S. Federal Government.

T2 United States Office of Personnel Management, at https://www.opm.gov/policy-data-oversight/data-analysis-documentation/federal-employment-reports/reports-publications/profile-of-federal-civilian-non-postal-employees/.

T3 Ronald Johnson and Gary D. Libecap, *The Federal Civil Service System and the Problem with Bureaucracy* (Chicago: University of Chicago Press, 1994), 98–99.

T4 Hugh M. Heclo, *A Government of Strangers: Executive Politics in Washington* (Washington, DC: Brookings Institution, 1977), 111–12.

T5 Department of State, at http://www.state.gov/r/pa/ei/rls/ dos/99494.htm.

T6 Department of the Interior, at http://www.doi.gov/bureaus/.

T7 Cornelius M. Kerwin, Rulemaking: *How Government Agencies Write Law and Make Policy* (Washington, DC: CQ Press, 1994), 6.

T8 Data from *Historical Statistics of the United States, Colonial Times to 1970, Bicentennial Edition* (Washington, DC: U.S. Dept. of Commerce, Bureau of the Census, 1975), series Y308; and *Statistical Abstract of the United States: 1987*, Table 741; 1997, Table 537; 1999, Table 539.

T9 James Q. Wilson, *Bureaucracy: Why Government Agencies Do and Why They Do It* (New York: Basic Books, 1989) 319–320.

T10 Ibid., 318–319.

The Judiciary

CHAPTER 12

Copyright: Tinnaporn Sathapornnanont/Shutterstock.com

Learning Objectives

When you have completed this chapter, you should be able to:

- Explain why the judiciary has less power than the other branches of the federal government.
- Define judicial review as it was established in *Marbury v. Madison*, and explain how it greatly enhanced the powers of the Supreme Court.
- Illustrate the three-tiered judicial structure in place at the federal and state levels, and explain the appeals process.
- Discuss how the Supreme Court selects, hears, and decides cases.
- Describe the judicial confirmation process, and explain why it has been contentious in recent years.
- Characterize the level of gender, racial, and religious diversity on the Supreme Court both historically and today.
- Explain how the Supreme Court relies on legitimacy and public opinion to bolster its weak political position.
- Define *stare decisis*, and explain the importance of continuity to the Supreme Court.
- Contrast judicial activism with judicial restraint.

12.1 Introduction

Quick: What do you think of when someone says the judiciary? The Supreme Court, perhaps? Justices in long black robes? An imposing marble building? Something totally removed from your everyday experience?

judiciary: The federal and state court systems charged with resolving legal and personal disputes and interpreting the law.

The **judiciary** has always been the branch of government that seems different from the rest of the political system: more secretive and distant, and removed from the body blows of politics. Its devotion to the law distinguishes the judiciary from the other institutions we've been discussing, not in the sense that it doesn't engage in the process of deciding who gets what, when, and how, but in the way it goes about doing this. The judiciary is the place where laws are interpreted and disputes are resolved. It rests at the heart of the **legal system**, which includes members of Congress and the president, who create laws that others may challenge; the bureaucracy, which implements laws in a manner that may cause disputes; individuals or interest groups with grievances; attorneys who argue legal issues on behalf of individuals or interest groups with grievances; and even police officers, who bring conflicts to the attention of the judicial system by enforcing the law on the street.[1]

legal system: The web of institutions and individuals involved in bringing legal and personal disputes to the attention of the courts.

Its involvement with matters of justice seems to put the judiciary above raw politics, and there are characteristics of the judiciary that you simply won't find anywhere else in the political process. Take the U.S. Supreme Court as an example. Its members are not elected (justices are appointed by the president and confirmed by the Senate). They serve for life, and never have to hire pollsters or media consultants to create a public image or position themselves for the next political campaign. Although they may be strong partisans, they shy away from involvement in partisan gatherings like political party conventions and do not stage media events like elected officials. They deliberate in private and never disclose what is said. This seems nothing like the other two branches of government, where popular participation in regularly scheduled elections is designed to keep officeholders accountable to the electorate.

The trappings of the Court only contribute to this mystique. We'd think it was silly if the president appeared in public in a dark robe, but on a Supreme Court justice, the robe evokes tradition and prestige, suggesting a certain respect for those who walk the imposing marble-laden corridors of the temple-like Supreme Court building. The Court's symbol of "Lady Justice," blindfolded as she balances scales, depicts objectivity and fairness—characteristics rarely on display when Republicans and Democrats face off in a political or policy debate. In form and content, the Supreme Court appears a world apart from the political system we've come to know.[2]

But is it? If Court actions were only influenced by legal criteria, the answer might be yes, but we will see that this is far from what really happens. As we read on, we'll come to perceive the Court as a highly political institution that may operate differently from other political institutions but that is nonetheless steeped in politics.

There are clues to the Court's political persona, some more obvious than others. For example, the president and senators consider their political agendas when selecting and acting on appointments to the Supreme Court and lower courts in the federal judicial system, and political disputes over appointment confirmations can be ferocious. Nominees themselves may be political figures or individuals with partisan activity in their pasts. Their judgments on the Court are invariably influenced by their political principles, and the decisions they render can put them at the heart of partisan disputes.[3] The Court may be a legal institution, but it exists in a political world.

Dark robes and sometimes somber expressions contribute to the mystique of the U.S. Supreme Court, which seems more distant and less political than the other two branches of government. Pictured here is the 2017 Roberts Court: (Back, left to right) Elena Kagan, Samuel Anthony Alito, Sonia Sotomayor, Neil Gorsuch. (Front, left to right) Ruth Bader Ginsburg, Anthony M. Kennedy, Chief Justice John G. Roberts, Clarence Thomas, Stephen G. Breyer.[T1]

12.2 A Judiciary without Power

By virtue of its position in this political world, the Court is at something of a disadvantage relative to the legislative and executive branches. The judiciary is, by design, the weakest of the three branches of the federal government. Alexander Hamilton, writing in Federalist #78, called it "the least dangerous to the political rights of the Constitution; because it will be least in a capacity to annoy or injure them." As Hamilton noted, the executive holds the power to enforce the law, and the legislature has the power to tax:

L.O. Explain why the judiciary has less power than the other branches of the federal government.

> The judiciary, on the contrary, has no influence over either the sword or the purse; no direction either of the strength or of the wealth of the society; and can take no active resolution whatever. It may truly be said to have neither FORCE nor WILL, but merely judgment; and must ultimately depend upon the aid of the executive arm even for the efficacy of its judgments.[4]

In other words, the Constitution's authors put the judicial function in an institution that would have to rely on a separate institution—the executive—to enforce its rulings. Simultaneously, the Constitution made the judiciary the branch that was to exercise judgment over the decisions of the executive, potentially putting the two branches at odds with each other while making the judiciary dependent on the executive to carry out rulings that could come at the executive's expense. Demystifying Government: A Weak Judiciary versus No Judiciary contrasts this weak judiciary with the earlier lack of a judiciary under the Articles of Confederation.

It took very little time after the ratification of the Constitution for Congress to flesh out the new judiciary, although it would be a while before the judicial and executive branches would come into conflict over the enforcement of judicial decisions. That's because it took a while for the nascent court system to find its bearings.

With little in the Constitution to guide them (Article III established the jurisdiction and tenure of justices, but otherwise is silent on the matter of how to organize the court system) and Federalists in command of the debate, Congress established a set of lower courts in the **Judiciary Act of 1789**. It set the number of Supreme Court justices at six (it is now nine), and assigned pairs of Supreme Court justices to each of three new circuit courts (occupying the lower level of the new court system).[5] So, not only would there be lower federal courts, but Supreme Court justices would have a hand in staffing them.

Judiciary Act of 1789: The act of Congress that established the federal court system. It initially called for a six-person Supreme Court and three circuit courts, each to be administered by two Supreme Court justices and one district judge.

Articles of Confederation: The first constitution of the United States, which created a loosely functioning national government to which the individual states were supreme. It addressed concerns about a strong national government undermining individual liberty, but it created a national government that was unable to regulate commerce or conduct foreign policy and was abandoned in favor of the United States Constitution just eight years after it was ratified.

DEMYSTIFYING GOVERNMENT

A Weak Judiciary versus No Judiciary

A weak judicial system designed under the doctrine of separation of powers was an upgrade from the mechanism in place for resolving national disputes under the Articles of Confederation. That's because there was no independent judiciary for resolving national disputes under the **Articles of Confederation**. Recall that the federal government under the Articles centered on a single legislature, which was composed of representatives of the states. The legislature could attempt to resolve conflicts, but the absence of a separate national judiciary left the young nation without an efficient forum for resolving the numerous disputes that arose among the states, and was widely considered a defect in need of correction by the delegates to the Constitutional Convention.

Like so much to emerge from the Convention, the judicial branch is the product of compromise between those who wished to establish strong federal institutions and those concerned about the rights of smaller states. Federalists who supported the **Virginia Plan** would have established a federal Supreme Court and a multitiered system of lower courts. Supporters of the **New Jersey Plan**, which called only for a federal Supreme Court to act as final arbiter in cases arising in state courts, were worried that a federal court system posed a threat to states' rights.[T2] The delegates resolved the issue by punting. In a characteristically vague passage, Article III of the Constitution vests the "judicial power" in the Supreme Court "and in such inferior Courts as the Congress may from time to time ordain and establish." It would be up to the new Congress to determine what, if anything, those "inferior Courts" would look like.

Serving on two courts at once probably sounds like a tall order, but the truth is that for the first decade of its existence, the Supreme Court didn't have much to do. It also didn't have a permanent home or staff, suffered from rapid turnover among justices, and didn't have much of an institutional identity or public prestige.[6] Consider the inaugural session of the Supreme Court, meeting in the Royal Exchange Building in New York City on February 1, 1790. Three justices were absent, and two of those missed the entire court session—which lasted all of ten days.[7] During that time, the justices who were present chose a seal for the Court and appointed a clerk. They didn't rule on any cases because no business was before the Court. In fact, they didn't rule on any cases for three years.[8]

As in so many other areas, George Washington supplied a model for his successors in the way he went about appointing justices to the Supreme Court. Faced with the opportunity to fill every slot on the Court, Washington did a few things that presidents still do today:

- *Appoint ideologically compatible judges.* All six Washington appointees were loyal Federalists. Even though the Federalists were not organized as a formal party, Washington nominated judges who shared his ideological penchant for a strong national government. Presidents throughout history have sought philosophically compatible judicial nominees from their political party.

- *Offer representation to key interests.* In the late eighteenth century, this meant providing geographic balance: Three of Washington's appointees were southerners, and three were northerners. As political interests changed, the particulars of offering representation to specific groups changed as well. In the twentieth and twenty-first centuries, religion, race, ethnicity, and gender have replaced regional concerns as factors in court appointments.

- *Don't expect the best.* Washington's Supreme Court nominees were uneven in their abilities and reputations. Subsequent presidents have found that they can't always get their top choices to serve on the Court, that political criteria like ideological compatibility or satisfying key interests may necessitate settling for a lesser candidate, and that nominees who seem promising may turn out to be disappointing.

- *Be especially careful when nominating the chief justice.* Washington's choice was John Jay, one of the authors of *The Federalist* and a New York lawyer and judge. Washington believed that the chief justice had to be a widely acclaimed jurist whose ethics were beyond reproach.[9]

For Washington, appointing justices was far from the contentious experience it is today, because sleepiness was the rule during the Court's first decade. With little prestige and an insignificant role in the federal government, the Court during this time was marked by high turnover and few responsibilities. It ruled on little more than fifty cases during that time and drew little attention to itself.[10] All of that changed with the dawn of the new century and the entrance on the scene of Chief Justice John Marshall, one of the most influential justices in Court history.

12.3 Judicial Review

John Marshall (see biography) was appointed chief justice by President Adams in 1801 and served in this capacity for thirty-four years, during which time he fashioned the Court into an equal partner with the executive and the legislature. Many of the procedures in place today were originated under Marshall's tutelage.[11] For instance, before Marshall, it was customary for every justice to write a separate opinion every time the Court ruled on a case, but Marshall recognized the political value of presenting a unified front for the Court by keeping differences among justices behind closed doors. He instituted the practice of hammering out disagreements in private deliberations, then handing down single opinions on cases.[12]

Marshall's most important and enduring contribution to the Court was the practice of **judicial review**. Today we take for granted that the Supreme Court has the authority to

JOHN MARSHALL

John Marshall was forty-five years old when President John Adams appointed him to be chief justice of the Supreme Court in 1801. The oldest of fifteen children, Marshall came from modest roots to distinguish himself in several fields of service. A captain in the Revolutionary War, Marshall studied law at the College of William and Mary and practiced law in his native Virginia. He served as a Federalist representative to the Virginia House of Delegates, as an American envoy to France, and briefly as a member of the U.S. Congress. In 1800, Adams tapped Marshall to be his secretary of state. The following year, as Adams's term was about to expire, he appointed Marshall to the Supreme Court, where Marshall served longer than almost anyone in history—until he died in 1835. Marshall was a bitter political enemy of the man who followed Adams in office, fellow Virginian Thomas Jefferson—who also, by a strange quirk of history, happened to be Marshall's second cousin. Jefferson, who never lacked for the ability to turn a phrase, referred to Marshall as "that gloomy malignity." Adams, in contrast, was more than satisfied with Marshall's long record of service on the Court. Just prior to his death, Adams proclaimed, "My gift of John Marshall to the people of the United States was the proudest act of my life."T3

review the actions of Congress or the president and declare them unconstitutional. In fact, many people think of constitutional interpretation as the essential purpose of the Supreme Court because the most important thing it does is validate or overturn the acts of others in the political system—but such authority is not expressly granted in the Constitution. It derives from a ruling in the 1803 case *Marbury v. Madison*. It's a complex and important case, involving political power plays, conflicts of interest, and a great twist ending. You can find the facts in the Demystifying Government box, *Marbury v. Madison*: The Brief Version.

Marbury v. Madison: The Supreme Court case, heard by the Marshall Court in 1803, that established judicial review.

The logic behind Marshall's ruling in *Marbury v. Madison*—that Congress over-reached by expanding the Court's jurisdiction, and so, the Court must strike down an act of Congress—requires a certain leap of faith. The rationale he gave for saying Congress overstepped its authority when it gave the Court the power to issue writs of *mandamus* in the Judiciary Act of 1789 was that the Constitution didn't stipulate that Congress had the authority to expand the Court's jurisdiction in this manner. Maybe so, but the Constitution also didn't stipulate that the Court could review an act of Congress and declare it unconstitutional—at least not directly. Marshall was asking us to accept a broad view of constitutional interpretation in the matter of judicial review while he was asking us to take a narrow view of constitutional interpretation in the matter of the Judiciary Act of 1789. Of course, what was anyone going to do about it? Because the Court could simply refuse the authority to issue writs of *mandamus*, it had the final say in the matter.

During his long tenure as chief justice, Marshall handed down several decisions that shaped the course of our national development by resolving questions about the key political issue of the day, the relationship between the federal government and the states, in favor of the federal government. When we were discussing federalism in Chapter 2, we profiled the case *McCulloch v. Maryland* (1819), which was a turning point in the establishment of federal dominance over state governments and an endorsement of a broad constitutional grant of power to the federal government. In *Gibbons v. Ogden* (1824), the Marshall Court established the supremacy of the federal government over matters of interstate commerce.

McCulloch v. Maryland: The 1819 Supreme Court case that established federal supremacy over the state governments.

Gibbons v. Ogden: The Supreme Court case, heard by the Marshall Court in 1824, that established the federal government's primacy in regulating interstate commerce, saying that the state of New York could not grant an exclusive license to a steamboat company operating between New York and New Jersey.

Marshall's durability was so great that he was still presiding over the Supreme Court at the start of Andrew Jackson's administration, during the transition to the second party system that we talked about in Chapter 6, and he was still frustrating chief executives who favored states' rights with his Federalist rulings. Marshall's opinion in the 1832 case *Worcester v. Georgia* upholding federal rather than state jurisdiction over Cherokee land

Marbury v. Madison: The Brief Version

In 1800, John Adams was defeated for re-election by his political rival Thomas Jefferson.

Before leaving office, Adams attempted to fill the federal judiciary with as many sympathetic Federalists as possible. This is also when he appointed John Marshall to be chief justice of the Supreme Court.

John Marshall was also Adams's secretary of state. In that role, it was Marshall's job to deliver Adams's judicial commissions for them to become official.

The commission had to be delivered before Jefferson was sworn in as president. Marshall ran out of time and failed to deliver several commissions, including the appointment of William Marbury, whom Adams had appointed justice of the peace for the District of Columbia. James Madison became secretary of state when Jefferson became president. For partisan reasons, he ignored the appointment of Marbury and his sixteen colleagues, which Marshall had failed to deliver in time. Marbury sued Madison, and the case went to the U.S. Supreme Court.

Marbury asked the Court to issue a **writ of mandamus**, a court order commanding an official to act—in this case an order to Secretary of State Madi-

son to deliver Marbury's judicial appointment. The Supreme Court was granted the authority to issue writs of *mandamus* as part of the Judiciary Act of 1789.

Setting aside the conflict of interest Marshall faced by having been the individual responsible for Marbury's dilemma, as chief justice, Marshall faced a dilemma of his own. Circumstances made it clear that Marbury was entitled to his appointment, but if Marshall issued the writ, President Jefferson most certainly would have told Secretary Madison to ignore it. And if he ruled against Marbury, the Court would have looked weak.

Marshall fashioned a solution in one of the most ingenious court decisions in American history. He agreed that Marbury was entitled to his appointment, but that Congress had exceeded its constitutional authority when it gave the Court the ability to issue writs of *mandamus*. He therefore struck down the provision of the Judiciary Act of 1789 that gave the Court that authority. It was a self-executing order that didn't require Jefferson's enforcement. Marbury didn't get to be justice of the peace, but Marshall had expanded the Court's reach by claiming the power of judicial review.

---

writ of *mandamus*: A court order commanding a public official to perform an official act.

L.O. Illustrate the three-tiered judicial structure in place at the federal and state levels, and explain the appeals process.

rights so angered President Jackson that the president is alleged to have said, "John Marshall has made his decision, now let him enforce it."[13]

12.4 The Court System

As we mentioned in Section 12.2, "A Judiciary without Power," a system of federal courts began to emerge in the 1790s, when a justice earned his keep by doubling as a judge on a lower "circuit" court since there wasn't much work for the Supreme Court to do. We noted that the Judiciary Act of 1789 created the first lower court system: three circuit courts corresponding to the eastern, middle, and southern sections of the country. The original arrangement called for each circuit to be staffed by two of the six Supreme Court justices, along with a permanent district judge.[14]

The court got its name because the justices would "ride circuit"—they literally covered the territory twice a year on horseback or carriage, hearing cases along the way. And they were miserable. Roads were horrendous, the weather was often bad, and justices had to be away from their families for long stretches of time. One justice, Levi Woodbury, who served in the 1840s, wrote of the "villaneous sea-sickness" he experienced riding circuit in a stagecoach:

I think I never again, at this season of the year, will attempt this mode of journeying. Besides the evils before mentioned I have been elbowed by old women—jammed by young ones—suffocated by cigar smoke—sickened by the vapours of bitters and w[h]iskey—my head knocked through the carriage top by careless drivers and my toes trodden to a jelly by unheeding passengers.[15]

Within ten years of their establishment, more circuits were added along with more district judges but the custom of riding circuit persisted through the nineteenth century, even though justices were required to do it less frequently. In the twentieth century, the circuit court system grew enormously. There are now eleven circuits plus the District of Columbia, as represented on the map in Figure 12.1.

Today, the federal system is a three-tiered system, with the circuit courts functioning as appeals courts. This parallels the structure in place in each of the fifty states, which have their own state court systems to hear cases arising out of violations of state law. Because each state has its own Constitution, the specifics of the court systems vary from state to state. It's reasonable to picture the federal court system existing in tandem with a system of fifty state courts.

One way to think of the differences among these courts is to consider the differences in their **jurisdiction**, or the types of cases each has the authority to hear. In both the federal and state systems, most cases originate at the bottom level and are appealed upwards.

There are exceptions. The Constitution grants the U.S. Supreme Court **original jurisdiction** over certain types of conflicts, meaning they can originate at the top rather than having to work their way through the system. The Supreme Court's original jurisdiction extends to cases where there is a dispute involving:

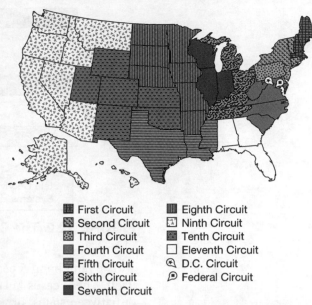

First Circuit	Eighth Circuit
Second Circuit	Ninth Circuit
Third Circuit	Tenth Circuit
Fourth Circuit	Eleventh Circuit
Fifth Circuit	D.C. Circuit
Sixth Circuit	Federal Circuit
Seventh Circuit	

FIGURE 12.1 United States Court System by Circuit

- The United States and a state
- Two or more states
- Citizens of different states
- A state and a citizen of another state
- Foreign ambassadors

The Supreme Court has **appellate jurisdiction** for all other cases, meaning the cases have to originate in lower courts and work their way through the judicial system on appeal.

Broadly speaking, state courts have jurisdiction over most criminal law and civil law—ranging from serious offenses like murder and robbery to minor offenses like traffic violations to civil issues like divorce and inheritance disputes—because most criminal and civil laws are state laws. For this reason, most trials are held in state courts, and 95 percent of judges are state judges.[16]

Federalism presents us with fifty state court systems that operate parallel to the federal system we've been discussing. Figure 12.2 demonstrates how the two systems are structured and how they operate. For the most part, each of these systems has three tiers. The trial level is where most cases originate. State trial courts hear cases involving state law, while federal district courts hear cases involving federal law. There are ninety-four federal district courts. Appellate courts hear cases appealed by those who lost at the trial level. In the federal court system, there are eleven circuit courts of appeals covering eleven geographic regions of the country, plus a court of appeals for the District of Columbia and one for the federal circuit. Federal courts also hear appeals of decisions by independent regulatory agencies. Every state has a top-tier court, which is typically the final stop for an appeal. Most—but not all—states call this the supreme court. Of course, the U.S. Supreme Court has the final word on cases appealed through the federal court system. About 65 percent of its cases come through this route.

Although the federal and state court systems have similar structures, their jurisdictions are so different that it's appropriate to think of them as separate entities. Their paths cross only in rare circumstances. If a case heard in state court raises a contested point of constitutional law, it can be appealed from the state court system to the federal court system, where it is heard directly by the U.S. Supreme Court. Roughly 30 percent of U.S. Supreme Court cases originate this way. Unless a constitutional question is raised in a state trial, there can be no appeal to the federal court system, and the state supreme court has the final word in the matter.

jurisdiction: The authority of a court to hear a case.

original jurisdiction: The authority of the U.S. Supreme Court to be the first court to hear a case, precluding the need for an appeal from a lower court. The Constitution grants original jurisdiction to cases involving a dispute between the United States and a state; two or more states; citizens of different states; a state and a citizen of another state; and foreign ambassadors.

appellate jurisdiction: The authority of a high court to hear cases only after the cases originate in and are appealed from a lower court.

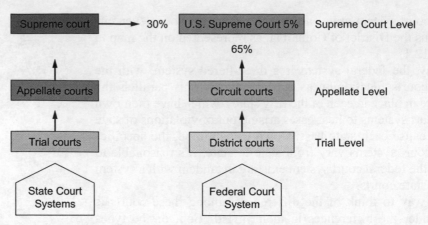

FIGURE 12.2 The Court System and Appeals Process[T4]

The remaining 5 percent of U.S. Supreme Court cases originate in the Supreme Court itself. These cases fall under the Court's original jurisdiction and involve disputes among or between states, or where the United States or a foreign nation or its representative is a party. Also, some cases involving civil rights or reapportionment claims can be appealed from the trial level directly to the U.S. Supreme Court.

When the Supreme Court refuses to hear a case on appeal, the word of the lower court is final. Because circuit courts operate under a wide range of judicial philosophies and ideological perspectives, the specific circuit court to hear a case can be critical to the outcome. So, blind justice only tells part of the story. Judicial outcomes can turn on the state or circuit in which a case is heard and the judicial philosophies of the individuals hearing it.

12.5 Deciding Cases

L.O. Discuss how the Supreme Court selects, hears, and decides cases.

When a court agrees to hear a case, it typically goes through several steps before issuing a judgment. Judges or justices hear arguments from attorneys representing the two sides of the matter, meet privately in conference to discuss the case, and draft their opinions on the case before the final vote is revealed. We'll look at the Supreme Court to get a sense of how this process works.

12.5a Oral Arguments

The first stage of the process is oral argument. Early in its history when the Supreme Court had little work to do, oral arguments could go on for hours or days. Today, unless there's an exception, oral arguments last one hour. They are held in the relatively small courtroom in the Supreme Court building, with the robed justices sitting on an elevated podium, looking down at the attorneys arguing the two sides of the case. You can visit if you like—oral arguments are open to the public. But you may have to wait in a long line for just several minutes of viewing because only about three hundred seats are reserved for the public.[17]

The atmosphere is solemn and the pace quick. Characteristically, justices will cut off the presenting attorneys in midsentence, challenging a statement they made or raising a related point. Other justices may jump in, taking the questioning in whatever direction they see fit. It's possible for time to expire before attorneys get to make the presentation they had prepared. The experience can be overwhelming and breathtaking, much like an intellectual contact sport.

The questions justices ask can supply clues to the way they're likely to rule. If a justice who is typically in the middle of the ideological spectrum on an issue appears to question one side more sternly than the other, it could be an indication of the way that justice is leaning—at least for the moment. Sympathetic justices may ask questions designed to elicit a response from the attorney arguing the side of the case they favor in order to get the record to reflect a point the justice will want to argue later on. Similarly, hostile justices may hammer the attorney arguing the side of the case they oppose in order to expose flaws in the attorney's reasoning.

Some justices find oral arguments decisive; others find them useless (Justice Oliver Wendell Holmes, who served during the first three decades of the twentieth century, would write letters or doze off while the attorneys were speaking).[18]

12.5b Conferences

Oral arguments are heard on Mondays, Tuesdays, and Wednesdays. Conferences to discuss the week's cases are held on Wednesdays and Fridays. Conferences are private, affording justices a closed setting for the frank exchange of opinions. With the huge workload the Court has to address, there is little time to deliberate at length about any particular case unless it is of exceptional magnitude. Instead, justices gather to see whether there is a consensus opinion. They may reason with each other about the case, or make emotional appeals. They may or may not take a formal vote. If they do, it's understood that their votes may be reversed at any time until the final decision is written and announced.[19]

Even though no one is privileged to the deliberation that occurs among justices, it's not unreasonable to assume that they think and act as strategically as anyone in elected office. This contention is in keeping with the idea of the Court as a political body, as well as with the idea that justices have a view of government and society that they want to advance. Because they don't have to run for office, they're free from the basic strategic decisions that face members of Congress and the president, like what their constituents desire and whether it's too close to an election to take a controversial position.

Instead, a justice's strategy can center on ways to move the law closer to his or her desired position. That entails assessing the likely actions of the other eight people in the room and deciding on a course of action that appears most likely to lead to the justice's desired outcome—an exercise that invariably takes into account the styles and personalities of the other justices as much as the abstract merits of an argument. From this type of reasoning, justices can decide whether their best choice is to advance the position they most desire or, if their position appears to be in the minority, compromise on something less in the hope of building a coalition with other justices.[20]

12.5c Writing Opinions

When justices write opinions, they state their vote on a case and the reasoning behind it. Justices will exchange drafts of opinions before they're made public as a form of negotiation, often making revisions to accommodate other justices they seek to have join them. It's part of a persuasive process in which justices try to get their colleagues to adopt their reasoning. Depending on the mixture of personalities on the Court at any time, this experience can range from collegial to contentious. As in any group of people, justices with a soft touch have often found themselves influential in bringing other justices on board, and have played the role of consensus-builder. In contrast, things can get ugly when dealing with justices who have lesser social skills.[21]

The majority opinion expresses the judgment of the Court, but it may not be the only word on a matter. The legal reasoning behind a decision is as important as the decision itself, and will determine how far reaching a decision will be. Justices who come to the same conclusion may do so for entirely different reasons—and even disagree with each other on the justification for their conclusions. Because of this, a justice may issue a **concurring opinion**, which supports the majority decision but provides a different legal justification for getting there. A justice who disagrees with the majority position explains his or her reasoning in a **dissenting opinion**.

concurring opinion: A statement issued by a justice who agrees with a vote of the Court but differs on the legal or constitutional rationale for the majority decision.

dissenting opinion: A statement issued by a justice who disagrees with a vote of the Court, offering a legal or constitutional rationale for that disagreement.

12.5d Staff

Considering the enormous workload of the Supreme Court—or any court for that matter—trained staff are brought in to assist with the burden. Much of a court's work falls to law clerks, who serve as assistants to justices and judges. There are over 2,000 law clerks in the federal system, working either for individual justices and judges or for an entire court. Law clerks typically engage in legal research, prepare background notes for oral arguments, and assist in drafting opinions.[22] The position of clerk on a high court is a prestigious and competitive one, and can be a valuable stepping stone for someone beginning a legal career. Perhaps because Supreme Court justices hail disproportionately from the Ivy Leagues, there is a strong tendency to select clerks from Ivy League law schools.

12.6 Selecting Cases

When feeling unfairly treated, people sometimes say, "I'll take my case all the way to the Supreme Court if I have to!" The assumption, of course, is that that's where we'll finally find justice, and the expectation underlying the claim is that we *could* take any case to the Supreme Court—that everyone who has a grievance is entitled to a hearing.

That's not exactly how it works. In fact, surprisingly few people who petition the Court get a hearing. The Supreme Court has a lot of latitude over its agenda. Sure, others have to bring suit before the Court can hear a case, but the Court can avoid cases in areas of law it doesn't want to address, and select cases in areas of law it wants to decide. It can turn aside cases that it believes raise a political rather than a constitutional question.

It can turn its head away from cases that it feels are not "ripe" because they were brought too early—for instance, if there are other legal avenues available to the person bringing the complaint—or if it feels a case is "moot" because the law has changed in a way that would settle the controversy. Who determines what's "ripe" and what's "moot"? The Supreme Court—and it can make these judgments broadly, using them to circumvent or delay wading into a controversy that it wants to avoid. It doesn't have to give a reason for rejecting a case, and the party bringing the case is out of luck if the Court refuses to listen.[23] Like Marbury, who never got the judgeship he was entitled to, individual outcomes matter less to the Court than legal judgments.

Sometimes, events force the Court to take a case. In 2003, the Supreme Court met in an unusual special session to rule on the constitutionality of the McCain-Feingold campaign finance law, in order to resolve any controversies about the new legislation before the 2004 primaries were held. Once the Court decided it had standing to intervene in the stalemated 2000 presidential election, it had no choice but to act before electoral votes were delivered to Congress. These salient cases are the exception, though. For the most part, the Court can decide its own agenda.

12.6a Reading Tea Leaves

docket: The list of cases pending before a court.

writ of *certiorari*: An order issued by the Supreme Court demanding a lower court turn over all records of a case that the Supreme Court has decided to hear on appeal.

The Court considers only a small number of cases on its **docket**, or list of cases. In a typical year, about 10,000 cases will be brought to the Supreme Court, and the Court will hear about 75 of them.[24] When the Court agrees to review a ruling of a lower court, it issues a **writ of *certiorari*** ordering the lower court to send all records of the case. If the Court denies *certiorari*, the appeal is not heard, and the ruling of the lower court stands.[25]

The choice of cases at the opening of the Court's annual term (on the first Monday of each October) is typically a strong clue as to the controversies the Court is prepared to consider, and "Court watchers" will speculate about what the justices' choices indicate about the direction the Court will take. This can be a little like trying to predict the future by reading tea leaves, but the Court does send signals that at least will make sense after the fact—by the following spring, when all the term's decisions have been handed down.

The selection of a case that challenges a landmark abortion ruling, for instance, would mean that the Court is prepared to revisit the abortion question. What's less clear is whether it would be looking to reinforce established law or to reconsider it. Overlooking a prominent case on abortion rights that was ripe for appeal would send the message that the Court does not wish to engage the issue at this time, although that may mean that the Court is entirely finished hearing cases on this matter, or simply not inclined to do so during the present term.

Members of the Court also send signals to the **solicitor general**, who argues cases on behalf of the administration, that the Court is interested in hearing a case on a particular question. The solicitor general will take these signals to mean that the Court is receptive to deciding a particular question in which the government has an interest and will take action to present an argument to the Court. The solicitor general is responsible for deciding which attorney in his or her office will argue a particular case and will personally argue high-profile cases and cases of particular concern to the administration.

The solicitor general operates out of the Department of Justice, so even though he or she represents "the government," his or her positions will reflect the administration's agenda. This gives the administration influence over the position the government takes before the Court, which in turn can influence the Court's judgment.[26]

solicitor general: The White House official responsible for arguing on behalf of the United States in Supreme Court cases where the United States is a party.

12.6b Interest Groups and Case Selection

More than ever before, interest groups of the wide variety we addressed in Chapter 8 engage the judicial system to advance or advertise their causes. This is a sensible strategy for a number of reasons. Interest groups have the resources to engage in protracted court fights as a result of their funding and organization. Legal victories hold the potential to be wide-ranging, broadly advancing the group's goals. Even legal defeats keep the interest group's concerns in the press and therefore on the public agenda. Also, a sympathetic judiciary can prove to be a swifter and more effective route to interest group objectives than working the political side of the federal government, with all its access points designed to slow progress. This was the rationale for the involvement of the National Association for the Advancement of Colored People (NAACP) in the *Brown v. Board of Education* case, discussed in Section 12.9b, "When the Court Overturns Itself," which resulted in advancing the cause of desegregation more swiftly than could have been done through the legislative process.[27]

As with the solicitor general, justices sympathetic to a particular cause may send signals to interest groups advancing that cause that the Court is prepared to hear a case on the issue. If the signal is sent to groups advancing one side of a contentious issue, it can be a strong indication of how the Court would like to rule. Because litigation is commonplace among interest groups, it typically takes little time for the group to get its legal team in place and take advantage of the opportunity the Court is giving them.

As part of an overall legal strategy, interest groups commonly file *amicus curiae* briefs with the Court, engaging in litigation as a third party to a suit that interests them. Literally "friend of the court," *amicus curiae* briefs can be solicited by a justice who intends to refer to them when writing an opinion in a case. More frequently, interest groups who have a stake in the outcome of a trial voluntarily submit them—and they can be influential. When justices make reference to the arguments in *amicus curiae* briefs in their written decisions on a case, you can tell which groups had an impact on their reasoning.[28]

amicus curiae: Briefs filed by interested parties to a case, whose opinions are offered in an effort to shape the Court's discussion and judgment.

12.7 Nomination Politics

Because the judicial philosophy of the people in the black robes matters so much to the direction of the Court, political battles can erupt whenever the president has an opportunity to name someone to the Supreme Court or to one of the lower federal courts. This is particularly true during times like the present, when the nation is deeply divided politically. It's why Senate Republicans took the unprecedented step of refusing to hold hearings on a presidential nominee to the Supreme Court when a vacancy arose on that body in early 2016. It is also why Republicans worked hard to delay confirmation hearings on President Obama's more liberal lower-court appointees, and why Democrats did the same when they controlled the Senate during the latter portion of the Bush administration. More than at any time in memory, divisive, strong-arm tactics have marked confirmation battles over nominees to every level of the federal bench.

In February 2016, Supreme Court Justice Antonin Scalia suddenly died, leaving a vacancy that if filled by President Obama could have dramatically shifted the Court's

L.O. Describe the judicial confirmation process, and explain why it has been contentious in recent years.

ideological direction. For thirty years, Scalia was the vocal leader of the Court's conservatives, who in many areas of jurisprudence held a slender but decisive 5–4 majority. His death jeopardized that balance.

President Obama nominated federal appeals court Judge Merrick Garland to fill the vacancy. Garland was a respected jurist with a reputation for moderation whose nomination by President Bill Clinton to the D.C. circuit court had been approved overwhelmingly by a Republican Congress. Still, Garland hailed from a liberal tradition, and his appointment to the Supreme Court promised to give liberals a majority for the first time in decades.

Republican congressional leaders fought back. Seeking to forestall the Court's pending ideological shift, the Senate refused to hold hearings on the Garland nomination, a prerequisite to holding a vote. Rather than claiming that Republicans were resisting Garland on the merits, Senate Majority Leader Mitch McConnell announced that he would oppose any Obama appointment on the grounds that a national election was under way to choose Obama's successor, and the American people, by way of their vote in November, "should have a voice in the selection of their next Supreme Court justice."[29]

McConnell's move generated a sharp rebuke from Democrats, but there was nothing they could do to force his hand. The Senate left Scalia's seat vacant for the remainder of the year, betting that they could win the 2016 election and salvage the Court's conservative majority. With Donald Trump's victory, they won that bet, and early in his term, President Trump nominated conservative judge Neil Gorsuch to fill the seat .

One of the questions to be resolved in the new Congress is how Democrats will respond. As the minority party, the only power they have to shape the Court in the new administration is the ability to filibuster President Trump's nominees. The filibuster is explained in Chapter 9, Section 9.4b (How the Senate Works). It is a procedure the minority can use to delay a measure by refusing to permit it to come to a vote. It is possible to end a filibuster with a supermajority of sixty senators, but Republicans have only fifty-two in their caucus.

Still, it is unclear how far Democrats might go to prevent Donald Trump from putting his mark on the Supreme Court. Not long ago, it would have seemed farfetched to imagine the Senate so hamstrung on partisan grounds that it could not confirm a Supreme Court justice. But in today's divided America, whichever side holds a Supreme Court majority has tremendous power to shape the country in its desired image.

This is why other recent Supreme Court nomination battles have been hotly contested. Just months after his inauguration, President Obama faced a vacancy on the Supreme Court with the resignation of Justice David Souter, a Republican appointed by the President George H. W. Bush who nonetheless tended to side with the Court's more liberal justices. Obama's nominee to replace Souter was Sonia Sotomayor, a federal appellate judge from New York. Conscious of the divisiveness of recent Supreme Court battles, President Obama recognized that his selection of Judge Sotomayor would make identity politics an important element of the confirmation hearings. As the first Latina and only the third female Supreme Court nominee, Sotomayor would present herself to the Senate as the embodiment of the American Dream: the daughter of Puerto Rican parents raised in a South Bronx housing project who earned a scholarship to Princeton and then graduated from Yale Law School before becoming a prosecutor and trial judge.[30]

But, identity politics can cut both ways, and some Senate Republicans grilled Sotomayor about remarks she had made suggesting that her upbringing and experience might guide her judicial judgment. The thrust of their criticism was that sympathies derived from her background might make her a partial arbiter of judicial questions. Their objections made for some pointed moments during Sotomayor's confirmation hearings, and in the end thirty-one Republican Senators voted against her, although that number fell far short of denying her a place on the Supreme Court.

Truthfully, the sort of jockeying and positioning that characterized the Sotomayor confirmation hearings isn't all that interesting to ordinary people, and with the exception of very heated nomination battles (which Sotomayor's was not) that occasionally play out on television, most of us don't pay attention to what goes on when the president sends the Senate a judicial nominee. However, interest groups pay a lot of attention, and if a nominee promises to alter the balance of a court, groups that stand to gain or lose from the shift will organize in a hurry.

In Chapter 9, we saw how the politically charged nominations of Robert Bork and Clarence Thomas to the Supreme Court generated intense resistance from Senate Democrats. They also generated strong lobbying efforts by groups on both sides of the ideological spectrum. In terms of sheer numbers, Bork was actively supported by twenty-one interest groups and actively opposed by seventeen in his unsuccessful bid to join the Supreme Court. Seventeen groups also mobilized to support Thomas, who was opposed by an unprecedented thirty-two interest groups in an unsuccessful effort to keep him off the Court. To put this in historical context, President Eisenhower's 1953 nomination of Earl Warren to be chief justice generated no interest group support and opposition from only two groups, and in the twenty-two years between Warren's nomination and President Ford's lone nomination to the Court (Justice John Paul Stevens) in 1975, a grand total of forty groups mobilized in support and forty-three groups mobilized against seventeen nominees.[31]

Then things heated up in the 1980s, as President Reagan acted on his pledge to appoint conservative justices who would counter the judicial liberals who had controlled the Court's agenda during the preceding three decades. Through the Reagan and first Bush administrations, interest groups battled fiercely over Court nominees. When two vacancies occurred on the Supreme Court in the summer of 2005 through the resignation of Justice Sandra Day O'Connor and the death of Chief Justice William Rehnquist, conservative and liberal interest groups geared up for what everyone expected to be an intense battle over their replacements. Historically, presidents get what they want even when there's a fight—but they don't get everything they want. President Reagan lost the fight over the Bork nomination, and President Nixon had two nominees—Clement Haynsworth, Jr. and G. Harrold Carswell—turned away following widespread questions about their qualifications. Overall, the Supreme Court scorecard favors the president, even if he has to fight hard for his nominee. See Table 12.1.

Presidents can increase the odds of confirmation by considering the prevailing political winds before making a nomination. President Obama had the advantage of a Senate dominated by Democrats to help propel his nominations of Sonia Sotomayor and Elena Kagan. President Bush may have been forced to appoint less conservative nominees to the Supreme Court than John Roberts and Samuel Alito, had the vacancies that led to their nominations occurred after Democrats regained control of the Senate in the 2006 election (for more discussion of the Roberts nomination, and for a look at how sometimes presidents are forced by political circumstances to back away from their nominees, see Demystifying Government: The Brief and Unlikely Nomination of Harriet Miers).

TABLE 12.1 Supreme Court Nomination Scorecard: Nixon (1969) through Obama (2013)

President	Number of Justices Nominated	Number of Justices Confirmed	Percent Confirmed
Nixon	6	4	66.7%
Ford	1	1	100%
Carter	0	--	--
Reagan	5	4	80%
G. H. W. Bush	2	2	100%
Clinton	2	2	100%
G. W. Bush	2	2	100%
Obama	3	2	66.7%

The Brief and Unlikely Nomination of Harriet Miers

When Justice Sandra Day O'Connor announced her retirement in the summer of 2005, the long-awaited battle over the direction of the Court appeared to have arrived. O'Connor had been a swing vote on a Supreme Court that had not lost a justice in eleven years—a remarkably long stretch without turnover. With the re-election of President Bush months earlier, many conservatives eagerly awaited the opportunity to replace O'Connor's moderate vote with a reliably conservative one.

President Bush initially nominated John G. Roberts to fill O'Connor's position. A Harvard-educated lawyer serving on the U.S. Court of Appeals for the District of Columbia, Roberts came with impeccable conservative credentials and a strong judicial background. Senate Democrats immediately objected to the nominee on grounds that O'Connor's replacement should not be someone who would shift the balance of the Court to the right. But, on the merits, they faced an uphill struggle opposing his confirmation.

Then, circumstances conspired to change everything. Shortly before Roberts' confirmation hearings were to begin, ailing Chief Justice William Rehnquist died, leaving a vacancy at the top of the Court. It would have been impossible for the president to nominate and Congress to confirm a replacement in time for the opening of the Court's new term one month later, especially with the hearings for the O'Connor seat scheduled to occur first. To complicate matters, President Bush was at this moment ensnared in the fallout of the administration's slow response to Hurricane Katrina, limiting both the political capital available to him for a brutal nomination fight and his ability to devote full attention to selecting a nominee.

Bush's solution to this problem was to elevate Roberts to the Rehnquist slot, withdrawing his nomination of Roberts to be O'Connor's replacement and instead nominating him to be chief justice. Although some Democrats objected, Roberts was considered to be no more conservative than the man he was replacing, and the long-anticipated fireworks over the chief justice appointment failed to materialize. Within one month of the nomination, Roberts took his seat at the head of the Supreme Court, in time for the start of its October session.

Of course, elevating Roberts necessitated a new nominee for the O'Connor seat, and when Bush selected White House Counsel Harriet Miers for the job, his conservative supporters were baffled. A Texas attorney whose ascendancy in Washington was the result of the support of the president she served, Miers was a largely unknown quantity with no judicial experience and—even more disconcerting to some of the president's strongest conservative supporters—a vague record on social issues. Key social conservatives spoke out in opposition to the nomination, while the strongest note of praise for the nominee came from Harry Reid—the Senate *Democratic* leader. The battle over the direction of the Court was finally on, but not in the way anyone anticipated: Conservatives were leading the charge against their own president.

And they succeeded. Before her confirmation hearings began, Miers withdrew her name from consideration. President Bush replaced her with Judge Samuel A. Alito, a conservative jurist serving on the U.S. Court of Appeals for the Third Circuit. Although Alito's nomination generated the kind of fireworks from liberals that Miers's nomination had generated from conservatives—and although liberals regarded him as more conservative than O'Connor—the president had the votes in the Senate to confirm him, and Justice Alito took his seat on the U.S. Supreme Court in late January 2006.

12.7a Senatorial Courtesy

senatorial courtesy: The custom that presidents will defer to the wishes of senators from a judicial nominee's home state before making a court appointment.

Regardless of the partisan composition of Congress, presidents as a matter of custom defer to the opinion of senators from the home state of a judicial nominee to one of the lower federal courts before sending the nomination to the full Senate. This custom is called **senatorial courtesy**, and it derives from the Senate's long history of institutional patriotism. Even though the Senate approves most judicial nominees, there's a sense among senators that they do not want to be a rubber stamp for any president. They take their constitutionally mandated role to offer advice and consent seriously, and the most direct way they can protect this is by permitting senators an informal veto over nominees from their home states.

Typically, a senator will object if the president is about to nominate a political adversary from back home. Senators can be particularly influential in derailing a nomination if they share a political party with the president, although senators of the opposing party have been known to influence presidential appointments. Remember, too, that even when a senator successfully blocks an appointment from his or her home state, there's no guarantee that the president will come back with another nominee from that state. In that regard, presidents always get to make the last move.[32]

The practice of senatorial courtesy goes back to the first president and the first Congress, when President Washington nominated Benjamin Fishbourn to serve as a naval officer in Savannah, Georgia. Both Georgia senators objected, and the full Senate made it clear that it intended to back its colleagues even though the nominee was qualified to serve. When Washington backpedaled and nominated someone else who was acceptable to the Georgians, he became the first president to engage in the dance of senatorial courtesy that has been repeated many times through history.[33]

12.7b Professional Influences

Senatorial courtesy is the most political of the external influences on the president's choice of a nominee, but it is not the only influence. Members of the court and members of the bar also have their say over nominees at every level of the court system. Presidents have been known to contact sitting judges and justices to solicit opinions about people who would become future colleagues, and it's not unheard of for the communication channels to work in the other direction, with members of the judiciary lobbying the president.

The American Bar Association (ABA), the preeminent legal professional association, routinely offers its opinion on whether a presidential choice is qualified. A favorable nod from the ABA's Federal Judiciary Committee lends a level of professional approval to the political business of judicial nominations. Strategically, it can give a president cover for a controversial nomination by permitting the president to point out that the nominee's peers consider him or her qualified for service. When President Reagan submitted the nomination of the deeply conservative Antonin Scalia, he knew it would be hard for liberal senators to oppose someone who by reputation was qualified to serve on the Supreme Court (the ABA endorsed him as "well qualified"). Reagan tried a similar strategy with the Bork nomination, but the ABA came back with a mixed verdict, with only ten of fifteen members of the Federal Judiciary Committee giving their approval.[34] This, in turn, gave Bork's opponents an opening to exploit.

A nominee without a strong network of professional allies and without a long legal history can run into trouble during the confirmation process. This contributed to the problem President Bush faced with the nomination of his White House Counsel Harriet Miers, which suffered in part because Miers had few allies in the legal community to come to her defense when opponents questioned her qualifications to sit on the Court. As the president's personal attorney, she found that Bush was her strongest and most enthusiastic supporter, but it wasn't enough to have the president urging senators and interest group leaders to support Miers because he believed in her.

12.7c Diversity

As presidents attempt to appeal to diverse constituencies, there is political advantage in selecting high-profile nominees who are not white male Protestants (which the overwhelming majority of Supreme Court justices have been). As a consequence, today's Supreme Court is more diversified than in the past with respect to religion, race, and gender.

L.O. Characterize the level of gender, racial, and religious diversity on the Supreme Court both historically and today.

Barriers to diversity fell slowly. Although President Jackson appointed the first Roman Catholic to the Court in 1836 (Chief Justice Roger B. Taney), it took until 1894 for President Grover Cleveland to appoint the second (Justice Edward D. White). An unprecedented five present justices are Roman Catholic—Roberts, Kennedy, Thomas, Alito, and Sotomayor—but they also represent almost half of all Catholic justices who have ever served on the Court.

Louis Brandeis was the first Jewish justice, appointed by President Wilson in 1916, and for many years thereafter, one seat on the Court was informally considered to be a "Jewish seat." This tradition was interrupted by President Nixon and restored by President Clinton, who appointed two of the present Court's three Jewish justices, Ginsburg and Breyer.[35]

TABLE 12.2 Roman Catholic and Jewish Supreme Court Justices through 2017

Roman Catholic Justices			Jewish Justices		
Justice	Appointed by	Dates of Service	Justice	Appointed by	Dates of Service
Roger B. Taney	Andrew Jackson	1836–1864	Louis D. Brandeis	Woodrow Wilson	1916–1939
Edward D. White	Grover Cleveland	1894–1921	Benjamin N. Cardozo	Herbert Hoover	1932–1938
Joseph McKenna	William McKinley	1898–1925	Felix Frankfurter	Franklin D. Roosevelt	1939–1962
Pierce Butler	Warren Harding	1922–1939	Arthur J. Goldberg	John F. Kennedy	1962–1965
Frank Murphy	Franklin D. Roosevelt	1940–1949	Abe Fortas	Lyndon B. Johnson	1965–1969
William J. Brennan	Dwight D. Eisenhower	1956–1990	Ruth Bader Ginsburg	Bill Clinton	1993–
Antonin Scalia	Ronald Reagan	1986–2016	Stephen G. Breyer	Bill Clinton	1994–
Anthony M. Kennedy	Ronald Reagan	1988–	Elena Kagan	Barack Obama	2010–
Clarence Thomas	George H. W. Bush	1991–			
John G. Roberts	George W. Bush	2005–			
Samuel A. Alito, Jr.	George W. Bush	2006–			
Sonia Sotomayor	Barack Obama	2009–			
Neil Gorsuch	Donald Trump	2017–			

Of 113 Supreme Court justices who served through 2017, a combined 21 have been Roman Catholic or Jewish (see Table 12.2).

The first African American on the Court was former civil rights attorney Thurgood Marshall, appointed by President Johnson in 1967. When he stepped down in 1991, President George H. W. Bush replaced him with Clarence Thomas, who is the Court's second African American justice. Although this appeared to establish a "black seat" on the Court, Thomas's conservative orientation couldn't have been more different from Marshall's liberalism, angering some African American activists who felt the Thomas appointment was a cynical ploy to use race to keep liberal senators from blocking the nomination of a conservative.

When President Reagan ran for office, he promised to nominate the first woman to the Court, and he kept his promise with the appointment of Sandra Day O'Connor in 1981. She is joined by Justice Ginsburg, Justice Sotomayor, and Justice Kagan as the only women to serve on the high court to date. As mentioned earlier, Justice Sotomayor is also the first Latino member of the Supreme Court.

Because of this history, the Court in 2017 looks far more diverse than at any other point in its history, with six Catholics, three Jews, three women, and one African American among its membership. For the first time in history, there are no Protestant justices. Viewed another way, however, there is a great deal of homogeneity. Seven justices are over sixty. Six are men; eight are white. Six attended Harvard Law School. The other three went to Yale. Take a second to look through their profiles in Figure 12.3 to get a sense of who is serving on the Court as of 2017.

Diversity on the lower federal courts is a less politically salient matter. Barack Obama made it a priority to diversify the federal courts, although his efforts received little attention. Forty-two percent of his appointments were women, and 37% were nonwhite.[36] In other instances, presidents made different choices than they did for the high-profile Supreme Court. President Reagan, for instance, may have made it a priority to put a

John G. Roberts
Title: Chief Justice
Appointed: 2005
By: George W. Bush
Political Party: Republican
Year of Birth: 1955
Religion: Roman Catholic
Law School Attended: Harvard

Anthony Kennedy
Title: Associate Justice
Appointed: 1988
By: Ronald Reagan
Political Party: Republican
Year of Birth: 1936
Religion: Roman Catholic
Law School Attended: Harvard

Clarence Thomas
Title: Associate Justice
Appointed: 1991
By: George H. W. Bush
Political Party: Republican
Year of Birth: 1948
Religion: Roman Catholic
Law School Attended: Yale

Ruth Bader Ginsburg
Title: Associate Justice
Appointed: 1993
By: Bill Clinton
Political Party: Democrat
Year of Birth: 1933
Religion: Jewish
Law School Attended: Harvard

Stephen Breyer
Title: Associate Justice
Appointed: 1994
By: Bill Clinton
Political Party: Democrat
Year of Birth: 1938
Religion: Jewish
Law School Attended: Harvard

Samuel Alito
Title: Associate Justice
Appointed: 2005
By: George W. Bush
Political Party: Republican
Year of Birth: 1950
Religion: Roman Catholic
Law School Attended: Yale

Sonia Sotomayor
Title: Associate Justice
Appointed: 2009
By: Barack Obama
Political Party: Democrat
Year of Birth: 1954
Religion: Roman Catholic
Law School Attended: Yale

Elena Kagan
Title: Associate Justice
Appointed: 2010
By: Barack Obama
Political Party: Democrat
Year of Birth: 1960
Religion: Jewish
Law School Attended: Harvard

Neil Gorsuch
Title: Associate Justice
Appointed: 2017
By: Donald Trump
Political Party: Republican
Year of Birth: 1967
Religion: Roman Catholic
Law School Attended: Harvard

FIGURE 12.3 Who Are the Supreme Court Justices?[T5]

woman on the Supreme Court, but fewer than 8 percent of his 368 lower-court appointments were female. Only one-fifth of George W. Bush's lower-court appointees were women.[37]

For a long time, the relative lack of diversity on the federal bench could be explained in terms of a long-standing lack of diversity in the elite legal community.[38] Justice Ruth Bader Ginsburg tells of attending a reception for her class while she was at Harvard Law School in the 1950s. There were over 500 students—and only nine women. She recounts the dean of the law school asking each of the nine "what we were doing at the law school occupying a seat that could have been filled by a man."[39]

12.7d Judicial Surprises

Republicans appoint Republicans and Democrats appoint Democrats, but that doesn't mean that presidents always get the results they expect from the people they place on the federal bench. There are numerous examples of presidents being surprised (or horrified) at the positions taken by their judicial appointees. Perhaps the most striking example from the twentieth century is President Eisenhower's appointment of Chief Justice Earl Warren, who led the most liberal and activist Court in modern times, particularly in the area of civil rights.

If the moderate Eisenhower had gotten what he was looking for in a chief justice, Earl Warren's activism never would have happened. Eisenhower, a Republican, considered several other moderate Republicans before settling on Warren as his nominee to preside over the Court. Two of these were his Secretary of State John Foster Dulles and New York Governor Thomas E. Dewey.[40] It's highly unlikely that either one would have been an activist chief justice committed to turning the Court into a forum for advancing civil rights the way Warren did.

Then again, few people suspected it of Warren—at least few in the Eisenhower administration suspected it. The president thought he was getting a centrist Republican like himself. Perhaps the broad support Warren had commanded from Republicans and Democrats in his three successful campaigns for California governor should have been a clue to his inherent activism, or the fact that his independent streak so distressed the leadership of the California Republican Party that they promoted Warren's appointment to get him out of the state. In any event, Eisenhower was in Warren's debt for the work the governor had done in moving the California delegation behind him in the 1952 Republican Convention, and it is of such political considerations that monumental decisions at times emerge. So, Eisenhower planted Earl Warren at the helm of the Supreme Court, believing he had chosen an experienced administrator with moderate tendencies.[41] He later called it the biggest mistake of his presidency.

There are good reasons for judicial surprises like Warren. A president often makes appointments based on the recommendations of aides (particularly to lower court positions) without personally knowing the nominee. While a dossier on a nominee's history can tell a lot, it can't always predict how he or she will behave on the bench. Perhaps nominees at the ideological extremes can be fairly predictable—Antonin Scalia, for instance, had a record of unfaltering conservatism going back to his youth—but between the extremes, where most nominees are found, it can be much harder to predict the future.

As mentioned earlier, Justice David Souter, who was replaced by Justice Sotomayor, had been a member of the Court's liberal bloc. That's not how President George H. W. Bush expected things to turn out when he nominated him. The president was looking for a conservative nominee who was likely to be an abortion opponent, but given the certainty that his nominee's record in adjudicating abortion cases would be a major factor in the pending confirmation battle, he preferred someone who hadn't left a lot of tracks on the issue. Bush's chief of staff John Sununu recommended Souter, a fairly obscure Appeals Court judge from Sununu's home state of New Hampshire. Souter fit the requirements perfectly, leaving little ammunition for congressional supporters of abortion rights to claim that Bush's nominee would tip the delicate Court balance away from the *Roe* decision.

The problem for Bush was that Souter was hard for everyone to judge—including Bush himself. He took it on faith (along with Sununu's judgment) that he had produced a reliably conservative vote for the Court—but Souter turned out to be much more independent than the president had bargained for and frequently voted with the Court's liberal justices. Souter surprised Bush and turned into a disappointment for his conservative supporters, who saw his appointment as one that got away.

Even when the president has a personal history with a nominee, it can be impossible to tell how the nominee will mature on the bench. Judicial philosophies can develop and change over time, and our perspectives on things sometimes alter with age. John Paul Stevens was considered a moderate conservative when President Ford appointed him in 1975, but as the Court became more conservative, he became more liberal.

It's equally impossible to know how a nominee will respond to issues that simply cannot be anticipated at the time of her or his confirmation. Lifetime appointments hold out the possibility, even the probability, that the issues of greatest concern to the president making the appointment will give way to an unexpected set of issues during the nominee's term of service. When Franklin D. Roosevelt named William O. Douglas to the Supreme Court in 1939, it would have been impossible to foresee that he would be at the center of an activist Court that would revolutionize civil rights law before his retirement in 1975. Justices named to the bench fifteen years ago could not have anticipated having to make judgments about privacy on the Internet or human cloning, although these are emerging as important areas of dispute. Knowing a nominee's position on abortion policy doesn't offer a clue as to how he or she might decide cases in other legal areas.

12.8 A Political Court

If justices must go through the political system to be nominated and confirmed, if personal background and judicial philosophy influence a justice's approach to the law, and if bargaining strategies shape court judgments, it should be clear that the Supreme Court—for that matter, any court—is hardly the neutral arbiter of conflict that its symbols would suggest. Justices may never have to face the judgment of voters, but they are enmeshed in a political process. Perhaps their biggest political challenge is reflected in the dilemma that presented itself to Chief Justice Marshall and which the Court continues to face centuries after *Marbury v. Madison*: In the end, it must rely on the president to enforce its decisions. Marshall may have established the Court as an equal branch of government and begun the long process of developing prestige and admiration for the Court, but at every point in its history the Court has had to be particularly attuned to the politics of the other branches to maintain its precarious place in the federal constellation.

Justice Felix Frankfurter (who served from 1939 to 1962) was attempting to protect the myth of an apolitical Court when he declared, "When a priest enters a monastery, he must leave—or ought to leave—all sorts of worldly desires behind him. And this Court has no excuse for being unless it's a monastery."[42] Frankfurter knew this was hardly the case. Far from being cloistered, the Court survives by reacting to the hardball pursuits of the elected officials populating government's other branches.

The resources it has to bring this about are intangible, but if properly used they can be extremely effective in protecting the Court's political position. One thing the Court has in its favor is the deep well of respect developed over the centuries with generations of Americans. Such legitimacy can make it difficult for presidents to disobey or disregard the Court, as their constituents would not look kindly on a president defying what would be widely perceived as a legitimate act of a respected institution.

Ironically, the symbols we talked about at the opening of the chapter that make the Court seem so removed from politics—the dark robes, the marble building, the secret deliberations—contribute to the mystique that is so much a part of the Court's legitimacy. Put another way, these "nonpolitical" characteristics serve a highly political purpose in protecting the reverence many people feel for the Supreme Court—an opinion that gives the Court leverage with the more powerfully equipped executive and legislative branches.

The Court Legalizes Same-Sex Marriage

Despite its conservative philosophical leanings, the Supreme Court has moved in recent years to put a judicial stamp of approval on rapidly changing attitudes toward same-sex marriage. At the start of the century, a majority of Americans opposed same-sex marriage, whereas only about one-third approved. By 2016 those figures were reversed.[T6] So when the Court ruled 5–4 in the landmark 2015 decision *Obergefell v. Hodges* that states could not deny same-sex couples the right to marry, it moved in line with trends in public opinion, even as the closeness of the decision reflected the controversy still generated by the issue.

As is so often the case with dramatic social shifts, the *Obergefell* decision had its roots in decades of political activism. Initially, LGBT rights groups demanded civil rights protections. It wasn't until the late 1990s that same-sex unions became part of that debate[T7] when a Hawaii circuit court judge opened the door to legalized same-sex marriage in that state and brought the issue to national attention. The 1996 case *Baehr v. Miike* established that Hawaii had no constitutional basis for denying a marriage license to a same-sex couple.[T8] With that judgment, Hawaii appeared on the verge of becoming the first state to recognize gay marriage. But the decision sparked a national backlash from groups seeking to preserve marriage as a heterosexual institution. By 2001, thirty-five states had passed laws prohibiting the recognition of same-sex unions that might be licensed in other states.

At this point, the battle shifted to Vermont. In late 1999, the Vermont Supreme Court unanimously ruled that the state had unlawfully denied three same-sex couples the rights afforded to heterosexual couples and instructed the state legislature to remedy the situation. The response was something legally different than same-sex marriage: a new institution called a "civil union," which had the effect of extending the benefits of marriage to gay couples living in Vermont without altering existing marriage laws.[T9]

In 2004, the Massachusetts Supreme Court ruled as Hawaii had earlier, finding nothing in the state constitution to prohibit gay marriage and giving the legislature six months to rewrite marriage laws to permit it. The Massachusetts ruling produced another wave of protests from gay marriage opponents, such as former President George W. Bush, culminating in the overwhelming approval in the 2004 election of measures banning gay marriage by voters in eleven states. The next ten years witnessed ballot, legislative, and court initiatives in states across the country on both sides of the issue: either codifying heterosexual marriage or extending greater rights to gay couples. Circuit courts were just as divided, signaling that the Supreme Court would eventually have to resolve the differences, but in the years leading up to the Court decision, public opinion had taken a decisive turn in support of same-sex marriage. By 2015, thirty-seven states and the District of Columbia had recognized same-sex marriage, at which point the Supreme Court made it legal nationwide.

No doubt, Frankfurter was trying to perpetuate this mystique by comparing the Court to a monastery.

To maintain this high level of legitimacy, justices throughout history have been attentive to political currents, often selecting and ruling on cases they feel the public is ready to accept. Recognizing that the large degree of popular goodwill invested in the Court could be threatened by rulings that took the country where it did not want to go, justices will often keep an eye on the same political trends that elected officials live by. Sometimes events force the Court to hear a controversial case of such magnitude that the results are likely to be met with disapproval from some quarters. By paying attention to popular opinion, the Court can defend its political position by squaring its legal positions with the politicians who will be called upon to enforce the Court's words. Take a look at Demystifying Government: The Court Legalizes Same-Sex Marriage, for an example of the Supreme Court taking a dramatic step on a contentious social issue in light of rapid changes in public opinion.

Public opinion and legitimacy interact in a delicate dance, each one reinforcing the other. We can see strains of this in Franklin Roosevelt's infamous "court packing scheme," where the Court's legitimacy was threatened by the actions of an enormously popular president, and in the harrowing case of *United States v. Nixon*, where a Court ruling directed President Nixon to commit political suicide.

12.8a Packing the Court

Although Franklin D. Roosevelt had large numbers of sympathetic Democrats in Congress to pass his New Deal programs during his first term, conservative justices appointed by Roosevelt's Republican predecessors dominated the Supreme Court. They were philosophically opposed to the New Deal, and during FDR's first four years in office, they struck down much of the president's program, often by a 5–4 vote. It was a classic case of how separation of powers works to impede rapid change, even when a landslide election gives one party control of the other two branches.

Roosevelt, of course, was uninterested in a textbook tutorial on separation of powers and was frustrated by how the Court was thwarting his initiatives. Following his landslide 1936 reelection, he decided to do something about it. Roosevelt asked Congress to give him the authority to expand the size of the Court by adding one new member for every sitting member over the age of seventy, a proposal that would have allowed Roosevelt to nominate six new justices and theoretically give his New Deal legislation a 10–5 majority on a new fifteen-member Supreme Court.[43] Supporters called it judicial reform. Opponents called it packing the Court.

Roosevelt's proposal failed even though he had a large partisan advantage in Congress. Democrats who embraced New Deal programs nonetheless had difficulty supporting a plan that would have so blatantly undermined the Court's legitimacy, even though it would have assured the legality of their legislation. Years of building the public's trust by appearing above politics worked to protect the Court from political tampering.

There's a postscript to the story, though. As the Senate Judiciary Committee was preparing to hold hearings on Roosevelt's plan in 1937, Justice Owen Roberts broke away from the anti–New Deal coalition and began ruling in favor of Roosevelt's programs. In *West Coast Hotel Co. v. Parrish*, he sided with the New Deal forces in support of a minimum wage law. In *National Labor Relations Board v. Jones and Laughlin Steel Corporation*, he voted to uphold the National Labor Relations Act.[44] Recognizing the direction the country was moving and tacitly acknowledging the importance of public opinion to preserving the Court's legitimacy, the conservative Roberts helped stave off a direct assault on the Court by aligning his judgments with public sentiment. It was called the "switch in time that saved nine."[45]

Even though his plan to pack the Court fell through, Roosevelt would exercise enormous influence over the Court's judicial direction. He would nominate eight justices during his tenure as president, leaving a judicial legacy that would outlast his administration. His first appointment came shortly after the Roberts switch. To get back at the Senate for failing to approve his judicial plan, and to make a point with the Court, Roosevelt nominated Senator Hugo Black, who had been at the forefront of the congressional fight in favor of packing the Court. Roosevelt knew that senators would never reject one of their own, and the Supreme Court would have no choice but to welcome one of its more vocal critics.[46]

12.8b The Nixon Tapes

On very rare occasions, the Court is called upon to render a judgment that threatens a confrontation with the president in a way that recalls Marshall's dilemma with *Marbury v. Madison*. It happened again in 1974, in *United States v. Nixon*, when the Supreme Court faced the prospect of issuing a ruling that would jettison President Nixon from office. One key difference between the two cases was the enormous legitimacy the Court could fall back on in making its judgment in the Nixon case. It turns out that it needed all the legitimacy it could muster.

The complex series of events that came to be known as the Watergate scandal originated with a burglary at the Democratic National Committee (DNC) headquarters in Washington's Watergate Hotel. It was 1972, and although President Nixon would win a second term in a landslide later that year, his reelection committee left nothing to chance. Documents had been copied and wiretaps had been placed on telephones at rival

United States v. Nixon: The 1974 case in which a unanimous Supreme Court ruled that President Nixon could not use executive privilege to protect the secrecy of incriminating tapes documenting his involvement in the cover-up of the Watergate break-in.

Democratic Party offices before a security guard caught five burglars at the DNC head-quarters one June evening. They had in their possession telephone numbers for the White House, establishing a connection between the burglars and the administration that would eventually reach to the highest level.

By the next year, congressional and public outcry forced Nixon to appoint a special prosecutor to investigate Watergate. Through that investigation, word surfaced that Nixon had secretly taped all his conversations with aides and visitors to the Oval Office. The audio record could prove vital to the work of the special prosecutor and members of Congress, who by 1973 were holding hearings into whether to impeach the president over his role in Watergate, but they would first have to get Nixon to hand over the tapes.

The scandal was spiraling out of control as it began attaching itself to high-ranking administration officials. Former Attorney General John Mitchell, once head of the Justice Department, was charged with obstruction of justice for his role in trying to block the investigation from reaching the Oval Office. To build his case against Mitchell, Special Prosecutor Leon Jaworski issued a subpoena for Oval Office tape recordings. Nixon refused, claiming his private conversations were protected by executive privilege. This made the matter a constitutional issue that would have to be resolved by the Supreme Court.[47]

Nixon knew the political damage that would result if the tapes were made public because they showed that he was instrumental in planning the cover-up of the Watergate break-in, implicating him in a scheme to obstruct justice. One tape, considered to be a "smoking gun," is a conversation between Nixon and his Chief of Staff H. R. "Bob" Haldeman, recorded just six days after the break-in. It shows that Nixon knew everything that was going on from the start and is chilling in the matter-of-fact way Nixon goes about plotting to obstruct justice in order to make sure the public never found out how much he knew. The plan he considered, as recommended by Attorney General Mitchell, involved getting the FBI's Watergate investigation "under control" to keep it from going in "directions we don't want it to go" by getting FBI Director L. Patrick Gray to "stay the hell out of this."[48] You'll find a transcript of a section of that tape in Figure 12.4. When you read it, you'll probably realize why Nixon fought so hard to keep it from becoming public.

Nixon's claim of executive privilege raised a constitutional question that would have to be resolved by the Supreme Court. Nixon argued that executive privilege provided the president with confidentiality so that he could speak openly with his confidants about matters of national importance. Jaworski contended that executive privilege did not protect a president from releasing private materials that potentially implicated him in a crime.

As the Supreme Court heard arguments in the case of *United States v. Nixon*, the president's political world was crumbling. Impeachment efforts were moving forward in the House, and the president's support was eroding in the Senate, even among members of his own party. Public opinion stood behind the position that Nixon should release the tapes, as the public widely believed that Nixon had something to hide. The Court would have the public on its side if it ruled against Nixon.

However, it would also have to rely on Nixon to enforce the ruling. There was little doubt that the tapes would incriminate Nixon, since he fought so hard to keep them secret. Would he comply with a court order to release them? What were his options if he did not?

The stakes could not have been higher. Failure to obey the Court would have thrown the nation into an unprecedented constitutional crisis, in which the president put his political survival above the rule of law. What then? Would Nixon use the ensuing crisis to clamp down on the justice system the way the tapes showed he tried to clamp down on the FBI, possibly suspending the Constitution and declaring martial law? That may sound ridiculous to us today, but plenty of people were worried about exactly that scenario. Nixon was under immense political pressure. Those close to him worried that he would see the Court as an enemy and lash out at it.

Under the circumstances, the Court needed to muster all its legitimacy and send the message that the president had no choice but to comply with an order that would lead to his political demise. It did so by ruling unanimously that executive privilege did not apply in this case, and that the president would have to hand over the tapes. Even one

AUDIO TEXT

This is the transcript of the recording of a meeting between President Nixon and his chief of staff, H. R. Haldeman, in the Oval Office on June 23, 1972.

Haldeman: Okay—that's fine. Now, on the investigation, you know, the Democratic break-in thing, we're back to the—in the, the problem area because the FBI is not under control because Gray doesn't exactly know how to control them, and they have, their investigation is now leading into some productive areas because they've been able to trace the money, not through the money itself, but through the bank, you know, sources—the banker himself. And, and it goes in some directions we don't want it to go. Ah, also there have been some things, like an informant came in off the street to the FBI in Miami, who was a photographer or has a friend who is a photographer who developed some films through this guy, Barker, and the films had pictures of Democratic National Committee letter head documents and things. So, I guess, so, it's things like that that are gonna, that are filtering in. Mitchell came up with yesterday, and John Dean analyzed very carefully last night and concludes, concurs now with Mitchell's recommendation that the only way to solve this, and we're set up beautifully to do it, ah, in that and that . . . the only network that paid any attention to it last night was NBC . . . they did a massive story on the Cuban . . .

Nixon: That's right.

Haldeman: thing.

Nixon: Right.

Haldeman: That the way to handle this now is for us to have Walters call [FBI director] Pat Gray and just say, "Stay the hell out of this . . . this is ah, business here we don't want you to go any further on it." That's not an unusual development, . . .

Nixon: Um huh.

Haldeman: . . . and, uh, that would take care of it.

Nixon: What about Pat Gray, ah, you mean he doesn't want to?

Haldeman: Pat does want to. He doesn't know how to, and he doesn't have, he doesn't have any basis for doing it. Given this, he will then have the basis. He'll call Mark Felt in, and the two of them . . . and Mark Felt wants to cooperate because . . .

Nixon: Yeah.

Haldeman: he's ambitious . . .

Nixon: Yeah.

Haldeman: Ah, he'll call him in and say, "We've got the signal from across the river to, to put the hold on this." And that will fit rather well because the FBI agents who are working the case, at this point, feel that's what it is. This is CIA.

President Richard Nixon (seated at right) meets with staff on March 13, 1970. H. R. Haldeman is to the left of the president.

FIGURE 12.4 The Smoking Gun Tape[T10]

dissenting opinion could have given Nixon an opening to make the claim that the Court had ruled in error, but the justices—including four Nixon appointees—did not give him that opportunity.

The nation waited breathlessly for Nixon's response. With popular opinion lined up against him and a Supreme Court that had placed on the line the full measure of public allegiance it had developed over nearly two centuries, the president succumbed to the order. Doing so left him without any more political options. The revelations in the tapes meant certain impeachment by the House and conviction by the Senate. Barely two weeks after the Court's ruling, on August 8, 1974, Nixon announced to the nation that he would become the first president in history to resign the office.

United States v. Nixon demonstrates that judgments can in fact be powerful—that words can have dramatic political repercussions. As with Roosevelt's attempt to pack the Court, it shows how public opinion factors directly into the Court's ability to make controversial rulings (or resist succumbing to the efforts of a popular president), provided that it has been able to build a reservoir of legitimacy with the public. Justices who have been sensitive to keeping the institution in good standing with the public, like Owen Roberts, have been willing to put their judicial philosophy and personal beliefs aside, or at least engage in compromise with other justices, in order to protect the Court's political standing. In rare circumstances where the Court is not able to bridge ideological differences among its members, justices put the Court's legitimacy at risk. We witnessed such an event following the 2000 presidential election.

12.8c Squandering Legitimacy?

In December 2000, the Supreme Court walked into the middle of an entirely different tempest—the biggest presidential election controversy in 124 years—when it agreed to hear the Bush campaign's request to put a halt to manual recounts of Florida ballots that did not clearly register a vote for president. George W. Bush and his Democratic rival Al Gore were separated in the final Florida count by several hundred votes out of millions cast, with the eventual winner to receive all of Florida's electoral votes, and with them the presidency. For weeks America was riveted by the recount battle, as several Florida counties manually reviewed unmarked and poorly marked ballots, using different standards for determining the intent of the voter.

The election battle ended abruptly when the U.S. Supreme Court terminated all recounts in the controversial case of *Bush v. Gore* (2000). Seven of the justices felt that the inconsistent recount standards employed in different counties were unconstitutional, but only five of them—all Republican appointees and the Court's most conservative members—argued that the calendar permitted no remedy to correct the inconsistencies because the time had come for electors to report. Four justices with a more liberal voting record strongly disagreed. Unlike the case of *United States v. Nixon*, the Court split into two camps, unable to find common ground on which to build consensus. The final vote was 5–4; the recounting would stop, and Bush would become president.

The ruling left the nation as divided as the Court, and it left the Court bitter about what it had done. For a brief time, the Court's veil of secrecy was lifted as justices uncharacteristically displayed their feelings in public, revealing deep disagreements and great resentment. Justice Clarence Thomas, a member of the conservative majority, appeared on C-SPAN within a day of the ruling to deny that partisan considerations had influenced the decision. Chief Justice Rehnquist made the same assertion to reporters.[49]

Meanwhile, the four dissenting justices angrily castigated the majority, writing that the decision "inevitably cast a cloud on the legitimacy of the election."[50] Some openly questioned if the decision would have the same effect on the Court. Justice Ginsburg, who sided with the minority, saw the ruling as a political victory for "the home crowd"—a reference to the conservative majority fashioning what she believed to be a legally questionable ruling in order to put the candidate they preferred in the White House. Justice Breyer, also on the losing side of the case, worried that the partisan overtones of the ruling would undermine the legitimacy of the judicial process, and by extension, the legitimacy of the Court.[51]

12.9 Consistency and Legitimacy?

To dissenters, one of the more disturbing components of the Court's ruling in *Bush v. Gore* was the requirement that it not be applied to any subsequent case. In other words, the majority made it clear that it was settling a contested election but that it was not establishing a legal precedent. This appeared odd because throughout its history, the Court has operated on the assumption that the collective body of constitutional interpretation contained in the Court's previous rulings provides the basis for making present-day judgments.

This has led the Court to place a premium on consistency. The Court puts a lot of stock in the doctrine of *stare decisis*, or "let the decision stand." *Stare decisis* encourages the Court to use its previous rulings as the basis for making present-day judgments and makes justices generally reluctant to overturn previous decisions, especially judgments that have become part of established law. This can lead justices who disagree with previous Court judgments to uphold them, even as they proclaim their differences with the interpretations of their predecessors.

At the same time, the Court does reverse course, especially in less than monumental matters. By one count, the Court overturned an average of four precedents per year between 1960 and 1999.[52] It's generally easier for the Court to reverse itself on a newly decided matter than on long-standing constitutional interpretation. See Demystifying Government: Abortion Rights and Established Law.

Bush v. Gore: The controversial 2000 Supreme Court case in which a sharply divided Court ended manual ballot recounts in Florida, following which George W. Bush became president.

L.O. Define stare decisis, *and explain the importance of continuity to the Supreme Court.*

stare decisis: Literally, "let the decision stand," it is a guiding principle of judicial interpretation that places a premium on letting previous judicial rulings guide current rulings.

Abortion Rights and Established Law

Prior to 1973, abortion was prohibited in many states. The landmark ruling in the case of *Roe v. Wade* changed that. The Court found that a constitutional right to privacy prohibited states from restricting the availability of abortions during the first three months of pregnancy, and struck down all laws that did so. Abortions were suddenly legal across the country.

Prior to the ruling, the abortion issue was not at the top of the national political agenda, but that quickly changed. As we know, the best way to influence the political process is to organize, and following *Roe v. Wade*, groups seeking to recriminalize abortions organized rapidly. They focused initially on a political and legal strategy, whereby they worked against the election of candidates for high office who were on record as supporting abortion rights, and challenged abortion laws in an effort to get the Supreme Court to reverse or chip away at its decision in *Roe*. The effort eventually bore fruit, and by the early 1980s a sizable congressional contingent and the president, Ronald Reagan, favored reversing the *Roe* decision.[T11]

This did not lead the Court to make an about-face, however. Advocates of reversal argued before the Court that the reasoning used to reach the *Roe* decision was faulty, but this was initially rejected. In *City of Akron v. Akron Center for Reproductive Health* (1983), the Court overturned restrictions imposed on abortion rights by the city of Akron, and in so doing, acknowledged the importance of precedent. In the majority opinion in the *Akron* case, Justice Powell wrote, "Arguments continue to be made . . . that we erred in interpreting the Constitution. Nonetheless, the doctrine of *stare decisis*, while perhaps never entirely persuasive on a constitutional question, is a doctrine that demands respect in a society governed by the rule of law. We respect it today, and reaffirm *Roe v. Wade*."[T12]

As the 1980s progressed, groups pressing to overturn *Roe* benefited from an effective campaign to keep the abortion issue at the forefront of the political agenda. Meanwhile, President Reagan had the opportunity to appoint to the Supreme Court justices who were philosophically opposed to legal abortion. When the Court again considered the issue in *Webster v. Reproductive Health Services* (1989), advocates of a Missouri law restricting abortions attacked the trimester language in *Roe* that decriminalized abortion in the first three months of a pregnancy, contending that it was unworkable, arbitrary, burdensome, and flawed. If their argument held sway in what had become a far more sympathetic Supreme Court, they hoped it would provide the legal rationale for undermining the *Roe* decision. A majority of five justices upheld the Missouri law, but they were divided on the issue of whether their verdict should be used to overturn *Roe*, so the 1973 decision survived what had been its biggest test to date.

We can derive several lessons from this history:

- *Precedent matters:* On major decisions, it takes a lot to move the Court to change what it has established. However, even if the Court is unwilling to reverse itself, it may well be open to chipping away at previous decisions.
- *Politics matters:* Who sits on the Supreme Court (a function of who serves as president), whether an interest is well organized, and the climate of public opinion all factor into the receptivity of the Court to a line of argument.
- *Argument matters:* Even when justices come down on the same side of a case, they may do so for different reasons. The way a case is presented to the Court can mean the difference between victory and defeat.

Reliance on precedent provides the Court with stability that contributes to its legitimacy. Reluctance to make dramatic changes to past rulings despite shifts in the Court's ideological composition distinguishes the Court from the other two federal branches, where swift changes of direction typically characterize partisan shifts. Even when given to ideological motivation, astute justices move slowly to project the appearance of allowing precedent to triumph over self-interest.

The same principle can hold true when the Court is asked to review a major act of Congress, as it did in 2012 when in a 5–4 vote it upheld the constitutionality of the individual mandate at the heart of the Affordable Care Act, the health-care reform law commonly called "Obamacare." The Court's four liberal justices cited long-standing precedent to argue that the mandate was constitutional under Congress's authority to regulate interstate commerce, but four of the five conservative justices disagreed and stood ready to strike down the entire law. The act was saved when Chief Justice Roberts, perhaps with an eye toward the gravity of striking down such major legislation, broke with his fellow conservatives and upheld the mandate as a tax—well within congressional power to

Roe v. Wade: The 1973 Supreme Court case that found a constitutional right to privacy applied to reproductive issues, striking down all state laws that prohibited abortions during the first trimester of pregnancy.

levy—sidestepping the question of how to apply years of precedent about the Interstate Commerce Clause.

Cautious tendencies such as these can paradoxically pose a dilemma when the Court is faced with a previous ruling that was simply a bad judgment. Following *stare decisis* means the Court may take a long time to reverse a burdensome decision, sometimes allowing changes in public opinion to make the outdated ruling untenable. In such cases, the Court eventually protects its legitimacy by changing course or finds its legitimacy tarnished and its judgments discarded by history.

12.9a When Events Overturn the Court

Sometimes, events conspire to reverse a bad judgment of the Court. The case of *Dred Scott v. Sanford* (1857) is a profound example. Dred Scott was a slave who had been taken by his owner to Illinois and the Wisconsin territory, where slavery was prohibited under the terms of the Missouri Compromise. When he was returned to the slave state of Missouri, he petitioned the Court to maintain his freedom on the grounds that he had been residing previously in a free state. A judgment in his favor would have undermined the institution of slavery throughout the Union.

Chief Justice Roger Taney had no intention of allowing this to happen. His Court ruled that no person of color, be they free or enslaved, could be considered a citizen of the United States, and therefore Scott had no legal basis to bring suit. Taney's decision referred to Scott (and all black persons) as "an ordinary article of merchandise" that had no rights. Furthermore, in the first direct challenge to Congress since *Marbury v. Madison*, Taney overturned the key provision of the Missouri Compromise that precluded slavery in northern states and territories, effectively making slavery legal nationwide.[53]

Legal scholars widely consider the *Dred Scott* decision to be the Court's lowest moment. Charles Evans Hughes, chief justice during the 1930s, called the ruling one of the Court's "self-inflicted wounds."[54] It destroyed the Court's legitimacy in the eyes of abolitionists as it intensified irreparable national divisions over slavery. Within three years, in part because of the effect of the Court's decision, the nation would explode into civil war.

Ultimately, the *Dred Scott* ruling was reversed, not by the action of a future Court, but by constitutional amendments approved in a different political climate. With the passage of the Thirteenth and Fourteenth Amendments following the Civil War, slavery was abolished and blacks were granted full citizenship. Taney's decision was rendered moot and his reasoning discredited, but the *Dred Scott* case remains as a warning about the lasting dangers inherent in any case where the Supreme Court establishes a bad precedent.

12.9b When the Court Overturns Itself

It took almost sixty years, but the Supreme Court eventually jettisoned another racially charged ruling, this time by establishing a new precedent in a subsequent case. The original case in question was *Plessy v. Ferguson* (1896), which established the constitutionality of separate public facilities for whites and nonwhites.

Homer Plessy was arrested in 1892 for sitting in the "whites only" car on a Louisiana railroad. Because he had black ancestors, he was considered black under Louisiana law and required to travel in the "coloreds only" car. Plessy went to court to challenge the constitutionality of the segregated railroad, contending it violated the Thirteenth and Fourteenth Amendments. The Court disagreed. Writing for the majority, Justice Henry Billings Brown asserted that the Fourteenth Amendment "could not have been intended to abolish distinctions based on color, or to enforce social, as distinguished from political equality."[55] As long as the facilities available to blacks were on par with those available to whites, segregation was legal.

In a lone dissent that proved to be generations ahead of its time, Justice John Harlan contended, "our Constitution is color-blind, and neither knows nor tolerates classes among citizens. . . . In my opinion, the judgment this day rendered will, in time, prove to be quite as pernicious as the decision made by this tribunal in the *Dred Scott* case."[56]

Dred Scott v. Sanford: The 1857 Supreme Court case that legalized slavery nationwide, while holding that people of color had no rights or protection under the Constitution. The ruling hastened the Civil War; it was subsequently overturned by constitutional amendment.

Plessy v. Ferguson: The 1896 Supreme Court case that upheld racial segregation. It was reversed in 1954 in the case of *Brown v. Board of Education*.

Harlan was right on target. However, it would take until 1954 before a majority of the Supreme Court would agree.

The vehicle for overturning its stand on legal segregation was ***Brown v. Board of Education*** (1954), which revolved around the case of a grade-school girl named Linda Brown, who had to walk to a distant all-black school even though there was an all-white school in her Topeka, Kansas, neighborhood. Her father tried to enroll her in the nearby all-white school but was turned down. With legal assistance from the National Association for the Advancement of Colored People (NAACP), the Browns sued the Topeka Board of Education, asking the courts to strike down barriers to integration. Because the ruling in the *Plessy* case clearly made separate educational facilities legal, the lower courts sided with the Board of Education.

Brown v. Board of Education: The landmark 1954 Supreme Court case that declared racial segregation unconstitutional, overturning the Court's ruling in *Plessy v. Ferguson*.

It was left to the Supreme Court to stand up to its past, and the politics of the moment made this possible. Earl Warren, just two months into his term as chief justice, had an opportunity to correct what the Court had done in 1896 and change the direction of American politics. In a unanimous decision, the Warren Court overturned fifty-eight years of constitutionally sanctioned segregation in a landmark ruling that began breaking down racial barriers in American institutions.

Taking direct aim at *Plessy*, Warren wrote, "Does segregation of children in public schools solely on the basis of race, even though the physical facilities and other 'tangible' factors may be equal, deprive the children of the minority group of equal educational opportunities? We believe that it does. . . . We conclude that in the field of public education the doctrine of 'separate but equal' has no place. Separate educational facilities are inherently unequal."[57]

With those words, the Court made a rare about-face in the wake of changing political conditions, propelling the groundbreaking work of the civil rights movement of the 1950s and 1960s. See Appendix F for excerpts of key civil rights decisions.

12.10 Activism and Restraint

It's probably evident by now that the competing philosophical approaches to the role of the Court that justices hold can make an enormous difference in how much the Court contributes to social change. In this regard, the people wearing the robes matter a lot. John Marshall and Earl Warren were activists who expanded the role of the Court in the political process and in American life. More restrained justices serving during the same periods in history would have done it differently, resulting in less development of federal power in the early nineteenth century and in fewer civil rights advancements in the twentieth century.

L.O. Contrast judicial activism with judicial restraint.

12.10a Judicial Activism

As a proponent of **judicial activism**, Warren presided over a revolutionary expansion in minority group rights, criminal defendant rights, voting rights, equal representation, and personal expression. Between 1953 and 1969, the Warren Court acted aggressively, among other things, to

judicial activism: The philosophy that the Court should take an aggressive posture toward politics and the law, striking down presidential and congressional actions whenever it is deemed necessary and instituting far-reaching remedies to social wrongs.

- Desegregate schools.
- Draw legislative boundaries so they reflected the "one person, one vote" principle.
- Protect individuals accused of crimes from self-incrimination (the famous "Miranda Rights" that police read to suspects prior to arresting them come from the 1966 case *Miranda v. Arizona*).
- Guarantee legal representation to criminal defendants who could not afford it.
- Forbid mandatory prayer in public schools.
- Expand press freedom by requiring public figures to prove that reporters acted with malice to support a claim of libel.[58]

If you're thinking that all this was controversial, you're right. Critics charge that judicial activists are less interested in interpreting the law than in making it, a role that is constitutionally reserved for Congress. Warren's critics repeatedly charged him with usurping powers that were reserved for others, which—along with the agenda his activism promoted—instigated sales of "impeach Earl Warren" bumper stickers.

If the Court takes a measure of public opinion before acting, though, it should be remembered that the Warren Court served during a period of social upheaval that suited it well. Certainly, the Court's activism contributed to the upheaval, and without a doubt, public opinion was sharply divided over a lot of what it did. Then again, public opinion was sharply divided over everything important happening during the 1960s, when rights for African Americans, women, and young people were at the forefront of the political agenda. It's hard to envision an activist Court taking the positions that the Warren Court did in an era that's more conducive to conservative politics, like what we saw in the decades after Warren left the Court.

Still, it would be a mistake to equate judicial activism with political liberalism. The aforementioned Felix Frankfurter, whose long service included a stint on the Warren Court before his retirement in 1962, was an economic conservative who advanced his preferences by striking down laws that conflicted with his agenda—in other words, through judicial activism.[59] Members of today's conservative Supreme Court who have worked to reverse some of what the Warren Court did could also be seen as conservative activists. It is not uncommon for the Roberts Court to overturn precedent, as they did in 2010 with campaign finance law in the *Citizens United v. Federal Election Commission* case. Often these votes rest on a narrow 5–4 majority, with the Court's most conservative justices voting with the majority.[60]

12.10b Judicial Restraint

judicial restraint: The philosophy that the Court should defer to the other branches of government and only overturn legislation when it is clearly unconstitutional.

The bookend to judicial activism is **judicial restraint**, or the philosophy that the judiciary should yield to the actions of the legislature and executive unless they are blatantly unconstitutional. To a justice who practices judicial restraint, a bad policy, an unnecessary policy, even an unfair policy that is permitted under the Constitution should be left alone.[61] Clearly, someone who takes this approach to the judiciary would never think of using the Court as a vehicle for advancing an activist political agenda. This became a point raised ironically by liberals during the Roberts and Alito confirmation hearings, as they sought assurances that these conservative jurists would regard *Roe v. Wade* as established law and not seek to overturn it. Although restraint and conservatism seem to go hand-in-hand, it's possible for conservative judges to make activist rulings.

constructionists: Those who hold to the judicial philosophy that the Constitution should be interpreted strictly and literally, and in the context in which it was written.

Some of the justices who practice judicial restraint are also **constructionists** when it comes to interpreting the Constitution. Constructionists believe that the Constitution should be subject to a literal or narrow interpretation, and understood within the context in which it was written.[62] So, for instance, strict constructionists might oppose the reasoning behind the *Roe* decision, which legalized abortion on the basis of a constitutional right to privacy, on the grounds that the Constitution does not enumerate privacy as a right, and that the framers of the Constitution did not intend for there to be such a right. A constructionist philosophy is conservative in nature and stands in clear opposition to judicial activism. However, it can result in far-reaching decisions should justices undermine or overturn existing law in the name of reinterpreting past rulings. Not surprisingly, recent conservative presidents like Nixon, Reagan, and both Bushes have favored judicial nominees who hold to this philosophy.

Despite the prevalence of Republican justices, the Supreme Court in recent years has been actively engaged in reversing its own decisions, acts of Congress, and state laws. The period since Chief Justice Warren took over the Court in 1953 through the present has been an unparalleled era of judicial activism, in which the Court as a whole has injected itself regularly into the political process. Between 1953 and 2005, the Court reversed 132 of its earlier rulings. In the previous century and a half, it had only done this eighty-eight times. Table 12.3 provides the details. Despite the conservative direction the Court has taken since Warren's departure, it has remained an activist branch of government.

TABLE 12.3 The Growth of Judicial Activism through Two Centuries, 1801–2005[T13]

Court	Years	Supreme Court Decisions Overturned	Acts of Congress Overturned	State Laws Overturned
Marshall	1801–1835	3	1	18
Taney	1836–1864	4	1	21
Chase	1865–1873	4	10	33
Waite	1874–1888	13	9	7
Fuller	1889–1910	4	14	73
White	1910–1921	5	12	107
Taft	1921–1930	6	12	131
Hughes	1930–1940	21	14	78
Stone	1941–1946	15	2	25
Vinson	1947–1952	13	1	38
Warren	1953–1969	45	25	150
Burger	1969–1986	52	34	192
Rehnquist	1986–2005	44	34	85

As an equal participant in the political process, the cumulative actions of the courts at every level have tremendous bearing on how we live our lives. The way the courts exercise this influence is itself determined by things beyond the control of the judiciary—like other political actors and the political climate of the times—and by the philosophical leanings of the people in the dark robes. Would the federal government be weaker today if John Marshall had not been chief justice for the first three decades of the nineteenth century, when clashes over federalism were being resolved? Would the Civil War have occurred when it did had Chief Justice Taney not tried to codify slavery as the law of the land? Would the civil rights agendas of the 1960s have been different without Earl Warren? Would Al Gore have become president had one justice voted differently?

In the courts as everywhere else in the political system, the rules of the game and the way they're interpreted by people in authority determines who gets what—who wins and who loses. Nowhere is this more evident than in the area of public policy, the outcomes produced by the political process in the form of domestic and foreign policy and laws regarding individual rights and liberties. We'll look at those outcomes and what they mean to us personally in the final part of the book, beginning with civil rights policies in Chapter 13.

Chapter Review

Explain why the judiciary has less power than the other branches of the federal government.

Define judicial review as it was established in *Marbury v. Madison*, and explain how it greatly enhanced the powers of the Supreme Court.

The judiciary resolves disputes arising from other branches of government, but it does so without the formal powers of the other branches and has to rely on the executive branch to enforce its rulings. This initially placed the United States Supreme Court in a weak position, which was strengthened enormously with the establishment of the Court's power of judicial review in the 1803 case *Marbury v. Madison*. Other rulings of the Marshall Court helped establish the supremacy of the federal government over the states.

Illustrate the three-tiered judicial structure in place at the federal and state levels, and explain the appeals process.

The federal court system is a three-tiered structure with trial courts, circuit courts of appeals, and the Supreme Court. Most cases work their way up this system through an appellate process, although the Supreme Court has original jurisdiction over cases involving the federal government, states, and foreign officials as detailed in the Constitution. State court systems follow this three-tiered structure and have jurisdiction over state criminal and civil law. Cases can only be appealed from a state court to the U.S. Supreme Court if they raise a point of constitutional law.

Discuss how the Supreme Court selects, hears, and decides cases.

Courts have a lot of latitude in the cases they select for review, although interest groups try to influence case selection. Deciding cases is a complicated process that starts with oral arguments in court, proceeds with closed conferences, and continues with a period of writing decisions, during which justices attempt to influence each other's opinions and may even change their votes.

Describe the judicial confirmation process, and explain why it has been contentious in recent years.

Judicial nominations can cause contentious battles between the president and Congress because the direction of the judiciary depends on the philosophy and ideology of the people the president appoints. Historically, presidents get most of the appointments they want, but the Senate takes its consent function seriously and has blocked nominations considered controversial. Presidents will also defer to senatorial courtesy and avoid appointing justices and judges who are not acceptable to their home-state senators.

Characterize the level of gender, racial, and religious diversity on the Supreme Court both historically and today.

Although the vast majority of Supreme Court appointees have been white Protestant men, today's Supreme Court reflects more religious, ethnic, and gender diversity. This is less evident on lower federal courts, where President Clinton is alone among his immediate predecessors in the diversity of his appointments.

Explain how the Supreme Court relies on legitimacy and public opinion to bolster its weak political position.

In order to turn its relatively weak political position to advantage, the Court plays on its mystique to bolster its legitimacy with the public, making it difficult for political officials to defy Court rulings. It also pays attention to public opinion, often taking pains not to get ahead of what the public will accept. So, when Franklin D. Roosevelt attempted to pack the Court with sympathetic justices, the public recoiled at his efforts to play politics with a revered institution, and the scheme failed. However, a justice who had been holding up Roosevelt's New Deal legislation acknowledged its broad public support and began changing his vote, which brought the Court in line with public sentiment.

Define *stare decisis*, and explain the importance of continuity to the Supreme Court.

Justices put a lot of stock in the doctrine of *stare decisis*, making dramatic reversals unusual. But as public opinion changes, the Court may become willing to revisit past rulings. The Court may overturn some of its earlier bad judgments, the way *Plessy v. Ferguson* (1896) was reversed by *Brown v. Board of Education* (1954). Events may conspire to reverse the Court, as when the decision affirming slavery in *Dred Scott v. Sanford* (1857) was overturned by constitutional amendment following the Civil War.

Contrast judicial activism with judicial restraint.

Justices differ in judicial philosophy. Judicial activists believe the Court should be a forum for correcting social wrongs. Justices advocating judicial restraint feel the Court should defer to the actions of Congress and the president unless they are blatantly unconstitutional.

Key Terms

amicus curiae Briefs filed by interested parties to a case, whose opinions are offered in an effort to shape the Court's discussion and judgment. (p. 375)

appellate jurisdiction The authority of a high court to hear cases only after the cases originate in and are appealed from a lower court. (p. 371)

Articles of Confederation The first constitution of the United States, which created a loosely functioning national government to which the individual states were supreme. It addressed concerns about a strong national government undermining individual liberty, but it created a national government that was unable to regulate commerce or conduct foreign policy and was abandoned in favor of the United States Constitution just eight years after it was ratified. (p. 367)

Brown v. Board of Education The landmark 1954 Supreme Court case that declared racial segregation unconstitutional, overturning the Court's ruling in *Plessy v. Ferguson*. (p. 391)

Bush v. Gore The controversial 2000 Supreme Court case in which a sharply divided Court ended manual ballot recounts in Florida, following which George W. Bush became president. (p. 388)

concurring opinion A statement issued by a justice who agrees with a vote of the Court but differs on the legal or constitutional rationale for the majority decision. (p. 373)

constructionists Those who hold to the judicial philosophy that the Constitution should be interpreted strictly and literally, and in the context in which it was written. (p. 392)

dissenting opinion A statement issued by a justice who disagrees with a vote of the Court, offering a legal or constitutional rationale for that disagreement. (p. 373)

docket The list of cases pending before a court. (p. 374)

Dred Scott v. Sanford The 1857 Supreme Court case that legalized slavery nationwide, while holding that people of color had no rights or protection under the Constitution. The ruling hastened the Civil War; it was subsequently overturned by constitutional amendment. (p. 390)

Gibbons v. Ogden The Supreme Court case, heard by the Marshall Court in 1824, that established the federal government's primacy in regulating interstate commerce, saying that the state of New York could not grant an exclusive license to a steamboat company operating between New York and New Jersey. (p. 369)

judicial activism The philosophy that the Court should take an aggressive posture toward politics and the law, striking down presidential and congressional actions whenever it is deemed necessary and instituting far-reaching remedies to social wrongs. (p. 391)

judicial restraint The philosophy that the Court should defer to the other branches of government and only overturn legislation when it is clearly unconstitutional. (p. 392)

judicial review The authority of the Supreme Court to overrule actions of Congress or the president by declaring them to be unconstitutional. (p. 368)

judiciary The federal and state court systems charged with resolving legal and personal disputes and interpreting the law. (p. 366)

Judiciary Act of 1789 The act of Congress that established the federal court system. It initially called for a six-person Supreme Court and three circuit courts, each to be administered by two Supreme Court justices and one district court judge. (p. 367)

jurisdiction The authority of a court to hear a case. (p. 371)

legal system The web of institutions and individuals involved in bringing legal and personal disputes to the attention of the courts. (p. 366)

Marbury v. Madison The Supreme Court case, heard by the Marshall Court in 1803, that established judicial review. (p. 369)

McCulloch v. Maryland The 1819 Supreme Court case that established federal supremacy over the state governments. (p. 369)

New Jersey Plan A proposal for the new Constitution, supported by small states, that would have provided for equal representation of large and small states in the national legislature, while limiting the power of the national government over the states. (p. 367)

original jurisdiction The authority of the U.S. Supreme Court to be the first court to hear a case, precluding the need for an appeal from a lower court. The Constitution grants original jurisdiction to cases involving a dispute between the United States and a state; two or more states; citizens of different states; a state and a citizen of another state; and foreign ambassadors. (p. 371)

Plessy v. Ferguson The 1896 Supreme Court case that upheld racial segregation. It was reversed in 1954 in the case of *Brown v. Board of Education*. (p. 390)

Roe v. Wade The 1973 Supreme Court case that found a constitutional right to privacy applied to reproductive issues, striking down all state laws that prohibited abortions during the first trimester of pregnancy. (p. 389)

senatorial courtesy The custom that presidents will defer to the wishes of senators from a judicial nominee's home state before making a court appointment. (p. 378)

solicitor general The White House official responsible for arguing on behalf of the United States in Supreme Court cases where the United States is a party. (p. 375)

stare decisis Literally, "let the decision stand," it is a guiding principle of judicial interpretation that places a premium on letting previous judicial rulings guide current rulings. (p. 388)

United States v. Nixon The 1974 case in which a unanimous Supreme Court ruled that President Nixon could not use executive privilege to protect the secrecy of incriminating tapes documenting his involvement in the cover-up of the Watergate break-in. (p. 385)

Virginia Plan A proposal for the new Constitution, supported by large states, that would have based representation on population and provided for a centralized national government that could overrule the states. (p. 367)

writ of *certiorari* An order issued by the Supreme Court demanding a lower court turn over all records of a case that the Supreme Court has decided to hear on appeal. (p. 374)

writ of *mandamus* A court order commanding a public official to perform an official act. (p. 370)

Resources

You might be interested in examining some of what the following authors have said about the topics we've been discussing:

Abraham, Henry J. *Justices, Presidents, and Senators: A History of the U.S. Supreme Court Appointments from Washington to Bush II,* 5th ed. Lanham, MD: Rowman & Littlefield, 2007. A colorful account of the nominating process and the Supreme Court through history.

Baum, Lawrence. *The Supreme Court*, 10th ed. Washington, DC: CQ Press, 2009. Baum offers a thorough exploration of the extent to which the Supreme Court operates as a political institution despite appearances to the contrary.

Carp, Robert A., and Ronald Stidham. *The Federal Courts*, 4th ed. Washington, DC: CQ Press, 2001. A detailed overview of the federal court system.

Epstein, Lee, and Jack Knight. *The Choices Justices Make.* Washington, DC: CQ Press, 1998. The authors offer a rational approach to the way Supreme Court justices reach decisions, which should appeal to anyone interested in strategic decision-making.

Epstein, Lee, Jeffrey A. Segal, Harold J. Spaeth, and Thomas G. Walker. *The Supreme Court Compendium: Data, Decisions, and Development*, 4th ed. Washington, DC: CQ Press, 2006. If you have a factual question about the Supreme Court, chances are you can find the answer here. It's everything you've ever wanted to know about the Supreme Court.

O'Brien, David M. *Storm Center: The Supreme Court in American Politics*, 8th ed. New York: W. W. Norton, 2008. An accessible account of the Supreme Court that emphasizes how the Court functions as a political branch of government.

Toobin, Jeffrey. *The Nine: Inside the Secret World of the Supreme Court*. New York: Doubleday, 2008. Toobin pulls back the veil of secrecy on the Supreme Court to reveal a world that's heavily influenced by personalities and politics.

You may also be interested in looking at the Supreme Court's website, at http://www.supremecourt.gov. You can browse the Court's docket, read about the rules and history of the Court, and even plan a visit if you're going to be in Washington, DC.

Notes

1 Herbert Jacob, *Law and Politics in the United States*, 2nd ed. (New York: HarperCollins, 1995), 6–18.

2 You can take a virtual tour of the Supreme Court, and even virtually visit a justice's chambers, by going to oyez.org at http://www.oyez.org/tour.

3 Lawrence Baum, *The Supreme Court*, 7th ed. (Washington, DC: CQ Press, 2001), 2–4.

4 Alexander Hamilton, *The Federalist*, No. 78. See http://www.constitution.org/fed/federa78.htm.

5 Robert A. Carp and Ronald Stidham, *The Federal Courts*, 4th ed. (Washington, DC: CQ Press, 2001), 4.

6 David M. O'Brien, *Storm Center: The Supreme Court in American Politics*, 6th ed. (New York: W. W. Norton, 2003), 105.

7 Ibid., 106.

8 Carp and Stidham, *The Federal Courts*, 6.

9 Ibid, 6–7.

10 Ibid.

11 Baum, *The Supreme Court*, 23–24.

12 Carp and Stidham, *The Federal Courts*, 7–8.

13 Ibid., 71. Jackson may not have actually spoken these words, but there's little doubt that they expressed how he felt about Marshall's Federalist tendencies.

14 Ibid., 16–17.

15 O'Brien, *Storm Center*, 105.

16 Carp and Stidham, *The Federal Courts*, 46–47.

17 Ibid., 248.

18 Ibid., 255.

19 Ibid., 257–267.

20 Lee Epstein and Jack Knight, *The Choices Justices Make* (Washington, DC: CQ Press, 1998), 1–21.

21 O'Brien, *Storm Center*, 267–296.

22 Carp and Stidham, *The Federal Courts*, 32–34.

23 O'Brien, *Storm Center*, 164–182.

24 U.S. Courts: The Federal Judiciary, at http://www.uscourts.gov. See also Supreme Court of the United States, at http://www.supremecourt.gov/faq.aspx#faqgi9.

25 If you're curious about the types of cases pending before the Supreme Court right now, you can access the Court's docket

at http://www.supremecourt.gov/docket/docket.aspx. At the search bar, type in an area that interests you, like "environment," "transportation," or "tax." The website will return all pending and recently decided cases pertaining to that area. If you're a budding lawyer, you can click on the docket number of a case and you'll find the path the case has taken to reach the Supreme Court, and the action taken (or lack thereof), expressed in language only a lawyer could love.

26 You can read more about the solicitor general online at http://www.justice.gov/osg/.

27 O'Brien, *Storm Center*, 222–225.

28 Ibid., 225.

29 Burgess Everett and Glenn Thrush, "McConnell Throws down the Gauntlet: No Scalia Replacement under Obama," *Politico*, February 13, 2016. http://www.politico.com/story/2016/02/mitch-mcconnell-antonin-scalia-supreme-court-nomination-219248.

30 See http://www.whitehouse.gov/the_press_office/Background-on-Judge-Sonia-Sotomayor.

31 Lee Epstein and others, *The Supreme Court Compendium: Data, Decisions, and Development*, 2nd ed. (Washington, DC: CQ Press, 1996), 329.

32 Abraham, *Justices, Presidents and Senators*, 18–19

33 Ibid., 19.

34 Ibid., 21–28.

35 Ibid., 46–47.

36 "How Obama Reshaped the Federal Courts," Law.com, October 31, 2016. http://www.law.com/sites/almstaff/2016/10/31/how-obama-reshaped-the-federal-courts/?slreturn=20170003182838.

37 Federal Judicial Center, at http://www.fjc.gov/.

38 Carp and Stidham, *The Federal Courts*, 69–78.

39 Ibid., 78.

40 Abraham, *Justices, Presidents and Senators*, 191–192.

41 Ibid., 191–194.

42 O'Brien, *Storm Center*, 87.

43 Ibid., 56.

44 Ibid.

45 Yes, that's really what it was called.

46 O'Brien, *Storm Center*, 58.

47 Jacob, *Law and Politics*, 79–80.

48 When you're looking at the transcript, note the reference to Mark Felt, who is described by Haldeman as "ambitious." Those familiar with the Watergate case may recognize Felt as the secret source, dubbed "Deep Throat," who helped *Washington Post* reporter Bob Woodward crack the Watergate case, and whose identity remained a mystery for thirty years.

49 O'Brien, *Storm Center*, 87.

50 Ibid., 251.

51 Ibid., 88 and 96.

52 Baum, *The Supreme Court*, 143.

53 O'Brien, *Storm Center*, 29.

54 Ibid., 115.

55 A summary of the case may be found at http://www.oyez.org/cases/1851-1900/1895/1895_210/, while the full text of the ruling may be found at http://supreme.justia.com/us/163/537/case.html.

56 O'Brien, *Storm Center*, 115.

57 The full text of the ruling may be found at http://supreme.justia.com/us/347/483/case.html.

58 O'Brien, *Storm Center*, 195–197.

59 Lee Epstein and Thomas G. Walker, *Constitutional Law for a Changing America: A Short Course* (Washington, DC: CQ Press, 1996), 39–41.

60 See, for instance, Segal, Daniel, and Maya Nayak, "High Court's End-of-Term Opinions Erode Precedent and Stare Decisis." *The Legal Intelligencer* (August 7, 2007); and Linda Greenhouse, "Precedents Begin Falling for Roberts Court," *New York Times*, June 21, 2007.

61 Abraham, *Justices, Presidents and Senators*, 271.

62 O'Brien, *Storm Center*, 14–15.

Table, Figure, and Box Notes

T1 Image of Supreme Court is in the Public Domain and is the property of the U.S. Federal Government. Courtesy Steve Petteway, Collection of the Supreme Court of the United States.

T2 Robert Carp and Ronald Stidham, *The Federal Courts*, 4th ed. (Washington, DC: CQ Press, 2001), 3–4.

T3 Henry J. Abraham, *Presidents, and Senators: A History of the U.S. Supreme Court Appointments from Washington to Clinton* (Lanham, MD: Rowman and Littlefield, 1999).

T4 David M. O'Brien, *Storm Center: The Supreme Court in American Politics*, 6th ed. (New York: W. W. Norton, 2002), 172 (table).

T5 The images of the Supreme Court justices are in the Public Domain and are the property of the U.S. Federal Government.

T6 "Changing Attitudes on Gay Marriage," Pew Research Center, May 12, 2016. http://www.pewforum.org/2016/05/12/changing-attitudes-on-gay-marriage/.

T7 William R. Eskridge, Jr., *Equality Practice: Civil Unions and the Future of Gay Rights* (New York: Routledge, 2002), 1–3.

T8 Robert M. Baird and Stuart E. Rosenbaum (eds.), *Same-Sex Marriage: The Moral and Legal Debate* (Amherst, NY: Prometheus Books, 1997), *Same Sex Marriage*, 9–10.

T9 Eskridge, *Equality Practice*, 6–82.

T10 Audio available through the National Archives and Records Administration. Photo is courtesy of the Nixon Library.

T11 Herbert Jacob, *Law and Politics in the United States*, 2nd ed. (New York: Harper Collins College Publishers, 1995), 232–233.

T12 Lee Epstein and Joseph F. Kobylka, *The Supreme Court and Legal Challenge: Abortion and the Death Penalty* (Chapel Hill, University of North Central Press, 1992), 244–245.

T13 David M. O'Brien, *Storm Center: The Supreme Court in American Politics*, 6th ed. (New York: W. W. Norton, 2003); and Lori A. Ringhand, "The Rehnquist Court: A 'By the Numbers' Retrospective," University of Georgia Law School, April 1, 2007.

Establishing Civil Rights

CHAPTER 13

Copyright: Billion Photos/Shutterstock.com

Chapter Outline

Learning Objectives

When you have completed this chapter, you should be able to:

- Define civil rights, and explain the importance of the equal protection clause of the Fourteenth Amendment.

- Express familiarity with the civil rights struggle of African Americans—from Reconstruction to Jim Crow laws to the civil rights movement of the 1950s and 1960s.

- Identify the purpose and range of affirmative action policies.

- Appreciate the discrimination faced by Native Americans during the centuries following the arrival of European settlers.

- Understand the history of Latinos in the United States as it relates to worker rights, education, and immigration issues.

- Recognize the work of women's rights advocates in establishing voting rights, attempting to pass the Equal Rights Amendment, and promoting policies on sexual harassment and workplace rights.

- Appreciate the Americans with Disabilities Act as civil rights legislation.

- Place the contemporary debate over gay marriage in the context of previous civil rights struggles.

13.1 Introduction

Some people feel passionately about the kind of country they want the United States to be. Others are content to sit on the sidelines as decisions are made about who gets what. For some people, social concerns are of great importance. For others, the stuff of daily experience is enough to keep them occupied, even if that experience is shaped in part by political choices that don't interest them.

Which kind of person are you? Do you think a lot about the kind of society you're living in? Do you think about ways you'd like to maintain it or change it? Do you engage in political action to try to bring it about?

Or do you find questions like these to be uninteresting? Maybe you feel government is too distant from your everyday life to matter much. Do you think that even if you got involved on behalf of what you believe, it wouldn't make much of a difference?

Questions like these are really about values. If you believe we should be a society where we spend heavily on the military, that's a value. If you believe we should be a society where abortions are available to women who want them, that's also a value. If you believe capital punishment is a deterrent to crime, you probably value the death penalty. If you believe traditionally disadvantaged groups should be given extra consideration in college admission decisions, you probably value affirmative action.

It's easy to see how values can conflict with one another because those who want to spend less tax money on the military will clash with those who want to spend more, those who believe abortion is morally wrong will clash with those who feel it is a matter of personal choice, and so on.

People who feel strongly about some of these things and see their positions as moral absolutes might object to having them defined as values. This complicates the battles that ensue when people with different visions of society clash in the political process because it's not unusual for people on *both sides* of an issue to believe that they are simply right. In one regard, the safeguards to the system that we talked about in the first part of the book put a drag on the most aggressive advocates of a political position and deter factions from imposing their will on others. But that doesn't stop the political debate from being intense and ferocious—even if you're not personally involved in it.

Regardless of your personal involvement in politics, all of us live with the results of those who get the political system to successfully respond to their values and their view of society. Politics creates winners and losers. In your parents' generation, advocates of government as a vehicle for bringing about social justice won a lot of battles. Your generation has witnessed the success of those who felt that approach was ineffective or misguided. Even if you didn't participate, if you hold a position on any of the wide range of things government touches, you are a winner or a loser, too.

We're going to explore four arenas where the fury of policy debate determines whose values receive official acknowledgment. It's a fluid process, where winners at one moment could turn into losers at another, and where winners in one area could be losers in another. So, as we look at policies affecting civil rights, civil liberties, domestic affairs, and international relations, consider the kind of country you would like to live in, and see how it compares with the kind of country we choose to be. Along the way, think about the things you value, and whether there is any way that you can imagine your voice contributing to the debate over any of the issues we will discuss.

We'll start with issues of civil rights.

L.O. *Define civil rights, and explain the importance of the equal protection clause of the Fourteenth Amendment.*

civil rights: The promise of equal treatment under the law, regardless of one's race, gender, ethnic group affiliation, sexual preference, or age.

13.2 Civil Rights

The Declaration of Independence says, "all men are created equal." **Civil rights** policies are about making sure this is enforced as a matter of law: that the law treats everyone equally, regardless of differences in race, gender, ethnic background, sexual preference, or anything people might be inclined to discriminate against. Because equal treatment does not naturally materialize, ensuring civil rights can be a challenge. Even among people who agree with the principle of equal treatment under the law, there can be strong disagreements over the means to that end. Some would treat everyone the same in order to treat them equally, whereas others would make exceptions for those who have long been the object of discriminatory treatment. This can be the cause of fierce policy disputes.

As we first noted in Chapter 1, there are different ways to define equality, and because they are not entirely compatible with one another, advocates of different conceptions of equality readily clash. Some of the early civil rights struggles were about affording disadvantaged groups the same political rights as others, such as African Americans, who for years were kept out of the political process through legal and violent means, and women, who struggled for decades to win the right to vote. These groups sought **political equality**, which you may recall is a form of **equality of opportunity** because it creates a level playing field for all participants. Although struggles by these groups were ferocious and met with intense resistance by those whites or men who felt threatened by opening the political process to blacks and women, subsequent generations have largely embraced the political gains they made. That's because Americans tend to support equality of opportunity, and widely value the evenhanded application of political rights.

Some of the more recent civil rights battles, however, have been fought over outcomes, which we know to be problematic for many Americans. These battles have sparked enormous controversy because by attempting to advance **equality of outcome**, disadvantaged groups have run headlong into the widely held American preference for not using government to produce **economic equality** or **social equality**. So, people who argue for policies like affirmative action, meant to compensate for past and present discrimination in hiring or college admissions, meet defiance from those who see it as a misguided attempt to mandate economic equality. Women face similar resistance when they argue for comparable-worth legislation, mandating equal pay for jobs predominantly performed by women that require similar skill levels and training as other jobs predominantly performed by men.

Compounding matters is the issue of who qualifies as a disadvantaged group. In recent years, Native Americans, Latinos, Asian Americans, gays, people with disabilities, and seniors have prominently organized to demand consideration for past and present discrimination. To some, having so many groups claiming redress for discriminatory practices makes a mockery of civil rights by creating a culture of victimization, whereby anyone with a grievance about how others treat them can turn to the government to rectify it. Their resistance is fueled by the fact that many of these civil rights agendas raise controversial questions about social equality: Should Spanish be used in schools with large Latino populations in order to treat Spanish-speaking children equally, or are Spanish-speaking children treated equally when schools require they learn English? Should monogamous homosexual relationships be treated the same as monogamous heterosexual relationships, with gays being allowed to marry? Should seniors be protected from discrimination by employers who may prefer to hire younger people?

In theory, most Americans would agree that everyone should have equal rights before the law and that all people should be treated with equal dignity. In practice, civil rights struggles are always controversial. People do not always accept the legitimacy of a group's grievances, and the aggrieved group's demands for a change in the economic or social order can be perceived to cut against widely held beliefs about equality of outcome. This serves to make civil rights issues among the most heated—and important—controversies that government has to address.

13.3 Equal Protection

The key to civil rights in the United States is laid out in Part 1 of the Fourteenth Amendment, which says "No state shall . . . deny to any person within its jurisdiction the equal protection of the laws." The intent of this **equal protection clause** is that all laws should be applied evenly and without prejudice to all citizens. Note that it is not a mandate for equality of outcomes: The Constitution is silent on the matter of equal results. Rather, the Fourteenth Amendment makes a statement about equal treatment, that everyone is equal in the eyes of the law. This approach is consistent with the long-standing American value of equal opportunity, which is secured in part by equal application of the law.

political equality: Establishing political and legal rights on the basis of the individual, so that everyone has the same right to vote and is equal under the law. An alternative would be to grant political rights to elite individuals based on wealth or social standing.

equality of opportunity: One of several ways of understanding equality, this way values giving people comparable advantages for succeeding in life, regardless of the unequal outcomes that may result.

equality of outcome: One of several ways of understanding equality, this way values leveling the social and economic inequities among people, rather than attempting to give people comparable advantages for succeeding in life.

economic equality: A form of equality of outcome that values using government policy to minimize the economic disparities found in society.

social equality: A form of equality of outcome that values using government policy to minimize social class distinctions found in society.

equal protection clause: The constitutional restriction against state laws that discriminate, as stated in the Fourteenth Amendment. The equal protection clause served as the legal basis for eliminating laws that permitted racial discrimination.

Groups that have experienced discrimination have used the equal protection clause to rectify inequities. Most prominently, it has been used by African Americans to fight legalized segregation. The Fourteenth Amendment established full citizenship for former slaves while guaranteeing them equal protection of the law. It is one of a trio of post–Civil War amendments designed to give African Americans a legal basis for equal rights. The Thirteenth Amendment abolished slavery in the United States, and the Fifteenth Amendment gave African American males the right to vote.

We saw in Section 12.9a, "When Events Overturn the Court," how slaves prior to the Civil War were treated as property, and how the Supreme Court had affirmed the institution of slavery in the case of *Dred Scott v. Sanford* in 1857, just four years before the South seceded from the Union, and just five years before President Lincoln issued the Emancipation Proclamation of 1862, granting freedom to all slaves living in the states of the Confederacy. With the passage of the Thirteenth Amendment in 1865, a revolution in the legal status of African Americans had transpired over the course of eight wrenching years.

Note also how the Fourteenth Amendment says that no state shall deny equal protection of the laws to any of its citizens. Not trusting the states of the Confederacy to grant equal protection to freed slaves, the federal government retained the ability to impose the conditions of all three post–Civil War amendments on the states. This language, along with the Union victory in the Civil War, constituted a turning point in a key matter of **federalism** by settling the question of federal supremacy that had been one of the country's hottest political issues since the ratification of the Constitution.

13.4 Civil Rights and African Americans

For many African Americans, who make up 13 percent of the U.S. population (see Figure 13.1), the story of contemporary citizenship has deep roots in an enduring struggle for civil rights that was shaped by the way southern states treated emancipated slaves. The authors of the post–Civil War amendments were wise to distrust southern states to implement laws that defied the political culture of the region. Immediately following the Civil War, when Union troops occupied the South, they could impose terms for **Reconstruction** of the Union. Officials of the former Confederacy were initially barred from exercising political power, and could only sit by and watch as the first African Americans were elected to Congress as Republicans from such states as South Carolina, Mississippi, and Louisiana.

Southern whites did their best to strike back. In 1865, the **Ku Klux Klan** was established in Tennessee as a secret white supremacist organization that regarded freedom for

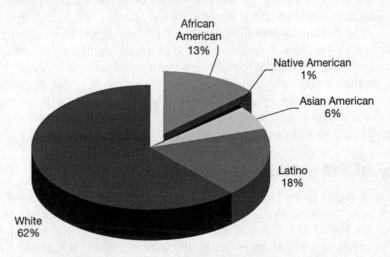

In 2015, about 13 of every 100 Americans were of African American ancestry.

FIGURE 13.1 African Americans in the Population[T1]

African Americans as a threat to whites. For decades, white-hooded Klansmen would terrorize, torture, and kill blacks, sometimes freely, sometimes despite tepid federal efforts to stop the violence.[1] The Klan disbanded in 1871, only to reemerge in 1915.[2]

Also in 1865, a number of southern states implemented **"Black Codes"** designed to restrict the civil rights of emancipated slaves. Although the details varied, Black Codes attempted to reinstate the social order that had existed before the Civil War by regulating where African Americans could work, live, and travel, and by preventing them from owning or renting land or from working as anything but laborers.[3] Federal civil rights laws struck down the Black Codes in 1866,[4] but this did not change the fact that millions of newly freed men and women still lived in a white-dominated society that continued to regard them as property and required their cheap, previously free labor to prop up a devastated economy.

When Abraham Lincoln sought a second term as president in 1864, he looked ahead to the conclusion of the Civil War and the need to reconstruct a unified nation. With this in mind, Lincoln—a Republican—selected as his running mate Andrew Johnson, a southern Democrat who believed in states' rights. Johnson represented Tennessee in the Senate even after his state seceded, making him something of a hero to northerners. Even so, Lincoln's move was significant because Democrats at the time were regarded as the party of the South and secession, and Republicans viewed Democrats as the enemy in war.

In one of the great ironies of American history, when Lincoln was assassinated in 1865, Johnson became president of the United States, and the job of reconstructing the Union fell to this southern Democrat. Whatever sympathies he felt toward his home region came through in his approach to reconstruction, or at least were apparent to a Congress dominated by radical Republicans who objected to Johnson's offer of pardons to southerners willing to swear allegiance to the United States and implementation of a reconstruction program while Congress was out of session.

Congress saw the rise of Black Codes across the South and the return of southern prewar political leaders as clear indications that Johnson's program would undermine efforts to extend civil rights to former slaves. They quickly fought back, with civil rights legislation banning Black Codes, by refusing to seat any member of Congress who had joined the Confederacy, and by strengthening the Union's military presence in the South. Radical Republicans so dominated Congress that they were able to impose their plan over Johnson's veto, the first time in history that Congress overrode the president on a consequential matter.

They went further, attempting to hamstring Johnson by placing restrictions on his office that were of questionable constitutionality. When Johnson violated one of these restrictions by firing the secretary of war—a member of Johnson's cabinet—without congressional authorization, he was impeached by the House—another first—and tried in the Senate, where he was acquitted by one vote in 1868.[5] His anguished tenure in office ended shortly thereafter. Republicans regained the White House with the election of President Ulysses S. Grant and did not relinquish it until 1885.

In 1876, the disputed election between Democrat Samuel Tilden and Republican Rutherford B. Hayes appeared to have put a Democrat in the White House for the first time since the start of Reconstruction. Tilden claimed an Electoral College majority, but results from several states were challenged by Republicans. With the election in doubt, a compromise was hammered out in which Hayes would be given the presidency in exchange for the withdrawal of Union troops from the South. This marked the end of Reconstruction and the start of a long period in which African Americans saw their civil rights taken away. As Reconstruction ended, the plight of African Americans faded as a political issue in the North. African American representation in Congress began to tail off.[6] Southern blacks were left with few viable avenues for the protection of their civil rights, despite the constitutional protections that had been granted a decade earlier.

From this point on, African Americans in the South faced decades of disenfranchisement and institutionalized segregation at the hands of whites who never accepted the terms of Reconstruction. With the Union army and northern Republicans out of the way,

Reconstruction: The period following the Civil War, from 1865 to 1877, during which Union troops occupied the South as states of the Confederacy were readmitted to the Union under conditions established in Washington.

Ku Klux Klan: The secret white supremacist society that terrorized and killed African Americans for decades following the Civil War.

Black Codes: An effort by white southerners immediately following the Civil War to restrict the civil rights of emancipated slaves. The codes were overturned by federal civil rights laws, only to become standard practice in the South following Reconstruction.

Jim Crow laws: Laws in place in the South through the middle portion of the twentieth century that legalized segregation in virtually every facet of life.

repressive measures took hold. Institutionalized segregation in the form of **Jim Crow laws** made discrimination a way of life in the South.

Jim Crow was a character from minstrel shows, performed by white entertainers who covered their faces in burnt cork and acted out demeaning stereotypes of African Americans, depicting them as childish and incompetent. By the Civil War, the Jim Crow character was an established part of American popular culture. The exact connection between the racist minstrel show character and the racist laws of the same name is a matter of historical dispute.[7]

Because you likely never experienced it, you may have trouble imagining just how total and repressive the Jim Crow laws were. Everything from the simplest everyday experiences like going to the park or using a public telephone, everything from birth to schooling to marriage to death was legally segregated. Table 13.1 should give you a sense of how this segregation permeated society and denied African Americans their basic civil rights. As you read the table, try to imagine being an African American subjected to Jim Crow laws. Ask yourself what your life would have been like and how you would have felt about yourself if you acquiesced to these laws. There would have been enormous pressures on you to conform, sometimes life-threatening pressures—and a tremendous loss of dignity for doing so. Can you even imagine how you might have behaved?

By the start of the twentieth century, legal segregation so pervaded the South that separate public facilities from restrooms to drinking fountains to public transportation waiting rooms were marked with "Colored Only" signs. As we know from Chapter 12, the Supreme Court had upheld this type of segregation in the 1896 case *Plessy v. Ferguson*. In some southern states, African Americans traveling by train were forced to sit in a separate "Jim Crow car." Interracial marriage was criminalized. Voting rights were taken away through high poll taxes, impossible literacy tests, and laws prohibiting grandchildren of slaves from voting. As a result of these barriers, the number of African Americans casting ballots in South Carolina and Georgia fell by half between 1880 and 1888.[8] Whatever thoughts African Americans may have had about standing up to these racist provisions were dispelled on the one hand through the debilitating effects of widespread illiteracy and poverty, and on the other hand by terrorist acts committed by white lynch mobs.[9]

Plessy v. Ferguson: The 1896 Supreme Court case that upheld racial segregation. It was reversed in 1954 in the case of *Brown v. Board of Education*.

Although it wasn't as institutionalized, overt, or brutal, color barriers existed nationwide. As industrialization transformed the country in the early twentieth century, manufacturing jobs prompted a mass migration of African Americans from the South to the North and Midwest. There, blacks met with a more subtle form of discrimination. They remained for the most part low-wage earners, confined to live in urban ghettos, often in poor or run-down housing. Job opportunities that held the promise of a better life were not forthcoming. Social attitudes in many cities were not much different than they had been in the South.

13.4a The Civil Rights Movement

The Supreme Court ruling in *Brown v. Board of Education* (1954) declaring segregated schools unconstitutional, which we discussed in Chapter 12, foreshadowed one and a half decades of activism on behalf of African American civil rights. It would culminate in the elimination of Jim Crow laws, the triumph of federal over state power, and full implementation of the Fourteenth Amendment one hundred years after its passage. As with any wrenching social change, the human cost was great, both in lives of civil rights activists lost to assassins and lives shattered by riots that decimated African American neighborhoods from Harlem in New York to Watts in Los Angeles.

It started innocuously enough. One year after the *Brown* decision, a forty-two-year-old seamstress named Rosa Parks boarded a bus in Montgomery, Alabama, and sat in the first row of what was called the "Colored" section at the back of

A bus station in Durham, North Carolina, in 1940[T2]

TABLE 13.1 Life under Jim Crow Laws[T3]

Subject	Restriction
Nurses	No person or corporation shall require any white female nurse to nurse in wards or rooms in hospitals, either public or private, in which Negro men are placed. (Alabama)
Pool and billiard rooms	It shall be unlawful for a Negro and a white person to play together or in company with each other at any game of pool or billiards. (Alabama)
Barbers	No colored barber shall serve as a barber (to) white women or girls. (Georgia)
Amateur baseball	It shall be unlawful for any amateur white baseball team to play baseball on any vacant lot or baseball diamond within two blocks of a playground devoted to the Negro race, and it shall be unlawful for any amateur colored baseball team to play baseball on any vacant lot or baseball diamond within two blocks of a playground devoted to the white race. (Georgia)
Burial	The officer in charge shall not bury, or allow to be buried, any colored persons upon ground set aside for the burial of white persons. (Georgia)
Textbooks	Books shall not be interchangeable between the white and colored schools, but shall continue to be used by the race first using them. (North Carolina)
Child custody	It shall be unlawful for any parent, relative, or other white person in this State, having the control or custody of any white child, by right of guardianship, natural or required, or otherwise, to dispose of, give, or surrender such white child permanently into the custody, control, maintenance, or support of a Negro. (South Carolina)
Buses	All passenger stations in this state operated by any motor transportation company shall have separate waiting rooms or space and separate ticket windows for the white and colored races. (Alabama)
Intermarriage	The marriage of a person of Caucasian blood with a Negro, Mongolian, Malay, or Hindu shall be null and void. (Arizona)
Parks	It shall be unlawful for colored people to frequent any park owned or maintained by the city for the benefit, use, and enjoyment of white persons . . . and unlawful for any white person to frequent any park owned or maintained by the city for use and benefit of colored persons. (Georgia)
Housing	Any person . . . who shall rent any part of any such building to a Negro person or a Negro family when such a building is already in whole or in part in occupancy by a white person or white family, or vice versa when the building is in occupancy by a Negro person or Negro family, shall be guilty of a misdemeanor and on conviction thereof shall be punished by a fine of not less than twenty-five ($25.00) nor more than one hundred ($100.00) dollars or be imprisoned not less than 10, or more than 60 days, or both such fine and imprisonment in the discretion of the court. (Louisiana)
Telephone booths	The Corporation Commission is hereby vested with power and authority to require telephone companies . . . to maintain separate booths for white and colored patrons when there is demand for such separate booths. That the Corporation Commission shall determine the necessity for said separate booths only upon complaint of the people in the town and vicinity to be served after due hearing as now provided by law in other complaints filed with the Corporation Commission. (Oklahoma)
Promotion of equality	Any person . . . who shall be guilty of printing, publishing, or circulating printed, typewritten, or written matter urging or presenting for public acceptance, or general information, arguments or suggestions in favor of social equality or of intermarriage between whites and Negroes, shall be guilty of a misdemeanor and subject to a fine not exceeding five hundred ($500.00) dollars or imprisonment not exceeding (6) months or both. (Mississippi)

the bus. Montgomery's law required that blacks pay their fare at the front of the bus, then leave the bus, reboard in the rear, and sit in the back. If a white patron boarded when the "White" section was full, black passengers seated in the front of the "Colored" section were required to give up their seats and move further back. This happened to Rosa Parks: When a white passenger boarded the crowded bus, the white bus driver insisted that she relinquish her seat as required by law. She refused and was arrested.

Rosa Parks had been locally active in the National Association for the Advancement of Colored Persons (NAACP) and knew the organization was looking for an opportunity to challenge Montgomery's segregation laws. She presented the organization with an ideal political symbol for the challenge: soft-spoken, demure, gainfully employed, happily married—in short, an utterly sympathetic figure to contrast the brutality of segregation. When Parks agreed to challenge the law, the NAACP immediately organized a boycott by African Americans of Montgomery buses, led by the minister of a local Baptist church, the Reverend Dr. Martin Luther King Jr. The boycott lasted for more than a year, until the Supreme Court ruled bus segregation unconstitutional in December 1956.[10] With that victory, the **civil rights movement** was born. A brief timeline emphasizing key events in the civil rights movement may be found in Table 13.2.

The actions undertaken by Dr. King and other prominent leaders on behalf of civil rights were nonviolent forms of **civil disobedience**, along the lines of Rosa Parks disobeying what she believed to be an illegitimate law. College students were heavily involved. The **Student Nonviolent Coordinating Committee (SNCC)** formed in 1960 and organized **"sit-ins"** at "Whites Only" lunch counters, where black students would simply sit down in seats reserved for whites, to focus national attention on segregated facilities. African Americans and sympathetic whites engaged in **"freedom rides"** throughout the South in 1961, where whites would take the seats at the back of the bus and use "Colored Only" facilities at highway rest stops, while African Americans sat up front and used "Whites Only" facilities.

These activities proved dangerous. Angry mobs attacked the demonstrators, often causing serious harm. Local authorities, sympathetic to the mobs, looked the other way, while local judicial officers sent protesters to prison. The actions of the demonstrators might have gone unnoticed if not for the fact that television, now a decade old and with national reach, was there to record the cruelty of segregation, broadcast it to the country, and help put pressure on the national government to act. Small victories began to pile up, like a 1961 order by the Kennedy Justice Department that outlawed discrimination on interstate buses that was issued in direct response to the treatment of the freedom riders.

As the stakes built, violence escalated. In 1963, civil rights leader Medgar Evers was assassinated. Dr. King organized peaceful demonstrations in Birmingham, Alabama, which were met with violence from angry white mobs. Four black girls attending Sunday school were murdered in the bombing of a Birmingham church. The first of many race

civil rights movement: The organized, largely nonviolent, and widely successful efforts of the 1950s and 1960s to bring about social change on behalf of African Americans in the South, whose civil rights were denied by a century-old system of Jim Crow laws.

civil disobedience: A peaceful means of protest whereby individuals draw attention to laws they consider unjust by disobeying them and being arrested for their actions.

Student Nonviolent Coordinating Committee (SNCC): The organization that involved college students in acts of civil disobedience to advance the cause of civil rights for African Americans.

sit-ins: A type of civil disobedience popular with civil rights protesters that involved African Americans peacefully sitting at "Whites Only" lunch counters, to focus attention on the injustice of segregation policies.

TABLE 13.2 Civil Rights Timeline[T4]

1954: School segregation ruled unconstitutional in *Brown v. Board of Education* Supreme Court decision.

1955: Dr. Martin Luther King, Jr. (below) leads boycotts against segregated transportation facilities after Rosa Parks (right) defies Montgomery, Alabama, law requiring African Americans to sit at the back of public buses; bus desegregation is eventually declared unconstitutional.

1957: President Eisenhower sends federal troops to Little Rock, Arkansas, after Governor Orval Faubus orders the Arkansas National Guard to block nine black students from integrating Central High School.

1960: African American students begin staging "sit-ins" at southern lunch counters that refuse to serve blacks.

1962: President Kennedy sends federal troops to the University of Mississippi to stop riots so that the first black students can attend; all military reserve units are integrated.

1963: Dr. Martin Luther King, Jr. delivers "I have a dream" speech to hundreds of thousands of civil rights protesters who have converged on Washington, D.C.

1964: Congress passes Civil Rights Act following a 75-day-long filibuster by southern senators; race riots erupt in Philadelphia and New York.

1965: Civil rights protesters march from Selma to Montgomery, Alabama, to demand voting rights; Congress passes the Voting Rights Act; race riots erupt in Los Angeles.

1968: Dr. Martin Luther King, Jr. is assassinated in Memphis, Tennessee.

riots began in African American sections of major cities, leaving urban centers in ruin for decades to come.

In 1964, SNCC, in conjunction with the NAACP and the largely white-run Congress of Racial Equality (CORE), organized "Freedom Summer," which centered on a voter registration drive in Mississippi to undermine the laws that prevented blacks from voting. White college students from the North were recruited to join southern blacks in a state where fewer than 7 percent of African Americans were registered to vote, the lowest percentage in the country. It drew an enormous amount of media attention, in part because the students were met with a violent response that resulted in over one thousand arrests, at least eighty beatings at the hands of white mobs or police officers, and three murders.[11]

Just as the civil rights movement was generating national sympathy, it was also beginning to fray. The political success of "Freedom Summer" masked racial tensions between black and white activists, as black workers were angered by what they felt was an attitude of superiority among white workers.[12] A radical faction of SNCC, angered at the violence they endured and what they felt was a slow rate of progress, rejected civil disobedience practices in exchange for confronting violence with violence. As the 1960s progressed, violence began to overtake peaceful resistance as a means for change. In 1968, the most visible advocate of peaceful social change, Dr. King, was assassinated in Memphis.

13.4b Legislative Success

Through it all, the civil rights movement realized stunning successes in the legislative arena that effectively ended segregation and stopped voting rights violations. Congress had considered—and failed to pass—civil rights legislation every year from 1945 to 1956. Then in 1957, in reaction to the changing climate of public opinion brought about by the civil rights movement, Congress passed the first civil rights bill in eighty years. The Civil Rights Act of 1957 was narrow in scope, establishing a federal Civil Rights Commission to hear complaints about voting irregularities. It was bolstered three years later by the Civil Rights Act of 1960, which prohibited states from destroying voter registration records.[13] In reality, complaints about voting irregularities took years to process and did not affect practices that disenfranchised African Americans, but these federal acts were valuable for what they presaged.

By 1964, political pressure largely generated by media coverage of the violent response to tactics of peaceful resistance served to bolster public support for legislation that only several years earlier would have been impossible to imagine moving through Congress. The fact that many Americans are naturally sympathetic to the notion of political equality was working to the long-term benefit of the protesters. A coalition of Republicans and non-southern Democrats fought an epic battle in the House and Senate on behalf of this legislation, culminating in a cloture vote that ended a two-month-long Senate filibuster. The result was the landmark **Civil Rights Act of 1964**, which:

- Outlawed discrimination in restaurants, hotels, motels, and all public accommodations involved in interstate commerce.

- Outlawed discrimination in hiring by businesses employing more than twenty-five people (serving as the basis for the affirmative action policies we'll talk about soon).

- Established the Equal Employment Opportunity Commission (EEOC) to hear complaints about workplace discrimination.

- Undermined practices designed to disenfranchise African Americans by mandating the equal application of voter registration requirements.

- Authorized withdrawing federal funds from institutions that practiced discriminatory policies.

- Authorized the attorney general to file suit when necessary to desegregate public schools.[14]

Although the law was not all encompassing—for instance, it still permitted discrimination in private clubs—it was sweeping in scope and represented a profound political

freedom rides: A type of civil disobedience popular with civil rights protesters, where mixed-race groups of bus passengers would ride through the South and disobey laws on racially segregated travel, often at the expense of submitting to mob violence.

Civil Rights Act of 1964: Landmark legislation arising from the civil rights movement that made racial discrimination a federal crime in the workplace and in public accommodations, while giving the federal government greater power to strengthen voting rights and desegregate public schools.

transformation in the area of civil rights. For the first time since Reconstruction, the federal government took an active role against discriminatory policies aimed at African Americans. A sympathetic Supreme Court upheld the legislation. Jim Crow could be heard in the distance, gasping for air.

Voting Rights Act of 1965: Landmark legislation arising from the civil rights movement that gave federal officials the power to oversee election practices in southern states where Jim Crow laws disenfranchised African American voters.

The following year, when Congress passed the **Voting Rights Act of 1965**, Jim Crow was effectively dead. By providing for direct federal intervention in state voting and registration procedures, the Voting Rights Act put an end to requirements that disenfranchised African Americans. Specifically, the law empowered the attorney general to send inspectors to supervise voter registration in states that required literacy tests and where fewer than 50 percent of qualified residents had registered or voted in 1964. By authorizing inspections instead of permitting voters with a complaint to file suit, as had been the case in previous civil rights legislation, the effects were immediate and dramatic.[15]

As with the Civil Rights Act of 1964, the success of the Voting Rights Act could be measured in the rapid changes it brought about. African American voter registration increased markedly. For the first time since Reconstruction, African Americans were returning to Congress and being elected to other offices, in the South and elsewhere. In 1966, Edward Brooke of Massachusetts became the first African American senator in eighty-five years. In 1967, Carl Stokes of Cleveland became the first African American mayor of a major U.S. city; six years later, when Maynard Jackson became the mayor of Atlanta, he became the first African American to lead a southern city.[16] In 1971, there were enough African Americans in the House of Representatives to establish the Congressional Black Caucus, which coordinates the legislative strategy of black members.[17] The first African American governor, Douglas Wilder, was elected in 1989 in Virginia, the state that once housed the capital of the Confederacy.[18] Nineteen years later, Barack Obama would carry the state of Virginia along with North Carolina and Florida on his way to the White House.

13.4c Affirmative Action

L.O. Identify the purpose and range of affirmative action policies.

Although Jim Crow laws have been buried for so long that you may not have been familiar with the term before encountering it in school, today's civil rights advocates charge that the legacy of Jim Crow lingers in unequal access by African Americans to high-quality education, high-paying jobs, and affordable housing. From this perspective, although the turbulence of the 1950s and 1960s is long behind us, Dr. King's dream of a color-blind America remains beyond our grasp. As unequal treatment of African Americans became less blatant than it was during the time of Jim Crow, and as the black civil rights agenda turned from advancing equality of opportunity to equality of outcome, American public opinion began to divide over the remedies to present-day injustices, making solutions to discriminatory practices such as **affirmative action** highly controversial. In Demystifying Government: Affirmative Action, you'll have an opportunity to read about affirmative action policies, and see what supporters and opponents say about them.

affirmative action: Federal policies requiring employers to address inequities in hiring and advancement if they appear to unfairly treat disadvantaged groups on the basis of race, religion, gender, national origin, sexual preference, physical disabilities, or Vietnam veteran status.

As racial attitudes evolved over time, some white conservatives expressed the position that discrimination was no longer the problem it once had been. In 2013, the Supreme Court overturned a key portion of the Voting Rights Act, permitting a number of largely southern states to implement or modify election laws without federal approval. Writing for the majority, Chief Justice John Roberts asserted that "our country has changed," and the federal government needed to adjust its laws to recognize "current conditions." Liberal Justice Ruth Bader Ginsberg, writing for the minority, called the decision a disservice to Dr. King's legacy.[19]

13.5 Civil Rights and Native Americans

L.O. Appreciate the discrimination faced by Native Americans during the centuries following the arrival of European settlers.

If the civil rights situation of African Americans is distinctive because they were the only immigrant group brought to North America involuntarily, the civil rights situation of Native Americans (see Figure 13.2) is unique because of their presence in North America prior to its colonization by European settlers. Before there were states or colonies, there were Native American tribes operating on their own governing principles with a well-

Affirmative Action

Affirmative action is a policy requiring employers to address racial, ethnic, or gender inequalities by ensuring equal opportunities for employment and advancement.[T5] It has been a matter of law since passage of the Civil Rights Act of 1964, which allowed the judiciary to battle discrimination by ordering "such affirmative action as may be appropriate." The following year, President Lyndon Johnson vastly expanded that mandate with an executive order requiring all employers who do business with the federal government to apply affirmative action principles.[T6]

Originally designed to address past discrimination against racial minority groups, affirmative action has been expanded over the years to include women, people with disabilities, gays, and Vietnam veterans. As affirmative action policies have grown to include more individuals, so have the methods of implementing them. Affirmative action law forbids artificial barriers to the hiring and advancement of people in the targeted groups, and if employers underutilize group members, they have to take steps to remedy the situation. Affirmative action policies range from relatively uncontroversial activities like minority recruitment to more explosive approaches like preferential hiring of underrepresented group members and targeted hiring of minority individuals.[T7]

All of these methods aim to address the same objective—correcting past discriminatory practices—but they cover the spectrum from offering equality of opportunity to historically disadvantaged groups (through recruitment procedures, for instance) to compensating for past inequalities with the promise of equal outcomes (preferential hiring). That's where affirmative action is most controversial—when group characteristics are placed ahead of individual talent and ability—because it conflicts with the long-standing American preference for favoring opportunity over outcomes.

The Supreme Court took up the controversy in the 1978 case *Regents of the University of California v. Bakke*. The University of California at Davis medical school denied admission to a white applicant while accepting less well-qualified minority applicants under a program that set aside a specific number of slots for members of traditionally disadvantaged groups. Bakke, the white student, claimed the policy itself was discriminatory and the Court agreed, backing away from unqualified support of affirmative action policies while upholding the constitutionality of using race as a factor (just not the primary factor) in college admissions.[T8]

Since the *Bakke* decision, the debate over affirmative action has simply grown more heated. In 2003, the Supreme Court revisited the issue in twin cases involving admissions procedures at the University of Michigan. In *Gratz v. Bollinger*, two white applicants rejected by the University of Michigan, despite having been deemed qualified for admission, sued the school, claiming its use of racial preferences in making admissions decisions violated the Fourteenth Amendment's equal protection clause.[T9] In *Grutter v. Bollinger*, a white applicant rejected by the University of Michigan law school filed a similar claim to the one made in the *Gratz* case, asserting that she had been turned aside because of an application process that treated race as a "predominant" factor in admissions.[T10]

The Court narrowly reaffirmed that race can be used as a criterion in admissions decisions in the interest of achieving diversity on campus, upholding the flexible procedures used by the law school, which considered race as one of a number of "soft" criteria for admission. However, it overturned the approach used by the university to admit undergraduates, which consisted of assigning a fixed number of points to minority group applicants. In 2016, the Court upheld the affirmative action policy used by the University of Texas for college admissions, contending that it was necessary for the university to achieve greater diversity.[T11]

Divisions in the Court reflect divisions in society. Although opponents of affirmative action may still claim a commitment to redressing racist and sexist policies of the past, that's not how it's always viewed by supporters. While supporters may argue that affirmative action is not about favoritism or quotas, that's not how opponents always see it.

established system of rights. When western political structures were superimposed on the territories inhabited by Native Americans, conflict erupted between two sets of values.

For centuries, the flashpoint for hostility and tension has been the lack of respect and recognition accorded the rights of Native Americans by the federal government. The most basic right that was abridged was tribal sovereignty, or the right of Native American tribes to self-government. Colonial settlers sharply limited tribal sovereignty so that it applied only to internal matters, subjugating tribal autonomy over land rights and affairs with other nations to the will of the colonists and later to the federal government. In many cases, settlers acquired land through treaties that left only hunting and fishing rights to native tribes, in exchange for a promise of protection by settlers that ultimately left

Regents of the University of California v. Bakke: The 1978 Supreme Court case that marked a reversal in unlimited support for affirmative action policies by backing the claim of discrimination by a white University of California medical school applicant who was denied admission in favor of less well-qualified minority applicants.

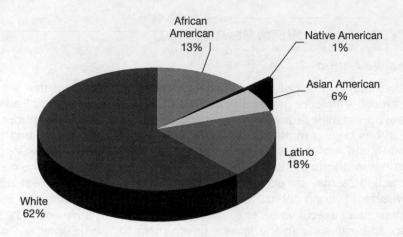

African American 13%

Native American 1%

Asian American 6%

Latino 18%

White 62%

In 2015, 1 of 100 Americans were of Native American heritage.

FIGURE 13.2 Native Americans in the Population[T12]

once-autonomous Native American nations as wards of the United States. Today, some members of existing tribes practice self-rule on lands set aside by the federal government and at the same time are subject to the laws and practices of the United States as American citizens.[20] That arrangement was generations in the making.

13.5a Early Policies: Containment and Relocation

The original policy of the American government toward native tribes was to contain them on undeveloped land. It was often implemented violently. In 1830, Congress passed the controversial **Indian Removal Act**, which called for relocating Native American tribes situated east of the Mississippi so that American expansion could continue unabated into that territory. Under the terms of the act, any Native Americans remaining on their land would be forced to leave their tribal nation to become citizens of the state in which they resided. Some moved willingly and some assimilated, although Native Americans who decided to remain sometimes found themselves cheated out of their land by white settlers.

Others resisted and were forced to move or go to war with the United States. Three Seminole wars were fought between 1817 and 1858 over the issue of relocation (fugitive slaves who had been given refuge by the Seminoles fought alongside them in the first two). Ultimately, the Seminoles were killed, driven out, or paid to leave.[21]

In 1836, the Cherokee were given two years to leave their homes in Georgia or face forced relocation. The Supreme Court, in the case of *Worcester v. Georgia* (1832), actually recognized the Cherokee as a sovereign nation, but President Jackson (as we previously learned in Section 12.3, "Judicial Review") had no regard for the decision and negotiated a removal treaty with a small faction of Cherokee, and then used it as the legal basis for evicting the entire tribe.

The 17,000 Cherokee who wished to remain in their homeland were compelled to leave at gunpoint by American troops as whites looted their belongings. On their forced march west, four thousand Cherokee men, women, and children died of illness and exposure along what became known to Native Americans as the **"Trail of Tears."**[22]

Many whites in the early nineteenth century felt that relocation would resolve territorial issues with Native Americans because they believed the United States would never expand beyond the Mississippi River. Once it did, the idea of separate nations was no longer viable, and national policy embraced reclaiming or dividing up reserved lands in the West and doing battle with Native American tribes.

13.5b Later Policies: "Civilizing" and Assimilating

In the 1890s, the government initiated an effort to "civilize" Native Americans as a means of incorporating them into white Christian society. Children were forced to attend boarding schools where their hair was cut short, they were given Anglo-American clothes, and

Indian Removal Act: Legislation passed in 1830 that led to the forced and sometimes violent transfer of Native American nations to areas west of the Mississippi River.

"Trail of Tears": A 1,000-mile forced march of Cherokee men, women, and children carried out in 1838 to satisfy a federal relocation policy.

they were required to speak English. This approach culminated in passage of the **Citizenship Act of 1924**, which made all Native Americans born on American soil citizens of the United States. Passage of the Citizenship Act gave Native Americans rights they lacked before, like the right to vote (a western concept, which not every state honored), but it was really a means of forcing assimilation, viewed by some Native Americans as another step toward undermining the sovereignty of native peoples.[23]

These efforts at assimilation largely failed. Generations of exploitation had left many Native Americans with deplorable living conditions. Poverty, malnourishment, and disease were rampant on reserved lands. In 1934, Congress tried to address this with the passage of the Indian Reorganization Act, which aimed at restoring traditional languages and practices in an effort to reverse the deleterious effects of forced relocation and forced assimilation.

Citizenship Act of 1924: An effort to assimilate Native Americans into white culture and society through the granting of American citizenship.

13.5c 1960s and 1970s Activism

By the late 1960s, a growing social awareness of civil rights issues gave rise to the "Red Power" movement: waves of activism designed to call attention to discrimination against Native Americans. In 1969, protesters landed on Alcatraz Island in San Francisco Bay and occupied it for nineteen months in a symbolic reclamation of lost native lands. In the decade that followed, activists occupied scores of other federal facilities, including a sit-in at Mount Rushmore, to bring attention to the political and social plight of Native Americans.[24] In 1973, armed members of the American Indian movement staged a seventy-one-day siege at Wounded Knee, South Dakota, the scene of a Sioux massacre eighty-three years earlier.

Native American civil rights activists successfully trained public attention on the long history of discriminatory practices that many white Americans would like to ignore because it is so uncomfortable to acknowledge. In some respects, their work brought about improvements in the status of Native American rights. For instance, while remaining subject to the jurisdiction of the United States government, the Indian Civil Rights Act of 1968 extended to tribal governing bodies the protections granted in the Bill of Rights. Courts upheld the continued legal force of century-old treaties, interpreting ambiguities in a way that favored Native American interests. In 1992, Colorado elected the first Native American to the U.S. Senate: Ben Nighthorse Campbell, who is also a chief of the northern Cheyenne tribe.[25]

During this period, the courts also began to recognize tribal sovereignty and the right of self-government on reserved lands,[26] including freedom from some state hunting and fishing regulations and special water rights.[27] Exemptions from state gaming regulations have in recent years provided an important (albeit controversial) source of revenue for over two hundred Native American tribes operating casinos and gambling ventures on reserved lands.[28]

Gambling has been an economic windfall for increasing numbers of Native American tribes, although it can hardly be considered a panacea for centuries of civil rights abuses. Poverty, unemployment, and alcoholism are still huge problems in many Native American communities, which bear little resemblance to the stable and thriving civilizations that Europeans encountered when they arrived in North America. Also, notwithstanding protests like Alcatraz and Wounded Knee that attract the national press, the concerns of Native Americans remain relatively low on the national civil rights agenda.

13.6 Civil Rights and Hispanic Americans

Hispanic Americans (the term used by the U.S. Census to describe individuals with roots in a Spanish-speaking country) and Latino Americans (more generally, individuals whose families hail from Latin America) are the largest minority group in the United States (see Figure 13.3). With origins from places as diverse as Mexico, Cuba, Puerto Rico, the Caribbean, and Central America, Hispanic Americans share a Spanish-speaking heritage even though the paths that brought them to the United States are quite varied. Figure 13.4 illustrates the diverse migration patterns of Latino groups in the United States. Mexican

L.O. Understand the history of Latinos in the United States as it relates to worker rights, education, and immigration issues.

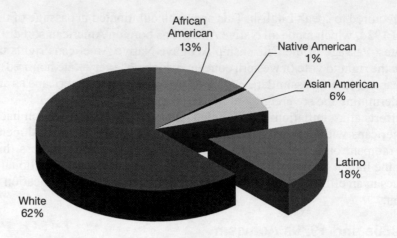

The largest minority group, Latinos constituted 17.6 percent of the American population in 2015.

FIGURE 13.3 Latinos in the Population[T13]

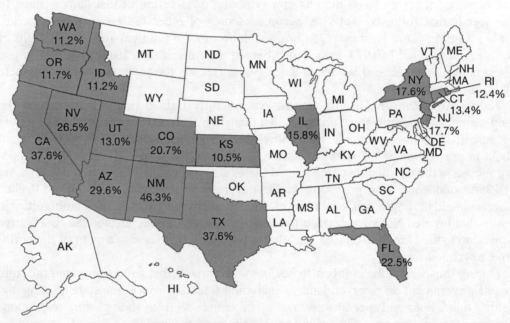

FIGURE 13.4 Where Latinos Have Settled[T14]

This map illustrates the diverse migration patterns of Latino groups in the United States. The shaded states have the largest Latino communities. The percentages shown indicate the percentage of Latinos in that state's population.

Americans, for instance, are most likely to have moved to the Southwest, notably California and Texas, and are likely to have come to the United States seeking economic opportunity. Cuban Americans are concentrated in southern Florida, where many arrived seeking political freedom following Fidel Castro's rise to power during the Cuban communist revolution of 1959. Large Puerto Rican communities may be found in the big cities of the Northeast, notably New York. Puerto Ricans hold U.S. citizenship because Puerto Rico is a self-governing commonwealth (it has an elected governor and legislature and its residents participate in federal programs like Social Security and welfare, but it is not represented in Congress or the Electoral College).

Latinos are also a diverse group economically and politically. Cuban Americans are more likely to be better educated and better off financially, and older Cuban Americans are more likely than other Latino groups to be Republicans. Many Mexican Americans are agricultural workers and, along with Puerto Ricans, experience a higher rate of poverty than the population as a whole.

13.6a Political Struggles and Victories

Although these differences point to a diversity of experiences among Latino groups, discrimination has been a widespread phenomenon. Many Hispanics are Caucasian, but dark skin, Spanish surnames, and a language difference have through the years been a source of discrimination in educational and work opportunities. Widespread unauthorized immigration by Mexican Americans is an ongoing source of harassment and discrimination toward Latino citizens by resentful Anglos living in areas with large Latino populations, particularly in states bordering Mexico, and was one of the prevalent themes of Donald Trump's presidential campaign. Parents of Latino schoolchildren have been confronted with demands for proof of U.S. citizenship by school officials, a form of discrimination that can dissuade them from enrolling their children in school.[29] In 2012, Arizona implemented a measure requiring law enforcement officials to check the residency status of anyone they suspected of being in the state illegally, a move opponents called racial profiling.

The general public first became aware of harassment against Latinos during the civil rights movements of the 1960s. The National Council of La Raza was established in 1968 as an advocacy group to reduce poverty and end discrimination against Latino groups.[30]

Agribusiness is vital to California's economy, and for years, vegetable and grape growers relied heavily on itinerant Mexican American labor, paying them dirt wages and forcing them to live in deplorable conditions. In 1965, typical Latino farm workers were paid ninety cents an hour and charged by their employers to live in shacks with no plumbing or cooking facilities. Child labor was commonplace. Dangerous conditions led to injury and death. The average life expectancy of a Latino farm laborer was forty-nine years.[31] Despite laws against these conditions, the plight of Latino agricultural workers did not register on the national political agenda.

This changed because of the work of Cesar Chavez, a former itinerant worker who painstakingly organized the first union for Latino laborers, the United Farm Workers (UFW). Inspired by the success of the African American civil rights movement, Chavez used nonviolent techniques like hunger strikes and boycotts to focus media attention on the working conditions of Mexican American agricultural workers and to put economic pressure on the businesses that exploited their labor. From the union's inception in 1962 until his death in 1993, Chavez effected social change by successfully raising levels of public awareness about how Latinos were being treated in order to force employers to enter into labor agreements with the union. At the height of the UFW's success between 1973 and 1975, millions of Americans participated in a boycott against Gallo wine for its continued use of nonunion labor.

Workplace discrimination against Latinos continues to be an issue, however. In 2003, the Mexican American Legal Defense and Education Fund and the Equal Employment Opportunity Commission filed suit against a Texas ductworks factory for segregating Mexican American workers into a department where the wages were less and the working conditions far more dangerous than in other departments. When the workers tried to strike, the company moved against them and attempted to have them fired, only to back off in the face of political pressure.

Recent years have brought some political milestones, notably the confirmation of Sonia Sotomayor to the Supreme Court. In 2002, both major parties nominated Latino gubernatorial candidates in New Mexico, with Democrat and former Clinton Energy Secretary Bill Richardson defeating Republican State Representative John Sanchez. Six years later, Richardson was a candidate for the Democratic presidential nomination, and he was followed in office by Republican Susana Martinez. In 2012, Texas voters elected Ted Cruz to the Senate, where he joins fellow Cuban American Senator Marco Rubio of Florida.

Republicans and Democrats recognize that by virtue of their rapidly growing numbers, Latinos have become an important political force. In 2008 and 2012, the Latino vote was instrumental in helping Barack Obama comfortably win states that had previously been reluctant to support a Democrat, including Colorado, Nevada, and Virginia. However, issues such as immigration that have great resonance in many Latino communities continue to be highly charged politically. After Mitt Romney lost Latino voters by a 3–1 margin in 2012, a number of Senate Republicans signed on to a comprehensive bipartisan immigration reform bill. However, House Republican leaders refused to consider the legislation because of resistance among some of their members to opening a pathway to citizenship for undocumented immigrants. Since that time, reform efforts have stalled, and in 2016, Donald Trump made building a wall along the Mexican border a cornerstone of his campaign.

13.6b Bilingual Education

Because language skills are critical to educational achievement, Hispanic Americans have faced roadblocks to advancement in cases where they speak little or no English. One approach to the language barrier is bilingual education, where classroom learning is conducted in English and Spanish. The rationale for bilingual education is that students who do not comprehend the language of instruction will quickly fall behind in the development of academic skills and are more likely to drop out of school, keeping them trapped in poverty or retarding the economic advancement that education makes possible.

Legally, bilingual education is a permissible alternative when English is a second language because the courts have determined that the circumstances fall under the equal protection umbrella. In the Supreme Court case *Lau v. Nichols* (1974), school districts were ordered to accommodate the needs of non-English-speaking students in order to assure equal access to educational opportunities. This permitted bilingual teaching, but it did not mandate it.[32]

Bilingual education is a controversial solution, even among Latinos. Some oppose it because they fear it will have the opposite effect to what advocates contend: that students schooled in Spanish and English will simply not learn English the way they would in an all-English environment. Some Anglos oppose it for the same reason, although often in the belief that Spanish-speaking Americans should learn the dominant language of the United States on their own and without what seems like special consideration. This gives the debate over bilingual education a sharp edge because it plays on the emotional issues of assimilation and cultural heritage.

13.7 Civil Rights and Asian Americans

As we saw in Chapter 4, Asian Americans are the fastest-growing minority group in the United States (see Figure 13.5). Particularly in the states of the Pacific Rim, the number of Americans of Japanese, Chinese, Vietnamese, and Filipino heritage, among others, has been growing. In 2015, 14.7 percent of California's population was of Asian origin, as was 8.4 percent of the population of the state of Washington (in Hawaii, which as a chain of Pacific islands has always had a large population of Asian Americans, the figure was 37.3 percent).[33] Asian Americans, many of whom have high socioeconomic status and are politically active, have been able to exercise influence in these regions. When Gary Locke was elected governor of the state of Washington in 1996, he became the first Chinese American governor and the only governor of Asian descent in the United States.

Still, Asian Americans have faced a long history of discrimination in housing, employment, and education at the hands of Caucasians. The most notorious incident was the forced internment of Americans of Japanese descent into "relocation camps" around the country during World War II. The official rationale for rounding up American citizens who showed no loyalty to Japan was to defend against Japanese spying, which was widely feared by American military leaders and ordinary citizens. To Asian Americans, forced relocation was a racist policy. The United States was also at war with Germany and Italy, but American citizens with these European origins were not targeted for removal.

The action appeared to violate the equal protection of Japanese Americans because it was based on a racial classification. In fact, the Supreme Court has been fairly consistent about striking down laws based on group categories as violations of the civil rights of the group singled out for differential treatment. This case was the exception, however.

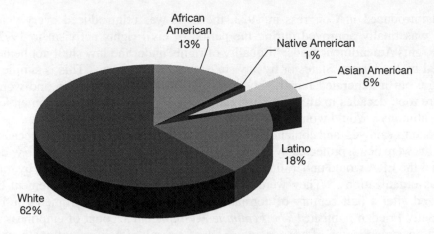

African American 13%

Native American 1%

Asian American 6%

Latino 18%

White 62%

The fastest-growing minority group, Asian Americans constituted 5.6 percent of the American population in 2015, up from 3.7 percent in 2000.

FIGURE 13.5 Asian Americans in the Population[T15]

In *Korematsu v. United States* (1944), the Court held that the "military urgency" of the situation justified permitting Congress and the president to use their war powers to justify the relocation.[34] Essentially, because the nation was at war, security arguments bested equal protection arguments. Today, many Americans look back at the government's policy toward Japanese Americans during World War II and regard it as one of the more shameful moments in the nation's history. In 1993, President Clinton formally apologized and offered reparations to internment victims.

13.8 Gender Issues

Imagine that you didn't have the right to vote. You owned some property, but once you got married, control over that property shifted to your husband. If you were fortunate enough to hold a job and earn a salary, chances are it was at a fraction of the pay that a man would earn, and your husband would control that income, too. The larger society believed that you did not have the capability or the right to engage in meaningful work outside the home, and that the proper (or divinely directed) order of things required that you have the protection and guidance of a man, who in turn controlled every significant aspect of your life.

Woman faced these circumstances well into the nineteenth century. Although women were afforded more rights and social standing than slaves, there were enough parallels between the relationship of slave to master and woman to man that it may not be surprising that the original women's rights movement was born of the antislavery movement. When the Civil War ended and the Fifteenth Amendment extended voting rights to freed slaves but not to women, a separate women's rights movement emerged. Through writing, speaking, petitioning, and tireless organizational work, Susan B. Anthony was instrumental in convincing New York State to extend property rights to married women in 1860. In 1869, abolitionists Elizabeth Cady Stanton and Lucretia Mott formed the National Woman Suffrage Association. The right to vote, however, was not extended to women nationwide until the Nineteenth Amendment was adopted in 1920.

L.O. Recognize the work of women's rights advocates in establishing voting rights, attempting to pass the Equal Rights Amendment, and promoting policies on sexual harassment and workplace rights.

13.8a The Equal Rights Amendment

Securing voting rights did not translate into equal rights for women, who faced social and legal obstacles to full equality under the law. Women's rights advocates turned their attention to full constitutional protection for women's civil rights by attempting to win passage of an **Equal Rights Amendment (ERA)**. In so doing, women's rights advocates shifted their agenda from political to social and economic equality, introducing a new degree of controversy as their objectives moved from equal opportunity to equal outcomes.

Equal Rights Amendment (ERA): A proposed constitutional amendment assuring equal rights for women that was first introduced in Congress in 1923, approved by Congress in 1972, and fell three states short of ratification in 1982.

First introduced in Congress in 1923, the ERA was reintroduced every year since, until it was finally approved during the period of civil rights activism in 1972.[35] The Equal Rights Amendment reads: "Equality of rights under the law shall not be denied or abridged by the United States or by any state on account of sex." This is simple enough language, but it generated remarkably stiff opposition from both men and women and therefore took decades to attract mainstream support. Would divorced women lose their right to alimony? Would women be sent into military combat?

Opponents said yes, and contended that the amendment was unnecessary because women's rights were being protected by favorable court decisions. They tapped into widely held fears that the ERA would undermine family structures, a position advocated by traditional religious organizations.[36] They were opposed by a women's rights movement that was revitalized after a half century of dormancy following passage of women's suffrage. In 1963, Betty Friedan published *The Feminine Mystique*, an account of emptiness and dissatisfaction some women of her generation felt as a result of being emotionally and financially dependent on men. The book caused an about-face in mainstream thinking about traditional values and women's roles at a time when civil rights activism was on the rise. In 1966, the **National Organization for Women (NOW)** was formed to advocate for women's equality and became an influential force for passage of the Equal Rights Amendment.

National Organization for Women (NOW): The largest women's rights organization in the United States, which has been an active force for advancing social and economic equality for women.

Congress gave the ERA a seven-year window for ratification and extended it in 1979 by three years. During that period, the political climate changed dramatically. Ronald Reagan was elected president on a platform that opposed the ERA, and opposition lobbying efforts had taken hold in the few states that had not ratified the amendment, many of which were in the culturally traditional South. When 1982 ended, the ERA was three states short of the three-quarters necessary for ratification. Proponents have tried to keep it alive by introducing it in states that failed to ratify, prepared to challenge the time limit imposed by Congress should three of them sign on, but they have faced an uphill battle in a conservative political climate.

That said, NOW has a long record of successful activism. It has been behind legal changes protecting women from sexual harassment and discrimination, encouraged unprecedented numbers of female candidates to seek public office, strived to improve conditions for women in the workplace, and promoted equal opportunity for women and men in campus athletics and education (see Demystifying Government: Universities and Title IX).

DEMYSTIFYING GOVERNMENT

Universities and Title IX

The federal government has taken action in matters of sex discrimination on campus. Title IX of the Education Amendments of 1972 (commonly referred to simply as "Title IX") prohibits gender discrimination in education programs receiving federal assistance. Because most colleges and universities receive federal assistance, the language of Title IX effectively makes sexual harassment on campus a federal matter. The same is true of most public school districts. Title IX requires that school officials take action when sexual harassment is severe or ongoing.

Perhaps the most publicized influence of Title IX has been on women's college athletics because it requires colleges and school districts accepting federal funds to provide equal opportunities in sports. The Department of Education has interpreted this provision to mean that the percentage of female athletes at colleges and universities should reflect the percentage of female undergraduates, and that male and female athletics should receive equal funding.[T16]

This interpretation has been controversial and difficult for some universities to implement. Football programs are expensive to run and often provide schools that support them with a large share of the income generated by athletics. With no female counterpart to football, college administrators with football programs face a dilemma of how to control the costs of a profitable venture in order to equalize expenditures with women's athletics. At the same time, Title IX has improved the situation of female student athletes while helping to put some women's sports programs on the map. The growing popularity of women's basketball and gymnastics, for instance, can be attributed in part to decisions universities made to invest in these programs as a result of Title IX regulations.

13.8b Sexual Violence and Harassment

One NOW-affiliated activity with which you may be familiar is the Take Back the Night march. These rallies are held periodically across the country and on many college campuses to draw attention to the issue of violence against women.[37] The issue has also been the subject of legislative action. The 1994 Violence Against Women Act provides for federal penalties for sex crimes and for federal assistance to reduce violent crimes against women and to curb domestic violence.

The political system has also responded to long-standing complaints by women about sexual harassment in the workplace. The U.S. Supreme Court has determined workplace harassment to be a form of discrimination and, as such, it is prohibited by the Civil Rights Act of 1964. It has established that a "hostile and abusive" work environment should be the standard for determining whether sexual harassment exists. Although this standard is to be applied with reason, so that any sensible observer would perceive that a hostile environment exists, determining the presence of sexual harassment in the workplace has been a complex matter subject at times to widely varying perceptions of what qualifies as abusive. This has caused the issue to be hotly debated, and has precipitated an ongoing and evolving public dialogue about how coworkers and subordinates should be treated in the workplace.

13.8c Workplace Rights

Harassment on the job is one of a cluster of work-related women's rights issues to occupy a central place on the recent political agenda. Although the 1964 Civil Rights Act forbids gender discrimination in hiring, firing, and promoting workers, practical barriers to this objective still exist. Under the law, companies have to demonstrate a compelling business reason for providing disparate treatment to men and women. This means pregnancy, childbirth, and marital status are not supposed to be reasons for making employment or promotion decisions.[38]

In practice, obstacles to women's employment and advancement abound. It's not uncommon for women to feel they have to trade-off career opportunities if they want to have a family, or for female employees to comment to each other that their company has an unspoken "mommy track" with fewer opportunities for advancement flowing to women who choose family before career. Companies with a preponderance of men in high-level managerial positions are evidence for those who feel there is an organizational "glass ceiling" above which few women can rise. Typically, conditions such as these exist informally, as part of an amorphous "corporate culture" that favors the advancement of men. In such an atmosphere, unequal treatment may be apparent to those who feel disadvantaged by it, but difficult to rectify through the legal system.

Family and medical leave is one place where legislative advances have worked to protect the employment concerns of women who need to devote attention to seriously ill loved ones or who need time away from work after a pregnancy. Under the **Family and Medical Leave Act of 1993**, eligible employees at companies with more than fifty people have the right to up to twelve weeks of unpaid leave in any calendar year to care for a newborn child, or a spouse, child, or parent with a serious medical condition. Under the terms of the act, a woman who leaves her job for three months after giving birth is assured that her job will still be there when she comes back.[39] In 2009, it was expanded to provide leave for relatives of military personnel caring for loved ones who were injured while on active duty.

Family and Medical Leave Act of 1993: Legislation designed to permit women working in medium or large companies up to twelve weeks of unpaid leave following childbirth. It also permits employees to take unpaid leave time to care for an ailing relative.

Laws requiring equal pay for equal work have been on the books since the Equal Pay Act of 1963, but intervening factors like differences in seniority between a male and female employee can confound attempts to demonstrate that two circumstances are comparable. Despite the law, women continue to earn on average less than men, although the gap is narrowing.[40] In 2009, President Obama signed the Lilly Ledbetter Fair Pay Act, which makes it easier for women to file pay discrimination suits. The act is named after a former supervisor at the Goodyear Tire Company who won a pay discrimination verdict against the company only to have it overturned by the Supreme Court because the statute of limitations for filing the suit had expired.[41] Under the terms of the law, every new discriminatory paycheck is regarded as a separate act of discrimination, and a 180-day window for filing suit is permitted from the time of the last paycheck.

Related to the issue of equal pay is the politically charged matter of comparable worth, which deals with matters of pay equity for comparable labor performed by men and women in different but comparable jobs. This shouldn't be confused with equal pay for performing the same job. Instead, **comparable worth** deals with disparities between jobs held mostly by women that pay less than jobs held mostly by men, despite the fact that the two jobs require comparable skills and training. This makes it a civil rights issue.[42] In Washington State, for instance, the job of legal secretary is considered to require a comparable level of skill and training to the job of heavy equipment operator. Legal secretaries are overwhelmingly female. Heavy equipment operators are overwhelmingly male. If legal secretaries earn less than heavy equipment operators, there's an issue of comparable worth.[43]

The controversy over comparable worth derives partly from differences in how people interpret the evidence of pay disparities and partly from value differences. Comparable-worth advocates point to persistent gaps in the pay of "female" and "male" occupations. Opponents cite data that suggest negligible or nonexistent differences between pay in "female" and "male" jobs by considering intervening factors, such as the fact that men average more hours annually on the job than women.[44] The question of how to determine comparability remains open for debate.

13.9 People with Disabilities

L.O. Appreciate the Americans with Disabilities Act as civil rights legislation.

Try for a moment to envision what a staircase looks like to someone in a wheelchair, or what a cell phone sounds like to someone who is hearing impaired. For years, most of us were unaware of the obstacles posed by ordinary objects to people with disabilities, and were largely oblivious to the discriminatory treatment that impaired individuals faced in the workplace or in navigating public and private buildings. In fact, the Civil Rights Act of 1964 did not cover people with disabilities.

Over time, lobbying efforts on behalf of disabled individuals helped to bring the circumstances faced by people with disabilities to the forefront of the national agenda, and in 1990 Congress passed the landmark **Americans with Disabilities Act**. The key provisions of the Act:

comparable worth: A manner of determining pay equity by equalizing pay between jobs held mostly by women that demand comparable training and labor to jobs held mostly by men.

Americans with Disabilities Act: The landmark 1990 legislation extending equal protection in the workplace and in public accommodations to people with physical and mental disabilities.

- Provide civil rights protection to persons with disabilities on a par with existing protections against discrimination on the basis of race, color, religion, national origin, and gender.

- Prohibit job discrimination against persons with disabilities, including discrimination in hiring, firing, compensating, and promoting disabled individuals who can perform essential job functions. Employers are required to make "reasonable accommodations" to the work environment to accommodate the needs of disabled individuals, provided that such changes do not impose "undue hardship" on the employer's business.

- Mandate all state and local government agencies to provide disabled individuals with equal access to programs and activities, and make public buildings readily accessible to disabled individuals.

- Require equal access to public accommodations, such as restaurants, hotels, theaters, stores, doctor's offices, parks, and private schools. Individuals operating such facilities are instructed to modify them for use by disabled individuals, provided that making such modifications does not present the owner with an "undue burden."[45]

The Americans with Disabilities Act is sweeping in scope, covering a wide range of physical and psychological conditions. These conditions include people with impairments that limit major life activities, such as walking, hearing, seeing, and breathing, as well as ailments such as epilepsy, HIV infection, and AIDS. Cancer survivors are protected against discrimination resulting from their medical history, as are people with a history of mental illness. People with learning disabilities are covered by the Act, as are recovering alcoholics. Close relatives of people with disabilities are included, so that the spouse of someone with a disability cannot be denied employment out of the concern that he or she might have to spend large quantities of time caring for a partner instead of working.[46]

If the Americans with Disabilities Act is sweeping, so is it vague, and this has made it controversial. Although the Act specifically excludes protection to people with short-term ailments like the flu or a broken leg, there's a large gray area between people who obviously are disabled and people who obviously are not, and this has generated controversy about how broadly to implement the act.

Controversy can be particularly acute when it comes to people with psychological conditions. Should the law cover people with Attention Deficit Disorder (ADD), for instance, who have trouble focusing on their job? The law is broad enough to cover this condition. Supporters say this is appropriate, and that psychological conditions should be afforded the same protection as physical conditions. Opponents contend that conditions like ADD are too frequently diagnosed, and that covering them dilutes the purpose of extending equal protection to people who in their view are obviously disabled.

The Americans with Disabilities Act is equally vague about remedies. At what point does a retail store begin to realize an "undue burden" as it attempts to accommodate people with disabilities? Might an employer have to permit flexible work schedules, modify office equipment, or hire an interpreter to protect disabled employees against workplace discrimination? The Act says yes: Any of these could be an appropriate remedy to discrimination and is considered to be a "reasonable accommodation." Employers who have to pay the bill may experience it differently.

13.10 LGBT Rights

As we mentioned in Chapter 12, attitudes toward lesbian, gay, bisexual, and transgender (LGBT) individuals have evolved over the past two decades, lending cultural support to the Supreme Court's narrow 2016 ruling in *Obergefell vs. Hodges* legalizing same-sex marriage nationwide. Nonetheless, the issue of homosexuality remains emotionally charged for many Americans. Homophobia is widespread in our culture, leading some people to fear or despise gay men and women. Some believe homosexuality is an abomination against God, whereas others see it as an abnormality of nature. Sometimes these attitudes provide the basis for discrimination against gays, who face covert and direct obstacles in every walk of life.

L.O. Place the contemporary debate over gay marriage in the context of previous civil rights struggles.

At the same time, even conservative estimates suggest that homosexuality is fairly prevalent in our society, and is not bounded by socioeconomic status, race, religion, or gender. The exact percentage of LGBT Americans is impossible to know because some keep their sexual orientation a secret to protect against discrimination and social reprisals. Others, however, have mobilized and organized in an effort to generate public attention that can translate into political action. Same-sex parenting and discrimination against LGBT individuals in public schools, employment, and housing remain prominent civil rights issues, as does the use of public restrooms by transgender inviduals.[47]

For a sense of how LGBT rights have evolved in the political process, consider the 1993 "Don't Ask, Don't Tell" policy, regarded as significant at the time for its challenge to a military culture that considered homosexuality at odds with service. In keeping with the emotionally charged nature of the issue, this policy was born of great controversy and protest. Fashioned as a compromise between President Clinton, who wanted to end discrimination based on sexual orientation, and military leaders operating in a culture where feelings about homosexuality were strong and at times hostile, "Don't Ask, Don't Tell" precluded military officials from asking service members to reveal their sexual orientation. Essentially, the policy said that gay or lesbian service members who kept their homosexuality private would not be asked about it or discharged because of it by their commanding officers. But "Don't Ask, Don't Tell" fell short of the equal rights standard, and as attitudes toward LGBT individuals evolved, so did attitudes toward the policy. President Obama promised to sign legislation to end "Don't Ask, Don't Tell" during the 2008 campaign, permitting gays and lesbians to serve openly, which he did in late 2010.

13.11 Senior Citizen Rights

Donald Trump was elected president in 2016 at the age of seventy. Ronald Reagan was elected president in 1980 at the age of sixty-nine. John McCain was the Republican presidential nominee at the age of seventy-two. John Glenn, the first American to orbit the earth in 1962, joined the crew of the Space Shuttle Discovery thirty-six years later—at age seventy-seven. Americans are living longer—demographically, people over eighty are the fastest-growing group—and as baby boomers begin to get on in years, the generation weaned on the civil rights movement could be expected to turn its attention and political clout to the rights of seniors.

Age Discrimination in Employment Act: The 1967 law that made it illegal for employers to discriminate against people over age forty in hiring, firing, and promotion decisions.

Age discrimination in its most widespread form occurs in the workplace, where employers are sometimes reluctant to hire older people. This type of discrimination has been illegal since the passage of the **Age Discrimination in Employment Act of 1967**, which makes it a crime to discriminate against people over forty in hiring, firing, and promotion decisions. Additionally, job notices cannot specify age limits or preferences, and benefits cannot legally be withheld from older employees.[48] Originally, these protections were extended to workers until they reached retirement at age sixty-five. As longevity increased, the mandatory retirement age was raised to seventy in 1978, and eliminated entirely in 1986.

It's not too difficult to expect that as people continue to live and work longer, civil rights for seniors will continue to emerge as an important political issue. In a time that has witnessed an expansion of the personal rights agenda, with groups not previously recognized as disadvantaged speaking out for equal rights, it is easy to imagine a growing, energetic movement supporting the rights of senior citizens.

Chapter Review

Define civil rights, and explain the importance of the equal protection clause of the Fourteenth Amendment.

Civil rights policies are designed to ensure that the law treats everyone equally, regardless of differences in race, gender, ethnic background, or anything people might be inclined to discriminate against. The key to civil rights in the United States is the equal protection clause of the Fourteenth Amendment, which says "No state shall . . . deny to any person within its jurisdiction the equal protection of the laws." The intent of the equal protection clause is that all laws should be applied evenly and without prejudice to all citizens.

Express familiarity with the civil rights struggle of African Americans—from Reconstruction to Jim Crow laws to the civil rights movement of the 1950s and 1960s.

When African Americans were granted citizenship following the Civil War, southern states used Black Codes and physical intimidation to deny former slaves their civil rights, even as those states were being reconstructed into the union. Until the 1950s, Jim Crow laws made segregation a way of life in the South. Then the civil rights movement drew national attention to segregation's abuses. A long period of civil disobedience, which was often met

with violence, culminated in landmark federal civil rights legislation, notably the Civil Rights Act of 1964 and the Voting Rights Act of 1965.

Identify the purpose and range of affirmative action policies.

Since the 1960s, affirmative action programs have been the primary way to address inequalities left from the long history of discriminatory practices against African Americans and other historically disadvantaged minority groups. Under the law, affirmative action requires that there be no artificial barriers to the hiring and advancement of people in groups that have been targets of past discrimination, and that if employers underutilize group members, they have to take steps to remedy the situation. In practice, affirmative action policies can range from minority recruitment to preferential hiring of underrepresented group members and targeted hiring of minority individuals.

Appreciate the discrimination faced by Native Americans during the centuries following the arrival of European settlers.

Native Americans have suffered discriminatory treatment since the arrival of European settlers in North America.

Colonists sharply limited Native American tribal sovereignty so that it applied only to internal matters, subjugating tribal autonomy over land rights and affairs with other nations to the will of the settlers and later to the federal government. For centuries, the federal government tried to subdue Native Americans by alternately containing them on reservations, relocating them to land that settlers hadn't developed, and westernizing them in an effort to get them to assimilate into American culture.

Understand the history of Latinos in the United States as it relates to worker rights, education, and immigration issues.

Latino groups have also faced discrimination, notably in education and the workplace. Mexican American farm laborers faced deplorable conditions, leading to the rise of the United Farm Workers Union under Cesar Chavez. Additionally, widespread illegal immigration by Mexican Americans is an ongoing source of harassment and discrimination toward Latino citizens by resentful Anglos living in areas with large Hispanic American populations. Parents of Latino schoolchildren have been confronted with demands for proof of U.S. citizenship by school officials, a form of discrimination that can dissuade them from enrolling their children in school.

Recognize the work of women's rights advocates in establishing voting rights, attempting to pass the Equal Rights Amendment, and promoting policies on sexual harassment and workplace rights.

At the dawn of the republic, women faced a male-dominated society that felt they were not capable of making decisions for themselves—an attitude manifested in laws restricting married women from owning property or managing finances. These restrictions began to come down in the mid-nineteenth century because of the work of activists like Susan B. Anthony and Elizabeth Cady Stanton. By 1920, women won the right to vote. A second wave of activism in the 1960s led to the establishment of the National Organization for Women, which works to end sexual violence and harassment, promote gender equality in the workplace and on campus, and advance the cause of women in politics.

A number of other minority groups face or have faced violations of equal protection. Japanese Americans were moved to detention centers during World War II without evidence that they posed a national security risk.

Appreciate the Americans with Disabilities Act as civil rights legislation.

Disabled individuals face discrimination in the workplace, although the Americans with Disabilities Act makes such discrimination illegal and attempts to eliminate barriers to navigating public accommodations.

Place the contemporary debate over gay marriage in the context of previous civil rights struggles.

Widespread homophobia is the source of discrimination against gays and lesbians, who face housing and workplace discrimination. Senior citizens may face employers who do not want to hire them because of their age, an act that is illegal under the Age Discrimination in Employment Act, which makes it a crime to discriminate against people over forty in hiring, firing, and promotion decisions.

Key Terms

affirmative action Federal policies requiring employers to address inequities in hiring and advancement if they appear to unfairly treat disadvantaged groups on the basis of race, religion, gender, national origin, sexual preference, physical disabilities, or Vietnam veteran status. (p. 408)

Age Discrimination in Employment Act The 1967 law that made it illegal for employers to discriminate against people over age forty in hiring, firing, and promotion decisions. (p. 420)

Americans with Disabilities Act The landmark 1990 legislation extending equal protection in the workplace and in public accommodations to people with physical and mental disabilities. (p. 418)

Black Codes An effort by white southerners immediately following the Civil War to restrict the civil rights of emancipated slaves. The codes were overturned by federal civil rights laws, only to become standard practice in the South following Reconstruction. (p. 403)

Citizenship Act of 1924 An effort to assimilate Native Americans into white culture and society through the granting of American citizenship. (p. 411)

civil disobedience A peaceful means of protest whereby individuals draw attention to laws they consider unjust by disobeying them and being arrested for their actions. (p. 406)

civil rights The promise of equal treatment under the law, regardless of one's race, gender, ethnic group affiliation, sexual preference, or age. (p. 400)

Civil Rights Act of 1964 Landmark legislation arising from the civil rights movement that made racial discrimination a federal crime in the workplace and in public accommodations, while giving the federal government greater power to strengthen voting rights and desegregate public schools. (p. 407)

civil rights movement The organized, largely nonviolent, and widely successful efforts of the 1950s and 1960s to bring about social change on behalf of African Americans in the South, whose civil rights were denied by a century-old system of Jim Crow laws. (p. 406)

comparable worth A manner of determining pay equity by equalizing pay between jobs held mostly by women that demand comparable training and labor to jobs held mostly by men. (p. 418)

Dred Scott v. Sanford The 1857 Supreme Court case that legalized slavery nationwide, while holding that people of color had no rights or protection under the Constitution. The ruling hastened the Civil War; it was subsequently overturned by constitutional amendment. (p. 402)

economic equality A form of equality of outcome that values using government policy to minimize the economic disparities found in society (p. 401)

equal protection clause The constitutional restriction against state laws that discriminate, as stated in the Fourteenth Amendment. The equal protection clause served as the legal basis for eliminating laws that permitted racial discrimination. (p. 401)

Equal Rights Amendment (ERA) A proposed constitutional amendment assuring equal rights for women that was first introduced in Congress in 1923, approved by Congress in 1972, and fell three states short of ratification in 1982. (p. 415)

equality of opportunity One of several ways of understanding equality, this way values giving people comparable advantages for succeeding in life, regardless of the unequal outcomes that may result. (p. 401)

equality of outcome One of several ways of understanding equality, this way values leveling the social and economic inequities among people, rather than attempting to give people comparable advantages for succeeding in life. (p. 401)

Family and Medical Leave Act of 1993 Legislation designed to permit women working in medium or large companies up to twelve weeks of unpaid leave following childbirth. It also permits employees to take unpaid leave time to care for an ailing relative. (p. 417)

federalism The division of power between a sovereign federal government and sovereign state governments, which provides that some functions will be performed by the national government, some by the state governments, and some by both the national and state governments. As a feature designed to limit the strength of government, federalism works to decentralize power by creating dual levels of authority. (p. 402)

freedom rides A type of civil disobedience popular with civil rights protesters, where mixed-race groups of bus passengers would ride through the South and disobey laws on racially segregated travel, often at the expense of submitting to mob violence. (p. 406)

Indian Removal Act Legislation passed in 1830 that led to the forced and sometimes violent transfer of Native American nations to areas west of the Mississippi River. (p. 410)

Jim Crow laws Laws in place in the South through the middle portion of the twentieth century that legalized segregation in virtually every facet of life. (p. 404)

Ku Klux Klan The secret white supremacist society that terrorized and killed African Americans for decades following the Civil War. (p. 402)

National Organization for Women (NOW) The largest women's rights organization in the United States, which has been an active force for advancing social and economic equality for women. (p. 416)

Plessy v. Ferguson The 1896 Supreme Court case that upheld racial segregation. It was reversed in 1954 in the case of *Brown v. Board of Education*. (p. 404)

political equality Establishing political and legal rights on the basis of the individual, so that everyone has the same right to vote and is equal under the law. An alternative would be to grant political rights to elite individuals based on wealth or social standing. (p. 401)

Reconstruction The period following the Civil War, from 1865 to 1877, during which Union troops occupied the South as states of the Confederacy were readmitted to the Union under conditions established in Washington. (p. 402)

Regents of the University of California v. Bakke The 1978 Supreme Court case that marked a reversal in unlimited support for affirmative action policies by backing the claim of discrimination by a white University of California medical school applicant who was denied admission in favor of less well-qualified minority applicants. (p. 409)

sit-ins A type of civil disobedience popular with civil rights protesters that involved African Americans peacefully sitting at "Whites Only" lunch counters, to focus attention on the injustice of segregation policies. (p. 406)

social equality A form of equality of outcome that values using government policy to minimize social class distinctions found in society. (p. 401)

Student Nonviolent Coordinating Committee (SNCC) The organization that involved college students in acts of civil disobedience to advance the cause of civil rights for African Americans. (p. 406)

"Trail of Tears" A 1,000-mile forced march of Cherokee men, women, and children carried out in 1838 to satisfy a federal relocation policy. (p. 410)

Voting Rights Act of 1965 Landmark legislation arising from the civil rights movement that gave federal officials the power to oversee election practices in southern states where Jim Crow laws disenfranchised African American voters. (p. 408)

Resources

You might be interested in examining some of what the following authors have said about the topics we've been discussing:

On Affirmative Action

Lawrence, Charles R. III, and Mari J. Matsuda. *We Won't Go Back: Making the Case for Affirmative Action.* Boston, MA: Houghton Mifflin, 1997.

Thomasson, Richard F., Faye J. Crosby, and Sharon D. Herzberger. *Affirmative Action: The Pros and Cons of Policy and Practice.* Lanham, MD: Rowman and Littlefield, 2001.

On Comparable Worth

England, Paula. *Comparable Worth: Theories and Evidence.* New York: Aldine de Gruyter, 1992.

Notes

1 For more details, see http://afroamhistory.about.com/library/weekly/aa121900a.htm.

2 See CNN Interactive, "The Civil Rights Movement," at http://www.cnn.com/EVENTS/1997/mlk/links.html.

3 See http://afroamhistory.about.com/library/weekly/aa121900a.htm.

4 For a full timeline of the major events of Reconstruction, see http://www.pbs.org/wgbh/amex/reconstruction/states/sf_timeline.html.

5 See a full account of the Johnson biography at the White House website, http://www.whitehouse.gov/about/presidents/andrewjohnson.

6 See http://www.africana.com/research/encarta/tt_333.asp.

7 For a history of Jim Crow, see http://www.pbs.org/wnet/jimcrow/.

8 Ibid.

9 Ibid.

10 You can read more about Rosa Park's story at Time.com: http://www.time.com/time/specials/packages/article/0,28804,2029774_2029776_2031835,00.html.

11 See the Congress of Racial Equality website, at http://www.core-online.org/History/freedom_summer.htm. The murders were later the subject of the film Mississippi Burning.

12 Ibid.

13 See CongressLink at http://www.congresslink.org/print_teaching_glossary.htm#cR57.

14 See CongressLink at http://www.congresslink.org/print_basics_histmats_civilrights64text.htm.

15 See CongressLink at http://www.congresslink.org/print_basics_histmats_votingrights_contents.htm.

16 CNN Interactive, "The Civil Rights Movement," at http://www.cnn.com/EVENTS/1997/mlk/links.html.

17 See LawHelpMN.org, Indian Tribal Sovereignty at http://www.lawhelpmn.org/MN/StateChannelResults.cfm/County/%20/demoMode/%3D%201/Language/1/State/MN/TextOnly/N/ZipCode/%20/LoggedIn/0/iSubTopicID/1/iProblemCodeID/1920600/sTopicImage/feather.gif/iTopicID/272/bAllState/0/ichannelid/3.

18 CNN Interactive, "The Civil Rights Movement," at http://www.cnn.com/EVENTS/1997/mlk/links.html.

19 Adam Liptak, "Supreme Court Invalidates Key Part of Voting Rights Act," *New York Times*, June 25, 2013. http://www.nytimes.com/2013/06/26/us/supreme-court-ruling.html.

20 See http://www.tribal-institute.org/lists/nations.htm.

21 See http://www.seminolewars.us/history.html.

22 North Georgia history, at http://ngeorgia.com/history/nghisttt.html.

23 For an overview, see http://www.nebraskastudies.org/0700/frameset_reset.html?http://www.nebraskastudies.org/0700/stories/0701_0146.html.

24 See http://www.nps.gov/archive/alcatraz/indian2.html.

25 See http://bioguide.congress.gov/scripts/biodisplay.pl?index=C000077.

26 See, for instance, *United States v. Wheeler* (1978).

27 See http://www.usbr.gov/native/naao/water/index.html.

28 See http://www.indiangaming.org/info/about.shtml. One prominent example is the Foxwoods Casino in Connecticut, operated by the Mashantucket Pequot nation. The story of the nation that operates it may be found at http://www.mptn-nsn.gov//.

29 See the NCLR website at http://www.nclr.org/index.php/issues_and_programs/education/.

30 You can get information on La Raza at http://www.nclr.org.

31 See the United Farm Workers website at http://www.ufw.org/_page.php?menu=about&inc=about_vision.html.

32 See the National Association for Bilingual Education website at http://www.nabe.org/.

33 Figures are from the 2000 U.S. Census, http://www.census.gov/quickfacts/table/PST045216/00.

34 *Korematsu v. United States*, 321 US 760 (1944).

35 See the Equal Rights Amendment website, at http://www.equalrightsamendment.org/era.htm.

36 Ibid.

37 See the National Organization for Women website, at http://www.now.org/history/history.html.

38 See http://www.archives.gov/education/lessons/civil-rights-act/.

39 The U.S. Department of Labor, at http://www.dol.gov/whd/fmla/index.htm.

40 Dennis Cauchon, "Gender Pay Gap is Smallest on Record," *USA Today*, September 14, 2010.

41 *Ledbetter v. Goodyear Tire & Rubber Co.*, 550 US 618 (2007).

42 Paula England, *Comparable Worth: Theories and Evidence* (New York: Aldine de Gruyter, 1992), 1–2, 23–24.

43 Ibid.

44 "What Is Comparable Worth?" Employment Policy Foundation paper.

45 U.S. Equal Employment Opportunity Commission, "Americans with Disabilities Act Questions and Answers," http://www.ada.gov/q&aeng02.htm.

46 Ibid.

47 American Civil Liberties Union statement on gay and lesbian rights, at http://www.aclu.org/lgbt-rights/lgbt-discrimination.

48 Equal Employment Opportunity Commission, "Facts about Age Discrimination," at http://www.eeoc.gov/facts/age.html.

Table, Figure, and Box Notes

T1 U.S. Census Bureau 2015 Population Estimates, at https://www.census.gov/quickfacts/table/PST045216/00.

T2 Image is a work of an employee of the U.S. Farm Security Administration or Office of War Information domestic photographic units, created during the course of the person's official duties. As a work of the U.S. federal government, the image is in the public domain.

T3 Adapted from http://afroamhistory.about.com/gi/o.htm?zi=1/XJ&zTi=1&sdn=afroamhistory&cdn=education&tm=8&f=00&tt=14&bt=0&bts=1&zu=http%3A//www.ferris.edu/jimcrow/what.htm.

T4 Adapted from CNN.com at http://www.cnn.com/EVENTS/1997/mlk/links.html. Rosa Parks image: This work was obtained from the now defunct United States Information Agency. In 1999 the agency was merged into the Bureau of Public Affairs, which is part of the U.S. Department of State. This work is in the public domain in the United States because it is a work of the U.S. federal government under the terms of 17 U.S.C. § 105. Martin Luther King, Jr. image: Source: Library of Congress. New York World-Telegram & Sun Collection. http://hdl.loc.gov/loc.pnp/cph.3c26559; author: Dick DeMarsico, World Telegram staff photographer. No copyright restriction known. Staff photographer reproduction rights transferred to Library of Congress through Instrument of Gift.

T5 Richard F. Thomasson, Faye J. Corsby, and Sharon D. Hertberger, *Affirmative Action: The Pros and Cons of Policy and Practice* (Washington, DC: American University Press, 1996), 5–6. The first story in this section is true; the second story is fictional.

T6 Ibid., 12.

T7 Ibid., 12–15 and 135–136.

T8 Ibid., 18–19.

T9 *Gratz v. Bollinger*, 539 US 244 (2003).

T10 *Grutter v. Bollinger*, 539 US 306 (2003).

T11 National Conference of State Legislators, June 2016, at http://www.ncsl.org/research/education/affirmative-action-court-decisions.aspx.

T12 U.S. Census Bureau 2015 Population Estimates, https://www.census.gov/quickfacts/table/PST045216/00.

T13 Ibid.

T14 Data from U.S. Census Bureau, 2010 Census.

T15 U.S. Census Bureau 2015 Population Estimates, at https://www.census.gov/quickfacts/table/PST045216/00.

T16 U.S. Department of Education, Office for Civil Rights, at http://www2.ed.gov/policy/rights/reg/ocr/edlite-34cfr106.html.

Protecting Civil Liberties

Copyright: Victor Moussa/Shutterstock.com

Learning Objectives

When you have completed this chapter, you should be able to:

- Define civil liberties, and explain how they are protected by the Constitution, the Bill of Rights, and judicial precedent.
- Define due process, and explain why it is central to the protection of civil liberties.
- Identify the establishment clause, and explain how it can be applied to different interpretations of the separation between church and state.
- Understand the limits to constitutionally protected free speech.
- Appreciate why the press is granted constitutional protections.
- Distinguish the right to assemble from the right to associate.
- Recognize the political controversy surrounding the Second Amendment right to bear arms.
- Explain the origins and applications of the right to privacy.

14.1 Introduction

L.O. Define civil liberties, and explain how they are protected by the Constitution, the Bill of Rights, and judicial precedent.

civil liberties: Constitutional and legal protections against government infringement on a host of personal freedoms.

Bill of Rights: The first ten amendments to the Constitution, which limit government from denying us a range of personal liberties.

Some of the most important and controversial questions debated in our political system involve matters of personal liberty. Although few of us question the need to protect individual freedom, actually doing so sometimes requires holding our noses and permitting behaviors we find distasteful or reprehensible. It's not easy to stand by and allow someone to make hostile statements aimed directly at our religious or ethnic group, for instance, much less stand up for their right to do so. You might even say it goes against human nature to defend those who attack us. That's why many people object to the specific liberties people are allowed, even if we agree in the abstract on the importance of maintaining them.

At the most fundamental level, there is little debate about the value of protecting **civil liberties**. The Constitution very clearly restricts government from denying us the liberty to express ourselves, congregate, worship, and protest, affording us the freedom to speak out against the government if we so desire. Remember, the authors of the Constitution were concerned that government be strong enough to protect the weakest among us but not so strong as to overwhelm personal liberty. That's why civil liberties are expressed in the Constitution as actions denied to government.

Most of these liberties were added to the Constitution in the **Bill of Rights**. Toward the end of the Philadelphia convention, George Mason of Virginia moved to include a Bill of Rights in the original document, offering to write one in short order. The delegates were fatigued, however, and in the case of some southerners, concerned that a written declaration of human liberty would conflict with their position on slavery. So, they opted to rely on the protections already included in state constitutions and not include a Bill of Rights in the final document.[1]

As we saw in Chapter 2, the new Constitution was rapidly amended to include a Bill of Rights as a political maneuver to win support for ratification. Table 14.1 is a reprint of the table you saw in Chapter 2 summarizing the contents of the Bill of Rights. Before we move on, take a minute and review the table as a refresher on the range of liberties that are protected from government interference by the Bill of Rights.

TABLE 14.1 The Bill of Rights

First Amendment	The First Amendment prevents government from interfering with several key personal freedoms, including the freedom to worship, speak, and assemble peacefully. It also prevents the government from restricting freedom of the press and the freedom to petition government.
Second Amendment	The Second Amendment protects the right to bear arms.
Third and Fourth Amendments	The Third and Fourth Amendments provide a right to privacy from government interference. The Third Amendment prevents government from forcing citizens to house soldiers during peacetime—addressing one of the complaints the colonists had against the British. The Fourth Amendment protects against unreasonable searches and seizures of property or personal effects.
Fifth through Eighth Amendments	The Fifth through Eighth Amendments establish a host of protections for individuals accused of a crime. These include the right not to be tried twice for the same crime, the right to be indicted by a grand jury before being tried for a capital crime, the right not to be forced to testify against yourself, the right to due process of law, and the right not to have property confiscated by government without compensation (all in the Fifth Amendment); the right to a speedy and impartial trial, the right to be informed of charges against you, the right to call and confront witnesses, and the right to a lawyer (all in the Sixth Amendment); the right to a jury in civil trials (Seventh Amendment); and the right to be free from excessive bail and from the infliction of cruel and unusual punishments (Eighth Amendment).
Ninth and Tenth Amendments	The Ninth Amendment is a safety net establishing that any rights not specifically mentioned in the first eight amendments are not necessarily denied. The Tenth Amendment establishes that any powers not granted to the federal government or prohibited to the states are reserved for the states.

14.1a Due Process

The civil liberties provided constitutional protection include the important right to **due process**, or protection against arbitrary actions of the government. The Fifth Amendment states that no person shall "be deprived of life, liberty, or property, without due process of law." The Fourteenth Amendment echoes this language and applies it to the states. The presumption behind due process is that conflict between individuals and the government is inevitable and should be resolved through a defined set of legal procedures, where the rules are written to protect the individual from government power.[2]

Some of these requirements are set down in the Constitution itself, while others appear in the Bill of Rights or have been established by the Supreme Court and applied to the states through interpretation of the due process clause of the Fourteenth Amendment. They are outlined in Table 14.2.

L.O. Define due process, and explain why it is central to the protection of civil liberties.

due process: The protection of individual liberty from the arbitrary or capricious actions of government through a defined set of legal procedures designed to protect the rights of the accused.

TABLE 14.2 Due Process

Item	Key Term	Constitutional Origin	What This Means
Right to a writ of *habeas corpus*	**writ of *habeas corpus*:** From the Latin for "you have the body," *habeas corpus* puts the burden on the courts to demonstrate that a defendant's rights have not been violated prior to sentencing. People who believe they have been imprisoned against their constitutional rights have the privilege to petition for their release.	Article 1, Section 9	Before you can be sent to prison, the government has the burden of assuring that your rights were not violated during trial. *Habeas corpus* gives you the right to petition the court if you believe you have been wrongfully imprisoned. It may only be suspended in extreme cases of domestic rebellion or foreign invasion.
Freedom from bills of attainder	**bills of attainder:** Declarations of guilt by legislative decree without benefit of a trial.	Article 1, Section 9	Congress or other legislatures cannot find you guilty of a crime by passing legislation that convicts you.
Freedom from *ex post facto* laws	***ex post facto* laws:** From the Latin for "after the fact," legislation that makes something a crime that was legal when it occurred.	Article 1, Section 9	If the drinking age was 18 before it was raised to 21, anyone who purchased alcohol legally at age 18 cannot subsequently, through legislation, be found guilty of a crime.
Protection against unreasonable searches and seizures		Fourth Amendment	You cannot be arrested or your person or possessions searched without a court warrant. Note the *unreasonable* qualifier: courts have determined it is *reasonable* for airport guards to frisk you at security checkpoints or for state troopers to search your car for drugs if you're pulled over for speeding.
Protection in the form of the exclusionary rule	**exclusionary rule:** To protect against unreasonable searches and seizures, the Supreme Court has established that evidence obtained illegally is not admissible in court.	Judicial Interpretation	To reinforce the protection against unreasonable searches and seizures, the Supreme Court ruled that evidence acquired in violation of Fourth Amendment protections is inadmissible in court.
Grand jury indictments for capital crimes		Fifth Amendment	The protection from being charged with a capital or "infamous" crime without an indictment from a grand jury is a way of dispersing the power to prosecute. It places the ability to charge someone with a serious crime in the hands of a jury of citizens.

TABLE 14.2 Due Process *(continued)*

Item	Key Term	Constitutional Origin	What This Means
Protection against double jeopardy	**double jeopardy:** Protection against the state using its power to repeatedly prosecute someone until the person is convicted. Double jeopardy precludes the prosecution of someone for the same crime in the same jurisdiction more than once.	Fifth Amendment	No one may be tried twice in the same jurisdiction for the same crime. However, someone who commits a crime that violates federal and state law can be tried in both jurisdictions, and someone who violates criminal and civil law can be tried in criminal and civil courts.
Protection against self-incrimination		Fifth Amendment	No one may be compelled to take the witness stand in a trial and testify against oneself, or confess to a crime involuntarily.
Miranda rights	**Miranda rights:** The Court requirement, following a judgment in the case *Miranda v. Arizona* (1966), that apprehended individuals know and understand that they have a right against self-incrimination and a right to be represented by an attorney.	Judicial Interpretation	Before questioning may begin, arresting officers must inform suspects that they have the right to remain silent; that if they speak, anything they say may be used against them in court; and that they have a right to have a lawyer present during interrogation.
Right to a speedy public jury trial		Sixth Amendment	You have the right to a speedy and public trial in criminal cases by an impartial jury in the place where the crime was committed. This keeps a prosecutor or judge from convicting someone unilaterally.
Right to be informed of a charge against you		Sixth Amendment	This includes the right to confront your accuser and to present witnesses in your defense.
Right to an attorney	*Gideon v. Wainwright:* The 1963 Supreme Court case that established the right to have an attorney appointed at no charge by the court to defendants unable to afford representation. It was brought by Clarence Earl Gideon, who was sentenced to five years in prison for breaking into a pool hall. From prison, Gideon filed a *habeas corpus* petition, claiming his right to an attorney was violated because he was forced by poverty to represent himself at his trial.	Sixth Amendment	Originally, the Constitution simply gave defendants the right to counsel, but it was of little practical use to the vast majority who could not afford to hire a lawyer. Following the 1963 case *Gideon v. Wainwright*, the Supreme Court ruled that an attorney must be provided to anyone who cannot afford one.
Protection against excessive bail		Eighth Amendment	This precludes incarceration prior to conviction and allows the accused the freedom to prepare a defense.
Protection against cruel and unusual punishment		Eighth Amendment	Although the Constitution does not specify what makes a punishment cruel and unusual, the Court has interpreted it to mean arbitrary punishment, punishment disproportionate to the crime committed, or torture.

How the Justice System Often Works

In a **plea bargain**, defendants plead guilty to a lesser crime than the one for which they have been charged and accept a lesser sentence than what they might have expected had they been convicted on the original charge. Instead of a trial, everyone moves right to sentencing. Plea bargains are the result of negotiations where, typically, each attorney tells his or her version of the story, with prosecutors pointing out the most serious facts of the case and defense attorneys minimizing the incident. Sometimes, judges enter the negotiations and explicitly state the sentence they intend to impose. A compromise is hammered out, and if the defendant accepts it, the deed is done. Most felony and misdemeanor cases end in guilty pleas, many of which are the direct result of negotiation.[T1]

Plea bargains serve the interests of the court officers, but we can ask how well they serve the interests of defendants and society as a whole. Because defendants waive their due process rights in accepting a plea bargain, there is no impartial finding of guilt or innocence. In a sense, plea bargaining turns the assumptions behind due process upside-down, presuming guilt on the part of defendants and foregoing the opportunity to permit them to wage a defense. It's possible to imagine innocent people being pressured into accepting a guilty plea by busy defense attorneys who convince them not to take their chances at trial. Maybe it's easier to imagine guilty parties getting a lighter sentence than they would face if they had been convicted in a trial. Does either outcome seem just to you?

You can think of due process as establishing the groundwork for resolving conflicts and protecting civil liberties, based on the presumption that individuals accused of a crime are innocent until proven guilty by the state. The theory is that by following clearly defined and evenly applied procedures, guilt can be assessed while the power of the state is held in check. Of course, this means that in some cases, guilty individuals will be set free because their rights were (purposely or inadvertently) violated at or before trial. This is the consequence of a fundamental choice made by the Constitution's authors: that it is better to let the guilty occasionally go free in the interest of protecting personal liberties than to inadvertently—or purposely—condemn the innocent.

In practice, the constitutionally defined system for a timely, impartial jury trial where defendants have a clear and full set of rights contrasts with the way justice is handled in many courtrooms. Because due process is slow, and courtrooms across the country are overburdened with cases, court officers with nominally adversarial roles will conspire in ways that move defendants through the system without time-consuming trials. Pressure to process a heavy caseload motivates judges to look for shortcuts. Prosecuting attorneys are evaluated for the cases they win and often jump at the chance to avoid the uncertainty of a trial. Defense attorneys, particularly those appointed by the court, tend to be overburdened and wish to avoid the work of a trial. Both can advance their professional interests by striking a plea bargain with the defendant. Demystifying Government: How the Justice System Often Works discusses plea bargaining, which requires that a defendant waive his or her due process rights.

plea bargain: A compromise between a defendant, defense attorney, and prosecutor, whereby the defendant foregoes due process and agrees to plead guilty without a trial to a lesser charge in exchange for a more lenient punishment.

14.1b Due Process and Capital Punishment

The death penalty is one place where the protection against cruel and unusual punishment has been controversial. Although the Court has established the constitutionality of capital punishment, the issue continues to divide Americans as much today as it did early in our history.

Some opponents contend that it is an inhumane violation of fundamental civil liberties for the state to take a life under any circumstances. They bolster their argument by pointing to economic and racial disparities in who is sentenced to death, claiming most death-row inmates are poor individuals lacking in funds to pay expensive lawyers who could have effectively saved their lives through more capable representation. Most of these individuals are African American, and most victims in capital cases are white. According to the American Civil Liberties Union, between 1976 and 2015, 76% of executions involved crimes with white victims.[3]

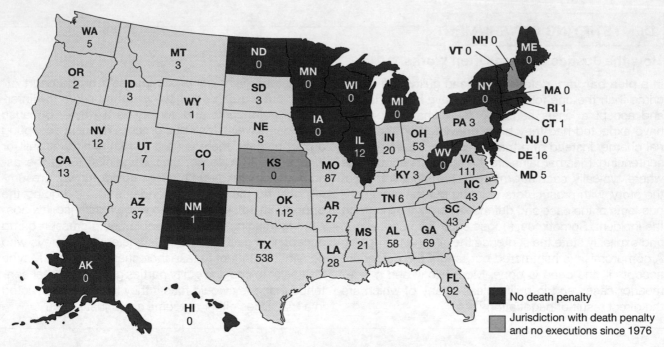

No death penalty

Jurisdiction with death penalty and no executions since 1976

FIGURE 14.1 Does Where You Live Influence If You Will Live?[T2]

There have been 1,442 executions in the United States since 1976, almost all of them in the South and Southwest. This map shows the number of executions by state as of December 2016.

Opponents also argue that the death penalty is carried out in a capricious way that depends largely on the state where you were convicted. The map in Figure 14.1 displays how the number of executions in the forty years since 1976 varies by state. Be sure to compare Texas with everyone else.

Nonetheless, a majority of Americans continue to support the death penalty, either because it is viewed as just or as a deterrent to crime, or both. Take a few minutes to read about the history of capital punishment in America in Demystifying Government: Capital Punishment.

14.2 Religious Freedom

L.O. Identify the establishment clause, and explain how it can be applied to different interpretations of the separation between church and state.

Americans traditionally have been a religious people. Despite the decline in religious identification we discussed in Chapter 3 as a result of lower levels of religious identity among Millennials, the 2014 General Social Survey found that 43 percent of Americans have a strong or somewhat strong religious identity, and a comparable percentage attend religious services at least once a month.[4] The United States also boasts a great deal of religious diversity, with Americans claiming to follow over a dozen religions with many denominations.[5] Such a wide range of affiliations can cause trouble when religious practices and customs come into conflict with each other and, at times, with nonreligious social values. Constitutional assurances of free religious worship, widely believed to be absolute, have at times been curtailed by the Court to provide for the rights of those opposed to public displays of religious expression or to uphold conflicting social standards.

establishment clause: The language in the First Amendment that serves as the basis for the constitutional separation of church and state.

free exercise clause: The language in the First Amendment that limits government interference in private religious beliefs and practices.

The First Amendment makes twin statements about religious freedom, which offer two distinct constitutional protections: "Congress shall make no law respecting an establishment of religion, or prohibiting the free exercise thereof." The first of these, the **establishment clause**, is the basis for the widely discussed separation between church and state. The second, typically called the **free exercise clause**, restricts government from interfering with private religious practices. Both of these clauses have been open to interpretation and therefore have been a source of controversy.

Capital Punishment

In January 2003, as one of his final official acts, Illinois Governor George Ryan commuted the death sentences of all 167 inmates on death row to life in prison, saying the system by which people are sentenced to death was "arbitrary and capricious—and therefore immoral."[T3] The sweeping move—unprecedented in its scope—followed an exhaustive study of Illinois death row cases that revealed, among other things, that people had been sentenced to death on the basis of questionable evidence, and that African Americans were far more likely to receive the death penalty than whites. Capital punishment opponents were overjoyed. Victims' rights groups were shocked and appalled.[T4]

Governor Ryan's action was one of the more recent turns in America's conflicted history with capital punishment. Through the nineteenth and twentieth centuries, as western countries like England, West Germany, Italy, Switzerland, Norway, Sweden, and Denmark abolished the death penalty, many American states vacillated between abolishing it and reinstating it. The number of executions in the United States plummeted in the 1960s, as the American public, strongly supportive of the death penalty for much of the twentieth century, became less sympathetic. Then, in the 1972 case *Furman v. Georgia*, a fragmented Supreme Court (nine separate opinions were issued) ruled all existing death penalty laws to be unconstitutional, saying they were instituted arbitrarily and capriciously.[T5]

The ruling came at a time when public opinion was beginning to swing back toward support of the death penalty, and it caused a backlash. Many states moved quickly to enact new capital punishment statutes. Within four years of the *Furman* verdict, a more conservative Supreme Court reinstated the death penalty in the case of *Gregg v. Georgia* (1976), ruling that capital punishment does not violate the Eighth Amendment's ban on cruel and unusual punishment and that statutory corrections made by Georgia and other states satisfactorily addressed the inequities that the Court had expressed concern about in its earlier ruling.[T6] But *Gregg* didn't put an end to questions about how equitably the death penalty was imposed. In fact, inequities in meting out capital punishment were the reason Governor Ryan commuted all Illinois death sentences twenty-seven years later.

Subsequent rulings have placed restrictions on how the death penalty may be implemented. *Coker v. Georgia* (1977) banned capital punishment for people convicted of rape, and *Atkins v. Virginia* (2002) did the same for mentally retarded criminals.[T7] In recent years, the public opinion pendulum has been swinging the other way. Support for capital punishment has diminished from a high of 80 percent in 1996 to 60 percent in 2016,[T8] and the number of states without a death penalty has grown to nineteen.[T9]

Throughout America's uneasy history with the death penalty, the positions taken by opponents and advocates have remained remarkably consistent. Opponents point to what they see as a double standard in the application of the death penalty to rich and poor, white and nonwhite; contend that it does not deter crime; and despite the opinion of the Court in *Gregg v. Georgia*, consider it cruel and unusual punishment. Supporters regard it as an appropriate penalty for the most violent crimes, a form of justice for crime victims, and a deterrent to violence.

This gurney is used to perform executions by lethal injection at a Terre Haute, Indiana, prison.[T10]

14.2a No Establishment of Religion

In the most fundamental sense, the establishment clause precludes the government from sanctioning a national religion, although it is often taken to mean much more. Thomas Jefferson wrote that the establishment clause built "a wall of separation between church and State." In *Everson v. Board of Education* (1947), Justice Hugo Black elaborated in great detail:

> The "establishment of religion" clause of the First Amendment means at least this: Neither a state nor the Federal Government can set up a church. Neither can pass laws which aid one religion, aid all religions, or prefer one religion over another. Neither can force nor influence a person to go to or to remain away from church against his will or

force him to profess a belief or disbelief in any religion. . . . No tax in any amount, large or small, can be levied to support any religious activities or institutions, whatever they may be called, or whatever form they may adopt to teach or practice religion. Neither a state nor the Federal Government can, openly or secretly, participate in the affairs of any religious organizations or groups, and vice versa.[6]

At the same time, the phrase "In God We Trust" appears on the quarter you have in your pocket. A chaplain offers a prayer to start congressional sessions. In fact, the *Everson* decision, in which Justice Black reaffirms Jefferson's "wall of separation," upheld the right of the state of New Jersey to provide public bus service to students of a Catholic school, saying the First Amendment intended government to be neutral—not adversarial—in matters of religion. These are places where religion mixes with government that fall short of establishment. Depending on how thick you feel the wall of separation should be, they may also be points of controversy.

No doubt, the place where the barrier between church and state is put to the greatest test is over the issue of whether prayer should be permitted in public school. Does religious freedom mean having the right to pray in public schools? Or does having religious freedom protect us from public school prayer? The way you answer this question is partly a matter of what you value and partly a matter of how you interpret the constitutional separation of church and state.

Some view religion as something the government should nurture and support on an evenhanded basis, without establishing a national religion or requiring people to participate in prayer. They see this as a tolerant interpretation of religious freedom consistent with the original intent of the First Amendment.[7] Others view religion as a private matter and understand the establishment clause in the First Amendment to be a statement of every individual's private right to worship or not to worship as he or she pleases. From this perspective, if a teacher leads a class in prayer, social and institutional pressures make it difficult for students who object to express their unwillingness to participate, effectively forcing them to pray against their First Amendment rights.[8]

The Supreme Court has tended to side with the latter interpretation of the First Amendment. In the 1962 case *Engle v. Vitale*, the Court ruled that the New York State Board of Regents could not give public school teachers the option of leading classes in a voluntary, nondenominational prayer, which read, "Almighty God, we acknowledge our dependence upon Thee, and we beg Thy blessings upon us, our parents, our teachers and our country."[9] In the Court's opinion, any prayer, no matter how neutral, is a religious activity and violates the First Amendment.

The next year, the Court issued a pair of rulings that, together with *Engle v. Vitale*, established the legal framework for school prayer. The Court struck down a Pennsylvania law in *Abington Township School District v. Schempp* (1963) that required the school day to start with Bible readings and the recital of the Lord's Prayer. In the companion case *Murray v. Curlett* (1963), the Court struck down a similar Maryland law that required unison prayer and Bible reading in public school.[10]

However, none of these cases made mention of voluntary private personal prayer in public schools, which remained constitutional, and in the *Schempp* decision, the Court recognized the importance of teaching about religion in the context of history as part of a well-rounded public school education.

More recent Court decisions have interpreted religious freedom the same way. In 1985, the Court struck down an Alabama law in *Wallace v. Jaffree* that required the school day to begin with a moment of silent meditation or voluntary prayer, on the grounds that prayer, even if voluntary, has a religious purpose. In *Lee v. Weisman* (1992), the Court struck down the recital of a prayer at public school graduation ceremonies as a form of coerced religious participation.[11]

14.2b Free Exercise of Religion

The idea behind the free exercise clause is that the practice of individual worship should be free from government interference. This is fairly easy to do when religious worship doesn't violate other social values, but since that's not always the case, free exercise has been a matter of dispute over the years, as the Court has held that the free exercise of religion is not absolute.

An early battle of great significance took place between federal authorities and the Mormon Church over the practice of polygamy in the Utah territory. The conflict dated to an 1852 pronouncement by Brigham Young, prophet of the Church of Jesus Christ of Latter-Day Saints, that Mormons would practice polygamy or plural marriage as a part of their religious beliefs. This position enraged official Washington, which found the whole idea of polygamy to be an abomination and criminalized it. The dispute ended up in the Supreme Court in 1878, in the case of *Reynolds v. United States*.[12]

The Mormon Church expected the Court to uphold its right to free exercise of religion as expressed in the Constitution. They were wrong. The Court contended that the Constitution did not define the term "religion," and proceeded to offer its own explanation of the concept, distinguishing between principles and actions. Under this interpretation, the First Amendment protected religious beliefs but not behaviors taken in the name of religion that violated the law. Writing for the Court, Chief Justice Waite asked rhetorically,

> Suppose one believed that human sacrifices were a necessary part of religious worship, would it be seriously contended that the civil government under which he lived could not interfere to prevent a sacrifice? Or if a wife religiously believed it was her duty to burn herself upon the funeral pile of her dead husband, would it be beyond the power of the civil government to prevent her carrying her belief into practice?[13]

The logic of the decision makes practical sense if the objective is to maintain the superiority of the law over personal religious practices, or to prohibit behaviors carried out in the name of worship that the broader society finds abhorrent. However, if the goal is to protect one's religious beliefs from government interference, the Court's distinction between beliefs and behaviors may appear a bit academic, for how does one hold a belief if it is not practiced? That dilemma runs through the body of law on the free exercise doctrine.

Other, more recent rulings have limited free exercise of religion when it clashes with deeply held social values. In *Employment Division, Department of Human Resources of Oregon v. Smith* (1990), the Supreme Court ruled that two Native Americans could be fired from their jobs at a drug rehabilitation organization and denied unemployment benefits for using peyote, a controlled substance with important religious significance that could be used legally on Native American reservations but not off those reservations in the state of Oregon, where the pair worked. Writing for the majority, Justice Antonin Scalia contended that the free exercise of religion can be limited as the incidental result of a law whose primary purpose is to set legal boundaries for everyone.[14] In other words, Oregon did not make peyote illegal in order to limit Native American worship, but if it has that effect, the rights of a religious minority must take a backseat to broader social interests.

Civil rights issues clashed with religious practices in the 1983 case *Bob Jones University v. United States*. Bob Jones University is a conservative Christian university that forbade interracial dating on religious grounds. Because of this policy, the Internal Revenue Service refused the school tax-exempt status on the basis of federal civil rights laws prohibiting tax exemptions for institutions that practiced discriminatory policies. Bob Jones University sued, claiming that its interracial dating policy was a matter of free exercise of religion, not racial discrimination. The Court disagreed, saying the government's overriding interest in ending discrimination outweighed the school's religious position.[15]

However, when the issue has been something narrower than polygamy, drug policies, and civil rights, the Court has sided with religious groups. In *Cantwell v. Connecticut* (1940), the Court held that states couldn't require religious groups to get a special permit to solicit for religious purposes, even if the group's message is unpleasant to those who hear it. In *Wisconsin v. Yoder* (1972), Amish children were granted the right to be taken out of public school after eighth grade in order to comply with religious teachings. The interest of the state in universal education was in this case considered secondary to Amish religious values. As in many cases involving the free exercise clause, the outcome often depends on how sharply religious practices clash with broader social norms.

14.3 Freedom of Expression

L.O. Understand the limits to constitutionally protected free speech.

No liberty is more central to an open society than freedom of expression. Even though the First Amendment is unequivocal in stating that "Congress shall make no law . . . abridging the freedom of speech," the issue in practice—like freedom of worship—has many variations. Justice Oliver Wendell Holmes may have penned the most famous line about the margins of free expression when he wrote, "Even the most stringent protection of free speech would not protect a man in falsely shouting fire in a crowded theatre and causing a panic."[16]

14.3a Dangerous and Unpopular Speech

Holmes was writing in the 1919 case *Schenck v. United States*, which arose out of the prosecution of Charles Schenck, a Socialist leader who had printed pamphlets urging young men to resist the draft during World War I. Schenck's actions violated provisions of the Espionage Act of 1917, which made it a crime to call for draft resistance or utter disloyal statements about the United States.

Schenck petitioned the Court to have the Espionage Act declared in violation of the First Amendment, but his efforts were unsuccessful. Nonetheless, in upholding the constitutionality of the Espionage Act as a measure the government was permitted to take during wartime, Holmes set out a specific rule for determining when government could limit free expression: the standard of **clear and present danger**.[17] Government could stifle dissent, Holmes argued, when words "are used in such circumstances and are of such a nature as to create a clear and present danger that they will bring about the substantive evils that Congress has a right to prevent. It is a question of proximity and degree."[18] Wartime created such a circumstance, Holmes argued, when unpopular speech became dangerous. Even if Schenck's pleas to avoid the draft were unsuccessful, the fact that he made them was in the Court's view sufficient to present a public danger.

clear and present danger: The standard established by Justice Oliver Wendell Holmes for determining when the government could limit speech.

Not surprisingly, people with unpopular ideas are typically the ones caught in the middle of court cases testing free expression. The same year as the Schenck decision, Eugene Debs, the Socialist Party presidential candidate, criticized American involvement in World War I and spoke out publicly against the draft. At a 1918 speech in Canton, Ohio, Debs urged his audience to oppose the war. Drawing distinctions between leaders who declare war and workers who die in war, he said (to a blue-collar audience), "You have your lives to lose; you certainly ought to have the right to declare war if you consider a war necessary."[19]

Debs was arrested under the terms of the Espionage Act and charged with inciting disloyalty, insubordination, and mutiny against the armed forces of the United States. He admitted to the statements he had made in the speech, was convicted, and was sentenced to ten years in prison. The Supreme Court upheld the conviction, using the clear and present danger standard established in Schenck, noting that the First Amendment protected the general socialist message in the speech but not the call to resist the draft.

Debs continued his 1920 presidential campaign from prison. He received 2.4 million votes.

Eight years after the *Schenck* decision, Justice Louis Brandeis elaborated on and in the process altered the clear and present danger standard. Brandeis contended that unpopular speech is critical to maintaining democratic freedom, and that for people to feel secure about democratic participation, they have to be assured that unpopular speech will not be punished. To this end, he said an idea has to be dangerous and not just disliked to pose a threat to society, and that if there is time to engage in a full discussion of an idea—which is always the case unless the country faces an immediate crisis—it can never pose a clear and present danger. To Brandeis, the way to defuse the danger posed by most threatening ideas is through more discussion, not suppression of speech.[20]

Brandeis's movement toward greater acceptance of free speech set the stage for Court decisions in the 1960s and 1970s that increased First Amendment protection for unpopular speech. The 1969 case *Brandenberg v. Ohio* established the strict standard that speech had to incite "imminent lawless action" in order for government to have the ability to suppress it. Otherwise, First Amendment protections apply, even to speech that advocates violence (but does not actually instigate violence).[21]

14.3b Unpopular Speech in a Difficult Time

During periods of national tension, though, strict protections on speech have been hard to maintain. The close of World War II found the United States settling into a protracted period of uneasy coexistence with the Soviet Union that would last forty-five years. The start of the cold war brought a hysterical reaction to Communism that was exacerbated and exploited by Republican Senator Joseph McCarthy of Wisconsin, who crusaded against Communists in government and the private sector.

McCarthy made baseless accusations without evidence, but with the backing of the FBI and congressional investigators, he wielded immense power. Employers fired people who were tainted by McCarthy's charges, leaving them blacklisted and unable to get work. People were encouraged to turn in their friends and associates to demonstrate their loyalty to America—and to save their own skin. Moderate voices were silenced by the fear that questioning McCarthy's charges would brand them Communist sympathizers, and that McCarthy would next turn his inquisition on them.[22] The publisher of this book would have placed itself at risk for printing this paragraph. For a period of time, our system failed its most basic test, as an intense minority was able to use the mechanisms of government to tyrannize the majority, quashing criticism of the government.

During this period, it was particularly dangerous to be directly affiliated with the American Communist Party. In 1940, Congress passed the Smith Act (technically the Alien Registration Act), which made it a crime to advocate the violent overthrow of the government—the position taken by the American Communist Party leadership during the time of McCarthy's Red Scare. In this climate, party leaders were prosecuted under the Smith Act, and the Court—in a momentary departure from the trend toward protecting unpopular speech—upheld the constitutionality of the Smith Act and the convictions of the Communist Party leadership. This happened despite the fact that the American Communist Party was small and ineffectual, making it highly unlikely that its advocacy would turn to action.

In dissent, Justice William O. Douglas anticipated the turn the Court would take in the next decade, stating, "Free speech has occupied an exalted position because of the high service it has given our society. Its protection is essential to the very existence of a democracy. The airing of ideas releases pressures which otherwise might become destructive."[23] This was a difficult argument to accept in the icy climate of 1951.

As we move deeper into a time when the fear of terrorism is making inroads into our national psyche, and when free expression facilitates the planning and execution of terrorist plots, we might ask ourselves whether we can embrace Douglas's rationale for the benefits of free expression, or whether we will react as our grandparents' generation did to a different but equally penetrating threat.

14.3c Symbolic Expression

Protesters through the ages have resorted to the use of images to make strong, emotional statements. Designed to be hard to take and often disrespectful, symbolic expression can be a potent and effective way to lash out at policies and policy makers that people find objectionable. Maybe you've seen footage—there's lots of it—of crowds in foreign cities protesting American policy by burning an effigy of the president. During the Vietnam War, hippies grew their hair long in defiance of the buttoned-down values of their parents' generation—the group that most strongly supported the war. A few desecrated national symbols like the flag as a way of expressing their opposition to the actions of political elites.

How much symbolic expression should be permissible under the First Amendment? The most emotional debate revolves around the question of whether flag burning should be condoned. As you will see in Demystifying Government: Flag Burning, the Court has

Flag Burning

Few symbols move Americans like the flag. To many it is a special icon: an emblem that represents the living nation, which should be accorded the utmost respect. Consequently, few acts of civil disobedience gall Americans like burning the American flag. It's an action that has happened rarely in our history—about two hundred times in over 225 years[T11]—but in the 1960s it became the most powerful symbol of anger and protest against the Vietnam War. During that time, many who supported the war felt American values were under attack by a militant counterculture for which flag burning became a potent form of protest. In some important respects, the social wounds opened by that conflict have yet to heal, and the sense of permissiveness and diminished respect for authority, which some people see as stemming from that time, still rubs raw. The intensity surrounding the flag-burning debate may be understood in this context.[T12]

In 1989, the Supreme Court issued a 5–4 decision in the case of *Texas v. Johnson*, upholding the right of a protester to burn the American flag at the 1984 Republican National Convention in Dallas, overturning a Texas law that had made flag burning a crime punishable by a $2,000 fine and a year in prison. The Court held that flag burning is a constitutionally protected form of political expression, and Texas could not prosecute Johnson for burning the flag without violating his First Amendment rights.[T13]

Congress responded immediately by passing the Flag Protection Act of 1989, which cleared both houses by a lopsided margin and was signed into law by President George H. W. Bush. The next year, the Court struck down the Flag Protection Act as unconstitutional by the same one-vote margin. That set in motion an organized lobbying campaign determined to overturn the *Johnson* decision with a constitutional amendment. Since 1994, an organization called the Citizens Flag Alliance has been waging a grassroots campaign in conjunction with a coalition of 120 other interest groups to recruit local and national legislative candidates who would support a flag protection amendment permitting federal, state, and local authorities to make it a crime to desecrate the flag.[T14]

Members of the Citizens Flag Alliance have been persistent, but they have fallen short of their goal. Bolstered by surveys showing that large majorities of Americans supported their position, they were successful in winning House approval for the amendment in 1995 by a vote of 312–120, far surpassing the two-thirds majority required for passage. The amendment failed in the Senate, but only by three votes. Since then, it has failed several more times by wider margins, although its supporters reintroduce it on a regular basis. The American Civil Liberties Union, which opposes the amendment as an infringement on First Amendment freedoms, connects the decline in congressional support to vocal opposition to the amendment by prominent Americans like former Secretary of State Colin Powell and the late senator and astronaut John Glenn.[T15]

narrowly upheld flag burning as a constitutionally permissible form of expression, but opponents have mounted a spirited counterattack by trying to win approval of a constitutional amendment that would overrule the Court.

14.4 Freedom of the Press

L.O. Appreciate why the press is granted constitutional protections.

The press carries a key constitutional responsibility as the source of the information we need to stay informed and make responsible public choices. Even though we questioned how effectively the press performs this function when we discussed the mass media in Chapter 5, the obligation to keep readers and viewers informed is so critical to democracy that news organizations are the only private, for-profit institutions afforded constitutional protection.

14.4a Prior Restraint

prior restraint: Censorship of the news by government officials before it is published or broadcast.

Press freedom stems from protection against a practice called **prior restraint**, or censorship of the news by government officials before it is printed or broadcast. The practice dates back to the seventeenth century, when the English king could censor the news before it was published. The rationale behind protecting the press against prior restraint is that the executive, legislature, or courts wield too much power if they are allowed to prevent ideas from entering circulation. Once information is circulated, however, the press is responsible for the consequences of its actions and can be held accountable for any misstatements of fact.[24] Protection from prior restraint was confirmed in the case of *Near v. Minnesota* (1931), when the Supreme Court struck down a Minnesota law that had been used to stop publication of embarrassing information about local political figures in a tabloid called the *Saturday Press*. In issuing the order, Chief Justice Hughes made it clear that even "miscreant purveyors of scandal" have the constitutional right to publish without government interference.[25] Prior restraint could only be imposed where the public interest was clearly jeopardized by publication, such as in the case of information that would create a major national security breach if released.

The Court has set the national security bar very high. Perhaps the most serious call for prior restraint on national security grounds occurred during the Nixon administration, which tried to block the *New York Times* and the *Washington Post* from publishing a scathing, classified study of the decisions that contributed to American involvement in Vietnam. The Pentagon Papers, as the study was known, showed how a series of presidential administrations had knowingly misled the public about the war. Daniel Ellsberg, a disillusioned senior Defense Department employee who was one of the report's authors, leaked it to the *New York Times* in 1971, and the Nixon administration—which was still prosecuting the Vietnam War—immediately moved to have a series of stories about it suppressed. The Court refused in a 6–3 decision that reaffirmed the need for an urgent national security breach to be threatened before prior restraint could be imposed.[26]

14.4b Libel

Of course, granting the press freedom from prior restraint puts a great responsibility in the hands of publishers, and gives them the power to inflict harm if that power is mishandled. The remedy available to individuals who feel they have been harmed by press coverage lies in **libel** laws, which we discussed in Chapter 5. As we noted, though, libel is difficult to prove—particularly for public figures, who have to show that false statements were published with malice.

In rare situations where sloppy reporting leads to damaging misstatements, the press can get hit hard. For instance, in 1990 the *Philadelphia Inquirer* was ordered to pay $6 million to a Pennsylvania Supreme Court judge for incorrectly accusing him of influence peddling. A year later, a Dallas television station lost a libel suit to a Texas district attorney for falsely reporting he had taken bribes. The station was ordered to pay $58 million.[27] Such judgments, though, are unusual.

libel: The legal restriction against the malicious publication of material that knowingly damages an individual's reputation.

14.4c Publishing on the Internet

The advent of the Internet as a device for publishing and communicating has added new wrinkles to traditional notions of press freedom. As neither a print nor an electronic medium, the Internet cuts across previous legal distinctions as it permits us to be our own publishers, sending our ideas across national boundaries where laws on press freedom vary widely.[28] From the standpoint of libel, early indications are that self-publishers can claim to be public figures, requiring those who might sue to restrict cyber content to demonstrate the presence of malice as if they were suing a newspaper or television station.[29]

The Internet is also home to a wide variety of distasteful, troubling, and hateful websites. This can prove to be a difficult test of our tolerance, or of Justice Douglas's remedy to allow expression of offensive ideas, because much of this speech is constitutionally protected.[30] A range of material published on the Internet might be considered obscene by some observers, although traditional law is vague and confusing when it comes to identifying obscenity, and Internet postings simply confound the situation. The First Amendment does not protect obscene communication, but there's little agreement over what obscene communication is or the standards that should be used to identify it. Those who have attempted to classify material as obscene can agree on little more than the standard that was penned by Justice Potter Stewart, who wrote in a frustrated effort to define pornography: "I know it when I see it."[31]

Other justices have hardly done better. The Supreme Court has used language like "prurient,"[32] "patently offensive," and "utterly without redeeming social value"[33] as a test

Obscenity on the Internet

Barbara Nitke is on the faculty of the School of Visual Arts in New York. She was president of the historic Camera Club of New York, a prestigious 130-year-old institution. Her photography has been critically acclaimed as sensitive in its depiction of sometimes graphic or disturbing subjects. She had been using the camera to reveal the trust and love exhibited by couples engaged in sadomasochistic sex. And she wanted to post her images on the Internet.[T16]

She knew that doing so would raise legal issues about whether her work is considered obscene because the law permits obscenity to be determined by local community standards—the same criterion applied to other media. But what are local community standards on the Internet? Nitke decided to raise that question in court, with the help of the National Coalition for Sexual Freedom, an organization that bills itself as dedicated to equal rights for "consenting adults who practice forms of alternative sexual expression."[T17]

There are a number of ways you could conceivably understand local standards on the Internet. Perhaps the entire Internet is a community. That would be the most general interpretation of the law and would allow virtually anything to be posted. Maybe local community standards are the ones in effect in New York, where she would post her material, or maybe the individuals who self-select to view her work constitute a community. Any of these interpretations would permit Nitke to post her work online for anyone in the world to see. Would these criteria be too permissive, affording constitutional protection to work that some people would definitely find objectionable?

Instead, what if "community" were defined as any place in the world where someone could access her pictures? That would be the most restrictive interpretation of the law because surely there are places were her work would be considered obscene, resulting in her having to remove it from the Internet. Would imposing that standard constitute censorship?

It's a difficult question because the Internet is so different from any communications medium to come before it. The first attempt to regulate Internet communication came in the form of the **Communications Decency Act of 1996**, which prohibited the posting of "patently offensive" or "indecent" material online. The language it employs is similar to that applied to broadcast media like radio and television to determine what constitutes offensive material. Of course, the Internet does not function like a television network, where content is broadcast to receivers for any viewer to watch. Social media sites and weblogs can take the form of a public gathering place, an electronic public park where freedom of speech is protected. People who post material on the web could be considered publishers, with their freedom of expression guaranteed.[T18]

These distinctions were not lost on the Supreme Court, which didn't take long to throw out most provisions of the Communications Decency Act on the grounds that it was an unconstitutional attempt to limit free expression. By a vote of 7–2, the Court ruled in the case of *Reno v. ACLU* (1997) that Internet communication was entitled to the same strict constitutional protection as print media because of its decentralized structure with many contributors and no strict gatekeepers.[T19]

However, the Court left in place the section of the law that permitted "local community standards" to determine if something was obscene, without clarifying the issue of what constitutes a community online. Hence Barbara Nitke's dilemma: Should the Internet be viewed as a global or self-selecting community where expression should be tolerated even if some communities with access to the web would find it obscene? Or should any community with access to the web have the right to veto a posting it considers obscene?

Communications Decency Act of 1996: A legislative attempt to regulate the transmission of "offensive" or "indecent" material over the Internet. The Supreme Court overturned most of the provisions of the Communications Decency Act.

of whether something is obscene, leaving it to "the average person, applying contemporary community standards"[34] to determine if something fits this definition. It's problematic how this test applies to the Internet, where in addition to defining obscenity, you have to define the community.

Consider the discussion in Demystifying Government: Obscenity on the Internet, which details a specific example of an Internet posting considered obscene by some, art by others. As you do, see if you can decide where and how you would set the standard for posting potentially obscene material online.

14.5 Freedom of Assembly and Association

L.O. Distinguish the right to assemble from the right to associate.

In January 2017, millions of demonstrators across the country joined hundreds of thousands gathered in Washington, D.C., to protest the inauguration of President Trump. In August 2009, hundreds of thousands of demonstrators gathered in Washington to protest the Obama administrator's efforts to expand goverment involvement in health care. In both instances, protesters were protected from government retribution by the First Amendment guarantee of "the right of the people to peaceably assemble, and to petition the government for redress of grievances." This may be something we take for granted, but the authors of the Constitution certainly did not. In seventeenth-century England, you could be put in prison for peacefully assembling to advocate ideas that were opposed by the crown.

The Supreme Court has affirmed that the First Amendment protects assembly for the purpose of the lawful exchange of ideas, no matter how unpopular the assembled group may be. This provision has been used to permit meetings of the Communist Party[35] and to enable African Americans to peacefully assemble in southern states during the Civil Rights movement.[36] It has also extended rights to unions, allowing them to form picket lines during labor disputes, provided they do so in an orderly manner.[37]

The right to assemble also covers the right to protest peacefully without repercussions, even if the protest is repugnant to the general public. This is probably the most controversial application of the freedom of assembly because it can require tolerance of visible displays of vile and hateful expression. When the American Nazi Party chose Skokie, Illinois, as the location for a march in support of fascism in 1977, they knew they were going to evoke a hostile reaction from the residents of the heavily Jewish Chicago suburb, some of whom were Holocaust survivors. Village residents were predictably outraged and went to court to block the march, but the Supreme Court upheld the constitutional rights of the Nazis to stage a public demonstration.[38]

The freedom to associate is closely related to the freedom to assemble. We devoted a lot of attention in Part 3 to group membership in political parties and interest groups, and we talked a little about how Americans like to join organizations. All of this is made possible by the freedom to associate.

While not explicitly stated in the First Amendment, freedom of association has been protected by the Court as an implied right, on the grounds that in order to petition government, people first need the freedom to gather in groups with like-minded citizens. Underlying this logic is the belief that groups of private citizens are necessary to advocate political positions and are valuable mechanisms for checking the power of government.[39]

14.6 Right to Bear Arms

The Second Amendment is one sentence long. It states, "A well-regulated militia, being necessary to the security of a free state, the right of the people to keep and bear arms, shall not be infringed." Those twenty-six simple words have been the basis for some of the most intense political battles in our recent history. The way you interpret them determines where you stand on gun ownership and probably says a lot about how you see the world.

L.O. Recognize the political controversy surrounding the Second Amendment right to bear arms.

Some people regard the Second Amendment as an unequivocal grant of freedom to possess firearms for everything from hunting to self-defense. They interpret gun ownership as a personal right. Others contend that the amendment's authors had only public defense in mind. They interpret gun ownership as a collective right, one that permits states to form militias—and nothing else.

Attitudes toward gun ownership and gun control are complex. At the turn of the century, Americans by better than two-to-one margins felt it was more important to regulate gun ownership than protect the rights of Americans to own guns. By 2013, those positions had drawn even.[40] Yet, Americans overwhelmingly support basic gun control policies, such as a waiting period on the purchase of handguns.[41]

14.7 Right to Privacy

The Constitution never mentions a **right to privacy**. Neither does the Bill of Rights. Over time, though, the Court has determined that there is an implied right to privacy that may be found in several constitutional passages, and from this construction, it has secured rights ranging from legal contraceptive use to legalized abortion.

L.O. Explain the origins and applications of the right to privacy.

right to privacy: The protection against government interference in private matters, which is not specifically guaranteed by the Constitution but which has been established by the Court and used to legalize contraception and abortion.

The road to this destination was uneven and bumpy. In 1902, a man living in Cambridge, Massachusetts, refused to participate in a smallpox vaccination program that was administered by city officials who feared an outbreak of the disease. He was tried, convicted, fined five dollars, and told that he would have to get a shot. The case reached the Supreme Court, where a judgment was rendered in favor of Massachusetts on the grounds that when any individual refuses to be vaccinated against a contagious disease, he or she passes the risks of vaccination to neighbors but assumes the benefits of immunity by living in an area where an outbreak is unlikely. The Court regarded the situation as a social contract issue, where individuals have to surrender some of their freedom in order for society to function effectively.[42]

However, the Court also recognized that not every situation fits this pattern, and in so doing, established that citizens have the constitutionally guaranteed freedom to be left alone by government, which comes into play when it is not outweighed by prevailing social concerns (like making sure a city is vaccinated against a deadly disease). This was the first step to establishing a right to privacy, which was articulated sixty-three years later in *Griswold v. Connecticut*.[43]

14.7a Privacy and Birth Control

In the early 1960s, Estelle Griswold, the executive director of the Planned Parenthood League of Connecticut, was convicted along with a Yale University medical professor of violating a Connecticut law against advising others in the use of contraceptive devices when they counseled and prescribed birth control for a married couple at the Planned Parenthood offices. They petitioned the Supreme Court to overturn the conviction on the grounds that the Connecticut law violated their civil liberties.

The Court agreed. Writing for the majority, Justice Douglas acknowledged that the right to marital privacy is not mentioned in the Constitution, but—as we've seen—neither is the right to associate, even though the First Amendment has been interpreted to include that right. Furthermore, Douglas argued that there are places in the Constitution where "Various guarantees create zones of privacy," including:

- The right of association implied by the First Amendment
- The Third Amendment prohibition against being forced by the government to house soldiers during peacetime
- The Fourth Amendment guarantee against unreasonable searches and seizures
- The Fifth Amendment protection against self-incrimination
- The Ninth Amendment assurance that personal rights should not be construed to be limited to those enumerated in the Constitution[44]

Douglas concluded that the evidence pointed to a constitutional right to marital privacy, which, while not expressed in the Constitution, is in keeping with the intent of its authors. "We deal," he wrote, "with a right of privacy older than the Bill of Rights."[45]

The immediate effect of the *Griswold* decision was to legalize the use of contraceptives among married couples. This right was soon extended to unmarried persons.[46]

14.7b Privacy and Abortion Rights

As we saw in Section 12.9, "Consistency and Legitimacy?," the right to privacy was also the basis for legalizing abortion. In the controversial case *Roe v. Wade*, Justice Blackmun established that the right to privacy was "broad enough to encompass a woman's decision whether or not to terminate her pregnancy."[47]

This line of reasoning has become a fault line in the abortion controversy because it has generated passionate debate about when or whether a fetus should be considered part of a woman's body, permitting abortion to be a private decision. The Court addressed this issue by assigning different conditions to each of pregnancy's trimesters. An unfettered right to privacy was applied to the first trimester, when the abortion decision may be left to a woman in private consultation with her physician. In the second trimester, the state may intervene in the decision for reasons involving the health of the mother. The state can prohibit abortion in the final trimester.[48]

The rationale behind this decision is that at some point the fetus becomes viable, and the choice to have an abortion is no longer without consequences for the developing child. In the absence of a definitive medical determination about when life begins, the Court acted to protect the privacy rights of the mother without making those rights absolute. The problem this generated is that many people have strong beliefs about when life begins despite the absence of medical proof, and those who believe it begins at conception reject as immoral the application of a right to privacy over abortion decisions at any term. Those who subscribe to the Court's logic argue passionately about the immorality of permitting the state to make intimate decisions about a woman's body when a pregnancy is not viable.[49]

Whether the Constitution may be interpreted to include a right to privacy was a major point of contention during the 2005 and 2006 confirmation hearings for Chief Justice John Roberts and Justice Samuel Alito. With the ideological balance of the Supreme Court at stake, abortion opponents pressed for justices who might question the right to privacy as a basis for reversing *Roe v. Wade*. Abortion supporters worried that President Bush's nominees might not agree that there is an implied right to privacy in the Constitution, threatening the *Roe* decision and perhaps *Griswold* as well.

14.7c Privacy and Physician-Assisted Suicide

The right to privacy is also a factor in the controversy over whether critically ill individuals should have the right to end their lives. The debate about physician-assisted suicide raises questions arising at the end of life that echo the issues raised in the abortion debate about the start of life: Is it a form of murder or a personal decision without repercussions for anyone but the individual involved?

Physician-assisted suicide involves doctors giving terminally ill patients the means for death, usually in the form of a prescription drug. Physician-assisted suicide is not euthanasia because the doctor does not actively participate in the patient's death. The patient must be of sound mind and make a rational decision to approach a doctor for a medical means to suicide, which the patient then applies without assistance.

In a culture that celebrates life and tends not to talk about issues surrounding death, it's not surprising that physician-assisted suicide is controversial. It flies against widely held religious beliefs about the sanctity of life and appears to invert the role of the doctor to do everything possible to save lives, although advocates contend that it is consistent with the physician's obligation to end suffering and that it is a compassionate choice for terminally ill patients in unbearable pain. Opponents worry that it will be abused, with patients who lack access to good medical treatment being forced into it, and patients suffering from depression rather than pain being most interested in it. This gives assisted suicide a complex moral and ethical dimension.

The Hemlock Society, an organization advocating the right to die, secured a spot on the 1994 Oregon ballot for an initiative to legalize physician-assisted suicide. Lobbying on both sides of the measure was intense, with groups as diverse as estate lawyers and the Catholic Church in opposition. Voters divided closely on the issue, opting to approve it by a slender 51–49 margin. Opponents went to court to block implementation, but their case was dismissed by the U.S. Circuit Court. Opponents then tried to overturn the law with a referendum of their own, but that measure failed by a wide margin, and Oregon became the first state in the union to legalize assisted suicide.[50] Ten months after the law went into effect, only eight people had taken advantage of it, suggesting that the Oregon experiment with physician-assisted suicide had not turned the state into a destination for large numbers of people looking for a final alternative to painful terminal illness.[51]

When the George W. Bush administration took office, the Justice Department moved to overturn the Oregon law. However, the lower courts repeatedly kept the law in place.

Finally, the Supreme Court agreed to decide the matter. In 2006, the Court ruled in favor of physician-assisted suicide in *Gonzales v. State of Oregon*, and the Oregon law was allowed to remain on the books.[52] Oregon has since been joined by five other states, including California, in legalizing physician-assisted suicide.

Chapter Review

Define civil liberties, and explain how they are protected by the Constitution, the Bill of Rights, and judicial precedent.

Civil liberties are constitutional and legal protections against government infringement on personal freedoms. Many civil liberties are protected by the Bill of Rights, although some are found in the Constitution and others were established through judicial precedent.

Define due process, and explain why it is central to the protection of civil liberties.

Due process, or protection against the arbitrary actions of government, is central to our civil liberties. Due process guarantees fixed and equitable procedures for being charged with and prosecuted for a crime, including the right to a swift jury trial and protection against double jeopardy, unreasonable searches and seizures, and self-incrimination. Due process also carries constitutional guarantees against cruel and unusual punishment. Opponents of capital punishment have argued that it should be classified as cruel and unusual, although the Court has disagreed.

Identify the establishment clause, and explain how it can be applied to different interpretations of the separation between church and state.

The First Amendment guarantees a host of personal liberties: religious freedom, freedom of speech, freedom of the press, and freedom of assembly. The First Amendment's establishment clause is the basis for the separation of church and state. This is accepted to mean that the federal government cannot establish a church or force people to attend or not attend a church, but there is disagreement about the height of the barrier between church and state. For instance, advocates of school prayer understand religious freedom to be the freedom to permit prayer in school; opponents of school prayer understand it to mean protection from prayer in school. The First Amendment's free exercise clause restricts government from interfering with religious practices, but this right is not absolute.

Understand the limits to constitutionally protected free speech.

Similarly, free expression is constitutionally protected—but not in all instances. The government can limit speech that poses a clear and present danger to others, and in the 1960s, the Court tightened that standard to speech that incited "imminent lawless action." The Court has also affirmed that constitutional safeguards apply to symbolic speech, like flag burning, although the Court was divided over the matter. Efforts to pass a constitutional amendment banning flag burning have come close to passage on several recent occasions. Unpopular expression may be the most difficult to deal with. Speech codes established at some universities in a "politically correct" effort to contend with offensive expression have met opposition in the courts because of the restrictions they placed on free expression.

Appreciate why the press is granted constitutional protections.

The press is the only for-profit private business granted constitutional protection because its obligations to keep people informed and to provide a check on government power are of central importance to democracy. The First Amendment protects the press from prior restraint, or government censorship. Publishing on the Internet adds a new dimension to free expression, especially when it entails hateful material or material some may deem obscene. The Communications Decency Act of 1996 attempted to set guidelines, but the Internet's global reach confounds the traditional legal test of applying contemporary community standards to determine if public communication is protected speech.

Distinguish the right to assemble from the right to associate.

The First Amendment also protects freedom of assembly and the right to petition the government, provided that it occurs peacefully. The Court has extended the First Amendment to protect the freedom to form associations, like interest groups and political parties.

Recognize the political controversy surrounding the Second Amendment right to bear arms.

The Second Amendment right to bear arms has been understood in different ways over the years, either as an individual grant of freedom to possess firearms or as a collective right to form state militias. The Court has been reluctant to weigh in on the matter, and the controversy over gun control has played out largely in the legislative arena.

Explain the origins and applications of the right to privacy.

One place where the Court has been quite proactive is in establishing a right to privacy, which is not addressed specifically in the Constitution. The right to privacy has been applied to the legalization of contraceptive devices and was the foundation for the *Roe v. Wade* decision that legalized abortion.

Key Terms

Bill of Rights The first ten amendments to the Constitution, which limit government from denying us a range of personal liberties. (p. 426)

bills of attainder Declarations of guilt by legislative decree without benefit of a trial. (p. 427)

civil liberties Constitutional and legal protections against government infringement on a host of personal freedoms. (p. 426)

clear and present danger The standard established by Justice Oliver Wendell Holmes for determining when the government could limit speech. (p. 434)

Communications Decency Act of 1996 A legislative attempt to regulate the transmission of "offensive" or "indecent" material over the Internet. The Supreme Court overturned most of the provisions of the Communications Decency Act. (p. 438)

double jeopardy Protection against the state using its power to repeatedly prosecute someone until the person is convicted. Double jeopardy precludes the prosecution of someone for the same crime in the same jurisdiction more than once. (p. 428)

due process The protection of individual liberty from the arbitrary or capricious actions of government through a defined set of legal procedures designed to protect the rights of the accused. (p. 427)

establishment clause The language in the First Amendment that serves as the basis for the constitutional separation of church and state. (p. 430)

ex post facto **laws** From the Latin for "after the fact," legislation that makes something a crime that was legal when it occurred. (p. 427)

exclusionary rule To protect against unreasonable searches and seizures, the Supreme Court has established that evidence obtained illegally is not admissible in court. (p. 427)

free exercise clause The language in the First Amendment that limits government interference in private religious beliefs and practices. (p. 430)

Gideon v. Wainwright The 1963 Supreme Court case that established the right to have an attorney appointed at no charge by the court to defendants unable to afford representation. It was brought by Clarence Earl Gideon, who was sentenced to five years in prison for breaking into a pool hall. From prison, Gideon filed a *habeas corpus* petition, claiming his right to an attorney was violated because he was forced by poverty to represent himself at his trial. (p. 428)

libel The legal restriction against the malicious publication of material that knowingly damages an individual's reputation. (p. 437)

Miranda rights The Court requirement, following a judgment in the case *Miranda v. Arizona* (1966), that apprehended individuals know and understand that they have a right against self-incrimination and a right to be represented by an attorney. (p. 428)

plea bargain A compromise between a defendant, defense attorney, and prosecutor, whereby the defendant foregoes due process and agrees to plead guilty without a trial to a lesser charge in exchange for a more lenient punishment. (p. 429)

prior restraint Censorship of the news by government officials before it is published or broadcast. (p. 436)

right to privacy The protection against government interference in private matters, which is not specifically guaranteed by the Constitution but which has been established by the Court and used to legalize contraception and abortion. (p. 439)

writ of *habeas corpus* From the Latin for "you have the body," *habeas corpus* puts the burden on the courts to demonstrate that a defendant's rights have not been violated prior to sentencing. People who believe they have been imprisoned against their constitutional rights have the privilege to petition for their release. (p. 427)

Resources

You might be interested in examining some of what the following authors have said about the topics we've been discussing:

On Capital Punishment

Epstein, Lee, and Joseph F. Kobylka. *The Supreme Court and Legal Change: Abortion and the Death Penalty*. Chapel Hill, NC: University of North Carolina Press, 1992.

On School Prayer

Alley, Robert S. *Without a Prayer: Religious Expression in Public Schools*. Amherst, NY: Prometheus Books, 1996.

On Flag Burning

Goldstein, Robert Justin. *Flag Burning and Free Speech: The Case of Texas v. Johnson*. Lawrence, KS: University Press of Kansas, 2000.

On Hate Speech and Political Correctness

Heumann, Milton, and Thomas W. Church, eds. *Hate Speech on Campus*. Boston: Northeastern University Press, 1997.

On Gun Control

Vizzard, William J. *Shots in the Dark: The Policy, Politics, and Symbolism of Gun Control*. Lanham, MD: Rowman & Littlefield Publishers, 2000.

On Physician-Assisted Suicide

Urofsky, Melvin I. *Lethal Judgments: Assisted Suicide and American Law*. Lawrence, KS: University Press of Kansas, 2000.

Notes

1 Howard N. Meyer, *The Amendment That Refused to Die: Equality and Justice Deferred: The History of the Fourteenth Amendment* (Lantham, MD: Madison Books, 2000), 4–5.

2 J. Roland Pennock and John W. Chapman (eds.), *Due Process* (New York: New York University Press, 1977), 3–4.

3 American Civil Liberties Union website, at https://www.aclu.org/issues/capital-punishment.

4 General Social Survey 2014, Cross-Section and Panel Combined, at http://www.thearda.com/Archive/Files/Analysis/GSS2014/GSS2014_Var145_1.asp.

5 Ibid.

6 *Everson v. Board of Education of the Township of Ewing*, 330 US 1 (1947).

7 Center for Religious Freedom, "Questions and Answers about the Religious Freedom Amendment," at http://crf.hudson.org/index.cfm?fuseaction=about_detail.

8 United States Department of State, "Facts about America."

9 William K. Muir, Jr., *Prayer in the Public Schools* (Chicago: University of Chicago Press, 1967), 15.

10 *Abington Township School District v. Schempp*, 374 US 203 (1963).

11 Robert S. Alley, *Without a Prayer: Religious Expression in Public Schools* (Amherst, NY: Prometheus Books, 1996), 128–138.

12 Sarah Barringer Gordon, "The Mormon Question: Polygamy and Constitutional Conflict in Nineteenth Century America," *Penn Law Journal*, Spring 2002.

13 *Reynolds v. United States*, 98 US 145 (1878).

14 *Employment Division, Oregon Department of Human Resources v. Smith*, 494 US 872 (1990).

15 *Bob Jones University v. United States*, 461 US 574 (1983).

16 *Schenck v. United States*, 249 US 27 (1919).

17 Nicholas Capaldi, *Clear and Present Danger: The Free Speech Controversy* (New York: Pegasus, 1969), 71–75.

18 *Schenck v. United States*, 249 US 27 (1919).

19 *Debbs v. United States*, 249 US 211 (1919).

20 *Whitney v. California*, 274 US 357 (1927).

21 *Brandenberg v. Ohio*, 395 US 444 (1969).

22 Ellen Schrecker, *The Age of McCarthyism* (Boston: Bedford Books, 1994), 92–94.

23 *Dennis v. United States*, 341 US 494 (1951).

24 Jerome A. Barron and C. Thomas Dienes, *First Amendment Law in a Nutshell* (St. Paul, MN: West Publishing Company, 1993), 47–48.

25 Ibid., 48.

26 Ibid., 52–54.

27 Steven Pressman, "Libel Law in the United States," Department of State International Information Programs at http://usa.usembassy.de/etexts/media/unfetter/press08.htm.

28 Jeremy Harris Lipschultz, *Free Expression in the Age of the Internet: Social and Legal Boundaries* (Boulder, CO: Westview Press, 2000), 10–11. See also 277–304.

29 Mike Godwin, *Cyber Rights: Defending Free Speech in the Digital Age* (New York: Times Books, 1998), 73–100.

30 Ibid., 101–132.

31 Barron and Dienes, *First Amendment Law*, 88.

32 *Roth v. United States*, 354 US 476 (1957).

33 *A Book Named "John Cleland's Memoirs of a Woman of Pleasure" v. Attorney-General*, 383 US 413 (1966). See also *Miller v. California*, 413 US 15 (1973).

34 Ibid.

35 *De Jonge v. Oregon*, 299 US 353 (1937).

36 *Edwards v. South Carolina*, 372 US 229 (1963).

37 *Thornhill v. Alabama*, 310 US 88 (1940).

38 *National Socialist Party of America v. Skokie*, 432 US 43 (1977).

39 Barron and Dienes, *First Amendment Law*, 238–239.

40 Andrew Kohut, "Despite Lower Crime Rates, Support for Gun Rights Increases," Pew Research Center. http://www.pewresearch.org/fact-tank/2015/04/17/despite-lower-crime-rates-support-for-gun-rights-increases/.

41 John Sides, "Gun Owners vs. the NRA: What the Polling Shows," *Washington Post*, December 23, 2012. https://www.washingtonpost.com/news/wonk/wp/2012/12/23/gun-owners-vs-the-nra-what-the-polling-shows/?utm_term=.92bb2fa79e00.

42 *Jacobson v. Commonwealth of Massachusetts*, 197 US 11 (1905).

43 James E. Leahy, *Liberty, Justice and Equality: How These Constitutional Guarantees Have Been Shaped by United States Supreme Court Decisions Since 1789* (Jefferson, NC: McFarland & Co., 1992), 19.

44 *Griswold v. Connecticut*, 381 US 479 (1965).

45 Quoted in Leahy, *Liberty, Justice, and Equality*, 20.

46 *Eisenstadt v. Baird*, 405 US 438 (1972).

47 Quoted in Leahy, *Liberty, Justice, and Equality*, 22.

48 Ibid., 23.

49 L. J. Macfarlane, *The Theory and Practice of Human Rights* (New York: St. Martin's Press, 1985), 22–23.

50 Melvin I. Uroofsky, *Lethal Judgments: Assisted Suicide and American Law* (Lawrence, KS: University Press of Kansas, 2000), 101–104.

51 Ibid., 158–159.

52 *Gonzales v. State of Oregon*, 546 US 243 (2006).

Table, Figure, and Box Notes

T1 Herbert Jacob, *Law and Politics in the United States*, 2nd ed. (New York: HarperCollins College Publishers, 1995), 163–175.

T2 Data from http://people.smu.edu/rhalperi/summary.html.

T3 Robert E. Pierre and Kari Lyderson, "Illinois Death Row Emptied," *Washington Post*, January 12, 2003, sec. A.

T4 Ibid.

T5 Lee Epstein and Joseph F. Kobylka, *The Supreme Court and Legal Change: Abortion and the Death Penalty* (Chapel Hill: University of North Carolina Press, 1992), 34–82.

T6 Ibid.

T7 *Coker v. Georgia*, 433 US 584 (1977); and *Atkins v. Virginia*, 536 US 304 (2002).

T8 Gallup Poll, at http://www.gallup.com/poll/1606/death-penalty.aspx.

T9 Death Penalty Information Center, at http://www.deathpenaltyinfo.org/states-and-without-death-penalty.

T10 Gurney image is in the public domain in the United States because it is a work of the United States Federal Government under the terms of Title 17, Chapter 1, Section 105 of the US Code.

T11 American Civil Liberties Union, at http://www.aclu.org/free-speech/flag-desecration.

T12 Robert Justin Goldstein, *Flag Burning and Free Speech: The Case of Texas v. Johnson* (Lawrence, KS: University Press of Kansas, 2000) xii–xiv.

T13 Ibid., xi.

T14 Citizens Flag Alliance, at http://www.cfa-inc.org/about.

T15 American Civil Liberties Union, at http://www.aclu.org/free-speech/flag-desecration.

T16 Dean Schabner, "Love or Obscenity?: S/M Photographer Challenges Internet Decency Standards," ABCNews.com, June 29, 2002.

T17 The National Coalition for Sexual Freedom website at www.ncsfreedom.org/.

T18 Yousuf Dhamee, "Obscenity and the Internet: The Communications Decency Act," at http://www.cyberartsweb.org/cpace/politics/decency.html.

T19 See the Center for Democracy and Technology, at http://cdt.org/.

Domestic Policy and Policy Making

Copyright: Dima Sobko/Shutterstock.com

Learning Objectives

When you have completed this chapter, you should be able to:

- Define and distinguish between competitive and protective regulatory policies, and give examples of each.
- Explain why some regulatory policies can be controversial.
- Define and distinguish between distributive and redistributive or social welfare policies, and give examples of each.
- Explain why distributive policies are generally less controversial than redistributive policies.
- Define entitlements.
- Correctly identify which groups benefit most from social welfare policies.
- Identify major sources of tax revenue.
- Explain why the American tax code has a progressive structure.
- Identify the major sources of government spending.
- Explain deficit spending, and distinguish deficits from debt.

15.1 Introduction

Should the government spend more money to protect the environment? In one recent survey, 60 percent of Americans said yes. What about more money for health care? That was supported by 58 percent of the population. Education? Seventy-four percent said spend more on that. Almost half want to spend more on law enforcement. Over half want to spend more on Social Security.

How about taxes to pay for all these spending increases? Should taxes be raised? Hardly. Fifty-seven percent of survey respondents said taxes are *too high* and should be lowered.[1]

Welcome to the world of domestic policy making, where we ask government officials to make choices on our behalf about how to spend our tax money. Collectively, the guidance we give them is a bit confusing. We want our representatives to support popular programs that benefit a lot of people, like Social Security, and spend money dealing with problems that concern a lot of us, like education and the environment. We also tend to feel we're paying *too much* in taxes and that a lot of that money gets wasted on things that government shouldn't be doing. This feeling is compounded by the fact that we don't have the option of stipulating how we want our tax dollars spent.[2]

Things aren't any less murky when it comes to whether or how government should regulate the way we go about our lives. Many things of value, like clean drinking water, safe workplaces, and cars that don't explode on impact, won't happen without a guiding hand (or a firm shove) from government. Still, many people recoil from the idea of having government place restrictions on their freedom.

You can make the argument that domestic policies should not be the product of a popularity contest. Some programs that assist disadvantaged people, like welfare and Medicaid, are controversial because the taxpayers who support them are not the ones receiving the benefits. That may not be sufficient reason, though, to curtail them. Instead, controversial policies are best developed (or rejected) following protracted political debates about what and how much government should do to assist the needy, or fight crime, or encourage the use of fuel-efficient cars.

We'll focus our attention on those debates because they represent the place where we can have the most influence over the political process. We'll emphasize two controversial types of domestic policy, where the decisions we make define what we're like as a society. The first is regulatory policy, which revolves around issues of how much the government should intervene in the operation of free markets. The second is social welfare policy, which you may be surprised to find is about a lot more than simply helping people in need. We'll also look at the budgetary process and discuss federal taxing and spending policies—two political buzzwords that are often heard in domestic political debates.

15.2 Regulatory Policies

L.O. Define and distinguish between competitive and protective regulatory policies, and give examples of each.

If everything the free market produced were beneficial for society, we wouldn't be talking about government managing private affairs, but the quest to maximize self-interest can have undesirable consequences for society as a whole. If you run a manufacturing plant where the cheapest way for you to dispose of industrial waste is to dump it in the river, you're probably going to do it unless someone stops you. If you run an airline and decide you want to fly from Denver to Cleveland, imagine the danger and confusion that would result if you just started flying jets without regard to who else might be sharing the skies.

regulatory policies: Domestic policies designed to protect the public from harmful conditions that could result from unrestrained free-market competition or to ensure the benefits of a level playing field for private competition.

This is where government steps in with **regulatory policies** designed to maximize benefits or minimize hazards that private enterprise alone will not address. You may remember regulatory policies from Chapter 11 (Section 11.5b, "Regulation,"), when we addressed regulations as being among the things the bureaucracy implements.

There are several reasons why government might regulate private activity:

- The market can cause confusion that undermines the public interest.
- The market may not give consumers important, beneficial information that could influence their choices.

- The market may produce undesirable personal outcomes.
- The market may produce undesirable social outcomes.

Let's look at each of these possibilities.

15.2a Serving the Public Interest

Let's say you wanted to operate a radio station in Salt Lake City. You have the necessary financing, so you proceed to put in place the hardware you'll need to set up your station. To give yourself the best possible market position, you'll of course want to broadcast on the most desirable frequency. No doubt, so will your competition. If you and the others were to go ahead and start broadcasting without regard to one another, the result would be chaotic. You know this, of course, and so do your competitors, but why should you be the one to back off and take a less desirable frequency?

Enter government and the requirement that you have to apply for a license before you operate a radio station. The Communications Act of 1934 protected the broadcast spectrum as a public resource and established the Federal Communications Commission (FCC) to issue public licenses to private organizations wishing to operate radio and television frequencies.

With the authority to regulate the airwaves by granting broadcasting licenses, the federal government can hold broadcasters to a set of standards that promote the "public interest." If protection against monopoly control of the media is considered to be in the public interest, as it was through the 1980s, the FCC can place limits on the number of licenses it will grant to a single corporation that wants to operate multiple television and radio stations in a given city. If public affairs programming is considered to be in the public interest, the FCC can require that television and radio stations devote a percentage of their broadcast time to news and information programs as a condition of keeping their license. If increased minority ownership of broadcast outlets is considered to be in the public interest, as it has been in recent years, the FCC can give licensing priority to minority-run organizations.[3]

As with any domestic policy, regulation produces winners and losers. When the government regulates in the effort to serve the public interest by determining who can provide a public service like operating a broadcast outlet, winners and losers are narrowly constrained to those elite groups—for instance, broadcast organizations—that apply for government licenses. This type of regulation is called a **competitive regulatory policy** because not every applicant to operate a television or radio station will be granted a license (of course, a corporation denied a license to broadcast in one city can apply to broadcast in another). As part of its regulatory function, a regulatory agency can assess applicants against established "public interest" standards and decide which applications will be approved.

competitive regulatory policy: A type of regulatory policy designed to protect the public interest by restricting the provision of a service or good to organizations that win federal licensing approval.

15.2b Providing Beneficial Information

Do you smoke cigarettes? Even if you don't, you're probably familiar with the warning label that appears on every pack, informing you of the risks of smoking. Warning labels have appeared on cigarettes in some form since the 1960s, when cigarette manufacturers were required to publish the qualified message that "cigarette smoking may be hazardous to your health." The tobacco industry opposed the move to tag their product as a health risk, but Congress authorized the labels under its obligation to notify the public about product hazards once evidence began to mount that cigarette smoking might be linked to health problems. Their intent was to keep cigarettes on the market but to notify smokers that using them could be risky, in order to give consumers the information they would need to make an informed purchasing decision.[4]

This type of **protective regulatory policy** comes into play when government officials decide the public is best served by being provided with information that would not be supplied voluntarily by manufacturers or service providers. In the case of cigarettes, the requirement to instruct the public about smoking perils falls far short of a policy that

protective regulatory policy: Regulations that supply consumers with information needed to make informed purchasing decisions about such things as cigarettes and home loans or that prevent undesirable personal or social conditions like child labor or unsafe food.

Got Milk?

In 1998, the Food and Drug Administration (FDA) issued new regulatory guidelines to standardize the use of the terms "fat free," "reduced fat," and "low fat" in food products. The move was designed to make it easier for shoppers to know exactly what they were getting when they bought an item and to compare the fat content of that item with other products.

The change had the effect of replacing some old, familiar terms with new ones. Take the case of milk labeling. The new FDA regulations provided that:

- "Skim milk" would be known as "fat-free milk." It may also be called "nonfat" milk.
- "Two percent fat-free milk" would be known as "reduced fat milk."
- "One percent fat-free milk" would be known as "low-fat milk." It may also be called "light milk."
- "Whole milk" would be known as . . . "whole milk."[T1]

  Got that?

would prohibit the sale of cigarettes entirely, resting instead on the principle that consumers can make intelligent purchasing decisions provided they are informed about potential product risks.

Similar logic guides the requirement that food products carry nutrition fact labels, which state how much fat, sodium, cholesterol, and the like is contained in a serving of every packaged item you can find on supermarket shelves. Regulations stipulate that product servings have to be standardized for ease of comparison and dictate the standards a product has to meet before it can be designated "low fat" or "fat free" (see Demystifying Government: Got Milk?).

Some beneficial information is regulated so that business competition is carried out in an open environment. The Securities and Exchange Commission (SEC) has a long list of requirements for establishing public access to investment information. For instance, if you look for a home loan one day, you'll find that all lending institutions need to make their rates public. That protects you by making sure you've got access to the full range of information you need to find the best terms for your loan.

15.2c Preventing Undesirable Personal Outcomes

Some of our most far-reaching labor laws were protective regulatory provisions that emerged out of the sweatshop conditions found in many industrial facilities during the early part of the last century. Child labor, long a fixture in agrarian, nineteenth-century America, took on a gruesome quality as children as young as six years old would perform factory work for up to thirteen hours a day. Adults and children alike had no choice but to work for measly wages in dirty and often unsafe factories. Today, we would consider these circumstances unthinkable, but at the time, they were the natural outgrowth of an industrial market that required a lot of cheap labor.

It wasn't until 1938 that Congress passed the Fair Labor Standards Act, which imposed meaningful regulations on such things as child labor and compensation. Among other things, it established a minimum wage, overtime pay for long hours, and a minimum age of sixteen for entering the nonagricultural labor force.[5] As a consequence of federal regulation, things we take for granted as being fundamental to the structure of the contemporary workplace—like guaranteed minimum pay, overtime, and safe working conditions—have become commonplace.

15.2d Preventing Undesirable Social Outcomes

An unregulated market can also produce conditions that are harmful or undesirable to society. The pressure to maximize profits can make cutting corners an attractive option to some companies, provided they don't go too far and undermine public confidence in their products. When producers make decisions about how unsafe to make a product, the temptation remains to push the limits too far, with the consequences being dangerous consumer products, unhealthy food, and unsafe drugs.

The rationale behind imposing government safety standards on everything from kitchens in restaurants to the construction of automobiles is to take safety decisions out of the hands of those who supply goods and services, who must bear the cost of making their products safer, and put them in the hands of government regulators who are positioned to think about the public interest rather than profitability. The next time you hear about a product recall or a restaurant that was shut down for health violations, you'll know it's because of a violation of regulatory guidelines that may not have been picked up if the manufacturer or restaurant had been permitted to self-police.

Regulations also require manufacturers to assume the cost of the unwanted by-products of production that would otherwise be passed along to everyone in the form of pollution. Environmental contamination produced by factory exhaust, toxic waste, and water pollution is a collective problem without a natural market solution. It's rational for producers to forego the often considerable cost and effort of environmental cleanup if they can. Regulatory policies requiring industrial polluters to constrain or repair environmental damage impose a form of social responsibility on industries that otherwise would, out of self-interest, exercise their liberty to avoid or ignore these costs. Essentially, government regulations coerce producers to pay the social costs of doing business rather than permit that cost to be passed on to society.

15.2e How Much Regulation?

We mentioned in Chapter 11 that regulations can be controversial, and you can probably see why. If you're the cigarette manufacturer who has to post warning labels that encourage people not to buy your product or the industrial plant that has to pick up the cost of antipollution devices, you're likely to balk at government regulations. Even if you're not, you may find yourself averse to the idea of regulation. The public has decidedly mixed attitudes toward regulatory policies. We generally want the benefits of clean air and safe food, but many people experience regulatory restrictions as unwelcome government interference—an attitude rooted in our fundamental embrace of liberty.

L.O. Explain why some regulatory policies can be controversial.

So environmental interest groups make a popular case when they argue in support of regulatory policies that would promote clean air and water, while former President George W. Bush also would get applause when he advocated fewer government regulations. You may even be philosophically inclined toward regulation in general but oppose particular regulations that are personally burdensome. A supporter of clean air who rides a bicycle to work is likely to be more supportive of a $2-per-gallon gasoline tax designed to regulate automobile use than is an environmentalist in an SUV. Your position on regulatory matters may well come down to whether you benefit more than you pay.

Some people don't object to the cost or philosophy of regulation so much as they have a problem with the way regulations are made and the sometimes undesirable effects they have. Their complaints have more to do with regulations that misunderstand and therefore fail to treat the problems they're designed to regulate and with unintended side effects of regulations.

Take the example of a thirty-five-page Environmental Protection Agency regulation that required oil refineries to filter smokestacks for the pollutant benzene. An Amoco refinery in Virginia complied with the regulation at a cost of $31 million, only to find that their investment did virtually nothing to cut down on the benzene being emitted by the plant. That was because the pollution was coming from fumes escaping from gasoline being pumped into barges on the loading docks. The regulation missed this simple point.[6]

There are plenty of other examples available to anyone who wants to make the case that regulations written in Washington run the risk of missing what's going on in the places where they are to be implemented. Critics point to such things as the unanticipated consequences of regulations designed to scrub toxic waste from land to be reused for industrial purposes. To avoid the expense of complying with this requirement, industries rationally seek to locate on clean sites farther away from highly developed urban areas. To reach them, workers have to spend more time in their cars. The result: more pollution.[7]

Critics of regulatory policies sometimes object to the process by which regulations are developed and implemented. They see individual initiative being hamstrung by rules written by lawyers and feel the evils that regulations are designed to address could be fought more successfully by the commonsense insights of those who are close to the problem.[8]

Some regulatory costs and benefits are intangible, leaving decisions about whether to regulate open to nonmonetary considerations. The question of whether to open the Arctic National Wildlife Reserve in Alaska to oil drilling is a sensitive issue that pits regulatory tendencies against free-market interests over a course of action that's filled with intangibles. Read on for a discussion of the matter in Demystifying Government: Environment vs. Oil.

15.3 Distributive Policies

distributive policies: Domestic policies primarily aimed at directing tax money to a range of public works items. Distributive policies tend not to be controversial because benefits are widely shared.

pork barrel: Wasteful or unnecessary spending that can result from logrolling. Whether something is a pork-barrel project or a valuable use of taxpayer dollars may depend on whether you stand to benefit from it.

public works: Civic projects built with tax dollars.

Regulatory policies are controversial because they create clear winners and losers, and because they invoke the debate over how much government should do to manage private affairs. **Distributive policies** are much less contentious. They entail spending tax dollars on a large host of items that individually benefit specific constituencies but, when taken collectively, offer something for just about everyone. This makes it hard to identify true winners and losers, inasmuch as the costs and benefits of distributive policy are spread around, and easy to make the claim that, in the aggregate, everyone benefits to some degree from distributive policies.[9]

To be sure, some of what we call distributive policy is the end result of **pork-barrel** politics, but that's not to say that distributive policies are simply wasteful. Many distributive policies are **public works** projects: infrastructure development that is undertaken exclusively or predominantly by government. Many of these are built and maintained by states and localities, and include such facilities as roads, bridges, schools, hospitals, sewer systems, airports, and municipal water plants. However, the federal government supports a long list of public works projects as well, sometimes operating on its own and sometimes providing federal funds to offset the cost of state projects.

In 2009, President Obama signed a stimulus bill designed to jump-start the sagging economy by, in part, spending federal money on a host of public works projects, including:

- $1.3 billion for highway, bridge, and road repairs
- $1.1 billion for airport improvements
- $8 billion for high-speed rail development
- $220 million for levee repairs on the Rio Grande
- $650 million for watershed and Forest Service improvements[10]

In one way or another, we all benefit from expenditures on national infrastructure. Even if you don't drive a car, you benefit indirectly from expenditures on highways and roads whenever you buy products at a store that were shipped by truck (see Demystifying Government: Interstate Highways and the Politics of Distribution). You may never fly on a plane, but you benefit from public expenditures on airports every time you send or receive an overnight package. Because most people recognize these benefits, expenditures on distributive policies of this nature are typically easy to accept.

There are places, though, where the question of how much to spend becomes a matter of public debate. One such place is the military budget. National defense is one of the most important services provided by the government, something we all contribute to through our taxes and something we all benefit from. Because we make it a major national priority, procurement of military items takes up a big portion of the federal budget. In fact, our military budget is the largest on Earth, which leads some people to ask how much military spending we need in order to assure our security. We'll take up the issue in Chapter 16, when we talk about defense policy.

Environment vs. Oil

In the farthest reaches of northeastern Alaska, beyond the majestic mountains of the Brooks Range, lies 19 million acres of wilderness called the Arctic National Wildlife Refuge (ANWR). Most Americans will never see it, but it's home to over 160 species of birds, 36 types of land mammals, and a wide assortment of marine life sharing what the U.S. Fish and Wildlife Service says is "among the most complete, pristine, and undisturbed ecosystems on earth."[T2]

Wandering caribou share the land with musk oxen, grizzly bears, and wolverines; snow geese and golden eagles dot the horizon. Coastal lagoons, tundra, boreal forests, and snow-capped mountains create an unmatched habitat that supports the rich diversity of wildlife. It is home to the Gwich'in people, who sustain themselves with food and clothing provided by the caribou of the Porcupine River and sustain their culture through intricate links to the coastal plain, which is their sacred ground. All have lived under the protection of the U.S. government, which has maintained the refuge under the direction of the Department of the Interior and has protected it from development.

None of this would be controversial if the Arctic National Wildlife Refuge wasn't sitting on top of a large deposit of oil. Americans, of course, depend heavily on oil to sustain themselves and their culture. In the wake of the attacks of September 11, 2001, President Bush made the argument that the United States would become less dependent on oil from the Middle East by drilling for oil in the Arctic Refuge. At the time, the United States was more reliant on foreign oil than it is today, and legislation to drill in ANWR was approved by the House of Representatives in 2001 before dying in the Senate,[T4] but the idea never fully disappeared. John McCain made oil drilling a key component of his 2008 campaign's energy plan, and his running mate, Alaska Governor Sarah Palin, was supportive of drilling in ANWR. Taking the opposite approach, President Obama attempted to have ANWR protected as a wilderness area, which would forever preclude drilling, but a Republican Congress rejected his efforts.[T5] President Trump has signaled that he is supportive of drilling.

Environmental groups like the Alaska Wilderness League warn of catastrophic regional and global damage if oil-drilling equipment is permitted in the Arctic Refuge. They assert that oil drilling would destroy the delicate balance of the regional ecosystem by altering the historic migratory patterns of birds and land animals, threatening species that are dependent on them, and destroying the habitat that sustains the Gwich'in people. The potential for damage from oil spills and drilling-induced temperature increases have environmentalists fearing an epic disaster that could lead to

The Arctic National Wildlife Refuge (ANWR)[T3]

the disappearance of wildlife, lakes, and forests as the permafrost melts due to the effects of accelerated climate change.[T6]

Oil interests paint a different picture. Chris Kelley, a representative of the American Petroleum Institute, told the British Broadcasting Corporation that oil drilling is now handled in a manner that's safe for the environment, pointing to the smaller size of oil rigs that can drill multiple wells from one location, minimizing the amount of land surface that's affected.[T7] In his view, the environmental risks of drilling are trivial compared to the potential benefit of having the oil.

Still, critics of drilling question whether ANWR would produce enough oil to make a dent in American demand. Journalist and environmentalist Mark Lynas writes that all the oil in ANWR would only keep American homes and industries running for half a year.[T8] A far better alternative for environmentalists would be to encourage energy conservation measures at home. Simply improving car mileage efficiency by 3 mpg would in one year save double the amount of oil that the most optimistic projections say is under ANWR.

Oil interests dispute these claims. They say that energy conservation can only be one part of a national strategy that includes looking for new sources of oil and natural gas, and that ANWR is perhaps the most promising untapped domestic source. They emphasize the benefits of additional oil drilling, which produces more jobs in the oil industry and throughout the economy from companies that do business with oil interests. They also make the point that residents of Alaska share the economic benefits of oil drilling through payments made by the state from oil royalty funds. These jobs and revenues extend to the Gwich'in, helping to compensate for whatever disruption drilling may cause in their lives.

Interstate Highways and the Politics of Distribution

One of the more ambitious public works projects this country ever attempted is the Interstate Highway System, which makes it possible for you to drive from New York to San Francisco, or from Canada to Mexico, without stopping for a traffic light. The idea for an integrated system of highways dates back to the Great Depression (the 1939 New York World's Fair had an exhibit touting the "highway of the future"), but preoccupation with World War II kept plans from moving forward until years later.

The Federal-Aid Highway Act of 1944 authorized the development of a national system of interstate highways, setting the stage for future work. Half the cost of the project was to be funded with federal money, but plans were to be developed and implemented by individual state highway departments, pitting urban against rural interests over the issue of whether federal money would be allocated according to population density or the number of miles that had to be covered. Construction began in 1947, but was bogged down as states diverted federal highway money to other pressing local needs, complained that funding was too low to cover costs, or simply found federal construction guidelines to be too onerous.

The project received a major boost in 1954, as President Eisenhower committed his administration to the completion of a national highway network, couching the initiative in terms of economic need (to promote the transportation of goods and recover billions of dollars in labor lost to traffic jams), safety (to reduce highway deaths), and not insignificantly, national security (as a method of evacuating cities in the event of nuclear war). The latter point may seem ridiculous in today's post–Cold War world (or silly to anyone who's been stuck in a highway traffic jam on a holiday weekend). In the political environment of its day, however, Eisenhower's case helped break the political logjam.

It took two years for Congress to work through the contentious issues of how much the federal government would spend, how the funding would be allocated to the states, which taxes would be assessed to pay for the program, and how to calibrate a pay scale for construction workers operating in different parts of the country with widely varying wage rates. Compromises on these matters made possible the Federal-Aid Highway Act of 1956, which produced within a decade the Interstate Highway System that is now a fixture on the American landscape.[T9]

15.4 Social Welfare Policies

L.O. Define and distinguish between distributive and redistributive or social welfare policies, and give examples of each.

L.O. Explain why distributive policies are generally less controversial than redistributive policies.

redistributive policies: Domestic policies, like those promoting social welfare, that take resources from one group in the form of taxes and provide goods or services for another group, typically those in need.

transfer payments: The direct payment of public money to individuals who qualify for it under the terms of a social welfare program.

Possibly the most contentious domestic policy issues involve promoting social welfare. This is because social welfare policies are **redistributive policies**, where one group (such as working taxpayers) covers the costs while another group (such as the unemployed or poor) receives the benefits. Table 15.1 provides a quick overview of the major federal social welfare policies, including who's eligible for them and how they're funded.

Redistributive policies sound like the same thing as distributive policies, but they are entirely different. Remember, with distributive policies, there are no clear "winners" or "losers" because the costs and benefits of distributive policies are spread around. In contrast, redistributive policies redistribute resources from one group (which bears the cost) to another (which receives the benefit).

If redistributive policies sound like an attempt to address outcome disparities, you're right, and that adds another layer to the conflict produced by having one group of "winners" and a different group of "losers." Given our historical choice of equal opportunity over equal outcomes, many Americans are uneasy with the government getting heavily involved in programs that redistribute resources, at least up to a point. Welfare, for instance, is at its most controversial when people view it as a "way of life" rather than as short-term assistance, less so when it's viewed as a way to offer greater opportunity to traditionally disadvantaged groups.

There are exceptions to this controversial quality of redistributive policies. Social Security—perhaps the most popular federal program—is redistributive. It's just that most people don't know it (more on this in Section 15.4b, "Social Welfare for Everyone").

Social welfare policies usually involve making **transfer payments** from federal coffers directly to qualifying individuals. Typically, these are direct cash payments to individuals who meet the eligibility requirements for programs like unemployment compensa-

TABLE 15.1 Social Welfare Policies

Policy	Who Benefits	Who Pays	Cost	How It Works
Temporary Assistance to Needy Families (TANF)	The poor	Federal taxpayers	$17 billion in 2013	Federal money is provided to states through block grants for the purpose of moving welfare recipients into the workforce. Using federal guidelines, states determine eligibility and benefits.
Medicaid	The poor	Federal and state taxpayers	$545.1 billion in 2015	Jointly funded by the federal and state governments, Medicaid provides medical services to low-income individuals and families, including the elderly and disabled.
Food Stamps	The poor	Federal taxpayers	$75 billion in 2015	Recipients receive coupons that can be redeemed like cash for food in grocery stores in order to provide the means for a healthy diet. The program is run by the Federal Department of Agriculture but administered by the states.
Earned Income Tax Credit	The working poor	Federal taxpayers who do not receive the credit	$66.7 billion in 2014	Low-income wage earners are eligible for a payment when they file their federal income tax return. The payment either reduces the amount of income tax owed or provides the taxpayer with a refund check that exceeds the amount of tax owed.
Supplemental Security Income (SSI)	The elderly, blind, and disabled	Federal taxpayers	$53 billion in 2013	Money from general tax revenues is provided in the form of monthly cash payments to eligible seniors, the blind, and disabled individuals with limited income. People who get SSI usually also get Medicaid and food stamps.
Social Security	Retired and disabled workers, regardless of income	Workers and employers, through payroll taxes	$888 billion in 2015	Social Security provides retirement benefits in the form of monthly cash payments to workers over age 62 (full benefits kick in at age 65) who have worked a required number of years and to insured families of deceased workers. Social Security also provides disability payments to people under age 65 who cannot work because of physical or mental impairment.
Medicare	The elderly and disabled, regardless of income	Workers and employers, through payroll taxes; federal taxpayers; and Social Security recipients	$646.2 billion in 2015	Medicare Part A provides hospital insurance to persons over 65 and the disabled, with benefits paid to participating hospitals, emergency rooms, and nursing facilities. Workers and employers support it through payroll taxes. Medicare Part B provides voluntary supplementary medical insurance, covering up to 80 percent of outpatient medical expenses in exchange for a monthly premium and a small deductible. Medicare Part C offers a subsidized private insurance alternative, and Part D offers a subsidized prescription drug benefit.
Unemployment Insurance	Unemployed people, regardless of income	Employers, through federal and state taxes	$93 billion in 2012	Workers who lose their jobs involuntarily and are able to work are entitled to payments to offset part of their lost wages for a temporary period of time, up to a maximum of 26 weeks in most states. Recipients pay income tax on the benefits. Each state, under the direction of the Federal Department of Labor, administers its own version of the program.

tion, veteran's pension and life insurance, Social Security, or welfare benefits. Transfer payments also take the form of food stamps and assistance for medical services offered through Medicare and Medicaid.

15.4a Social Welfare for the Poor

L.O. Define entitlements.

The chief rationale for social welfare policies that aid the disadvantaged is found in the large income disparities that exist in the United States—disparities that grew larger in the last two decades of the twentieth century. As Figure 15.1 demonstrates, income during this period increased for Americans across the board, but the richest group got so much richer that the poorest Americans saw their share of total income decline. Disparities in wealth—what people own—are even greater.

In order to design government programs to assist the poor, you need a standardized definition of poverty. This is easier said than done because defining an income boundary that separates the poor from everyone else is an arbitrary exercise, no matter how or where that limit is set. The first to attempt it was a social worker named Robert Hunter, who studied the poor in America at the turn of the twentieth century and determined that an average (for those days) family of five lived in poverty if they earned less than $460 annually in industrial regions of the North, or $300 in the rural South. This was the minimum income that Hunter estimated was necessary to provide subsistence food, clothing, and shelter. To earn less than that, he said, was to live by the "same standard that a man would demand for his horses or slaves."[11]

poverty line: A statistical determination of poverty based on income and family size that is used to establish eligibility for some social welfare programs designed to assist those in need.

There have been many attempts since Hunter to calculate a **poverty line**. Under a formula in use for the past two generations, the U.S. Department of Health and Human Services placed the poverty line for a family of four at $24,036 in 2015.[12] This figure does not account for people who are living just above the poverty line, who could easily slip below it through an unforeseen reversal of fortune. It also does not indicate how many of these individuals are permanently poor and how many might be able to climb above the poverty line with an improvement in their financial circumstances.

Measured against the poverty line, 43.1 million Americans, or 13.5 percent of the population, lived in poverty in 2015. The rate was almost double this figure for African Amer-

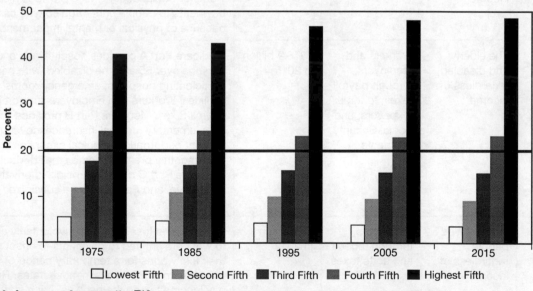

FIGURE 15.1 Income Inequality[T10]

Full income equality would mean that everyone's earnings were the same: The top one-fifth of the population would earn the same as the bottom one-fifth, so all the bars in the figure would rest on the horizontal line at the 20 percent mark. In reality, income inequality in the United States is pronounced, and has grown over the past four decades. In 1975, the top 20 percent claimed slightly more than 40 percent of all income. By 2015, that figure had increased to nearly 50 percent. The monumental income growth of the top 5 percent is one big reason for the shift. The top 5 percent earned 20.9 percent of aggregate income in 2015, up from 14.9 percent in 1975.

icans and considerably higher for Hispanics (21.4 percent) and among people under the age of 18 (19.7 percent). Poverty especially afflicts female-headed households severely. Regardless of whether they are white, African American, or Hispanic, women raising children without partners are more likely than any group to find themselves without the means to make ends meet.[13]

Determining who qualifies as impoverished is only part of the problem surrounding the design and administration of social welfare programs meant to aid the poor. The way you go about dealing with the effects of poverty has a lot to do with what you believe the causes of poverty to be, and on this point there is a great deal of disagreement. Is poverty the result of the actions of the impoverished or of the situation in which they find themselves? There are several schools of thought, among them:

Individual Explanations

- The poor lack the skills or motivation necessary to climb out of poverty.
- With well-paying jobs out of reach, the poor lack the motivation to get the training that would make them marketable.

Economic Explanations

- Social programs are generous enough to serve as a disincentive to finding work because they make minimum-wage jobs look like an unappealing alternative to welfare.
- The economy does not produce enough well-paying jobs to employ everyone.

Cultural Explanations

- The chronically poor develop a "culture of poverty" apart from mainstream culture, in which initiative and hard work are not valued.[14]

These arguments tend to divide along ideological lines. Conservatives traditionally attributed poverty to the personal characteristics of the poor, whose perceived lack of personal skills or motivation is reinforced by social programs that create a "culture of poverty" that discourages initiative. Liberals traditionally believed poverty was rooted in economics and were more likely to shy away from attributing poverty to cultural attributes, while believing motivational obstacles to overcoming poverty are rooted in a lack of opportunity caused by an economy that cannot produce enough jobs for the poor.

This has caused the two groups to talk past each other. One prominent conservative social theorist called the social welfare programs of the 1960s and 1970s a "trap" that "tried to provide more for the poor and produced more poor instead"[15] by substituting handouts for hard work. Liberals responded by accusing conservative critics of trafficking in mythology about cultural, individual, and economic characteristics when they assert that success comes to those with better values and the free market is the best mechanism for creating economic winners and losers.[16]

These traditional positions shifted a bit in response to changing economic conditions. Liberals, who in the 1960s tended to blame poverty on bad economic times, were more inclined during the boom years of the 1980s and 1990s to say the changing global economy undermined the desire of the poor to find work because it produced well-paying jobs that they had no hope of attaining. Conservatives, who once derided the poor as lacking initiative, later spoke of how increasingly generous welfare benefits provided a disincentive to working. In essence, the two sides swapped perspectives on how the economy and human nature contributed to poverty, with conservatives speaking more about the economic irrationality of welfare policy and liberals emphasizing the personal effects of poverty.[17]

If this looks to you like an inconclusive and even confusing debate, you probably won't be surprised to learn that public opinion has also fluctuated considerably on the issue of how we view the poor. The moral dimension of poverty leads some to believe that the poor are unworthy of assistance. People holding this view tend to equate welfare recipients with laziness because of their perceived dependence on the state, with socially undesirable behaviors like crime and drug use, or with behaviors that disregard family values, like out-of-wedlock childbirth. Yet, these attitudes vary in prominence in the public debate about poverty, tending to receive more attention during periods when public officials talk about "getting tough" on welfare.[18]

The same uneven pattern of public opinion applies to whether people feel we spend too much money on welfare programs. From 1976 to 1996, majorities twice found welfare spending to be too high: in the late 1970s and again in the early 1990s, with a peak near 60 percent in 1994, just before federal welfare programs were overhauled. These peaks in popular opposition to welfare coincide with peaks in the number of people on welfare. So, while it's possible these fluctuations in public opinion reflect shifting attitudes toward the poor, it's also possible that attitudes toward the poor follow attitudes about the cost of public support for the poor.[19]

It's reasonable to assume that people are aware of increases in spending on social programs for the poor because transfer payments to those in need automatically increase as more people qualify for assistance. Social welfare programs are **entitlements**, meaning everyone who fits a benefit category is eligible for support. The government places a **means test** on programs aiding the poor, like Medicaid, food stamps, and Supplementary Security Income, so that as more individuals fall below the poverty line (or a similar statistical measure of eligibility), they automatically qualify for transfer payments. In contrast, programs designed to address temporary setbacks (like unemployment insurance) or support seniors (like Social Security and Medicare) are entitlements without means tests: If you become unemployed or reach the legal age designated for retirement benefits, you're eligible for those benefits regardless of whether you're rich or poor. As entitlements, social welfare policies are expensive and open-ended.

15.4b Social Welfare for Everyone

In an age when many people have little faith in the government to operate successful social programs, **Social Security** stands out as the great exception. Created by the Social Security Act of 1935 during the Great Depression to assure a basic level of subsistence to people in their retirement years, Social Security is arguably the most successful federal program in history. It has achieved its stated purpose and provided generations of seniors with a social safety net that has enabled them to anticipate a basic level of economic stability after retirement. Working people have come to expect that they will not have to endure sudden poverty in old age. It is so popular, in fact, that some people don't realize it's a government program! Many others have no idea that it's a form of social welfare, a redistributive program that transfers resources from young to old. But it is.

Many of us think Social Security works like a pension or retirement account where the money we pay into the Social Security system during our working years accumulates in value and is there for us to live on after we retire. If that were the case, Social Security would be a distributive program. Instead, Social Security is funded by a payroll tax on workers and employers, which goes into a trust fund that makes payments to people who have reached retirement age, immediate family members of a covered worker who dies before retirement, and injured workers who are eligible for disability payments. The tax is automatically deducted from every eligible worker's paycheck. When a worker becomes eligible for benefits, the Social Security Trust Fund pays out, but the dollars paid out today are the dollars collected today, making Social Security a redistributive program—essentially a welfare program that doesn't disqualify people based on need and that transfers resources from the young to the old.[20]

Together with the hospital and medical insurance provided to the elderly and disabled through **Medicare**, millions receive a level of government support that protects them from having to worry that age or injury will leave them destitute. As entitlements, Social Security and Medicare are available to all, regardless of income or wealth.

Of course, as entitlements, Social Security and Medicare are open-ended government commitments, and that's at the heart of a major political debate. Our aging population and rising medical costs make both programs increasingly expensive. Some officials would

---

entitlements: Social welfare programs targeted to specific groups of individuals, like senior citizens or the unemployed. Benefits are available to all who meet the program requirements, although some entitlements for the poor impose a means test.

means test: Eligibility requirements placed on social welfare programs aiding the poor, which restrict participation to individuals whose incomes fall below set levels.

L.O. Correctly identify which groups benefit most from social welfare policies.

Social Security: The popular social welfare program that provides benefits to retirees regardless of need. Social Security also offers insurance payments to families of deceased workers and disability payments to impaired workers.

Medicare: The federal social welfare program that provides hospital and supplementary medical insurance to senior citizens and the disabled.

like to address these costs by adding market mechanisms to the mix through the partial privatization of Social Security, but this is controversial, as you will see when you read Demystifying Government: Is It Still a Government Program If It's Private? Think about the alternatives available for maintaining the solvency of the Social Security program, and the advantages and disadvantages of partial privatization of Social Security—an option that holds the promise of finding new revenues for retirees at the cost of changing the ironclad commitment of a retirement safety net.

DEMYSTIFYING GOVERNMENT

Is It Still a Government Social Program If It's Private?

Social Security has been called the "third rail of politics"—touch it and you die. Historically, the program has been so popular that for many years, no serious public official would have suggested changing it. But as the long-term solvency of Social Security has become a political issue, ideas once considered radical have entered the mainstream.

One reason for the popularity of Social Security is that as a redistributive program dressed up to look like a distributive program—the separate trust fund helps recipients feel like they're getting their own money and not a handout from government coffers—it is palatable to middle-class recipients who might otherwise object to participating in anything resembling welfare (along with Medicare, it's the reason why most social welfare spending goes to the middle class, not the poor). However, the program's structure makes Social Security sensitive to changes in population dynamics. In 1940, the first year the trust fund paid monthly benefits, 222,488 people received a combined $35 million. Since then, an explosion in the population, greater longevity, and cost-of-living adjustments (COLAs) made annually so that payments keep pace with inflation have combined to place a tremendous strain on the system. In 2016, nearly 61 million beneficiaries received a combined $918 *billion* in payments.[T11]

That's an awful lot of voters receiving an awful lot of money, hence the "third rail" problem. However, long-term demographics are not kind to Social Security, and everyone across the political spectrum expects that at some point modifications will have to be made to this popular program. As baby boomers have begun to retire, demand on the system has only increased, and with fewer workers to replace them, the tax base available to provide for this large batch of retirees will shrink. In 1950, when birth rates were high and life expectancy much lower than it is today, there were 16.5 workers to pay for every Social Security recipient. In 1990, each retiree was supported by 3.4 workers. By 2050, it's projected that there will be fewer than 2 workers to pay for every retiree—and more than one-third of those retirees is expected to be over age 80.[T12] Opinion surveys suggest that if you're like 70 percent of

eighteen- to thirty-four-year-olds, you're not confident that Social Security will be solvent when you reach retirement.[T13] It's an expression of doubt about the ability of politicians to address the problems that lie ahead.

When the system first faced the prospect of a shortfall as a result of a period of rapid inflation in the 1970s, officials addressed the situation by increasing payroll taxes slightly and cutting benefits at the margins. That was enough to keep the program solvent for a projected fifty years. As we reach the end of that window, the principal choices for restoring the program this century are the same as they were in the 1970s—raise taxes, cut benefits, or push back the retirement age, making people ineligible for benefits until they're older.

There is one alternative to tax increases and benefit cuts, but it's controversial. What if Social Security were restructured so that it operated more like a traditional retirement account? In other words, what if some of that payroll tax money were freed up for investment so that it could potentially grow over the course of time, rather than be transferred to today's recipients? There are a number of ways to do this, with the most widely discussed involving partial privatization of the Social Security system.

Under partial privatization plans that have circulated around Washington, a percentage of Social Security taxes would be diverted to private accounts that workers would individually control. Depending on the plan, there might be limits on how it could be invested, but workers would have control over what to do with the money. Unlike the transfer payments that characterize the present program, these funds could be invested, leaving them free to rise and fall with the market. The balance of the payroll tax would continue to be used to cover transfer payments to present-day Social Security beneficiaries, but by necessity, at a sharply lower level than what is currently provided.

Partial privatization plans had a lot of public support in the late 1990s, when the booming stock market was providing middle-class investors with annual double-digit returns. Some people looked at the taxes they were required to pay to the Social Security Trust Fund and complained loudly that if the government

(continued)

Is It Still a Government Social Program If It's Private? (continued)

would only let them invest that money, they could really make it grow.[T14] Then, when the high-tech bubble burst at the turn of the century, market forces no longer seemed so friendly, and some who had been enthusiastic about partial privatization had second thoughts, feelings only reinforced when the market crashed in 2008.

Opponents doubt that partial privatization will save money, arguing that the transition from a pay-as-you-go system to a partially private investment system would take hundreds of billions of dollars (some say as much as $1 trillion) out of present-day benefits so funds could be shifted for private investment. They fear today's retirees would bear the brunt of that cost. They also doubt that Americans would quickly abandon the psychology of a social safety net for seniors, and would resist permitting grandma and grandpa to live out in the cold because they invested poorly or suf-

fered a market downturn at the wrong time. This could mean there would be political pressure for an expensive government bailout of hard-luck investors, just as the financial crisis generated intense pressure for a government bailout of banks.[T15]

One thing both sides agree on is that partially privatizing Social Security would signal a dramatic change from the intent of the original Social Security Act. Instead of having government provide a guaranteed retirement safety net, it would only require that everyone save something for retirement, leaving everyone's bottom-line retirement package up to the way they invest and the direction of the market. These are vastly different social commitments. When we think about which direction to take, it's important to think about the underlying promise we want government to make to us and the nature of the obligation we want to make to one another.

15.4c "Corporate Welfare"

What would you call a government cash payment to large corporations that protects them from uneven market conditions? Supporters call it a safety net for businesses that otherwise could be unfavorably affected by circumstances they cannot control. Critics call it "corporate welfare." This difference of perspective is at the core of the debate over agricultural subsidies, an issue that you may be more familiar with if you live in a rural area. Agricultural subsidies don't grab national headlines, which means Congress can address them in relative anonymity. This gives interested parties greater freedom to operate behind the scenes to lobby for government support.

Agriculture is a risky and uncertain business. Drought, floods, temperature extremes, and other natural disasters can play havoc with this critical industry—and with the lives of people dependent on it. So government can step in to try to add an element of stability to agriculture, and has been doing so since the Depression. The Agricultural Adjustment Act of 1933 was the New Deal response to an oversupply of crops that was keeping prices low. Farmers voluntarily agreed to decrease production of such staples as corn, wheat, rice, and cotton in exchange for payments from the government. This was followed a year later by establishment of the Commodity Credit Corporation, a government corporation charged with making favorable loans to farmers in exchange for agreements to control crop production. The Agricultural Adjustment Act of 1938 introduced price supports, or payments to farmers to make up the difference for low market prices.[21]

Farm prices rebounded as a result of these measures, and ever since, farm subsidies have been a part of domestic policy and politics. A subsidy is a government payment for which nothing is expected in return. Such payments have been used to keep farmers from producing a crop that's in abundant supply and to maintain crop price stability. Over time, they've come to be regarded in the agricultural sector as a safety net for farmers akin to welfare for the poor and Social Security for retirees.

They are also highly controversial. In large part, that's because of the changing nature of agriculture and the way farm subsidies are allocated. In recent years, the small, independent farmer has become increasingly rare, as large corporate farms have come to dominate an industry now known as "agribusiness." Because subsidies are distributed on the type and amount of crop a farm produces, big corporate farms that produce more corn, wheat, rice, cotton, and soybeans (the most heavily subsidized crops) can claim a disproportionate share of the subsidy. Small farmers who produce these crops are only eligible for a tiny subsidy, and small farmers who produce other crops are not eligible for anything.[22]

The result: 60 percent of farmers do not get a penny of assistance, while past top recipients include farms owned by the John Hancock Life Insurance Company, Chevron Oil, banker David Rockefeller—even basketball millionaire Scottie Pippen.[23] You can probably see why critics call it corporate welfare.

In an effort to address this imbalance, Congress in 1996 passed the Federal Agriculture Improvement and Reform Act, which set limits on how much individual farms could receive from the federal government. However, supporters of farm subsidies argued these limits shredded the agricultural safety net—after all, 40 percent of farmers *did* receive something—and they have had enough political clout to get Congress to bypass its own limits by passing annual emergency supplemental bills every year since 1998. In 2016, supplemental farm subsidies were estimated at $13.9 billion.[24]

Still, advocates of farm subsidies point out that the serendipitous nature of the weather is a risk that no other industry faces, making it an economic necessity for the government to regulate agricultural prices. They note that other nations do the same thing, many to a greater extent than the United States,[25] and contend that without government aid, thousands of farmers would go under. If that happened, advocates argue that land prices would plummet, and businesses that rely on farmers would be pulled down with them. From this perspective, there is too much riding on agriculture subsidies for the government to pull them back.

Opponents counter with the argument that other industries that are just as vital to the economy and just as risky do not receive support. From this vantage point, there's no obvious reason to bolster farmers, especially as the one-time reality of the small, independent, hard-working farmer recedes into myth. Even if lifting agricultural subsidies hurts businesses that rely on income from farmers, opponents argue that the extra money in our pockets from not having to pay for agricultural relief would more than compensate for the damage to the economy.

The interesting political wrinkle in the farm-subsidy debate is that supporters cut across geographic as well as ideological and partisan lines. Big-government Democrats from rural states regularly team up with limited-government Republicans from rural states to advocate assistance for farmers. In principle, you might expect some of these supporters—those who see government as an instrument for helping the disadvantaged and those who espouse the virtues of the free market—to oppose government aid to agribusiness. Instead, the overarching principle in play is more practical than philosophical.

15.5 Taxing and Spending

Apart from decisions about war and peace, writing a budget and deciding how to pay for it are the most important choices Congress and the president make. That's because budgeting drives substantive determinations about who gets what. Choices about how the tax code is structured and how money is appropriated are often made out of public view. They involve a lot of small, technical, and detailed decisions. Nonetheless, they are worth paying attention to because they determine how the burden of supporting the government is distributed across economic groups and how much money is (or is not) available for government to do the things we say we want it to do. In this regard, taxing and spending decisions may be viewed as social welfare choices that determine how and how much government will redistribute wealth.

We discussed how the federal budget is drafted as part of our discussion of Congress in Chapter 9. Before moving on, you may wish to review the process, which is described in Demystifying Government: Making Budgets.

15.5a Tax Policy

Raising revenue is often controversial. Figure 15.2 should give you a sense of where the money comes from to power the federal government.

L.O. Identify major sources of tax revenue.

Making Budgets

If you've ever tried to save for something or figure out how you're going to spend limited funds on a bunch of needs, then you know how tricky it can be to write a budget. Add the individual wishes of hundreds of members of Congress and the president into the mix, and it shouldn't be hard to see how writing a budget is one of the most complex, sensitive, and important things Congress has to do. Members who sit on committees with a hand in budget writing find that they are rarely lonely.

Budget writing is an annual affair that typically takes an entire year to complete. A number of committees get into the act, in keeping with the decentralized way the House and Senate function. The process has been more coordinated though, ever since the passage of the **Congressional Budget and Impoundment Control Act of 1974**. A lot of the action happens in the House and Senate Appropriations Committees, which are charged with reporting bills that determine how much money government agencies and programs will have to spend (**appropriations** refer to legislation authorizing the government to spend money).

The procedure is complex, but it follows this outline: First, the House and Senate budget committees set guidelines and budgetary priorities. Then the appropriations committees are supposed to allocate money in line with those priorities. They approve spending bills to cover the variety of items in the federal budget. If the sum of these expenditures exceeds the budgetary guidelines, the expenditures are brought into line with the budget targets through a process called **reconciliation**. For both houses to end up with the same budget, differences between them are resolved in a conference committee, after which final approval on a budget can be sought in both houses.[T16]

If budget guidelines necessitate changes in tax law, the House Ways and Means Committee and the Senate Finance Committee get into the act. As the tax-writing committees of Congress, they draft legislation specifying which taxes will be raised and by how much.

Congressional Budget and Impoundment Control Act of 1974: An act designed to centralize the congressional budgeting process, which established current procedures and timetables for writing a budget.

appropriations: Legislation permitting the government to spend money that determines how much will be spent and how it will be spent.

reconciliation: A procedure in the budget-writing process, whereby appropriations made in a number of congressional committees and subcommittees need to be brought in line with spending targets established early in the process.

It's pretty clear that the federal government depends heavily on people like you and me for revenue. Here's how it breaks down:

- In 2015, the federal government raised $3.2 trillion, almost half of which came from personal income taxes.

- Another one-third came from Social Insurance payroll taxes, such as Social Security and Medicare taxes, and unemployment insurance taxes.

- Slightly more than one in ten federal dollars came from corporate income tax payments.

- Other taxes include a miscellaneous group of revenues, such as customs duties, estate taxes, gift taxes, and excise taxes, which are collected on specific products and services such as alcohol, tobacco, gasoline, and telephone services. Next time you look at your telephone bill, find the line that lists the federal tax owed—it's a small but regular feature of your bill.

If you're like most Americans, you probably think that income tax rates are very high. Think again: In comparison to other western nations, the U.S. Treasury makes relatively

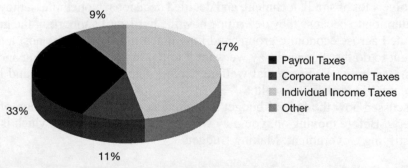

FIGURE 15.2 Where the Money Comes From[T17]

Federal Government Revenues, 2015
Receipts: $3.2 Trillion

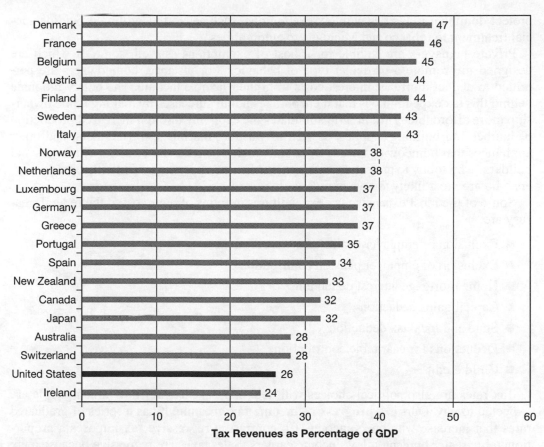

Tax Revenues as Percentage of GDP

FIGURE 15.3 Government Tax Revenues as a Percentage of GDP, 2015[T18]

few demands on our bank accounts. The United States tax burden ranks second from the bottom in comparison to twenty other industrialized nations, as Figure 15.3 attests.

Not convinced that our taxes are comparatively low? Neither are most Americans. If you were to track attitudes about the appropriate size and scope of government, you'd find that Americans rank at the top of industrialized nations in the belief that private or individual initiative is often preferable to public solutions to social problems. It's a belief with deep roots in the individualistic strains of our political culture that we discussed in Chapter 4, and it helps explain why Americans frequently feel that government takes too much of our hard-earned money, when in fact we pay less in taxes than almost anyone else.[26]

Then there's the issue of how the tax code is structured, which compounds questions about the extent of the tax burden with issues of tax equity and fairness. There is no single or obvious way to tax people. In fact, people were once taxed on the number of windows in their home, on the assumption that more windows meant greater wealth, and windows were harder to hide from the tax collector than assets like money or livestock.[27]

The way government defines what forms of wealth and income are taxable is a political matter that determines how much various social groups will have to pay. Typically, groups with more political power are able to protect their interests most effectively. At the turn of the twentieth century, when the influx of immigrants produced enormous demand for new public works projects, upper-income citizens maneuvered to have their wealth declared tax exempt out of fear that they would have to pay the bill. These efforts hit a roadblock as the Progressive movement gained steam and advanced laws taxing wealth.[28]

Even when tax laws are on the books, officials can tinker with them by creating exemptions targeted at particular groups of taxpayers. Tax exemptions are officially called **tax expenditures** because, from the government's standpoint, they amount to lost revenue that would have been collected if the exemption had not been in place. Corporate tax breaks go to industries that lobby for favorable treatment, and it's common for states to

tax expenditures: Tax breaks in the form of exemptions targeted at groups of taxpayers or, in the case of corporate taxes, at specific industries.

protect dominant industries with tax exemptions, such as North Carolina providing special treatment to tobacco and Michigan to automobiles.

Private taxpayers are eligible for a host of exemptions as well, some of which are designed to promote a particular type of behavior. For instance, homeowners are permitted to deduct mortgage interest costs from their taxable income. The policy rationale behind this tax expenditure is that it encourages home purchases by making home ownership more affordable. This, in turn, stimulates the economy through increased production of lumber and building supplies, as well as washing machines, refrigerators, and other appliances that homeowners need. Of course, it also benefits the interests of realtors and builders (who lobby to protect it), and is skewed to the upper- and middle-income taxpayers who are most likely to own homes.[29]

Some of the most expensive tax expenditures in terms of their cost to the federal treasury are:

- Exclusion of employer health-care contributions
- Exclusion of employer pension contributions
- Home mortgage interest deduction
- Capital gains deduction
- State and local tax deduction
- Deductions for charitable contributions
- Child credit[30]

L.O. *Explain why the American tax code has a progressive structure.*

progressive income tax: A tax structure with graduated income rates designed to increase the tax burden on higher-income earners.

regressive tax: A tax structure that increases the tax burden on lower-income earners. Sales taxes are regressive because as incomes decline, the tax becomes a larger percentage of total income, and therefore, a greater burden.

Tax rates are also political choices with real consequences for how much people are expected to pay. Ours is a **progressive income tax**, meaning it has a series of graduated rates that increase with one's income. (In contrast, a **regressive tax** imposes a proportionately greater burden on low-income earners. Sales taxes are regressive because a tax everyone pays on food or clothes represents a bigger share of the incomes of low-wage individuals.) In general, the tax structure is redistributive because lower-income groups pay proportionately less than upper-income groups, and most Americans fall into the lower groups.

Some officials have claimed the tax structure is too progressive. Mitt Romney famously noted during the 2012 presidential campaign that almost 47 percent of Americans did not pay any federal income tax. Although that figure held true in 2011, it was also the case that 60 percent of these individuals paid federal payroll taxes, and the remaining 40 percent were largely elderly individuals or individuals with incomes under $20,000.[31] The average American earned $71,600 that year and paid 27.9 percent of it in combined federal, state, and local taxes, including income and payroll taxes. And tax policy can be written to mitigate the effects of progressive taxation. With the advantage of deductions and tax shelters, individuals in the top 1 percent of income paid only a slightly higher percentage—29 percent—on an average income of $1,371,000.[32]

15.5b Spending Policy

L.O. *Identify the major sources of government spending.*

If you've ever had to cover your expenses with money you've earned from working, you know what it's like to budget funds in order to make ends meet. In an ideal world, the amount of money you take in would bear some resemblance to the amount you spend. In the real world, you might have to borrow to pay for a major necessity like tuition or a car, or to afford a luxury you really want, like a spring break vacation. You might take out a loan or run up an unpaid balance on your credit card. In either case, you pay for having additional funds now by making interest payments later. The longer you go without making interest payments, the more you have to pay out over time.

The federal budget works pretty much the same way. Federal budget numbers may be staggeringly large—can you visualize a $3.7 trillion budget?—but the temptation to spend beyond our means applies just as much to the public sphere as to our private exploits with credit cards, and the issue is compounded by the fact that hundreds of lawmakers with

Deficits and Debts

When the government takes in less than it spends in a given year, it runs a **deficit**. This is easily confused with the **national debt**, but they are different. The deficit is an imbalance between revenues and expenditures in a given year. After climbing out from under years of deficit spending in the late 1990s, the federal government became heavily indebted again during the second Bush administration; in 2015, the Congressional Budget Office projected a deficit of $439 billion, way down from $1.6 trillion in 2009 but still far from the surpluses realized briefly at the end of the Clinton administration. When the government runs a deficit, it has to borrow to bridge the gap and to make interest payments on the money it borrows, just like you or I would. The amount the government borrows is its debt, and interest on the debt becomes a budgetary expense. As the government continues to run a deficit, it has to keep borrowing, which increases both the size of the debt and the portion of the budget that goes to paying interest on the debt.

As of January 1, 2017, the national debt was $14.428 trillion, or $14,428,038,035,992,[T19] to be precise. The debt is owed mostly to domestic banks and financial institutions, and to holders of treasury bonds and savings bonds, although state, local, and foreign governments hold a portion of the debt.[T20] You can get an exact account of the national debt today from the Treasury Department, at http://www.treasurydirect.gov/NP/BPDLogin?application=np.

---

different interests have a say over what goes in the budget. The all-too-human tendency to spend now and worry about how to pay for it later has been at the center of national political debate for a generation.

One point of confusion in this debate is the difference between the federal deficit and the national debt. Many people confound the two, but as Demystifying Government: Deficits and Debts points out, they're different—and recognizing the difference is fundamental to establishing a reasoned opinion on deficit spending.

Except for a few years in the late 1990s, the government has run a deficit every year since 1969. There are a number of reasons for deficit spending, some of them arguably more justifiable than others. Sometimes the government runs a deficit accidentally because expenditures or revenue projections were incorrectly estimated when the budget was written. Emergencies like war, a terrorist strike, or a major natural disaster can cause the government to run a deficit because it has no choice but to spend money that wasn't budgeted to address these unexpected circumstances. Congress and the president may even intentionally run a deficit during economic downturns in order to stimulate the economy through increased spending (this was part of the logic behind the stimulus package passed by Congress during the first weeks of the Obama administration). Each of these circumstances is short-lived and does not add considerably to the national debt.[33]

Sometimes, though, Congress and the president are unwilling to make difficult choices to keep the budget in balance, resulting in long-term deficit spending. This happened in the 1980s, when President Reagan sought to reduce the size of the federal government through cuts in taxes and domestic expenditures while spending more on national defense. Politically popular tax cuts and added defense money proved easy to institute, but curtailing domestic spending meant confronting constituents who benefited from government programs. The result was a policy that spared many domestic programs and looked the other way as deficits climbed to unprecedented levels that regularly surpassed $200 billion per year, which simply deferred the problem for future generations (which means you). The roaring economy of the late 1990s brought the government a windfall of unexpectedly high tax revenues and helped end deficit spending temporarily; by 1998, the government was running a small surplus. This was short-lived, however, as large deficits returned with the economic slowdown that set in at the turn of the twenty-first century, coupled with expensive tax cuts favored by the Bush administration, high defense needs following the September 11 terror attacks, the Iraq War, the cost of recovery after Hurricane Katrina, the price of bailing out large banks that teetered on the edge of bankruptcy following the 2008 financial meltdown, and the cost of President Obama's 2009 stimulus package.

deficit: The gap created in the federal budget when the government takes in less than it spends in a given year.

L.O. Explain deficit spending, and distinguish deficits from debt.

national debt: The amount the government borrows to pay for accumulated budget deficits.

Strong political and ideological forces make deficit spending hard to stop once it gets started. Although many of us support the idea of a balanced budget in theory, we are more likely to be moved to political action to keep Congress from cutting programs that benefit us rather than to rise up in protest against red ink on a ledger sheet. Interest groups will keep the pressure on legislators to protect their programs, and as we saw in Chapter 8, they have the resources and relationships they need to be persuasive. Consequently, members of Congress are more likely to feel constrained to maintain or increase spending in the face of large deficits while acknowledging the importance of fiscal responsibility in their public remarks. Their words address the widespread constituent desire for responsible budgeting, but they avoid taking actions that would extract a great political cost. As politicians of both parties realized in the 1980s, it's easy to run against an incumbent who voted to cut back a popular program, but it's hard to run against an incumbent who helped run up large, abstract deficit numbers.[34]

Philosophically, arriving at a balanced budget pits different conceptions of the appropriate size and role of government against each other. This, too, can hinder action. Liberals who support social welfare spending are more likely to favor tax increases over spending cuts to achieve balance. Conservatives prefer spending cuts, and some favor tax reductions in part to force the issue of reducing the size of government, hoping to leave Congress with no choice but to reduce domestic spending as a result of lower revenues and higher deficits.[35] This difference reflects a deep philosophical division over what government should be doing and is a way of using tax policy to legislate social outcomes.

The matter of cutting the budget is complicated by the fact that large portions of it cannot go under the axe. A host of expenditures are mandatory, which means they cannot be touched. These include Social Security and Medicare payments, unemployment insurance, federal retirement benefits, and means-tested entitlements. Interest on the debt is also a fixed cost. With these expenses removed from consideration, you're left with 35 percent of the total budget for discretionary items, and about half of that is earmarked for defense, which is politically unpopular to cut.

Figure 15.4 shows the major spending categories in the 2015 budget. A look at the chart should show you how much of the budget is beyond the control of the budgeters. As more people retire, the percentage of the budget dedicated to Social Security will grow with it. The same is true of Medicare. Programs that help the needy and unemployed become more costly during economic downturns—precisely when tax revenues drop because fewer people are working. The easiest way to pay these costs is to borrow,

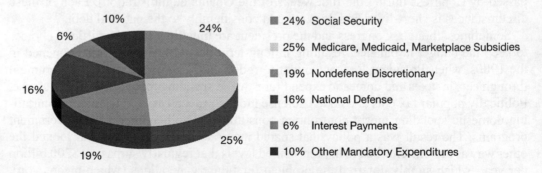

Nondefense discretionary spending includes items not earmarked for the military, including all programs for education, training, science, technology, transportation, housing, and foreign aid. Other mandatory expenditures include unemployment insurance, payments to farmers, federal retirement and insurance programs, and other means-tested entitlements, including food stamps, Supplemental Security Income (SSI), veterans' pensions, and the child nutrition program.

FIGURE 15.4 Where the Money Goes[T21]

Federal Government Expenditures, 2015

but as deficits grow, the portion of the budget dedicated to interest payments grows, too, squeezing out the relatively small set of discretionary expenditures. These economic limitations constrain the political options available to the elected officials who write the budget, contributing to the high-stakes nature of budgetary politics.

Chapter Review

Define and distinguish between competitive and protective regulatory policies, and give examples of each.

Regulatory policies depend on government action to minimize hazards or maximize benefits that will not be attended to by the free market. Competitive regulatory policies restrict the provision of a service or good, like operating a television station, to organizations that win federal licensing approval. Protective regulatory policies provide the public with information the government believes is beneficial to disseminate, like health warnings on cigarette packs.

Explain why some regulatory policies can be controversial.

Regulation can be controversial because of widely held beliefs about limiting government involvement in the marketplace, even when the results of regulation, like clean air and safe food, are extremely popular.

Define and distinguish between distributive and redistributive or social welfare policies, and give examples of each.

Explain why distributive policies are generally less controversial than redistributive policies.

Distributive policies are typically less controversial because they benefit everyone to some degree. Many distributive policies are public works projects financed by state and local governments, sometimes with federal support like the Interstate Highway System.

In contrast, social welfare policies are redistributive because the beneficiaries are different from the people who pay the bill. Many social welfare policies, like unemployment compensation, veteran's benefits, Social Security, and Temporary Assistance to Needy Families, involve transfer payments of federal dollars to qualifying individuals. Social welfare policies for the poor are controversial among people who believe they contribute to a "culture of poverty."

Define entitlements.

As entitlements, social welfare programs deliver benefits to everyone who meets the eligibility requirements, like being unemployed or retired. Some programs are means-tested, such that eligibility is dependent on meeting a statistical standard, like having an income below the poverty line in order to receive welfare benefits.

Correctly identify which groups benefit most from social welfare policies.

Contrary to popular belief, most social welfare dollars do not go to support the poor. Social Security, which benefits retired workers, is the largest social welfare program and arguably the most popular government program. It is redistributive because today's workers provide the money used to support today's retirees.

Explain why the American tax code has a progressive structure.

Substantive decisions about domestic policy are made through budgetary politics involving raising and spending tax money. The structure of the tax code is a political matter that determines how the tax burden will be shared across income groups. The American tax code is progressive, as higher levels of income are taxed at higher rates, although deductions, or tax expenditures, permit individuals with higher incomes to reduce their payments.

Identify major sources of tax revenue.

Most government revenue comes from individual income taxes and social insurance receipts. A much smaller share comes from corporate income taxes. Many Americans consider income taxes to be very high, although the tax burden in the United States is near the bottom of industrialized nations.

Identify the major sources of government spending.

Most government spending goes to entitlement programs like Social Security and Medicare, defense, and other mandatory expenditures. Less than one-fifth of the budget is discretionary, making it difficult for Congress to make cuts without also making hard political choices.

Explain deficit spending, and distinguish deficits from debt.

Because tax cuts are politically popular and it's hard to cut funds for programs with a constituency, the federal budget has run a deficit, or spent more than it has taken in, almost every year since 1969. Deficit spending contributes to the national debt, which is the accumulated money owed—with interest—on past deficits. A large percentage of mandatory expenditures, like money earmarked for transfer payments and interest on the debt, compounds the difficulty of making spending cuts and contributes to deficit spending.

Key Terms

appropriations Legislation permitting the government to spend money that determines how much will be spent and how it will be spent. (p. 462)

competitive regulatory policy A type of regulatory policy designed to protect the public interest by restricting the provision of a service or good to organizations that win federal licensing approval. (p. 449)

Congressional Budget and Impoundment Control Act of 1974 An act designed to centralize the congressional budgeting process, which established current procedures and timetables for writing a budget. (p. 462)

deficit The gap created in the federal budget when the government takes in less than it spends in a given year. (p. 465)

distributive policies Domestic policies primarily aimed at directing tax money to a range of public works items. Distributive policies tend not to be controversial because benefits are widely shared. (p. 452)

entitlements Social welfare programs targeted to specific groups of individuals, like senior citizens or the unemployed. Benefits are available to all who meet the program requirements, although some entitlements for the poor impose a means test. (p. 458)

means test Eligibility requirements placed on social welfare programs aiding the poor, which restrict participation to individuals whose incomes fall below set levels. (p. 458)

Medicare The federal social welfare program that provides hospital and supplementary medical insurance to senior citizens and the disabled. (p. 458)

national debt The amount the government borrows to pay for accumulated budget deficits. (p. 465)

pork barrel Wasteful or unnecessary spending that can result from logrolling. Whether something is a pork-barrel project or a valuable use of taxpayer dollars may depend on whether you stand to benefit from it. (p. 452)

poverty line A statistical determination of poverty based on income and family size that is used to establish eligibility for some social welfare programs designed to assist those in need. (p. 456)

progressive income tax A tax structure with graduated income rates designed to increase the tax burden on higher-income earners. (p. 464)

protective regulatory policy Regulations that supply consumers with information needed to make informed purchasing decisions about such things as cigarettes and home loans or that prevent undesirable personal or social conditions like child labor or unsafe food. (p. 449)

public works Civic projects built with tax dollars. (p. 452)

reconciliation A procedure in the budget-writing process, whereby appropriations made in a number of congressional committees and subcommittees need to be brought in line with spending targets established early in the process. (p. 462)

redistributive policies Domestic policies, like those promoting social welfare, that take resources from one group in the form of taxes and provide goods or services for another group, typically those in need. (p. 454)

regressive tax A tax structure that increases the tax burden on lower-income earners. Sales taxes are regressive because as incomes decline, the tax becomes a larger percentage of total income, and therefore, a greater burden. (p. 464)

regulatory policies Domestic policies designed to protect the public from harmful conditions that could result from unrestrained free-market competition or to ensure the benefits of a level playing field for private competition. (p. 448)

Social Security The popular social welfare program that provides benefits to retirees regardless of need. Social Security also offers insurance payments to families of deceased workers and disability payments to impaired workers. (p. 458)

tax expenditures Tax breaks in the form of exemptions targeted at groups of taxpayers or, in the case of corporate taxes, at specific industries. (p. 463)

transfer payments The direct payment of public money to individuals who qualify for it under the terms of a social welfare program. (p. 454)

Resources

You might be interested in examining some of what the following authors have said about the topics we've been discussing:

Harris, Richard A., and Sidney M. Milkis. *The Politics of Regulatory Change: A Tale of Two Agencies*. New York: Oxford University Press, 1996. An examination of the politics behind regulation and deregulation.

Hayes, Sharon. *Flat Broke with Children: Women in the Age of Welfare Reform*. New York: Oxford University Press, 2004. A look at welfare policy from the perspective of single mothers dealing with the environment created by welfare reform.

Howard, Philip K. *The Death of Common Sense: How Law Is Suffocating America*. New York: Random House, 1996. The author makes a case against regulatory policy, contending that regulations written in Washington routinely miss their intended mark while stifling local initiatives that could be far more creative and effective.

Kelso, William A. *Poverty and the Underclass: Changing Perceptions of the Poor in America*. New York: New York University Press, 1994. Kelso considers the changing arguments made by liberals and conservatives about the reasons for poverty in America.

Murray, Charles A. *Losing Ground: American Social Policy, 1950–1980*. New York: Basic Books, 1994. A controversial and influential conservative critique of the social welfare programs of the 1960s and 1970s.

Rubin, Irene S. *The Politics of Public Budgeting: Getting and Spending, Borrowing and Balancing*, 6th ed. Washington, DC: CQ Press, 2009. Rubin provides an accessible overview of budgetary politics.

Notes

1 General Social Survey, "Trends in National Spending Priorities, 1973–2014," March 2015. http://www.norc.org/PDFs/GSS%20Reports/GSS_Trends%20in%20Spending_1973-2014.pdf. Data are from 2014.

2 The one notable exception is a federal income tax checkoff that routes three dollars of your tax return to a fund for publicly financing presidential candidates without increasing your overall tax payment. Some states also have tax checkoffs for a variety of publicly financed causes like wildlife protection, child-abuse protection, and senior-citizen support.

3 For an overview of the history and procedures of broadcast licensing, see the Museum of Broadcast Communications website at http://www.museum.tv/eotvsection.php?entrycode=license.

4 There are questions about the effectiveness of warning labels. Canada goes much further than the United States to draw the connection between smoking and illness, by requiring the placement of pictures of diseased lungs, gums, and hearts over large portions of its cigarette packs.

5 See the Bureau of Labor Statistics, "Child Labor Laws and Enforcement," *Report on the Youth Labor Force* (U.S. Dept. of Labor, November 2000), at http://www.bls.gov/opub/rylf/pdf/chapter2.pdf.

6 Phillip K. Howard, *The Death of Common Sense: How Law Is Suffocating America* (New York: Random House, 1994), 7–8.

7 Ibid., 8

8 Ibid.

9 Theodore Lowi, "American Business, Public Policy, Case Studies, and Political Theory," *World Politics* 16:4 (July 1964), 677–715.

10 Propublica.org, at www.propublica.org/special/the-stimulus-plan-a-detailed-list-of-spending.

11 James T. Patterson, *America's Struggle against Poverty, 1900–1994* (Cambridge, MA: Harvard University Press, 1994), 7.

12 The 2012 Health and Human Services Poverty Guidelines, at https://aspe.hhs.gov/computations-2016-poverty-guidelines.

13 U.S. Census Bureau, at http://www.census.gov/data/tables/2016/demo/income-poverty/p60-256.html.

14 William A. Kelso, *Poverty and the Underclass: Changing Perceptions of the Poor in America* (New York: New York University Press, 1994), 31–45.

15 Charles Murray, *Losing Ground: American Social Policy, 1950–1980* (New York: Basic Books, 1984), 9.

16 Arnold Vedlitz, *Conservative Mythology and Public Policy in America* (New York: Praeger, 1988), 1–15.

17 Kelso, *Poverty and the Underclass*, 42–43.

18 Joel F. Handler, *The Poverty of Welfare Reform* (New Haven, CT: Yale University Press, 1995), 1–6.

19 Elaine B. Sharp, *The Sometime Connection: Public Opinion and Social Policy* (Albany, NY: State University of New York Press, 1999), 177–207.

20 History Page, Social Security Online, at http://www.ssa.gov/history/briefhistory3.html.

21 Senate Agriculture Committee website, at http://ag.senate.gov/site/.

22 Brian Riedl, "How Farm Subsidies Become American's Largest Corporate Welfare Program," The Heritage Foundation Policy and Research Analysis, February 25, 2002.

23 Environmental Working Group Farm Subsidy Database, at http://farm.ewg.org/index.php.

24 Alan Bjerga, "Farmers Get Biggest Subsidy Check in Decades as Prices Drop," *Bloomberg News*, April 11, 2016, https://www.bloomberg.com/news/articles/2016-04-11/farmers-get-biggest-u-s-subsidy-check-in-decade-as-prices-drop.

25 Reported on the American Embassy in Paris website.

26 John W. Kingdon, *America the Unusual* (New York: Worth Publishers, 1999).

27 Irene S. Rubin, *The Politics of Public Budgeting: Getting and Spending, Borrowing and Balancing*, 3rd ed. (Chatham, NJ: Chatham House Publishers, 1997), 42.

28 Ibid., 42–43.

29 Ibid., 43–53.

30 Businessinsider.com.

31 Taxpolicycenter.org.

32 Citizens for Tax Justice, at http://ctj.org/ctjreports/2012/04/who_pays_taxes_in_america.php.

33 Rubin, *Politics of Public Budgeting*, 177–179.

34 Ibid., 182–183.

35 Ibid.

Table, Figure, and Box Notes

T1 "Milk Gets a Makeover—New Labels Help Make Shopping a Snap." American Dietetic Association, June, 1999.

T2 U.S. Fish and Wildlife Service, at http://arctic.fws.gov/index.htm.

T3 Image Source: Steven Chase, U.S. Fish and Wildlife Service. This image or recording is the work of a U.S. Fish and Wildlife Service employee, taken or made during the course of an employee's official duties. As a work of the U.S. federal government, the image is in the public domain.

T4 BBC Reports, "Head to Head: Arctic Oil Drilling," August 2, 2001, BBC.

T5 Brian Palmer, "The Long, Long Battle for ANWR," Natural Resources Defense Council, July 13, 2016. https://www.nrdc.org/stories/long-long-battle-anwr.

T6 Alaskan Wilderness League, "Oil Drilling."

T7 BBC Reports, "Head to Head."

T8 Alaskan Wilderness League, "Oil Drilling."

T9 Richard R. Weingroff, "Creating the Interstate System," U.S. Department of Transportation Federal Highway Administration.

T10 Data from the U.S. Census Bureau, at http://www.census.gov/data/tables/time-series/demo/income-poverty/historical-income-inequality.html.

T11 Social Security Fact Sheet, at https://www.ssa.gov/news/press/factsheets/basicfact-alt.pdf.

T12 Susan A. MacManus, *Young v. Old: Generational Combat in the 21st Century* (Boulder, CO: Westview Press, 1996), 3–9.

T13 "Social Security Politics," *Cato Daily Comment*, May 12, 2000. Data originally cited in May 11 *Roll Call*.

T14 Ibid.

T15 "Bush and Social Security: The Full Facts," Washington State Democrats online newsroom.

T16 Barbara Sinclair, *Unorthodox Lawmaking: New Legislative Process in the U.S. Congress* (Washington, D C: CQ Press, 1997), 63–69.

T17 Center on Budget and Policy Priorities, at http://www.cbpp.org/research/policy-basics-where-do-federal-tax-revenues-come-from.

T18 Data from Organization for Economic Cooperation and Development, 2015.

T19 As of midnight, January 30, 2013.

T20 The U.S. Treasury Department has a website for answering frequently asked questions about deficits and the national debt, at http://www.treasurydirect.gov/govt/resources/faq/faq_publicdebt.htm.

T21 Center on Budget and Policy Priorities, at http://www.cbpp.org/research/federal-budget/policy-basics-where-do-our-federal-tax-dollars-go?fa=view&id=1258.

Foreign and Defense Policies

Copyright: Africa Studio/Shutterstock.com

Learning Objectives

When you have completed this chapter, you should be able to:

- Understand how the president's worldview can influence foreign policy.
- Identify key actors in the American foreign policy establishment.
- Explain the influence of international organizations in shaping American foreign policy.
- Conceptualize the role of economic policies such as trade and foreign aid in the conduct of foreign affairs.
- Identify key actors in the conduct of diplomatic relations.
- Appreciate the size of American defense expenditures relative to the rest of the world, and understand the arguments for and against maintaining a large defense budget.
- Recognize key strategic assumptions behind American foreign policy as they relate to the acquisition and deployment of resources.
- Explain the role of strategy in crisis response.
- Understand how domestic political considerations can influence foreign policy decisions.

16.1 Introduction

In the winter of 2003, as America and the world readied for war in Iraq, the foreign policy apparatus of the United States went into full swing. On the diplomatic front, having won the support of Congress for an invasion, the Bush administration intensely engaged in efforts to get allied nations to endorse its decision to go to war with Iraq by declaring Saddam Hussein in violation of United Nations dictates that he disarm. Simultaneously, on the military front, tens of thousands of American troops gathered in the Persian Gulf, preparing to receive invasion orders. In Washington, battle plans were developed to leverage American military superiority in the pursuit of strategic objectives: removing Hussein from power and replacing his regime, finding and destroying Iraqi weapons of mass destruction, minimizing civilian casualties, and doing it all in the shortest possible time. A successful war, the administration argued, would promote a host of American strategic objectives by bringing democracy to the Middle East, keeping dangerous weapons from terrorists, facilitating a settlement of the Israeli-Palestinian crisis, and stabilizing oil markets.

These simultaneous initiatives represent the full reach and scope of American foreign and domestic policy, which is designed to advance American security interests in an increasingly interdependent world. The buildup to war in Iraq engaged the full weight and attention of the domestic political actors who have a hand in developing and executing foreign policy—the president, American diplomats overseas, and Congress—as well as the American foreign policy establishment, including the Departments of State and Defense, the National Security Council, and the Joint Chiefs of Staff. Likewise, it actively engaged prominent world actors, like the United Nations, NATO, and the European Union.

The American effort encompassed economic, diplomatic, and military planning. Provisions were made for protecting Iraqi oilfields from destruction in the event of an invasion, and for rebuilding Iraq's infrastructure in the aftermath of fighting. On the diplomatic front, the State Department engaged in a months-long, ultimately unsuccessful effort to convince traditional allies France and Germany to back American invasion plans in the United Nations, attempted unsuccessfully to negotiate a foreign aid package with Turkey in exchange for permission from that reluctant nation to house American invasion forces, and stared down Iraqi claims of disarmament, which the United States termed hollow posturing. As diplomacy ran its course, military planners were preparing invasion scenarios in the event that weapons replaced words.

Long-term strategy shaped this diplomatic and military planning. Foreign policy is about first articulating goals for American security, then enacting policies designed to attain them. Strategic interests are typically easy to identify, and historically have been shared by Republican and Democratic lawmakers and by most Americans. During the Cold War, there was bipartisan support for containment of the Soviet Union and preventing a Soviet nuclear first strike (see Demystifying Government: The Cold War). In the 1990s, liberals and conservatives saw the need to make the American economy competitive in a period of economic globalization. After September 2001, no one questioned the need to protect America from further terrorist attacks.

Articulating goals is typically the easy part of foreign policy development. The challenge comes from reaching agreement on how to achieve them, which is why the real juice in foreign policy making comes from confronting differences over strategies. When the Reagan administration advocated a military buildup to contain the Soviet Union, detractors argued that their policies would lead to a dangerously militarized world and increase the risk of nuclear war. When the Clinton administration pressed for free trade to enhance global markets for American goods, critics said these policies would cost American workers their jobs. When the Bush administration pursued an unprovoked attack on Iraq as a way of making the world safer from terrorism, it sparked global protests with millions of dissenters.

In the pages ahead, we'll look more closely at the people and institutions engaged in foreign policy formulation, at the economic, diplomatic, and military initiatives they undertake, and at the sometimes controversial strategies they employ to advance their objectives abroad and at home.

The Cold War

For over two generations, global politics was defined by the standoff between the United States and the Soviet Union. Allies during World War II when faced with a common threat, the two nations settled into a frosty peace following the defeat of Germany and Japan. Each saw the other as having designs on global expansion and conquest. Each felt threatened by the other's ideology—American capitalism and Soviet communism—and each saw the other as attempting to export its ideology around the globe. Each had nuclear weapons and therefore was limited in its ability to fight a "hot" war with the other.

Instead, numerous proxy wars were fought between nations aligned with the two sides, with direct or indirect assistance from the superpowers. The Vietnam War can be understood in terms of the United States coming to the assistance of South Vietnam in its struggle to prevent a takeover by the forces of communist North Vietnam. Additionally, there were ongoing propaganda battles between the two sides, each trying to convince the world that its system was superior. During the 1960s, Americans and Soviets were consumed with the "space race," a show of strength through technology measured by which side would be the first to orbit the earth, send satellites into space, and ultimately land a man on the moon.

The Cold War divided the globe into two camps, with many democratic nations of Western Europe aligned with the United States through the NATO treaty, and many communist nations of Eastern Europe aligned with the Soviet Union through the Warsaw Pact. In fact, although people still refer to the president of the United States as the "leader of the free world," it's really an outdated Cold War term that invokes the split between the communist East and capitalist West (not every regime aligned with the United States during the Cold War permitted freedom for its people, but the term fit well into the propaganda battle).

Generations raised during this time regarded the Cold War struggle between the United States and the Soviet Union as an accepted fact of life. It dominated literature, film, and art; fear of nuclear annihilation was a chronic reality. In fact, the nuclear standoff between the two nations made it seem inconceivable that the Cold War would ever end, which made the collapse of the Soviet Union in 1991 a surreal experience for the millions who had been weaned on superpower tensions and a divided world.

With the collapse of the Soviet Union, the nations of the Warsaw Pact were free to determine their futures without Soviet influence. German reunification saw the end to the division of that country, which had been in place since the end of World War II, with formerly communist East Germany incorporated into the democratic west. Other nations that had been in the Soviet orbit during the Cold War opted for democratic governance, and a large number of countries that constituted the Eastern Bloc during the Cold War became NATO nations, including Poland, the Czech Republic, Hungary, Bulgaria, Estonia, Latvia, Lithuania, Romania, Slovakia, and Slovenia.[T1] By 2007, these nations were all members of the European Union as well (we'll discuss NATO and the European Union later in the chapter), another indication that the deep ideological differences that had turned Europe into two armed and opposite camps during the forty-plus years of the Cold War had evaporated into history.

16.2 The Players at Home

Ultimate responsibility for foreign policy formulation—and for its success and failure—rests with elected officials in the executive and legislative branches. They are joined by an extensive foreign policy establishment that bridges the diplomatic and military functions of foreign affairs.

16.2a Domestic Policy Makers

As we saw in Chapter 10, the president maintains chief responsibility for American foreign policy, with vast diplomatic and military authority. The president appoints all American ambassadors, but he also functions as chief diplomat through his constitutional ability to negotiate treaties with other nations and through the power to enter into **executive agreements** on behalf of the United States. In his role as commander-in-chief, the president is civilian head of the armed forces and has final authority to commit troops to combat.

Placing primary responsibility for national security in the hands of one person leaves vital decisions about our national welfare at the mercy of how that person views the world.

L.O. Understand how the president's worldview can influence foreign policy.

executive agreements: Legally binding presidential agreements with other nations that do not require congressional approval.

The assumptions the president makes about the intentions, motivations, and actions of our friends and adversaries—beliefs rooted in his approach to human nature—can structure his thinking and, with it, the policies he develops in our name. A lot of things can contribute to the development of a president's "worldview," particularly the experiences he has growing up and in previous offices that permit him to draw conclusions about what makes people tick.[1] In the end, these remain assumptions and cannot be demonstrated to be definitively right or wrong, even though that is exactly how history will view the actions taken in the name of a worldview.

President George W. Bush was heavily influenced by his experience fighting in World War II, in the years after European appeasement permitted Adolph Hitler to begin his pursuit of global conquest, and the surprise Japanese attack on Pearl Harbor caught America off guard. Experience taught Bush to be strong and be prepared, and during one of his biggest foreign policy crises, when Iraq invaded Kuwait, these principles guided his reaction. Comparing Saddam Hussein to Hitler, Bush assembled an international coalition and, with America in the lead, launched a war to push back Hussein's aggressive move.

His successor had an entirely different formative experience. Bill Clinton witnessed the debacle of Vietnam, where strength and preparedness led America into a costly guerilla war for reasons many people did not understand. Clinton personally wrestled with serving in that war—some believe he evaded the draft—and like many of his generation, he regarded military solutions as a last resort to solving complex problems, perhaps even as a failure of policy. When Clinton spoke of disseminating humanitarian aid as a way of avoiding conflict, he was expressing a worldview that placed diplomacy and economic assistance ahead of military action.

George W. Bush was more like his father than his predecessor, although he was more inclined to see the world in absolute terms. Following the September 11 attack, he issued his call to other nations that in the fight against terror, you were either "with us or against us." This view of the world explains his belief that a good regime (the United States) could replace an evil regime (Saddam Hussein's Iraq) with another good regime, and that the Iraqi people would see the difference and embrace the change. It also explains his determination to head toward war even though it meant alienating allies who were bitterly opposed to the American policy (reasoning in absolute terms, he believed they would come around when they saw the United States was successful).

After the 2008 election, strategic decisions on the course of the wars in Iraq and Afghanistan fell to Barack Obama, whose formative experiences were quite different from the experiences of those who came before him. Coming of age in the 1970s, he neither fought in a war like the first President Bush nor wrestled with serving in Vietnam. Born to a Kenyan father and an American mother, Obama spent a portion of his childhood in Indonesia. During his presidential campaign, he pointed to this background and promised that as president he would reach out to portions of the Muslim world that he felt were alienated by American policy during the Bush years, suggesting that his personal experiences would inform a more nuanced approach to foreign policy. Political rhetoric during the 2016 campaign suggests President Trump will change course again, demonstrating how a change in presidencies can bring with it a dramatic reshaping of foreign policy reflecting the worldview of the new Oval Office occupant.

Although a president's worldview will shape his foreign policy judgments, it's impossible to know if a worldview accurately describes the world and predicts how other national actors will behave. It's entirely possible that worldviews are suited to some situations but are not "one size fits all," leaving little room for knowing how likely it is that policies will be effective. Even after the fact, if things go badly, the side whose view is not supported by events will be tempted to rationalize away what happened. That's because worldviews are so fundamental that it's sometimes easier to challenge what happened than to challenge what we believe.

We mentioned in Chapter 10 that the president has over time acquired more range than Congress over the conduct of international affairs. The Constitution gave Congress the power to declare war in a time when formal declarations preceded military action, but as we said in Chapter 10, since World War II, the pattern has been to wage war without declaring it. This is the reason why Congress passed the **War Powers Act of 1973**, in an effort to regain lost authority in military affairs.

Although Congress is not irrelevant to military policy—after all, President Bush asked Congress for formal approval of his Iraq policy to bolster its legitimacy—the blueprint for where and when to use force comes from the executive branch. It was President Bush's decision to disarm Iraq; he approved the plans and gave the go-ahead. Congress had the more constrained function of offering its consent, operating in an important but subsidiary role that is typical of its place in foreign policy making.[2]

War Powers Act of 1973: A congressional attempt to reassert the role of the legislature with respect to the president in military affairs by restricting the president's ability to wage war.

16.2b The Foreign Policy Establishment

Presidents make the call on what our foreign policy should be, but they have a lot of assistance in deciding what to do. Some presidents might say they have *too much* assistance because members of the vast foreign policy establishment have been known to fight among themselves and jockey for influence in the Oval Office.

L.O. Identify key actors in the American foreign policy establishment.

We already know a bit about the major institutions of foreign policy making from our work in Chapter 10, where we discussed the Departments of State and Defense, the National Security Council, the CIA, and the Joint Chiefs of Staff. Let's take a closer look at how officials in foreign policy organizations operate and how they work together (or go after each other's throats).

Department of State

The president's foreign policy is formulated and implemented at the State Department. Headed by the **secretary of state**, who is the president's chief foreign policy advisor, the State Department coordinates the activities of federal agencies that have dealings with other nations and is responsible for allocating money to other agencies engaged in foreign affairs. The Department of State is also the lead diplomatic institution, where it represents the president's policies to other nations through the efforts of the secretary of state and through a diplomatic corps operating at over 260 embassies, consulates, and international organization offices in over 180 nations.[3]

secretary of state: The head of the Department of State, who functions as the president's chief foreign policy advisor.

Department of Defense

What the State Department is to diplomacy, the Department of Defense is to military and national security concerns. The army, navy, air force, and marine corps all report to the Defense Department for matters involving equipping, training, and recruiting personnel. This includes procuring weapons systems for national defense. Overall, the Department of Defense houses 1.3 million active-duty forces and 818,000 reserves.[4]

Joint Chiefs of Staff

The heads of the army, air force, navy, and marine corps also serve as the president's key military advisors in their capacity as members of the **Joint Chiefs of Staff**. Working with an extensive staff, they perform an important research and advisory function, informing the civilian commander-in-chief about the military contingencies of any potential defense policy. As President Bush was developing his policy toward Iraq, former Secretary of State Colin Powell and Defense Secretary Donald Rumsfeld weighed in on the *desirability* of a diplomatic versus military approach to Saddam Hussein; the joint chiefs contributed an analysis of *how* a military approach should be implemented, including estimates of the size and composition of the force, the timing and duration of the conflict, and how it would best be carried out.

Joint Chiefs of Staff: The group of military advisors comprised of the heads of the army, air force, navy, and marines.

At the same time, the civilian leaders were not without a voice on military questions. Widely circulated press reports told of disagreements between Rumsfeld and the joint chiefs over the size of the Iraqi invasion force, with the defense secretary rejecting the joint chiefs' recommendation for a larger troop buildup than what the United States eventually put in place. In the first week of the campaign, as administration hopes for a smooth march to Baghdad faded against initially tenacious Iraqi resistance, Rumsfeld was bombarded with questions by reporters who suggested the American advance might have been more swift and less costly had he not overruled the military advisors. This critique faded from discussion days later when American troops waged a rapid assault on the Iraqi capital; it reemerged during the occupation of Iraq, when a thinly stretched American presence necessitated extending the tour of duty of many soldiers.

National Security Council

National Security Council (NSC): The group of senior policy advisors responsible for helping the president shape national security policy.

Established by President Truman in 1947 to coordinate foreign policy in the White House, the **National Security Council (NSC)** is an advisory body to the president that pulls together high-level representatives of the diplomatic and defense establishment. Its purpose is to review national security issues and offer advice on how the president might address them.[5] By bringing together the president, the secretaries of state and defense, the chairman of the Joint Chiefs of Staff, and the Director of National Intelligence, among others, all major diplomatic and military perspectives are represented.

national security advisor: The president's counselor on national security matters. In some administrations, the national security advisor has competed with the secretary of state for the president's attention.

This arrangement can be fruitful when disagreements among the participants are minimal or can be effectively managed. As with the case of Secretary Rumsfeld and the joint chiefs, however, infighting is not uncommon. In some administrations, the president's **national security advisor** (who serves as a personal advisor to the president on national security matters) and the secretary of state have found themselves in competition with each other for the president's attention. Tension derives from the overlapping responsibilities of the two positions, which can place their occupants on a collision course when they have major differences over the direction of foreign policy.

L.O. Explain the influence of international organizations in shaping American foreign policy.

16.2c Players on a Global Stage

International alliances have long been a staple of foreign relations, but international organizations today play a critical role in shaping national policy perhaps more than at any time in history. President Bush spent months trying to win the support of allied nations opposed to an invasion of Iraq, in part because of the desirability of sharing the costs of war and reconstruction, in part because global public opinion matters. The president wanted the legitimacy that comes from having the backing of influential world leaders, and he delayed American invasion plans in February 2003 in an effort to get it.

There are limits, of course, to the restrictions other countries can place on a determined head of state; failing to win the support he sought, Bush forged ahead with his plans anyway. However, in an interdependent world there are also ramifications for unilateral action; as critics in France, Germany, and Russia viewed the American invasion of Iraq as blatantly disregarding their wishes, they made it plain that a lot of repair work would have to be done in order for them to put relations with the United States back on track. This came to pass when Secretary of State Powell struggled to get these nations to contribute to the costs of rebuilding Iraq after the major fighting ended.

Global influences on American foreign policy come from major organizations like the United Nations, NATO, and the European Union. They can also come from interest groups with a multinational base.

The United Nations

Although it cannot make laws or guarantee enforcement of its resolutions, the United Nations (UN) is the voice of international opinion and a forum for working through international conflict. With a membership list that includes almost every country on Earth, the UN has been the center of international discussion on some of the most problematic conflicts of our time. Established in 1945 in a world that had seen two global wars in the course of thirty years, the UN charter aimed at four objectives: maintaining peace, fostering cooperation among nations, resolving international disputes, and promoting human rights.[6]

Even though the United Nations encompasses a host of organizations to advance its objectives, and all member nations are represented in the large General Assembly, the main diplomatic work takes place in the Security Council. There, the United States is one of five permanent members with the power to veto any resolution (China, France, Russia, and Great Britain are the others). Along with ten other nations who serve two-year terms, the Security Council tries to resolve international hostilities by establishing guidelines for conflict resolution, working to arrange cease-fires between warring parties, and in some cases, sending peacekeeping troops to separate hostile armies.

Since 1948, the Security Council has sent peacekeeping forces to intervene in sixty-nine conflicts.[7] In recent years, the Security Council has supported the successful struggle to end apartheid in South Africa, advanced the cause of human rights in Cambodia, negotiated an end to the fighting and supported relief efforts in the former Yugoslavia, overseen free elections in Nicaragua, worked to rebuild Afghanistan following the fall of the Taliban government, and brokered the transition from American occupation to an interim government in Iraq.[8]

Like much of the work of the Security Council, these were all long-term efforts that defied immediate success. Intractable problems can remain before the world community for generations. Security Council Resolutions 242 and 338 are still widely considered to be central components of a potential resolution to the Israeli-Palestinian conflict even though they were passed, respectively, in 1967 and 1973, and a solution to that crisis is nowhere in view.

NATO

The **North Atlantic Treaty Organization (NATO)** is a throwback to the Cold War, when it served as a common security pact for North America and Western Europe against the Warsaw Pact alliance of the Soviet Union and Eastern Europe. The NATO alliance initially maintained that a Soviet attack on any member nation would be regarded as an attack on the entire alliance in an effort to prevent Soviet expansion in Europe. After the Cold War, NATO maintains its relevance by virtue of its size (which has grown to include some former Warsaw Pact members) and strategic position.[9]

North Atlantic Treaty Organization (NATO): An alliance of the United States, Canada, and Western European nations originally designed as a military pact to counter Soviet expansion. Following the Cold War, it has grown to include European nations once aligned with the Soviet Union.

The European Union

An economic counterpart to NATO, the **European Union (EU)** has integrated the previously disparate economies of European nations into a single market with clout in the international economy. Originally a small federation of nine countries when it was established in 1950, the EU grew in size and importance toward the end of the Cold War. In May 2004, ten countries—mostly former communist nations of Eastern Europe—joined the EU.[10] In January 2007 they were joined by Bulgaria and Romania, and in 2013 by Croatia, bringing its membership to twenty-eight countries with over a half-million people. The EU formally established a single European market in 1993. In 2002, it introduced a single European currency—the euro—which is recognized as the official currency of many member nations.[11]

European Union (EU): The framework for integrating previously disparate European economies into a single market.

The future of the European Union was clouded in 2016 when Great Britain voted to withdraw from the EU in what has been termed the "Brexit" (British Exit) referendum. Economic concerns and worries about immigration drove the vote to leave, which passed by a narrow 52–48 margin. As a consequence of the vote, the British government needs to enter into treaty negotiations to set the terms of withdrawal, a complex process that could take until 2019.

Nongovernmental Organizations (NGOs)

A host of nonprofit, voluntary **nongovernmental organizations (NGOs)** bring local involvement to international concerns. NGOs may perform a number of functions. They lobby governments individually or through the United Nations, encourage participation in matters of international importance, monitor government actions in international affairs, or perform humanitarian work around the world. Many NGOs are issue-oriented and organized around a specific policy area with international applications, like the human rights group Amnesty International or the environmental group Greenpeace.[12] These organizations are probably familiar as some of the interest groups that we talked about in Chapter 8, and some NGOs can be classified in this way. You might think of NGOs as nonprofit interest groups advancing solutions to problems that lie beyond international boundaries. NGOs are based in countries around the world.

nongovernmental organizations (NGOs): Nonprofit organizations that promote interests with global ramifications on the world stage.

The tactics used by NGOs range from organizing international protests to working quietly in diplomatic circles. Operating as they do beyond national borders, NGOs are likely to use the Internet to mobilize international support behind their agendas. In fact, their influence is such that they may be regarded as nonstate actors on the international scene. In recent years, NGOs have engaged in successful efforts to strengthen women's and children's rights around the globe, influence arms control and disarmament agreements, improve the well-being of poor and indigenous people, win international approval to ban land mines, and address numerous other global social and economic concerns.[13]

Corporate Interests

Multinational corporations are, like NGOs, transnational actors with great influence over the structure of international affairs. Many of these groups will be familiar from Chapter 8 as well, as corporate interests heavily involved in lobbying Congress and the president. As more and more corporations have become global entities, their lobbying efforts have extended to the international arena, and their influence can be strong because of the resources they command. Multinational energy corporations, for instance, have an interest in maintaining or establishing friendly governments in the oil-rich Middle East and will want a say over policies influencing that region. Corporations doing business around the globe have a direct interest in international business regulations and will lobby to protect their interests in the way these regulations are formulated and implemented.

16.3 Economic Policies

L.O. Conceptualize the role of economic policies such as trade and foreign aid in the conduct of foreign affairs.

protectionism: The policy of raising the price of imported goods through tariffs in order to make them less attractive than domestic products.

tariff: A tax on imports designed to raise their cost and make them less competitive than domestic products, in an effort to protect the jobs of domestic workers.

World Trade Organization (WTO): The international organization responsible for promoting free trade among nations and settling trade disputes.

General Agreement on Tariffs and Trade (GATT): The 1948 treaty establishing the rules for free trade, which has been revised and dramatically expanded, most recently during the Uruguay Round of trade negotiations (1986–1994). GATT was also the name of the international organization that oversaw the treaty; the World Trade Organization (WTO) replaced it in 1995.

With national borders becoming increasingly smaller obstacles to international trade and finance, economic policies are becoming a more important component of international relations. Global computer networks make it possible for assets to be moved instantaneously around the world, connecting financial markets in a web of interdependency. Trade in services—like telecommunications, banking, and insurance—and trade in ideas—like inventions and other "intellectual property"—have vastly expanded the traffic in international markets, which following World War II, was limited primarily to goods.[14] These changes have moved nations to renegotiate the terms under which they do business.

16.3a Protectionism and Free Trade

Through the first half of the twentieth century, nations commonly followed a policy of **protectionism**, designed to boost the sales of domestic goods in order to protect the jobs of the workers who produced them. The main instrument of protectionism is the **tariff**, or a tax on imports designed to make them more costly and therefore less competitive than domestic products. Protectionism appealed to many policy makers in a world with distinct borders, where nations traded far fewer commodities far less frequently than they do today and where corporations resided within national boundaries. Today, multinational corporations defy those boundaries; a Toyota automobile that appears to be an import could easily have been manufactured in Kentucky by American workers using Japanese parts. Arrangements like these have promoted free trade policies aimed at reducing barriers between nations.

The vehicle for negotiating trade agreements is an international body called the **World Trade Organization (WTO)**, which establishes the rules for trade among nations, hosts trade negotiations, and settles trade disputes. The WTO was created in 1995 as part of a major overhaul of the **General Agreement on Tariffs and Trade (GATT)**, an international treaty that had been in effect since 1948. Between 1948 and 1995, GATT was the source of rules about world trade, implemented on a provisional basis by an international organization also called GATT. Over the years, several rounds of negotiations updated GATT, primarily by reducing tariffs. Then, between 1986 and 1994, the Uruguay Round of negotiations—quite possibly the largest trade negotiation ever—culminated in almost all of the 125 participants agreeing to reduce trade barriers and apply free trade principles to services and intellectual property in addition to goods.[15]

GATT requires all trading partners to be treated equally, so, for instance, if a country wants to do another country a favor and lower the customs duty assessed against one of its products, it would have to extend that treatment to every other WTO nation.[16] One exception to this rule is the case of regional trade zones, like North America, where nations can agree to separate free trade agreements applying only to nations in the region.

A highly controversial effort to create a regional free trade zone in North America, called the **North American Free Trade Agreement (NAFTA)**, was negotiated with Canada and Mexico by President George H. W. Bush and, following an intense lobbying effort by the Clinton administration, was approved by Congress in 1993. NAFTA phased out tariffs on most items traded among the three countries; opened previously protected agricultural, automobile, and textile products to free trade; and provided for free trade in finance and telecommunications services.

North American Free Trade Agreement (NAFTA): A landmark free trade agreement setting up a regional free trade zone in North America.

16.3b The Trade Deficit

The debate over free trade takes place against the backdrop of a stark imbalance between the value of the goods and services the United States imports and the value of the goods and services it exports. Since the early 1980s, the United States has run an annual **trade deficit**, meaning that American consumers and businesses have purchased more goods and services from foreign nations than foreign nations have purchased from the United States. This makes the United States a debtor nation because it owes more than it brings in, and contrasts with the situation in place prior to 1980, in which there was a **balance of trade**, or a rough equivalence between the value of American exports and the value of imports.

trade deficit: A negative balance between the value of goods and services purchased from foreign nations and the value of goods and services sold to foreign nations.

balance of trade: Equilibrium between the value of imports and exports.

Whether or not the trade deficit is a huge problem depends a lot on your outlook. Some see the trade deficit as a sign of American prosperity, an indication that low interest rates and low inflation have made the United States an appealing destination for foreign investment. At the same time, American trading partners are relatively weak, explaining why exports are increasing at a much lower rate than imports. Others see in the trade imbalance the deleterious effects of global trade posing a long-term threat to America's standard of living. They blame the trade deficit on unequal rules that give countries like China and Japan access to American markets while maintaining barriers to U.S. imports, multinational corporations moving manufacturing plants to other countries where labor is cheaper, and unfair competition from developing nations that maintain low prices for goods by exploiting workers and disregarding costly environmental standards.[17]

Of course, different perspectives on the meaning of the trade deficit lead to different conclusions about what, if anything, American policy makers should do about it. Conservatives who see the trade imbalance as a sign of American global economic strength do not believe that it will produce long-term, adverse consequences. They do not believe that corrective measures are necessary. Rather, they credit the current trade imbalance with contributing to recent periods of economic growth, job creation, low inflation, and high levels of productivity built on foreign investments. Some liberals who regard the trade deficit as problematic advocate policies to regain balance in order to reverse what they see as the detrimental effects of the trade deficit, including rising income inequality, the loss of manufacturing jobs, and declining U.S. competitiveness in world markets because of America's position as the world's largest debtor nation.[18]

16.3c Foreign Aid

Apart from trade policy, money figures into foreign relations in the form of aid to other nations. Foreign aid tends to be one of the least appreciated components of foreign policy.

You're not alone if you don't know a lot about foreign aid. Most Americans believe we give far more than we do in foreign aid, and when asked their opinion on what the proper level of aid should be, often demand cuts in spending—to amounts far greater than what we really give. Foreign aid works against an isolationist streak in American public opinion—a streak that advocates that other nations solve their own problems—which is why it can be controversial for representatives to propose increases in aid to other nations. Private contributions from U.S. corporations and foundations are more palatable to some. The argument in favor of foreign aid is that it is a relatively inexpensive way to maintain international stability and advance national interests, particularly by addressing poverty in developing nations, promoting international economic growth, and advancing the cause of human rights abroad.[19]

16.4 Diplomatic Policies

L.O. Identify key actors in the conduct of diplomatic relations.

Diplomatic relations are managed through an extensive network of ambassadors to other nations and representatives to organizations like the United Nations, NATO, and the WTO. Although you may (correctly) think of diplomacy as being the first line of defense in a crisis, the primary purpose of diplomacy is proactive. Effective diplomacy promotes stability in parts of the world where the United States maintains vital security interests, in conjunction with allied nations who have common concerns. In this regard, diplomacy is an ongoing endeavor whose success is often measured by what does not happen, as when regional tensions are prevented from bubbling into regional conflict and war.

Promoting stability also involves using diplomatic means to combat global challenges. Diplomacy is an integral part of the government's attempt to fight terrorism, as well as the war on drugs. American diplomats work to prevent the development and transport of nuclear, biological, and chemical weapons. When humanitarian concerns are an administration priority, diplomats carry them out, and in recent years, diplomats have worked to battle the African AIDS epidemic and fight international trafficking in women and girls.[20] Diplomats, along with foreign service workers, labor to assure the safety of Americans traveling abroad.

Foreign service workers are civilians stationed at American embassies and consulates overseas to assist American citizens who are traveling or living abroad. This may involve anything from arranging emergency funds for U.S. citizens to providing aid to American travelers who become ill while in another country to assisting Americans during an overseas crisis. Foreign service work can be highly rewarding and highly demanding. Workers have to be ready to serve for unspecified periods of time in any country where the United States has diplomatic relations and may have to be prepared to endure hardships. At times, their work may involve risk, as when the American consulate in Benghazi, Libya, was attacked in 2012.

Diplomatic activities are also a means for carrying out economic policies. Trade agreements like NAFTA, GATT, and over 250 others finalized in the past two decades were negotiated through diplomatic means, as a way of implementing the policy of expanding free trade. The 1994 Summit of the Americas was a diplomatic function engaging Western Hemisphere nations in negotiations for hemispheric free trade. The Asia-Pacific Economic Cooperation partnership is a long-term diplomatic effort to open trade among Pacific Rim nations.[21] Diplomacy led to agreement among 196 countries in 2015 to reduce greenhouse gas emissions to combat global warming.[22]

16.5 Military Policies

L.O. Appreciate the size of American defense expenditures relative to the rest of the world, and understand the arguments for and against maintaining a large defense budget.

As we said in Chapter 15, national defense is one of the most important functions the government performs. We acknowledge this claim by devoting close to one-fifth of the federal budget to military spending. The manner in which we spend it determines what our military capabilities will be, which in turn is the result of a debate about the type of challenges our military is likely to be asked to confront.

During the Cold War, there was consensus over what those challenges were. The United States pursued a policy of containment toward the Soviet Union designed to check the spread of communism around the globe. This required a large, conventional military equipped to fight regional conflicts on behalf of countries like South Vietnam and South Korea as they opposed Soviet-backed communist regimes in North Vietnam and North Korea. It also required a large nuclear force to check the large Soviet nuclear force, following an approach called Mutual Assured Destruction (MAD)—the theory being that the best way to avoid nuclear war between rival superpowers with large nuclear arsenals was to assure that a first strike by either side would be met with a fatal response by the other.[23]

During the forty-five years of the Cold War, the United States spent heavily on national defense to secure these goals. In fact, during the Kennedy administration, defense spending accounted for half the federal budget.[24] The end of the Cold War brought about widespread discussion of a "peace dividend" in the form of lower defense spending, and in fact, the percentage of federal money spent on defense declined slightly during the 1990s, as policy makers tried to determine what our defense needs would be in a world where we were the only remaining superpower.

However, the notion of a "peace dividend" was controversial. As an ideological matter, some conservative members of Congress argued that even without the Soviet threat, the United States risked being unprepared for unforeseen acts of aggression if it permitted the military to atrophy. Liberals, eager to redirect funds to domestic priorities, took the opposite position, arguing that defense budgets had become bloated during the Cold War and that national security could be maintained for less money. At the same time, practical considerations cut across ideological lines. Defense contractors are powerful interest groups with an investment in maintaining lucrative government business, and they don't have to remind members of Congress that military equipment is built in congressional districts across the country, providing jobs for constituents. Liberals and conservatives alike recognize the value of keeping these jobs secure.[25]

The September 11 terror attacks brought clarity to national defense policy and provided the basis for a steady increase in defense spending. The fiscal year 2003 military budget of $355 billion, drafted in the year following the attacks, represented an increase of 10.6 percent from the previous year. What kinds of things did it provide for? Highlights include:

Intelligence and Surveillance

- The largest one-year increase in spending for the National Foreign Intelligence Program in two decades

Ballistic Missile Defense

- Patriot missile defense system
- Airborne laser development
- Total funding: $7.4 billion

Strategic Mobility

- Fifteen C-17 transport aircraft, totaling $3.3 billion

Personnel

- $93.6 billion to support 1.4 million active duty and 865,000 guard and reservists

Operation and Maintenance

- $114.8 billion for training, spare parts, real property, and maintenance

Major Acquisitions

- Aircraft, including nineteen Blackhawk helicopters, forty-six F/A-18 fighters, and twenty-three F-22 fighters
- Munitions, including Tomahawk cruise missiles and JDAM precision-guided bombs
- Ships, including two AEGIS destroyers and one attack submarine[26]

By any measure, this is an extensive menu of items. Whether it is enough is, of course, a matter of debate. Take a few minutes to see what people on both sides of that debate have to say. You'll find a discussion in Demystifying Government: Defense Spending.

Defense Spending

At what level have we committed sufficient resources to ensure our national security? When have we spent too much? Are we willing to trade off spending on domestic programs so that we can spend on national defense? Is defense money best spent on the military or on global aid projects?

Questions like these arise every year as Congress and the president negotiate the federal budget, and in an age when homeland security is a top priority, they take on an urgency not seen since the Cold War.

Regardless of whether the American military budget is increased or held steady, the United States far outspends everyone else in the world. The military budget for fiscal year 2015 of $596 billion was three times the military budget of China, and China ranks number two in the world. The combined military budgets of Great Britain, Japan, Russia, and Germany are one-third that of the United States. There is no question that, as a matter of dollars, the United States is in a league by itself.[T2]

The military budget is traditionally viewed as so untouchable that in 2012 Congress included extreme defense cuts as part of a sequester measure designed to force members into a deficit reduction compromise on the assumption that across-the-board defense cuts would be harder for members to bear than tax increases or cuts to entitlement programs. The cuts were designed to go into effect in early 2013 only if members couldn't come up with a better deficit reduction plan.

Still, many people feel we do not spend enough on national defense. They contend that national security is our number one priority, for which we should spare no expense to protect ourselves. They point out that we live in a complex age when our military faces a wide range of demands, including fighting two major regional wars simultaneously, monitoring military threats in the Middle East and North Korea, participating in peacekeeping missions in the Balkans, and disrupting terrorist activities around the world.[T3]

Opponents of increased military spending fall into two groups: those who think a larger military budget is unnecessary and those who think it is misguided. Those in the first group point to the fact that defense spending still averages 95 percent of what it did during the Cold War.[T4]

Those who believe increased military spending is misguided generally take one of two positions. Some look at the unconventional nature of the terrorist problem and advocate a smaller, flexible, and well-trained military tailored to meet targeted threats. They say massive force is a relic of the Cold War and does not make us safer today, and they would supplement downsized forces with better intelligence capabilities and diplomacy.

Others take the position that a military as large as ours is a threat to world peace. They invite Americans to try to imagine how provocative our military position looks to the rest of the world, and contend that it will only aggravate global tension. They point to the relatively small amount of money the United States devotes to foreign aid and argue that if we spent even a fraction of what we devote to the military toward humanitarian assistance to combat disease, illiteracy, poverty, and hunger, we would reap the benefits of a safer world.[T5]

No matter which way you come down, you should see military spending as a choice we make as a nation. Whether or not you support an increase in defense spending, remember that every dollar spent on defense is a dollar that is not spent on something else, a dollar that contributes to budget deficits, or a dollar that is not returned to us in tax relief. Because of the stakes involved in protecting national security, military spending is an expense many people are willing to assume. Because the defense budget is so vast, it's a choice that generates resistance in others.

16.6 Strategic Policies

L.O. Recognize key strategic assumptions behind American foreign policy as they relate to the acquisition and deployment of resources.

As we said in the previous section, policy makers try to design the military budget to meet what they consider to be the most likely threats to our security. Doing so requires long-term strategic planning, which by necessity is a matter of making assumptions about the challenges that are likely to come along. If we expect the United States to fight two long-term regional wars simultaneously, we need to have the capacity to do so. If we believe that intelligence information will provide security against terrorist groups, then we need to make the appropriate investments. If we believe that strong alliances—like NATO during the Cold War—advance our national security, then we will target the necessary money and diplomatic effort to keep those alliances strong.

16.6a Strategies and Resources

Military and intelligence capabilities and international alliances are among the tools of strategy, some of the things that policy makers can employ in order to chart a course for advancing national interests. Our foreign policy objectives have to be built on a realistic assessment of the resources we have to work with, and, in turn, we make judgments about the size, scope, and allocation of resources with our foreign policy objectives in mind.

When strategic objectives can only be met with resources we don't have, policy debate will center on questions of resource acquisition. President Reagan wanted to counter the Soviet nuclear arsenal with an antiballistic missile capability that would seek and destroy inbound nuclear warheads before they could reach their target. However, the capability to implement this strategy did not exist. Thus began a protracted debate about the strategic desirability and technical feasibility of what became popularly known as "Star Wars" technology. The debate over whether to embark on an expensive research and development campaign to create a missile shield centered on both the rightness of President Reagan's strategy (would it make the United States safer or destabilize the existing nuclear balance of power?) and resource issues (did the huge price tag and uncertain outcome of a missile defense program make "Star Wars" a bad investment?).

Similarly, for several years after the 2001 attack on the World Trade Center and Pentagon, policy makers wrestled with how best to organize American intelligence capabilities to maximize effectiveness against an elusive terror threat. In 2004, an independent commission looking into the September 11 attack suggested restructuring the intelligence community around a new director of national intelligence, setting off a heated political battle with the Pentagon and CIA over their place in the new intelligence bureaucracy. Ultimately, political pressures to address the nation's most pressing foreign policy problem were enough to overcome bureaucratic resistance to change, and Congress approved the restructuring plan in late 2004.[27]

In contrast, when strategic objectives can be met with existing resources, debate will center exclusively on questions of strategy. During the buildup to the Iraq War, questions about resource availability were not at issue. America's military capability was clear. Policy planners in the Bush administration knew they had the personnel and hardware necessary to give the United States an overwhelming advantage in any conflict with Saddam Hussein. As a consequence, the debate within the administration and in the press centered on whether it was strategically advisable for the United States to use its military power against Iraq.

16.6b Strategies and Assumptions

The debate over Iraq was passionately engaged, as advocates of two different approaches faced off against each other in the administration, in homes across America, in the United Nations, and around the world (see Global Topics: Dueling Strategies). At home, the dividing line was whether a military or a diplomatic strategy would best advance American interests in the Middle East. The military strategy called for quick use of American forces in Iraq, which for logistical reasons would have to occur before international support could be won. The diplomatic strategy called for avoiding rifts in time-tested alliances by not going to war without international support. It was not a simple choice. As is typical of strategic decisions, assumptions by domestic policy makers about how best to advance national interests shaped the debate and its outcome.

16.6c Strategies and Crisis Response

Some strategies are long-term and enduring, like the Cold War strategy of containment. Others are developed in response to a crisis. During the Cold War, the United States faced periodic international crises and had to fashion its response with long-term strategic interests in mind—foremost among them containing Soviet expansion without triggering nuclear war. For this reason, whenever hostility broke out in a region of the world involving client states of the two superpowers, the United States was constrained in its actions.

L.O. Explain the role of strategy in crisis response.

Dueling Strategies

As a military matter, timing was everything to the Iraqi campaign. Eager to avoid fighting a war in the scorching desert summer, the Bush administration calibrated the military buildup in the Persian Gulf to coincide with Iraq's cooler winter months, with the aim of having a fighting force in place by February 2003. In order to meet this strategic aim, the administration needed to move an invasion force to the region while it was engaged in diplomatic efforts to resolve matters peacefully, creating a sense among nations opposed to war, like France and Germany, that American military strategy was at odds with American diplomatic efforts.

It was an open secret in Washington and at the United Nations that the American military was following a timetable, even though the Bush administration publicly denied it. Diplomats understood America's strategic military needs, but the sense that American military strategy was driving American diplomatic efforts fueled resistance by nations that felt the United States was not taking their interests seriously. France, Germany, and Russia led the charge for giving UN weapons inspectors—who were in Iraq under the terms of Security Council Resolution 1441—more time to do their work, claiming that they were slowly but effectively disarming Iraq. The United States brushed this off, aware that negotiating more time for weapons inspections would upend its military strategy.

As a diplomatic matter, the model for building a multinational coalition was the 1991 Persian Gulf War. Following Iraq's march into Kuwait, President George H. W. Bush took time to build a global coalition against Saddam Hussein, using diplomacy backed by the threat of force to pressure Iraq to relinquish Kuwait.

On the surface, the second Bush administration appeared to be doing the same thing, but because there had not been a hostile action by Iraq to precipitate war in 2003, President George W. Bush had a far more difficult time selling allied nations on the idea of an invasion than did his father. This would be a preemptive action, designed to forestall what American officials said was an ongoing Iraqi program to develop weapons of mass destruction. With some nations doubting the existence of such weapons and questioning the moral authority of carrying out an attack under these circumstances, advocates of continued weapons inspections found a receptive audience.

Internal administration divisions about the desirability of diplomacy further complicated matters. Secretary of State Colin Powell, as the head of the department responsible for American diplomacy, was an early advocate of building a coalition. Secretary of Defense Donald Rumsfeld, as the head of the department responsible for orchestrating the military campaign, advocated action on a schedule that favored American troops.

Underlying these different departmental perspectives was something deeper: fundamental differences in the strategic *desirability* of building a coalition or going it alone. This is where the assumptions that strategists made about the world most influenced their strategic choices.

Advocates of alliances emphasized the importance of *legitimacy* in international affairs. They believed that a broad group of like-minded nations acting in concert diminished political resistance from opponents, and that a worldwide invasion force would look less to the Islamic world like an imperialist action by the United States, making the invasion less likely to precipitate a new wave of terrorism against American interests. For this reason, they believed that American security was advanced by multilateral diplomatic efforts rather than through a unilateral show of strength.

Advocates of unilateral military action emphasized the importance of *strength* in international affairs. They believed that actions determine how nations respond, that it is more important to be feared than liked, and that while the Islamic world might not like the presence of American troops on Iraqi soil, they would respect the results. Nations opposed to American military action before the war would have no choice but to grudgingly accept the results of the invasion, which would leave the United States in a strong position to dictate the terms of Iraqi reconstruction. For this reason, they believed that American security was advanced by a unilateral show of strength rather than through multilateral diplomatic efforts.

As America's traditional allies began to perceive that unilateralists were in charge of American policy, they came to regard the press for war as more than a matter of military strategy, and they dug in their heels. In the end, advocates of strength carried the day. The effectiveness of their strategy depended, like any strategy, on how clearly and accurately their underlying assumptions captured global dynamics. As America faced mounting casualties in Iraq, they came under fire from advocates of coalition-building, who argued that American power had not been sufficient to shape conditions in postwar Iraq.

For instance, Israel and neighboring Arab countries fought four wars during the Cold War era, in which the Soviet Union supported the Arab combatants and the United States supported Israel (in Cold War language, Israel was always described as the Middle East's only democracy). The United States was able to offer Israel economic support and weaponry, but had to temper its involvement to avoid creating a direct conflict with the Soviet Union. Likewise, the "hot" wars America fought in Korea and Vietnam did not threaten to undermine broader national interests as long as they remained surrogate conflicts in the struggle with the USSR.

Not surprisingly, the most frightening crises of the Cold War period came when American and Soviet interests directly clashed. Try to imagine what things felt like in October 1962 when President Kennedy announced to the American public that the Soviet Union was in the process of placing nuclear weapons in Cuba, and that the American response would be a naval quarantine of the island to prevent Soviet ships from reaching Cuban ports. An American invasion of Cuba was threatened if the Soviets disobeyed the quarantine, an act certain to start World War III. Pressure to invade was immense; the chairman of the Joint Chiefs of Staff argued that it was America's only option. Secretary of Defense Robert McNamara reportedly looked closely at the sun shining in the White House Rose Garden, believing he would never see it again.[28]

Never before had the world been as close to nuclear war as during the Cuban missile crisis. What most of Kennedy's advisors didn't know, however, was that the president was engaged in back-channel communications with Soviet Premier Nikita Khrushchev, and was ready to remove antiquated American missiles in Turkey as a fallback compromise had the Soviets rejected outright American demands that they remove their missiles from Cuba. It was an action that would have cost Kennedy prestige and left him vulnerable to political attack from hardliners, but the president saw the need to keep his options open and not embark on an irreversible course to global destruction.

The crisis ended peacefully and victoriously for the United States when the Soviets abandoned their position in Cuba. There was a lot of self-congratulating among the president's advisors, who believed their hard line was the reason why "the other fellow blinked," in Secretary of State Dean Rusk's phrase, or gave in first. In fact, it was strength coupled with flexibility and the willingness to avoid going past the brink of nuclear war that enabled Kennedy to escape the Cold War's most dangerous moment.[29]

The American reaction to the September 11 terror attacks constituted a different type of crisis response. When the reality of what had happened settled in, many Americans instinctively agreed with President Bush that we were suddenly at war with a previously unknown adversary. When we learned that the adversary was named al-Qaeda and that they were granted safe haven by a radical Islamic regime in Afghanistan, there was little debate about the Bush administration's decision to invade Afghanistan with the objective of removing the Taliban government and dismantling the terrorists' leadership structure.

However, this crisis reaction created new policy questions for the United States, requiring new strategies to meet the circumstances of living in a world that seemed to have changed in one day. This is not unusual in crisis situations, as every action creates fallout—both intended and unexpected. One of the key questions raised by the American invasion of Afghanistan was what to do once the crisis response had been carried out. Indications were that the United States would have to find a way to put the political structures of Afghanistan back together again, but Americans who objected to maintaining a long-term presence in other nations recoiled at this possibility. By 2013, owing in part to the strategic risk of withdrawing American military personnel, Afghanistan had become America's longest war.

16.7 Foreign Policy and Domestic Politics

Because every major foreign policy decision has political ramifications, it shouldn't be surprising that politically sensitive administrations pay careful attention to the domestic fallout of the actions they take. Public response to foreign policy choices can cut many ways. As we saw in Section 10.3c, "Malleable Public Opinion," the public regularly rallies behind the president immediately following a national crisis or when the president first commits

L.O. Understand how domestic political considerations can influence foreign policy decisions.

troops to military action. We also saw, however, that rally events are typically short-lived. And protracted war without a favorable conclusion can deeply erode presidential support, as President Bush learned as the Iraq War continued inconclusively into his second term.

Where a president's popularity lands depends on how the public experiences the effectiveness of the administration's response.

Foreign policy decisions are unpredictable because they are only as good as the assumptions behind them and because their outcomes depend on the actions of leaders of other nations. So, presidents will do their best to spin events to their liking. Nowhere is the urge to manage the media message more evident than in wartime, when events are at their most unpredictable and the stakes are at their highest. The more an administration is able to exercise control over war coverage, the more likely it is to convince the public to experience conflict on its terms. Working in its favor is the tendency for domestic reporters to identify with the American cause when troops are in battle, but should things go sour for the United States, as they did in Vietnam, pictures of dead and injured American soldiers can have a negative impact on domestic public opinion. The Bush administration embargoed news photos of coffins of dead American soldiers returning to the United States, ostensibly out of respect for the dead but with awareness of the political risks posed by these images. This policy was overturned by the Obama administration.

Presidents can also try to use the political circumstances created by international events to advance their domestic agenda. In the run-up to war with Iraq, President Bush saw his job approval ratings sag under the weight of the uncertainty many Americans felt about the impending conflict, but his political advisors correctly anticipated that he would get a short-term boost in popularity once the war started. Mindful of the overwhelming job approval Bush's father received following the first Persian Gulf War, White House strategists anticipated that a successful conclusion to the impending conflict would enhance the president's long-term approval, and that he could use his refreshed public standing to enhance his clout with Congress on domestic matters.[30]

In fact, President Bush didn't wait until the end of the war to advance an important component of his domestic agenda. During the first few days of fighting, while national attention was focused overseas and public debate on domestic matters appeared unseemly, Republican congressional leaders worked with the White House to slowly advance the president's proposed $726 billion tax cut through a sharply divided legislature. In peacetime, this would have been a big story, and opponents of the controversial tax cut would have felt emboldened to speak out against it. Instead, the president was able to find cover for his tax plan while the media agenda was saturated with war issues.

By the early months of President Bush's second term, the interplay of foreign policy and presidential job approval were working in reverse. A majority of the public had soured on the war, and questions about the administration's veracity about the danger posed by Saddam Hussein led a growing number of Americans to question the president's honesty. Americans continued to die in Iraq, and despite administration claims to the contrary, the Iraqi political process was not showing promise as a stabilizing force that would end the fighting. Under these circumstances, President Bush found himself losing control of his domestic agenda. By early 2006, congressional Republicans began to worry that identification with the administration and the war effort would complicate their re-election efforts the following fall. The unity that Republicans demonstrated when the Iraq invasion was popular began to dissipate under the weight of strong public disapproval of the administration's conduct of the war, paralyzing the president's ability to set the domestic agenda.

Foreign policy decisions can also have ramifications for domestic policy rather than politics. In the period following the attack on the World Trade Center and the Pentagon, the administration wrestled with how to handle individuals who have been detained as suspected terrorists. The issue pits safety imperatives against civil rights concerns. The more leeway law enforcement officials are given to imprison suspects, the more efficiently they can do their jobs. However, we have seen how efficiency can be the enemy of liberty, and in this case, the liberty of potentially innocent suspects was in the crosshairs. How far should we go to protect their liberty when we believe terrorists are plotting to strike again in the United States?

Take a few minutes to read Demystifying Government: Detaining Terror Suspects, and see if you can sharpen your opinion on what the government should do to balance the rights of the individual against the needs of the community.

Detaining Terror Suspects

When the president swears an oath to uphold the Constitution, he pledges to defend the rights that document entitles us to. He also promises to "faithfully execute his office," which includes doing his best to keep us safe. You could make the case that there are no two greater responsibilities for a president—which makes it all the more complicated when the two conflict. Presidents George W. Bush and Barack Obama had deeply conflicting ideas about the measures they needed to take in order to defend our rights and keep us safe. Bush believed that extraordinary dangers called for extraordinary security measures. Obama articulated the belief that strength comes from adhering to legal principle.

It was inevitable following the September 11, 2001 attacks that there would be a dragnet for individuals who were suspected of having knowledge of or involvement with known terror organizations. It was equally inevitable that many of these individuals would be innocent of the charges made against them. In order to defend the country, it would be necessary to detain them until officials could sort through the evidence against them and determine if they were security risks. This is a laborious and time-consuming job, though, and detainees have a right to a speedy trial or to be released pending trial if the government cannot give the courts a compelling reason to hold them in custody. This poses a serious dilemma in which the rights of the accused are in direct conflict with national security interests.

Initially, the Bush Justice Department asked Congress for unilateral powers to indefinitely detain illegal aliens it believed were involved in terrorist activity. Congress refused. The attorney general would have to demonstrate that there were "reasonable grounds" to believe that a suspect was involved in terrorism, unless he could present the court with evidence of the suspect's involvement in a crime. Otherwise, the suspect could only be legally detained for a few days.

This proved complicated. If the Justice Department had evidence against a suspect that came from secret intelligence sources, it would be unable to present it in court without compromising the source. The same problem would arise from evidence that the Justice Department wanted to keep secret so as not to compromise the search for other suspects.[T6]

In the confusion of the ensuing weeks, it was hard to keep track of the more than 1,000 people who were detained by the United States. Many, it turned out, had no terrorist connections, but some were disappearing from public view, and suspicion grew among civil rights groups that suspects were being held against their legal rights. In December 2001, nineteen civil rights groups filed suit against Attorney General Ashcroft under the Freedom of Information Act, asking for immediate release of the records of everyone detained in connection with the September 11 attacks. A lawyer for the American Civil Liberties Union (ACLU) said, "It is absolutely critical that the American public has the information it needs to decide whether the Justice Department's actions are consistent with the freedoms we are now fighting to defend."[T7]

Months passed, but the tension between protecting America and protecting suspects' rights did not dissipate. Hundreds of suspects were detained indefinitely at the U.S. military base at Guantanamo Bay, Cuba, under a controversial policy in which the Justice Department labeled them "unlawful combatants," denying them the rights of prisoners of war. However, the United States was having difficulty putting together a legal case against many of them. The dilemma posed by these detainees, said the State Department ambassador-at-large for war crimes, was that "as long as they live and breathe, they are devoted to killing Americans, yet there is insufficient information to prosecute some of them. We would hate to . . . release such a person, and he's out there on the next plane heading into another tower in the United States."[T8]

In 2004, the issue went before the Supreme Court in the twin cases of *Rasul v. Bush* and *al Odah v. United States*. In these cases, relatives of Kuwaiti, British, and Australian prisoners being held at Guantanamo Bay argued that their family members were innocent victims being held indefinitely for no reason. The Court agreed, holding that the detainees had a right to challenge the legality of their detention at Guantanamo Bay and that federal courts have jurisdiction to hear their complaints even though they were being held at a facility outside the United States.[T9] During his campaign for president, Barack Obama pledged to end indefinite detentions and prosecute those accused in the September 11 attacks through usual legal means. As president, he moved forward haltingly on both fronts. In 2009, the Obama Justice Department announced it was going to prosecute Khalid Shaikh Mohammed, who described himself as the mastermind of the September 11 attack, and four co-conspirators in a New York City federal court just blocks from where the World Trade Center once stood. The announcement sparked controversy among those who questioned the security risks of holding the accused on American soil and hearing the case through the civilian justice system,[T10] and the administration decided to reverse course in response to public pressure.

16.8 Completing the Circle

The first question we raised in this book was, "Should we care about politics?" It was raised with the promise that it would not be answered for you, that you would in the end decide for yourself whether any form of political involvement—the big and small ways available for you to interact with the political process—is a valuable use of your time.

We've now reached the end of the discussion, which makes this a good time to think back over the range of issues we discussed along the way, and consider how closely your view of America aligns with the reality of what our policy makers do. If there are places where the United States is moving in a direction you don't like, ask yourself if you feel that any action on your part might make a difference. If you're largely content with the direction of the country, remember that political situations are fluid, and ask yourself if you feel that any political activity would be warranted to counter those who seek to change course.

The sixth edition of this book went to press as Donald Trump was taking the presidential oath of office in the shadow of the divisive 2016 election and following a year in which politics could be characterized as chaotic. Consider the events leading up to the Trump administration, which are without parallel in recent times.

There is no precedent in your lifetime or mine for the public to elect a novice to the presidency, or for Congress to deny an incumbent president the right to appoint a qualified Supreme Court nominee, or for the press to fail to set the agenda for a national election. New presidents often meet with opposition, but it is rare for those on the losing side of an election to use the language of resistance, as we have seen in 2017. Political party leaders have struggled to hold on to fraying coalitions in the past, but it has been decades since we have seen the decay of party coalitions that we witnessed in 2016. It has been 130 years since the Electoral College "misfired" twice in close proximity. Many Americans harbor doubts about the viability of our institutions; the public shares a sense that the country is off track but cannot agree on a direction.

Dramatic social and economic changes can drive disruptive politics. At other dislocating times in our history we have experienced difficult moments, and at each juncture, the political process has proved resilient. How we manage in the times ahead will depend in part on the strength and durability of a constitutional system designed to decentralize power, moderate dramatic change, and make it possible to endure the momentary passions of a tumultuous age. And that requires political engagement because the system only responds to those who make demands on it.

Even if you don't believe you're in a position to make a difference, think about whether you believe any action on your part would be meaningful. When you do, remember that not all participation is noisy, and not all participation is all-encompassing. True, millions of Americans have taken to the streets in vocal demonstrations against the Trump administration, and tens of thousands protested against government-centered policies during the Obama administration and against the Iraq War during the Bush administration. This may be the most visible form of participation, but it is far from the most common. Sending an email to a senator, voting, and even advocating political action to a friend are all ways to advance your views and make your mark. There are many ways for your voice to be heard.

Remember also that not acting is a choice, for there will always be others ready to take the space that you could fill, others who may differ with your objectives and desires. You've got to decide how much that matters. Some of us hold beliefs about what America should look like, but we don't hold to them very strongly. Some of us care deeply about one or two things. Some are motivated to speak out in moments of crisis. Some are universally committed and actively involved.

And some of us are turned off when we don't get what we want, when the rewards of participation are not forthcoming. This can be discouraging, as we know from considering the plight of individuals without many resources who do not feel the efficacy necessary for participation. Is political participation worth it anyway, even when we lose—even when we fail to achieve our objectives? Is there value in the process, or satisfaction in knowing that our voice was expressed, even if it was not ultimately heard?

The answers to these questions are personal. Ultimately, they shape the choices we make about how or whether to voice our views, the sum total of which determines the kind of future we will have.

Chapter Review

Understand how the president's worldview can influence foreign policy.

American foreign and defense policy is influenced by domestic and global actors. The president is the leading domestic figure in developing and executing foreign policy, and the way he views the world will shape the policy choices he makes.

Identify key actors in the American foreign policy establishment.

The president is supported in his decisions by an extensive foreign policy establishment. He receives diplomatic support from the Department of State, military advice from the Department of Defense and the Joint Chiefs of Staff, and policy coordination from the National Security Council. Because of their different missions, perspectives, and ambitions, these actors do not always work together harmoniously.

Explain the influence of international organizations in shaping American foreign policy.

Globally, American policy is influenced by international organizations. Foremost among these is the United Nations, a diplomatic union that provides a forum for discussing international disputes and engages in peacekeeping work, but that cannot back its decisions with the force of law. Regionally, NATO remains an important strategic organization even though it no longer serves its original Cold War purpose as a security pact for Western Europe and North America. Additionally, nongovernmental organizations and multinational corporations function like interest groups on a global scale, operating cross-nationally to advance agendas that go beyond national borders.

Conceptualize the role of economic policies such as trade and foreign aid in the conduct of foreign affairs.

Foreign policy encompasses a wide range of economic, diplomatic, and military concerns. Significant steps away from protectionism and toward free trade were made in the 1990s with the creation of the World Trade Organization and the negotiation of the North American Free Trade Agreement. Supporters claim free trade is good for economic growth, while detractors assert that it causes corporations to move American jobs to countries where labor is cheap. The debate over free trade takes place against the backdrop of a sharply rising trade deficit, the result of American imports far outpacing exports. Foreign aid is also a controversial item, although as a percentage of gross domestic product, the United States gives less foreign aid than any of the world's wealthiest nations, and far less than most Americans believe.

Identify key actors in the conduct of diplomatic relations.

Diplomatic relations are managed through an extensive network of ambassadors to other nations and representatives to international organizations. Effective diplomacy promotes stability in parts of the world where the United States maintains vital security interests.

Appreciate the size of American defense expenditures relative to the rest of the world, and understand the arguments for and against maintaining a large defense budget.

Military policy is supported by a large defense budget that is protected by advocates of a strong defense and by lawmakers responding to the lobbying efforts of defense contractors. The defense budget is also influenced by assumptions about the country's future strategic needs, just as strategic concerns shape the way the United States relates to other nations and responds to crises.

Recognize key strategic assumptions behind American foreign policy as they relate to the acquisition and deployment of resources.

Strategic assumptions about foreign policy need to be based on an appraisal of available resources, like military and intelligence capabilities and international alliances. When strategic objectives can only be met with resources we don't have, debate will center on resource acquisition.

Explain the role of strategy in crisis response.

While some strategies are long-term and enduring, others are developed in response to a crisis, albeit with long-term national interests in mind. For instance, during the Cold War, American responses to crises in the Middle East and Southeast Asia needed to be measured against whether they would trigger a larger crisis with the Soviet Union.

Understand how domestic political considerations can influence foreign policy decisions.

Domestic political strategy may enter into foreign policy considerations, with presidents aware that their effectiveness in handling important international incidents may constrain or enhance the public support they need to advance their domestic agenda.

Key Terms

balance of trade Equilibrium between the value of imports and exports. (p. 479)

European Union (EU) The framework for integrating previously disparate European economies into a single market. (p. 477)

executive agreements Legally binding presidential agreements with other nations that do not require congressional approval. (p. 473)

General Agreement on Tariffs and Trade (GATT) The 1948 treaty establishing the rules for free trade, which has been revised and dramatically expanded, most recently during the Uruguay Round of trade negotiations (1986–1994). GATT was also the name of the international organization that oversaw the treaty; the World Trade Organization (WTO) replaced it in 1995. (p. 478)

Joint Chiefs of Staff The group of military advisors comprised of the heads of the army, air force, navy, and marines. (p. 475)

national security advisor The president's counselor on national security matters. In some administrations, the national security advisor has competed with the secretary of state for the president's attention. (p. 476)

National Security Council (NSC) The group of senior policy advisors responsible for helping the president shape national security policy. (p. 476)

nongovernmental organizations (NGOs) Nonprofit organizations that promote interests with global ramifications on the world stage. (p. 477)

North American Free Trade Agreement (NAFTA) A landmark free trade agreement setting up a regional free trade zone in North America. (p. 479)

North Atlantic Treaty Organization (NATO) An alliance of the United States, Canada, and Western European nations originally designed as a military pact to counter Soviet expansion. Following the Cold War, it has grown to include European nations once aligned with the Soviet Union. (p. 477)

protectionism The policy of raising the price of imported goods through tariffs in order to make them less attractive than domestic products. (p. 478)

secretary of state The head of the Department of State, who functions as the president's chief foreign policy advisor. (p. 475)

tariff A tax on imports designed to raise their cost and make them less competitive than domestic products, in an effort to protect the jobs of domestic workers. (p. 478)

trade deficit A negative balance between the value of goods and services purchased from foreign nations and the value of goods and services sold to foreign nations. (p. 479)

War Powers Act of 1973 A congressional attempt to reassert the role of the legislature with respect to the president in military affairs by restricting the president's ability to wage war. (p. 475)

World Trade Organization (WTO) The international organization responsible for promoting free trade among nations and settling trade disputes. (p. 478)

Resources

You might be interested in examining some of what the following authors have said about the topics we've been discussing:

Graebner, Norman A., Richard Dean Burns, and Joseph M. Siracusa. *America and the Cold War, 1941–1991: A Realist Interpretation*. New York: Praeger, 2010. A sweeping look at the origins and significance of the Cold War.

Halberstam, David. *The Best and the Brightest*. New York: Random House, 1993. The title is an ironic reference to the highly capable and experienced elite that led the United States into the Vietnam War. Halberstam's journalistic account provides insight into a time that continues to cast a shadow over American foreign policy.

Lindsay, James M. *Congress and the Politics of U.S. Foreign Policy*. Baltimore: Johns Hopkins University Press, 1994. Lindsay presents a comprehensive account of the secondary but important role Congress plays in the conduct of American foreign policy.

Nathan, James A. *Anatomy of the Cuban Missile Crisis*. Westport, CT: Greenwood Press, 2001. With the assistance of declassified information, Nathan provides context and meaning for one of history's most dangerous crises.

Wilson, George C. *This War Really Matters: Inside the Fight for Defense Dollars*. Washington, DC: CQ Press, 2000. An inside account of the political maneuvering that shapes the nation's defense budget.

You may also be interested in looking at this resource site:

If working abroad for the government sounds interesting to you and you'd like to get more information, contact the State Department online at http://www.state.gov/careers/.

Notes

1 For a discussion of the development of presidential "worldview" in the context of the development of a president's character and style, see James David Barber, *The Presidential Character: Predicting Performance in the White House*, 4th ed. (Englewood Cliffs, NJ: Prentice Hall, 2008).

2 See James M. Lindsay, *Congress and the Politics of U.S. Foreign Policy* (Baltimore: Johns Hopkins University Press, 1994). Lindsay contends that Congress plays the secondary but essential role of legitimizing and criticizing presidential policy decisions.

3 See the U.S. Department of State website, at http://www.state.gov/.

4 See United States Department of Defense, at https://www.dmdc.osd.mil/appj/dwp/dwp_reports.jsp.

5 For background on the National Security Council, see: http://www.whitehouse.gov/nsc/.

6 See the United Nations website, at http://www.un.org/en/documents/charter/index.shtml.

7 See the United Nations website, at http://www.un.org/en/peacekeeping/operations/history.shtml.

8 Ibid.

9 See the NATO website, at http://www.nato.int.

10 The new additions are Cyprus, the Czech Republic, Estonia, Hungary, Latvia, Lithuania, Malta, Poland, the Slovak Republic, and Slovenia. These nations joined Austria, Belgium, Denmark, Finland, France, Germany, Greece, Ireland, Italy, Luxembourg, the Netherlands, Portugal, Spain, Sweden, and the United Kingdom. See http://europa.eu/abc/history/2000_today/index_en.htm.

11 See the European Union website, at http://ec.europa.eu/economy_finance/euro/index_en.htm.

12 See information from the UN on NGOs at http://www.un.org/dpi/ngosection/index.asp.

13 James A. Paul, "NGOs and Global Policy-Making," *Global Policy Forum*, June 2000.

14 See "What is the World Trade Organization?" at http://www.wto.org/english/thewto_e/whatis_e/tif_e/fact1_e.htm.

15 See the World Trade Organization, at http://www.wto.org/english/thewto_e/whatis_e/tif_e/fact4_e.htm.

16 Ibid.

17 "The U.S. Trade Deficit: Causes, Consequences and Recommendations for Action," U.S. Trade Deficit Review Commission report, November 14, 2000, 17–18.

18 Ibid., 84–85.

19 "Foreign Aid in the National Interest," United States Agency for International Development, at http://www.usaid.gov/fani/.

20 U.S. Department of State website, at http://www.state.gov/g/drl/hr/index.htm.

21 Ibid, at http://www.state.gov/e/eeb/tpp/bta/fta/index.htm.

22 Joby Warrick and Chris Mooney, "196 Countries Approve Historic Climate Agreement," *Washington Post*, December 12, 2015. https://www.washingtonpost.com/news/energy-environment/wp/2015/12/12/proposed-historic-climate-pact-nears-final-vote/?utm_term=.2767b0b9577d.

23 For a complete account of the personalities and events that shaped the Cold War, see Benjamin Frankel, ed., *The Cold War, 1945–1991* (Washington, DC: Gale Research, 1992).

24 Defense spending declined following the Vietnam War but remained high by present levels. With increases during the Reagan years, defense spending totaled slightly more than one-quarter of federal spending during the 1980s. See Office of Management and Budget, Budget of the United States Government: Historical Tables, Table 3-1.

25 See George C. Wilson, *This War Really Matters: Inside the Fight for Defense Dollars* (Washington, DC: CQ Press, 2000).

26 Almanac of Policy Issues: Defense Spending, at http://www.policyalmanac.org/world/defense_spending.shtml.

27 Philip Shenon, "New Phase Begins in Push to Reorganize Intelligence," *New York Times*, December 20, 2004.

28 James A. Nathan, *Anatomy of the Cuban Missile Crisis* (Westport, CT: Greenwood Press, 2001), 93–101.

29 Ibid.

30 In fact, the second Bush administration was looking over its shoulder at the first Bush administration to apply political and policy lessons learned during the first Persian Gulf War. For a look at some of the lessons learned by students of the conflict, see Joseph S. Nye, Jr. and Roger K. Smith, eds., *After the Storm: Lessons from the Gulf War* (Lanham, MD: Madison Books, 1992).

Table, Figure, and Box Notes

T1 See http://www.nato.int/structur/countries.htm.

T2 Deidre McPhillips, "U.S. a Global Leader in Military Spending," *US News*, November 11, 2016. http://www.usnews.com/news/best-countries/articles/2016-11-11/10-countries-with-the-largest-military-budgets.

T3 See Network Justice Watch, at www.thirdworldtraveler.com.

T4 See "Making Sense of Defense," at Council for a Livable World, http://livableworld.org.

T5 See "Why the Military Budget Should Be Cut," at Council for a Livable World, http://livableworld.org.

T6 Joseph A. D'Agostino, "Detaining Foreign Terror Suspects Difficult," *WorldNet Daily*, October 15, 2001.

T7 "U.S. Government Sued for Detaining Hundreds of Terror Suspects," *Agence France-Presse*, December 6, 2001.

T8 Frank Davies, "Detaining Suspect Brings Many Legal Questions," *Miami Herald*, May 9, 2002.

T9 *Rasul v. Bush*, 542 U.S. 466 (2004).

T10 Charlie Savage, "Accused 9/11 Mastermind to Face Civilian Trial in NY," *New York Times*, November 13, 2009.

The Declaration of Independence

In Congress, 4 July 1776

The Unanimous Declaration of the Thirteen United States of America

When, in the course of human events, it becomes necessary for one people to dissolve the political bands which have connected them with another, and to assume, among the powers of the earth, the separate and equal station to which the laws of nature and of nature's God entitle them, a decent respect to the opinions of mankind requires that they should declare the causes which impel them to the separation.

We hold these truths to be self-evident: That all men are created equal; that they are endowed by their Creator with certain unalienable rights; that among these are life, liberty, and the pursuit of happiness; that, to secure these rights, governments are instituted among men, deriving their just powers from the consent of the governed; that whenever any form of government becomes destructive of these ends, it is the right of the people to alter or to abolish it, and to institute new government, laying its foundation on such principles, and organizing its powers in such form, as to them shall seem most likely to effect their safety and happiness. Prudence, indeed, will dictate that governments long established should not be changed for light and transient causes; and accordingly all experience hath shown that mankind are more disposed to suffer, while evils are sufferable, than to right themselves by abolishing the forms to which they are accustomed. But when a long train of abuses and usurpations, pursuing invariably the same object, evinces a design to reduce them under absolute despotism, it is their right, it is their duty, to throw off such government, and to provide new guards for their future security. Such has been the patient sufferance of these colonies; and such is now the necessity which constrains them to alter their former systems of government. The history of the present King of Great Britain is a history of repeated injuries and usurpations, all having in direct object the establishment of an absolute tyranny over these states. To prove this, let facts be submitted to a candid world.

He has refused to assent to laws, the most wholesome and necessary for the public good.

He has forbidden his governors to pass laws of immediate and pressing importance, unless suspended in their operation till his assent should be obtained; and, when so suspended, he has utterly neglected to attend to them.

He has refused to pass other laws for the accommodation of large districts of people, unless those people would relinquish the right of representation in the legislature, a right inestimable to them, and formidable to tyrants only.

He has called together legislative bodies at places unusual, uncomfortable, and distant from the depository of their public records, for the sole purpose of fatiguing them into compliance with his measures.

He has dissolved representative houses repeatedly, for opposing, with manly firmness, his invasions on the rights of the people.

He has refused for a long time, after such dissolutions, to cause others to be elected; whereby the legislative powers, incapable of annihilation, have returned to the people at large for their exercise; the state remaining, in the mean time, exposed to all dangers of invasions from without and convulsions within.

He has endeavored to prevent the population of these states; for that purpose obstructing the laws for naturalization of foreigners; refusing to pass others to encourage their migration hither, and raising the conditions of new appropriations of lands.

He has obstructed the administration of justice, by refusing his assent to laws for establishing judiciary powers.

He has made judges dependent on his will alone, for the tenure of their offices, and the amount and payment of their salaries.

He has erected a multitude of new offices, and sent hither swarms of officers to harass our people and eat out their substance.

He has kept among us, in times of peace, standing armies, without the consent of our legislatures.

He has affected to render the military independent of, and superior to, the civil power.

He has combined with others to subject us to a jurisdiction foreign to our constitution, and unacknowledged by our laws, giving his assent to their acts of pretended legislation:

For quartering large bodies of armed troops among us;

For protecting them, by a mock trial, from punishment for any murders which they should commit on the inhabitants of these states;

For cutting off our trade with all parts of the world;

For imposing taxes on us without our consent;

For depriving us, in many cases, of the benefits of trial by jury;

For transporting us beyond seas, to be tried for pretended offenses;

For abolishing the free system of English laws in a neighboring province, establishing therein an arbitrary government, and enlarging its boundaries, so as to render it at once an example and fit instrument for introducing the same absolute rule into these colonies;

For taking away our charters, abolishing our most valuable laws, and altering fundamentally the forms of our governments;

For suspending our own legislatures, and declaring themselves invested with power to legislate for us in all cases whatsoever.

He has abdicated government here, by declaring us out of his protection and waging war against us.

He has plundered our seas, ravaged our coasts, burned our towns, and destroyed the lives of our people.

He is at this time transporting large armies of foreign mercenaries to complete the works of death, desolation, and tyranny already begun with circumstances of cruelty and perfidy scarcely paralleled in the most barbarous ages, and totally unworthy the head of a civilized nation.

He has constrained our fellow-citizens, taken captive on the high seas, to bear arms against their country, to become the executioners of their friends and brethren, or to fall themselves by their hands.

He has excited domestic insurrections among us, and has endeavored to bring on the inhabitants of our frontiers the merciless Indian savages, whose known rule of warfare is an undistinguished destruction of all ages, sexes, and conditions.

In every stage of these oppressions we have petitioned for redress in the most humble terms; our repeated petitions have been answered only by repeated injury. A prince, whose character is thus marked by every act which may define a tyrant, is unfit to be the ruler of a free people.

Nor have we been wanting in our attentions to our British brethren. We have warned them, from time to time, of attempts by their legislature to extend an unwarrantable jurisdiction over us.

We have reminded them of the circumstances of our emigration and settlement here. We have appealed to their native justice and magnanimity; and we have conjured them, by the ties of our common kindred, to disavow these usurpations, which would inevitably interrupt our connections and correspondence. They, too, have been deaf to the voice of justice and of consanguinity. We must, therefore, acquiesce in the necessity which denounces our separation, and hold them, as we hold the rest of mankind, enemies in war, in peace friends.

We, therefore, the representatives of the United States of America, in General Congress assembled, appealing to the Supreme Judge of the world for the rectitude of our intentions, do, in the name and by the authority of the good people of these colonies, solemnly publish and declare, that these United Colonies are, and of right ought to be, FREE AND INDEPENDENT STATES, that they are absolved from all allegiance to the British crown, and that all political connection between them, and the state of Great Britain is, and ought to be, totally dissolved; and that, as free and independent states, they have full power to levy war, conclude peace, contract alliances, establish commerce, and do all other acts and things which independent states may of right do. And for the support of this declaration, with a firm reliance on the protection of Divine Providence, we mutually pledge to each other our lives, our fortunes, and our sacred honor.

John Hancock [President]

New Hampshire
Josiah Bartlett • William Whipple • Matthew Thornton

Massachusetts Bay
Samuel Adams • John Adams • Robert Treat Paine • Elbridge Gerry

Rhode Island
Stephen Hopkins • William Ellery

Connecticut
Roger Sherman • Samuel Huntington • William Williams • Oliver Wolcott

New York
William Floyd • Philip Livingston • Francis Lewis • Lewis Morris

New Jersey
Richard Stockton • John Witherspoon • Francis Hopkinson • John Hart • Abraham Clark

Pennsylvania
Robert Morris • Benjamin Rush • Benjamin Franklin • John Morton • George Clymer • James Smith • George Taylor • James Wilson • George Ross

Delaware
Rodney George • Read Thomas M'Kean

Maryland
Samuel Chase • William Paca • Thomas Stone • Charles Carroll, of Carrollton

Virginia
George Wythe • Richard Henry Lee • Thomas Jefferson • Benjamin Harrison • Thomas Nelson, Jr. • Francis Lightfoot • Lee Carter Braxton

North Carolina
William Hooper • Joseph Hewes • John Penn

South Carolina
Edward Rutledge • Thomas Heyward, Jr. • Thomas Lynch, Jr. • Arthur Middleton

Georgia
Button Gwinnett • Lyman Hall • George Walton

Constitution of the United States

We the People of the United States, in Order to form a more perfect Union, establish Justice, insure domestic Tranquility, provide for the common defense, promote the general Welfare, and secure the Blessings of Liberty to ourselves and our Posterity, do ordain and establish this Constitution for the United States of America.

Article I

Section 1

All legislative Powers herein granted shall be vested in a Congress of the United States, which shall consist of a Senate and House of Representatives.

Section 2

The House of Representatives shall be composed of Members chosen every second Year by the People of the several States, and the Electors in each State shall have the Qualifications requisite for Electors of the most numerous Branch of the State Legislature.

No Person shall be a Representative who shall not have attained to the age of twenty-five Years, and been seven Years a Citizen of the United States, and who shall not, when elected, be an Inhabitant of that State in which he shall be chosen.

Representatives and direct Taxes shall be apportioned among the several States which may be included within this Union, according to their respective Numbers, which shall be determined by adding to the whole Number of free Persons, including those bound to Service for a Term of Years, and excluding Indians not taxed, three fifths of all other Persons. The actual Enumeration shall be made within three Years after the first Meeting of the Congress of the United States, and within every subsequent Term of ten Years, in such Manner as they shall by Law direct. The Number of Representatives shall not exceed one for every thirty Thousand, but each State shall have at Least one Representative; and until such enumeration shall be made, the State of New Hampshire shall be entitled to chuse three, Massachusetts eight, Rhode-Island and Providence Plantations one, Connecticut five, New-York six, New Jersey four, Pennsylvania eight, Delaware one, Maryland six, Virginia ten, North Carolina five, South Carolina five, and Georgia three.

When vacancies happen in the Representation from any State, the Executive Authority thereof shall issue Writs of Election to fill such Vacancies.

The House of Representatives shall chuse their Speaker and other Officers; and shall have the sole Power of Impeachment.

Section 3

The Senate of the United States shall be composed of two Senators from each State, chosen by the Legislature thereof, for six Years; and each Senator shall have one Vote.

Immediately after they shall be assembled in Consequence of the first Election, they shall be divided as equally as may be into three Classes. The Seats of the Senators of the first class shall be vacated at the Expiration of the second Year, of the second Class at the Expiration of the fourth Year, and of the third Class at the Expiration of the sixth Year, so that one third may be chosen every second Year; and if Vacancies happen by Resignation, or otherwise, during the Recess of the Legislature of any State, the Executive thereof may make temporary Appointments until the next Meeting of the Legislature, which shall then fill such Vacancies.

No Person shall be a Senator who shall not have attained to the Age of thirty Years, and been nine Years a Citizen of the United States, and who shall not, when elected, be an Inhabitant of that State for which he shall be chosen.

The Vice President of the United States shall be President of the Senate, but shall have no Vote, unless they be equally divided.

The Senate shall chuse their other Officers, and also a President pro tempore, in the Absence of the Vice President, or when he shall exercise the Office of President of the United States.

The Senate shall have the sole Power to try all Impeachments. When sitting for that Purpose, they shall be on Oath or Affirmation. When the President of the United States is tried the Chief Justice shall preside: and no Person shall be convicted without the Concurrence of two thirds of the Members present.

Judgment in Cases of Impeachment shall not extend further than to removal from Office, and disqualification to hold and enjoy any Office of honor, Trust or Profit under the United States: but the Party convicted shall nevertheless be liable and subject to Indictment, Trial, Judgment and Punishment, according to Law.

Section 4

The Times, Places and Manner of holding elections for Senators and Representatives, shall be prescribed in each State by the Legislature thereof; but the Congress may at any time by Law make or alter such Regulations, except as to the Places of choosing Senators.

The Congress shall assemble at least once in every Year, and such Meeting shall be on the first Monday in December, unless they shall by Law appoint a different Day.

Section 5

Each House shall be the Judge of the Elections, Returns and Qualifications of its own Members, and a Majority of each shall constitute a Quorum to do Business; but a smaller Number may adjourn from day to day, and may be authorized to compel the Attendance of absent Members, in such Manner, and under such Penalties as each House may provide.

Each House may determine the Rules of its Proceedings, punish its Members for disorderly Behavior, and, with the Concurrence of two thirds, expel a Member.

Each House shall keep a Journal of its Proceedings, and from time to time publish the same, excepting such Parts as may in their Judgment require Secrecy; and the Yeas and Nays of the Members of either House on any question shall, at the Desire of one fifth of those Present, be entered on the Journal.

Neither House, during the Session of Congress, shall, without the Consent of the other, adjourn for more than three days, nor to any other Place than that in which the two Houses shall be sitting.

Section 6

The Senators and Representatives shall receive a Compensation for their Services, to be ascertained by Law, and paid out of the Treasury of the United States. They shall in all Cases, except Treason, Felony and Breach of the Peace, be privileged from Arrest during their Attendance at the Session of their respective Houses, and in going to and returning from the same; and for any Speech or Debate in either House, they shall not be questioned in any other Place.

No Senator or Representative shall, during the Time for which he was elected, be appointed to any civil Office under the Authority of the United States, which shall have been created, or the Emoluments whereof shall have been increased during such time; and no Person holding any Office under the United States, shall be a Member of either House during his Continuance in Office.

Section 7

All Bills for raising Revenue shall originate in the House of Representatives; but the Senate may propose or concur with Amendments as on other Bills.

Every Bill which shall have passed the House of Representatives and the Senate, shall, before it become a Law, be presented to the President of the United States; If he approve he shall sign it, but if not he shall return it, with his Objections to that House in which it shall have originated, who shall enter the Objections at large on their Journal, and proceed to reconsider it. If after such Reconsideration two thirds of that House shall agree to pass the Bill, it shall be sent, together with the Objections, to the other House, by which it shall likewise be reconsidered, and if approved by two thirds of that House, it shall become a Law. But in all such Cases the Votes of both Houses shall be determined by yeas and Nays, and the Names of the Persons voting for and against the Bill shall be entered on the Journal of each House respectively. If any Bill shall not be returned by the President within ten Days (Sundays excepted) after it shall have been presented to him, the Same shall be a Law, in like Manner as if he had signed it, unless the Congress by their Adjournment prevent its Return, in which Case it shall not be a Law.

Every Order, Resolution, or Vote to which the concurrence of the Senate and House of Representatives may be necessary (except on a question of Adjournment) shall be presented to the President of the United States; and before the Same shall take Effect, shall be approved by him, or being disapproved by him, shall be repassed by two thirds of the Senate and House of Representatives, according to the Rules and Limitations prescribed in the Case of a Bill.

Section 8

The Congress shall have Power To lay and collect Taxes, Duties, Imposts and Excises, to pay the Debts and provide for the common Defence and general Welfare of the United States; but all Duties, Imposts and Excises shall be uniform throughout the United States;

To borrow Money on the credit of the United States;

To regulate Commerce with foreign Nations, and among the several States, and with the Indian Tribes;

To establish a uniform Rule of Naturalization, and uniform Laws on the subject of Bankruptcies throughout the United States;

To coin Money, regulate the Value thereof, and of foreign Coin, and fix the Standard of Weights and Measures;

To provide for the Punishment of counterfeiting the Securities and current Coin of the United States;

To establish Post Offices and post Roads;

To promote the Progress of Science and useful Arts, by securing for limited Times to Authors and Inventors the exclusive Right to their respective Writings and Discoveries;

To constitute Tribunals inferior to the Supreme Court;

To define and punish Piracies and Felonies committed on the high Seas, and Offenses against the Law of Nations;

To declare War, grant Letters of Marque and Reprisal, and make Rules concerning Captures on Land and Water;

To raise and support Armies, but no Appropriation of Money to that Use shall be for a longer Term than two Years;

To provide and maintain a Navy;

To make Rules for the Government and Regulation of the land and naval Forces;

To provide for calling forth the Militia to execute the Laws of the Union, suppress Insurrections and repel Invasions;

To provide for organizing, arming, and disciplining, the Militia, and for governing such Part of them as may be employed in the Service of the United States, reserving to the States respectively, the Appointment of the Officers, and the Authority of training the Militia according to the discipline prescribed by Congress;

To exercise exclusive Legislation in all Cases whatsoever, over such District (not exceeding ten Miles square) as may, by Cession of particular States, and the Acceptance of Congress, become the Seat of the Government of the United States, and to exercise like Authority over all Places purchased by the Consent of the Legislature of the State in which the Same shall be, for the Erection of Forts, Magazines, Arsenals, dock-Yards and other needful Buildings; And

To make all Laws which shall be necessary and proper for carrying into Execution the foregoing Powers, and all other Powers vested by this Constitution in the Government of the United States, or in any Department or Officer thereof.

Section 9

The Migration or Importation of such Persons as any of the States now existing shall think proper to admit, shall not be prohibited by the Congress prior to the Year one thousand eight hundred and eight, but a Tax or duty may be imposed on such Importation, not exceeding ten dollars for each Person.

The Privilege of the Writ of Habeas Corpus shall not be suspended, unless when in Cases of Rebellion or Invasion the public Safety may require it.

No bill of Attainder or ex post facto Law shall be passed. No Capitation, or other direct, Tax shall be laid, unless in Proportion to the Census or Enumeration herein before directed to be taken.

No Tax or Duty shall be laid on Articles exported from any State. No Preference shall be given by any Regulation of Commerce or Revenue to the Ports of one State over those of another; nor shall Vessels bound to, or from, one State, be obliged to enter, clear or pay Duties in another.

No Money shall be drawn from the Treasury, but in Consequence of Appropriations made by Law; and a regular Statement and Account of the Receipts and Expenditures of all public Money shall be published from time to time.

No Title of Nobility shall be granted by the United States.

And no person holding any Office of Profit or Trust under them, shall, without the Consent of the Congress, accept of any present, Emolument, Office, or Title, of any kind whatever, from any King, Prince, or foreign State.

Section 10

No State shall enter into any Treaty, Alliance, or Confederation; grant Letters of Marque and Reprisal; coin Money; emit Bills of Credit; make any Thing but gold and silver Coin a Tender in Payment of Debts; pass any Bill of Attainder, ex post facto Law, or Law impairing the Obligation of Contracts, or grant any Title of Nobility.

No State shall, without the Consent of the Congress, lay any Imposts or Duties on Imports or Exports, except what may be absolutely necessary for executing its inspection Laws: and the net Produce of all Duties and Imposts, laid by any State on Imports or Exports, shall be for the Use of the Treasury of the United States; and all such Laws shall be subject to the Revision and Control of the Congress.

No State shall, without the Consent of Congress, lay any Duty of Tonnage, keep Troops, or Ships of War in time of Peace, enter into any Agreement or Compact with another State, or with a foreign Power, or engage in War, unless actually invaded, or in such imminent Danger as will not admit of delay.

Article II

Section 1

The executive Power shall be vested in a President of the United States of America. He shall hold his Office during the Term of four Years, and, together with the Vice President, chosen for the same Term, be elected, as follows

Each State shall appoint, in such Manner as the Legislature thereof may direct, a Number of Electors, equal to the whole Number of Senators and Representatives to which the

State may be entitled in the Congress: but no Senator or Representative, or Person holding an Office of Trust or Profit under the United States, shall be appointed an Elector.

The Electors shall meet in their respective States, and vote by Ballot for two Persons, of whom one at least shall not be an Inhabitant of the same State with themselves. And they shall make a List of all the Persons voted for, and of the Number of Votes for each; which List they shall sign and certify, and transmit sealed to the Seat of the Government of the United States, directed to the President of the Senate. The President of the Senate shall, in the Presence of the Senate and House of Representatives, open all the Certificates, and the Votes shall then be counted. The Person having the greatest Number of Votes shall be the President, if such Number be a Majority of the whole Number of Electors appointed; and if there be more than one who have such Majority, and have an equal Number of Votes, then the House of Representatives shall immediately chuse by Ballot one of them for President; and if no Person have a Majority, then from the five highest on the List the said House shall in like Manner chuse the President. But in chusing the President, the Votes shall be taken by States, the Representation from each State having one Vote; a quorum for this Purpose shall consist of a Member or Members from two thirds of the States, and a Majority of all the States shall be necessary to a Choice. In every Case, after the Choice of the President, the Person having the greatest Number of Votes of the Electors shall be the Vice President. But if there should remain two or more who have equal Votes, the Senate shall chuse from them by Ballot the Vice President.

The Congress may determine the Time of chusing the Electors, and the Day on which they shall give their Votes; which Day shall be the same throughout the United States.

No Person except a natural born Citizen, or a Citizen of the United States, at the time of the Adoption of this Constitution, shall be eligible to the Office of President; neither shall any person be eligible to that Office who shall not have attained to the Age of thirty five Years, and been fourteen Years a Resident within the United States.

In Case of the Removal of the President from Office, or of his Death, Resignation, or Inability to discharge the Powers and Duties of the said Office, the Same shall devolve on the Vice President, and the Congress may by Law provide for the Case of Removal, Death, Resignation or Inability, both of the President and Vice President, declaring what Officer shall then act as President, and such Officer shall act accordingly, until the Disability be removed, or a President shall be elected.

The President shall, at stated Times, receive for his Services, a Compensation, which shall neither be encreased nor diminished during the Period for which he shall have been elected, and he shall not receive within that Period any other Emolument from the United States, or any of them.

Before he enter on the Execution of his Office, he shall take the following Oath or Affirmation: "I do solemnly swear (or affirm) that I will faithfully execute the Office of President of the United States, and will to the best of my Ability, preserve, protect and defend the Constitution of the United States."

Section 2

The President shall be Commander in Chief of the Army and Navy of the United States, and of the Militia of the several States, when called into the actual Service of the United States; he may require the Opinion, in writing, of the principal Officer in each of the executive Departments, upon any Subject relating to the Duties of their respective Offices, and he shall have Power to grant Reprieves and Pardons for Offences against the United States, except in Cases of Impeachment.

He shall have Power, by and with the Advice and Consent of the Senate, to make Treaties, provided two thirds of the Senators present concur; and he shall nominate, and by and with the Advice and Consent of the Senate, shall appoint Ambassadors, other public Ministers and Consuls, Judges of the supreme Court, and all other Officers of the United States, whose Appointments are not herein otherwise provided for, and which shall be established by Law: but the Congress may by Law vest the Appointment of such inferior Officers, as they think proper, in the President alone, in the Courts of Law, or in the Heads of Departments.

The President shall have Power to fill up all Vacancies that may happen during the Recess of the Senate, by granting Commissions which shall expire at the End of their next Session.

Section 3

He shall from time to time give to the Congress Information of the State of the Union, and recommend to their Consideration such Measures as he shall judge necessary and expedient; he may, on extraordinary Occasions, convene both Houses, or either of them, and in Case of Disagreement between them, with Respect to the Time of Adjournment, he may adjourn them to such Time as he shall think proper; he shall receive Ambassadors and other public Ministers; he shall take Care that the Laws be faithfully executed, and shall Commission all the Officers of the United States.

Section 4

The President, Vice President and all civil Officers of the United States, shall be removed from Office on Impeachment for, and Conviction of, Treason, Bribery, or other high Crimes and Misdemeanors.

Article III

Section 1

The judicial Power of the United States, shall be vested in one supreme Court, and in such inferior Courts as the Congress may from time to time ordain and establish. The Judges, both of the supreme and inferior Courts, shall hold their Offices during good Behaviour, and shall, at stated Times, receive for their Services, a Compensation, which shall not be diminished during their Continuance in Office.

Section 2

The judicial Power shall extend to all Cases, in Law and Equity, arising under this Constitution, the Laws of the United States, and Treaties made, or which shall be made, under their Authority; to all Cases affecting Ambassadors, other public Ministers and Consuls; to all Cases of admiralty and maritime Jurisdiction; to Controversies to which the United States shall be a Party; to Controversies between two or more States; between a State and Citizens of another State; between Citizens of different States; between Citizens of the same State claiming Lands under Grants of different States, and between a State, or the Citizens thereof, and foreign States, Citizens or Subjects.

In all Cases affecting Ambassadors, other public Ministers and Consuls, and those in which a State shall be Party, the supreme Court shall have original Jurisdiction. In all the other Cases before mentioned, the supreme Court shall have appellate Jurisdiction, both as to Law and Fact, with such Exceptions, and under such Regulations as the Congress shall make.

The Trial of all Crimes, except in Cases of Impeachment, shall be by Jury; and such Trial shall be held in the State where the said Crimes shall have been committed; but when not committed within any State, the Trial shall be at such Place or Places as the Congress may by Law have directed.

Section 3

Treason against the United States, shall consist only in levying War against them, or in adhering to their Enemies, giving them Aid and Comfort. No Person shall be convicted of Treason unless on the Testimony of two Witnesses to the same overt Act, or on Confession in open Court.

The Congress shall have Power to declare the Punishment of Treason, but no Attainder of Treason shall work Corruption of Blood, or Forfeiture except during the Life of the Person attainted.

Article IV

Section 1

Full Faith and Credit shall be given in each State to the public Acts, Records, and judicial Proceedings of every other State. And the Congress may by general Laws prescribe the Manner in which such Acts, Records and Proceedings shall be proved, and the Effect thereof.

Section 2

The Citizens of each State shall be entitled to all Privileges and Immunities of Citizens in the several States.

A person charged in any State with Treason, Felony, or other Crime, who shall flee from Justice, and be found in another State, shall on Demand of the executive Authority of the State from which he fled, be delivered up, to be removed to the State having Jurisdiction of the Crime.

No Person held to Service or Labour in one State, under the Laws thereof, escaping into another, shall, in Consequence of any Law or Regulation therein, be discharged from such Service or Labour, but shall be delivered up on Claim of the Party to whom such Service or Labour may be due.

Section 3

New States may be admitted by the Congress into this Union; but no new State shall be formed or erected within the Jurisdiction of any other State; nor any State be formed by the Junction of two or more States, or Parts of States, without the consent of the Legislatures of the States concerned as well as of the Congress.

The Congress shall have Power to dispose of and make all needful Rules and Regulations respecting the Territory or other Property belonging to the United States; and nothing in this Constitution shall be so construed as to Prejudice any Claims of the United States, or of any particular State.

Section 4

The United States shall guarantee to every State in this Union a Republican Form of Government, and shall protect each of them against Invasion; and on Application of the Legislature, or of the Executive (when the Legislature cannot be convened) against domestic Violence.

Article V

The Congress, whenever two thirds of both Houses shall deem it necessary, shall propose Amendments to this Constitution, or, on the Application of the Legislatures of two thirds of the several States, shall call a Convention for proposing Amendments, which, in either Case, shall be valid to all Intents and Purposes, as Part of this Constitution, when ratified by the Legislatures of three fourths of the several States, or by Conventions in three fourths thereof, as the one or the other Mode of Ratification may be proposed by the Congress; Provided that no Amendment which may be made prior to the Year One Thousand eight hundred and eight shall in any Manner affect the first and fourth Clauses in the Ninth Section of the first Article; and that no State, without its Consent, shall be deprived of its equal Suffrage in the Senate.

Article VI

All Debts contracted and Engagements entered into, before the Adoption of this Constitution, shall be as valid against the United States under this Constitution, as under the Confederation.

This Constitution, and the Laws of the United States which shall be made in Pursuance thereof; and all Treaties made, or which shall be made, under the Authority of the United States, shall be the supreme Law of the Land; and the Judges in every State shall be bound thereby, any Thing in the Constitution or Laws of any State to the Contrary notwithstanding.

The Senators and Representatives before mentioned, and the Members of the several State Legislatures, and all executive and judicial Officers, both of the United States and of the several States, shall be bound by Oath or Affirmation, to support this Constitution; but no religious Test shall ever be required as a Qualification to any Office or public Trust under the United States.

Article VII

The Ratification of the Conventions of nine States, shall be sufficient for the Establishment of this Constitution between the States so ratifying the Same.

Done in Convention by the Unanimous Consent of the States present the Seventeenth Day of September in the Year of our Lord one thousand seven hundred and Eighty seven and of the Independence of the United States of America the Twelfth In witness whereof We have hereunto subscribed our Names,

G° WASHINGTON—*Presid^t And Deputy From Virginia*

New Hampshire	JOHN LANGDON NICHOLAS GILMAN		GEO: READ GUNNING BEDFORD jun
Massachusetts	NATHANIEL GORHAM RUFUS KING	*Delaware*	JOHN DICKINSON RICHARD BASSESTT
Connecticut	W^M SAM^L JOHNSON ROGER SHERMAN		JACO: BROOM
New York	ALEXANDER HAMILTON	*Maryland*	JAMES M^C HENRY DAN OF S^T THO^S JENIFER DAN^L CARROLL
New Jersey	WIL: LIVINGSTON DAVID BREARLEY W^M PATERSON JONA: DAYTON	*Virginia*	JOHN BLAIR— JAMES MADISON JR.
Pennsylvania	B FRANKLIN THOMAS MIFFLIN ROB^T MORRIS GEO. CLYMER THO^S FITZSIMONS JARED INGERSOLL JAMES WILSON GOUV MORRIS	*North Carolina*	W^M BLOUNT RICH^D DOBBS SPAIGHT HU WILLIAMSON
		South Carolina	J. RUTLEDGE CHARLES COTESWORTH PINCKNEY CHARLES PINCKNEY PIERCE BUTLER
		Georgia	WILLIAM FEW ABR BALDWIN

Amendments to the Constitution

Amendment I *[The first ten amendments, known as the "Bill of Rights," were ratified in 1791]*

Congress shall make no law respecting an establishment of religion, or prohibiting the free exercise thereof; or abridging the freedom of speech, or of the press; or the right of the people peaceably to assemble, and to petition the Government for a redress of grievances.

Amendment II

A well regulated Militia, being necessary to the security of a free State, the right of the people to keep and bear Arms, shall not be infringed.

Amendment III

No Soldier shall, in time of peace, be quartered in any house, without the consent of the Owner, nor in time of war, but in a manner prescribed by law.

Amendment IV

The right of the people to be secure in their persons, houses, papers, and effects, against unreasonable searches and seizures, shall not be violated, and no Warrants shall issue, but upon probable cause, supported by Oath or affirmation, and particularly describing the place to be searched, and the persons or things to be seized.

Amendment V

No person shall be held to answer for a capital, or otherwise infamous crime, unless on a presentment or indictment of a Grand Jury, except in cases arising in the land or naval forces, or in the Militia, when in actual service in time of War or public danger; nor shall any person be subject for the same offence to be twice put in jeopardy of life or limb; nor shall be compelled in any criminal case to be a witness against himself, nor be deprived of life, liberty, or property, without due process of law, nor shall private property be taken for public use, without just compensation.

Amendment VI

In all criminal prosecutions, the accused shall enjoy the right to a speedy and public trial, by an impartial jury of the State and district wherein the crime shall have been committed, which district shall have been previously ascertained by law, and to be informed of the nature and cause of the accusation; to be confronted with the witnesses against him; to have compulsory process for obtaining witnesses in his favor, and to have Assistance of Counsel for his defence.

Amendment VII

In Suits at common law, where the value in controversy shall exceed twenty dollars, the right of trial by jury shall be preserved, and no fact tried by a jury, shall be otherwise reexamined in any Court of the United States, than according to the rules of the common law.

Amendment VIII

Excessive bail shall not be required, nor excessive fines imposed, nor cruel and unusual punishments inflicted.

Amendment IX

The enumeration in the Constitution, of certain rights, shall not be construed to deny or disparage others retained by the people.

Amendment X

The powers not delegated to the United States by the Constitution, nor prohibited by it to the States, are reserved to the States respectively, or to the people.

Amendment XI *[Ratified in 1795]*

The Judicial power of the United States shall not be construed to extend to any suit in law or equity, commenced or prosecuted against one of the United States by Citizens of another State, or by Citizens or Subjects of any Foreign State.

Amendment XII *[Ratified in 1804]*

The Electors shall meet in their respective states and vote by ballot for President and Vice President, one of whom, at least, shall not be an inhabitant of the same state with themselves; they shall name in their ballots the person voted for as President, and in distinct ballots the person voted for as Vice President, and they shall make distinct lists of all persons voted for as President, and of all persons voted for as Vice President, and of the number of votes for each, which lists they shall sign and certify, and transmit sealed to the seat of the government of the United States, directed to the President of the Senate; The President of the Senate shall, in the presence of the Senate and House of Representatives, open all the certificates and the votes shall then be counted; The person having the greatest number of votes for President, shall be the President, if such number be a majority of the whole number of Electors appointed; and if no person have such majority, then from the persons having the highest numbers not exceeding three on the list of those voted for as President, the House of Representatives shall choose immediately, by ballot, the President. But in choosing the President, the votes shall be taken by states, the representation from each state having one vote; a quorum for this purpose shall consist of a member or members from two-thirds of the states, and a majority of all the states shall be necessary to a choice. And if the House of Representatives shall not choose a President whenever the right of choice shall devolve upon them, before the fourth day of March next following, then the Vice President shall act as President, as in the case of the death or other constitutional disability of the President.

The person having the greatest number of votes as Vice President, shall be the Vice President, if such number be a majority of the whole number of Electors appointed, and if no person have a majority, then from the two highest numbers on the list, the Senate shall choose the Vice President; a quorum for the purpose shall consist of two-thirds of the whole number of Senators, and a majority of the whole number shall be necessary to a choice. But no person constitutionally ineligible to the office of President shall be eligible to that of Vice President of the United States.

Amendment XIII [Ratified in 1865]

Section 1

Neither slavery nor involuntary servitude, except as a punishment for crime whereof the party shall have been duly convicted, shall exist within the United States, or any place subject to their jurisdiction.

Section 2

Congress shall have power to enforce this article by appropriate legislation.

Amendment XIV [Ratified in 1868]

Section 1

All persons born or naturalized in the United States and subject to the jurisdiction thereof, are citizens of the United States and of the State wherein they reside. No State shall make or enforce any law which shall abridge the privileges or immunities of citizens of the United States; nor shall any State deprive any person of life, liberty, or property, without due process of law; nor deny to any person within its jurisdiction the equal protection of the laws.

Section 2

Representatives shall be apportioned among the several States according to their respective numbers, counting the whole number of persons in each State, excluding Indians not taxed. But when the right to vote at any election for the choice of electors for President and Vice President of the United States, Representatives in Congress, the Executive and Judicial officers of a State, or the members of the Legislature thereof, is denied to any of the male inhabitants of such State, being twenty-one years of age, and citizens of the United States, or in any way abridged, except for participation in rebellion, or other crime, the basis of representation therein shall be reduced in the proportion which the number of such male citizens shall bear to the whole number of male citizens twenty-one years of age in such State.

Section 3

No person shall be a Senator or Representative in Congress, or elector of President and Vice President, or hold any office, civil or military, under the United States, or under any State, who, having previously taken an oath, as a member of Congress, or as an officer of the United States, or as a member of any State legislature, or as an executive or judicial officer of any State, to support the Constitution of the United States, shall have engaged in insurrection or rebellion against the same, or given aid or comfort to the enemies thereof. But Congress may by a vote of two-thirds of each House, remove such disability.

Section 4

The validity of the public debt of the United States, authorized by law, including debts incurred for payment of pensions and bounties for services in suppressing insurrection or rebellion, shall not be questioned. But neither the United States nor any State shall assume or pay any debt or obligation incurred in aid of insurrection or rebellion against the United States, or any claim for the loss or emancipation of any slave; but all such debts, obligations and claims shall be held illegal and void.

Section 5

The Congress shall have power to enforce, by appropriate legislation, the provisions of this article.

Amendment XV *[Ratified in 1870]*

Section 1

The right of citizens of the United States to vote shall not be denied or abridged by the United States or by any State on account of race, color, or previous condition of servitude.

Section 2

The Congress shall have power to enforce this article by appropriate legislation.

Amendment XVI *[Ratified in 1913]*

The Congress shall have power to lay and collect taxes on incomes, from whatever source derived, without apportionment among the several States, and without regard to any census or enumeration.

Amendment XVII *[Ratified in 1913]*

The Senate of the United States shall be composed of two Senators from each State, elected by the people thereof, for six years; and each Senator shall have one vote. The electors in each State shall have the qualifications requisite for electors of the most numerous branch of the State legislatures.

When vacancies happen in the representation of any State in the Senate, the executive authority of such State shall issue writs of election to fill such vacancies: Provided, That the legislature of any State may empower the executive thereof to make temporary appointments until the people fill the vacancies by election as the legislature may direct.

This amendment shall not be so construed as to affect the election or term of any Senator chosen before it becomes valid as part of the Constitution.

Amendment XVIII *[Ratified in 1919]*

Section 1

After one year from the ratification of this article the manufacture, sale, or transportation of intoxicating liquors within, the importation thereof into, or the exportation thereof from the United States and all territory subject to the jurisdiction thereof for beverage purposes is hereby prohibited.

Section 2

The Congress and the several States shall have concurrent power to enforce this article by appropriate legislation.

Section 3

This article shall be inoperative unless it shall have been ratified as an amendment to the Constitution by the legislatures of the several States, as provided in the Constitution, within seven years from the date of the submission hereof to the States by the Congress.

Amendment XIX *[Ratified in 1920]*

The right of citizens of the United States to vote shall not be denied or abridged by the United States or by any state on account of sex.

Congress shall have power to enforce this article by appropriate legislation.

Amendment XX *[Ratified in 1933]*

Section 1

The terms of the President and Vice President shall end at noon on the 20th day of January, and the terms of Senators and Representatives at noon on the 3rd day of January, of the years in which such terms would have ended if this article had not been ratified; and the terms of their successors shall then begin.

Section 2

The Congress shall assemble at least once in every year, and such meeting shall begin at noon on the 3rd day of January, unless they shall by law appoint a different day.

Section 3

If, at the time fixed for the beginning of the term of the President, the President elect shall have died, the Vice President elect shall become President. If a President shall not have been chosen before the time fixed for the beginning of his term, or if the President elect shall have failed to qualify, then the Vice President elect shall act as President until a President shall have qualified; and the Congress may by law provide for the case wherein neither a President elect nor a Vice President elect shall have qualified, declaring who shall then act as President, or the manner in which one who is to act shall be selected, and such person shall act accordingly until a President or Vice President shall have qualified.

Section 4

The Congress may by law provide for the case of the death of any of the persons from whom the House of Representatives may choose a President whenever the right of choice shall have devolved upon them, and for the case of the death of any of the persons from whom the Senate may choose a Vice President whenever the right of choice shall have devolved upon them.

Section 5

Sections 1 and 2 shall take effect on the 15th day of October following the ratification of this article.

Section 6

This article shall be inoperative unless it shall have been ratified as an amendment to the Constitution by the legislatures of three-fourths of the several States within seven years from the date of its submission.

Amendment XXI [Ratified in 1933]

Section 1

The eighteenth article of amendment to the Constitution of the United States is hereby repealed.

Section 2

The transportation or importation into any State, Territory, or possession of the United States for delivery or use therein of intoxicating liquors, in violation of the laws thereof, is hereby prohibited.

Section 3

This article shall be inoperative unless it shall have been ratified as an amendment to the Constitution by conventions in the several States, as provided in the Constitution, within seven years from the date of the submission hereof to the States by the Congress.

Amendment XXII [Ratified in 1951]

Section 1

No person shall be elected to the office of the President more than twice, and no person who has held the office of President, or acted as President, for more than two years of a term to which some other person was elected President shall be elected to the office of the President more than once. But this Article shall not apply to any person holding the office of President when this Article was proposed by the Congress, and shall not prevent any person who may be holding the office of President, or acting as President, during this term within which this Article becomes operative from holding the office of President or acting as President during the remainder of such term.

Section 2

This article shall be inoperative unless it shall have been ratified as an amendment to the Constitution by the legislatures of three-fourths of the several States within seven years from the date of its submission to the States by the Congress.

Amendment XXIII *[Ratified in 1961]*

Section 1

The District constituting the seat of Government of the United States shall appoint in such manner as the Congress may direct: A number of electors of President and Vice President equal to the whole number of Senators and Representatives in Congress to which the District would be entitled if it were a State, but in no event more than the least populous State; they shall be in addition to those appointed by the States, but they shall be considered, for the purposes of the election of President and Vice President, to be electors appointed by a State; and they shall meet in the District and perform such duties as provided by the twelfth article of amendment.

Section 2

The Congress shall have power to enforce this article by appropriate legislation.

Amendment XXIV [Ratified in 1964]

Section 1

The right of citizens of the United States to vote in any primary or other election for President or Vice President, for electors for President or Vice President, or for Senator or Representative in Congress, shall not be denied or abridged by the United States or any State by reason of failure to pay any poll tax or other tax.

Section 2

The Congress shall have power to enforce this article by appropriate legislation.

Amendment XXV *[Ratified in 1967]*

Section 1

In case of the removal of the President from office or of his death or resignation, the Vice President shall become President.

Section 2

Whenever there is a vacancy in the office of the Vice President, the President shall nominate a Vice President who shall take office upon confirmation by a majority vote of both Houses of Congress.

Section 3

Whenever the President transmits to the president pro tempore of the Senate and the Speaker of the House of Representatives his written declaration that he is unable to discharge the powers and duties of his office, and until he transmits to them a written declaration to the contrary, such powers and duties shall be discharged by the Vice President as Acting President.

Section 4

Whenever the Vice President and a majority of either the principal officers of the executive departments or of such other body as Congress may by law provide, transmit to the President pro tempore of the Senate and the Speaker of the House of Representatives their written declaration that the President is unable to discharge the powers and duties of his office, the Vice President shall immediately assume the powers and duties of the office as Acting President.

Thereafter, when the President transmits to the President pro tempore of the Senate and the Speaker of the House of Representatives his written declaration that no inability exists, he shall resume the powers and duties of his office unless the Vice President and a majority of either the principal officers of the executive department[s] or of such other body as Congress may by law provide, transmit within four days to the President pro tempore of the Senate and the Speaker of the House of Representatives their written declaration that the President is unable to discharge the powers and duties of his office. Thereupon Congress shall decide the issue, assembling within forty-eight hours for that purpose if not in session. If the Congress, within twenty-one days after receipt of the latter written declaration, or, if Congress is not in session, within twenty-one days after Congress is required to assemble, determines by two-thirds vote of both Houses that the President is unable to discharge the powers and duties of his office, the Vice President shall continue to discharge the same as Acting President; otherwise, the President shall resume the powers and duties of his office.

Amendment XXVI *[Ratified in 1971]*

Section 1

The right of citizens of the United States, who are 18 years of age or older, to vote shall not be denied or abridged by the United States or by any State on account of age.

Section 2

The Congress shall have power to enforce this article by appropriate legislation.

Amendment XXVII *[Ratified in 1992]*

No law, varying the compensation for the services of the senators and representatives, shall take effect until an election of representatives shall have intervened.

Federalist 10

James Madison

22 November 1787

To the People of the State of New York

Among the numerous advantages promised by a well constructed Union, none deserves to be more accurately developed than its tendency to break and control the violence of faction. The friend of popular governments, never finds himself so much alarmed for their character and fate, as when he contemplates their propensity to this dangerous vice. He will not fail therefore to set a due value on any plan which, without violating the principles to which he is attached, provides a proper cure for it. The instability, injustice and confusion introduced into the public councils, have in truth been the mortal diseases under which popular governments have every where perished; as they continue to be the favorite and fruitful topics from which the adversaries to liberty derive their most specious declamations. The valuable improvements made by the American Constitutions on the popular models, both ancient and modern, cannot certainly be too much admired; but it would be an unwarrantable partiality, to contend that they have as effectually obviated the danger on this side as was wished and expected. Complaints are everywhere heard from our most considerate and virtuous citizens, equally the friends of public and private faith, and of public and personal liberty; that our governments are too unstable; that the public good is disregarded in the conflicts of rival parties; and that measures are too often decided, not according to the rules of justice, and the rights of the minor party; but by the superior force of an interested and overbearing majority. However anxiously we may wish that these complaints had no foundation, the evidence of known facts will not permit us to deny that they are in some degree true. It will be found indeed, on a candid review of our situation, that some of the distresses under which we labor, have been erroneously charged on the operation of our governments; but it will be found, at the same time, that other causes will not alone account for many of our heaviest misfortunes; and particularly, for that prevailing and increasing distrust of public engagements, and alarm for private rights, which are echoed from one end of the continent to the other. These must be chiefly, if not wholly, effects of the unsteadiness and injustice, with which a factious spirit has tainted our public administrations

By a faction I understand a number of citizens, whether amounting to a majority or minority of the whole, who are united and actuated by some common impulse of passion, or of interest, adverse to the rights of other citizens, or to the permanent and aggregate interests of the community.

There are two methods of curing the mischiefs of faction: the one, by removing its causes; the other, by controlling its effects.

There are again two methods of removing the causes of faction: the one by destroying the liberty which is essential to its existence; the other, by giving to every citizen the same opinions, the same passions, and the same interests.

It could never be more truly said than of the first remedy, that it is worse than the disease. Liberty is to faction, what air is to fire, an ailment without which it instantly expires. But it could not be a less folly to abolish liberty, which is essential to political life, because it nourishes faction, than it would be to wish the annihilation of air, which is essential to animal life, because it imparts to fire its destructive agency.

The second expedient is as impracticable, as the first would be unwise. As long as the reason of man continues fallible, and he is at liberty to exercise it, different opinions will be formed. As long as the connection subsists between his reason and his self-love, his opinions and his passions will have a reciprocal influence on each other; and the former will be objects to which the latter will attach themselves. The diversity in the faculties of men from which the rights of property originate, is not less an insuperable obstacle to a uniformity of interests. The protection of these faculties is the first object of Government. From the protection of different and unequal faculties of acquiring property, the possession of different degrees and kinds of property immediately results: and from the influence of these on the sentiments and views of the respective proprietors, ensues a division of the society into different interests and parties.

The latent causes of faction are thus sown in the nature of man; and we see them every where brought into different degrees of activity, according to the different circumstances of civil society. A zeal for different opinions concerning religion, concerning Government and many other points, as well of speculation as of practice; an attachment to different leaders ambitiously contending for preeminence and power; or to persons of other descriptions whose fortunes have been interesting to the human passions, have in turn divided mankind into parties, inflamed them with mutual animosity, and rendered them much more disposed to vex and oppress each other, than to cooperate for their common good. So strong is this propensity of mankind to fall into mutual animosities, that where no substantial occasion presents itself, the most frivolous and fanciful distinctions have been sufficient to kindle their unfriendly passions, and excite their most violent conflicts. But the most common and durable sources of factions, has been the various and unequal distribution of property. Those who hold, and those who are without property, have ever formed distinct interests in society. Those who are creditors, and those who are debtors, fall under a like discrimination. A landed interest, a manufacturing interest, a mercantile interest, a monied interest, with many lesser interests, grow up of necessity in civilized nations, and divide them into different classes, actuated by different sentiments and views. The regulation of these various and interfering interests forms the principal task of modern Legislation and involves the spirit of party and faction in the necessary and ordinary operations of Government.

No man is allowed to be a judge in his own cause; because his interest would certainly bias his judgment, and, not improbably, corrupt his integrity. With equal, nay with greater reason, a body of men, are unfit to be both judges and parties, at the same time; yet, what are many of the most important acts of legislation, but so many judicial determinations, not indeed concerning the rights of single persons, but concerning the rights of large bodies of citizens, and what are the different classes of legislators, but advocates and parties to the causes which they determine? Is a law proposed concerning private debts? It is a question to which the creditors are parties on one side, and the debtors on the other. Justice ought to hold the balance between them. Yet the parties are and must be themselves the judges; and the most numerous party, or, in other words, the most powerful faction must be expected to prevail. Shall domestic manufactures be encouraged, and in what degree, by restrictions on foreign manufactures? Are questions which would be differently decided by the landed and the manufacturing classes; and probably by neither, with a sole regard to justice and the public good. The apportionment of taxes on the various descriptions of property, is an act which seems to require the most exact impartiality; yet, there is perhaps no legislative act in which greater opportunity and temptation are given to a predominant party, to trample on the rules of justice. Every shilling with which they overburden the inferior number, is a shilling saved to their own pockets.

It is in vain to say, that enlightened statesmen will be able to adjust these clashing interests, and render them all subservient to the public good. Enlightened statesmen will not always be at the helm: Nor, in many cases, can such an adjustment be made at all, without taking into view indirect and remote considerations, which will rarely prevail over the immediate interest which one party may find in disregarding the rights of another, or the good of the whole.

The inference to which we are brought, is, that the causes of faction cannot be removed; and that relief is only to be sought in the means of controlling its effects.

If a faction consists of less than a majority, relief is supplied by the republican principle, which enables the majority to defeat its sinister views by regular vote: It may clog the administration, it may convulse the society; but it will be unable to execute and mask its violence under the forms of the Constitution. When a majority is included in a faction, the form of popular government on the other hand enables it to sacrifice to its ruling passion or interest, both the public good and the rights of other citizens. To secure the public good, and private rights, against the danger of such a faction, and at the same time to preserve the spirit and the form of popular government, is then the great object to which our enquiries are directed: Let me add that it is the great desideratum, by which alone this form of government can be rescued from the opprobrium under which it has so long labored, and be recommended to the esteem and adoption of mankind.

By what means is this object attainable? Evidently by one of two only. Either the existence of the same passion or interest in a majority at the same time, must be prevented; or the majority, having such co-existent passion or interest, must be rendered, by their number and local situation, unable to concert and carry into effect schemes of oppression. If the impulse and the opportunity be suffered to coincide, we well know that neither moral nor religious motives can be relied on as an adequate control. They are not found to be such on the injustice and violence of individuals, and lose their efficacy in proportion to the number combined together; that is, in proportion as their efficacy becomes needful.

From this view of the subject, it may be concluded, that a pure Democracy, by which I mean, a Society, consisting of a small number of citizens, who assemble and administer the Government in person, can admit of no cure for the mischiefs of faction. A common passion or interest will, in almost every case, be felt by a majority of the whole; a communication and concert results from the form of Government itself; and there is nothing to check the inducements to sacrifice the weaker party, or an obnoxious individual. Hence it is, that such Democracies have ever been spectacles of turbulence and contention; have ever been found incompatible with personal security, or the rights of property; and have in general been as short in their lives, as they have been violent in their deaths. Theoretic politicians, who have patronized this species of Government, have erroneously supposed, that by reducing mankind to a perfect equality in their political rights, they would, at the same time, be perfectly equalized and assimilated in their possessions, their opinions, and their passions.

A republic, by which I mean a government in which the scheme of representation takes place, opens a different prospect, and promises the cure for which we are seeking. Let us examine the points in which it varies from pure democracy, and we shall comprehend both the nature of the cure and the efficacy which it must derive from the union.

The two great points of difference, between a democracy and a republic, are, first, the delegation of the government, in the latter, to a small number of citizens, elected by the rest; secondly, the greater number of citizens, and greater sphere of country, over which the latter may be extended.

The effect of the first difference is, on the one hand, to refine and enlarge the public views, by passing them through the medium of a chosen body of citizens, whose wisdom may best discern the true interest of their country, and whose patriotism and love of justice, will be least likely to sacrifice it to temporary or partial considerations. Under such a regulation, it may well happen, that the public voice, pronounced by the representatives of the people, will be more consonant to the public good, than if pronounced by the people themselves, convened for the purpose. On the other hand the effect may be inverted. Men of factious tempers, of local prejudices, or of sinister designs, may by intrigue, by corruption, or by other means, first obtain the suffrages, and then betray the interest of the people. The question resulting is, whether small or extensive republics are most favorable to the election of proper guardians of the public weal, and it is clearly decided in favor of the latter by two obvious considerations.

In the first place, it is to be remarked that, however small the republic may be, the representatives must be raised to a certain number, in order to guard against the cabals of a few; and that however large it may be, they must be limited to a certain number, in order to guard against the confusion of a multitude. Hence, the number of representatives in the two cases not being in proportion to that of the constituents, and being proportionally greatest in the small republic, it follows, that if the proportion of fit characters be not less in the large than in the small republic, the former will present a greater option, and consequently a greater probability of a fit choice.

In the next place, as each Representative will be chosen by a greater number of citizens in the large than in the small Republic, it will be more difficult for unworthy candidates to practise with success the vicious arts, by which elections are too often carried; and the suffrages of the people being more free, will be more likely to center on men who possess the most attractive merit, and the most diffusive and established characters.

It must be confessed, that in this, as in most other cases, there is a mean, on both sides of which inconveniences will be found to lie. By enlarging too much the number of electors, you render the representative too little acquainted with all their local circumstances and lesser interests; as by reducing it too much, you render him unduly attached to these, and too little fit to comprehend and pursue great and national objects. The Federal Constitution forms a happy combination in this respect; the great and aggregate interests being referred to the national, the local and particular, to the state legislatures.

The other point of difference is, the greater number of citizens and extent of territory which may be brought within the compass of Republican, than of Democratic Government; and it is this circumstance principally which renders factious combinations less to be dreaded in the former, than in the latter. The smaller the society, the fewer probably will be the distinct parties and interests composing it; the fewer the distinct parties and interests, the more frequently will a majority be found of the same party; and the smaller the number of individuals composing a majority, and the smaller the compass within which they are placed, the more easily will they concert and execute their plans of oppression. Extend the sphere, and you take in a greater variety of parties and interests; you make it less probable that a majority of the whole will have a common motive to invade the rights of other citizens; or if such a common motive exists, it will be more difficult for all who feel it to discover their own strength, and to act in unison with each other. Besides other impediments, it may be remarked, that where there is a consciousness of unjust or dishonorable purposes, communication is always checked by distrust, in proportion to the number whose concurrence is necessary.

Hence it clearly appears, that the same advantage, which a Republic has over a Democracy, in controlling the effects of faction, is enjoyed by a large over a small Republic—is enjoyed by the Union over the States composing it. Does this advantage consist in the substitution of Representatives, whose enlightened views and virtuous sentiments render them superior to local prejudices, and to schemes of injustice? It will not be denied, that the Representation of the Union will be most likely to possess these requisite endowments. Does it consist in the greater security afforded by a greater variety of parties, against the event of any one party being able to outnumber and oppress the rest? In an equal degree does the increased variety of parties, comprised within the Union, increase this security? Does it, in fine, consist in the greater obstacles opposed to the concert and accomplishment of the secret wishes of an unjust and interested majority? Here, again, the extent of the Union gives it the most palpable advantage.

The influence of factious leaders may kindle a flame within their particular States, but will be unable to spread a general conflagration through the other States: a religious sect, may degenerate into a political faction in a part of the Confederacy but the variety of sects dispersed over the entire face of it, must secure the national Councils against any danger from that source: a rage for paper money, for an abolition of debts, for an equal division of property, or for any other improper or wicked project, will be less apt to pervade the whole body of the Union, than a particular member of it; in the same proportion as such a malady is more likely to taint a particular county or district, than an entire State.

In the extent and proper structure of the Union, therefore, we behold a Republican remedy for the diseases most incident to Republican Government. And according to the degree of pleasure and pride, we feel in being Republicans, ought to be our zeal in cherishing the spirit, and supporting the character of Federalists.

Publius

Federalist 51

James Madison

6 February 1788

To the People of the State of New York

To what expedient then shall we finally resort for maintaining in practice the necessary partition of power among the several departments, as laid down in the constitution? The only answer that can be given is, that as all these exterior provisions are found to be inadequate, the defect must be supplied, by so contriving the interior structure of the government, as that its several constituent parts may, by their mutual relations, be the means of keeping each other in their proper places. Without presuming to undertake a full development of this important idea, I will hazard a few general observations, which may perhaps place it in a clearer light, and enable us to form a more correct judgment of the principles and structure of the government planned by the convention.

In order to lay a due foundation for that separate and distinct exercise of the different powers of government, which to a certain extent, is admitted on all hands to be essential to the preservation of liberty, it is evident that each department should have a will of its own; and consequently should be so constituted, that the members of each should have as little agency as possible in the appointment of the members of the others. Were this principle rigorously adhered to, it would require that all the appointments for the supreme executive, legislative, and judiciary magistracies, should be drawn from the same fountain of authority, the people, through channels, having no communication whatever with one another. Perhaps such a plan of constructing the several departments would be less difficult in practice than it may in contemplation appear. Some difficulties however, and some additional expense, would attend the execution of it. Some deviations therefore from the principle must be admitted. In the constitution of the judiciary department in particular, it might be inexpedient to insist rigorously on the principle; first, because peculiar qualifications being essential in the members, the primary consideration ought to be to select that mode of choice, which best secures these qualifications; secondly, because the permanent tenure by which the appointments are held in that department, must soon destroy all sense of dependence on the authority conferring them.

It is equally evident that the members of each department should be as little dependent as possible on those of the others, for the emoluments annexed to their offices. Were the executive magistrate, or the judges, not independent of the legislature in this particular, their independence in every other would be merely nominal.

But the great security against a gradual concentration of the several powers in the same department, consists in giving to those who administer each department, the necessary constitutional means, and personal motives, to resist encroachments of the others. The provision for defense must in this, as in all other cases, be made commensurate to the danger of attack. Ambition must be made to counteract ambition. The interest of the man must be connected with the constitutional right of the place. It may be a reflection on human nature, that such devices should be necessary to control the abuses of government. But what is government itself but the greatest of all reflections on human nature? If men were angels, no government would be necessary. If angels were to govern men, neither external nor internal controls on government would be necessary. In framing a government which is to be administered by men over men, the great difficulty lies in this: You must first enable the government to control the governed; and in the next place, oblige it to control itself. A dependence on the people is no doubt the primary control on the government; but experience has taught mankind the necessity of auxiliary precautions.

This policy of supplying by opposite and rival interests, the defect of better motives, might be traced through the whole system of human affairs, private as well as public. We see it particularly displayed in all the subordinate distributions of power; where the constant aim is to divide and arrange the several offices in such a manner as that each may be a check on the other; that the private interest of every individual, may be a sentinel over the public rights. These inventions of prudence cannot be less requisite in the distribution of the supreme powers of the state.

But it is not possible to give to each department an equal power of self defense. In republican government the legislative authority, necessarily, predominates. The remedy for this inconveniency is, to divide the legislature into different branches; and to render them by different modes of election, and different principles of action, as little connected with each other, as the nature of their common functions, and their common dependence on the society, will admit. It may even be necessary to guard against dangerous encroachments by still further precautions. As the weight of the legislative authority requires that it should be thus divided, the weakness of the executive may require, on the other hand, that it should be fortified. An absolute negative, on the legislature, appears at first view to be the natural defense with which the executive magistrate should be armed. But perhaps it would be neither altogether safe, nor alone sufficient. On ordinary occasions, it might not be exerted with the requisite firmness; and on extraordinary occasions, it might be perfidiously abused. May not this defect of an absolute negative be supplied, by some qualified connection between this weaker department, and the weaker branch of the stronger department, by which the latter may be led to support the constitutional rights of the former, without being too much detached from the rights of its own department?

If the principles on which these observations are founded be just, as I persuade myself they are, and they be applied as a criterion, to the several state constitutions, and to the federal constitution, it will be found, that if the latter does not perfectly correspond with them, the former are infinitely less able to bear such a test.

There are moreover two considerations particularly applicable to the federal system of America, which place that system in a very interesting point of view.

First, in a single republic, all the power surrendered by the people, is submitted to the administration of a single government; and usurpations are guarded against by a division of the government into distinct and separate departments. In the compound republic of America, the power surrendered by the people, is first divided between two distinct governments, and then the portion allotted to each, subdivided among distinct and separate departments. Hence a double security arises to the rights of the people. The different governments will control each other; at the same time that each will be controlled by itself.

Second, it is of great importance in a republic, not only to guard the society against the oppression of its rulers; but to guard one part of the society against the injustice of the other part. Different interests necessarily exist in different classes of citizens. If a majority be united by a common interest, the rights of the minority will be insecure. There are but two methods of providing against this evil: The one by creating a will in the community independent of the majority, that is, of the society itself, the other by comprehending in the society so many separate descriptions of citizens, as will render an unjust combination of a majority of the whole, very improbable, if not impracticable. The first method prevails in all governments possessing an hereditary or self appointed authority. This at best is but a precarious security; because a power independent of the society may as well espouse the unjust views of the major, as the rightful interests, of the minor party, and may possibly be turned against both parties. The second method will be exemplified in the federal republic of the United States. While all authority in it will be derived from and dependent on the society, the society itself will be broken into so many parts, interests and classes of citizens, that the rights of individuals or of the minority, will be in little danger from interested combinations of the majority. In a free government, the security for civil rights must be the same as for religious rights. It consists in the one case in the multiplicity of interests, and in the other, in the multiplicity of sects. The degree of security in both cases will depend on the number of interests and sects; and this may be presumed to depend on the extent of country and number of people comprehended under the same government. This view of the subject must particularly recommend a proper federal system to all the sincere and considerate friends of republican government: Since it shows that in exact proportion as the territory of the union may be formed into more circumscribed confederacies or states, oppressive combinations of a majority will be facilitated, the best security under the republican form, for the rights of every class of citizens, will be diminished; and consequently, the stability and independence of some member of the government, the only other security, must be proportionally increased. Justice is the end of government. It is the end of civil society. It ever has been, and ever will be pursued, until it be obtained, or until liberty be lost in the pursuit. In a society under the forms of which the stronger faction can readily unite and oppress the weaker, anarchy may as truly be said to reign, as in a state of nature where the weaker individual is not secured against the violence of the stronger. And as in the latter state even the stronger individuals are prompted by the uncertainty of their condition, to submit to a government which may protect the weak as well as themselves: So in the former state, will the more powerful factions or parties be gradually induced by a like motive, to wish for a government which will protect all parties, the weaker as well as the more powerful. It can be little doubted, that if the state of Rhode Island was separated from the confederacy, and left to itself, the insecurity of rights under the popular form of government within such narrow limits, would be displayed by such reiterated oppressions of factious majorities, that some power altogether independent of the people would soon be called for by the voice of the very factions whose misrule had proved the necessity of it. In the extended republic of the United States, and among the great variety of interests, parties and sects which it embraces, a coalition of a majority of the whole society could seldom take place on any other principles than those of justice and the general good; and there being thus less danger to a minor from the will of the major party, there must be less pretext also, to provide for the security of the former, by introducing into the government a will not dependent on the latter; or in other words, a will independent of the society itself. It is no less certain than it is important, notwithstanding the contrary opinions which have been entertained, that the larger the society, provided it lie within a practicable sphere, the more duly capable it will be of self government. And happily for the republican cause, the practicable sphere may be carried to a very great extent, by a judicious modification and mixture of the federal principle.

Publius

Anti-Federalists and the Constitution

Anti-Federalists opposed ratification of the Constitution because they feared it would create a strong national government that would trample the rights of individual citizens. In the following selection, George Mason, a leading Anti-Federalist who participated in the Constitutional Convention but who refused to sign the final document, systematically details his objections to the Constitution. Like most Anti-Federalists, Mason concentrates his criticisms on the risks of giving too much power to the national government.

George Mason, "Objections to the Constitution," *Virginia Journal* (Alexandria), November 22, 1787

There is no declaration of rights; and the laws of the general government being paramount to the laws and constitutions of the several States, the declarations of rights in the separate States are no security. Nor are the people secured even in the enjoyment of the benefits of the common law, which stands here upon no other foundation than its having been adopted by the respective acts forming the constitutions of the several States.

In the House of Representatives there is not the substance, but the shadow only of representation; which can never produce proper information in the Legislature, or inspire confidence in the people; the laws will therefore be generally made by men little concerned in, and unacquainted with their effects and consequences.

The Senate have the power of altering all money-bills, and of originating appropriations of money, and the salaries of the officers of their own appointment in conjunction with the President of the United States; although they are not the representatives of the people, or amenable to them.

These with their other great powers (viz. their power in the appointment of ambassadors and other public officers, in making treaties, and in trying all impeachments) their influence upon and connection with the supreme executive from these causes, their duration of office, and their being a constant existing body almost continually sitting, joined with their being one complete branch of the Legislature, will destroy any balance in the government, and enable them to accomplish what usurpations they please upon the rights and liberties of the people.

The judiciary of the United States is so constructed and extended as to absorb and destroy the judiciaries of the several States; thereby rendering law as tedious, intricate and expensive, and justice as unattainable by a great part of the community, as in England, and enabling the rich to oppress and ruin the poor.

The President of the United States has no constitutional council (a thing unknown in any safe and regular government). He will therefore be unsupported by proper information and advice; and will be generally directed by minions and favorites—or he will become a tool to the Senate—or a Council of State will grow out of the principal officers of the great departments; the worst and most dangerous of all ingredients for such a council in a free country; for they may be induced to join in any dangerous or oppressive measures, to shelter themselves, and prevent an inquiry into their own misconduct in office; whereas had a constitutional council been formed (as was proposed) of six member, viz. two from the eastern, two from the middle, and two from the southern States, to be appointed by vote of the States in the House of Representatives, with the same duration and rotation in office as the Senate, the Executive would always have had safe and proper information and advice, the President of such a council might have acted as Vice-President of the United States, pro tempore, upon any vacancy or disability of the chief Magistrate; and long continued sessions of the Senate would in a great measure have been prevented.

From this fatal defect of a constitutional council has arisen the improper power of the Senate, in the appointment of public officers, and the alarming dependance and connection between that branch of the Legislature and the supreme Executive.

Hence also sprung that unnecessary and dangerous officer the Vice-President; who for want of other employment is made President of the Senate; thereby dangerously blending the executive and legislative powers; besides always giving to some one of the States an unnecessary and unjust preminence over the others.

The President of the United States has the unrestrained power of granting pardons for treason; which may be sometimes exercised to screen from punishment those whom he had secretly instigated to commit the crime, and thereby prevent a discovery of his own guilt.

By declaring all treaties supreme laws of the land, the Executive and the Senate have, in many cases, an exclusive power of legislation; which might have been avoided by proper distinctions with respect to treaties, and requiring the assent of the House of Representatives, where it could be done with safety.

By requiring only a majority to make all commercial and navigation laws, the five southern States (whose produce and circumstances are totally different from that of the eight northern and eastern States) will be ruined; for such rigid and premature regulations may be made, as will enable the merchants of the northern and eastern States not only to demand an exorbitant freight, but to monopolize the purchase of the commodities at their own price, for many years: To the great injury of the landed interest, and impoverishment of the people: And the danger is the greater, as the gain on one side will be in proportion to the loss on the other. Whereas requiring two-thirds of the members present in both houses would have produced mutual moderation, promoted the general interest and removed an insuperable objection to the adoption of the government.

Under their own construction of the general clause at the end of the enumerated powers, the Congress may grant monopolies in trade and commerce, constitute new crimes, inflict unusual and severe punishments, and extend their power as far as they shall think proper; so that the State Legislatures have no security for the powers now presumed to remain to them; or the people for their rights.

There is no declaration of any kind for preserving the liberty of the press, the trial by jury in civil causes; nor against the danger of standing armies in time of peace.

The State Legislatures are restrained from laying export duties on their own produce.

The general Legislature is restrained from prohibiting the further importation of slaves for twenty odd years; though such importations render the United States weaker, and more vulnerable, and less capable of defence.

Both the general Legislature and the State Legislatures are expressly prohibited making *ex post facto* laws; though there never was nor can be a Legislature but must and will make such laws, when necessity and the public safety require them, which will hereafter be a breach of all the constitutions in the Union, and afford precedents for other innovations.

This government will commence in a moderate aristocracy; it is at present impossible to foresee whether it will, in its operation, produce a monarchy, or a corrupt oppressive aristocracy; it will most probably vibrate some years between the two, and then terminate between the one and the other.

Race and the Constitution

Race has been a fundamental issue in American politics since the founding of the Republic. As these summaries of three landmark Supreme Court rulings show, our understanding of the civil rights guaranteed by the Constitution has changed dramatically over the past two centuries.

Dred Scott v. Sanford 19 How. 393 (1857)

Dred Scott was an African American slave who moved with his owner from Missouri, a slave state, first to Illinois, a free state, and then to the Wisconsin territory, where slavery was illegal under the terms of the Missouri Compromise of 1820. In 1846, Scott asked a state court in Missouri to grant him his freedom on the grounds that he had lived for two years in a free state and a free territory. Scott initially won his case, but the judgment was overturned on appeal and eventually made its way to the Supreme Court. In 1857, the Court's southern majority ruled against Scott, arguing that the Missouri Compromise was unconstitutional because Congress had no power to ban slavery in federal territories. As the following excerpt shows, the Court went even further and argued that African Americans descended from slaves were not American citizens and thus had no right to sue in court:

> The question is simply this: Can a Negro, whose ancestors were imported into this country, and sold as slaves, become a member of the political community formed and brought into existence by the Constitution of the United States, and as such become entitled to all the rights, and privileges, and immunities, guaranteed by that instrument to the citizen? One of which rights is the privilege of suing in a court of the United States in the cases specified in the Constitution. . . .

> The words "people of the United States" and "citizens" are synonymous terms, and mean the same thing. They both describe the political body who, according to our republican institutions, form the sovereignty, and who hold the power and conduct the Government through their representatives. They are what we familiarly call the "sovereign people," and every citizen is one of this people, and a constituent member of this sovereignty. The question before us is, whether the class of persons described in the plea in abatement compose a portion of this people, and are constituent members of this sovereignty? We think they are not, and that they are not included, and were not intended to be included, under the word "citizens" in the Constitution, and can therefore claim none of the rights and privileges which that instrument provides for and secures to citizens of the United States. On the contrary, they were at that time considered as a subordinate and inferior class of beings, who had been subjugated by the dominant race, and, whether emancipated or not, yet remained subject to their authority, and had no rights or privileges but such as those who held the power and the government might choose to grant them. . . .

> [T]he court is of opinion, that, . . . Dred Scott was not a citizen of Missouri within the meaning of the Constitution of the United States, and not entitled as such to sue in its courts

Plessy v. Ferguson 163 U.S. 537 (1896)

In 1890, the Louisiana state legislature followed the lead of several other southern states and passed a law requiring that "all railway companies carrying passengers in their coaches in this State, shall provide equal but separate accommodations for the white, and colored, races." Homer Adolph Plessy, who was one-eighth African American by descent, was arrested for violating the statute. He was tried in the Criminal District Court of New Orleans, where Judge John H. Ferguson found him guilty. In 1896, the Supreme Court upheld Ferguson's verdict, finding that "separate but equal" laws did not violate the Fourteenth Amendment, as Plessy had argued. In dissent, Justice Harlan denounced the ruling and anticipated the direction the Court would take six decades later:

> In view of the Constitution, in the eye of the law, there is in this country no superior, dominant, ruling class of citizens. There is no caste here. Our Constitution is color-blind, and neither knows nor tolerates classes among citizens. In respect of civil rights, all citizens are equal before the law. The humblest is the peer of the most powerful. The law regards man as man, and takes no account of his surroundings or of his color when his civil rights as guaranteed by the supreme law of the land are involved. . . . The arbitrary separation of citizens, on the basis of race, while they are on a public highway, is a badge of servitude wholly inconsistent with the civil freedom and the equality before the law established by the Constitution. It cannot be justified upon any legal grounds.

Brown et al. v. Board of Education 347 U.S. 483 (1954)

In 1950, Oliver Brown, a railroad worker in Topeka, Kansas, attempted to enroll his daughter Linda in the third grade at the Sumner School, a public school for whites located only four blocks from his home. When school officials refused to admit Linda because she was African American, Brown sued the Board of Education for the city of Topeka. Brown's lawsuit eventually reached the Supreme Court, where it was considered along with several other cases challenging the constitutionality of segregated public schools. In 1954, a unanimous Court ruled that segregated school systems denied African American children equal protection under the law, thereby violating the Fourteenth Amendment. The Court's decision in *Brown et al. v. Board of Education* effectively overturned the decision it had reached fifty-eight years earlier in *Plessy v. Ferguson*. Chief Justice Warren's landmark ruling illustrates how dramatically the Court's understanding of race had changed since the *Dred Scott* decision:

> Does segregation of children in public schools solely on the basis of race, even though the physical facilities and other "tangible" factors may be equal, deprive the children of the minority group of equal educational opportunities? We believe that it does. . . . To separate them from others of similar age and qualifications solely because of their race generates a feeling of inferiority as to their status in the community that may affect their hearts and minds in a way unlikely ever to be undone. The effect of this separation on their educational opportunities was well stated by a finding in the Kansas case by a court which nevertheless felt compelled to rule against the Negro plaintiffs: "Segregation of white and colored children in public schools has a detrimental effect upon the colored children. The impact is greater when it has the sanction of the law; for the policy of separating the races is usually interpreted as denoting the inferiority of the Negro group. A sense of inferiority affects the motivation of a child to learn. Segregation with the sanction of law, therefore, has a tendency to retard the educational and mental development of Negro children and to deprive them of some of the benefits they would receive in a racially integrated school system." Whatever may have been the extent of psychological knowledge at the time of *Plessy v. Ferguson*, this finding is amply supported by modern authority. Any language in *Plessy v. Ferguson* contrary to this finding is rejected.

> We conclude that in the field of public education the doctrine of "separate but equal" has no place. Separate educational facilities are inherently unequal. Therefore, we hold that the plaintiffs and others similarly situated for whom the actions have been brought are, by reason of the segregation complained of, deprived of the equal protection of the laws guaranteed by the Fourteenth Amendment.

Presidents and Vice Presidents

Year	President	Vice President	Party
1789–1797	1 George Washington	John Adams	None
1797–1801	2 John Adams	Thomas Jefferson	Federalist
1801–1809	3 Thomas Jefferson	Aaron Burr (to 1805)George Clinton (to 1809)	Democratic-Republican
1809–1817	4 James Madison	George Clinton (to 1813) Elbridge Gerry (to 1817)	Democratic-Republican
1817–1825	5 James Monroe	Daniel D. Tompkins	Democratic-Republican
1825–1829	6 John Quincy Adams	John C. Calhoun	Democratic-Republican
1829–1837	7 Andrew Jackson	John C. Calhoun (to 1833) Martin Van Buren (to 1837)	Democratic
1837–1841	8 Martin Van Buren	Richard M. Johnson	Democratic
1841	9 William H. Harrison	John Tyler	Whig
1841–1845	10 John Tyler	(vacant)	Whig
1845–1849	11 James K. Polk	George M. Dallas	Democratic
1849–1850	12 Zachary Taylor	Millard Fillmore	Whig
1850–1853	13 Millard Fillmore	(vacant)	Whig
1853–1857	14 Franklin Pierce	William R. King	Democratic
1857–1861	15 James Buchanan	John C. Breckinridge	Democratic
1861–1865	16 Abraham Lincoln	Hannibal Hamlin (to 1865) Andrew Johnson (1865)	Republican
1865–1869	17 Andrew Johnson	(vacant)	Democratic
1869–1877	18 Ulysses S. Grant	Schuyler Colfax (to 1873) Henry Wilson (to 1877)	Republican
1877–1881	19 Rutherford B. Hayes	William A. Wheeler	Republican
1881	20 James A. Garfield	Chester A. Arthur	Republican
1881–1885	21 Chester A. Arthur	(vacant)	Republican
1885–1889	22 Grover Cleveland	Thomas A. Hendricks	Democratic
1889–1893	23 Benjamin Harrison	Levi P. Morton	Republican

Year	President	Vice President	Party
1893–1897	24 Grover Cleveland	Adlai E. Stevenson	Democratic
1897–1901	25 William McKinley	Garret A. Hobart (to 1901) Theodore Roosevelt (1901)	Republican
1901–1909	26 Theodore Roosevelt	(vacant to 1905) Charles W. Fairbanks (to 1909)	Republican
1909–1913	27 William Howard Taft	James S. Sherman	Republican
1913–1921	28 Woodrow Wilson	Thomas R. Marshall	Democratic
1921–1923	29 Warren G. Harding	Calvin Coolidge	Republican
1923–1929	30 Calvin Coolidge	(vacant to 1925) Charles G. Dawes (to 1929)	Republican
1929–1933	31 Herbert Hoover	Charles Curtis	Republican
1933–1945	32 Franklin D. Roosevelt	John N. Garner (to 1941) Henry A. Wallace (to 1945) Harry S Truman (1945)	Democratic
1945–1953	33 Harry S Truman	(vacant to 1949) Alben W. Barkley (to 1953)	Democratic
1953–1961	34 Dwight D. Eisenhower	Richard M. Nixon	Republican
1961–1963	35 John F. Kennedy	Lyndon B. Johnson	Democratic
1963–1969	36 Lyndon B. Johnson	(vacant to 1965) Hubert H. Humphrey	Democratic
1969–1974	37 Richard M. Nixon	Spiro T. Agnew (to 1973) Gerald R. Ford (to 1974)	Republican
1974–1977	38 Gerald R. Ford	Nelson A. Rockefeller	Republican
1977–1981	39 Jimmy Carter	Walter Mondale	Democratic
1981–1989	40 Ronald Reagan	George H. W. Bush	Republican
1989–1993	41 George H. W. Bush	Dan Quayle	Republican
1993–2001	42 Bill Clinton	Al Gore	Democratic
2001–2009	43 George W. Bush	Richard Cheney	Republican
2009–2017	44 Barack Obama	Joseph Biden	Democratic
2017–	45 Donald Trump	Mike Pence	Republican

Presidential Election Results, 1789–2016

Year	Winner	Defeated	Party	Popular Vote (%)	Electoral Vote
1789	**George Washington**				69
1792	**George Washington**				132
1796	**John Adams**	Thomas Jefferson	Federalist		71
1800	**Thomas Jefferson**	John Adams	Democratic-Republican		73
1804	**Thomas Jefferson**	Charles C. Pinckney	Democratic-Republican		162
1808	**James Madison**	Charles C. Pinckney	Democratic-Republican		122
1812	**James Madison**	DeWitt Clinton	Democratic-Republican		128
1816	**James Monroe**	Rufus King	Democratic-Republican		183
1820	**James Monroe**	John Quincy Adams	Democratic-Republican		231
1824	**John Quincy Adams**	Andrew Jackson	Democratic-Republican	30.5%	84*
1828	**Andrew Jackson**	John Quincy Adams	Democratic	56.0%	178
1832	**Andrew Jackson**	Henry Clay	Democratic	55.0%	219
1836	**Martin Van Buren**	William H. Harrison	Democratic	50.9%	170
1840	**William H. Harrison**	Martin Van Buren	Whig	53.1%	234
1844	**James K. Polk**	Henry Clay	Democratic	49.6%	170
1848	**Zachary Taylor**	Lewis Cass	Whig	47.4%	163
1852	**Franklin Pierce**	Winfield Scott	Democratic	50.9%	254
1856	**James Buchanan**	John C. Fremont	Democratic	45.4%	174
1860	**Abraham Lincoln**	Stephen A. Douglas	Republican	39.8%	180
1864	**Abraham Lincoln**	George B. McClellan	Republican	55.0%	212
1868	**Ulysses S. Grant**	Horatio Seymour	Republican	52.7%	214
1872	**Ulysses S. Grant**	Horace Greeley	Republican	55.6%	286
1876	**Rutherford B. Hayes**	Samuel J. Tilden	Republican	48.0%	185*
1880	**James A. Garfield**	Winfield S. Hancock	Republican	48.3%	214

Year	Winner	Defeated	Party	Popular Vote (%)	Electoral Vote
1884	Grover Cleveland	James G. Blaine	Democratic	48.5%	219
1888	Benjamin Harrison	Grover Cleveland	Republican	47.8%	233*
1892	Grover Cleveland	Benjamin Harrison	Democratic	46.0%	277
1896	William McKinley	William J. Bryan	Republican	50.8%	271
1900	William McKinley	William J. Bryan	Republican	51.7%	292
1904	Theodore Roosevelt	Alton B. Parker	Republican	56.4%	336
1908	William Howard Taft	William J. Bryan	Republican	51.6%	321
1912	Woodrow Wilson	William Howard Taft	Democratic	41.8%	435
1916	Woodrow Wilson	Charles E. Hughes	Democratic	49.3%	277
1920	Warren G. Harding	James M. Cox	Republican	61.0%	404
1924	Calvin Coolidge	John W. Davis	Republican	54.1%	382
1928	Herbert Hoover	Alfred E. Smith	Republican	58.2%	444
1932	Franklin D. Roosevelt	Herbert Hoover	Democratic	57.3%	472
1936	Franklin D. Roosevelt	Alfred Landon	Democratic	60.7%	523
1940	Franklin D. Roosevelt	Wendell Wilkie	Democratic	54.7%	449
1944	Franklin D. Roosevelt	Thomas E. Dewey	Democratic	52.8%	432
1948	Harry S Truman	Thomas E. Dewey	Democratic	49.5%	303
1952	Dwight D. Eisenhower	Adlai E. Stevenson	Republican	55.2%	442
1956	Dwight D. Eisenhower	Adlai E. Stevenson	Republican	57.4%	457
1960	John F. Kennedy	Richard M. Nixon	Democratic	49.9%	303
1964	Lyndon B. Johnson	Barry Goldwater	Democratic	61.1%	486
1968	Richard M. Nixon	Hubert H. Humphrey	Republican	43.4%	301
1972	Richard M. Nixon	George McGovern	Republican	61.3%	520
1976	Jimmy Carter	Gerald R. Ford	Democratic	50.1%	297
1980	Ronald Reagan	Jimmy Carter	Republican	50.7%	489
1984	Ronald Reagan	Walter F. Mondale	Republican	58.8%	525
1988	George H. W. Bush	Michael Dukakis	Republican	53.4%	426
1992	Bill Clinton	George H. W. Bush	Democratic	43.0%	370
1996	Bill Clinton	Robert Dole	Democratic	49.2%	379
2000	George W. Bush	Al Gore	Republican	47.9%	271*
2004	George W. Bush	John F. Kerry	Republican	50.7%	286

Year	Winner	Defeated	Party	Popular Vote (%)	Electoral Vote
2008	**Barack Obama**	John McCain	Democratic	52.9%	365
2012	**Barack Obama**	Mitt Romney	Democratic	51%	332
2016	**Donald Trump**	Hillary Clinton	Republican	46.1%	304*

*Denotes the winning candidate lost the popular vote.

Party Control of Congress, 1901–2017

Congress (no.)	Years	President	Senate			House		
			Dem	Rep	Other	Dem	Rep	Other
57	1901–1903	McKinley/ T. Roosevelt	29	**56**	3	153	**198**	5
58	1903–1905	T. Roosevelt	32	**58**	–	178	**207**	–
59	1905–1907	T. Roosevelt	32	**58**	–	136	**250**	–
60	1907–1909	T. Roosevelt	29	**61**	–	164	**222**	–
61	1909–1911	Taft	32	**59**	–	172	**219**	–
62	1911–1913	Taft	42	**49**	–	**228**	162	1
63	1913–1915	Wilson	**51**	44	1	**290**	127	18
64	1915–1917	Wilson	**56**	39	1	**231**	193	8
65	1917–1919	Wilson	**53**	42	1	210	**216**	9
66	1919–1921	Wilson	47	**48**	1	191	**237**	7
67	1921–1923	Harding	37	**59**	–	132	**300**	1
68	1923–1925	Coolidge	43	**51**	2	207	**225**	3
69	1925–1927	Coolidge	40	**54**	1	183	**247**	5
70	1927–1929	Coolidge	47	**48**	1	195	**237**	3
71	1929–1931	Hoover	39	**56**	1	163	**267**	1
72	1931–1933	Hoover	47	**48**	1	216	**218**	1
73	1933–1935	F. Roosevelt	**59**	36	1	**313**	117	5
74	1935–1937	F. Roosevelt	**69**	25	2	**322**	103	10
75	1937–1939	F. Roosevelt	**75**	17	4	**333**	89	13
76	1939–1941	F. Roosevelt	**69**	23	4	**262**	169	4
77	1941–1943	F. Roosevelt	**66**	28	2	**267**	162	6
78	1943–1945	F. Roosevelt	**57**	38	1	**222**	209	4
79	1945–1947	Truman	**57**	38	1	**243**	190	2
80	1947–1949	Truman	45	**51**	–	188	**246**	1

Congress (no.)	Years	President	Senate			House		
			Dem	Rep	Other	Dem	Rep	Other
81	1949–1951	Truman	**54**	42	–	**263**	171	1
82	1951–1953	Truman	**48**	47	1	**234**	199	2
83	1953–1955	Eisenhower	46	**48**	2	213	**221**	1
84	1955–1957	Eisenhower	**48**	47	1	**232**	203	–
85	1957–1959	Eisenhower	**49**	47	–	**234**	201	–
86	1959–1961	Eisenhower	**64**	34	–	**283**	154	–
87	1961–1963	Kennedy	**64**	36	–	**262**	175	–
88	1963–1965	Kennedy/ Johnson	**67**	33	–	**258**	176	–
89	1965–1967	Johnson	**68**	32	–	**295**	140	–
90	1967–1969	Johnson	**64**	36	–	**248**	187	–
91	1969–1971	Nixon	**58**	42	–	**243**	192	–
92	1971–1973	Nixon	**54**	44	2	**255**	180	–
93	1973–1975	Nixon/Ford	**56**	42	2	**242**	192	–
94	1975–1977	Ford	**61**	37	2	**291**	144	–
95	1977–1979	Carter	**61**	38	1	**292**	143	–
96	1979–1981	Carter	**58**	41	1	**277**	158	–
97	1981–1983	Reagan	46	**53**	1	**243**	192	–
98	1983–1985	Reagan	46	**54**	–	**268**	167	–
99	1985–1987	Reagan	47	**53**	–	**253**	182	–
100	1987–1989	Reagan	**55**	45	–	**258**	177	–
101	1989–1991	G. H. W. Bush	**55**	45	–	**260**	175	–
102	1991–1993	G. H. W. Bush	**56**	44	–	**267**	167	1
103	1993–1995	Clinton	**57**	43	–	**258**	176	1
104	1995–1997	Clinton	47	**53**	–	202	**230**	1
105	1997–1999	Clinton	45	**55**	–	207	**227**	1
106	1999–2001	Clinton	45	**55**	–	211	**223**	1
107	2001–2003	G. W. Bush	**50**	49	1	212	**221**	2
108	2003–2005	G. W. Bush	48	**51**	1	205	**229**	1
109	2005–2007	G. W. Bush	44	**55**	1	202	**232**	1
110	2007–2009	G. W. Bush	**49**	49	2	**233**	202	–
111	2009–2011	Obama	**58**	40	2	**255**	180	–

Appendix I Party Control of Congress, 1901–2017

Congress (no.)	Years	President	Senate			House		
			Dem	Rep	Other	Dem	Rep	Other
112	2011–2013	Obama	**51**	47	2	193	**242**	–
113	2013–2015	Obama	**53**	45	2	201	**234**	–
114	2015–2017	Obama	44	**54**	2	188	**247**	–
115	2017–2019	Trump	46	**52**	2	194	**241**	–

Bold denotes the majority party.

Justices of the Supreme Court Since 1900

Justice	Nominated by	Service	Justice	Nominated by	Service
John M. Harlan	Hayes	1877–1911	Harlan F. Stone	F. Roosevelt	1941–1946
Horace Gray	Arthur	1882–1902	James F. Byrnes	F. Roosevelt	1941–1942
Melville W. Fuller	Cleveland	1888–1910	Robert H. Jackson	F. Roosevelt	1941–1954
David J. Brewer	Harrison	1890–1910	Wiley B. Rutledge	F. Roosevelt	1943–1949
Henry B. Brown	Harrison	1890–1906	Harold H. Burton	Truman	1945–1958
George Shiras, Jr.	Harrison	1892–1903	Fred M. Vinson	Truman	1946–1953
Edward D. White	Cleveland	1894–1910	Tom C. Clark	Truman	1949–1967
Rufus W. Peckham	Cleveland	1895–1909	Sherman Minton	Truman	1949–1956
Joseph McKenna	McKinley	1898–1925	Earl Warren	Eisenhower	1953–1969
Oliver W. Holmes	T. Roosevelt	1902–1932	John M. Harlan	Eisenhower	1955–1971
William R. Day	T. Roosevelt	1903–1922	William J. Brennan	Eisenhower	1956–1990
William H. Moody	T. Roosevelt	1906–1910	Charles E. Whittaker	Eisenhower	1957–1962
Horace H. Lurton	Taft	1910–1914	Potter Stewart	Eisenhower	1958–1981
Edward D. White	Taft	1910–1921	Byron R. White	Kennedy	1962–1993
Charles E. Hughes	Taft	1910–1916	Arthur J. Goldberg	Kennedy	1962–1965
Willis Van Devanter	Taft	1911–1937	Abe Fortas	Johnson	1965–1969
Joseph R. Lamar	Taft	1911–1916	Thurgood Marshall	Johnson	1967–1991
Mahlon Pitney	Taft	1912–1922	Warren E. Burger	Nixon	1969–1986
James C. McReynolds	Wilson	1914–1941	Harry A. Blackmun	Nixon	1970–1994
Louis D. Brandeis	Wilson	1916–1939	Lewis F. Powell, Jr.	Nixon	1971–1987
John H. Clarke	Wilson	1916–1922	William H. Rehnquist	Nixon	1971–1986
William H. Taft	Harding	1921–1930	John Paul Stevens	Ford	1975–2010
George Sutherland	Harding	1922–1938	Sandra Day O'Connor	Reagan	1981–2006
Pierce Butler	Harding	1922–1939	William H. Rehnquist	Reagan	1986–2005
Edward T. Sanford	Harding	1923–1930	Antonin Scalia	Reagan	1986–2016

Justice	Nominated by	Service	Justice	Nominated by	Service
Harlan F. Stone	Coolidge	1925–1941	David H. Souter	G. H. W. Bush	1990–2009
Charles E. Hughes	Hoover	1930–1941	Clarence Thomas	G. H. W. Bush	1991–
Owen J. Roberts	Hoover	1930–1945	Ruth Bader Ginsburg	Clinton	1993–
Benjamin N. Cardozo	Hoover	1932–1938	Stephen G. Breyer	Clinton	1994–
Hugo L. Black	F. Roosevelt	1937–1971	John G. Roberts, Jr.	G. W. Bush	2005–
Stanley F. Reed	F. Roosevelt	1938–1957	Samuel A. Alito, Jr.	G. W. Bush	2006–
Felix Frankfurter	F. Roosevelt	1939–1962	Sonia Sotomayor	Obama	2009–
William O. Douglas	F. Roosevelt	1939–1975	Elena Kagan	Obama	2010–
Frank Murphy	F. Roosevelt	1940–1949	Neil Gorsuch	Trump	2017–
Anthony M. Kennedy	Reagan	1988–			

Gray boxes denote the chief justice.

Glossary

A

access The ability to maintain personal contact with public officials. Many lobbying strategies depend on maintaining an open door to contacts in the legislative and executive branches.

administration The bureaucratic function of tending to the details of executing public policy.

administrative presidency A strategic approach to the bureaucracy relying on ideological political appointees and tight presidential management to combat the tendency for political appointees to "go native."

affective Existing in the realm of emotion or feeling.

affirmative action Federal policies requiring employers to address inequities in hiring and advancement if they appear to unfairly treat disadvantaged groups on the basis of race, religion, gender, national origin, sexual preference, physical disabilities, or Vietnam veteran status.

Age Discrimination in Employment Act The 1967 law that made it illegal for employers to discriminate against people over age forty in hiring, firing, and promotion decisions.

agenda setting The tendency for topics given great weight by the media to be given equally great weight by those who use the media, such that the people and events considered important by those who determine media coverage will become the people and events that the public considers important.

agents of socialization External influences that shape the way we are socialized to politics, including parents and siblings in the home, friends and coworkers outside the home, and institutions like schools and the media.

Americans with Disabilities Act The landmark 1990 legislation extending equal protection in the workplace and in public accommodations to people with physical and mental disabilities.

amicus curiae Briefs filed by interested parties to a case, whose opinions are offered in an effort to shape the Court's discussion and judgment.

apathy A sense of indifference to or lack of interest in politics.

appellate jurisdiction The authority of a high court to hear cases only after the cases originate in and are appealed from a lower court.

apprenticeship The legislative norm that says freshmen members of Congress should limit their activity and defer to senior members as they learn the ways of the institution. Apprenticeship is no longer enforced in Congress.

appropriations Legislation permitting the government to spend money that determines how much will be spent and how it will be spent.

Articles of Confederation The first constitution of the United States, which created a loosely functioning national government to which the individual states were supreme. It addressed concerns about a strong national government undermining individual liberty, but it created a national government that was unable to regulate commerce or conduct foreign policy and was abandoned in favor of the United States Constitution just eight years after it was ratified.

attack journalism A form of aggressive coverage in which reporters latch onto an allegation of misdoing by a candidate or public official and engage in a "feeding frenzy" in which they cover it intensely and to the exclusion of other news.

attitudes A component of public opinion that measures people's orientations toward politics.

authority The right to act in an official capacity by virtue of holding an office like president or member of Congress.

B

backgrounders Off-the-record exchanges between the president or administration officials and reporters. Whatever a reporter learns at a backgrounder can be used in a story, but the source of the information cannot be revealed.

balance of trade Equilibrium between the value of imports and exports.

beliefs A component of public opinion that measures what people think is true about politics.

bicameral A legislature composed of two houses.

Bill of Rights The first ten amendments to the Constitution, which limit government from denying us a range of personal liberties.

bills of attainder Declarations of guilt by legislative decree without benefit of a trial.

Black Codes An effort by white southerners immediately following the Civil War to restrict the civil rights of emancipated slaves. The codes were overturned by federal civil rights laws, only to become standard practice in the South following Reconstruction.

Boston Massacre A precursor to the war that was still five years away, it was the first mortal conflict between colonists and British troops in Boston and resulted in the deaths of five colonists in 1770.

Boston Tea Party A protest against the Tea Act of 1773 in which fifty colonists dressed as Native Americans boarded British trade ships loaded with tea and threw the contents into the water.

Brown v. Board of Education The landmark 1954 Supreme Court case that declared racial segregation unconstitutional, overturning the Court's ruling in *Plessy v. Ferguson*.

Budget and Accounting Act of 1921 The act providing the legal basis for presidential participation in the budget process, by requiring the president to submit an annual budget to Congress for its consideration.

bureaucracy Another name for the executive branch of government, the institutional component of the presidency, which is charged with carrying out laws passed by Congress.

Bush v. Gore The controversial 2000 Supreme Court case in which a sharply divided Court ended manual ballot recounts in Florida, following which George W. Bush became president.

C

cabinet The name given to the collection of secretaries of the executive departments. Despite commonly held beliefs to the contrary, the cabinet rarely serves as an advisory body to the president.

casework Service performed by members of Congress for constituents with individual problems or complaints that they would like the government to address.

caucus A method of candidate selection in which party identifiers gather in a series of meetings to select delegates to the national convention.

census An accounting or, as Article I Section 2 of the Constitution puts it, an "actual Enumeration" of the residents of the United States, taken every ten years by constitutional decree to assess population growth and population shifts. Census figures are used to determine representation in Congress, as states that lose population between censuses stand to lose House seats to states that gain population.

checks and balances The ability of any one of several equal and independent branches of government to keep the others from acting, designed to prevent power from being consolidated in any one branch. Because any branch can put a check on the others, government can only act when there is cooperation between the branches, a situation that necessitates compromise.

chief diplomat A constitutional role of the president, in which he has the power to recognize ambassadors from other nations.

chief executive The role the president plays as head of the executive branch, in which he carries out the constitutional directive to "take Care that the Laws be faithfully executed."

chief legislator The role the president plays when he offers a legislative agenda and attempts to win congressional approval for it.

chief of staff One of the president's top political advisors and the formal head of the White House staff.

chief of state The role the president plays as ceremonial head of the United States.

Citizenship Act of 1924 An effort to assimilate Native Americans into white culture and society through the granting of American citizenship.

civic responsibility A sense of duty or obligation to society that some people believe comes along with citizenship.

civil disobedience A peaceful means of protest whereby individuals draw attention to laws they consider unjust by disobeying them and being arrested for their actions.

civil liberties Constitutional and legal protections against government infringement on a host of personal freedoms.

civil rights The promise of equal treatment under the law, regardless of one's race, gender, ethnic group affiliation, sexual preference, or age.

Civil Rights Act of 1964 Landmark legislation arising from the civil rights movement that made racial discrimination a federal crime in the workplace and in public accommodations, while giving the federal government greater power to strengthen voting rights and desegregate public schools.

civil rights movement The organized, largely nonviolent, and widely successful efforts of the 1950s and 1960s to bring about social change on behalf of African Americans in the South, whose civil rights were denied by a century-old system of Jim Crow laws.

civil servants Career employees who staff the bureaucracy in a wide range of positions and who get their jobs independent of political considerations.

Civil Service Commission The commission established by the Pendleton Act to oversee the hiring of career civil servants.

classical liberalism A term given to the philosophy of John Locke and other seventeenth- and eighteenth-century advocates of the protection of individual rights and liberties by limiting government power.

clear and present danger The standard established by Justice Oliver Wendell Holmes for determining when the government could limit speech.

cloture The procedure for ending a filibuster. A cloture vote requires a 60 percent majority of the Senate.

coalition A government formed as a partnership among several victorious parties in a multiparty system, following negotiations about the agenda that each party will be allowed to pursue in exchange for its participation in the new government.

coattails The ability of a victorious presidential candidate to sweep congressional candidates of the same party into office on the strength of people voting for one political party.

Coercive Acts Called the Intolerable Acts in the colonies, the Coercive Acts represented the British attempt to clamp down on the colonies following the Boston Tea Party.

cognitive A factual awareness or appreciation of someone or something. Cognition implies knowledge and the ability to exercise judgment. This is why we would say that a young child's understanding of the president is not cognitive because kids' awareness of the president as an important figure lacks appreciation of what the president does and why he is important.

collective goods Benefits stemming from the work of an interest group that are available to everyone, whether or not they join the group.

commander-in-chief The president's constitutional role as civilian leader of the armed forces.

committee chair The member of Congress responsible for running a committee, who can have great influence over the committee agenda and, by extension, the legislative process.

Communications Decency Act of 1996 A legislative attempt to regulate the transmission of "offensive" or "indecent" material over the Internet. The Supreme Court overturned most of the provisions of the Communications Decency Act.

Communications Office The White House office responsible for coordinating the president's media operations, including speechwriting and liaison with national and local reporters.

comparable worth A manner of determining pay equity by equalizing pay between jobs held mostly by women that demand comparable training and labor to jobs held mostly by men.

competitive regulatory policy A type of regulatory policy designed to protect the public interest by restricting the provision of a service or good to organizations that win federal licensing approval.

compromise A form of reciprocity in which members of Congress exhibit flexibility over their legislative objectives in exchange for future flexibility from their colleagues.

concurring opinion A statement issued by a justice who agrees with a vote of the Court but differs on the legal or constitutional rationale for the majority decision.

confederal system An arrangement for establishing a government out of a set of component states, in which the national government is the creation of the states and subservient to them. The Articles of Confederation established a system like this in the United States. In today's world, the United Nations may be the most prominent example of a confederation.

conference committee A committee made up of members of both houses of Congress, assembled when the House and Senate pass different versions of the same legislation. If the conference committee can iron out the differences, a compromise version of the legislation is sent back to both houses for final passage. If it cannot arrive at a compromise, the legislation dies.

Congressional Budget and Impoundment Control Act of 1974 An act designed to centralize the congressional budgeting process, which established current procedures and timetables for writing a budget.

Connecticut Compromise A compromise between the Virginia and New Jersey Plans that broke the deadlock over representation at the Constitutional Convention by providing for a bicameral legislature. Large states would get their demand for representation based on population in the House of Representatives, while every state, regardless of size, would have two senators, which pleased small states.

conservatism An ideology that advocates limits on government power to address economic and social problems, relying instead on economic markets and individual initiative to address problems like health care and education, while promoting government involvement in moral matters to, for instance, minimize or eliminate abortions or permit prayer in public schools.

constituents Individuals living in a district represented by an elected official.

Constitutional Convention A meeting of representatives from twelve of the thirteen states held in Philadelphia in 1787, which produced the federal system of government outlined in the United States Constitution.

constructionists Those who hold to the judicial philosophy that the Constitution should be interpreted strictly and literally, and in the context in which it was written.

cooperative federalism One of several perspectives on federalism, popular during the first two-thirds of the twentieth century, which was defined by joint endeavors between the federal and state governments. Typically, state governments would carry out federal initiatives, using federal money and federal guidelines.

courtesy The legislative norm that members of Congress should treat each other with respect and avoid personal attacks, regardless of how much they may disagree.

critical election An election that heralds a realignment, during which large numbers of voters deviate from their traditional party allegiances in what turns out to be a lasting change.

cue taking Looking to other members of Congress for guidelines on how to cast a vote on a technical or unfamiliar matter.

cynicism A pervasive attitude of mistrust about politics that may lead people to withdraw from political participation.

D

dealignment The weakening of party affiliation, signified by an increase in the number of people who call themselves independents.

Declaration of Independence The document drafted by Thomas Jefferson and approved by the Continental Congress in July 1776, stating the reasons for the Revolutionary War and declaring a formal break with Great Britain.

deficit The gap created in the federal budget when the government takes in less than it spends in a given year.

delegate A philosophy of representation that says officials are elected to carry out constituent interests, even when these interests conflict with what the representative believes is the right thing to do.

democracy A government created by the people over whom it rules.

deregulation The lifting of federal regulations that had been previously imposed on private industry.

diplomatic recognition Formal acceptance of the legitimacy of another nation or its representatives.

direct democracy Democracy without representation, where each eligible individual participates in decision making.

directional An aspect of public opinion that measures whether people feel favorably or unfavorably toward a political figure, institution, or policy.

discharge petition A House procedure that forces a floor vote on legislation stalled in committee. To succeed, a discharge petition must be signed by half the House membership.

disenfranchised Losing or being denied the legal right to vote by intentional or unintentional means.

dissenting opinion A statement issued by a justice who disagrees with a vote of the Court, offering a legal or constitutional rationale for that disagreement.

distributive policies Domestic policies primarily aimed at directing tax money to a range of public works items. Distributive policies tend not to be controversial because benefits are widely shared.

divided government Partisan division of the national government, in which each of the two major parties can claim control of one branch (or one legislative house) of the federal government.

docket The list of cases pending before a court.

double jeopardy Protection against the state using its power to repeatedly prosecute someone until the person is convicted. Double jeopardy precludes the prosecution of someone for the same crime in the same jurisdiction more than once.

Dred Scott v. Sanford The 1857 Supreme Court case that legalized slavery nationwide, while holding that people of color had no rights or protection under the Constitution. The ruling hastened the Civil War; it was subsequently overturned by constitutional amendment.

dual federalism One of several perspectives on federalism, popular during the early years of the republic, which stated that the federal and state governments operated concurrently in separate arenas, and that each had the final say in those areas where it had a clear grant of authority.

due process The protection of individual liberty from the arbitrary or capricious actions of government through a defined set of legal procedures designed to protect the rights of the accused.

E

economic equality A form of equality of outcome that values using government policy to minimize the economic disparities found in society.

efficacy The attitude that you can be effectual and effective in your dealings with government.

electorate The portion of the public eligible to vote in elections.

elitism The theory that government responds to a small, stable, centralized hierarchy of corporate and academic leaders, military chiefs, people who own big media outlets, and members of a permanent government bureaucracy. People who subscribe to this position believe the actions of regular citizens, like voting and joining groups, simply mask the real power exercised by elites.

empirical Any statement based on the assessment of data or the analysis of information, without regard to value judgments.

entitlements Social welfare programs targeted to specific groups of individuals, like senior citizens or the unemployed. Benefits are available to all who meet the program requirements, although some entitlements for the poor impose a means test.

enumerated powers Powers directly granted to Congress by the Constitution .

equal protection clause The constitutional restriction against state laws that discriminate, as stated in the Fourteenth Amendment. The equal protection clause served as the legal basis for eliminating laws that permitted racial discrimination.

Equal Rights Amendment (ERA) A proposed constitutional amendment assuring equal rights for women that was first introduced in Congress in 1923, approved by Congress in 1972, and fell three states short of ratification in 1982.

equal time provision The federal requirement that broadcast outlets selling commercial time to a political candidate must make equal time available to other candidates running for office.

equality of opportunity One of several ways of understanding equality, this way values giving people comparable advantages for succeeding in life, regardless of the unequal outcomes that may result.

equality of outcome One of several ways of understanding equality, this way values leveling the social and economic inequities among people, rather than attempting to give people comparable advantages for succeeding in life.

establishment clause The language in the First Amendment that serves as the basis for the constitutional separation of church and state.

European Union (EU) The framework for integrating previously disparate European economies into a single market.

ex post facto laws From the Latin for "after the fact," legislation that makes something a crime that was legal when it occurred.

exclusionary rule To protect against unreasonable searches and seizures, the Supreme Court has established that evidence obtained illegally is not admissible in court.

executive agreements Legally binding presidential agreements with other nations that do not require congressional approval.

executive branch The institutional component of the branch of government we think of as the presidency, charged with carrying out laws passed by Congress. Sometimes, the executive branch is referred to as the bureaucracy.

Executive Office of the President (EOP) The large staff of advisors to the president that comprises the president's political and policy operation.

executive orders Presidential directives to the bureaucracy that are legally binding and do not require congressional approval.

executive privilege The power of the president, established by custom, to keep Congress, the courts, and the public from having access to presidential documents and communications.

expectations The benchmark for how well a campaign needs to perform in presidential primaries in order to receive positive horserace coverage, based on reporter assessments of the campaign's viability.

F

faction A group of individuals who are united by a desire that, if realized, would threaten the liberty of the larger community—in James Madison's words, individuals who are "united and actuated by some common impulse of passion, or of interest, adverse to the rights of other citizens, or to the permanent and aggregate interests of the community." A faction may be defined by size, such as when a majority of citizens threatens the liberty of the minority, or by intensity, such as when a minority of citizens with intensely held preferences threatens the liberty of a disinterested majority.

Fair Deal The name given to the domestic policies of President Harry S Truman, which built on the popularity of the New Deal.

fairness doctrine The FCC requirement, no longer in force, that electronic media provide a balanced forum for controversial public discourse.

faithless elector A member of the Electoral College who does not cast a vote for the plurality winner of the popular vote in his or her state.

Family and Medical Leave Act of 1993 Legislation designed to permit women working in medium or large companies up to twelve weeks of unpaid leave following childbirth. It also permits employees to take unpaid leave time to care for an ailing relative.

fascism A militant, ultra-nationalistic ideology of the extreme right that rejects liberal ideas about personal rights.

Federal Communications Act of 1934 The act of Congress that established the Federal Communications Commission (FCC) and the equal time provision.

Federal Communications Commission (FCC) The federal agency responsible for regulating broadcast communications, including radio, television, wire, satellite, and cable transmissions. The FCC is directed by five commissioners who are appointed by the president and confirmed by the Senate for five-year terms.

Federal Election Campaign Act The 1974 act aimed at limiting the influence of big-money contributions on political campaigns.

Federal Election Commission (FEC) The federal regulatory agency that administers and enforces campaign finance laws.

Federal Register A publicly available list of all proposed and existing federal regulations.

federal system The arrangement created by the United States Constitution, in which the national government and the states share authority over citizens. States may act autonomously to do such things as create school districts, levy taxes, or assemble a police force; at the same time, powers are reserved for the national government, which is supreme to state laws. In addition to the United States, only Canada, Germany, India, and a small group of other nations have federal systems.

Federal Wage System (FWS) The system used to determine salaries for blue-collar civil servants.

federalism The division of power between a sovereign federal government and sovereign state governments, which provides that some functions will be performed by the national government, some by the state governments, and some by both the national and state governments. As a feature designed to limit the strength of government, federalism works to decentralize power by creating dual levels of authority.

The Federalist A collection of essays written by Alexander Hamilton, James Madison, and John Jay in an effort to persuade a reluctant public to support the Constitution.

filibuster The strategy available to senators to delay or derail legislation by refusing to relinquish their time on the Senate floor. The filibuster is possible only in the Senate, where rules permit unlimited time for debate.

fireside chats The term given to Franklin Roosevelt's radio addresses to the American public, which demonstrated Roosevelt's ability to master the medium and build a sense of rapport with ordinary Americans.

First Continental Congress A gathering of representatives from twelve of the thirteen colonies in Philadelphia in 1774 to protest the Coercive Acts and chart a unified colonial response.

focus groups A small group of voters chosen by a political campaign for their demographic similarities who are brought together to gauge how the group they represent feels about the candidate.

frame The frame of reference for a news story, or the context around which the facts of a story are organized. If a news story is thematic, like most television news stories, the frame determines what the specific theme of the story will be.

free exercise clause The language in the First Amendment that limits government interference in private religious beliefs and practices.

free media The news coverage that major candidates for high office can expect to receive on a regular basis. Although free, candidates cannot control the content of this coverage or guarantee that it will be favorable.

free rider Someone who is sympathetic to the objectives of an interest group and enjoys the benefits produced by that group without making a contribution. Accordingly, he or she "rides free" on the backs of dues-paying members.

freedom rides A type of civil disobedience popular with civil rights protesters, where mixed-race groups of bus passengers would ride through the South and disobey laws on racially segregated travel, often at the expense of submitting to mob violence.

front-runner The presidential candidate who leads the primary horserace, based on media assessments of the campaign.

G

gatekeepers Television producers, newspaper editors, and prestigious reporters and anchors who make the decisions about what stories will be published or aired. Think of the imagery of a guard who decides who will be allowed to pass through a gate. In this case, news gatekeepers determine which information will be allowed to pass through the medium.

gender gap A difference in the voting pattern of men and women, evident since 1980, whereby men are more likely than women to support Republican presidential candidates.

General Agreement on Tariffs and Trade (GATT) The 1948 treaty establishing the rules for free trade, which has been revised and dramatically expanded, most recently during the Uruguay round of trade negotiations (1986–1994). GATT was also the name of the international organization that oversaw the treaty; the World Trade Organization (WTO) replaced it in 1995.

General Service (GS) The system of eighteen grade levels (GS1 through GS18) that determine the pay level of white-collar civil servants.

generational effects Historical influences felt by an entire generation during their formative years, which shape the way they are socialized to politics .

gerrymandering Drawing district lines in a way that favors the electoral prospects of the party in power.

Gibbons v. Ogden The Supreme Court case, heard by the Marshall Court in 1824, that established the federal government's primacy in regulating interstate commerce, saying that the state of New York could not grant an exclusive license to a steamboat company operating between New York and New Jersey.

Gideon v. Wainwright The 1963 Supreme Court case that established the right to have an attorney appointed at no charge by the court to defendants unable to afford representation. It was brought by Clarence Earl Gideon, who was sentenced to five years in prison for breaking into a pool hall. From prison, Gideon filed a *habeas corpus* petition, claiming his right to an attorney was violated because he was forced by poverty to represent himself at his trial.

"go native" The tendency for political appointees to adhere to the organizational culture of the department they are sent to run, making them advocates of the department rather than advocates of the president.

going public The presidential strategy of using the media to appeal directly to the public to support presidential initiatives.

goldplating Government purchasing of top-of-the-line items at maximum cost, which can happen when bureaucrats overseeing purchasing decisions have an interest in the items being purchased.

government corporations Corporations established by Congress to perform important services, like delivering the mail and operating rail lines, which could not be or were not profitably provided by private corporations.

Great Society The name given to the programs of President Lyndon B. Johnson, which elevated the federal government to the most prominent role it would play in the twentieth century. The philosophy of the Great Society was that government should try to solve large social problems like hunger and poverty.

gridlock The term given to legislative inaction, when members of Congress are unable to reach agreement and legislation stalls.

gross domestic product (GDP) A measure of national productivity, the gross domestic product is the total value of goods and services produced by a nation during a fixed period of time.

H

hard money Funds contributed directly to candidates or national parties by individuals or PACs for the purpose of electing candidates to federal office. Federal law regulates hard-money contributions.

hard news Traditional news items that derive their value from recent, relevant events that have some bearing on the lives of readers or viewers.

Hatch Act Legislation enacted in 1939 that prohibits civil servants from engaging in political activities.

Hobbes, Thomas (1588–1679) The seventeenth-century British social thinker and author of *Leviathan* who believed that people need to trade off liberty for a strong government that can protect their fundamental right to live.

home style The way legislators approach constituents, determined partly by how they size up their support in the district.

honeymoon The initial weeks of a new presidential administration when enthusiasm and good press typically translate into high public-approval ratings.

horserace That element of a political campaign that deals with winning and losing, whether a candidate is leading or trailing an opponent, and what the candidate may be doing to improve or solidify his or her electoral prospects.

I

ideological parties Third parties that form around a broad ideology not represented by the two major American parties. They endure from election to election despite the fact that they rarely achieve electoral success.

ideology A wide-ranging set of beliefs that logically fit together.

impeachment The power granted to Congress to remove from office the president, vice president, judges, and other federal officials.

implementation The bureaucratic function of taking the legal language of legislation and turning it into functioning programs.

implied powers The broad constitutional grant of power to Congress that allows it to make all laws that are "necessary and proper" to carry out its enumerated functions.

incumbent An official presently serving in office.

independent agencies Bureaucratic organizations that report directly to the president rather than through cabinet secretaries, and whose administrators serve at the pleasure of the president.

independent regulatory commissions and boards Panels designed to oversee the conduct of various segments of the economy. Members are appointed by the president and confirmed by the Senate. They serve fixed terms and cannot be removed by the president.

Indian Removal Act Legislation passed in 1830 that led to the forced and sometimes violent transfer of Native American nations to areas west of the Mississippi River.

influence The ability to shape political outcomes to your liking.

infotainment News reports and information-based programs that use information to entertain by playing on sensational topics, such as celebrities, violence, and the like.

inside strategies Lobbying approaches that rely on direct relationships between lobbyists and officials.

institutional patriotism The legislative norm that precludes members of Congress from acting or speaking in ways that would discredit the institution.

integrity A key component of reciprocity in which members of Congress are expected to keep their word with each other and honor their commitments.

intensity An aspect of public opinion that measures how strongly people feel toward a political figure, institution, or policy.

interest aggregation The process by which groups with different and potentially conflicting agendas are brought together under the umbrella of a political party.

interest groups Organized associations that seek to promote common objectives through government action.

inverted pyramid A style of reporting typical of twentieth-century newspaper coverage, in which stories were constructed with the most important factual material in the first paragraph, followed by successively less important facts.

iron triangle The ongoing, mutually beneficial relationship among an interest group, members of Congress sharing the interest group's objectives, and bureaucrats in federal agencies responsible for carrying out legislation pertaining to the interest group's field. Iron triangles can develop in any policy area, and many distinct iron-triangle relationships form because the federal government is responsible for a large number of policies.

issue network A fluid policy community permeable to a wide range of interest groups, permitting a broad array of policy outcomes.

issue voting Choosing a candidate in an election on the basis of his or her proximity to your position on an issue or issues you consider important.

J

Jim Crow laws Laws in place in the South through the middle portion of the twentieth century that legalized segregation in virtually every facet of life.

Joint Chiefs of Staff The group of military advisors comprised of the heads of the army, air force, navy, and marines.

joint committees Committees composed of members of the House and Senate that consider matters of interest to both houses.

judicial activism The philosophy that the Court should take an aggressive posture toward politics and the law, striking down presidential and congressional actions whenever it is deemed necessary and instituting far-reaching remedies to social wrongs.

judicial restraint The philosophy that the Court should defer to the other branches of government and only overturn legislation when it is clearly unconstitutional.

judicial review The authority of the Supreme Court to overrule actions of Congress or the president by declaring them to be unconstitutional.

judiciary The federal and state court systems charged with resolving legal and personal disputes and interpreting the law.

Judiciary Act of 1789 The act of Congress that established the federal court system. It initially called for a six-person Supreme Court and three circuit courts, each to be administered by two Supreme Court justices and one district court judge.

jurisdiction The authority of a court to hear a case.

K

"Know-Nothing" movement An anti-Catholic movement that formed in the 1840s as a reaction to the first large wave of Irish immigration.

Ku Klux Klan The secret white supremacist society that terrorized and killed African Americans for decades following the Civil War.

L

legal system The web of institutions and individuals involved in bringing legal and personal disputes to the attention of the courts.

legislative liaison White House lobbyists who maintain regular contacts with members of Congress and congressional committees, in order to help guide the president's legislative agenda.

legislative work The legislative norm that members of Congress should stay on top of the work required by the committee that deals with their area of specialization.

legitimacy Widespread public acceptance of the official standing of a political figure or institution.

libel The legal restriction against the malicious publication of material that knowingly damages an individual's reputation.

liberalism An ideology that advocates the use of government power to address economic and social problems, like unemployment and environmental protection, while limiting government involvement in moral matters like abortion rights and prayer in public schools.

libertarianism An ideology centered on the reduction of government power to advance personal liberty.

liberty The ability to pursue your ends and objectives, tempered by socially defined boundaries and limited government impediments.

life cycle effects Changes to the way we relate to politics and society that naturally occur during the course of aging, which typically leave us less open to political and social change as we get older.

limited government The idea that power can be denied to government and the people who serve in it, in order to restrict those in positions of authority from infringing upon individual liberty.

lobbying Attempting to influence the content of policy by exerting influence on government officials.

lobbyists Professionals hired by interest groups to influence the political process on behalf of the group.

Locke, John (1632–1704) A seventeenth-century British social contract theorist whose ideas about government getting its authority from the consent of the governed in order to protect fundamental human rights greatly influenced the leaders of the American Revolution.

logrolling A form of reciprocity in which members of Congress exhibit mutual cooperation for each other's pet projects.

long shot A presidential candidate who is not expected to fare well in the primary horserace, based on media assessments of the campaign.

M

majoritarian principle Procedures, such as those in place in the House of Representatives, that limit the ability of the minority party to influence the shape of legislation or the direction of the legislative agenda.

majority Winning more than half the votes in an election, or 50 percent plus one.

majority leader The number-two leadership position in the House of Representatives and the number-one leadership position in the Senate. In the House, the majority leader is the chief assistant to the Speaker; in the Senate, the majority leader is the chief leader on a par with the House Speaker.

majority whip The number-three leadership position in the House of Representatives and the number-two leadership position in the Senate. In both instances, the whip is responsible for mobilizing party members to support the leadership on key issues.

mandate A directive by voters to the president to move ahead with the program he promised when he was a candidate. A large mandate produced by a lopsided vote gives the president a strong bargaining position with respect to Congress to set and advance the agenda in Washington.

Marbury v. Madison The Supreme Court case, heard by the Marshall Court in 1803, that established judicial review.

mass media Vehicles, such as television, radio, newspapers, magazines, and the Internet, capable of rapidly communicating information to large numbers of people over large distances. Note that *media* is the plural form of *medium*: Television is a medium, whereas television and the Internet are media.

McCain-Feingold Act The name commonly used to describe the Bipartisan Campaign Reform Act of 2002, which prohibits the use of soft money in federal elections in an attempt to close a loophole in the 1974 Federal Election Campaign Act.

McCulloch v. Maryland The 1819 Supreme Court case that established federal supremacy over the state governments.

McGovern-Fraser Commission The commission organized by the Democratic Party following its 1968 convention to democratize the process of delegate selection to party conventions.

means test Eligibility requirements placed on social welfare programs aiding the poor, which restrict participation to individuals whose incomes fall below set levels.

media events Activities staged by campaigns or political officials that have enough news value to draw press attention to a message the politician wants to communicate.

Medicare The federal social welfare program that provides hospital and supplementary medical insurance to senior citizens and the disabled.

merit system Procedures for hiring civil servants based on objective evaluations of their performance rather than on their political connections.

minority leader The number-one leadership position for the opposition party in the House of Representatives and Senate, whose responsibilities mirror those of the majority leader but without the ability to set or advance the legislative agenda.

minority rights Procedures, such as those in place in the Senate, that permit members of the minority party the opportunity to resist legislative actions they oppose.

minority whip The number-two leadership position for the opposition party in the House of Representatives and Senate, whose responsibilities mirror those of the majority whip.

Miranda rights The Court requirement, following a judgment in the case *Miranda v. Arizona* (1966), that apprehended individuals know and understand that they have a right against self-incrimination and a right to be represented by an attorney.

momentum The ability of a presidential campaign to maintain viability by meeting or exceeding press-generated expectations during the long primary period.

Montesquieu, Baron de (1689–1755) An eighteenth-century French political theorist whose ideas about decentralizing power to ensure personal liberty greatly influenced the government created by the Constitution.

muckraking Investigative reporting prevalent during the turn of the twentieth century, which centered on uncovering corruption in government and industry for the purpose of promoting progressive reforms.

multimember district The structure of electoral districts in proportional representation systems, in which each electoral district sends several representatives to the legislature.

multiparty system Political systems in which more than two parties have a realistic chance to win representation in government.

N

name recognition An informal measure of how much the public is aware of a candidate or elected official, based on how widely people are able to identify the candidate or official.

narrowcasting Programming oriented to a small segment of viewers, like that found on cable television stations. It contrasts with broadcasting, like that found on traditional television networks, which seeks to reach a larger audience with programming that has wide appeal.

nation-centered federalism One of several perspectives on federalism, which argues for the supremacy of the Constitution and federal law over state actions.

national debt The amount the government borrows to pay for accumulated budget deficits.

National Organization for Women (NOW) The largest women's rights organization in the United States, which has been an active force for advancing social and economic equality for women.

national security advisor The president's counselor on national security matters. In some administrations, the national security advisor has competed with the secretary of state for the president's attention.

National Security Council (NSC) The group of senior policy advisors responsible for helping the president shape national security policy.

national supremacy The doctrine that the federal government has the final word in disputes with the states. National supremacy was established through court rulings, precedent, and the victory of the North in the Civil War, eventually resolving the conflict between nation-centered federalism and state-centered federalism in favor of the former.

National Voter Registration Act Passed in 1993 to simplify and standardize voter registration requirements, the "Motor Voter Act" allows residents of most states to register to vote at the same time as they apply for or renew their driver's license. It also provides for a standardized, national registration form that can be downloaded from the Internet.

natural rights Inalienable rights inherent to every individual that cannot be taken away by individuals or government, and that government should be designed to protect.

"necessary and proper" clause A constitutional provision (Article I, Section 8) giving Congress a broad grant of authority to make laws that are binding on the states.

neutral competence The philosophy guiding nineteenth-century civil service reform, which states that bureaucrats should be chosen strictly for their ability to perform their job, without political criteria influencing their selection or their actions.

New Deal The name given to the programs of President Franklin D. Roosevelt, which vastly expanded the role of the federal government in an effort to deal with the debilitating effects of the Great Depression on American society.

New Federalism The name given to the programs of Presidents Richard M. Nixon and Ronald Reagan, which started as an effort to streamline the federal government produced by the Great Society and ended up as a movement to reverse fifty years of federal growth by returning authority to the states.

New Jersey Plan A proposal for the new Constitution, supported by small states, that would have provided for equal representation of large and small states in the national legislature, while limiting the power of the national government over the states.

news cycle The time between when an event happens and when it gets press coverage. With twenty-four-hour news services setting the pace, the demand for new information is enormous and immediate, greatly accelerating the news cycle.

news leaks The tactic used widely by White House officials of releasing information to the press on an anonymous basis when it serves their interests to have the information publicized. Some leaks are unauthorized and unwanted by the White House.

newsworthy The conditions under which a story warrants publication or dissemination, based on a set of values applied by newspaper editors and television producers. Newsworthy stories typically have conflict, proximity, and relevance to the audience, timeliness, and familiarity.

nomination The official endorsement of a candidate by a political party, making that candidate the one whose name will appear on the ballot next to the party label in the next general election.

nongovernmental organizations (NGOs) Nonprofit organizations that promote interests with global ramifications on the world stage.

normative Any statement that invokes a judgment or evaluation. Think of the word *norm*, which implies a standard for evaluating something.

norms Unspoken rules of behavior that people adhere to in an institution like Congress that allow people to fit in and help the institution run smoothly.

North American Free Trade Agreement (NAFTA) A landmark free trade agreement setting up a regional free trade zone in North America.

North Atlantic Treaty Organization (NATO) An alliance of the United States, Canada, and Western European nations originally designed as a military pact to counter Soviet expansion. Following the Cold War, it has grown to include European nations once aligned with the Soviet Union.

O

Office of Management and Budget (OMB) The executive office responsible for developing the president's annual budget proposals by evaluating requests for funding among departments and setting the president's spending priorities.

original jurisdiction The authority of the U.S. Supreme Court to be the first court to hear a case, precluding the need for an appeal from a lower court. The Constitution grants original jurisdiction to cases involving a dispute between the United States and a state; two or more states; citizens of different states; a state and a citizen of another state; and foreign ambassadors.

outside strategies Lobbying approaches that rely on mobilizing group members to influence the actions of officials.

override The congressional power to overturn a presidential veto by a two-thirds vote of both houses of Congress.

oversight The process of congressional review of the bureaucracy.

P

paid media Radio and television ads paid for and produced by political campaigns.

pardon power The unilateral power of the president to grant unconditional clemency to anyone for any reason.

party caucus The group of all members of a political party in the House or Senate that meets to discuss and formulate legislative priorities.

party identification An individual's association with a political party. The most common parties Americans identify with are the two major parties, Republican and Democrat. Party identification—also called party I.D.—varies in intensity such that it may be strong or weak. Those who do not identify with any party are typically called independents.

party in government That component of political parties composed of elected officials that organizes and runs our governing institutions like Congress, the presidency, state governorships and assemblies, and the like.

party in the electorate Party identifiers who make up the rank-and-file membership of the political parties.

party press Newspapers functioning as an arm of a political party, communicating information about partisan politics from party leaders to their supporters. Newspapers functioned in this capacity from the inception of political parties in America around 1790 through the 1830s.

party system The regular, over-time competition of the same major political parties, composed of the same groups of identifiers.

patronage Jobs, favors, and other resources that party officials provide in exchange for people's political support.

Pendleton Act The 1883 law requiring that merit-based criteria be used to hire public employees, ending the tradition of patronage appointments.

penny press High-circulation newspapers, emerging after 1830, that kept costs down by selling advertising. These newspapers brought in large numbers of readers with lurid and sensational reporting.

persuasion An informal source of presidential power that gives skilled presidents the opportunity to influence the decisions of members of Congress and others in Washington whose support the president needs to accomplish his political objectives.

photo opportunities Staged appearances by politicians in visually appealing settings designed to produce images that will be widely disseminated in the press.

platform The official document produced at the major party conventions that serves as a philosophical and policy blueprint for the party's presidential nominee.

plea bargain A compromise between a defendant, defense attorney, and prosecutor, whereby the defendant foregoes due process and agrees to plead guilty without a trial to a lesser charge in exchange for a more lenient punishment.

Plessy v. Ferguson The 1896 Supreme Court case that upheld racial segregation. It was reversed in 1954 in the case of *Brown v. Board of Education*.

Plum Book The congressional publication listing all top-level political positions in the bureaucracy.

pluralism The theory that government responds to individuals through their memberships in groups, assuring that government is responsive to a wide range of voices. People who subscribe to this position believe that the wide distribution of resources in society drives the decisions government officials make.

plurality Winning the most votes in an election, or at least one more vote than the next closest candidate or party.

pocket veto The presidential prerogative to veto a bill without taking action. Presidents may issue pocket vetoes only if Congress has passed legislation within ten days of adjournment. A pocket veto cannot be overridden.

political action committees (PACs) Organizations formed by interest groups such as labor unions, businesses, and ideological groups for the purpose of contributing money to political candidates.

political appointees Top-level bureaucratic officials whom the president appoints, typically pending Senate confirmation, and who serve at the pleasure of the president.

political culture The common set of attitudes, beliefs, and values that provide the foundation of support for a political system.

political equality Establishing political and legal rights on the basis of the individual, so that everyone has the same right to vote and is equal under the law. An alternative would be to grant political rights to elite individuals based on wealth or social standing.

political machines The name given to urban political parties that used patronage to overrun their competition and maintain power.

political participation The range of activities people can engage in to influence the political process. While voting is the most commonly performed political act, participation encompasses a host of things—from writing letters to public officials to contributing time or money to a campaign or protesting the actions of government.

political party An organized group of individuals with common interests seeking to gain power in government by electing officials to public office.

political socialization The process by which we acquire political knowledge, attitudes, and beliefs.

politics The process of determining who gets what, when, and how.

popular sovereignty Rule by the people based on the consent of the governed.

popular vote The votes individuals cast in a presidential election. Technically, these are votes for a slate of electors representing the candidate. A candidate who wins a plurality of the popular vote in a state gets all the electoral votes allocated to that state.

pork barrel Wasteful or unnecessary spending that can result from logrolling. Whether something is a pork-barrel project or a valuable use of taxpayer dollars may depend on whether you stand to benefit from it.

poverty line A statistical determination of poverty based on income and family size that is used to establish eligibility for some social welfare programs designed to assist those in need.

power The ability to make others act in a way that they otherwise might not have done.

president *pro tempore* The senator charged with the honorary duty of presiding over the Senate in the absence of the vice president of the United States.

press briefings Formal exchanges of information between the press secretary and the national press covering the president.

press conferences Scheduled meetings between reporters and political figures like the president, which give the press access to the official and an opportunity to ask him or her questions firsthand.

press secretary The liaison between the White House and the national press covering the president.

pressure groups Another term for interest groups that emphasizes the demands interest groups make on the political system.

primary A method of candidate selection in which party identifiers vote for the candidate who will run on the party label in the general election. In presidential primaries, voters select delegates to the national convention.

primary agent of socialization Parents and siblings exert disproportional influence on the political development of children by virtue of the initial influence they have on kids, giving the family a primary role in the process of political socialization.

priming A media effect whereby the context in which a political figure is presented in the news can create a positive or negative cue for how viewers think about and evaluate that figure.

prior restraint Censorship of the news by government officials before it is published or broadcast.

professional reputation The sense among Washington officials of the president's political skills and abilities. It is one of the keys to effective persuasion, as it enhances the president's ability to bargain.

progressive income tax A tax structure with graduated income rates designed to increase the tax burden on higher-income earners.

proportional representation Electoral systems that encourage the participation of many parties by awarding representation on the basis of the share of the vote won by each party in an electoral district.

protectionism The policy of raising the price of imported goods through tariffs in order to make them less attractive than domestic products.

protective regulatory policy Regulations that supply consumers with information needed to make informed purchasing decisions about such things as cigarettes and home loans or that prevent undesirable personal or social conditions like child labor or unsafe food.

public opinion A collection of opinions people hold on matters relating to government, politics, and society.

public prestige The sense among Washington officials about whether the president is well regarded by the public. It is one of the keys to effective persuasion, as it enhances the president's ability to bargain.

public works Civic projects built with tax dollars.

purposive benefit The gratification an interest group member gets by contributing to a cause.

push polls Surveys that appear legitimate but in fact are a dirty campaign trick designed to generate negative opinion about an opponent in a political contest.

Q

Quartering Act An act of the British Parliament requiring colonists to house British troops; first imposed in 1765 and then again in 1774 as part of the Coercive Acts.

R

racial gerrymandering Drawing district lines in a way that combines disparate populations of minority groups in order to guarantee representation by those groups in Congress.

rally effect The tendency for Americans to unite around the president during a crisis, temporarily bolstering his job-approval ratings.

random sample The basis for a scientifically accurate public opinion poll, in which everyone in the community being polled has an equal chance of being selected to give their opinions to pollsters. In a poll of national opinion, everyone in the country would have to have an equal chance of being selected to participate in it.

ranking minority member The minority party counterpart to the committee chair, but without the power to influence the direction of the committee .

realignment A shift from one party system to another, the result of a lasting, long-term adjustment in the groups that identify with the major political parties.

recess appointments The constitutional power granted to the president to make nominations while Congress is out of session that do not require Senate approval. The appointments stand until the end of the congressional term.

reciprocity The legislative norm that encourages members of Congress to support each other's initiatives, even if there is no direct political benefit in doing so.

reconciliation A procedure in the budget-writing process, whereby appropriations made in a number of congressional committees and subcommittees need to be brought in line with spending targets established early in the process.

Reconstruction The period following the Civil War, from 1865 to 1877, during which Union troops occupied the South as states of the Confederacy were readmitted to the Union under conditions established in Washington.

redistributive policies Domestic policies, like those promoting social welfare, that take resources from one group in the form of taxes and provide goods or services for another group, typically those in need.

redistricting The process by which congressional districts are redrawn every ten years following the release of new census data.

Reform Party The organization built by businessman Ross Perot in a mostly unsuccessful attempt to create a competitive third party.

Regents of the University of California v. Bakke The 1978 Supreme Court case that marked a reversal in unlimited support for affirmative action policies by backing the claim of discrimination by a white University of California medical school applicant who was denied admission in favor of less well-qualified minority applicants.

regressive tax A tax structure that increases the tax burden on lower-income earners. Sales taxes are regressive because as incomes decline, the tax becomes a larger percentage of total income, and therefore, a greater burden.

regulation The bureaucratic function of placing standards or restrictions on the actions of private individuals or companies in order to protect the general welfare of the public.

regulatory policies Domestic policies designed to protect the public from harmful conditions that could result from unrestrained free-market competition or to ensure the benefits of a level playing field for private competition.

Reinventing Government The name given to President Bill Clinton's initiative to make the federal government smaller by making it more efficient.

Religious Right Ideological interest groups promoting a conservative political agenda consistent with an evangelical religious perspective.

representative democracy A form of democracy in which eligible individuals choose others to make decisions on their behalf.

republic Any nation with provisions for the selection of representatives who make decisions on behalf of those who select them. James Madison said a republic was "a government in which the scheme of representation takes place," as compared to direct democracy.

resources Anything of value to others that can be used to sway another individual.

responsible parties Political parties whose legislative members act in concert, taking clear positions on issues and voting as a unit in accordance with their stated positions.

retrospective voting Evaluating the past performance of an incumbent to make a judgment about the future—whether the incumbent should be retained or replaced.

revolving door A consequence of the close relationships between interest groups and government officials that makes it possible for lobbyists to become government officials charged with regulating the organizations they once worked for, or for government officials to become lobbyists who influence friends in their former agency.

right to privacy The protection against government interference in private matters, which is not specifically guaranteed by the Constitution but which has been established by the Court and used to legalize contraception and abortion.

Roe v. Wade The 1973 Supreme Court case that found a constitutional right to privacy applied to reproductive issues, striking down all state laws that prohibited abortions during the first trimester of pregnancy.

Rules Committee The committee of the House that channels legislation to the floor for debate and a vote on passage.

S

Second Continental Congress A gathering of representatives from the colonies in Philadelphia in 1775, necessitated by the need to coordinate planning during the Revolutionary War, that functioned as the first central government in colonial America.

secondary agent of socialization Schools and the media have an effect on political socialization, but the effect is less than from primary agents like the family because we do not form close interpersonal bonds with either institution.

secretary of state The head of the Department of State, who functions as the president's chief foreign policy advisor.

select committee A House or Senate committee established on a temporary basis to review a specific matter. Typically, select committees make recommendations but do not move legislation.

selective benefits Incentives offered exclusively to interest group members as a means of getting people to join.

selective exposure The tendency to pay attention to messages that are consistent with existing attitudes or beliefs, while overlooking messages that conflict with them.

selective perception An unconscious process by which we filter information that we deem irrelevant, uninteresting, or inconsistent with our attitudes and beliefs, while absorbing information that conforms to our self-perception.

senatorial courtesy The custom that presidents will defer to the wishes of senators from a judicial nominee's home state before making a court appointment.

Senior Executive Service (SES) The payment scale used for a small group of upper-level government managers and technical experts. Most positions covered by the Senior Executive Service are in the civil service, although the SES covers select political appointees whose jobs do not require Senate confirmation.

seniority The custom of awarding committee chairs on the basis of length of service.

separation of powers The division of political power among several equal and independent branches of government to prevent power from being consolidated in any one branch.

Shays' Rebellion A rebellion by debtor farmers in western Massachusetts, led by Revolutionary War Captain Daniel Shays, against Boston creditors. It began in 1786 and lasted half a year, threatening the economic interests of the business elite and contributing to the demise of the Articles of Confederation.

single-issue parties Third parties that form to advance a specific issue agenda, like environmentalism, that members feel is not being adequately addressed by the two major American parties. They endure from election to election despite the fact that they rarely achieve electoral success .

single-member district The structure of electoral districts in winner-take-all electoral systems, in which each electoral district sends only one representative to the legislature.

sit-ins A type of civil disobedience popular with civil rights protesters that involved African Americans peacefully sitting at "Whites Only" lunch counters, to focus attention on the injustice of segregation policies.

social contract The arrangement in which people agree to give up some of their liberty to establish a government that will protect basic rights that are threatened in the state of nature.

social desirability bias A form of error in public opinion polls, whereby opinions or behaviors that could be considered undesirable are not fully reported in the data.

social equality A form of equality of outcome that values using government policy to minimize social class distinctions found in society.

social responsibility Concern for the protection of the rights of individuals in a community or society, at the expense of some degree of personal liberty.

Social Security The popular social welfare program that provides benefits to retirees regardless of need. Social Security also offers insurance payments to families of deceased workers and disability payments to impaired workers.

socialism A left-leaning ideology centered on the use of government power to advance equal outcomes.

socioeconomic status (SES) A measure of an individual's social position based primarily on education, income, and occupation. High socioeconomic status individuals are more likely to have advanced education, high incomes, and occupations that award high status and demand great responsibility, like professional or managerial work. The abbreviation for socioeconomic status is SES.

soft money Funds contributed to state and local parties or to national parties for the purpose of running state elections or conducting local "grassroots" political activity.

soft news Feature stories, stories about celebrities, and other news items that do not derive their news value from proximity, timeliness, or relevance to the reader or viewer.

solicitor general The White House official responsible for arguing on behalf of the United States in Supreme Court cases where the United States is a party.

Speaker of the House The leader of the majority party in the House of Representatives who exercises control over the operation of that branch through formal and informal means.

special interest groups Another term for interest groups that emphasizes the narrow scope of their concerns.

specialization The legislative norm that members of Congress should become experts in a legislative field.

spin A technique used by political figures to characterize events in a favorable way in order to get the media to report them in a favorable way—regardless of what the facts of a story may indicate.

splinter parties Third parties that split away from one of the major parties in protest against the direction taken by the Republicans or Democrats. They often form around a charismatic leader and last a short time, after which the major parties address their concerns and they lose their reason to continue.

spoils system The method of staffing the federal bureaucracy, commonplace in the nineteenth century, in which the president offered patronage appointments to political supporters.

stability An aspect of public opinion that measures how much change or variability there is in the way people feel toward a political figure, institution, or policy.

Stamp Act A particularly vexing tax levied by the British on scores of legal documents, which led to a colonial boycott of British goods.

standard operating procedures (SOPs) Guidelines that provide uniformity to bureaucratic decision making.

standing committees Permanent congressional committees that handle matters related to a specific legislative topic.

stare decisis Literally, "let the decision stand," it is a guiding principle of judicial interpretation that places a premium on letting previous judicial rulings guide current rulings.

state of nature The condition of total liberty in which people are free to act on their impulses, but where individual rights are afforded no protection.

state-centered federalism One of several perspectives on federalism, which argues that the Constitution and the federal government are creations of the states and therefore can be overruled by the states.

structural bias The possibility that news stories are skewed toward the limited set of sources and topics selected by gatekeepers for publication and broadcast.

Student Nonviolent Coordinating Committee (SNCC) The organization that involved college students in acts of civil disobedience to advance the cause of civil rights for African Americans.

subcommittees Subunits of standing committees that do the detail work involved in writing legislation.

subgovernments Another term for iron triangles, which captures the specialized (and often hidden) relationship among lobbyists, members of Congress, and bureaucrats, who share mutual professional and policy interests and objectives.

substantive representation The ability of a legislator to represent the agenda or interests of a group to which he or she does not personally belong.

Sugar Act The first in a string of taxes levied by Great Britain on the American colonies. Formally called the American Revenue Act of 1764, it taxed a number of colonial imports, including sugar.

supremacy clause A constitutional provision (Article VI) establishing the relationship between the federal and state governments. The supremacy clause asserts that any conflict between the federal government and the states will be decided in favor of the federal government.

T

tariff A tax on imports designed to raise their cost and make them less competitive than domestic products, in an effort to protect the jobs of domestic workers.

tax expenditures Tax breaks in the form of exemptions targeted at groups of taxpayers or, in the case of corporate taxes, at specific industries.

Telecommunications Act of 1996 Legislation that overhauled the Federal Communications Act of 1934 by deregulating a range of communications technologies in an effort to promote competition in the development and provision of telecommunications services. If your local telephone company offers long-distance service, or if your cable television provider also offers high-speed Internet access, it's because the opportunity for them to do so was made possible by this law.

tenure Job security afforded to civil servants following a probationary period, to protect them against losing their jobs for political reasons.

Three-Fifths Compromise A compromise between northern and southern states that broke the deadlock over how slaves should be counted for purposes of representation. Three-fifths of slaves would be included in population totals, benefiting southern states that had the largest concentration of slaves by inflating their representation in the House of Representatives .

ticket splitting Voting for candidates of different parties for different offices, rather than voting a "party line" for all Republicans or all Democrats. Ticket splitting, which has increased in recent years, is a sign of how Americans have been growing independent from political parties.

trade associations Groups that advance the concerns of specific business interests, such as banks, energy companies, real estate firms, and car manufacturers.

trade deficit A negative balance between the value of goods and services purchased from foreign nations and the value of goods and services sold to foreign nations.

"Trail of Tears" A one-thousand-mile forced march of Cherokee men, women, and children carried out in 1838 to satisfy a federal relocation policy.

transfer payments The direct payment of public money to individuals who qualify for it under the terms of a social welfare program.

trustee A philosophy of representation that says officials are elected for their wisdom and to exercise their judgment of the national interest, even when it is at odds with their constituents' wishes.

two-party system A political system, like ours in the United States, in which only two parties have a realistic chance to win most elections.

tyranny The denial of liberty to individuals through the actions of a faction or through the actions of government.

U

unitary system The inverse of a confederal system, in which a centralized national government creates subnational units like states, provinces, and counties, which derive their authority from the national government. Most nations are unitary systems. In the United States, the relationship between each individual state and its counties, townships, and cities is a unitary relationship, with the states creating and empowering the local governments.

United States v. Nixon The 1974 case in which a unanimous Supreme Court ruled that President Nixon could not use executive privilege to protect the secrecy of incriminating tapes documenting his involvement in the cover-up of the Watergate break-in.

V

veto power The constitutional power granted to the president to block an act of Congress. It takes a two-thirds vote of both houses of Congress to override a presidential veto.

Virginia Plan A proposal for the new Constitution, supported by large states, that would have based representation on population and provided for a centralized national government that could overrule the states.

Voting Rights Act of 1965 Landmark legislation arising from the civil rights movement that gave federal officials the power to oversee election practices in southern states where Jim Crow laws disenfranchised African American voters.

W

War Powers Act of 1973 A congressional attempt to reassert the role of the legislature with respect to the president in military affairs by restricting the president's ability to wage war.

White House Office That portion of the Executive Office of the President organized to serve the president's immediate needs.

winner-take-all system The electoral system in use in the United States, whereby the candidate of the party receiving the most votes in an electoral district gets to represent that district.

World Trade Organization (WTO) The international organization responsible for promoting free trade among nations and settling trade disputes.

writ of *certiorari* An order issued by the Supreme Court demanding a lower court turn over all records of a case that the Supreme Court has decided to hear on appeal.

writ of *habeas corpus* From the Latin for "you have the body," *habeas corpus* puts the burden on the courts to demonstrate that a defendant's rights have not been violated prior to sentencing. People who believe they have been imprisoned against their constitutional rights have the privilege to petition for their release.

writ of *mandamus* A court order commanding a public official to perform an official act.

Y

yellow journalism The term given to the sensational newspaper coverage prevalent during the turn of the twentieth century, noteworthy for its emphasis on violence, sex, human-interest stories, and exposés of official corruption.

Z

zero-sum policy A policy debate in which any victory by one side comes at the expense of the opposing side, negating the possibility of compromise.

Name Index

W

Wagner, John, 162*n*T4
Walker, Jack, 254*n*25
Walker, Thomas G., 396, 397*n*59
Walsh, Deirdre, 295*n*19
Walters, Everett, 192*n*T5
Warrick, Joby, 491*n*22
Washington Post, 6, 148–149, 203, 245, 335*n*47, 397*n*48
Washington Representatives, 245
Washington State Democrats online newsroom, 470*n*T15
Watson, Libby, 225*n*14
Watson, Mary Ann, 161*n*56
Wattenberg, Martin P., 191, 192*n*23
Weber, Max, 7, 339
Weigel, David, 295*n*7
Weinger, Mackenzie, 124*n*37
Weingroff, Richard R., 470*n*T9
Welsh-Huggins, Andrew, 226*n*T10
White House, 192*n*13, 423*n*5
White, Graham J., 161*n*55
Wicker, Tom, 193*n*T9

Wildavsky, Aaron, 225, 225*nn*19, 20, 23, 226*n*T6, 320–321, 335*nn*41, 42, 46
Wilentz, Sean, 192*n*T3
William McKinley Biographical Resources, 192*n*T5
Wilson, David, 226*n*T2
Wilson, George C., 490, 491*n*25
Wilson, James Q., 339, 340, 363, 363*nn*7, 8, 33, 34, 37, 38, 364*nn*T9, T10
Wilson, Joan Hoff, 192*n*T6
Winfield, Betty Houchin, 161*n*53
Winkler, Allan M., 193*n*T7
Wittenberg, Elisabeth, 255*n*33
Wittenberg, Ernest, 255*n*33
Woliver, Laura R., 255*n*T10
Wolpe, Bruce C., 246, 254, 254*n*31, 255*nn*47, T9
Women's Bureau, 23*n*11
World Trade Organization, 491*nn*14, 15
Wright, David, 23*n*T4
WXYZ-TV-Detroit, 160*n*14

Z

Zeleny, Jeff, 161*n*42

Subject Index

Page numbers in italics identify illustrations. An italic *t* next to a page number (e.g., 241*t*) indicates information that appears in a table. An italic *n* and number following a page number (e.g., 241*n*13) indicate information that appears in an end-of-chapter note and the number of the note where the material can be found.

A

AARP, 238, 240
ABC News, 128
ABC television network, 143, *144*
Ablington Township School District v. Schempp, 432
Abortion debate
 entry of new interest groups, 249
 as issue in Supreme Court nomination, 382, 389, 392, 441
 judicial precedents in, 389
 language of, 39
 lobbying in, 234, 249
 as privacy issue, 440–441
 varying beliefs in, 71–72
Access to public officials, 238–239
Accounting scandals, 228
Activism, judicial, 391–393
Adams, John, 222, 322, 334*n*5, 369, 370
Administration, as function of bureaucracy, 353
Administrative assistants, 284
Administrative presidency, 343, 345
Advertising
 influence on media coverage, 139–140
 negative, 216–217
 political, 145
Affective awareness, 102
Affirmative action, 408, 409
Affluence, politics of, 101–102
Affordable Care Act, 62, 209, 389
Afghanistan War
 Bush administration and, 9, 485
 civil rights and, 30, 486–487
 Obama administration and, 474
 public opinion on, 2–3, 61–62, 30
 rebuilding after, 477, 485
AFL-CIO, 232, 250
Africa, immigration from, 96
African Americans
 census undercount, 98
 civil rights struggles, 402–408, 409
 congressional caucus, 282
 death penalty discrimination, 429, 431
 earning power of, 15
 political liberalism, 98
 political participation, 109–113
 political socialization of, 105–106
 as presidential candidates, views of, 67–69
 reduced opportunity for, 17
 slavery abolished, 402
 on Supreme Court, 379–382
AFSCME (American Federation of State, County and Municipal Employees), 232
Age Discrimination in Employment Act, 420
Agenda setting, 105, 144, 154
Agents of socialization, 103–106

Agnew, Spiro, 335*n*T13
Aging, 102, 108–109
Agribusiness, 232, 460–461
Agricultural Adjustment Act of 1933, 460
Agricultural groups, 232
Agricultural subsidies, 460–461
Airline deregulation, 352–353
Alabama, current voter registration requirements, 115
Alabama Literacy Test, 112
Alaska Wilderness League, 453
Alcatraz protest, 411
Alexander, Lamar, 206
Alien Registration Act, 435
Alito, Samuel, *366*, 377, 378, 379, *381*, 392, 441
Alliances with news media, 312–313
al Odah v. U.S., 487
al-Qaeda, 70, 485
Amazon Prime, 142
Ambiguous legislation, 349–350
Amendments to Constitution
 basic provisions, 40*t*, 43*t*
 Bill of Rights origins, 40
 full text, A-11–A-17
 ratification process, 39–41
American Association of Retired Persons, 238
American Bar Association, 230, 254*n*9, 318, 379
American Ceramic Society, 229
American Civil Liberties Union, 233, 254*n*15, 487
American Communist Party, 435, 439
American Conservative Union, 243
American creed, 92–93, 97
American Farm Bureau Federation, 232
American Federation of State, County and Municipal Employees (AFSCME), 232
American flag, 93
American Institute of Certified Public Accountants, 228
American Medical Association, 230, 233, 254*n*9
American National Election Studies (ANES), 62, 63, 65, 117
American Nazi Party, 439
American Petroleum Institute, 453
American Political Science Association, 192*n*26, 237
American Political Science Review, 237
American Revenue Act, 27*t*
American Revolution, 26–28
American Society of Home Care Inspectors, 229
Americans with Disabilities Act, 418–419
The American Voter, 74
America Online, 143
Amicus curiae briefs, 375
Amtrak, 349
Anderson, John, 167, 171*t*, 171–172
ANES (American National Election Studies), 62, 63, 65, 117
Annenberg Public Policy Center, 135
Anthony, Susan B., 415
Anti-Federalists, 39–41, 45, A-25–A-26
Anti-immigration movements, 97
Apathy, 113–114
Appellate courts, 371, *372*
Appellate jurisdiction, 371
Appointments
 to bureaucracies, 340–341
 congressional confirmation, 275, 359

race and, A-27–A-28
 state-federal power distribution, 39–44
Constitutional Convention, 33–37
Constructionists, 392
Continental Congress, 27–28
Contraceptives, 440
Contract with America, 184, 250
Contribution limits, 201–205
Conventional political participation, 107
Conventions (party)
 activities, 212–214
 delegate selection, 196–201
 evolution of, 198–201
Cooperative federalism, 46
CORE (Congress of Racial Equality), 407, 423n11
Corporation for Public Broadcasting (CPB), 140
Corporate income taxes, 461–464
Corporate reform legislation, 250–251
Corporate scandals, 228
Corporate welfare, 460–461
Corporation for Public Broadcasting, 140
Corporations, foreign policy influence, 478
Cornyn, John, *280*
Costa, Antonio, 319
Council of Economic Advisors, 333
Council on Environmental Quality, 333
Courtesy, congressional norm, 264t, 265
Court system. *See also* Judiciary; Supreme Court
 influence on bureaucracy, 360
 media coverage, 153–154
 overview, 370–372
Cozy triangles, 246
CPB (Corporation for Public Broadcasting), 140
Crisis management, 300–301, 483–485
Critical elections, 173
Cronkite, Walter, 131t, 143
Cruel and unusual punishment, 426t, 428t, 429
Cruz, Ted, 146, 208, *210*, 413
C-SPAN, 153, 290, 296n49, 388
Cuban Americans, 412
Cuban immigrants, 97–98
Cuban missile crisis, 485
Cue taking, 286
Cultural explanations for poverty, 457
Cynicism
 of children, 103
 of electorate, 64–65, 68
 of reporters, 149–150
Czech Republic, 319

D

Dahl, Robert, 12
The Daily Show, 138
Daisy ad, 217
Dangerous speech, 434–435
Deadlines, ballot filing, 167
Dealignment, 180, 251
Dean, Howard
 fund-raising success, 131t203
 Internet-based support, 67, 68, 95, 131t
 Kerry vs., 208
Death penalty, 429–430, 431
Debates
 in Congress, 266–268
 presidential, 217–219
Debs, Eugene V., 434
Debts, deficits versus, 465
Deceptive reporting, 135
Declaration of Independence, 13, 29, 31, 34, A-1–A-3
Deductions, tax, 464
Defense Department, foreign policy role, 475
Defense policies, 472–478, 481–485
Defense spending
 factors guiding, 481–482
 as percentage of federal budget, *466*, 491n24
 strategic interests and, 482–485
Deficit spending, 465–467

Deficits, trade, 479
Delegates
 activities of, 212–214
 elected officials as, 287, 307
 selection processes, 196–201
Democracy
 approaches to, 4–5
 authority and legitimacy in, 5–10
 defined, 4
 fairness in, 13–18
 individuals' stake in, 19–20
 power in, 10–13
 prerequisites, 4
 social responsibility versus liberty, 18–19
 taxation in, 17
Democracy in America (Tocqueville), 94
Democratic National Committee, 385–387
Democratic Party
 congressional party committees, 281–283
 convention of 1968, 198–199, 225n5
 delegate selection rules, 196–201
 demographics, *187*
 early discrimination by, 111
 economic lobby contributions to, 231t
 factions in, 168
 identification with, 117
 noneconomic lobby contributions to, 233t
 origins and evolution, 173–182
 PAC contributors to, 243t
 segregationist splits from, 171
 2016 platform, 213t
 union support for, 232
Democratic-Republican Party, 173, *183*
Denmark, 166, 319
Departmental organizations, 345–347
Department of Agriculture, 354
Department of Commerce, 354
Department of Defense, 354
Department of Energy, 338
Department of Labor, 354
Department of Homeland Security, 321–322, 333, 340
Deregulation
 effects of, 352–353
 of media, 140–141
de Sousa, Rebelo, 319
de Tocqueville, Alexis, 94
Detachment phase, 313
Detainment policies, 486–487
Dewey, Thomas E., 382
Diplomatic recognition, 320
Diplomatic policies, 480
Direct democracy, 5
Directionality of public opinion, 56
Disabilities, people with, 418–419
Disadvantaged groups, 400. *See also* Minorities
Discharge petitions, 268
Discrimination. *See also* Civil rights
 age, 420
 civil disobedience in response to, 108
 in death penalty, 429, 431
 in earning power, 15
 in voting rights, 109–113
Disenfranchisement, 6, 26
Disney Corporation, 143–144
Disputed elections, 2, 8–9, 221–222
Dissent in American political culture, 93
Dissenting opinions, 373
Distributive policies, 452, 454
District of Columbia, proposed amendment on, 42, 54n8
Districts, congressional, 258–261
Diversity
 equal opportunity and, 15–16
 as feature of political culture, 97–99
 immigration and, 95–97
 of judiciary, 379–382
 tolerance of, 67–70
Divided government, 181
Divine right of kings, 29, 36

Idealism, 106
Ideological interest groups, 235
Ideological parties, 170
Ideologies, impact on public opinion, 73–77
Illinois death row cases, 431
Immigration
    hostility toward, 3, 97, 414–415
    influence on U.S. political system, 14
    political culture and, 95–97
    political struggles of Hispanics and, 413–414
    reform, 414
    Trump rhetoric, 3, 30
Impeachment, 9, 275–277
Imperial presidency, 327–328
Implementation, as function of bureaucracy, 349–351
Implied powers of Congress, 266
Income inequality, 15–16, 454–460
Income level, effect on views of government efficacy, 66, 67
Income taxes, 461–464
Incumbents, 259, 291–292
Independent agencies, 347, 348t
Independent regulatory commissions and boards, 347–348
Independents in electorate, 180, 180–181
Indian Civil Rights Act of 1968, 411
Indian Removal Act, 410
Indian Reorganization Act, 411
Individual explanations for poverty, 457
Individualism, 26–27
Industry, economic lobby contributions and, 231t
Infertility treatments, 249
Influence, presidential, 250–251, 327–330
Informal presidential powers, 304–309
Information
    bureaucratic shortages, 351
    entertainment versus, 138–139
    from lobbyists, 238–239
    as power, 11
Infotainment, 138–139
Infrastructure projects, 452, 454
Inside strategies, 238–239, 242
Instagram, 290
Institute for Advanced Studies in Culture, 92
Institutional patriotism, 264t, 378
Institutional presidency, 323–325
Integrity in Congress, 264
Intelligence activities, presidential supervision, 321–322
Intensity of public opinion, 56
Interest aggregation, 169
Interest group liberalism, 248
Interest groups
    cooperation with government officials, 245–249, 344, 351
    defined, 229
    economic lobbies, by sector, 231t
    as factions, 228–229
    "Five Commandments" of, 246
    influence, 250–251
    input on judicial nominations, 376–377
    joining, 236–238
    legal actions by, 375
    lobbying strategies and resources, 238–245, 254n2
    lobbyist qualifications, 245
    noneconomic lobbies, 231t
    nongovernmental organizations as, 477–478
    overview of, 228
    pluralism and, 229, 230, 248–249, 250–251
    polling by, 81
    types, 230–236
Interest on national debt, 466
Interior Department, 347
Intermarriage, Jim Crow laws, 405t
International Brotherhood of Electrical Workers, 243
International Dairy Foods Association, 232
International organizations, foreign policy role, 476–478
Internet. See also Social media
    Big Data, 206, 207
    campaign fund-raising, 203
    children's access to, 103

civic engagement via, 94–95
effect on views of government efficacy, 67, 68
growth of, 142, 160n29
Obama's use of, 67, 68, 95, 131t, 203
obscenity on, 437–438
press freedom on, 437–438
questionable accuracy of sites, 128–129
role in Dean's success, 95, 203
use by congressional representatives, 290–291
validity of news on, 135–135, 156–157
video streaming, 142
Interstate Commerce Clause, 390
Interstate highways, 452, 454
Inverted pyramid, 135–136
Investigative reporting, 134
Investment scandals, 228
Iowa caucuses, 197t, 201, 207
Iraq invasion
    Bush administration and, 273, 305, 308, 321, 474–475, 476, 483, 484, 486, 491n30
    congressional support, 273, 288, 305, 321, 474–475
    Joint Chiefs of Staff and, 475–476
    media coverage, 155
    policy efforts preceding, 472, 474–475, 476, 483, 484, 486
Ireland, 319
Irish immigration, 96–97
Iron triangles, 245–249, 344
Israel, political parties, 166
Israeli-Arab conflicts, 485
Issue ads, 204
Issue networks, 249–250
Issues coverage decline, 150
Issue voting, 118–119, 184
Italian immigration, 96
Italy, 166, 319

J

Jackson, Andrew, 9, 174, 175, 192n13, 222, 302, 326, 370, 396n13
Jackson, Jesse, 143
Jackson, Maynard, 408
Japanese American internment, 414–415
Jay, John, 37, 368
Jefferson, Thomas
    criticisms of, 299
    Declaration of Independence, 13
    Electoral College tie, 220
    faction aligned with, 173–174
    Locke's influence, 29
    opposition to Marshall, 369
    two-term limit and, 334n5
Jeffords, Jim, 271, 278
Jewish immigration, 96–97
Jewish justices, 379–382
Jim Crow laws, 404, 405t, 423n7
Jindal, Bobby, 209, 210
John Hancock Life Insurance Company, 461
Johnson, Andrew, 277, 403, 423n5
Johnson, Gary, 170
Johnson, Lyndon B.
    affirmative action and, 409
    bad advice to, 328
    biography, 180
    character, 309
    commander-in-chief role and, 322
    Daisy ad, 217
    Democratic Convention of 1968 and, 198
    federalism of, 47, 49, 178
    misinformation about Vietnam, 63, 131t
    public mandate, 316
    Supreme Court nominations of, 380
    use of presidential authority, 302
Johnson, Richard M., 326
Joint Chiefs of Staff, 321, 475–476
Joint committees, 270
Journalism, political history in U.S., 130–134. See also Media
Judicial activism and restraint, 391–393

National Education Association, 230
National Election Studies survey, *57, 62, 63t, 64, 66t, 67*
National Gazette, 130t
National Highway Traffic Safety Administration, 345
National Labor Relations Act, 385
National Labor Relations Board, 348t
National Labor Relations Board v. Jones and Laughlin Steel Corporation, 385
National Milk Producers Federation, 229
National Organization for Women (NOW), 416
National Public Radio (NPR), 140
National Rifle Association (NRA), 241, 242
National Right to Life Committee, 234, 249
National Security Act of 1947, 321
National security advisor, 476
National Security Council
    basic functions, 321
    foreign policy role, 476
    website, 333, 335n45
National supremacy, 46
National Voter Registration Act, 115
National Woman Suffrage Association, 415
Nation-centered federalism, 44–45
Native Americans, 95–96, 98, 408–411, 433
NATO (North Atlantic Treaty Organization), 477
Natural rights, 29
NBC radio, 131t, 133
NBC television network, 143, 144–145
Near v. Minnesota, 437
"Necessary and proper" clause, 47
Negative campaigning, 216–217
Negative news, 149
NES Guide to Public Opinion and Election Behavior,124n40
Netflix, 142
Neuropersonality poll, 80
Neutral competence, 356
Nevada primary, 201
New Deal
    agricultural subsidies, 460
    court-packing plan and, 385
    Democratic coalition supporting, 178
    fireside chats and, 150–151
    government corporations and, 349
    impact on bureaucracy, 354
    as new era of federalism, 47–49
New Deal coalition, 178
New Federalism, 49
New Hampshire primary, 197t, 201, 207
New Jersey Plan, 33–34, 367, 368
News
    criteria for, 134–137
    entertainment versus, 132–134
    management of, 310–313
    from official "leaks," 311, 334n24
News Corporation, 143–144
News cycle, 147
News media. *See* Media
Newspapers
    circulation figures, 140
    political history, 130–134
    recent resurgence, 143
Newsworthiness, 136–137, 290, 338
Newt Gingrich, 60
New York, ratification of Constitution, 41
New York Herald, 132
New York Journal, 130t, 133
New York Sun, 130t
New York Times, 143, 437
New York Tribune, 130t, 132
New York World, 130t, 133
Nielson Media Research, 139
Nineteenth Amendment, 43t, A-15
Ninth Amendment, 40t, 426t, 440, A-12
Nitke, Barbara, 438
Nixon, Richard
    administration secrecy, 328, 437
    approach to bureaucracy, 343

character, 309
commander-in-chief role and, 322
debate with Kennedy, 131t, 217, 218
federalism of, 49
mandate of, 316
pardon, 304
resignation, 131t, 277, 300, 387
Supreme Court nominations of, 377, 379, 392
use of presidential authority, 302, 328
as vice president, 335nT12
Watergate scandal (*see* Watergate scandal)
Nominations
    campaign momentum for, 205–212
    defined, 196
    rules for, 196–201
    spending to attain, 201–205
Noneconomic interest groups, 232–236
Nongovernmental organizations, 477–478
Nonideological liberals and conservatives, 77
Normative judgments, 13t, 56
Norms of Congress, 263–265
North American Free Trade Agreement (NAFTA), 478–479
North Atlantic Treaty Organization (NATO), 477
North Dakota, lack of registration requirement, 115
NOW (National Organization for Women), 416
NPR (National Public Radio), 140
NRA (National Rifle Association), 241, 242
Nuclear weapons
    Cuban missile crisis, 485
    GE manufacture, 144–145
    Mutual Assured Destruction, 481
Nurses, Jim Crow laws, 405t
Nutrition labeling regulations, 450

O

Obama, Barack
    acceptance speech staging, 212
    on ANWR oil drilling, 453
    appointees of, 175, 341
    approval ratings, 8, 58, 306, *308*
    cabinet of, 247–248, 314
    congressional membership, 292
    on detaining of terror suspects, 487
    "Don't Ask, Don't Tell" policy, 419
    fund-raising efforts, 323
    health-care reform, 48, 60, 75, 99, 102, 151, 230, 238, 269–270, 291, 306
    image building, 146
    Internet-based support and fund-raising, 67, 68, 95, 131t, 203
    Iraq invasion and, 273, 474
    mandate, 305–306
    news leaks, 311
    Nobel Peace Prize, 320
    poll predictions about, 82
    popularity in suburbs, 101
    regulation legislation, 353
    relations with news media, 152, 312
    second-term agenda, 310, 316, 317
    support for Hillary Clinton, 323
    support from Latinos, 413
    support from young people, 108, 109
    Supreme Court nominations of, 176, 375–376, 377
    2008 inauguration crowd size, 128
    2008 election, 3, 305
    2012 reelection, 3, 119–120
    view of federalism, 48, 49
    weekly addresses, *311*
    worldview, 48, 49, 474
Obama, Michelle, 325
"Obamacare," 60, 76, 99, 389
Obergefell v. Hodges, 384, 419
Objectivity in reporting, 132
Obscenity, 437–438
Occupational Safety and Health Act, 350
Occupational Safety and Health Administration, 350
Occupy Wall Street movement, 3, 15

political turmoil and, 3–4, 488
popular vote, 2, 7, 8–9, 222
populist ideology of, 168, 209, 214, 271
predicted loss of, 2, 7, 211
press conferences, 152
public support and, 330
social media use, 68, 131*t*, 139, 145
support for ANWR drilling, 453
Supreme Court nominations, 376
tolerance and, 67
tradition and, 8
Trustees, elected officials as, 287, 307
Trust in government, 63–65
Turner Communications, 143
Twelfth Amendment, 43*t*, 220, A-12–A-13
Twentieth Amendment, 43*t*, A-15
Twenty-first Amendment, 42, 43*t*
Twenty-fifth Amendment, 43*t*, 302, A-17
Twenty-fourth Amendment, 43*t*, A-16
Twenty-second Amendment, 43*t*, 334*n*5
Twenty-seventh Amendment, 43*t*, A-17
Twenty-sixth Amendment, 43*t*, A-17
Twenty-third Amendment, 43*t*, A-16
Twitter, 8, 39, 59, 68, 131*t*, *136*, 139
Two-party systems
    conditions favoring, 164–170
    major eras in U.S., 173–182
Two-term limit, 302, 334*n*5
2000 presidential election
    factors in Gore loss, 326
    Florida ballot dispute, 2, 222
    Supreme Court ruling, 2, 388
    vote swapping, 216
2016 presidential election
    congressional majority, 278–280
    Democratic candidates, 211–212
    divisiveness of, 7, 488, 489
    electoral/popular vote split, 2, 7, 8–9, 20, 216, 220, 221, 222
    entertainment vs. news and, 138–139
    false claims during campaign, 134–137, 155–157
    gender differences in voting, 181
    House and Senate leaders following, *280*
    minor parties in, 170
    negative coverage of, 117, 147, 148–149, 156, 217
    nomination and selection process, 197–198, 201, 205–212
    overview of, 2–4
    PAC contributions to, 202–203, 232, 244
    party platform planks, 213*t*
    party system challenges, 182
    political culture and, 92–93
    Republican candidates, 208–211
    social media use in, 68, 131*t*, 139, 145
    strategies, 215–216
    tolerance of diversity and, 67
    voter ID laws, 6
Tyranny, 37, 173

U

Unconventional political participation, 107–108
Undercounted groups, 98
Undersecretaries in State Department, *346*
Unemployed people, political participation by, 113
Unemployment insurance, 455*t*
Unions, 232, 238, 243, 244
Unitary systems, *32*, 33
United Arab Emirates, political parties prohibited, *166*
United Auto Workers, 232
United Farm Workers, 413, 423*n*31
United Mine Workers of America, 232
United Nations, 273, 275, 476–477
United States Chamber of Commerce, 230
United States Postal Service, 349*t*
United States v. Nixon, 384, 385–387
United States v. Wheeler, 423*n*26
United We Stand America, 172
Unit rule, *199*

Unpopular speech, 434–435
Unreasonable searches and seizures, 426*t*, 427*t*
Unsafe at Any Speed (Nader), 233
Urban sprawl, *100*
Uruguay Round, 478
USA Today, 143
U.S. Census Bureau, 98
U.S. Communist Party website, 192*n*7
U.S. Department of Education, 416
U.S. Department of Labor, 16
U.S. Fish and Wildlife Service, 453
U.S. Green Party website, 192*n*7
U.S. Libertarian Party website, 192*n*7
U.S. Socialist Party website, 192*n*7
U.S. Treasury Department, 247

V

Vaccination, 440
Value judgments, 13–16, 400
Van Buren, Martin, 326
Ventura, Jesse, 172
Versailles Treaty, 321
Vetoes, 303, 317–318, 334*n*39, 335*n*40
Viacom, 143
Vice presidency
    candidate selection, 214
    list of vice presidents, A-29–A-30
    political outcomes for, 325–326, 327*t*
    Senate leadership, 279
    traditional disengagement of, 325–326
video streaming, 142
Vietnam War
    commander-in-chief role and, 322
    impact on trust in government, 63
    political dissent during, 93, 198, 435, 436
    presidential advisors, 328
    as proxy war between superpowers, 473
Violence against women, 417
Violent protests, 406–407
Virginia Plan, 33–34, 367, 368
Virtual civic engagement, 95
Voter focus groups, 215
Voter ID laws, 6, 14, 115
Vote swapping, 216
Voting
    constitutional amendments affecting, 43*t*
    disenfranchisement, 6
    early, 115
    factors that govern choices, 116–120
    inequities in, 6, 109–113
    making it easier, 115
    participation rates, 107, 114
    political knowledge and, 58–61
    polls predicting outcomes, 81–82
    registration requirements, 114–115
    2000 election dispute over, 2, 222
Voting Rights Act of 1965, 259, 406*t*, 408
Voting rights of women, 415

W

Walker, Scott, 208, *210*
Wallace, George, 171*t*, 171–172
Wallace v. Jaffree, 432
Wall Street Journal, 143
Wal-Mart, 15
Warner Communications, 143
"War of the Worlds" broadcast, 133
War on terrorism. *See* Terrorism
War Powers Act of 1973, 322, 327, 328, 475
Warren, Earl, 382, 391–392
Warsaw Pact, 473
Washington, George
    cabinet of, 334*n*33
    Constitutional Convention role, 34
    criticisms of, 299